W9-ABI-175

CRITICAL SURVEY

OF

POETRY

CRITICAL SURVEY

OF

POETRY

Second Revised Edition

Volume 8
Essays

Research Tools

Indexes

Editor, Second Revised Edition
Philip K. Jason
United States Naval Academy

Editor, First Edition, English and Foreign Language Series
Frank N. Magill

SALEM PRESS, INC.
Pasadena, California   Hackensack, New Jersey

Editor in Chief: Dawn P. Dawson
Managing Editor: Christina J. Moose
Developmental Editor: Tracy Irons-Georges
Research Supervisor: Jeffry Jensen
Acquisitions Editor: Mark Rehn
Photograph Editor: Philip Bader
Manuscript Editors: Sarah Hilbert, Leslie Ellen Jones,
Melanie Watkins, Rowena Wildin
Assistant Editor: Andrea E. Miller
Research Assistant: Jeff Stephens
Production Editor: Cynthia Beres
Layout: Eddie Murillo

Library of Congress Cataloging-in-Publication Data

Critical survey of poetry / Philip K. Jason, editor.—2nd rev. ed.

p. cm.

Combined ed. of: Critical survey of poetry: foreign language series, originally published 1984, Critical survey of poetry: supplement, originally published 1987, and Critical survey of poetry: English language series, rev. ed. published 1992. With new material. Includes bibliographical references and index.

ISBN 1-58765-071-1 (set : alk. paper) — ISBN 1-58765-079-7 (v. 8 : alk. paper) —

1. Poetry—History and criticism—Dictionaries. 2. Poetry—Bio-bibliography. 3. Poets—Biography—Dictionaries. I. Jason, Philip K., 1941 -   .

PN1021 .C7 2002
809.1′003—dc21   2002008536

First Printing

CONTENTS

COMPLETE LIST OF CONTENTS

VOLUME 1

VOLUME 2

VOLUME 3

VOLUME 4

Critical Survey of Poetry

VOLUME 5

VOLUME 6

VOLUME 7

VOLUME 8

CRITICISM AND THEORY

POETRY AROUND THE WORLD

RESEARCH TOOLS

INDEXES

ESSAYS

CRITICISM FROM PLATO TO ELIOT

The criticism of poetry has always played an influential role in the development of poetry in Western civilization, from the time of the ancient Greeks and Romans up through the Renaissance, neoclassic, and Romantic periods and into the twentieth century. By articulating the general aims and ideals of poetry and by interpreting and evaluating the works of particular poets, critics throughout the ages have helped to shape the development of poetry. Poets, for their part, have often attempted to meet—or to react against—the stated aims and ideals of the prevailing critical theories. Some poets have also formulated and practiced the criticism of poetry, producing a closer and more vital relationship between criticism and poetry. For the student, the study of poetic theory and criticism can be not only an interesting and fruitful study in itself, but also a valuable aid in the attempt to understand the historical development of poetry.

The following review is organized chronologically, divided into six main sections: Classical critics; Renaissance critics; Neoclassic critics; Romantic critics; Victorian critics; and Modern critics. The focus is primarily on English critics, though the ancient Greeks and Romans are included because they represent the classical tradition inherited and built upon by the English. Significant American contributors to the mainstream of poetic theory and criticism are, with the exception of Edgar Allan Poe, restricted to the twentieth century. In this essay, T. S. Eliot is the only American critic treated in depth, though even his contributions are seen as a continuation of the English tradition.

Criticism of poetry can appear in many different forms, but can be categorized one of two basic ways: Theoretical criticism, or poetic theory, is the articulation of general principles and tenets of poetry, usually regarding the nature, aims, and ideals of poetry, but also covering techniques and methods. Practical criticism, on the other hand, is the application of these principles and tenets to the tasks of interpreting and evaluating particular works of poetry. Both theoretical and practical criticism can be focused on any of four different aspects of poetry: first, the poem itself; second, the relationship of the poem to that which it imitates; third, the poet's relationship to the poem; and finally, the relationship of the poem to the audience. M. H. Abrams designated these four types of criticism as objective, mimetic (after the Greek work *mimesis*, for imitation), expressive, and pragmatic. A recognition of the critic's orientation as either theoretical or practical and as objective, mimetic, expressive, or pragmatic can help the student of criticism to comprehend the contribution of the critic to the history of criticism.

CLASSICAL CRITICS

Four works of poetic theory by ancient Greek and Roman theorists have had a profound influence on the course of Western literature in general and poetry in particular: Plato's *Politeia* (c. 399-390 B.C.E.; *Republic*), Aristotle's *De poetica* (c. 334-323 B.C.E.; *Poetics*, 1705), Horace's *Ars poetica* (13-8 B.C.E.; *The Art of Poetry*), and Longinus's *Peri hypsous* (*On the Sublime*). In these four works are found many critical theories that make up the classical tradition inherited by English letters. The two most important of these theories address the relationship of poetry to that which it imitates and the relationship of poetry to its audience. The central Greek concept of poetry is that of *mimesis*: Poetry, like all forms of art, imitates nature. By nature, the Greeks meant all of reality, including human life, and they conceived of nature as essentially well ordered and harmonious and as moving toward the ideal. Hence, poetry seeks to imitate the order and harmony of nature. Of equal importance to the mimetic concept of poetry is the Greek belief that poetry has a moral or formative effect on its audience. Poetry achieves this effect by making the reader more aware of reality and thereby more aware of his own nature and purpose. The Roman theorists, in turn, accepted these basic concepts of poetry. Neither the Greeks nor the Romans were very interested, however, in the expressive relationship between the poet and the poem (involving such questions as what takes place in the poet during the creative act of writing poetry), though they do make occasional comments on this aspect of poetry.

PLATO

In Book X of the *Republic*, Plato (427 B.C.E.-347 B.C.E.), the great Greek philosopher, discusses the role of poets and poetry in the ideal society. His ideas regarding poetry are valuable, not because they clarify poetic issues, but because they raise serious objections to poetry that later critics are forced to answer. Indeed, Plato states that poets and poetry should be banished from the ideal society for two reasons: Poetry represents an inferior degree of truth, and poetry encourages the audience to indulge its emotions rather than to control them. The *Republic* is written in the form of a dialogue, and in Book X Socrates (speaking for Plato) convinces Glaucon of these two objections to poetry. He arrives at the first objection by arguing that poetry, like painting, is an imitation of an imperfect copy of reality, and therefore is twice removed from ultimate truth. Reality, or ultimate truth, Plato believed, exists in universal ideas or eternal forms and not in the particular concrete objects of this world of matter. A table or a bed, for example, is a concrete but imperfect copy of the eternal form of the table or the bed. A painter who paints a picture of the particular table or bed is thus imitating, not the reality (the eternal form), but an imperfect copy of the eternal form. The poet, in writing a poem about the table or the bed—or about any other imperfect concrete manifestation of reality—is also removed from reality, and therefore his poem represents an inferior degree of truth.

The second objection to poetry raised by Plato stems from his belief that human lives should be governed by reason rather than by emotions. Poetry, Plato believed, encourages the audience to let emotions rule over reason. As an example, Socrates cites the fact that those who listen to tragic passages of poetry "delight in giving way to sympathy, and are in raptures at the excellence of the poet who stirs [their] feelings most" (translated by Benjamin Jowett). Yet, if similar tragic events took place in their own lives, they would strive to be stoical and would be ashamed to be so emotional.

Plato's objections to poetry raise serious questions: Does poetry represent an inferior degree of truth? Does it have a harmful social or moral effect? More generally, and in a sense more important, his objections raise the question of whether or not poetry can be interpreted and evaluated on grounds other than the philosophical, moral, and social grounds he uses. In other words, can poetry be interpreted and evaluated on poetic grounds? Later critics, beginning with Aristotle, argue that it is

possible to construct a general theory by which to interpret and evaluate poetry on poetic grounds.

ARISTOTLE

The *Poetics* of Aristotle (384 B.C.E.-322 B.C.E.), as W. J. Bate has remarked, stands out not only as the most important critical commentary of the classical period but also as the most influential work of literary criticism in the entire period of Western civilization. Thus it is essential for the student of poetic theory and criticism to have a grasp of Aristotle's basic ideas concerning poetry, especially those that refute Plato's objections and those that help to establish a general theory by which poetry can be interpreted and evaluated on poetic grounds.

The title *Poetics* means a theory or science of poetry, and accordingly Aristotle begins in a scientific manner:

> I propose to treat of Poetry in itself and of its various kinds, noting the essential quality of each; to inquire into the structure of the plot as requisite to a good poem; into the number and nature of the parts of which a poem is composed; and similarly into whatever else falls within the same inquiry. (This and following quotations of the *Poetics* are translations by S. H. Butcher.)

It is important to note that the word "poetry" (the Greek word is *poiesis*, which means "making") is used by Aristotle in a generic sense, to refer to all forms of imaginative literature, including drama, and not in the specific sense in which it is used today to refer to a form of literature distinct from drama and fiction. Unfortunately, the *Poetics* is not complete (either Aristotle never finished it or part of it was lost). As it now stands, the work contains an extensive analysis of tragedy, an account of the sources and history of poetry, and scattered remarks on comedy, epic poetry, style, and language. It also contains an evaluative comparison of tragedy and epic poetry and a discussion of critical difficulties in poetry. Yet, despite its incompleteness and its lack of any discussion of lyric poetry, the *Poetics* is an extremely important document of poetic theory.

First of all, the *Poetics* is important because it refutes Plato's objections to poetry, though it is uncertain whether Aristotle considered the *Poetics* to be a direct reply to Plato. (As a student of Plato at Athens, he must have been aware of Plato's objections, but the *Poetics* may have been written long after Plato's death and therefore not intended as a direct reply.) The key to Aristotle's refutation of Plato's first objection—that poetry represents an inferior degree of truth—is in his interpretation of the Greek concept that poetry is an imitation of nature. It is known from Aristotle's philosophical works that he believed that reality exists, not solely in universal ideas or eternal forms (as Plato believed), but rather in the process by which universal ideas work through and give form and meaning to concrete matter. For example, the reality of a table for Aristotle is not in the universal idea of a table but in the process by which the idea of a table gives form to the wood that goes into the particular table. Hence, in observing the process of nature the poet observes reality, not an inferior copy of it. Furthermore, the poet's act of imitation, for Aristotle, is not mere slavish copying, as it seems to be for Plato. (Plato implies that the poet is concerned with making realistic copies of the objects of the world of matter rather than with representing universal ideas.) Rather, Aristotle apparently saw the act of poetic imitation as a duplication of the process of nature or reality. That is, poetry is an imitation of the process of universal ideas or forms working through concrete matter. For example, a universal idea of human suffering gives shape to language, characters, and action in a tragic poem.

Poetry for Aristotle is both *poiesis* and *mimesis*, making and imitating. Hazard Adams, in *The Interests of Criticism* (1969), explains it in this way:

> To Aristotle, then, there is no contradiction between poet, or maker, and imitator. The two words, in fact, define each other. The poet is a maker of plots, and these plots are imitations of actions. To imitate actions is not to mirror or copy things in nature but to make something in a way that nature makes something—that is, to have imitated nature.

As for Plato's second objection to poetry—that it encourages emotional and irrational responses—Aristotle's theory of catharsis provides a means of refutation. Catharsis (*katharsis*), a term used by the Greeks in both medicine and religion to mean a purgation or cleansing, is apparently used by Aristotle (there is some disagreement) to mean a process that the audience of a tragedy

undergoes. Tragedy excites the emotions of pity and fear in the audience and then, through the structure of the play, purges, refines, and quiets these emotions, leaving the audience morally better for the experience. While Aristotle's comments on catharsis are restricted to tragedy, they seem to be applicable to various kinds of literature. Poetry, Aristotle's ideas suggest, does not simply encourage its audience to indulge their emotions, as Plato contended, but rather it engages their emotions in order that they may be directed and refined, thus making the audience better human beings.

The *Poetics*, then, is a significant document in the history of poetic theory because it refutes the specific objections to poetry raised by Plato. It has another significance, however, just as important and closely related to the first: It demonstrates the possibility of establishing a general theory by which poetry can be analyzed and evaluated on poetic grounds, rather than on the philosophical, moral, or social grounds used by Plato. Aristotle's analysis of tragedy, his evaluative comparison of tragedy and epic poetry, and his discussion of critical difficulties in poetry all contribute to establishing such a general theory of poetry.

In his analysis of tragedy, which takes up the better part of the *Poetics*, Aristotle enumerates the parts of tragedy (plot, character, thought, diction, song, and spectacle), ranks them in importance, and analyzes each (though he devotes most of his discussion to plot, which he calls "the soul of a tragedy"). In addition to breaking down the parts of a tragedy, he explains how the parts must interrelate with one another and form a unified whole, "the structural union of the parts being such that, if any one of them is displaced or removed, the whole will be disjointed and disturbed." While his structural analysis is largely restricted to tragedy (he touches on epic poetry), it has the far-reaching effect of demonstrating that every form of literature, including all types of poetry, is made up of parts that ideally should interrelate with one another and form a harmonious and unified whole that is aesthetically pleasing to the audience.

In comparing tragedy with epic poetry, Aristotle concludes that tragedy is the higher art because it is more vivid, more concentrated, and better unified than epic poetry, and that it "fulfills its specific function better as an art—for each art ought to produce, not any chance pleasure, but the pleasure proper to it." Aristotle thus demonstrates, in making this judgment, that poetry can be judged by its poetic elements (such as vividness, concentration, and unity) and its aesthetic effects (the pleasure proper to it).

In one of the last sections of the *Poetics*, Aristotle discusses five sources of critical objections to artistic works, including poetry. Works of art are censured for containing things that are (1) impossible, (2) irrational, (3) morally hurtful, (4) contradictory, and (5) contrary to artistic correctness. Aristotle shows that each of the critical objections can be answered, either by refuting the objection or by justifying the presence of the source of the objection. In several cases the refutation or justification is made on aesthetic grounds. For example, he says that the artist or poet may describe the impossible if the desired artistic effect is achieved. Here also, then, Aristotle shows that poetry can be analyzed and judged as poetry according to a general theory of poetry.

In summary, the *Poetics* of Aristotle is of primary importance in the history of criticism because it answers Plato's charges against poetry and because it demonstrates to later critics how a general theory of poetry can be established.

HORACE

The greatest Roman contribution to the history of poetic theory is a work by the poet Horace (65 B.C.E.-8 B.C.E.), usually titled *Ars poetica* (*The Art of Poetry*) but known originally as *Epistle to the Pisos* because it was written as a verse letter to members of the Piso family. Perhaps because it was written in the form of a letter, Horace's work lacks the systematic approach and profundity of Aristotle's treatise and the vigorous thought of Plato's dialogue. Despite these differences, as well as a lack of originality (Horace was restating—perhaps actually copying from an earlier treatise—already accepted poetic principles and tenets), *The Art of Poetry* is valuable for its influence on later ages, in particular the Renaissance and the neoclassic age. Poets and critics of those times found in Horace's graceful verse letter many of the classical poetic aims and ideals, such as simplicity, order, urbanity, decorum, good sense, correctness, good taste, and respect for tradition. In addition, Horace's urbane style and witty tone provided his admirers with a writing model.

Horace comments on a wide variety of literary concerns, ranging from the civilizing effect of poetry to the poet's need for study and training as well as genius and natural ability, though he does not explore any of these in appreciable depth. Some of the concerns are specific to drama (for example, a play should have five acts), but others relate to poetry in general. The most famous statement in *The Art of Poetry* is that "[t]he aim of the poet is to inform or delight, or to combine together, in what he says, both pleasure and applicability to life. . . . He who combines the useful and the pleasing wins out by both instructing and delighting the reader" (translated by W. J. Bate). This idea that poetry is both pleasing and formative extends back to the Greeks and has retained a central position in poetic theory through the ages. Another important concept that pervades Horace's letter is that of decorum, which is defined as the quality of fitness or propriety in a literary work. All elements in the work should be fitted to one another: character to genre, speech and action to character, style of language to genre, and so on. Horace's statements on decorum, the separation of poetic genres, the use of past models for imitation, and the formative effect of poetry became cornerstones of neoclassic theory in the seventeenth and eighteenth centuries.

LONGINUS

The fourth classical work to have an important influence on English poetry and criticism is *Peri hypsous*, usually translated as *On the Sublime*, a fragmentary treatise generally attributed to Longinus, a Greek philosopher and rhetorician of the third century C.E. The work, however, shows evidence of having been written in the first half of the first century C.E. (though the oldest extant manuscript is from the tenth century C.E.), and therefore the authorship is questionable. While the work is mostly a treatise on the principles of rhetoric, it does contain passages of poetic theory.

The author lists five sources of the "sublime," which Bate defines as an "elevation of style, or that which lifts literary style above the ordinary and commonplace to the highest excellence" (*Criticism: The Major Texts*, 1970). The effect of the sublime on the audience is the result of characteristics possessed by the poet: "the power of forming great conceptions" and "vehement and inspired passion" (translated by W. Rhys Roberts). The other three sources are poetic techniques, which the poet must practice and execute: figurative language, noble diction, and the dignified and elevated arrangement of words.

On the Sublime was first published in the sixteenth century by an Italian critic, and its popularity among poets and critics of Europe and England reached a peak in the later half of the eighteenth century. Commentators attribute the popularity of *On the Sublime* to its combined appeal to the traditional classical interests and to the emerging romantic interests of the eighteenth century. That is, the author of *On the Sublime* stresses, on the one hand, the classical values of studying and practicing the techniques of writing poetry, of imitating past models, and of creating balanced and unified works of poetry, while on the other hand he stresses the Romantic values of inspiration, imagination, and emotion, both in the poet who creates the poetry and in the reader who is emotionally transported by sublime passages.

RENAISSANCE CRITICS

During the Middle Ages scholars had little interest in the literary elements of poetry and valued it, if at all, for its religious and philosophical meanings. Even the great Italian poets of the late Middle Ages—Dante, Petrarch, and Giovanni Boccaccio—state in their critical works that the value of poetry is in its religious and moral teachings.

With the Renaissance, however, there came a renewed interest in the literary qualities of poetry. At first, the interest was restricted to studies of technical matters, such as meter, rhyme, and the classification of figures. These studies did not, however, solve what J. E. Spingarn, in *A History of Literary Criticism in the Renaissance* (1899), called "the fundamental problem of Renaissance criticism": the justification of poetry on aesthetic or literary grounds. The solution to the problem was contained in classical literary theory, so that, with the rediscovery of Aristotle's *Poetics* (it had been lost to Western Europe during the Middle Ages) and with the study of Horace's *The Art of Poetry*, Renaissance critics were able to formulate a theory that justified poetry on literary grounds and that demonstrated its value for society. In Italy, this theory was developed by such critics as Antonio Minturno, Bernardino Daniello,

and Francesco Robortelli. In England, it was most eloquently and persuasively articulated in the late sixteenth century by Sir Philip Sidney in the *Defence of Poesie* (1595), which Bate calls "the most rounded and comprehensive synthesis we have of the Renaissance conception of the aim and function of literature" (*Criticism: The Major Texts*).

Sir Philip Sidney (1554-1586) was neither a full-time poet nor a full-time critic; nevertheless, he is recognized as the first great English poet-critic. The *Defence of Poesie*, written in the early 1580's and published posthumously, is Sidney's sole piece of sustained literary criticism, but it so well provided the needed aesthetic defense of poetry that Sidney's reputation as the foremost English critic of the Renaissance rests securely on it. The essay is an impressive reflection of Sidney's classical education both in its structure and style and in its ideas. The structure, as Kenneth Myrick (*Sir Philip Sidney as a Literary Craftsman*, 1935) pointed out, is that of a classical oration, and the graceful and persuasive style is adapted perfectly to the structure. The ideas, while shaped by Sidney's mind, are derived from the great classical theorists: Aristotle, Plato, and Horace. In addition, the essay shows the influence of Italian literary criticism and contemporary Christian religious thought.

The *Defence of Poesie* (also published as *An Apologie for Poetry*) is a justification of poetry in the generic sense, that is, of all imaginative literature, and was occasioned by various puritanical attacks on poetry, such as Stephen Gosson's *The School of Abuse* (1579), which was dedicated to Sidney. Not only does Sidney refute the puritanical charges against poetry, but he also argues that poetry is the most effective tool of all human learning in leading humankind to virtuous action. His essay is devoted to establishing proof for this thesis.

Sidney begins to line up his proof by presenting a historical view of poetry, in which he asserts that poetry is the most ancient and esteemed form of all learning. Poetry, he says, was "the first light-giver to ignorance, and first nurse, whose milk by little and little enabled [peoples] to feed afterwards of tougher knowledges." The first books were books of poetry, and these led to other kinds of books, such as history, philosophy, and science. Hence, poetry is the great educator. Accordingly, poets have enjoyed a place of esteem in most civilizations throughout history. The names given to poets (such as the Roman name *vates*, meaning prophet or diviner) is further proof of the honor accorded poets and poetry.

Following his historical view, Sidney offers a definition of poetry and an analysis of the nature and function of poetry—all of which is designed to buttress his argument that poetry, more than any other kind of learning, leads humankind to virtuous actions. It is important to notice in this part of Sidney's argument that he is making a direct connection between the aesthetic quality of poetry and its moral effect—a connection that has its origin in classical theory.

With obvious debts to Aristotle and Horace, Sidney defines poetry as "an art of imitation . . . that is to say, a representing, counterfeiting, or figuring forth—to speak metaphorically, a speaking picture; with this end, to teach and delight." In imitating, Sidney says, the poet is not restricted to nature. He may "mak[e] things either better than Nature bringeth forth, or, quite anew, forms such as never were in Nature," such as demigods and other fantastic creatures. The result is that the poet creates a "golden" world, whereas nature's world is of brass. Poetry, in other words, creates an ideal world and, thereby, "maketh us know what perfection is." In giving us a "speaking picture" of perfection, poetry moves us to virtuous action. The various genres of poetry—epic, satire, elegy, pastoral, comedy, and so on—present various versions of the ideal.

Neither history nor philosophy, according to Sidney, is equal to poetry in its ability to move humankind to virtuous action. History is tied to the actual, "the particular truth of things" or "what is," and philosophy, conversely, is concerned with the universal or the ideal, "the general reason of things" or "what should be." Hence, history fails to show humankind a universal truth or ideal for which to aspire, and philosophy, while possessing the universal truth or ideal, presents it in abstract and general terms, rather than in concrete and particular terms, and thus fails to reach most of humankind. Poetry, on the other hand, "coupleth the general notion with the particular example," that is to say, embodies the universal truth in a concrete image or situation, and, in so doing, affects its readers emotionally as well as intellectually and moves them to virtuous action.

After establishing proof for his thesis that poetry is the most effective tool of human knowledge in leading humankind to virtuous action, Sidney turns to a refutation of the charges against poetry. He lists four specific charges: first, that there are "more fruitful knowledges" than poetry; second, that poetry is "the mother of lies"; third, that poetry is "the nurse of abuse, infecting us with many pestilent desires"; and fourth, that "Plato banished [poets] out of his Commonwealth." Sidney overturns the first charge by stating that, since no knowledge "can both teach and move [mankind to virtue] so much as Poetry," then none can be as fruitful as poetry. As for the second charge, that poetry lies, Sidney states that the poet does not lie because he does not affirm anything that is false to be true. By this, Sidney means that the poet does not attempt to deceive his audience into believing that what his poetry presents is actual or real. Rather, he offers his poem as an imaginary picture of the ideal, or "what should be." Sidney refutes the third charge, the puritanical charge that poetry is harmful because it increases sinful desires, by asserting that the fault lies, not in poetry itself, but in the abuse of poetry. When poetry is abused, it is harmful; but, used rightly, it is beneficial. In refuting the fourth charge, that Plato banished the poets, Sidney argues that Plato was "banishing the abuse, not the thing"; that is, Plato was upset by the mistreatment of gods in poetry. In *Ion*, Sidney claims, Plato gave "high and rightly divine commendation to Poetry."

The *Defence of Poesie* also expresses many of the neoclassic ideas and concerns that were to be treated more fully by critics in the seventeenth and eighteenth centuries: the separation and ranking of genres, the need for decorum in poetry, and the use of ancient classical models and critical authorities. It is, however, in the defense and justification of literature on aesthetic as well as moral grounds that Sidney's essay deserves its high place in the history of criticism.

NEOCLASSIC CRITICS

In the two centuries following Sidney's *Defence of Poesie*, neoclassic poetic theory flourished in England. During this period, and especially from the mid-seventeenth to the late eighteenth century, England produced a number of able exponents of neoclassicism. Some of these critics, following the lead of French critics, insisted on a rather strict form of neoclassic theory and critical practice, turning the ancient classical principles into hard-and-fast rules. The two greatest critics of this period, however, rose above this rule-mongering and inflexibility, so that their criticism has been of permanent value. They are John Dryden and Samuel Johnson.

JOHN DRYDEN

John Dryden (1631-1700) is known as "the father of English criticism," an honorary title given to him by Samuel Johnson because he was the first English critic to produce a large body of significant literary criticism. Almost all of it, however, is practical criticism, that is, criticism that examines particular literary works and particular problems in literary technique and construction. (Dryden often wrote about his own poems and plays.) Dryden rarely, if ever, treated in depth the larger theoretical issues of literature, such as the aims and ideals of literature, the nature of imitation, the creative process, and the moral and aesthetic effects of literature on the audience. He did write on these issues, but in passing rather than in depth. Furthermore, in no one piece of criticism did Dryden develop a general theory of literature (as Aristotle and Sidney did) as a standard by which to investigate particular works of literature.

Some literary historians are repelled by Dryden's lack of an explicitly stated general theory of literature, especially because his scattered remarks on theoretical issues are sometimes inconsistent or even contradictory. For example, on the matter of the ends of poetry, he says several times that delight is the most important end. This statement from "A Defence of *An Essay of Dramatic Poesy*" (1668) is typical: "for delight is the chief, if not the only, end of poesy: instruction can be admitted but in second place, for poesy instructs as it delights." In other pieces, however, he expresses a different opinion: "Let profit [instruction] have the pre-eminence of honour, in the end of poetry" (*A Discourse Concerning the Original and Progress of Satire*, 1693); and "The chief design of Poetry is to instruct" ("A Parallel of Poetry and Painting," 1695). In still other pieces, Dryden merges the two ends: "To instruct delightfully is the general end of all poetry," he states in "Preface to *Troilus and Cressida* Containing 'The Grounds of Criticism in Tragedy' " (1679).

While some commentators see Dryden's lack of an explicitly stated general theory of literature to be a weakness that results in inconsistent statements and judgments, others see it as a strength that affords him flexibility and allows him to evaluate individual pieces of literature on their own merits rather than against a theoretical standard. These latter commentators point out that much questionable neoclassic criticism resulted from an inflexible adherence to general principles and rules.

Most of Dryden's criticism, as well as being practical rather than theoretical, pertains to drama rather than to poetry and is, therefore, outside the purview of this essay. His best and most famous piece, for example, is *Of Dramatic Poesie: An Essay* (1668), a comparative analysis of ancient, modern, French, and English drama, examined in the light of neoclassical dramatic principles and rules by four different speakers. It might be argued that it is his criticism of drama that gives Dryden his high ranking among literary critics; nevertheless, he is also at times an astute reader and judge of poetry.

"Preface to *The Fables*" (1700) is Dryden's best-known commentary on poetry. Written in an informal, discursive style that Dryden perfected, the essay serves as an introduction to Dryden's translations of fables by Homer, Ovid, Boccaccio, and Geoffrey Chaucer. Dryden's method is largely comparative: He compares Homer to Vergil, Ovid to Chaucer, and Chaucer to Boccaccio, revealing the characteristics of the poets and the beauties of their poems. In addition, Dryden comments on the history and the development of poetry, pointing out relationships among various poets, such as Dante, Petrarch, Edmund Spenser, and John Milton, as well as those mentioned above. In doing all of this, Dryden gives a sense of the achievement of poetry in general and of Chaucer in particular. Chaucer, Dryden says, is "the father of English poetry." He was "a perpetual fountain of good sense," and he "follow'd Nature everywhere." In examining *The Canterbury Tales* (1387-1400), Dryden finds a rich variety of characters representing "the whole English nation." It is to Chaucer's magnificent cast of characters that Dryden applies the proverb: "Here is God's plenty."

Although it is impossible to summarize Dryden's critical position because it frequently shifted and because it was not explicitly stated, it is possible to summarize his critical concerns and to list the characteristics he values as a critic of poetry. First, he was concerned more with the practice of poetry than with theory. He liked to examine particular poems and specific literary problems. Second, in examining particular poems he felt that the critic's business is not "to find fault," but "to observe those excellencies which should delight a resonable reader" ("The Author's Apology for Heroic Poetry and Poetic License," 1677). Third, he was interested in genres—satire, epic poetry, and so on. He considered, as did most neoclassic critics, heroic (epic) poetry to be the highest type of poetry (partially because of the mistaken neoclassic notion that Aristotle ranked epic over tragedy). In "The Author's Apology for Heroic Poetry and Poetic License," an essay influenced by Longinus's *On the Sublime*, Dryden calls heroic poetry "the greatest work of human nature."

The characteristics that Dryden values as a critic of poetry are unity, simplicity, decorum, wit, grace, urbanity, good sense, and the like. As a poet, he often embodied these characteristics in his own poetry. Thus, in both his poetry and his criticism Dryden stands out as the preeminent model of neoclassic poetic theory of the seventeenth century.

JOSEPH ADDISON AND ALEXANDER POPE

Between Dryden and Samuel Johnson, there were two English critics who deserve mention. Joseph Addison (1672-1719) contributed to English neoclassic criticism through the essays he wrote for popular periodicals of his day, such as *The Tatler* (1709-1710) and *The Spectator* (1711-1712, 1714), which he published with Richard Steele. Addison wrote both theoretical pieces on such poetic matters as wit, taste, and imagination, and pieces of practical criticism on such poems as Milton's epic, *Paradise Lost* (1667), and the medieval ballad "Chevy Chase." As a body, the essays express the prevailing notions of English neoclassic criticism.

Alexander Pope (1688-1744), a poet of the first rank, is the author of *An Essay on Criticism* (1711), a verse essay written in heroic couplets and modeled on Horace's *The Art of Poetry* and such contemporary pieces as *L'Art poétique* (1674), by the French critic Nicolas Boileau-Despréaux. Pope's essay contains no new critical ideas, nor does it explore traditional ideas in any appreciable

depth. It is, however, commendable for its expression of the prevailing neoclassic principles and tenets and for its liberal interpretation. Pope's couplet on wit is a good example of his ability to express ideas succinctly: "True wit is Nature to advantage dress'd;/ What oft' was thought, but ne'er so well express'd." His discussion ranges from the characteristics and skills needed by the critic to various critical methods and principles. A reading of Pope's essay is an excellent introduction to English neoclassic criticism.

SAMUEL JOHNSON

Samuel Johnson (1709-1784) has been called the "Great Cham" of eighteenth century English literary criticism. If to Sidney belongs the honor of writing the first great piece of English literary criticism, and to Dryden that of being the first great practicing English critic, then to Johnson belongs the honor of being the first "complete" English literary critic. Johnson was expert in all forms of literary criticism: He formulated and explained literary theory; he edited texts and practiced the principles of sound textual criticism (criticism that seeks to date texts, to settle questions of authorship, and to establish the author's intended text, free from errors and unauthorized changes); he explained the historical development of poetry; he examined and evaluated particular literary works in relation to genre and in terms of literary aims and ideals; and he wrote literary biography. Johnson's criticism appears in a variety of sources, ranging from the monumental *The Lives of the Poets* (1779-1781) to the preface and notes to *The Plays of William Shakespeare* (1765), from the narrative *Rasselas, Prince of Abyssinia* (1759) to the essays in *The Rambler* (1750-1752) and *The Idler* (1758-1760), two periodicals he published. In addition to his critical work, he wrote poetry, a play (*Irene: A Tragedy*, 1749), a long narrative referred to above, and a great many moral and social essays and meditative works; he also compiled a dictionary of the English language and edited a collection of Shakespeare's works.

Johnson believed firmly in the classical idea that poetry is an imitation of nature, having as its ends instruction and delight. The nature that the poet imitates, however, should be "general nature." In the preface and notes to *The Plays of William Shakespeare*, he states: "Nothing can please many, and please long, but just representations of general nature." By general nature, John-son means what is universal and permanent, that is, what is true for all people in all ages. In *Rasselas*, the philosopher Imlac explains:

> The business of a poet . . . is to examine, not the individual, but the species; to remark general properties and large appearances; he does not number the streaks of the tulip, or describe the different shades in the verdure of the forest. He is to exhibit in his portraits of nature such prominent and striking features, as recall the original to every mind. . . . [He] must disregard present laws and opinions, and rise to general and transcendental truths, which will always be the same.

By imitating general nature, the poet instructs and delights the audience. Johnson believed that instruction, or what Bate calls "the mental and moral enlargement of man," was the more important end of poetry, but he realized that poetry could best instruct by delighting. Hence, he repeatedly makes such statements as that "the end of poetry is to instruct by pleasing" (preface and notes to *The Plays of William Shakespeare*).

As a practicing critic, Johnson examined and evaluated poetry primarily in the light of this principle that poetry is an imitation of general nature with the purpose of instructing and delighting. He also investigated poetry in terms of the prevailing neoclassic notions regarding the conventions and techniques of the various genres. He believed, however, that "there is always an appeal open from criticism to nature" (preface and notes to *The Plays of William Shakespeare*), so that he never approved of conventions and techniques for their own sakes. In fact, he frequently rejected the rigid neoclassic rules as being in violation of the laws of nature. The poet's duty, he felt, was to imitate nature and life, not to follow critical rules. It was on this principle that Johnson rejected Milton's "Lycidas," a pastoral elegy. The pastoral elements, he felt, divorced the poem from nature, truth, and life. Finally, as a practicing critic Johnson strove for impartiality, seeking to discover "the faults and defects" of a poem, as well as its "excellencies." By giving a balanced and impartial account of a poet's work, Johnson established credibility as a critic.

The Lives of the Poets is a set of fifty-two critical biographies of English poets, varying greatly in length and written as prefaces to the works of these poets collected and published by a group of London booksellers. The poets are all from the seventeenth and eighteenth centuries and range from Abraham Cowley to Thomas Gray, Johnson's contemporary. Johnson's general method is to sketch the poet's life and character, analyze his works, and estimate his achievement; but he also discusses a variety of poetic issues, such as diction, wit, and the conventions of genre, and by covering the poets of more than a century he effectively establishes the history of English poetry from the mid-seventeenth to the mid-eighteenth century. A review of several of the more famous biographies will give an idea of Johnson's methods and critical prowess.

In the biographical account of Pope in *Life of Pope*, Johnson includes a description of Pope's method of composition. It serves as a description of the quintessential neoclassic poet (and may be compared to that of the Romantic poet found in various pieces of Romantic criticism). Johnson says that Pope's method of poetic composition "was to write his first thoughts in his first words, and gradually to amplify, decorate, rectify, and refine them." Pope's nearly exclusive use of the heroic couplet resulted in "readiness and dexterity," and his "perpetual practice" led to a "systematical arrangement" of language in his mind. Johnson recounts the rumor that, before sending a poem to be published, Pope would keep it "under his inspection" for two years, and that he always "suffered the tumult of imagination to subside, and the novelties of invention to grow familiar." Johnson's description of Pope emphasizes the neoclassic poet's belief in the importance of practice, labor, revision, and the use of reason over imagination.

Johnson devotes a great part of his *Life of Milton* to a long analysis of *Paradise Lost*, Milton's epic. In neoclassic fashion, he examines the poem in light of the requirements of the epic genre: moral instruction, fable or plot, significance of subject matter, characters, use of the probable and marvelous, machinery, episodes, integrity of design, sentiments, and diction. His judgment is that, in terms of fulfilling the requirements of an epic, *Paradise Lost* ranks extremely high. There are faults in the poem, however, the chief one being "that it comprises neither human actions nor human manners. The man and woman [Adam and Eve] who act and suffer are in a state which no other man or woman can ever know." The result is that the reader cannot identify with the characters or the actions, so that the poem lacks "human interest." Nevertheless, *Paradise Lost*, in Johnson's final judgment, "is not the greatest of heroick poems, only because it is not the first."

In the *Life of Cowley*, Johnson gives an account of the seventeenth century "Metaphysical poets," a term he is credited with coining. His account of them is to a great extent denigrating: They "will, without great wrong, lose their right to the name of poets, for they cannot be said to have imitated anything; they neither copied nature nor life." They were, however, men of learning and wit, and this admission leads Johnson to a penetrating examination of the essence of wit. After rejecting Pope's definition of wit ("What oft' was thought, but ne'er so well express'd") because it "reduces [wit] from strength of thought to happiness of language," Johnson offers his own definition as that "which is at once natural and new" and "though not obvious . . . acknowledged to be just." He finds, though, that the Metaphysical poets do not possess wit defined as such. Rather, their wit is "a kind of *discordia concors*; a combination of dissimilar images, or discovery of occult resemblances in things apparently unlike. . . . The most heterogeneous ideas are yoked by violence together." It is a tribute to Johnson's critical powers that this definition of Metaphysical wit continues to be applied, despite the fact that his general estimate of Metaphysical poetry is no longer accepted.

Johnson is the last—and arguably the greatest—of the neoclassic critics of poetry. In another sense, though, he is apart from them. By appealing to nature and reason and common sense—in other words, by returning to classical literary principles—he almost singlehandedly overturned the tendencies of extreme neoclassic critics to codify and regularize all aspects of literature. Johnson is, in effect, a great proponent of the classical view of poetry.

ROMANTIC CRITICS

Romantic criticism represents a sharp movement away from the concerns and values of neoclassic criticism. Whereas the neoclassic critic is concerned with the mimetic relationship of poetry to the nature or reality that it imitates and with the pragmatic relationship of poetry to its audience, the Romantic critic focuses primarily on the expressive relationship of the poet to poetry. The neoclassic critic sees poetry as an imitation of nature designed to instruct and delight; the Romantic critic sees poetry as an expression of the creative imagination. In examining poetry, the neoclassic critic turns to matters of genre, techniques, conventions, and effects of poetry; the Romantic turns back to the poet, the imagination, and the creative process. When the Romantic critic does turn to the mimetic relationship, he focuses on the organic and beneficent qualities of nature, and when he looks at the pragmatic relationship, he is especially interested in the connection between feelings and moral response.

WILLIAM WORDSWORTH

In 1798, William Wordsworth (1770-1850) published, with Samuel Taylor Coleridge, a volume of poetry titled *Lyrical Ballads*. For many literary historians, this publication is the watershed between neoclassicism and Romanticism, and the preface that Wordsworth wrote for the second edition (1800) of *Lyrical Ballads* is the manifesto of the English Romantic Movement. In this preface, Wordsworth presents definitions and descriptions of the poet, the creative process, and poetry. He also discusses, among other things, the differences between poetry and prose and the effect of poetry on its readers.

Wordsworth defines the poet as "a man speaking to men," suggesting by this phrase that the poet does not differ in kind from others. He does, however, differ in degree: He has "a more lively sensibility, . . . a greater knowledge of human nature, . . . a greater promptness to think and feel without immediate external excitement, and a greater power in expressing such thoughts and feelings as are produced in him in that manner." In short, the poet is, for Wordsworth, one who responds to life and nature with intense feelings and thoughts and is capable of expressing his feelings and thoughts poetically.

"[A]ll good poetry," Wordsworth says, "is the spontaneous overflow of powerful feelings," a definition that, at first glance, seems to be the very antithesis of the neoclassical view that poetry is the expression of restrained emotion and clear thought and the result of labor and revision. This definition of poetry is, however, sharply qualified by Wordsworth's description of the creative process. The poet, he says, does not compose poetry spontaneously upon the occasion of having an emotional experience. Rather, the emotional experience of the poet must first resolve itself into tranquillity, during which the poet reflects on his emotional experience:

> the emotion is contemplated till, by a species of reaction, the tranquility gradually disappears, and an emotion, kindred to that which was before the subject of contemplation, is gradually produced, and does itself actually exist in the mind. In this mood successful composition generally begins.

In other words, raw emotion is not enough for poetic composition. The emotion must be refined in a period of tranquillity by thoughts, which themselves are the representatives of past feelings. When the tranquillity modulates back into emotion, composition can begin.

Though Wordsworth does not make it explicit in this passage on the creative process, it can be inferred from the passage and from statements he makes in his poems that the faculty by which the poet creates poetry is the imagination. Like the other Romantics, Wordsworth exalts imagination over reason (itself exalted by the neoclassics) and assigns to it a variety of functions, which Bate sums up in his introduction to Wordsworth in *Criticism: The Major Texts*:

> We have, then, in the imagination, an ability to draw upon all the resources of the mind: to centralize and unify sense impressions, to combine them with intuitions of form and value, and with realizations won from past experience.

In *The Prelude* (1850), his long, autobiographical poem, Wordsworth says that the imagination "Is but another name for absolute power/ And clearest insight, amplitude of mind/ And Reason in her most exalted mood."

One of Wordsworth's principal aims in the preface to *Lyrical Ballads* is to explain the poetic and philosophical bases for the kind of poems he had written. The purpose, he says, "was to choose incidents and situations from common life, and to relate or describe them . . . in a selection of language really used by men." The incidents would be made interesting by "a certain coloring of imagination, whereby ordinary things should be presented to the mind in an unusual aspect" and "by tracing in them . . . the primary laws of our nature." He goes on to say that he chose to depict "[h]umble and rustic life" in

his poems because those who live in such circumstances are closer to nature and its formative and beneficial influences. Their feelings and passions reach a maturity from being "incorporated with the beautiful and permanent forms of nature," and their language is purified because they "hourly communicate with the best objects [that is, those of nature] from which the best part of language is originally derived." The effect of reading such poetry as Wordsworth has prescribed is that "the understanding of the Reader must necessarily be in some degrees enlightened, and his affections strengthened and purified." This poetic and philosophical notion—that poetry should imitate the purified language and the beautiful passions and feelings of those who live simple lives in a close relationship to nature—is known as Romantic Naturalism. Wordsworth's idea that a poetry of Romantic Naturalism will have a profound moral effect on its readers is a central tenet of Romantic poetics.

Wordsworth's poetry of "[h]umble and rustic life" is in opposition to the eighteenth century poetry that depicted a polite, urban society. His espousal of a "language really used by men" is in opposition to the language of eighteenth century poets, known as "poetic diction." Poetic diction is marked by personification, periphrasis, Latinisms, archaisms, invocations, and the like, and is based on the notion that, as Thomas Gray put it, "the language of the age is never the language of poetry." Wordsworth sought, in his poetry and in his preface, to break down the prevailing distinction between the language of poetry and the language of everyday life because he believed that an artificial poetic language prevents the poet from capturing "the essential passions of the heart." For Wordsworth, "the language of a large portion of every good poem, even of the most elevated character, must necessarily, except with reference to the metre, in no respect differ from that of good prose." This idea, in turn, leads him to the controversial notion that meter and rhyme are superadditions to the poem. They are added by the poet in order to increase the reader's pleasure and to balance the emotional excitement produced by imagery and language with the calmness produced by the regularity of meter and rhyme. This notion that meter and rhyme are superadditions to a poem conflicts, however, with the more accepted concept that all elements of a poem are essential to forming a unified whole.

Wordsworth's importance as a literary critic does not go much beyond the contribution of the preface to *Lyrical Ballads*. Nevertheless, the role that this document played in the Romantic movement and the importance that it has in the total body of Romantic criticism are great indeed.

SAMUEL TAYLOR COLERIDGE

Samuel Taylor Coleridge (1772-1834) is, by far, the greatest of the Romantic critics of poetry: He wrote more theory and practical criticism; he ranged farther across critical terrain; and he pondered critical problems more deeply than did the other Romantic critics. It is also true, however, that he is not always clear about his ideas, that some of his ideas are left incomplete, and that he borrowed some concepts from critics and philosophers, especially the Germans, without proper attribution. The fact that his literary ideas frequently move into philosophical areas also makes it difficult for the student of literature to grasp fully his literary positions. His key literary concepts appear in a variety of publications, the major ones being *Biographia Literaria* (1817) and his lectures on William Shakespeare.

Like the other Romantic critics, Coleridge is interested less in the rules and conventions of poetry than in the nature of the poet, the imagination, and the creative process. He is also deeply interested in the question of what makes a poem a poem.

Poetry for Coleridge is the product of the creative imagination of the poet. He makes this clear when he states in Chapter XIV of *Biographia Literaria* that the question "What is poetry? is so nearly the same question with, what is a poet? that the answer to the one is involved in the solution to the other." He then describes the poet, not by what he *is*, but by what he *does:*

> The poet, described in *ideal* perfection, brings the whole soul of man into activity, with the subordination of its faculties to each other, according to their relative worth and dignity. He diffuses a tone and spirit of unity, that blends, and (as it were) *fuses*, each into each, by that synthetic and magical power, to which we have exclusively appropriated the name of imagination.

Coleridge has thus moved from poetry back to the poet and then to the imagination.

Coleridge spent a great deal of critical effort in attempts to define the imagination because he felt that a concept of the imagination was central to his poetic theory. Some of his key statements, besides the one quoted above, are that the imagination is the "reconciling and mediatory power" that joins reason to sense impressions and thereby "gives birth to a system of symbols" (*Statesman's Manual*, 1816); that it is "that sublime faculty by which a great mind becomes that on which it meditates" ("Shakespeare as a Poet Generally"); and that it "reveals itself in the balance or reconciliation of opposite or discordant qualities" (*Biographia Literaria*, Chapter XIV). He also distinguishes between the primary and secondary imagination in Chapter XIII of *Biographia Literaria*. The primary imagination is "the living Power and prime Agent of all human Perception, and as a repetition in the finite mind of the eternal act of creation in the infinite I AM." By this latter phrase, he apparently means that the imagination is godlike in its ability to create. The secondary imagination, he explains, differs in degree but not in kind from the primary imagination. Essentially, Coleridge seems to say that the imagination is creative, empathetic, perceptive, harmonizing, synthesizing, symbolizing, and reconciling.

One of Coleridge's key literary concepts that has been fully embraced by modern critics is that of organic form. Although the theory is not original with Coleridge (Aristotle advocated it), he was the first important English critic to elaborate on it. In one of his Shakespeare lectures, Coleridge distinguishes between "organic" form and "mechanic" form:

> The form is mechanic, when on any given material we impress a pre-determined form, not necessarily arising out of the properties of the material; as when to a mass of wet clay we give whatever shape we wish it to retain when hardened. The organic form, on the other hand, is innate; it shapes, as it develops, itself from within, and the fulness of its development is one and the same with perfection of its outward form. Such as the life is, such is the form. ("Shakespeare's Judgment Equal to His Genius")

Nature, for Coleridge (as for Aristotle), is the model of organic form. Poetry imitates nature's organic process of giving unifying form to all of its diverse elements. A poem, for Coleridge, is like a plant, a living organism, synthesizing all of its diverse elements—imagery, rhythm, language, and so on—into a harmonious and organic whole.

Coleridge also wrote a great amount of criticism on particular poets—Dante, Shakespeare, John Donne, Milton, Wordsworth, and many others. The greater part of it, however, is on Shakespeare and Wordsworth. Much of his criticism on Wordsworth is negative. He objects (in *Biographia Literaria*) to Wordsworth's preface, in particular to what he sees as Wordsworth's attempt to present his poetic theory as applicable to all poetry rather than to a particular kind. Despite his objections, Coleridge considers that his fellow Romantic poet ranks just behind Shakespeare and Milton in greatness.

Coleridge's investigations of particular poets are almost always interesting, but his greatness as a critic lies in his contributions to the theories of the creative imagination and the organic nature of poetry.

PERCY BYSSHE SHELLEY

The poetic theories of Percy Bysshe Shelley (1792-1822) are contained, for the most part, in his essay *A Defence of Poetry* (1840), which he wrote in response to Thomas Love Peacock's satirical attack on poetry in an essay titled "The Four Ages of Poetry." Shelley's essay shows the influence of Neoplatonism combined with Romantic notions of the organic character of nature, and it bears a resemblance to Sidney's *Defence of Poesie*, especially in its defense of poetry on moral and aesthetic grounds. Although the greater part of the essay is given over to a descriptive history of poetry, it is typically Romantic in its discussion of the nature of the poet, the poetic process, the creative imagination, and the importance of sympathy and feeling in the development of the moral faculty.

Shelley's claims for the poet are very grand: "A poet participates in the eternal, the infinite, and the one." The poet unites the two vocations of legislator and prophet, not in the sense of making social laws and foretelling the future, but in the sense that the poet "beholds intensely the present as it is, . . . [and] beholds the future in the present." Hence, "[A] poem is the very image of life expressed in its eternal truth."

The faculty by which the poet discovers these Platonic laws that govern nature is not reason (which Plato championed) but imagination. Reason, for Shelley, is the "principle of analysis" that dissects, divides, enumerates, and distinguishes objects of nature, whereas imagination is the "principle of synthesis" that grasps the totality of nature in all of its organic character and perceives its value and quality. Poetry, for Shelley, is "the expression of the imagination"; it is not "produced by labour and study," as it was for the neoclassicists. The poet cannot create poetry at will, "for the mind in creation is as a fading coal," which is blown into "transitory brightness" by a power within the poet that comes and goes without warning. Even as the poet is composing, his inspiration is waning, and because inspiration is so fleeting, "the most glorious poetry . . . is probably a feeble shadow of the original conceptions of the poet." This Romantic notion—that the conception is perfect and the execution or composition is imperfect according to its distance from the conception—is the very opposite of the neoclassic notion that the poet approaches perfection through labor and revision.

The effect of poetry on the reader is, according to Shelley, morally formative, not because poetry is or should be didactic, but because it engages the reader's emotions. Shelley echoes the other Romantic critics, especially William Hazlitt, when he states that "[t]he great instrument of moral good is the imagination." The imagination—strengthened and enlarged by reading poetry—enables the reader to move away from his own selfish concerns and sympathetically identify with others, thus developing his moral faculty.

JOHN KEATS

John Keats (1795-1821) was not a professional critic nor did he set down his critical ideas about poetry in a systematic fashion, as did Wordsworth, Coleridge, and Shelley. He expressed his poetical ideas—which are profound and suggestive—sporadically in his personal letters to family and friends. In a letter concerning a personal matter, he would suddenly express his ideas about poetry, the poet, the creative imagination, and other related issues in which he was passionately interested.

Keats describes the nature of the poet to his friend Richard Woodhouse, in a letter of October 27, 1818. The poet, he says, "has no Identity"; rather, he is always "filling some other Body," that is, identifying with someone or something else with which he is poetically engaged—a character, a tree, the sun, a bird, autumn. The poet, for Keats, is like the chameleon: He changes his color to adjust to his environment. Keats distinguishes this sort of poet from "the Wordsworthian or egotistical sublime," by which he seems to mean the poet who is intent on projecting his own feelings onto other things, instead of entering into the nature of other things.

The power by which the poet is capable of sympathetically identifying with other people and things is labeled by Keats "negative capability." At its simplest, negative capability allows the poet to negate his own personality in order to identify with and understand another person or thing. The understanding, however, is not one of reason but of feeling. Keats says that negative capability is at work "when a man is capable of being in uncertainties, Mysteries, doubts, without any irritable reaching after fact & reason" (December 21 or 27, 1817). Stated another way (in the same letter): "With a great poet the sense of Beauty overcomes every other consideration."

Beauty and truth are the chief aims of art and poetry, according to Keats. He says that "[t]he excellence of every Art is its intensity, capable of making all disagreeables evaporate, from their being in close relationship with Beauty and Truth" (December 21 or 27, 1817). Another function of the imagination for Keats (besides that of negative capability) is that of apprehending beauty and translating it into truth. In a letter of November 22, 1817, he states that "What the imagination seizes as Beauty must be truth." Abstract truth—truth gained through "consequitive reasoning"—is not as valuable for Keats as truth embodied in the concrete forms of beauty and experienced with the senses and emotions. This belief that truth must be concretely experienced leads Keats to state that if poetry "is not so fine a thing as philosophy—[it is] For the same reason that an eagle is not so fine a thing as a truth" (March 19, 1819).

Several other Romantic critics deserve mention, though there is not space to describe their contributions in detail. In England William Hazlitt wrote widely on literary matters and promulgated many of the ideas that make up the Romantic theory of poetry. In Germany

A. W. von Schlegel and his brother Friedrich articulated the aims and accomplishments of German Romanticism. Edgar Allan Poe is recognized as the leading American Romantic critic, though there is substantial disagreement about the real value of his critical ideas. His most famous critical work is "The Poetic Principle" (1848), which urges that beauty, and not truth, is the proper aim of poetry.

VICTORIAN CRITICS

Criticism of poetry in the last century and a half has been extremely diverse. In the last half of the nineteenth century, it ranged from the classical, moral, and humanist interests of Matthew Arnold to the impressionistic, "art for art's sake" theories of Walter Pater and Oscar Wilde and the historical, sociological, and biographical methods of the French critics Hippolyte Taine and Charles Sainte-Beuve. The diversity has increased in the twentieth century, as critics have applied methods and terminology from a variety of other disciplines to the history and interpretation of literature. This diversity makes it difficult to identify the "great" critics of poetry in the Victorian and modern periods, but certainly two in particular stand out: Matthew Arnold and T. S. Eliot.

MATTHEW ARNOLD

Matthew Arnold (1822-1888) is the major literary critic of the last half of the nineteenth century. He was a poet, a professor of poetry at Oxford, and an inspector of schools. Furthermore, he perceived his role as critic as extending far beyond literary matters into social, educational, moral, and religious areas, so that he is, in effect, a critic of culture in a broad sense. For this reason, it is imperative to understand his ideas about culture in order to understand his ideas about poetry and criticism.

In "Sweetness and Light" (a chapter from *Culture and Anarchy*, 1869), Arnold defines culture as "a study of perfection, and of harmonious perfection, general perfection, and perfection which consists in becoming something rather than in having something, in an inward condition of the mind and spirit, not in an outward set of circumstances." In other words, culture is not, as it is often thought of today, the possession of certain knowledge or information; rather, it is a condition or habit of being that can be applied to everyday life. Arnold equates the "pursuit of perfection," which is the goal of culture, with the "pursuit of sweetness and light," metaphors for beauty and truth.

The way to culture's goal of perfection, to beauty and truth, is "to know the best which has been thought and said in the world." (Arnold repeats this phrase with some variations in different essays.) When Thomas Huxley, a scientist, accused Arnold of limiting the sources of culture to literature (Huxley believed that scientific knowledge is as effective as literary knowledge in attaining culture), Arnold responded in "Literature and Science" (1882) by stating that all literature—including scientific, social, political, as well as imaginative—contributes to the pursuit of culture. Nevertheless, Arnold goes on to say, a literary education is in fact superior to a scientific education. There is a need in life, Arnold says, for knowledge, and science satisfies this need by providing one with facts about man and nature. There is also, however, a great need to relate knowledge to "our sense for conduct" and "our sense for beauty," and this, Arnold contends, science cannot do. Literature, on the other hand, does have the power of relating new knowledge to people's senses of conduct and beauty. Arnold means that literature, because it unites the universal with the particular and because it affects the emotions as well as the intellect, can show people how to apply new ideas morally in their conduct and aesthetically in the way they perceive the world.

Arnold's most famous definition of literature is that it is "a criticism of life," a definition that he repeatedly uses in his critical works and consistently applies to poetry under his inspection. Arnold means by this phrase that poetry should address the moral question of "how to live." It should provide an ideal by which people can measure their own lives. In another famous phrase that Arnold uses in various essays, he says that great poetry is "the noble and profound application of ideas to life." The purpose of poetry, he says in "The Study of Poetry" (1880), is "to interpret life for us, to console us, to sustain us," a function that he likens to that of religion. Indeed, to an age in which religious faith had been badly shaken by the findings of science, Arnold solemnly offered poetry as a source of consolation and sustenance.

Criticism, as well as poetry, plays a central role in Arnold's concept of culture. In "The Function of Criticism at the Present Time" (1864), Arnold defines criticism as "a disinterested endeavor to learn and propagate the best that is known and thought in the world, and thus to establish a current of fresh and true ideas." Arnold is speaking here of all types of criticism, not only literary criticism, and the ideas generated by disinterested criticism will be ideas relating to all fields of knowledge and will contribute to the attainment of culture. The task in every critical endeavor, according to Arnold, is "to see the object as in itself it really is," and in evaluating new ideas the duty of the critic is "to be perpetually dissatisfied . . . while they fall short of a high and perfect ideal."

Arnold's method as a practicing critic of poetry is seen in a number of essays. The most famous—and most controversial—of these is "The Study of Poetry," an introduction to a collection of English poetry. In the essay, Arnold rejects two traditional methods of evaluating poetry: the "historic estimate," which judges a poem by its historical context, and the "personal estimate," which relies on a critic's personal taste and preferences to judge a poem. In place of these, Arnold proposes the "touchstone" method: The critic compares lines of the poem under consideration with "lines and expressions of the great masters"—Homer, Dante, Shakespeare, Milton. Such lines, which the critic should keep stored in his mind, will serve as "an infallible touchstone for detecting the presence or absence of high poetic quality, and also the degree of this quality, in all other poetry which we may place beside them."

The chief objection raised to Arnold's "touchstone" method is that it appears to place more value on the individual parts (lines) than on the interrelationship of the parts and the total design and unity of the poem. This may not, in fact, have been Arnold's intention. In other critical works, he emphasizes the importance of total design and unity. For example, in his preface to *Poems* (1853), he praises the quality of total design in poems, and he disparages "poems which seem to exist merely for the sake of single lines and passages; not for the sake of producing any total-impression." He cites Keats's *Isabella* (1820) as a poem without total design. In *Matthew Arnold: A Survey of His Poetry and Prose* (1971), Douglas Bush suggests that Arnold may have meant that "a line or two [the touchstone] may recall the texture and total character of a long poem—which he assumes that his readers know," so that in effect the critic using the touchstone method is not comparing individual lines but complete poems.

"The Study of Poetry" is also controversial in some of its judgments of English poets. In the latter half of the essay, Arnold uses the touchstone method to evaluate most of the major English poets from Chaucer to Robert Burns. In examining each poet, Arnold looks for "high seriousness," a quality he does not define but which is obviously related to his notion that poetry should be "a criticism of life." Shakespeare and Milton, in Arnold's view, are classics of English poetry because they possess "high seriousness." Chaucer, on the other hand, is not a classic of English poetry because he lacks "high seriousness." This judgment conflicts with past judgments of Chaucer (such as Dryden's), and it is all the more controversial in the light of the fact that Arnold judges Thomas Gray to be a classic poet with "high seriousness." Also controversial is Arnold's judgment that Dryden and Pope are not classics of English poetry. Instead, "they are classics of our prose" because they possess the qualities of great prose: "regularity, uniformity, precision, balance."

The survey of English poetry in "The Study of Poetry" stops with Burns (who falls short of being judged a classic), but Arnold makes judgments of later English poets in other essays, most of which can be found in the two volumes of *Essays in Criticism* (1865 and 1888). He ranks Wordsworth directly behind Shakespeare and Milton in poetical greatness because Wordsworth "deals with more of *life* than [other poets] do; he deals with *life*, as a whole, more powerfully" ("Wordsworth"). Lord Byron, in Arnold's opinion, ranks right behind Wordsworth. The strengths of Byron are his "splendid and puissant personality, . . . his astounding power and passion . . . and deep sense for what is beautiful in nature, and for what is beautiful in human action and suffering." Byron lacks, however, the "great artist's profound and patient skill in combining an action or in developing a character." This and his other faults—such as "his vulgarity, his affectation"—keep him from achieving in his poetry "a profound criticism of life" ("Byron").

Of Keats's poetry, Arnold's opinion is that it "is abundantly and enchantingly sensuous" and possesses "natural magic" equal to that of Shakespeare. He lacks, on the other hand, the "faculty of moral interpreta-

tion" and "high architectonics" (by which Arnold means the ability to create a total design) necessary for the great poet. Had Keats not died early, he might, in Arnold's view, have developed into a great poet because he undoubtedly had the "elements of high character" ("Keats"). Arnold's essay on Shelley is a review of a recent biography of the Romantic poet. Arnold rejects the biographer's unqualified veneration of Shelley and "propose[s] to mark firmly what is ridiculous and odious in . . . Shelley . . . and then to show that our former beautiful and lovable Shelley nevertheless survives." He concludes the essay by repeating his now-famous description of Shelley (first used in his essay on Byron): Shelley is "a beautiful *and ineffectual* angel, beating in the void his luminous wings in vain" ("Shelley").

Arnold's literary interests extended beyond English poetry. He also wrote about Celtic literature, the poetry of Homer, of Heinrich Heine and Johann Wolfgang von Goethe, and the works of Count Leo Tolstoy, as well as about many other authors and literary topics. Through all of his critical writings, Arnold maintained the position of the classicist, asserting the broad moral value of humane arts and letters in a world in which proponents of science, on the one hand, and proponents of the "art for art's sake" movement, on the other, were threatening to eclipse classical literary ideals.

MODERN CRITICISM: T. S. ELIOT

T. S. Eliot (1888-1965) deserves the title of "great critic" because of the range and depth of his criticism. A gifted poet and playwright who gave up his American citizenship to become a naturalized British subject, Eliot wrote on a diversity of literary topics. Because of this diversity, his critical work is very difficult to summarize. Rather than attempting to encompass all of his views regarding poetry and criticism, the following discussion presents a rough classification of his critical works and a detailed explanation of several of his key poetic concepts. If Eliot's critical works on drama and dramatists and those dealing with topics other than literature, such as culture and religion, are excluded, most of the remaining works can be classified into three groups: first, works dealing with the nature of criticism; second, works dealing with the nature of poetry; and third, works dealing with individual poets.

The first group includes such works as "The Perfect Critic" and "Imperfect Critics" (both from *The Sacred Wood*, 1920), "The Function of Criticism" (1923), and *The Use of Poetry and the Use of Criticism* (1933). One of the purposes of the latter work is to explore "the relation of criticism to poetry" from the Elizabethan age to the modern period, and it includes essays on many of the great critics of poetry. Eliot's ideas about the criticism of poetry are many and diverse, but on the whole they contributed greatly to modern formalistic or New Criticism by insisting on the primacy of the poem itself. In the introduction to *The Use of Poetry and the Use of Criticism*, Eliot states that criticism addresses two questions: "What is poetry?" and "Is this a good poem?" At a time when literary critics were often concerned with historical and biographical aspects, Eliot's statement served to remind critics that poetry itself should be the primary concern of the critic.

The second group of critical works includes such essays as "The Social Function of Poetry," "The Music of Poetry," and "The Three Voices of Poetry" (all contained in the first section of *On Poetry and Poets*, 1957). As with the first group, Eliot's range in this group is wide. Almost any aspect of poetry interests him—relatively small matters such as the use of blank verse to larger issues such as the difference between "classic" and "romantic." Probably the two most influential essays in the group are "Tradition and the Individual Talent" and "The Metaphysical Poets" (both in *Selected Essays*, 1932, 1950).

The English poets about whom Eliot writes in the third group of critical works include Andrew Marvell, Milton, Dryden, William Blake, Byron, Algernon Charles Swinburne, and William Butler Yeats, as well as many more. Especially noticeable in these works is Eliot's extensive use of quotations from the poetry to illustrate his observations. This practice is in keeping with his idea that the critic should focus on the poetry. Also noticeable are Eliot's attempts to reshape the reigning view of English poets (especially to downgrade Milton and to elevate the Metaphysical poets and Dryden). Eliot believed that one of the ends of criticism is "the correction of taste."

Several of Eliot's poetic concepts have become very important in modern poetics and therefore deserve spe-

cial attention. These concepts concern the nature of the poet and the poetic process, the nature of poetry, and the idea of tradition. Eliot developed these ideas throughout several works, the most important of which are "Tradition and the Individual Talent" and "The Metaphysical Poets."

In "Tradition and the Individual Talent" Eliot says that "[t]he poet's mind is in fact a receptacle for seizing and storing up numberless feelings, phrases, images, which remain there until all the particles which can unite to form a new compound are present together." The difference between a poet and an ordinary person, Eliot explains, is that the poet has the ability to form these chaotic elements into a unified whole:

> When a poet's mind is perfectly equipped for its work, it is constantly amalgamating disparate experience; the ordinary man's experience is chaotic, irregular, fragmentary. The latter falls in love, or reads Spinoza, and these experiences have nothing to do with each other, or with the noise of the typewriter or the smell of cooking; in the mind of the poet these experiences are always forming new wholes. ("The Metaphysical Poets")

To explain the actual creative process of composing poetry, Eliot uses a scientific analogy, which has the effect of emphasizing the objectivity and intensity of the process. He compares the creative act of composing poetry to the scientific act of forming sulphurous acid:

> When the two gases previously mentioned [oxygen and sulphur dioxide] are mixed in the presence of a filament of platinum, they form sulphurous acid. This combination takes place only if the platinum is present; nevertheless the newly formed acid contains no trace of platinum, and the platinum itself is apparently unaffected; has remained inert, neutral, and unchanged. ("Tradition and the Individual Talent")

The two gases represent the emotions and feelings and other experiences that the poet has stored up. The filament of platinum represents his mind or creative faculty, and the sulphurous acid is the poem. The objectivity of the process is stressed in the fact that the poem (the sulphurous acid) shows "no trace" of the poet's mind (the platinum) and that his mind is "unchanged" by the experience of writing the poem. Eliot further emphasizes this objectivity (called "aesthetic distance" by formalistic critics) in his statement, following the analogy that "the more perfect the artist, the more completely separate in him will be the man who suffers and the mind which creates."

Eliot calls this process of composing poetry the "process of depersonalization" because it deemphasizes the poet's personality and personal emotions. "Poetry," he states in "Tradition and the Individual Talent," "is not a turning loose of emotion, but an escape from emotion; it is not the expression of personality, but an escape from personality." This does not mean, however, that poetry for Eliot is not intense. There is intensity involved, but "it is not the 'greatness,' the intensity, of the emotions, the components, but the intensity of the artistic process, the pressure, so to speak, under which the fusion takes place, that counts." The result of such an intense artistic process is an impersonal aesthetic emotion, that is, an "emotion which has its life in the poem and not in the history of the poet." Eliot expounds on this idea of an impersonal aesthetic emotion in his essay "Hamlet and His Problems":

The only way of expressing emotion in the form of art is by finding an "objective correlative"; in other words, a set of objects, a situation, a chain of events which shall be the formula of that *particular* emotion; such that when the external facts, which must terminate in sensory experience, are given, the emotion is immediately evoked.

The ideal poet for Eliot, then, is one who keeps his creative self separate from his personal self and who creates an impersonal artistic emotion in his poetry through the "objective correlative" formula. In order to be such a poet, it is necessary for him to "surrender . . . himself . . . to something which is more valuable," that is, to tradition. Tradition, for Eliot, involves the "historical sense," that is, "a perception, not only of the pastness of the past, but of its presence." The historical sense gives the poet a feeling for the "simultaneous existence" and "simultaneous order" of all literature from Homer on, and it will make clear to him how his own work must fit into this literary tradition while at the same time expressing his "individual talent."

With regard to the English literary tradition, Eliot worked to overturn the prevailing opinion that the line of great English poets extended from Shakespeare to Milton to Wordsworth and excluded the Metaphysical poets (Donne, Marvell, and others) and the neoclassic poets, especially Dryden. (Arnold was the critic most responsible for the prevailing opinion, especially by his designation of Dryden and Pope as "classics of prose" and not of poetry, and his praise of Wordsworth, but Johnson's view that the Metaphysical poets were more "wits" than poets had stuck through the nineteenth century and contributed to the prevailing opinion.) Eliot argues that the Metaphysical poets "were the direct and normal development of the precedent age," that is the Elizabethan age, and not "a digression from the main current" of English poetry. These poets, like their Elizabethan predecessors, "possessed a mechanism of sensibility which could devour any kind of experience." They had the ability to unite thought and feeling, so that in their poetry "there is a direct sensuous apprehension of thought, or a recreation of thought into feeling." After the Metaphysical poets, "a dissociation of sensibility set in, from which we have never recovered" ("The Metaphysical Poets").

This "dissociation of sensibility"—the separation of thought and feeling in poetry—was "aggravated," Eliot says, by Milton and Dryden. Milton perfected an impassioned language but dispensed with wit, whereas Dryden developed an intellectual wit lacking an emotional element. Both were fine poets, but their followers lacked their poetic qualities and only "thought and felt by fits, unbalanced." Eliot touches on this thesis again in his essays on Milton, Dryden, and Marvell, but he does not develop it further in his essays on the Romantic poets. Nevertheless, his theory of poetic sensibility has become one of the leading theories regarding the historical development of English poetry.

Other modern critics of poetry perhaps deserve to be ranked as great critics, but it is fitting to end this essay with Eliot because he is the latest in a long line of great English critics who are also poets. It is not essential, of course, that a critic also be able to write poetry, but the fact that so many of the great English critics—from Sidney to Eliot—have also been poets has undoubtedly increased the perception, sensitivity, range, and flexibility of English criticism.

BIBLIOGRAPHY

Ashton, Rosemary. *The Life of Samuel Taylor Coleridge: A Critical Biography.* Cambridge, Mass.: Blackwell Publishers, 1996. Examines Coleridge's complex personality, from poet, critic, and thinker to feckless husband and guilt-ridden opium addict. Coleridge's life is placed within the context of both British and German Romanticism.

Baines, Paul. *The Complete Critical Guide to Alexander Pope.* New York: Routledge, 2000. An introduction that offers basic information on the author's life, contexts, and works. Outlines the major critical issues surrounding Pope's works, from the time they were written to the present.

Barfield, Owen. *What Coleridge Thought.* Middletown, Conn.: Wesleyan University Press, 1971. One of the most lucid expositions of Coleridge's philosophical thought, which is explained in its own terms rather than in its connections with other systems of thought. Emphasizes Coleridge's concept of "Polar Logic" and fully discusses such Coleridgean topics as fancy and imagination, understanding and reason. Assumes that Coleridge's later philosophy was implicit in the earlier, an assumption that has been questioned by other Coleridge scholars.

Bate, Walter Jackson. *Samuel Johnson.* New York: Harcourt Brace Jovanovich, 1979. This Pulitzer prize-winning biography has shrewd psychological assessments of Johnson's early and major poems.

Bloom, Harold, ed. *John Dryden.* New York: Chelsea House, 1987. Plays, prose, and poetry are discussed side by side in this collection of essays by leading Dryden scholars, focusing on Dryden's place in the Restoration, ideologically and poetically. Contains a chronology, a bibliography, and an index.

_____, ed. *William Wordsworth.* New York: Chelsea House, 1985. This collection of eleven previously published critical essays includes some of the most advanced and influential work on Wordsworth. Bloom's introduction is a lively and persuasive overview. Other important essays include Frederick A. Pottle's "The Eye and the Object in the Poetry of Wordsworth," Paul de Man's "Intentional Structure of the Romantic Image" (which presents an opposing view to that of Pottle), Geoffrey H. Hartman's "The Romance of Nature and the Negative Way," and M. H. Abrams's "Two Roads to Wordsworth," which examines different critical approaches.

Bond, Donald Frederic *The Spectator.* 5 vols. Oxford: Clarendon Press, 1987. This multivolume set contains writings from the original *Spectator* of Joseph Addison and Richard Steele, with an introduction and notes by Donald F. Bond. It includes writings that spanned the length of the publication, which began in March, 1711, and continued intermittently until in December, 1714.

Boswell, James. *Life of Johnson.* Edited by R. W. Chapman. New York: Oxford University Press, 1998. A massive and exhaustive edition of Boswell's 1791 biography. Boswell has littered the book with countless quotes including Johnson's definitions of oats and lexicographer, his love for his cat Hodge, as well as thousands of bons, and mals, mots.

Cameron, Kenneth Neill. *Shelley: The Golden Years.* Cambridge, Mass.: Harvard University Press, 1974. This major, lengthy work of biography and criticism covers the later period of Shelley's life, from 1814 to 1822, when all of his great poetry was written. Cameron examines Shelley's prose works and gives crystal-clear readings of all the major poems. He views Shelley's work in a historical context, and this acts as a necessary counterweight to Wasserman's philosophical readings.

Carritt, E. F. "Addison, Kant, and Wordsworth." *Essays and Studies* 22 (1937): 26-36. This landmark study reveals Addison's anticipation of the succeeding era of poets. Shows how Immanuel Kant, often connected with the first Romantic generation in England, was influenced by Addison and how Samuel Taylor Coleridge is the catalyst between Kant and William Wordsworth.

Christensen, Allan C. *The Challenge of Keats: Bicentenary Essays, 1795-1995.* Atlanta, Ga.: Rodopi, 2000. Contributors to this volume reexamine some of the criticisms and exaltations of Keats in order to find a new analysis of his achievement. Delivers an appraisal of the historical and cultural contexts of Keats's work and an in-depth discussion of the influences and relationships among Keats and other poets.

Damrosch, Leopold, Jr. "The Significance of Addison's Criticism." *Studies in English Literature* 19 (1979): 421-430. Shows Addison's humanistic viewpoint and concentrates on Addison's own view of the critic as an aid to the reader for purposes of clarification, rather than the deviser of meaning for a text.

Donoghue, Denis. *Words Alone: The Poet, T. S. Eliot.* New Haven, Conn.: Yale University Press, 2000. A wide-ranging critical examination in the form of an intellectual memoir, and an illuminating account of Donoghue's engagement with the works of Eliot. Includes bibliographical references and an index.

Evert, Walter H. *Aesthetic and Myth in the Poetry of Keats.* Princeton, N.J.: Princeton University Press, 1965. An important and frequently cited study of Keats's aesthetic ideas and his use of a mythic structure to express them. Argues persuasively that the Greek myth of Apollo gave Keats a vision of human life operating in harmony with the cycle of life and growth in nature. The longest discussion is of *Endymion*, but Evert also provides illuminating readings of most of the other major poems.

Gelber, Michael Werth. *The Just and the Lively: The Literary Criticism of John Dryden.* Manchester, England: Manchester University Press, 1999. Gelber provides a complete study of Dryden's criticism. Through a detailed reading of each of Dryden's essays, the book explains and illustrates the unity and the development of his thought.

Greene, Donald. *Samuel Johnson.* 2d ed. Boston: Twayne, 1989. This updated biography offers a vigorous summing-up of Johnson's poetic genius. A solid introduction to the life and thought.

Levi, Peter. *Horace: A Life.* New York: Routledge, 1998. Biography of the poet, intended for general readers with little understanding of classical life or literature. Emphasizes the personal relationships that inspired his poetry; provides insight into the historical events that shaped Horace's thought. Offers close textual analysis of key works, including an extensive discussion of *Ars Poetica*.

Machann, Clinton. *Matthew Arnold: A Literary Life.* New York: St. Martin's Press, 1998. This study is a succinct and well-articulated exposition of Arnold's intellectual and literary concerns, spanning his career in chronological chapters. Emphasizes Arnold's achievement as an essayist: His ethical, interpretive, and instructional concerns are given full play, and due allowance is made for both the scope and limitations of his vision.

Mazzeno, Laurence W. *Matthew Arnold: The Critical Legacy.* Rochester, N.Y.: Camden House, 1999. Mazzeno surveys the critical response to Arnold. Resembling an annotated bibliography in that it treats its material item by item, this is a book for persons wanting to acquaint themselves with the scholarship on Arnold.

Murray, Chris, ed. *Encyclopedia of Literary Criticism.* 2 vols. Chicago, Ill.: Fitzroy Dearborn, 1999. Based on Salem Press's four-volume *Critical Survey of Literary Theory* (1987), this indispensable reference expands on the original publication, adding 117 new entries. It covers more than 250 world critics through the ages in lengthy essays that survey their lives, introduce their literary theory, and list both primary and secondary works. Articles on concepts, chronological periods, and movements range from ancient times to the present and are worldwide in scope. Copious finding aids (alphabetized, chronological, and categorized lists) and a thorough subject index make the wealth of information completely accessible to both students and scholars.

Noyes, Russell. *William Wordsworth.* New York: Twayne, 1971. Several short introductory studies of Wordsworth exist, and this is one of the best. Noyes possesses a deep understanding of Wordsworth, and his elegant prose gets to the heart of the poetry. The book is arranged chronologically to show Wordsworth's development, and Noyes smoothly integrates biographical information with literary analysis. Includes a chronology and an annotated bibliography.

Pulos, C. E. *The Deep Truth: A Study of Shelley's Scepticism.* Lincoln: University of Nebraska Press, 1954. This brief volume can still be recommended as one of the best introductions to Shelley's philosophical thought. Pulos reads Shelley in the light of the skeptical tradition, and this acts as a corrective to studies which may have overemphasized Shelley's Platonism. Written when it was still necessary to rescue Shelley from charges of incoherence, Pulos shows that apparent inconsistencies in Shelley's thought can be attributed to his refusal to be dogmatic and to his attempt to balance idealism and empiricism.

Schuchard, Ronald. *Eliot's Dark Angel: Intersections of Life and Art*. New York: Oxford University Press, 1999. A critical study demonstrating how Eliot's personal voice works through the sordid, the bawdy, the blasphemous, and the horrific to create a unique moral world. Schuchard works against conventional attitudes toward Eliot's intellectual and spiritual development by showing how early and consistently his classical and religious sensibility manifests itself in his poetry and criticism.

Weinbrot, Howard. *Alexander Pope and the Traditions of Formal Verse Satire*. Princeton, N.J.: Princeton University Press, 1982. Pope's greatest achievements as a poet were in the genre of satire, and he and his contemporaries were very aware of the rich satiric traditions bequeathed them by such classical predecessors as Horace, Juvenal, and Persius. Weinbrot thoroughly examines these traditions and considers their influence on Pope and the satiric enterprise in general in early eighteenth century England.

Wellek, René. *A History of Modern Criticism: 1750-1950*. 8 vols. New Haven, Conn.: Yale University Press, 1992. This work is a behemoth and still considered a standard history of literary criticism. Wellek conceives of literary study as comprising three areas: criticism, theory, and history. His volumes cover the later eighteenth century; the Romantic age; the "age of transition"; the later nineteenth century; the first half of the twentieth century in England; the first half of the twentieth century in America; German, Russian, and Eastern European criticism in the first half of the twentieth century; and French, Spanish, and Italian criticism in the same period.

Michael L. Storey

ARCHETYPAL AND PSYCHOLOGICAL CRITICISM

Historically, an archetypal approach to poetry is derived from Sir James Frazer's work in comparative anthropology, *The Golden Bough* (1890-1915), and from the depth psychology of Carl G. Jung. Frazer discovered certain repetitive cultural patterns which transcended time and place appearing in widely different myths and literatures. Jung posited the existence of a collective unconscious within each individual, a racial memory which held a variety of archetypes. The archetypes or recurrent patterns and images had to do with birth, death, rebirth, marriage, childhood, old men, magnanimous mothers, heroes and villains, male and female, love and revenge, and countless others. A type of person, a type of action, a type of relationship were so embedded within an individual's history that any new appearance was imbued with the force and richness of every past occurrence. When literature possesses such archetypes, its potency is magnified.

An archetypal critic of poetry can employ Jungian psychology as an extraliterary body of knowledge, in contrast to the archetypal criticism represented by Northrop Frye, in which archetypes do not refer to anything outside literature but to a larger unifying category within literature itself. Even though the term "archetypal" is relevant to both Jung and Frye, their critical intentions differ. A Jungian approach to poetry seeks to wrest meaning from the poem by referring specific images, persons, and patterns to broader, richer archetypes. A Frye approach assumes that there is a totality of structure to literature represented by a variety of common literary archetypes. It is the critic's job to connect individual works to the total structure of literature by way of the recognition of archetypes. Thus, one archetypal approach, Jungian, involves content and meaning, and the other, derived from Frye, involves systematic literary form.

It is only the Jungian variety of archetypal criticism that has relevance for a distinctively "psychological" approach to literature. A Jungian archetype is an inherited racial pattern or disposition residing in a layer of the unconscious which all persons share. It is brought to light by the poet's imaginative transformation of the archetype into a symbol, a symbol which appears in the poem. All depth psychologies, which postulate the existence of an unconscious, are predicated on the notion that a symbol emerging from an unconscious level may manifest itself in a poem. Freudians, however, do not interpret man's psychological base as the collective unconscious; their symbols emerge from the personal unconscious and therefore have no connection with archetypes. Within the psychoanalytic group, there are a number of schools and therefore a number of psychological approaches to poetry. After discussing the Jungian approach (which is both archetypal and psychological), Frye's approach, and the varieties of psychoanalytic approaches, and the phenomenological approach, which owes nothing to archetype or symbol, will be discussed.

A JUNGIAN APPROACH TO POETRY

Carl G. Jung deals specifically with literature in the following essays: "The Type Problem in Poetry," "The Phenomenology of the Spirit in Fairytales," "On the Relation of Analytical Psychology to Poetry," and "Psychology and Literature." What ties Jung's discussion of literature to psychology is the symbol. The inexplicable part of the symbol is, according to Jung, a manifestation of certain "inherited" structural elements of the human psyche. These elements or "archetypes" are revealed in dreams, visions, or fantasies and are analogous to the figures one finds in mythology, sagas, and fairytales.

In "Psychology and Literature," Jung mentions those "visionary artists" who seem to allow us "a glimpse into the unfathomed abyss of what has not yet become." Beyond Jung's specific focus on symbol as revealed in literature as a basis for certain hypotheses and finally for an entire depth psychology which may be applied in turn to literature itself, Jung's study of the nature of symbol gives him an especially perceptive understanding of the nature of literature. Jung has no concern for the specific form, the presentation of symbols in literature; it is not possible to distinguish the symbolic processes of the poet from those of anyone else. The symbolic richness of a work as illuminated by the Jungian approach, therefore, does not itself make the work successful. A Jungian methodology, however, can be said to reinforce the notion of a symbolic unity of a work in the sense that it can make explicit certain image-patterns which may be obscure.

The Freudian attacks upon Jung's view of art are strident and somewhat muddled. Frederick Crews believes that invoking the Jungian system is contradictory—a view presented at length in Edward Glover's *Freud or Jung* (1950). For Jung, art represents necessary contact with the personal unconscious, as in the case of psychological art, and with the collective unconscious, as in the case of visionary art. While Sigmund Freud's artist is a man who turns from the real world to a fantasy life that permits him to express his erotic wishes, Jung's artist is not driven to art because of such unfulfilled desires but achieves his art through a natural encountering of energies existing on two levels of the unconscious and through a manifestation of archetypal energy by means of unique symbols.

With Freud, no universal, inherited archetypes exist; therefore no continuum of comparable symbols can be traced in literature except those that refer to the personal unconscious and specifically to repressed energy therein. Symbols in Freud's view represent instinctual needs and are always defined within a limited model of the human personality—one in which no real growth beyond childhood takes place. On the other hand, Jung's consideration of archetype and symbol as emerging from a nonpathological relationship between consciousness and two levels of the unconscious goes beyond Freud's notion that all art is the sublimation of repressed drives.

The Jungian approach has been criticized for reducing the artist to a mere instrument of the archetype. This criticism, however, is based on a confusion between the archetype and the symbol, the observable image representing the archetype; it is an image which cannot be fully grasped and which does not fully realize the archetype. The archetype may be considered autonomous, since it does not depend on the conscious mind. The symbol that the imagination grasps, however, is manifested in accord with the volitions of the conscious mind. Actual pictorial and verbal images owe their aesthetic aspects not to the uncontrollable forces of the archetype but to the forming disposition of the conscious mind. A Jungian approach to literature casts light on the symbolic aura of a literary work as well as on the creative process itself. Such revelation in turn, from a psychological view, acquaints us with unconscious levels that we ourselves cannot reach and encourages a continuation of our own growth. As in Norman Holland's reader-response approach, the Jungian critic-reader possesses a personality which develops through literature, although the literary text in the Jungian view is certainly a repository for symbols which transcend the personal.

A JUNGIAN APPROACH TO "THE SICK ROSE" BY BLAKE

> O Rose, thou art sick!
> The invisible worm
> That flies in the night,
> In the howling storm,
>
> Has found out thy bed
> Of crimson joy,
> And his dark secret love
> Does thy life destroy.

The design accompanying the poem pictures the worm in human form. Two other human figures are pictured in lamenting postures. A Jungian interpretation of this poem brings in archetypes of Anima and Animus and Shadow. In Jung's view, the human male must assimilate his contrasexual self, his female Anima, and the human female must assimilate her contrasexual self, her male Animus. The totally individuated person is androgynous on the psychic level and is able to utilize energies from male and female contrasexual portions of the psyche. In this poem, the worm is the rose's Animus and she is his Anima. Both are clearly divided, obdurate in their own sexual identities. Divided so, there is no mutual sexual interaction, no sexual dynamic. Instead, the rose has a "bed of crimson joy" which obviously must have been hidden, since the worm has to journey to find it. The Shadow archetype is formed in the personal unconscious by repressed desires. In this poem, the rose has clearly repressed sexual desire since she hides from her male counterpart and thus allows him but one entrance—as a ravager. His love is dark and secret from the perspective of the rose. He is indeed a shadow figure emerging from the night, a shadow of the rose's own unconscious.

NORTHROP FRYE'S ARCHETYPAL CRITICISM

Frye's archetypes connect "one poem with another and thereby [help] to unify and integrate our literary experience" (*Anatomy of Criticism*, 1957). Literature, in Frye's view, is an expression of man's imaginative transformation of his experiences. Ritual and myth were the first creative expression, beginning as stories about a god and developing into "a structural principle of storytelling" (*The Educated Imagination*, 1964). Essential mythic patterns or archetypes manifested themselves in literature. Writers in various periods drew upon these archetypes, modifying them in accordance with the conventions of their own day and the force of their own personalities.

The archetypal literary critic views the entire body of literature as a self-contained universe of these archetypes, an autonomous and self-perpetuating universe which is not effectively interpreted by extraliterary analogues. Frye believes that by confining criticism to an exploration of essential archetypes recurring throughout literature, he is developing a "science" of literary criticism, a science which recognizes that literature, like all art, is self-referential and that the function of criticism is to bring past imaginative transformations of human experiences into the present and to explore the parameters of present transformations. According to Frye, the critic is scientific in his study of literature, although his mission is not to proclaim literature as science but to make man's imaginative transformations of his experience, his literature, "a part of the emancipated and humane community of culture."

Frye discerned four basic types of imaginative transformations of experience in literature. These types first developed as mythic patterns expressing man's attempt to humanize the world around him. The imagination fuses the rhythms of human life with the cycle of nature and then invests the whole with variable emotional import. The fused natural-human cycle is one in which a youthful spring declines into winter and death. Frye then relates literature to the following mythic structure: Romance is synonymous with dawn, spring, and birth; comedy is synonymous with the zenith, summer, and marriage; tragedy is synonymous with sunset, autumn, and death; satire is synonymous with darkness, winter, and dissolution.

Frye defines commentary as "the translating of as much as possible of a poem's meaning into discursive meaning" ("Literary Criticism"). Such allegorical commentary, however, is not the aim of *criticism*, which, in Frye's view, is to identify the poem. Like a cultural anthropologist, the literary critic places the poem within its proper literary context. The first context is the total canon produced by the poet under consideration. The second context is historical. For example, John Keats's poetry must be understood within the broader context of Romanticism. Beyond considering the poet's historical context, the critic must consider the genre. Tragedy, Frye says, is a "kind of literary structure," a genre exemplified throughout literary history. The critic must also pay attention to the allusions within the poem itself. John Milton's "Lycidas" for example, reveals historical ties both in its form—pastoral elegy—and in its imagery. These ties are within literature itself. Allusions in a poem by Milton are to a poem by Vergil.

Poems in Frye's Romantic mode possess a vision of the heroic, either religious or secular, with which the poet himself is identified. Gerard Manley Hopkins's "The Windhover" presents a view of Jesus as hero, while Walt Whitman's *Passage to India* (1871) presents the poet as hero. The poet of the romantic mode seeks the imaginative transformation of the natural world, as do Andrew Marvell in "The Garden" and William Butler Yeats in "Sailing to Byzantium." The poets in the comic mode, however, are satisfied with the world as it is, as in Keats's major odes. The tragic mode involves loss and reconciliation through some effort to make sense out of loss, as in Milton's "Lycidas," Percy Bysshe Shelley's *Adonais* (1821), and Hopkins's "The Wreck of the *Deutschland*." The ironic poet does not achieve imaginative transformation of the world through supernatural help but rather achieves a vision of a shattered world. Emily Dickinson's poetry, T. S. Eliot's *The Waste Land* (1922), and Robert Frost's "Stopping by Woods on a Snowy Evening" are examples.

In Frye's criticism, mythic images were the first and clearest expressions of a relationship between man and his world. Literature is thus a "direct descendant of mythology," and biblical and classical mythologies are central myths in Western literature. What the poetry critic of archetypal persuasion ultimately does is to explore archetypal connections, recurrent patterns, in literature. As criticism continues to explore the structure of literature rather than its content, it eventually encompasses literature as a whole as its content. Once this is achieved—when criticism has a hold on literature as a whole—questions regarding the purpose of literature, its relationship to society, and its connections with discursive literature can be tackled.

Frye has been criticized for ignoring the critic's task of evaluation, for separating literature from life, for ignoring the individuality of a work by emphasizing its archetypal relations with other literature, and for creating, in *Anatomy of Criticism*, a literary work rather than a critical theory which has practical applications. Frye is criticized for assuming that literary discourse and poetic vision are unique and separable from all modes of "extraliterary" thought and discourse. Frye's views here are traced to the German idealist tradition, in which the words of the poet are somehow autonomous, free of referential meaning. Frye's view of literature is criticized because literature is seen as the ultimate goal of culture, as superior to the objective world because it transcends it by way of the imagination. The liberally educated person has replaced an unsatisfying world with its imaginative transformation—literature. What is celebrated in Frye "is a fantastical, utopian alternative to the perception of a degraded social existence: a human discoursing free of all contingency, independent of all external forces, a discoursing empowered by unconditioned human desire" (Frank Lentricchia).

A FRYE APPROACH TO "THE SICK ROSE"

In Frye's essay "Blake's Treatment of the Archetype," he comments on William Blake's powerfully integrated theory of art and of the unity of symbol and archetype in Blake's work. Frye places Blake in the anagogic phase of symbolic meaning, in which the total ritual of man, the total dream of man is represented. Blake's "The Sick Rose" is interlocked with Blake's entire canon; in itself it re-creates the "total form of verbal expression" of Blake's work ("Levels of Meaning in Literature"). Blake's symbols are anagogic symbols, symbols which turn outward toward the macrocosm of Blake's entire myth and inward toward any individual

work (in this case "The Sick Rose") which expresses the unity of desire and reality, of dream and ritual.

Only religious myths have achieved this combination of personal dream or desire and reality or ritual. Romance, a phase just below the anagogic phase, reflects a conflict rather than a unity of desire and reality. It also employs archetypes which do not have a limitless range of reference as do the "monads" of the anagogic phase. If "The Sick Rose" is placed within a mythical rather than anagogic phase of symbolic meaning, the rose and the worm would have correspondences to other roses and worms in literature but would not be true representations of the visionary apocalyptic kind of poetry that Blake's is. The location of the poem within Frye's anatomy depends upon a proper location of Blake's entire work within that anatomy. All the richness of the proper fit can be brought to bear on "The Sick Rose." Thus, finding the proper niche for the poem rather than interpreting it as a unique, unconnected entity is the task of Frye's critical anthropologist.

PSYCHOANALYTIC APPROACHES TO POETRY: FREUD

Sigmund Freud's views of the relationship between art and psychoanalysis were presented in his "Delusion and Dreams in Jensen's *Gradiva*" and in "The Relationship of the Poet to Daydreaming." The forbidden wishes of dream, associated with the psychosexual stages (oral, anal, phallic, and genital), appear in the literary work but are disguised by distracting aspects of aesthetic form. The superegos of both reader and author are circumvented, and art serves to release unconscious forces which might otherwise overwhelm the ego. The critic's job is to delve below the surface of a distracting literary facade and point out the lurking fantasies. Freud himself began, in his book on Leonardo da Vinci, a stage of psychoanalytic criticism which has been termed "genetic reductionism," or the discussion of a work in terms of the author's neurosis.

Genetic reductionism has been and remains a primary focus of psychoanalytic criticism in spite of a general recognition that the danger for psychoanalysis is the lure of a simplistic and mechanistic interpretation. The dispute here is between those who hold that literature is autonomous, existing independently of a creator's emotional disposition, and those who hold that a psychoanalytic critic can "show how a writer's public intention was evidently deflected by a private obsession" (Frederick Crews). A psychoanalytic examination of the author's wishes and anxieties, in the view of antipsychoanalytic criticism, ignores the variety and ontology of literature. Crews argues, nevertheless, that there does exist a certain range of problems which psychoanalytic assumptions illuminate.

Freud also initiated a psychoanalytic interpretation of particular characters in his work on Wilhelm Jensen's _Gradiva_ (1918) and in his discussion of oedipal complexes displayed by certain characters in Sophocles' _Oedipus Tyrannus_ (c. 429 B.C.) and William Shakespeare's _Hamlet_ (c. 1600-1601). While most contemporary psychoanalytic critics deplore genetic reductionism, there is debate regarding the treatment of characters as real people. Critics on one side of the spectrum tend to put a character on the analyst's couch, talk about the character's childhood, and totally neglect other aspects of the literary work. Opposing critics contend that while readers do indeed experience characters as human beings, the critic must use psychoanalysis so as to understand fully the character in relation to other aspects of the work.

In Freud's view, literature was like dream—a symbolic expression of the unconscious whose original meaning could be interpreted. This interest in the relationship between the writer and his work, in the creative process itself and its importance in interpreting a work, remains an interest of contemporary psychoanalysts and psychoanalytic critics. Freud's original view of creativity has been refashioned in various ways, and psychoanalytic critics now fall into various camps. Freud's view of the work of literature as a product of the author's sublimated desires has been challenged by an emphasis upon the literary work as "the potential space between the individual and the environment," by an emphasis upon the reader whose own "identity theme" fashions meaning from a work of art, and by an emphasis on preconscious and conscious involvement with literary creation (Donald W. Winnicott). These views have been termed, respectively, Object-Relations, Reader-Response (based on the work of Norman Holland), and Ego Psychology. The psychoanalyst Jacques Lacan has also created a unique approach to literature.

A FREUDIAN APPROACH TO "THE SICK ROSE"

The focus in this approach is immediately upon the poet. The question is: What "dark secret" repressed by the poet has found release in this poem? The poem is a mere symptom of the poet's neurotic desires. The rose can be viewed as a female whose "bed of crimson joy" is "found out." This is no healthy, natural sexual act, however, because the "worm" or phallus "flies in the night," in a "howling storm," and destroys his beloved with "his dark secret love." At the root of the poem, therefore, is the incestuous desire of the poet. The secret love of the poet is his mother.

EGO PSYCHOLOGY

Freud's view of literature-as-symptom emerging from the id is modified by ego psychologists who recognize creativity as a function of the ego. For the ego psychologists, literature in the service of the ego reflects the ego's mission of mediating between self and others, between id and super-ego. Symbols from the id are therefore shaped in literature so as to be communicable beyond the intrapsychic level. The movement in ego psychology is away from literature as raw wish fulfillment of the author and toward the literary text as a manifestation of id instinct and ego-monitoring. Literary critics utilizing ego psychology seek in the text not the disguised wish or wishes of the author but their transformation by the ego in the direction of something beyond the personality of the author, something of thematic import, communicable and succeeding or not succeeding depending upon the author's gifts or skills.

The ego psychoanalyst analyzing poetry emphasizes ego functions rather than id impulses. In what ways, this critic asks, does the poem display the ego's assertion of control by allowing repressed instincts an outlet? A discovery of what instincts are latent does not lead the critic into the entire poem, but a study of the poem as a manifestation of an ego directing the release of repressed instincts does.

AN EGO PSYCHOLOGIST'S APPROACH TO "THE SICK ROSE"

For the critic applying the theories of ego psychology, incest may remain the repressed desire of the poem, but the ways in which the conscious ego expresses that hidden desire in the form of the poem itself is the proper subject matter of the critic. The poet distances himself from the poem by adopting a censorious tone. The directness and clarity of poetic style also reveal the wise perceptiveness of the poet with regard to the sexual plight of rose and worm. Thus, both tone and style point to the ego's mastery over a repressed desire of the id, and a search for such ego mastery results in an analysis of the poem. The poet's perceptiveness does not lie in the core fantasy of incest but in his view of love which must be invisible, which must emerge only at night. The poet's perceptiveness lies in his understanding that a covert sexuality injures and ultimately destroys both sexual partners. His censoriousness lies in his view that such clandestine sexuality is "unethical," that it works against humanity and the individual human life. The instinctual base remains incest but it has been controlled by the ego's fashioning of the poem, making the poem something other than the wish which inspired it.

READER-RESPONSE CRITICISM

Norman Holland, in *The Dynamics of Literary Response* (1968), emphasizes the instinctual drives of the id rather than the monitoring, controlling powers of the ego, although, unlike early Freudian interpreters of literature, he posits an ego which mediates between the id and the superego and whose mediation is the form of the work itself. The form of a literary work is indeed comparable to the ego defenses against the assault of the id, but it is this assault which is the hidden, determining root of the work. A core fantasy is the base of every literary work and the writer, through form, defends against it, tries to shape it in the direction of redeemable social, moral, and intellectual value. The eye of the critic, in Holland's view, is on the core fantasy, on the id, while the eye of the ego psychologist-critic is on the ego's manipulation of the id through literary form. The core fantasy critic seeks out the core fantasy and demonstrates the author's artistry in shaping and disguising it. The reader accepts both the core fantasy, which he or she may share, and the devices employed to contain the fantasy. Thus, the reader achieves pleasure by possession of the fantasy as well as by having it controlled. The reader, in the view of the ego psychologist-critic, attains plea-sure primarily through the pattern of ego control expressed in the literary work.

In Holland's later work (*Poems in Persons*, 1973, and *Five Readers Reading*, 1975), he places the pertinent core fantasy in the mind of the reader rather than in the text. Readers extract meaning from the text in accordance with their "identity themes." Readers may be directed by their own desires to seek such themes in the texts they read. Finding them, readers may deal with them as they do in their own lives. They may also attend the author in transforming a core fantasy into something socially acceptable or intellectually significant. Holland believes that through the literary text the readers confront themselves, engaging in acts of self-discovery by analyzing what they as readers have said about a text. Throughout the three faces of psychoanalysis that Holland identifies—psychology of the unconscious (id), of the ego, and of the self—readers have always been structuring the text by means of their own intentions. A realization of this fact enables readers to make use of literature as an opportunity to gain self-knowledge.

A critical approach to poetry based on Holland's later work would begin with a description of the critic-reader's own responses to the poem. These responses, determined by the critic-reader's "identity theme," direct an analysis of the poem. A dialectic then takes place between the objective reality of the poem, a common store of shareable realities, and the critic.

A READER-RESPONSE CRITIC'S APPROACH TO "THE SICK ROSE"

The reader-response critic approaches the poem by focusing on those personal connections made in the poem. Such an interpretation is not necessarily the same thing as a literal interpretation, for example, that the poem is about the perils of gardening. From the reader-response view, this poem would be seen as a poem only about gardening by a gardener. It is quite possible in the first line of the poem, "O Rose, thou art sick," for a reader to think of someone named Rose, perhaps a mother or a sister or a lover, who was or is or may be sick. The "invisible worm" becomes a disease, such as cancer, that has struck the reader-critic's beloved suddenly, perhaps in the full bloom of life, in bed of "crimson joy." Now, this cancer slowly destroys the beloved.

Given this personal reading, what can the poem do to assert its own existence? The reader-critic must first be willing to entertain the notion that perhaps the poem is not about Rose's bout with cancer. The poet has used the word "love." The poem asserts itself, if given a chance, by its words, and the word here is "love." This "love" "flies in the night" "in the howling storm"—it emerges from Nature. Thus, in spite of the apparent ludicrousness of such a subjective beginning, the reader-critic is led toward an acceptance of this "love" as natural. It is in the nature of things to die, or to love sexually. Neither death nor sexuality can be repressed wisely. In this instance, the path of subjectivity is modified by the poem itself. As this dialectic continues, the original subjectivity of the reader-critic is modified, and the interpretation becomes more "objective" though determined by the identity theme of the reader-critic. What the poem is connects with what the reader is and the result is a thoroughly human form of comprehension.

OBJECT-RELATIONS THEORY

Object-relations theory does not hold, as do traditional psychological and ego psychological theories, that a literary work is the product of psychic conflict. It holds, rather, that a literary work is the place where the writer's wishes and the culture around him meet. Rather than emphasizing the literary work as narcissistic wish fulfillment, object-relations critics emphasize those aspects of a literary work which are not the author's self, which lead toward a world outside the writer. This outside world of convention and tradition is transformed by the writer, he having accepted what is outside his own self. The literary work as an object is an extension of the writer somewhat as a teddy bear is an extension of a child. Both teddy bear and literary work are invested with illusions; yet they are objects in the world. In the case of the child, the teddy bear is something like the mother's breast, although significantly it is another object. Similarly, the literary work is wish fulfillment and yet an object which is not pure wish fulfillment but a place where wishes and world meet, an object representing a "collective love affair with the world."

A critical approach to poetry based on an object-relations theory would not focus on the poem as an expression of intrapsychic conflict but as the ground in which

the poet's wishes and the outside world meet. In what ways does the poem signify what the internal desires of the poet are? In what ways does it stand as a transformation of those desires into what is outside the poet? The meeting of internal and external is the poem.

AN OBJECT-RELATIONS CRITIC'S APPROACH TO "THE SICK ROSE"

The object-relations critic views the poem as a meeting ground of the poet's fantasies and the surrounding environment—in this case, late eighteenth century England. If incest is on the unconscious mind of the poet, he has presented it as nothing more specific than "dark secret love," a phrase that has meaning in the context of an England in which hypocrisy with regard to sexuality was increasing. If the poet were really expressing a desire to unite sexually with his mother, then the poem would serve as an illusionary connection between himself and his mother. The poem as object, however, is clearly a transitional object rather than a complete illusion of the poet. The poem is a transition between the poet's desire for uncensored sexuality and the moral prohibitions against sexuality that were prevalent in the poet's day.

JACQUES LACAN

Lacanian psychoanalysis once again resurrects the sole supremacy of the id in the creative process. Indeed, the unconscious itself is structured as a language, and therefore both the conscious and the unconscious are identically rooted. Literary discourse, like ordinary discourse, is symbolical and subjective. Rather than the id being a source of instinctual drives which appear disguised in literature, specifically in the language of literature, the Lacanian id is a reservoir of words which determine perceptions.

Lacanian literary interpretation depends upon tracing literary language to a constitutive language of the unconscious. It depends upon relating significant words in the literary text to words signified in the unconscious. The unconscious is structured not according to innate laws but originally according to the image of another, someone whom the child is dependent upon (usually the mother). This desire to remain secure is fulfilled when the child constructs his unconscious in accordance with the significant other. The "discourse" of the other becomes the discourse of the child's unconscious, which is fictional insofar as it is not the child's but another's.

In Lacan's view, the ego is composed of a *moi*, which is unconscious, overriding the other but determined by it, and the *je*, which is identified with spoken language and culture. The discourse of the *moi* permeates the discourse of the *je*. The symbolic, subjective *moi* permeates the apparent logical discourse of the *je*. The Lacanian literary critic seeks to go from the discourse of the *je* to the discourse of the *moi*, from a symbolical consciousness to a symbolical unconsciousness. The discourse of the *moi*, of the unconscious, is weakly and elusively manifest in the surface of the literary text. Both signifiers and signifieds are available in the surface of the text, and the act of literary interpretation attempts to reconstruct, wherever possible, the connection between signifiers and signifieds. It is an act which seeks to uncover what unconscious desires determine the details of the literary text.

A LACANIAN APPROACH TO "THE SICK ROSE"

A Lacanian interpretation attempts to break through the language of the *je* and reach the symbolical unconscious of the *moi*. The literal language of the *je* in this poem has to do with gardening, with the destruction of a rose by a worm which is invisible to the naked eye. When readers probe more deeply, they discover that the poem is really "talking" about human sexuality. The poet, Blake, clearly reveals his symbolic intent in his depiction of human figures in the design accompanying the poem. A Lacanian analysis probes below the level of the language of the *je* in poems apparently not symbolical and not intended to be symbolical by the poet, whose surface language seems to mean no more than it says. The "invisible worm" as a phallus signifies a flaccid phallus. The erect, firm phallus *lies* not *flies* in the night. The "dark secret love" cannot be consummated with the flaccid phallus and thus the *moi*, formed by a desire to please the mother, describes in this poem the fulfillment in words of a desire the reality of which the words themselves belie.

PSYCHOANALYTIC APPROACHES: CRITICAL OVERVIEW

Alan Roland and Frederick Crews, among others, have provided criticism of various psychoanalytic approaches to literature. Roland objects to the correlation of literary work and daydream. The literary work, in his view, goes far beyond the author's fantasies and the imagery of dream. Poetic metaphor and the structure of paradox are essential components of the literary work but not of dream. According to Roland, literary form must be freed from the notion that it is synonymous with the ego's defenses. Defense is viewed as only part of form. Object-relations critics do not limit the author's fantasies to those of a psychosexual stage, but they fail, in Roland's view, to integrate their exploration of fantasies with what the work may mean on its highest level. In opposition to Holland's view of the reader, Roland feels that, besides a core fantasy, a literary work possesses an abstract meaning, a total vision formally created. The relationship between these two levels should be described by the critic. In Roland's view, the core fantasy within the reader's mind is apparently affected by the critic's efforts.

Frederick Crews sees as reductionist the views that Holland expresses in *The Dynamics of Literary Response*, although he admits that Holland is sensitive to literary form and very cautious about making "armchair diagnosis of authors." Holland's reductionism lies in his view of literature as subterfuge for forbidden thoughts. Crews also maintains that no one goes to criticism to discover the "identity theme" of the critic but rather to learn more about literature as a meaning-creating enterprise.

In the final analysis, according to Crews, Holland's focus on the reader is yet another example of academic objectivity being attacked by subjectivists, by those who argue that the interpretation of literature is a private affair. Crews finds no real remedy for contemporary psychoanalytic criticism, not even ego psychology. Eventually, all psychoanalytic critics realize that their interpretations say more about themselves than about the text, that "they have reduced literature to the rigid and narrow outlines of their own personalities." A psychoanalytic critic, according to Crews, must bear in mind that his method is reductive and that there are many aspects of a work excluded from his approach.

In an essay titled "Anaesthetic Criticism," Crews goes beyond a discussion of the dangers of reductionism in psychoanalytic criticism and defends it against antideterministic critics. He considers the "informal taboo" placed on extraliterary theories by many academic critics. Northrop Frye, the most influential antideterministic critic, in Crews's view, advocates an inductive survey of literary works, in which no external conceptual framework is considered. Literature, in Frye's archetypal view, is its own progenitor; although Crews terms such a belief "a common fantasy among writers, a wish that art could be self-fathered, self-nurturing, self-referential, purified of its actual origins in discontent." Such a "fantasy," of course, is no less common among critics than among writers. In essence, critics who deplore the search for causes and effects are anti-intellectual, preferring a literary approach in which references to extraliterary analogues are at once disclaimed. Finally, in Crews's view, criticism which ignores the affective element of literature and accentuates the role of form over chaos, of genre conventions and the like, is anaesthetic criticism. Crews concludes that regardless of the dangers of reductionism in the application of psychoanalysis to literature, the approach is more efficacious than that of such antideterministic critics as Frye.

PHENOMENOLOGICAL PSYCHOLOGY

In the case of a phenomenological psychology, a delineation of a *Lebenswelt*, or human life-world of a character, a speaker in a poem, or an author, is in each case a delineation of consciousness. The phenomenologist's desire is to return to lived experiences and "bracket," or set aside, presuppositions. Such experiences are not understood by an examination of external behavior but by an examination of psychic reality, or consciousness. Since consciousness is always consciousness of something, intentionality with regard to external reality being always implicit, a focus on a person in literature or on the author himself, on various self-revelations, reveals the *Lebenswelt*. To the phenomenological psychologist, literary accounts—poetry, drama, or fiction—are personal records, descriptions of psychic reality which aid in achieving a psychological understanding of both behavior and phenomenal experience. Through a phenomenological approach to poetry, which emphasizes various portrayals of self by both poetic speakers and the

poet (portrayals of others, of objects and time), it is possible both to define and to reveal meaning in the poem as a whole.

The poetic consciousness involves the poet's own intentions, which are tied to his own human life-world and his own particular arrangement of phenomena. Although such an arrangement is unique to each poet, a patterning presided over by his own poetic consciousness, such consciousness, by virtue of its intentionality, is directed to and tied to objects comprising the reader's natural universe. The very process of poetic construction and patterning reveals the experiential foundation of the reader's world and illuminates rather than mirrors disparate objects and impressions. The critic of poetry has little interest in poetry as a source of phenomenal experience, as an exploration of psychic-subjective reality. Rather, he utilizes the phenomenological perspective to define the relationship between intentionality and aesthetic patterning or form.

The relationship between intentionality and form cannot be defined until the *Lebenswelt* of each speaker or persona in the poem is defined, leaving the poet's own *Lebenswelt* discernible. Thus, the phenomenological perspective enables the critic to analyze speakers and personae by means of their perceptions of the world and eventually to distinguish aspects of the poem which are derived from intentions not of any speaker or persona but of the poet. Nothing less than the entire poem is revealed.

A PHENOMENOLOGICAL PSYCHOLOGICAL APPROACH TO "THE SICK ROSE"

In "The Sick Rose" it is possible to discern two "characters" almost immediately—worm and rose. It is also possible to discern a speaker, who may or may not be the poet, and, somewhere behind it all, the poet. Neither worm nor rose is a true character since they do not reveal their own perceptions. Focus must be placed on the speaker of the poem, who reveals himself in his revelation regarding the worm and the rose. In spite of the conventional perception that a rose is beautiful, the speaker finds, in the very first line, that this rose is sick. She is sick because her life is being destroyed by the dark secret love of an invisible worm. In the mind of the speaker of the poem, the worm is "the" and not "a" worm; in the mind of the speaker of the poem, the worm is obviously someone or some specific thing. If "someone" is first considered, it is someone up to no good, someone evil. That evil has been created not through hate but through love, although a dark secret love. A bright, open love is a love which can be displayed in society without fear of censure. A dark, secret love is that sexual love which must go on behind closed doors, which cannot be lawfully witnessed. The worm in this speaker's mind is a diabolical figure bringing death through sexuality to the rose. When one begins to separate poet from speaker, it is clear that the speaker himself is "sick."

The poet's *Lebenswelt* is not restricted to this one poem. In the case of Blake, it is revealed in the totality of the work he has titled *Songs of Innocence and of Experience* (1794). "The Sick Rose" is a song of experience. Most often the speakers within poems of experience are themselves victims of what Blake considered to be the "evils" of experience. In the phenomenological approach, critics employ what is known of the poet as revealed in his other work as a gloss on the poem under consideration. Biographical information becomes important so that the *Lebenswelt* of the poet can be defined. The reader-critic's intention is to know enough about the poet's mode of perception to be able to distinguish the poet from speakers or personae in his poems. The richness of the poem is then revealed as a rhetorical juxtaposition of victimized speaker and critical poet.

In another experience poem, "The Garden of Love," a speaker returns to the garden of love, which previously bore so many sweet flowers, and discovers that it is filled with graves, that priests have bound with briars the speaker's joys and desires. This bound speaker is the speaker of "The Sick Rose." In the poet's view, "the" worm may be a priest, or he may be conventional religion's notion of god. The rose of perfect beauty, in its bed of crimson joy, is destroyed by a priest's or a conventionally perceived god's repressive dark secret love—a love which binds the speaker's joys and desires, a love which is fatal. A dark secret love makes love dark and secret. Only man victimized as this speaker is victimized can construct a god for himself who binds and shackles and is then considered loving because of those acts. The love of an institutionalized religion's god, a god outside man himself, is, in this poet's view, not love but death.

BIBLIOGRAPHY

Ackerman, Robert. *The Myth and Ritual School: J. G. Frazer and the Cambridge Ritualists*. New York: Garland, 1991.

Benvenuto, Bice, and Roger Kennedy. *The Works of Jacques Lacan: An Introduction*. New York: St. Martin's Press, 1986.

Bodkin, Maud. *Archetypal Patterns in Poetry*. 1934. Reprint. New York: AMS Press, 1978.

Cobb, Noel. *Archetypal Imagination: Glimpses of the Gods in Life and Art*. Hudson, N.Y.: Lindisfarne Press, 1992. Figures who are examined include Dante, Rumi, Rainer Maria Rilke, and Gabriel García Lorca.

Ellmann, Maud, ed. *Psychoanalytic Literary Criticism*. New York: Longman, 1994.

Felman, Shoshana, ed. *Literature and Psychoanalysis: The Question of Reading, Otherwise*. Yale French Studies 55/56. New Haven, Conn.: Yale University, 1977.

Frazer, James George, Sir. *The Golden Bough: A Study in Magic and Religion*. 1890-1915. Rev. ed. New York: Viking Penguin, 1997. The monumental study of comparative folklore and religion that gave impetus to archetypal criticism.

Frye, Northrop. *Anatomy of Criticism: Four Essays*. Princeton, N.J.: Princeton University Press, 1957.

Hamilton, A. C. *Northrop Frye: Anatomy of His Criticism*. Toronto: University of Toronto Press, 1990.

Holland, Norman. *Poems in Persons: An Introduction to the Psychoanalysis of Literature*. 1973. Reprint. New York: Columbia University Press, 1989.

Kofman, Sarah. *Freud and Fiction*. Boston: Northeastern University Press, 1991.

Lauter, Estrella. *Women as Mythmakers: Poetry and Visual Art by Twentieth-Century Women*. Bloomington: Indiana University Press, 1984.

Lauter, Estella, and Carol Schreier Rupprecht, eds. *Feminist Archetypal Theory: Interdisciplinary Revisions of Jungian Thought*. Knoxville: University of Tennessee Press, 1985.

Meurs, Jos van, and John Kidd. *Jungian Literary Criticism, 1920-1980: An Annotated Critical Bibliography of Works in English*. Metuchen, N.J.: Scarecrow Press, 1988.

Natanson, Maurice Alexander. *The Erotic Bird: Phenomenology in Literature*. Princeton, N.J. : Princeton University Press, 1998.

Pratt, Annis V. *Archetypal Patterns in Women's Fiction*. Bloomington: Indiana University Press, 1981.

Ray, David, ed. *Archetypal Process: Self and Divine in Whitehead, Jung, and Hillman*. Evanston, Ill: Northwestern University Press, 1989.

Storr, Anthony, ed. *The Essential Jung: Selected Writings*. Rev. ed. Princeton, N.J.: Princeton University Press, 1999.

Vice, Sue, ed. *Psychoanalytic Criticism: A Reader.* Cambridge, Mass.: Polity Press, 1996.

Vickery, John B., ed. *Myth and Literature: Contemporary Theory and Practice*. Lincoln: University of Nebraska Press, 1966.

Wright, Elizabeth. *Psychoanalytic Criticism: A Reappraisal*. New York: Routledge, 1998.

Joseph Natoli

FEMINIST CRITICISM

Any survey of feminist criticism is fraught with difficulties, the most serious of which is the avoidance of reductionism. This introduction to feminist work attempts to identify key figures, central concerns, and general "movements." Such an attempt is a strategic move to organize a vital and growing body of work into some sort of scheme that can be collated and presented. Despite the existence of American, French, and British "feminisms," for example, no such clear-cut schools or movements exist in a fixed way. The various writers included in this essay, and the various trends and movements discussed, share many positions and disagree on many important points. Such agreements and disagreements have less to do with nationality than with the rapid changes occurring in feminist criticism. Three general perspectives on feminism are summarized here, as reflected in the work of American, French, and British writers. The work of two pivotal feminist writers, Simone de Beauvoir and Virginia Woolf, is discussed at some length, and there is also an attempt to isolate a few general trends and issues within the feminist movement.

Feminism has diverse goals, many of which overlap in the work of individual writers. This work is filled with pitfalls and temptations: Because women have been participants in their cultures, feminine thinking and writing cannot be separated from the methods of the cultures in which they have lived. Nor can a woman be separated from her race or sexual orientation. Furthermore, feminist criticism may be combined with other methods of criticism, such as deconstruction, psychoanalytic criticism, and Marxist criticism. Generally, however, feminist writers are concerned with encouraging the equality of women—political equality, social equality, and aesthetic equality—and researching the impact of gender upon writing—determining how the writing of women differs from the writing of men.

GENDER SYSTEMS

Feminist critics have produced a variety of models to account for the production, reproduction, and maintenance of gender systems. They discuss the female writer's problems in defining herself in the conventional structures of a male-dominated society, structures that restrict the possibilities of women and impose standards of behavior upon women personally, professionally, and creatively. Again, to generalize, once women experience themselves as subjects, they can attempt to undermine the social, cultural, and masculine subject positions offered them.

Feminist critics may, for example, reexamine the writing of male authors (an approach associated with American feminists) and, in particular, reexamine the great works of male authors from a woman's perspective in an attempt to discover how the great works reflect and shape the ideologies that hold back women. In this reexamination, feminist critics will carefully analyze the depictions of female characters to expose the ideology implicit in such characterizations. They may also seek to expose the patriarchal ideology that permeates great works and to show how it also permeates the literary tradition. This particularly American approach is seen in the work of Kate Millett, Judith Fetterley, and Carolyn Heilbrun.

GYNOCRITICISM

A second approach used by American feminists is termed "gynocriticism." This method of inquiry takes as its subject the writings of women who have produced what Elaine Showalter, who coined the term "gynocriticism," calls "a literature of their own." A female literary tradition is examined to discover how women writers have historically perceived themselves and their cultures. Other goals of gynocriticism are to preserve and chronicle the history of women's writing and to rediscover lost or neglected women writers. Showalter describes feminine writing as a form of the general experience of minority cultures, cultures that are also "Others" and whose members are struggling to find a place usually reserved for white males. This leads to the problem of multiple marginalization, since some men and women may be Others in terms of ethnicity and sexual orientation. In particular, the place within feminism of women of color is a controversial issue, as black writers such as Phillis Wheatley, Toni Morrison, Gwendolyn Brooks, Nikki Giovanni, and others challenge and enter the canon. Other practitioners of gynocriticism include Patricia Meyer Spacks and Susan Gubar.

LANGUAGE

Feminist writers may also focus on language, defining it as a male realm, and exploring the many ways in which meaning is created. This language-based feminism is typically associated with French feminism. Such feminists may conceive of language as phallocentric, arguing that it privileges the masculine by promoting the values appreciated by the male culture. Such a language-based approach typically attempts to reveal a relationship between language and culture, or, more specifically, the way the politics of language affects and even determines women's roles in a culture. Radical French feminists may associate feminine writing with the female body, so that the repression of female sexual pleasure is related to the repression of feminine creativity in general. They insist that once women learn to understand and express their sexuality, they will be able to progress toward a future defined by the feminine economy of generosity as opposed to the masculine economy of hoarding. Such a position has drawn criticism from other feminists, since it seems to reduce women to biological entities and fosters (though it reverses) a set of binary oppositions—female/male. Julia Kristeva, Annie Leclerc, Xaviere Gauthier, and Marguerite Duras are four French feminists.

Interestingly, differences between the French and English languages involve complicated feminist issues. The English language distinguishes between sex and gender, so that human beings are either female or male by sex and feminine or masculine by gender. The feminine/masculine opposition permits some fluidity, so that androgyny can become a central, mediating position between the two extremes. The distinction between male and female, however, is absolute. The way the English language categorizes people has itself created a debate within feminism, over naming. In French, by comparison, the concepts of femininity and femaleness are included in the same word.

POLITICAL AND SOCIAL AGENDAS

Finally, British feminists have tended to be more historically oriented than French and American feminists.

These British critics tend to be materialistic and ideological; they look carefully at the material conditions of historical periods and consider such conditions as central to understanding literature. Literature, in this model, is culturally produced. Some British feminists consider that an American opposition to male stereotypes has produced a feminine reaction that has led to an ignorance of real differences among women's races, social classes, and cultures. British feminists also emphasize that women's development of individual strategies to obtain real power within their political, social, or creative arenas is actually a negative move. They argue that such examples mystify male oppression and perpetrate the myth that, somehow, male oppression creates for women a world of special opportunities.

Generally, the British position encourages historical and political engagement to promote social change. This model of activism contrasts with the American and French models, which focus primarily on sexual difference. A typical strategy of the British approach is to examine a text by first placing the text in its historical context and then exposing the patriarchal ideologies that structure the text and govern the depiction of women characters. Because of historical oppression, the women characters tend to be either silent or mouthpieces for men's myths. Judith Newton and Deborah Rosenfelt are two examples of British feminists.

HISTORY

Feminist criticism owes much to the work of Simone de Beauvoir and Virginia Woolf, two founders of contemporary feminist thought. De Beauvoir explored many ways in which women are defined and limited in relation to men. Her most important work is probably *The Second Sex* (1949). Such limiting, de Beauvoir contends, cannot be avoided in a male-dominated culture; even women perceived as "independent" are still negatively affected by the ideas and the relations of the male society. Western society in general, for de Beauvoir, is patriarchal and denies freedom of expression to women. In this patriarchal society, women become Others, viewed not as they are but as projections of male needs and subordinate to male expectations. Her approach tends toward a Marxist model in identifying an economic and political limiting of women with sexism in literature. De Beauvoir finds in literature reflections of a more general socioeconomic oppression of women. Her approach emphasizes art's mimetic quality: Through its powers of reflection, art yields valuable insights into the sexism that is culturally prevalent.

The otherness examined by de Beauvoir and other feminist writers is a condition of women, so that the characteristic of identity for women is separation. Constituted through a male gaze, the feminine exists as something that is inexpressible. Women function as objects of the male gaze. Therefore, women's bodies are vehicles for ambivalent feelings toward the mother. These problems extend into the Western philosophical tradition, so that Western (usually male) thinkers express their philosophical positions as essential and universal while embracing a center that is unexamined and male.

In her essay *A Room of One's Own* (1929), Virginia Woolf introduced many topics that have become vital to feminist critics. She contends that art is a collective product, incorrectly romanticized in theory as individual and personal. Woolf's conceptualization of a metaphorical "room," a female place, merges the introspection often associated with female discourse and the social sanctuary within which a woman may achieve her potential. Woolf helped to establish the broad range of feminist criticism, from cultural critique to discourse. The most important portion of *A Room of One's Own* ironically and satirically traces the lost career of "Shakespeare's sister," whose creativity had no outlet in the sixteenth century. Woolf problematizes the structures of the male ego, its rituals, titles, and institutions, which are created at the expense of Others. This ironic introduction sets the stage in the text for a historical discussion of women writers and the problems they had in pursuing their careers. Furthermore, in her discussion of women novelists of the nineteenth century, especially George Eliot, Charlotte Brontë, and Jane Austen, Woolf foreshadowed contemporary research on language.

Woolf argued that a woman writer should write as a woman writer and as a woman who is not self-conscious of her gender. She strove to be aware of the alienating and repressive effects of the myths created around women and also to avoid creating alternative myths. She set forth the attempt to discover a collective concept of subjectivity that would foreground identity constructs and argued that such a concept of subjectivity is a characteristic of women's writing. Other women writers, however, are more interested in the alienation created by structures that permit women only very restricted and repressive roles, roles as Others, in society.

In her writing, Woolf is striving, like later feminists, to uncover the effects of a phallocentric culture that idolizes the autonomous and rational ego. She also attempts to offer an alternative to this idolatry, an alternative that emphasizes subjectivity and connectedness, if in a historically fluid context. Through her struggle to redefine women, she tries to avoid simply reversing the binary oppositions that polarize men and women into specific categories. She does not argue for a reversal of the categories.

GENDER RULES AND RELATIONS

Since de Beauvoir and Woolf, the naming and interrogating of phallocentrism has become more assured. Feminist critics are challenging the stereotypical masculine virtues, no longer accepting them as measures of virtue and excellence. One strategy many feminist critics adopt is to locate both men and women within a larger context, as both being captives of gender in vastly different, but interrelated, ways. Though men may appear to be the masters under the rules of gender, they are not therefore free, for like women they remain *under* gender rules.

If both men and women are influenced by gender, then the conceptualizations of women and the conceptualizations of men must be examined in terms of gender relations. Feminist critical models are complex and often contradictory. Claims about the centrality of gender relations in the formation of self, knowledge, and power relations, and the relationships of these areas to one another, continue to be debated. Feminist critics have developed many theories on how gender systems are created, continue, dominate, and maintain themselves. Each of the theories, however, identifies a single process or set of processes as vital to gender relations. Influential feminist theorists have suggested the centrality of the sexual division of labor, childbearing and child-rearing practices, and various processes of representation (including aesthetic and language processes, for example). Such positions address the meanings and nature of sexuality and the relationship of sexuality to writing, the importance and implications of differences among women writers, and the effects of kinship and family organizations. Each of these many theories and debates has crucial implications for an understanding of knowledge, gender, power, and writing.

Juliet Mitchell has argued for the importance of Freudian theories to feminist theories of gender relations. Her work entails a defense of Lacanian psychoanalysis. She argues that Sigmund Freud's work on the psychology of women should be read as a description of the inevitable effects on feminine psychic development of patriarchal social power. Dorothy Dinnerstein and Nancy Chodorow contribute to this psychoanalytical approach a larger account of the unconscious and its role in gender relations. They also examine the traditional sexual division of labor in the West, how this tradition has been passed on, and how it influences male-female relations.

MALE VS. FEMALE DISCOURSE

Helen Cixous and Luce Irigary find fundamental psychological differences between men and women. They have concluded that women are more influenced by pre-Oedipal experience and believe that the girl retains an initial identification with her mother, so that the relationship between mother and daughter is less repressed than that of the mother and son. This retention affects women's selves, so that they remain fluid and interrelational. As a result of this difference between men and women, masculine writing has an ambivalent response to women. Women tend to remain outside or on the fringes of male discourse, and feminine pleasure poses the greatest challenge to masculine discourse. Masculine discourse is also logocentric and binary; its meaning is produced through hierarchal, male-dominated, binary oppositions. Masculine discourse creates a situation in which feminine discourse is characterized by omissions and gaps. Latent in these gaps and omissions are conflicting feelings regarding sexuality, motherhood, and autonomy.

An important question raised by feminist criticism iswhether there is a gender-based women's language that is significantly and inevitably different from the language of men. In *Language and Woman's Place* (1975), Robin Lakoff argues that there is more to "speaking like a woman" than vocabulary. Examining syntactical patterns of a typical female and evaluating the frequency with which women use tag questions, she concludes that the traditional powerlessness of women in a Western society is reflected in many aspects of women's language. Other theorists who are interested in differences between male and female languages explore sociolinguistic issues, such as the practice of women assuming their fathers' names at birth and their husbands' names when married, the frequency with which women are addressed by familiar names, the frequency of interruption in speech between men and women, and the large number of pejorative terms applicable to women. Writers interested in these latter linguistic areas are Cheris Kramarae and Julia Penelope Stanley.

In this conflict between male and female discourse, writing may be an anticipatory, therapeutic experience of liberation. Writing may return woman's repressed pleasure to her. It may also create a collective space in which women writers may speak of and to women. Gayatri Chakravorty Spivak explores discourse and literature in general as discursive practices. In *In Other Worlds* (1987) she shows the tendency in Western cultures to universalize particular examples into human examples. Spivak examines feminism in relation to British imperialism in India and then situates feminist criticism within middle-class academia. This approach argues that what has been assumed to be universal truth is in fact the Western colonial or male conception of truth, a perspective that distorts or ignores the experiences of Others. The goal of such a critical perspective is to authenticate the expression of Others based on individual experience and shared understanding and to call into question the accepted definitions of truth and meaningful discourse.

DIFFERENCES AMONG WOMEN

Another concern that has become important in feminist criticism is the differences among women themselves. A model that presumes a universal feminine experience requires that women, unlike men, be free from cultural and racial determination. Under such a model, the barriers to shared experience created by race and class and gender are somehow cleared away when one is a woman. Women critics of color, such as Barbara Smith, argue that it is incorrect to assume that there is one universal feminine experience or writing. For example, the sexuality of black women tends to be represented as natural, primitive, and free from traditional cultural inhibitions. Yet this assumption has been invoked both to justify and to deny the sexual abuse of black women and the lack of respect given to them. In general, Smith criticizes fellow feminists for excluding or ignoring women of color. She also observes that both black and white male scholars working with black authors neglect women.

Furthermore, it is not possible to discuss a universal experience of motherhood. Racism affects women of color differently from the way it affects white women, especially in the effort to rear children who can be self-sufficient and self-respecting. These troubles are inherent in a culture that holds as natural the binary opposition white/black, wherein white is the privileged term. This opposition is deeply rooted in the colonial history of Western civilization. Women of color cannot be exempt from the insidious consequences of this binary opposition, and white women cannot participate in productive dialogue with women of color whenever this traditional opposition is ignored.

LESBIAN CRITICISM

Another friction within the feminist movement involves lesbian feminist criticism. Just as women of color have considered themselves excluded, lesbian feminists consider themselves excluded, not only by the dominant white male culture but also by heterosexual females. Authors concerned with this problem include Bonnie Zimmerman and Adrienne Rich. In fact, Rich provides a definition of lesbianism so broad that it encompasses most of feminine creativity.

FEMINIST PSYCHOANALYTIC CRITICISM

In the 1970's a general movement toward psychoanalysis and toward women's reading men and one an-

other occurred within feminism. This movement is exemplified in the writings of such feminists as Mary Jacobs, Jane Gallop, and Juliet Richardson. For feminist theorists, the limitations of traditional theories accounting for the origins of oppression had been uncovered. Writers in the 1970's became very interested in, for example, the positioning of women within repressive sexual and political discourses. Many feminist writers have become interested in the establishment of an identity that involves both separation and connection, so that a binary relationship is not created and one is not perceived as a threat. In such a new relationship, women would no longer need, for example, to attempt to create an Oedipal triangle through their children. Each of the sexes might develop less threatening relations to the other.

READING DIFFERENCES

In regard to women's reading men and one another, Annette Kolodny investigated methodological problems from an empiricist stance. She concludes that women, in fact, do read differently from men. Her "A Map for Re-reading" (1980) examines how the two contrasting methods of interpretation of men and women appear in two stories and how the differences between masculine and feminine perspectives are mirrored in the reaction of the public to the two stories (Charlotte Perkins Gilman's "The Yellow Wallpaper" and Susan Keating Glaspell's "A Jury of Her Peers"). Judith Fetterley's work also presents a model for gender differences in reading. Her book *The Resisting Reader* (1978) argues against the position that the primary works of American fiction are intended, and written, for a universal audience and that women have permitted themselves to be masculinized in order to read these texts. One of the first steps, Fetterley contends, is for women to become resisting, rather than assenting, readers.

VARIETIES OF FEMINISM

Feminism has engaged in and with other branches of criticism, including Marxist criticism and deconstruction. Nancy K. Miller and Peggy Kamuf, for example, have incorporated deconstructive approaches in their work. Judith Lowder Newton and Lillian Robinson have incorporated Marxism.

The movement toward alternative ways of writing, however, involves drastic changes in the relationship between public and private and the traditional opposition between emotional and rational. Such an attempt in literature was heralded by Woolf's writing (for example, *The Waves*, 1931 and *To the Lighthouse*, 1927) and may be read in the work of Muriel Spark (*The Hothouse by the East River*, 1973), Angela Carter (*The Passion of New Eve*, 1977), Toni Morrison (*The Bluest Eye*, 1970), Alice Walker (*Meridian*, 1976), Marge Piercy (*Women on the Edge of Time*, 1976), Margaret Atwood (*The Edible Woman*, 1969), Joanna Russ (*The Female Man*, 1975), and Fay Weldon (*The Life and Times of a She-Devil*, 1983), among others since.

Perhaps the most agreed-upon accomplishment of feminist criticism (though even in this agreement there is caution) has been to find and identify a variety of feminine traditions in literature. Numerous women writers have been "rediscovered," introduced into the literary canon, and examined as important to the literary tradition. This interest in expanding the study of literature by women has had a significant impact in colleges and universities. Indeed feminist criticism, by the beginning of the twenty-first century, had joined with other traditions—Native American, African American, Asian American, gay and lesbian—in an ongoing effort to celebrate and express diversity in the ongoing investigation of identity.

BIBLIOGRAPHY

Beauvoir, Simone de. *The Second Sex*. 1949. Reprint. New York: Random House, 1990.

Belsey, Catherine. *Critical Practice*. New York: Methuen, 1980.

Butler, Judith. *Gender Trouble: Feminism and the Subversion of Identity*. New York: Routledge, 1990.

Delany, Sheila. *Writing Women: Women Writers and Women in Literature, Medieval to Modern*. New York: Schocken, 1984.

Eagleton, Mary, ed. *Feminist Literary Theory: A Reader*. New York: Blackwell, 1988.

Fetterley, Judith. *The Resisting Reader: A Feminist Approach to American Fiction*. Bloomington: Indiana University Press, 1978.

Finkle, Laurie A. *Feminist Theory, Women's Writing*. Ithaca, N.Y.: Cornell University Press, 1992.

Gilbert, Sandra M., and Susan Gubar. *The Madwom,an in the Attic: The Woman Writer and the Nineteenth-Century Literary Imagination*. New Haven, Conn.: Yale University Press, 1979.

Greer, Germaine. *The Female Eunuch*. New York: McGraw-Hill, 1970.

_____. *Slip-Shod Sibyls: Recognition, Rejection, and the Woman Poet*. London: Viking, 1995.

Harvey, Elizabeth D. *Ventriloquized Voices: Feminist Theory and English Renaissance Texts*. New York: Routledge, 1992.

Jackson, Stevie, and Jackie Jones. *Contemporary Feminist Theories*. New York: New York University Press, 1998.

Kitch, Sally L., and Catharine R. Stimpson. *Higher Ground: From Utopianism to Realism in American Feminist Thought and Theory*. Chicago: University of Chicago Press, 2000.

Lakoff, Robin. *Language and Woman's Place*. New York: Harper & Row, 1975.

Millett, Kate. *Sexual Politics*. Garden City, N.Y.: Doubleday, 1970.

Mills, Sara. *Feminist Stylistics*. New York: Routledge, 1995.

_____. *Gendering the Reader*. New York: Harvester Wheatsheaf, 1994.

_____. *Language and Gender: Interdisciplinary Perspectives*. New York: Longman, 1995.

Mills, Sara, et al., eds. *Feminist Readings/Feminists Reading*. Charlottesville: University of Virginia Press, 1989.

Moi, Toril. *Sexual/Textual Politics: Feminist Literary Theory*. New York: Methuen, 1985.

Rich, Adrienne. *Blood, Bread, and Poetry: Selected Prose, 1979-1985*. New York: Norton, 1986.

_____. *On Lies, Secrets, and Silence: Selected Prose, 1966-1978*. New York: Norton, 1979.

_____. *What Is Found There: Notebooks on Poetry and Politics*. New York: Norton, 1993.

Roszak, Theodore, and Betty Roszak, eds. *Masculine/Feminine: Readings in Sexual Mythology and the Liberation of Women*. New York: Harper & Row, 1969.

Schneir, Miriam, ed. *Feminism: The Essential Historical Writings*. New York: Vintage Press, 1994.

Showalter, Elaine, ed. *The New Feminist Criticism: Essays on Women, Literature, and Theory*. New York: Pantheon, 1985.

_____. *Speaking of Gender*. New York: Routledge, 1989.

Smith, Barbara. *Toward a Black Feminist Criticism*. Brooklyn, N.Y.: Out and Out, 1977.

Spivak, Gayatri Chakravorty. *In Other Worlds*. New York: Methuen, 1987.

Woolf, Virginia. *A Room of One's Own*. 1929. Reprint. New York: Harcourt, 1991.

David L. Erben

FORMALISTIC CRITICISM

The formalist approach to poetry was the one most influential in American criticism during the 1940's, 1950's, and 1960's, and it is still often practiced in literature courses in American colleges and universities. Its popularity was not limited to American literary criticism. In France, formalism has long been employed as a pedagogical exercise in reading literature in the universities and in the *lycées*. In England in the 1940's and in the 1950's, formalism was associated with an influential group of critics writing for a significant critical periodical, *Scrutiny*, the most prominent of whom was F. R. Leavis. There was also a notable formalist movement in the Soviet Union in the 1920's, and, although championed by René Wellek in the United States, its influence at that time was primarily limited to Slavic countries.

The formalist approach in America was popularized by John Crowe Ransom, Allen Tate, Robert Penn Warren, and Cleanth Brooks, all four Southerners, all graduates of Vanderbilt University, and all, in varying degrees, receptive to the indirections and complexities of the modernism of T. S. Eliot, James Joyce, and William Butler Yeats, which their critical method—known as the New Criticism—was, in part, developed to explicate. A fifth critic, not directly associated with the Vanderbilt group, R. P. Blackmur, made important contributions to the formalist reading of poetry in *The Double Agent* (1935) and in essays in other books. He did not, however, develop a distinctive formalist method.

FORMALISM IN THE HISTORY OF LITERARY CRITICISM

Formalism is clearly a twentieth century critical phenomenon in its emphasis on close reading of the literary text, dissociated from extrinsic references to the author or to his or her society. There had been formalist tendencies before in the history of literary criticism, but it did not, as in twentieth century formalism, approach exclusivity in its emphasis on the structure of the work itself. Aristotle's analysis in *De poetica* (c. 334-323 B.C.E.; *Poetics*, 1705) of the complex tragic plot as having a tripartite division of reversal, recognition, and catastrophe is one of the most valuable formalist analyses of the structure of tragedy ever made.

That Aristotle's approach to poetics was not intrinsic but extrinsic, however, was made clear by his twentieth century followers, the Chicago Neo-Aristotelians, Ronald S. Crane and Elder Olson. They were the harshest critics of what they regarded as the limited critical perspective of modern formalists, pointing out that an Aristotelian analysis was characteristically in terms of four causes. These were the formal cause (the form that the work imitates), the material cause (the materials out of which the work is made), the efficient cause (the maker), and the final cause (the effect on the reader or audience). Crane charged in *Critics and Criticism: Ancient and Modern* (1952) that the New Criticism is concerned with only one of these causes, language, in order to distinguish poetic from scientific and everyday uses of language, but was unable to distinguish among the various kinds of poetry. It is true that formalism is largely concerned with literature as a verbal art. This single-mindedness has been its strength in explication as well as its weakness as a critical theory.

Two key concepts in the literary theory of the English Romantic period may have been influential on twentieth century formalism. Although the New Critics were professedly anti-Romantic, following T. S. Eliot's call for impersonality in modern poetry, their stress on the meaning of the total poem, rather than the meaning centered in a specific part, probably owes something to the concept of organic form, assumed by most Romantics and stated explicitly by Samuel Taylor Coleridge in his defense of William Shakespeare. This is the concept that a poem grows like a living organism, its parts interrelated, its form and content inseparable; the total work is thus greater than the sum of its parts. This concept was assumed by all the New Critics except Ransom, who viewed "texture" as separate from structure.

The formalist view of creativity is of a "rage" brought to "order" through submission to the discipline of form. A good poem is characterized by tensions that are usually reconciled. The most detailed statement of this view by a New Critic is in Robert Penn Warren's essay "Pure and Impure Poetry," in which Warren gives a long list of resistances or "tensions" in a good poem. The origin of this idea lies in Romantic critical theory. Warren's statements, as well as Allen Tate's discussion of tension in his essay "Tension in Poetry," undoubtedly owe much to chapter 14 of Coleridge's *Biographia Literaria* (1817), in which he describes the distinctive quality of the creative imagination of the poet as revealing itself "in the balance or reconciliation of opposite or discordant qualities."

The strongest twentieth century influences on formalism in America and in England were the early essays of T. S. Eliot, especially those in *The Sacred Wood* (1920), and two books by I. A. Richards, *Principles of Literary Criticism* (1924) and *Practical Criticism* (1929). Eliot, influenced by the anti-Romanticism of T. E. Hulme in *Speculations* (1924), called for a theory of the impersonal in the modernist view of poetry to rectify the personality cults of Romantic and Victorian poetry, and he even detailed how to impersonalize personal emotions through the use of "objective correlatives." Eliot's intention was to redirect critical attention from the poet to the work of art, which he declared to be "autotelic," self-contained, a fictive world in itself. It was this pronouncement of Eliot's, more than any statement in his essays in the 1920's, which had the strongest influence on the development of formalist criticism.

Eliot also devised his own version of a Cartesian "split" between logic and untrustworthy feelings, his theory that a dissociation of sensibility took place in English poetry in the late seventeenth century. John Donne had a unified sensibility capable of devouring any kind of experience. In the Metaphysical poets "there is a direct sensuous apprehension of thought": They could think feelings and feel thoughts. The New Critics were to develop a formalist approach to poetry that could show this kind of sensibility at work. To a formalist such as Cleanth Brooks in *Modern Poetry and the Tradition* (1939), Metaphysical poetry was the proper tradition in which to fit modern poetry, and critical techniques were needed in order to explicate the complexities of poetry in the tradition. He provided a model for formalist explication in a brilliant analysis of parallelisms and ironic contrasts utilized functionally by Eliot in *The Waste Land* (1922).

THE FORMALIST DEFENSE OF POETRY

Formalism in America and England may have evolved in reaction to nineteenth century literary thought and practice as a method of understanding a modernist literature that was indirect, impersonal, complex, and "autotelic." As far as the New Critics were concerned, however, their formalism was a defense of poetry in an age of science. Their criticism can quite properly be regarded as an "apology" for poetry in the tradition of Sir Philip Sidney and Percy Bysshe Shelley. An "apology" is a formal defense of poetry in an age thought to be hostile to the poetry of its own time. Sidney "apologized" for poetry at a time when Puritans were attacking drama and voicing suspicions as to whether poetry could and did advance morality. Shelley defended the value of poetry in an age that was beginning to turn to prose, assuming that the golden age of poetry was over. In this tradition the New Critics "apologized" for poetry in an age of logical positivism, when scientific method was regarded as the sole means to truth, and poetry was being limited to mere emotive effects.

In his *Principles of Literary Criticism*, I. A. Richards sought to find a place for poetry in an age of science by emphasizing the psychological effects of poetry on the personality of the reader. In *Practical Criticism* he documented the helplessness of his graduate students when confronted with an unidentified poem to explicate, making a case for a literary criticism that specialized in explicating the text. Richards seemed, however, at least in the earlier book, to be in agreement with the positivistic view that poetry was a purely emotive use of language, in contrast to science, which was the language of factual assertion. Although influenced by Richards, the New Critics attempted to counter his apparent denial of a cognitive dimension of poetry. They did this through their formalism, staying inside the poem in their explications and declaring it characteristic of the poet's use of language to direct the reader to meanings back inside the poem rather than to referents outside the poem.

Cleanth Brooks contended that poets actually block too direct a pinpointing to everyday referents outside the poem and that the meanings of a poem cannot be wrenched outside the context of the poem without serious distortions. He was making a case for meaning in the poem and at the same time was keeping poetry out of direct competition with science. In a poem, he asserted, apparently referential statements are qualified by ambiguities, paradoxes, and ironies so that the knowledge offered cannot stand as a direct proposition apart from the poem itself. This is why it does not matter that John Keats in a famous sonnet credits Hernando Cortes, not Vasco de Balboa, with the first sighting by a European of the Pacific Ocean. What Keats writes is true to the poem, not to historical fact, and he does not intend a truth claim to be taken outside the poem and examined for factual accuracy. Murray Krieger argued quite plausibly in *The New Apologists for Poetry* (1956) that the New Critics might be called "contextualists" because of their insistence on getting meaning from and in the context.

Each major New Critic was in his own way trying to establish that poetry offers a special kind of knowledge and does not compete with the more referential knowledge that Richards found characteristic of scientific assertions. Their "apology" for poetry committed them to formalism, to directing critical attention intrinsically to the structure of the poem rather than extrinsically to referents outside. Ransom, in *The World's Body* (1938) and *The New Criticism* (1941), even departed from the concept of organic form to argue that the main difference between scientific and poetic language was that while both had "structure," only the latter had "texture," details that are interesting in themselves. Through his "texture" the poet expresses his revulsion against the inclination of science to abstract and to categorize by giving his reader the particulars of the world, the "sensuous apprehension of thought" that Eliot had admired in the Metaphysical poets. To Ransom, this was knowledge of "the world's body." Ransom's single most important contribution to formalism was his often anthologized essay, "Poetry: A Note on Ontology."

The most philosophically inclined of the New Critics, Allen Tate, also made a specific claim that literature offers a special kind of knowledge, more complete than the knowledge of science; it is experiential knowledge rather than the abstracted, shorthand version of experience given by science. Tate argued that a special characteristic of poetic language is the creation of "tension," a kind of balance between the extremes of too much denotation and literalness and too much connotation and suggestiveness. A good poem possesses both a wealth of suggestiveness and a firm denotative base. In his essay "Tension in Poetry," he provided exam-

ples of tension as a kind of touchstone for critical judgments.

In "Pure and Impure Poetry," Robert Penn Warren presented his own version of the concept of "tension," one closer to Coleridge's than Tate's was. Warren was also influenced by Richards's concept of a "poetry of inclusion" (in turn derived from Coleridge), a poetry that contains its own oppositions. Warren believed that such an "impure" poet writing today must "come to terms with Mercutio," that is, use irony to qualify direct propositions, much as William Shakespeare used the realistic, bawdy jests of Mercutio to counter the sentimental love poetry in *Romeo and Juliet* (1594-1596). Such irony is accessible only through formalist analysis of the poem itself, a close reading of the text. As a formalist, Warren believed, as the other New Critics did, in a less accessible meaning beyond the usual public meaning.

THE PRACTICE OF FORMALISM

Cleanth Brooks was the most consistent practicing formalist and the most influential as well, whether in collaboration with Robert Penn Warren, in their popular textbooks, *Understanding Poetry* (1950) and *Understanding Fiction* (1943) or in his own studies in formalism, *Modern Poetry and the Tradition* and *The Well Wrought Urn* (1947). In *Modern Poetry and the Tradition*, Brooks extended Eliot's concept of tradition to a selective history of poetry from seventeenth century Metaphysical poetry to twentieth century modernism. The proper tradition for the modern poet was the Metaphysical tradition because "hard" Metaphysical conceits conveyed both thought and feeling and maintained a proper balance, in contrast to the excessive emotion in much Romantic poetry and the excessive rationalism in much neoclassical poetry. Brooks wrote the book to show the relationship between Metaphysical and modern poetry and to explain modern poetry to readers whose understanding of poetry was primarily based on Romantic poetry.

His next book, *The Well Wrought Urn*, was slightly revisionist, expanding the tradition to include some of the best works of Romantic and Victorian poetry, and even a major poem of the neoclassical period, Alexander Pope's *The Rape of the Lock* (1712). The test for admission to the tradition is again a careful formalist analysis, revealing, in unexpected places, tensions and para-doxes—although the formalist technique has been re-fined and even expanded. Brooks contended that poetry is "the language of paradox," evident even in a poem such as William Wordworth's "Composed upon West-minster Bridge." The paradox central to the structure of the poem is that a city, London, is enabled to "wear the beauty of the morning," a privilege that Wordsworth usually reserves for nature. The city is also paradoxi-cally most alive with this surprising beauty when it is asleep, as it is on this occasion. Brooks conceded that Wordsworth's employment of paradox might have been unconscious, something he was driven to by "the nature of his instrument," but paradox can also be conscious technique, as it was in John Donne's "The Canoniza-tion."

Brooks's analysis of "The Canonization" is a model of formalist method, as his analysis of Eliot's *The Waste Land* had been in his previous volume. The poem is complex but unified, an argument dramatically pre-sented but a treatise on the important subject of divine and profane love as well. The tone, an important element of meaning, is complex, scornful, ironic, and yet quite serious. Also central in the poem is the "love metaphor," and basic to its development is the paradox of treating profane love as if it were divine love. Such a treatment permits the culminating paradox in the speaker's argu-ment for his love: "The lovers in rejecting life actually win to the most intense life." In this poem, technique has shaped content: The only way in which the poet could say what the poem says is by means of paradox.

Brooks made another major contribution to formalist practice in *The Well Wrought Urn.* He demonstrated the importance of the dramatic context as the intrinsic refer-ent for meaning in a poem. Even the simplest lyric has some of the drama of a play. There are within a poem a speaker, an occasion, sometimes an audience, and a con-flict—in a lyric usually a conflict of attitudes. Brooks declared in "The Problem of Belief and the Problem of Cognition" that a poem should not be judged by the truth or falsity "of the idea which it incorporates, but rather by its character as drama. . . ." The formalist as New Critic, most fully represented by an explication ac-cording to Brooks's formula, is concerned with this drama in the poem, with how the conflict of attitudes is resolved, with paradox and how it is central to argument in poetry, with metaphor and how it may be the only per-missible way of developing the thought of the poem. He is concerned with technique in a verbal art, and these techniques make possible the poetic communication of what becomes the content.

Ranking with *The Well Wrought Urn* as a major formalist document is René Wellek and Austin Warren's *Theory of Literature* (1949). When it was published, the intention of the book was to argue for the use of intrinsic approaches to literature, drawing on the New Criticism, Russian Formalism, and even phenomenology, in con-junction with literary history and the history of ideas, then the dominant approaches. Its value today is as a source book of formalist theory, just as Brooks's *The Well Wrought Urn* is a source book of formalist practice. Wellek and Warren make the distinction between the scientific use of language, ideally purely denotative, and the literary use of language, not merely referential but expressive and highly connotative, conveying the tone and attitude of speaker and writer. Form and content are regarded as inseparable: Technique determines content. Reference to the Russian Formalists reinforces the New Critics on this point. Meter, alliteration, sounds, imag-ery, and metaphor are all functional in a poem. Poetry is referential but the references are intrinsic, directed back inside the fictive world that is being created.

THE DECLINE OF FORMALISM

The influence of formalism reached its peak in the 1950's and began to decline in the 1960's. In England, *Scrutiny* suspended publication; although F. R. Leavis continued to publish, his criticism became less formal-istic and more Arnoldian. In America, the New Critics also became less formalistic, and their formalism was taken over by followers who lacked the explicative ge-nius of Ransom, Tate, Brooks, and Warren.

Warren had always published less formal criticism than his colleagues, and in the 1960's he turned his at-tention even more to fiction and, especially, to writing poetry. Allen Tate, never as fond as the others of critical explications, continued to write essays of social and moral significance, moving in and out of Catholicism and the influence of Jacques Maritain. His best critical explication remained that of his own poem, "Ode to the

Confederate Dead," an exploration of the creative process as well as a formalistic analysis. He died in 1979. Ransom continued to edit the most important new critical journal, *The Kenyon Review*, until his retirement from Kenyon College; then he returned to something he had put aside for many years—his poetry. In the few essays that he wrote in the years just before his death in 1974, his Kantian interests preoccupied him more and more. Cleanth Brooks wrote one more book that might be called formalistic, *A Shaping Joy* (1971), but he turned most of his attention to his two major books on William Faulkner, *William Faulkner: The Yoknapatawpha Country* (1963) and *Toward Yoknapatawpha and Beyond* (1978). In these works, Brooks brilliantly discusses Faulkner's novels, but it is clear that his interest is more in the relationship of Faulkner's fiction to his Southern society than in formalist analysis.

Newer critical approaches appeared, none of which was content to remain within the structure of the poem itself—the archetypal criticism of Northrop Frye, the phenomenological criticism of Georges Poulet and Hillis Miller, the structuralism of Roland Barthes, and the deconstruction of Jacques Derrida. The latter were influential but were more concerned with the modes of literary discourse than with the explication of texts, and better with fiction than with poetry.

During the protest movement of the later 1960's, formalism fell into disrepute because of its lack of concern for the social and political backgrounds of literary works. Ironically, the New Critics were accused of empiricism and scientism in the analysis of literature. Nevertheless, twentieth century formalism has had a seemingly permanent influence on the teaching of literature in the United States, just as it has in France. Most literature introductory courses remain primarily formalistic in their approaches.

The New Critics taught a generation of students the art of close reading of the text. They warned readers against fallacies and heresies in reading and teaching poetry, and the lessons seem to have been widely learned. Although they used paraphrase masterfully themselves, they warned against "the heresy of paraphrase." The prose statement should not be regarded as the equivalent of the "meaning" of the poem. They attacked and seemingly permanently damaged the

positivistic view that would limit poetry to the emotions only—what they called the "affective fallacy." As Brooks declared in *The Well Wrought Urn*: "Poetry is not merely emotive . . . but cognitive. It gives us truth. . . ." Formalism did not prevent, but did restrict, practice of the biographical fallacy, studying the poet instead of his or her works.

The most controversial fallacy exposed by the New Critics was the intentional fallacy, against which all the formalists warned. Monroe C. Beardsley and William K. Wimsatt, who stated (in *The Verbal Icon*, 1954) what was implicit in formalism all along, may have gone too far in seeming to exclude the poet from throwing any light at all on the meaning of his poem; they did, however, warn against finding the meaning of a work in some prose statement by the author before or after he wrote it. Formalism has made the point that the actual intention of a poem can be determined only from an explication of the poem itself. Few literary critics today would regard the poem as a fictive world that is sufficient unto itself. Poems have thematic and psychological contexts as well as verbal and dramatic contexts. Formalist analyses were too innocent of the linguistic structures of the language that poetry used. Nevertheless, no modern critical approach has revealed more of the richness of meaning potentially available within a poem.

BIBLIOGRAPHY
Brooks, Cleanth. *Modern Poetry and the Tradition*. Chapel Hill: University of North Carolina Press, 1939.
Brooks, Cleanth, and Robert Penn Warren. *Understanding Poetry*. 3d ed. New York: Holt, Rinehart, and Winston, 1976.
_____. *The Well Wrought Urn: Studies in the Structure of Poetry*. New York: Harcourt Brace, 1947.
De Man, Paul. "Form and Intent in the American New Criticism." In *Blindness and Insight*. 2d rev. ed. Minneapolis: University of Minnesota Press, 1983.
Empson, William. *Seven Types of Ambiguity*. 1930. 3d ed. New York: New Directions, 1966.
Krieger, Murray. *The New Apologists for Poetry*. Minneapolis: Univeristy of Minnesota Press, 1956.
Lentricchia, Frank. *After the New Criticism*. Chicago: University of Chicago Press, 1980.

Ransom, John Crowe. *The New Criticism.* 1941. Reprint. Westport, Conn.: Greenwood Press, 1980.

Richards, I. A. *Practical Criticism: A Study of Literary Judgement.* 1929. Reprint. New York: Harcourt Brace, 1978.

_____. *Principles of Literary Criticism.* 1924. Reprint. New York: Harcourt Brace, 1980.

Tate, Allen. *Essays of Four Decades.* 1968. 3d ed. Wilmington, Del.: ISI Books, 1999.

Wellek, René. *American Criticism, 1900-1950.* Vol. 6 in *A History of Modern Criticism, 1750-1950.* New Haven, Conn.: Yale University Press, 1992.

Wellek, René, and Austin Warren. *Theory of Literature.* 3d ed. New York: Harcourt Brace Jovanovich, 1984.

Wimsatt, W. K., Jr. *The Verbal Icon: Studies in the Meaning of Poetry.* 1954. Reprint. Lexington: University Press of Kentucky, 1989.

Richard J. Calhoun

LINGUISTIC CRITICISM

In many ways, the area called "linguistic criticism" is a legacy of the work done in the early twentieth century by Ferdinand de Saussure, the great French theorist whose posthumously published work has been the point of departure for all modern structuralism, not only in linguistics but also in anthropology and other disciplines as well. American structural linguistics, the principles and research program for which were laid down by Leonard Bloomfield in his *Language* (1933), was concerned with establishing the structure—phonological, morphological, syntactical, and semantic—of languages conceived as systematic wholes. It dealt with what Saussure's *Cours de linguistique generale* (1916; *Course in General Linguistics*) called the *langue*, the system of a limited repertoire of sounds, on whose differentiation differences of meaning depend, and of a limited number of kinds of sentence elements that can be combined in certain orders and hierarchical relationships, as distinguished from *parole*, particular utterances. To elicit these elements and rules of combination for a given language, linguists depended primarily on speech rather than on written texts. Furthermore, Bloomfieldian linguists tended to concentrate their efforts on the description of exotic languages rather than of English. Meanwhile, literary critics focused their attention on particular written texts, deemed literary, and were concerned with the interpretation and evaluation of these works of individual writers.

Poems and other literary works are, of course, works of verbal art whose medium is language, and this fact suggested to some linguists a potential for the application of linguistics to the study of literature. The techniques developed by linguists for the analysis of language could be applied to the language of literary texts. The linguist could bring to bear on these texts an expertise that the literary critic did not have. Much of the work that has been done involving the application of linguistics to the study of literary texts falls under the heading of "stylistics," the study of literary style. Early contributions in linguistic stylistics tended to carry the animus of bringing a new objectivity to a field that had hitherto been merely impressionistic in its methods; however, later work has generally recognized both the inevitability and the value of a subjective component in stylistic analysis. While the interest of literary criticism and, for the most part, stylistics, is in particular literary texts, modern poetics, which traces its roots to Russian Formalism (a movement in literary scholarship originating in Russia around 1915 and suppressed there about 1930), is instead interested in the question of the nature of literariness or poeticity. The study of poetics is closely related to the study of linguistics.

Besides application of the specific techniques and categories of one or another kind of linguistics for studying the language of literary texts, another kind of application of linguistics to the study of literature has been of great importance: Linguistics has been taken as a model for the study of literary structures, such as narrative, that are not intrinsically linguistic but are translatable into other media, and students of literature have identified constituents of such structures and formalized descriptive rules for their combination by analogy with linguists' descriptions of the structure of a language (*langue*). In thus adopting the structuralist approach derived from Saussure, literary critics have participated in a transdisciplinary movement affecting all the human sciences. A discussion of structuralism in literary studies, however, is outside the scope of this survey of linguistic approaches to poetry, which will be limited to applications of the techniques and categories of linguistic analysis to the language of poetic texts. Even within these limits, this survey does not purport to cover all the significant work. The contributions discussed below—which include both general, programmatic pieces and specific, descriptive studies—do not by any means represent all the important figures in the field or even the full range of relevant work by those cited; they are simply examples of various linguistic approaches to poetry from the early 1950's to the early 1980's.

BEGINNINGS

When, in 1951, the linguists George L. Trager and Henry Lee Smith, Jr., published *An Outline of English Structure*, a description of English phonetics, morphology, and syntax such as had been made of many exotic languages, the linguist Harold Whitehall immediately saw the possibility of application to the study of English literature, and went so far as to say that "no criticism can go beyond its linguistics." Specifically, he saw that Trager and Smith's account of stress, pitch, and juncture—as each having four functionally distinguishable levels in English—would be valuable to students of meter and rhythm of English verse. The rhythm of lines could presumably be much more precisely described in terms of four levels of stress rather than in the two normally recognized in traditional metrics. Such an application of Trager and Smith's findings for modern American speech to the study of verse in English was actually made by Edmund L. Epstein and Terence Hawkes, who found in a body of iambic pentameter verse a vast number of different stress-patterns according to the four-level system. The question of the relevance of such descriptive analysis to the meaning and aesthetic value of the poetry in question was not raised in these early applications of linguistics to literature.

Archibald A. Hill, who did practical work in the application of linguistics to literature in the 1950's, saw linguistic analysis of a text in terms of such factors as word-order and stress as operating on a preliterary level, but considered them to be a useful preliminary to analysis in terms of literary categories such as images. Not unlike the New Critics, he approached a poem as a structured whole and sought to interpret it with minimal reference to outside knowledge such as biographical information, but he differed from the New Critics in thinking it best to begin with specifically linguistic formal details. In a 1955 discussion of Gerard Manley Hopkins's "The Windhover," he took an analysis of Hopkins's stress and word-order, considered in relation to general English usage, as the basis for resolving ambiguities and determining emphases at particular points—and applied it, as an aid to interpretation of at least local meaning.

ROMAN JAKOBSON

In 1958 a Conference on Style was held at Indiana University, in which a group of linguists, literary critics, and psychologists presented and discussed papers on issues relevant to the matter of style in language. This conference, the papers of which were published in 1960 in a collection titled *Style in Language*, edited by Thomas A. Sebeok, proved to be something of a water-

shed for the application of linguistics to the study of poetry. Roman Jakobson's presentation on the relation of linguistics to poetics still remains a point of reference for work on the language of poetry. While the focus of the New Critics and some linguists working on literature was on the individual poem considered as an autonomous structured whole, the concern of poetics, as Jakobson sets it forth, is with the differentiating characteristics of poetic language. He argues that inasmuch as poetics deals with problems of verbal structure, it lies wholly within the field of linguistics, "the global science of verbal structure." He offers a functional definition of poetic language in terms of the constitutive factors of any act of verbal communication, enumerating six such factors—the addresser, the message, the addressee, the context, the contact between addresser and addressee, and the code (the rules of the language, also of a certain register, dialect, and so on) in accord with which the message is constructed. In any given utterance or text, focus will be on one of these factors primarily, though to a lesser extent on others, and the predominant function of the utterance or text can be defined accordingly. Jakobson defines the poetic function of language as "focus on the message for its own sake," stressing that the poetic function is not confined to poetry (appearing also, for example, in political slogans and advertising jingles) and that poetry involves functions of language other than the poetic; different genres, for example, are partially characterized by the relative importance of the referential, emotive, or conative (focus on the addressee) functions.

Contending that "the verbal structure of a message depends predominantly on [its] predominant function," Jakobson then studies the effect of the poetic function on the linguistic structure of a text. His famous account of the differentiating feature of language in which the poetic function predominates over the other functions depends on the fact that making an utterance or constructing a text always involves two operations: (1) *selection* from among a series of items that are syntactically and semantically equivalent and (2) the *combination* of the selected items into a meaningful sequence of words. "The poetic function," runs Jakobson's formulation, "projects the principle of equivalence from the axis of selection into the axis of combination." In verse, for example, every syllable becomes equivalent to every other syllable, every stress to every other stress, as units of measure. A passage of verse is characterized by the repetition of equivalent units.

Jakobson goes on to cite some of the kinds and operations of equivalence in a broad range of poetry of many different languages, in the process providing what amounts to a program for research on poetic language. All metrical systems, he says, use "at least one (or more than one) binary contrast of a relatively high and relatively low prominence"; he gives examples of meters "based only on the opposition of syllabic peaks and slopes (syllabic verse)," meters based "on the relative levels of the peaks (accentual verse)," and meters based "on the relative length of the syllabic peaks or entire syllables (quantitative verse)." Besides features invariably present in lines in a given meter, optional features will be likely to occur, and these, Jakobson maintains, form part of the metrical system to be described by the linguist. A full description should not, as traditional descriptions of meters typically do, exclude any linguistic feature of the verse design. Jakobson cites, as an example of a feature that ought not to be ignored, the "constitutive value of intonation in English meters," "the normal coincidence of syntactic pause and pausal intonation" with line-ending, such that, even when frequent, enjambment is felt as a variation. Word boundaries and grammatical boundaries may also be among the defining characteristics of a line in a given verse tradition, even if such boundaries are not marked by any distinguishable phonetic features. (He does not specify a method for ascertaining that the enumeration of relevant features has been exhaustive.) What have generally been treated as deviations from a metrical pattern should, according to Jakobson, form part of the description of the pattern, for they are variations allowed by the rules of the given meter.

For rhyme as well as meter Jakobson emphasizes that linguistic analysis should not be limited to sound alone. The similarity of sound between rhyme words throws into relief their grammatical and semantic relations. Whether rhyme words are of the same or different grammatical classes, whether their syntactical functions are the same or different, whether they have a semantic relationship of similarity or antithesis, are all questions relevant to the operation of rhyme in the poetry in question. Poets and schools of poetry that use rhyme differ in favoring or opposing rhyming words of the same grammatical class and function, and grammatical rhymes operate differently from anti-grammatical ones.

While repetition is an important aspect of the sound of poetry, a sound can be important, Jakobson points out, without being repeated: A sound with a single occurrence in a prominent position against a contrasting background and in a thematically important word should not be neglected. Analysis of the sound in poetry must take into account both the phonological structure of the language in question and which of the distinctive features of phonemes (voiced/voiceless, nasal/oral, and so on) are taken into account in the particular verse convention. Besides meter, rhyme, alliteration, and other forms of reiteration that are primarily of sound, though also involving syntactic and semantic aspects, poetic language is characterized by other forms of parallelism. For example, lines may be grammatically parallel, inviting semantic comparison between words in corresponding positions, which may be perceived as having a metaphorical or quasimetaphorical relationship. Concentration on lexical tropes to the exclusion of the syntactical aspect of poetic language is, according to Jakobson, not warranted: "The poetic resources concealed in the morphological and syntactic structure of language, briefly the poetry of grammar, and its literary product, the grammar of poetry, have been seldom known to critics and mostly disregarded by linguists but skillfully mastered by creative writers."

MICHAEL RIFFATERRE

Jakobson asserted "the right and duty of linguistics to direct the investigation of verbal art in all its compass and extent," and provided a program for such research. At about the same time, Michael Riffaterre was concerning himself with the problem that a linguistic analysis of a poetic text could provide only a linguistic description of it and could not distinguish which of the features isolated were operative as part of the poem's style. In a 1959 paper, "Criteria for Style Analysis," he endeavored to supply a technique for distinguishing stylistic features of a text from merely linguistic features without stylistic function.

Riffaterre's argument is based on the dual assumption—diametrically opposed to Jakobson's notion of the nature of poetic language—that the literary artist works to ensure the communication of his meaning, and that this end can be achieved through reduction of the predictability of elements, so that the reader's natural tendency to interpolate elements that seem predictable from the context will be frustrated, and he will be held up and forced to attend to unpredictable elements. The linguistic elements that are to be taken into account in the stylistic analysis of a literary work are precisely these unpredictable elements, which Riffaterre calls "stylistic devices" or "SD's." While he is apparently confident of the efficacy of this means for getting reader-attention, at least one investigator of style in poetry (Anne Cluysenaar) cites an instance where readers failed to notice an unpredictable phrase, simply substituting what they would have expected for what was actually there in the text. Not content that the analyst of style should rely simply on his own subjective impressions as to the location of stylistic devices in a literary text, Riffaterre recommends the use of informants, readers of the text in question, including critics and editors of the text as well as lay readers. In using informants' responses, the analyst of style should, according to Riffaterre, empty them of such content as value judgments and take them as mere indicators of possible sites of stylistic devices. The resultant enumeration should then be verified, by checking whether the points identified coincide with points where a pattern established by a preceding stretch of text has been broken; if so, they are stylistic devices and should be submitted to linguistic analysis by the stylistician.

In choosing to compare parts of a given text with each other, Riffaterre departed from the practice, become common at the time, of taking "ordinary language"—a very vague entity—as a norm with which to compare the text. His examples show, however, that he has not been able to dispense altogether with reference to language usage outside the text in question, for items can be interpreted as unpredictable in a given context only with respect to knowledge or experience of usage in similar context elsewhere. Besides the fact of departure from a pattern established by a preceding stretch of text, another phenomenon can, according to Riffaterre,

help confirm the identification of a stylistic device: This is the presence of a cluster of independent stylistic devices, which together highlight a particular passage.

In a well-known paper published in *Yale French Studies* in 1966, Riffaterre assesses an analysis by Jakobson and Claude Lévi-Strauss of the poem "Les Chats" of Charles Baudelaire. Jakobson and Lévi-Strauss had scanned the text on several levels—meter, phonology, grammar, and meaning—discovering equivalences of various kinds, which they took as constitutive of several simultaneous structural divisions of the poem. Riffaterre contends that many of the linguistic equivalences they identify cannot be taken as stylistic features, as elements of the poetic structure, because they would not be perceived in the process of reading. Only such equivalences as would be perceptible should be taken as pertaining to the poetic structure of the text. Equivalences on one level alone generally will not be perceived as correspondences; grammatical parallelism, for example, will need to be reinforced by correspondence in metrical position.

TRANSFORMATIONAL-GENERATIVE GRAMMAR

With the development of transformational-generative grammar by Noam Chomsky and others, beginning with Chomsky's 1957 book *Syntactic Structures*, came new kinds of linguistic approaches to literature. The theory of transformational-generative grammar is based on the assumption that native speakers of a language internalize grammatical rules for their language such that they are able to produce unlimited numbers of grammatical sentences they have never heard before and to judge a given sentence as grammatical or ungrammatical (or as more or less grammatical, more or less complex). There is the further assumption that the grammar should reflect native speaker intuitions of relation between superficially different sentences, as between a given declarative sentence in the active voice and its passivization, and of ambiguity as to the construction of certain sentences: In the former case, the superficially different sentences are taken as having the same "deep structure"; in the latter, the surface structure of the given sentence is taken as able to have been reached by two or more different routes, from two or more different deep structures. A transformational-generative grammar of a given language ideally consists of an ordered set of rules for the generation of all possible grammatical sentences in the language; besides phrase-structure rules, it includes ordered series of obligatory and optional transformational rules that transform an underlying "kernel sentence" or set of kernel sentences into a surface structure.

The surface structure/deep structure distinction was taken, in early efforts at the application of transformational-generative grammar to the study of literary texts such as Richard Ohmann's, as a confirmation and clarification of the traditional distinction between form and content. A writer's style could be accounted for by the nature of the optional transformations he chose. Ohmann adheres to the position of early transformational-generative theory that different surface structures produced by the choice of different optional transformations have the same content, but he contradicts himself when he says that each writer will make characteristic choices and that these choices correlate with the writer's way of looking at experience. Likewise, regarding deviance in poetic language from usage restrictions on categories of words, he holds that the kinds of deviance employed by a poet will reflect his vision; the kinds of deviance found in Dylan Thomas's poetry, Ohmann suggests, reflect his sense of nature as personal, the world as process.

One of the first linguists to apply transformational-generative grammar to the study of style in poetry was Samuel Levin. Levin was interested in the fact that poetry contains sentences and phrases that a native speaker might consider ungrammatical or semigrammatical. In a 1965 paper called "Internal and External Deviation in Poetry," he takes external deviation in syntax, that is, deviation from a norm of syntactical usage lying outside the text in question, as ungrammaticality; in other words, he assumes that it involves sentences that the grammar of the language in question would not generate. Among such sentences he recognizes degrees of deviance or ungrammaticality. He does not find the notion of the probability of a given element at a given point in the text (transitional probability) helpful in rationalizing this sense of degrees of deviance because of the unfeasibility of calculating transitional probabilities for the occurrence of a given word after a given sequence of preceding words. His approach is to determine what kinds of changes would have to be made in the rules of the grammar to make it generate the deviant sentences or phrases, assuming that it does not do so. These would be deemed more or less grammatical depending on the number of ungrammatical sentences that the changes entailed would generate.

In the case of a phrase such as E. E. Cummings's "a pretty how town," the number would be large, since either "how" would have to be added to the class of adjectives, or adverbs would have to be allowed to occur in the place of the second adjective in the sequence determiner plus adjective plus adjective plus noun, changes involving large classes. In the case of Dylan Thomas's phrase, "Rage me back," however, "rage" would simply have to be added to the subclass of transitive verbs taking "back" (mostly verbs of motion). Hence, the Cummings example is less grammatical than the Thomas. In like manner, the Thomas example produces a sense of richness through the conflation of the verb "rage" with notions of transitivity and motion, while Cummings's phrase leaves a sense of diffuseness because what is added to "how" is so unspecific. Levin notes that the former kind of ungrammaticality occurs more frequently than the latter in poetry and considers it akin to metaphor in its operation.

J. P. Thorne shares Levin's interest in the occurrence in poetry of sentences that would not be generated by the grammar; indeed, he says at one point that such sentences form the subject matter of stylistics. Where Levin takes single sentences and phrases from poetry and considers how the grammar would have to be modified to generate each sentence, however, Thorne proposes taking whole poems and constructing a grammar for the language of each poem. The grammar for a poem should be constructed on the same principles as the grammar for the language as a whole, the point being to compare the two and discover how the one differs from the other. A good poet, in Thorne's view, will invent a new language, differing from the standard language not (or not primarily) in surface structure, but in deep structure, that is, on the level of meaning. The poet will invent a new language in order to be able to say things that cannot be said in the standard language. In reading a good poem, the reader learns a new language. The grammar that one constructs for this new language will make explicit one's intuitions about its structure. One must decide which features of the poem's language are features of that language and which are features merely of the sample, when the sample (the poem) is all of the language there is. One's assignments of words to categories in this grammar and formulation of selection rules for their co-occurrence will reflect one's interpretation of the poem.

In a 1965 paper, "Stylistics and Generative Grammars," Thorne sketches a grammar for Cummings's poem, "anyone lived in a pretty how town." He also suggests that it may be illuminating to construct grammars for poems in which the language does not seem so manifestly ungrammatical, such as John Donne's "Nocturnal upon St. Lucy's Day," where animate subjects have verbs normally selected by inanimate subjects, and inanimate subjects have verbs normally selected only by animate subjects. In a 1970 paper, "Generative Grammar and Stylistic Analysis," he finds a similar deviation from the selection rules for Standard English in Theodore Roethke's poem "Dolour," where there are constructions such as "the sadness of pencils," which attach to concrete, inanimate nouns adjectives that normally select animate nouns or a subcategory of abstract nouns including "experience" and "occasion"; he points out that the decision whether to assimilate "pencils" and the other nouns so used in the poem to the category of animate nouns or to the particular subcategory of abstract nouns will depend on how one reads the poem.

Early efforts at applying transformational-generative grammar to literature have been recognized as limited by (1) the theory's separation of syntax from semantics (that is, of consideration of sentence structure from questions of meaning); (2) the assumption in early versions of the theory that the transformations that produced different surface structures from a single underlying structure did not affect the meaning; (3) the failure to extend analysis beyond the level of the sentence; and (4) the treatment of literary (especially poetic) language as characterized by ungrammatical constructions, deviations from the supposed norm of everyday speech. With these limitations, transformational-generative grammar could not illuminate the relation between form and content in poetry or relate formal description to interpretation. It did not offer a means of discussing the connections within and cohesiveness of a text as a whole. It had

nothing to say about poetry in which the language was not in any sense ungrammatical. Much of the irritation of literary critics with early applications of transformational-generative grammar to literature is attributable to limitations in the applications resulting from limitations in the early versions of the theory.

CATEGORY-SCALE GRAMMAR

Besides transformational-generative grammar, other modes of syntactical analysis developed by modern linguistics have been used in approaches to poetry. One of these is category-scale grammar, developed by M. A. K. Halliday and set forth in his 1961 paper "Categories of the Theory of Grammar." Category-scale grammar analyzes English syntax in terms of a hierarchically ordered enumeration or "rank-scale" of units: sentence, clause, group, word, morpheme. Halliday introduces the notion of "rank-shift" to refer to cases where a unit operates as a structural member of a unit of the same or lower rank; for example, a clause can be part of another clause or of a group (phrase). Category-scale grammar has been commended to students of literary style as making possible a clear and accurate description of the infrastructuring of the language and helping to discover and specify where the structural complexity of a text resides. Halliday himself has advocated the linguistic study of literary texts, arguing that this should be a comparative study and that it is not enough to discover, say, the kinds of clause structures in a given text, but that their relative frequencies in that text should then be compared with those in other texts, other samples of the language.

In a 1964 paper, he illustrates the sort of treatment he recommends with a discussion of two features of the language of William Butler Yeats's "Leda and the Swan"—the use of "the" and the forms and nature of the verbs. "The" is a deictic (a word that points to or identifies); its particular function is to identify a specific subset, by reference to the context (either of the text itself or of the situation of its utterance), to elements of the rest of the modifier or of the qualifier of the noun it modifies, or to the noun modified itself. In nominal groups where there are other modifying elements preceding the noun or a qualifier following it, "the" usually (in samples of modern English prose referred to by Halliday) specifies by reference to the rest of the modifier or the qualifier.

While "Leda and the Swan" has a high proportion of such nominal groups in comparison with another Yeats poem, in only one of them does "the" function in the usual way; in all the rest it specifies by reference not to anything else in the nominal group, but to the title. "Leda and the Swan" is also found to differ markedly in the handling of verbs from both another Yeats poem and a poem by Alfred, Lord Tennyson. A high proportion of verbs, including especially the lexically more powerful, are "deverbalized" by occurring as participles in bound or rank-shifted clauses or as modifiers of a noun (rather than as finite verbs in free clauses).

John Sinclair's 1966 paper, "Taking a Poem to Pieces," is the sort of analysis recommended by Halliday. Further, it represents an effort to remedy linguists' neglect of poetry in which the language is not describable as ungrammatical or deviant. Sinclair hypothesizes that even in poetry, where the language is apparently unremarkable, grammatical and other linguistic patterns are operating in a more complex way than could be described—or even perceived—with traditional terms. He uses the terms of category-scale grammar to describe the language of a short poem by Philip Larkin called "First Sight."

Beginning with the highest unit of syntax, the sentence, Sinclair sets forth the syntactical structure of Larkin's text: first the sentence structure (the nature and arrangement of the constituent clauses), then the clause structure (the nature and arrangement of the constituent groups and rank-shifted clauses), then the structure of the groups (the arrangement and relations of the constituent words and rank-shifted higher structures). He shows that the language of Larkin's poems represents a restricted selection from among the wide range of possibilities afforded by the language. Its stylistic character can be in part accounted for by the persistent selection of certain constructions normally occurring with lower frequency.

It is on the level of the clausal constitution of its sentences that Larkin finds the particular quality of the language of "First Sight" to lie. In what he calls "everyday English," in sentences that contain a free clause and a bound clause, the most common arrangement is an uninterrupted free clause followed by a bound clause; discontinuous structure (that is, a free clause interrupted by a bound clause) and the sequence of bound clause followed by free clause are both less common. Of the four

sentences in Larkin's poem, only the last has the generally most common arrangement of free clause followed by bound clause. Thus, while this poem's language is not deviant in such a way as to require a special grammar to describe it, it is distinguished by the relative frequency of certain otherwise unremarkable structures.

In a 1972 paper, "Lines About 'Lines,'" Sinclair attempts to integrate stylistic description with interpretation and develop theoretical principles and a methodology for stylistic analysis. He assumes that the analyst must *begin* with a critical understanding of the text; then look for patterns at successive levels; in each case where a pattern is found, relate it to the meaning; and finally synthesize the findings of form-meaning relationships. Sinclair hypothesizes that there will be "intersection points" of form and meaning and adopts the term "focusing categories" or "focats" for such points. The focats found in the analysis of a given text will be initially taken as pertaining to that text alone, but assumed to be general if subsequently encountered in numerous texts.

In this case, Sinclair takes as his example for analysis William Wordsworth's famous "Lines Composed a Few Miles Above Tintern Abbey." He finds two focats operative in the poem. One, the introduction of an optional element in a syntactical structure not yet complete, he calls "arrest." The other, which he calls "extension," is essentially the continuation of a potentially completed structure by an element not syntactically predictable from any of the preceding elements. Sinclair argues convincingly that arrest and extension do indeed represent instances of significant interrelation of formal structure and meaning in "Tintern Abbey." These two focats also seem to be likely candidates for generality (occurence in numerous texts).

GENERATIVE METRICS

Many of the examples of linguistic approaches to poetry so far considered here have been studies of the language, especially the syntax, of individual poems. Besides focusing on individual texts, however, linguists have also addressed themselves to more general phenomena of poetic language, such as meter and metaphor.

Beginning with a 1966 paper by Morris Halle and Samuel Jay Keyser, a "generative metrics" was developed, devoted almost exclusively to accentual-syllabic verse, principally iambic pentameter. Halle and Keyser draw an analogy between the native speaker of a language, who has internalized a set of logically ordered rules in accord with which he produces grammatical sentences, and the poet, whom they assume to have similarly internalized a set of rules in accord with which he produces metrical lines. Generative metrics does away with the notion of the metrical foot and replaces the hodgepodge of rules and exceptions of traditional metrics with a brief and ordered sequence of systematically related rules. This sequence of rules governs the realization of an abstract pattern in an actual text. The pattern is represented as consisting of positions rather than feet, each position corresponding to a single syllable. The rules for actualization of the pattern are presented as alternatives arranged in an order from least to greatest metrical "complexity" (greatest to least strictness).

DAVID CRYSTAL: TONE-UNITS

A very different approach to metrics has been taken by the British linguist David Crystal, who, in a 1971 paper, proposed a model for the description of English verse that is supposed to encompass both accentual-syllabic and free verse and to distinguish both from prose. He takes the line, rather than the syllable or the foot, as the basic unit of verse, and hypothesizes that the line normally consists, in performance, of a single complete "tone-unit." A tone-unit is the basic unit of organization of intonation in an utterance; since intonation functions in part to signal syntactical relations, tone-unit boundaries coincide with syntactical—generally clause—boundaries.

SPEECH-ACT THEORY

Transformationalists have approached metaphor as deviance through violation of "selection restriction rules" (rules formalizing acceptable collocations—for example, that for verbs with certain semantic features the subject must be animate). One interprets metaphors, according to this view (espoused, for example, by Robert J. Matthews in a 1971 paper), by deemphasizing those semantic features entailed in the selection restriction violation.

In the 1970's and 1980's, there was a growing recognition that properties such as metaphoricity, previously assumed to be peculiar to literary language, pertain as

well to conversational usage; also, not only the formal features of a text but also the situational context and the speaker-hearer (or writer-reader) relationship were now seen as relevant to its operation.

Growing interest in speech-act theory (developed by J. L. Austin and John Searle) is a reflection of the concern for context-sensitive analysis of utterances or texts. According to speech-act theory, besides performing a locutionary act (that is, producing a grammatical utterance), a speaker will perform one or another kind of illocutionary act (such as asserting, ordering, promising) and possibly a perlocutionary act (that is, bringing about a certain state in the hearer). Besides being grammatical or ungrammatical, an utterance will be appropriate or inappropriate in the given situation; appropriateness conditions—internalized rules of language use that speakers assume to be in force—can be formulated.

While the Austinian treatment of appropriateness conditions is to define them in relation to particular speech acts in particular contexts, H. Paul Grice has generalized the notion of appropriateness, developing rules intended to apply to all discourse. His "cooperative principle," which a participant in a speech exchange supposedly will normally assume his interlocutor to know and to be trying to observe and expecting him to observe also, is: "Make your conversational contribution such as is required, at the stage at which it occurs, by the accepted purpose or direction of the talk-exchange in which you are engaged." At the same time, linguists have been extending the purview of their discipline in ways that bring it into close accord with speech-act philosophy. Since 1968, post-Chomskyan generative semantics (as developed by George Lakoff, Robin Lakoff, Charles Fillmore, and others) has extended the notion of speaker competence to embrace the ability to perform appropriate speech acts in particular situations, as well as phonology and syntax. In addition, sociolinguists are concerned with language *use*.

How do these developments in linguistics and allied fields relate to the study of literature, particularly poetry? Mary Louise Pratt claims (*Toward a Speech Act Theory of Literary Discourse*, 1977) that, with these developments, linguistics is for the first time able to describe literary discourse in terms of the literary speech situation, to define it in terms of use rather than of intrinsic features, and to relate it to other kinds of language use. She cites studies showing that features assumed by poeticians to be exclusively attributes of literary discourse occur in conversation as well; specifically, structural and stylistic features such as are found in fiction also occur in "natural narratives." These formal similarities, she thinks, can be in part explained by the fact that with both natural narratives and literary works, the speech exchange situation is one in which the hearer or reader is a voluntary, nonparticipant audience. She also considers it important to take into account that the reader normally knows that a literary work was, and was intended to be, published, and assumes it was composed in writing with an opportunity for deliberation, hence that it is more likely to be worthwhile than casual utterances; because of these assumptions on the part of the reader, a literary work can get away with being "difficult," and with making considerable demands on its audience.

Pratt attempts to adapt the categories of speech act theorists to accommodate literary discourse and relate it to other kinds of speech acts. She considers that many, if not all, literary works, together with exclamations and natural narratives, fall into the class of speech acts that have been characterized as thought-producing (as opposed to action-producing), representative (representing a state of affairs), or world-describing (as opposed to world-changing). She sees exclamations, natural narratives, and literary works together as constituting a subclass of representative speech acts that are characterized by "tellability," that is, by the unlikelihood or problematical nature of the state of affairs represented (whether fictional or not). This characteristic she holds to pertain as much to lyric poetry as to novels and short stories. The subclass is further characterized by (1) detachability from any immediate speech context (this is obvious for literary works, which generally have no immediate relation to the situation in which the reader happens to find himself) and (2) a tendency to elaborate on the state of affairs represented. Indeed, elaborating on the state of affairs they posit, may be taken, Pratt suggests, as what literary works chiefly do.

SOCIOLINGUISTICS

Roger Fowler, a British linguist, has been advocating and practicing the application of linguistics to the study of literary texts since the 1960's; his early work in this field includes a paper (published in the 1966 collection, *Essays on Style and Language,* which he edited) showing, with a rich variety of examples, that verse of a given meter can have very different rhythmical movements, depending on the relationships of the grammatical units with the lineation. In his 1981 volume *Literature as Social Discourse: The Practice of Linguistic Criticism,* Fowler argues that linguistic description of literary texts should concern itself with the sociocultural context. He exemplifies the sort of description, essentially sociolinguistic, that he advocates in a treatment (in the same volume) of Wordsworth's poem "Yew-Trees."

Fowler's treatment is in answer to a reading of this poem by Michael Riffaterre. Riffaterre concentrates on the lexical aspect of the poem's language, showing that it consists basically of variations on "yew-tree" through translation of certain of its semantic components from "tree-code" into other codes—for example, "snake-code" in the lines, "Huge trunks! and each particular trunk a growth/ Of intertwisted fibres serpentine/ Upcoiling, and inveterately convolved." Fowler contends that by neglecting the matters of register (and what it implies of the activity of the speaker of the poem vis-à-vis an addressee) and of the reader's sequential experience of the text, Riffaterre has failed to give sufficient weight to the shift from a geographical guide register to Miltonic loftiness in these lines. This and other shifts of register in the poem are, he contends, significant, central to its meaning.

NEW DIRECTIONS

Besides speech-act theory and sociolinguistics, later work on the development of a linguistic theory of discourse saw applications to literature. Teun van Dijk, for example, has done work on a grammar taking the text, rather than the sentence, as the structure to be described, and including a "pragmatic" component that would specify appropriateness conditions for discourses.

BIBLIOGRAPHY
Austin, J. L. *How to Do Things with Words.* Cambridge, Mass.: Harvard University Press, 1962.
_____. *Sense and Sensibilia.* Oxford, England: Clarendon Press, 1962.

Bloomfield, Leonard. *Language.* New York: Holt, Rinehart and Winston, 1933.

Carter, Ronald, and Paul Simpson, eds. *Language and Literature: An Introductory Reader in Stylistics.* Boston: Allen & Unwin, 1982.

Chatman, Seymour, ed. and trans. *Literary Style: A Symposium.* New York: Oxford University Press, 1971.

Chomsky, Noam. *Syntactic Structures.* The Hague: Mouton, 1957.

Dijk, Teun van. *Discourse Studies.* 2 vols. Newbury Park, Calif.: Sage Publications, 1997.

_____. *Some Aspects of Text Grammars: A Study in Theoretical Linguistics and Poetics.* The Hague: Mouton, 1972.

_____, ed. *Discourse and Literature.* Philadelphia: J. Benjamins, 1985.

Fowler, Roger, ed. *Essays on Style and Language.* New York: Humanities Press, 1966.

_____. *Linguistic Criticism.* New York: Oxford University Press, 1986.

_____. *Literature as Social Discourse: The Practice of Linguistic Criticism.* Bloomington: Indiana University Press, 1981.

Grice, H. Paul. *Studies in the Way of Words.* Cambridge, Mass.: Harvard University Press, 1989.

Halle, Morris, ed. *Roman Jakobson: What He Taught Us.* Columbus, Ohio: Slavica, 1983.

Halle, Morris, and Samuel Jay Keyser. *English Stress: Its Form, Its Growth, and Its Role in Verse.* New York: Harper & Row, 1971.

Halliday, M. A. K. "Categories of the Theory of Grammar." In *Literary Style: A Symposium.* New York: Oxford University Press, 1971.

Lee, David. *Competing Discourses: Perspective and Idology in Language.* New York: Longman, 1992.

Levin, Samuel. *Linguistic Structures in Poetry.* New York: Mouton de Gruyter, 1973.

Pratt, Mary Louise. *Toward a Speech Act Theory of Literary Discourse.* Bloomington: Indiana University Press, 1977.

Riffaterre, Michael. *Semiotics of Poetry.* Bloomington: University of Indiana Press, 1978.

Saussure, Ferdinand de. *Course in General Linguistics.* 1916. Translated and annotated by Roy Harris, edited by Charles Bally and Albert Sechehaye with the collaboration of Albert Riedlinger. LaSalle, Ill.: Open Court, 1986.

Searle, John R. *Expression and Meaning: Studies in the Theory of Speech Acts.* New York: Cambridge University Press, 1979.

_____. *Speech Acts: An Essay in the Philosophy of Language.* London: Cambridge University Press, 1969.

Sebeok, Thomas A., ed. *Style in Language.* 1960. Reprint. Cambridge, Mass.: M.I.T. Press, 1971.

Sinclair, John. "Taking a Poem to Pieces." In *Essays on Style and Language,* edited by Roger Fowler. New York: Humanities Press, 1966.

Toolan, Michael. *Narrative: A Critical Linguistic Introduction.* 1988. 2d ed. New York: Routledge, 2001.

Trager, George L., and Henry Lee Smith, Jr. *An Outline of English Structure.* 1951. New York: Johnson Reprint, 1970.

Weber, Jean Jacques, ed. *The Stylistics Reader.* New York: St. Martin's Press, 1996.

Eleanor von Auw Berry

MARXIST CRITICISM

Marxist criticism uses the terms and tools of Marxist philosophy to explain the production and meaning of literature. Based on the writings of Karl Marx and Friedrich Engels from the middle of the nineteenth century, Marxist criticism flourished in the 1920's and 1930's (Vladimir I. Lenin, Leon Trotsky, and Mao Zedong all wrote on literature) and was refined after World War II using more sophisticated poststructuralist theory and the rediscovered writings of Georg Lukács, Walter Benjamin, Mikhail Bakhtin, Antonio Gramsci, and other European critics.

Marx and Engels left no systematic study of literature, although they both discussed literature extensively in reviews and letters, but later critics have built their theory on Marx and Engels's understanding of the crucial roles of social class and class struggle in every phase of human history, and the interdependence of the socioeconomic foundations or "base" of any society and its "superstructure" of law, religion, art, and other manifestations of culture and civilization. In Marxist criticism, social class is a key determining factor. An understanding of medieval poetry, for example, might start with the aristocratic and feudal class structure of that society. History is the story of the struggles between social classes—in modern times, and in Western culture, between a dominant bourgeoisie and an emerging proletariat. Literature, like all cultural products, plays a role in that struggle, whether the makers of literature are aware of that role or not.

Given such sweeping historical and political views, it is not surprising that Marxist criticism is often best at explaining larger literary movements: for example, how the development of the novel followed the emergence of the middle class (and thus increased leisure time for reading) in the eighteenth century; the rise of modernism in Anglo-American literature at the beginning of the twentieth century; or the function of a literary canon in any culture. Marxist criticism may be closest in practice to sociological criticism, in its study, for example, of the actual social conditions and relations that produce works of art; to New Historicism, in the understanding of the layers of meaning in any society; and to feminist criticism, because both feminist and Marxist criticism challenges power structures—feminist critics usually in the name of gender issues and Marxists more generally in terms of social class. All four of these critical schools have come to be subsumed by the end of the twentieth century under what is usually called "cultural studies," and many contemporary literary critics use analytical tools from all four, especially in talking about issues of race, gender, and social class in literary works and movements.

The Marxist critic is best at showing the important role that ideology plays in any literary work. "Ideology" is the term used to identify the shared beliefs and values held by any particular culture, and one of its functions, as the British critic Terry Eagleton has defined it,

> is to legitimate the power of the ruling class in society; in the last analysis, the dominant ideas of a society are the ideas of its ruling class.

Marxist critics attempt to identify the key ideological concepts at play in any work (the anti-Semitism and bizarre economic views of the American poet Ezra Pound in the 1930's, for example) at the same time that they try to avoid reductive critical interpretations (for example, that those horrific political views must necessarily cripple the poetry he produced in that period). Since all literature is finally ideological—even when the author denies it—the task of the Marxist critic is to evaluate a literary work in part as the transcription of a complex reaction among a writer and the prevailing material conditions, class relations, and dominant values of that writer's world. This Marxist literary practice—particularly the use of ideological analysis—has become influential on nearly all other critical disciplines.

THE EMERGENCE OF POETRY

Given its interest in larger socioliterary movements and its belief in the interdependent relationship between literature and society, it is not surprising that much earlier Marxist criticism focused, not on individual poems, but on the emergence of poetry as a literary genre. One of the first full-length studies of the origins of poetry was Christopher Caudwell's *Illusion and Reality: A Study of the Sources of Poetry* (1937), in which the young British Marxist, who died fighting in the Spanish Civil War near the time his book was published, mixed insights into the sources of poetry with some rather crude analyses. George Thomson was a major disciple of Caudwell, and his *Marxism and Poetry* (1945) was a much more developed study that argued the organic relationships between work and consciousness, between inspiration and collective expression. Even the rhythm of poetry, Thomson argued, could finally be traced to the use of tools in work.

Probably the best study of the origins of poetry appeared in the Austrian critic Ernst Fischer's *Von der Notwendigkeit der Kunst* (1959; *The Necessity of Art: A Marxist Approach*, 1963), which described the history of the arts from a Marxist perspective and included, in its analysis of everything from the collective origins of art to the modern conditions of alienation and mystification, a number of poetry topics, including William Shakespeare and the Romantic poets. (See "The world and language of poetry," in Fischer's chapter "Content and Form.") A similarly valuable work a few years later was Raymond Williams's *The Country and the City* (1973), a study of English literature that touched on various poets and poetic forms over thousands of years. Fischer and Williams proved how valuable Marxism could be in exploring the complex and symbiotic relationship between art and literature (including poetry), on one hand, and the societies out of which they came, on the other.

THEORIES OF POETIC FORM

The development of theories of poetic form, beyond the study of the emergence of poetry as a genre, has been more recent. The prolific American critic Margaret Schlauch wrote *Modern English and American Poetry: Techniques and Ideologies* (1956), which illustrated, as much as anything, the multiple pressures Marxist criticism suffered during the Cold War years between 1947 and 1991. A few years later, however, Peter Demetz published *Marx, Engels, und die Dichter: Zur Grundlagenforschung des Marxismus* (1959; *Marx, Engels, and the Poets: Origins of Marxist Literary Criticism*, 1967), which established the interest in poetry the founders of Marxism had, looking in particular at Marx and Engels's comments on Shakespeare, Johann Wolfgang

von Goethe, and Honoré de Balzac. Henri Arvon's *L'Esthéthique marxiste* (1970; *Marxist Esthetics*, 1973) firmly established the importance of formal questions in Marxist criticism, and the following year, Fredric Jameson published his groundbreaking *Marxism and Form: Twentieth-Century Dialectical Theories of Literature* (1971), a work that would have a profound influence, not only on Marxist critics, but on much poststructuralist criticism as well. Drawing on the twentieth century Marxist theory of T. W. Adorno, Walter Benjamin, Herbert Marcuse, Ernst Bloch, Jean-Paul Sartre, and other critics, Jameson developed what he called a "dialectical criticism." Jameson established the primacy of theoretical and formal issues in Marxist criticism. Dismissing earlier crude and reductive Marxist practice, Jameson built an aesthetic theory that was sophisticated (if at times difficult to understand) and that built on the best of his European models.

Another important Marxist theorist has been Terry Eagleton, who, in a dozen books in the last quarter of the twentieth century, incorporated the theory of Pierre Macherey, Theodor Adorno, and other critics to create a poststructuralist Marxist criticism that is both theoretically supple and capable of dealing with a wide range of literature, including poetry. His best works include *Criticism and Ideology: A Study in Marxist Literary Theory* (1976), *Marxism and Literary Criticism* (1976), and *Literary Theory: An Introduction* (1983).

The Marxist study of individual poems operates of course under the same requirements as any critical approach and often begins by resembling formalist criticism—that is, by trying to understand the particular pattern of words, lines, and stanzas that make up the poem, and the structure of its meaning. Only after this kind of formal analysis has been completed (or at least acknowledged) does the Marxist critic turn to the larger ideological questions that tend to define the discipline to produce the distinctive analyses Marxist criticism can make.

POETRY AND IDEOLOGY

Rarely does literature reveal its own ideological biases, but older poetry tends to give them up more easily than contemporary verse. In 1839, for example, the American Henry Wadsworth Longfellow published "A Psalm of Life," and this hymn of faith and courage

("Life is real! Life is earnest!/ And the grave is not its goal") was to become one of the most popular poems in the English language over the next century, with its famous concluding stanza,

> Let us, then, be up and doing,
>   With a heart for any fate;
> Still achieving, still pursuing,
>   Learn to labor and to wait.

Viewing the poem in terms of its ideological content, the Marxist critic would be able to link the poem's values to an emergent industrial capitalism in the first half of the nineteenth century, for the poem was clearly encouraging the development of a work ethic needed in the textile mills of New England, as elsewhere. Forty years later, Eliza Cook, in a poem titled "Work" that appeared in *McGuffey's Fifth Eclectic Reader* in 1879, urged—

> Work, work, my boy, be not afraid;
>   Look labor boldly in the face;
> Take up the hammer or the spade,
>   And blush not for your humble place.

which may strike the modern reader as a rather crude job-recruitment poster for child labor. By the twentieth century, such blatant hymns to work would be harder to find. More common might be a poem like "The Golf Links" (1917), where Sarah N. Cleghorn could write, with much irony,

> The golf links lie so near the mill
>   That almost every day
> The laboring children can look out
>   And see the men at play.

Here social classes and the tensions between them are revealed, and the inequities that gap signifies are made the subject of the poem, heightened by the incongruous inversion of roles (boys working, adults playing). The ideological assumptions of Longfellow and Cook and other earlier American writers have been turned on their heads in Cleghorn's poem, to reveal what an unchecked industrial capitalism had become by the end of the nineteenth century—and how few good writers can any longer subscribe to its values.

Even narrative poetry is ideological, according to the precepts of Marxist criticism. In one of the most popular poems produced at the end of the nineteenth century, the American poet Edward Rowland Sill (in imitation of his master, the British Victorian poet Alfred, Lord Tennyson) could create the heroic battle scene depicted in "Opportunity" (1880), in which, in a dream, the narrator sees the troops of the "Prince" forced back in a "furious battle." A cowardly foot soldier compares his plight to the Prince's—"Had I a sword of keener steel—/ That blue blade that the king's son bears"—throws away his sword, "And lowering crept away and left the field":

> Then came the king's son, wounded, sore bestead,
> And weaponless, and saw the broken sword,
> Hilt-buried in the dry and trodden sand,
> And ran and snatched it, and with battle-shout
> Lifted afresh he hewed his enemy down,
> And saved a great cause that heroic day.

Translated into the socioeconomic conditions of the late nineteenth century, this heroic narrative clearly becomes a cry of encouragement to the working masses: Take your "opportunity" while you can, and ignore the horribly inequitable conditions around you. The poem urges workers to apply themselves in spite of class differences and working conditions: Do not *as*pire, the poem argues, *per*spire. Clearly, these are the values of a dominant capitalist class, which needs a willing proletarian workforce to operate its machines; the fewer complaints, the better the machines will run. Late nineteenth century American poetry is filled with such encouragements to those toiling in mill and mine. Like the Horatio Alger myth circulating through dime novels, or Russell Conwell's lecture "Acres of Diamonds," delivered thousands of times during the same period, the values of the author of "Opportunity" and other poets—like their belief in the work ethic—came from the dominant ideology of a capitalist ruling class. Poetry is never free of ideology, the Marxist critic argues; here, at the end of the nineteenth century and before the advent of labor unions and other protections for workers, it was in full display.

It is harder of course to do this kind of Marxist analysis on poetry at the turn of the twenty-first century (since reader, poet, and critic are all part of the same ideological moment), but the Marxist critic strives to do something similar on any poem: to recognize its formal structures, the patterns of sound and meaning that make up the totality of the poem, but to go beyond and beneath these to uncover the underlying ideological values and assumptions out of which this poem has emerged. Such an analysis demands sensitivity to formal questions, but additionally an awareness of the role that class values and ideals, along with the assumptions and stereotypes of race and gender, play in any society, including the present one.

BIBLIOGRAPHY

Eagleton, Terry. *Criticism and Ideology*. London: New Left Books, 1976. Eagleton's early attempt to build a "materialist" criticism and practice. In chapter 4 ("Ideology and Literary Form"), Eagleton analyzes several English poets, including T. S. Eliot. The form Eliot's poem *The Waste Land* (1922), Eagleton argues, is in contradiction to its conservative content, and "it is precisely in this conjuncture of 'progressive form' and 'reactionary content' that the ideology of *The Waste Land* inheres."

Goldstein, Philip. *The Politics of Literary Theory: An Introduction to Marxist Criticism*. Tallahassee: The Florida State University Press, 1990. A comprehensive overview of both Marxist theory and opposed critical theories, from the New Criticism of Cleanth Brooks and René Wellek, through those of feminism, reader-response, Raymond Williams and Fredric Jameson, to recent "Marxist versions of deconstruction" (Terry Eagleton, Michael Ryan, Gayatri Chakravorty Spivak).

Haslett, Moyra. *Marxist Literary and Cultural Theories*. New York: St. Martin's Press, 2000. Divided into two parts, "Key Theories" and "Applications and Readings." The second section includes the long chapter "A Labouring Woman Poet in the Age of Pope: Mary Leapor's 'Crumble-Hall' (1751)," which propounds a Marxist reading of this eighteenth cen-tury poem, and then "possible critiques of this reading." (The poem in its entirety is printed in an appendix.) An annotated bibliography describes sixteen seminal Marxist theoretical works, including volumes by Eagleton, Jameson, and Williams.

Jameson, Fredric. *Marxism and Form: Twentieth-Century Dialectical Theories of Literature*. Princeton, N.J.: Princeton University Press, 1971. This work established Marxist aesthetics as a legitimate form of poststructuralist literary theory. Includes chapters on T. W. Adorno, "Versions of a Marxist Hermeneutic" (Walter Benjamin, Herbert Marcuse, Friedrich Schiller, and Ernst Bloch), Georg Lukács, and Jean-Paul Sartre, and ends with an essay, "Towards Dialectical Criticism," which attempts to build a modern Hegelian model for literary criticism.

Venuti, Lawrence. *Our Halcyon Days: English Prerevolutionary Texts and Postmodern Culture*. Madison: University of Wisconsin Press, 1989. Venuti's study is "a Marxist intervention into Renaissance studies" that includes the chapter "Cavalier Love Poetry and Caroline Court Culture," in which Thomas Carew, Richard Lovelace, John Suckling, Ben Jonson, and other period poets are examined in depth and detail.

Williams, Raymond. *The Country and the City*. New York: Oxford University Press, 1973. A study of country and city as subject and theme in literature from Andrew Marvell to D. H. Lawrence, this is also a polemic against a "loss of the organic society" nostalgia toward the past. Capitalism as a mode of production, Williams argues, "is the basic process of most of what we know as the history of country and city." Considers pastoral poetry, dark views of the city, and stereotypes of "innocent" country and "wicked" town.

David Peck

STRUCTURALIST AND POSTSTRUCTURALIST CRITICISM

Space and spatial form traditionally bear directly upon the visual arts, and only metaphorically, by virtue of the tradition of the Sister Arts (*Ut pictura poesis*), upon literature. The language of literary criticism is rich in spatially metaphorical terms such as "background," "foreground," "local color," "form," "structure," "imagery," and "representation." The opposition of literal and metaphorical spatiality in literature could be accounted for as a residual effect of Gotthold Ephraim Lessing's classic and influential attack in the eighteenth century on the *Ut pictura poesis* tradition.

Lessing maintained an absolute distinction between the verbal and visual arts based on a belief that an essential difference between poetry and painting is the divergent perceptions of their signs: The proper domain of language is temporal, since its signs are sequential, unfolding one by one in linear fashion along a time line, whereas the proper domain of painting, whose signs are simultaneous images juxtaposed in space, is spatial.

The modern mind, nurtured in Einsteinian physics, would have no trouble collapsing the mutual exclusivity of Lessing's categorization by way of the notion of space-time, in which the description of an object consists not merely of length, width, and height but also of duration. The fourth dimension is the inclusion of change and motion; space is defined in relation to a moving point of reference.

If time and space are not viewed as mutually exclusive, then Lessing's categories cannot maintain the absolute distinction he desired to establish between the verbal/temporal and the visual/spatial arts. A painting, in fact, is simply not perceived as a whole instantaneously; rather the eye moves across the picture plane, assimilating and decoding in a process not unlike that of reading, which likewise entails movement over spatial form: the words written on the page. Given this interpretation of space and time, literary criticism of the second half of the twentieth century has radically redefined the nature of the relationship between the Sister Arts.

The seminal theoretical work in Anglo-American studies on literature as a spatial art is Joseph Frank's essay "Spatial Form in Modern Literature" (1945). Frank asserts that in the literature of modernism (Gustave Flaubert, James Joyce, T. S. Eliot, Ezra Pound), spatial juxtaposition is favored over normal linear chronology, marking the evolution toward a radical dislocation of the theory that language is intrinsically sequential. The formal method of modern literature is architectonic-spatial rather than linear-temporal, in that meaning is seen to arise ex post facto from the contiguous relation among portions of a work, rather than simply being represented in a temporal and progressive unfolding. The theory that the *modern* text has its own space by virtue of the simultaneous configuration of its elements—words, signs, sentences—in temporal disposition, is then extended to language in general in the model of meaning predominant in the critical movement known as structuralism.

STRUCTURAL LINGUISTICS: SAUSSURE

Structuralism is a method of investigation which gained popularity in the 1960's in Paris and in the 1970's in the United States through the writings of the anthropologist Claude Lévi-Strauss, the social historian and philosopher Michel Foucault, the critic Roland Barthes, and the psychoanalyst Jacques Lacan, among others. The diversity of the list is accounted for by the fact that structuralism grew out of structural linguistics, whose methods were considered applicable to several disciplines. Analysis is structuralist when the meaning of the object under consideration is seen to be based on the configuration of its parts, that is, on the way the elements are structured, contextually linked.

The linguistic theory grounding structuralism, and, by extension, literary criticism in the structuralist vein, is that of Ferdinand de Saussure (1857-1913). Saussurian linguistics considers the basic unit in the production of meaning to be the sign, an entity conceived of as a relationship between two parts; the *signified* or mental, conceptual component, lies behind the *signifier*, or phonetic, acoustical component. The signifier is a material manifestation of what is signified, of a meaning. Any given sign will be conceived of spatially, inasmuch as it always occupies a particular semantic and phonetic territory whose boundaries mark the limits of that space, thus allowing meaning to *take place*; that is, allowing the sign to function. For example, the phonetic space within which "tap" remains operable is always relative to a limit beyond which it would no longer differ from "top" or "tape." Likewise, its semantic space would be defined in terms of differentiation from other signs verging on "tap" semantically, such as "strike," "knock," "hit," and "collide." Thus, the value of the sign is neither essential nor self-contained but rather is contingent upon its situation in a field of differential relations, in the absence of which meaning would not arise.

Comparable to Frank's attribution of spatial form to modern literature by virtue of its atemporality, Saussurian linguistics renders language spatial in promoting synchrony over diachrony as its procedural method. The synchronic study of language, whose basic working hypothesis is that there exists an underlying system structuring every linguistic event, would reconstruct language as a functional, systematic whole at a particular moment in time, in contrast to the diachronic method of nineteenth century linguists interested in etymologies, the evolution of language over the course of time. Space becomes a linguistic activity in structural linguistics through investigation under ahistorical conditions of the synchronic structures governing the language system and through the notion of the sign as constitutive of a space of differential relations. Applied to the analysis of poetic texts, this theoretical groundwork accords the written work a space of its own in which meaning is produced. The pervasive influence of structural linguistics, specifically in the analysis of poetic texts, might be traced to the investigation in the early 1960's by Roman Jakobson of what he termed the *poetic function* of language.

ROMAN JAKOBSON

Jakobson designates the poetic function (one of six possible functions fulfilled by any utterance) as "the focus on the message for its own sake"; it is distinct from the referential or mimetic function dominating in normal linguistic usage where the meaning to which signs refer is directly conveyed (represented) by virtue of a univocal rapport between signifier (sound) and signified (meaning). The exchange of signs (communication) is not problematic. Whereas referential or mimetic language would focus on an exterior referent, the nature of the poetic function is introversion. The

poetic function reaches its apex in poetry, according to Jakobson: "a complex and indivisible totality where everything becomes significant, reciprocal, converse, correspondent . . . in a perpetual interplay of sound and meaning."

The poetic text is characterized by a high degree of patterning; its principal technique of organization is parallel structure: Patterns of similarity are repeated at each level of the text (phonetic, phonological, syntactic, semantic, and so on), such that the grammatical structure is seen as coextensive with the level of meaning or signification. In his analysis of William Blake's "Infant Sorrow," for example, Jakobson uncovers a network of ten nouns contained in the poem—evenly divided into five animates and five inanimates, and distributed among the couplets of the poem's two quatrains according to a principle of asymmetry:

> Anterior couplets: 3 animates, 2 inanimates
> Outer couplets: 3 animates, 2 inanimates
> Posterior couplets: 2 animates, 3 inanimates
> Inner couplets: 2 animates, 3 inanimates

Recalling "a remarkable analogy between the role of grammar in poetry and the painter's composition," Jakobson compares what he terms the manifestly spatial treatment opposing animates and inanimates in the poem to the converging lines of a background in pictorial perspective. The tension in the grammatical structure between animate and inanimate nouns underscores the tension between birth and the subsequent experience of the world on the poem's semantic level.

This type of structural analysis is characterized by the codification and systematization of the structural patterns grounding textual space, resulting in an immanent rather than transcendent reading of that space, one which reconstructs the rules governing the production of meaning rather than uncovering an essential meaning of that text. The tendency is toward all-encompassing systematic accountability in which every detail supplies information. The poem is interpreted as a highly structured network of interacting parts; it is a space closed off from "normal" language, a polysemic discourse whose semiotic play eventuates meaning within its borders, and not by virtue of an exterior referent or a priori idea that the poem is to convey. Structuralism thus implies the rejection of a purely phenomenological approach to language as expression, as denotation. As Vincent Descombes remarks in *Modern French Philosophy* (1980),

> . . . if a poetic utterance presents the construction that it does, this is not at all that some lived state (regret, desire) has elicited this particular form of expression in which to speak its meaning. . . . The poet listens not so much to the stirrings of his heart as to the prescriptions of the French language, whose resources and limitations engender a poetics which governs the poem.

The poem as productive textual space signals the dissolution of the notion of the author as a univocal source of meaning and intentionality situated outside the text and, thus, marks a radical shift away from critical analysis that would determine meaning as controlled by authorial intent or ultimately by the sociological, historical, and/or psychological influences structuring that intent.

POSTSTRUCTURALISM: DECONSTRUCTION

A tendency in literary criticism of the 1970's to examine the unquestioned assumptions of structuralism has come to be labeled deconstruction, or poststructuralism. It is largely influenced by the writings of Jacques Derrida, whose examination of the Western concept of representation (of language as referential, mimetic) is responsible in large part for the highly philosophical bent of poststructuralist criticism.

Poststructuralism does not offer an alternate comprehensive system of textual analysis as a replacement for structuralist methodology; it supplements tenets of structuralism. It is not a system, but rather a particular use of language which recognizes the involvement of any discourse, itself included, in paradoxes which may be repressed but cannot be resolved. Whereas structuralism tends to view textual space in the final analysis as the configuration of a unified and stable semantic space—a system actualized by its structure in which every detail is functional—for the poststructuralist a fully coherent and adequate system is impossible. The system in which all coheres depends on exclusion: the repression of elements which will not fit. For example, in the analysis of "Infant Sorrow" on the basis of grammatical categories, Jakobson is able to ignore the *pronoun* "I" in his discussion of animate and inanimate *nouns*. Taken into ac-

count, "I" alters Jakobson's numeric scheme, undermining the specific nature of the parallel structures claimed to function in the poem.

When textual space is made to function systematically, it is only by the synthesis or exclusion of elements otherwise disruptive of the system. Such unified totality and closure are illusory from a poststructuralist point of view, which sees textual space effecting a meaning that is always at least double, marked by unresolvable tension between what a discourse would appear to assert and the implications of the terms in which the assertions are couched. Inscription, the writing per se, is thereby not seen as a neutral form at the service of meaning, but a signifying force threatening the determination of signification. In its attention to the graphic force of a word, its "letteral" meaning, poststructuralism would not pass off writing as mere transcription of the spoken word. In some sense dealing with any discourse as if it were concrete poetry, it recognizes the participation of the medium—the letter, the word as plastic form—in its own definition. Signification would be seen to be constantly displaced along a multiplicity of signifying trajectories whose transformations "anagrammatically" engender new possibilities: A signifier might verge on another, perhaps contradictory, signifier that it resembles phonetically or graphically; it may disengage other signifiers by way of semantic similarity; the visual impact of the word or letter on the page might cut a significant figure; signifying combinations might arise from mere juxtaposition of elements without any other apparent connection.

No longer conceived as the transparent carrier of a message, the signifier/word/inscription menaces the establishment of ultimate signification. Poststructuralism thus supplements the structuralist attack on the authority of the writing subject to include the dissolution of the illusion of mastery on the part of the critic. To the poststructuralist, the text is a space of semantic dispersal, a space of dissemination forever in flux, never to be completely controlled and mastered. From this standpoint, structuralist methodology is thought to be overly reductionist in its resolution of the text into a set of structuring components, too akin to the effort of archetypal criticism, or to Romantic notions of the work as an organic whole, albeit in structuralism an architectural one. Although it might be said in defense of structuralism that the analysis of structure is purely formal, that an essence (meaning, nature of being) is not ascribed to particular structures, structuralist readings imply essentiality by the air of puzzle-solving involved in their uncovering of the semiotic unity of a work, its essential governing principles. Structures are implicitly privileged with the status of eschatological presence; language's suggestive power, the disruptive force of its inscription, is attenuated for the sake of form: that is, of defining the system.

Poststructuralism would regard, for example, the emphasis in structuralist linguistics on synchrony as an attempt to exclude linguistic force and change that might undermine the fixity of systematic analysis. Following the implications of structuralism's principle of difference, of meaning produced by virtue of relational differences, one cannot escape the conclusion that the practice of language is implicitly diachronic, temporal, historical, since the principle is undeniably one of combination, selection, and exclusion. If meaning for the structuralist is the product of relational differences rather than derivative of an intrinsic permanent value attached to a word in itself, then it can never be fully present all at once at a given moment; no single word/gesture/expression/ signifier is in and of itself capable of initiating the difference necessary for significance to operate. Like motion, meaning cannot be completely grasped in a present moment that would exclude a past and a future moment, and thus the structuralist principle of difference implies a paradoxically double movement at the "origin" of meaning which is repressed in favor of the oneness and synchrony establishing textual space as an unproblematic domain of simultaneous, systematic relationships.

The structuralist concept of textual space does attribute spatiality to language and not merely to a particular use of it ("modern literature"). It establishes a synchronic stable space containing the movement of signification guaranteeing that the text will be something other than nonsense. Language is dealt with as a spatial phenomenon, but to the exclusion of temporal movement and flux which might trigger disorder or nonsense. In other words, a protest against Lessing's separation of the verbal and visual arts by way of structuralism seems only to reverse the categories of space and time and thus remain within the mode of oppositional think-

ing: Language is synchronic when diachronicity is ignored, spatial when temporal movement is repressed. In an effort to exceed the limitations of oppositional thinking, poststructuralism supplements the principle of difference with what Jacques Derrida terms the *différance* operative in the textual dissemination of signification.

DIFFERENCE = DIFFÉRANCE

Différance is a neologism whose graphic play—in French—combines the meaning of "différ*ance*" (difference), with which it is exactly equivalent phonetically, and "deferring." It articulates meaning as a complex configuration incorporating both a passive state of differences and the activity of differing and deferring which produces those differences. *Différance* is consequently inconceivable in terms of binary opposition: Like motion, it is neither simply absent nor present, neither spatial (differing in space) nor temporal (deferring in time). "Espacement" (spacing), a comparable Derridean term, indicates both the passive condition of a particular configuration or disposition of elements, and the gesture effecting the configuration, of distributing the elements in a pattern.

Like the Einsteinian concept of space-time, *différance* and spacing (articulated along the bar of binary opposition that would separate space and time, active and passive) disrupt the comfort of thinking within a purely oppositional mode. Derrida demonstrates such lack of guarantees in his reading of "hymen" in the poetry of Stéphane Mallarmé. An undecidable signifier whose meaning cannot be mastered, hymen is both marriage and the vaginal membrane of a virgin. Whereas hymen as virginity is hymen without hymen/marriage, hymen as marriage is hymen without hymen/virginity. Hymen, then, articulates both difference (between the interior and exterior of a virgin, between desire and its consummation), and, at the same time, the abolition of difference in the consummation of marriage; it is the trace of a paradoxical abolition of difference between difference and nondifference.

Within a structuralist framework, meaning produced by textual space, albeit ambiguous or polysemic, is in the final analysis recuperable. Ambiguity is controlled as the various strands of meaning are enumerated and accounted for. Poststructuralism views the implications of such practice as problematic. On the one hand, meaning is claimed to be the product of semiotic play governed by a principle of difference (signaling the dissolution of the control of the writing subject) that implicates a definition of the sign in which meaning floats among signifiers rather than existing a priori as an essence—the signified. On the other hand, by enclosing this textual play within the boundaries of the "poetic" and seeking out and privileging structures informing that play, a very classical definition of the sign is implied in which the signifier serves ultimately as a vehicle representing an eschatological presence: an ultimate signified which arrested play and closes off the movement of signification. Dissemination, *différance*, and spacing would splay the fixed borders that characterize criticism's structuring of the movement of signifiers within poetic space so as to explicate texts.

Sign, like symbol, ultimately refers back to a single source, a signified assuring of the determination of meaning; with the poststructuralist gloss on signifier as signifying trace, there can be no return to a simple origin. Signifying trace would articulate an effect of meaning without the illusion of understanding provided by binary opposition. Trace (again, like motion), cannot be determined as simply either present or absent. Giving evidence of an absent thing which passed by, trace "in itself" contains its other which it is not (the absent thing). It paradoxically "is" what it is not, inasmuch as its presence (its identity) depends on alluding to an absence (its nonidentity to the absent thing leaving the trace) from which it distinguishes itself. Its meaning or identity is thus split from the beginning, already always involved in a paradoxical movement of *différance*. The origin of meaning or identity is then not single; the first trace of anything is first only in deferring to a second in relation to which it becomes first—and in that sense it is more of a third. The poststructuralist endeavor is a recognition of the intractable paradox of the nonsingle point of origin of the difference which inaugurates any signifying system. *Différance* is, then, not so much a concept as an opening onto the possibility of conceptualization.

IMAGE AND DIFFÉRANCE

A recapitualization of Ezra Pound's theory of the Image as a generative and dislocating force in Joseph

Riddel's "Decentering the Image" is a useful gloss on *différance*. Like spacing, which is both configuration and the gesture effecting that configuration, Pound's Image is both a visual representation (form) and a displacement or trope (force); it is a cluster of figures in a space of relational differences and a transformative machine articulating movement across the differential field. The Image is not an idea, not the mere signifier of a signified, but rather a constellation of radical differences, a vortex whose form as radiating force resists the synthesis and collapse of differences into oneness and unity. Whereas formalist, archetypal, and structuralist criticism tends to privilege implicitly master structures, assuring a totalization of the poem's fragments, Pound's vortex would disrupt the assurance of an originating signified in its refusal to be resolved into the unity of presence, to be fully present at a given moment. As the signifying trace is always already split at its origin, constituted in a present moment/space by absence, so too is Pound's vortex always already an image; that is, a field of relations, originally a text, the reinscription of a past into a present text, a vector, a force always already multiple and temporalizing.

There is, then, no continuity between origin and image as there is with symbol and the conventional sign. A poem is not recuperable in synthesizing totality and must be read somewhat in the manner of a rebus, whose play of signifiers annuls/refuses a simple reading, provoking, instead, reinterpretations and reopenings.

POSTSTRUCTURALISM VS. STRUCTURALISM

The poststructuralist critique of the frame that structuralism would draw around poetic discourse provokes reinterpretation of structuralist discourse. Since the principle of difference provides for theoretically unlimited play of the sign within the textual space, what prevents that movement from exceeding its borders, that force from spilling out of its form? How can one unproblematically draw borders around different language functions, keeping the play of the poetic—that introverted self-referential "focus on the message for its own sake"—framed off from the mimetic referential space of common linguistic usage?

The controversy between structuralism and poststructuralism indicated by such questioning is not a simple dispute over methodological technique in the analysis of poetry. Deconstruction of structuralist discourse betrays the ideological move involved in fixed framing: the strategy of setting up distinctions to shelter "rational" discourse from the vagaries of the poetic.

Relegation of textual play to the poetic seemingly protects the language of critical discourse from irrational forces, guarantees it the possibility of lucidity, of the impression that language is under control—mastered by the critic. Meaning as *différance*/spacing dissolves the illusion of the possibility of purely logical discourse unfettered by the anomolies of the poetic, of a purely literal language unhampered by figural machinations. Furthermore, *différance* annuls the very distinction classically affirmed between literal and figurative. Signification would be neither purely literal nor metaphoric; there would be no literal truth represented by a sign because the very possibility of representation depends on metaphor: In representing an absent in a present, in transferring the literal reference signified, the sign "tropes" and metaphorizes (*metapherein*—to carry over, transfer). Likewise, if purely metaphoric meaning were possible, then there would be a literal meaning of metaphor to which metaphor would refer metaphorically.

Whereas for structuralism, space structures meaning, delineating its borders and giving it form, poststructuralism demonstrates that closure of meaning is illusory. Meaning as spacing/*différance* is neither fixed nor absolute but kept in motion by the figural, the figural both as metaphor usurping the position of the sign's would-be literal referent, and as inscription, whose graphic impact on the page engenders disruptive anagrammatic combinations. Poststructuralism traces the catachresis at play in the space of discourse, be it poetic, philosophic, or critical. The signifying traces at play in the text are catachrestic in their deconstruction of the illusion of literal terms whose eschatological presence would stop the movement of signification. Catachresis—the metaphor created when there is no literal term available (such as the foot of the table)—is traditionally considered a form of abuse and misapplication. Poststructuralism demonstrates such misapplication as the condition of language: The sign necessarily fails to hit the mark; the signifier is always something other than its signified in order that language might operate.

BIBLIOGRAPHY

Arac, Jonathan, Wlad Godzich, and Wallace Martin, eds. *The Yale Critics: Deconstruction in America.* Minneapolis: University of Minnesota Press, 1983.

Bloom, Harold, Paul de Man, Jacques Derrida, and Geoffrey Hartman. *Deconstruction and Criticism.* New York: Seabury Press, 1979.

Baran, Henryk, ed. *Semiotics and Structuralism: Readings from the Soviet Union.* White Plains, N.Y.: International Arts and Sciences Press, 1976.

Barthes, Roland. *Critical Essays.* 1972. Translated by Richard Howard. New York: Hill & Wang, 1980.

_____. *Elements of Semiology.* 1967. Translation by Annette Lavers and Colin Smith. New York: Hill & Wang, 1968.

Berman, Art. *From the New Criticism to Deconstruction: The Reception of Structuralism and Post-Structuralism.* Urbana: University of Illinois Press, 1988.

Caputo, John D. *Deconstruction in a Nutshell: A Conversation with Jacques Derrida.* New York: Fordham University Press, 1997.

Cornell, Drucilla. *The Philosophy of the Limit.* New York: Routledge, 1992.

Cornell, Drucilla, Michael Rosenfeld, and David Gray Carlson. *Deconstruction and the Possibility of Justice.* New York: Routledge, 1992.

Critchley, Simon. *The Ethics of Deconstruction: Derrida and Levinas.* 1992. Reprint. West Lafayette, Ind.: Purdue University Press, 1999.

Culler, Jonathan. *Structuralist Poetics: Structuralism, Linguistics, and the Study of Literature.* Ithaca, N.Y.: Cornell University Press, 1975.

Derrida, Jacques. *Acts of Literature.* New York: Routledge, 1992.

_____. *Dissemination.* Chicago: Chicago University Press, 1981.

_____. *Of Grammatology.* Corrected ed. Baltimore: Johns Hopkins University Press, 1998.

_____. *Positions.* Chicago: University of Chicago Press, 1981.

_____. *The Post Card: From Socrates to Freud and Beyond.* 1987.

_____. *Writing and Difference.* Chicago: University of Chicago Press, 1978.

Eco, Umberto. *The Role of the Reader: Explorations in the Semiotics of Texts*. Bloomington: University of Indiana Press, 1979.

_____. *A Theory of Semiotics*. Bloomington: University of Indiana Press, 1976.

Ehrmann, Jacques, ed. *Structuralism*. Garden City: Anchor Books, 1976.

Galan, F. W. *Historic Structures: The Prague School Project, 1928-1946*. Austin: University of Texas Press, 1985.

Greimas, A. J. *Structural Semantics: An Attempt at Method*. Lincoln: University of Nebraska Press, 1983.

Jakobson, Roman. *Selected Writings, 1962-1987*. 8 vols. New York: Mouton de Gruyter, 1994.

Jameson, Fredric. *The Prison-House of Language: A Critical Account of Structuralism and Russian Formalism*. Princeton, N.J.: Princeton University Press, 1972.

Johnson, Barbara. *A World of Difference*. Baltimore: Johns Hopkins University Press, 1987.

Lane, Michael, ed. *Introduction to Structuralism*. New York: Basic Books, 1970.

Lévi-Strauss, Claude. *Structural Anthropology*. 1963. Reprint. New York: Basic Books, 1999.

Lotman, Iurii. *The Structure of the Artistic Text*. Ann Arbor: University of Michigan Press, 1977.

Prince, Gerald. *Narratology: The Form and Functioning of Narrative*. New York: Mouton, 1982.

Riffaterre, Michael. *Semiotics of Poetry*. Bloomington: University of Indiana Press, 1978.

Saussure, Ferdinand de. *Course in General Linguistics*. 1916. Translated and annotated by Roy Harris, edited by Charles Bally and Albert Sechehaye with the collaboration of Albert Riedlinger. LaSalle, Ill.: Open Court, 1986.

Scholes, Robert. *Structuralism in Literature: An Introduction*. New Haven, Conn.: Yale University Press, 1974.

Selden, Raman, ed. *From Formalism to Poststructuralism*. Vol. 8 in *The Cambridge History of Literary Criticism*. New York: Cambridge University Press, 1995.

Todorov, Tzvetan. *The Fantastic: A Structural Approach to a Literary Genre*. 1973. Reprint. Ithaca, N.Y.: Cornell University Press, 1975.

Nancy Weigel Rodman

AFRICAN AMERICAN POETRY

The struggle for freedom—social, psychological, and aesthetic—is the distinguishing attribute of African American poetry from its origins during slavery through its pluralistic flowering in the twentieth century. Although the impact of the struggle has only intermittently been simple or direct, it has remained a constant presence both for writers concentrating directly on the continuing oppression of the black community and for those forging highly individualistic poetic voices not primarily concerned with racial issues.

Generally, two basic "voices" characterize the African American poetic sensibility. First, black poets attempting to survive in a literary market dominated by white publishers and audiences have felt the need to demonstrate their ability to match the accomplishments of white poets in traditional forms. From the couplets of Phillis Wheatley through the sonnets of Claude McKay to the modernist montages of Robert Hayden to the rap and hip-hop stylings of Queen Latifah, Public Enemy, IceT, Mos Def, Tupac, and KRS1, African American poets have mastered the full range of voices associated with the evolving poetic mainstream. Second, black poets have been equally concerned with forging distinctive voices reflecting both their individual sensibilities and the specifically African American cultural tradition.

This dual focus within the African American sensibility reflects the presence of what W. E. B. Du Bois identified as a "double-consciousness" that forces the black writer to perceive himself or herself as both an "American" and a "Negro." The greatest African American poets—Langston Hughes, Sterling Brown, Gwendolyn Brooks, Robert Hayden, Imamu Amiri Baraka, Maya Angelou, Rita Dove, Yusef Komunyakaa, and Kevin Powell—draw on this tension as a source of both formal and thematic power, helping them to construct a poetry that is at once unmistakably black and universally resonant.

CAGED EAGLES: EARLY POETS

From the beginning, African American poets have continually adjusted to and rebelled against the fact of double consciousness. To be sure, this rebellion and adjustment have varied in form with changing social circumstances. Nevertheless, Baraka's statement in his poetic drama *Bloodrites* (pr. 1970) that the aware black artist has always been concerned with helping his or her community attain "Identity, Purpose, Direction" seems accurate. Over a period of time, the precise emphasis has shifted between the terms, but the specific direction and purpose inevitably reflect the individual's or the era's conception of identity. To some extent, this raises the issue of whether the emphasis in "African American" belongs on "African" or on "American." Some poets, such as Baraka during his nationalist period, emphasize the African heritage and tend toward assertive and frequently separatist visions of purpose and direction. Others, such as Jean Toomer in his late period, emphasize some version of the "American" ideal and embrace a variety of strategies for the purpose of reaching a truly integrated society.

Phillis Wheatley, the first important African American poet, was forced to confront this tension between African and American identities. As an "American" poet of the eighteenth century—before the political entity known as the United States was formed—her writing imitated the styles and themes of British masters such as John Milton, John Dryden, and Alexander Pope. Brought to America at age six, she experienced only a mild form of slavery in Philadelphia, because her owners Thomas and Susannah Wheatley felt deep affection for her and respected her gifts as a writer. Unlike other Wheatley servants, Phillis, treated more as a stepdaughter than as a servant, was exempted from routine duties and had a private room, books, and writing materials. At the same time, her career was hobbled by the blatant discrimination heaped on all "African" people. For example, in 1772, Susannah Wheatley sought patrons to help publish the then eighteen-year-old Phillis's first collection of twenty-eight poems. Colonial whites rejected the proposal because she was a slave. Phillis was forced to seek a publisher in London.

Although her poem "On Being Brought from Africa to America" views slavery as a "mercy," because it led her from "pagan" darkness to Christian light, she was never accepted as a poet on her own merits. However, in England, whose antislavery movement was stronger than that of the colonies, people of wealth and stature such as the countess of Huntingdon and the earl of Dartmouth embraced the poet. Lady Huntingdon, to whom Wheatley's first volume, *Poems on Various Subjects, Religious and Moral* (1773), was dedicated, financed the publication and put Phillis's picture on the frontispiece. Wheatley's work was advertised as the product of a "sable muse" and she was presented as a curiosity; the blind racism of the times made it impossible for her to be accepted as a poet who was as accomplished as her white contemporaries. That sentiment was made clear by Thomas Jefferson in his *Notes on the State of Virginia* (1777): "Religion indeed has produced a Phyllis Whately [sic] but it could not produce a poet. The compositions published under her name are below the dignity of criticism." Those sentiments are counterbalanced by a contemporary, Jupiter Hammon, also a slave poet, who in "An Address to Miss Phillis Whealy [sic]" praised her talent and influence as part of God's providence:

> While thousands tossed by the sea,
> And others settled down,
> God's tender mercy set thee free,
> From dangers that come down.

Other early writers, such as George Moses Horton and Frances Watkins Harper, shared a common purpose in their antislavery poetry but rarely escaped the confines of religious and political themes acceptable to the abolitionist journals that published their work. The pressures on the African American poet became even more oppressive during the post-Reconstruction era as the South "reconquered" black people, in part by establishing control over the literary image of slavery. "Plantation Tradition" portrayed contented slaves and benevolent masters living in pastoral harmony. Paul Laurence Dunbar attained wide popularity in the late nineteenth and early twentieth centuries, but only by acquiescing partially in the white audience's stereotypical preconceptions concerning the proper style (slave dialect) and tones (humor or pathos) for poetry dealing with black characters.

A VOICE OF THEIR OWN

Spearheading the first open poetic rebellion against imposed stereotypes, James Weldon Johnson, a close friend of Dunbar, mildly rejected Dunbar's dialect poetry in his preface to *The Book of American Negro Poetry* (1922), which issued a call for "a form that will express the racial spirit by symbols from within rather than by symbols from without." He explained:

> The newer Negro poets discard dialect; much of the subject matter which went into the making of traditional dialect poetry, 'possums, watermelons, etc., they have discarded altogether, at least, as poetical material. This tendency will, no doubt, be regretted by the majority of white readers; and indeed, it would be a distinct loss if the American Negro poets threw away this quaint and musical folk-speech as a medium of expression. And yet, after all, these poets are working through a problem not realized by the reader, and perhaps, by many of these poets themselves not realized consciously. They are trying to break away, not from the Negro dialect itself, but the limitations on the Negro dialect imposed by the fixing effects of long convention.

> The Negro in the United States has achieved or been placed in a certain artistic niche. When he is thought of artistically, it is as a happy-go-lucky, singing, shuffling, banjo-picking being or as a more or less pathetic figure. The African American poet realizes that there are phases of Negro life in the United States which cannot be treated in the dialect either adequately or artistically. Take, for example, the phases rising out of life in Harlem, that most wonderful Negro city in the world. I do not deny that a Negro in a log cabin is more picturesque than a Negro in a Harlem flat, but the Negro is here, and he is part of a group growing everywhere in the country, a group whose ideals are becoming increasingly more vital than those of the traditionally artistic group, even if its members are less picturesque.

HARLEM RENAISSANCE

This call was heeded by the poets of the Harlem Renaissance, who took advantage of the development of large black population centers in the North during the Great Northern Migration of blacks from the rural South to the urban North during the 1910's and 1920's. Where earlier poets lived either among largely illiterate slave populations or in white communities, the "New Negroes"—as Alain Locke, one of the first major black critics, labeled the writers of the movement—seized the opportunity to establish a sense of identity for a sizable black audience. Locke viewed the work of poets such as Claude McKay, Countée Cullen, and Jean Toomer as a clear indication that blacks were preparing for a full entry into the American cultural mainstream.

The support given Harlem Renaissance writers by such white artists and patrons as Carl Van Vechten and Nancy Cunard, however, considerably complicated the era's achievement. On one hand, it appeared to herald the merging predicted by Locke. On the other, it pressured individual black writers to validate the exoticism frequently associated with black life by the white onlookers. Cullen's "Heritage," with its well-known refrain "What is Africa to me?" reflects the sometimes arbitrarily enforced consciousness of Africa that pervades the decade. African American artists confronted with white statements such as Eugene O'Neill's "All God's Chillun Got Wings" could not help remaining acutely aware that they, like Wheatley 150 years earlier, were cast more as primitive curiosities than as sophisticated artists. However, an expansion in the U.S. literary canon and evolution in African American literature could not be denied. It was celebrated in the March, 1925, issue of Van Vechten's literary journal *Survey Graphic*, guest-edited by Locke, who was then a Howard University philosophy professor.

The first flowering of Harlem as an artistic center came to an end with the Great Depression of the 1930's, which redirected African American creative energies toward political concerns. The end of prosperity brought a return of hard times to the African American community and put an end to the relatively easy access to print for aspiring black writers.

THE 1930'S: NEW DIRECTIONS

If the Harlem Renaissance was largely concerned with questions of identity, the writing in Hughes's *A New Song* (1938) and Brown's *Southern Road* (1932) reflects a new concern with the purpose and direction of both black artists and black masses. Hughes had earlier addressed the caution in an essay, "The Negro Artist and the Racial Mountain," published in the June 23, 1926, issue of *The Nation*:

The Negro artist works against an undertow of sharp criticism from his own group and unintentional bribes from the whites. But in spite of the Nordicized Negro intelligentsia and the desires of some white editors we have an honest American Negro literature already with us. . . . I am ashamed for the black poet who says, "I want to be a poet, not a Negro poet," as though his own racial world were not as interesting as any other world. An artist must be free to choose what he does, certainly, but he must also never be afraid to do what he might choose.

Where many of the Harlem Renaissance writers had accepted Du Bois's vision of a "talented tenth" who would lead the community out of cultural bondage, the 1930's writers revitalized the African American tradition that perceived the source of power—poetic and political—in traditions of the "folk" community. Margaret Walker's "For My People" expresses the ideal community "pulsing in our spirits and our blood." This emphasis sometimes coincided or overlapped with the proletarian and leftist orientation that dominated African American fiction of the period. Again external events, this time World War II and the "sell-out" of blacks by the American Communist Party, brought an end to an artistic era.

THE POSTWAR ERA: UNIVERSALISM

The post-World War II period of African American poetry is more difficult to define in clear-cut terms. Many new poets became active, especially during the 1960's and 1970's, while poets such as Hughes and Brown, who had begun their careers earlier, continued as active forces. Nevertheless, it is generally accurate to refer to the period from the late 1940's through the early 1960's as one of universalism and integration, and that of the mid-1960's through the mid-1970's as one of self-assertion and separatism.

The return of prosperity, landmark court decisions, and the decline of legal segregation in the face of nonviolent protest movements created the feeling during the early postwar period that African American culture might finally be admitted into the American mainstream on an equal footing. Poets such as Brooks, who became the first black to win the Pulitzer Prize for Poetry—for *Annie Allen* (1949)—and Hayden, who later became the first black Library of Congress poet, wrote poetry that was designed to communicate to all readers, regardless of their racial backgrounds and experiences. Neither poet abandoned black materials or traditions, but neither presented a surface texture that would present difficulties for an attentive white reader. Brooks's poem "Mentors" typifies the dominant style of the "universalist" period. It can be read with equal validity as a meditation on death, a comment on the influence of artistic predecessors, a commitment to remember the suffering of the slave community, and a character study of a soldier returning home from war.

The universalist period also marked the first major assertion of modernism in black poetry. Although both Hughes and Toomer had earlier used modernist devices, neither was perceived as part of the mainstream of experimental writing, another manifestation of the critical ignorance that has haunted black poets since Wheatley. Hayden and Melvin B. Tolson adopted the radical prosody of T. S. Eliot and Ezra Pound, while Baraka, Bob Kaufman, and Ted Joans joined white poets in New York and San Francisco in forging a multiplicity of postmodernist styles, many of them rooted in African American culture, especially jazz.

THE BLACK ARTS MOVEMENT

As in the 1920's, however, the association of black poets with their white counterparts during the 1950's and 1960's generated mixed results. Again, numerous black writers believed that they were accepted primarily as exotics and that the reception of their work was racially biased. With the development of a strong Black Nationalist political movement, exemplified by Malcolm X (who was to become the subject of more poems by African American writers than any other individual), many of the universalist poets turned their attention to a poetry that would directly address the African American community's concerns in a specifically black voice. LeRoi Jones changed his name to Imamu Amiri Baraka and placed the term Black Arts in the forefront as an indicator of a new cultural aesthetic in the poem, "Black Dada Nihilismus." Brooks announced her conversion to a pan-Africanist philosophy, and community arts movements sprang up in cities throughout the United States.

A major movement of young black poets, variously referred to as the New Black Renaissance or the Black Arts movement, rejected involvement with Euro-American culture and sought to create a new "black aesthetic" that would provide a specifically black identity, purpose, and direction. Poets such as Haki R. Madhubuti (Don L. Lee), Sonia Sanchez, Nikki Giovanni, and Etheridge Knight perceived their work primarily in relation to a black audience, publishing with black houses such as Broadside Press of Detroit and Third World Press of Chicago. Most poets of the Black Arts movement remained active after the relative decline of the Black Nationalist impulse in the late 1970's and 1980's, but, with such notable exceptions as Madhubuti, their tone generally became more subdued. They have been joined in prominence by a group of poets, many of whom also began writing in the 1960's, who have strong affinities with the modernist wing of the universalist period. If Madhubuti, Knight, and Giovanni are largely populist and political in sensibility, poets such as Michael Harper, Ai, and Jay Wright are more academic and aesthetic in orientation. Although their sensibilities differ markedly, all the poets asserted the strength of both the African American tradition and the individual voice.

A new pluralism began to emerge, testifying to the persistence of several basic values in the African American sensibility: survival, literacy, and freedom. The publication of the anthology *Black Fire* (1968), coedited by Baraka and Larry Neal, signaled the emergence of the new age. The shift in goals, simply put, was from the uplift of the black community to the transformation of U.S. society. The collection made it clear that African American artists had moved beyond cultural navel gazing. The poets now defined themselves as a Third World people engaged in a global struggle. Neal's essay "The Black Arts Movement" became the period's manifesto:

National and international affairs demand that we appraise the world in terms of our own interests. It is clear that the question of human survival is at the core of contemporary experience. The black artist must address himself to this reality in the strongest terms possible. Consequently, the Black Arts Movement is an ethical movement. Ethical, that is, from the viewpoint of the oppressed. And much of the oppression confronting the Third World and black America is directly traceable to the Euro-American cultural sensibility. This sensibility, antihuman in nature, has, until recently, dominated the psyches of most black artists and intellectuals. It must be destroyed before the black creative artist can have a meaningful role in the transformation of society.

Even highly idiosyncratic poets, such as Toomer in "Blue Meridian" and Ishmael Reed in his "neo-hoo-doo" poems, endorsed those basic values, all of which originated in the experience of slavery. In his book *From Behind the Veil: A Study of Afro-American Narrative* (1979), Robert B. Stepto identifies the central heroic figure of the African American tradition as the "articulate survivor," who completes a symbolic ascent from slavery to a limited freedom, and the "articulate kinsman," who completes a symbolic immersion into his cultural roots. The articulate survivor must attain "literacy" as defined by the dominant white society; the articulate kinsman must attain "tribal literacy" as defined by the black community.

In the 1960's and 1970's, the U.S. Civil Rights movement and subsequent Black Power movement breathed life into human rights struggles throughout the world. Poets in other parts of the African world began to be heard in the United States during the 1970's, which gave evidence that black bids for survival, literacy, and freedom were indeed universal. Derek Walcott of St. Lucia, South African Dennis Brutus, and Nigeria's Wole Soyinka were among the most important voices.

Walcott, like McKay a Jamaican, almost half a century before him showed a reverence for the native Caribbean cultures. Another theme in his early work was outrage at the injustices of colonial rule. Beginning with, *The Gulf and Other Poems* (1969), the poet begins to grapple with ideological and political questions. The strength of the reflection grows in *Sea Grapes* (1976) and comes to full potency in *The Star-Apple Kingdom* (1979).

Brutus's first volume of poems, *Sirens, Knuckles, Boots* (1963) was published while he was doing an eighteen-month stretch on Robben Island, apartheid South Africa's most infamous jail. The equivalent of the Alcatraz, it was considered escape-proof because of the water that separated its inmates from the mainland. After release in 1965, he was exiled to London. The poet joined the Northwestern University English faculty in

1970. Three years later, *A Simple Lust* detailed for American audiences the horror of South African prisons and apartheid's injustices. The collection was also influenced by medieval European sensibilities and images. In the first poem of the collection, Brutus speaks in the voice of a troubadour who fights for his beloved against social injustice and betrayal. Even though outwardly European, the poem reverberates the sense of the heroic found in many American-born black writers' works.

Like these Caribbean and South African counterparts, U.S. poets of African descent made reference to, but transformed, European influences. Maya Angelou's "Still I Rise" and Mari Evans's "Vive Noir!" convey the drama of knighthood's quests against an unjust society through plain language and images drawn from black environments. The works also tossed aside traditional notions of grammar, spelling, and punctuation as a means to emphasize the rejection of conventional European sensibilities. Evans, for example, sick of the language of oppressors as much as the slums of Inner Cities, asserts she is

> weary
> > of exhausted lands
> > sagging privies
> > saying yessuh yessah
> > yesSIR
> > in an assortment
> > of geographical dialects

The Black Arts movement faded in the mid-1970's, without changing the world or stabilizing the growth it gave to African American consciousness. New Orleans poet Kalamu ya Salaam, in an essay in *The Oxford Companion to African American Literature* (1997), traced the beginning of the swan song to 1974:

As the movement reeled from the combination of external and internal disruption, commercialization and capitalist co-option delivered the coup de grace. President Richard Nixon's strategy of pushing Black capitalism as a response to Black Power epitomized mainstream co-option. As major film, record, book and magazine publishers identified the most salable artists, the Black Arts Movement's already fragile independent economic base was totally undermined.

A SHIFT IN EMPHASIS: 1970'S-1990'S

As in the 1930's, after the Renaissance subsided most of the independent publications, public forums, and other outlets for African American cultural expression had evaporated. Lotus Press and Broadside Press in Detroit and Third World Press in Chicago would continue to create outlets for excellent literature. White-owned book companies and magazines shifted focus to the movements for women's equality and against the Vietnam War. That set the stage for the emergence of Audre Lorde, Lucille Clifton, and Yusef Komunyakaa.

Lorde's *The Black Unicorn* (1978) used African symbols and myths to explore the dimensions within her existence. Adrienne Rich acknowledged the volume as a kind of declaration of independence: "Refusing to be circumscribed by any single identity, Audre Lorde writes as a Black woman, a mother, a daughter, a Lesbian, a feminist, a visionary." In an interview with editor Claudia Tate in *Black Women Writers at Work* (1983), Lorde averred the Black Arts movement's stress on representation of the global experience of blacks and the oppressed. Tossing aside previous notions that true African American art is political at its core, she sketched a vision of poetry as a reflection of the personal:

> Black men have come to believe to their detriment that you have no validity unless you're "global," as opposed to personal. Yet our *real power* comes from the personal; our real insights about living come from the deep knowledge within us that arises from our feelings. Our thoughts are shaped by our tutoring. We were tutored to function in a structure that already existed but that does not function for our good. Our feelings are our most genuine path to knowledge. Men have been taught to deal only with what they understand. This is what they respect. They know that somewhere feeling and knowledge are important, so they keep women around to do their feeling for them, like ants do aphids.

The African American poets who rose in prominence during the 1980's, employed stylistic traditions that stretched back to Langston Hughes and other Harlem Renaissance writers. The themes of survival and freedom remained pronounced in their works. The major difference was that, instead of grappling with outside forces, they confronted their nightmares.

Komunyakaa took on Vietnam. The Bogalusa, Louisiana, native won a Bronze Star for his service during the war as a writer and editor of the military newspaper *The Southern Cross*. His poem "Facing It," which reflects on a visit to the Vietnam Veterans Memorial in Washington, D.C., exposes the war as a personal bad dream: "My clouded reflection eyes me like a bird of prey, the profile of the night slanted against the morning." The poet becomes the black granite slab and the archetype of the tens of thousands of visitors. As the poem unfolds, it becomes clear that the conflict is a ghost that will haunt every American for generations.

In September, 1994, the largest gathering of black poets since the end of the Black Arts period was held in Harrisonburg, Virginia, at James Madison University. Thirty of the top black poets since the 1960's—old voices such as Baraka, Madhubuti, Sanchez, Giovanni, and Evans, and new voices such as E. Ethelbert Miller and Toi Derricotte—came together with more than 250 scholars, reporters. and critics. According to a report in *The Washington Post* (October 1), the one subject none of the writers wanted to discuss was what qualities set African American poetry apart from the mainstream. The reporter said that the poets "hate the question, because it reminds them of days when black poetry was relegated to the 'Negro' section of anthologies." Yet each of these poets was living with the deep awareness that African American poets were still not equal members of an elitist literary establishment.

Literacy, frequently illegal under the slave codes, both increases the chance of survival and makes freedom meaningful. Tribal literacy protects the individual's racial identity against submersion in a society perceived as inhumane and corrupt. "The literature of an oppressed people is the conscience of man," wrote Lance Jeffers in an essay printed in the January, 1971, issue of the journal *Black Scholar*:

> [N]owhere is this seen with more intense clarity than the literature of Afroamerica. An essential element of Afroamerican literature is that the literature as a whole—not the work of occasional authors—is a movement against concrete wickedness. The cry for freedom and the protest against injustice are a cry for the birth of the New Man, a testament to the Unknown World (glory) to be discovered, to be created by man.

To a large extent, black poets writing in traditional forms established their literacy as part of a survival strategy in the white literary world. Those concerned with developing black forms demonstrate their respect for, and kinship with, the culturally literate African American community.

JUST PLAIN FOLKS

Against this complex of values and pressures, folk traditions have assumed a central importance in the development of the African American sensibility. Embodying the "tribal" wisdom concerning survival tactics and the meaning of freedom, they provide both formal and thematic inspiration for many black poets. African American poets have become extremely adept at manipulating various masks. Originating with the trickster figures of African folklore and African American heroes such as Brer Rabbit, these masks provide survival strategies based on intellectual, rather than physical, strength.

Existing in a situation during slavery in which open rebellion could easily result in death, the slave community capitalized on the intimate knowledge of white psychology encouraged by the need to anticipate the master's wishes. The white community, conditioned not to see or take into account black needs and desires, possessed no equivalent knowledge of black psychology. Lacking knowledge, whites typically turned to comfortable stereotypes—the loyal mammy, the singing darkie, the tragic mulatto, the black beast—for their interpretation of black behavior. The observant slave found it both easy and rewarding to manipulate white perceptions of reality by appearing to correspond to a stereotypical role while quietly maneuvering for either personal or community gain. The nature of the mask, which exploits a phenomenon of double consciousness by controlling the discrepancy between black and white perspectives, is such that the true goal must always remain hidden from the white viewer, who must always feel that he is making the "real" decisions. Brer Rabbit asks not to be thrown in the briar patch; he will be allowed to escape, however, only if Brer Bear, the symbolic white man, believes that Brer Rabbit's mask is his true face.

This folk tradition of masking adds a specifically African American dimension to the standard poetic manip-

ulation of persona. African American poets frequently adopt personas that, when viewed by white audiences, seem transparent incarnations of familiar stereotypes. Dunbar's dialect poetry and Hughes's Harlem street poems, for example, have been both accepted and dismissed by white readers as straightforward, realistic portraits of black life. An awareness of the complex ironies inherent in the African American folk traditions on which each drew, however, uncovers increasingly complex levels of awareness in their work. Dunbar's melodious dialect songs of plantation life contrast sharply with his complaint against a world that forced him to sing "a jingle in a broken tongue." Similarly, his classic poem "We Wear the Mask" expresses the anguish of a people forced to adopt evasive presentations of self in a nation theoretically committed to pluralism and self-fulfillment. Less agonized than Dunbar, Hughes manipulates the surfaces of his poems, offering and refusing stereotypical images with dazzling speed. "Dream Boogie" first connects the image of the "dream deferred" with the marching feet of an army of the dispossessed, only to resume the mask of the smiling darkie in the sardonic concluding lines:

> What did I say?
> Sure,
> I'm happy!
> Take it away!
> Hey, pop!
> Re-bop!! Mop!
> Y-e-a-h!

The critical record gives strong evidence that Hughes is frequently taken at "face" value. His mask serves to affirm the existence of a black self in control of the rhythm of experience, as well as to satirize the limitations of the white perception.

Throughout the history of African American poetry, poets choosing to address the black political experience without intricate masks have been plagued by the assumption that their relevance was limited by their concentration on racial subject matter. Particularly in the twentieth century, a new stereotype—that of the "angry black" writer—has developed. The conditions of black life frequently do, in fact, generate anger and protest. African American poets, from Wheatley through

Alberry Whitman in the late nineteenth century to Cullen and Giovanni, frequently protest against the oppression of blacks. McKay's sonnet "If We Must Die" embodies the basic impulse of this tradition, concluding with the exhortation: "Like men we'll face the murderous, cowardly pack,/ Pressed to the wall, dying, but fighting back!" Far from being limited by its origins in the African American experience, such poetry embraces a universal human drive for freedom. Winston Churchill quoted lines from the poem (ironically written partially in response to British exploitation of McKay's native Jamaica) during the early days of World War II. The stereotype of the angry black, while based on a limited reality, becomes oppressive at precisely the point that it is confused with or substituted for the full human complexity of the individual poet. Giovanni, at times one of the angriest poets of the Black Arts Movement, pinpoints the problem in her poem "Nikki-Rosa":

> I really hope no white person ever has cause to write about me because they never understand Black love is Black wealth and they'll probably talk about my hard childhood and never understand that all the while I was quite happy.

The drive for freedom transcends any single tone or mode. While frequently connected with the protest against specific conditions limiting social, psychological, or artistic freedom, the impulse modifies a wide range of poetic voices. At one extreme, explicitly political poems such as Baraka's "Black Art" call for "Poems that shoot/ guns." Even Baraka's less assertive poems, such as "For Hettie" or the more recent "Three Modes of History and Culture," seek to envision a world free from oppression. At another extreme, the drive for freedom lends emotional power to "apolitical" poems such as Dunbar's "Sympathy," with its refrain, "I know why the caged bird sings." Although the poem does not explicitly address racial issues, the intense feeling of entrapment certainly reflects Dunbar's position as a black poet subject to the stereotypes of white society. Similar in theme, but more direct in confronting racial pressures, Cullen's sonnet "Yet Do I Marvel," a masterpiece of irony, accepts the apparent injustices of creation, concluding: "Yet do I marvel at this curious thing/ To make a poet

black, and bid him sing." Hughes's "Mother to Son" and "I, Too" with their determination to keep moving, reflect a more optimistic vision. Despite the hardships of life in a country which forces even the "beautiful" black man to "eat in the kitchen," Hughes's characters struggle successfully against despair. Significantly, many of Hughes's poems are very popular in the Third World. "I, Too," for example, has become a kind of anthem in Latin America, which honors Hughes as a major poet in the Walt Whitman tradition.

Where Hughes and Walker frequently treat freedom optimistically, Sterling Brown's "Memphis Blues" provides a stark warning of the ultimate destruction awaiting a society that fails to live up to its ideals. McKay's sonnet "America," with its echoes of Percy Bysshe Shelley's "Ozymandias," strikes a similar note, envisioning the nation's "priceless treasures sinking in the sand." Perhaps Robert Hayden best embodies the basic impulse in his brilliant "Runagate Runagate," which employs a complex modernist voice to celebrate the mutually nourishing relationship between the anonymous fugitive slaves and the heroic figure of Harriet Tubman, who articulates and perpetuates their drive for freedom. Blending the voices of slavemasters, runaway slaves, the spirituals, and American mythology, Hayden weaves a tapestry that culminates in the insistent refrain, "Mean mean mean to be free."

Hayden's use of the anonymous voice of the runaway slave with the voice of the spirituals underscores both the drive for freedom and the nature of the individual hero who embodies the aspirations of the entire community. It exemplifies the importance of folk traditions as formal points of reference for the African American poetic sensibility.

MUSIC AND MESSAGE

Poets seeking to assert a specifically black voice within the context of the Euro-American mainstream repeatedly turn to the rhythms and imagery of folk forms such as spirituals and sermons. During the twentieth century, the blues and jazz assume equal importance. As Stephen Henderson observes in *Understanding the New Black Poetry* (1973), these folk traditions provide both thematic and formal inspiration. Hayden's "Homage to the Empress of the Blues," Brown's "Ma Rainey,"

Brooks's "Queen of the Blues," and poems addressed to John Coltrane by Harper ("Dear John, Dear Coltrane," "A Love Supreme,"), Madhubuti ("Don't Cry, Scream"), and Sanchez ("A Coltrane Poem") are only a few of countless African American poems invoking black musicians as cultural heroes. Bluesmen such as Robert Johnson (who wrote such haunting lyrics as "Crossroads," "Stones in My Passageway," and "If I Had Possession over Judgement Day") and singers such as Bessie Smith frequently assume the stature of folk heroes themselves. At their best they can legitimately be seen as true poets working with the vast reservoir of imagery inherent in African American folk life. Du Bois endorsed the idea by montaging passages of African American music with selections of Euro-American poetry at the start of each chapter of *The Souls of Black Folk* (1903). Similarly, Johnson's poem "O Black and Unknown Bards" credits the anonymous composers of the spirituals with a cultural achievement equivalent to that of Ludwig van Beethoven and Richard Wagner.

These folk and musical traditions have suggested a great range of poetic forms to African American poets. Johnson echoed the rhythms of black preaching in his powerful volume *God's Trombones: Seven Negro Sermons in Verse* (1927), which includes such classic "sermons" as "The Creation" and "Go Down Death—A Funeral Sermon." Hughes and Brown used their intricate knowledge of black musical forms in structuring their poetry. Early in his career, Hughes was content simply to imitate the structure of the blues stanza in poems such as "Suicide." As he matured, however, he developed more subtle strategies for capturing the blues impact in "The Weary Blues," which establishes a dramatic frame for several blues stanzas, and "Song for Billie." The latter mimics the subtle shifts in emphasis of the blues line by altering the order of prepositions in the stanza:

> What can purge my heart
>   of the song
>   and the sadness?
> What can purge my heart
>   But the song
>   of the sadness?
> What can purge my heart
>   of the sadness
>   of the song?

The persona moves from a stance of distance to one of identification and acceptance of the blues feeling. In merging emotionally with the singer, he provides a paradigm for the ideal relationship between artist and audience in the African American tradition.

Brown's blues poem "Ma Rainey" incorporates this "call and response" aspect of the blues experience into its frame story. Ma Rainey attains heroic stature because her voice and vision echo those of the audience that gathers from throughout the Mississippi Delta to hear its experience authenticated. Brown's attempt to forge a voice that combines call and response points to what may be the central formal quest of African American poetry. Such an ideal voice seeks to inspire the community by providing a strong sense of identity, purpose, and direction. Simultaneously, it validates the individual experience of the poet by providing a sense of social connection in the face of what Ralph Ellison refers to as the "brutal experience" underlying the blues impulse. Both Ellison and Hughes, two of the most profound critics of the blues as a literary form, emphasize the mixture of tragic and comic world-views in the blues. Hughes's definition of the blues attitude as "laughing to keep from crying" accurately reflects the emotional complexity of much blues poetry.

Like the blues, jazz plays a significant formal role in African American poetry. Poets frequently attempt to capture jazz rhythms in their prosody. Ambiguous stress patterns and intricate internal rhyme schemes make Brooks's "We Real Cool" and "The Blackstone Rangers" two of the most successful poems in this mode. Brown's "Cabaret" and Hughes's "Jazzonia" employ jazz rhythms to describe jazz performances. On occasion, poets such as Joans ("Jazz Must Be a Woman") and Baraka ("Africa Africa Africa") create "poems" which, like jazz charts, sketch a basic rhythmic or imagistic structure that provides a basis for improvisation during oral performance. Jazz may be most important to African American poetry, however, because of its implicit cultural pluralism. In his critical volume *Shadow and Act* (1964), Ellison suggests a profound affinity between the aesthetics of African American music and Euro-American modernism: "At least as early as T. S. Eliot's creation of a new aesthetic for poetry through the artful juxtapositioning of earlier styles,

Louis Armstrong, way down the river in New Orleans, was working out a similar technique for jazz." As Ellison suggests, jazz provides an indigenous source for an African American modernism incorporating voices from diverse cultural and intellectual sources. In effect, this enables the African American poet to transform the burden of double consciousness, as manifested in the traditions of masking and ironic voicing, into sources of aesthetic power.

Many of the masterworks of African American poetry, such as Hughes's "Montage for a Dream Deferred," Brooks's "In the Mecca," Hayden's "Middle Passage," and Jay Wright's "Dimensions of History," accomplish precisely this transformation. Choosing from the techniques and perceptions of both Euro-American and African American traditions, these works incorporate the dreams and realities of the American tradition in all its diversity. Aware of the anguish resulting from external denial of self and heritage, the African American tradition recognizes the potential inherent in all fully lived experience. Hughes's vision of individuals living out a multiplicity of dreams within the American dream testifies to his profound respect and love for the dispossessed.

The blend of the spoken word, politics, and music in the 1970's laid the foundations for rap music to become a major art form for social criticism. From Gil Scott-Heron's "The Revolution Will Not Be Televised" to Public Enemy's "Fight the Power," the rhymed critiques of life in America move beyond racial icons to indict anyone who turns away from the plight of the oppressed as the enemy. There is debate outside the community as to whether rappers are poets or song stylists. Even some successful African American writers look upon the rap and hip-hop as clever wordplay, but lacking the discipline of traditional poetry. Yet, anthologies edited by up-and-coming African American poets such as Kevin Powell and Clarence Gilyard give works by some artists credibility as voices of dissent outside the "American" canon.

Focusing on concrete human experience rather than on abstract universals, the African American sensibility distrusts the grandiose rhetoric that has too frequently glossed over the materialism, racism, and solipsism that disfigure the American democratic ideal. The African American tradition seeks to provide a sense of identity,

purpose, and direction connecting the visions of Frederick Douglass and Malcolm X with those of Thomas Jefferson and Walt Whitman. Drawing on folk roots and forging a complex pluralism, it reaffirms the values of universal survival, literacy, and freedom.

BIBLIOGRAPHY

Chapman, Abraham, and Gwendolyn Brooks, eds. *Black Voices: Anthology of African-American Literature*. New York: Signet Classics, 2001. A reissue of a classic anthology. The book, first produced in two volumes in the late 1960's and early 1970's, was the first great collection on black writing. It pulls together poetry, fiction, autobiography and literary criticism, with informative, concise author biographies.

Gilbert, Derrick I. M., and Tony Medina, eds. *Catch the Fire!!! A Cross-Generation Anthology of Contemporary African-American Poetry*. Riverhead Books, 1998. *Catch the Fire!!!* Introduces a new generation of African American poets, showcased by established writers who include June Jordan, Amiri Baraka, Abiodun Oyewole (of the Last Poets), Ntozake Shange, and Sonia Sanchez. It gives the reader an understanding of what is happening in coffee houses and clubs throughout the country as gifted spoken-word artists tie into the rap and hip-hop cultures.

Liggins Hill, Patricia et al., eds. *The Riverside Anthology of the African American Literary Tradition*. New York: Houghton Mifflin, 1998. It took more than a decade to pull together this ground-breaking anthology. The book is hefty (more than 2,000 pages and 550 selections), but for the serious student of the culture, it will prove indispensable. Traces the literary tradition from the seventeenth century with discussions of African proverbs, folktales, and chants to contemporary writers such as Rita Dove and August Wilson.

Miller, E. Ethelbert, ed. *In Search of Color Everywhere: A Collection of African American Poetry*. New York: Stewart, Tabori and Chang, 1997. This was one of the best of a new wave of anthologies published in the 1990's, and includes works by classic artists such as Phillis Wheatley, Paul Laurence Dunbar,

Countée Cullen, and Langston Hughes, as well as younger poets such as Elizabeth Alexander, Jacquie Jones, and Kevin Young. Organized by themes. For example, The "Freedom" section is followed by "Celebrations of Blackness."

Powell, Kevin, ed. *Step into a World: A Global Anthology of the New Black Literature.* John Wiley & Sons, 2000. The broadest collection of hip-hop generation writers available. Includes fiction writers, poets, journalists, and commentators, as well as es-tablished authors such as Junot Diaz, Edwidge Danticat, Danyel Smith, and Paul Beatty.

Powell, Kevin, and Ras Baraka, eds. *In the Tradition: An Anthology of Young Black Writers.* New York: Writers&Readers, 1993. This is a good place to sample poetry and stories from authors whose names will be better known in the twenty-first century.

Craig Werner,
updated by Vincent F. A. Golphin

AFRICAN POETRY

African literature, including poetry, finds its roots in a long tradition of oral literature in native languages. With European colonial intrusions between the fourteenth and twentieth centuries, much literature from the continent was expressed in English, French, Portuguese, and other foreign languages, particularly Arabic in North Africa. Postcolonial literatures continue in a variety of languages and a combination of traditions.

ORAL TRADITIONS

Traditionally, oral poetry was produced by specialized, trained poets who were connected to kings, chiefs, spiritual figures, or secret societies. In addition, certain groups, such as hunters, farmers, cattle herders, and warriors, had designated poets. Oral poets were often descended from family lineages. A large body of oral poems from Africa has been recorded, translated, and published. Traditional oral poets recited in indigenous languages, such as Hausa, Yoruba, Ewe, Kongo, Igbo, Mandika, Fulani, Wolof, Zulu, Tswana, Gikuyu, and Swahili. Performance artistry—memorization, improvisation, and gesture—and audience response are part of the oral presentation, which has social and cultural significance. The oral poet who recites well-known pieces can introduce self-inspired innovations.

Used to honor and criticize, the most widely discussed form of oral poetry is the praise poem, generally associated with royal courts but also applicable to other social strata. Praise poetry is designated by such names as *oriki* (Yoruba), *maboko* (Tswana), *izibongo* (Zulu), and *ijala*, poetry of professional Yoruba hunters. Among the Akan, women are known for their proficiency in the funeral dirge. Usually, the praise poem of the court poet rendered historical lineage and stressed positive characteristics, but a poem of this nature could also remind the celebrated figure of responsibilities to the community. A "freelance" oral poet can offer praise and possibly criticism of individuals of lesser status. There are a number of names for oral poets: *griot* (Mandinka), *kwadwumfo* (Asante), *imbongi* (southern Africa), *azmaris* (Ethiopia), and *umusizi* (central Africa). The *umusizi* of Rwanda recited at ceremonial occasions such as births, initiations, and funerals. The spiritual role of certain oral poets is exemplified by the Yoruba *babalawo*, whose verse is distinctly musical. Yoruba *Ifa* divination, associated with the *Ifa* oracle, is expressed in verses. Among the forms of oral poetry, which can be accompanied by drums and stringed instruments, are elegies, lyrics, political pieces, and children's songs. In addition, such African epics as *Sundjata* (Gambia) and *The Epic of Liyongo* (Kenya) display oral influences. Though the authorship of older oral poetry is often unknown, certain individuals have been recognized, such as the eighteenth century Somali poet Ugaas Raage.

EARLY WRITTEN POETRY

The earliest written poetry can be represented by Egyptian hieroglyphs such as the obelisk inscriptions of Queen Hatshepsut, Eighteenth Dynasty. Other early written poetry by writers of African descent is in such languages as Arabic, Latin, Portuguese, Swahili, Amharic, and Hausa. Antar (born c. 550) and Rukn al-Din Baibars (born c. 1268) wrote in Arabic, suggesting the Islamic influence; Juan Latino (born c. 1516), in Latin; and Domingos Caldas Barbosa (born c. 1738 on a slave ship bound for Brazil from Angola), in Portuguese. The Kenyan woman poet Mwana Kupona binti Msham, who wrote in Swahili, composed "Poem of Mwana Kupona" (1858), addressed to her daughter. Ethiopian Blatta Gābrā Egzi'abeher (born c. 1860), educated in Eritrea, is reputedly the first to have written Amharic poetry.

COLONIAL PERIOD

Paralleling the legacy of oral verse, modern African written poetry developed through a series of generations, each coming to prominence in successive eras encompassing the colonial, liberation, and independence periods. As a result of the political and cultural impact of European colonialism during the first half of the twentieth century, the path to poetic recognition involved writing in the dominant colonial languages, which influenced poetic style and form: English (anglophone), French (francophone), and Portuguese (lusophone). Some of the principal poets born between 1900 and 1930 were the Madagascan (francophone) Jean-Joseph Rabéarivelo; the Senegalese (francophone) Annette M'Baye d'Erneville; Ghanaians (anglophone) Gladys May Casely-Hayford, Michael Dei Anang, R. E. G. Armattoe, and Kwesi Brew; Nigerians (anglophone) Dennis Chukude Osadebay and Gabriel Okara; the Kenyan (anglophone) Marjorie Oludhe Macgoye; and South Africans (anglophone and indigenous language) H. I. E. Dhlomo, Benedict Wallet Vilakazi (who published poems in Zulu), and Dennis Brutus. Highly recognized, Rabéarivelo employed Madagascan song forms and techniques of the French Symbolists. In 1953, Okara's poem "The Call of the River Nun" earned for him the Nigerian Festival of Arts award. Banned under apartheid, Brutus's *Sirens, Knuckles, Boots* appeared in 1963. The lusophone poets of this period include Jorge Barbosa of Cape Verde, Antonio Agostinho Neto and Antonio Jacinto, of Angola, Alda do Espírito Santo of São Tomé, and Noémia de Sousa of Mozambique, the first African woman poet to be internationally recognized. North Africa also produced a number of poets, such as imprisoned and tortured Algerian Anna Gréki (1931-1966), who published in Arabic and French.

NEGRITUDE

One of the most important developments was the negritude movement, at its height from the 1930's through the 1960's and influenced by America's Harlem Renaissance. The movement had Caribbean and African cadres. Decidedly francophone, negritude, a valorization of African racial identity and anticolonialism, was represented by such poets as Aimé Césaire of Martinique, Léon Damas of French Guiana, Jacques Roumain of Haiti, Édouard Maunick of Mauritius, Tchicaya U Tam'si of Congo, Birago Diop and Leopold Sédar Sénghor of Senegal, and David Diop, born in France of Cameroonian and Senegalese parentage. Born in 1906, Sénghor, to become president of Senegal in 1960, emerged as one of the leading African poets writing in French. His advocacy of negritude is evident in his 1945 poem "Femme noire" ("Black Woman"): "And your beauty strikes me to the heart, like the flash of an eagle."

LIBERATION PERIOD

In the 1950's and 1960's, the period in which African countries gained liberation, there emerged a dynamic group of poets publishing in English, many of whom were born in the 1930's; some of them directly criticized negritude as romantic. This group included Ghanaian Kofi Awoonor; Ugandans Okot p'Bitek and Taban Lo Liyong; Nigerians Christopher Ifekandu Okigbo (influenced by T. S. Eliot and Ezra Pound), Wole Soyinka (a vocal critic of negritude), and John Pepper Clark-Bekederemo, who founded the poetry magazine *The Horn*; Malawian David Rubadiri; and Gambian Lenrie Peters. Okigbo's first collection, *Heavensgate* (1962), contributed to his legendary reputation as a committed liberation poet, and indeed he was killed in the Biafran War. Okot p'Bitek's *Song of Lawino* (1966), translated into English from Acholi, was one of the most influential poems challenging Western cultural values. Kofi Awoonor authored many volumes of poetry, including *Night of My Blood* (1971). Among the South African writers were Mazisi Kunene (who wrote in both Zulu and English), Cosmo Pieterse, Keorapetse Kgositsile, Arthur Nortje, and Amelia Blossom Pegram. Titles such as Kgositsile's *Spirits Unchained* (1969) and Pegram's *Our Sun Will Rise: Poems for South Africa* (1989) exemplify the protest voice.

Many poets were published in such magazines as *Présence africaine*, *Transition*, and *Black Orpheus*. Certain poets have also been accomplished in other literary genres. Novelists Chinua Achebe, Ayi Kwei Armah, Ama Ata Aidoo, and Ben Okri, and dramatists Femi Osofisan and Nobel laureate Soyinka, author of *Idanre and Other Poems* (1967), have published poetry of note. By the 1960's and 1970's, critical works and edited collections of African poetry began to appear, produced by such advocates as Janheinz Jahn, Gerald Moore, Ulli Beier, Donald Herdeck, Soyinka, and Langston Hughes. Among later editors of African poetry are Awoonor, Isidore Okpewho, Jack Mapanje, Frank and Stella Chipasula, Musaemura Zimunya, and Adewale Maja-Pearce.

POST-INDEPENDENCE POETRY

With independence, African poets accelerated their poetic production. By the 1980's numerous anthologies, representing various regions and scores of poets, had been published. Many of the poets born after World War II were especially concerned with political and social issues relating to their newly independent governments. Critical of the state, certain poets were imprisoned or forced into exile. Among those imprisoned for political reasons were Soyinka, Awoonor, Brutus, and, from the then "younger" generation, the highly acknowledged Mapanje of Malawi, who published, among other works, *Of Chameleons and Gods* (1981). South African poets such as Mongane Wally Serote and Frank Chipasula of Malawi chose exile. Serote's *Third World Express* (1992) is an extended poem with a global scope. Representing North Africa, Abdellatif Laâbi of Morocco published numerous collections in French. Political commitment to the "nation" and beyond is a distinguishing feature of post-independence poets.

A good number of post-independence poets have come from anglophone countries. Their poetic production has been furthered by the establishment of writers' organizations in such countries as Ghana, Nigeria, and Kenya. Among the most prolific and highly recognized poets are Niyi Osundare, Tanure Ojaide, Chimalum Nwankwo, Lemuel Johnson, Catherine Acholonu, and Ifi Amadiume, of Nigeria; Atukwei Okai, Kofi Anyidoho, Kojo Laing, and Kobena Eyi Acquah, of Ghana; Mapanje, Steve Chimombo, Lupenga Mphande, and Frank Chipasula, of Malawi; Syl Cheney-Coker of Sierra Leone; Serote of South Africa; Tijan Sallah of Gambia; Jared Angira of Kenya; and Zimunya and Chenjerai Hove, of Zimbabwe. Holding advanced degrees, many of these poets have written critically, have been editors, and have taught at academic institutions in the United States, Europe, or Africa. For a variety of personal and political reasons, a good number of the post-independence-generation poets reside in the West. Anyidoho addresses the African diaspora in *AncestralLogic and CaribbeanBlues* (1993), and Ojaide, a well-published literary critic, was the recipient of the Alliance Africa Okigbo Prize for Poetry. Ojaide's *The Fate of Vultures and Other Poems* (1990) contains the award-winning title poem "The Fate of Vultures," a striking critique of political materialism. Amadiume's *Passion Waves* (1986) was followed by her critical work *Male Daughters, Female Husbands* (1987). Commonwealth Poetry Prize recipient Osundare was recognized for such works as *The Eye of the Earth* (1986), concerned with the environment. The end of the twenti-

eth century generated still-to-be-recognized poets such as Solomon Omo-Osagie II of Nigeria and Kwame Okoampa-Ahoofe, Jr., of Ghana.

Most important, the 1980's and 1990's were marked by the recognition of women poets, who address gender and patriarchy, themes generally overlooked by their male counterparts. Representative of this group are Pegram, Lindiwe Mabuza, and Zindzi Mandela, of South Africa; Amina Saïd of Tunisia; Ama Ata Aidoo, Naana Banyiwa Horne, and Abena Busia, of Ghana; Molara Ogundipe-Leslie, Rashidah Ismaili, Amadiume, and Catherine Acholonu, of Nigeria; Kristina Rungano of Zimbabwe; Stella Chipasula of Malawi; and Micere Githae Mugo of Kenya. Micere Mugo's "Wife of the Husband," from *Daughter of My People, Sing* (1976), questions traditional marriage symbolized by "His snores," and Busia's *Testimonies of Exile* (1990) voices African feminism, expressed in the poem "Liberation": "For we are not tortured/ anymore." Concerned with state injustices, Mabuza's "Death to the Gold Mine!" (1991) recalls the shooting of mine workers by South African police through such images as "the calcified bones in the ridges." The younger guard of women poets includes Iman Mirsal of Egypt and Mabel Tobrise of Nigeria.

FORMS AND THEMES

The form of oral poems is not limited to set patterns of lines or rhythms. A good number of them are literally songs containing poetic elements such as rhyme, assonance, and alliteration. However, when transcribed and printed in European languages, oral poetry resembles free verse. Repetition is a common device of the praise poem, whose rhythm can reflect the tonal qualities of certain African languages. Written poetry of the colonial era borrows from oral poetry and European style; there is a modernist quality to the body of twentieth century African poetry—most notably the absence of rhyme. The Hausa oral poem "Ali, Lion of the World!" uses repetition effectively, as does modernist Cheney-Coker in "The Hunger of the Suffering Man" (1980).

A functional art, African poetry in its oral and written forms has addressed a variety of themes, including worldview, mysticism, values, religion, nature, negritude, personal relationships, anticolonialism, pan-Africanism, neocolonialism, urbanism, migration, exile, the African diaspora, and patriarchy, as well as such universals as valor, birth, death, betrayal, and love. Religious poetry is exemplified by Islamic influences in such languages as Arabic, Hausa, and Swahili and in *Ifa* oral verses. A primary motif is the spiritual world often reflected in a praise or evocation of ancestors.

Imagery in African poetry frequently evokes the natural environment, as in Brutus's "Robben Island Sequence," in which the poet alludes to "the blood on the light sand by the sea," ironically blending imprisonment and seascape. Neto implies the hardships of colonization in "The African Train" through the image of "the rigorous African hill," and another lusophone writer, Sousa, suggests pan-Africanism in "Let My People Go," with references to "Negro spirituals," Paul Robeson, and Marian Anderson. Negritude is observable in U Tam'si's "Brush Fire" (1957): "my race/ it flows here and there a river."

Furthermore, the sometimes problematic experience of westernization is echoed in Macgoye's "Mathenge" (1984), which juxtaposes cultural memory and Western modernity: "the neon light, the photo flash." Similarly, Zimunya contrasts the urban and rural in "Kisimiso," which describes a son "boastful of his experiences in the city of knives and crooks." African poets have also mined their experiences outside the continent, suggested in Anyidoho's "The Taino in 1992" (1993), which remembers "a hurricane of Arawak sounds" in the Caribbean.

Gender themes appear in a line from a Zulu woman's oral self-praise poem, "I am she who cuts across the game reserve," and in the straightforward poem "Abortion," by an Egyptian poet born in the 1960's, Iman Mirsal, who evokes the image "lots of foetuses." Acholonu's "Water Woman" blends orality with natural imagery evoking a "daughter of the river."

Although most of the poetry in European languages uses standard grammar, Nigerian Ezenwa-Ohaeto composed "I Wan Bi President" (1988) in pidgin; earlier poets Casely-Hayford and Nigerian Frank Aig-Imoukhuede also wrote in africanized English. For the most part, African poets writing after the independence era have remolded free-verse forms and have borrowed or incorporated elements of oral poetry, using folklore,

songs, rhythms, words, or concepts from indigenous languages. Osundare uses animal imagery in *Waiting Laughters* (1989):

> Ah! *Aramonda* [wonder of wonders]
> The mouth has swallowed something
> Too hard for the mill of the stomach

Furthermore, certain poets, who valorize African languages, compose initially in indigenous languages, such as Kenyan Gitahi Gititi (Gikuyu) and Eritrean (Tigrinya) Reesom Haile.

Modern African poets have strived for a poetic voice that recognizes orality and evocative metaphors, demonstrating how the imposed colonial languages along with African mother tongues can be honed to express relevant social and cultural images. Because written poetry may also be performed, African poets have worked for a balance between abstract and accessible metaphors in order to continue the functional and communal art of their poetic forebears.

BIBLIOGRAPHY

Anyidoho, Kofi, Peter Porter, and Musaemura Zimunya, eds. *The Fate of Vultures: New Poetry of Africa*. Oxford, England: Heinemann, 1989. This compilation brings together a selection of poems drawn from the 1988 Arts and Africa Poetry Competition, sponsored by the British Broadcasting Corporation.

Chipasula, Stella, and Frank Chipasula, eds. *The Heinemann Book of African Women's Poetry*. Oxford, England: Heinemann, 1995. This extremely important collection focuses on underrepresented women poets. The introduction critically investigates this publishing oversight.

Finnegan, Ruth. *Oral Literature in Africa*. London: Oxford University Press, 1970. One of the first comprehensive treatments of African oral literature, containing a substantial section devoted to poetry.

Hughes, Langston, ed. *An African Treasury*. New York: Pyramid, 1961. Perhaps the first collection by an African American to recognize the emergence of modern African writing. The section devoted to poetry includes such poets as Sénghor, Soyinka, Okara, and Rabéarivelo.

Maja-Pearce, Adewale, ed. *The Heinemann Book of African Poetry in English*. Oxford, England: Heinemann, 1990. Arranged chronologically, this collections includes poets from the "first generation," beginning with Brutus and continuing through the 1980's.

Mapanje, Jack, and Landeg White, eds. *Oral Poetry from Africa: An Anthology*. Burnt Mill, Essex, England: Longman, 1983. This important anthology groups oral poetry by theme and designates countries of origin.

Moore, Gerald, and Ulli Beier, eds. *The Penguin Book of Modern African Poetry*. 4th ed. New York: Penguin, 1998. First published in 1963, this extensive volume was one of the first to focus exclusively on "modern" African poets, who are presented by country.

Ojaide, Tanure. *The Poetic Imagination in Black Africa: Essays on African Poetry*. Durham, N.C.: Carolina Academic Press, 1996. By a leading Nigerian critic and poet, this is an excellent collection of critical essays emphasizing African aesthetics.

Ojaide, Tanure, and Tijan M. Sallah, eds. *The New African Poetry: An Anthology*. Boulder, Colo.: Lynne Rienner, 1999. Organized by region and country, this collection focuses on the "third generation" of African poets, who came to the fore after independence.

Okpewho, Isidore, ed. *The Heritage of African Poetry*. Burnt Mill, Essex, England: Longman, 1985. A valuable thematic textbook-anthology on oral and written African poetry. The collection contains a critical introduction and analyses of poems.

Soyinka, Wole, ed. *Poems of Black Africa*. New York: Hill and Wang, 1975. Organized thematically, this is a comprehensive collection edited by a foremost African writer.

Joseph McLaren

ASIAN AMERICAN POETRY

"Asian Americans" are in fact diverse groups of people whose ethnicity cannot be pinned down by a single label. As immigrants or descendants of immigrants from various regions of Asia and at different junctures in the history of the United States, Asian American poets bring with them heterogeneous cultural values, practices, and expressions that interact with the "mainstream" Anglo- and Euro-American culture in various ways. Asian American poetry, the product of such interactions for more than a century, is therefore inherently pluralistic and polyphonic.

CHINESE AMERICAN POETRY

Chinese American poetry can be traced back to the mid-nineteenth century. In the isolated culture of Chinatown, Chinese immigrants began to compose poetry in Chinese. The earliest volumes in English that can be tracked down are Hsi Tseng Tsiang's *Poems of the Chinese Revolution* (1929) and Moon Kwan's *A Chinese Mirror: Poems and Plays* (1932), both of which have an ostensibly Chinese component. A preliminary breakthrough came when two Chinese-born poets, Stephen Shu Ning Liu (born 1930) and David Raphael Wang (born 1931), began publishing in English and continued to do so for several decades. Both Wang and Liu naturalize Chinese formats, sensibilities, and stylistics into idiomatic English, demonstrating that Chinese Americans fluent in both languages can be versatile poets capable of imbuing their work with either an American or a Chinese flavor.

Wang and Liu also epitomize the inevitable movement between two cultures that would become characteristic of the younger generation of Chinese American poets, especially those who have been directly exposed to the cultures of both China and the United States. Diana Chang (born 1934), for example, was American-born but was reared in China until 1945; she had authored half a dozen novels before turning out two volumes of poetry. Chang is constantly reminded of her cultural duality: "To me, it occurs that Cézanne/ Is not a Sung painter." Like many people of multicultural upbringing, she enjoys an immense personal freedom ("I shuttle passportless within myself,/ My eyes slant around both hemispheres") yet acknowledges a deep longing to be "accustomed,/ At home here." Embedded in the poetry of Liu, Wang, and Chang there is an acute awareness of global tensions between East and West, First World and Third World, tradition and modernity.

Most Chinese American poetry collected in book form is an outgrowth of the immigration experience, which is not only a collective memory but also a collective reality of the struggle for survival in an uncongenial environment. Authors intent on delineating inexhaustible vignettes of the immigration experience include Nellie Wong, Fay Chiang, Alan Chong Lau, Kitty Tsui, Amy Ling, Marilyn Chin, and Genny Lim. In their books, the poems are arranged according to thematic concerns such as ancestors, family, childhood, adulthood, and marriage. At times helpless, bitter, and outraged, at others respectful, nostalgic, and humorous, they join their variegated voices into a sonorous chorus for the combined elegy and eulogy of an ethnic destiny that has taken more than a century to be reckoned with.

When Chinese American poets speak of themselves as American citizens, the immigrant background heightens their sense of identity, as in Genny Lim's "Yellow Woman":

> I am the daughter of
> seafarers, gold miners, quartz miners
> railroad workers, farm workers
> garment workers, factory workers
> restaurant workers,
> laundrymen
> houseboys, maids, scholars
> rebels, gamblers, poets
> paper sons

The background may be a stigma, but it can also be a means of self-definition, as in Kitty Tsui's "A Celebration of Who I Am": "I am afraid only of forgetting/ the chinese exclusion act of 1882."

In any case, thanks to their self-awareness, the generation of native-born American Chinese who survived the immigration predicament of their forebears took pride in being living contradictions to the stereotypes perpetuated by racist Americans. Daryl Ngee Chin, for example, expresses this pride in "Skin Color from the Sun."

The world of Chinese American poetry is fast becoming more dazzling in its wide variety, Mei-mei Berssenbrugge (born 1947) and John Yau (born 1950), who have published voluminously, are virtuosos of poetic form. Li-Young Lee's *Rose* (1986) deals mainly with haunting memories of a deceased father and a tender, loving relationship between husband and wife, and is exemplary in its seamless amalgamation of the best in both Chinese and Western poetry. While others shuttle between dualities, Li blends the two cultures subtly and organically into a mellow brew.

At the beginning of the twenty-first century, younger poets began to reflect an interdisciplinary trend toward combining poetry, drama, and performance art. Lim, for example, wrote in a number of genres, including fiction and drama, and became a member of the performance group Unbound Feet. In an interview, she complained about the labels that have been applied to her and other artists: "I am what I am. Chinese, American, woman . . . labeling is a preoccupation of mass media, marketers, and politicians. . . . My priority has never been to fit in a box." Whereas Chinese Americans once were confined to literal ghettos in the United States, now, Lim notes, they and many other cultural and racial groups have graduated to academic and literary ghettos, as represented by labels such as "Asian American" and "African American." Lim therefore seeks to escape the box of labels. In poems like "Ahmisa" and "Bardo," she addresses universal themes. On stage, her multimedia performance pieces have incorporated Butoh, sculpture, live music, poetry, and video.

Beau Sia (born 1977) gives further proof of the desire to encompass more than one art form. Author of edgy confessionals that touch on fame, money, sex, and Asian cultural stereotypes, Sia has released a spoken-word compact disc, *Attack Attack Go!* (1998), that makes references to popular culture—Nike shoes, timeshares, the role-playing game Dungeons & Dragons, and the *Transformers* television show. Sia is known for brutally honest, aggressive, and humorous performances in a deadpan delivery reminiscent of comedian Stephen Wright. He befriended Beat poet Allen Ginsberg, who,

echoing other poets, taught him the interconnectedness of all: "He taught me how to be positive and genuine and connect everything universally," said Sia. Like other poets, Sia credits a wide variety of sources for his inspiration—rap music as well as Frank O'Hara and William Carlos Williams.

JAPANESE AMERICAN POETRY

Writing in the early twentieth century, the first generation of Japanese American poets, Yone Noguchi (1875-1947), Carl Sadakichi Hartman (born 1867), and Jun Fujita, employed Japanese forms such as *tanka* and *haiku* in their often nostalgic works. Later generations of Japanese American poets continued to explore Japanese poetic forms. After the great divide of World War II, however, Japanese American poetry began to be marked by a decisive sense of identity and coherence.

The trauma of the internment of Japanese Americans during World War II served as the rallying point for their literary expression. Lawson Fusao Inada's seminal collection of poems revolving around the relocation experience, *Before the War* (1971), is paradigmatic. Similarly conceived collections include James Masao Mitsui's *Journal of the Sun* (1974), Mitsuye Yamada's *Camp Notes and Other Poems* (1976), and Lonny Kaneko's *Return from the Camp* (1986). Though not all have drawn their inspiration explicitly from the internment experience, through it Japanese American poets have consolidated a collective memory and established an ethnic identity for themselves. Yet rather than simply musing upon the wrongs they suffered in their incarceration, they have moved on to explore its various ramifications.

The result of such explorations is epitomized by the phrase "breaking silence." In *Shedding Silence* (1987), Janice Mirikitani develops the idea that "the strongest prisons are built/ with walls of silence" ("Prisons of Silence"). In the widely anthologized poem "Breaking Silence," she articulates the mission for an entire generation of younger Japanese American poets. The poem could very well be regarded as a manifesto in verse. In the first place, to break silence is to come to terms with the turmoils of the incarceration that Japanese Americans before the 1970's had generally avoided discussing:

We were made to believe our faces
betrayed us.
Our bodies were loud with yellow screaming flesh
needing to be silenced
behind barbed wire.

. . . .

We must recognize ourselves at last.

As a corollary, to break silence is also to learn a lesson about the body politic of racist America. In "Block 18, Tule Relocation Camp," Mitsui describes "a quiet man," by day surrounded by Italians and Germans, who by night retreats to a boiler room. There he fashions a samurai sword from scrap metal: "A secret edge/ to hold against the dark mornings." Mitsui is well aware of the stereotypes perpetuated about his race:

White voices
claim the other side of the ocean
is so crowded
the people want to find death
across the phantom river.

By extension, then, to break silence is to sympathize with other peoples of color. Many of these poets look beyond the United States to discover an alliance with the Third World; many of them also condemn the warlike mentality that led to the great devastations of World War II and the Vietnam War. See, for example, Geraldine Kudaka's *Numerous Avalanches at the Point of Intersection* (1979), Mirikitani's "We the Dangerous," and David Mura's "The Hibakusha's Letter."

Above all, to break silence is to dare to critique and dissent in a country that, through legal instruments of exclusion, antimiscegenation laws, segregation, and discrimination, stubbornly refused to practice what it taught. In order to establish this voice, Japanese American poets such as Mura in *After We Lost Our Way* (1989) began to memorialize the details of the family lives of generations past and present. Others aimed to establish a sense of origins and direction (Garrett Hongo, *Yellow Light*, 1982, and *The River of Heaven*, 1988) or to assess the everyday life of Americans at large (Ai, *Cruelty*, 1973, *Killing Floor*, 1979, and *Sin*, 1986). Especially worthy of attention is the fact that Japanese American poets looked toward the past of their immigrant forebears (Mura, *After We Lost Our Way*) and

proudly but judiciously retraced their cultural roots and heritage (Yamada, *Desert Run*, 1988; Hongo, *The River of Heaven*).

In the midst of these developments, an interesting discord can be detected among those who hold opposite views of "tradition," which must be broken for a Japanese American to be American (Mirikitani, "Breaking Tradition") but at the same time must be preserved so as to retain one's distinctive voice as an American of color. The resolution of this conflict will probably continue to be a major issue in Japanese American poetry.

KOREAN AMERICAN POETRY

Korean American poetry is a very young literature, coming to the fore mainly in the second half of the twentieth century. In the 1970's, when memories of the Korean War were still fresh and were in fact heightened by the ongoing Vietnam War, there emerged a distinct voice centering on the historical and psychological issue of Koreans as a "lost" people whose destiny has been unfulfilled. This voice was often a questioning one, singing of the inexplicable predicament of a strong-spirited but disempowered people under oppression or in exile. In Gail Whang Desmond's "Korean Declaration of Independence" (appended to her "Memories of My Grandfather: Rev. Whang Sa Sun"), she describes her attempt to understand her grandfather:

Korean Declaration of Independence
yellow from age
brittle from usage

. . . .

How many times has he read it?
Why does he read it?

. . . .

Who are Koreans?

She explains how her grandfather arrived in the United States in 1913, full of dreams for a "good life," for an "education." Yet he has endured "nothing but pain, struggle." She wonders about the tiny lapel pin of a flying goose that he never takes off: "Why?" Her poem is plaintive: "It's the end of our first generation./ Will anyone ever understand?"

The questioning voice at times becomes an indictment, as in Kim Tong Il's poems, which sing of dreams about an independent, unified "Morning Calm" (literal translation of *Korea*) turned into nightmares of "the land of oppressed calm":

> Tell me the silent hills,
> Isn't it time for us
> To break down the barbed wire
> and determine our own destiny?
> I hear only a roaring
> Of gunfire

To be American is often a tragic irony to a Korean, because Americans have caused much suffering to Korea. In "Your Name Is Chang-Mee" Kim Tong Il describes one visible form of such oppression:

> you're pretty being found
> among the thorny bush and helpless,
>
> .   .   .   .
>
> your Yankee daddy
> abandoned you long ago, and
> your mother has to sell her body
> to another Yankee tonight

Myung Mi Kim's "A Rose of Sharon" is a more refined poem along similar lines. This tragic irony looms large in many poems that depict an American-born Korean yearning to understand and internalize a historical and political background with which he or she has little familiarity.

Reading these poems, one is led to participate in the poets' efforts to understand the destiny of the first generation and later generations. For example, in "Leaving Seoul: 1953" (appearing in Joseph Bruchac's anthology *Breaking Silence*, 1983), Walter Lew (born 1955) describes how he discovered a familial duty, or burden, that was never explained to him. A family of three is leaving Seoul on an airplane. The father has told the mother to leave behind a number of urns. Secretly and with much difficulty, however, the mother, who is a doctor, smuggles them along:

> We have to bury the urns,
> Mother and I. We tried to leave them in a back room,
> Decoyed by a gas lamp, and run out
> But they landed behind us here, at the front gate.

Decades later, "tapping the tall glowing jars," the speaker finds that "they contain all that has made/ The father have dominion over her." This poem powerfully encapsulates the conflict between the imperative to preserve traditional values (ancestral worship, male supremacy) and the necessity of surviving in a time of turmoil. Yet this conflict could not have been understood at the time it took place. A conflict between two generations is also present: The son, though he knows about the mother's action, does not see the point of it at that time. The father, described as "waiting at the airfield in a discarded U.S. Army/ overcoat" and "smoking Luckys like crazy," also serves to epitomize the calamitous tragedy to which an entire people falls victim. The series of urn poems that follow "Leaving Seoul: 1953" suddenly take on epic proportions.

Cathy Song, a Chinese Korean born in Hawaii in 1955, has attracted attention since the 1980's. Her work is both a continuation of and a departure from her three-cultured Asian heritage. In *Picture Bride* (1983), she finds in her grandmother a matrilineal archetype. The archetype, above all, allows her to define her own being by weaving calmly recollected family memories and patiently mediated everyday observations together into a fabric of life. Her poems focusing on her own experience of womanhood and motherhood are not only lyrical but also, in the light of this archetype, mythical. Yet as is clear from the multilayered design (memory, family, art, history, culture, geography, and botany, to name a few) in which the poems of *Picture Bride* are arranged, Song is moving ahead to explore a new world grounded in, but transcending, ethnicity. Her multifaceted background has facilitated this move, and her *Frameless Windows, Squares of Light* (1988) and *School Figures* (1994) are further attempts in this direction.

FILIPINO AMERICAN POETRY

Filipino American literature is a direct offshoot of a continuous modern Filipino literature, which features a number of mature writers already versatile in Spanish and English and familiar with the Western tradition. José García Villa (1914-1997), who came to the United States in 1930, was a prolific poet. Steeped in the Western tradition and making little reference to his ethnic background, his poetry won the acclaim of American and European critics. He was a favorite of Edith Sitwell and other British critics, who found his poetry dealing with the mysterious beauty of God to be Blakean ("Be Beautiful, Noble, Like the Antique Ant"; "Imagine God a Peacock"). In contrast to Villa, Carlos Bulosan, arriving in America in 1931, felt compelled to scrutinize in his poetry (*Letters from America*, 1942, and *American Is in the Heart*, 1943), as in his prose, his Filipino heritage and his American life.

Filipinos often suffer from a perpetual identity crisis resulting from their four-century experience of colonization. In the spirit of Bulosan, younger generations of Filipino poets have examined their backgrounds carefully. They are generally acutely aware of their ethnicity—or more precisely, their anonymity. As Alfred Robles (born 1944) hilariously dramatizes his marginality in "It Was a Warm Summer Day" (in *Asian American Authors*, edited by Kai Yu Hsu and Helen Palubinskas, 1972), he is asked about his identity in a long series of questions that becomes a "laundry list" of American minorities. Upon his return to the Philippines, however, his alienation evaporates and gives way to a rejuvenating excitement ("Manong Federico Delos Reyes and His Golden Banjo," in *Breaking Silence*). Virginia Cerenio captures, in "You Lovely People," the same marginality and the same nostalgia, but in a more poignant manner:

> like indios, we are
> lost
> not in india or middle america
> or the wrong side of a carabao nickel
> but on a boat
> between oceans
> between continents.

Yet she affirms her people's strength:

> your old brown hands
> hold life, many lives
> within each crack
> a story

The marginality delineated by Robles and Cerenio constitutes an important theme in Filipino American literature. It is further defined by Jeff Tagami, who suggests that Filipino Americans may be anonymous ("Without Names") but nevertheless can still be identified by their contribution to the development of Hawaii as menial la-

borers—an episode that he memorializes and celebrates in *October Light* (1987).

Meanwhile, in the continuing search for a positive ethnic identity against a background of anonymity, Filipino American poetry was blessed with the arrival of Jessica Hagedorn (born 1949) from Manila, a city where, as Hagedorn says in her poem "Souvenirs" in reference to the Marcos regime,

> the president's wife
> dictates martial law
> with her thighs
> sanctity n piety
> is her name
> as she sips tea

In the United States, "the loneliest of countries," she is entangled, like Robles, in mixed-up identities, as in this passage from "Song for My Father":

> in new york
> they ask me if i'm puerto rican
> and do i live in queens?
> i listen to pop stations
> chant to iemaja
> convinced i'm really brazilian

She identifies closely with other peoples of color and particularly comes to value the indigenous music of Latin America ("Latin Music in New York"; "The Woman Who Thought She Was More than a Samba"). For Hagedorn, the sense of self is also built upon the sense of insecurity: "there are rapists/ out there/ some of them don't like asian women" ("Solea"). Increasingly, identity is impossible without an awareness of the negative aspects of American life, such as cheapened love ("Seeing You Again Makes Me Wanna Wash the Dishes"), televised sensationalism ("Justifiable Homicide"), pervasive violence ("The Song of Bullets"), and women's vulnerability to men's lust ("The Leopard"). On the whole, Hagedorn has developed most of the themes central to Filipino American poetry and has added new ideas and stylistic expressions of her own that are geared to the problematics and aesthetics of modernity.

Russell Gonzaga, in the Philippines and raised in San Francisco, also reflects the interdisciplinary work being done by so many poets at the beginning of the twenty-first century. He is a spoken word poet and community activist who mixes street life and the academic world. He grew up in a community rich in oral tradition and was interested in rap music as a teenager. He realized rap was just a structure, regular metered rhyming verse, so he freed it up. He sees the interconnectedness of rap music and the spoken word and cites his inspiration from widely divergent sources: hip-hop, the Qu'ran, science fiction, and *The Autobiography of Malcolm X* (1965). Like other Asian Americans of his generation, he expresses a distaste for labels and a belief in universality and blending:

> . . . it's part of the western philosophical paradigm to chop everything up and put it into compartments . . . but I think people of color aren't like that. . . . we understand everything informs everything else.

Gonzaga is a three-time winner of the San Francisco Poetry Slam Championship, in which poets read their works to an enthusiastic audience and are evaluated by a panel of judges.

SOUTHEAST ASIAN AMERICANS

In the 1990's and at the beginning of the twenty-first century, one thing many Asian American poets of many ethnic backgrounds shared was an ability to blend their work and their ethnicities with other groups and methods of communication, capitalizing on the interest in multiculturalism in the United States. Such a tendency is evident among many young poets of the turn of the century, including Chinese Americans Genny Lim and Beau Sia, and Filipino American Russell Gonzaga.

Le Thi Diem Thuy (born 1972), a Vietnamese American, shares this interest in blending her work with other forms of presentations. She grew up in South Vietnam during fierce fighting. She left the country in 1979 and settled in the United States. As a performance artist, she has become well known for *Red Fiery Summer* (pr. 1995), which covers the period of terrible attacks from North Vietnam. On stage she attempts to embody her father, to "express his presence," as she puts it. The presentation combines prose, poems, and monologues that reflect on war and its aftermath, from the days of the French involvement in Vietnam. Her passionate, terrify-

ing stories are understated. She says, "I go about things in an oblique way." She gets to the point, but she feels the approach can be just as satisfying. She was selected by the *Village Voice* as a Writer on the Verge. Her powerful look at the way Vietnam still haunts its victims can be seen in a passage from "Shrapnel Shards on Blue Water," in which she compares first-generation Vietnamese Americans who relocated to the United States in the 1970's with the "shards" of war and then denies that self-identity with war to transform it, embracing and defending the image of her homeland as not war but rather "a piece of us":

> we are fragmented shards
> blown here by a war no one wants to remember
> in a foreign land
> with an achingly familiar wound
> our survival is dependent upon
> never forgetting that vietnam is not
> a word
> a world
> a love
> a family
> a fear
> to bury
>
> . . . . . .
> let people know
> VIETNAM IS NOT A WAR
> but a piece
> of
> us . . .

Li-Young Lee (born 1957), born in Jakarta, Indonesia, represents another culture that has added to the American experience. Genny Lim says of Lee, "He is a wonderful poet and his work deeply reflects his affinity for Chinese poetry, consistent with western expectations." Her comments show again the blending that occurs when two cultures meet. For example, Lee writes repeatedly of his father, who at one time was Chinese leader Mao Zedong's personal physician but in the United States became a Presbyterian minister. Lee explores the dramatic differences in these two extremes. The poet writes of love, family, ordinary experiences, and his specific past.

In "Persimmons," for example, Lee recalls childhood experiences typical of the immigrant child: his teacher punishing him for not knowing the difference between the words "persimmons" and "precision"; then the precise method for choosing and eating a persimmon ("This is precision"); early sexual experimentation with an Anglo neighbor girl whom he teaches a few words of Chinese; and the difficulty of pronouncing the language ("Other words/ that got me into trouble were/ *fight* and *fright, wren* and *yarn*"). Each stanza's recalled experience leads to and interweaves with that of the next, mimicking the process of memory and displaying the constant interplay of the poet's dual cultural and ethnic experiences. Yet at the same time that these experiences are shaped by the poet's cultural and linguistic background, that are nevertheless familiar to all readers, inviting and binding readers in the common obstacles and challenges of growing up.

BIBLIOGRAPHY

Bruchac, Joseph, ed. *Breaking Silence: An Anthology of Contemporary Asian-American Poets*. Greenfield Center, N.Y.: Greenfield Review Press, 1983. Bruchac, a prolific writer himself, heads up a groundbreaking collection. The poems here include a wide range of authors, including Diana Chang, Gail Harada, Yuri Kageyama, Joy Kogawa, Genny Lim, Janice Mirikitani, Arhtur Sze, and Nellie Wong.

Carbo, Nick, ed. *Returning a Borrowed Tongue: Poems by Filipino and Filipino American Writers*. Minneapolis: Coffeehouse Press, 1996. Contains translations of established writers such as Gemino Abad, Eugene Gloria, Catalina Cariaga, and Jessica Hagedorn. Newer poets such as Jaime Jacinto are also represented.

Chang, Juliana, ed. *Quiet Fire: Asian American Poetry*. New York: Asian American Writers' Workshop, 1996. This first book published by the Workshop has become a landmark anthology as the first historical survey of Asian American poetry. It contains early works of Joy Kogawa, Jessica Hagedorn, and Lawson Fusao Inada, and others, selected to reflect both the high quality and wide range of Asian American poetic discourse through the mid-1990's. Bibliography. An indispensable collection.

Cheung, King-Kok, ed. *An Interethnic Companion to Asian American Literature*. New York: Cambridge University Press, 1997. The publisher notes that the volume surveys the work of "North American writers of Asian descent, in terms of both national origins (Chinese, Filipino, Japanese, Korean, South Asian, Vietnamese) and shared concerns. It introduces readers to the distinctive literary history of each group of writers and discusses issues that connect or divide these different groups." Bibliography, index.

Cheung, King-Kok, and Stan Yogi, eds. *Asian American Literature: An Annotated Bibliography*. New York: Modern Language Association of America, 1988. A useful resource that directs students to additional source material.

Hongo, Garrett, ed. *The Open Boat: Poems from Asian America*. New York: Anchor, 1993. Edited by one of the best known poets of the Asian American experience, this major collection includes work by Maxine Hong Kingston, David Mura, Marilyn Chin, John You, and twenty-seven other contemporary poets representing a variety of perspectives on the Asian American experience.

Kim, Elaine H. *Asian American Literature: An Introduction to the Writings and Their Social Context*. Philadelphia: Temple University Press, 1982. Writing for *Choice*, reviewer David L. Heiserman notes that "the author demonstrates how the roles of men and women have been inevitably changed through the American experience. Well documented, the book has 82 pages of helpful notes, bibliography, and index. This study should help to introduce a host of excellent writers such as Louis Chu, Carlos Bulosan, and Hisaye Yamamoto, among others."

Lew, Walter, ed. *Premonitions: The Kaya Anthology of New Asian North American Poetry*. New York: Kaya Production, 1995. This major anthology (six hundred pages long) focuses on writers of the post-1970's era.

Lim, Shirley Geok-Lin, et al., eds. *The Forbidden Stitch: An Asian American Women's Anthology*. Corvallis, Oreg.: Calyx Books, 1989. Works by seventy Asian American women are collected here: poetry, stories, art, reviews. Among the writers represented are Diana Chang, Cathy Song, and Elaine Kim.

Mahony, Phillip, ed. *From Both Sides Now: The Poetry of the Vietnam War and Its Aftermath*. New York:

Simon & Schuster, 1998. Poems included here come from Vietnamese and Americans, adults and children, combatants and protesters. Much is from Vietnamese Americans and Amerasian poets.

Rustomji-Kerns, Roshni, ed. *Living in America: Poetry and Fiction by South Asian American Writers*. Boulder, Colo.: Westview Press, 1995. This major compilation of Asian American writers includes the native-born, immigrants, refugees, and expatriates. Some are well known (Ved Mehta, Meena Alexander), and many are new voices. All authors contribute a statement with the works they wrote.

Sunoo, Brenda Paik, ed. *Korean American Writings: Selected Material from "Insight," Korean American Bimonthly, by First, Second, and Third Generation Koreans Living in the United States, 1972-1975.* New York: Insight, 1975. Includes graphics and a bibliography.

Tabios, Eileen, ed. *Black Lightning: Poetry in Progress.* New York: Asian American Writers' Workshop, 1998. Follows the early drafts of poems through to their final forms. Works by Meena Alexander, Mei-mei Berssenbrugge, Marilyn Chin, Jessica Hagedorn, Garrett Hongo, Timothy Liu, David Mura, Arthur Sze (who wrote an introductory essay for the book), and John Yau are presented.

Tran, Barbara, ed. *Watermark: Vietnamese American Poetry and Prose.* Philadelphia: Temple University press, 1998. Tran gives voice to Vietnamese American writers in this anthology of work, collecting fiction, prose, and poetry, both previously published and never before published. The poems cover more than the war. Includes work of both first-generation and second-generation Vietnamese Americans. Authors include Linh Dinh, Andrew Lam, and Christian Longworthy.

Balance Chow, updated by
Gary Zacharias and Christina J. Moose

CARIBBEAN POETRY

From its earliest beginnings in the eighteenth century, Caribbean, or West Indian, poetry has been an elusive but dynamic art. Though sometimes static, it has always been an evolving art form. According to one scholar, Lloyd W. Brown, the first 180 years of West Indian poetry were uneven at best; however, Brown was apprising only the formal aspect of Caribbean poetry, a poetic tradition that was imposed on the peoples of the West Indies first by a slaveocracy and later by an imperialist regime. There has always been an oral tradition in the Caribbean, and although this tradition has been suppressed, it could never be destroyed. It has existed in children's ring games, in calypso, and in the combined arts of carnival, Junkanoo, and other folk and religious celebrations. Then too, the unwritten tradition of the Amerindians has enriched the art of Caribbean poetry. Ironically, after years of suppression it is the folk/oral tradition, combined with other aspects of Afro-Caribbean cultural experiences, that Edward Kamau Brathwaite theorizes is the wellspring of "nation language."

EIGHTEENTH CENTURY

Slavery in the Caribbean was extremely harsh, and people of African descent had very little opportunity to develop the art of composing poetry. Therefore the first poems to be published by an Afro-Caribbean came as a result of an experiment centered in the noble savage concept. Francis Williams of Jamaica, a free black, was the first to publish a poem. John, the second duke of Montagu (and at one time Jamaica's governor), believed that if blacks were given the same educational opportunities as Caucasians they would be able to compete successfully with Caucasians. Williams, under the patronage of the duke, was educated in England. On his return to Jamaica, the duke was unable to establish his protégé in Jamaican society, so Williams opened a school in Spanish Town.

In 1759, Williams wrote "An Ode to George Haldane, Governor of the Island of Jamaica" to celebrate the arrival of the governor at his new office. Written in Latin, the poem, the only extant work of Williams, attests to the poet's abilities, but it also suggests the subservient position in which Williams found himself:

> Established by a mighty hand (God the creator gave the same soul to all his creatures without exception), virtue itself, like wisdom, is devoid of color. There is no color in an honorable mind, nor in art.

Williams then bids his black muse not to hesitate but to "mount to the abode of [the new governor] the Caesar of the setting sun," and bid him welcome.

The other acknowledged poet of the eighteenth century is James Grainger, a Scottish physician who made his home in Jamaica. His extended poem *The Sugar-Cane* (1766) is often described as a pastoral epic that discusses the vicissitudes of life on the island. The poem is based Western European forms that underscore European stereotypes, as in this description of the slaves:

> Annon they [slaves] form; nor inexpert
> A thousand tuneful intricacies weave,
> Shaking their sable limbs; and oft a kiss
> steal from their partners; who, with neck reclin'd
> and semblant scorn resent the ravish'd bliss.

Grainger depicts a Romantic pastoral but also indicates that, should the slaves drink alcohol or hear the drum they will immediately revert to their savage ways, and "bacchanalian frenzy" will ensue. Despite the idealistic picture presented in *The Sugar-Cane*, the poem has come to typify the long-lived tradition of the Caribbean pastoral.

NINETEENTH CENTURY

Williams and Grainger represent the poetry of the eighteenth century; the poets who typify the tradition during the nineteenth century are the Hart sisters of Antigua and Egbert Martin of Guyana. Elizabeth Hart Thwaites and Anne Hart Gilbert were two women of African descent who have not received much exposure. Their parents, Anne Clerkley Hart and Barry Conyers Hart, were free African Caribbeans. The father, a plantation owner, was also a poet who published his poems in the local newspaper. Although slavery prevailed in Antigua, both sisters married white men and devoted their lives to educating other African Caribbeans. The sisters were known for writing religious poems and hymns. Anne Hart Gilbert affirms that, although race prejudice was pervasive, her light complexion exempted her and her family from racial prejudices. In her poem "On the Death of the Rev. Mr. Cook," Elizabeth Hart Thwaites praises the missionary for his work among all races:

> With rapture [he] heard the diff'rent tribes converse,
> In Canaan's tongue redeeming love rehearse,
> And Afric's sable sons in stammering accents tell
> Of Jesu's love, immense, unspeakable.

Like the Hart sisters, Egbert Martin had his roots in the Caribbean Basin and was considered the most prominent poet of his day. The son of a Guyanese tailor, Martin wrote poetry that followed the traditional modes of European models. He did, at times, paint realistic word-pictures of Guyanese landscapes, and in some of his better poems he makes his readers aware of the poverty of his people. Perhaps he is not as patriotic as his poem "National Anthem" suggests, but in it he calls for Britain to close her "Far-reaching wings" over all her "Colonial throng." Written for Queen Victoria's Jubilee in 1887, the poem won an award for his patriotic efforts.

TWENTIETH CENTURY

Caribbean poetry came into its own during the twentieth century. The nineteenth century poets were cautious. They protested against the oppressive rule of the colonials, but they saw themselves as British. The poets of the early part of the twentieth century were militant. They were nationalistic. The poets who best represent this period are Jamaica's Claude McKay, Jamaica's Louise Bennett, Guyana's A. J. Seymour, St. Lucia's Derek Walcott, and Barbados's Edward Kamau Brathwaite.

One of the strongest voices to come out of the Caribbean during the early twentieth century is that of Claude McKay, born in 1889 in Sunny Ville, Jamaica. Before leaving his home, he published two volumes of dialect poetry *Constab Ballads* (1912) and *Songs of Jamaica* (1912). Shortly after publishing these volumes, McKay migrated to the United States, where he became the voice of oppressed blacks not only in the Caribbean but throughout the world. He insisted that he was "never go-ing to carry the torch for British colonialism or American imperialism." Using the sonnet as his major mode of expression, McKay describes America as a vicious tiger that "sinks into my throat her tiger's tooth/ stealing my breath of life. . . ." The poet warns America that he "sees her might and granite wonders. . . . Like priceless treasures sinking in the sand." The poet insists that if America kills him, she will be killing herself because it is he who makes America strong. In "If We Must Die," McKay's persona encourages the oppressed not to die "like hogs/ Hunted and penned in an inglorious spot," but to die nobly facing the enemy: "Pressed to the wall, dying but fighting back!" Although McKay was probably not thinking of the British as oppressed (the British for Mckay were always the colonizers, the oppressors), during World War II, when the Germans were blitzing London, Prime Minister Winston Churchill quoted McKay's poem in the House of Commons to rally the nation, and British soldiers carried copies of the poem in their pockets.

Although McKay never returned to Jamaica to live, he did write about the beauty of the island. In "Flame Heart" he admits that he has forgotten much about Jamaica, but what he has never forgotten is "the poinsettia's red, blood red in warm December." His romantic nostalgia is also evidenced in "The Tropics in New York": In passing a store that displayed tropical fruits in a window the persona admits: "And, hungry for the old, familiar ways,/ I turned aside and bowed my head and wept." McKay, then, represents the new thrust in Caribbean poetry that came to the fore in the early part of the twentieth century. He is sophisticated enough to use the traditional British literary tradition, but instead of writing romantic pastorals he instructs the oppressed to fight and he warns the oppressors of disastrous times should they continue their oppression.

Louise Bennett (born in Jamaica in 1919) is an important poet in the development of Caribbean poetry because she had the courage not to develop her talents in the accepted English literary tradition. Bennett admits that she was not taken seriously as a poet. She started out writing in the traditional Caribbean pastoral tradition, but she was not doing what she wanted to do, so she followed the folk/oral tradition. A nationalist and a womanist, Bennett makes her philosophical statements through humor. In "Colonization in Reverse" the poet informs Miss Mattie, a persona in much of her poetry, that England is in for a surprise because Jamaicans now have the whip hand. They "Jussa pack dem bag and baggage;/ An tun history upside dung." The Jamaicans are giving Britain a dose of its own medicine by moving to Britain. The poet insists that the British folk are known for being calm when faced with adversity, yet she muses: "But ah wonder how dem gwine stan/ Colonization in reverse." In "Jamaican Oman" Bennett explains that Island women have always been liberated and have always supported their men. Long before other women of the world sought to be liberated "Jamaican women wassa work/ Her liberation plan!" Bennett was not always held in high esteem as a poet, especially prior to the 1960's. However, with independence, poets became more concerned with finding their own voices rather than imitating British models. Bennett became the spirit of the age.

Arthur J. Seymour, from Guyana (born 1914), is pivotal to the development of poetry in the Caribbean as both a writer and a publisher. As a poet, his longevity allows us to see the transition that was occurring in the Caribbean. His poetry of the 1930's has very little if any protest and is tempered by a "colonial quiescence." Later, however, Seymour combines his Guyanese nationalism with an embracing of the entire Caribbean. In the poem "For Christopher Columbus" the reader, like Columbus, sees weaving palm trees in the tropical breezes "And watches the islands in a great bow swing/ From Florida down to the South American coast." While he seems to fall back on the earlier English model of the Caribbean pastoral, Seymour does not forget to remind his audience of the degradation of slavery and of the suffering that African Caribbeans have endured.

Derek Walcott of St. Lucia and Edward Brathwaite of Barbados are the two writers who bridge the gap between poets of the colonial period and the New World poets. These artists have witnessed the harshness of colonialism. They have known what it means to be isolated as artists and as individuals, for they came into adulthood and began their writing when the Caribbean nations were still crown colonies. As a poet and a dramatist, Walcott has used his talents to accentuate Caribbean speech patterns and cultural traditions in works such as *Omeros* (1990) and *The Odyssey: A Stage Version* (pr.

1992). He has used the Homeric legends and Homeric characters to crystallize the Caribbean experience. In 1992 he won the Nobel Prize in Literature, thereby bringing great visibility to Caribbean writers as a whole.

Brathwaite, also a poet of international fame, has brought notoriety to Caribbean poetry not only through his writing and his oral presentation but also through his scholarly endeavors in Caribbean language and culture. Both Walcott and Brathwaite have transcended their Caribbean ethos to become world-renowned poets, and both have brought Caribbean poetry from its colonial vision into the international arena and have turned Caribbean dialect into what Brathwaite calls "nation language" of the Caribbean.

POST-INDEPENDENCE PERIOD

The poetry of the post-independence period in the Caribbean is more exuberant than the poetry of the colonial era. Brathwaite affirms that Caribbean poets have found a new mode of expression that he calls "nation language." This New World language might sound like English, "but in its contours, its rhythm and timbre, its sound explosions, it is not English. . . ." Three poets who demonstrate this new language are Grace Nichols, Fred D'Aguiar, and Bongo Jerry.

Nichols (born in Guyana in 1950), whose roots are in Guyana, insists that her poetry comes out of "a heightened imagistic use of language that does things to the heart and head." She is at ease with both languages, standard English as well as creole or nation language, because for her, the two languages are "constantly intercepting." The blending of these languages is evident in the poem "I is a Long-Memoried Woman." Here the persona states:

> From dih pout
> of mih mouth
> from dih
> treacherous
> calm of mih smile
> you can tell
> I is a long-memoried woman.

D'Aguiar (born in 1960 in London, England, and sent to Guyana as a child) fuses folk tradition with standard English and nation language. In "Mama Dot

Learns to Fly," D'Aguiar explores the myth of the flying African. Mama Dot, looking at a film of inventors trying to fly, decides that she wants to see an ancestor, so with "Her equipment straightforward/ Thought-up to bring the lot/ To her: *come leh we gaff girl.*" The idea here, as Toni Morrison suggests in *Song of Solomon* (1977), is that people of African descent do not need the invention of flying machines because they have the natural ability to fly. Much of the flying concept is suggested in the final line of the poem when Mama Dot says: "Come let us go off, girl."

Unlike Nichols and D'Aguiar, who fuse standard English and nation language, Bongo Jerry, a Rastifarian poet, uses a language that Braithwaite calls "the roots and underground link of all the emerging forces" of the New World literature. Bongo sees the new language as a liberating tool for people of the Caribbean. In the poem "MABRAK" the poet proclaims:

Save the YOUNG
from the language that MAN teach,
the doctrine Pope preach
skin bleach
HOW ELSE? . . . MAN must use MEN language to
   carry this message.

The message is that the language that has been taught by the European, "BABEL TONGUES," must be silenced, and the poets of the Caribbean must "recall and recollect BLACK SPEECH."

Caribbean poetry has evolved from an imitation art into a dynamic expression of the cultural traditions of the people. In reclaiming their submerged language, a language of African origins, poets are affirming their heritage and their pride in their newfound freedom. In the past, artists left their native lands to find success in foreign countries. With the development in communication technology, the Caribbean is no longer isolated from the rest of the world. Also, Caribbean poets are less likely to migrate to foreign lands. Indeed, independence has resulted in an affirmation of cultural liberation and has nurtured a spirit of creativity in Caribbean poets.

BIBLIOGRAPHY
Barksdale, Richard, and Kenneth Kinnamon, eds. *Black Writers of America: A Comprehensive Anthology.* New York: Macmillan, 1972. Includes the work of major black writers from Olaudah Eqinano to Eldridge Cleaver. With an extensive bibliography on literary history and criticism, the text has excellent examples of McKay's poetry.

Brathwaite, Edward Kamau. *A History of the Voice: The Development of National Language in Anglophone Caribbean Poetry.* London: New Beacon Press, 1984. The text explores Brathwaite's theory of the development of a Caribbean language that is centered in an African rather than a British tradition.

Brown, Lloyd. *West Indian Poetry.* Boston: Twayne, 1978. Brown's text is a scholarly work that evaluates Caribbean poetry from its beginnings through the independence period. A must for anyone studying Caribbean poetry.

Burnett, Paula, ed. *The Penguin Book of Caribbean Verse.* London Penguin Books, 1986. This comprehensive anthology of Caribbean poetry from the eighteenth century to the mid-1980's offers biographical and explanatory notes, as well as an invaluable glossary.

Burns, Sir Allen. *History of the British West Indies.* London: George Allen and Unwin, 1954. With copious maps and appendices, the text narrates the history of the Caribbean from the arrival of Christopher Columbus to 1952.

Dance, Daryl Cumber. *Fifty Caribbean Writers: A Bio-bibliographical Critical Sourcebook.* New York: Greenwood Press, 1979. As the title suggests, the text offers bibliographical as well as biographical reference notes on fifty of the most important Caribbean writers.

Dathorne, O. R., ed. *Caribbean Verse.* London: Heinemann Educational Books, 1967. Collects works of poets of the colonial period.

Ferguson, Moira, ed. *The Hart Sisters: Early African Caribbean Writers, Evangelicals, and Radicals.* Linds, Nebraska: University of Nebraska Press, 1993. Contains an extended critical introduction, the major works of the Hart sisters, and an appendix with information about people who were involved with the sisters.

Hammer, Robert D., ed. *Critical Perspectives on Derek Walcott.* Boulder, Colo.: Three Conntinents, 1997.

This text has both criticisms by Walcott and criticism of his works by other scholars. It is an invaluable tool for the Walcott scholar.

Herdeck, Donald E. *Caribbean Writers: A Bio-bibliographical-cultural Encyclopedia*. Washington, D.C.: Three Continents, 1979. Herdeck's work is a comprehensive study of English, Spanish, French, and Dutch writers of the Caribbean. It is not as detailed as Dance's text, but it covers more territory.

King, Bruce, ed. *West Indian Literature*. Hamden, Conn.: Shoe String Press, 1979. A series of articles, by different scholars, on Caribbean writers.

Livingstone, James T., ed. *Caribbean Rhythms: An Emerging English Literature of the West Indies*. New York: Washington Square Press, 1974. This anthology of Caribbean writers offers many of the works of post-independence literary artists.

Markham, E. A., ed. *Hinterland: Caribbean Poetry from the West Indies and Britain*. Glasgow, Scotland: Bloodaxe Books, 1989. The anthology is the work of post-independence Caribbean poets; many of them, as the title suggests, live in England.

Salky, Andrew, ed. *Breaklight: The Poetry of the Caribbean*. New York: Doubleday, 1971. Deals with poets of the colonial period. The introduction is brief but helpful.

Ralph Reckley, Sr.

CATALAN POETRY

Catalan, a romance language that serves as a bridge between the Ibero-Romanic and the Gallo-Romanic languages, is spoken today mainly in Spain, in the regions of Catalonia, Valencia, and the Balearic Islands. In addition, it is the official language of the tiny nation of Andorra, which lies in the Pyrenees Mountains on the border between Spain and France. Although clearly related to its sister Romance languages, it is not a dialect but a fully developed language with a venerable history and literature of its own. It flourished from the Middle Ages through to the twentieth century, but during Francisco Franco's totalitarian rule (1939-1975) was banned from use in schools, government agencies, and the media. It did not die, however, but was reborn, along with a sometimes radical sense of nationalism, in the late 1970's after Franco's death. In 1979, both Spanish and Catalan were officially recognized in Catalonia, and in 1983 the Linguistic Normalization Act reinvigorated the language's use in official and commercial contexts. In 1997, the Catalan Language Act actually required broadcast media in Catalonia to offer programming in Catalan. Schools expose children to Catalan from a young age. This rebirth of the language has given rise to a revived interest in Catalan poetry both new and old.

MIDDLE AGES: PROVENÇAL VS. CATALAN

Catalan first produced its own poetry in the thirteenth century. Prior to that time, and for the next two hundred years, many powerful poets whose vernacular was Catalan chose instead to write in Provençal. The Provençal poets, neighbors geographically, had provided the forms and the lexicon of courtly love and had developed the prestige of *amour courtois* in lyric poetry. Although some Catalan poets of this period did occasionally write in Catalan, their best-known works are in the more prestigious Provençal. The troubadour "Catalan school" began to flourish in the late twelfth century; among its members were Count Ramon Berenguer IV, Guillem de Cabestany, Guerau de Cabrera, Guillem de Bergadà, Cerverí de Girona, and Ramon Vidal de Besalú. The latter two were jongleurs or troubadours. Their sensitive love lyrics and highly sophisticated rhyme schemes were faithful to earlier Provençal models; among their themes were *amour courtois* of a political nature and satiric social verse.

Provençal, the language of art, was noticeably different from daily speech in Catalan. An important factor in maintaining the predominance of Provençal was the poetic Consistory of Toulouse, "de la Gaya Sciencia," at which Catalan poets writing in Provençal were winning contestants more often than not. This poetic contest, later named the Jocs Florals, has been revived in Toulouse and Barcelona since the nineteenth century, although Provençal is no longer the requisite language.

RAMON LLULL

A chronological study of the masterpieces of Catalan poetry begins with the *Cancó de Santa Fe* (c. 1075), which represents an early, still formative Catalan that nevertheless resembles modern Catalan much more closely than the language of *La Chanson de Roland* (c. 1100; *Song of Roland*) resembles modern French. Into the formless genre of Catalan poetry there suddenly burst the most brilliant, fecund author and thinker of all Catalan literature, Ramon Llull (c. 1235-1316). His stature in Catalan letters is comparable to that of Dante, Giovanni Boccaccio, and Petrarch in Italian literature.

Although Llull's writings encompass a broad literary range, he is particularly appreciated for his poetry, including *Llibre d'amic e amat* (c. 1285; *The Book of the Lover and Beloved*, 1923), *Lo desconhort* (c. 1295; lamentation), and *Cant de Ramon* (c. 1299; song of Ramon). Llull, a Franciscan, wrote almost innumerable philosophical and theological treatises in Latin, Arabic, and Catalan. His Catalan novel, *Libre d'Evast e Blanquerna* (c. 1284; *Blanquerna: A Thirteenth Century Romance*, 1926), composed in five parts which symbolize the five wounds of Christ, is considered his masterpiece; embedded in this novel is the highly poetic, internally rhyming prose poem, *The Book of the Lover and Beloved*, which echoes the biblical Song of Songs and anticipates Saint John of the Cross in its celebration of the mystic ecstasy of lover and beloved.

Llull's encyclopedic *Llibre de contemplació en Deu* (c. 1282) is a doctrinal work, while his *Felix e llibre de meravelles* (c. 1288) is concerned with the revelation of

God in nature, particularly in the section titled *Libre de les bèsties* (c. 1290; *The Book of the Beasts*, 1927), in which animals assume anthropomorphic roles. Among his other Catalan texts is the *Llibre de l'orde de cavalleria* (c. 1292; *The Book of the Ordre of Chyualry*, 1484), which became a manual for medieval knighthood and which was closely imitated by Don Juan Manuel in Castilian. Llull's *Opera latina* is principally theological and rigorously Scholastic in approach, while *Llibre del gentil e los tres savis* (c. 1274; the book of the Gentile and the three wise men) is a balanced discussion of the respective religious positions of a Christian, a Jew, and a Moslem. Llull produced many other works in both Latin and Arabic.

A noble and amoral courtier as a young man, Llull underwent a dramatic conversion at the age of thirty. He left wife, children, and rank to become a Franciscan, dedicating himself to study, teaching, and writing and to converting Muslims and Jews. He traveled and taught widely, writing in different languages for widely divergent audiences. He made more than one trip to Tunis, perhaps dying while he was there or soon thereafter as a martyr, stoned by a mob. He is venerated not only as a great scholar, thinker, and poet but also as a religious figure, having attained the rank of Blessed.

Llull was the first great poet to write in Catalan. It is almost certain that, during his dissolute and courtly youth, he practiced versifying in Provençal, but after his conversion, he wrote in Catalan, using poetic forms borrowed from Provençal, except in *The Book of the Lover and Beloved*. In addition to being the first champion of Catalan poetry and prose, Llull was the first Catalan poet to delineate the Franciscan approach to God through nature, a tradition which has persisted in Catalan poetry to the present day. Llull's desire to demonstrate the rationality of the Christian faith and to recognize the universe as a manifestation of the Divine informed his philosophical and poetic quest.

Lo desconhort is one of Llull's best-known poems. Written in monorhymed Alexandrines, it is a highly personal analysis of his failures, imbued with pessimism and personal frustration. Readers today sense the poet's personality quite strongly, while recognizing the theme of unfulfilled personal aspirations as universal and timeless.

Llull employed poetic form not to exhibit his artistry but merely to provide a vehicle for his deeply felt religious expression. Concept and emotion take precedence over art, which had become hollow to him after his conversion. He was perceived during his own lifetime as a scholar, theologian, and prose writer, and a full appreciation of his poetry has developed over the past century. Llull was able to free himself from ritual Provençalisms and artistic rigidity precisely because of his overwhelming religious purpose.

After the uniquely personal poetry of Llull, the fourteenth century passed without the emergence of another significant Catalan poet. While the popular vernacular lyric did exist, the more erudite court poets continued the Provençal tradition, and the Catalan epics of the period were written exclusively in prose.

THE RENAISSANCE

The Catalan Renaissance began with the reign of Martí L'Humà in 1396, extending to 1516 and covering the reigns of Ferdinand Alfons IV of Catalonia, Alfons V of Aragon, Joan II, and Ferdinand II. Under Alfons, the center of the Catalan kingdom was Naples, which served as a meeting ground for Catalan and Italian poets and other intellectuals. Italian poets and writers, particularly Dante, Petrarch, and Boccaccio, were influential in the middle and late phases of the Catalan Renaissance in both poetry and prose. Provençal influences continued to be dominant in the early stage of the Renaissance, especially in the poems of Gilabert de Pròixita and Andreu Febrer, the latter also a translator of *La divina commedia* (c. 1320; *The Divine Comedy*) in terza rima.

Jordi de Sant Jordi (c. 1400-1424), poet, courtier, and soldier, was the outstanding poet of the young Catalan Renaissance. His love poetry appears in his collection *Estramps* (c. 1420; free verses). The flavor of his unrhymed, decasyllabic verse is Petrarchan, though still with a hint of Provençal. He was much appreciated for his adaptation of Italianate love themes, reminiscent of the *dolce stil nuovo*. The elegance of his Catalan was innovative and raised Catalan poetic diction and versification to new heights of expressiveness and sensitivity, achieved through sophisticated harmonizing of vocabulary and syntax.

The greatest poet of the Catalan Renaissance was Ausiàs March (1397-1459). His influence has been so far-reaching that he is still the most highly respected poet of classic Catalan literature. Catalan poets of the nineteenth and twentieth centuries have continuously studied, imitated, and drawn inspiration from March's controlled emotional torment. Among the Renaissance Castilian poets who admired and cited him were the Marqués de Santillana, Garcilaso de la Vega, Gutierre de Cetina, and Francisco de Herrera.

March, poet and soldier-statesman, came from a noble literary family. He sings of the paradox of carnal love and its purification, the path from *eros* to *caritas*. His verse is poetically intense, involved actively in the Renaissance, but retaining vestiges of the late Middle Ages. His profound suffering in the course of a carnal and impossible love, followed by the death of his youthful mistress, provided him with his single, obsessive subject. What remained to be done after his personal tragedy was to replace *eros* with *caritas* in the manner of Dante and Beatrice. The death of the beloved created the possibility of this replacement, but since March was sincere in his moral code, this death was not a sufficient expiation; it robbed him of the possibility of attaining a "perfect" love in the course of life in this world. His expiation then became a unique experience, interiorized and always present to conscience and consciousness.

In March's *Cants d'amor* (c. 1450; songs of love), love is carnal, forbidden, guilty. His preoccupation with sinful love marked a transition in Catalan poetry. In March's time, many Catalan poets were still writing in Provençal, following the traditional precepts of courtly love. In contrast, March was absolutely sincere in his recognition of the iniquity of carnal love, but hesitant to deny it totally in his desire for the unattainable Teresa Bou, who assumed for him a role very similar to that of Beatrice for Dante.

March renounced the cult of form to write a dense, cerebral poetry. His language, like his style, is sober, measured, direct, nakedly expressing his tortured passion. His preferred form is the decasyllabic line, the same form later used by Maurice Scève in the sixteenth century. March's poems are a conversation, a dialogue and debate between the lover and his soul; their concerns are as vital in the twentieth century as they were in the fifteenth.

After March, two other Valencian poets of note appeared in the Catalan Renaissance: Joan Roiç de Corella and Jaume Roig. Roiç de Corella wrote *Tragèdia de Caldesa* (fifteenth century), lyric love poetry devoted to his beloved, Caldesa; he also wrote religious poetry devoted to the Virgin.

Roig is remembered for the narrative poem *Spill o llibre de les dones* (c. 1460; *Mirror: Or, Book of Women*), the most violent misogynistic diatribe of the Hispanic peninsula and one of the most extreme antifeminist works written in any century. Composed in a brusque, five-syllable line, it is full of crude descriptions which contrast radically with the tradition of lyric poetry; indeed, its content is essentially novelistic, and the choice of form has made the work an oddity in Catalan letters.

In the fifteenth century, Catalan literature and culture fell into a decline that continued into the nineteenth century. With the ascendancy of Castile, power shifted away from the Catalan-speaking lands. As a result, Catalan poetry suffered; typical was the case of Joan Boscan, a Catalan who wrote only in Castilian. Only Pere Serafí (c. 1505-1567), Francesc Vicenç Garcia (1582-1623), and, in the seventeenth century, Francesc Fontanella attempted to keep formal Catalan poetry alive during the Decadence. Poetry continued on the popular level, however, particularly in the sixteenth century. It has survived in the anonymous *Romancer/Canconer* (poem collection), which contains many famous ballads, such as "Els estudiants de Tolosa" (the students of Tolosa), "El testament d'Amelià" (Amelia's will), "El Comte Arnau" (Count Arnau), and "La dama d'Aragó" (the lady of Aragon); many of these ballads are written in a fourteen-syllable line of rhyming couplets with a caesura at the hemistich.

THE RENAIXENÇA

The nineteenth century brought a renewed sense of patriotism to Catalonia, and this renewal had intellectual overtones. Poetry was to play a great part in the Catalan cultural resurgence; indeed, it can be said that the lifeblood of modern Catalan literature is its poetry, which has nourished the culture with regular infusions of contemporary masterpieces.

One must begin an appreciation of modern Catalan poetry with the remarkable poetic event that initiated the

Renaixença (rebirth) of Catalan letters: the newspaper publication in 1833 of "La Pàtria," an ode by Bonaventura Carles Aribau (1798-1862). After a lapse of three centuries, Aribau had captured the spirit of Catalonia in a nostalgic, Romantic evocation of landscape. The Catalan population had continued speaking Catalan during the three centuries since Pere Serafí, and scholarly interest in the language had increased in the eighteenth century. The nineteenth century brought a renewed interest in the Middle Ages and in past grandeur; in this climate, "La Pàtria" provided the necessary impulse for the Renaixença. Once under way, the Catalan cultural revival was eagerly supported by intellectuals, scholar-poets such as Milà i Fontanals, archivists, and the Catalan people in general.

One consequence of the Renaixença was the reestablishment of the Jocs Florals in 1859, with the stipulation that Catalan be used exclusively. One of the winners was the epic and lyric poet Jacint Verdaguer (1845-1902). Verdaguer, often called Mossén Cinto, is the best known and most highly esteemed poet of the Renaixença. His complete works were available during his lifetime, and he was a living inspiration to and symbol of the Catalan people during the nineteenth century. Catalan scholars now consider Verdaguer's works to represent the long first flowering of the Renaixença, with its Romantic, religious, patriotic, and epic tendencies. Verdaguer's Franciscan humanism, his enrichment of the Catalan language, and his evocation of Catalan history and landscape combine in a formula that has given him a unique place as the patriarch of modern Catalan literature.

THE MALLORCAN SCHOOL

While Verdaguer was writing near Barcelona, Maria Aguilo was laying the foundations for poetry and literature in Mallorca in the nineteenth century, influencing Valencian poetry as well. Teodor Llorenc and Vicent Querol were nineteenth century poets of the simple life. Josep Lluis Pons i Gallarça, another Mallorcan poet, led the way for Miquel Costa i Llobera (1854-1922), the most famous Mallorcan poet of the early twentieth century. Costa i Llobera, a priest and admirer of Horace, combined a sensitivity to the beauty and serenity of Mallorca with Christian fervor. His poetic intensity is refined, controlled, but deeply felt. Joan Alcover, Gabriel

Alomar, Llorenç Riber, Miquel dels Sants Oliver, Maria Antònia Salvà, Bartomeu Rosselló-Pòrcel, and J. M. Llompart are other Mallorcan poets who followed the example of Costa i Llobera.

MODERNISM AND THE TWENTIETH CENTURY

After the initial impact of the Renaixença and the reestablishment of Catalan as a literary and cultural language, the younger Catalan writers came under foreign influences such as French poetry, Surrealism, and modernism.

Juan Maragall (1860-1911) was a contemporary of Verdaguer but differed from him as much as the Mallorcan school did in its own way. Maragall was concerned with aesthetics and the act of creating poetry, and his personal wealth, happy marriage, and social status allowed him the luxury of composing on his own terms. He relied on the moment of inspiration for his lyric poetry, not on forms, styles, or foreign influences. More of an intellectual than Verdaguer, his themes are love, death and resurrection, and Catalonia.

Maragall's admiration for German and Greek literature led him away from the Romantic tendencies of the Jocs Florals. His inner fire and his belief in his own inspiration helped him to create his own style, highly personal, negligent in form, and new in approach. His "Canto espiritual" has been compared by numerous scholars to works of March and Llull. Maragall remains a pivotal figure in Catalan letters, because he moved Catalan poetry forward aesthetically and stylistically.

Maragall's influence brought about an explosion of Catalan poetry in the early and mid-twentieth century; Josep Carner, Jaume Bofill i Mates, and Josep Maria López-Picó were particularly indebted to Maragall. Joaquim Folguera (1894-1919), Joan Salvat-Papasseit (1894-1924), and the Mallorcan Bartomeu Rosselló-Pòrcel (1913-1938) were unable to fulfill their great potential; all three died young. Salvat-Papasseit's soul-wrenching intensity gives his verse a peculiarly modern flavor and makes it among the most powerful in Catalan literature of any period. Other outstanding poets who were contemporaries of Salvat-Papasseit are Agustí Esclasans, Clementina Arderiu, J. V. Foix, Marià Manent, Josep Maria de Sagarra, Tomàs Garcés, Ventura Gassol, Carles Riba, and Josep Sebastià Pons of Roussillon, a

Catalan in that now-French region. Several of these poets were associated with the movement known as *Noucentisme* (1900-ism), which rejected the late Romanticism of Verdaguer and the provincialism of nineteenth century Catalan culture.

Josep Carner (1884-1971) spent much of his life outside Catalonia, but his influence still places him at the apex of modern Catalan poets. Whereas Maragall sought the "living word" of inspiration, Carner, a lover of wordplay, was a master of form and controlled emotion. He was a "poet's poet" of great inner serenity. Carles Riba (1893-1959) ranks with Carner in importance. Riba, a professor of Greek, was a highly intellectual poet, yet his work is informed by a deep sensitivity to human concerns.

J. V. Foix (1893-1987) was the outstanding figure of twentieth century Catalan literature. Many of his works defy categorization in traditional genres. His poetry is an extraordinary fusion of native Catalan elements with influences assimilated from the European avant-garde. He was particularly influenced by Surrealism and maintained a lifelong interest in the visual arts; his close association with Joan Miró and other painters in the post-World War I period had an important impact on his work.

Foix was a major force in introducing the European avant-garde to Barcelona and Catalonia through his extensive journalistic writing. Many of his poems have been immortalized in paintings of Salvador Dalí, Miró, Joan Ponç, and Antoni Tàpies, who recognized in him a kindred spirit. Foix regards the poet as an "investigator," a "researcher," whose medium is words. He is an anguished twentieth century poet who combines the syntax and emotion of Ausiàs March with the vision of Giorgio de Chirico, René Magritte, Dalí, and Miró.

Salvador Espriu (1913-1985), author of *La pell de brau* (1960; *The Bull-Hide*, 1977) and *El llibre de Sinera* (1963; the book of Sinera), is perhaps the best-known modern Catalan poet—one of the few whose works are known outside Catalonia. Whereas Foix was a writer of "pure poetry," Espriu was concerned with political actualities. Foix's poems are sung in cathedrals by choirs, while Espriu's are sung by the modern "troubadours" of popular music. His eclectic use of literary and cultural influences and his satiric wit contribute to his unique appeal.

REVIVAL OF INTEREST

What is most significant about Catalan poetry is that it has been able to renew itself after a significant historical lacuna. In the 1980's, the Spanish government agreed to the demands of Catalan nationalists, supported by a majority of the Catalan-speaking populace, to make Catalan the official language of their region, and legislation since then such as the Catalan Language Act of 1997 has furthered those goals. Even though Spanish remains dominant, poets have continued to appear on the scene: Maria Àngels Anglada (1930-1999), Miquel Martí i Pol (born 1929), Marta Pessarrodona, and Francesc Parcerisas are only a few.

BIBLIOGRAPHY

Barkan, Stanley H., ed. *Four Postwar Catalan Poets.* 1978. Rev. ed. Translated by David H. Rosenthal. Merrick, N.Y.: Cross-Cultural Communications, 1994. Provides translations and critical commentary of twentieth century Catalan poets.

Carner, Josep. *Nabi.* Translated by J. L. Gili, edited by Jaume Coll. London: Anvil Press Poetry, 2001. Offers a translated version of Carner's Christian-themed poetry and an introduction by Arthur Terry.

Espriu, Salvador. *Selected Poems of Salvador Espriu.* New York: W. W. Norton, 1991. A bilingual collection that includes selections from all nine of Espriu's books of poetry. Also includes an introduction by the Catalan poet Francesc Vallverdu, which provides valuable insight into Espriu, the man and the artist.

Fauriel, C. C. *History of Provençal Poetry.* New York: Haskell House, 1966. Examines those factors which influenced Provençal poetry as well as the evolution of poetry forms peculiar to Provençal literature.

Foix, J. V. *When I Sleep Then I See Clearly.* Translated by David Rosenthal. New York: Persea Books, 1988. The selection spans the entire career of Catalonia's major avant-garde poet, J. V. Foix, who won Spain's 1985 National Prize for Literature.

Gaunt, Simon. *The Troubadors: An Introduction.* London: Cambridge University Press, 1999. Leading scholars in Britain, the United States, France, Italy, and Spain trace the development of the troubadour tradition (including music), engage with the main trends in troubadour scholarship, and examine the reception of troubadour poetry in manuscripts and in Northern French romance. A series of appendices offer an invaluable guide to more than fifty troubadours, to technical vocabulary, to research tools, and to surviving manuscripts.

Llull, Ramon. *Romancing God: Contemplating the Beloved*. Edited by Henry L. Carrigan. Brewster, Mass.: Paraclete Press, 1999. Contains *The Art of Contemplation* and *The Book of the Lover and the Beloved*. Editor Carrigan's commendable "mild modernizations" slightly alter the syntactic difficulties and archaisms of the originals while allowing them to retain both their otherness and their rhetorical power.

McNerny, Kathleen, and Cristina Enriques de Salamanca, eds. *Double Minorities of Spain: A Biobibliographic Guide to Women Writers of the Catalan, Galician, and Basque Countries*. New York: Modern Language Association of America, 1994. Alphabetically arranged listings provide brief biographies of a heretofore neglected group of authors, with evaluative descriptions of their work. Following each entry is a listing of books and other publications in which their writing has appeared, works that have been translated into Castilian or English, and critical studies.

Rosenthal, David H. *Postwar Catalan Poetry*. Lewisburg, Pa.: Bucknell University Press, 1991. Critically examines the trends in twentieth century Catalan poetry. Includes bibliography and an index.

Solà-Solé, Josep M., ed. *Modern Catalan Literature: Proceedings of the Fourth Catalan Symposium*. New York: Peter Lang, 1995. Presents the topics and discussions of the Fourth Catalan Symposium, held at the Catholic University of America in 1993. Topics range from general surveys of modern Catalan poetry to studies of specific poets, poems, novels, and modern folktales. Also discusses women writers and stylistic relationships between writers. Includes translations of two new collections by poets Olga Xirinacs and Miquel Martí i Pol.

Terry, Arthur. *Catalan Literature*. In *A Literary History of Spain*. New York: Barnes & Noble, 1972. One of the richest histories available in English, taking readers to the mid-twentieth century.

Triadú, Joan. *Anthology of Catalan Lyric Poetry*. Berkeley: University of California Press, 1953. Critically examines and provides translations of the works of Catalan's lyric poets.

_____. *Spanish, Catalan, and Galician Literary Authors of the Eighteenth and Nineteenth Centuries: An Annotated Guide to Bibliographies*. Metuchen, N.J.: Scarecrow Press, 1995. Provides a comprehensive index to published bibliographies that list a literary author's works and critical studies about the works. In addition to novelists, playwrights, poets, and short story writers, the guide also covers bibliographies for linguists, literary critics, and historians who lived in the eighteenth or nineteenth centuries and who wrote in Spanish, Catalan, or Galician.

Patricia J. Boehne

CHINESE POETRY

China has traditionally been a nation of poets. From ancient times through the first decade of the twentieth century, Chinese poetry held a position of importance unequaled by that of any other nation. By virtue of several important factors—linguistic, cultural, social, educational, and political—Chinese poetry, until the downfall of the monarchy in 1911, manifested certain characteristics that are unique.

ANCIENT CHINESE WRITING

The earliest known examples of Chinese script were inscribed on tortoise shells and animal bones around 1300 B.C.E., the time of the Shang Dynasty (c. 1600-1066 B.C.E.). These objects are referred to as "oracle bones" because they were employed by shamans, or priests, to predict future events. Later in the Shang, inscriptions were made on bronze vessels. When the Zhou (Chou) Dynasty (1066-221 B.C.E.) succeeded the Shang, its bronzes were also inscribed. A series of hunting songs carved on boulders, erroneously termed "stone drums," dates to around 400 B.C.E. In 219 B.C.E., by order of Shi Huangdi (Shih Huang Ti), the first emperor of the Qin (Ch'in) Dynasty (221-206 B.C.E.), the Chinese script underwent a standardization process. Two new types of script were devised: One, to be used for formal and official purposes, was called *xiao juan* (*hsiao chüan*); the other, intended for general use, was called *li shu* (clerk's style). Because it was found that the speediest and most efficient way of writing *li shu* was with brush and ink, such writing soon developed into an art in itself, the art of calligraphy. By the time of the Han Dynasty (206 B.C.E.-220 C.E.), calligraphy had achieved equality as an art with painting and poetry. Not only were calligraphy and painting seen as twin arts of the brush, but also they were intimately associated with poetry. This attitude is shown in the famous remark made by Su Tongpo (Su T'ung-p'o) about the great Wang Wei, who was outstanding as a calligrapher, a painter, and a poet: "In his poetry there is painting, and in his painting, poetry."

The distinctive visual properties of Chinese script that made its writing an art transcend its pictographic origins. Although Chinese writing began with pictographic word-signs, these word-signs were soon conventionalized into almost complete abstractions. Single characters were then combined to form not only compound but also complex characters, many simply with determinants of the broadest meaning and others with signs to indicate sound. The Chinese written language thereby expanded from around twenty-five hundred characters in early times to between forty and fifty thousand by the Qing (Ch'ing) Dynasty, which was founded in the seventeenth century.

Writing such characters demands skill in drawing, a sense of form and proportion, and a sensitivity to the qualities of line, dot, and hook. Although a number of single characters can be combined into one, the resulting character must occupy the same amount of space and have the same square appearance as that of any other character. Furthermore, calligraphers tended to view the strokes in their characters in terms of natural objects and forces. To them, a horizontal stroke was a mass of clouds; a hook, a bent bow; a dot, a falling rock; a turning stroke, a brass hook; a drawn-out line, an old dry vine; a free stroke, a runner on his mark; and so on. Painters considered calligraphy their training ground, and poets saw their art as a kind of word-painting. The three arts of calligraphy, painting, and poetry can be seen woven together in that school of composite art known as *wenrenhua* (*wen-jen-hua*), or "literary men's painting." Here, the scholar-artist would display his calligraphy in the brushstrokes he used to fashion trees, rocks, or bamboo shoots. Then he would balance his picture with a poem inspired by his painting, written in his best calligraphy, as an integral part of his composition. Later, his friends or other connoisseurs might write additional poems or laudatory inscriptions on his painting that would add to its value.

Although the visual was preeminent in the development of Chinese poetry, it must not be thought that the musical quality of the words, even in silent reading, was ignored or considered unimportant. The sounds of spoken Chinese in its various dialects have their phonetic systems of vowels and consonants and also their distinctive tonal systems, which depend on the movement of or the holding of the pitch of the voice.

At the same time, however, classical Chinese written characters are independent of any particular pronunciation or dialect. The origins of this literary language can be traced to a period sometime after the establishment of the Zhou Dynasty, when a new class of men began to replace the Shang priesthood as magical religion gave way to a philosophy of history. This new class was the scholar class; only such men could memorize the large number of characters that their language by then comprised. These scholars, later called the "literati," were responsible for the transmission of China's cultural heritage to future generations.

CLASSICAL CHINESE

By the fall of the Han Dynasty in 220 C.E., the literati had so monopolized the Chinese script that it had broken away from the vernacular language and gone its separate way. Soon, it was recognized that writing need not be restricted to utilitarian purposes—that it was capable of producing aesthetic pleasure. This view elevated the status of belles letters to a high position for the first time in Chinese history. In this way, *wenli* (*wen-li*), or *wenyan* (*wen-yan*), "literary Chinese," became the only form of the written language used everywhere for all serious purposes, quite divorced from the spoken language. Such written Chinese has no pronunciation of its own but is pronounced in as many different ways as there are dialects. All Chinese poetry considered as literature has been written in *wenli*, or classical Chinese, from its formulation until the advent of the Chinese literary renaissance in 1917, when it was almost entirely replaced by *bai hua* (*pai hua*), or the living language of the people, used for literary as well as practical purposes.

Regardless of the independence of *wenli* with respect to the sounds that are attached to it, Chinese poetry has its own peculiar sound structure, which includes metrical forms as well as rhyme and other auditory effects. In short, there is a "music" of Chinese poetry that has its own rules of versification relative to genre and purpose. Indeed, this sound structure of Chinese poetry is so peculiar to itself that it is impossible to render in translation.

CHINESE VERSIFICATION

Chinese versification is based on two principal auditory qualities that may be attached to the Chinese word-

signs. Every character is monosyllabic when sounded, and each monosyllable has a fixed pitch, called a "tone," which is semantic—that is, gives a clue to its meaning. Hence, generally speaking, the number of syllables in a poetic line is equivalent to the number of characters in that line. The number of characters and their monosyllables, however, is not invariably equal to the number of "words" in a given line, because there are some characters that never appear alone and make up "words" of two or more characters. The regularity or the variation of the number of characters (or syllables) and the regularity or the variation of their fixed tones are the basis of Chinese poetic meter and play the major role in Chinese versification, together with some incidence of rhyme.

During the Tang (T'ang) Dynasty (618-907), classical Chinese had eight tones, which could be reduced to four pairs. By the Yuan (Yüan) Dynasty (1279-1368), the eight tones had been reduced to four. These pitches were distinguished, ranging from one to four, as "level" (*ping*, or *p'ing*), "rising" (*shang*), "falling" (*qu*, or *ch'ü*), and "entering" (*ze*, or *tse*). These four tones, however, were arbitrarily reduced for poetic purposes to two, the first being regarded as level while all the rest were simply considered as deflected. For example, in the demanding form of the *lüshi* (*lü-shih*, regulated poem), the requirement was that a poem be made up of eight lines of equal length with each line comprising either five or seven characters. The poet had at his disposal various "tone patterns" from which he could choose, depending on whether he first chose five or seven characters. His first full line might call for the following tone pattern: deflected (but level permitted), deflected, level, level, deflected. Each of the rest of his lines would have its specific tone pattern. Such regulated verse also required a particular rhyme scheme. In addition to varieties of pitch, the poet had at his disposal contrasts in the length or quantity of syllables, because the tones differ in length and movement. All this sound variation gives the recitation of a Chinese poem a singsong quality.

MUSIC AND FOLK SONGS

From the beginning, Chinese poetry has been intimately connected with music. The folk poems collected in the earliest anthology, *Shi Jing* (or *Shi Ching*, songbook), were originally songs meant to be chanted or sung. Some were popular songs, others courtly songs or sacrificial and temple songs. The popular songs were intended to be sung to the accompaniment of music with group dancing. Early commentators on the *Shi Jing* were musicians as well as literary critics.

The history of Chinese poetry shows the marked influence of folk songs. The *Shi Jing* established a poetic tradition that was to be followed by serious poets until the twentieth century. Its typical four-line character poem became an esteemed and standard form. Its tone of refined emotional restraint, its sympathy with human nature, and its general lack of malice toward others became a poetic ideal followed by many later poets. A number of other standard Chinese poetic forms were derived from folk songs, such as the Han *yuefu* (*yüeh-fu*), the Tang *ci* (*tz'u*), and the Yuan *qu* (*ch'ü*). All these standard forms were derived from the songs of the people, but once they became the standard fare of the literati, the words and music were divorced from each other, and the poetry was written to be read rather than sung, with little or no regard for its musical potential. Yet the history of Chinese poetry also shows that once a form became too refined and overly artificial—too far removed from normal reality—poets would return to folk traditions for new inspiration.

THE POLITICS OF POETRY

Certain cultural factors peculiar to China, quite apart from the nature of its language and the relation of that language to the other arts, have also shaped Chinese poetry. Although philosophy and religion have played important roles (particularly Confucianism, but also Daoism and Buddhism), perhaps the major role has been played by government. From the time of the early Zhou Dynasty, the Chinese state took a decided interest in poetry. The government realized that the popular songs of the people could serve as an index to the ways in which the people felt about the government and their lives under it. Rulers or their emissaries would travel over the feudal states collecting popular songs and their musical scores. A department of music called the Yuefu (Yüeh-fu, or music bureau) was established for this purpose. Although it languished for a time, it was revived by Emperor Wudi in 125 B.C.E. Thus, folk poems were

written down and preserved, inspiring sophisticated poets to imitate them in their own work.

Because the difficulty of the Chinese written script had led to the formation of a scholar class from whose ranks the government was obliged to select its officials, teachers such as the great Confucius (551-479 B.C.E.) were engaged primarily in educating and training students as prospective government servants. Confucius believed that the study of poetry had an important role in the development of moral character, a prerequisite of just and efficient government. For this reason, he selected from the government collections of the feudal states the poems that make up the *Shi Jing*, which he edited and used as a textbook in his seminars. After his death and the official sanction of the Confucian doctrine during the Han Dynasty, the *Shi Jing* became one of the Five Official Classics, which, together with the Four Books, made up the Nine Official Classics considered indispensable to the education of the scholar-official.

During the Han Dynasty, the government decided that the best way to discover "men of talent" suitable for public service was on the basis of merit, and a merit system based on competitive examinations was established. The government began to employ the Confucian-trained graduates of the National University. This practice indissolubly linked an education in the Confucian classics with an official career, and by the time of the Tang Dynasty, a nationwide system of public competitive examinations to recruit officials on the basis of merit had been established. Theoretically, these competitive examinations were open to all Chinese citizens except those who followed certain occupations classified as "mean" (in the sense of base or common). The subsequent major Chinese dynasties relied on these public examinations to obtain the best possible government officials until as late as 1905, when the system was abandoned as obsolete. Thus, for many centuries, the civil-service examination system provided the ruling class with an influx of new talent that had undergone intensive intellectual and artistic training, including skill in the writing of poetry.

The system required a candidate to acquire three successive degrees—taken, respectively, at the county, province, and national capital levels—before being eligible for official appointment. The first degree, that of *shengyuan* (*sheng-yüan*, government student), and the second degree, that of *xiucai* (*hsiu-ts-ai*, budding talent), were simply preparatory for the third and highest, that of *jinshi* (*chin-shih*, metropolitan graduate), the acquisition of which entitled the graduate to be appointed to some official post in the government. The *jinshi* degree required a thorough knowledge of the Confucian classics, skill in calligraphy, and the ability to write poems as well as essays. The standards were high, and only a few of the many candidates were passed by the examiners.

The prevalence of this system of competitive examinations had a profound effect not only on Chinese society, education, and politics but also on literature. Apart from its role in perpetuating poetic conventions from generation to generation, the civil-service experience furnished themes that are common to Chinese poetry as a whole. Indeed the vast majority of Chinese poets were government officials.

GRAMMAR AND SYNTAX

The grammar and syntax of Chinese have also played their part in the shaping of China's poetry. Some writers have declared that the Chinese language has no grammar and that its words may serve as any part of speech. Neither of these allegations is correct. Although Chinese has no inflection of number, case, person, tense, or gender—and more words in Chinese than in English have multiple functions—Chinese verbs do have aspects, and some words are normally nouns, whereas others are normally verbs. Although the basic pattern of the Chinese sentence is subject followed by predicate, the Chinese "subject" is the topic of the sentence, not necessarily the agent that performs the action of the verb. In addition, the subject or the verb of the Chinese sentence is often omitted, and coordinate constructions frequently lack conjunctions.

The Chinese language is, therefore, more compact and concise than English. In economy of expression, it resembles a telegram in English, and *wenli*, or classical Chinese, is even more abbreviated than *bai hua*, or everyday speech. If Chinese is more sparing in its words than English, however, it is also less precise. If this feature is a disadvantage in prose concerned with the particular, it is a distinct advantage in Chinese poetry, which is concerned essentially with the universal. Chinese poetry can therefore exploit its compactness and economy of expression in conjunction with its grammatical and syntactic fluidity to enhance its power to mean far more than it says.

ZHOU DYNASTY (1066-221 B.C.E.)

The earliest great monument of Chinese poetry is the *Shi Jing*, an anthology of folk poems selected and edited by Confucius around 500 B.C.E. The poems themselves come from the earlier period of the Zhou Dynasty, from between 1000 and 700 B.C.E. Their collection and preservation by Confucius, China's greatest teacher, shows the importance he attached to the study of poetry, which he believed was essential to the proper moral development of man, and since his time, the *Shi Jing* has been regarded as one of the great classics of Chinese literature.

The *Shi Jing* not only possesses great aesthetic value but also is an important historical document which strongly influenced all subsequent Chinese poetry. Revealing the minds and hearts of the Chinese people during the ancient Zhou times, it established a poetic tradition that was followed by later Chinese poets down to modern times. Throughout the history and development of Chinese poetry, the *Shi Jing* has served as a model of poetic eloquence, a storehouse of words, images, themes, and poetic forms (its typical four-character line became a standard form), and a continual source of inspiration to later poets.

By the beginning of the fifth century B.C.E., the power of the feudal state of Zhou had begun to wane, and new national states emerged whose rulers appropriated the title *wang* (king). Of these new states, two emerged as the most powerful—Ch'u in the south and Qin in the northwest. Ch'u had become a prosperous and beautiful state with a high degree of refined culture. The leisurely cultivation resulting from its economic prosperity eventually produced a series of popular religious songs that were collected under the title *Jiu Ge* (*Chiu Ko*, nine songs). These elegant songs dating from the fifth century B.C.E. became the model for an irregular and flexible type of elegy that was to inspire sophisticated poets to create a new poetic genre, the *Chu ci* (*Ch'u tz'u*, Chu elegy).

By the next century, an identifiable person emerged from the anonymity of collective authorship to become

China's first known poet. This was Qu Yuan (Ch'ü Yüan, c. 343-290 B.C.E.), author of the distinctive masterpiece *Li Sao* (encountering sorrow). A son of the nobility, he had served his king as second in rank to the prime minister. Having for some reason lost his political office, however, Qu Yuan was exiled to wander throughout the land. Deciding to devote his life to poetry, he eventually composed the *Li Sao*, a poem that significantly influenced the course of Chinese poetry. Qu Yuan's work conferred distinction on the new genre of the *Chu ci* and inspired a school of poetry responsible for the establishment of a Chinese elegiac tradition that continued to exist until modern times. This tradition eventually led directly to the creation of another new genre, the Han *fu*.

QIN AND HAN DYNASTIES (221 B.C.E.-220 C.E.)

A struggle for power went on among the feudal states during what is called the Warring States Period (475-221 B.C.E.). This struggle was concluded when the state of Qin succeeded in crushing all opponents to form the first unified empire in Chinese history. Prince Zheng of Qin, who ascended the throne in 221 B.C.E. as Emperor Shi Huang Di, was a man of authoritarian mold: During his reign, all literature of which he disapproved was burned, and the Chinese script was standardized.

The earliest examples of Qin poems appear in the *Shi Jing*, but they do not differ significantly from the rest of the poetry in the collection. Other specimens of Qin poetry appear in the hunting songs carved on the so-called stone drums. The most important Qin scholar and poet was Li Si (Li Ssu, 280-208 B.C.E.), who was the scholar the emperor assigned to standardize the Chinese script and who initated a new poetic genre—the *song ci* (*sung tz'u*), or panegyric. When the emperor toured the country, large stone tablets were erected on which were carved panegyrics to commemorate his visits to various places. These imperial panegyrics were composed and inscribed by Li Si.

The Qin Dynasty did not last long. When Shi Huang Di died in 210 B.C.E., rebellions broke out, resulting in internal warfare. This anarchy was resolved with the establishment of the Han Dynasty in 207 B.C.E.

During the Han Dynasty, two new poetic genres made their appearance—the *fu* and the *yuefu*. Generally,

the word *fu* means "to display," and specifically, it means "to chant or to narrate." As a poem, the *fu* originally was one to be chanted rather than sung—that is, performed without musical accompaniment. Under the Han, the *fu* became a poem of social criticism, but later this motive was replaced by the desire to treat its subject in an elegant or refined manner. This later motive eventually resulted in cutting the poem off from the real world, and even some of the best writers of such *fu* considered them frivolous exercises, worthless as literature. Nevertheless, the *fu* dominated the Han period.

At its best, the *fu* is characterized by flowing rhythm, pleasant rhyme, and splendid imagery. An offshoot of the *Chu ci*, the form came to prominence when Emperor Wu Di (reigned 140-87 B.C.E.) became fascinated by the work of the great Han *fu* writer, Sima Xiangru (Ssu-ma Hsiang-ju, c. 180-117 B.C.E.). Author of such *fu* as "Zi xu fu" ("Master Nil"), "Shang lin fu" ("Supreme Park"), "Meiren fu" ("The Beautiful Lady"), and "Chang men fu" ("Long Doors"), Sima Xiangru was rewarded for his skill by appointments to important government posts.

The Han *yuefu* emerged from the popular folk songs collected by the government's Music Bureau. This sophisticated type came to maturity about 200 C.E., by which time it had been discovered that the form was particularly suited to narration. Perhaps the most famous writer of the narrative type was a woman, Cai Yan (Ts'ai Yen, fl. 206 C.E.), who composed two "Songs of Distress," which became famous. Taken captive by the Huns and forced to become the consort of a Hun chieftain for twelve years before she was ransomed, she tells of her life during her captivity and reflects on her experiences. Another Han narrative *yuefu* (author unknown), titled "Kong jue dongnan fei" ("Southwest the Peacock Flies"), is generally considered a masterpiece and is the longest medieval poem of China at 353 lines. Later, poems of this type based on the folk style and rendered in five- or seven-character lines became known as *gushi* (ancient verse).

SIX DYNASTIES AND SUI DYNASTY (220-618 C.E.)

With the end of the Han Dynasty, China again lapsed into disunity. Three independent kingdoms struggled with one another for power. Wei had retained much of the power it had usurped from Han, but soon it was challenged by Shu and Wu. This period of political contention is known as the Three Kingdoms period (220-265). The powerful house of Jin then arose and eliminated both Shu and Wu to found the Jin (Chin) Dynasty (265-419). By 420, China had divided itself into the South and North Dynasties; this division lasted until 589. Finally, the Sui Dynasty took over and ruled China until 618.

Despite the political confusion and social unrest resulting from the power struggles of the Six Dynasties period (220-588 C.E.), it was an age of rapid development in poetry, in both form and content. Beginning in the third century, a profound change took place in the intellectual climate of China, the positivism of Han Confucianism being replaced by mystical Confucianism supported by the *yin-yang* cosmology. With this change, a new attitude toward poetry as an art emerged. The *Shi Jing* was interpreted in terms of mystical philosophy, the *Lun yu* (*Lun yü*, late sixth or early fifth century B.C.E.; *Analects*) of Confucius was interpreted on Daoist principles, and the *Yi Jing* (or *I Ching*; *Book of Changes*, 1986), the classic of spiritual or psychological transformation, became the dominating Confucian text. In short, a fusion was effected between Confucianism and Daoism, and Indian Buddhism was integrated into Chinese intellectual life. Buddhists and Daoists came to the fore, and a number of poets were predominantly one or the other.

During the time of the last Han emperor, the five- or seven-character poetic line had replaced the old four-character pattern of the *Shi Jing*. Although the irregular verse form of the popular folk song had been rejected, the poets had not entirely lost contact with the spontaneity of these songs. A master of this new type, called *shi* (later *gushi*; *ku-shih*), was Cao Zhi (Ts'ao Chih, 192-232), perhaps the most important member of the group called the Seven Masters of Jian An (Chien An). Another significant group, the Seven Worthies of the Bamboo Grove, was composed of poets who had abandoned the city for the country to escape the political confusion of the time. Ruan Ji (Juan Chi, 210-263) was the most outstanding member of this group; his eighty-two *yonghuai shi* (*yung-huai shih*, poems expressing feelings) express the new attitude that poetry should be an honest disclosure of the poet's feelings and emotions. Poets termed this attitude *tou*, and *tou qing qing* (*t'ou*

ch'ing ch'ing) means "to call up and expose one's inmost feelings."

In accord with the mysticism of the time, this attitude was linked to *tong* (*t'ung*), the ability to see into the nature of things—literally, "to go through things." At the same time, a number of poets rejected the orthodox Confucian idea that the main purpose of poetry was didactic and moralistic, a view that emphasized content over form. The poet and critic Lu Chi (261-303), for example, in his *wen fu* (literary *fu*), adamantly declared that form is as important as content and insisted that poetry has an intrinsic aesthetic value.

In addition to the five- or seven-character *shi*, another genre was developed during the Six Dynasties period: a new kind of *fu*, a shorter version that omitted dialogue and tried to capture the lyric quality of the *Chu ci*. It also employed the rhetoric of *pian wen* (*p'ien wen*, balanced prose). Lu Chi as well as Zuo Si (Tso Ssu, fl. 265-305) were both great masters of this new kind of *fu*. Later came the literary giant Tao Qian (T'ao Ch'ien, 365-427), also known as Tao Yuanming (T'ao Yüan-ming), a many-sided man. The scion of a great official family, he joined the civil service, but loving his freedom and independence more than official rewards, he resigned at the age of thirty-three and never returned to public life. His poem on retirement, "Homeward Bound," has been much admired, but he is most famous for his *fu* "The Scholar of Five Willows" and "Peach Blossom Spring." He is the greatest of the recluse poets of the Six Dynasties period.

Although China was unified once again under the Sui Dynasty (581-618), little need be said about that dynasty's poetry. No significant developments took place and no great poets emerged. The two best poets were Yang Guang (Yan Kuang, 580-618), who succeeded his father on the throne in 605, and the Lady Hou, one of Yang Guang's concubines.

T'ANG AND FIVE DYNASTIES (618-960)

The T'ang Dynasty, founded by Li Yuan (Li Yüan, 565-635) after he crushed the Sui regime, was the golden age of Chinese poetry. Li Yuan reigned as Gao Zu (Kao Tsu), then voluntarily stepped down in 626 in favor of his second son, Li Shimin (Li Shih-min, 597-649), who reigned as Tai Zong (T'ai Tsung) and was a great patron of literature. Under these rulers and their successors, a new system of land tenure was put into effect, and the competitive trade that developed on a wide scale produced a new social class, the urban bourgeoisie. Changes also took place in the realms of philosophy, religion, the arts, and literature. Orthodox Confucianism was modified by the inclusion of mystical elements, new religions such as Nestorian Christianity came on the scene, and two new forms of *shi* made their appearance and became very popular: *jueju* (*chüeh-chü*, literally "cut short") and *lüshi* (*lü-shih*, literally "ruled verse"). Until the Rebellion of An Lushan in 755, during the reign of the Emperor Xuan Zong (Hsüan Tsung), also known as Ming Huang (reigned 712-756), the nation enjoyed unprecedented peace, prosperity, and cultural development. The Tang Dynasty produced China's two greatest poets, Li Bo (Li Po, also known as Li Bai, 701-762) and Du Fu (Tu Fu, 712-770), as well as a host of other major poets: Wang Wei (701-761), Han Yu (Han Yü, 768-824), Bo Juyi (Po Chü-yi, 772-846), Yuan Zhen (Yüan Chen, 779-831), Du Mu (Tu Mu, 803-852), and Li Shangyin (Li Shang-yin, 813-858). Although poetry flourished at the court of the early Tang, it was mostly of the occasional type, inspired by festivals and sumptuous banquets. With the appearance of the *jueju* and the *lüshi* forms, poetry was taken more seriously. The *jueju* was a poem of four lines of equal length, with either five or seven characters to the line, a set tone pattern, and a rhyme scheme. The *lüshi* was a poem of eight lines of equal length, again with either five or seven characters to the line, contrasting intonations in each pair of lines, and a rhyme scheme. Parallel construction was required in the four middle lines of the eight-line poem, rhyme was required in the even-numbered lines, and a set tonal sequence was required in all eight lines. Two masters of court poetry, Shen Juanqi (Shen Chüan-ch'i, c. 650-713) and Song Zhiwen (Sung Chih-wen, c. 660-712), are credited with crystallizing the *lüshi* form.

The Emperor Xuan Zong (reigned 712-756) was a lover of beauty and the arts, and he succeeded in bringing the best poetic talent of China to his court. Two of the poets he employed turned out to be the two greatest poets China has produced: Li Bo and Du Fu.

Li Bo came from Changming in Sichuan Province. As a boy, he developed two consuming interests—poetry and swordsmanship. At the age of ten, he was writing poetry and studying fencing. He apparently never entertained any political ambitions and did not study the Confucian classics in preparation for taking the examinations. Rather, he was a dabbler in Daoism and alchemy. He left home at the age of nineteen to seek adventure and wandered from place to place. Occasionally he sought employment as a bodyguard, and it is said that he thrust his sword through a number of opponents; otherwise, he indulged his passion for writing poetry. He eventually arrived at Changan, where his poetic talent was brought to the attention of the emperor, who employed him as a court poet for a brief period (742-744).

Emperor Xuan Zong found that Li Bo was as fond of drinking wine as he was of writing poetry, and the two activities frequently went hand in hand. Independent in spirit and incapable of sycophancy, Li Bo soon lost his position and resumed his wandering. According to legend, he drowned while boating on a lake; having grown intoxicated from drinking wine, he tumbled out of his boat into the water in an effort to embrace the moon's reflection. True or false, this legend accurately reflects the spirit of Li Bo, a lover of nature and beauty who continually sought to plunge into the unknown.

A poetic genius in the romantic mold, Li Bo was intent on being himself, yet he sought to transcend the self as well. A visionary poet, he never lost his humanity. If he ascended the mountain to touch the stars, he descended to enjoy a bowl of rice and the welcoming pillow of a farmer friend. He relished listening to a Buddhist monk playing his lute as much as he did fencing or drinking wine. Poetry was always foremost in his mind.

China's other great poet, Du Fu, was a man and a poet of a character quite different from that of Li Bo. A native of Xiangyang County in what is today Honan Province, he was descended from a family of scholars and writers. He studied the Confucian classics with the object of qualifying himself for an official career, and at the age of twenty-five, he journeyed from his home to the capital of Ch'ang to take the *jinshi* examinations. Failing to receive his degree, however, he decided to take up the career of poet and journeyed about the country riding on a donkey. At the age of thirty-eight, he submitted three *fu* compositions to Emperor Xuan Zong.

Impressed, the monarch rewarded him with an official appointment. Soon, however, the An Lushan Rebellion drove Xuan Zong from power and Du Fu into exile. The shock of the rebellion had a pronounced effect on him and on his subsequent poetry.

Following the accession of Emperor Su Zong (Su Tsung), Du Fu returned to the capital to accept the dangerous office of imperial censor. His critical memorials to the throne, however, displeased the emperor, who, in effect, banished him by appointing him governor of a small town in Shensi. Consequently, Du Fu resigned and retired to the country. Called out of retirement to serve on the Board of Works, Du Fu resigned again after six years and retired to the country, this time permanently. Dedicating his life to poetry, he grew old before his time and died in poverty at the age of fifty-eight.

Li Bo was a romantic, "a heavenly immortal in temporary exile on earth." His poetry tends to move away from the real toward the unreal; he sought not to reform the society of his time but to escape from it. Du Fu was a classicist, an earth-rooted man, a mortal with a social consciousness, a serious man with a heart full of sorrow and passionate indignation. His poetry tends to concentrate on the real and to avoid the unreal. He faced up to the hard facts of life: the suffering of the masses, social injustice, corruption in government, the extravagances of the rich, the horrors of war, the ravages of time, and the desires and fears of living people in the everyday world. He was a critical realist with a tragic sense of life. Yet despite the sorrow he carried in his heart, he had his light side and never lost his sense of humor.

Du Fu's poetry can be divided into an early, a middle, and a late period. His early period (c. 750-755), that prior to the Rebellion, is characterized by such poems as "The Eight Immortals of the Wine Cup," a clever piece of lighthearted satire, and the glittering satirical ballads "The Ballad of the Beauties" and "The Ballad of the War Chariots." The middle period (755-765), that of the rebellion and its aftermath, is characterized by such poems as "Lament of the River Bank" and "Lamenting of the Imperial Heir," both of which feature nostalgia, sadness, and cynicism. The late period (766-770) is characterized by poems such as "My Thatched Roof Whirled Away by an Autumn Gale," a vivid picture of the hardships of poverty and old age. Du Fu called Li Bo the

"unrivaled poet," yet Du Fu surpasses his friend in intellectual power and emotional range. No Chinese poet has displayed more mastery of the regulated form.

Of the other major T'ang poets, Bo Juyi stands above the rest. A very successful government official, he rose to high rank under Emperor Xuan Zong. He was a leader in the development of the long narrative poem called the *xin yuefu* (*hsin yüeh-fu*), or "new lyric ballad." Despite their length, his two poems "Song of Everlasting Sorrow" and "Song of the Lute" were in their day extremely popular with both commoner and aristocrat. Wang Wei, poet, painter, calligrapher, and musician, followed a political career. His devotion to the Chan (Japanese Zen) school of Buddhism is evident in both his painting and his poetry. He was noted for his mastery of the *jueju* form. Han Yu was a highly successful government official and a noted essayist and writer of short romances as well as a poet. He was the leader of a reform movement that sought to free literature from its artificialities. His poems "Mountain Stones" and "Poem on the Stone Drums" were particularly admired.

Yuan Zhen is as famous for his thirty-year friendship with the greater Bo Juyi as for his own poetry. A government official, his career was not very successful, but he is known for the poems and letters that passed between him and Bo Juyi. Du Mu (Tu Mu) had a moderately successful official career. He is regarded as a transitional figure between the middle and late Tang periods and was a sharp critic of both Li Bo and Du Fu. He is noted for the descriptive talent displayed in his "Traveling in the Mountains."

Li Shangyin also pursued a moderately successful political career while achieving a considerable literary reputation. In his poetry, he makes much use of myth, symbolism, and classical allusions, and his work is regarded by some as obscure. He is noted especially for his love poems and funeral elegies.

After the T'ang restoration, which followed the suppression of the An Lushan Rebellion in 757, the imperial administration experienced increasing difficulties in maintaining control over the empire. Finally, in 907, a local military commander murdered the T'ang emperor and proclaimed himself the founder of a new dynasty, the Liang. This dynasty, however, was short-lived and was followed by four others before China was reunited with the establishment of the Song (Sung) Dynasty in 960. This period between 907 and 960, known as the Five Dynasties period, did not produce distinguished poetry.

SONG DYNASTY (960-1279)

Under Emperor Tai Zu (T'ai Tsu), China became an empire again, with its capital at Kaifeng (K'ai-feng, then called Pien-ching, or Bianjing), just south of the Yellow River in East Central China. In 1126, the Jin Empire invaded the North China Plain, captured Kaifeng, and held the emperor prisoner. The Chinese court fled southward to establish a new capital at Hang (present Hangchow) on the lower Yanzi Plain, not far from the East China Sea. Hence, the Song is divisible into the Northern Song (960-1127) and the Southern Song (1127-1279).

Although the Song was a period of turmoil, warfare, and chaos, in many ways it was also an age of great culture and refinement. The dynasty is noted for its landscape painters as well as for its writers. Indeed, in the arts and literature, the Song nearly equaled the accomplishments of the T'ang. The chief poets of the Song Dynasty were Ouyang Xiu (Ou-yang Hsiu, 1007-1072), Wang Anshi (Wang An-shih, 1021-1086), Su Tongpo (Su T'ung-p'o, pen name of Su Shi, 1036-1101), Li Qingzhao (Li Ch'ing-chao, 1084-c. 1151), and Lu You (Lu Yu, 1125-1210).

Ouyang Xiu was both a major political figure—he was president of the Board of War—and the acknowledged leader of the literary world of his time. A great prose master and a major poet, he was a reformer and innovator. His position of influence and his own exemplary prose style were largely responsible for the success of the *guwen* (*ku-wen*) prose movement, which had originated with Han Yu several hundred years earlier. As for *shi* (*shih*), or regulated poetry, he was a master of the *jueju*, or quatrain. This can be seen in his "The Pavilion of Abounding Joy" and "Returning Home in the Rain," which are direct, simple, and fluent. Although he closely followed tradition in these works, his individual voice is apparent. His *ci*, or poems based on musical scores, are short but produce a distinctive musical effect. His most outstanding *fu* is "Qiu shenfu" ("Sounds of Autumn"). Ouyang Xiu was a painstaking writer and a tireless reviser of his work.

Wang Anshi was a powerful political figure and a controversial social reformer. As prime minister under Emperor Shen Zong, who ascended the throne in 1068, Wang instituted a reform program that caused great controversy and resulted in his resignation. He became the governor of what is now Nanking and received many subsequent honors, but he never regained his former political power. He was an outstanding prose writer as well as a superb poet and was particularly famous for his direct and clear-cut memorials to the throne and for his funeral inscriptions. He invented the "five-legged essay," the precursor of the famous "eight-legged essay" later required in the public examinations. In poetry, his *jueju* were much admired. Poems such as "Night Duty" and "Early Summer" present concrete images in swift sequence with vivid realism.

The most original poet of the Song was Su Tongpo, an important public official and an outstanding calligrapher and painter as well as a major poet. He opposed Wang Anshi's reforms and was therefore banished. Su returned to the capital in 1085, after Wang's fall. From 1089 to 1091, Su was the governor of Hang. He returned to the capital but was soon banished again, first to Huizhou in Guangdong Province and then to Hainan Island. As a poet, he was a keen student of such previous literary greats as Tao Qian, Du Fu, and Han Yu. He was also a great admirer of his contemporary, Ouyang Xiu. He deliberately strove to break out of the limitations of Tang poetry and succeeded more spectacularly than his contemporary Wang Anshi. With a view toward perpetuating his technique, he drew around him some of the outstanding poets of his time. His "school" succeeded in dominating *shi* poetry for the remainder of the Song period.

Su Tongpo liked to write regulated poetry of the kind that allowed him maximum freedom—long, freewheeling *fu* or short, seven-character *jueju*. His twin *fu* on the "Red Cliff" are memorable descriptions and meditations on history. His quatrain "Mid-Autumn Moon" shows his disciplined economy of expression. He broke away entirely from the conventions of the *ci* and wrote a meditative kind of poetry without much regard for its musical possibilities. Whatever kind of poems he wrote, he was always original. His poetry is noted for its range of vision, its inclusion of vernacular language, and its organic form.

Li Qingzhao and Lu You are perhaps the two most interesting poets of this group because of their unusual personalities and the peculiar circumstances of their lives. Li Qingzhao has been called the greatest woman poet of China. She was a native of Shandong Province, and her father was the renowned scholar and writer Li Gefei (Li Kei-fei). Having married a scholar and antiquarian, Zhao Mingcheng (Chao Ming-ch'eng), Li Qingzhao apparently had found an ideal relationship. When the Jin invasion forced the Chinese court to flee southward, she and her husband did likewise, but her husband died on the way, and she was obliged to continue her flight alone, a sad widow. This tragic loss profoundly affected Li Qingzhao for the rest of her life. After a few years in Hang, she removed herself to Zhejiang, where she spent the rest of her days. Li Qingzhao wrote both prose and verse, but the vast majority of her writings have been lost. She enjoyed a high reputation in her time, particularly for her *ci*. Her poetry displays a sensibility that is distinctively feminine. Many of her *ci* express her feelings regarding her widowhood and increasing age. Her images are precisely selected and her poems show a capacity for deep feeling.

Lu You, a native of Zhejiang Province, has been regarded as the greatest poet of the Southern Song. At the age of twelve, he wrote prose and verse sufficiently distinguished to attract the attention of the highest officials in the government, including the emperor himself. Lu You began a career in public life, but he soon encountered difficulties. His independent spirit and pronounced talent excited the envy of many, who spread malicious gossip about him; furthermore, he found great difficulty in conforming to the expectations of others. An ardent patriot who felt deeply dishonored by China's loss of its former territory, he consequently took a strong interest in the military. He served on the staff of Fan Chenda when that renowned poet was the military commander of Sichuan Province. He wrote a large body of nature poetry, but despite its high quality, the keys to his work are his patriotism and his respect for the art of war. He saw a special dignity in the profession of soldier and held that warfare was indispensable to national defense. He yearned to be a man of action but never could find the proper context in which to act. The most prolific poet in the history of Chinese literature, Lu You lived to the advanced age of eighty-five.

Although the Song Dynasty is noted for the production of some great *shi* and *fu*, the dominant poetic genre of the period was the *ci*. The *ci* was the most popular form of the age, despite the fact that it was rated below the *shi* and *fu* in terms of literary merit.

YUAN DYNASTY (1279-1368)

The ruling class of the Southern Song had believed in negotiation, appeasement, and opportunistic alliances rather than an aggressive foreign policy and a strong national defense. Militarily weak, its treasury exhausted by the payment of exorbitant tribute, the government sought an alliance with the Mongols against their common enemy, the Jin Tartars. This policy backfired when Kublai Khan, the grandson of Genghis Khan, suddenly grown powerful, blatantly annexed China to the Mongol Empire. The Chinese people awakened from their long dream to find themselves under the heel of a foreign conqueror.

To the imperialistic Mongols, China was simply a colony for exploitation. Ignoring Chinese tradition and customs, they did whatever they thought necessary to maintain control over the country. In place of the traditional Chinese class hierarchy of scholars, farmers, merchants, and soldiers, the Mongols instituted a hierarchy based on race: Mongols, useful foreigners, Northern Chinese, and Southern Chinese. At first, the Chinese as a whole were excluded from participating in the government, but, soon realizing the enormity of its mission, the Mongol regime decided that such a policy might have dire results. Accordingly, the regime began depending heavily on the Chinese official class. Many Chinese scholars, however, refused to cooperate with the Mongols and retreated to the country to become recluses and wanderers.

Thus, energies that might have been exerted in governmental administration were channeled into the arts, particularly into painting and musical drama. The Yuan Dynasty was a great age of *wenrenhua*, the art that combined painting, calligraphy, and poetry into a single unit and produced the Four Great Masters of the Yuan Dynasty: Huang Gongwang (Huang Kung-wang), Ni Zan (Ni Tsan), Wang Men, and Wu Zhen (Wu Chen). It was also the golden age of the Chinese opera, the Mongols being particularly fond of this theatrical form, and it produced four great masters of the Northern school: Guan Hanqing (Kuan Han-ch'ing, c. 1220-1307), Wang Shifu (Wang Shih-fu, c. 1250-1337), Ji Junxiang (Chi Chün-hsiang, fl. 1260-1280), and Ma Zhiyuan (Ma Chih-yüan, c. 1265-1325). Although the Northern style of drama predominated during the Yuan period, a Southern style had developed under the leadership of Gao Ming (Kao Ming, fl. 1345-1375).

In the realm of nondramatic poetry, the most important Yuan form was a new kind of lyric that developed from the *qu* (*ch'ü*), or dramatic verse, and was known as the *sanqu* (*san-ch'ü*), or "unattached song." Poets who were not dramatists began to write these "unattached songs" based on the style of dramatic verse but not intended to be part of any play. This new type of lyric was looser in its requirements than *shi* with respect to rhythm, diction, and treatment of subject matter. The most prominent author of *sanqu* after the year 1300 was Zhang Kejiu (Chang K'o-chiu, fl. 1275-1325). A songwriter who occupied various civil-service posts under the Mongols, he wrote mainly about his disappointments in life and his efforts to console himself.

MING DYNASTY (1368-1644)

The last years of the Yuan Dynasty were plagued by rebellions, the work of military adventurers and quasi-religious leaders; behind the scenes were the wealthy gentry, ambitious for political power. A Buddhist monk named Zhu Yuanzhang (Chu Yüan-chang), crafty and ruthless, was able to best all opponents and oust the Mongols at the same time. He became the founder of the Ming Dynasty and reigned as Emperor Hong Wu (Hung Wu) from 1368 to 1399. An absolute monarch, he tightened the hold of the government on the everyday life of the nation.

Free of Mongol domination, the Chinese people welcomed native rule and reacted strongly against foreign practices. The emperor himself led this pro-Chinese movement by reviving ancient Chinese customs and ceremonies and emphasizing agricultural pursuits. He revised the civil-service examinations and introduced the very rigid format of the "eight-legged essay," which was

required of all degree candidates. As a consequence, candidates were driven away from poetry, which previously had been their main preoccupation, to concentrate on this rigid essay format. Indeed, the spirit of originality and innovation was suppressed altogether in favor of maintaining tradition and observing established conventions.

Although for a time the Ming experienced considerable trouble in keeping the Mongols at bay, the third emperor of the Ming Dynasty, Yong Luo (Yung Lo, reigned 1402-1424), succeeded in frustrating all their efforts, reestablishing the empire in most of the northwest. With peace restored, interest in art and literature increased. The technique of block printing was perfected, publishing flourished, and scholars were put to work selecting the best literature of the past and present for preservation and circulation. Illustrated encyclopedias, dictionaries, collections of stories, plays, and poems; treatises and monographs on the arts and sciences; and critical studies of art and literature were prepared and printed. It was an age of *tongshu* (*t'ung-shu*), or "collectanea." There was great activity in the writing and production of drama and in the writing of vernacular fiction. Much nondramatic poetry was written in the *shi* and *ci* forms, but it was the Southern *sanqu* that became a universal fad. Although superb craftsmen, the nondramatic poets were generally imitative and bound by tradition and conventions.

QING (OR MANCHU) DYNASTY (1644-1911)

In 1644, China was invaded by the Manchus, a nomadic Mongolian people. Unlike the Mongols, the Manchus were interested in China for its own sake, not merely as a colony to be exploited. They admired Chinese culture and gradually became completely assimilated, losing their own cultural distinctiveness. The second Qing emperor, Kang Xi (Ka'ang Hsi), was not only a strong military leader and an able administrator but also a scholar and a lover of the arts and literature. From an early age, he had loved the Chinese language, Chinese literature, and Confucian philosophy. He encouraged Chinese scholarship to such a degree that scholarship became the dominating force of his time. Because of him, a great dictionary of more than forty thousand Chinese characters was compiled.

Massive compendia such as the *Tushu Zhicheng* and the *Siku Quanshu* came into being. The former classified all the significant writings of the empire; the latter reedited all the major writings of the empire for inclusion and was so voluminous that it was never printed, although seven copies were made by hand. Interest in classical literature flourished, and vigorous creative efforts were made in drama and fiction. In poetry, all previous literary types were revived: the Tang *shi*, the Song *ci*, the Yuan dramatic and lyric *Chu ci*, and the Han *fu*. A similar revival took place in classical prose, with interest directed at the *guwen* of the Tang and Song Dynasties. Vernacular prose produced perhaps the greatest Chinese novel, Cao Xueqin's (Ts'ao Hsueh-ch'in's) *Honglou-meng* (1792; *Dream of the Red Chamber*, 1958).

Most of the Qing poets were fine technicians, but few were able to free themselves from the old masters such as Li Bo, Du Fu, Bo Juyi, and Su Tongpo. Nevertheless, there were some poets whose independence of spirit penetrated their imitations so that they spoke in their own voice. The most outstanding of them were Qian Qianyi (Ch'ien Ch'ien-yi, 1582-1664), Wu Weiye (Wu Wei-yeh, 1609-1671), Wang Shizhen (Wang Shih-chen, 1634-1711), and Yuan Mei (Yüan Mei, 1715-1797). Important but lesser poets were Chen Zulong (Ch'en Tsu-lung, 1608-1647), Chen Weisong (Ch'en Wei-sung, 1626-1682), and Nara Singde, a Manchu (1655-1685), all of whom were noted for their *ci* during the early Qing. Among the noteworthy writers of *ci* during the late Qing were playwright Jiang Shiquan (Chiang Shih-ch'üan, 1725-1785), Wang Pengyun (Wang P'eng-yün, 1848-1904), and Huang Xing (Huang Hsing, 1874-1916).

By the end of the nineteenth century, Western ideas and the aggressive dynamics of Western power and technology had brought fear, dismay, turmoil, violence, and shame to the people of China. Despite pleas from its wise men for reforms that would enable China to survive as a nation and a civilization, the Dragon Throne and the power around it blindly opposed all change as capitulation to Western ideas and methods. Such intransigence brought about the revolt of the people in 1911, when, led by the revolutionary firebrand Sun Yat-sen, they overthrew the old autocratic system and established the Chinese Republic the following year.

POST-QING PERIOD (1911-1949)

In 1905, the civil-service examination system was abolished, and modern education along Western lines was introduced into China. Large numbers of students went abroad to study—to Japan, to North America, and to Europe. Depending on where they studied, they absorbed the influences of various foreign authors. They returned to their homeland with all sorts of Western ideas. In 1917, Hu Shi (Hu Shih), a philosopher trained in the United States, and Chen Duxiu (Ch'en Tu-hsiu) launched a radical literary movement advocating that literature be written exclusively in *bai hua*, the vernacular, and no longer in *wenli*, or classical Chinese. Furthermore, old genres, diction, and themes were to be abandoned, and a new value was to be placed on those novels, plays, and folk poems of the past that had been written in the everyday language of the people.

With the acceptance of this doctrine and the historical circumstances surrounding Chinese poets from 1917 to 1927, Chinese literature fell into in turmoil. In 1923, a group of young writers gathered around Xu Zhimo (Hsü Chih-mo, 1895-1931) to form the Crescent Society. The aesthetic theoretician of this group was Wen Yiduo (Wen I-to, 1899-1946), who, under the influence of the French writer Théophile Gautier, championed the use of measured prosodic units to achieve a musical effect in the vernacular similar to that of the best classical poetry. Another group, interested in expressing the relationship of man to the universe, is represented by such poets as Feng Zhi (Feng Chih, born 1905) and Bian Zhilin (Pien Chih-lin, born 1910?) advocating the use of metaphor to express metaphysical ideas. Under the influence of French Symbolists such as Paul Verlaine and Stéphane Mallarmé, a group led by Li Jinfa (born 1900?) and Dai Wangshu (Tai Wang-shu, 1905-1950?) attempted to suggest through symbols that only man's impressions of the world have substantial reality. In this period of ferment and experimentation, the theme common to all was freedom from the old classical restraints.

From 1927 to 1932, revolutionary ideas were in the air, and social protest became the watchword behind the slogan "From literary revolution to revolutionary literature." Many radical writers were imprisoned and executed as a result of their overt protests. Around 1932, revolutionary writing began to be replaced by what was called the New Realism; the sufferings of the masses were realistically described without recommendations for revolutionary action. The poetry of Zang Kejia (Tsang K'o chia, born 1910?), Ai Qing (Ai Ch'ing, the pen name of Chiang Hai-ch'eng, or Jiang Haicheng, born 1910?), and Ren Jun (Jen Chün, born 1912?) is typical of this period.

From 1937 to 1947, China was at war. In 1942, the Communist leader and poet Mao Zedong (Mao Tsetung, 1893-1976) issued his famous dictum from Yenan calling for "Social Realism" in literature. By 1947, most writers had purged themselves entirely of classical ornament as well as of the conventions of Western literature, and the new vernacular medium had assumed its own Chinese shape. With the establishment of the People's Republic of China in 1949, however, Chinese literature became shackled in another manner: by communist ideology. It assumed the stereotyped role of supporting the new communist society in ways approved by the party leaders.

In looking back over the period from 1917 to 1949, at least one Chinese poet stands out above all the rest: Wen Yiduo (Wen I-to), a poet who believed in art free of politics, an orientation for which he was attacked by some. His volume *Sishui* (the dead water), published in 1928, has been admired as one of the finest volumes of poetry produced anywhere in the 1920's. Wen Yiduo may be the greatest Chinese poet of the twentieth century.

THE MAOIST ERA (1949-1976)

Though his regime was harshly repressive of poetic creativity, Mao himself fancied his own poetic abilities and took a general interest in the state of Chinese poetry. The delicacy, precision, and suggestiveness of traditional Chinese poetry made an uneasy fit with the sloganeering and propaganda of the Maoist belief system, but Mao nonetheless produced many fervid poems that inevitably received much comment from Chinese literary organs. In Maoist ideology, the cultural sphere was an important vehicle for disseminating the ideology of the state. Yet the modernist poets of the Guomindang era were not entirely silenced under Mao. Guo Moruo (1892-1978), who wrote in free verse, bridged several generations and was a living link between past and present. Although he served as a functionary in the commu-

nist government (he was head of the Chinese academy of science) Guo's poetic integrity was never compromised; he continued to range widely over aesthetic, historical, and philosophical concerns. Even the harsh repression of the Cultural Revolution of the 1960's failed to extinguish the spark of poetic imagination totally. The underground poetry of this era erupted, ironically, as an enthusiastic echo of government-sponsored frenzy; the initiative and spirit that was generated, however, was felt to be threatening by the leadership despite its apparent ideological conformity. Poets such as Huang Xiang and Quo Lusheng suffered terribly for their independence during this era. Though poetry did not entirely grind to a halt, creativity was trammeled.

THE POST-MAO ERA (AFTER 1976)

The literary generation immediately following the Cultural Revolution produced what is known as "scar literature" (*shanghen wenxue*), whose main purpose was to provide a testimony to the ravages of the immediate past. Scar literature emerged particularly after the death of Mao and after the April 5, 1976, protests occasioned by the death of Mao's colleague Zhou Enlai. Although as far as politically possible it excoriated the crimes of the government, scar literature was still overwhelmingly public in orientation, and it continued, if perhaps only in the mode of trauma, the idea that literature is a rendition of external reality.

Around 1978, several poets decided to go a step further than scar literature. *Meng long* ("misty" or "obscure") poetry that sprang up in this era went in tandem with the "Democracy Wall" movement of 1978-1979, yet paradoxically turned away from public expression into a more indirect and introspective mode, concentrating on the self in natural surroundings. Misty poetry in this way seemed to resemble traditional landscape poetry, but it often contained hidden symbols of ideological dissent from the communist government. Misty poetry produced the major names that dominated Chinese poetry into the twenty-first century: Bei Dao, Gu Cheng, Shu Ting, Yang Lian, Mang Ke. Bei Dao (born 1949) was the first of the misty poets to come to public light with his poem "The Answer" (1979); still the most famous living Chinese poet at the end of the century, Bei and his work made new demands of the reader, not remaining within the customary conventions of Chinese lyric, although its influence by Western models did not at all equate to mere imitation. Gu Cheng is contemporary Chinese poetry's *poète maudit*; his psychological turmoil eventually led him to kill both himself and his wife in exile in New Zealand in 1993. Simpler and more confrontational in his language than Bei Dao, Gu wrote poems whose final meaning is nonetheless elusive. Shu Ting (born 1952) was the only major woman poet in the misty group; her signature poem "To the Oak Tree" reveals more rhythmical and musical tendencies than do the poems of her contemporaries. Yang Lian's (born 1955) poetry is often rhapsodic and dense with natural images, yet replete with an underlying cynicism; he has tended to write about Tibet and the western portions of China itself. In later years, he became more interested in the roots of Chinese identity. Mang Ke (born 1950), with Bei Dao, was founding coeditor of *Jin Tian* (today), the leading magazine of misty poetry. Mang Ke was one of the first of his generation to publish serious poetry, and his images, most famously that of the sunflower, are vivid and bridge the gap between objectivity and subjectivity, nature and human desire.

The government began to react against misty poetry in the "anti-spiritual pollution" campaign of 1983, and some of the poets went underground or into exile. The misty poets nevertheless were still the most prominent group at the beginning of the twenty-first century, drawing increasing international attention. Their stature sometimes led to resentment on the part of less well known poets, many of whom began to adopt a more discursive and colloquial approach, one focusing less on the individual ego than on the intermittently intolerable conditions of human existence itself. Others, though, went in the opposite direction and introduced spiritual, sometimes explicitly Christian themes into their verse.

Chinese poetry in the 1990's was impacted by a specific event and a long-term process: the Tiananmen Square massacre of June, 1989, and the onslaught of globalization that led Shanghai to be changed virtually overnight into a gleaming postmodern megalopolis. Although the communists adamantly retained control, Chinese writers were much more in touch with their counterparts abroad, especially in the Chinese diaspora. The government allowed freedom of expression in strictly

literary matters, no longer aspiring to intervene in the cultural sphere or codifying a prescribed aesthetic, as in the Mao era. At the turn of the twenty-first century, the main tension in Chinese poetry was between "vulgar," or *minjian* poets, who used the banalities of everyday life to express a pulse of authenticity, and more intellectual poets who sought to plug into advanced Western philosophical debates. The underground journal *Shi Can Kao*, edited by Zhong Dao, tended to promote the *minjian* poets, especially Yi Sha, who in "My Ancestors" took a completely anti-idealistic and antinostalgic view of his own relation to tradition. The *minjian* poets espoused an aesthetic that would have been out of fashion in the West, had they been Western, and thus provided a counterpoise to the inevitable cross-fertilization between Chinese and Western aesthetics. This cross-fertilization was expedited by the number of Chinese writers who, whether for political or for economic reasons, emigrated to Western countries.

Ouyang Yu, for instance, not only moved to Australia but also (in volumes such as *Songs of the Last Chinese Poet*, 1997) saw himself as much as an Australian poet as a Chinese one and founded a bilingual journal *Yuan Xiang* (otherland). The translator Mabel Lee, also based in Australia, translated both Chinese poetry and fiction into English, making it more internationally visible. Other overseas poets, such as Bei Ling (born 1959), continued to be active in calling attention to human rights concerns within China. Bei Ling, with fellow exile Meng Lang (born 1961), in 1993 founded the literary periodical *Qing Xiang* (tendency), the most spirited and imaginatively comprehensive Chinese literary journal of its era. Bei Ling, who first left China in the late 1980 s, returned to China and was arrested there in the summer of 2000 for his literary activities, being liberated only after international pressure. Bei Ling's poetry, praised by Western luminaries such as Joseph Brodsky, Seamus Heaney, and Susan Sontag, is measured in its diction and stance yet is written with considerable emotion—one example of the many available new syntheses in the age-old tradition of Chinese poetry.

BIBLIOGRAPHY

Barnstone, Tony. *Out of the Howling Storm: The New Chinese Poetry*. Hanover, N.H.: University Press of

New England, 1993. History and criticism; includes a bibliography and an index.

Birrell, Anne, trans. *Chinese Love Poetry: New Songs from a Jade Terrace, a Medieval Anthology.* 2d ed. London: Penguin, 1995. Collects poems from the Chinese medieval period; Birrell adds an introduction, notes, and a map.

_____. *Popular Songs and Ballads of Han China.* Honolulu: University of Hawaii Press, 1993. Birrell's anthology of poems from the period from 221 B.C.E. to 220 C.E. offers illustrations, a substantial section of bibliographical references, and an index.

Burnett, David, and John Cayley, trans. *Mirror and Pool: Translations from the Chinese.* London: Wellsweep Press, 1991. Cayley adds notes and an afterword; illustrations by Bronwyn Borrow.

Cai, Zong-qi. *The Matrix of Lyric Transformation: Poetic Modes and Self-Presentation in Early Chinese Pentasyllabic Poetry.* Ann Arbor: Center for Chinese Studies, University of Michigan, 1996. A scholarly study of poetry from the Qin and Han Dynasties, including Cao Zhi (192-232), Ruan Ji (210-263), and *yuefu*. Bibliography, index.

Cao, Zuoya. *The Asian Thought and Culture: The Internal and the External, a Comparison of the Artistic Use of Natural Imagery in English Romantic and Chinese Classic Poetry.* New York: Peter Lang, 1998. An examination of the different ways that the English Romantic poets and the Classic Chinese poets connected the inner and outer worlds, as well as their different poetics—correcting previous wrong notions about Chinese nature poetry. Close readings of more than thirty poems. Notes, bibliography.

Chang, Kang-i Sun, and Huan Saussy, eds. *Women Writers of Traditional China: An Anthology of Poetry and Criticism.* Stanford, Calif.: Stanford University Press, 1999. Women have long played a role in Chinese literature; this massive (nearly nine-hundred-page) work is important to literary, Chinese, and women's studies. Bibliography, index, maps.

Crevel, Maghiel van. *Language Shattered: Contemporary Chinese Poetry and Duoduo.* Leiden, Netherlands: Research School CNWS, 1996. Chinese experimental poetry of the twentieth century and the work of Duoduo are the subjects of this study. Chinese texts appear in appendices. Bibliographical references, index.

Finkel, Donald, and Carolyn Kizer, trans. *A Splintered Mirror: Chinese Poetry from the Democracy Movement.* San Francisco: North Point Press, 1991. Two well-known poets translate democracy-movement poems from the late twentieth century for this anthology.

Goh, Robbie B. H., ed. *Memories and Desires: A Poetic History of Singapore.* Translations by Chitra Sankaran, Sharifah Maznah Syed Omar, and Robin Loon. Singapore: UniPress, 1998. A rare anthology of English translations of southern Chinese, Malay, and Tamil poetry.

Hamill, Sam, trans. *Crossing the Yellow River: Three Hundred Poems from the Chinese.* Rochester, N.Y.: BOA Editions, 2000. Hamill's introduction and a preface by poet W. S. Merwin make this a valuable compendium.

Harris, Peter, ed. *Zen Poems.* New York: Alfred A. Knopf, 1999. Includes translations from Korean and Japanese, along with Chinese.

Hightower, James Robert, and Florence Chia-ying Yeh. *Studies in Chinese Poetry.* Cambridge, Mass.: Harvard University Press, 1998. This monograph of more than six hundred pages covers the history of Chinese poetry and poetics into the twentieth century. Bibliography, index.

Hockx, Michel. *A Snowy Morning: Eight Chinese Poets on the Road to Modernity.* Leiden, Netherlands: Research School CNWS, 1994. Twentieth century Chinese poetry, in English and Chinese; bibliographical references, index.

Holden, Kren. *Book of Changes: Poems.* Berkeley, Calif.: North Atlantic Books, 1998. Translations from the *Yi Jing* (*I Ching*).

Holzman, Donald. *Immortals, Festivals, and Poetry in Medieval China: Studies in Social and Intellectual History.* Brookfield, Vt.: Ashgate, 1998. Valuable social and historical context for Chinese medieval poetry. Bibliography, index.

_____. *Landscape Appreciation in Ancient and Early Medieval China: The Birth of Landscape Poetry.* Hsin Chu, Taiwan: Program for Research of Intellectual-

Cultural History, College of Humanities and Social Sciences, National Tsing Hua University, 1996. Scholarly study of an important element of early Chinese poetry, and Chinese attitudes toward literature.

Hsu, Kai-Yu, ed. *Twentieth Century Chinese Poetry: An Anthology.* Ithaca, N.Y.: Cornell University Press, 1970. A massive compendium of more than five hundred pages.

Huang, Yunte. *Shi: A Radical Reading of Chinese Poetry.* New York: Roof Books, 1997. Slim volume of translations into English.

Kwong, Charles Yim-tze. *Tao Qian and the Chinese Poetic Tradition: The Quest for Cultural Identity.* Ann Arbor, Mich.: Center for Chinese Studies, University of Michigan, 1994. Examines the poetry of the Six Dynasties literary giant who left government office to devote his life to poetry. Bibliography, index.

Landau, Julie, trans. *Beyond Spring: Tz'u Poems of the Sung Dynasty.* New York: Columbia University Press, 1994. Poetry from the tenth and eleventh centuries. Bibliography, index.

Lin, Julia C., trans. *Women of the Red Plain: An Anthology of Contemporary Chinese Women's Poetry.* New York: Penguin, 1992. A valuable collection of twentieth century Chinese poems by women, in English translation. Index.

Lynn, Richard John, and Roger B. Bailey. *Guide to Chinese Poetry and Drama.* 2d ed. New York: Macmillan, 1984. A good introduction for students.

McCandless, Bonnie, ed. *Chinese Poetry Through the Words of the People.* New York: Ballantine, 1991. Translations into English; bibliographical references.

Min, Pyong-su, trans. *Korean Poetry in Classical Chinese: Encounters Between Man and Nature.* Seoul, Korea: Somyong, 1999. Bilingual in both English and Korean, a collection of a tradition in "Chinese" poetry that has not received much study in Western schools. Illustrated.

Murck, Alfreda. *Poetry and Painting in Song China: The Subtle Art of Dissent.* Cambridge, Mass.: Harvard University Asia Center for the Harvard-Yenching Institute, 2000. Based on the author's thesis for Princeton University, an analysis of the interplay of painting and literature in the tenth through twelfth centuries in China. Bibliography, index, illustrations, maps.

Ping, Wang, ed. *New Generation: Poems from China Today.* Brooklyn, N.Y.: Hanging Loose Press, 1999. Late twentieth century poems from modern China, translated into English.

Owen, Stephen. *The End of the Chinese "Middle Ages": Essays in Mid-Tang Literary Culture.* Stanford, Calif.: Stanford University Press, 1996. An examination of Chinese literary and intellectual life during the Tang Dynasty. Bibliographical references, index.

Seaton, Jerome P., and Dennis Maloney, eds. *A Drifting Boat: An Anthology of Chinese Zen Poetry.* Translations by Tony Barnstone et al. Fredonia, N.Y.: White Pine Press, 1994. Poems from an important Buddhist tradition in China. Bibliographical references.

Seth, Vikram. *Three Chinese Poets: Translations of Poems by Wan Wei, Li Bai, and Du Fu.* Boston: Faber, 1992. Seth, a poet in his own right, offers translations of three of the most important poets in eighth century China.

Soong, J. S., ed. and trans. *Pearls in the Shell: Best Loved Short Verses from the Chinese Language.* Fremont, Calif.: Asian Humanities Press, 1999. A collection of short lyrics for popular audiences. Index, illustrations.

Sun, Cecile Chu-chin. *Pearl from the Dragon's Mouth: Evocation of Scene and Feeling in Chinese Poetry.* Ann Arbor: Center for Chinese Studies, University of Michigan, 1995. A scholarly examination of nature and human emotions in Chinese poetry. Bibliography, index, Chinese appendix.

Sze, Arthur, trans. *The Silk Dragon: Translations from the Chinese.* Port Townsend, Wash.: Copper Canyon Press, 2001. Translations into English of Chinese poems from the fourth through the twentieth centuries.

Wawrytko, Sandra A., and Catherine Y. Woo. *Crystal: Spectrums of Chinese Culture Through Poetry.* New York: Peter Lang, 1995. A look at Chinese traditions, values, and themes (Dao, family-centeredness, nature, social protest) as expressed by poetry and poetic technique, up through the end of the twentieth century. Includes a chapter on Chinese culture, language, and poetry. Tables.

Wu, Fusheng. *The Poetics of Decadence: Chinese Poetry of the Southern Dynasties and Late Tang Periods*. Albany: State University of New York Press, 1998. Includes examination of Hsiao Kang, Wen T'ing-yün, Li Ho, Li Shang-yin, and other poets of the fourth to tenth centuries. Bibliographical references, index.

Yeh, Michelle. *Modern Chinese Poetry: Theory and Practice Since 1917*. New Haven, Conn.: Yale University Press, 1991. Scholarly study of the philosophy, poetics, and history of twentieth century Chinese poetry. Bibliography, index.

Yeh, Michelle, and N. G. D. Malmqvist, eds. *Frontier Taiwan: An Anthology of Modern Chinese Poetry*. New York: Columbia University Press, 2001. A substantial (nearly five-hundred-page) anthology of Taiwanese poetry. Bibliography and a map.

Yip, Wai-lim. *Diffusion of Distances: Dialogues Between Chinese and Western Poetics*. Berkeley: University of California Press, 1993. Chinese-language versification is examined in comparison with English poetics. Bibliographical references, index.

_____, ed. and trans. *Anthology of Modern Chinese Poetry*. New Haven, Conn.: Yale University Press, 1992. Twentieth century Chinese poems in English. Bibliography, index.

_____, trans. *Lyrics from Shelters: Modern Chinese Poetry, 1930-1950*. New York: Garland, 1992. Yip's anthology collects poems from the period leading up to the Maoist era. Introduction, bibliographical references.

Yu, Pauline, ed. *Voices of the Song Lyric in China*. Berkeley: University of California Press, 1994. Examines *ci* (*tz'u*) poetry from the Tang period. Bibliography, index.

Zhao, Henry Yiheng, Yanbing Chen, and John Rosenwald, eds. *Fissures: Chinese Writing Today*. Brookline, Mass.: Zephyr Press, 2000. Collects contemporary works, both short stories and poems, in English translation.

Zhong, Xu Yuan, trans. *Song of the Immortals: An Anthology of Classical Chinese Poetry*. New York: Penguin, 1994. A bilingual collection. Bibliography.

Richard P. Benton,
updated by Nicholas Birns

COMMONWEALTH POETRY

As the British Empire spread to all corners of the world, so did the English language and literature. The Empire faded after World War II, but what had become the international tongue and medium for creative writing survived and even prospered. English and its literature had long been enriched by speech and writing from Africa, the West Indies, Canada, India, Australia, and New Zealand. The dismantling of the Commonwealth neither subordinated nor silenced the distinctive voices that had arisen and that continue to arise. Traditionally, this body of fiction, drama, and poetry has been referred to as "Commonwealth literature" to distinguish it from the mother literature and from its elder brother, American writing. It is often still called that for want of a better name, but as the old British Commonwealth recedes into history, so does a once-significant but now largely meaningless political term. These days, names such as "post-colonial literature," "world literature written in English," or "international literature in English" are more common. Some critics envision a time when all literature in English, including that of England and the United States, will blend into a single body, a time when no literary works will receive preference because of their national origins and all literature will be judged entirely on merit.

The circumstances in which poetry grew out of the one-time Commonwealth affected all aspects of the poetry's development. Such effects were felt in the poetry both of the "settler" countries—Australia, Canada, New Zealand, and South Africa—and that of the colonized areas—great parts of Africa, India, and the West Indies. The distinction between "settler" and "colonized" is simple: The settlers came to stay, taking over the land from those they considered primitives—the Aboriginals in Australia, the Indians in Canada, the Maoris in New Zealand, and the Blacks in South Africa—and these peoples were variously ignored, enslaved, or exterminated. During the last two decades, the descendants of the dispossessed natives have added their poetic voices to those of the settlers, who had through the years created their own exclusionary literature. The colonizers, on the other hand, went forth from England to rule and to exploit, not to settle; of course some did settle, but once the Empire dissolved their descendants left, unlike

those in the settler countries. During the heyday of colonialism, the British set up schools for select groups of the natives they colonized; although those they educated in such places as Kenya, Nigeria, or India were intended to help rule their fellows, some became writers instead, thus giving Commonwealth poetry a third voice.

The writers in all three voices had available the centuries-old British literary tradition from which to draw forms, standards, and inspiration. Always, though, this fully developed text—a part of the colonial baggage—set up a creative tension that both benefited and hindered the poets.

AUSTRALIA, SOUTH AFRICA, CANADA, NEW ZEALAND: SETTLER POETS AND THEIR DESCENDANTS

How were the settlers to express in poetry the peculiarities of a new land and the life there? Could English poetry alone serve as a model? The emu had replaced the skylark; the flamboyant blossoms of the frangipani had dimmed the daffodil and primrose. Colonial outposts like Cape Town or Sydney bore little resemblance to London. Makeshift towns or isolated homesteads on the bleak veld of South Africa or in the vast outback of Australia contrasted starkly with the villages, meadows, copses, and moors of England. As the settlers communicated less with their former home, even their language changed: New words came into usage to describe unfamiliar things, accepted grammar fell by the wayside, and indigenous expressions crept in. Neither could the heterogeneous and structured English society survive intact among those in the isolated pockets of the Empire; no matter how hard the settlers tried to preserve their traditions, they faced lives in altered societies where rules and conduct adjusted to circumstance.

Yet the poetic impulse loomed strong among the early settlers. Perhaps the writing of poetry served as a comfort, as a way to overcome loneliness and isolation, a way to grasp the radical changes the settlers experienced. For example, even though Australia's convict pioneers were not literate for the most part, they were the colony's first poets. Soon after their arrival in 1788, they altered familiar English and Irish ballads to express the despair and misery that marked their lives. Like the literate free settlers who followed them to Australia and like those who went to Canada, South Africa, and New Zealand, they drew from the established text, imitating it and adding a new dimension. In 1819, an Australian judge named Barron Field (1786-1846) published two poems in a booklet titled "First Fruits of Australian Poetry," in which he claimed to be the colony's first poet: "I first adventure; follow me who list/ And be Australia's second harmonist." Traditional in form, these two poems—"Kangaroo" and "Botany Bay Flowers"—are typical of much early settler poetry. While Field finds the unfamiliar flora and fauna intriguing, he neither captures it wholly in his imitation of English verse nor refrains from recording his amusement over such oddities.

On the other hand, an anonymous Canadian settler expresses greater appreciation for his new land in "The Lairds of Esquesing," which appeared in 1826. This poem celebrates "Canada's wild woody shore" and "The Oak and the Hemlock and Pine" as the means of a better life for those who "are still coming o'er;/ In hopes of a good situation." Yet pride and delight in the potential exploitation of natural resources, not in their beauty, lies at the center of the poem. These examples—like the early poetry from New Zealand and South Africa—express not a national identity but rather a colonial mentality. Such was the case with the abundant verse that continued to be written well into the twentieth century. Some was brazenly nationalistic in its celebration of the heroic pioneers, those hardy individuals who conquered the land; although the pioneers have long been admired for destroying the forests or eroding the veld and killing the natives, later generations have questioned whether these acts deserve epic status. Some records of pioneer exploits, usually too mundane for true heroic stature, have found posterity as folk verse, such as the work of Australia's Banjo Paterson (1864-1941). Yet much of the poetry was far removed in spirit from the place where it originated, a pale imitation of distant literary fashions. For example, while there was no dearth of localized nature poetry, too often the poets saw the New World, the antipodes, or Africa through a Romantic sensibility they inherited from earlier English nature poetry. A true voice had not yet emerged, and for the most part this poetry has been forgotten, deservedly so.

The established text continued both to bless and to debilitate, for that which came from England was considered the real literature and that written in the colonies a shadow of the original. Those who had never seen a daffodil or a skylark were strictly schooled in a poetry that celebrated such phenomena and were led to believe that the literature of their own country was second-rate. After all, it was not until the 1950's that the national literatures entered into the school curriculum of the settler countries, which after World War II were at last breaking their ties with England. Further, as the political and economic influence of the United States spread during the postwar period, so did its literature, which had long ago rebelled against the British tradition. The maturing of poetry in these countries, then, has come about during the twentieth century and in particular since 1945.

One exception is Roy Campbell (1901-1957), South Africa's major English-language poet. Born in Durban, South Africa, of British descent and schooled in English literature, Campbell broke away from his heritage. Revolted by South African racial attitudes, he became one of the country's first literary exiles and spent most of his life abroad, mainly in France, Spain, and Portugal. At times he satirized South African settler society, as in the biting wit of a poem like "The Wayzgoose," whose opening stanza contains the lines: "Where having torn the land with shot and shell/ Our sturdy pioneers as farmers dwell,/ And twixt the hours of strenuous sleep, relax/ To shear the fleeces or to fleece the blacks." Campbell experienced a divided relationship with his native land, calling it "hated and adored" in his poem "Rounding the Cape." This dichotomy continues to haunt South African writers and consequently dominates much of the country's literature. Campbell, a major lyric poet and one of the first Commonwealth writers to attain an overseas reputation, also wrote about his homeland with fervor and captured its essence in poems like "The Zebras" and "Zulu Girl."

Another poet of international standing is the Australian writer Judith Wright (1915-2000), who discovered her homeland as a metaphorical entity from which she could draw meaning and through extending the metaphor express that meaning to others. For Wright, nature serves as a bridge to universal understanding, and the landscape she explores to attain this knowledge is purely Australian;

she approaches nature with a sensibility untainted by the inherited text of English literature. Her first book of poems, *The Moving Image*, appeared in 1946. One of her major themes is the relationship between humankind and nature, which led her to become a public figure fighting to protect the environment: "a landscape that the town creeps over;/ a landscape safe with bitumen and banks," she laments in one of her poems, "Country Town." Some critics have observed that Wright's later poetry suffered from her political involvement with environmental issues. However this work might be judged, Wright helped to show the generation of poets who followed how they could be Australian without being provincial, how they could express an Australian sensibility without cringing, and how they could examine the landscape honestly. Wright is also the first poet of Anglo-Saxon origin to treat the Australian Aboriginal in an understanding way. One of the best of these poems is "Bora Ring," in which she mourns the loss of the ancient rites of those who inhabited the country for forty thousand years before the white man came: "The song is gone; the dance/ is secret with the dancers in the earth,/ the ritual useless, and the tribal story/ lost in an alien tale."

A. D. Hope (1907-2000), the third poet from a settler country who gained an international reputation, was Australian as well. Yet he made no effort to explore the metaphysical dimension of his native land as a basis for poetry; instead he followed the dictates of eighteenth century neoclassicism. Damning free verse, modernism, and lyricism, Hope wrote in a highly structured, witty, cosmopolitan way. For him the inherited text was not to be discarded but to be utilized and improved upon. He rarely mentioned Australia, for he felt more at home in Greece than he did in a place where, as he wrote in his poem "Australia," "second-hand Europeans pullulate/ Timidly on the edge of alien shores."

The Australian poet Les Murray (born 1938) gained recognition around the world, receiving numerous international awards, and regularly publishing overseas. In 2000, a collection of his poems called *Learning Human: Selected Poems* appeared in New York. His poetry, noted for its verbal intensity and lyrical qualities, is undergirded by conservative political and religious views. A dichotomy marks his work. On one hand, it celebrates the strength and character of ordinary people and assumes

an anti-intellectual pose. At the same time, though, it is extremely erudite in its references and allusions.

Canada and New Zealand have strong poetic traditions, and both have many poets widely admired in their own countries, but who have not yet achieved the stature of Campbell, Wright, Hope, or Murray. Contemporary Canadian poets have moved far from the anonymous nineteenth century versifier who exulted in the pioneers' despoilment of the land. One of Canada's best-known poets, Al Purdy (born 1918), for example, sees the necessity of reinventing a poetic tradition divorced from the colonial past, a tradition that takes into account Canada's geographical vastness, a primary theme in his own work. While Margaret Atwood (born 1939) has established a worldwide reputation as Canada's leading fiction writer, her considerable achievement as a poet is little recognized outside of the country.

New Zealand, too, has produced a wide array of poets, the best-known being James K. Baxter (1926-1972). An old-fashioned poet by some standards, Baxter gained his popularity and lasting fame through a rare ability to meld language and location, for his was truly a national voice that spoke apart from the established British text. The far more sophisticated work of another New Zealander, Allen Curnow (born 1911), is also highly regarded, for both its rich language and its handling of the metaphysical aspects of the remote country; for instance, in "House and Land," he speaks of the "great gloom" that "Stands in a land of settlers/ With never a soul at home." A New Zealand poet who has received attention overseas is Bill Manhire (born 1946). His poetry is simple and direct yet sophisticated and dense in its suggestiveness. It takes varied forms, covers a wide variety of subjects, and draws its material both from his native country and from places abroad.

AUSTRALIA, SOUTH AFRICA, CANADA, NEW ZEALAND: INDIGENOUS POETS

Silent, or silenced, for the two hundred or so years since the white man invaded their lands, the indigenous people of the settler countries have added their voices to Commonwealth poetry. They are the victims of a secondary colonialism, for they have long been subjected and in the past often murdered by the settlers who saw them as one more pest on the landscape. Also secondary to the indigenes is the English language and literature, which was forced onto them for survival on the fringes of the white world. Beset by a borrowed written text and an oral literature that has eroded during two centuries of assimilation, the indigenous writers face peculiar problems as they set out to create a tradition that is not a third-hand version of the British text. Should they write in the conqueror's language at all? If not, what language should they use, considering that their own languages have been corrupted and sometimes lost? Should they follow standard English usage or the creolized language that many indigenes speak as a result of poor education and segregation? How can they incorporate the remnants of their oral traditions? How can they reach the largest audience?

The last question often seems the most important, for much of the poetry protests the second-class citizenship to which the natives have been relegated. At first, the main audience for such writing was white liberals, so English became the mandatory language. In the 1970's, though, the poetry began to play a more direct role in the lives of those it talked about, as the land-rights campaigns and the consciousness movement gained momentum, inspired in part by the Civil Rights movement in the United States. Because English stood as the common language among the indigenes, most of the writing was of necessity done in the borrowed language.

One of the first such voices to be heard was that of Kath Walker (1920-1993), an Australian Aboriginal later known by her tribal name, Oodgeroo Noonuccal. In 1965, she published the volume of poetry *We Are Going*, and asked in one of the poems, "Aboriginal Charter of Rights," "Must we native Old Australians/ In our own land rank as aliens?" Widely admired by black Australians as well as by their oppressed fellows in other settler countries, Oodgeroo's poetry helped to awaken these long-silent people. White readers also discovered her work, which made them realize that something new was afoot. The poems in *We Are Going* now seem tame and have in recent years been called too conciliatory by some activist Aboriginals, who have taken a harsher stance toward the white world in their poetry. Later Aboriginal poets such as Lionel Fogarty (born 1958), Archie Weller (born 1957), and Kevin Gilbert (1933-1993) take a stronger approach to the Aboriginal cause. In their work and that of emerging poets, the protest

rings loud and the anger erupts. Often, though, a comic strain runs through the poems and makes them even more immediate. As well, these poets tend to mix Aboriginal words and slang terms into standard English, which is an effective technique.

The South African poet and novelist Dennis Brutus (born 1924) is another early and widely acclaimed writer of protest poetry. In particular, his poems from prison, *Letters to Martha* (1968), describe vividly the abuse he and other political prisoners suffered. In "This Sun on this Rubble," he writes: "Under jackboots our bones and spirits crunch/ forced into sweat-tear-sodden slush/ — now glow-lipped by this sudden touch." Other black South African poets include Oswald Mbuyiseni Mtshali (born 1940), who published *Sounds of a Cowhide Drum* in 1971, and Mongane Wally Serote (born 1944), who in "Ofay-Watcher Looks Back" observes that "jails are becoming necessary homes for people." Although it is too soon to make judgments or to name major poets, the post-apartheid era in South Africa has unleashed a vast amount of poetry by those formerly oppressed by the political system. For one thing, publishing opportunities and financial support have become more available. This work addresses the triumph over apartheid as well as its lingering effects, taking up the challenges, problems, and disappointments facing the majority native population after a century of submission.

New Zealand poets Rosemary Kohu (born 1947), Robert DeRoo (born 1950), and Hone Tuwhare (born 1922) express in their work what it is like to be a Maori among the "Pakehas"—the Maori word for the Anglo-Saxon settlers. In "Taken," for example, Kohu recalls how as a child she was placed in the Bethlehem Native School, which methodically stripped away her heritage so she might become a "Pakeha-thinking Maori." Between each stanza of the poem appears the refrain: "'To get on in this world you must be Pakeha.'" In "Aotearoa/ New Zealand/Godzone?" DeRoo speaks to the land, calling it "Aotearoa," its name before the colonial "New Zealand" and the affectionate "Godzone" were affixed. He sees history as "conquest" where "we claw each other for rights" to the land, then concludes that as an inhabitant of Aotearoa he can claim no single piece of the land but must embrace it all, telling Aotearoa that "my mind's birth-knot ties me irrevocably to you." Another

Maori, Tuwhare is one of New Zealand's most popular poets. Neither didactic nor angry, his work is full of warmth and wit. Still, he speaks strongly for his community and its marginal place in New Zealand society.

The work of the early Canadian activist-poet Duke Redbird (born 1939) condemns white society for its insensitive treatment of the native people. "I Am the Redman," one of his best-known poems, became a rallying cry in the 1970's for the long-silent Indians. Another native poet, Rita Joe (born 1932), articulates her people's plight in a more conciliatory fashion—reminiscent of Oodgeroo in some ways—saying, for example, in one of her untitled poems published in *Poems of Rita Joe* (1978), "Pray/ meet me halfway—/ I am today's Indian." Other poets in this group include Chief Dan George (1899-1981), Daniel David Moses (born 1952), and George Kenny (born 1951).

It would be misleading, though, to leave the impression that indigenous poetry constitutes nothing more than protest. As the years have passed, some rights have been gained and certainly consciousness has been raised, and many indigenous poets have moved toward familiar topics of poetry: love, home, nature, and spiritual quest. They have also combined with English-language forms their oral heritage, which has been retrieved through great effort. These writers are thus in the process of establishing a poetic tradition that echoes the borrowed literature and at the same time imbues it with their own ancient text.

One of the writers who has combined the two texts most impressively is the Australian poet Mudrooroo Narogin (born 1939), who published as Colin Johnson before taking a tribal name. His volume of poetry *Dalwura* (1988) records the travels of the Black Bittern, a totemic bird from Aboriginal mythology. Like the poet himself, this bird sets out on a spiritual quest, visiting Singapore, India, the United Kingdom, and other parts of Asia before returning to his native Australia. In the introduction to *Dalwura*, Mudrooroo describes the work as a way of showing how ancient Aboriginal song cycles can serve as the framework for poems in English, adding that by using such traditional materials the poet is to some degree disciplined by them.

The highly original poetry of Mudrooroo, of such Maori writers as Keri Hulme, born 1947, (who is better known abroad for her novel *The Bone People*, 1983, than for her poetry), and of emergent South African and Canadian poets promises that this new voice in Commonwealth poetry will prevail.

INDIA, AFRICA, WEST INDIES: COLONIAL AND POSTCOLONIAL POETS

The most important poet of this group, Derek Walcott (born 1930), is of African descent but was born and grew up in the West Indies when his remote Caribbean island still formed part of the Empire. In the poem "A Far Cry from Africa," he speaks of "the English tongue I love" but then asks a question common to many postcolonial poets who are not Anglo-Saxon but whose heritage and language is largely English: "Where shall I turn, divided to the vein?" While the West Indies has produced a number of poets, Walcott overshadows the others and to a great degree represents international poetry in English at its very best. He received the Nobel Prize in Literature in 1992. Walcott has incorporated his native Caribbean into a metaphor of universal proportions. Although some of his work takes up other locales and subjects, his best poetry returns to the land of his birth, with all its seductive beauty and internal decay.

Like Walcott, many of the postcolonial writers spent their first years as colonials, then at maturity found themselves in young nations set free from the imperial fetters of the past. Were they at that point to continue writing in English, thus building a national literary tradition based on the language and text of the departed conquerors? Should they not turn their backs on the English tongue they loved and write in the native languages of, say, Kenya, Nigeria, or India? By writing in English were they not pandering to the Western world rather than speaking to their own people, thereby creating what some have called "tourist literature"? While these questions have been debated by critics and writers in the half century since the era of independence, an English-language literature has continued to develop in Africa, India, and the West Indies. "Develop" carries significance: What has emerged in all the genres is not a postcolonial facsimile but a sturdy hybrid, which grows out of what West Indian novelist Wilson Harris (born 1921) calls "the universal imagination," be its source

African, ancient Greek or Roman, British, European, or American; its mythology Hindu, Buddhist, Muslim, or Christian; its forms expressionistic, romantic, neoclassic, or indigenous.

The first major poet from India, Sarojini Naidu (1879-1961), long preceded independence. Born into an Anglicized Indian family at the height of the British Raj and educated in England, Naidu published her first book of poems in English, *The Golden Threshold*, in London in 1905 and received immediate recognition at home and abroad. She published three more books of poems that still hold charm—and immense promise—with their curious blend of Romantic and Victorian forms with Indian imagery and subject matter. Her poetry reveals a passionate love for India along with an Eastern preoccupation with death and immortality, as in "Imperial Delhi," which celebrates the ancient city of so many past glories: "But thou dost still immutably remain/ Unbroken symbol of proud histories,/ Unageing priestess of old mysteries/ Before whose shrine the spells of Death are vain." Yet Naidu gave up her poetic career in "the English tongue" she loved to join Gandhi's freedom movement and became one of the Mahatma's closest associates throughout India's struggle for independence, which was finally gained in 1947. Had she been born later her story might have been different.

In postcolonial India one of the major poets is also a woman, Kamala Das (born 1934). Her work, infinitely more modern in form, sophisticated in tone, and confessional in nature, still brings to mind Naidu's poetry as it blends Indian imagery, Western forms, and the universal concerns of love, passion, alienation, spirituality, and death. Although Das writes in both the Indian language Malayalam and English, she describes language in her poem "An Introduction" as nothing more than a tool for expression, a way of communicating what is said in the other language of nature and experience, which she calls "the deaf blind speech/ Of trees in storm or of monsoon clouds or of rain or the/ Incoherent mutterings of the blazing/ Funeral pyre." While the imagery is purely Indian, the idea it expresses reaches far beyond its source. Das validates her use of English by divorcing language from superficial nationalism and seeing it as just one form of human expression, which she calls in the same poem "the speech of mind that is/ Here."

Another important Indian poet in English, Nissim Ezekiel (born 1924), is considered a pioneer figure who introduced European expressionistic forms into Indian poetry but at the same time diffused what he borrowed to express a purely Indian sensibility. His often-experimental work encompasses a wide range: Some of it is highly personal in its revelation of the inner experience, as in "Two Images," and some in its frank treatment of sexuality, as in "Nudes"—two of his best-known poems. In a work like "Poster Poems," he creates collages of the subcontinent's variegated human landscape. Some Indian critics, however, have found Ezekiel's work—and that of Das as well—too Western in orientation, objecting, for instance, to the use of Christian imagery; these poets and others writing in English should, the critics say, rely more heavily on Indian mythology, history, and literature even if their language is non-Indian.

To a great extent, contemporary African poets have been more faithful than their sometimes all-too-literary Indian counterparts at integrating the African languages and heritage into English poetry. Many African poets write first in an African language and then render their work into English, often retaining many of the African words. Some write in pidgin to reproduce the flavor that English has acquired in Africa. Others attempt to evoke through verbal effects traditional drum or flute poetry, or the chanted verses that are a part of tribal ceremonies. A single poem may refer to Christian mythology alongside allusions to African religion, or may contain lines from Ezra Pound or echo the rhythms of Gerard Manly Hopkins while focusing on a purely African subject. The Western hero Odysseus might be mentioned in the same breath as Chaka, the legendary African warrior.

The colonial African poets concentrated on subject matter, often protest, and let technique take care of itself, usually adhering to the forms and diction set by the British text. In contrast, postcolonial writers have exercised admirable craft in their work; from a technical standpoint, they do not write in a vacuum but show a keen awareness of the current trends in English-language poetry. Of course, many were educated abroad, in England, Europe, or the United States. Still, they do not sacrifice their Africanness in order to be fashionable or acceptable on the international scene. Finally, African writers, whatever their genre, have never indulged in art for art's sake, but see a high seriousness and purpose in what they do. The Somali novelist Nuruddin Farah (born 1945) expresses this intent forcefully in his 1981 address "Do Fences Have Sides?": "The writer in Africa and the Third World countries is looked upon as the contributor to and/or creator/shaper of the nation's enlightened opinion . . . he is, to a great number of people, the light whose beams guide the ark to safety."

Certainly the approach to literature espoused by the Nigerian writer Wole Soyinka (born 1934) exemplifies Farah's statement. Receiving the Nobel Prize in 1986, Soyinka is better known for his poetic drama than for his separate poems, even though he has excelled in the latter form, as well as in fiction and the essay. Soyinka's work is sometimes described as creatively eclectic; a single play or poem may bring together such disparate elements as African purification ceremonies, the rhythms of Shakespearean verse, folk narrative of the Yoruba people (Soyinka's tribal identity), and the dramatic techniques of Bertolt Brecht. His work represents brilliantly the subtle interaction that takes place when a writer borrows from and responds to a wide variety of texts. While nationalist critics and theorists in Africa and elsewhere may denounce such interdependence and call it artistic neocolonialism, the artists apparently—and fortunately—realize that they do not create within set boundaries.

Another such poet is Christopher Okigbo (1932-1967), who was born in Nigeria and was killed in the Biafran war. Lyrical, cryptic, intense, and frequently obscure, his highly personal work blends the sounds of African music and the performance of ancient ritual with Western artistic and literary elements. Okigbo is usually considered the most modern of the African poets, and the fusion of sound and symbol makes his work extremely difficult—at times incomprehensible—on an intellectual level, but it is always resonant and exciting.

Okot p'Bitek (1931-1982) was born in Uganda but spent the last decade of his life in Kenya after his criticism of the Ugandan government made him *persona non grata* in his homeland. Trained as an anthropologist, p'Bitek received international attention when his four "Songs" were published, the first in 1961, the last in 1971. The overriding theme of the "Songs"—actually dramatic monologues in which various Africans

speak—is the conflict between Western influence and African ways. For example, in the *Song of Lawino* (1966), the speaker laments her husband's desertion of her, complaining that the "manhood" of all the young African men "was finished/ In the class-rooms,/ Their testicles/ Were smashed/ With large books!" Witty, at times satirical toward both African and Western ways, the "Songs" record in addition to the lament of the African woman the observations and sometimes the desperation of a Europeanized African man, a prisoner, and a prostitute. The poems serve to supplement anthropologist p'Bitek's scholarly writing on African culture.

Along with their counterparts in India and the West Indies, the Africans join the settler poets and emergent indigenous writers to lend contemporary poetry in English voices that are unmistakably international.

BIBLIOGRAPHY

Adcock, Fleur, ed. *The Oxford Book of Contemporary New Zealand Poetry*. New York: Oxford University Press, 1982.

Adelaide, Debra. *Bibliography of Australian Women's Literature, 1795-1990: A Listing of Fiction, Poetry, Drama, Non-Fiction Published in Monograph Form Arranged Alphabetically by Author*. Port Melbourne, Australia: D. W. Thorpe, 1991.

Alvarez-Pereyre, Jacques. *The Poetry of Commitment in South Africa*. Translated by Clive Wake. London: Heinemann, 1985.

Berry, James, ed. *News for Babylon: The Chatto Book of West Indian-British Poetry*. London: Chatto & Windus, 1984.

Besner, Neil Kalmen, Deborah Schnitzer, and Alden Turner, eds. *Uncommon Wealth: An Anthology of Poetry in English*. New York: Oxford University Press, 1999.

Breiner, Laurence A. *An Introduction to West Indian Poetry*. New York: Cambridge University Press, 1998.

Brown, Lloyd Wellesley. *West Indian Poetry*. London: Heinemann, 1984.

Brown, Stewart. *Caribbean Poetry Now*. 2d ed. London: Edward Arnold, 1994.

Brown, Stewart, and Mervyn Morris, eds. *Voiceprint: An Anthology of Oral and Related Poetry from the Caribbean*. Chicago: Dearborn Financial, 1995.

Coplan, David B. *In the Time of Cannibals: The Word Music of South Africa's Basotho Migrants.* Chicago: University of Chicago Press, 1994.

DiGioanni, Caroline M., ed. *Italian Canadian Voices: An Anthology of Poetry and Prose, 1946-1986.* New York: Mosaic Press, 1994.

Espinet, Ramabai. *Creation Fire: A CAFRA Anthology of Caribbean Women's Poetry.* Toronto: Sister Vision Press, 1990.

Gill, John, ed. *New American and Canadian Poetry.* Boston: Beacon Press, Press, 1971.

Habekost, Christian. *Verbal Riddim: The Politics and Aesthetics of African-Caribbean Dub Poetry.* Atlanta, Ga.: Rodopi, 1993.

House, Amelia. *Our Sun Will Rise.* Illustrated by Selma Waldman. Washington, D.C.: Three Continents Press, 1989.

Hurley, E. Anthony. *Through a Black Veil: Readings in French Caribbean Poetry.* Trenton, N.J.: Africa World Press, 1997.

Jaffa, Herbert C., ed. *Modern Australian Poetry: A Guide to Information Sources.* Detroit: Gale Group, 1979.

Kellman, Anthony, ed. *Crossing Water: Contemporary Poetry of the English-Speaking Caribbean.* Greenfield Center, N.Y.: Greenfield Review Press, 1994.

Lecker, Robert, and Jack David, eds. *The New Canadian Anthology: Poetry and Short Fiction in English.* Scarborough, Ont.: Nelson Canada, 1988.

Lindfors, Bernth. *Contemporary Black South African Literature: A Symposium.* Ithaca, N.Y.: Cornell University Press, 1985.

Luca, Rose, and Lyn McCredden. *Bridgings: Readings in Australian Women's Poetry.* New York: Oxford University Press, 1997.

McDonald, Ian, and Stewart Brown, eds. *The Heinemann Book of Caribbean Poetry.* Portsmouth, N.H.: Heinemann, 1992.

Markham, E. A. A. *Hinterland: Caribbean Poetry from the West Indies and Britain.* Washington, D.C.: Dufour, 1992.

Marshall, Tom. *Multiple Exposures, Promised Lands: Essays on Canadian Poetry and Fiction.* Kingston, Ontario, Canada: Quarry Press, 1992.

Maver, Igor. *Readings in Contemporary Australian Poetry.* New York: Peter Lang, 1997.

Narain, Denise Decaires, ed. *Contemporary Caribbean Women's Poetry: Making Style.* New York: Routledge, 2001.

Ndebele, Njabulo S. *South African Literature and Culture: Rediscovery of the Ordinary.* New York: St. Martin's Press, 1994.

Norris, Ken, ed. *Canadian Poetry Now: Twenty Poets of the Eighties.* Buffalo, N.Y.: Anansi, 1984.

Pierce, Lorne, and Vernon Blair Rhodenizer. *Canadian Poetry in English.* Edited by Bliss Carman. Westport, Conn.: Greenwood, 1976.

Ray, David. *Kangaroo Paws: Poems Written in Australia.* Kirksville, Mo.: Thomas Jefferson University Press, 1994.

Schurmann-Zeggel, Heinz. *Black Australian Literature: A Bibliography of Fiction, Poetry, Drama, Oral Traditions and Non-Fiction, Including Critical Commentary, 1900-1991.* New York: Peter Lang, 2000.

Shapiro, Norman R. *Negritude: Black Poetry from Africa and the Caribbean.* New York: October House, 1970.

Smith, Arthur J., ed. *The Book of Canadian Poetry.* 3d ed. Toronto: W. J. Gage, 1957.

Wallace, Ann, ed. *Daughters of the Sun, Women of the Moon: Poetry by Black Canadian Women.* Stratford, Ont.: Williams-Wallace, 1991.

Wevers, Lydia, ed. *Yellow Pencils: Contemporary Poetry by New Zealand Women.* New York: Oxford University Press, 1988.

Robert L. Ross, updated by Ross

CROATIAN POETRY

The beginnings of Croatian poetry coincided with the introduction of Christianity to the Croats in the ninth century, when the disciples of the missionaries Cyril and Methodius came to the South Slavic lands, bringing with them writings in Old Church Slavonic concerning church rituals. Unfortunately, most Croatian literary works of that period have been lost. The earliest extant Croatian poetry is contained in *Misal Kneza Novaka* (1368; the missal of Prince Novak), written in *glagolitsa*, a special alphabet devised by the missionaries on the basis of the local tongue. Numerous church songs from the fourteenth and fifteenth centuries show a great variety of rhymed and unrhymed metrics—from seven to twelve syllables—but there are also songs in free verse. All of this poetic activity, limited though it was in subject matter and scope, constituted the necessary preparation for, and transition to, the blossoming of artistic literature in general, and poetry in particular, in cultural centers along the Adriatic coast from the second half of the fifteenth century to 1835.

The Croatian territories on the Adriatic coast escaped Turkish rule and, as a result, were able to develop in every respect. This was especially true of the Republic of Dubrovnik (Ragusa). Culturally, this area was under the direct influence of Italian Humanism and Petrarchan poetry. Many Croatian poets were educated in Italy and wrote for the most part, or exclusively, in Latin. More important, even though the general tenor and spirit of their poetry were unmistakably under the Italian influence, the Croatian poets of Dalmatia were able to give their poetry a native slant and color, not only in language and setting but also in their own understanding of the function and purpose of literature and poetry.

FOURTEENTH TO SIXTEENTH CENTURIES

The first writer of stature who excelled in both Latin and Croatian was Marko Marulić (1450-1524). His many writings on religious and moral issues were widely circulated throughout Europe in the first half of the sixteenth century. Marulić was at times suspicious of the secular spirit of the Renaissance; his poetry is steeped in piety and Christian morality, often touching upon the social problems of his time, especially the immoral behavior of some members in the hierarchy of the Catholic Church. He also warned repeatedly about the danger of the advancing Turks, who had besieged his native Split. His most ambitious work, the epic *Judita* (1501; Judith), uses a biblical story to reflect on conditions in Dalmatia in his time, particularly the Turkish threat and the need to preserve freedom.

Šiško Menčetić (1457-1527) and Džore Držić (1461-1501) were two of the early Dubrovnik writers who laid the foundations of Croatian medieval poetry with their somewhat scant poetic contributions. Menčetić was a patrician and Držić a priest; they complemented each other in that the former was a more conventional and the latter a more spontaneous poet. Menčetić's lyric poetry follows closely the spirit of Petrarch, while that of Držić reflects the spontaneity and freshness of folk poetry.

The works of these two poets soon began to exert influence upon the second generation of Dalmatian poets in the first half of the sixteenth century. Hanibal Lucić (1485-1553) and Petar Hektorović (1487-1572) wrote love poems in the Petrarchan tradition and incorporated that tradition even in their longer works, the play *Robinja* (1520; the slave girls) by Lucić, and the epic *Ribanje i ribarsko prigovaranje* (1568; fishing and fishermen's talk) by Hektorović. A strong influence of folk poetry is also evident in their works; like many writers of their generation, they had begun to assert themselves as Croatian writers even as they assimilated foreign influences. One of the most fascinating poets in this respect is Andrija Ćubranović, of whose life very little is known but who, in his love poem "Jedjupka" (the Gypsy), embellished his Petrarchan model with the octosyllabic line, which had become synonymous with the young but rapidly growing Croatian tradition.

Other noteworthy poets of the sixteenth century expanded the scope of their poetry while branching out into other genres; in fact, some of them are better known for their work in other genres. Mavro Vetranović (1482-1576), after starting in the religious and moralistic vein of his predecessors, developed into a pure lyric poet who was not reluctant to dwell on his personal concerns in a highly reflective manner. Marin Držić (c. 1508-1567), the author of many pastoral plays and comedies, expresses in his love poems, as in his drama, the joy of life, indulging in an unabashed glorification of youth, pleasure, and beauty. Dinko Ranjina (1536-1607) and Dinko Zlatarić (1558-1609) also endeavored to break away from the traditions established by older poets; although they lacked the strength to complete such an important task, they pointed in the direction that Croatian literature would take in the next century.

RENAISSANCE

On the strength of the solid foundation laid by almost a century of unhindered growth, Croatian poetry of the Renaissance reached its pinnacle in the seventeenth century. The greatest Croatian poet of the century, and indeed of the entire era, was Ivan Gundulić (1589-1638). Continuing in the Christian tradition of his predecessors, Gundulić added a pronounced nationalism in order to present the life of Dubrovnik and of his people in general. In *Suze sina razemetnoga* (1622; the tears of the prodigal son), his deep religiosity is reflected in the realization of the transience of all things and of the need to seek God. It is the long, unfinished epic poem *Osman* (1651), however, that qualifies Gundulić as one of the greatest poets in all the South Slavic literatures. *Osman* reflects Gundulić's preoccupation with the freedom of his people in their struggle against the Turks. The defeat of the Turkish sultan Osman by Poland is used by the poet to instill hope in the Slavs. What makes the epic outstanding is an artistic quality not previously seen in Croatian poetry: a richness of poetic expression, a strong rhythm and deft rhyming, and a skillful mixture of lyric and realistic elements.

SEVENTEENTH CENTURY

After Gundulić, the literature of Dubrovnik began a slow decline. There were only two other poets of note: Ivan Bunić Vučić (1591-1658) wrote Anacreontic poems with an emphasis on love and other sensuous experiences, composed in flowing octosyllables and couched in picturesque images. Ignjat Djurdjević (1675-1737) wrote most of his poetry in the eighteenth century, but in spirit he belonged to the preceding century and, as such, concluded the golden age of the literature of Dubrovnik. Like Vučić, Djurdjević wrote love lyrics stressing sensuality and the unhappy ending of the love experience.

While Dubrovnik relinquished its leading position in Croatian literature, other parts of Croatia began to assert themselves. In the seventeenth century, there were three noteworthy poets in Croatia proper: Petar Zrinski (1621-1671), Fran Krsto Frankopan (1643-1671), and Pavao Ritter Vitezović (1652-1712). The first two belonged to aristocratic families, which furnished the leaders of Croatian society at that time. They were involved in a conspiracy against Austrian rule and because of this lost their lives while still very young. They managed to write only a few poems each, drawing from their great knowledge of foreign literatures and concentrating on translation from these literatures. In their own poetry, they were influenced by folk traditions and by the fashionable poetry of their time, including that of Dubrovnik. Vitezović, the first professional writer in Croatia, distinguished himself by his work in cultural matters and by his efforts toward the unification of all the Southern Slavs.

EIGHTEENTH CENTURY

In the eighteenth century, the poets of Croatia proper failed to match the achievements of the Dubrovnik literature of the past, but they prepared the ground for greater achievements that would soon follow. Andrija Kačić Miošić (1704-1760), for example, imitated folk poetry in a versified historical chronicle, *Razgovor ugodni naroda slovinskoga* (1756; a pleasant account of the Slavs), thus foreshadowing the importance of folk poetry during the national revival of the Southern Slavs in the next century. Matija Antun Reljković (1732-1798), primarily a didactic poet, endeavored in his main work, *Satir* (1762; the Satyr), to help his people free themselves from foreign rule as well as from ignorance. Tito Brezovački (1757-1805) also wrote primarily to educate his people and, in the process, used their own language.

FOLK TRADITIONS

During these centuries, there was another literature—folk literature—which existed like an underground river. The folk poetry of the Croats developed simultaneously with that of the Serbs; sometimes it is impossible to tell them apart unless they deal with clearly identifiable historical events and figures. Like their Serbian counterparts, Croatian folk poems concern themselves with the basic conflict of the medieval history of the Southern Slavs—the struggle of Christendom against Islam. Croatian lyric folk poems are almost identical with those of the Serbs in that they, too, depict the everyday concerns of the common people. They are also rich artistically. While the Serbian folk lyrics are mostly decasyllabic, Croatian folk lyrics employ a greater variety of meters, most of them in a twelve-syllable meter known as *bugarštica*.

NINETEENTH CENTURY ROMANTICISM

Folk poetry gave a strong impetus to the national revival in all the South Slavic lands at the beginning of the nineteenth century. The sense of oneness among the Serbs and Croats, as evidenced by folk poetry that could be read and appreciated in all parts of the Serbo-Croatian linguistic and ethnic domain, led to the reawakening of national identity and to the formation of the so-called Illyrian movement. This movement originated in Croatia, where it also had its strongest and most eloquent support. It consisted of people from all walks of life, although writers, especially poets, predominated. The movement was influenced, somewhat belatedly, by Western European Romanticism, notably that of German literature. Nationalistic aspirations to free the country from the suffocating domination of Austrian, Hungarian, German, Italian, and Turkish rulers also contributed considerably to the birth of this movement. Its main leader, Ljudevit Gaj (1809-1872), proposed that the *štokavian* dialect, the language of the vast majority of Serbo-Croatian folk poems, should serve as the official language of all the Southern Slavs, and many writers began to use this dialect exclusively.

The Illyrian movement in Croatia produced three excellent poets: Ivan Mažuranić (1814-1890), Stanko Vraz (1810-1851), and Petar Preradović (1818-1872). Mažuranić is best known for his epic poem *Smrt Smail-age Čengijića* (1846; the death of Smail-aga Chengich), which glorifies the struggle of the Montenegrins against the Turks while presenting a dark picture of the Turkish atrocities. The epic embodies many elements of Croatian culture, even though it depicts the plight of another South Slavic nation, thus underscoring one of the basic themes of the Illyrian movement. The influence of epic folk poetry is reflected in the simplicity and immediacy

of Mažuranić's language, in the poem's dramatic action, and in its decasyllabic meter. Stanko Vraz, a Slovene by birth and upbringing, started to write in Slovenian but then accepted the call of the Illyrians for a common language. He wrote his best works in Croatian, chiefly love poems collected in *Djulabije* (1840; red apples). Like most Illyrians, he believed that a poet should create artistic literature based on folk poetry, but he also wrote sonnets, ghazels (a form of Middle Eastern love poem popular among the Romantics), romances, ballads, satiric poems, and epigrams, introducing a more cosmopolitan spirit to Croatian literature. Peter Preradović, an officer in the Austrian army who had almost forgotten his native language and had begun to write poems in German, "awoke" in later years and in the process, became one of the best-loved Croatian poets. He wrote love poems and reflective verse, but he particularly excelled in patriotic poems, which expressed his faith that one day, all Slavs would unite to form a single nation. The message of his poetry is complemented by an artistic prowess of a kind never seen before in Croatian literature.

Croatian Romanticism was carried on by the generation of poets around the middle of the nineteenth century, although without the intensity and high accomplishments of the Illyrians. The unsuccessful Revolution of 1848, when hopes for independence and a better future were dashed, also had a dampening effect. Of several Romantics during this phase (Mirko Bogović, 1816-1893; Luka Botić, 1830-1863; Franjo Marković, 1845-1914; Josip Eugen Tomić, 1843-1906), the most powerful was August Šenoa (1838-1881). A prolific writer of fiction and prose in other genres, he wrote poetry with the same attitude as he did his prose, combining a realistic method with many Romantic elements, including a preoccupation with the past, the rediscovery of folk literature and folklore, the primacy of emotion, and nationalistic pride.

NINETEENTH AND EARLY TWENTIETH CENTURY REALISM

During the period of realism (1881-1895), there were only two significant poets: August Harambašić (1861-1911) and Silvije Strahimir Kranjčević (1865-1905). While Harambašić wrote light, musical poems in which he extolled freedom and exhorted his people to fight for it, Kranjčević developed into a poet of fiery spirit. His four books of poetry constitute one loud cry of protest against the injustice and senselessness of contemporary social conditions and of human existence in general. Nevertheless, he expressed the hope that somehow conditions would improve. The author of several outstanding poems, he enriched Croatian literature like no other poet in the nineteenth century, and with his spotlight on human relationships and on the inequities contained therein, he made a sharp turn toward modernity in Croatian poetry.

MODERNISM

The modern spirit came into full recognition and expression with the next generation of poets, grouped around the movement fittingly calling itself *Moderna*. *Moderna* was keenly attuned to contemporary problems and concerns; it also welcomed the influence of foreign authors to a degree unprecedented in Croatian letters. Poetry was its strongest voice, although other genres and arts were also involved. Long strides were made in matters of form and poetics. The movement did much to free Croatian poetry from its provincial confines and to make it a worthy though still neglected partner on the international scene. There were several competent poets in the *Moderna* movement. One of the first to achieve recognition was Milan Begović (1876-1948). His love poetry, collected in *Knjiga boccadoro* (1900; the book of the golden word), is bold, innovative, rebellious, uninhibited; it shocked older readers but endeared itself to the younger generation. Begović later became more active in drama and fiction and abandoned poetry altogether. Dragutin Domjanić (1875-1933), who made a more important contribution to the poetry of *Moderna* than did Begović, reached his zenith in *Pesme* (1907; poems). He led a secluded and self-effacing life, reflected in his rather private and pessimistic poetry. Vladimir Vidrić (1875-1909) was the exact opposite of Domjanić, in both his upbringing and his approach to poetry. He wrote only about forty poems, in which he roamed the world and its history, from classical antiquity and Slavic mythology to the present, giving full vent to his Dionysian joy of life. Sparse in quantity but refreshing in quality, Vidrić's poetry has steadily gained in esteem and popularity. Ante Tresić Pavičić (1867-1949), during his long life and career, belonged for a

while to *Moderna* and with his broad erudition, attempted to adopt classical meters to contemporary Croatian. His importance lies more in his influence on younger poets than in his own output. Perhaps the most significant representative of *Moderna* was Antun Gustav Matoš (1873-1914), although his contribution was more important in other genres than in poetry. He wrote poems relatively late in his life, paying strict attention to form and the high aesthetic criteria he advocated in all of his works. His influence on subsequent Croatian writers has been considerable; he was one of the most important Croatian men of letters in the first two decades of the twentieth century.

Vladimir Nazor (1876-1949) also began to write during this period and espoused modernistic tendencies, but because he was able to outgrow many literary periods and movements, it is difficult to tie him down to a single one. He wrote in many genres, but he was at his best in poetry, of which he published more than ten collections. Central to Nazor's poetic outlook is his pantheistic reverence and love for nature in all its forms. His ebullient optimism and faith in man despite all the seamy aspects of life, of which he was not oblivious, made him a bard of faith and hope. He undoubtedly derived his sunny disposition from his place of birth, an island in the Adriatic where he had grown up and spent his youth, and from the fact that his long life passed without much trouble. With his somewhat idealized depiction of the Croatian people, Nazor won favor with the broad reading public, who readily overlooked his shortcomings and lack of depth.

THE WORLD WARS

The advent of World War I brought about a decisive change in Croatian poetry, just as it did in other South Slavic literatures. New faces and forces occupied the central stage during and after the war, elbowing out the older ones, even the writers of *Moderna*. Most of the new poets considered it their first duty to protest against the horrors and madness of war. The strongest new voice belonged to Miroslav Krleža (1893-1981), a writer of remarkable power and breadth who would dominate Croatian letters for seven decades. A politically engaged intellectual, an insistent advocate of social justice, a passionate polemicist, a writer of unusual prowess and broad erudition, Krleža expounded his views in a highly artistic manner in all of his works, of which poetry constituted only a small part. He led Croatian literature during the period of feverish activity and artistically satisfying creativity between the two world wars.

There were other poets worth mentioning (in addition to prewar poets such as Domjanić and Nazor): Tin Ujević (1891-1955), Antun Branko Šimić (1898-1925), Gustav Krklec (1899-1978), Dobriša Cesarić (1902-1980), and Dragutin Tadijanović (born 1905), to name only some of the most accomplished. The first two should be singled out. Ujević was a Bohemian by nature and a highly original poet of intense, mostly pessimistic experiences. In his eight books of poetry, he trod the tortuous path of an often misunderstood loner in his struggle for inner freedom and identity. Šimić's poems strike a similarly tragic chord, intensified by illness and premonitions of early death. Both of these poets have exerted a strong influence on their younger counterparts and on contemporary Croatian poetry.

During World War II, most poets were silent, but a few gave expression to the tragic experiences of their people. Vladimir Nazor joined the partisans and wrote poems extolling their struggle in his usual positive fashion. Those were the last noteworthy poems he wrote; he died soon after the war. A young poet, Ivan Goran Kovačić (1913-1943), also joined the partisans and gained prominence with his long poem *Jama* (1944; the pit). It is written in a very strict form, full of magnificent imagery and powerful use of language, raising to a tragic level the theme of human suffering and the horrors of war. Kovačić himself was a victim of the war.

POSTWAR AND LATE TWENTIETH CENTURY

In the first postwar years, several older poets—Ujević, Nazor, Krklec, Cesarić, Tadijanović, and others—reappeared with new works, but in almost all cases, their earlier poetry is much better. In the first postwar generation, Vesna Parun (born 1922) and Jure Kaštelan (1919-1990) occupy prominent positions. In 1947, Parun published her first book, *Zore i vihori* (daybreaks and whirlwinds), a collection that was influential among young poets and was at the same time denounced by the Socialist Realist critics. Primarily a poet of love, she combines sensuousness and great compassion with the rich texture of her

spiritual intuition. For her, love is a redeeming force which can rescue the world, but from the beginning, one also detects a dark streak in her poetry, for ultimately she is a realist. The ideal she reaches for remains unattainable, and her numerous collections attest this struggle. Kaštelan brought a new, specifically personal tone into Croatian poetry, especially in his elegiac war poems. On one hand, he laments the dead; on the other hand, he reflects on the fate of those who survived. In his most recent poems, Kaštelan sought to find a new voice, replacing the themes of war with the problems of modern man as a social being.

The next generation produced a crop of excellent poets. Slavko Mihalić (born 1928) writes in an idiom remarkable for its simplicity, precision, and lyric fluency. His poetry is that of a contemporary man with a rich personal experience who is at the same time well aware of the whole range of intellectual history. His spirit is critical and self-conscious. Mihalić the poet can forget neither that he is writing a poem nor that he lives in the twentieth century. His poems are meditations on the fate of the individual attempting to find a synthesis in a world which feels no pressing need for one. It is the seriousness of his commitment that makes Mihalić one of the most impressive figures in contemporary Croatian literature.

Milivoj Slaviček (born 1929) reveals a certain intellectual kinship with Mihalić, although his emphasis on rationalism and nonconformism is much greater. The intentional prosiness and even awkwardness of his lines result in poetry that is not devoid of emotion and that has its own original intensity. Slaviček at his best has the ability to bring out the absurd details of everyday life and give them poetic luminosity. He seems to carry on a running dialogue with his fellow man and himself about the basic problems of existence, expressed in colloquial language.

Ivan Slamnig (born 1930) is probably the most tireless experimenter in contemporary Croatian literature. Each of his poems is a subtle reworking of some aspect of traditional style, form, and imagery. What guides him in these experiments is his impeccable ear as well as his sense of the absurd. The result is a blend of black humor and high seriousness. Essentially an intellectual, he creates a kind of metaphysical vaudeville, at once terrifying and comical, cool yet not lacking in compassion. Antun Šoljan (1932-1993), who has of late turned to fiction and drama, has probably the greatest imagistic talent in postwar Croatian literature. The clarity and the resonance of his images give his poems an anonymous, timeless quality. At best, they appear to be parables of an intense inner life. Both Šoljan and Slamnig have been influenced by, and have translated, English and American poetry.

Zvonimir Golob (born 1927) shares Šoljan's interest in the image, although he leans toward Surrealism and those who influenced him are to be found among Spanish and South American poets. Parallel to this imagistic tendency, there is in Croatian literature a profound wish to write a poetry of ideas. The prime example of this tendency is the poetry of Vlado Gotovac (1930-2000). His poetry is terse, austere, reduced to an absolute economy of expression whereby each line is almost a separate unit, a kind of epigrammatic building block of the poem. Still, beyond the hermeticism of these poems there is an authentic lyric voice, in tone not unlike that of the Serbian poet Borislav Radović.

Dubravko Horvatić (born 1939), Danijel Dragojević (born 1934), and Dubravko Škurla (1933-1957) belong to the next generation of poets. Horvatić has steadily evolved his own universe of symbols, exploring the situation and the fate of modern man. Dragojević is a poet of intellectual parables, and Škurla a lyricist of great directness and purity. In addition to these poets, there are many younger poets who are slowly acquiring their own poetic profile and carving their own niche in Croatian poetry. The completion of that process is still some time away. As in Serbian poetry, there is bustling activity in contemporary Croatian poetry that bodes well for its future.

BIBLIOGRAPHY

Barac, Antun. *A History of Yugoslav Literature.* Ann Arbor, Mich.: Joint Committee on Eastern Europe Publication Series, 1973. A standard history of all Yugoslav literatures and poetry, including Croatian, by a leading literary scholar. Although somewhat outdated, it still provides reliable information, especially on the older periods.

Debeljak, Aleš. "Visions of Despair and Hope Against Hope: Poetry in Yugoslavia in the Eighties." *World Literature Today* 68, no. 3 (1992): 191-194. Debeljak looks at Yugoslav poetry, including Croatian, on the eve of tumultuous events and changes in Yugoslavia in the 1990's. Poetry of the 1980's in some ways foreshadows those events, giving vent to despair and forlorn hope.

Eekman, Thomas. "Form and Formlessness in Contemporary Serbian and Croatian Poetry." *Southeastern Europe* 9, nos. 1/2 (1982): 84-94. An expert analysis of formalistic aspects of Croatian poetry, based on copious examples and citations.

Kadić, Ante. "Postwar Croatian Lyric Poetry." *Slavic Review* 17 (1958): 509-529. Kadić examines the first post-World War II generation of poets and their output, emphasizing their efforts to preserve their artistic freedom under political pressure to conform to non-artistic dictates.

Torbarina, Josip. *Italian Influence on the Poets of the Ragusan Republic.* London: Williams & Norgate, 1931. Torbarina traces the Italian influence on the poets of this very important period, that led to the blossoming of the literature of Dubrovnik in the Middle Ages.

Žmegač, Viktor. "On the Poetics of the Expressionist Phase in Croatian Literature." In *Comparative Studies in Croatian Literature.* Zagreb: Zavod za znanost i književnost Filozofskog fakulteta u Zagrebu, 1981. A skillful treatment of expressionism in Croatian poetry in the 1920's and 1930's, covering a very important period.

Vasa D. Mihailovich, updated by Mihailovich

CZECH POETRY

The oldest Czech poetry dates to the fourteenth century, although the literary history of Bohemia extends further back by several centuries, to include the Old Church Slavonic and medieval Latin poetry written in Bohemia before the use of the vernacular in literature. Arne Novák, the doyen of Czech literary historiography, includes even works written in German in his survey of Czech literature. A less controversial course, however, is to discuss only poetry written in Czech, considering it as Czech even if written by a Slovak, as was the case with Ján Kollár (1793-1852).

An overview of Czech poetry encourages an imperfect division into roughly four periods: the Golden Age (to 1409); the Age of Struggle (1409-1774); the Age of Revival (1774-1918); and the Modern Age (1918 to the present). In a terminology that includes the entire Western European cultural context, the four periods parallel the Gothic, the Baroque, the Romantic, and the modernist periods; clearly missing is the Renaissance, marginalized in the religious wars, in the Reformation and Counter-Reformation. (Paradoxically, it was only in the second half of the nineteenth century that a "Renaissance" poet, Jaroslav Vrchlický, 1853-1912, appeared in Czech poetry.) Nevertheless, such schematic divisions should not be rigidly respected; they merely provide convenient orientation markers.

THE GOLDEN AGE (TO 1409)

The magnificence of fourteenth century Czech literature lies in the breadth and quality of poetry that appeared so suddenly, situating Bohemia firmly in the Western European literary context. Verse chronicles, epics, didactic literature and satire, courtly love poetry, sacred hymns, profane lyrics—such was the rich spectrum of Czech poetry in the fourteenth century, unequalled in any other Slavic literature at the time. For today's readers, this rich poetic tradition serves as a reminder of the cultural unity of Bohemia with Western Europe; like other Central European cultures, Bohemia has always been oriented toward the West, something that the unfortunate political locution "Eastern Europe" managed to obfuscate.

The rich treasury of fourteenth century Czech poetry was the product of many well-educated and practiced poets working at the court in Prague, at the Caroline University, or in the monasteries. The oldest attested Czech hymn, from the fourteenth century, was based on a Greek refrain and bears some traces of Old Church Slavonic forms. This hymn, "Hospodine, pomiluj ny" ("Lord Have Mercy on Us"), was preserved as an integral part of the coronation ceremony of the Czech kings, which explains its antiquity. The typical fourteenth century hymn appears in rhymed octosyllabic quatrains, or even longer stanzas, as in "Kunhutina modlitba" ("The Prayer of Lady Kunhuta"). More interesting and indeed regarded as representative of the best poetry of the century is the sophisticated fourteenth century epic poem *Legenda o svaté Kateřióe* (*The Legend of St. Catherine*). The poem combines religious, Scholastic, and secular themes, perhaps reflecting the new situation of Prague, where, in 1348, Charles IV had established the Caroline University (Saint Catherine was the patron saint of its faculty of arts) and his magnificent court. In *The Legend of St. Catherine*, the story of the martyrdom of Saint Catherine and her miracles is supplemented both by skillful rhetorical arguments and by elements reminiscent of the Provençal love song.

In its synthesis of sacred and secular elements, the poem marks the transition from versified lives of the saints to the courtly love poetry then sweeping Western Europe. The Provençal love song, and the German *Minnesänger* were not perceived as exotic imports in Prague. Rather, because of the cosmopolitan atmosphere encouraged by Charles IV, courtly love poetry developed almost simultaneously in Western Europe and in Bohemia, having found in Prague a fertile soil. In the work of the homegrown Czech love poet Záviš, a Master of the Caroline University, there is proof of such encouragement of genre, as well as an indication that at least some poets of the period were connected with the university.

Apart from religious and scholarly poetry, the Golden Age also produced satirical poems that castigate shoemakers, blacksmiths, butchers, bakers, and others. These "satiry o řemeslnících" (satires about tradesmen) are simple moralistic exempla; much more elaborate are other satirical poems from the same collection of fourteenth century manuscripts, including the twelve hundred lines of the satirical *Decalogue*, wherein adaptations from *Gesta Romanorum* abound.

The art of poetry was only one facet in the many-sided jewel of Czech Gothic culture: the cathedrals, the painting, the advances of learning which, collectively, form the Golden Age. They all flourished in the fourteenth century, and it is difficult to say which of them was preeminent.

THE AGE OF STRUGGLE (1409-1774)

After the magnificence of the fourteenth century, the fifteenth century seems disappointing. Hymnal poetry was all that remained from the rich fourteenth century heritage, but in the religious strife brought about by Hussite Wars, the hymn was forced to assume a military function, and poetry suffered accordingly.

The period of religious strife was not, however, completely unsuited for literature of any kind: Pamphlets were produced in large numbers, as befitted an age of controversy. Particularly rich, too, is the satirical poetry of the period. Here, the medieval form of the satirical exemplum combines with a new content, the fruit of the fifteenth century religious pamphleteering of such Hussite thinkers as Petr Chelčický (1390-1460). The didacticism of this satire works against its metaphorical elements to the extent that the latter are suppressed; the allegory in such works seems heavy-handed, so subservient is it to the propagandistic function of the Hussite cause. The Catholic cause did not remain undefended, and the result was a battle of pamphlets, and even a battle of satirical poems, in which both causes were ridiculed.

After the Hussite Wars, Bohemia found itself in a paradoxical position. Nationally—that is, from the point of view of the advancement of the Czech cause, Czech control of the main cities, the use of the vernacular, and so on—there was a clear victory. At the same time, the Czechs isolated themselves from the European context as heretics. This cultural isolation was sadly accompanied by the decline of the Caroline University, by the inability of the main European cultural movements of the Renaissance to establish themselves in Bohemia, and by the destruction of much of the Gothic heritage, including artworks of all kinds, but particularly manuscripts.

Thus, the Czech literary tradition was interrupted, and it was only at the end of the fifteenth century that a cultural revival began, under the influence of Italian Humanism. At first, this influence appeared primarily in translations from classical literature, and only later in original work. At the turn of the fifteenth century, there was a small poetic movement of Czech noblemen, some of whose works are preserved in the *Neuberg Anthology* (c. 1500). There, along with Humanistic irony and Renaissance *joi de vivre*, the reader encounters compositions of a medieval character close in spirit to the courtly lyric. Further developments—after the Habsburg Dynasty assumed control over Bohemia—strengthened the Humanistic influence, but at the price of turning Bohemia, culturally, into a German province. Humanism inspired the writing of original Latin poetry, while infusions of Italians and Spaniards further discouraged the production of Czech literature. Given this situation, it is difficult to overestimate the impact made on Czech literature by the Kralická Bible (1579-1593).

This landmark Czech translation of the Bible was comparable in its influence to Martin Luther's German translation: It standardized the Czech language, providing a model of usage and style. Its concreteness of expression, its precision, and its lively use of colloquial language make the Kralická Bible the acme of the literary production of its time. It has been partricularly influential—indeed incalculably so—on Czech poetry.

The defeat of the Protestant cause and with it the Czech nationalist cause at the Battle of White Mountain in 1620 ushered in a period of religious intolerance that forced many into exile. Jan Ámos Komenský (1592-1670), better known as Comenius, was representative of this Czech exile. A pioneer of modern educational methods and a lexicographer, he was also the author of many Protestant hymns and the last bishop of the Czech Brethren Church.

The greatest personality of the Catholic period was the Jesuit Bohuslav Balbín (1621-1688), whose historical and linguistic works as well as his poetry were written in Latin. A small group of Catholic Baroque poets wrote in Czech: Adam Michna z Otradovic (1600-1670), Felix Kadlinský (1613-1675), and—the most talented of the group—Bedřich Bridel (1619-1680).

Bridel illustrates the positive aspect of the cultural situation that developed after the defeat of the Protestant and nationalist causes. There was in this period a strong Spanish influence under the sign of the victorious Counter-Reformation. Bridel, like Balbín, was a Jesuit, and his work can serve as a good example of Baroque poetry. His transcendentalism and mysticism are evident in such works as "Verše o nebeském paláci" (1658; verses about the celestial palace). This was also the age of hymnbooks, and the same Jesuits were highly productive in offering the people rich collections of hymns, an enormously popular genre at the time.

Worth noting among the various types of literature of the time is Czech folk poetry, which was discovered by the literate Czech writers at the end of the seventeenth century and gradually became the object of a Romantic cult. Assiduously collected, published, propagated, and eventually imitated, the folktales and folk songs of the Czech people are among the most impressive cultural achievements of the Slavs and deserve to be studied in their own right. It is not an exaggeration to say that Czech Romanticism without Czech folk literature would be unthinkable, for the revivalists needed something to revive.

THE AGE OF REVIVAL (1774-1918)

Rather than a revolution from below, a fiat from above—in the form of an imperial edict on religious tolerance—stands at the beginning of the Czech national revival. The revival of Czech as a literary language was also given impetus by the pan-European fascination with folk culture which preceded the Romantic movement. In particular, Johann Gottfried Herder's collection of folk songs, *Volkslieder* (1778-1779), directly influenced, after a delay of several decades, such Czech folklorists as Václav Hanka and František Ladislav Čelakovský. Hanka could not withstand the temptation to provide Czechs with an ancient epic comparable to Ossian and so produced two forgeries of ancient epics. This basically Romantic impulse was rewarded, surprisingly, by an impressive result that played a positive role in firing the imagination of other revivalists.

The literary revival of Czech language was given further impetus by the nationalist reaction against the Germanizing tendency at the end of the eighteenth cen-

tury, but the movement directly responsible for bringing into play all the forces conducive to revival was the Enlightenment. The Enlightenment brought the Counter-Reformation to a decisive end, symbolized by the suppression of the Jesuit Order. Those active in the Enlightenment were also active in the nationalist, revivalist movement following the 1774 clash over the compulsory use of German in Czech schools—an edict that provoked massive resistance and heightened national consciousness.

As an overview of the entire revivalist period, Arne Novák's periodization seems particularly helpful: Enlightenment (1774-1815), Classicism (1815-1830), early Romanticism (1830-1848), and late Romanticism (1848-1859). (Novák omits the period from 1860 to World War I, for by 1860 the revival was an accomplished fact.) In the period of Enlightenment inaugurated by the reforms of Emperor Joseph II, the literary revival profited from historical and linguistic scholarship; notable is the work of the learned Jesuit Josef Dobrovský (1753-1829), whose *Geschichte der bömischen Sprache und Literatur* (1792; history of Czech language and literature) laid the foundation for such revivalists as Josef Jungmann and Pavol Jozef Šafárik.

The revival of Czech poetry began with the Puchmajer group of poets. Antonín Jaroslav Puchmajer (1769-1820), influenced by Dobrovský, published *Sebrání básní a zpěvů* (1795; collection of poems and songs), an anthology of poems by young Czech poets.

At a time when Romanticism had already conquered Western Europe, Czech poetry went through a brief phase of classicism, exemplified in poetry by Jungmann (1773-1847) and his poetic school. Jungmann translated widely from both classical and modern European literature; his translations from English, French, and German poetry had an enormous impact on young Czech poets, although this impact was largely limited to formal imitation of Jungmann's hexameters. Jungmann's school included scholars and poets such as the professional soldier Matěj Milota Zdirad Polák (1788-1856), the author of a rare and precious lyric poem in six cantos, *Vznešenost přírody* (1813; the nobility of nature). The greatest poet associated with Jungmann, eclipsing him as the personification of the Age of Revival, was Ján

Kollár (1793-1852), a Slovak writing in Czech and thus claimed, not unreasonably, by both nations as their national poet. His magnum opus is *Slávy dcera* (1824, 1832; the daughter of Sláva), organized into five cantos that situate the poem geographically and mythologically at the foci of five rivers: Elbe, Rhine, Moldau, Lethe, and Acheron. Following the form of the Petrarchan sonnet with trochaic meter, Kollár manages to be most inspiring when mourning the fate of the Lusatian or Sorbian Slavs' fate—those Western Slavs who, by Kollár's time, had been almost completely absorbed by Germany.

František Palacký (1798-1876) and—a Slovak—Pavol Jozef Šafárik (1795-1861) were two other outstanding figures in the national revival: Palacký mainly as a cultural and literary historian, Šafárik as a Slavist, the author of the first comparatist history of Slavic literatures, published in 1826.

Palacký, folklorist Čelakovský, and others were much impressed by Bernard Bolzano (1781-1848), a Prague thinker of Italian origin but a German patriot. Bolzano influenced Czech religious thought and poetry in the rationalist direction, and his influence explains in part the distinctive character of the late-blooming Czech Romantic movement.

Unlike Western European Romanticism, which began as a reaction against the rationalist sensibility of the Enlightenment, Czech Romanticism, hampered by the Hussite heritage as well as by the influence of Catholic thinkers like Bolzano, was of a decidedly rationalist orientation. Folklore, which played an important role in the Romantic movement throughout Europe, was particularly significant in Czech Romanticism. Many Czech Romantics began as collectors of folktales and folk songs, and their immersion in the folk tradition and the poetics of folk literature distinguishes them from the scholarly classicists, with their finely honed versifying and precision of poetic expression.

Karel Jaromír Erben (1811-1870) is known as the greatest poet of the ballad, a folk genre he enriched through his wide ethnographic experience. He was also an author who, aware of many native and foreign influences, was able to elevate a humble folk genre into a sophisticated vehicle of poetic expression. Of particular importance is the first part of his *Kytice z pověstí národních* (1853; a bouquet of folktales), containing twelve ballads that were immediately recognized as treasures of Czech poetry.

A contemporary of Erben, Karel Hynek Mácha (1810-1836) elevated Czech Romanticism to new heights. Within the Romantic period, widely regarded as the richest in the history of Czech poetry, Mácha reigns as the undisputed leader, largely on the strength of his poem *Máj* (1836; *May*, 1973), influenced as much by the native ballad as by his wide readings in Romantic literature: Lord Byron, Victor Hugo, Friedrich Schiller, Adam Mickiewicz. The poem is a mixture of lyric and epic built around two balladic motifs: the fate of a jealous murderer and the tragedy of a parricide who avenged the seduction of his beloved. Among Mácha's innovations were his fresh diction and imagery, his discovery of the iambic potential of the Czech language, and his novel combination of the philosophical reflection (often with nihilistic undertones) with a sensational plot (imperfectly developed) derived from tragic ballads. Uniformly rejected on its publication by established critics, *May* was passionately accepted by the young generation, who turned it into a sort of manifesto and even founded a literary journal, *Máj*, named after it. Mácha's masterpiece is still considered to be the greatest single Czech poem. After Mácha's death, pilgrimages to his grave were organized, and an entire cult of Mácha developed. Few Czech poets of subsequent generations (a notable exception is Jan Neruda) escaped Mácha's influence.

In the 1850's a transitional period, poets gave way to translators and popularizers, with a few notable exceptions: the belated publication of Erben's *Kytice z pověsti národních*, Božena Němcová's lyric novel *Babička* (1855; granny), and the satiric poetry of Karel Havlíček Borovský (1821-1856). Havlíček's poetry was a harbinger of the new, rationalist, critical age to come, paralleled on the ideological level by the switch from individualism to the collectivizing faith of socialism. Still, other movements were also present on the scene; such was the Mladá Čechie (Young Bohemia) movement, vaguely fashioned after the Young Germany movement, and the tendency to take into account more fully the works of foreign literatures and thus move away from the narrow, Slav-centered direction of the older revivalists.

Havlíček represents another awakening as well: Starting from the premise, so dear to the older revivalists, of the liberating potential of Russia, he became disenchanted after visiting Russia and bitterly opposed Russophilism in Bohemia. His great satire of sacred and profane absolutism, though unfinished, sounded a new note in Czech satiric poetry, particularly in *Křest svatého Vladimíra* (1876; the baptism of Saint Vadimir). Feuerbachian materialism and virulence reminiscent of the satiric polemics of the Hussite age join in this low burlesque based on the grotesque treatment of the legendary beginnings of Russia. The poem is a literary equivalent of Gustav Doré's *Histoire pittoresque, dramatique, et caricaturale de la Sainte Russie* (1854; *The Rare and Extraordinary History of Holy Russia*, 1971), though arguably less comical than the latter. Havlíček also excelled in the genre of epigram and was a journalist of genius, all of which is clearly reflected in his poetry.

Havlíček's acidic satire marked the end of the Romantic and revivalist period proper—which came to a close in 1860 when an imperial edict proclaimed constitutional liberties guaranteeing the Czechs the national freedoms (without the full national independence that was to come in 1918) for which the earlier revivalists fought so long and hard. Thus, the foreign tendencies—not merely literary influences—that appeared in literary movements as a full-fledged cosmopolitan orientation began to compete seriously with the narrower nationalist pan-Slav orientation that had characterized the revivalists. This development coincided with the rise of realistic convention in European literature and with the availability in Bohemia of a rapidly growing and increasingly sophisticated readership. The problem of "catching up with the rest of Europe" suddenly became more pressing than the problem of preserving and strengthening the national identity. Of the latter, there were fewer doubts after 1860, and Czech poets began to look around more inquisitively.

The distinct national and cosmopolitan movements had their own literary journals: *Máj*, the tribune of the nationalistic and Romantic movements, and *Lumír*, the forum of the more cosmopolitan but also tendentiously realistic movement. *Máj*, however, was not neglectful of foreign literature, and if it idolized first of all Mácha, Erben, and Havlíček, one should note that these three writers exemplified three quite different literary tendencies: a diversity challenging such simplifications as the national-cosmopolitan division. Thus, a "cosmopolitan" author, Jan Neruda (1834-1891), published in *Máj*, though he was a *Lumír* author par excellence. His *Hřbitovní kvítí* (1857; graveyard flowers), distinguished by its social motifs, its critique of hypocrisy, and its irony and skepticism reminiscent of the late verse of Heinrich Heine; his ballads after Erben; and his *Písně kosmické* (1878; cosmic songs), full of positivist zeal, all led to his final collection, *Zpěvy pátecní* (1896; Friday hymns), an amalgam of messianic and religious-patriotic hymns celebrating the future national victory in a manner found in Polish messianic poetry. The tortuous development of Neruda's poetry gives an indication of the complexity of this literary period.

Neruda's complex development can be contrasted with the career of his friend, the lyric poet Adolf Heyduk (1835-1923), a member of the *Máj* circle. Heyduk produced poetry that is remarkably even, influenced by Erben and by Slovak culture, which Heyduk grew to love and promoted among fellow Czechs. His forte was the intimate lyric, exemplified in *Cigánské melodie* (1859; Gypsy melodies), though his Slovakophile *Cymbal a husle* (1876; cymbalo and violin) complements Kollár's *Slávy dcera*.

The contrast of Neruda and Heyduk was repeated in the next period by the contrasting pair of Jaroslav Vrchlický (1853-1912) and Svatopluk Čech (1846-1908). The latter has been called the last revivalist poet, influenced by Mácha, Mickiewicz, Aleksandr Pushkin, and Byron, as were many revivalist poets before him. Čech's tendentious, nationalistic work often suffers from an artificial, academic, heavily periphrastic style. Thus, his ideological importance in Czech poetry outweighs his artistic contribution. Indeed, this late revivalist was not a match for Vrchlický in any sense other than a narrowly partisan one: Vrchlický was a giant and Čech his contemporary.

In his enormous output, erudition, awesome scope, and fundamental importance for subsequent Czech poetry, Vrchlický has no rivals. His output alone dwarfs that of an entire poetic generation, including some eighty-odd volumes of original poetry, drama, and prose and an incredibly rich treasure chest of translations that in turn dwarfs his original work. It would be easier to list the names of those world authors whom he failed to translate than to enumerate those whom he rendered into Czech. Above all, Vrchlický preferred Italian literature, from which he translated Dante, Petrarch, Torquato Tasso, Ludovico Ariosto, and many others. From French, he translated Victor Hugo, Charles Baudelaire, Pierre Corneille, Molière, and Edmond Rostand; from English, an anthology ranging from James Thomson to Alfred, Lord Tennyson, as well as Percy Bysshe Shelley, Edgar Allan Poe, Walt Whitman, and William Shakespeare's *Sonnets*; from German, Johann Wolfgang von Goethe, Schiller, and so on. Then there are the odds and ends: Henrik Ibsen, Mickiewicz, János Arany, Sándor Petőfi, Hafiz, and the Chinese *Shi Jing* (c. 600 B.C.E.; book of odes). In addition, Vrchlický did a number of prose translations. Vrchlický was a cosmopolitan figure of world stature whose literary orientation was a matter of daily practice and a practical vocation: He was a professor of comparative literature in Prague. The range of Vrchlický's translations suggests what was and was not available to the Czech reader before his time and gives a clear indication of the increasing cosmopolitanism of Czech literature. Vrchlický's immersion in foreign literature as well as in foreign life (he lived in Italy for a year and traveled widely in Western and Northern Europe) made him a figure without precedent in Czech poetry.

Vrchlický (like Mácha before him) inspired a poetic school and a new generation of translators whose appetites Vrchlický had whetted. At the same time, poets such as Josef Svatopluk Machar (1864-1952) went in another direction entirely, following the realistic orientation of Havlíček and Neruda. Machar, in his attempt to follow Neruda, pushed Czech poetic diction closer to prose by purposely making it dissonant and ugly. Machar's poetry of social protest was echoed by a regional poet Petr Bezrucč (1867-1958), the author of *Slezské písně* (1903; Silesian songs).

In turn, a reaction against this poetry of social protest was initiated by a group of poets known as Katolická Moderna (modern Catholic movement), the most important of whom were Antonín Sova (1864-1928) and Otokar Březina (1868-1929). This group eclipsed, by both their artistic strength and their numbers, the movement of social protest.

Sova was an anti-Parnassian and thus was at odds with the Vrchlický school as well as with the school of social protest. A strong individualist, he crafted intimate lyrics, rejecting social values. With Březina, Czech poetry gained a fresh and original voice worthy of the fine tradition of Czech Catholic verse. Religious poets in today's Bohemia still find Březina refreshing and profound, for he is a poet of mystery, a reflective poet whose verse reveals his study of ancient and modern philosophy. In some literary histories, both Sova and Březina are mentioned in connection with the Symbolist movement, an identification made tenuous by the fact that in Bohemia, Symbolism appeared simultaneously with realism, metaphysical Romanticism, and other movements.

By the end of the nineteenth century, the Czech literary situation was complicated by a proliferation of movements under the general heading of modernism. The age of manifestos began in 1895 with the proclamation of the *Manifest ceské moderny*. This was the era of the decadents, such as Jirí Karásek ze Lvovic (1871-1951), Hlaváček, and later, Otakar Theer (1880-1917): a period characterized by the glorification of death and of free love; by Satanism, irony, and nihilism; by the so-called Illusionist Baroque of Hlaváček and the tragic metaphysical vision of Theer's sensuous lyrics. Here, at the beginning of the modern age, one can find the origin of a basic division that has continued to plague twentieth century poetry: modernism versus social protest.

THE MODERN PERIOD

The year 1918 saw revolutionary changes: The Czechoslovak Republik was established after generations of poets and patriots had spent centuries hoping, dreaming, and writing about the day of independence. When independence finally came, however, euphoria was mixed with deep shame and despair following the moral disaster of World War I, which ushered in modernity in a way that few had expected. If anything, the fact of independence intensified many social problems, for there was no more national oppression to be used as a scapegoat. These social problems paled, however, when compared to the huge human losses that came twenty years later, following the debacle of the Munich Treaty of 1938 and subsequent occupation of Bohemia and

Moravia by the Nazis in 1939. Czechoslovakia was re-established in 1945, but in 1948 the communists took over and ruled until the collapse of communism in Europe in 1989. The democracy was reestablished. By 1993, the Czech and Slovak Federation broke up in an amicable divorce brokered by the political elite motivated by economic (Czech) and nationalist (Slovak) reasons. Since January 1, 1993, there have been separate Czech and Slovak republics. At the beginning of the new millennium, the Czech Republic, having joined the North Atlantic Treaty Organizaion, was poised to join the European Community, of which it had been a firm member already during its Golden Age, some six hundred years before.

During the twentieth century, for some poets, a red star was beckoning from Moscow, offering promises that were never fulfilled. For others, indeed for most, a far more attractive symbol was the Eiffel Tower: Paris, its poets and its avant-garde. Finally, the Catholic Church and the rich tradition of Czech religious verse nourished another line of poets. The various movements of modern Czech poetry can largely be located with reference to these three trends.

The movements themselves can be briefly enumerated: the Proletarian movement, Poetism, Surrealism, and Socialist Realism. The last was a caricature of the original Proletarian phase, consisting of already forgotten "courtly" poetry (in honor of Joseph Stalin) and poetry about socialist construction, in which tractors, foundries, and mines, together with collective farms, were amply featured. As for Poetism and Surrealism, both were avant-garde movements of French origin. Poetism attracted a wider group of Czech poets than did its more widely known counterpart. By 1934, when the Surrealist movement reached the Czechs, the situation in poetry was highly polarized, politically and ideologically, and only a few of the Poetists became Surrealists. With Socialist Realism, matters were simpler still: Whatever was published was, by definition, Socialist Realist poetry, because during this reign of Stalinist dogma, only such poetry was deemed acceptable. Thus, poets had to acquire the new way of writing or be imprisoned or worse, unless they chose to remain silent.

It is a different story when one considers individual poets. Here a neatly schematic approach is inadequate,

for a single poet may be associated with diverse and even contradictory movements. Stanislav Kostka Neumann (1875-1947), for example, spanned the spectrum from the Satanism of his decadent youth to anarchism, Naturalism, and on to Marxism, ending his life as a model Socialist Realist.

A more talented poet, Jiří Wolker (1900-1924), began his career with *Host do domu* (1921; a guest in the house), wherein he reflected on the miracle of existence, on the harmony of life in which the numinous penetrates the objects of everyday reality. Soon, however, he joined the Proletarian poets grouped around the communist literary journal *Devětsil*. His next collection, *Těžká hodína* (1922; difficult hour), became a classic of Proletarian poetry, although it eschews the superficial contempt for tradition which the Proletarians shared with the avant-garde, harking back as it does to the ballads of Erben. A more interesting, if not more talented, member of *Devětsil* was František Halas (1901-1949), whose pro-worker sympathy is belied by his meditative, complex poetry collected in *Tvář* (1931; face), *Dokořán* (1936; wide open), and *A co?* (1957; so what?).

Instead of social commitment and collective spirit, the Poetists offered unbridled individualism and irresponsibility. This disdain of convention was personified in Vítězslav Nezval (1900-1958), whose individuality was apparent in his first collection. *Most* (1922; *Bridge*), and particularly in *Podivuhodný kouzelník* (1922; *The Amazing Magician*). By 1930, the macabre and the graveyard atmosphere—all the rage in Czech poetry at the time—claimed him in *Poems of the Night*, which anticipated the advent of Surrealism in Czechoslovakia. Between 1934 and 1938, when the Surrealist movement in Czechoslovakia was dissolved (though continuing in Slovakia during the war with much success), Nezval published *Žena v množném čísle* (1936; woman in the plural), *Praha s prsty deště* (1936; Prague with fingers of rain), and *Absolutní hrobař* (1937; a total gravedigger). After the war, and some forgettable collections of Socialist Realist poetry, Nezval returned with a modest volume of patriotic poems in the old style, *Z domoviny* (1951; from my homeland), subdued, without a trace of his Surrealist sparkle.

When Wolker was idolized after his untimely death, Jaroslav Seifert (1901-1986) coined the slogan "Down with Wolker"; in his view, Wolker's ballads were radically unsuited to the demands of the new age. In Seifert's *Sama láska* (1923; love alone), traditional art is dead (including the ballad), and love and revolution meet. Seifert's *Na vlnách TSF* (1925; on the radio waves) is completely Poetist, but by 1933, he had broken with Poetism and the morbid death poetry of the period with his *Jablko z klína* (an apple from the lap). Seifert rejected social commitment as well as the iconoclasm of Poetism, devoting himself to the ideal of good art in the traditional sense, as in *Sbohem a šáteček* (1934; farewell and a handkerchief), where there are no avant-garde tricks, no morbidity, no conflict. The strongest feature of Seifert's poetry becomes his very personal lyric voice, and nowhere in his thirty collections is it as poignant as in his *Morový sloup* (1971,1977; the plague column), great poetry based on mature reflection against the stark background of his country's tragic history. In 1984, Seifert was the first Czech author awarded the Nobel Prize in Literature.

Vladimír Holan (1905-1980) would have amply deserved that prize, but he was a unique and controversial figure, towering with his talent above the discordant fray of Czech poetry. Movements were not to his liking, and after 1945 he refused to have anything to do with his epoch, isolating himself as if in solidarity with those who, like the fine poet Jan Záhradníček (1905-1960) the author of the apocalyptic *La Saletta* (1947), were imprisoned by the authorities. Holan's great poetry is meditative, prosodically demanding, and complex; his mastery was evident as early as in *Triumf smrti* (1926; triumph of death), and he continued to work at a high level in *Vanutí* (1932; breezing) and *Oblouk* (1934; the arch). His *Panychida* (1946; vigil) treats in a prophetic manner the monsters of "Satanocracy" and "Titanomania," while his *Noc s Hamletem* (1964; night with Hamlet) is widely translated and increasingly seen as a masterpiece of European, if not world, literature.

The following generation produced a trio of significant poets: Jan Skácel (born 1922), Miroslav Holub (1923-1998), and Karel Šiktanc (born 1928). Of interest are Skácel's collection *Hodina mezi psem a vlkem* (1962; the hour between the dog and the wolf), Holub's *Achilles a zelva* (1960; Achilles and the turtle), and

Šiktanc's *Slepá láska* (1968; blind love). Catholic poets such as Zahradníček and the older Jakub Deml (1878-1961) reentered the Czech literary consciousness in the 1990's after a long period of neglect and suppression during communism. This holds true as well for Václav Renc (1911-1973), Zdenek Rotrekl (born 1920), and Josef Palivec (1886-1975).

Poetry by women, who became more visible in the 1980's, made a strong contribution. The work of Marcela Chmarová, Marta Gärtnerová (born 1948), and Marta Chytilová should be mentioned. The exile, not always a good place for poets, nevertheless enabled publication of such poets as Jirí Gruša and Ivan Diviš (born 1924). It also helped popularize authors of protest songs, forbidden at home during the communist rule, such as Karel Kryl (1944-1994), Jaroslav Hutka (born 1947), and Svatopluk Karásek (born 1942).

BIBLIOGRAPHY

Cejka, Jaroslav, Michael Cernik, and Karel Sys. *The New Czech Poetry*. Chester Springs, Pa.: Dufour Editions, 1992. The works of these three poets from the generation after Holub, all born during the 1940's.

French, Alfred. *The Poets of Prague: Czech Poetry Between the Wars*. New York: Oxford University Press, 1969. Historical and critical overview. Illustrations, bibliography.

_____, ed. *Anthology of Czech Poetry*. Introduced by René Wellek. Ann Arbor: Czechoslovak Society of Arts and Sciences in America, 1973. Translations into English with original Czech text. Illustrated.

_____, ed. *The Czech Avantgardists*. Rockville, Md.: Kabel Publishers, [1994?]. English translations of late twentieth century avant-garde Czech poets. Includes illustrations.

Novák, Arne. *Czech Literature*. Translated by Peter Kussi. Ann Arbor: Michigan Slavic Publications, 1976. A rare English-language history. Includes a bibliography and an index.

Pynsent, Robert. *Czech Prose and Verse*: A Selection with an Introductory Essay. 1979. Atlantic Highlands, N.J.: Humanities Press, 1979. Czech text with an English introduction. Index.

Peter Petro

EAST GERMAN POETRY

DEFINITION AND GENERAL CONSIDERATIONS

Any study of the literature of the German Democratic Republic (GDR) must tackle the problem of definition. What, exactly, is East German poetry? The question may appear trivial and the answer self-evident: This term is intended to apply to the verse literature produced in the German Democratic Republic, the socialist state that came into being on October 7, 1949, and that ceased to exist on October 3, 1990, when its member states joined the Federal Republic of Germany (FRG). Such a facile definition, however, is inadequate. To begin with, it fails to comprehend the literature produced between 1945 and 1949 in what was then the Soviet Occupation Zone of Germany. Another problem relates to residency and publishing conditions. Does the definition include writers who were expelled from the country, such as Wolf Biermann; who voluntarily left it permanently, such as Peter Huchel, Reiner Kunze, and Sarah Kirsch; who were granted long-term visas enabling them to take up residency in the West, such as Günter Kunert; or who had written their works in East Germany but could get them into print only in the FRG, as was the case with Biermann?

For the purpose of this essay, then, East German poetry will be defined very broadly as the poetry written (although not necessarily published) from April, 1945, to September, 1990, in the territory that once constituted the German Democratic Republic. This definition excludes works by writers such as Bertolt Brecht and Johannes R. Becher which were produced before the authors settled in East Germany and those written by poets such as Kunze and Thomas Brasch after their departure from the GDR.

Another important preliminary question to be addressed is whether the literatures of East and West Germany did indeed represent two separate and essentially dissimilar literatures or whether they formed one body of writing, exhibiting only superficial differences as the result of external conditions. No agreement exists on this matter. The official East German position, formulated in 1956 by Walter Ulbricht, then first secretary of the ruling Socialist Unity Party of Germany (Sozia-listische Einheitspartei Deutschlands, SED), was that there are two German states with two different cultures. That had not always been the East German view. When the first all-German convention of writers gathered in Berlin in 1947, the lyric poet Johannes R. Becher, who was to serve as the country's minister of culture from 1954 to his death in 1958, condemned attempts to bring about confrontations between the East and the West and to play off the Germans in the different occupation zones against one another. Becher declared emphatically:

> Thus, there is no West German or East German literature in this sense, neither a South German nor a North German one, but only a single one, a German one which does not allow itself to be hemmed in by the boundaries of occupation zones.

From a different vantage point, the East German novelist and dramatist Rolf Schneider, who was granted a long-term visa in 1979 and thereafter resided in the West, gave a similar assessment, although he phrased it much more polemically: "There is only one German literature, that of West Germany. Some of its authors are living in the GDR."

On the other hand, Fritz J. Raddatz, who had also chosen to move to the Federal Republic, started his 1972 book on East German literature with the flat statement: "There are two German literatures." As he explained, the political division of the country had so strongly affected what used to be the common language of the two German states that it was no longer possible to consider the literatures based on those differing modes of communication as one and the same. The present study, while not completely agreeing with Raddatz's premise, is also based on the conviction that the literature of East Germany, largely as the result of political and social factors, constituted an entity that developed separately and was relatively independent of trends and developments in the nonsocialist world, including the FRG. Obviously, East German poetry did not evolve in a vacuum, yet on the whole, the differences between the literatures of the two Germanies appeared more pronounced than those between contemporary works written in West Germany and in Austria or Switzerland. It is interesting that the Soviet critic Lev Kopelev (who was stripped of his Soviet citizenship in 1981 and later resided in Western Germany) maintained in 1965 that there were *three* German literatures: one characteristic of the GDR, one typical of the FRG, and a third one that, by reason of generality of theme and interest (and of artistic quality), transcended any political division.

PHASE OF DEVELOPMENT IN LITERATURE
AND SOCIETY

The Marxist position that all literature ought to be viewed in its economic, social, and political context may be debatable, but it is impossible to assess the work of the poets of a socialist society such as the GDR without regard to the environment in which they live. The SED and its cultural policies had an immediate impact on all creative writing, and the East German poets' attitude toward their audience often differed from that of their Western counterparts. While German literature has always had a strong didactic bent, East German novelists and dramatists, and also lyrical poets, have followed Brecht's example in defining their function as that of educators of the nation to a much greater extent than have writers in the West.

East German poetry, then, should be seen in direct relation to the evolution of a socialist ideology in the GDR. Several successive phases of this evolution can be distinguished. The years from 1945 to 1949 represent the period of building, of laying the foundation for a "socialist national literature." It was important to understand what had happened during the period when Adolf Hitler was chancellor and what had paved the way for the National Socialist movement. A new ideology had to be firmly anchored in the minds of the people. Thus, "anti-Fascist and democratic renewal" was the political as well as the cultural goal. With the formal establishment of the GDR, this first—and largely preparatory—phase was completed.

From 1949 to the early 1960's, the concept of a "socialist national literature" within an autonomous socialist state crystallized. In part, literature served to rally the people behind the effort to build a strong economy, although poetry played a less important role in this effort

than did the other genres. In the light of this declared goal of literature, the 1959 writers' conference in the industrial town of Bitterfeld was an important attempt to forge a strong alliance between authors and workers. The "Bitterfeld movement" encouraged industrial and agricultural workers to become writers, and urged writers to gain direct experience in factories and collective farms. Socialist Realism was seen as the most appropriate stylistic approach, and Soviet literature provided models.

While the overall goals to be attained were fairly clear, this period was by no means one of consistent and planned cultural development. Like all the countries in the communist bloc, East Germany was affected by Joseph Stalin's death in 1953 and the subsequent official denunciation of the "personality cult." In the summer of 1953, widespread expressions of dissatisfaction with economic and social conditions led to unrest, labeled an "attempted Fascist putsch" by the SED. The Twentieth Congress of the Soviet Communist Party of February, 1956, and the discussions at the Fourth Writers' Congress in Berlin a month earlier seemed to signal a more flexible cultural policy. This "thaw" came to an end, however, with the October, 1956, uprising in Hungary. The construction of the Berlin Wall on August 13, 1961, and which was not breached until November 9, 1990, marked the conclusion of the phase of developing and protecting the new socialist state.

"Literature within a developed socialist society" is the label frequently attached to the works of authors since the early 1960's. This period has been characterized by growing self-confidence on the part of the government and by decreasing popular interest in a reunification of Germany. By the end of 1962, the lyric poet Peter Huchel had been replaced as the editor of the highly respected and influential journal *Sinn und Form*. He and many intellectuals in both German states had considered it one of the last cultural bridges between East and West. Under Huchel's successors, the character of this publication changed drastically, and any potential West German influence was eliminated. The Second Bitterfeld Conference in April, 1964, was unable to repeat the impact of the Bitterfeld movement of five years earlier, although the phenomenon of the "writing worker" was still a factor in contemporary East German literature.

The Eighth Convention of the SED, in the summer of 1971, marked the beginning of a period of cultural liberalization. A few months later, Erich Honecker, first secretary of the Party's Central Committee, made clear that the restrictions imposed by the doctrine of Socialist Realism had at least been eased: "As far as I am concerned, no taboos can exist in the realm of art and literature, provided that one proceeds from the firm postion of Socialism." He emphasized that he was referring both to the choice of topics and to artistic style. That "firm position of Socialism," however, was by no means clearly defined, and it was the Party that determined the extent to which an author might have strayed from that basis. In November, 1976, Wolf Biermann, who had moved to East Germany from Hamburg in 1953, was considered to have gone too far in his satiric poems and songs. He was allowed to leave the country for a concert in West Germany but was then denied permission to return and stripped of his East German citizenship. This action provoked strong protests from many of his fellow writers, prompting, in turn, official reprisals.

In June, 1979, Honecker repeated his 1971 statement about taboos having no place in literature, but he added a warning:

> However, what matters most is to know where one stands in the political struggles of our times. . . . The position between the fronts of the warring classes has always been the losers' position, a position that is as hopeless as it is ignominious, opposing the interests of the people who are the true patrons of the arts.

In the 1980's, official repression coincided with the government's willingness to let oppositional poets emmigrate to West Germany, often under cover of long-term visas to the West. Other poets managed to have their poems published in the West and smuggled back into East Germany. As popular unrest grew against the socialist government, many poets who had remained in the East took part in the mass demonstrations which finally persuaded the authorities to open East Germany's borders on November 9, 1989, and permit free elections which swept them from power and led to the demise of the GDR in October, 1990.

THE GENERATIONS OF EAST GERMAN POETS

One problem with generalizations about trends in East German poetry—apart from the implied disregard for the writers' individuality—was the coexistence of several different generations of poets, with each age-group representing different experiences and conceptions.

When the Nazi regime collapsed at the end of World War II, a number of outstanding writers returned to Germany from their wartime exile in the United States, in Mexico, in the Soviet Union, and elsewhere. Many of them had been supporters of communist ideology before Hitler came to power, and they saw a chance to help create a new society that would reflect their political philosophy. The role of these writers in the development of a "socialist national literature" is important. In West Germany, the year 1945 was considered "point zero," a new beginning after the near-total destruction of the country and much of its culture. East German writers and ideological leaders, on the other hand, emphasized the importance of the inheritance of progressive trends in bourgeois literature since the turn of the century and, even more significant, of a socialist tradition in German culture. Wolfgang Joho stated that position most clearly when he titled his 1965 article in the journal *Neue Deutsche Literatur* (new German literature), "We Did Not Begin in the Year Zero."

Thus, Brecht, Anna Seghers, Arnold Zweig, and a number of other writers provided an important link between positive aspects of the past and the hoped-for better future. Best known among these poets of the "first generation" were Erich Weinert (1890-1953), Johannes R. Becher (1891-1958), Bertolt Brecht (1898-1956), Peter Huchel (1903-1981), Erich Arendt (1903-1984), René Schwachhofer (1904-1970), Georg Maurer (1907-1971), Louis Fürnberg (1909-1957), and Max Zimmering (1909-1973).

For most of the writers of the "second generation," the Nazi period and World War II had been a traumatic experience. Some had left Germany at an early age, others had fought in the war, and several had spent time as prisoners of war in the Soviet Union, where they had been exposed to a new ideology. Franz Fühmann's autobiographical novel *Das Judenauto* (1962; the Jews' car) is perhaps the best document of the inner changes that these authors experienced. Characteristic of this group is the attempt to look both to the past and into the future. In prose narratives and dramas, but also in poetry, they attempted to come to terms with what had happened in the period of the Third Reich. At the same time, those who had lived through such dark years believed that the future held great promise, and many of their poems reflect this faith. Prominent among these writers, many of whom are still active, were Kuba (Kurt Barthel, 1914-1967), who had gone into exile when he was nineteen; Stephan Hermlin (1915-1997), who had left Germany in 1936; Johannes Bobrowski (1917-1965); Hanns Cibulka (born 1920); Franz Fühmann (1922-1984); Paul Wiens (1922-1982), who had emigrated with his parents in 1933; Günther Deicke (born 1922); Walter Werner (born 1922); and Helmut Preissler (born 1925).

The "third generation" is made up of East German poets who were between ten and twenty years old when Hitler's Reich ended. These writers came to maturity in a socialist society, and the war, which played a large role in the thinking of those only a few years older, was not as much of a decisive experience for most of them. They were diligent students, though by no means mere imitators, of the poets who had already established a reputation. Their works frequently praised the society in which they lived, combining personal expression with an affirmation of the socialist system. On the other hand, a significant number of writers from this group eventually chose to live in the West.

Well-known representatives of this generation are Christa Reinig (born 1926), Werner Lindemann (born 1926), Uwe Berger (born 1928), Günter Kunert (born 1929), Eva Strittmatter (born 1930), Heinz Kahlau (born 1931), Reiner Kunze (born 1933), Uwe Gressmann (1933-1969), Wulf Kirsten (born 1934), Rainer Kirsch (born 1934), Sarah Kirsch (born 1935, for several years Rainer Kirsch's wife), Karl Mickel (born 1935), Helga M. Novak (born 1935), and Heinz Czechowski (born 1935). Reinig, Kunert, Kunze, Sarah Kirsch, and Novak all eventually moved to the West before the end of the GDR. Adolf Endler (born 1930) belongs to the same age group, although his background is different; he moved from West Germany to the GDR in 1955.

Often the authors of the "fourth generation," those who were not yet ten years old at the end of the war or who were born after it, are not considered a separate group because much of their work is similar in character to that of the writers who are slightly older. Yet these writers, unlike their near-contemporaries, never knew a society other than the socialist German state, and that fact alone sets them apart. Furthermore, many of them were instrumental in bringing about what critics like to call the "new wave of lyrical poetry" of the early 1960's, a period marked by experimentation and an increased emphasis on personal modes of expression. A landmark poetry reading in December, 1962, at the Academy of Arts, organized by Stephan Hermlin and featuring among other young poets Sarah Kirsch, Volker Braun, and Wolf Biermann, focused attention on these attempts. Some politicians strongly objected to the "fear of life, nihilism, and skepticism" of these poets and condemned the "excessive individualism, ambiguity, and symbolism" exhibited in their works as essentially non-Marxist. With the 1966 discussion on the meaning and purpose of poetry in the journal *Forum*, in which Party leaders and established critics eventually specified these objections, the new wave had come to an end.

Well known or very important among this last generation of GDR poets—although certainly not in every case representative of the new wave—are Biermann (born 1936), Jochen Laabs (born 1937), Peter Gosse (born 1938), Kito Lorenc (born 1938), Braun (born 1939), Harald Gerlach (born 1940), Andreas Reimann (born 1946), Kristian Pech (born 1946), and Gabriele Eckart (born 1954). Biermann, as mentioned above, lived in West Germany after 1976, although he continued to consider the GDR his real home. Eckhart belongs to those poets who were allowed to leave for the West in the 1980's. Lorenc holds a unique position within this group; he writes poetry both in German and in Sorbian (or Wendish), the West Slavic language of a small ethnic minority in the GDR that received special attention and encouragement from the government after 1945.

From the mid-1980's toward the end of the socialist regime, a group of young, urban poets, many of whom lived in the hip, working-class district Prenzlauer Berg of East Berlin, established a poetic "underground." Utilizing a loophole in state censorship, which required publication permits if only one hundred or more copies were printed, the poets published their verses in magazines and folders of just five to ninety-nine copies. These mini-collections, which were often widely shared among readers, quickly became known by their Soviet name, samizdat (meaning self-publication). Among these young, oppositional poets, Elke Erb (born 1939), an accomplished poet herself, guided the work of writers like Uwe Kolbe (born 1957), who left the GDR in 1987, shortly before its demise. Among the exiles like Kolbe was another underground poet, Sascha Anderson, (born 1953) who later was revealed to have worked as an informer for the "Stasi" (East Germany's secret police). While the government barely tolerated and, as Anderson's case proves, tried to infiltrate the community of underground poets, their impact and influence grew as that of the regime faltered. When Andreas Hegewald wrote of "frozen mummies" in his poetry, his readers caught the reference to the GDR's superannuated leadership. Soon, the "mummies" were gone, and the samizdat magazines, which bore titles like *Anschlag* (assault), *Ariadnefaden* (Ariadne's tread), or *Grenzfall* (border case), became prized collectors' items.

THEMES OF EAST GERMAN POETRY

Any comparison between East German poetry and that produced by authors in the FRG tends to be an oversimplification. All works of literature are statements by individuals, reflecting their personal temperaments, insights, and experiences. Yet all the writers under discussion lived and created poetry within a socialist society. Some broad generalizations may be warranted in view of that fact. Certain trends in East Germany did not appear to have parallels in the West.

Perhaps the most obvious difference between East German and West German poetry was the choice of explicitly political themes by some East German writers. Poems praising the Party and glorifying great leaders of the socialist movement, both dead and living, have no equivalents in West German literature. It should be pointed out, however, that such paeans became rare after the 1950's and that they are not representative of more modern East German poetry, either in quality or—contrary to the impression created by certain one-sided anthologies—in quantity.

In line with the clearly perceived goals of creating a new political consciousness after the Third Reich had

collapsed and of pointing to new role models that would symbolize the ideals of socialism, the authors of the First Generation and those beginning to write in 1945 and shortly thereafter produced a large amount of poetry that can be classified only as political propaganda. (It may be worth noting here that the term "propaganda" had essentially positive connotations in the East German vocabulary.) Their poems related important events in the history of socialism or praised the accomplishments of workers devoted to the welfare of the masses. Brecht's long narrative poem of 1950, "Die Erziehung der Hirse" ("The Education of Millet"), could serve as an example. It describes the developments leading to Soviet grain production sufficient to feed the Red Army during its defense of the homeland. Max Zimmering's "Die grosse Kraft" (the great power) celebrated the ambitious "Stalin Plan" to irrigate large areas of Siberia and to generate electric power by controlling and rerouting Russian rivers. A revival of this type of literature occurred in connection with the successful launching of the first Soviet Earth satellite. Typical of the flood of "Sputnik poetry" is Becher's "Planetarisches Manifest" (planetary manifesto), which hails the technical achievement of the Sputnik—the first artificial satellite placed in orbit around Earth—as the culmination of the revolutionary development that had started in Russia in 1917.

Other works glorify the heroes of socialism. Brecht, Becher, and many others related in their poems the sufferings and the unbroken spirit of Resistance fighters against the Third Reich during World War II. Martyrs for the communist cause, such as Rosa Luxemburg and Karl Liebknecht, who were murdered by right-wing army officers in 1919, or Ernst Thälmann, who died in a Nazi concentration camp in 1944, were the topics of poems by Brecht, Becher, Bobrowski, Weinert, and other writers. Some of the poetry in praise of great communist leaders consciously evoked religious associations. Becher lauded Vladimir Ilich Lenin as the man who "touched the sleep of the world/ With words that became bread," and Kuba's "Kantate auf Stalin" ("Stalin Cantata") said about the Soviet leader: "The book in his hands, his eyes fixed on it,/ he stood against a world full of evil./ Upright he ascended the via dolorosa/ filled with compassion, with wrath, and with love." Stalin's death signified the demise of this type of poetry, which then largely disappeared from later East German anthologies. It is difficult to read such poems today without a sense of embarrassment, and one has to agree with the insight of Hans Magnus Enzensberger's important essay on poetry and politics that "authority, stripped of its mythical cloak, can no longer be reconciled with poetry."

When workers rebelled against increased work quotas on June 17, 1953, and the ensuing uprising had to be quelled by Soviet tanks to rescue the East German government, Brecht wrote "Die Lösung" (1953; "The Solution"), one of his few critical poems challenging the socialist government which had welcomed him with wide open arms. Brecht's angry poem quotes the official statement of the Secretary of the Writers Union that the people have lost the confidence of their government and can win back this confidence only through twice the work effort. With an irony worthy of Jonathan Swift, the poem proposes the following solution:

> Would it not be
> easier if the government
> dissolved the people and
> elected a new one?

In a similar vein, the young worker-poet Volker Braun wrote in 1956, "Oh Lord, create space in my congested chest!" a clear cry for more political freedoms. Since the mid-1960's, fewer and fewer poems of a blatantly propagandistic, political nature have been published in the GDR. This does not mean, however, that political philosophy no longer has a significant impact. Characteristically, Sarah Kirsch said in connection with her 1973 collection *Zaubersprüche* (magic spells), which contains mainly love poems, "If I had no political interests, I could not write any verse." To many authors, socialism was an established and accepted fact in their society and in their lives, and it was no longer necessary to sing its praise or to educate the public about it.

Political poetry that criticizes and accuses could be found, too, but it was understandably not very common in an open forum, unless such criticism was veiled, published privately, or clearly directed against conditions and phenomena in capitalist society. Biermann's 1963 "Ballade von dem Briefträger William L. Moore" ("Ballad of the Letter-Carrier William L. Moore"), about the murder of a civil rights demonstrator in the United States, was made available to a wide audience. His satiric poems about shortcomings in GDR society, about pettiness and doctrinaire rigidity among Party functionaries, could be published only in the West. There, the poems were welcomed as ammunition in the propaganda war against the East, although the author had intended them as contributions toward the improvement of socialist society. The state he had chosen, however, saw his writings as attacks on the foundations of Marxism-Leninism and would not tolerate lines such as the following from his 1962 "Rücksichtslose Schimpferei" ("Reckless Abuse"):

> I am the individual
> the collective has
> isolated itself from me
> Don't stare at me with such understanding!
> Oh, I know
> You are waiting with serious assuredness
> for me to float
> into your net of self-criticism.

The partisan interpretation of Biermann's poetry in the FRG points to a serious problem in the Western response to GDR literature. Western observers tended to read a rejection of socialism into many poems that actually convey no such message. It may be legitimate to see the five-line poem by Kunert, "Unterschiede" ("Differences"), as an expression of the writer's concern about a position that depends on official praise and is threatened by government sanctions:

> Sadly I hear a name called out:
> not mine.
> With a sigh of relief
> I hear a name called out:
> not mine.

Much more questionable, however, is the attempt to use some of Bobrowski's late poems as evidence of the author's alienation from his society. Bobrowski, a convinced Christian and an active member of the East German Christian Democratic Party, repeatedly expressed his basic agreement with the goals and principles of the Marxist state in which he lived.

It was not until the mid-1980's that poems expressing political protest gained a large audience. In 1988, Volker

Braun, the regime's previously celebrated worker-poet, wrote in "Verheerende Folgen mangelnden Anscheins innerbetrieblicher Demokratie" (disastrous consequences of a lack of appearance of intra-factory democracy):

> It is too soon. It is too late
> Summer is waiting outside the door
> A lighter time. But frozen still
> everything flowers, all thought. With what little
>   freedom
> do we go out, lingering instead
> in our homes.

When the poem was published, *glasnost* (openness) and *perestroika* (restructuring) were propagated in the Soviet Union, but the East German leadership tried to freeze its country in the pre-Gorbachev past.

At first glance, much of the nonpolitical poetry by East German writers appears somewhat more provincial than the work of their Western counterparts. Many poems clearly reflect very specific and often narrowly defined geographical and cultural settings. Frequently an attempt is made, however, to relate the specific to the general. Georg Maurer, whom many younger poets consider their teacher, demonstrated this relationship when he referred to a definite area near Leipzig where he lived: "I am sitting in the universe/ on a bench in the Rosental."

There are many references to recent history and present social and economic conditions and, even with writers outside the Bitterfeld movement, frequent attempts to re-create the atmosphere of the industrial or agricultural workplace. While the many mediocre poems in praise of the tractor and its role in the battle for food are rightfully forgotten today, more modern authors often—consciously or unconsciously—employed the vocabulary of an industrialized world. In the poem that introduced his first volume of poetry, *Provokation für mich* (1965; provocation for myself), Volker Braun compared the poems of his generation with "high pressure valves in the pipeline network of our longings" and "telegraph wires that endlessly vibrate with electricity." It is doubtful that such metaphors would have occurred to his West German counterparts.

In such cases, it is often difficult or even pointless to distinguish between political and nonpolitical poetry. In general, history—especially twentieth century history—was a popular theme. Bobrowski, who grew up in the region of East Prussia, where Germans and Slavs had lived together and struggled with each other for centuries, again and again inserted into his poems references to German oppression of other cultures and to the heritage of guilt he shared. What for him was a general theme was treated by Führmann as a personal experience in his long poem of 1953, "Die Fahrt nach Stalingrad" ("Journey to Stalingrad"), the lyric companion piece to his *Das Judenauto*.

Related to the focus on the immediate surroundings, there was a greater emphasis on nature poetry than in the West. Huchel and Bobrowski (who saw himself as Huchel's pupil) wrote some of the finest German nature poems of his day. Occasionally, the tendency to depict nature and landscapes has been interpreted by outside observers as an escape from a stifling society, yet it is remarkable that in Huchel as well as in Bobrowski, nature does not exist for its own sake but becomes meaningful only through humanity's relationship to it. Consequently, few of the landscapes they describe are without a reference to humanity. Maurer said about his *Dreistrophenkalender* (three-stanza calendar) of 1951: "When, through Marx, I understood something about the essence of humanity, I comprehended the essence of nature at the same time. In this way, I personified it and sealed the relationship between me and it."

Beginning in the 1960's, however, the cityscape replaced the landscape in much East German poetry, and Gressmann's "Moderne Landschaft" ("Modern Landscape") of 1966 evokes a characteristic image:

> Steel trees are growing on the sidewalks
> And wires branch
> From tree to tree.
> Below, the electric animals
> With people in their hearts
> Are roaring past.

The passerby finds the sight quite normal, "For the landscape of stone/ Is his mother as well." In the industrialized world of the GDR, an unabashed nature poet such as Eva Strittmatter has become the exception rather than the rule.

FORMS OF EAST GERMAN POETRY

Much of East German poetry in the early years after World War II was marked by an attempt to adapt traditional forms to new ideological content. Classical patterns and the structures once developed as vehicles for religious expression served to give dignity to socialism and the new world it appeared to open up. Numerous cantatas, oratorios, and hymns were created by Becher, Fürnberg, Kuba, Hermlin, Zimmering, and others. Their texts are virtually interchangeable and lack any mark of artistic individuality. Some authors also attempted to create modern "folk songs" in order to popularize political ideas. While those works found their way into the songbooks of the youth organizations of the GDR, few have enriched the literature of the country. Brecht's simple language and direct approach were often used as models, but few imitators approached the quality of his verse.

Other traditional forms were still far more popular in East Germany than in the West. East German poets wrote sonnets and adapted the classical ode to the language of the twentieth century. Similarly, the ballad, a convenient tool for the effective presentation of scenes from history, retained a firm position in the country's poetry and became a vehicle of antigovernment protest by the late 1980's. Brecht, Hermlin, Biermann, and many others wrote ballads to illustrate political and philosophical views. Even the metric form of the medieval epic was revived, as in Fühmann's reinterpretation of the Nibelungen myth.

As a rule, East German writers are less given to formal experimentation and thus tended to produce more immediately accessible and concrete statements than some of the more adventurous poets of West Germany. It may be worth mentioning in this context that the very term "concrete" with respect to poetry assumed two quite different meanings in the two German states. Although some East German poets, such as Kunert or Endler, showed an inclination toward the condensation of a poem's idea into a few brief lines, the reduction to isolated words or even letters so characteristic of Western "concrete poetry" can hardly be found in East Germany. A perusal of East German magazines and anthologies suggests that even the renunciation of uppercase letters was seen as a daring experiment.

It is evident that the formal conservatism of East German poetry sprang from two distinct although closely connected sources. One was the tradition established by the Party and its cultural policies. When the State Commission for Artistic Concerns was established in 1951, it listed among its goals "overcoming formalism" and carrying on the "fight against decadence." Despite Hermlin's 1964 statement that it is a sad sight indeed if the representatives of the world's most modern social order recoil when they come across the word "modern," there was little official encouragement of formal experimentation. Alexander Abusch's denunciation of poetry, "which stammers linguistic fragments, assembles combinations of letters and juggles with them," thus creating poetic "ephemeral sensations, written for the snobbish amusement of a bourgeois 'elitist' audience," remained the official SED position to the end.

It would be wrong, however, to attribute the formal conservatism of East German literature solely to government pressure. Many authors themselves had little appreciation for the self-centered, hermetic poetry of some "elitist" Western writers who show disdain for their audience and who have consciously robbed poetry of its communicative function. Indeed, quite a few East German writers agreed with the lines from Fürnberg's poem "Widmung" ("Dedication"): "Oh, those who call themselves pure poets—/ if they only knew how poor they are!"

EAST GERMAN POETS AND THEIR AUDIENCE

Whereas lyric poetry is generally a much more private vehicle of expression than the other literary genres and thus tends to be monologic, East German lyric poets showed a definite inclination toward dialogue. With remarkable frequency, their works aim for a partnership with the reader and attempt to engage him or her directly. This popular view of the poem as a means of two-way communication was emphasized through the many public readings and discussions of poetry held throughout the country. More important, however, is its impact on the literary works themselves in terms of their language and structure.

Lorenc started his poem "Versuch über uns" ("Attempt About Us") with the—not completely rhetorical—question, "Or in which Language should I speak from us to us?" His ethnic and linguistic background adds a special meaning to this question, but many East German writers pondered the same problem. The plural "us" is also quite appropriate: The poet is addressing the people, the collective, of which he, too, is a part. This is important, because the poet no longer saw himself as a teacher, above and apart from the people, as in the earlier years of the GDR. Eva Strittmatter and Kunert stated explicitly that they did not have any didactic purposes in writing poetry, but Kunert added that he was not engaging in a monologue. Poets had the feeling that they were needed by their audience, that poet and readers are searching for the same thing—which, according to Kunert, could be defined by reference to the African American term "soul food." Braun similarly saw himself as a "good friend" of his reader, not as a "barker." He and his colleagues did believe, however, that the poet has to transcend the merely personal and private to say something of relevance to the audience. Thus, as Kahlau's love poems show, even the intimate emotional relationship between two human beings can become part of a dialogue with the reader.

No dialogue can occur if the ideas to be discussed are obscured by linguistic patterns out of the grasp of one of the partners. This realization made many writers strive for *Volkstümlichkeit* (folksiness, or popular comprehensibility of poetry). In some cases, this attempt has led to an impoverishment of language. Hermlin's early poems, for example, demonstrate his skill in translating the idioms of German Expressionism and French Symbolism into an artistic vehicle for the communication of his philosophy. His language was widely criticized as esoteric and obscure, and perhaps partly in response to such attacks, but surely also out of a desire to reach a broader audience and not merely an "elite," he deliberately changed his style, much to the detriment of his art.

HISTORICAL PARALLELS

Most of the specific features of East German poetry discussed above were directly related to the role of the writer in a socialist society, yet many of these phenomena also have a long-standing tradition in German literature. Political poetry has been written in Germany since the Middle Ages. Many authors were opposing prevailing conditions, to be sure, but from Walther von der

Vogelweide (c. 1170-c. 1230) through Johann Wolfgang von Goethe (1749-1832) and Heinrich von Kleist (1777-1811) to some of the minor bards of the Third Reich, poets have sung the praise of the mighty.

The poetry of the *Biedermeier* period as well as that of German Realism emphasized the writers' immediate environment, but even before the nineteenth century, the outstanding lyric poet Friedrich Hölderlin (1770-1843) was able to embrace the universe by focusing on his South German surroundings. Nature poetry has been popular with German writers and their audiences from Friedrich Gottlieb Klopstock (1724-1803), whom Bobrowski called his "taskmaster," and Goethe to the Romantics and the Realists, with the works of Annette von Droste-Hülshoff (1797-1848) constituting an artistic peak. Some parallels exist between the poetry of certain East German authors, particularly Huchel, and the nature poetry of the 1920's and 1930's.

One of the outstanding accomplishments of the great German writers of the eighteenth century—from Klopstock and Hölderlin to Gotthold Lessing, Friedrich Schiller (1759-1805), and Goethe—was their successful adaptation of traditional literary forms to their language and their times. Some of those classical forms were still popular among the poets of the GDR. The Romantic writers not only collected folk songs but also imitated their style in their own creative efforts. Fühmann's interesting experiment of retelling fairy tales in linguistically simple poems, while giving them a contemporary socialist interpretation, is also reminiscent of Romantic literature. Historical ballads, elevated to a high level of lyric expression by Goethe and Schiller, were among the most characteristic literary forms of the last century. On the other hand, the conservative trend in German poetry is by no means a new phenomenon, and writers as well as critics have again and again eschewed experimentation and rejected "empty" formalism. The denunciation by the old Goethe of what he considered "unhealthy" in Romantic writing can serve as an example. Finally, the already-mentioned didacticism of much of German literature, from medieval polemical pieces to the exhortations of the Expressionists, has always implied the reader's role as a silent partner in a dialogue.

These historical parallels are hardly surprising. The GDR considered itself the true heir to the cultural values of the German classical tradition. It assumed the role of guardian of a heritage that, so it claimed, was neglected and destroyed in the FRG. This attitude helps to explain why much East German poetry, especially that of the late 1940's and of the 1950's, strikes outside observers as dated and old-fashioned.

FINAL PHASE

By the 1980's, many of the old masters—Brecht, Bobrowski, and Huchel the most important among them—were gone. Some poets, such as Hermlin and Fühmann, had turned to other forms of literature. In reaction to government repression and swelling popular unrest and dissatisfaction with the socialist government, an increasing number of poets was leaving the country right up to the fall of the Wall in Berlin. Yet, among the younger generation, talents did emerge that were well worth watching. The number of books of verse that were published in the GDR would amaze most Western observers, and even more so the fact that this poetry found readers. Politics played a heavy role in the literary life of the country, and the massive political changes bringing an end to the GDR saw many poets at the vanguard of popular opposition and protest. Before the 1980's, many poems never made it into print for reasons unrelated to their artistic quality.

The English-speaking reader is handicapped still by the relative scarcity of East German poetry in translation. Except for much of Brecht's work, some of Bobrowski's poetry, isolated poems by other East Germans, and a few good anthologies of Eastern and Western German poetry, there is still relatively little opportunity for those who cannot read the originals to acquaint themselves with a once thriving and interesting verse literature.

The English-speaking reader is often further handicapped by ideological preconceptions. If John Flores, in an important 1971 study, singles out two 1947 poems, "Die Zeit der Wunder" (the time of miracles) and "Ballade nach zwei vergeblichen Sommern" (ballad after two futile summers), as "perhaps the finest Hermlin has written" and then adds that they are "poems of disappointment and disillusion," one cannot escape the impression that there is a causal connection between those two statements. Unless the reader in the

West is willing to accept East German poetry within its own context, the mere availability of translations will not matter much.

BIBLIOGRAPHY

Deicke, Günter, ed. *Time for Dreams: Poetry from the German Democratic Republic*. Translated by Jack Mitchell. Berlin: Seven Seas Press, 1976. A good collection of East German poetry up to the mid-1970's.

Flores, John. *Poetry in East Germany: Adjustments, Visions, and Provocations, 1945-1970*. New Haven, Conn.: Yale University Press, 1971. Older and staunchly anticommunist, still a valuable discussion of the role of poetry in East Germany during the height and the eventual waning of the Cold War. Shows how in the West, East German poetry was often considered either propaganda or secret opposition to the socialist regime.

Hartung, Harald. "Lyric Poetry in Berlin since 1961." Translated by Lorna Sopcak and Gerhard Weiss. In *Berlin Culture and Metropolis*, edited by Charles W. Haxthausen and Heidrun Suhr. Minneapolis: University of Minnesota Press, 1990. A brief but very important article shedding light on, among other things, the flourishing of an alternative, underground East German poetic culture in East Berlin. Poets from East Berlin were in the vanguard of those intellectuals demanding change from the socialist regime, resulting in its ultimate peaceful overthrow.

Ives, Rich, ed. *Evidence of Fire: An Anthology of Twentieth Century German Poetry*. Seattle, Wash.: Owl Creek Press, 1988. Contains some significant and important East German poems. Nicely places East German Poetry in the overall context of modern German poetry. A useful complement to Charlotte Melin's anthology.

Leeder, Karen J. *Breaking Boundaries: A New Generation of Poets in the GDR, 1979-1989*. New York: Oxford University Press, 1996. A comprehensive analysis that focuses on both official and underground poetry of the last decade of the GDR. Well written and critically informed, this is a very important study for any student of the topic. Includes bibliographical references and index.

Melin, Charlotte. *German Poetry in Transition, 1945-1990*. Hanover: University Press of New Hampshire, 1999. One of the best anthologies for readers ready to acquaint themselves with East German poetry. Excellent, informative introduction, valuable author biographies, good bibliography, index.

Sax, Boria. *The Romantic Heritage of Marxism: A Study of East German Love Poetry*. New York: Peter Lang, 1987. A perceptive study of the topic. Marxist positions on the topic are clearly expressed, and discussion, criticism, and analysis of the poems are of remarkable clarity and distinction. Bibliography and index.

Dieter P. Lotze, updated by R. C. Lutz

ENGLISH AND CONTINENTAL POETRY
IN THE FOURTEENTH CENTURY

Whan that Aprill with his shoures soote
The droghte of March hath perced to the roote . . .
Thanne longen folk to goon on pilgrimages,
And palmeres for to seken straunge strondes,
To ferne halwes, kowthe in sondry londes;
And specially from every shires ende
Of Engelond to Caunterbury they wende,
The hooly blisful martir for to seke,
That hem hath holpen whan that they were seeke.

With these words Geoffrey Chaucer begins *The Canterbury Tales* (1387-1400), arguably the poetic masterpiece of fourteenth century England and certainly a stout cornerstone in the monumental edifice of the English literary tradition. Critics have long praised Chaucer's choice of the pilgrimage as the overarching frame for a highly varied collection of individual tales, and readers are often advised of its particular virtues of providing a theme of religious renewal and community enterprise against which are set, for example, the delightful boorishness of the Miller, the outrageous iconoclasm of the Wife of Bath, the earnest pondering of how man and woman are to live together in what G. L. Kittredge called the "Marriage Group," and the insouciant extortion of the wily Pardoner. Yet perhaps readers are not often enough reminded of the milieu in which *The Canterbury Tales* was created, the context which it in part reflects. It is crucial to a faithful reading of any literary work that readers take a moment to review its cultural and historical background, and never is such a review more needed than for this tumultuous period that proved to be the poetic flowering of the late Middle Ages.

HISTORICAL CONTEXT

The fourteenth century was an era of great literary achievement in the face of governmental, economic, and religious near-apocalypse. No sooner had Boniface VIII declared his own gaudy papal jubilee in the year 1300 than his chief secular opponents, Philip IV of France and Edward I of England, began to contest his power. Working from the solid church and state amalgam that was the bequest of the thirteenth century, Boniface had aroused the kings' resistance in 1296 with the *Clericis laicos* papal bull, which asserted the Church's right to levy taxes. Two years after the jubilee he issued the more famous *Unam sanctam*, intended to establish the primacy of the Church in unambiguous terms by subordinating all human creation to the authority of the pope in Rome. This anachronistic attempt at absolutism, destined to fail in an era in which social and political evolution was ever accelerating, precipitated the withdrawal of the Papacy from Rome to Avignon, initiating in 1309 the "Babylonian Captivity" of popes that was to last until 1376 and presaging the ultimate schism in the Church, which was healed only two decades into the fifteenth century at the Council of Constance. With the loss of a generally accepted central government for Christianity, as well as numerous other disasters, many of the philosophical and religious syntheses of the previous century also foundered.

As prominent as any dogma inherited from the thirteenth century was Thomas Aquinas's apparent reconciliation of faith and reason in his *Summa theologiaea* (c. 1265-1273; *Summa Theologica*, 1911-1921). Blending the newly rediscovered Aristotelian logic and his own brand of Christian humanism, Thomas erected a cathedral-like intellectual monument to celebrate the fusion of human reason and divine grace. John Duns Scotus (c. 1265-1308), a Franciscan, had begun to pry faith and reason apart, however, and William of Ockham (c. 1280-1350) finished the dismantling through the application of his well-known "razor." Ockham insisted that human knowledge should be restricted to the immediately evident, thus making it necessary to discard the grand latticework of categories assembled by Aquinas and others. The Nominalist movement, so called because of its dismissal of the Thomistic *nominae* (or categories), also provided the impetus for a series of scientific developments at the universities of Oxford and Paris. To replace the Aristotelian notions of streams of air as the medium for physical motion, for example, John Buridan (c. 1300-1358) offered a theory of original forces that was to be transferred fruitfully to studies of heavenly bodies. Remarkably, Nicholas of Oresme (c. 1330-1382) described the universe as a mechanical clock, an idea all the more brilliant since such time-pieces had been perfected only in his century. Along with these discoveries, and others such as the cannon, eyeglasses, and the mariner's compass, came the evolution of modern scientific method in the nominalist emphasis on observed phenomena.

To be sure, however, Ockham's was not the only heresy to come to prominence in the vacuum of formal religious authority created by the withdrawal of the Papacy. As rationalism lost its footing in the Christian world-view, mysticism increased markedly and became a pan-European movement, finding its focus in Germany, for example, with the writings of Meister Eckhart (c. 1260-1327). Interest in astrology and alchemy was likewise on the rise; and Chaucer especially revealed a fascination with the courses of the stars and planets and their supposed influence on the world of men. One of the more engaging and curiously modern heresies involved the professions of the Free Spirit reformers, who advocated unrestrained sexual freedom and other apparent vices in the pursuit of individually achieved deification. Nearly as influential as Ockham's nominalist beliefs were the attacks of John Wycliffe (c. 1320-1384) on the presumptions of the Avignon popes. Refusing to credit any clergy with the power they claimed unless they were in a state of divine grace, he championed the Englishmen who resisted the financial demands of the Papacy and later questioned the existence of Church government and even the Eucharist itself. In many ways Wycliffe, a strident religious dissenter and yet the originator of the first English Bible, well represents the maelstrom that was Christianity in the age of Chaucer and his contemporaries.

As religion passed through a series of challenges, reforms, and counter-reforms, losing in the process the comparatively well-regulated syntheses of the preceding century, secular developments followed suit. England and France entered the fourteenth century with their governments reasonably intact, but in both cases a succession of less-than-qualified leaders and a sequence of catastrophic events brought the countries to their political knees and, not inconsequently, to the Hundred Years' War. On the French side, Philip the Fair (Philip IV), opponent of Boniface, had placed the monarchy in a position of strength at the cost of considerable financial

strain on his constituency. When he died in 1314, his successor Louis X was quickly forced to agree to charters limiting his power and transferring a great deal of authority to a confused baronial system. After two more Capetian kings of unremarkable achievement, the rule passed to the inept Philip VI, who set about establishing an adversary relationship with his English counterpart Edward III, an ongoing conflict that led eventually to open warfare. In mid-century, John the Good assumed the throne, only to be taken prisoner at the Battle of Poitiers. Even as these monarchs followed one another to death or infamy, Edward III was in the process of declaring himself king of France; the French, in a weakened condition, had to curb his presumptuousness in 1360 by consenting to the conditions of the Treaty of Brétigny, awarding Gascony, Calais, and Ponthieu to the English in return for Edward's renunciation of his claim to their monarchy. While John's son Charles V (ruled 1364-1380) was able to reorganize his country and help the English to exhaust themselves and relinquish newly won territories, the century ended with France in the hands of the incompetent Charles VI and the advantage once more passed to her opponent.

England likewise started the fourteenth century struggling with Boniface. Edward I (ruled 1272-1307) fostered a typical thirteenth century cooperation between the monarchy and the legislative powers, reformed the judicial system, gave order to ecclesiastical activity, and controlled feudal tendencies. His son Edward II, however, was at best a shadow of his father. He suffered a humiliating defeat by the Scots at Bannockburn in 1314 and gave no evidence whatever that he was qualified for leadership. In 1327, he was forcibly deposed by the parliament, and his fourteen-year-old son, Edward III, was appointed the nominal regent. At first the young man was only a figurehead manipulated by his mother Queen Isabella and her lover Roger Mortimer, but three years after his accession he toppled them both, sentencing Mortimer to death and stripping the queen of all power and holdings. With the monarchy in hand, this English Orestes then set about providing a focus for growing English nationalism by erasing the "Shameful Peace" with Scotland from popular memory through a series of successful battles to the north. Thus, Edward III showed his ambitions and talents early in his fifty-year reign and also revealed, not incidentally, a penchant for nationalistic assertion that was to lead to severe, even crippling, problems for the nation he so stoutly defended.

The most serious and debilitating result of this martial activity was the Hundred Years' War with France, which opened in 1337 when Edward ordered the Gascon fleet to attack shipping in the ports of Normandy. As mentioned above, a context for these actions already existed in the quarrel over the French crown and the efforts of Flanders to gain its independence, and this single event was merely one of many subsequent skirmishes along the English Channel. Important events included the naval encounter of 1340, the Treaty of Brétigny in 1360, and the gradual reversal in favor of the French in the late fourteenth century. At the same time, the spirit of British nationalism that fueled Edward's war machine also manifested itself in other ways: The Statute of Praemuniere (1353) forbade Englishmen to bring their appeals to a foreign (that is, papal) court, and the first of the Navigation Acts (1382) stipulated that English goods must be carried by domestic ships only. When the official change from French to English as the language of the law courts (1361) is added to this list, it becomes apparent that the rising tide of nationalism was nearing its peak. Unfortunately, the advent of Richard II in 1377 created another incompetent monarch to rival Edward II. The century closed in an undistinguished manner, with Richard desperately resorting to execution of his enemies in 1397 and suffering his own death two years later.

In Germany the political situation was even worse. The inheritor of an unwieldy coalition of states headed by scheming princes and under attack by the Papacy, Albert of Habsburg tried to bring order to the empire but was murdered in 1308 by his nephew. The puppet emperor Henry of Luxemburg (VII) made a foolish expedition to Rome in an attempt to bring Italy back into the fold but was poisoned in 1313. His successor, Charles of Bohemia, dismissed papal claims with his Golden Bull of 1356, but his concentration on Bohemia at the expense of the Empire as a whole left his nation vulnerable to attack, and the French and Swiss made steady gains throughout the fourteenth century. Notwithstanding this unrest, the German cities made some strides forward in

urban management in the form of administrative innovations, paved streets, fire protection, and public health. At about the same time, the Serbian people made their first heroic effort to throw off the Ottoman yoke at the celebrated Battle of Kosovo (1389), where the Serbs and their leader Knez Lazar went down to a defeat that was to serve as the seedbed of a fierce nationalism and an extensive cycle of heroic poems.

In Italy, the internal strife characteristic of the period stemmed primarily from the withdrawal of the popes to Avignon. With Philip IV and Edward I in open defiance of Boniface's edicts, and with the time of absolute clerical authority on the wane, there was little choice but to abandon the politics of Rome and to seek refuge under the French imperial banner. Meanwhile, the customary infighting in Italy grew worse, with the merest and most superficial unity existing between the southern Kingdom of Naples and the northern despots. A touch of neoclassicism emerged for a moment in the reforms of Cola di Rienzi, who rose to power in 1347, but the age made his visions of reinstating antiquity anachronistic, and he was driven into exile and murdered in 1354. The popes began to try to return to Rome and reinstall themselves in 1367; nine years later, when Urban VI resisted all attempts to depose him, and his "successor" Clement VII retreated to Avignon to establish a rival Papacy, the Great Schism was begun. All in all, Italy was not a pleasant place to live in the fourteenth century, as the writings of Dante confirm.

Almost precisely in the middle of the century the Black Death struck Europe, reducing the total population of most countries by half to two-thirds. As the frequency of themes of morbidity, pessimism, and death in all the arts indicates, this pestilence had a profound effect on the medieval mind, in addition to its decimation of the populace. Traveling along trade routes from China through Italy, Spain, and southern France, by July, 1348, it had reached Normandy and the English coast. Medieval medicine was apparently powerless against the more virulent of the disease's two forms and it passed unchecked into Ireland and Wales over the next two years, only to return periodically throughout the rest of the century. In addition, people had earlier had to contend with the disastrous crop failure and famine of 1315, caused by floods which were also to recur regularly for many years to come. For these and other reasons, economic disaster became the rule of the day, and overtaxed market systems, alternating surpluses and shortfalls of agricultural and manufactured goods, the backsliding of emancipated serfs into the feudal equivalent of slavery, and general social upheaval led to the Peasants' Revolt of 1381.

As the authority of the Church and of secular government languished, the Thomistic unity of faith and reason unraveled, the Black Death claimed half of Europe, antifeminist and anti-Semitic movements gained momentum, and the economic and social institutions of the thirteenth century trembled and then fell, people were forced to experiment and adapt in order to survive. Reform and renovation proceeded in all areas, with various degrees of success and almost no visible effect until the fifteenth century. Yet, in the middle of the worst confusion and turmoil the Middle Ages was to know, the arts underwent truly radical change and produced a remarkable number of discoveries and true masters.

Artistic and literary context

Emblematic of this transformation was the Italian painter Giotto (c. 1266-1337), a genius who cast aside his shepherd's crook to become the first great postclassical painter. What Giotto accomplished was phenomenal: He replaced the formal, stylized, two-dimensional Byzantine representations with a more realistic artistic idiom that imitated nature in all her beauty and with all her flaws. His *Madonna Enthroned* (c. 1310) and *Death of St. Francis* (c. 1318-1320), for example, illustrate his technique of creating depth, movement, and fidelity to nature. While the Italo-Byzantine style continued in a modest way on a separate line (an example is Simone Martini's *Annunciation* of 1333), Giotto's techniques spread north rather quickly, first in the form of manuscript illumination (as in the work of Jean Pucelle, beginning c. 1325) and later in architecture and portraiture. Giotto's painting played a large part in bringing Europe to the brink of the Renaissance.

As the conventional use of Latin declined and the vernaculars became more prominent all over Europe, great authors began to mold the new tongues for literary purposes. Like Giotto, the Italian poet Dante (1265-1321) reached beyond traditional models and the tenor of the times to create his masterpiece, *La divina commedia* (c. 1320; *The Divine Comedy*, 1802). Dante wrote his epic poem while he was a political exile wandering through northern Italian cities in search of a patron; however, even though topical allusions to the political and social problems of his beloved Florence abound, his work rises above contemporary strife to glimpse the path to God: in the hands of his guides, Vergil, representing human reason, and then Beatrice, who as the symbol of divine love leads the pilgrim Dante to the heaven where reason cannot take him, he accomplishes the journey of Everyman and allegorically points the way to the Christian's true reward. Dante's countryman Francisco Petrarch (1304-1374), who, in addition to establishing so many of the Italian sonnet conventions, contributed to most of the literary and philosophical genres of his day, stressed the importance of human mortality in the face of theological dogma and displayed an atavistic tendency to return to the ancient philosophers in his search for truth.

Giovanni Boccaccio (1313-1375), author of *Decameron: O, Prencipe Galetto* (1349-1351; *The Decameron*, 1620), a collection of ten "days" of ten stories each, tried to develop a more worldly poetic language. His famous tales are told by seven young women and three young men who flee Florence to escape the ravages of the Black Death and for ten days amuse themselves with stories of cuckolding, murder, and other fantastic pursuits. Especially since it now appears that Chaucer had not read *The Decameron* and thus conceived the analogous structure of his *The Canterbury Tales* independently, the genre of tales unified by a framing story should be considered a typically fourteenth century form in its originality and response to the demands of individuality upon traditional genres.

Medieval texts

Some characteristics of medieval texts were particularly prominent in this age of experimentation and reaction to change. Authors in this period suffered very little from the more modern "anxiety of influence," and there were compelling reasons for their resistance to this literary disease. In the fourteenth century—and virtually throughout the Middle Ages—no special value was placed on "originality": Stories, characters, events, and situations were almost always borrowed, either from another source or from the word hoard of convention, or simply translated from Latin or one of the vernacular tongues, in whole or selectively. Poets did not so much strive after fresh and mysteriously engaging material as they molded known material to their own designs; they were in the main retellers rather than creators, and this procedure characterized not only their subject matter but also the ways in which they shaped it. As has been shown time and again, the rhetoric of medieval poetry was codified by such writers as Geoffrey of Vinsauf, Bernard Silvestris, and Alanus de Insulis. Fourteenth century poets had available to them handbooks concerning such topics as the proper method of picturing a woman's beauty—proceeding vertically through a catalog of her features from "tip to toe." These conventional methods of description were advocated by poets and expected by their audiences, as were what Ernst R. Curtius has called *topoi*, or narrative commonplaces, such as the ubiquitous garden of earthly delights, the *locus amoenus*. Form as well as content was traditional, and each aspect of the poetry was all the more expressive because of its typicality in other works and consequent connotative power. Twice-told tales and time-tested rhetoric were the order of the day, and so modern notions of aesthetics must be adjusted to take faithful account of these medieval values.

Such stories and established methods of telling them imply a particular kind of text no longer extant in a modern literary milieu consisting of finely crafted objects virtually complete in themselves. The Romantic legacy of originality marks the end of texts with an active history behind them, but the poem that reaches out into its traditional context to complete its form and content is, par excellence, a medieval phenomenon. The process had begun with earlier medieval oral traditions—Anglo-Saxon, Old French, and Hispanic; in the case of the oldest texts, such as *Beowulf* (c. 1000) and the *Chanson de Roland* (c. 1100; *The Song of Roland*), the tradition is paramount and the poet is a member of a succession of bards who transmit more than they compose. With later medieval texts, the individual author is firmly the master of his or her own literary fate, and yet the debt to tradition is still great. The medieval text, in short has diachrony: It reaches back to earlier narratives or lyric moments and it speaks through a grammar of commonplaces and rhetorical figures assembled and approved by tradition. The more innovative writers of the fourteenth century grasped tradition with consummate ease, reformulating its lexicon of tales and grammar of rhetoric, and passed beyond it to create formerly unheard harmonies on the basic melodies of the canon. These original melodies remain, however, and give the newer compositions a fundamental strength. Indeed, it is well to remember that even the great iconoclast and innovator, Chaucer, was the inheritor of a rich traditional legacy, which he invested brilliantly with his often startlingly fresh ideas for literary works, and that both the intensely dramatic and psychological *Troilus and Criseyde* (1382) and the great send-up of medieval romance "Sir Thopas" bear testimony to his creative use of poetic tradition.

Arthurian legend

One of the strongest of medieval traditions, and one that was to reach forward to the Medieval Revival of the Victorian nineteenth century, to the classic American tale-telling of Mark Twain, and beyond, into the modern era, was the cycle of legends surrounding King Arthur and his knights. This central character of countless tales was probably a sixth century historical figure celebrated in Britain for his heroic defense against Saxon invaders; like the Serbian Knez Lazar after his fall at Kosovo in the late fourteenth century, Arthur was especially revered after the Celts were defeated and subjugated by the Germanic attackers. Of his earliest history little is known—some Welsh sources from about 600 (such as the elegy *Gododdin*) refer to his martial accomplishments, and the priest Nennius chronicles the victories over the Saxons as well as local legends, but by 1100 in Wales he had become a full-blown legendary hero of romantic adventure and the leader of a band of men who were themselves larger than life. From this Welsh origin, the legend of Arthur spread to the Cornish, who claimed him for their own, and then to the Bretons, who through their French-Celtic bilingualism were able to spread the insular tradition to the Continent: Largely by means of oral transmission, a medium that was to remain a channel for diffusion of romance materials throughout the Middle Ages, the tales soon passed from Wales to

France, Provence, Italy, Sicily, Germany, and parts of Asia Minor. Even the great Arthurian masterworks of Chrétien de Troyes in France and Wolfram von Eschenbach and Gottfried von Strassburg in Germany trace their origins to this Breton connection.

Arthurian legend entered the learned tradition through Geoffrey of Monmouth's *Historia regum Britanniae* (c. 1136, Vulgate version; *History of the Kings of Britain*, 1718), a delightful, wholesale fabrication that passed as the standard historical account until the sixteenth century and was even adapted into French by the Norman poet Wace in 1155 (*Le Roman de Brut* or *Geste des Bretons*), in which form it also enjoyed wide currency as a source for English romances, directly and through Layamon's *Brut* (c. 1205). Meanwhile, the French romancers were developing the attached legends of Lancelot, Tristram, Gawain, and the Grail. In the twelfth century, Arthur's knights and court occupied the center of their attentions, while in the thirteenth they combined individual tales, greatly expanded the contemporary cycles of tales, and further Christianized the originally animistic and magical Grail stories. It is from this French efflorescence that the English tales of Arthur begin to develop in the second half of the thirteenth century, the legends having come full circle back to their origins in Britain, albeit in much modified form.

Of the considerable number of fourteenth century poems concerning Arthur or his knights, a handful stand out as deserving of special attention. Perhaps foremost among them are *Sir Gawain and the Green Knight* (c. 1375-1400) and the two poetic tales of Arthur's death, the alliterative *Morte Arthure* (c. 1400) and the stanzaic *Morte Arthur* (c. 1360). The former, composed in alliterative long lines in the same Northwest Midlands dialect that characterizes *Sir Gawain and the Green Knight* and the stanzaic version, derives mainly from Wace's translation of Geoffrey and legends of Alexander, and presents its portrait in both epic and tragic terms. Because of its relatively high density of conventional diction and typical scenes, it has been described as either a memorized or a traditionally composed poem; it is not far removed from the oral tradition that spawned its phraseology and narrative design. The alliterative poem represents what Larry Benson calls the "chronical tradition," an ostensibly historical account of battles and

warriors rather than of romance and carefully drawn, individualized characters. The stanzaic version, on the other hand, is a true romance composed in eight-line stanzas of four-stress lines and represents a deftly managed condensation of the French prose *La Mort Artu* (c. 1225-1230). It includes Lancelot's encounter with the maid Astolat, his defense of the queen, the usurpation of the kingdom by Mordred, and the events leading up to Arthur's death. Unlike the alliterative version, this poem depends more on a fast-paced, streamlined narrative with emphasis on action rather than on conventional romance tropes, an economical texture that no doubt played a part in attracting the close attention of Sir Thomas Malory as he composed his classic Arthurian works in the next century.

GAWAIN POEMS

While no fourteenth century poems specifically about the wizard Merlin survive, owing perhaps to the lesser influence of Geoffrey's *Vita Merlini* as compared to his seminal *History of the Kings of England*, and while the only verse tale involving Lancelot in any significant role is the stanzaic *Le Morte Arthur*, a great many poems about Arthur's knight Gawain survive from the late medieval period. Primarily because Gawain was prominent in both Geoffrey and Wace, as well as in the French romances of Chrétien de Troyes, the English romancers celebrated his chivalric prowess and, it may be safely said, by their literary attention assigned him the highest rank of all who honored Arthur at the famous Round Table. Apart from *Sir Gawain and the Green Knight*, the best known of these tales is *Ywain and Gawain* (c. 1300-1350), a translation and condensation of Chrétien de Troyes's *Yvain: Ou, Le Chevalier au lion* (c. 1170; *Yvain: Or, the Knight with the Lion*, c. 1300) and the only extant Middle English version of any of the great French romancer's works. As is the general rule with Anglo-Norman or French originals and their English descendants, the continental poem bristles with sophisticated literary conventions which reflect its intended courtly audience, while the English adaptation often uses proverbial or colloquial expressions more in keeping with its popular constituency. *Syre Gawene and the Carle of Carelyle* (c. 1400) is also aimed at a popular audience and shares with its better-known counterpart the elements of temptation and beheading. In addition, the second episode of *The Awntyrs off Arthure at the Terne Wathelyne* (after 1375) consists of the common challenge to Gawain and incorporates the hunting scenes that are juxtaposed to scenes of courtly wooing in *Sir Gawain and the Green Knight*. Finally, the *Libeaus Desconus* (c. second quarter of the fourteenth century), not much read today but extremely popular in its time, included the story of Gawain's bastard son Guinglain, whose emergence from personal obscurity combines the biographies of his father and Perceval. Possibly the work of Thomas Chestre, the author of *Sir Launfal* (c. 1430), this romance is ordinary enough in its execution but boasts a fair number of analogues, among them the Middle High German *Wigalois* (c. 1209) by Wirnt Von Grafenberg and the Italian *Carduino* (c. 1375) in addition to the inevitable French parallel *Le Bel Inconnu* (c. 1190).

PERCEVAL, GRAIL, AND TRISTAN POEMS

The Perceval legend is rare in the medieval English poetic tradition, but alongside Malory's later prose is found the fourteenth century romance *Sir Perceval of Galles* (c. 1300-1340) and the more ambitious and justly famous German *Parzival* (1200-1212) of Wolfram and the French *Le Conte du graal* (c. 1182), the last romance composed by Chrétien. The Grail poems, Christianized in twelfth century French versions by association of the magic platter, and later cup, with already existing legends surrounding the Eucharist, are likewise few in English during this period, the only avatar being the fragmentary *Joseph of Arimathie* (c. 1350). Tales of Sir Tristram prove scarcer still, the sole examples being found in the thirteenth century *Sir Tristram*, in Thomas Malory's *Le Morte d'Arthur* (1485), and in a phantom twelfth century text by one Thomas of Britain that provided the basis for Gottfried von Strassburg's monumental but incomplete *Tristan* (c. 1210). If the relative paucity of Arthurian poems in certain areas is frustrating, caused in part by the eternal problem of damaged, destroyed, and lost manuscripts, it should be remembered how freely and widely these tales circulated, even without the aid of writing, throughout the Middle Ages, and therefore how rich the Arthurian tradition must have been.

ALLITERATIVE REVIVAL

Part of the richness of poems such as the Alexander fragments, the alliterative version of the death of Arthur, *Sir Gawain and the Green Knight*, *The Vision of William, Concerning Piers the Plowman* (A text 1362, B text 1377, C text 1393), and other works by the *Gawain*-poet stems from a literary phenomenon or movement that proceeded hand in hand with the development of Arthurian legend in the latter half of the fourteenth century: the burgeoning of unrhymed alliterative verse commonly called the Alliterative Revival. Like many terms canonized by usage in literary histories, this rubric is in some ways a misnomer. In the absence of hard and unambiguous information, it is customarily assumed that the rejuvenation of the alliterative verse form reflects a kind of continuity not only with the thirteenth century *Brut* of Layamon but also with the poems in the Anglo-Saxon type of alliterative meter five centuries earlier. Although the former connection is generally acknowledged, the latter is much more tenuous and cannot at present be demonstrated. It would be better to consider the Revival essentially a Middle English phenomenon, a poetic renaissance that took place when the cultural, linguistic, and historical time was right.

To appreciate the explosion that took place about the year 1350, one should note Derek Pearsall's striking observation that, while only twenty-eight lines of unrhymed alliterative verse survive from the period of 1275 to 1350, the figure rises to more than forty thousand lines during the period from 1350 to 1425. Clearly something significant happened to precipitate this poetic deluge, and scholars have long been laboring to uncover and describe the forces that were or might have been at work. One suggestion is primarily historical, although with innumerable ramifications in other areas: It explains the rapid rise of English alliterative poetry as a response to the vacuum created by the demise of the Anglo-Norman tradition, a reflex of the progressive reaffirmation of things English, and especially English language and literature. Other critics locate the impetus of the Revival in the activity of monastic orders, which in the later Middle Ages were much involved in the social and economic as well as religious spheres. Still others have attributed this resurgence to the patronage of the ruling classes of the west of England, and some have found the verse to be propagandistic of this or that group or opinion.

Whatever the complex of origins at the root of the movement, however, most critics agree that the Revival was a phenomenon that began in the north and soon spread to the Northwest and Southwest Midlands areas, that it was a typically fourteenth century flowering of literary excellence far outstripping anything immediately before or after it, that the movement was transitional between oral and written composition and transmission in its often consciously artistic permutations of traditional conventions and patterns, and that it represents the increasingly English character of literary tradition.

POETIC GENRES

Literary traditions seldom follow well-worn or predictable pathways; rather, they seem to meander this way and that, ever evolving and changing their own defining characteristics. As so many editors of anthologies and teachers of medieval survey courses have come to recognize, this truism is particularly apt for the fourteenth century. Although the period was never at a loss for models in the various European literatures, and although not a few contemporary writers were content to follow unquestioningly the rules of composition bequeathed to them implicitly in the assortment of genres at hand and explicitly in sources such as the handbooks mentioned above, many poets struck out bravely beyond the frontiers of generic and rhetorical propriety to discover new modes of artistic expression.

The result of this iconoclasm is at once a rich legacy of experimentation and a correspondingly heterogeneous mix of poetic types. In confronting this achievement one must be careful not to diminish its richness and complexity by insisting on too rigid a taxonomy to contain it. Some of the commonly used labels, such as the venerable "romance," do have bona fide literary identities and deserve the title of genre on the basis of classical critical criteria. Others, such as "didactic poetry," are obviously the offspring of descriptive necessity and can lay no claim to constituting an integral group within the poetic tradition; clearly, it would be difficult to locate many medieval poems that are not in some manner didactic. With this caveat in mind, then, some

general remarks about the maze of fourteenth century genres can be made.

THE ROMANCE

Although it may boast of being the most widespread and significant poetic form of the fourteenth century, the romance is not a genre that lends itself easily to brief definition. A general profile of the English romance can be assembled, however, and certain cycles or groups among its extant representatives can be distinguished. The English romance, a creature of the mid-thirteenth through the fifteenth century, was composed in a bewildering variety of verse forms as well as in prose, the major types of versification being the four-stress couplet, the tail-rhyme stanza (with a large number of different rhyme schemes), and the four-beat alliterative meter, sometimes in stanzaic format. The romancer followed the typical medieval method of borrowing par excellence, the source most often being a French original that was adapted into English, with original touches added by the poet, or simply translated in whole or in part. Stories concerned the adventures, both martial and amorous, of knights and their opponents and ladies, and were told with the greatest "willful suspension of disbelief" imaginable, a fantastic quality that fairly characterizes the genre as a whole. The narrative voice of most romances leads one to the conclusion that the primary aim of their composers was entertainment, and in fact there is evidence that many of the poems were meant to be read before audiences, both popular and courtly. This tendency did not, however, absolutely preclude a didactic intent; in some of the more finely crafted romances, such as *Sir Gawain and the Green Knight*, the chivalric and religious undercurrents are plain in the overall design of the work.

Hand in hand with the fantasy element in medieval romance goes idealization, readily transmuted to instructive purpose, and convention. Because the genre made use of oral traditional forms by cultivating stock characters, attitudes, and action patterns, it tended to present the immediate and particular against the larger canvas of the generic. Commonplaces, story patterns, verbal tags and formulas, and stock scenes were all among the elements at the romancer's disposal, and the fantastic, the ideal, and the typical merge in a text enlivened by its traditional context. The responses of heroes, the undertaking of quests, the wooing of ladies, and the games of courtly love are expected subjects; the audience read (or better, listened) to the story of Sir Launfal or Morgan Le Fay with a deep sense of its "reality" in the romance tradition and without nagging worry that its content was in modern terms quite unrealistic. To enter the world of medieval romance, to join the poet's quest, was willfully to renounce the corporeal and mundane in favor of the mysterious, the adventurous, and the magical.

More often than not the quest proved successful, the journey culminating in the medieval equivalent of a Hollywood ending. Innocence and even naïveté prevail, as the Perceval tradition well illustrates, and virtue is almost always rewarded. With little regard for historical accuracy, the romancer felt free to embroider a dull sequence of events either with his own personal literary design or, more frequently, with a pattern that was part of his poetic inheritance. He favored feasts and public ceremonies of all sorts for his courtly audience, more worldly embellishments for a popular group. In either case, however, his English poems were, as remarked above, generally less sophisticated than their French originals, in part because their intended audience was also less sophisticated.

As the useful taxonomy in *Manual of the Writings in Middle English* (1967) by John Wells and J. Burke Severs indicates, the great variety of English romances can profitably be viewed in ten groups: poems that derive from legends concerning (1) early Britain, (2) King Arthur, (3) Charlemagne, (4) Godfrey of Bouillon, (5) Alexander the Great, (6) Troy, (7) Thebes, (8) the long-suffering Eustace, Constance, Florence, or Griselda, (9) the Breton lay, and (10) a miscellaneous category that includes works of Eastern origin, historical poems, and didactic pieces. An alternate method for classifying and interrelating romances is the approach of Laura H. Loomis and Maldwyn Mills, a tripartite division of chivalric, heroic, and edifying. The first group contains those verse tales most like earlier French romances in their primary concern with love and chivalry, inorganic combination and recombination of stock elements, and typical location in a magical or exotic domain. The second type characteristically treats the hero as a member

of a collective force and highlights societal expectation in addition to heroic achievement. In the third group the most important values are suffering and endurance in the face of just or unjust punishment, with the possibility of eventual transcendence as the protagonist's reward.

The most famous entry in the first Wells/Severs category, that of native English romances, must certainly be *King Horn* (c. 1225), a tale told and retold in many forms throughout the medieval period. Within the fourteenth century are *The Tale of Gamelyn* (c. 1350-1370) and *Aethelston* (c. 1355-1380), two poems that are probably English in origin and for which, unlike most other works in this group, no surviving sources in French have been discovered. *The Tale of Gamelyn* presents a lively composite of a number of familiar folktale elements, most prominently the benevolent outlaw behavior associated in the popular imagination with Robin Hood, and contemporary social commentary, as imaged in the hero's overturning of a corrupt judge and court. Moreover, there are criticisms of monastic and mendicant orders of clergy, humor, psychological realism, and the cherished happy ending, the last perhaps as much the gift of folktale as the emblem of the romance genre as a whole. The quite Anglo-Saxon *Aethelston*, a patently unhistorical tale of the victorious leader at the Battle of Brunanburh, is even more qualified for inclusion in the Loomis-Mills group of "heroic" romances, for not only is it unrelieved by episodes of love and chivalry but it also figures forth community values and obligations at the expense of individuals. Aethelston stands falsely accused until a trial by fire proves his innocence; the same trial determines the treason of his blood brother Wymound, and matters are soon set right through execution. A third verse romance, *William of Palerne* (c. 1350-1361), amounts to a popularized translation of the French *Guillaume de Palerne* (1194-1197) and follows the return pattern so common in this and other categories.

THE LYRIC

The miscellany of surviving Middle English lyrics extends throughout the period 1200-1500 and resists the application of general ordering principles and specific dating. Many of these works, however, take on a variety of identifiable aspects, even though the poets are themselves generally anonymous, and with good reason since many of the poems and virtually all of the constituent motifs and phraseology were in the public domain. As Raymond Oliver puts it, the poems have three intentions: to celebrate, to persuade, and to define. In the first case, the setting is a ritual occasion, such as the spring season, a wedding, Easter, or, preeminently, Christmas; the large collection of traditional carols belongs to this category. Lyrics intended to persuade customarily adopt a stance on particular actions and explain them in a coherent fashion, the *contemptus mundi* theme being a common subject for treatment. The third case, definition, bears on a position or doctrine and is almost always religious in nature. Other characteristics of the lyrics include their impersonal, generalized attitude and lack of interest in personality and psychology, features reflecting the poems' presentation in oral performance.

Many of the topics and themes common to other fourteenth century literature can be found in much abbreviated form in the lyrics. An example is the courtly lover's plaint, such as the justly famous "Blow, Northern Wynd" (c. 1320), or, perhaps most classically, in "Now Springs the Spray" (c. 1300): "Nou sprinkes the sprai./ Al for love Icche am so seek/ That slepen I ne mai." The employing of a seasonal marker to impart an archetypal momentum to a brief narrative, another familiar medieval device, also typifies many of the lyrics, such as this one (c. 1320):

> Somer is i-comen in,
> Loude syng cuckow!
> Groweth seed and bloweth meed
> And spryngeth the wode now. . . .

This famous poem preserves, as do others of the period, an elaborate set of instructions for performing its music. More than other contemporary genres, however, these poems manifest the influence of French and Latin traditions in their multilingual phraseology: Where they are not straighforwardly macaronic, they are often brimful of borrowings. Their rhetoric is also very different from that of other forms; again in keeping with their customary composition for oral performance, the rhetorical figures ordering the poems lean toward the paratactic in structures such as anaphora, parallelism, and repetition of words and phrases. Larger patterns follow suit, with emphasis on stanzaic organization, narrative patterns

based on ritual, liturgical, or seasonal events, and repetition of segments. Alliteration and assonance occur frequently, and the meter is accentual; as a rule, Rossell Hope Robbins's suggestion that the levels of prosody and versification are commensurate with the complexity of the subject well summarizes the matter and takes account of the whole spectrum of lyrics, from the plainest and most popular song to the most sophisticated tract on human mutability.

As Oliver notes, surviving Middle English lyrics differ considerably from contemporary continental traditions in their anonymity and lack of concern with individual psychology. German, Latin, and French lyrics of the period often treated ostensibly biographical or other personal issues, most notably the poems of François Villon (c. 1431-1463?) written in the form of a last will and testament, but also the works of Walther von der Vogelweide (c. 1170-1230), Hugh Primas of Orléans (wrote c. 1150), and the German "Archpoet" (died c. 1165). Comparisons with Old English material, particularly with elegiac lyrics and gnomic poetry, show a large number of alliterative and rhetorical features in common, and the further development of the Middle English lyric can be seen in the poetry of John Skelton and William Dunbar in the late fifteenth and early sixteenth centuries. Those lyrics that can be placed in the fourteenth century (at least on the evidence of surviving manuscripts) show a representative spread of topics and concerns, from the sometimes vulgar recountings of nature in all its earthiness, to Christmas carols that have managed to survive to this day, to celebrations of spring and religious renewal, to earnest contemplations of the transience of human life and meditations on liturgical moments and their meaning. The lyrics constitute a rich miscellany, a backdrop of tradition that helps to contextualize the entire medieval period.

DIDACTIC POETRY

Under this heading are grouped, for the sake of convenience, poems whose intent is chiefly religious and instructional and that do not easily stand alongside better-defined counterparts in other genres. Although it is quite true that much of fourteenth century verse could be called didactic, this category should include only works not generically appropriate for inclusion elsewhere. One such work is Robert Mannyng's *Handlyng Synne* (1303-c. 1317), a thorough recasting of the Anglo-Norman *Le Manuel des péchés* (by William of Wadington in the thirteenth century). The subject of Mannyng's poem is vast: A good deal of Christian church doctrine, including the Ten Commandments, the Seven Deadly Sins, the Sins of Sacrilege, the Seven Sacraments, the Twelve Points of Shrift, and the Eight Joys of Grace, comes under his scrutiny. He occasionally leavens his theological lessons, perhaps intended for a specific audience of novices of Sempringham, with realistic detail and reaction, and, like Chaucer after him, he knows the edifying potential of a good story:

> For lewde men Y undyrtoke
> On Engylssh tunge to make thys boke;
> For many ben of swyche manere
> That talys and rymys wyl blethly here.

Mannyng also composed *The Story of England* (c. 1338), a chronicle of historical events from the Flood to the reign of Edward I, and he may be responsible for an adaptation of St. Bonaventure's *Meditations on the Life of Christ* (mid-thirteenth century).

Another primarily didactic poem of this century is the anonymous *Parlement of the Three Ages* (c. 1350), which employs two of the most characteristic medieval narrative devices, the dream vision and the debate. An example from the Alliterative Revival described earlier, this tale concerns the Nine Worthies and thus connects itself with the Alexander legends and their form as romances, but the most fundamental structure of the poem is as a moral lesson on the transience and mutability of all things earthly. The poet reviews the Worthies, wise men, and lovers, all from the perspective of the "vanity of human wishes," combining tried and true stories, topoi, and narrative patterns with a vigorous alliterative language that recalls at points the hearty realism of Anglo-Saxon heroic poetry as well as the later *Sir Gawain and the Green Knight*.

Less realistic but perhaps more rewarding stylistically and aesthetically, the elegiac *Pearl* (c. 1380), attributed to the anonymous *Gawain*-poet, concerns the author's infant daughter who dies in her second year and inspires in her father a debate over divine wisdom and mortal expectation. After ascending to heaven, she tells him of her spiritual happiness and explains temporal misconceptions in God's ordering of the universe. Just as he tries to cross over to her, the poet awakes from his dream vision with his head on her grave, forever reconciled to her loss. A highly allegorical work, *Pearl* recalls numerous biblical figurations from Revelations and elsewhere and presents its simple dream-vision narrative and complex allegorical latticework in a style both nominally typical of the Alliterative Revival and yet uniquely its own in the concomitant development of stanzaic patterns. Many critics have sought, and arguably found, numerological sequences that relate in some way to biblical and patristic sources, a not uncommon phenomenon in medieval texts. Other poets likewise turned to the dream and debate as methods for active mediation of the earthly and spiritual worlds, but few achieved the delicate interweaving of alliterative idiom and theological instruction that the Pearl-Poet displays.

The same author is also credited with two other poems in the *Gawain* manuscript, *Cleanness* and *Patience*. The former presents the tales of the Flood, a popular subject since Anglo-Saxon times and usually thought to prefigure the Apocalypse, the destruction of Sodom and Gomorrah, and the fall of the sacrilegious Belshazzar, concerning itself chiefly with the impurity of the situations that incurred God's punishment. The poet counterposes the sinful figures in these three biblical stories—and again the numerology seems more than accidental—to the three positive figures of Noah, Abraham, and Nebuchadnezzar, whose respect toward God is rewarded with mercy. Although not so intensely allegorical as *Pearl*, *Cleanness* still motivates the reader to compare the three main stories with other biblical sources and, perhaps most of all, to consider the tropological implications for his own life. Similarly, *Patience*, the fourth of the poems in the *Gawain* manuscript, retells the narrative of the Book of Jonah, although the general medieval fascination with steadfast faith throughout the worst imaginable adversity, as evidenced so widely in the edifying romances of Griselda and company, must also serve as a background for this alliterative expatiation. This shorter poem is also the most personal of the four, portraying each of its characters with considerable realism and finesse, and offering a glimpse into the psychology of Jonah, particularly his human frailty. As a whole, the works of the Pearl-Poet must be numbered among both the best and most memorable of the didactic poems of the fourteenth century and the most complicated representatives of the Alliterative Revival.

POLITICAL-HISTORICAL POETRY

During the fourteenth century there arose a fair number of poems that chronicled various historical epochs and events with a political purpose in mind. The earliest of these are eleven poems by Laurence Minot, written between 1333 and 1352, on the successful campaigns by Edward III against the Scots and the French. Responding to earlier English defeats, in particular the "Shameful Peace" with Scotland following Edward II's defeat at Bannockburn in 1314, Minot sought to eulogize the king's achievement and foster the cause of nationalism. The first and best known of his works, *Halidon Hill* (c. 1333), commemorates the young monarch's retributive victory that regained control of the northern border and soothed the political as well as territorial wounds inflicted on the English psyche but warns against thoughtless celebration lest the nation be deceived by Scottish "gile."

John Barbour's *The Bruce* (c. 1375), on the other hand, celebrates Scottish nationalism in an account of the heroic actions of King Robert the Bruce and his faithful comrade-in-arms Sir James Douglas that stretches to more than thirteen thousand lines. Beginning with historical facts and bringing to his work classical and medieval models as well as a lively sense of mythic narrative, Barbour recounts the heroic accomplishments of Robert, including the Battle of Bannockburn, and Douglas's unsuccessful attempt to bear the fallen king's heart to the Holy Land. As Charles Dunn and Edward Byrnes observe in *Middle English Literature* (1973), the poem finds its thematic center in Robert as the quintessential defender of Scottish liberty and in Douglas as the equally paradigmatic loyal follower. In this and other ways, *The Bruce* eludes categorization, whether as chronicle, political poem, epic, or myth; in the final analysis it remains a work *sui generis*, one most typical of the mélange of later fourteenth century verse forms.

The anonymous author of *Thomas of Erceldoun* (c. 1388-1401) also combined a number of stock medieval generic characteristics to forge a unique kind of narrative. Although parts of the story share with *Halidon Hill* and *The Bruce* certain real battles as subjects, and although the hero of the work, one Thomas Rymor of Earlston, is historical, the poem also interweaves common folktale elements and other features typical of medieval romance. The main narrative frame concerns Thomas's love affair with an underworld queen and his consequent ability to foretell the future. As well as the queen's predictions about clashes between Scotland and England, the poet presents certain other auguries of indistinct relation to the first group. Dunn and Byrnes note that *Thomas of Erceldoun* typifies a pan-European medieval technique in its assignment of known historical facts to the visions of a seer or prophet and attachment of especially attractive prophecies not yet fulfilled to the historical record; once assembled, the entire package was apparently submitted as a political tour de force.

PRECURSORS TO CHAUCER

Apart from the many engaging and accomplished poems treated above under various generic categories stand some individual authors and works that, by virtue of both their own artistic excellence and their influence and modern appeal, deserve special attention. Among this latter group are William Langland's *The Vision of William, Concerning Piers the Plowman*, the anonymous *Sir Gawain and the Green Knight*, and John Gower's *Confessio Amantis* (1386-1390, *The Lover's Confession*). Each in its own way helps to set the standard of poetic achievement that is the legacy of the late fourteenth century or "Ricardian" period, as J. A. Burrow has named it, and together these three poems constitute a crucial context for the genius of Chaucer.

WILLIAM LANGLAND: PIERS PLOWMAN

The Vision of William, Concerning Piers the Plowman is extant in three recensions, labeled the A, B, and C texts. The three combined are divided into two parts, "The Vision of William, Concerning Piers the Plowman" and "The Life of Do-Well, Do-Better, and Do-Best," which articulate, respectively, general and individual problems of evil and corruption, both offering solutions for the good Christian during his stay on earth. The vision portrays the ruin of contemporary society in allegorical terms and, perhaps responding in part to the social upheaval that wracked the everyday lives of four-teenth century humanity, suggests the humble and sim-ple virtue and obedience of the plowman as an antidote to temporal discord. In the second section, the poet con-ducts an allegorical search for the ideal Christian exis-tence, starting within himself and then undertaking a quest through various liturgical and philosophical do-mains under the guidance of a series of mentors. With his journey complete, the dreamer's vision turns from its focus on higher abstract truths to their practical imple-mentation in contemporary society.

Langland's poem is, as much as any medieval work, uniquely his own, but one can trace a few analogues and parallels to fill out its literary context. Tracts such as Mannyng's *Handlyng Synne*, described above in the sec-tion on didactic poetry, are typical of many such instruc-tional poems and prose works of the period; some of the most familiar include Dan Michel of Northgate's *Ayenbite of Inwyt* (1340, a translation of *La somme des vices et des vertues* by Laurentius Gallus) and Chaucer's "Parson's Tale." These poems and similar works were commonly consulted by writers for liturgical details and traditional literary accounts associated with church dogma. Also of influence was the well-developed ser-mon tradition of the later Middle Ages, which became a learned craft memorialized in handbooks (*Ars prae-dicandi*), much like the *Ars rhetoricae* or *Ars poeticae* employed by poets in search of commonplaces of de-scription or narrative action. In fact, several whole works are at least formally similar to *The Vision of William, Concerning Piers the Plowman*, such as Guillaume de Deguileville's *The Pilgrimage of Human Life, of the Soul, and of Jesus Christ* (c. 1330-1358), as well as more general classical and other foreign models of alle-gorical quests and seeking after divine truth. Although superficially *The Vision of William, Concerning Piers the Plowman* and *Sir Gawain and the Green Knight* appear to be strange bedfellows, the fact remains that Langland's poem is also a manifestation, and a bril-liantly executed one, of the Alliterative Revival. Even so, as with all of the best works of the late fourteenth century, *The Vision of William, Concerning Piers the Plowman* is best assessed on its own merits as an earnest and able contemplation of its time, in this instance against the backdrop of the Christian drama.

To appreciate the earnestness of this finely crafted al-legorical latticework, it is necessary to view the poem in its literary historical milieu. Recalling the desperate state of affairs in late fourteenth century England—the Church in corrupt disarray since the preceding century, the Avignon Papacy just coming to an end, the Black Death having run rampant only twenty-five years be-fore, the longstanding social discontent crystallizing in the Peasants' Rebellion of 1381, the condemnation of Wycliffe's teaching in 1382, and the blatantly incompe-tent rule of Richard II, one can well imagine how a poem such as *The Vision of William, Concerning Piers the Plowman* came to be composed and why, if the ex-tremely large number of extant manuscripts is any testi-mony, it found a large and sympathetic audience long before being taken up by scholars and critics as one of the masterpieces of its time. In a century wracked by un-certainty, the spiritual journey of Everyman in search of truth must have served a social as well as aesthetic pur-pose; given the prevailing problems, it may not be too daring to characterize one function of this "poem of apocalypse," as Morton Bloomfield calls it, as cathartic or therapeutic. In the medium of poetic art, Langland and, vicariously, his countrymen could respond to a sometimes corrupt and vacuous clergy with satire and wit; they could counter a monumentally intransigent and self-centered government with lessons on taming Lady Meed; and, most crucial, they could combat the socially exacerbated sickness of mortality by imagining, in great allegorical detail, a religious restorative. Langland pro-posed a journey not unlike that of Dante, a dream of transcendence of the earthly sphere, and a vision of God uncomplicated and unsullied by the catastrophic events of his time. Even if *The Vision of William, Concerning Piers the Plowman* ends with the Antichrist in power, the Church under attack, and the world as yet unre-deemed, the dreamer has a new understanding of what lies beyond his immediate environment as a defense against apocalypse. The search will continue.

Sir Gawain and the Green Knight

Another of the jewels in the crown of the Alliterative Revival, *Sir Gawain and the Green Knight* represents a very different sort of literary masterpiece from *The Vision of William, Concerning Piers the Plowman*.

Melding together games and story patterns from Celtic folklore, attitudes and values from a highly developed and thoughtful Christianity, and the ritualistic procedures of courtly love, it achieves a fusion of medieval ideas unique in the fourteenth century. An Arthurian hero, Gawain, in place of his monarch, takes up the challenge to behead the Green Knight and, should the marvelous fellow survive, to allow him the same privilege a year hence. Gawain accepts what critics have viewed as both a Christmas prank and the initial act in a story of vegetative renewal and cleanly lops off the Green Knight's head; not the least discouraged, his adversary gathers up his lost part and, reminding Gawain of his pledge, rides off to unknown regions. Too soon the annual cycle is complete and the day arrives for the honorable knight's departure to fulfill the bargain; Gawain leaves Arthur's court and eventually finds himself at the castle of one Bercilak and his lady, an honored guest enjoying their hospitality. Here the plot begins to thicken ominously. While the lord and master is off on his daily hunting expedition, not incidentally for three successive days, his wife acts as courtly temptress of their guest. Gawain finds himself suspended between two medieval romantic codes: Either he must follow the precepts of chivalric behavior and, refusing the lady's advances, honor his host's hospitality as a true knight of the Round Table, or he must gallantly bow to the pressures of courtly love and, accepting the lady, fulfill another set of expectations. Of course he cannot do both, especially since he agreed with Bercilak to exchange any booty won on their respective hunts, and so he is caught in a logically insoluble quandary. After weakening the third day and accepting a kiss, Gawain leaves the castle and soon encounters the Green Knight, who turns out to be Bercilak in disguise. Submitting to the promised return blow, the hero flinches once, receives a second feint, and on the third swing of the ax is slightly injured, just enough to compensate for his minor indiscretion on the third day of the earlier test. The Green Knight then gives him the lady's "girdle" or sash, a symbol of femininity since classical times, to wear around his belt in remembrance of the whole affair, and Gawain heads back to Arthur's court with his life and his knighthood intact.

The sources behind this lively tale include a mixture of originally Celtic elements and common romance motifs, but whatever the actual source materials with which he worked, the artistic achievement of the *Gawain*-poet remains uniquely his own. The archetypal frame provided by the self-renewing Green Knight promotes ideas of recurrence and inevitability and is made to surround a series of ironic and playful games engaged in by the much-tried hero, the lady temptress, and the lord Bercilak. There is clearly no escape for Gawain, nor is there meant to be: The fall of Gawain as Everyman is in fact remarkably innocuous given the pressing circumstances, as the Green Knight's mercy (but justice) with his sharp edge illustrates. Gawain loses a battle as, from one point of view, the entrapment made inevitable by his mortality eventually draws blood; the Green Knight must be repaid, just as surely as the next Christmas season will announce the rebirth of God. Yet the hero's fallibility also becomes his religious and moral sinecure. Chastised by a natural, postlapsarian error, he shows himself—and in the process humanity—to be the better for the test. What he loses with a kiss and a flinch from the blade he repays, Christ-like, with his wound, and ever afterward the girdle remains as a symbol of his transcendence of mere mortal frailty. Gawain, like Oedipus, solves a riddle and wins a contest; by surviving the complex contest of conventions and circumstances, he comes to epitomize the triumph not only presaged by Christ but also, optimally, mirrored in Everyman's experience of earthly life. For all this, the vehicle for this highly serious investigation of mysteries remains a virtual *cadeau*, a Christmas jest: When all is over, when the tale is done and the poet adds "Honi soyt qui mal pence" ("Evil be to him who thinks evil"), Chaucer's immoral morality and playful hermeneutics seem very near indeed.

JOHN GOWER'S *CONFESSIO AMANTIS*

John Gower's much praised *Confessio Amantis* forms one third of a trilogy of poems by Gower on the evils that assail the individual and state and on methods for overcoming them and achieving virtue. He first completed the Anglo-Norman *Mirour de l'Omne* (1374-1378), and the Latin *Vox Clamantis* followed in 1381; the first version of *Confessio Amantis*, universally proclaimed his masterpiece, was finished in 1390. A straightforwardly and severely moral work, it functions chiefly through a barer and more economical allegory than does *The Vision of William, Concerning Piers the Plowman*, but one that is in its way equally powerful. Again, there is the familiar dream-vision structure in Book I, with the poet Gower imagining a meeting with the God of Love, the Queen of Love, and the Queen's priest Genius. The priest then treats the dangers of earthly love and the Seven Deadly Sins, one after the other, for most of the remainder of the work, teaching the poet-lover in good medieval style through a series of illustrative stories. Finding himself absolved of his afflictions, the poet is able to bid Venus farewell, turn to reason for guidance, and pursue the lasting spiritual rewards of moral virtue.

Several features of the *Confessio Amantis* deserve special comment. First, in addition to the dream vision, allegorical commonplaces, and discussion of the Seven Deadly Sins, the poem is thoroughly medieval in its juxtaposition of human versus divine love, a topic as old as the Anglo-Saxon elegies *The Wife's Lament* or *The Seafarer* (both c. tenth century). Of course, no poem could well function more differently from *Sir Gawain and the Green Knight*, but the two works do share the story of medieval man learning his human shortcomings and profiting from the lesson. The *Confessio Amantis* delivers its instruction in a less immediate, more austere manner, agreeing in tone and structure with *The Vision of William, Concerning Piers the Plowman*, but it seems worthwhile to note that John Gower's moral allegory and the *Gawain*-poet's romance do affirm the same values and, once the particulars deriving from generic differences are deemphasized, can be seen to offer similar prescriptions for getting on in the world. At the same time, one should remember that the *Confessio Amantis* is not, like *The Vision of William, Concerning Piers the Plowman* and *Sir Gawain and the Green Knight*, a product of the Alliterative Revival, and that both its subject and the rhymed couplets of its verse hark back to foreign as well as native models, as indicated by the vision's considerable debt for its story-line to the *Roman de la Rose* (the first portion written in the first half of the thirteenth century by Guillaume de Lorris, the second portion written between 1275 and 1280 by Jean de Meurq). As an obviously well-educated and widely read man, Gower had no shortage of models for his poetry, and he turned his conception of proper human attainments into

a clear and readable narrative intended both to instruct and to entertain. That such a work, rigorously formal in attitude and design yet a paragon of literary attractiveness, could exist beside *Sir Gawain and the Green Knight* and even complement its purpose is a measure of the poetic cornucopia of the fourteenth century.

GEOFFREY CHAUCER'S THE CANTERBURY TALES

Towering over all of fourteenth century poetry are the poems of Geoffrey Chaucer. In nearly every imaginable manner Chaucer epitomizes his age and its literature: In the midst of social anguish and turmoil he focused his genius on matters of supreme and permanent importance; as a thoroughly medieval author he borrowed freely and imaginatively from English, French, Italian, and Latin sources; refusing even more than his contemporaries to be hide-bound by generic or rhetorical constraints, he frequently pushed the rules of genre and poetic composition to the breaking point, creating in the process some works that defy classification in their brilliant originality; and, especially typical of late fourteenth century or Ricardian masters, he managed to achieve affecting and enduring *aperçus* into the pilgrimage of humanity and the ceaseless ritual games between men and women.

Chaucer's most ambitious work is also the most typical literary document of its age. At a time when uncertainty and doubt threatened to send most social and political institutions careening into disaster or disrepute, when Langland was composing his monumental allegory of salvation as a bulwark against religious and cultural apocalypse, Chaucer managed to assemble a company of remarkably disparate individuals and to lead them on a pilgrimage of hope, a journey that would discover their common humanity in a startlingly novel fashion. If creative response to the breakdown of hard-won but outmoded syntheses was an important theme in this period, then *The Canterbury Tales* epitomizes that solution: In presenting his panorama, Chaucer uses most of the major contemporary genres but subordinates them to a new design; he introduces God's plenty of personalities but finds a way to integrate them into a believable community; he has his pilgrims discuss many of the burning social, religious, and philosophical issues of the day but never lets debate or pedantry obtrude on the collective function of the group; and he achieves a realism and naturalism of characterization far beyond that of any contemporary work without ever abandoning either his finely crafted, brilliantly conceived narrative voice or the structure, large and small, of the stories themselves and the work as a whole. When one adds the tremendous range of his learning, so apparent in the variety of sources and the skill with which he re-creates them, and the outright appeal of the poem for generations of audiences, it becomes no exaggeration to call *The Canterbury Tales* both Chaucer's masterpiece and the masterwork of the entire fourteenth century.

As might be expected, such a poem seems to have been largely the product of the poet's later years, of his mature style. Still influenced by the French tradition of romances and *dits amoureux* which served so importantly as models in his earlier writings, and having digested the contributions of the Italian poets and transmuted this literary gold into an indigenous English coin, Chaucer struck out on the kind of creative, original venture that only a lifetime of exposure to experience with traditional materials could foster. Scholars customarily associate the year 1386 with his conception of the plan for *The Canterbury Tales*, but he may well have been working on the project beforehand. Perhaps the next year he composed the immortal "General Prologue," from a textual viewpoint the key to all that follows. Opinions on other aspects of chronology vary as well, but the tales themselves probably occupied Chaucer for most of the rest of his life. The unfinished state of the work and its tangle of manuscripts indicate that he probably composed significant parts of the poem up until his death, but one should also remember that *The Canterbury Tales* was, like most medieval poetry, intended for oral performance and not primarily as a written text.

One of the influences on Chaucer's poem was the Italian *novelle* tradition, a loose aggregation of tales brought together by an outwardly unifying fiction. Although Giovanni Sercambi did write such a collection in the general form of a pilgrimage about 1374, it is important to note that neither this nor any other group of *novelle* could have provided more than a suggestion for the complex and dynamic frame of *The Canterbury Tales*. Likewise, the richness of the "General Prologue" derives not from the considerable number of sketches

written at the time, but most vitally from Chaucer's genius for weaving conventional topoi, rhetorical rules, character types, and at least some real personalities into a fabric distinctly his own. Of the sources and analogues for the tales themselves, it may be said that the mélange of genres and possible parallels is as diverse as the company of pilgrims, including, besides the *novelle*, the French *fabliau* tradition, the romance, the saint's life, the folktale, the medieval sermon, the miracle story, the epic, and the mock-heroic poem. No form passed through Chaucer's hands without considerable elaboration or some sort of modification; often his contribution consisted of turning the genre to his favorite purpose of social satire, and at times his reworking was so complete that, as in the case of the superbly farcical "Sir Thopas," he created a virtually new genre.

To surround his tales of life and love, Chaucer constructed what is frequently called a frame but which might better be labeled a purpose or context. Unlike the Italian analogues that postulate a nominal unifying fiction and leave the matter quite undeveloped, the pilgrimage is ever evolving, with the poet shifting the focus this way and that to sustain the fiction and to allow his characters their remarkable range of expression and interaction. Intimately allied to the pilgrimage conceit is the naïve, impressionable narrator who keeps it alive—the poet-pilgrim Chaucer who mourns his lack of literary aptitude ("My wit is short, ye may wel understonde"). Behind this wide-eyed, good-natured fellow, of course, stands the poet Chaucer, manipulating the unbounded enthusiasm of his narrator with consummate skill and a keen sense of irony, allowing his audience a double perspective on characters and events. Indeed, it is impossible to separate the pilgrimage context from its somewhat clumsy but ever-willing rhapsode. If Chaucer's characters come alive and interact in ways unique to *The Canterbury Tales*, a large part of the credit is due to a combination of his narrator's unfailing and irrepressible humanity with the poet's own perspectives on the fascinating heterogeneity of humankind.

From this union of authorial design and naturalistic narration springs the vivacity of the "General Prologue." After setting the scene and creating the rationalizing fiction, the narrator begins an exacting introduction of his society in microcosm, epitomizing each character type and endowing each pilgrim with a memorable individuality. His small community allegorizes fourteenth century society—and it does not: Taking advantage of traditional associations, Chaucer not infrequently adorns a character with the "tell-tale detail," such as the Prioress's brooch, the Miller's wart, the Wife's deafness or scarlet hose, or the Pardoner's waxy yellow hair. Details and the actions and habits that they either imply or actually represent come nimbly into play, as the narrator balances expectations based on character types against the exceptions to those *règles du jeu*. Such is Chaucer's mastery of the poetic medium, however, that he expresses even these singularities in the form of medieval rhetorical commonplaces. Drawing on conventional techniques of poetic description, and especially on the *notatio-efficito* method of portraying inner qualities or liabilities in a character's specific physical features, he encodes some of his most subtle and iconoclastic observations on a character in the metalanguage prescribed by poetic handbooks. Sometimes an overabundance of one of the four humors—blood, phlegm, yellow bile, and black bile, postulated since the Greek physician Galen and common in medieval medical lore—leads to a judgment on a person; in another case a term with lascivious associations, such as the Wife's quality of being "gat-toothed," mitigates or seconds other aspects of a description. Employing to the hilt the narrator's unremittingly naïve euphemisms (only he could call as notorious a swindler and reprobate as the Pardoner a "noble ecclesiaste"), Chaucer delicately balances traditional expectation and individual design, managing to make time for implicit commentary that ranges from ironic to bawdy to sincerely religious.

Chaucer's portraits are elaborately crafted, to be sure, and just as certainly very carefully hung. Critics have pointed out various possible schemes for the arrangement, many of them founded on the ideas of the various estates or social classes of medieval provenance. Donald Howard suggests that the order of presentation is a mnemonic structure or *aide-mémoire* analogous to medieval formulations reported by Frances Yates; that is, three groups of seven, each group headed by an ideal figure: the Knight, followed by the Squire, Yeoman, Prioress, Monk, Friar, and Merchant; the Clerk, followed by the Man of Law, Franklin, Guildsman, Shipman,

Physician, and Wife; and the Parson and Plowman (brothers), followed by the Miller, Manciple, Reeve, Summoner, Pardoner, and Host. Howard argues that these mnemonic constructs were so much a part of medieval literary consciousness that it would be only natural for Chaucer to employ them in his art. This scheme for the introduction of the characters seems credible enough. It does, however, leave out a character who is in many ways the most important of all: Chaucer the pilgrim. Throughout the "General Prologue," but particularly in the thirty-two lines that intervene between the introductions of the Pardoner and the Host, the narrator is introduced as another in the company, an appealing fellow who begs his readers not to hold him directly responsible for what he reports because he can only repeat what was said by others. It is very much in the innocent nature of Chaucer the pilgrim to issue such a disclaimer before he begins the recital of romance, *fabliau*, and the other genres that make up *The Canterbury Tales*, and the reader may also sense the guiding hand of the poet finishing off the characterization of yet another pilgrim, the narrative liaison between poet and poem and the lifeblood of the pilgrimage frame.

Harry Bailly, the Host, soon takes nominal charge of the enterprise, sets the rules for tale-telling (two while riding to Canterbury and two on the way back from each pilgrim), and has the participants draw lots to determine who will start. The cut falls to the Knight, and the tales begin as they should in the social sphere of fourteenth century England with the pilgrim of highest rank opening the proceedings. "The Knight's Tale" turns out to be a story and a type of poem appropriate both to its teller and to its position in the work as a whole. As an adventurer in the service of the Christian God, and as "a verray, parfit gentil knyght" quite the opposite of that over-courtly *bon vivant* his Squire, he lends dignity and a sense of purpose to the community by relating an intricate Boethian romance that reaffirms the social order that he leads. Drawn primarily from Boccaccio's *Teseida* (1340-1345), or epic of Theseus, with a great deal of the favorite medieval device of compression, this chivalric tale was probably first composed as a separate piece unconnected with *The Canterbury Tales* and only later fitted into its present place. Whatever the nature of the lost version mentioned in the prologue to *The Leg-*

end of Good Women (1380-1386), the extant tale chronicles the tragic and eventually ennobling love of the young knights Palamon and Arcite for a lady Emelye. The misfortunes of earthly life are seen as "perturbations of the spheres" and the story moves like Chaucer's *Troilus and Criseyde* from mortal myopia to a larger perspective under the aegis of Theseus. The variety of contributions to follow are to an extent rationalized by this tale, which remains a philosophical anchor and moral standard for the entire work.

No sooner has the stately knight finished justifying the ways of God to his fellow pilgrims than the drunken Miller counters the propriety and high style of the initial tale with his coarse, irreverent *fabliau* of carpenter John's cuckolding. The Miller is so impatient and rude, in every way the antithesis of the first teller, that he interrupts the Host's request that the Monk be next and, ever so characteristically, barges straight ahead to "quite the Knyghtes Tale." His own words introduce an important structural principle, that of "quiting" or repaying, which will account for the presence of the tale to follow as well. This low-life character offers the furthest remove imaginable from the philosophical complexity of "The Knight's Tale" by telling an uproarious story of how Nicholas the clerk planned and carried off the seduction of the carpenter's wife virtually before her husband's eyes. Not only is the Miller "quiting" the Knight; in addition, the lower class is challenging the views and values of the upper, animal instincts and scheming are being played off against higher passions and earnest moral deliberations, and, perhaps most significantly, the dynamics of the community of pilgrims—both as individuals and as representatives of their vocations or types—is starting to take shape. "The Miller's Tale" deals not with Boethius but with bawdiness: the clever Nicholas, the doltish John, the unspeakably fey parish clerk Absolon, and the concupiscible young wife Alison engage in a fast-paced charade that rides roughshod over courtly love, religious duty, matrimonial fidelity, and all available aspects of contemporary morality. At the same time, the Miller stumbles through a real, if homely, alternative to the deep pondering and austerity of "The Knight's Tale" and helps to set the tone and outer limits of Chaucer's investigation of humanity.

The lonely Reeve, who brings up the rear of the assemblage, then reacts violently against what he judges to be the Miller's personal insult of a trade he has practiced and, "quiting" his foe, responds with a *fabliau* about the cuckolding of a dishonest miller. Some tales later Chaucer introduces a justly famous character, Dame Alys or the Wife of Bath, as vigorous, self-serving, and lecherous as the Reeve is biting, sarcastic, and "colerik." Her prologue consists of a boisterous, happy biography complete with accounts of her five husbands and how she achieved mastery over all of them. Often linked to the antifeminist sentiment of the period, ironically evident in her fifth husband's book of misogynist exempla, the Wife commands the stage of *The Canterbury Tales* by misquoting and misapplying biblical and patristic authorities, by celebrating the lustful nature that led her to ogle Jankyn (her fifth husband) during her fourth mate's funeral, by discoursing on male and female genitalia with a crudity that would do the blockhead Miller proud, and generally by providing the community of pilgrims with an inextinguishable source of gleeful iconoclasm, good will, and high spirits. Very rarely in any literary period is there so vivacious and singular a character as the Dame; like a medieval Falstaff, she stands astride the work of which she is a part, to be remembered and cherished as a patroness of its art.

As the Wife boasts of her conquests in the prologue, the reader begins to understand that she is offering one possible solution to the problem of the contest for mastery between men and women. "The Wife of Bath's Prologue and Tale" is one in a series of seven tales that Kittredge identified as the "Marriage Group," a sequence that, he argued, was intended to present various possibilities for the seat of authority in marriage. The four most important members of this group are the Wife, the Clerk, the Merchant, and the Franklin. The Clerk tells a story of male dominance over a painfully patient Griselda which "quites" the Wife, and the Merchant spins the ubiquitous medieval tale of the elderly January and his young wife May, warning of the consequences that such a doomed alliance must bring. For her part, the Wife fashions a prologue that finds distant analogues in the very antifeminist writings that it parodies, but which remains after all a brilliant original; her tale, on the other hand, is the common story of the Loathly Lady and her miraculous transformation, analogues of which are found in Gower's *Confession Amantis* and numerous contemporary romances. With the Knight under the thumb of the hag, whom he has promised to marry after she saves his life, Dame Alys makes her exit, no doubt supremely confident of the influence of her words on the audience she has been both entertaining and instructing. Even so, the reader may ask how well she has succeeded in making the patently outrageous palatable.

If the Wife, Clerk, and Merchant offer what are finally unsatisfactory alternatives for the problem of sovereignty in marriage, the Franklin, "Epicurus owene sone" and knight of the shire, provides a final solution in a tale that Chaucer adapted from Boccaccio's *Il Filostrato* (1335-1340), with elements from Geoffrey of Monmouth, the Breton lay tradition, and the common folktale motif of the rash promise. As Paul Ruggiers puts it in *Art of The Canterbury Tales* (1965), "The view of marriage which has in a sense been dismembered is reconstituted in terms of a balance between service and dominance, between human weakness and strength of character, between respect for self and respect for others." Even the announced genre of the tale, a Breton lay, promotes the resolution by creating a fairy-tale world wherein forbidding complexities can be magically simplified and the nagging temporal concerns of an imperfect world dissolved in a romantic suspension of disbelief. Taking as his topic and argument the already demonstrated reality that "Love wold not been constreyned by maistrye," the Franklin tells the story of Arveragus and his faithful wife Dorigen, whom Aurelius, the courtly lover *par excellence*, is, characteristically enough, pursuing. In resisting his suit, a rare abstinence in the world of *The Canterbury Tales*, she sets him a seemingly impossible task, saying that she will accede only if he manages to remove each and every stone from the coast of Britain. By consulting a clerk versed in Chaucer's favorite science of astronomy, the resourceful Aurelius accomplishes the task and calls the lady's hand.

The dilemma that now presents itself to Arveragus and Dorigen is clear-cut but morally insoluble: If she refuses Aurelius's love, she violates her solemn promise; if she accepts him, he violates her contract of fidelity with her husband. As much as the outcome seems "agayns the proces of nature," the quandary is real, at least for people as honorable and devoted to each other as this couple. Arveragus selflessly counsels his wife to uphold her part of the bargain and she reluctantly agrees, but such is the self-correcting nature of the world of "The Franklin's Tale" that the once crafty and unabashed suitor takes pity on Dorigen's obvious suffering and releases her from the promise, even proclaiming her fidelity as a virtue implicitly superior to the code of courtly love. True to its genre, the poem then completes the resolution by releasing Aurelius from his financial obligations through the kindness and mercy of the clerk he had surreptitiously hired to perform the impossible feat. *Gentilesse*, the Chaucerian idiom for nobility and delicacy of character, replaces *governance* as the ruling principle of conjugal relations, and the Marriage Group finds the answer it has been seeking throughout the community of pilgrims. "The Franklin's Tale" thus represents a kind of testament to order in the world of man as well as a coda to a set of literary preludes. In the midst of real and expectable social chaos there is a bit of magic, a moment of harmony in a generally discordant world.

That discord is never more baldly evident than in the shameless words of the Pardoner, a marvelously vile and altogether reprehensible character who will offer, so he claims, a "moral tale." It is difficult to see how such a man could bring it off: A seller of bogus absolutions and false relics, he takes as his theme the oft-quoted aphorism "Radix malorum est Cupiditas" ("The root of all evils is Greed") and goes on to make a case for himself as the contemporary personification of Cupiditas. He straightforwardly and pridefully boasts of swindling well-meaning people searching for religious comfort in the form of supposedly genuine pardons, happy to deprive even the poorest widow of the money that would keep her children from starvation. Ironically true to his claim to be able to instruct although he is himself fast-fettered by sin, the Pardoner launches into a moral exemplum presented as a sermon. His tale, designed to illustrate the eventual retribution to be visited on gluttons and revelers and, by extension, on all those guilty of the deadly sins, is crudely told and leads into hollow apostrophes against what are of course his own flaws, followed by his customary shameless plea for money. His direct address of the Host as the pilgrim most in need of his services inflames Bailly and evokes his memorable threat to denature the Pardoner, a sentiment that the audience—especially the contemporary audience, who had to deal more and more with false sellers of writs as the authority of the Church continued to decline—must have applauded. It remains for the Knight, the embodiment of honor and social protocol and a tale-teller whose words have already served as balm for the ephemeral wounds of Everyman, to brave the verbal fray between these two and restore order to the pilgrim's community.

As an entire work, *The Canterbury Tales* seems to stand incomplete. Only twenty-three of the thirty pilgrims mentioned actually tell a tale, even though the Host's original arrangement called for no fewer than four apiece. The framing device, however, is a fiction that provides unity to a heterogenous collection; it is not a legal document. Especially since *The Canterbury Tales* were composed primarily for reading aloud before an audience, individual stories or groups of stories may well have enjoyed an existence of their own apart from the text as a whole. Chaucer may never have intended to "complete" his most lasting poem at all; having invented the fiction that would cause any number of tales to cohere, he may simply have turned his hand to those characters, issues, genres, and narratives that most attracted him. It seems more than a little pedantic, then, to insist that *The Canterbury Tales* remains incomplete, in the sense of "partial," for Chaucer's vision reached far beyond anything created by even his most talented contemporaries, and the tales he did compose bear eloquent testimony to the fertility of his design.

At the close of "The Parson's Tale" there is one final twist of the narrative thread in *The Canterbury Tales*. Here Chaucer places his "retraction," ostensibly a profession of faith accompanied by a confession of self-proclaimed wrongdoings in some of his poetic works. Critics have pointed out how the retraction has numerous literary precedents and analogues, perhaps the most striking of which is Boccaccio's own rejection of his often bawdy tales in Italian in favor of learned Latin treatises. A reader may also take Chaucer's protestation as another in a series of clever manipulations of his audience, accepting his prayer at face value as both a pious expostulation and a traditional tour de force but recog-

nizing the retraction itself as a form of disclaimer—only this time on the part of Chaucer the poet rather than Chaucer the pilgrim. As has been seen, the narrator is more than adequate to the task of presenting *The Canterbury Tales* in a naturalistic and blameless way, and now the poet further relativizes not only this work but also all others that treat in any way lecherous, scatological, or otherwise irreligious subjects. If Chaucer's retraction honestly professes faith in Christ and hope for eternal salvation, it also allows the poet and audience yet another perspective on the wonderful variety of pilgrims who have trod the stage of *The Canterbury Tales:* They are real, they are complete in themselves, and they collectively figure forth a uniquely engaging pastiche of characteristics, attitudes, values, and beliefs typical of the fourteenth century in particular and of humanity in general. Chaucer cannot retract that achievement.

BIBLIOGRAPHY

Andrew, Malcolm, and Robert Waldron, eds. *Poems of the Pearl Manuscript.* 3d ed. Exeter, Devon: University of Exeter Press, 1997. This collection is updated with notes that take into account some of the more important textual and interpretative scholarship since the appearance of the first edition in 1978. The bibliography has also been updated, and a number of older works have been discreetly removed from the lists.

Bisson, Lillian M. *Chaucer and the Late Medieval World.* New York: St. Martin's Press, 1999. Examines the fourteenth century societal issues that Chaucer explored in his work. Bisson provides lively interpretations of Chaucer's texts, especially *The Canterbury Tales*, in the context of the paradigmatic shifts taking place around him, and offers a broad historical overview—often going back to the early Christian period—to help the reader grasp the significance of those shifts.

Chaucer, Geoffrey. *The Canterbury Tales.* Translated by R. M. Lumiansky. New York: Pocket Books, 1991. Chaucer's various tales come appealingly alive in this version, translated into modern English. The Middle English is explained, yet the beauty of the meter and rhymes remains intact. A good introduction to Chaucer's masterpiece.

　　　　　Critical Survey of Poetry

_____. *The Works of Geoffrey Chaucer.* Edited by F. N. Robinson. 2d ed. Boston: Houghton Mifflin, 1957. Robinson's is the classic edition of Chaucer, including all his extant works. A lengthy introduction surveys the poet's life, works, language, meter, and textual issues. Copious notes throughout. Glossary, index of proper names.

Curtius, Ernst Robert. *European Literature in the Latin Middle Ages.* Translated by Willard R. Trask. 1953. Reprint. Princeton, N.J.: Princeton University Press, 1973. This classic offers coverage of literature on the Continent in the language that dominated written literature in the Western world until the fifteenth century. A must for those investigating the intellectual, spiritual, and social framework for fourteenth century literature.

Luria, Maxwell S., and Richard L. Hoffman, eds. *Middle English Lyrics: Authoritative Texts, Critical and Historical Backgrounds, Perspectives on Six Poems.* New York: W. W. Norton, 1990. Offers one of the largest collections of Middle English lyrics. In all there are 245 lyrics, arranged thematically.

Malory, Thomas. *Mallory: Works.* Edited by Eugène Vinaver. London: Oxford University Press, 1954, The standard edition, which has seen many reprintings since. Vinaver provides an introduction and a glossary.

_____. *Le Morte d'Arthur.* New York: Random House, 1999. Edited and first published by William Caxton in 1485, Thomas Malory's unique and splendid version of the Arthurian legend tells an immortal story of love, adventure, chivalry, treachery, and death. The introduction by Elizabeth J. Bryan places the poem in historical context.

Putter, Ad. *The Gawain-Poet.* New York: Longman, 1996. Provides contextual interpretations and critical analysis of the Gawain Poet and related works. Examines alliterative aspects of, and romance and realism in, medieval poetry. Includes a bibliography and an index.

Saul, Nigel, ed. *The Oxford Illustrated History of Medieval England.* London: Oxford University Press, 2001. Provides a wealth of information on the social, cultural, and religious life of the period, covering topics as varied as the nature of national identity, the character of urban life, the great works of art and architecture, the details of religious practice, and the development of a vernacular literature. Illustrated with more than one hundred pictures—including twenty-four pages of color plates.

Thomas Aquinas. *Selected Philosophical Writings.* Translated by Timothy McDermott. New York: Oxford University Press, 1993. Offers selections of Aquinas's famed works, including *Summa Theologica* and *Summa contra gentiles.* Includes a select bibliography, notes on sources and text, and an index.

Tolkien, J. R. R., trans. *"Sir Gawain and the Green Knight," "Pearl," and "Sir Orfeo."* Edited by Christopher Tolkien. Boston: Houghton Mifflin, 1975. Tolkien is known today mainly as the author of the *Lord of the Rings* cycle, but he was better known during his lifetime as a medievalist and professor of English literature at Oxford University. His translations of Anglo-Saxon works are considered classics. His son Christopher includes a glossary and an appendix on verse forms.

Turville-Petre, Thorlac, ed. *Alliterative Poetry of the Later Middle Ages: An Anthology.* London: Routledge, 1989. Provides critical interpretation of medieval alliterative poems, presented here in Middle English. Introduction and notes in Modern English. Includes a bibliography.

John Miles Foley

ENGLISH POETRY IN THE FIFTEENTH CENTURY

Dwarfed by the mighty accomplishments of Geoffrey Chaucer at one end and the great Elizabethans at the other, fifteenth century poetry has often seemed to stretch like a lesser plain between mountain ranges. There is some truth to this view: By no standard was this a distinguished age in the history of English verse. The English Chaucerian tradition, running from John Lydgate and Thomas Hoccleve to Stephen Hawes, can boast no major poet and only a paucity of significant minor ones, and rarely did fifteenth century works in the well-established popular genres of metrical romance, saint's life, and lyric match the high achievements of the century before. Indeed, the best-known literary productions of the 1400's—the prose Arthurian romances of Thomas Malory and the dramatic cycles of the Corpus Christi season—belong to genres other than poetry. On the other hand, poetry in this period may have suffered a general undervaluation owing to comparisons that it cannot sustain.

If one approaches fifteenth century poetry with chastened expectations and sensitivities attuned to the artistic aims of this period as distinct from others, one can find work of real interest and value. For example, although the age found little original stimulus in matters of poetic form, the carol attained its fullest development during this time, and the ballad was beginning to take shape. Finally, at the turn of the century, three Scots "makars"—Robert Henryson, William Dunbar, and Gavin Douglas—produced verse of a sufficiently high order to warrant labeling the reign of James IV a brief "golden age" of literary Scotland.

HISTORICAL CONTEXT

Although it is always hazardous to speculate on the connections between history and artistic felicity, it remains true that the political and social climate in the fifteenth century did not favor literary achievement. The international stage was still dominated by the Hundred Years' War with France; Henry V's successful invasion, crowned by the victory of Agincourt in 1415, committed his successors to a costly, protracted, and ultimately futile defense of this new French territory against the onslaughts of Joan of Arc and the French king. Meanwhile, in England itself the weakness of Henry VI encouraged factionalism and intrigue which finally erupted in the Wars of the Roses between the Lancastrians and the Yorkists. It was a nation tired of war and depopulated of much of its nobility that welcomed the restoration of civil order in 1485 with the crowning of Henry VII and the establishment of the Tudor dynasty.

This political turbulence severely disrupted the patronage system upon which art throughout the Middle Ages and into the Renaissance had always relied. Early in the century Henry V had encouraged literary production, as had his brother, Humphrey of Gloucester. Yet the decimation and financial impoverishment that subsequently exhausted the aristocracy could hardly serve to foster an atmosphere of courtly refinement such as had supported Chaucer and John Gower. Indeed, it is notable that the fifteenth century witnessed a contraction in most aspects of intellectual and cultural life. Architecture, the visual arts, philosophy, and theology all declined; only in music did the English excel, principally through the harmonic innovations of John Dunstable (1370?-1453). At the same time, the role of the poet seems to have been evolving from that of an entertainer in the tradition of medieval minstrelsy to one of an adviser to princes. Thus the prestige of erudition rose while the indigenous oral traditions fell further into disrepute.

SOCIAL CONTEXT

The rise of the middle class was another factor in the determination of literary tastes. Though depressed economically by the disorders in the middle of the century, this constituency ultimately gained in power as the aristocracy depleted its own ranks and resources. Simultaneously, education and literacy were spreading down the social pyramid. The gradual infiltration of Humanism from the Continent, particularly during the 1480's and 1490's, had as yet made no impression on the literary sensibility: What this new, conservative readership demanded was the familiar and time-honored—such as the lives of saints, or works of the revered Chaucer. This appetite fueled extensive copying of manuscripts, an activity culminating, as chance would have it, in a technological revolution when William Caxton established England's first printing press in 1476. The advent of widespread printing, following Johann Gutenberg's invention of movable type for the printing press, radically and permanently altered the availability of literary works and finally established the written text as the principal medium of poetic exchange.

GENRES AND VERSIFICATION

In their cumulative effect, these factors produced a literary conservatism that persisted throughout the century. Poets of this era turned to their own native tradition, particularly to Chaucer and Gower, for their models and stimulus, a practice contrasting radically with that of Chaucer himself, who wove into his verse many Continental influences. Thus Chaucer's meters, the iambic pentameter and tetrameter, and his rhyme patterns, notably the ballade (*ababbcbc*) and rhyme royal (*ababbcc*) stanzas and the couplet, were widely imitated, even by poets with a most imperfect grasp of what they were imitating. These same poets likewise admired the poetic diction and the rhetorical elevation that Chaucer and Gower had standardized. This influence produced the inflated sententiousness, the rhetorical pomp, and the "aureation" (use of polysyllabic Latinisms) that modern readers often deplore in the verse of Lydgate and his followers.

Yet fifteenth century poets adopted larger poetic forms as well. The many allegories and dream visions of the period clearly model themselves on Chaucer's work and that of his contemporaries. Other genres, such as the romance and lyric, continued to draw upon the same reserve of verse forms, topoi, story patterns, and subjects. Nowhere is the conservative character of the period better revealed than in the inclination toward verse translation. Of course, this was nothing new: The Middle Ages always had great respect for authority, and most writers—even the best—worked from sources. Yet the sheer bulk of fifteenth century translation obtrudes nevertheless, particularly in the number of major works that fall into this class. Lydgate's 36,365-line *The Fall of Princes* 1430-1438, printed 1494), for example, was his longest poetic effort. Further, with the exception of Gavin Douglas's version of the *Aeneid*, seldom do the translations, despite their frequent expansion and sup-

plementation of the originals, stand as significant poetic works in their own right; John Walton's competent yet poetically uninspired rendering of Boethius's *The Consolation of Philosophy* (523) represents the best that the age produced. However sympathetically perceived, this widespread tendency to rely on the matter and inspiration of the past must ultimately be admitted as a weakness in much fifteenth century poetry, translated or otherwise. Rarely do the versifiers exhibit the ability of great traditional poets to return to and re-create the myths embedded in the traditional material.

THE CHAUCERIAN TRADITION

In the late fourteenth century Geoffrey Chaucer, drawing on the French tradition of courtly love and allegory that he found in *Roman de la Rose* (c. 1370; *Romaunt of the Rose*), brought courtly poetry in England to its fullest perfection. His precedent inspired many imitations; allegories, love-debates, and dream visions throughout the fifteenth century attempted to recapture the Chaucerian magic. Although several of these labors show talent, one finds in this tradition little innovation or development beyond the point that Chaucer had reached.

Chaucer's first and historically most significant heir was John Lydgate (1370?-1450?), the prolific monk of Bury St. Edmunds whose influence and prestige over the next two hundred years rivaled those of his master. Written in almost every form and mode available to him, Lydgate's poetic corpus is staggering in its volume and variety: Taken collectively, his many allegories, romances, histories, courtly love poems, fables, epics, lyrics, hymns, prayers, didactic and homiletic works, and occasional pieces total some 145,000 lines. Lydgate's debt to Chaucer and the courtly love tradition appears most plainly in his early work of the first decade of the 1400's. *Complaint of the Black Knight* (c. 1400) and *The Floure of Courtesy* (c. 1400-1402) both feature lovers' complaints in dream-vision garden settings; in the 1,403-line *Temple of Glas* (c. 1410, printed 1477) the poet in a dream visits a temple, styled after Chaucer's House of Fame, in which Venus joins a love-distressed knight and a lady. An allegorical cast and landscape in the manner of *Romaunt of the Rose* give texture to the narrative in *Reson and Sensuallyte* (c. 1408), a pleasant and unfinished 7,042-line translation of the beginning of a long French poem, *Les Echecs Amoureux*. To this early period also belong versions of seven of Aesop's fables, representative of several didactic works in this vein composed by Lydgate at various times. Tales of Mariolatry loosely strung amid much digressive material constitute the 5,932-line *The Lyf of Our Lady* (c. 1409), another early work, and the harbinger of many later efforts in the genre of the legend's or saint's life.

Yet Lydgate's major works were the prodigious translations completed in his later years. Undertaken at the behest of Henry V, the *Troy Book* (1513) rendered Guido delle Colonne's Latin prose history of Troy into 30,117 lines in decasyllabic couplets. The tale of Oedipus and the rivalry of his two sons furnished the matter of the 4,176-line *The Storye of Thebes* (c. 1500), a tale embedded in a narrative frame attaching it to Chaucer's *The Canterbury Tales* (1387-1400). Begun in France in 1426 and probably completed two years later, the 24,832-line *The Pilgrimage of the Life of Man* translates and slightly expands Guillaume de Deguileville's fourteenth century *Pèlerinage de la vie humaine* (c. 1340). The lengthy and popular *The Fall of Princes*, composed for Humphrey of Gloucester between 1430 and 1438, generously renders into English Laurent de Premierfait's version of Giovanni Boccaccio's *De Casibus Illustrium Virorum* (1358), a compendium of medieval "tragedies" of men of greatness whom fickle fortune humbled. In addition to these major works, one finds myriad shorter pieces of every description poured forth profusely throughout the poet's long career.

Time has not smiled upon Lydgate's literary reputation over the last two hundred years. Chief among his alleged sins is his prolixity, but critics also remark a prosodic weakness (especially in the prevalence of "broken-backed" lines), a tendency toward syntactic incoherence, and an infatuation with rhetoric and aureation. Other readers, however, finding these condemnations unduly harsh, note a human empathy, passages of lyric smoothness, and occasionally felicitous imagery, and a few have competently defended the poet's often-slandered craftsmanship. Although it is probable that Lydgate's poetic star will never rise to its former ascendency, it is also likely that future generations will find in his work merits that its amplitude has sometimes tended to obscure.

Less important historically yet in some regards more interesting is Thomas Hoccleve (1368?-1430?), a clerk of the Privy Seal whose attempts to secure patronage and pecuniary recompense would seem to have been less successful than desired. His magnum opus, the *Regement of Princes* (1412), occupies 777 stanzas of rhyme royal after the three-stanza envoy dedicating the work to Henry, Prince of Wales. The body of the *Regement of Princes*, conflating material from three Latin sources, urges the young prince by means of exemplary tales to aspire toward virtue and to eschew vice. Yet the most characteristic portion is the 288-stanza prologue, which amounts to an elaborate begging plea with many melancholy digressions and allusions to contemporary conditions. This autobiographical strain, allied with the many topical references and the poet's endearing love for Chaucer, whom he seems to have known personally, endows Hoccleve's verse with a human and historical interest that constitutes his main claim on posterity. On the other hand, his work lacks serious artistic intention, a sense of structural design, and stylistic distinction. Along with several shorter pieces, his other main poems are *La Male Règle* (1406), the *Letter of Cupid* (1402), and an autobiographically linked series including the *Complaint* (1422), the *Dialogue with a Friend* (1422), the *Tale of Jereslaus' Wife* (1422), *Knowing How to Die*, and the *Tale of Jonathas*.

Three other early "Chaucerians" require mention. Foremost among them is James I of Scotland (1394-1437), who spent most of his childhood as a prisoner of the English. Composed during his captivity, *The Kingis Quair* (1423-1424, *The King's Choir*) pays tribute in 197 stanzas of rhyme royal to Lady Joan Beaufort, whom James married the next year (1424). In the poem the young monarch, complaining about his bad fortune, sees a beautiful woman through his cell window and is smitten with love. That night in a dream he visits Venus, Minerva, and Fortune, the last of whom promises the betterment of his affairs; on this hopeful note he awakes. Betraying a clear debt to Boethius's *The Consolation of Philosophy*, Chaucer's "The Knight's Tale," and Lydgate's *Temple of Glas*, *The King's Choir* was written in the Scots dialect with Midlands admixtures and so occupies an important role in the emerging Scottish tradition.

Another captive nobleman, Charles d'Orleans (1391-1465) sprang directly from the French courtly tradition in which language and traditional idiom he wrote. The main English translation, which Charles may have authored, is a three-part sequence of ballads and rondels dealing conventionally with the progress of several love affairs.

One further work from this early period was Sir John Thomas Clanvowe's *The Boke of Cupide* (1391). This May-time dream vision is dominated by a debate between a cuckoo, who slanders lovers, and a nightingale, who lauds them; the nightingale prevails, and the dream concludes with an assembly of birds. Composed in an unusual five-line stanza (*aabba*), this poem recalls such earlier works in the bird-debate tradition as the thirteenth century *Owl and the Nightingale* (c. 1250) and Chaucer's *Parlement of Foules* (1380).

The allegorical tendency found in the *Temple of Glas* emerges again in a group of poems from the later fifteenth century, most of which were at one time or another apocryphally attributed to Chaucer. One of the finest of these, *The Flower and the Leaf*, depicts through the eyes of a female narrator an amusing incident involving the followers of the Leaf (the laurel) and the followers of the Flower (the daisy). Skillfully composed in 595 lines of rhyme royal, *The Flower and the Leaf* invests its lightly allegorized narrative with much charm of image and detail. Somewhat heavier in its allegorical machinery, the 756-line *Assembly of Ladies* features such characters as Perseverance, Diligence, Countenance, Largesse, Remembrance, and Loyalty. Less courtly and more didactic, the *Court of Sapience*, sometimes attributed to Stephen Hawes, confronts a traveler with a more scholastic variety of allegorical personifications—such as Peace, Mercy, Righteousness, Truth, and the seven arts. Hawes's *The Pastime of Pleasure*, composed shortly before its publication in 1506, recounts the allegorical adventures of Graunde Amour on his road toward knightly perfection and the love of La Belle Pucel. Another early sixteenth century work, *The Court of Love*, far more skillfully narrates Philogenet's visit with Alcestis and Admetus at the Court of Love and recounts his successful wooing of Rosiall; the action closes with a celebration and bird-songs of praise. Thoroughly Chaucerian in form and intention, these poems mark the end of the courtly tradition in medieval English literature.

THE LYRIC

The term "lyric" suggests to most modern readers a highly individualized expression of some personal feeling in concrete language treating a subject of the poet's choice, yet this notion proves misleading in the case of the medieval English lyric. Although this body of poems indeed concerns itself with feelings, the individuality of the poet has been largely effaced; thus most of the surviving pieces are anonymous, not merely because the names of the authors are unknown (with a few exceptions, such as John Audelay and James Ryman), but in the nature of the expression. Moreover, the subjects, the basis on which these poems are usually classified, belong to a common cultural word hoard that also provides much of the standard imagery and diction. The consequence is a poetic genre expressive of what might be called "public experience"—moods, thoughts, and emotions defined and recognized in the public mind.

The essential continuity of the English medieval lyric from its beginnings in the mid-thirteenth century to the closing of the Middle Ages reveals itself in the persistence of certain lyric types, such as the Passion poem (treating Christ's Passion), the hymn to Mary, and the praise and complaint of lovers. Yet the fifteenth century brought its share of changes. One new development was a growing literary self-awareness with a corresponding loss of freshness and spontaneity, characteristics that had distinguished early English lyrics from their more artificial French counterparts. New motifs came into prominence, such as the Marian lament; other poems elaborated old themes to greater lengths with an increasingly aureate diction.

The fifteenth century's most distinctive contribution lay in the flowering of a relatively new lyric form, the carol. Medieval English lyrics in general, employing a variety of metrical and stanzaic patterns, share no defining formal characteristics. The carol differs in this regard: R. L. Greene, the editor of the standard anthology, defines this lyric type as "a song on any subject, composed of uniform stanzas and provided with a burden." Sung at the beginning and repeated after every stanza, the burden is a group of lines, most often a couplet, that usually signals a major theme or subject in the poem. Some claim that the carol originated as a dance song. In any event, it is clear that during the fifteenth century the carol was developing a connection with the Christmas season; many explicitly celebrated the Nativity in a manner familiar to modern readers from Christmas carols of the present era. The genre was not restricted to this subject, however; one of the most beautiful and haunting of all carols is a Passion elegy whose burden runs, "Lulley, lulley, lulley, lulley;/ The fawcon hath born my mak away."

Medieval lyrics are usually classified on the basis of subject into two groups, the religious and the secular, with the religious poems being far more numerous. The most popular subject was the Virgin, whose cult still flourished in the late Middle Ages. Some of these Marian poems, adopting the conventions of secular love verse, proclaimed her inexpressible beauty, or praised her bodily parts, or begged for her mercy, or presented her with a Valentine's Day offering. More often, however, these lyrics derived from the Latin liturgical tradition. Many such pieces celebrated various of the Virgin's five joys—the Annunciation, the Nativity, the Resurrection, the Ascension, and the Assumption; "The Maiden Makeles" is a particularly famous Nativity song. God and Christ were often the objects of address; "Close in my Breast thy Perfect Love" harks in its intimate tenderness back to the fourteenth century mystical tradition of Richard Rolle. Christ's Passion provided another major subject in poems that tended toward a more extended narrative treatment and greater didacticism than in previous periods. In one common and distinctive type of Passion poem, Christ Himself addresses humanity directly from the Cross. A new fifteenth century trend introduced the theme of Mary's compassion and her participation in Christ's suffering. Lyrics in the *planctus* mode give expression to her grief; other poems present this theme through dialogues between the Virgin and Son.

Turning to the secular lyrics, one finds in the fifteenth century, as in most ages, a preponderance of love songs. All the expected types appear: praise to a lady and enumeration of her beauties, complaints about her cruelty and fickleness, laments on a lover's absence, and epistles, such as the one that opens "Go, litull bill, and command me hertely/ Unto her. . . ." Some lyrics take the form of antifeminist diatribes; others are plainly pornographic. One interesting anonymous series, *The Lover's Mass*, tastefully mimics the liturgy in fine love poems bearing such titles as the *Introibo*, *Kyrie*, and *Gloria*. A dramatic framework informs the highly praised "Nut Brown Maid," a debate between a woman and an earl's son disguised as a knightly outlaw which culminates in a self-revelation and a marriage offer. Other types of secular lyrics include drinking songs, charms and gnomes, and poems on historical events. In the meditations on fortune and worldly happiness, one can once more discern a growing religious tone in the contemplation of human affairs, a tone that emerges explicitly in the songs on death, the penitential confessions, and the homilies on virtue and vice. Cutting across this entire dichotomy of the secular and the religious are lyric types distinguishable by their objects of address. Poems addressed to the reader tend toward didacticism; lyrics addressing a third party (such as the Virgin or a human beloved) define themselves between the polarities of celebration and of complaint or petition. An appreciation for both strains, the didactic and the celebratory, is an essential prerequisite to any competent reading of medieval lyrics.

POPULAR NARRATIVE: ROMANCES AND BALLADS

During the fifteenth century two forms of popular narrative overlapped as the metrical romance declined and the ballad rose to supplant it. Though the relationship between these genres remains unsettled, both were probably circulated orally, and the traveling minstrel performers may have provided a line of continuity between them. This context of oral performance helps to explain in both cases the frequent verbal and narrative formulas that overly sophisticated readers are likely to condemn as "trite" and "stereotyped." At the same time, differences in subject matter and narrative technique clearly distinguish the two forms.

The first English romances appeared in the middle of the thirteenth century, at the very time when this aristocratic form had begun its decline in France. Descended from the *chanson de geste*, the French romance was a tale of knightly adventure that celebrated the ideals of bravery in battle, chivalric honor, courtesy, and service to a lady. Showing little concern for verisimilitude or psychological realism, these stories pitted their shallowly portrayed heroes against frequently supernatural and fabulous adversaries in a string of encounters joined less by a sense of "organic unity" than by a technique of narrative interlace. The English romances were regularly "translations" of such French works and exhibit many of these same characteristics. They also borrow most of their stories from the French cycles, specifically the "matters" of Britain (including the Arthurian cycle and unrelated "English" tales such as *Haveloc* written in the early thirteenth century), France (the Charlemagne cycle), and antiquity (including the cycles of Alexander, Troy, and Thebes). Other tales deal with the Orient, and a few bear no relation to any major cycle.

Fifteenth century romances have been relatively neglected in favor of Sir Thomas Malory's *Le Morte d'Arthur* (c. 1469, printed 1485), the greatest of the many prose narratives published by Caxton, yet the metrical romance persisted as a popular form: According to the *Wells Manual*, some thirty can be dated roughly from the fifteenth century, with a growing number from Scotland in the later decades. Lengths ranged from 516 lines in the cases of *The Grene Knight*, an unhappy condensation of *Sir Gawain and the Green Knight* (c. 1370), to the 27,852 lines of Henry Lovelich's *Merlin*, a translation of the prose French Vulgate. The most common verse patterns were rhyming octosyllabic couplets and tail-rhyme stanzas, although occasionally other forms, such as the rhyme royal or ballade stanza, made their appearance. Although the Alliterative Revival had passed its prime, alliterative tendencies still persisted in Northumbria and Scotland, yielding late in the century such Middle Scots works as *Golagrus and Gawain* (c. 1500) and *The Taill of Rauf Coilyear*.

In their choice of subjects, fifteenth century romancers followed the established channels described earlier. One of the best-known Arthurian romances is the stanzaic *Morte Arthur* (c. 1360), a 3,969-line account of Lancelot's role in Arthur's downfall. Most of the romances from the Arthurian cycle depict the deeds of Gawain, who in the English tradition (unlike the French) remained for the most part a model knight. Two of the best Gawain romances are *The Avowynge of King Arthur, Sir Gawan, Sir Kaye, and Sir Bawdewyn of Bretan* (c. 1425), which follows each knight's separate path of adventure, and *Golagrus and Gawain*, whose plot hinges on a noble act of self-effacement by Gawain. Af-

ter the Arthurian cycle, the next most popular source of lore for romance was the life of Alexander. *The Alliterative Alexander Fragment C* (c. 1450) verges on the epic manner; far more leisurely and episodic in its narrative style, the 11,138-line *Scottish Alexander Buik* (1438) is surpassed in length by another bulky Middle Scots poem, Gilbert Hay's 20,000-line *Buik of Alexander*. In other areas, the wars of Troy and Thebes inspired a handful of romances, two by Lydgate; a small group, including only *The Taill of Rauf Coilyear* and a Middle English *Song of Roland* (c. 1100), belong to the Charlemagne cycle; five or six others, such as *Eger and Grime* (c. 1450) and John Metham's *Amoryus and Cleopes* (c. 1448), treat miscellaneous subjects. By 1500, the 250-year-old English metrical romance tradition had, with a few minor exceptions, reached an end.

David Fowler has argued that in the late Middle Ages, as the medieval minstrels were increasingly denied access to the courts of the higher nobility, the romance converged with the folk song to produce a shorter, simplified, less episodic narrative form that we now call the ballad. While origins of balladry remain a controversial subject, it is certainly the case that the ballad is one of the few medieval forms that did not perish with the Renaissance and its aftermath, and as such it has a special claim to modern interest. The most thoroughly oral of the genres so far considered, the ballad could be defined as a short narrative poem, usually composed in two- or four-line stanzas, and distinguished by its concentration on a single event or episode. Unlike romances, which characteristically "tell" their stories, ballads tend to "show" their action directly through dramatic dialogue stripped of descriptive scene-setting. The ballad style is formulaic: Tags, phrases, motifs, and episodes are repeated throughout the ballad tradition, and the poems themselves have survived in multiple versions. The general impersonality of the formulaic style is reinforced by the absence of a distinctive narrative persona. Although current opinion favors individual and not group composition, in its cumulative effect balladry strikes one as reflecting the outlook of a community and tradition, not that of some particular person.

Although most extant ballads survive in collections from the seventeenth century and later, many of these poems may have originated in the fifteenth century or even before, for oral traditions have a well-demonstrated ability to transmit story patterns over remarkably long periods of time. The reconstruction of a specific ballad's evolution remains a speculative and subjective process, however, and there are a mere handful of documentably fifteenth century ballads, most of which narrate the adventures of Robin Hood. The choice of this legendary outlaw as a hero presents a departure from the usual practice of romancers with their knightly, aristocratic adventurers; indeed, later ballads do tend to draw subjects from middle-class life more often than romances had done. This point, however, should not be overemphasized: Ballads and romances retain many similarities of motif, story pattern, and even metrical form; in several cases, such as *Hind Horn* and *King Horn* (c. 1250), a ballad and romance relate the same story. Yet during the fifteenth century the ballad had begun a life of its own that would lead in its peregrinations down to the modern day to a point far from its medieval origins.

OTHER FIFTEENTH CENTURY POETRY

The prestige of the courtly tradition did not obscure the power that religious narrative continued to exercise over the popular imagination. Indeed, collections of saints' lives of the type represented in the *South English Legendary* and the *Golden Legend* enjoyed immense popularity throughout the century although original composition in this vein was on the decline. One of the most prolific of the religious versifiers, Osbern Bokenham, composed between 1443 and 1447 a group of thirteen saints' lives under the title *The Lives of Saints: Or, Legends of Holy Women.* The versatile Lydgate several times turned his hand to this genre; even John Capgrave, a learned friar who customarily wrote in prose, composed lives of Saint Norbert and Saint Katharine in rhyme royal. One must further note the numerous translations and verse paraphrases of books of the Bible, both Old and New Testaments, even if their literary achievement is slight.

A number of shorter poems address themselves to the events or conditions of the day. Major military conflicts such as the Battle of Agincourt and the Wars of the Roses inspired commemorative ballads and lyrics. A spirited series in prose and crude poetry, *Jack Upland, Friar Daw's Reply,* and *Jack Upland's Rejoinder,* ex-

change blows on the subjects of friars and Lollardy. Long attributed to Lydgate, *London Lickpenny* (1515) vividly depicts life in the late medieval metropolis. Other poems in this satirical vein lament the state of the clergy and the general evils of the age.

A considerable bulk of the surviving poetry seems to be little more than versified prose. *The Libel of English Policy*, for example, makes recommendations on foreign trade policy in couplets and rhymed royal stanzas totaling 1,141 lines. Similarly, pragmatic intentions appear in John Russell's *Book of Carving and Nature*, an *Ordinal of Alchemy*, and *The Babees Book*, the latter an instruction on points of etiquette. By far the longest of these poems is Peter Idley's 7,000-line *Instructions to His Son*, which gives advice on a variety of subjects.

THE SCOTTISH MAKARS

In the fifteenth century in Scotland, an era concluding in military cataclysm as England crushed James IV and his Scottish forces at the Battle of Flodden Field in 1513, one finds a burgeoning literature with several poets or "makars" of real greatness. John Barbour, in many respects the founder of the English-language poetic tradition in Scotland, had already sounded a patriotic note in *The Bruce* (c. 1375), an epic romance celebrating the deeds of Robert the Bruce, national liberator and victor at the Battle of Bannockburn (1314). In 1423-1424 James I introduced a courtlier, more Chaucerian strain in *The King's Choir*. Two other poems sometimes ascribed to James, *Christis Kirk on the Green* and *Peblis to the Play*, initiate a Scottish comic tradition that continues in such works as *Sym and His Brudir, The Wyf of Auchtiramuchty, Cockelbie's Sow,* and even the romance *The Taill of Rauf Coilyear*. Exhibiting the superb mastery of an intricate, interlocking stanzaic pattern, *Christis Kirk on the Green* and *Peblis to the Play* are both distinguished for their vividly sketched rustic settings and their rough-and-tumble humor.

Meanwhile, the nationalistic and historical tradition of Barbour was carried on by Andrew of Wyntoun (1350?-1424) in his *Orygynale Chronikil of Scotland*, a lifeless history of the nation from Creation to the time of writing. Composed in octosyllabic couplets, Wyntoun's chronicle is best known now as the source of the Macbeth story that William Shakespeare found in Raphael Holinshed's *Chronicles of England, Scotland, and Ireland* (1577). By far the most popular and influential Scottish poem of the century was *The Wallace*, ascribed to a certain Blind Harry and completed before 1488. A companion piece to *The Bruce*, Harry's eleven-book heroic romance is based on the life of William Wallace (1272-1305), an unsuccessful Scottish insurgent a generation before Robert the Bruce. The first sustained Scottish work in decasyllabic couplets, *The Wallace* often irks modern readers with its chauvinistic romanticization, its repetitiveness, and its lack of psychological depth. At the same time, the poem does not lack enthusiasm, and many passages show real poetic power.

The work of Robert Henryson (1430?-1506?) and William Dunbar (1460?-1520?) is unrivaled in fifteenth century poetry, Scottish or English. The label "Scottish Chaucerians" attached to these and other Middle Scots poets should be rejected, for it clouds their essential originality. Nevertheless, the poem for which Henryson is best known, *The Testament of Cresseid* (1532), is a 615-line continuation of the fifth book of Chaucer's *Troilus and Criseyde* (1382) in rhyme royal stanzas. Cresseid, rejected by Diomede, blasphemes against the gods, who accordingly punish her with leprosy. Troilus rides past one day and, pitying the wretched woman, whom he fails to recognize, tosses her a purse; learning the name of her benefactor, Cresseid repents, sends him a ring token, and dies. A poetic tour de force, *The Testament of Cresseid* presents a stern and uncompromising moral vision in which Cresseid falls as the result of her own wrongdoing; nevertheless, she ultimately finds redemption. Another major effort, the 633-line *Tale of Orpheus* (1508) interprets the Orpheus myth in a standard allegorical fashion. Of Henryson's some dozen minor poems, perhaps the best is "Robene and Makyne," a debate of wooing and rebuttal with an amusing dramatic reversal.

Henryson's magnum opus was his 2,975-line collection, *Fables* (1621). The didactic character of these thirteen fables of Aesop is reflected in the twenty to seventy-line *moralitas* following each one; composed in rhyme royal, the fables show in their ordering an awareness of total design. Henryson's poetry in general lacks the dazzling stylistic virtuosity of Dunbar's, although his meticulous craftsmanship cannot be faulted. His greatness

lies more in his moral profundity, his detached, ironic humor, and his ability to depict the small and commonplace. In the sources of his learning and the tendency to allegorize, Henryson looks more to the Middle Ages than to the Renaissance; despite the usual Chaucerian influence and a competence in handling aristocratic themes, he belongs more to the parish pulpit than to the court.

Henryson's temperamental opposite, William Dunbar, flourished in the court of James IV during the first decade of the sixteenth century until the demise of his royal patron at Flodden Field. Although he never attempted a work of much more than five hundred lines, his range of form and manner was otherwise matched only by the apparent fluctuations of his mood. "The Thrissill and the Rois" (1503), a dream vision in the Chaucerian allegorical fashion, celebrates the marriage of Margaret Tudor (the "Rose") and James IV (the "Thistle"). Another allegory of love, "The Goldyn Targe" (c. 1508), launches its poet-narrator into another dream vision before the court of Venus, where he is wounded by the arrows of Dame Beauty. Similar in spirit is *The Merle and the Nightingale*, in which the two birds debate on the subject of love. "The Tretis of the Tua Mariit Wemen and the Wedo" treats love more satirically, as these depraved discussants contemplate sex and their husbands. Satire turns to invective in "The Flyting of Dunbar and Kennedy," a distinctively Scottish form in which the poetic contestants hurl at one another volleys of extravagant verbal abuse.

Dunbar also had his darker moments, as in "The Dance of the Sevin Deidly Synnis" (c. 1503-1508), in which the dreaming poet watches Mohammed preside over the grotesque festivities of his fiendish crew (Christian versus Muslim "infidels" being a common theme during the Middle Ages). *Lament for the Makaris*, with its refrain "Timor Mortis conturbat me" ("the fear of death disturbs me"), evokes the elegiac strain and the theme of the world's ephemerality that recur again in *This World Unstabille* and *In Winter*; a sonorous musical power adds weight to poems on the Nativity and the Resurrection. Among Dunbar's numerous remaining shorter poems, many were addressed to the king and the royal family. Some readers find Dunbar deficient in human sympathy and in his vision, but none can deny his imaginative inventiveness, tonal and emotional range, satirical humor tending toward the grotesque, and prosodic and stylistic genius that finds few equals in any period.

Although Gavin Douglas (1475?-1522) turned to the classical world for his greatest literary attempt, the generality of his work, like that of his immediate peers and predecessors, belongs more to the Middle Ages than to the humanistic movements then stirring on the Continent and in England. His debt to the Chaucerian tradition appears in his early poems, *The Palice of Honour* and *King Hart*, both love allegories in the tired French and Chaucerian manner. His rendering of the *Aeneid* into heroic couplets, completed just before Flodden Field in 1513, was the first; it remains one of the finest of all verse translations of this Vergilian masterpiece. Matching poetic style to social degree, Douglas employed heavy alliteration in passages relating to rustic characters and reserved a "noble" style for aristocratic matters. He also contributed an original prologue to each book. The total result, less a translation than a re-creation of the Roman epic into the Middle Scots language and idiom, exerted a regrettably minor influence on later poetry because of Scotland's political collapse and the rapid linguistic changes that followed. Flodden Field sounded the death knell to a literary era, but even as it did, English-language poetry was about to experience fresh influences and the revitalization of the Renaissance.

BIBLIOGRAPHY

Boffey, Julia, and Jeremy Griffiths, eds. *Manuscripts of English Courtly Love Lyrics in the Later Middle Ages*. Dover, N.H.: D. S. Brewer, 1985.

Cooney, Helen, ed. *Nation, Court, and Culture: New Essays on Fifteenth Century Poetry*. Dublin, Ireland: Four Courts Press, 2001.

Ebin, Lois A. *Illuminator, Makar, Vates: Visions of Poetry in the Fifteenth Century*. Lincoln: University of Nebraska Press, 1988.

Furrow, Melissa M., ed. *Ten Fifteenth Century Comic Poems*. Garland Medieval Texts 13. New York: Garland Publishing, 1985.

Gittes, Katharine S. *Framing "The Canterbury Tales": Chaucer and the Medieval Frame Narrative Tradition*. Contributions to the Study of World Literature 41. New York: Greenwood Press, 1991.

Leonard, Francis McNeely. *Laughter in the Courts of Love: Comedy in Allegory, from Chaucer to Spenser*. Norman, Okla.: Pilgrim Books, 1981.

Morgan, Gwendolyn A., ed. *Medieval Ballads: Chivalry, Romance, and Everyday Life, a Critical Anthology*. New York: Peter Lang, 1996.

Scanlon, Larry. *Narrative, Authority, and Power: The Medieval Exemplum and the Chaucerian Tradition*. Cambridge, England: Cambridge University Press, 1994. Explores the political and ideological significance of the medieval exemplum, a brief narrative form used to illustrate a moral, by studying four major works in the Chaucerian tradition (*The Canterbury Tales*, John Gower's *Confessio Amantis*, Thomas Hoccleve's *Regement of Princes*, and Lydgate's *The Fall of Princes*).

Ward Parks

ENGLISH POETRY IN THE SIXTEENTH CENTURY

The poetry of the sixteenth century defies facile generalizations. Although the same can obviously be said for the poetry of other periods as well, this elusiveness of categorization is particularly characteristic of the sixteenth century. It is difficult to pinpoint a century encompassing both the growling meter of John Skelton and the polished prosody of Sir Philip Sidney, and, consequently, past efforts to provide overviews of the period have proven unhelpful. Most notably, C. S. Lewis in his *English Literature in the Sixteenth Century Excluding Drama* (1954) contrived an unfortunate division between what he called "drab" poetry and "Golden" poetry. What he means by this distinction is never entirely clear, and Lewis himself further confuses the dichotomy by occasionally suggesting that his own term "drab" need not have a pejorative connotation, although when he applies it to specific poets, it is clear that he intends it to be damaging. Furthermore, his distinction leads him into oversimplifications. As Lewis would have it, George Gascoigne is mostly drab (a condition that he sees as befitting a poet of the "drab" mid-century) though blessed with occasional "Golden" tendencies, while Robert Southwell, squarely placed in the "Golden" period, is really a mediocre throwback to earlier "drab" poetry. Such distinctions are hazy and not helpful to the reader, who suspects that Lewis defines "drab" and "Golden" simply as what he himself dislikes or prefers in poetry.

The muddle created by Lewis's terminology has led to inadequate treatments of the sixteenth century in the classroom. Perhaps reinforced by the simplicity of his dichotomy, teachers have traditionally depicted the fruits of the century as not blossoming until the 1580's, with the sonneteers finally possessing the talent and good sense to perfect the experiments with the Petrarchan sonnet form first begun by Sir Thomas Wyatt early in the century. Students have been inevitably taught that between Wyatt and Sidney stretched a wasteland of mediocre poetry, disappointing primarily because so many poets failed to apply their talents to continuing the Petrarchan experiments begun by Wyatt. Thus, indoctrinated in the "axiom" that, as concerns the sixteenth century, "good" poetry is Petrarchan and "bad" poetry is that which fails to work with Petrarchan conceits, teachers deal in the classroom mostly with the poets of the 1580's and later, ignoring the other poetic currents of the early and mid-century. It has been difficult indeed to overcome Lewis's dichotomy of "drab" and "Golden."

Fortunately, there have been studies of sixteenth century poetry that are sensitive to non-Petrarchan efforts, and these studies deserve recognition as providing a better perspective for viewing the sixteenth century. In 1939, Yvor Winters's essay "The Sixteenth Century Lyric in England: A Critical and Historical Reinterpretation" focused on some of the less notable poets of the period, such as Barnabe Googe, George Turberville, and George Gascoigne, who, until Winters's essay, had been dismissed simply because they were not Petrarchan in sentiment, and the essay also helped to dispel the notion that the aphoristic, proverbial content of their poetry was symptomatic of their simple-mindedness and lack of talent. By pointing out how their sparse style contributes to, rather than detracts from, the moral content of their poetry, Winters's essay is instrumental in helping the reader develop a sense of appreciation for these often overlooked poets. In addition to Winters's essay, Douglas L. Peterson's book *The English Lyric from Wyatt to Donne: A History of the Plain and Eloquent Styles* (1967), taking up where Winters left off, identified two major poetic currents in the sixteenth century: the plain style and the eloquent style. Peterson provided a more realistic and less judgmental assessment of the non-Petrarchans as practitioners of the "plain" rhetorical style, a term that was a welcome relief from Lewis's "drab." Thus, Winters's and Peterson's efforts were helpful in destroying the damaging stereotypes about the "bad" poets of the mid-century.

POETRY AS CRAFT

Despite the difficulties inherent in summarizing a century as diverse as the sixteenth, it is possible to discern a unifying thread running through the poetry of the period. The unity stems from the fact that, perhaps more than any other time, the sixteenth century was consistently "poetic"; that is, the poets were constantly aware of themselves as poetic craftsmen. From Skelton to Edmund Spenser, poets were self-conscious of their pursuits, regardless of theme. This poetic self-conscious-ness was manifested primarily in the dazzling display of metrical, stanzaic, and prosodic experimentation that characterized the efforts of all the poets, from the most talented to the most mediocre. In particular, the century experienced the development of, or refinement upon, for example, the poulter's measure (alternate twelve-and fourteen-syllable lines), blank verse, heroic couplets, rime royal, ottava rima, terza rima, Spenserian stanza, douzains, fourteeners—all appearing in a variety of gen-res. Characteristic of the century was the poet watching himself be a poet, and every poet of the century would have found himself in agreement with Sidney's assess-ment of the poet in his *Defence of Poesie* (1595) as prophet or seer, whose craft is suffused with divine in-spiration.

SOCIAL CONTEXT

This process of conscious invention and self-moni-toring is one key to understanding the poetry of the six-teenth century. It is a curious fact that whereas in other periods, historical and social factors play a large role in shaping poetic themes, in the sixteenth century, such extraliterary influences did little to dictate the nature of the poetry. Surprisingly, even though Copernicus's the-ory of a heliocentric universe was known by mid-cen-tury, the poetry barely nodded to the New Science or to the new geographical discoveries. Certainly, the century experienced almost constant political and religious tur-bulence, providing abundant fare for topical themes; a less apolitical period one can hardly imagine. It was the prose, however, more than the poetry, that sought to re-cord the buffetings created by the fact that the official re-ligion in England changed four times between 1530 and 1560.

It seems that the instability created by this uneasiness had the effect of turning the poets inward, rather than outward to political, social, and religious commentary (with the exceptions of the Broadside Ballads, pseudo-journalistic poems intended for the uncultivated, and the verse chronicle history so popular at the close of the cen-tury), bearing out the hypothesis that good satire can flourish only in periods of relative stability. For exam-ple, despite the number of obvious targets, the genre of political satire did not flourish in the sixteenth century,

and its sporadic representatives, in particular anticlerical satire, a warhorse left over from the Middle Ages, are barely noteworthy. A major figure in Spenser's *The Faerie Queene* (1590-1596) is Gloriana, a figure depict-ing Queen Elizabeth, but she is an idealized rendering, only one of many such celebrations in poetry of Queen Elizabeth, not intended to provide a realistic insight into her character.

RISE OF VERNACULAR LANGUAGES

Thus, to the poet of the sixteenth century, the pri-mary consideration of the poetic pursuit was not who or what to write about, but rather how to write. The reason for this emphasis on style over content is simple enough to isolate. By the middle of the sixteenth century, the En-glish language was experiencing severe growing pains. In fact, throughout Europe the vernacular was struggling to overthrow the tyranny of Latin and to discover its essen-tial identity. Nationalism was a phenomenon taking root everywhere, and, inevitably, the cultivation of native languages was seen as the logical instrument of expedit-ing the development of national identity. Italy and France were undergoing revolts against Latin, and Joachim du Bellay's *La Défense et illustration de la langue française* (1549; *The Defence and Illustration of the French Lan-guage*, 1939) proclaimed explicitly that great works can be written in the vernacular. In England, the invention of new words was encouraged, and war was waged on "inkhornisms," terms of affectation usually held over from the old Latin or French, used liberally by Skelton. Thus, George Puttenham, an influential critical theorist of the period, discusses the question of whether or not a poet would be better advised to use "pierce" rather than "penetrate," and Richard Mulcaster, Spenser's old head-master, was moved to announce, "I honor the Latin, but I worship English."

It was no easy task, however, to legislate prescribed changes in something as malleable as language, and the grandeur of the effort nevertheless often produced comic results. Sixteenth century English vernacular, trying to weed out both Latin and French influences, produced such inelegant and uneasy bastardizations as "man-nerlier," "newelties," "hable" (a hangover from Latin *habilis*), and "semblably," leading William Webbe in his *Discourse of English Poetry* (1586) to rail in a sneering pun about "this brutish poetry," with "brutish" looming as a veiled reference to "British." Although the sixteenth century was constantly discovering that the subtleties of perfecting a new language could not be mastered overnight, the effort was nevertheless sustained and paved the way for a future confidence in what the vernacular could achieve. Words that often strike the modern reader as outdated, stodgy pedantry are, in fact, the uncertain by-products of innovative experimentation.

Thus, to understand sixteenth century poetry is to ignore the stability of language, which is taken for granted in later centuries, and to understand the challenge that the poets experienced in shaping the new language to fit their poetry. Working with new words meant changes in the old classical syntax, and, in turn, changes in the syntax meant changes in the old classical versifications. These changes often resulted in frustration for the poet (and for the reader), but, depending on the skills of the poet, the result of all this experimentation could mean new rhyme schemes, new meters, and new stanzaic structures. In the wake of all the excitement generated by this constant experimentation, the poets cannot be blamed for often judging innovations in content as secondary to the new prosody. The volatility and flux of the language siphoned all energies into perfecting new styles not into content.

TRANSLATIONS

The zeal for metrical experimentation which characterized the sixteenth century is manifested not only in the original poetry of the period but also in the numerous translations that were being turned out. The primary purpose of the translations was to record the works of the venerable authorities in the new vernacular, and it is significant that Webbe refers to these works not as being "translated" but as being "Englished." Vergil's *Aeneid* (c. 29-19 B.C.E.) was a favorite target for the translators, with the Earl of Surrey publishing a translation in 1554, Thomas Phaer in 1558, and Richard Stanyhurst in 1582. Stanyhurst translated only the first four books, and he achieved a metrical monstrosity by attempting to translate Vergil in English hexameters, reflecting the tensions of cramming old subject matter into new forms. Ovid was another favorite of the translators. Arthur Golding translated the *Metamorphoses* in 1567, and also in that

year, George Turberville translated the *Heroides*, featuring elaborate experiments with the poulter's measure, fourteeners, and blank verse. Most of the translations of the period may be dismissed as the works of versifiers, not poets (with the exception of George Chapman's Homer, which has the power of an original poem), but they are valuable reflections of the constant metrical experimentations taking place and, subsequently, of the ongoing process of shaping the new vernacular.

LITERARY THEORY

An overview of the poetry of the 1500's would be incomplete without an introduction to the critical theory of the period and the ways in which it recorded the successes and failures of the new vernacular experimentations. Not surprisingly, critical theory of the age was abundant. An obvious representative is Sidney's *Defence of Poesie*. The elegance and polish of this argument for the superiority of poetry over any other aesthetic pursuit has made it the most outstanding example of Renaissance critical theory. The easy grace of the work, however, tends to obscure the fact that the new experiments in prosody had created a lively, often nasty debate in critical theory between the guardians of the old and the spokesmen for the new. There were many other works of critical theory closer than the *Defense of Poesie* to the pulse rate of the arguments.

The turbulent nature of the critical theory of the period (and, by implications, the turbulence of the poetry itself) is reflected by George Gascoigne, who in his "Certayne Notes of Instruction Concerning the Making of Verse" (1575) serves as a hearty spokesman for the new vernacular, advocating a more widespread use of monosyllables in poetry and a rejection of words derived from foreign vocabularies so that "the truer Englishman you shall seem and the less you shall smell of the inkhorn," and decrying poets who cling to the old Latin syntax by placing their adjectives after the noun. In his *Art of English Poesy* (1589), George Puttenham scolds those poets who "wrench" their words of fit the rhyme, "for it is a sign that such a maker is not copious in his own language." Not every critic, however, was so enchanted with the new experimentation. In his *Art of Rhetorique* (1553), Thomas Wilson called for continued practice of the old classical forms, and he sought to remind poets that words of Latin and Greek derivation are useful in composition. Contempt for new techniques in versification pervades Roger Ascham's *The Schoolmaster* (1570). He condemns innovations in rhyming, which he dismisses as derived from the "Gothes and Hunnes," and calls for renewed imitation of classical forms. In his *Discourse of English Poetry*, William Webbe is even less charitable. He scorns the new experiments in prosody as "this tinkerly verse," and he campaigns for keeping alive the old, classical quantitative verse, in which the meter is governed by the time required to pronounce a syllable, not by accentuation. Clearly the severity of the critical debate needs to be kept in the forefront as one begins consideration of the poetry of the period; to fail to do so is to overlook what the poets were trying to accomplish.

ALLEGORIES AND DREAM VISIONS

The opening of the sixteenth century, however, was anything but a harbinger of new developments to come. Like most centuries, the sixteenth began on a conservative, even reactionary note, looking backward to medieval literature, rather than forward to the new century. Allegories and dream visions written in seven-line stanzas, favorite vehicles of the medieval poets, dominated the opening years of the sixteenth century. Under Henry VII the best poets were Scottish—William Dunbar, Gavin Douglas, and Sir David Lindsay—and they were devoted imitators of Geoffrey Chaucer. The first English poet to assert himself in the new century was Stephen Hawes, who wrote *The Pastime of Pleasure* in 1509, representing uninspired medievalism at its worst. The work is constructed as a dream-vision allegory. An almost direct imitation of John Lydgate, *The Pastime of Pleasure* narrates the hero Grand Amour's instruction in the Tower of Doctrine, employing a profusion of stock, allegorical characters reminiscent of the morality plays. The old medieval forms, especially those combining allegory and church satire, were hard to die. In 1536, Robert Shyngleton wrote *The Pilgrim's Tale*, a vulgar, anticlerical satire directly evocative of Chaucer, and as late as 1556, John Heywood wrote *The Spider and the Fly*, a lengthy allegory depicting the Roman Catholics as flies, the Protestants as spiders, and Queen Mary as wielding a cleaning broom.

JOHN SKELTON

Another heavy practitioner of the dream allegory was John Skelton, one of the most puzzling figures of the century. Skelton has long been an object of negative fascination for literary historians—and with good reason. He deserves a close look, however, because, despite his reactionary themes, he was the first metrical experimenter of the century. His paradoxical undertaking of being both metrical innovator and medieval reactionary has produced some of the oddest, even comic, poetry in the English language. His infamous Skeltonic meter, a bewildering mixture of short, irregular lines and an array of varying rhyme schemes, relies on stress, alliteration, and rhyme, rather than on syllabic count, and as a result, the reader is left either outraged or amused. His subject matter was inevitably a throwback to earlier medieval themes. He wrote two dream-vision allegories, *The Bowge of Court* (1499), a court satire, and *The Garlande of Laurell* (1523). Skelton is still read today, however, because of his fractured meter. The theme of his *Collyn Clout* (1522), a savage satire on the corruption of the English clergy (whose title, incidentally, was the inspiration for Spenser's *Colin Clouts Come Home Againe*, 1591), is of interest to the modern reader not so much for its content as for its versification. In the work, Skelton describes his own rhyme as being "Tatterèd and jaggèd/ Rudely rain-beaten/ Rusty and moth-eaten." Skelton's rhyme arrives fast and furious, and it is possible to conclude that he may have been the object of Puttenham's attack on poets who "wrench" their words to fit the rhyme.

CONTINENTAL INFLUENCES

Despite his original metrical experimentation, Skelton was still entrenched in inkhornisms and looked backward for his themes. Paradoxically, as is often the case, it can be the poet with the least talent who nevertheless injects into his poetry vague hints of things to come. Alexander Barclay wrote no poetry of the slightest worth, but embedded in the mediocrity lay the beginnings of a new respect for the vernacular. To the literary historian, Barclay is of interest for two reasons. First, he was the sixteenth century's first borrower from the Continent. Specifically, in his *Certayn Egloges* (1570), he was the first to imitate the eclogues of Mantuan, which were first printed in 1498 and which revolutionized the genre of the pastoral eclogue by making it a vehicle for anticlerical satire, although such satire was of course nothing new in England at that time. Barclay's second importance, however (and perhaps the more significant), lies in the fact that he was the first to use the vernacular for the pastoral.

TOTTEL'S MISCELLANY

It was not until mid-century that English borrowings from the Continent were put on full display. In 1557, a collection of lyrics known as *Tottel's Miscellany* was published, and the importance of this work cannot be overemphasized. It was innovative not only in its function as a collection of poems by various authors, some of them anonymous, but also in the profusion of prosodic experimentation that it offered. *Tottel's Miscellany* represented nothing less than England's many-faceted response to the Continental Renaissance. In this collection, every conceivable metrical style (including some strange and not wholly successful experiments with structural alliteration) was attempted in an array of genres, including sonnets, epigrams, elegies, eulogies, and poems of praise and Christian consolation, often resulting in changes in the older Continental forms. Truly there is no better representation of poets self-consciously watching themselves be poets.

Nevertheless, unfair stereotypes about the collection abound. Perhaps because of Lewis's distinction between "drab" age and "Golden" age poetry, students are often taught that the sole merit of *Tottel's Miscellany* is its inclusion of the lyrics of Sir Thomas Wyatt and Henry Howard, Earl of Surrey (which had been composed years earlier)—in particular, their imitations of the amatory verse of Petrarch. The standard classroom presentation lauds Wyatt and Surrey for introducing Petrarch and his sonnet form into England. Students are further taught that the long-range effects of *Tottel's Miscellany* proved to be disappointing since no poet was motivated to continue Wyatt's and Surrey's experiments with Petrarch for decades thereafter. Thus, *Tottel's Miscellany* is blamed for being essentially a "flash in the pan" work lacking in any significant, literary influence. Such disappointment is absurdly unjustified, however, in view of what the publisher Richard Tottel and Wyatt and Surrey were try-

ing to accomplish. Tottel published his collection "to the honor of the English tong," and in that sense the work was a success, as the conscious goal of all its contributors was to improve the vernacular. Furthermore, its most talented contributors, Wyatt and Surrey, accomplished what they set out to do: to investigate fully the possibilities of the short lyric, something that had never before been attempted in England, and, in Surrey's case, to experiment further with blank verse and the poulter's measure.

By no stretch of the imagination did Wyatt view himself as the precursor of a Petrarchan movement in England, and he made no attempt to cultivate followers. In fact, despite the superficial similarity of subject matter, Wyatt's poetry has little in common with the Petrarchan sonneteers of the close of the century, and he most assuredly would have resented any implication that his poetry was merely an unpolished harbinger of grander efforts to come. As Douglas L. Peterson has pointed out, Wyatt used Petrarch to suit his own purposes, mainly to perfect his "plain" style; and Yvor Winters maintains that Wyatt is closer to Gascoigne than Sidney. Whereas the sonneteers of the close of the century composed decidedly in the "eloquent" style, Wyatt expressed contempt for trussed-up images and pursued the virtues of a simple, unadorned style.

PLAIN STYLE

Thus, far from attempting to initiate a new "movement" of Petrarchan eloquence, many of the poems in *Tottel's Miscellany* sought to refine the possibilities of the plain style. As Peterson defines it, the plain style is characterized by plain, proverbial, aphoristic sentiments. It is a style often unappreciated by modern readers because its obvious simplicity is often mistaken for simplemindedness. The practitioners of the plain style, however, were very skilled in tailoring their verse to fit the needs of the poem's message, the pursuit of simplicity becoming a challenge, not a symptom of flagging inspiration. Skelton unwittingly summarizes the philosophy of the plain style when, commenting on his rhyme in *Collyn Clout*, he instructs the reader: "If ye take well therewith/ It hath in it some pith."

Thus, a plain-style poet expressing disillusionment with the excesses of love or extolling the virtues of frugality, rather than adorning his poem with an abundance of extravagant images, he instead pared his sentiments down to the minimum, with the intense restraint itself illuminating the poet's true feelings about love or money. The desiderata of the plain style were tightness and disciplined restraint. In the hands of an untalented poet, like John Heywood, who published his *A Dialogue of Proverbes* in 1546 and a collection of epigrams in 1556, the aphoristic messages could easily become stultifying; but as practiced by a poet with the skill of Wyatt, the economy of rendering a truth simply could produce a pleasurable effect. Interestingly, near the close of the century, when the eloquent style was all the rage, Sir Walter Ralegh, Thomas Nashe, and Fulke Greville often employed the techniques of the plain style.

IMITATIONS OF TOTTEL'S MISCELLANY

The three decades following the publication of *Tottel's Miscellany* have been stereotyped as a wasteland when poetry languished desultorily until the advent of the sonneteers in the 1580's. Nothing could be more unfair to the poetry of the period than to view it as struggling in an inspirational darkness. Amazingly, such a stereotype manages to overlook the profusion of poetry collections that *Tottel's Miscellany* spawned. Though admittedly the poetry of some of these collections is forgettable, nevertheless the continual appearance of these collections for the next fifty years is an impressive indication of the extent to which Tottel's philosophy of prosodic experimentation continued to exert an influence.

The first imitation of Tottel to be published was *The Paradise of Dainty Devices* (1576), the most popular of the imitations. As its title would indicate, a number of amatory poems were included, but the predominant poems had didactic, often pious themes, which offered ample opportunity for further experimentation in the plain style. A number of reasonably accomplished poets contributed to the collection, including Sir Richard Grenville, Jaspar Heywood, Thomas Churchyard, and Barnabe Rich. Another successful collection was *Brittons Bowre of Delights* (1591), interesting for its wide range of metrical experimentation, especially involving poulter's measure and the six-line iambic pentameter stanza.

Imitations of Tottel's works did not always prove successful. In 1577, *A Gorgeous Gallery of Gallant Inventions* appeared, a monotonous collection of poems whose oppressive theme was the vanity of love and pleasure, and it was as plagued with affectations and jargon as *Brittons Bowre of Delights* was blessed with fresh experimentation. Not everyone was pleased, however, with the new direction the lyric was taking after Tottel. In 1565, John Hall published his *Court of Virtue*, an anti-Tottel endeavor designed to preach that literature must be moral. In his work the poet is instructed by Lady Arete to cease pandering to the vulgar tastes of the public and instead to write moral, instructive lyrics, an appeal which results in the poet's moralizing of Wyatt's lyrics.

The experimental spirit of Tottel carried over into the works of individual poets, as well. From such an unlikely source as Thomas Tusser's *A Hundreth Good Points of Husbandry* (1557), an unassuming almanac of farming tips, explodes a variety of metrical experimentation, including Skeltonics, acrostics, and other complicated stanzaic forms. Despite his willingness to experiment, however, Tusser was not an accomplished talent, and thus there are three poets, Barnabe Googe, George Turberville, and George Gascoigne, to whom one must turn to refute the stereotype of the mid-century "wasteland." Too often viewed as bungling imitators of Tottel, these poets deserve a closer look as vital talents who were keeping poetry alive during the so-called wasteland years.

GOOGE, TUBERVILLE, AND GASCOIGNE

In his *Eclogues, Epitaphs, and Sonnets* (1563), Barnabe Googe's explicit poetic mission was to imitate Tottel. Working mostly in the didactic tradition, he wrote some epitaphs and poems in praise of friends, but his eclogues are of primary interest to the literary historian. He revived the Mantuan eclogue, which had been lying dormant in England after Barclay, and his eclogues were good enough to offer anticipations of Spenser's *The Shepheardes Calender* (1579). Another noteworthy work is his *Cupido Conquered* (1563), a dream-vision allegory, which Lewis dismissed as "purely medieval." The dismissal is unfair, however, because, despite the throwback to medieval devices, the plot, in which the languishing, lovesick poet is chided by his muses for his shameful lack of productivity, reveals Googe's self-consciousness of himself as craftsman, a characteristic pose for a poet of the sixteenth century.

George Turberville's dexterity with metrics in his translation of Ovid has already been mentioned. Like Googe, Turberville, in his *Epitaphs, Epigrams, Songs, and Sonnets* (1567), carried on with Tottelian experimentation, primarily in didactic poems employing poulter's measure and fourteeners written in the plain style.

George Gascoigne has only recently received the attention that he deserves, his poetry serving as the most impressive evidence disproving the existence of a post-Tottel wasteland. Predictably, Lewis describes him as a precursor of golden age poetry, ignoring Gascoigne's contributions to the plain style. In his *A Hundreth Sundrie Flowres Bounde up in One Small Poesie* (1573), Gascoigne was the first to experiment with Petrarch and the sonnet form since Wyatt and Surrey, but he was no slavish imitator. Gascoigne's poetry is often coarser and more lewd than that of Petrarch, but he never sacrifices a robust wit. In addition, he is an interesting figure for his variations in the sonnet form, featuring the octave-sestet division of the Petrarchan form, but in an English, or abab rhyme scheme. Puttenham refers to his "good meter" and "plentiful vein."

ELIZABETHAN POETRY

Thus, the poetry of the latter part of the century, the great age of the eloquent style, must not be viewed as a semimiraculous phoenix, rising from the ashes between Wyatt's experiments with Petrarch and the advent of Sidney. Nevertheless, it must be noted that the Elizabethan era ranks as one of the outstanding poetic periods of any century, its development of the eloquent style ranking as an outstanding achievement. A valuable representative of what the eloquent style was trying to accomplish is Sir John Davies' *Orchestra: Or, A Poeme of Dauncing* (1596). In his *Elizabethan World Picture* (1943), E. M. W. Tillyard analyzes the poem at length as a fitting symbol of the Elizabethans' obsession with cosmic order. Though accurate enough, Tillyard's discussion places too much emphasis on the poem's content and does not pay enough attention to the style in which

the message is delivered. In the poem, the suitor Antinous launches an elaborate discourse designed to persuade Penelope, waiting for her Odysseus to return, to dance. Through Antinous's lengthy and involved encomium to cosmic order and rhythm, Davies was not attempting a literal plea to Penelope to get up and dance. Rather, he was using Antinous as a vehicle for an ingenious argument, ostentatious in its erudition and profusion of images; in effect, Antinous's argument is the repository of Davies' experiments in the eloquent style. It is the dazzling display of the process of argumentation itself, not the literal effort to persuade Penelope, that is the essence of the poem. The way in which the poem is written is more important than its content, and in that sense (but in that sense only) the goal of the eloquent style is no different from that of the plain style.

PETRARCHAN AND "ELOQUENT" STYLE

When one thinks of sixteenth century poetry and the eloquent style, however, one almost immediately thinks of the Petrarchan sonnet sequence, and one explanation for the almost fanatic renewal of interest in Petrarch was the inevitable shift of interests in poetic style. The plain style, so dominant for almost half a century, was beginning to play itself out, a primary indication being the decline in use of the epigram, whose pithy wit held little appeal for Elizabethan poets. The more skillful among them were anxious to perfect a new style, specifically the "eloquent" style, almost the total antithesis of the plain style. Not particularly concerned with expressing universal truths, the eloquent style, as practiced by Davies, sought embellishment, rather than pithy restraint, and a profusion of images, rather than minimal, tight expression. The eloquent style effected some interesting changes in the handling of the old Petrarchan themes, as well. It should be noted that in his experiments with Petrarch, Wyatt chafed at the indignities suffered by the courtly lover. By contrast, the sonneteers emphasized with relish the travails of the lover, who almost luxuriates in his state of rejection. In fact, there is no small trace of *fin de siècle* decadence in the cult of the spurned lover that characterized so many of the sonnets of the period, most notably Sidney's *Astrophel and Stella* (1591), and it decidedly signaled the end of the plain style.

SONNETS AMD SONNET SEQUENCES

The sonnet sequence, a collection of sonnets recording the lover's successes and failures in courting his frequently unsympathetic mistress, was practiced by the brilliant and mediocre alike. Of course, the two most outstanding poets of the century pioneered the form—Sidney in his *Astrophel and Stella*, who in the true spirit of the poetic self-consciousness of the century wrote sonnets about the writing of sonnets and wrote some sonnets entirely in Alexandrines, and Edmund Spenser in his *Amoretti* (1595), who, in addition to introducing refinements in the sonnet structure, also intellectualized the cult of the rejected lover by analyzing the causes of rejection.

In the next twenty years the contributions to the genre were dizzying: Fulke Greville's *Caelica* (written in 1577); Thomas Watson's *Passionate Century of Love* (1582); Samuel Daniel's *Delia* (1592); Henry Constable's *Diana* (1592); Thomas Lodge's *Phillis* (1593); Giles Fletcher's *Licia* (1593); Barnabe Barnes's *Parthenophil and Parthenophe* (1593); Bartholomew Griffin's *Fidessa* (1593); Michael Drayton's *Ideas Mirrour* (1594), noteworthy for its experiments with rhyme; *The Phoenix Nest* (1593), a collection of Petrarchan sonnets in a wide variety of meters by George Peele, Nicholas Breton, Thomas Lodge, and others—the list of accomplished poets and tinkering poetasters was almost endless.

By the close of the century, so many mediocre poets had turned out sonnet sequences, and the plight of the rejected lover had reached such lugubrious proportions that the form inevitably decayed. Not only was the cult of the masochistic lover becoming tediously commonplace, but also one of the major triumphs of the eloquent style, the Petrarchan paradox (for example, Wyatt's "I burn, and freeze like ice") lost its appeal of surprise and tension as it became overworked, predictable, and trite. The genre had lost all traces of originality, and it is interesting to consider the fact that the modern definition of a sonneteer is an inferior poet. As early as 1577, Fulke Greville in his *Caelica* had perceived how easily in the sonnet sequence numbing repetition could replace fresh invention, and to maintain some vitality in his sequence his subject matter evolves from the complaints of the rejected lover to a renunciation of worldly vanity and expressions of disappointment in the disparity between "ideal" love and the imperfect love that exists in reality. (For this reason, of all the sonneteers Greville is the only precursor of the themes so prevalent in seventeenth century devotional poetry.)

The success and subsequent decline of the sonnet sequence left it wide open to parody. Many of the sonnets of William Shakespeare, who himself revolutionized the sonnet structure in England, are veiled satiric statements on the trite excesses of Petrarchan images ("My mistress's eyes are nothing like the sun"), indicating his impatience with the old, worn-out sentiments. Sir John Davies' collection of *Gulling Sonnets* (1873) was an explicit parody of Petrarchan absurdities and weary lack of invention, and, following their publication, the genre spun into an irreversible decline.

MYTHOLOGICAL-EROTIC NARRATIVE

As the sonnet declined, however, another form of amatory verse was being developed: the mythological-erotic narrative. This form chose erotic themes from mythology, embellishing the narrative with sensuous conceits and quasipornographic descriptions. It was a difficult form to master because it required titillation without descending into vulgarity and light touches of sophisticated humor without descending into burlesque. Successful examples of the mythological-erotic narrative are Christopher Marlowe's *Hero and Leander* (1598), Shakespeare's *Venus and Adonis* (1593), Chapman's *Ovids Banquet of Sence* (1595), Drayton's *Endimion and Phoebe* (1595), and Lodge's *Scillaes Metamorphosis* (1589). Like the sonnet the mythological narrative fell into decline, as evidenced by John Marston's *The Metamorphosis of Pygmalion's Image and Certain Satires* (1598), in which the decadence of the sculptor drooling lustfully over his statue was too absurdly indelicate for the fragile limits of the genre.

SATIRIC AND RELIGIOUS VERSE

As the mythological narrative and the sonnet declined, both social satire and religious verse experienced a corresponding upswing. The steady growth of a middle-class reading audience precipitated an increased interest in satire, a genre which had not been represented with any distinction since Gascoigne's *The Steel Glass* (1576).

Understandably, though inaccurately, Joseph Hall labeled himself the first English satirist. Juvenalian satire flourished in his *Virgidemiarum* (1597), similar to Davies' *Gulling Sonnets*, followed by Everard Guilpin's *Skialetheia: Or, Shadow of Truth in Certain Epigrams and Satyres* (1598), which attacks the "wimpring sonnets" and "puling Elegies" of the love poets, and Marston's *The Scourge of Villainy* (1598).

Perhaps feeling reinforced by the indignation of the satirists, religious verse proliferated at the end of the century. Bedazzled by the great age of the sonnet, the modern reader tends to generalize that the latter decades of the century were a purely secular period for poetry. Such a view, however, overlooks the staggering amount of religious verse that was being turned out, and it should be remembered by the modern reader that to the reader of the sixteenth century, verse was typified not by a Sidney sonnet, but by a versified psalm. Throughout the century, experiments with Petrarch ebbed and flowed, but the reading public was never without religious writings, including enormous numbers of sermons, devotional manuals, collections of prayers and meditations, verse saints' lives, devotional verse, and, of course, an overflow of rhyming psalters. Versifying the psalter had begun as early as the fourteenth century, but its popularity and practice went unsurpassed in the sixteenth. Although many excellent poets tried their hand at the Psalms, including Wyatt, Spenser, and Sidney, who saw them as legitimate sources of poetry, these versifications were led by the Thomas Sternhold and John Hopkins edition of 1549, and it represents a mediocre collection of verse. Nevertheless, the uncultivated reading public hailed it as an inspired work, and people who refused to read any poetry at all devoured the Sternhold and Hopkins edition. Popular collections among the Elizabethans were William Hunnis's *Seven Sobs of a Sorrowfull Soule for Sinne* (1583) and William Byrd's *Psalmes, Sonnets, and Songs of Sadnes and Pietie* (1588).

By the close of the century, attempts at religious verse by more accomplished poets were surpassing the efforts of hack versifiers. While the satirists were ridiculing the atrophied sonnet sequence on aesthetic grounds, other writers were attacking it on moral grounds, and perceptions of what poetry should be and

do were shifting as the sonnet lost its influence. Having put a distance of four years between his *Astrophel and Stella* and the publication of his *Defence of Poesie*, Sidney authoritatively proclaimed in the latter work that poetry should celebrate God and Divine Love. Thomas Nashe attacks verse in which "lust is the tractate of so many leaves." Physical love was no longer *au courant*. In his "A Coronet for his Mistress Philosophy," George Chapman reflects the new vogue of Neoplatonism by carefully identifying the differences between divine and physical love, also investigated meticulously by Spenser in his *Fowre Hymnes* (1596). Joshua Sylvester's translations between 1590 and 1605 of the works of the French Huguenot poet Guillaume du Bartas helped to reinforce Protestant piety and further counteracted the Petrarchans. The most saintly poet of the period was a Jesuit, Robert Southwell. In his preface to his *St. Peter's Complaint* (1595), Southwell laments that the teachings of Christ go unheeded as poets would rather celebrate the glories of Venus. In *St. Peter's Complaint* itself, Peter excoriates himself for his denial of Christ, and the fact that the work is oddly adorned with sensuous conceits is an interesting indication that Petrarchan images managed to survive stubbornly, even in works inimical to their spirit. Finally, in 1599, Sir John Davies published his *Nosce Teipsum*, whose theme was self-knowledge, rather than carnal knowledge of one's mistress, as well as the proper relationship between the soul and the body.

EDMUND SPENSER

The tug of war between the sonneteers and the religious poets was only one of several noteworthy poetic developments near the close of the century. Spenser, the most talented poet of the century, contributed to both sides of the battle (the *Amoretti* and *Fowre Hymnes*), but his versatility as a poet enabled him to transcend any one category. Spenser's early poetic career is not without its mysteries. No literary historian would have predicted that at a time when a new poetry was being refined by means of the sonnet form, someone would choose to revive the old medieval forms, but that is what Spenser did. *The Shepheardes Calender* is a throwback to the Mantuan eclogues, at this point almost a century old, and *Colin Clouts Come Home Againe* is reminiscent of Skelton's anticlerical satires. His *Mother Hubberds Tale*

(1590) is an imitation of a medieval beast fable, and even *The Faerie Queene*, his most famous work, is essentially a compendium of medieval allegory and Italian epic forms derived from Ludovico Ariosto and Torquato Tasso. Furthermore, many of Spenser's works were written in a deliberately archaic style.

Thus a major contribution to Spenser's fame is not the originality of his themes but the range of his metrical and stanzaic experimentations. In a century characterized by poets self-consciously aware of themselves exercising their craft, Spenser was the apotheosis of the poetic craftsman. Though his archaic diction violated the tenets of many critics who believed that the vernacular must grow, Spenser's experiments in versification furthered the cause of making English more vital. Despite its reactionary themes, *The Shepheardes Calender* explodes with experimentation in poetic forms. The "January" eclogue is written in the six-line ballad or "Venus and Adonis" stanza, "February" is written in Anglo-Saxon accentual verse, "March" is written in the romance stanza of Chaucer's "Sir Topaz," "July" is written in a rough, vulgar ballad meter, and "August" is a contrast of undisciplined folk rhythms and elegant sestinas. Though not Spenser's most famous work, *The Shepheardes Calender* is nevertheless a remarkable symbol and culmination of the poetic self-consciousness of the sixteenth century and a fusion of the experiments in poetic versification that had helped to shape English as a suitable vehicle for poetry.

VERSE CHRONICLES

As the century was drawing to a close, a popular genre flourishing outside the continuing battle between amatory and religious verse was the verse chronicle history. Of all the genres popular in the sixteenth century, the verse chronicle history is probably the most difficult for the modern reader to appreciate, probably because of its excruciating length; but more than any other genre, it serves as a repository for Elizabethan intellectual, historical, and social thought, especially as it reflects the Elizabethan desire for political order, so amply documented by Tillyard in his *Elizabethan World Picture*.

The first treatment of English history in poetry was the landmark publication of *A Myrrour for Magistrates* in 1559. It was a collection of tragedies of famous leaders in the medieval tradition of people brought low by the turning wheel of Fortune and was written in rime royal, the favorite stanzaic vehicle of medieval narrative. The structure of its tragedies was imitated from Giovanni Boccaccio and from John Lydgate's *The Fall of Princes* (1494), and the constant themes of the tragedies were both the subject's responsibility to his king and the king's responsibility to God; if either the ruler or the subject should fail in his proper allegiance, disorder and tragedy would inevitably ensue. *A Myrrour for Magistrates* was extraordinarily popular with a reading public desiring both entertainment and instruction. It went through eight editions in thirty years, with Thomas Sackville's "Induction" being considered at the time the best poem between Chaucer and Spenser.

The major importance of *A Myrrour for Magistrates* is the fact that it fulfilled Sidney's mandate in his *Defence of Poesie* that the poet take over the task of the historian, and *A Myrrour for Magistrates* exerted a powerful influence on the late Elizabethan poets. Pride in the royal Tudor lineage led not only the prose chroniclers but also the poets of the Elizabethan period to develop a strong sense of Britain's history. Shakespeare's history plays are widely recognized as reflections of England's growing nationalistic fervor, and because of the magnitude of the plays, it is easy to overlook the contributions of the poets to English history, or, perhaps more accurately, pseudohistory. The troublesome murkiness of Britain's origins were efficiently, if somewhat questionably, cleared up by exhaustive embellishments of the legends of Brut and King Arthur, legends that spurred England on to a sharpened sense of patriotism and nationalism. An obvious example is Spenser's chronicle of early British history at the end of Book II of *The Faerie Queene*. In 1586 William Warner published his *Albion's England*, a long work ambitiously taking as its province all of historical time from Noah's Flood down to the execution of Mary, Queen of Scots.

The following years saw the publication of Samuel Daniel's *The First Fowre Bookes of the Civile Warres* (1595, 1599, 1601), whose books represented the apotheosis of all attempts at versified history. Like Shakespeare in his history plays, Daniel focused on a theme common in Elizabethan political theory, the evil that inevitably results from civil and moral disorder—specifically, the overthrow of Richard II. The modern reader has a natural antipathy toward the Elizabethan verse chronicles because of their length and because of the chroniclers' penchant for moral allegorizing, for their tedious accounts of past civil disorder as illustrative of present moral chaos, and for their far-reaching, interweaving parallels among mythological, biblical, and British history (for example, the Titans' defeat of Saturn being contrasted with the victory of Henry V at Agincourt in Thomas Heywood's *Troia Britannica*, 1609). Nevertheless, these versified histories and their championing of moral order and nationalism constituted much of the most popular poetry of the Elizabethan period, and their impact cannot be overemphasized.

Growth and transition

In retrospect, it is indeed astonishing to consider precisely how much the poetry of the sixteenth century grew after Stephen Hawes's allegories first limped onto the scene in 1509. The pressing need for most poets at the beginning of the century was to imitate medieval forms as faithfully as possible. There was no question as to the superiority of the classical authorities, and there was no "English" poetry as such. In 1531, Sir Thomas Elyot mentions Ovid and Martial but not English poets, and, as late as 1553, Thomas Wilson was defending the rhetoric of the authorities Cicero and Quintilian. Gradually, however, by struggling with the new language and continuing to experiment with verse forms both new and original, poets were starting to shape a new English poetry and were achieving recognition as craftsmen in their own right. By 1586, William Webbe respectfully addressed the preface to his *Discourse of English Poetry* to "the Noble Poets of England" and made mention of Skelton, Gascoigne, and Googe, finally recognizing Spenser as "the rightest English poet that ever I read." Thus, by the end of the century the question of whether there could be an English poesy had been replaced by the question of what were the limits of the great English poets.

Because of the struggle to shape the new vernacular, the sixteenth century differs from other centuries in that many innovations were coming from the pens of not particularly gifted poets. Thus, working in a period of volatility and flux in the language, such men as Barclay

and Skelton could exert an impact on the shaping of the poetry and earn their place in literary history. The first half of the sixteenth century did not witness the formation of new genres. The old reliables, dream-vision allegories, anticlerical satires, pastorals, ballads, versified psalms, and neomedieval tragedies, were the favorite vehicles of most poets. The extraordinary development of this period was the metrical experimentation, which never stopped, no matter how limited the poet. Perhaps more than any other period, therefore, the first half of the sixteenth century reveals as many noteworthy developments in its bad poets as in its talented ones.

After the publication of *Tottel's Miscellany*, poetry began to settle down somewhat from its pattern of groping experimentation as it gained confidence and stability working with the vernacular. Perhaps the surest indication that poetry had hit its stride in England was the parody of the Petrarchan sonnet. The parody of the first truly great lyric form in England was a significant landmark because only widely popular forms tend to serve as targets for parody. A further indication of the vitality of the poetry was the fact that its poets survived the parody and went on to create new forms. Furthermore, poetic tastes were flexible enough to produce a Spenser who, while forging ahead with prosodic experimentation, looked backward to the archaisms that English poetry had originally utilized.

As the sixteenth century waned and old genres, such as the sonnet, the pastoral, and the verse chronicle, faded, there were numerous hints of what the poets of the new century would be attempting. In particular, there were several suggestions of the Metaphysicals. The decline in popularity of the Petrarchan sonnet and its subsequent ridicule paved the way for John Donne's satires of the form in many of his secular lyrics. As was seen earlier, Greville's religious themes in his *Caelica* were a precursor of devotional poetry. The sensuous conceits of Southwell heralded the baroque extravagances of Richard Crashaw. The pastoral, a favorite Elizabethan genre, was fast fading, as indicated by Sir Walter Ralegh's cynical response to Christopher Marlowe's "The Passionate Shepherd to His Love," a plea for living a romantic life in pastoral bliss. In his "Nymph's Reply to the Shepherd," Ralegh makes it clear that such idyllic bliss does not exist. The pastoral was being replaced, however, by a less idealized, more rational mode, the theme of self-contained, rural retirement, as embodied at the close of the century in Sir Edward Dyer's "My Mind to Me a Kingdom Is," a theme that became increasingly popular in the new century. Finally, the proliferation of songs and airs, found in such collections as Nicholas Yonge's *Musica Transalpina* (1588), John Dowland's *The First Book of Songs or Airs* (1597), and Thomas Campion's *A Booke of Ayres* (1601), created a vogue that influenced the lyrics of Ben Jonson and his followers.

The true worth of the poetry of the sixteenth century, however, lies not in the legacies that were inherited from it by the next century but rather in the sheer exuberance for the poetic undertaking that characterized the century from beginning to end. Because of the continuing process of shaping the new vernacular, the tools of the poetic craft are evident in every work, and in no other century did the poets better embody the original etymology of the word "poet," which comes from the Greek word for "maker." To use Webbe's term, they "Englished" the old poetry and proved to be untiring "makers" of a new.

BIBLIOGRAPHY

Bush, Douglas. *Prefaces to Renaissance Literature.* New York: W. W. Norton, 1965. A slim volume that sketches a framework for understanding the social, historical, and literary context of English poetry in the sixteenth and early seventeenth centuries.

Campbell, Lily B. *Divine Poetry and Drama in Sixteenth-Century England.* Berkeley: University of California Press, 1959. An examination of religious influences on the literature of the sixteenth century, including Continental influences such as the Humanism of Desiderius Erasmus and the French poet Guillaume du Bartas.

Hardison, O. J., Jr., ed. *English Literary Criticism: The Renaissance.* Englewood Cliffs, N.J.: Prentice-Hall, 1963. A collection of writings from William Caston's 1484 preface to his edition of *The Canturbury Tales* to commentary by John Milton in the later half of the seventeenth century, this is a valuable collection of primary prose documents on poetics and literary theory.

Huntington, John. *Ambition, Rank, and Poetry in 1590's England.* Urbana: University of Illinois Press, 2001.

Jones, Emrys, ed. *The New Oxford Book of Sixteenth Century Verse.* London: Oxford University Press, 1992.

Lewis, C. S. *English Literature in the Sixteenth Century Excluding Drama.* The Oxford History of English Literature 3. Oxford, England: Clarendon Press, 1954.

Morotti, Arthur F. *Manuscript, Print, and the English Renaissance Lyric.* Ithaca, N.Y.: Cornell University Press, 1995.

Peterson, Douglas L. *The English Lyric from Wyatt to Donne: A History of the Plain and Eloquent Styles.* 1967. 2d ed. East Lansing, Mich,: Colleagues Press, 1990.

Rivers, Isabel. *Classical and Christian Ideas in English Renaissance Poetry.* 2d ed. London: Routledge, 1994.

Sidney, Philip. *"Defense of Poesie," "Astrophel and Stella," and Other Writings.* Edited by Elizabeth Porges Watson. New York: Charles E. Tuttle, 1997.

Sowerby, Robin. *The Classical Legacy in Renaissance Poetry.* Longman Medieval and Renaissance Library. New York: Longman, 1994.

Tillyard, E. M. W. *Elizabethan World Picture.* London: Chatto & Windus, 1943.

Waller, Gary F. *English Poetry of the Sixteenth Century.* 2d ed. New York: Longman Publishing Group, 1993.

Webbe, William. *The Discourse of Poetry.* Edited by Edward Arber. London: Ayer Company Publishers, 1977.

Whitney, Isabelle, Mary Sidney, and Amelia Lanyer. *Renaissance Women Poets.* New York: Viking, 2001. Explores three English women poets who wrote during the Renaissance.

Williams, John, ed. *English Renaissance Poetry: A Collection of Shorter Poems from Skelton to Jonson.* 2d ed. Fayetteville: University of Arkansas Press, 1990.

Elizabeth J. Bellamy

ENGLISH POETRY IN THE SEVENTEENTH CENTURY

A question that can be asked of any century's poetry is whether it owes its character to "forces"—nonliterary developments to which the poets respond more or less sensitively—or whether, on the other hand, the practice of innovative and influential poets mainly determines the poetry of the period. Clearly, great poets do not always shape the literature of their century, as the cases of the twin giants of seventeenth century England, William Shakespeare and John Milton, indicate. What Ben Jonson wrote of Shakespeare is true of both: They are "not of an age, but for all time!" John Donne and John Dryden, however, are poets who seem to have stamped their personalities on much of the poetry of their own and succeeding generations.

THE CENTURY'S ANTIPODES: DONNE AND DRYDEN

John Donne turned twenty-nine in the year 1601. John Dryden, busy to the last, died in 1700. Thus a century brimming with good poetry may be said to begin with Donne and end with Dryden. On most library shelves, Donne and Dryden are both literally and figuratively neighbors. If not the shaper of poetry in the first half of the century, Donne stands at least as its representative poet, while Dryden, born only a few months after Donne died in 1631, probably has an even more secure claim to the same position in the final decades of the century. They may indeed have determined the poetic climate; certainly they serve as barometers on which modern readers can see that climate registered. The distinctive differences between the writings of the two men testify to the diversity of seventeenth century poetry and to the likelihood that powerful forces for change were at work in the interim.

The differences are apparent even when—perhaps particularly when—roughly similar types of poems (and parallels between the two are inevitably rough) are chosen. Donne wrote two sequences of religious sonnets. One begins:

> Thou hast made me, and shall thy work decay?
> Repair me now, for now mine end doth haste,
> I run to death, and death meets me as fast,
> And all my pleasures are like yesterday.

Dryden is known for two longer religious poems, one of which, *Religio Laici: Or, A Layman's Faith* (1682), begins: "Dim as the borrowed beams of moons and stars/ To lonely, weary, wand'ring travelers,/ Is Reason to the soul. . . ." A long list of contrasts might be drawn up, most of which would hold true of entire poems and, for that matter, of the works of the two poets generally.

Donne addresses God directly, for example, and even ventures to command him, while neither in his opening nor anywhere else in 456 lines does Dryden apostrophize his maker, although several times he refers circumspectly to "God," "Godhead," or "Omnipotence." Donne not only personifies but also personalizes the abstraction *death*, which "runs fast" and "meets" the speaker. Dryden's chief abstraction, *Reason*, is grand but "dim," and another which he introduces soon thereafter, *Religion*, though described as "bright," remains inanimate. Donne's sonnet has an immediate, even urgent, quality; Dryden sets out in a more deliberate and measured way, as if any necessary relationships will be established in due time. Donne achieves that immediacy through a plain, simple vocabulary, thirty-one of his first thirty-five words having only one syllable. While there are no striking irregularities after the first line, rhetorical stresses govern the rhythm. Dryden's diction is also simple, but there are more polysyllables, and their arrangement, as in "lonely, weary, wand'ring travelers," creates a smoother, more regular cadence.

In other ways the poems elicit different responses. Donne is paradoxical. The reader senses in his third line that rigorous demands are being made on him. What does "I run to death" mean exactly? How can that be? Why is death said to do the same? Such questions have answers, no doubt, but the reader anticipates that he will have to work for them, that he must stay alert and get involved. Dryden, on the other hand, begins by making a statement that can be accepted without any particular mental activity (which is not necessarily to say that it should be, or is intended to be, so accepted). Whereas the person setting out to read Donne suspects that obscurities may lie ahead, the beginner at Dryden finds nothing to raise such expectations. (The reader will hardly be surprised to find Dryden saying, near the end of the poem: "Thus have I made my own opinions clear.")

Samplers of other poems by the two poets reveal similar contrasts right from the beginning. Frequently in Donne's poems a speaker is addressing someone or something—God, a woman, a friend, a rival, the sun—in a tone which is often abrupt, questioning, or imperious. The poems are often dramatic in the sense of implying a situation and a relationship. They make demands, both on the addressee and the reader, who is present in somewhat the same way as an audience in a theater. Dryden was a dramatist, and a highly successful one, but he seems to have reserved drama for his plays. In his poems he is inclined to begin, as in *Religio Laici*, with statements, often in the form of generalizations: "All human things are subject to decay." "From harmony, from heavenly harmony,/ This universal frame began." "How blest is he who leads a country life." While not condescending to his readers, Dryden is much more likely to go on to *tell* them something—something clear, measured, plausible.

THE ELIZABETHAN HERITAGE

The Renaissance came to England late. Sixteenth century Italian poetry is dotted with famous names—Ludovico Ariosto, Pietro Bembo, Michelangelo Buonarroti, Torquato Tasso—and French poets distinguished themselves throughout the century, Pierre de Ronsard and the Pléiade group overshadowing others of whom today's readers would hear much more but for that brilliant constellation of poets. The Elizabethan poets' debt to these older literatures, particularly to that created by their French elders and contemporaries, has been well documented.

From the time of Edmund Spenser's *The Shepheardes Calender* (1579), English poetry came on with a rush, while the post-Renaissance baroque movement was already rising on the European continent. By 1600, Spenser and Sir Philip Sidney, both born in the 1550's, were dead, but many of their contemporaries from the 1550's and 1560's worked on, with many of their brightest achievements still ahead. As relief from the earlier but continuing Elizabethan tradition of ponderous, prosaic moralizing exemplified by the incessantly reprinted and expanded *A Myrrour for Magistrates*, whose first

extant edition dates from 1559, the poets of later Elizabethan decades favored pastorals, love sonnets, mythological narratives, and of course songs and the verse drama.

As part of the last wave of poets to come of age under Elizabeth, Donne and Ben Jonson might have been expected to rebel against their elders. Fifteen years or so of hobnobbing with Hobbinol and other literary shepherds and of agonizing with woebegone Petrarchan lovers over their unattainable or recalcitrant golden ladies goaded the new generation into staking out new territory. The sweetness and naïveté of much Elizabethan verse cloyed their literary taste buds. The serious side of Elizabethan endeavor ran wearyingly to themes of transience and mutability. There was room for more realism and sophistication, and new forms and conventions.

Donne responded by parodying the ideal Petrarchan mistress in his paean to indiscriminate love, "I can love both fair and brown," meanwhile reserving that standard vehicle for love laments, the sonnet, for religious purposes. Jonson refused to write sonnets at all, coolly praised a goddess named Celia, and claimed, with some exaggeration, that he did not write of love. As mythologizers, Elizabethans were accustomed to plunder from Ovid and the Ovidians, but Donne did not conduct his raids on the *Metamorphoses*, with its wistful accounts of lovers vanished into foliage and feathers; instead, he concentrated on Ovid's saucy prescriptions for both lovemaking and love-breaking in the *Amores* (*Loves*), *Ars amatoria* (*Art of Love*), and *Remedium amoris* (*Love's Remedy*). Later (or perhaps just alternatively) he drew on the pre-Petrarchan traditions, including Platonism and Scholasticism, to write of love as a refining and exalting experience. As for Jonson, where the Elizabethans were amply decorous, he tended to be blunt and epigrammatic. More rigorously than Donne, he rejected the medieval trappings that clung to Elizabethan poetry.

Yet neither man made anything like a clean break with Elizabethan values. In satirizing Petrarchan conventions, Donne was only continuing a tendency implicit in the Petrarchan mode almost from its beginning, Shakespeare already preceding him in English poetry in his sonnet "My mistress's eyes are nothing like the sun." The man most responsible for the English sonnet-writing mania, Sir Philip Sidney, had, in his

Astrophel and Stella (1591) suggested all sorts of latent possibilities for the deployment of wit which the Elizabethans had barely begun to exploit. Elizabethan moral earnestness awaited poets who could bring fresh resources to its expression. The student of the drama can hardly escape the conclusion that Donne owed something of his penchant for dramatizing love and religious conflict to the fact that he grew up in London at a time of flourishing theatrical activity, when even writers deficient in dramatic talent strove to turn out plays. Jonson must have learned much about friendship from Sidney's *Arcadia* (1590), the Fourth Book of Spenser's *The Faerie Queene* (1590, 1596), and other romances of the sort before turning this subject to account in poetic forms more congenial to him. Again, Jonson's distinctive contribution to songwriting depended on his good fortune in maturing at a time when music was everywhere in the air, as Willa McClung Evans showed in *Ben Jonson and Elizabethan Music* (1929). In short, Elizabethan influences on these Jacobean poets were very far from exclusively negative ones.

SPENSERIAN TRADITION

Seventeenth century developments originating with Donne and Jonson have absorbed much of the attention of literary students, but the Spenserian tradition must not be underrated. Its master having been a many-faceted poet, it is a rich and diverse one. Michael Drayton carried his adaptations of Spenserian pastoral to the verge of the new century's fourth decade. The greatest English poet after Shakespeare found in *The Faerie Queene* the best model for his own epic. Some poets imitated Spenser's idealism, some his sensuous and even sensual music, some his achievement in romantic narrative, and some his demanding stanza. No one like Spenser wrote in the seventeenth century, but the rays of his genius shone over the century and long afterward. The twentieth century emphasis on Donne and the Metaphysical poets has had the unfortunate effect of obscuring the illumination that Spenser furnished generations of respectful and admiring followers.

LONDON BROTHERHOOD

In few European countries was there such a concentration of talent and creative energy as in Renaissance London. England had no city to rival it in size or cultural pretensions, and to the city or to the court came all aspiring writers and all ambitious men. Literary associations blossomed easily in its square mile, as did rivalries and jealousies. Although London did not boast a university, many of its creative men came to know one another in school. Beginning in the last quarter of the sixteenth century, for example, and extending over the next seventy years, the roster of poets who attended just one school, Westminster, includes Jonson, Richard Corbett, Giles Fletcher, Henry King, George Herbert, William Strode, Thomas Randolph, William Cartwright, Abraham Cowley, and Dryden. Half of these men later gravitated to one Cambridge college, Trinity. A similar list of poets who claimed residence at London's Inns of Court might be made. It is likely that the richness of late Elizabethan and seventeenth century English poetry owes much to the cross-fertilization that is almost inevitable when virtually all of the poets of any given time know one another more or less intimately. Although poets have always come together for mutual support and stimulation, in the seventeenth century the poets who did so were not beleaguered minorities without status in the intellectual world or insulated coteries intent on defending the purity of their theory and practice against one another. Poets constituted something of a brotherhood—although brothers are known to fight—and not a school or club where narrowness can prevail along with good manners.

Realizing the essentially close relationships among poets whose work scholars tend to classify and mark off from one another, modern commentators on seventeenth century poetry have emphasized the common heritage and shared concerns of writers once assumed to be disparate and even antagonistic. It is well to recall this shared heritage and common cause when distinguishing—as criticism must distinguish—among individual achievements and ascertainable poetic movements.

THE METAPHYSICAL SCHOOL

After Sir Herbert Grierson's edition of Donne's poems in 1912, critics spent some decades attempting to define and delineate "Metaphysical poetry." T. S. Eliot, in a 1921 essay, lent his prestige to the endeavor, and such studies as George Williamson's *The Donne Tradi-*

tion (1930), Joan Bennett's *Four Metaphysical Poets* (1934), J. B. Leishman's *Metaphysical Poets* (1934), Helen C. White's *The Metaphysical Poets* (1936), and Rosemond Tuve's *Elizabethan and Metaphysical Imagery* (1947) refined readers' understanding of the movement but created such a vogue that the term "metaphysical" came to acquire a bewildering variety of applications and connotations, with the understandable result that some critics, including Leishman, came to view it with suspicion. Nevertheless, it remains useful for the purpose of designating the kind of poetry written by Donne, Herbert, Richard Crashaw, Henry Vaughan, Thomas Traherne, Andrew Marvell (at least some of the time), and a considerable number of other seventeenth century poets, including the American, Edward Taylor. The earlier tendency to call these poets a "school" has also fallen into disrepute because the term suggests a much more formal and schematic set of relationships than existed among these poets. Douglas Bush, in his valuable contribution to the *Oxford History of English Literature* series, *English Literature in the Earlier Seventeenth Century, 1600-1660* (1962), refers to the Metaphysicals after Donne as his "successors," while Joseph H. Summers prefers another designation, as the title of his 1970 study, *The Heirs of Donne and Jonson*, indicates.

Because the bulk of English Metaphysical poetry after Donne tends to be religious, it has been studied profitably under extraliterary rubrics, especially by Louis L. Martz as *The Poetry of Meditation* (1954), in which the author demonstrates how many distinctive features of such poetry derive from the Christian art of meditation, especially from such manuals of Catholic devotion as Saint Ignatius Loyola's *Spiritual Exercises* (1548) and Saint Francis de Sales's *An Introduction to the Devout Life* (c. 1608). More recently, Barbara Kiefer Lewalski has argued for the importance of Protestant devotional literature in her *Protestant Poetics and the Seventeenth Century Religious Lyric* (1979). Donne and some of his followers have been profitably studied as poets of wit, a classification that connects them with Jonson and the Jonsonians, in later books by Leishman (*The Monarch of Wit*, 1951) and Williamson (*The Proper Wit of Poetry*, 1961), as well as in the aforementioned book by Summers.

Students of literature continue to be intrigued by the word "metaphysical," however, and by the challenge of pinpointing its essential denotation. One of the most distinctive traits of this poetry is the Metaphysical conceit, an image which, as its name suggests, is intended to convey an idea rather than a sensory quality. The conceit, as exemplified by Donne's comparison of the quality of two lovers' devotion to the draftsman's compass in "A Valediction: Forbidding Mourning," or the pulley image in Herbert's poem of that title used to express the speaker's sense of the relationship between God and man, is likely to be ingenious, unexpected, and apparently unpromising; the poet is inclined to develop it at considerable length (Donne uses three stanzas for his compass conceit, while Herbert builds his whole poem on the pulley image) and in a number of particulars; and the result, often arrived at through argumentation, justifies the seeming incongruity of the image. An interesting comparison between Donne's imagery and that of Shakespeare has been made by Cleanth Brooks (in *The Well Wrought Urn*, 1947) with the view of demonstrating the use of similar conceits by Shakespeare, who is never thought of as a Metaphysical.

Describers of Metaphysical poetry have most often cited a cluster of traits, no one of which differentiates this mode from others. Metaphysical poems are often dramatic, colloquial in diction and rhythm, and set forth in intricate and varied forms with respect to line lengths, rhyme schemes, and stanzaic configurations. Whether dealing with sexual or religious love, Metaphysical love poems develop the psychological aspects of loving which are always implicit, sometimes explicit in the Petrarchan tradition. Sexual, Platonic, and religious love are frequently explored in terms seemingly more appropriate to one of the other types. Thus Donne assures God that he will never be "chaste, except you ravish me," and a lady that "all shall approve/ Us canonized for love." Crashaw can refer to a mistress as a "divine idea" in a "shrine of crystal flesh," and, in another poem, to God as a rival lover of St. Teresa.

The chief trait of Metaphysical poetry in the eyes of Earl Miner (*The Metaphysical Mode from Donne to Cowley*, 1969) is its "private mode." He considers the most distinctive aspect of the love or religious experience in this poetry to be its individual and private character. Either because the poet senses a breakdown of social bonds or because these bonds threaten the integrity of private experience, the Metaphysical poet is in self-conscious retreat from the social realm. Thus Donne's love poems often evoke third parties only to banish them as early as the first line: "For God's sake, hold your tongue, and let me love." The earlier Metaphysicals, however, are familiar with the world that they reject, and its immanence contributes to the dramatic quality in their poetry. In later poets such as Vaughan and Traherne the interfering world has receded; as a result the dramatic tension largely disappears.

Metaphysical poetry's reputed taste for the obscure and the "far-fetched" has been overemphasized by critics from Dryden to the twentieth century. That it is intellectual and that its allusions are likely to necessitate numerous glosses for modern readers there can be little doubt. The ideal audience for Metaphysical poetry was small and select. To pre-Restoration readers, however, the poems probably did not seem especially difficult. It is simply that Renaissance learning was replaced by a different learning. As the century waned, a gap widened between the old and new learning; as a result Dryden had more difficulty reading Donne than do modern readers, who enjoy the benefit of modern scholars' recovery of much of that older learning. The continuing popularity of Metaphysical poetry demonstrates readers' continuing willingness to absorb glosses without which the richness of the poetry is lost.

European Metaphysical Poetry (1961), an anthology by Frank J. Warnke with a long critical introduction, presents French, German, Spanish, Dutch, and Italian texts of selected poems with facing verse translations. The volume includes a number of poems analogous to the works of Donne and his followers and distinguishes between the Metaphysical and baroque traditions, although clearly they overlap. A Mexican nun, Sor Juana Inés de la Cruz (1651-1695), rivals Edward Taylor, who came to America in 1668, as the first Metaphysical poet of the New World. Like Crashaw, Sor Juana writes emotional, sexually charged religious verse, but, also like him, she was a keen student of theology and something of an intellectual. In Taylor the Metaphysical manner and a Puritan religious outlook produced a body of poetry unique in the American colonies or elsewhere. The influence of Richard Baxter's famous book *The Saints' Everlasting Rest* (1692) is heavier on Taylor than on any

other Metaphysical poet, and many of his poems are cast as meditations. The language is that of a man who lived and worked on the late seventeenth century American frontier, cut off from the society of the learned and the artistic. Even his conceits, such as the one on which he bases "Huswifery"—"Make me, O Lord, thy spinning wheel complete"—have a homely, rough-hewn air.

Religious poetry and other trends

Finally, the seventeenth century produced a body of poetry not usually classified as Metaphysical but having some affinities with that tradition. Much of it is religious. Emblem poetry, best exemplified by Francis Quarles, was a mixed-media art including a print that depicted a scene of religious or moral significance, a biblical quotation, a related poem, another quotation, and, in most cases, a concluding epigram. The engravings in emblem books are frequently more interesting than the poems, but the form seems to have made its mark on Spenser, Shakespeare, and several of the Metaphysical poets, notably Herbert and Crashaw. Herbert's great book *The Temple* (1633) contains several poems which, arranged to form figures, become in effect emblems of their subject matter. Another poet, Henry More, in his fondness for allegory and the Spenserian stanza points to one large influence, but often reminds the reader of the Metaphysicals in his choice and handling of imagery, even though his work is more justly charged with obscurity than theirs. At the same time More is one of the few seventeenth century poets who is known to have studied René Descartes and to have been directly influenced by the Cartesian dualism of mind and matter. If, as Basil Willey has argued in *The Seventeenth Century Background* (1934), Cartesian thought undermined confidence in the "truth" of poetry, it is in More that one should be able to read the signs of the decline, but More seems as sure of the truth of his poetical utterances as of his *Divine Dialogues* (1668) in prose. Other Metaphysically tinged poetry will be considered as part of the "Mid-Century Transition" below.

Ben Jonson and Renaissance classicism

From a twentieth century perspective Ben Jonson was overshadowed by Shakespeare as a playwright and by Donne as a lyric and reflective poet, but his importance in his time is difficult to overestimate. Before his time England had produced classical scholars who edited texts, produced grammars and other educational tools, and wrote significant prose. Not until Jonson, however, did an Englishman combine classical learning with great poetic ability. Jonson's interpretation of the classical heritage, which involved (besides the drama) imitations of such distinctly classical forms as the epigram, ode, and verse epistle; the translation into verse of Horace's *Ars poetica* (c. 17 B.C.E.; *The Art of Poetry*) and the employment of poetry as an ethical, civilizing influence not only enriched poetry but also defined classicism itself for generations of Englishmen. Even today classicists are likely to conceive of its essential spirit as comprising such virtues as simplicity, clarity, symmetry, detachment, and restraint, although such qualities are hardly the hallmarks of Euripides, Pindar, Ovid, and any number of other Greek and Roman poets. Jonsonian classicism proved to be a timely antidote to Elizabethan verbosity and extravagance, however, and generated some of the best poetry of the seventeenth century.

All Jonson's favorite classical forms had been practiced in the sixteenth century, though often in an eclectic and self-indulgent way. Jonson showed that the discipline of strict classicism could be liberating. Douglas Bush has pointed out that his imitations of Martial not only capture the temper of the greatest Roman epigrammatist better than did any of his predecessors, but also display more originality than earlier poems in this genre. Although not a great love poet, Jonson wrote a series of song lyrics that are models of their type, one of them, "Drink to me only with thine eyes" being familiar to millions of people who know nothing of classicism or of Jonson himself. His verse letter "To Penshurst," though initially unexciting to a reader accustomed to Donne's pyrotechnics, achieves an unobtrusive but unforgettable effect. When, at the end he contrasts the Sidney family mansion with other houses—"their lords have built, but thy lord dwells"—he has accomplished a tribute worth all the fulsome compliments that Elizabethans heaped upon their benefactors. It was through his study of Horace, a quiet bastion of civility in the noisy Roman Empire, that Jonson was able to produce such an effect.

Like Donne, Jonson not only wrote fine poems but inspired others of a high order as well. Robert Herrick,

to whom Jonson was "Saint Ben," sometimes approached his master in the art of epigram and sometimes exceeded him in the writing of cool, elegant lyrics. Poets such as Edmund Waller who reached the heights only infrequently probably could not have done so at all without Jonson's example (and occasionally Donne's also). The delicacy of Waller's "Go, lovely rose" is an inheritance of the Tribe of Ben. If the same poet's Penshurst poems fall short of Jonson's, Andrew Marvell's "Upon Appleton House" is both marvelously original and indebted to Jonson. William Alexander McClung, in *The Country House in English Renaissance Poetry* (1977), has shown how the poets after Jonson were able to set forth both an ideal of environment and an ideal of virtue through their reflection in a house.

Neither Jonson nor his followers necessarily came by their Horatian restraint and moderation naturally. As a young man, Jonson flashed the same hot temper that many another Elizabethans did not bother to control. In 1598 he plunged a rapier six inches into the side of a fellow actor named Gabriel Spencer, killing him instantly. He escaped with a branding on the thumb by pleading benefit of clergy—a dubious privilege possible for an educated man in or out of holy orders. Pen in hand, however, he modeled his work on that of Horace, who counseled, and perhaps practiced, moderation as a "golden mean." Horace did not prevent Jonson from lashing out verbally at his critics from time to time, but the Roman poet probably saved the impetuous Jonson from many a poetical gaucherie.

Many of Jonson's followers were political conservatives, advocates of royal supremacy and others who had most to fear from the intransigent Puritans, whose power grew steadily throughout the first half of the century until they forced Charles I from his throne and, in 1649, beheaded him for treason. Thus Jonsonian classicists overlapped, but did not subsume, the Cavalier lyric poets, who celebrated the not particularly Horatian virtues of war, chivalry, and loyalty to the monarchy. Just as paradoxically, the great classicist of the generation after Jonson turned out to be Latin Secretary of Oliver Cromwell's Commonwealth, the militant Puritan John Milton.

At their best, the Jonsonians wrote graceful and civilized lyrics reflecting a philosophy that was, in the best sense of the term, Epicurean. Like the Elizabethans, they were attracted to the theme of man's mortality, but whereas the earlier poets had responded to the inevitability of decline and death with lugubrious melancholy, the Tribe of Ben had imbibed Horace's advice: *carpe diem*, "seize the day." They wrote the most beautiful lyrics on this theme ever written in English: Herrick's "To Daffodils," "To the Virgins, to Make Much of Time," and "Corinna's going A-Maying," Waller's "Go, lovely rose," and Andrew Marvell's "To His Coy Mistress."

Another subject dear to the heart of Jonsonians was one relatively rare in previous (and many later) eras: children. Jonson wrote, with deep feeling yet immense restraint, of the deaths of two children. "On My First Daughter" does not repeat the personal pronoun of the title, although the reader learns that her name was Mary. The parents, however, are referred to in the third person, only the final phrase, "cover lightly, gentle earth!" betraying the speaker's involvement in the child's demise. An even finer poem, "On My First Son," has only six couplets and yet achieves enormous poignancy through the most economical means. Jonson could have expressed his love no more forcefully than by saying: "Here doth lie/ Ben Jonson his best piece of poetry." The lesson he draws is more Horatian than Christian: "For whose sake, henceforth, all his vows be such/ As what he loves may never like too much." Although Jonson wrote a few religious lyrics, it seems to be the classical legacy that he cherished most deeply.

Among those who gathered with Jonson at the Mermaid Tavern, Richard Corbett also wrote of family members, including one poem "To His Son, Vincent" in which he characteristically sets forth moderate wishes for his offspring, "not too much wealth, nor wit," and on the positive side, the graces of his mother, friends, peace, and innocence at the last. Among the poets who wrote poems about other people's children was William Cartwright, who expressed wishes for a friend's newborn son, and Robert Herrick, who penned two short epitaphs and two graces for children to recite at meals. Obviously the range of childhood poems in the seventeenth century is very narrow, even if Traherne's mystical poems "Shadows in the Water," "Innocence," and others are included. Even so, that children figure in poetry at all

is an indication that Jonson's disciples do not consider commonplace subjects beneath their notice.

As might be expected of admirers of Horace and Martial, Jonsonians favored short lines and short stanzas, though without the intricacy and irregularity often seen in Metaphysical lyrics. They often wrote in couplets, though the form known as the heroic couplet does not appear much before mid-century and does not become important until the age of Dryden. The couplets mirror the unassuming quality of so much early English classicism but commonly betray careful craftsmanship. The diction is rather plain, the metaphors few and not often unusual. The words and images are carefully chosen, however, with an eye to precision and euphony. The tone is tender and affectionate toward friends and loved ones, sarcastic toward those who, like fools, deserve it. There are few high flights, but neither are Jonsonian lapses likely to be very gross. Speech, Jonson wrote, in *Timber: Or, Discoveries Made upon Men and Matter* (1641) is "the instrument of society." Furthermore, "words are the people's." The poet is someone who uses the people's resources for the people's good.

BAROQUE POETRY

Probably because it arose as a reaction against a Renaissance classicism that had no parallel in England before Ben Jonson, the movement called the "baroque," beginning around 1580 and continuing for the better part of a century, had few manifestations in English poetry. First applied to architecture and later to sculpture and painting, the term described in particular the style of certain sixteenth century Venetian painters, particularly Jacopo Robusti Tintoretto, and of those, such as El Greco, who were influenced by the Venetians. The baroque disdained formal beauty and placidity in favor of asymmetrical composition, rich color, energy, and even contortion.

Applied to prose style, "baroque" signifies the revolt against full and rounded Ciceronian elegance, a tendency to place the main sentence element first, the avoidance of symmetry by varying the form and length of constructions, and a greater autonomy for subordinate constructions, which tend to follow the main sentence element. English had developed a Ciceronian prose style, but a recognizably anti-Ciceronian prose arose in the seventeenth century, notably in such works as Robert Burton's *The Anatomy of Melancholy* (1621) and Sir Thomas Browne's *Religio Medici* (1642).

In poetry the baroque has some affinities with the Metaphysical, but the differences are suggested by the adjectives used to describe the baroque: "ornate," "sensuous," "pictorial," and "emotional." The baroque is more likely to reject logic and reason, which are useful to Metaphysical poets of an argumentative bent. In his *European Metaphysical Poetry* Frank J. Warnke distinguishes between a baroque inclination to use contrast and antithesis for the purpose of separating opposites and a Metaphysical preference for paradox and synthesis to produce a fusion of opposites. The baroque was cultivated chiefly—not exclusively—by Roman Catholics as an expression of the Counter-Reformation spirit; it stands in contrast to the austerity of much northern European Protestant art.

The only English poets commonly associated with the baroque are Giles Fletcher (1585-1623) and Richard Crashaw (c. 1612-1649). Although Crashaw left more than four hundred poems, he is best known for his Saint Teresa poems, especially his florid "Upon the book and picture of the seraphical Saint Teresa" called "The Flaming Heart." The poem blazes to a finish in a series of oaths that illustrate the baroque manner:

> By thy large draughts of intellectual day,
> And by thy thirsts of love more large than they;
> By all thy brim-filled bowls of fierce desire
> By thy last morning's draught of liquid fire. . . .

By these and other oaths he asked to be emptied of self and enabled to imitate her example. It is no surprise to learn that Crashaw lived for some years on the Continent, that he renounced his Anglican priesthood to become a Roman Catholic, and that he died in Italy. Fletcher, on the other hand, stands as a caution against too facile generalizations. He remained English and Anglican, and although his poetry reminds some readers of the baroque pioneer Guillaume du Bartas, he usually causes readers of Spenser to think of *The Faerie Queene*. The case of Giles Fletcher underlines the fact that English writers of the earlier seventeenth century felt no compulsion to wage war with the Renaissance, since its greatest nondramatic poet, far from being a

doctrinaire classicist, synthesized elements classical, medieval, and Renaissance.

The baroque style in poetry, as in the visual arts, contained more than the usual number of the seeds of decadence. Baroque poets were liable to grotesqueness, obscurity, melodrama, and triviality. Its excesses no doubt helped pave the way for the later neoclassical resurgence. Again by analogy with architecture, some literary historians have seen the baroque also leading to the rococo, understood as a fussy, overdecorative, playful style which nevertheless might serve a serious purpose for a neoclassicist engaged in playful satire. The most obvious example in English literature, Alexander Pope's *The Rape of the Lock* (1712), comes early in the eighteenth century.

MID-CENTURY TRANSITION

To argue for too neat a mid-century transition between the earlier classical, Metaphysical, and baroque styles, on the one hand, and the Neoclassical Age on the other, is perhaps to betray an obsession with the neoclassical virtue of symmetry, but in a number of ways the mid-century marks a turning point. England's only interregnum straddles the century's midpoint, while on the Continent the Thirty Years' War came to an end with the treaties of the Peace of Westphalia in 1648. Both of these political events involved poetry and poets, the English Civil War more strikingly. The continental wars, insofar as they involved Protestant-Catholic clashes, represented nothing new, but they exhibited several modern features. Because they involved most European states in one way or another and required a general congress of nations to achieve even temporary peace, these conflicts augured the modern situation, in which local conflicts can trigger unforeseen large-scale involvement. Armorers preparing soldiers for battle had to devise protection against traditional weapons such as the sword and also new ones such as the pistol; the latter were often used as a kind of last resort, as clubs, or thrown at enemies more often than they were fired. All over Europe men were getting a preview of the mass destruction they could expect in future wars. The necessity of compromise and toleration—never before recognized as virtues—was beginning to dawn. More and more it seemed essential that reason and judgment, not passion and force, reign.

England had embarked on its internal war in 1642. The Puritans, who had already succeeded in closing London's theaters, alarmed conservative Englishmen by closing down the monarchy itself. The execution of Charles I and the proclamation of the Commonwealth in 1649 culminated nearly a decade of violence that had driven Sir John Denham, Sir William Davenant, and Thomas Hobbes, among others, into exile, and the Cavalier poet Richard Lovelace into prison, where he penned several immortal poems. The political transition ended in 1660. Young John Dryden wrote *Astraea Redux* (1660), an elaborate poetic tribute to a great event: the return of Charles II, son of the executed king, in glory. The adjustments made by all the former belligerents signal a new era. The next revolution, in 1688, despite ingredients seemingly as volatile as those which had precipitated the mid-century war, was not bloody.

Earl Miner (*The Metaphysical Mode from Donne to Cowley*) has referred to the decade between 1645 and 1655 as a "microcosm" of the century as a whole. Certainly it was a productive time for poets. In only the first half of that decade appeared Waller's *Poems* (1645), Sir John Suckling's *Fragmenta Aurea* (1646), Crashaw's *Steps to the Temple* (1646), Herrick's *Hesperides* (1648), Lovelace's *Lucasta* (1649), and Vaughan's *Silex Scintillans* (1650, 1655), all studded with still familiar anthology favorites. Although Marvell's posthumous poems are difficult to date, at least some of his best are presumed to have been written in the early 1650's, as were a number of the finest of Milton's sonnets, while *Paradise Lost* (1667, 1674) was evolving in Milton's imagination. Miner's point, however, is that the poets at work at this time are difficult to classify as "Cavalier" or "Puritan" or "Metaphysical" or "neoclassical." The distinctive earlier voices—those of Donne and Jonson and Herbert—had been stilled, and the most distinctive later one had not yet developed. The teenage Dryden's notorious foray into Metaphysical imagery in his 1649 poem "Upon the Death of the Lord Hastings," where Hastings's smallpox blisters are compared to "rosebuds stuck in the lily-skin about," and where "Each little pimple had a tear in it/ To wail the fault its rising did commit," presages the great neoclassicist only in its use of rhymed pentameter couplets—and those are not yet particularly "heroic."

That particular form, the end-stopped couplet with its potential for balance, antithesis, and memorable precision, was being hammered out in the 1640's by such poets as Edmund Waller, Sir John Denham, and John Cleveland (otherwise remembered chiefly as a decadent Metaphysical) in a series of spirited anti-Puritan satires. The latter's 1642 poem, "Cooper's Hill," now faded, looks forward to the Augustan Age with its blend of Horatian and Vergilian sentiments, its lofty abstractions, and its skillful handling of rhythm. The pentameter couplet was as old as Geoffrey Chaucer, but as a distinct unit, sometimes virtually a stanza in itself, it was capable of generating quite different effects. Detachable, quotable, suited for uttering the common wisdom, the great truths apparent to all, it embodied the neoclassical concept of wit, which was variously defined from this period on, but most memorably (because so well-expressed in a couplet, of course) by Pope in 1711: "True wit is nature to advantage dressed,/ What oft was thought, but ne'er so well expressed."

At the very middle of the century appeared a work by a man whose profession was neither poet nor critic but whose terse genealogy of a poem marks off the distance between the ages of Donne and Dryden. Thomas Hobbes was responding to remarks on epic made by Sir William Davenant in the preface to his fragmentary heroic poem *Gondibert* (1651) when he wrote:

> Time and education beget experience; experience begets memory; memory begets judgment and fancy; judgment begets the strength and structure, and fancy begets the ornaments of a poem.

It is impossible to imagine Donne countenancing the splitting asunder of "structure" and "ornaments," or for that matter acknowledging "ornaments" at all—for where were they in his poetry?

The following year, 1651, saw the publication of Hobbes's magnum opus, the *Leviathan*. There he made explicit what his answer to Davenant had implied: "In a good poem . . . both judgment and fancy are required: but the fancy must be more eminent." In other words, "ornament" is more important than "structure." To be sure, Hobbes was only stating succinctly a view that had already surfaced in Francis Bacon's philosophy: Poetry is make-believe ("feigned history," as Bacon put it in

The Advancement of Learning back in 1605) and has nothing to do with truth. This reproach becomes more damning when seen in the context of the linguistic theories set forth elsewhere by Hobbes and by the Royal Society of London in the following decade.

Another work of the mid-century marks a beginning rather than a transition. In 1650 there was published in London a book with the title *The Tenth Muse Lately Sprung Up in America*. Supposedly the manuscript had been spirited across the Atlantic without its author's consent. It was the first book of poems by an American woman. Discounting the doggerel of such works of piety as *The Bay Psalm Book* (1640), it was in fact the first book of poems by any American. Over two hundred years would pass before another woman poet would do as well as the woman who had emigrated to Massachusetts as a teenage bride twenty years earlier, Anne Bradstreet.

POETRY AND THE SCIENTIFIC REVOLUTION

Of the nonliterary forces on seventeenth century poets, the New Science may well have been the most uniformly pervasive throughout the Western world. Whereas social, political, and even religious developments varied considerably in nature and scope, the scientists were busy discovering laws that applied everywhere and affected the prevailing worldview impartially. Some artists and thinkers discovered the New Science and pondered its implications before others, but no poet could fall very many decades behind the vanguard and continue to be taken seriously. The modern reader of, say, C. S. Lewis's *The Discarded Image* (1964) and E. M. W. Tillyard's *The Elizabethan World Picture* (1943) observes that the Elizabethan "picture" had not changed substantially from the medieval "image" described by Lewis. Between 1600 and 1700, however, the worldview of educated people changed more dramatically than in any previous century. Early in the century John Donne signaled his awareness of science's challenge to the old certitudes about the world. By Dryden's maturity the new learning had rendered the Elizabethan brand of erudition disreputable and its literary imagination largely incomprehensible.

In *The Breaking of the Circle* (1960) Marjorie Hope Nicolson uses a popular medieval symbol, the circle of perfection, to demonstrate the effect of the New Science on the poets' perception of their world. The universe was a circle; so was the earth and man's head. The circle was God's perfect form, unending like himself, and all its manifestations shared in the perfection. It was easy—one might almost say "natural"—for Donne to begin one of his sonnets: "I am a little world made cunningly." Significantly, Donne did not say that he was *like* a little world. Not only did he use a metaphor instead of a simile, but also he used the metaphor confident that he was expressing a *truth*. In another sonnet Shakespeare refers to his soul as "the center of my sinful earth." Two thousand years earlier Aristotle had said that "to make metaphors well is to perceive likeness," and this judgment still stood firm. Already, however, a succession of thinkers from Nicolaus Copernicus in 1543 to Sir Isaac Newton in 1687 were at work breaking up the circle of perfection.

A special irony attaches to the contribution of Copernicus, a pious Roman Catholic who took the concept of the circle of perfection for granted when he set forth his heliocentric theory of the solar system. His insight was to see the sun, not the earth, as the center of God's operations in the visible world. To him it was perfectly obvious that God would impart perfect circular motion to the planets. Unfortunately his new model provided even less accurate predictability of planetary motions than the old geocentric theory that it was intended to replace. Thus he had to invent an ingenious system of subordinate circles—"eccentrics" and "epicycles"—to account for the discrepancies between the simple version of his model and his observations of what actually went on in the heavens. Thus, although his heliocentric theory incurred condemnation by Protestant and Catholic alike, his cumbersome model did not attract many adherents, and for decades intelligent men remained ignorant of his theory and its implications.

Two contemporaries of Donne changed all that. In 1609 Galileo built a telescope; by the next year he was systematically examining not just our solar system but other suns beyond it. Johann Kepler discovered, virtually at the same time, the elliptical orbit of Mars. He did this by breaking the old habit—his own as well as humankind's—of regarding physical events as symbols of divine mysteries, and thereby swept Copernicus's eccentrics and epicycles into a rubbish heap. When Donne wrote his "First Anniversary" poem, *An Anatomy of the World*, in 1611, he showed his familiarity with the new astronomy:

> And new philosophy calls all in doubt,
> The element of fire is quite put out;
> The sun is lost, and the earth, and no man's wit
> Can well direct him where to look for it.

Even before the confirmation of Copernicus's theory, the greatest literary geniuses of his century raised in their masterpieces versions of the great question provoked by the new science. Michel de Montaigne put it most simply in his *Essais* (1580; *Essays*): "What do I know?" The word *essays* signifies "attempts," and the work can be described as a series of attempts to answer his question. Miguel de Cervantes, setting out with the rather routine literary motive of satirizing a particularly silly type of chivalric romance, stumbled on his theme: the difficulty of distinguishing appearance from reality—even for those who, unlike Don Quixote, are not mad. The second part of Cervantes' novel, written like the first out of an understandable but pedestrian literary ambition (to reclaim his hero from the clutches of a plagiarist), raises the disturbing possibility that the madman interprets at least some aspects of reality more sensibly than the "sane" people among whom the idealistic Don Quixote was floundering. Shakespeare, having already endorsed the ancient concept of the poet as a divinely inspired madman in *A Midsummer Night's Dream* (c. 1595-1596), created, at the very beginning of the new century, a "mad" hero who raises an even more profound question: Can knowledge of the truth, even if attainable (and Hamlet gains the knowledge of the truth that concerns him most—the circumstances of his father's death—through ghostly intervention), lead to madness and paralysis of the will?

Unlike T. S. Eliot's twentieth century figure of J. Alfred Prufrock, who asks, "Do I dare disturb the universe?," medieval man did not disturb, and was not disturbed by, the universe. Even the presumed decay of the world from its original golden age did not alarm him, for it was all part of the plan of a wise and loving Creator. In *An Anatomy of the World*, the decay of the world has become profoundly disturbing, for the very cosmic order

itself seems to be coming apart: "'Tis all in pieces, all coherence gone." Shortly before writing this poem—and perhaps afterwards—Donne was able to write poetry of the sort quoted earlier, in which he moves easily from macrocosm to microcosm; but he also recognized that the "new philosophy calls all in doubt."

Astronomical discoveries were not the only form of knowledge. In 1600 William Gilbert wrote a book on magnetism. He was, like Copernicus, a good sixteenth century man and could talk about lodestones as possessing souls; his important discovery, however, was that the earth *is* a lodestone. In 1628, when William Harvey published his findings on the circulation of the blood, he referred to the heart as the body's "sovereign" and "inmost home," but in the process he taught the world to regard it as a mechanism—a pump. The old worldview was being destroyed quite unintentionally by men whose traditional assumptions often hampered their progress, but whose achievement made it impossible for their own grandchildren to make the same assumptions or to take the old learning seriously. As a result of Robert Boyle's work, chemistry was banishing alchemy, a subject taken seriously not only by poets but also by the scientists of an earlier day. At century's end, to talk of a person as a "little world" was mere quaintness, for Harvey had taught everyone to regard the body as one sort of mechanism, while the astronomers insisted that the solar system was another. It was merely idle to make connections between them.

As the scientists focused more clearly on their subjects, the poets' vision became more blurred. Astronomy is only one such subject area, but it is a particularly useful one for the purpose of demonstrating the change. Around 1582 Sir Philip Sidney's Astrophel could exclaim: "With how sad steps, O moon, thou climb'st the skies,/ How silently, and with how wan a face." Astrophel is a disappointed lover, of course, and need not be taken too seriously. What strikes the reader is the ease with which his creator sees parallels between the moon and the earthbound lover. In a more serious context, George Herbert addresses a star: "Bright spark, shot from a brighter place/ Where beams surround my Savior's face." Herbert almost surely knew what Galileo had been doing, but his "brighter place" still lay, as it were, beyond the reach of the telescope. In 1650 Henry

Vaughan could begin a poem: "I saw Eternity the other night/ Like a great Ring of pure and endless light,/ All calm, as it was bright." The reader's first inclination is perhaps to marvel at the facility of the utterance, but is the tone as matter-of-fact as it seems? Might not Donne and Herbert have seen eternity every night? On second thought one wonders whether the moments of insight are getting rarer. Five years later Vaughan published "They are all gone into the world of light," a poem reflecting an awareness of the transience of the heavenly vision:

> And yet, as Angels in some brighter dreams
> Call the soul, when man doth sleep:
> So some strange thoughts transcend our wonted
>   themes,
> And into glory peep.

At the end of the poem the speaker begs God to "disperse these mists." Any reader can verify that in later Metaphysical poetry the view of heaven gets cloudier. Thomas Traherne, almost surely writing in the Restoration, sees heaven not through the earthly eye but mystically with a sight often blurred by dream, shadows, and mists. In "My Spirit," for example, his soul "saw infinity/ 'Twas not a sphere, but 'twas a power/ Invisible." In *Religio Laici*, Dryden can see none of this and counsels submission to the Church. By 1733 Pope has banished all thought of reading heavenly meanings in the heavens: "The proper study of Mankind is Man"—unless, of course, one happens to be an astronomer.

NEOCLASSICISM FROM 1660 TO 1700

By the Restoration the poets had turned their attention primarily to public and social themes. The comedy of this period has given readers the impression of a licentious age determined to bury the memory of Puritanistic domination and live as fast and loose an existence as possible. Such behavior could not have characterized more than a tiny percentage of the people of later Stuart England. It was an age struggling for order through compromise. Wit might entertain, but life required sober judgment.

The classical tradition survived the New Science better than did the Metaphysical. It did not aspire to compete with science in the realm beyond everyday human and social experience. The Jonsonian tradition of short lyric and reflective poems no longer flourished, but the neoclassicists of the Restoration rediscovered satire and the heroic poem—the latter primarily in the remarkable triad of Miltonic poems published between 1667 and 1671: *Paradise Lost*, *Paradise Regained*, and *Samson Agonistes*. Horace was not neglected, but the study and translation of the Homeric and Vergilian epics gained in popularity. The time might have been ripe for a great patriotic epic (Milton considered a true Arthurian epic that would rectify the deficiencies of Spenser's episodic one before he finally settled on the yet nobler idea of justifying God's way to men), but whether because Milton's accomplishment had preempted the field or because history as Restoration poets knew it could not be hammered into the Vergilian mold, it was not written.

Instead, Dryden produced something new: a political satire in a heroic style based on a contemporary controversy over the attempt to exclude Charles II's Roman Catholic brother James from the royal succession. It was a serious matter, laden with danger for the principal in the struggle, for Dryden, and for the nation. He did not use blank verse, as Shakespeare and Milton had in their greatest works, but the heroic couplet, a form which Dryden had been honing for twenty years. The result is a poem of peculiar urgency, yet by virtue of Dryden's skillful representation of Charles II as the biblical King David and of the earl of Shaftesbury as "false Achitophel," who attempts to turn Absalom (Charles's illegitimate son, the duke of Monmouth) against his father, the poem takes on universality. It is by far the most impressive poem of the period: *Absalom and Achitophel* (1681).

The drama aside, satire is the greatest literary achievement of the Restoration, and it is also the most diverse. From Samuel Butler's low burlesque of the Puritans in *Hudibras* (1663) to Dryden's sustained high style in *Absalom and Achitophel*, from a butt as small as one undistinguished playwright (Thomas Shadwell in Dryden's 1682 mock-epic *Mac Flecknoe*) to one as large as humankind, vain aspirer to the status of rational being (the earl of Rochester's "A Satire Against Mankind," printed in 1675), verse satire flourished, providing models for even greater achievements in the first part of the following century. The Renaissance notion of decorum as the delicate adjustment of literary means to ends, of the suitability of the parts to the whole, governed these diverse attempts at diminishing the wickedness and folly that Restoration poets considered it their duty to expose and correct. Even *Hudibras*, with its slam-bang tetrameter couplets and quirky rhymes, seems the perfect vehicle for flaying the routed Puritans, and its levels of irony are far more complex than superficial readers suspect. When satire began to invade prose, as it increasingly did in the eighteenth century, its narrative possibilities increased, but it lost subtle effects of rhythm, timing, and rhyme.

Compared with the first sixty years of the century, the Restoration seems a prosaic age. A considerable number of its most accomplished writers—John Bunyan, the diarists Samuel Pepys and John Evelyn, Sir William Temple, John Locke—wrote no poetry worth preserving, and Dryden himself wrote a large proportion of prose. Does the preponderance of prose and satire confirm T. S. Eliot's early charge that a "dissociation of sensibility" had set in by the time of the Restoration? Is it true that writers no longer could fuse thought and feeling, with the consequence that prose was used for conveying truth and poetry for the setting forth of delightful lies?

Hobbes, who had little use for poetry in general, praised the epic as conducive to moral truth, and he admitted that satire can be defended on moral grounds also. The Restoration poets in England were the successors of a classical tradition that emphasized the ethical value of poetry, so they might as plausibly be considered carrying out, on a somewhat larger scale, the dictates of Jonson as those of Hobbes. The Royal Society of London, of which Dryden was a member, was founded in 1662 for "the improving of natural knowledge," and among its ambitions it numbered the improving of the language by waging war against "tropes" and "figures" and "metaphors." One cannot imagine Donne having anything to do with such an organization, all the more because the Society on principle did not discuss "such subjects as God and the soul." It is difficult to see how Dryden's association with it substantiates the charge of dissociated sensibility, however, for there is certainly both thought and feeling together in *Absalom and Achitophel*, even if it is, like the Royal Society itself,

earthbound and relatively unmetaphorical, and, while it is no doubt instructive, generations of readers have taken delight in it also.

One is tempted to offer a different explanation for Restoration writers' greater attachment to prose and to satire. The reading audience expanded greatly in the seventeenth century, and increasingly it became the business of the writer to satisfy its interests, which for a variety of reasons were political and social. The early Metaphysical writers possessed a very small audience (one another and a few more who shared the same interests); very much the same situation obtained for Jonson and his followers. When the readership increased, poets modified their work accordingly. When Dryden did write of religion, he wrote of it as he and his contemporaries understood it. That Dryden took little delight in Donne's poetry is clear from his remarks in "A Discourse Concerning the Original and Progress of Satire" (1693):

Donne affects the metaphysics, not only in his amorous verses, where nature only should reign; and perplexes the minds of the fair sex with nice speculations of philosophy, when he should engage their hearts and entertain them with the softnesses of love.

Dryden did not understand Donne's intentions very well, but he understood his own political intentions very well indeed.

In his own and the century's final years Dryden worked primarily at translation, promising in his preface to *Fables Ancient and Modern* (1700) a translation of the whole *Iliad* (c. 800 B.C.E.), "if it should please God to give me longer life and moderate health." He added another provision: "that I meet with those encouragements from the public, which may enable me to proceed in my undertaking with some cheerfulness." This is the remark of a public figure—a former poet laureate, author of a stream of plays and published books since the 1600's, a veteran attraction at Will's Coffee House in London.

Poets had not always expected such encouragements. When Donne died in 1631, only four of his poems had been published. Herbert, Marvell, and Traherne saw few or none of their poems in print. Jonson, on the other hand, had offered his work to the public, even inviting ridicule in 1616 by boldly calling his volume *Works*. Like Dryden after him, he had developed a healthy sense of audience in his career as a playwright. He had even more reason to fear an unhappy audience than Dryden, for along with John Marston and George Chapman, he had been imprisoned and very nearly mutilated by a gang of Scots retainers of James I whom the trio had outraged by some of their jests in their play *Eastward, Ho!* (1605). Nevertheless, Jonson promised a translation of Horace's *The Art of Poetry*, with no provisions whatsoever, that same year. The fact that he did not deliver the translation until long afterward does not seem to have had anything to do with readers' wishes. Jonson usually conveyed the impression that whatever he had to say amounted to nothing less than a golden opportunity for any sensible reader or listener.

Even if one assumes that Dryden's hope for encouragement may have been only an expression of politeness, that politeness itself signifies a change of relationship with the "public." Most of the poetry written in the time of Donne and Jonson has the quality of being overheard. It is as if the poet is praying, making love, or rebuking a fool, and the reader has just happened to pass by. If the poem is a verse epistle, the reader experiences the uncomfortable feeling that he is reading someone else's mail—and quite often that is so. By 1700 the poet seems conscious of producing a document for public inspection and proceeds accordingly, with all the implications—fortunate and unfortunate—of such a procedure. He will not tax the public with too many difficulties, for some of them—too many, perhaps—will not understand. He had better polish his work, and he had better not be dull. He might produce one of those "overheard" lyrics once in a while, but the chances are that they will yield few excellences not imitative of earlier poets whose circumstances favored that type of poem.

The neoclassical sense of audience would continue, as the neoclassical period would continue, for nearly another century—at least in those poets with access to a public. The poet's public stance would give rise to more fine satire and reflective poems of great majesty and sustained moral power. The knack of lyric would be largely lost, and, when recovered, the lyrics would be romantic. No one would ever write poems like "A Valediction: Forbidding Mourning" or "To His Coy Mistress" again,

but poets would offer, in compensation, poems such as *The Dunciad* (1728-1743) and *The Vanity of Human Wishes* (1749).

BIBLIOGRAPHY

Baker, David J. *Between Nations: Shakespeare, Spenser, Marvell, and the Question of Britain*. Stanford, Calif.: Stanford University Press, 1997. Fusing historiography and literary criticism, this book places Renaissance England and its literature at a meeting of English, Irish, Scottish, and Welsh histories. It ranges from the late sixteenth through the late seventeenth centuries and deals with the "reigns" of three monarchs and one regicide.

Baker, Herschel Clay. *The Later Renaissance in England: Nondramatic Verse and Prose, 1600-1660*. Prospect Heights, Ill.: Waveland Press, 1996.

Barbour, Reid. *English Epicures and Stoics: Ancient Legacies in Early Stuart Culture*. Massachusetts Studies in Early Modern Culture. Amherst: University of Massachusetts Press, 1998. Portrays the intricate dialectical influence of the ancient Greek philosophies of Epicureanism and Stoicism on seventeenth century England and analyzes how these disparate legacies served as touchstones for discourse in the theater, poetry, and political, religious, and scientific literature of the period.

Bennett, Joan. *Four Metaphysical Poets: Donne, Herbert, Vaughan, Crashaw, Marvell*. 3d ed. Cambridge, England: Cambridge University Press, 1964.

Brooks, Cleanth. *Historic Evidence and the Reading of Seventeenth Century Poetry*. Columbia: University of Missouri Press, 1991.

Bush, Douglas. *English Literature in the Earlier Seventeenth Century, 1600-1660*. Rev. ed. Oxford, England: Clarendon Press, 1962.

Cunnar Eugene R., and Jeffrey Johnson. *Discovering and (Re)Covering the Seventeenth Century Religion Lyric*. Pittsburgh: Duquesne University Press, 2001.

Di Cesare, Mario A., ed. *George Herbert and the Seventeenth Century Religious Poets: Authoritative Texts*. New York: W. W. Norton, 1990.

Fallon, Stephen M. *Milton Among the Philosophers: Poetry and Materialism in Seventeenth Century England*. Ithaca, N.Y.: Cornell University Press, 1991.

Fowler, Alistair, ed. *The New Oxford Book of Seventeenth Century Verse*. London: Oxford University Press, 1992.

Guibbory, Achsah. *Ceremony and Community from Herbert to Milton: Literature, Religion, and Cultural Conflict in Seventeenth Century England*. Cambridge: Cambridge University Press, 1998.

Harvey, Elizabeth D., and Katharine Eisaman Maus, eds. *Soliciting Interpretation: Literary Theory and Seventeenth Century English Poetry*. Chicago: University of Chicago Press, 1990.

Hellegers, Desiree. *Handmaid to Divinity: Natural Philosophy, Poetry, and Gender in Seventeenth Century England*. Norman: University of Oklahoma Press, 1999.

Kramer, David Bruce. *The Imperial Dryden: The Poetics of Appropriation in Seventeenth Century England*. Athens: University of Georgia Press, 1994.

Leishman, J. B. *Metaphysical Poets: Donne, Herbert, Vaughan, Traherne*. 1934. Reprint. New York: Russell & Russell, 1963.

Lewalski, Barbara Kiefer. *Protestant Poetics and the Seventeenth Century Religious Lyric*. Princeton, N.J.: Princeton University Press, 1979.

Martz, Louis L. *The Poetry of Meditation: A Study in English Religious Literature of the Seventeenth Century*. New Haven, Conn.: Yale University Press, 1954.

Miner, Earl. *The Metaphysical Mode from Donne to Cowley*. Princeton, N.J.: Princeton University Press, 1969.

Morotti, Arthur F. *Manuscript, Print, and the English Renaissance Lyric*. Ithaca, N.Y.: Cornell University Press, 1995.

Post, Jonathan F. *English Lyric Poetry: The Early Seventeenth Century*. New York: Routledge, 1999.

Summers, Claude J., and Ted-Larry Pebworth. *Bright Shootes of Everlastingnesse: The Seventeenth Century Religious Lyric*. Columbia: University of Missouri Press, 1987.

_____, eds. *The Wit of Seventeenth Century Poetry*. Columbia: University of Missouri Press, 1995.

Summers, Joseph H. *The Heirs of Donne and Jonson*. New York: Oxford University Press, 1970.

Tuve, Rosemond. *Elizabethan and Metaphysical Imagery: Renaissance and Twentieth-Century Critics*. Chicago: University of Chicago Press, 1947.

White, Helen C. *The Metaphysical Poets: A Study in Religious Experience*. New York: Macmillan, 1936.

Williamson, George. *The Donne Tradition: A Study in English Poetry from Donne to the Death of Cowley*. Cambridge, Mass.: Harvard University Press, 1930.

Young, R. V. *Doctrine and Devotion in Seventeenth-Century Poetry: Studies on Donne, Herbert, Crashaw, and Vaughan*. Studies in Renaissance Literature 2. Rochester, N.Y.: D. S. Brewer, 2000.

Robert P. Ellis

ENGLISH POETRY IN THE EIGHTEENTH CENTURY

The eighteenth century in Britain saw the blossoming of seventeenth century poetic modes and the sprouting of modes that would blossom into Romanticism. It was an age of reason and sentiment, of political turbulence, of growing colonialism and wealth, of beautiful landscapes and parks, of gin addiction and Evangelicalism, of a burgeoning middle class and growing respect for middle-class values, of increasing literacy and decreasing dependence on patronage, and of cantankerous Tories and complacent Whigs. As England became the center of world commerce and power, so, too, it became the center of literary achievement.

John Dryden died in 1700, but his death signaled no dramatic change in poetic style. Poets walked in his footsteps, moving away from Metaphysical conceits—from the style of those poets who glittered "Like twinkling Stars the Miscellanies o'er"—to search for smoothness and a new style of thinking. Symptomatic of the eighteenth century's passion for order and regularization was Alexander Pope's tinkering with the poetry of John Donne: He made Donne's numbers flow melodiously and corrected his versification. Heroic couplets and lampoons and political satires such as Dryden's were written throughout the century. Common Restoration subjects such as the imperious mistress and the cacophony of critics continued to be used.

Dryden named William Congreve his poetical successor, but Pope was his true heir. From the appearance of his *Pastorals* in 1709 until William Wordsworth's *Lyrical Ballads* in 1798, Pope dominated poetry. His influence, for example, pervades Robert Dodsley's *Collection of Poems, by Several Hands* (1748), in William Mason's *Museaus* (1747), in the half dozen other poems concerned chiefly with Pope, and in the many others that refer respectfully to him. If the poets of the latter part of the century did not imitate him, they at least grudgingly admired him while reacting against him.

The "ancients"—Homer and Vergil in particular, but Horace, Pindar, Juvenal, Martial, and Anacreon, too—were devoutly followed. As school-boys, the poets did countless exercises translating Latin and Greek verse, and, like John Milton before them, poets such as Joseph Addison and Samuel Johnson began by writing Latin verse. In the middle of his career, Pope translated the *Iliad* in 1715-1718 and the *Odyssey* in 1725-1726; he spent his later career writing imitations of Horace. Johnson chose to write imitations of the other great Roman satirist, Juvenal. These imitations were not strict translations; rather, they picked up hints from the classics and made the subject relevant to contemporary life. Even at the end of the century, William Cowper translated Homer (1791), though his style was too heavily Miltonic.

William Shakespeare and other Elizabethans provided a third important example for eighteenth century poets. Both Pope and Johnson edited Shakespeare: Pope's edition was valuable chiefly for restoring "prose" passages to the original blank verse, Johnson's for his criticism founded upon common sense. Joseph and Thomas Warton and other mid-century poets appealed to the example of Shakespeare to free themselves from the classical doctrine of the superiority of judgment and taste to the imagination. Shakespeare helped inspire William Collins's *An Ode on the Popular Superstitions of the Highlands of Scotland, Considered as the Subject of Poetry* (1788), and even William Blake was drawn to Elizabethan poetry. For the eighteenth century, Shakespeare represented unlearned genius, and his quality of irregularity, of "great beauties and blemishes" was highly praised.

Although less influential than Shakespeare, Edmund Spenser had his followers. James Thomson's *The Castle of Indolence* (1748) imitated Spenserian melody and descriptive techniques, and William Shenstone parodied Spenser in *The Schoolmistress* (1742). James Beattie's *The Minstrel* (1771-1774) was one of the longest and best poems of the century written in Spenserian stanza. Another poet who owed much to Spenser was the tragic Thomas Chatterton. Like Spenser, Chatterton wrote vigorous lyrics and showed much metrical originality.

When eighteenth century poets sat down to write a poem, they did not pour forth images of their souls; they attempted certain genres and looked to the ancients for inspiration and example. Their voices and emotions were public rather than private, and they wrote about the present rather than about their own pasts. The poet was the spokesman for his age and his subject was man as a social creature. The personal did, however, creep into eighteenth century verse: Matthew Prior's best work was personal, if not autobiographical, and Pope used the epistle form to speak personally.

Eighteenth century poets valued elegant ease and noble urbanity. "Decorum" was a key word: The eighteenth century classicists sought to control the abundant energy which characterized earlier English classicists. Augustan poets tried to achieve the effect of apparent casualness of structure with definite coherence under the surface. Their use of noble Roman tone and classical patterns familiar throughout Europe gave them a Continental audience, something the Elizabethans never had.

EPICS AND MOCK-EPICS

The most popular genres were epic, ode, satire, elegy, epistle, and song. To show their fealty to Homer and Vergil, nearly every eighteenth century poet at least thought of writing an epic. Pope, for one, was planning an epic on Brutus when he died. None of the plans for writing epics or the epics that were written brought forth anything but sour fruit (Aaron Hill's biblical epic *Gideon*, 1749, is a prime example); however, the mock-epic form in this possibly nonheroic age brought forth delicious fruit, including Pope's *The Rape of the Lock* (1712, 1714) and *The Dunciad* (1728-1743).

ODES

Eighteenth century poets had more success writing odes than they did writing epics. In the early years of the century, poets looked to Pindar or to Horace as models for writing odes. They used Pindaric odes for exalted subjects and Horatian odes for various urbane, personal, and meditative themes. In the seventeenth century Abraham Cowley had popularized irregularities in the Pindaric odes; after Congreve denounced them in his *A Pindarique Ode on the Victorious Progress of Her Majesties Arms* (1706), most poets knew the duty of Pindaric regularity but still preferred the laxness of Cowley's form. Thomas Gray was an important exception: He wrote two Pindaric odes—"The Bard" and "The Progress of Poesy"—in rigidly correct form.

In the second quarter of the century, a new type of ode appeared, inspired by John Milton's "L'Allegro" and "Il Penseroso." The "descriptive and allegorical ode" centered around a personified abstraction, such as pity or simplicity, and treated it in a descriptive or pictorial way. Collins and the Warton brothers did much to popularize this mode in the 1740's.

SATIRE

The eighteenth century was, of course, the golden age of satire. Satirists such as Jonathan Swift and Pope attacked the frivolity of polite society, the corruption of politics, and false values in all the arts. The aim of satire, as Pope explained it, was not wanton destruction: Satire "heals with Morals what it hurts with Wit." Satirists, he claimed, nourished the state, promoting its virtue and providing it everlasting fame.

Eighteenth century poetry has been accused of monotony and weak feeling. The zeal of the satirists for truth and virtue, however, blazes through many lines, and the warmth of their compassion for the poor, the sick, the mistreated, and the aged glows through many others. Pope, in the *Moral Essays* (1731-1735), for example, pities the ancient belles of court: "See how the World its Veterans rewards!/ A Youth of Frolicks, an old Age of Cards." The age, particularly the state under the administration of Sir Robert Walpole, may not have been as black as the satirists painted it—it was an age of increasing wealth and progress—but the satirists were obsessed by the precariousness of intellect and of civilization, by the threat of fools and bores and pedants, by the fear of universal darkness burying all. In a world where man's intellect alone keeps society from the disintegration caused by unthinking enthusiasts and passionate pig heads, dullness is morally objectionable—an aspect of vice. Satirists thus became moral crusaders for truth, virtue, and intelligence. They believed in an ancient state of purity which man could not re-create; man could, however, "relume the ancient light" (in Pope's words) for the future.

ELEGIES

Elegies in Latin and Greek were composed in elegiac couplets rather than the hexameter lines of the epic and the pastoral. Donne wrote amatory elegies in the seventeenth century, but by the eighteenth century elegies were meditative pieces, often about death. Gray's *Elegy Written in a Country Churchyard* (1751), said by some to be the best poem of the eighteenth century, is an elegy for all "average" and obscure men. It achieves the ideals of its day in its attempt to work in universal terms and in its purity and harmony of diction; it approaches Romanticism in its placid melancholy and rustic setting. In "Elegy to the Memory of an Unfortunate Lady" (1717), the other important elegy of the eighteenth century and one of the only works of Pope which the Romantics could tolerate, Pope laments the mortality of a young suicide victim and his own mortality, stressing the threats to human feeling and the glory of its intensity.

EPISTLES

The epistle, or verse letter, an important form in the seventeenth century, reached its height in the epistles of Pope in the 1740's, and continued to be popular until the end of the nineteenth century. Horace provided the classical model for the verse epistle. The familiar form of the epistle allowed poets to seem to speak sincerely and intimately to a close friend while addressing the public about general issues. Almost all epistles were written in heroic couplets, began in a rather rambling way, and finally came to a point about halfway through the poem. Charles Churchill's *Epistle to William Hogarth* (1763), for example, begins with a miscellaneous discussion of satire. The effect of this structure is comic and optimistic: Order is brought out of disorder.

LYRIC POETRY

Lyric poets used the song to achieve brevity and, at times, elegance. Songs were collected and written throughout the period, but the greatest of the songwriters—Robert Burns—came at the end. He not only composed his own songs but also reconstituted and invigorated old Scottish songs, turning a drinking song into "Auld Lang Syne" and a disreputable ballad into "John Anderson my Jo."

EPIGRAMS

Other popular genres included the epigram, the fable, and verse criticism. The tradition of the epigram, modeled on Martial and on Horace, began in the Renaissance and appealed to the eighteenth century because of its conciseness and the opportunity it provided to display wit. The average epigram was at most six lines long, beginning with something to arouse curiosity or anticipation and closing with humor or surprise. Common topics included love and the characters of people, though some epigrams were obscene. A specialized form of the epigram was the epitaph, which several poets composed for themselves. John Gay's epitaph reads: "Life is a jest, and all things show it/ I thought so once; but now I know it," and Swift's Latin epitaph, roughly translated, says that he is now gone where bitter indignation no longer lacerates his heart.

FABLES

The fables of the eighteenth century demonstrate the ability of Augustan writers to enrich and vary a genre. The favorite form for the fables was the iambic tetrameter couplet. Gay wrote the best English fables (1727-1738), though Swift, Bernard Mandeville, Prior, Christopher Smart, Cowper, Beattie, and Johnson also wrote them. Far from being childlike, Gay's *Fables* (1727, 1738) expressed a disillusioned cynicism toward humankind, particularly emphasizing man's foolish pride. No English fable, however, could measure up to those written in France by Jean de La Fontaine in the seventeenth century.

CRITICAL POETRY AND *An Essay on Criticism*

The critical poem was popular in the Restoration and came into full bloom in the eighteenth century. Following the pattern set by Horace in his *Ars Poetica* (c. 17 B.C.E.; *The Art of Poetry*), the Italian poet Girolamo Vida wrote *De arte poetica* in 1527 and the French poet Nicolas Boileau-Despréaux wrote *L'Arte poetique* in 1674 (*The Art of Poetry*, 1683). In England, John Sheffield's *Essay on Poetry* (1682), Wentworth Dillon, Earl of Roscommon's *Essay on Translated Verse* (1684), and Lord Lansdowne's *Essay upon Unnatural Flights in Poetry* (1701) bore testimony to the increased interest in literary criticism and theory.

Pope's *An Essay on Criticism* (1711), the zenith of this genre, condensed eighteenth century poetic standards. *An Essay on Criticism* is actually a poem on how to judge a poem and on what morals are requisite for a critic. The first requirement is to follow nature, then to follow the ancients who "discov'red" and "Methodiz'd" the rules of nature. The "laws of Nature" to the Augustans meant, roughly, the right principles which every man of common sense and goodwill would follow in his thought and conduct. The French called nature "*la belle nature*," and Pope maintained that it is "the source, and end, and test of Art." The faith that man has in a world of universal human values underlies the concept of nature.

From *An Essay on Criticism* comes such neoclassic advice as: "The Sound must seem an Eccho to the Sense," "Avoid Extreams" (the Augustan ideal of the golden mean), "In all you speak, let Truth and Candor shine," and "Men must be taught as if you taught them not." The poem's merit lies in its compressed phrasing of current standards, not in any originality of thought. Early eighteenth century poets or their audiences were not as much impressed by originality as by memorable expression: Pope said that true wit is "What oft was *Thought*, but ne'er so well *Exprest*," and Joseph Addison in *The Spectator* 253 wrote that "wit and fine writing doth not consist so much in advancing things that are new, as in giving things that are known agreeable turn."

POETRY, PATRONAGE, AND POLITICS

Eighteenth century poets generally came from good families in much reduced circumstances. Prior, Swift, and Johnson fit this generalization, though Pope was the son of a wealthy linen draper. Poets still sought patrons, praising their parks and estates, but more and more their writings at least partially supported them. Prior, for example, apparently netted four thousand guineas from his *Poems on Several Occasions* (1707, 1709). The audience for literature was growing, thanks in large measure to the graduates of charity schools and the newly founded grammar schools. Political preferment also proved lucrative for poets. Addison served as undersecretary of state and later secretary to the lord-lieutenant of Ireland, and Robert Burns collected excise taxes. Samuel Johnson's letter to Lord Chesterfield on his tardy recognition of the *Dictionary of the English Language* (1755) is said to have given the final blow to patronage, though the letter was not printed until near the end of the century.

In the first half of the century, poets aligned themselves according to politics. Addison and Whigs such as Ambrose Philips reigned at Button's coffeehouse. The

Tories—Swift, Gay, Thomas Parnell, Pope, and John Arbuthnot—formed the Scriblerus Club and met at Arbuthnot's apartments in St. James's Palace. Thomas Parnell and John Gay both worked closely with Pope and yet remained independent: Parnell published his Miltonic poems chiefly in miscellanies, and Gay became the king of burlesque. Barbs flew back and forth between the Whig and Tory parties, the deadliest of which was Pope's portrait of Addison in *Epistle to Dr. Arbuthnot* (1735).

HUMOR AND SATIRE

Though there undoubtedly was venom in these attacks, there was also a good measure of humor written in the early decades of the century. Gay was a chief contributor with *Wine* (1708), a burlesque of Milton and John Philips's *Cyder* (1708) and *Trivia: Or, The Art of Walking the Streets of London* (1716). Swift, Lady Mary Wortley-Montagu, and others helped to popularize "town eclogues." The most delightfully imaginative and amusing of the exposés of society was Pope's mock-heroic *The Rape of the Lock*, with its sylphs and gnomes and diminution of Homeric epic. *The Rape of the Lock* is much more complicated than Dryden's *Mac Flecknoe* (1682): Pope reveals the confusion of moral values in society in such catalogs as "Puffs, Powder, Patches, Bibles, Billet-doux." Pope simultaneously laughs at the foibles of society and warns of the fragility of beauty.

Most poets wrote in heroic couplets, a pair of rhyming pentameter lines. In Shakespeare's time, couplets closed sonnets or scenes in blank verse dramas; in the later seventeenth century couplets were adapted to correspond to the elegiac couplet of classical verse and to the heroic, unrhymed Greek and Latin hexameter. Pope was the master of the heroic couplet; he knew how to build two or three couplets, each technically closed, into a unified, easy period. Throughout the century, poets in England and America tried to equal his artistry. By the end of the century, poets such as Cowper still attempted heroic couplets, but with little success. Cowper could achieve the Horatian simplicity admired in the eighteenth century, but his verses lacked Horatian polish and piquancy.

Even in the early part of the century, however, poets such as Swift and Prior ignored heroic couplets in favor of tetrameter couplets. Prior criticized the heroic couplet, complaining that it

> cuts off the Sense at the end of every first Line, which must always rhime to the next following, and consequently produces too frequent an Identity in the Sound, and brings every Couplet to the Point of an Epigram.

Short poems and irregular meters, on the whole, were not highly regarded.

THE NATURE OF HUMANKIND

After the 1640's, England's civil war left deep scars that lasted well into the eighteenth century. Religious and political factions still strained the country, and the atmosphere was at once one of compromise and tolerance and one of skepticism. It was a time when writers questioned and strove to understand the nature of man, human limitations, and the limitations that must be set on human passions. Answers to these questions differed significantly: Some optimistic moralists believed in the essential goodness of humankind, some satirists and cynics bemoaned humanity's incorrigible pride, which would forever keep people from the truth, and some realists insisted that humanity and the world must be accepted as they are, in all their ugliness.

In *Characteristics of Men, Manners, Opinions, Times* (1711), the earl of Shaftesbury promulgated a belief in the perfection of the universe and the naturalness of virtue in man. Opposing Thomas Hobbes's belief in the natural selfishness of man, Shaftesbury wrote that it is

> impossible to conceive that a rational creature coming first to be tried by rational objects, and receiving into his mind the images or representations of justice, generosity, gratitude, or other virtue, should have no liking of these or dislike of their contraries. . . .

He asserted that unselfishness is as natural to man as selfishness and that man has "social instincts" and "social passions" as well as egotism. Although Shaftesbury had many detractors, including Bernard de Mandeville in his *Fable of the Bees* (1714), his beliefs gained wide acceptance in England, France, and Germany.

Pope's *An Essay on Man* (1733-1734), another influential document on these ethical questions, reflects Pope's own attempts to balance optimism and a sense of

fact. He describes the "great chain of being" and man's placement in this "isthmus of a middle state,/ A Being darkly wise, and rudely great." He tried to build his rational system of ethics without denying religion but by being independent of it. Thomson, who was influenced by Shaftesbury, anticipated Pope in declaring in *The Seasons* (1730) that that which seems evil is seen only in part, because the whole is good, that order may be threatened yet will survive in a larger sense. He did not, however, attack the problems of evil and man's moral responsibility directly.

A corollary to the question about human nature was the problem of happiness. As the wealth of the citizenry increased, leisure time, sports, recreation, and the search for happiness became important. "Happiness" replaced "property" as one of the inalienable rights of man. In searching for happiness, man becomes disillusioned, and many a writer from Prior through Johnson to Oliver Goldsmith expressed the pessimism that neither knowledge, riches, pleasure, nor power can avail against the assault of time and human weakness. John Dyer voiced the feeling well in these lines from *Grongar Hill* (1726):

> A little Rule, a little Sway,
> A Sunbeam in a Winter's Day
> Is all the Proud and Mighty have,
> Between the Cradle and the Grave.

This pessimism led Prior to urge men to cherish fleeting joys as the only respite in the human world of suffering and led Edward Young in *Night Thoughts* (1742-1745) to insist upon the latent divinity of man and his power to fly above worldly claims to the blessed realms of infinity. Gray, in his "Hymn to Adversity" (1742), which Johnson termed both "poetical and rational," cautioned against expecting more of life than life can give. Chastising men for chasing "treacherous phantoms" and deluding themselves with visions of "airy good," Johnson in *The Vanity of Human Wishes* (1749) urged men to study, exertion, and prayer. All these men evince the increasing concern and compassion of the century with the lot of man.

LANDSCAPE AND PHILOSOPHICAL DISCOURSE

While Pope inherited satire and heroic couplets from Dryden, there was another poetic movement in the eighteenth century whose ancestors were Milton, reflective poetry, and blank verse. Poets increasingly used landscape as material for their poetry and wedded it to philosophical discourse. Thomson's *The Seasons* was both the crowning effort of this movement and a stimulus to its further development. Thomson patterned *Autumn* and *Winter* on the chronological progress of the season and *Summer* on the events of a typical day. The passages alternate between description and meditation, with description being the most innovative. Thomson excelled in the presentation of exuberant motion and tightly packed detail. Pope and Ambrose Philips had written lovely pastorals earlier in the century, and Gay incorporated much folklore and the sights and sounds of the country in his *Rural Sports* (1713) and *The Shepherd's Week* (1714); but Thomson's work differed sharply from the pastoral in its description of nature for its own sake, with human incidents as background rather than nature as background for human drama. *The Seasons* started a tradition of descriptive poetry which at its extreme became a love of what Shenstone called "odd picturesque description." The descriptive poem usurped the place of the epic as the most honored poetic form, and Thomson was invested as the preeminent English poet of nature until Wordsworth succeeded him.

Thomson has been accused of having an overly latinate style with false ornamentation. His strength lies in his minute observation of nature, in his almost scientific curiosity. A professed deist, Thomson saw in nature a revelation of the attributes of God; other deists, and even the more orthodox, upheld him in this belief. The scientist in Thomson admired the orderliness of the mathematical universe. Like Pope, Thomson insisted on intelligence and reason; he believed that a study of nature frees men from superstition and ignorance. He, too, reflected on the wants and miseries of human life.

DIDACTIC POETRY

Encouraged by *The Seasons* and *An Essay on Man*, many poets began to write in a moralizing, didactic manner, including William Somerville (*The Chace*, 1735), Henry Brooke (*Universal Beauty*, 1735), Dr. Mark Akenside (*The Pleasures of the Imagination*, 1744), and Edward Young (*Night Thoughts*). Akenside's *The Pleasures of the Imagination*, based on Addison's discussion

of the same subject in *The Spectator*, insists on the interconnection of truth, goodness, and beauty. Akenside's training in religion, philosophy, science, and art is evident throughout the poem, which is more a document for a historian of ideas than for an appreciator of poetic beauty.

Night Thoughts is essentially a Christian book of piety, but its appeal lay in its concentration on death and its autobiographical elements. Its main theme is that death's inevitability should sober both the reckless libertine and the complacent deist. Its moral reflections are addressed to a "silken son of pleasure" named Lorenzo, whose "fond heart dances while the siren sings." The pious gloom of *Night Thoughts*, which was mistranslated and misinterpreted, caused a sensation on the Continent and was gradually incorporated into the European tradition of romantic *Weltschmerz*.

SENSIBILITY AND MELANCHOLY

Another important movement in the literature of England and the Continent in the first half of the eighteenth century has been named "sensibility." By this is meant an exquisite sensitiveness to the beautiful and the good, a sensitiveness which induces melancholy or sorrow. All that is noble and generous in human conduct was thought to have its source in this exquisite sensitivity, and nature assisted as a moral tonic to the human heart. The pensive mood, even though it induced melancholy, also induced pleasure because it freed the emotions and the imagination from the conventions of civilization and from the vanity and corruption of humankind. Milton's "Il Penseroso" partly influenced this new mode, and Richard Steele promoted melancholy in *Tatler* 89: "That calm and elegant satisfaction which the vulgar call Melancholy, is the true and proper Delight of Men of Knowledge and Virtue." In *Grongar Hill* Dyer employed picturesque ruins and other devices to summon a mood of gentle melancholy, and Shenstone asserted his independence from the satirists and wits, writing that the eighteenth century had "discovered sweets in melancholy which we could not find in mirth." Thomas Warton's celebratory "The Pleasures of Melancholy" (1747) avoided the didacticism of some of Milton's followers and cultivated relaxed and idyllic moods instead. In some ways, sensibility was a natural reaction to the Restoration, to its moral cynicism and its exclusive culture. Sensibility was a movement toward moral feeling and conduct, toward middle-class values, and, politically, toward the Whigs.

FROM SOCIETY TO THE INDIVIDUAL

The latter half of the century produced no English poet equal to Pope, but it did produce a large number of important writers and did serve as a transition period from concentration on society as the preserver of the best in man to concentration on the nobility and potential of the individual. The beautiful city of Bath was built in the classical style, and the Adam brothers designed and built new streets and squares in Edinburgh. Advances were made in the art of writing history because men had come to believe with Pope that the "proper study of mankind is man." Shaftesbury's doctrine of man's natural goodness coupled with materialistic rationalism had led to optimistic political programs based on the perfectibility of man.

Writers did not rebel.overtly against the classical tradition but increasingly began to write about realistic matters of everyday life. Thomas Gray's *Elegy Written in a Country Churchyard* is one of the best examples of this new poetic material. Humble life is treated humorously as well as realistically and much less idyllically. Writers began to claim that absolute standards are impossible and to believe in progress and novelty. With increasing doubts about Pope's assertion that truth is "one clear, unchanged, and universal light," the pendulum swung from fear of individualism and enthusiasm (which had led to civil war) to love of diversity (which, in turn, led to revolutions).

Poets became expressers of mood rather than eloquent preachers of general truths. The poet was exalted as a mysterious and sacred natural force which mere intelligence could not comprehend and training could not bestow. "Genius" supplanted wit as the creative force in the poet's mind. Abbe Yart in his sketch of Pope distinguished between the two: "Wit consists in adorning well-known thoughts, but genius is creative." William Duff in his *Essay on Original Genius* (1767) wrote that genius combines a "plastic and comprehensive imagination" with "an acute intellect, and an exquisite sensibility and refinement of taste." Imagination, the key ingredient in genius, was for Johnson a lively, delightful faculty which objectifies truth, recombines experience, and produces

novelty by its varied combinations. For Blake, the imagination was the highest power in man, the organ of morality, art, and spiritual illumination. It had a demonic power and, indeed, was said to be the voice of Nature herself speaking through the poet's soul. Genius, which was subject only to its own laws, produced "natural" literature of wild irregularity or homely simplicity. Giving a suprarational source to poetic genius eventually created problems, particularly in Blake's works. It served to weaken the poet's powers of self-criticism and control.

Moving away from the Renaissance and neoclassic idea that poetic genius should be learned, mid-eighteenth century audiences believed in "natural" or unlearned genius. Johnson, however, while affirming that "no man ever became great by imitation," insisted that genius must be trained by study. Belief in "natural" genius went hand in hand with a return to folk and national literature. In Germany, Johann Gottfried von Herder developed his famous distinction between *Volkspoesie*, poetry that springs spontaneously from the people, and *Kunstpoesie*, poetry that the educated produce within the traditional culture. In England, Collins's *Ode on the Popular Superstitions of the Highlands of Scotland, Considered as the Subject of Poetry* (1750) used folklore to inspire the poetic imagination and voiced the view that literature should have its source in the indigenous folk culture rather than in Greco-Roman literary tradition.

The better poets imitated Horatian and French models inexactly. Even the conservative Goldsmith could write *The Deserted Village* (1770) without setting out to write an elegy or a pastoral. In Pope's time imitation was supposed to be creative rather than servile, but by mid-century critics such as Edward Young were writing that it is the poet's duty and highest possible achievement to be "original." Originality, not to be confused with novelty, meant going back to the originals of things, not going to the "copies" of others. As one newspaper critic wrote, "striking out new Paths" rather than "treading very circumspectly in old ones" is of primary importance (*Daily Gazetteer*, 1741). The classical soil had been tilled out.

GOTHICISM

In addition to the fertile soil found in humble, everyday life, poets found new material in the Middle Ages, in castles and ruins and anything "Gothic." The Frenchman Paul Henri Mallet and his work *Northern Antiquities* (1770) did more than any other individual to set Europe ablaze with enthusiasm for ancient Germanic mythology and the medieval manners and customs of the North. In England, Horace Walpole built his monument to Gothicism, Strawberry Hill. Thomas Warton, the elder, wrote "A Runic Ode," and Thomas Warton, the younger, wrote three volumes on the history of English poetry from the twelfth to the close of the sixteenth century (1774-1781). Pope earlier in the century had chronicled love pangs in an *Epistle from Eloisa to Abelard* (1717), though this also had its source in Ovidian elegy, Dyer described Welsh ruins in *Grongar Hill*, Thomas Warton set his "The Pleasures of Melancholy" in the yard of a partially ruined Gothic church, and Gray published two odes "from the Norse tongue"—"The Fatal Sister" and "The Descent of Odin"—and some translations of Welsh stories. The poetry of Gray, in fact, provides a useful example of the turn from Greco-Roman traditions to Northern antiquities: He began his career writing classically correct elegies and odes and finished his career imitating the primitive minstrelsy of the North.

Even though James Macpherson's Ossian tales were not authentic, they were extraordinarily successful, praised by Gray because they were "full of nature and noble wild imagination." The tales of Ossian reveal what eighteenth century audiences thought they saw in medieval writings: primitivism and sentimentalism. The idea of a Centic bard such as Ossian who could rival Homer thrilled Macpherson's contemporaries. They also enjoyed the sententious melancholy they could feel in such tales as that of the warrior Carthon whose father Clessámmoor unknowingly kills him. The sentimentality and melancholy of the tales is increased by double distancing: The tales themselves are supposedly old and the poet Ossian is writing longingly of a time past. Macpherson owed more to the Bible, Homer, Milton, and more recent authors, however, than he did to an oral tradition.

Ballads

Concurrent with the interest in medievalism came the reawakening interest in the ballad. Popular ballads in the first half of the century include Henry Carey's *Sally in Our Alley*, Gay's *'Twas When the Seas Were Roaring* (1715) and the ballads in his *The Beggar's Opera* (1728), and Henry Fielding's *Roast Beef of Old England* (1731). Even Swift's two saints found broadside ballads plastered on the walls of the cottage of Baucis and Philemon. Many of the ballad songs are narratives. Allan Ramsay, an important publisher of ancient Scottish ballads, modernized and "improved" the texts. In America, many complaints against the British took the form of ballads.

Considered a rather rude and plebeian amusement, the ballad gained respectability with the publication of Thomas Percy's collection, *Reliques of Ancient Poetry*, in 1765. The ballad's simple style profoundly affected the changing tastes of the writers and public of the eighteenth century. In the latter part of the century, Cowper's "The Diverting History of John Gilpin" had tremendous success; Cowper adapted it from the true story of a wild horseback ride taken by John Beyer, a Cheapside linen draper. Cowper credited the popularity of the ballad to its nationalism (he believed the ballad form was peculiar to England), its flexibility in being used for both humorous and tragic subjects, and its simplicity and ease.

Percy's *Reliques of Ancient Poetry* caught the imagination of its German readers. Addison, Swift, and Pope had had followers in Germany, and, then, Thomson, Milton, and Young. Sentimental verse won approval in the writings of F. G. Klopstock and Ewald Christian von Kleist. H. W. von Gurstenberg, F. F. Kretschmann, and Michael Denis (the translater of Ossian) led the "bardic" movement. It was Percy's collection, however, that directly influenced the poets who in 1772 founded Gottinger Hain, or the Brotherhood of the Grove, and who belonged mainly to the peasant or bourgeois classes.

Nature

The same yearnings that the eighteenth century felt for native poetry and nature stimulated the glorification of the "noble savage." Particularly in the latter half of the century, writers expressed longing for a "return to Nature" and brought primitivism into vogue. They contrasted the innocent child of the wilderness with the selfish man of artificial civilization. Urban life and civilization departed from the "natural." Jean-Jacques

Rousseau, the greatest European supporter of the "Return to Nature," believed that nature had originally made men good and happy but that civilization had made them criminal and miserable. Poets such as Cowper escaped to the countryside for tranquillity, and in those times nature was easily found: One could walk into the country even from central London, the largest of the few large towns in England. Cowper expressed the sentiments of many when he wrote, "God made the country, but man made the town."

The spread of education and the longing for innocence produced another new literary form, literature for children. Before the eighteenth century, poets wrote about children, particularly about their deaths, in hopes of parental patronage, but few poems were written for children. At the beginning of the century, Isaac Watts wrote *Divine and Moral Songs for Children* (1715) and at the end of the century William Blake wrote *Songs of Experience and of Experience* (1794) specifically for children. Blake did not condescend to children or indulge in humorous play to amuse the adults who read to children. His verses are childlike but never childish. Other writers for children include Ambrose Philips and Matthew Prior. Philips, a writer of pastorals, earned the nickname "Namby Pamby" for his syrupy children's verses. Much better were Prior's mock-serious verses like the one in which Kitty begged Mama for the chariot and "set the world on fire."

HYMNS

Another new flowering in the eighteenth century was hymn writing. As more and more sects formed in opposition to established churches, new music for worship had to be created. In the first part of the century, Watts was one of the best and most scholarly of the Dissenting writers. His hymns, including "God our help in ages past," expressed the popular view that the universe displays the Almighty's hand. With fresh and independent critical ideas, Watts believed that the cultivation of faith can elevate poetry. Watts's hymns and others in the early part of the century tended to be "congregational" in point of view.

In Germany, pietism revived and left its traces in the sphere of religious poetry. The main emphasis lay in the individual's spiritual experience, not in conformity. A comparable revival in England was Evangelicalism. Just as literature had reacted to excessive cynicism and rationalism by growing in emotional intensity, so religion, both within and without the Anglican Church, reacted to skepticism and deism by emphasizing the passions and conversion of the individual soul. John and Charles Wesley, ordained Anglican ministers, felt forced by the hostile Established Church to break off and form an independent sect of Methodism. Methodism rapidly gained converts, especially among the humble and less educated. It brought them solace for their sorrows, gave them a moral force and feeling of personal importance, and added to the stirrings of democracy within society. The Wesleys themselves wrote hymns, mostly personal in nature. Charles Wesley's most famous hymn is "Jesus, Lover of My Soul." Another famous hymn written at this time is "Rock of Ages, Cleft for Me" by the now unknown writer, Augustus Toplady. Many hymn writers, unfortunately, committed the error of mixing secular metaphor and symbolism, with ludicrous and unsavory results.

William Cowper, *the* poet of the Evangelical revival though still an Anglican, wrote sixty-five *Olney Hymns* (1779) in conjunction with Reverend John Newton, the most famous of which is "Light Shining Out of Darkness" ("God moves in a mysterious way"). For the most part, his hymns express the beauty and serenity of the religious experience, although self-doubts darken "Light Shining Out of Darkness." Cowper was obsessed by the idea that God's grace had been withheld from him and that his eternal damnation had already been decided. His poetry expressed despair and hope and made firm doctrinal assertions which were typical of his day.

PROGRESS POEMS

The two best poets of the new belief in secular progress were William Collins and Thomas Gray. Both accomplished scholars, they expressed their poetic ideals of liberty and simplicity in historical surveys or "progress poems." Collins excelled in writing odes: His "Ode to Evening" is particularly beautiful in its delicate "dying fall" of cadence. His "Ode Written in the Beginning of the Year 1746" has a delicate and pensive melody. Emotional apostrophes fill Collins's work, making it more exclamatory than reflective and making it less warm and personal. He chiefly appeals with his curious, ornate fantasies and his creation of dim and dreamlike effects.

Even though Gray and Collins resembled each other in temperament and literary principles, Gray was the better and more popular writer. Among the most learned of English poets, Gray read widely in Latin and Greek, in his English predecessors, and in Old Norse and Welsh. His range in various meters was unmatched in his century: He could write ceremonious heroic quatrains in *Elegy Written in a Country Churchyard*, energetic effluences in his Pindaric odes, and primitive chants in his later period. His poetry dealt with emotions more directly than Collins'. "The Bard" and "The Progress of Poesy," which combine tight organization with wild imaginative flights, approach the sublime as few other attempts at this time did. Gray's fastidiousness and habit of endless revision limited the number of poems he published.

LATER EIGHTEENTH CENTURY

Although the spring and summer of neoclassicism had passed, there still remained the colorful autumn in the writings of Johnson and his friends, writings which insisted on presenting life realistically. The impressive figure of Samuel Johnson dominates the later half of the eighteenth century. The last major Augustan figure, he excelled in writing poetry, essays, and criticism, and in compiling the great *A Dictionary of the English Language*. His first major poem, *London* (1738), satirized the city's corruption in imitation of Juvenal's denunciation of Rome. It came out on the same day as Pope's *Epilogue to the Satires* and was thought to compare favorably with it. In 1747 Johnson composed a prologue for the opening of the season at Drury Lane, a poem remarkable for its compressed and intelligent dramatic criticism. His greatest poem, *The Vanity of Human Wishes*, expressed Christian pessimism about man's earthly lot. Johnson opposed the currents of his age in criticizing Milton, the pastoral tradition, and blank verse, and in condemning the elevation of instincts and emotions over reason.

Johnson's friend Oliver Goldsmith displayed a similar range of talent in writing poetry, a novel, essays, and plays. In *The Traveller* (1764), representative of the "survey" convention of eighteenth century verse, he scrutinizes and judges the national temperaments and political constitutions of several European nations. He explains the doctrine of the principle of compensation, yet another eighteenth century exegesis on the idea of happiness: Every state has its own particular principle of happiness, which in each may be carried to "mischievous excess." In *The Deserted Village* he chastizes large estate owners for razing country villages and scattering the villagers to increase their holdings. He describes the economic plight of the villagers and warns of the dangers of luxury and "trade's unfeeling train." Both poems, written in heroic couplets, display the gentle humor and kindness of their author.

Another poet who insisted on portraying life realistically was George Crabbe. Crabbe despised the weak idealism of the pastoral and poured his energy into describing the sordid and humble life of the Suffolk villagers of his youth. Crabbe was no devotee of Shaftesbury: He had no sentimental confidence in the goodness of human nature. Unlike earlier classicists, he emphasized individual responsibility rather than societal responsibility for crime and distress.

Charles Churchill, a dissipated clergyman who turned poet in his later years, continued the classical tradition of satire with all the faults of Pope and fewer merits. In his first important poem, *The Rosciad* (1761), he vigorously attacked theatrical personalities (some critics have named this poem the best satire between Pope's *The Dunciad* and Lord Byron's *English Bards and Scotch Reviewers*, 1809). Churchill's satires have the energy and venom of Pope's satires, but they lack deftness and elegance. Churchill wrote many of his satires in support of his friend John Wilkes. Wilkes had condemned the Scottish people in *The North Briton*, a weekly political periodical; Churchill continued the outcry in *The Prophecy of Famine* (1763). William Hogarth had drawn a caricature of Wilkes in the courtroom; Churchill took revenge on him in *Epistle to William Hogarth*. Wilkes dueled with Samuel Martin; Churchill defended him in *The Duellist* (1763). The fourth earl of Sandwich was Wilkes's enemy; Churchill attacked his hypocrisy in *The Candidate* (1764). Contemporaries of Pope and Churchill could relish the frequent personal allusions, but to succeeding generations they have meant little.

William Cowper tried to add to the satirical tradition, but he was too gentle and gracious a man to be a great satirist. In "Table Talk" he commented on the poetry of the century; in "Retirement" and "The Progress of Error" he attacked the follies of high life; and in "Expostulation" he condemned patriotic poems, including the lyric "On the Loss of the Royal George."

Cowper could write moving realistic poetry. In *The Task* (1785) he accurately and delightfully sketched country life, recording the sights and sounds and shrewdly portraying human character. *The Task* satisfied the hunger of the eighteenth century for long poems (a hunger which soon began to be satiated), for rambling structure, and for reflective description. "Domestic happiness" and gardening, he rejoiced, give "blest seclusion from a jarring world." Humor at this time was becoming rare and precious in poetry. Cowper wrote *The Task* on the urging of his friend Lady Austen, who wanted him to try blank verse and who told him, when he complained of not having a subject, "Oh, you can never be in want of a subject; you can write upon any—write upon that sofa!"

Cowper's poetry blended and harmonized the new and sometimes disquieting elements of his era: evangelical religion, sensibility, and democratic rumblings. Unlike his predecessors, Cowper seldom philosophized about the abstraction "Nature" when he described and reflected about the landscape. Unlike his contemporaries, he did not follow the rationalist tradition of placing the "Book of Nature" beside the Bible, although he did believe in creation as "an effect whose cause is God." Unlike the Romantics, he found no strangeness in beauty and felt no intense passion for nature; he was simply and genuinely attached to it.

Unlike Thomson and Young, the other two great descriptive poets of the century, Cowper had a natural fluency and could choose his polysyllables well. He avoided the stereotypical "poetic diction" used for objective detail and wrote easy, graceful blank verse. Although his verse lacks the concentration and intensity of the greatest poetry, it nevertheless remains faithful to reality and does so in natural, nearly conversational diction.

Cowper and Burns were among the late bloomers of the cult of simplicity, writing of rural domesticity and using subjective, autobiographical material. More intimate and emotional than their predecessors, they saw their roles as poets more as individuals speaking to themselves or to small audiences about their own experience than as the loud voice of the public. As such, they were transitional poets. Although less intellectual than Dryden or Pope, Cowper wrote intelligently about prison reform, slavery, and the French Revolution, and Burns wrote cogently about the oppressive Church of Scotland. Unlike Dryden, Swift, or Pope, Cowper never zealously burned for causes, but he did defend George Whitfield, an eminent Methodist who had been slandered.

Like Cowper, Burns wrote satire and realistic verse in natural and spontaneous style. He too was a poet of domestic emotion, but he described his environment not for itself but for the human relationships implied in it. Although he lived among and wrote of the common people of the Scottish lowlands, he was a highly educated man and a worthy inheritor of the ancient tradition of vernacular song and poetry. He wrote about Scottish life and manners in Scottish dialect and used his local Ayrshire neighborhood for inspiration. His manner, though not original, struck his non-Scottish audience as fresh and unusual.

Earlier Scottish poets had been ignored in London. In the cases of Allan Ramsay and Robert Fergusson, this was perhaps understandable; they wrote unpretentiously about their native land. Ramsay's work resembled that of John Gay in many ways: He displayed hearty humor and shrewd observation for vivid rustic detail. Like Gay, he used the pastoral form for realistic ends and attempted a ballad opera, *The Gentle Shepherd* (1728). John Home, the author of *Douglas* (1756), who was known as the "Scottish Shakespeare," and William Wilkie, the author of *The Epigoniad* (1757), who was known as the "Scottish Homer," had also been slighted.

Working with stanzaic types popular with Scottish poets since the Middle Ages, Burns added vigor and musicality to his inheritance. (The stanza of "The Holy Fair," for example, is adapted from the old "Christis Kirk on the Green" stanza.) In his most effective satires—"Holy Willie's Prayer," "The Holy Fair," and "Address to the Unco Guild"—Burns savagely exposed religious hypocrisy. He wrote at the height of the liberal-minded rebellion against the doctrine of election and the impossibly strict rules of conduct enforced by the orthodox Presbyterian Church and its courts.

Like Cowper, Burns sympathized with the growing democratic tendencies: He believed in the essential worth of a man, whether rich or poor. His mind was free and modern, and his powers of observation accurate and penetrating. His nature poetry was the plain, simple observation of a Scottish farmer, not the reflective scientific musing of a devotee of Thomson. Above all, he was an extraordinarily gifted lyricist. He became the voice and symbol of his people, pleasing non-Scots with his "primitive" and "native" verse and focusing the national feelings of his own people.

TOWARD ROMANTICISM

The most significant event of the end of the eighteenth century was, of course, the French Revolution. In German literature it was regarded as a warning about the problem of liberty. In English literature it kindled enthusiasm in poets, but their celebratory poetry did not sparkle. Cowper and Burns saw in the revolution a declaration of the worth of all men, a manifesto of the political rights of the people. Beyond this, the revolution generated a millennial movement in English thought and life. William Blake was the greatest of the millennial prophets, imagining a day when a new Jerusalem would arise in England after the reconciliation of Urizen (reason) with Los (imagination) and Luvah (passion).

The classical myths were dead, but the millennial era provided a seedbed for new myths. In *The Book of Thel* (1789), Blake introduced his own myths to symbolize philosophical ideas, which he later expanded in his "Prophetic Books." Against the character Urizen, the spirit of reason, custom, and institutions, Blake could vent all his revolutionary ire.

It is easy to write generalizations about the poetry of a particular period; it is less easy to make the poetry fit the generalizations. One can say, though, that the eighteenth century is a garden of exotic and diverse blooms. (Any century which included Blake, Gray, and Pope would have to be.) With some reservations, one can generalize that the century began with the glories of satire, the desire for improvements in society, and ended with the uncertainties of a new individualism and emerging social order. In between grew the love of description, reflection, and moralizing; an apprecia-

tion for everyday life and the common man; a yearning to know man, his native land, his history, and his place in the universe; a burning for feeling as well as reason; and a search for truth and beauty. The garden was ready to blossom into the fresh colors of Romanticism.

BIBLIOGRAPHY

Broich, Ulrich. *The Eighteenth Century Mock-Heroic Poem.* Translated by David H. Wilson. Cambridge, England: Cambridge University Press, 1990. Comprehensive study of the theory, the conventions, and the history of the mock-heroic genre.

Dowling, William C. *The Epistolary Moment: The Poetics of the Eighteenth Century Verse Epistle.* Princeton, N.J.: Princeton University Press, 1991. Focuses on the internal audience in poetry—the audience "inside" the poem, created by its discourse and belonging to its world—that divides in epistolary poetry into a double or simultaneous register of address: the audience directly addressed by the letter-writer, and an epistolary audience listening in on the exchange from a point external to the discourse of the speaker but internal to the discourse of the poem.

Ferguson, Moira. *Eighteenth Century Women Poets: Nation, Class, and Gender.* Albany: State University of New York, 1995. Examines the poetry of Anne Yearsley, Janet Little, Mary Scott, and Mary Collier through various lenses, including women's labor, patriotism and resistance, and class identity.

Frushell, Richard C. *Edmund Spenser in the Early Eighteenth Century: Education, Imitation, and the Making of a Literary Model.* Pittsburgh, Pa.: Duquesne University Press, 1999. A study of eighteenth century imitations and adaptations of the works of Spenser.

Gerrard, Christine, and David Fairer, eds. *Eighteenth Century Poetry: An Annotated Anthology.* Blackwell Annotated Anthology Series. Oxford, England: Blackwell Publishers, 1999. Provides the widest possible range of texts and places work of the traditionally prominent figures (such as Alexander Pope, Jonathan Swift, Anne Finch, Christopher Smart, Robert Burns, and William Cowper) alongside work by other writers, particularly women with strong and distinctive voices (Sarah Egerton, Mary Jones, Mary Collier, Mary Leapor, Ann Yearsley, and Anna Laetitia Barbauld). All the poems have full annotations and generous head notes.

Goodridge, John. *Rural Life in Eighteenth Century English Poetry*. Cambridge, England: Cambridge University Press, 1996. Compares poetic accounts of rural labor by James Thomson, Stephen Duck, and Mary Collier, and explores the purpose of rural poetry, revealing an illuminating link between rural poetry and agricultural and folkloric developments of the time.

Irlam, Shaun. *Elations: The Poetics of Enthusiasm in Eighteenth Century Britain*. Stanford, Calif.: Stanford University Press, 1999. Examines the aesthetic theory of the period and reassesses the poetry of two poets seldom read today but very popular in their time, James Thomson and Edward Young. The book also explores the genesis and construction of moral authority through a variety of competing discourses appropriated by poetry.

Jackson, Wallace. *Probable and the Marvelous: Blake, Wordsworth, and the Eighteenth Century Critical Tradition*. Athens: University of Georgia Press, 1978.

Kaur, Savil. *Poems of Nations, Anthems of Empire: English Verse in the Long Eighteenth Century*. Charlottesville: University Press of Virginia, 2000. Describes the formal features and thematic concerns of the long poems written in the Restoration period of the mid-eighteenth century and how they tie in with England's, and Britain's, empire of the sea.

Nilsen, Don Lee. *Humor in Eighteenth and Nineteenth Century British Literature: A Reference Guide*. Westport, Conn.: Greenwood Press, 1998. Examines how British writers of the eighteenth and nineteenth centuries used humor in their works. An introductory chapter overviews humor in British literature of the era, and sections then treat humor in British literature of the eighteenth century and in three periods of the nineteenth century.

Rowland, Jon Thomas. *Faint Praise and Civil Leer: The "Decline" of Eighteenth Century Panegyric*. Newark: University of Delaware Press, 1995. Examines political poetry, showing how panegyrical writing developed into mock-panegyric and satire, increasingly as much in response to versions of events as to the events themselves.

Ann Willardson Engar

ENGLISH AND AMERICAN POETRY IN THE NINETEENTH CENTURY

The literary nineteenth century is commonly divided into periods or phases, more or less arbitrarily. There was clearly a Romantic period in England from about 1786 to 1832, however, followed by a more sedate Victorian reaction that itself began to disintegrate after 1860. American literature remained minor and derivative until about 1820, when William Cullen Bryant emerged. While the 1830's were comparable on both sides of the Atlantic, with significant interaction, Romanticism lasted longer in America—to which it was more applicable. The traumatic Civil War of 1861 to 1865, however, soon drew American letters toward the increasing pessimism already common in England. During the last third of the nineteenth century, British and American literature were widely separate, and the uniqueness of American writers was generally acknowledged. Nevertheless, the two literatures were deeply interdependent at the beginning of the century, with Britain's dominating, as the young United States of America were less united than a collection of states with strong ties to Britain and the Continent.

Despite its geographical separation from England, the East Coast of what is now the United States was very strongly British during the eighteenth century, not only politically but also culturally. The American Revolution (1776-1783), which justified itself on grounds derived primarily from British thought, changed nothing in that respect, for though American writers such as John Trumbull, Timothy Dwight, and Philip Freneau soon turned toward American subjects, they continued to see them through British eyes and to imitate British literary models, which were still of the neoclassical type. Neoclassicism was appropriate to a society in which religious and social values were well assured and stability was more evident than change. Yet this stability was vanishing rapidly throughout the latter eighteenth century, in both England and America.

REVOLUTIONS: POLITICAL, ECONOMIC, SOCIAL

It was an era of revolutions, through which much that has since characterized the West came into being. Not all of these revolutions were sudden or dramatic, but their cumulative force was irresistible. For example,

population increased enormously throughout the latter eighteenth century in England and America as better sanitation, nutrition, and medicine increased longevity and reduced infant mortality. This larger and healthier population strained available resources, pressured an outmoded economic system, and gave both countries unusually large numbers of the young, who utilized the increasing availability of books to effect political, agricultural, technological, scientific, and social revolutions on behalf of the abundance and freedom with which their own interests were identified.

Two of the most obvious revolutions were political, as America broke away from England in 1776 and France attempted to discard its outmoded monarchy and religious establishment in 1789. Less precipitously, agriculture was revolutionized by the development of improved plows, crop rotation schemes, selective breeding, and (in England) an improved network of canals and turnpikes that allowed farmers to market specialty crops over greater distances. The superior transportation of the latter eighteenth century was also broadly effective in extending the boundaries of urban culture beyond London to provincial and even rural centers, so that authorship (for example) was more widespread. As mail service improved, men of letters everywhere corresponded more meaningfully, and even American colonials such as Benjamin Franklin were effective participants in the European ferment. Other aspects of technological change were also rapid, as both England and America responded ever more fully to the development of mechanical power. The steam engine, developed by James Watt, inaugurated the first phase of the Industrial Revolution, which would then transform the two countries for a second time during the nineteenth century with the advent of railroads and steamships; these latter inventions made the territorial ambitions of Britain and America—Britain's, beyond its shores, and America's, toward the west—feasible. The factory system, with its emphasis on regulated labor and standardized parts, was not only of economic and social importance—it strongly influenced nineteenth century literature and thought as well. Prior to the American Revolution, however, because British law prevented the full development of American manufacture (finished goods had to be imported from England), much colonial ingenuity was devoted instead to improved nautical technology—at which New England quickly became outstanding—and eventually to exploring the resources of the constantly retreating western frontier.

The sea, the frontier, and foreign countries attracted young adventurers who would otherwise have been victimized by the economic inequities of hereditary wealth. Thus, in the nineteenth century the Industrial Revolution fostered a new entrepreneurial class that gained both economic and social prominence. These aggressive and often uncouth opportunists challenged the increasingly moribund landed aristocracies of England and America, wresting a larger share of political power and social respectability for themselves. If the eighteenth century was, at its beginning, dominated by hereditary nobility, its internal conflicts gave rise to a nineteenth century in which an aristocracy of talent was more important.

The internal conflicts of the eighteenth century derived in large part from a crosscurrent of ideas known as the Enlightenment, which originated in seventeenth century England with Francis Bacon, John Locke, and Isaac Newton, then spread during the next hundred years to France, where ideals of cosmopolitan urbanity, rational humanism, and religious toleration (if not outright disbelief) were popularized by Voltaire, Denis Diderot, and Jean-Jacques Rousseau, all of whom advocated freedom and change. A second eighteenth century center of Enlightenment initiative was Scotland (then experiencing a nationalistic revival), which contributed the skepticism of David Hume, the economic theories of Adam Smith, and an impressive series of historiographic, scientific, technological, and literary achievements. The American phase of the Enlightenment, including Benjamin Franklin, Thomas Jefferson, and James Madison, guided restless colonials toward independence, economic self-sufficiency, and a radically new theory of government. Yet both the Declaration of Independence and the Constitution of the United States were based on Enlightenment ideals that derived in large part from those of Republican Rome.

INFLUENCE OF THE PAST

Nineteenth century minds never forgot their indebtedness to the past, and one of the most reliable characteristics of nineteenth century literature is its historicism. The science of archaeology, for example, arose during the 1740's with systematic digging at Pompeii and Herculaneum, leading to a revival of visual classicism in architecture, sculpture, and painting. Then the nineteenth century began with French archaeological discoveries in Egypt, including the Rosetta stone. As a result, pyramids recur throughout nineteenth century arts as symbols of death, the sphinx and hieroglyphics appear as mysterious embodiments of knowledge denied to humanity, and Egypt itself becomes the new symbol (replacing Rome) of antiquarian grandeur. Incremental archaeological enthusiasm soon overwhelmed Europe and its more creative minds with statuary from the Parthenon, winged lions from Assyria, relics from Troy, many now-familiar classical masterpieces, and vast new sites, art forms, and religions from the Americas, Asia, and Africa. During the nineteenth century also, the concept of geological time was established, with all its vast duration and wondrous legacy of vanished giants. Thus, the nineteenth century past no longer began with Adam, but instead an immensely complex progression through incalculable time from uncertain beginnings to the illustrious present. No other century in the history of the West experienced such a readjustment of its time sense as did the nineteenth.

Although overwhelmingly Protestant, nineteenth century writers in England and America were often attracted to the Catholic Middle Ages. Gothic architecture was popularly revived in Britain, and there was a resurgence of medieval craftsmanship in the Pre-Raphaelite movement of Dante Gabriel Rossetti and William Morris, which (together with the aesthetic and social criticism of John Ruskin) did much to reduce the ugliness of overindustrialized Victorian minor arts. Poets likewise returned to the Middle Ages for inspiration, though seldom realistically. For Sir Walter Scott, John Keats, Alfred, Lord Tennyson, James Russell Lowell, William Morris, and other writers, medievalism was a utopian alternative to the deficiencies of the present, but one that the cold scrutiny of history could not fully corroborate.

To some extent, the same disparity characterizes the nineteenth century's image of classical Greece, which overshadowed Rome in cultural prestige and was accepted as a symbol of liberty, whether political, intellectual, or behavioral. For the many Hellenists of the nineteenth century, Greek mythology was a major inspiration. Among the most popular myths was that of Prometheus, which attracted William Blake, Thomas Campbell, Lord Byron, Elizabeth Barrett Browning, Robert Bridges, and especially Percy Bysshe Shelley, for whom Prometheus was the mythological embodiment of enlightened, technological man. In related contexts, Byron died on behalf of Greek independence, and Keats revered its artistic legacy. Mid-Victorian writers, such as Tennyson, valued Greece primarily for its writers, particularly Homer, while later ones such as Matthew Arnold and Thomas Hardy admired the realism of Greek tragedy. Greek lyric poetry found readers throughout the century and influenced A. E. Housman, especially. Combining the lyric and dramatic traditions of classical Greece, Shelley attempted two lyric dramas on Greek subjects, *Prometheus Unbound* (1820) and *Hellas* (1822), which would be imitated later by Arnold (*Empedocles on Etna*, 1852), Algernon Charles Swinburne (*Atalanta in Calydon*, 1865), and Hardy (*The Dynasts*, 1903, 1906, 1908). The pagan, libertarian, and sometimes erotic influence of Greece was taken very seriously.

Nineteenth century writers admired individuality and boldness. They found the heroic age of exploration particularly congenial, as poems about Christopher Columbus (for example) were written by Joel Barlow, Samuel Rogers, William Lisle Bowles, Alfred, Lord Tennyson, Walt Whitman, Joaquin Miller, and James Russell Lowell. Samuel Taylor Coleridge's *The Rime of the Ancient Mariner* (1798) was based upon exploration literature and the voyage of Magellan; Keats mistook Cortez for Balboa; while Bowles and Whitman celebrated Vasco da Gama and the spirit of discovery in general. Other heroes of the century included George Washington, Napoleon Bonaparte, the duke of Wellington, and Abraham Lincoln. There were also many poems and essays about writers, including Homer, Vergil, Dante, William Shakespeare, Torquato Tasso, John Milton, Johann Wolfgang von Goethe, the British Romantic poets, Ralph Waldo Emerson, and Whitman. Artists of the Italian Renaissance were often extolled for their individuality—the Renaissance as a whole was popular—and various Enlightenment figures (Bacon, Newton, Voltaire,

and Rousseau primarily) were either praised or damned, according to the religious preferences of the writer. Surprisingly little was written, however, in praise of religious heroes as such.

RELIGIOUS DOUBT

Traditional religion was sorely pressed throughout the nineteenth century (its latter half particularly) to retain credibility in the face of pervasive doubts which arose on all sides—from biblical criticism, undermining the literal word; from Enlightenment objections to religious authority and intolerance; from the diversity of religious observance and the insipidity of orthodox spirituality; and from the currently popular philosophies of materialism and utilitarianism, neither of which found much use for the inanities of a debased theological tradition which, during the eighteenth century, had clearly become part of an oppressive church-and-state establishment. One of the most pervasive features of nineteenth century literature, therefore, is religious doubt, which frequently resolved itself in any of several ways: by regarding history as a manifestation of God; by turning from God to man; by abandoning religion in favor of art; or by returning to orthodox belief. Though there were also a number of alternative faiths, including spiritualism, the guiding light of the century was science.

BRITISH ROMANTICISM

The century began with the English Romantics, who were influential in both England and America. Neoclassical literature, which dominated the first half of the eighteenth century in England, emphasized practical reason, social conformity, emotional restraint, and submission to the authority of classical literary techniques. It was generally allied to political and religious conservatism as well. As life in eighteenth century England was transformed by political, economic, social, and technological innovations, however, the old manner of literary expression seemed increasingly obsolete to younger and more audacious writers who had absorbed the Enlightenment philosophy of humanism and freedom.

Among the first of these new men in literature was Robert Burns (1759-1796). Though he did not live quite long enough to experience the nineteenth century at first hand, Burns strikingly exemplified a number of its tendencies. Far from apologizing for either his Scottish burr or his rural origins, at a time when both were disparaged in polite society, he appealed to the 1780's as a supposedly untutored genius, a *natural* poet whose verses arose not from the inkwell but from the heart. Beneath his colorful regionalism and earthy rural sensuality there remained a stubborn dignity, an antiaristocratic humanity, and a concentration upon his own emotions that favored meditative and lyric poetry. Burns's carefree morality and religious satire signaled the approaching end of religious orthodoxy in British poetry (it would last longer in America) and effectively countered the turgid morbidity into which so many mid-century versifiers had fallen. In his egalitarian social attitudes ("A man's a man for a' that"), Burns portended the imminent French Revolution of 1789. His literary influence throughout the next century extended to Scott, Tennyson, John Greenleaf Whittier, Lowell, Hardy, and Rudyard Kipling, all of whom profited from Burns's use of dialect in serious literature and from his revolutionary insistence that the right of an individual to worth and dignity is not dependent upon the urbanity of his speech.

If William Blake (1757-1827), of Burns's generation, was not so obviously an outsider as the Scottish poet, he soon became one through the seeming incomprehensibility of his highly individualistic poetry and art. A firm supporter of the American and French Revolutions, Blake was also the first important author to sense the underlying dynamism of his times. No other poet, for example, perceived the historical importance of either the Industrial Revolution or the political upheaval in America so clearly. Similarly, no other poet has influenced twentieth century theories of literature so much. Yet Blake was dismissed as a madman in his own times, and his influence on nineteenth century literature became important only toward the end, with Swinburne, Rossetti, James Thomson, and William Butler Yeats. It is now clear, however, that Blake's concerns with innovation, energy, myth, lyric, and sexuality were extremely prescient.

Though William Wordsworth (1770-1850) was more in accord with late eighteenth century restraint than Blake, he effected the most significant theoretical change ever seen in English literature and did more than any other individual to give nineteenth century literature

its distinctive character. With its explicit rejection of neoclassicism and the aristocratic tradition in literature, Wordsworth's *Lyrical Ballads* of 1798 (first American edition, 1800), written with Samuel Taylor Coleridge, is often considered the official beginning of the literary nineteenth century. Its famous preface, added to the English edition of 1800, outlined Wordsworth's new criteria for literature, to which virtually all the significant poets of his century would subscribe. His influence is evident in Coleridge, Byron, Shelley, Keats, Tennyson, Arnold, and Hardy, among major British poets, and in Bryant, Emerson, Henry David Thoreau, Whitman, Henry Wadsworth Longfellow, and Whittier, among American ones. He was the most written-about poet of the century. Wordsworth also had a significant impact upon non-poets such as John Stuart Mill; even Charles Darwin read him. Nineteenth century literature in all its forms is immensely indebted to Wordsworth's preoccupations with rural life, childhood, mental and emotional development, language, history, and nature.

Although Wordsworth's collaborator, Samuel Taylor Coleridge (1772-1834), was also an accomplished poet, his substantial influence on later writers (Emerson in particular) came primarily through his prose. As a poet, however, he influenced Wordsworth, Scott, Shelley, Keats, and Edgar Allan Poe, preceding the latter as a symbolist of sometimes uncanny power. Coleridge was also a foremost theorist and critic of English Romanticism, as well as an effective transmitter of German Romantic thought to both England and America.

Wordsworth and Coleridge now seem far greater poets, but Sir Walter Scott (1771-1832) and George Gordon, Lord Byron (1788-1824), were more immediately popular, not only in Britain and America but also throughout Europe. In his narrative poems and many novels (all too hastily written), Scott further popularized regionalism, historicism, and folk traditions. His novels influenced Washington Irving and James Fenimore Cooper, thus virtually beginning nineteenth century literature in America, and created an immense vogue for historical literature of all kinds; his poetic insistence on a nationalistic Scottish muse helped to inspire the Irish harp of Thomas Moore, the Indian one of Bankim Chatterjee, and the "barbaric yawp" of Whitman. Henry Wadsworth Longfellow (1807-1882) was also indebted to Scott's influence for his well-known longer poems on American themes, but went beyond Scott in the amazing cosmopolitanism of his literary sources. In his pseudo-medieval manor house at Abbotsford—much copied by his fellow artisans—Scott played the gracious host to innumerable literary visitors, several of them American. Throughout his lifetime, he was the kindest and most accessible major literary figure in Europe.

During the first decade of the nineteenth century, when Britain was preoccupied with its resistance to Napoleon and travel upon the Continent was scarcely possible, Scott was also his country's most popular poet. Byron dominated the following decade, the Regency, when from 1811 to 1820 England was governed by their heir apparent (later George IV), George III having been declared hopelessly insane. Byron's contradictory but forceful verses, cynical and witty as they were, appealed to a disillusioned younger generation who had seen its hopes for political reform quashed by the failure of the French Revolution and its taste for heroics eradicated by the unnecessary holocaust of the Napoleonic wars. After 1816, however, as England reverted to peacetime reconstruction, Byron's immorality and religious heterodoxy became too much. He was forced into exile on the Continent that year, soon to be followed by Percy Bysshe Shelley (1792-1822), against whom the same charges were leveled, and (primarily for reasons of health) by John Keats (1795-1821), who appeared to some imperceptive critics as nothing more than a sensuously explicit Cockney. These judgments, of course, did not prevail as Byron's influence extended to John Clare, Tennyson, Arthur Hugh Clough, Elizabeth Barrett Browning, Emily Brontë, Poe, Whitman, and Joaquin Miller; Shelley's to Arthur Henry Hallam, Thomas Lovell Beddoes, Tennyson, Browning, Swinburne, Thomson, Hardy, and Yeats; and Keats's to Tennyson, Thomas Hood, Rossetti, Morris, Emily Dickinson, Lowell, Swinburne, and innumerable minor poets. The Byronic hero also became a familiar type in Victorian fiction, Shelley had a major impact upon freethinkers and labor leaders, and Keats became almost a model for both writers and artists during the latter half of the century. Thus, the major English Romantic poets as a group were highly influential in and beyond literature throughout the nineteenth century.

AMERICAN TRANSCENDENTALISTS

The Transcendentalist movement in America during the 1830's and 1840's, centering on Ralph Waldo Emerson (1803-1882)—who disassociated himself from the term—was an awakening of new literary possibilities comparable to, and in part derived from, the literary revolution initiated by Wordsworth and Coleridge. Whereas British Romanticism was often a rebellion against social oppression within the country itself, however, much of its American equivalent was pitted against the tyranny of British literary predominance and European snobbishness generally. William Ellery Channing concluded in 1830 ("Remarks on National Literature") that a truly American literature did not yet exist, and there were many subsequent laments regarding the Yankee failure to achieve cultural independence. "We have listened too long to the courtly muses of Europe," proclaimed Emerson in his famous oration on "The American Scholar" in 1837. Nathaniel Parker Willis, a minor poet from New York, was even more emphatic two years later. "*In literature*," he claimed,

> *we are no longer a nation.* The triumph of Atlantic steam navigation has driven the smaller drop into the larger, and London has become the center. Farewell nationality! The English language now marks the limits of a new literary empire, and America is a suburb.

Like many desperate pronouncements, this one soon proved wrong, but it was by no means clear in 1839 that those then living would witness the remarkable effulgence of American letters that was to come.

The significant American poets whose emergence showed Willis to be a false prophet included Emerson, Thoreau, Jones Very, Poe, Whitman, Dickinson, Longfellow, Whittier, Oliver Wendell Holmes, and Lowell. Emerson himself was a major influence upon contemporary and later American poets, including Thoreau, Very, Whitman, and Dickinson. His essays influenced such remarkable British thinkers as Thomas Carlyle, Arnold, Clough, John Sterling, James Anthony Froude, Herbert Spencer, and John Tyndall. Poe, eventually a force in France, was significant in England only for Swinburne, Rossetti, and Thomson. Whitman appealed to a number of late Victorians, influencing Tennyson (in "Vastness"), Swinburne, William Rossetti, John Addington Symonds, Lionel Johnson, Edward Dowden, and even Robert Louis Stevenson. Those who appreciated his accomplishment were generally fond of Blake and Shelley also. Longfellow became the most popular poet in the English-speaking world around the mid-century, so beloved in Britain and elsewhere that hundreds of his editions appeared, including one of *The Song of Hiawatha* (1855) illustrated by Frederick Remington. Although now considered only a genial minor figure in world literature, Longfellow alone among American poets was accorded by his British admirers a memorial in "Poets' Corner," Westminster Abbey. As for the others, Whittier, Holmes, and Lowell had only moderate international appeal, while Thoreau, Very, Dickinson, and Herman Melville were virtually unknown. Even so, it could no longer be said that literary influences between England and America ran only in one direction.

ATTITUDES TOWARD NATURE

From certain Germanic sources, often transmitted through the philosophical prose of Coleridge and Carlyle, Emerson and his associates derived a fundamental conviction that all material facts are emblematic of spiritual truths, which led them to believe that religious revelation was continuous. This openness to factual and spiritual enlightenment prompted American writers to read widely, often in untraditional sources. Thus, classical works of Oriental religion, the *Bhagavadgītā* and others, were of interest. The Orientalism of Emerson, Thoreau, and Whitman, more serious and better informed than that to be found in the work of earlier English poets such as Thomas Moore (*Lalla Rookh*, 1817), helped them to accept the benevolent impermanence of nature.

Because of their belief in progressive revelation, American Transcendentalists were also more able than their British literary counterparts to accept the current findings of natural science—astronomy, geology, and biology—by which many nineteenth century writers were influenced. Though these three sciences were together discrediting the Creation narrative in Genesis (a task virtually completed by 1840), and suggesting the relative insignificance of man in a mechanistic world of vast time and space, the American Transcendentalists remained almost sanguine in denying the unique status

of any one religious tradition, for they regarded the world of nature (whose cruelty they overlooked) as God's most reliable revelation of himself and as a corrective to the mythological understanding of all earlier peoples.

Attitudes toward nature remained benign in America well after they had become suspect in Britain, where a skeptical tradition among the unorthodox had been articulated by Shelley and soon reasserted itself through Alfred, Lord Tennyson (1809-1892), who was the official and most influential poet of Victorian England. Yet just after Emerson had published his idealistic, Wordsworthian essay *Nature* (1836), he and Tennyson both read Charles Lyell's *Principles of Geology* (1830-1833), which emphasized the immensity of geological time and raised fundamental questions about the history of life. The book exhilarated Emerson, who regarded it as a demonstration of the pervasiveness of natural law, and hence of morality. Tennyson, however, had still not reconciled himself to the premature death of his friend Arthur Henry Hallam at the age of twenty-two and was led by Lyell into agonizing despair over a seemingly amoral world in which whole species perished routinely.

Tennyson's doubts were eventually assuaged by his reading of Goethe, his friendship with Carlyle, and a conviction (reinforced by several naturalists) that life's record in the rocks was purposeful and upward. Yet his literary resolution of the dilemma in *In Memoriam* (1850), the greatest long poem of its time, only temporarily delayed the specter of amoral, indifferent nature that would come to haunt the remaining half of the nineteenth century. In America, on the contrary, the prevailing attitude toward nature long remained that of Thoreau's *Walden* (1854) or even became symbolic of national greatness, as western exploration revealed mountains, rivers, and other scenic wonders unequaled in England; surely they were emblematic of the country and its future. The future that most concerned Americans at mid-century belonged to this life rather than the next, for their nation had been imperiled by issues of slavery and states' rights, despite the glitter of California gold.

VICTORIAN REFORMS AND DOUBTS

In general, the first third of the literary nineteenth century in England was preoccupied with political questions, as public concern responded in turn to the French Revolution and its failure; to the subsequent rise, threats, and necessary defeat of Napoleon; to the internal dislocations of the Regency; to the complicated international situation after Waterloo; and especially to needed reforms at home—for inequities between social classes were rife, and England seemed to be on the brink of insurrection. After 1832, however, when the first Reform Bill (enfranchising the middle class) was enacted, it became clear that social betterment would be achieved through legislation and education rather than revolution. Poets such as Ebenezer Elliott, Thomas Hood, Elizabeth Barrett Browning, and (in America) Lydia Huntley Sigourney joined Thomas Carlyle, Charles Dickens, and other writers of prose in depicting the hard lot of the underprivileged, particularly children and the working poor. Black slavery was no longer at issue in Britain because the slave trade had been abolished in 1807 and slavery itself (common only in the West Indies) in 1832. It would last until 1865 in America. There was also feminist agitation, but this was a social revolution for which the Victorian world was not yet prepared; Victoria herself (crowned in 1837) opposed it.

Even so, a remarkable transformation took place within mid-century England as enlightened advocates uncovered inequities old and new. Among the revolutionary bills passed by reforming parliaments were the Factory Act of 1833, regulating child labor; the Poor Law Amendment Act of 1834, regulating workhouses; the Municipal Reform Act of 1835, unifying town governments; an act of 1842 prohibiting the employment of women and children in mines; another in 1843 prohibiting imprisonment for debt; the first public health act in 1848; another factory act, shortening hours and days, in 1850; a second major political reform in 1868; and, finally, the great public schools act of 1870. If there were fewer reforming acts in less-developed America, it was in part because fewer were needed. Whatever the indigenous shortcomings of British industrialism, its problems were taken seriously by both workingmen and writers. One of the few European states to avoid armed revolution during the nineteenth century, Britain was perhaps the most socially advanced nation in the world, as well as the most industrialized, for humanitarianism and progress had become its prevailing creeds.

This humanitarianism increasingly superseded orthodox religion, which had begun to experience severe problems of credibility. The Oxford movement toward a more historical Christianity, less dependent upon the precise text of the Bible, had begun under John Keble in 1833, but this promising doctrinal initiative on the part of the Anglican Church (official in England) lost effectiveness when John Henry Newman, its most persuasive advocate, announced his conversion to Roman Catholicism in 1845. The high road to orthodoxy having proved disastrous, Anglican theology was afterward dominated by the Broad Church movement (to which the poets Coleridge and Clough were important), which scarcely emphasized doctrinal conformity at all. Except for Newman, Christina Rossetti, and Gerard Manley Hopkins, few English poets after 1850 were orthodoxly religious.

Tennyson's *In Memoriam* managed a dubious immortality for the young skeptic that it commemorated, but other poets of the time were less sure, as Clough and Arnold remained agnostics at best. In *Christmas Eve and Easter Day* (1850) Robert Browning rejected both doctrinal and evangelical Christianity in favor of a theistic religion of love, Arnold implying much the same in "Dover Beach" (1851). While meeting the equivalent American spiritual crisis with more gusto, Whitman observed in *Leaves of Grass* (1855) that "Creeds and schools" were "in abeyance." His own faith derived from all religions and did not include curiosity about God. In a poem of 1871 addressed to Whitman, however, Swinburne admitted that "God is buried and dead to us." Among American poets, Melville and Dickinson became religious seekers; Emerson, Whittier, and Longfellow, among others, remained relatively confident of supernatural goodness throughout the 1850's and 1860's, but their optimism (shared by Tennyson and Browning to some extent) seemed increasingly tenuous to younger readers.

One by one, traditional verities disappeared from English and American literature, and more rapidly in Britain. God was doubtful, Nature cruel, History vindictive, Love impossible, Man animalistic and corrupt. The poet who articulated the new disillusionment most forcefully, Matthew Arnold (1822-1888), saw himself as an isolated wanderer through a post-Christian, postrationalistic wilderness of historical and personal estrangement. Like Shelley's poet in *Alastor* (1816), Arnold sought for love and could not find it; of all men he wrote, "Thou hast been, shalt be, art, alone." Several later Victorian poets, including Browning (*Men and Women*, 1855), D. G. Rossetti, George Meredith, and Coventry Patmore, wrote extensively of their relationships with women, and of the failure of love; others turned from normal eroticism altogether. Compare these works with other long poems of the times which concentrate upon women, including Tennyson, *The Princess* (1847), and "Guinevere," taken from *Idylls of the King* (1859-1885); Clough, *The Bothie of Tober-na-Vuolich* (1848); Elizabeth Barrett Browning, *Aurora Leigh* (1856); Longfellow, *The Courtship of Miles Standish* (1858); and Morris, *The Defence of Guenevere* (1858).

INFLUENCE OF NATURAL SELECTION

As for nature, history, and man, all three had become suspect by mid-century and all three coalesced in the theory of natural selection publicized by Darwin's *On the Origin of Species by Means of Natural Selection* (1859), which transformed nineteenth century skepticism into disillusioned pessimism and savage exploitation. Darwin himself should not be held uniquely responsible for the capitalistic and imperialistic excesses mistakenly derived from his biological theories; his work inspired a major literary movement called naturalism and certainly ennobled the tragic sense of such powerful, effective poets as Thomas Hardy (1840-1928) and Stephen Crane (1871-1900). In both England and America, Darwin's harsh view of nature was coupled with the reality of war (India, 1857; Charleston, 1861; Havana, 1898). Perhaps even more disillusioning, however, was the incremental recognition in both countries that the optimism of previous decades regarding human nature was implausible. Throughout the last quarter of the nineteenth century authors repeatedly proclaimed, though usually in prose, that human beings are defiled on the surface and ugly to the core. Though the century could bear its religious losses with stoic fortitude, it could not maintain an essentially optimistic outlook against the pervasive antihumanism of its final years.

ALLIED WITH ART

Throughout the century literature had been closely allied with art. Much of its descriptive poetry, for exam-

ple, was based upon painted forebears or similar contemporary work; thus, Wordsworth is often compared with John Constable, Shelley with J. M. W. Turner, Coleridge with German Romantic art, Byron with Eugène Delacroix, and Browning with the Impressionists. Several important writers, including Blake, John Ruskin, Morris, and D. G. Rossetti, were authentic artists in their own right; others combined their verbal work with others' art to collaborate upon illustrated editions. That poets were makers of pictures, as the Roman poet Horace had declared, was assumed throughout the century. They became interpreters of pictures also, as can be seen in Bowles, Wordsworth, and especially Browning. For many later nineteenth century poets, however, the writer was no longer a prophet but a critic, concerned less with cosmic purpose than with man's revelation of himself through art.

TRANSITION TO A MINOR ART

It is symptomatic of the times that poetry became more personal, less prestigious, and even private (Dickinson, Hardy, Hopkins) as public utterances turned instead to evaluation of the literary past. Thus, Arnold virtually abandoned poetry for criticism of various kinds, while D. G. Rossetti, Lowell, Swinburne, and William Watson all reveal critical aspirations overtopping creative ones. Major anthologies of the time, edited by Edmund Clarence Stedman and Francis Palgrave, show that poetry appealed to the later nineteenth century more as conventional verbal prettiness than as original thought; a great deal of it was essentially decoration. Fanciful, but not imaginative (in the searching, Romantic sense), late Victorian poetry soon became, with only a few exceptions, a minor art, as statements of intellectual importance tended increasingly to be made in prose.

The Pre-Raphaelite Brotherhood of Dante Gabriel Rossetti (1828-1882) and his circle, which fostered both poetry and art, was a major attempt to defend creative imagination against the economic, social, and intellectual forces that were depressing it, which is to say, against the impersonality of manufacture, the bad taste of the rising middle class, and the unidimensional reality of empirical science. William Michael Rossetti (1829-1919) was, with his brother, largely responsible for bringing Whitman, Joaquin Miller, and Edward Fitz-

Gerald the *Rubáiyát of Omar Khayyám* (1859) to critical attention, while reviving interest in the work of Blake and Shelley. Only a small coterie in London, however, fully appreciated how desperate the artistic situation had become. From them emerged William Butler Yeats (1865-1939), an Irish cultural nationalist influenced by Thomas Moore and Sir Walter Scott, who based his major poems (mostly twentieth century) on the bold visions of Blake and Shelley, while rejecting Tennysonian doubt and the depressing outlook of scientific materialism. Tennyson, Browning, Whitman, Arnold, Hardy, and Yeats are now regarded as the most significant British poets of the latter part of the nineteenth century, and all have had their impact upon subsequent writers.

BIBLIOGRAPHY

Armstrong, Isobel, Cath Sharrock, and Joseph Brigtow, eds. *Nineteenth Century Women Poets: An Anthology.* Reprint. London: Oxford University Press, 1998. Presents the work of more than one hundred women writers and achieves range and depth by reprinting poems by working-class, colonial, and political poets, in addition to very substantial selections from the work of major figures.

Beach, Christopher. *Politics of Distinction: Whitman and the Discourses of Nineteenth Century America.* Athens: University of Georgia, 1996. Demonstrates how Walt Whitman differentiated his work from previous literary models while, at the same time, he sought to portray daily life and the concerns of the common people in an idiomatic, rather than a high-minded literary manner.

Blank, Kim G., and Margot K. Louis. *Influence and Resistance in Nineteenth Century English Poetry.* New York: St. Martin's Press, 1993. Explores the distinctions between Romantic and Victorian genres and demonstrates how well the Romantics thought, and with what ferocious diligence the Victorians explored, resisted, and reworked, the Romantic vision.

Everest, Kelvin. *English Romantic Poetry: An Introduction to the Historical Context and the Literary Scene.* Philadelphia: Open University Press, 1990. Presents the lives and careers of the major English Romantic poets—Blake, Wordsworth, Coleridge, Shelley, Keats, and Byron—in relation to the larger historical forces and circumstances of the period, and to the literary culture within and against which they worked and published.

Gray, Janet, ed. *She Wields a Pen: American Women Poets of the Nineteenth Century.* Iowa City: University of Iowa Press, 1997. Includes sixty-eight American women writers and their works, which appeared in print in the context of social purposes—the abolitionist movement, the temperance movement, the Hawaiian nationalist movement, the Sunday School movement, the Zionist movement, and the woman suffrage movement.

Harralson, Eric L., and John Hollander, eds. *Encyclopedia of American Poetry: The Nineteenth Century.* Chicago: Fitzroy Dearborn, 1998. Essays furnish not only useful facts and dates, biographical background, and information on the provenance of American poetry of the nineteenth century, but a critical discussion of the formal features, literary-historical significance, and cultural relevance of the verses being addressed.

Hodgson, John A. *Coleridge, Shelley, and Transcendental Inquiry: Rhetoric, Argument, and Metapsychology.* Lincoln: University of Nebraska Press, 1989. Integrates contemporary rhetorical, deconstructionist, and psychological approaches, offering new insights into English Romantic poetry and Freud's metapsychology.

Jackson-Houlston, C. M. *Ballads, Songs, and Snatches: The Appropriation of Folk Song and Popular Culture in British Nineteenth Century Realist Prose.* Brookfield, Vt.: Ashgate Publishing Company, 1999. Focuses on nineteenth century British literary allusions to folk songs and popular culture. Examines the work and attitudes of authors of the period who attempted to mediate the culture of the working classes for the enjoyment of middle-class audiences.

Lambdin, Laura Cooner, and Robert T. Lambdin. *Camelot in the Nineteenth Century: Arthurian Characters in the Poems of Tennyson, Arnold, Morris, and Swinburne.* Westport, Conn.: Greenwood Press, 1999. Examines how four poets used figures, events, and ideas from the Arthurian legends in their work and for their own ends. The authors conclude that the poets sought not to reflect historical reality but to produce religious, aesthetic, and political systems of representation.

Levere, Trevor Harvey. *Poetry Realized in Nature: Samuel Taylor Coleridge and Early Nineteenth Century Science*. Cambridge, England: Cambridge University Press, 1981. Establishes the fundamental importance of science in Coleridge's intellectual development, showing how it served as a source of imaginative insight. Offers a case study of the interactions between Romanticism and science.

McGann, Jerome. *The Romantic Ideology: A Critical Investigation*. Chicago: University of Chicago, 1990. Examines the role of Romantic ideology in the development of nineteenth century British poetry.

_____, ed. *The New Oxford Book of Romantic Period Verse*. London: Oxford University Press, 1994. Presents poetry from such noted Romantics as Byron, Shelley, Keats, Blake, Burns, Coleridge, and Wordsworth.

Nilsen, Don Lee. *Humor in Eighteenth and Nineteenth Century British Literature: A Reference Guide*. Westport, Conn.: Greenwood Press, 1998. Examines how British writers of the eighteenth and nineteenth centuries used humor in their works. An introductory chapter overviews humor in British literature of the era, and sections then treat humor in British literature of the eighteenth century and in three periods of the nineteenth century.

Olson, Steven. *The Prairie in Nineteenth Century American Poetry*. Norman: University of Oklahoma Press, 1995. Examines poetry of Herman Melville, Emily Dickinson, Walt Whitman, Oliver Wendell Holmes, James Russell Lowell, and Henry Wadsworth Longfellow. Explores the idea of the prairie as the principal metaphor for embodying the issues present in the political, social, and cultural life of nineteenth century America.

Storey, Mark. *The Problem of Poetry in the Romantic Period*. New York: St. Martin's Press, 2000. Examines the relationship between the various Romantic manifestos and the major poetry of the time, finding that despite the apparent confidence of many writers, there was an underlying unease about the validity of poetry.

Wagner, Jennifer Ann. *A Moment's Monument: Revisionary Poetics and the Nineteenth Century English Sonnet*. Madison, Wis.: Fairleigh Dickinson University Press, 1996. Argues that the history of the sonnet in the nineteenth century is more than a decorative strand in its literary fabric. This book is namely about William Wordsworth, who discovers, through Milton, that at the heart of the sonnet's power as a form is the trope of synecdoche, which he connects up with the very moment and act of representation—thereby "inventing" the visionary Romantic sonnet.

Dennis R. Dean

ENGLISH AND AMERICAN POETRY IN THE TWENTIETH CENTURY

Twentieth century poetry has been variously characterized as romantic, antiromantic, impersonal, highly personal, chaotic, orderly, classical, symbolist, wholly untraditional, reasoned and measured, or incomprehensible—depending upon the critic whom one reads. This radical diversity suggests a fundamental problem with poetry in the twentieth century: It has no clear path to follow. Finding previous poetry inadequate to deal with the situation in which they find themselves, modern poets must create anew, must, in Wallace Stevens's phrase, "find out what will suffice." The modern poem is an act of exploration. In the absence of givens, it must carve out its own niche, make its own *raison d'être*.

Not surprisingly, then, twentieth century poetry is marked by astonishing variety. What logic could successfully yoke together Robert Frost and Allen Ginsberg, Philip Larkin and William Carlos Williams, Sylvia Plath and Ezra Pound? None, so long as the category of modern poetry is understood to be a fixed entity; such definitions always aim at closure and exclusion. Nevertheless, it is possible to see all of modern poetry as a piece, and that possibility is what this essay hopes to explore.

THE RISE OF MODERNISM

Modern poetry began with a sense of discontinuity, a sense that the world of the twentieth century was not merely different as one century always is from another but decisively different, qualitatively different from all the centuries past. This sense of discontinuity was shared by the other arts; it was "on or about December 1910," Virginia Woolf wrote, that "human character changed." This shared conviction of radical change gave rise to the far-flung, loosely defined movement in the arts known as modernism, characterized in poetry by the fragmented, elliptical, allusive styles of Ezra Pound and T. S. Eliot.

To believe that the poetry of the Pound-Eliot school constitutes the whole of important modern poetry, however, or that modernism was a cohesive, unified movement, is to ignore many of its characteristic elements. As early as the first meetings of the Imagist group, gathered around Pound in England in 1912, the diversity of talent,

ideas, and aesthetics among modernist poets was already clear. Modernism was not a unified movement even in its early stages. Moreover, there were significant poets who did not buy into modernism at all. Against Pound's famous injunction to "compose in the manner of the musical phrase, not the metronome," there is Frost's equally well-known statement that writing free verse is like "playing tennis without a net." Against the heavily idea-laden poetry of Eliot and the New Critic/Fugitive poets—John Crowe Ransom and Allen Tate, in particular—stand William Carlos Williams's "no ideas but in things" and Archibald MacLeish's "a poem should not mean but be." The pillars of what is commonly regarded as modernism, then, found themselves flanked right and left by dissenters, as well as faced by independent thinkers within their camp. Modernist poetry, as commonly construed, represents a fairly limited if important range of the whole of modern poetry. If discussion of that entire range (and the diversity of British and American poetry is staggering) is to go forward, *modern* must be reclaimed from modernist. As distinguished from the self-consciously modernist, "modern poetry" can be understood to be roughly synonymous with twentieth century poetry, excepting the occasional reactionary or nostalgic poet and a few carryovers from Victorianism.

THE END OF VICTORIANISM

Modern literature is less united in what it stands for than in what it opposes. In a sense, almost all writing in the twentieth century attempts to throw over the nineteenth, particularly those aspects of it generally classified as Victorian. Both the sociopolitical and the literary elements of Victorianism come under fire from the modern artist, and the combination of targets should not be surprising, since politics and economics combine with literature in the nineteenth century to form what appears to modern eyes to be a uniform culture. While this uniformity may be largely mythical, it nevertheless has become one of the givens in discussions of Victorianism.

Behind most of the philosophical, social, and political inquiries of the nineteenth century, not merely in England and America but throughout the Western world, lies the idea of progress, of a goal toward which society is moving perceptibly. One of the clearest manifestations of this idea is Karl Marx's *telos*, the goal or endpoint of civilization's quest for utopia. Marxism depends on this idea as on no other; the supposition that one can chart the course of societies with certainty that each will follow the same line of development rests on the unstated assumption that all societies are moving in the same direction, and that therefore there must be some goal toward which all, willingly or not, tend. Marx is not alone, of course, in so thinking. The utilitarianism of Jeremy Bentham and John Stuart Mill, with its emphasis on "the greatest good for the greatest number," builds on similar foundations: That act is best which, since it offers maximum benefits to the most members of society, promotes the greatest social progress. Other progress-centered developments in thought range from American "manifest destiny" (and other nations' quest for empire, as well) to Mary Baker Eddy's "Every day in every way things get better and better."

Nor is this phenomenon limited to social thought; the single greatest scientific contribution of the century bears the mark of its time. Charles Darwin's evolutionary theory is every bit as dependent on the notion of *telos* as is Marx's: The result of the fittest members of the species surviving to mate with one another is that newer and fitter forms of life constantly come into being. The newest and fittest form, naturally, is the human being. That Darwinian thought is a logical extension of nineteenth century notions of progress is borne out by the readiness with which evolution was accepted not by biologists, but by social thinkers. Social Darwinism combines evolutionary thought with the already accepted mode of utilitarianism.

CULTURAL BREAKDOWN

Against this concept of progress lies its opposite, and what may even be seen as its necessary, complement. A society that is constantly progressing is undergoing constant change, which in turn means that traditional institutions and ways of life must break down. In *The Education of Henry Adams* (1907), Henry Adams expresses this idea in terms of the twin images of virgin and dynamo. The virgin, representative of traditional culture, symbolizes stability and order, a manageable, if static,

society. The dynamo, the modern society, spins constantly faster, changing incessantly, leaving its members with a sense of chaos and confusion. While modern society shows progress, it also falls into relativism, since the traditional institutions on which absolutes are based are breaking down. Whereas the idea of progress was a product of mid-nineteenth century thinkers, the time of the Great Exhibition in London, the notion of cultural breakdown achieved its widest circulation late in the nineteenth century and into the twentieth, receiving its fullest development, perhaps, in the work of T. S. Eliot.

Nineteenth century literature, particularly in England, mirrored the development of thought in the period. It should not be surprising, therefore, that the chief poet of High Victorianism, Alfred, Lord Tennyson, was tremendously popular as well as critically acclaimed, and that the same should be true for the novelist Charles Dickens. The artists of mid-century specialized in giving the people what they wanted. Walt Whitman, the nineteenth century poet to whom American moderns so often look, would seem to be an exception. One must remember, of course, that Whitman's work was largely ignored during his lifetime, that he was not a popular poet by any means when his work first appeared, and that the recognized poets of the era, such as John Greenleaf Whittier and Henry Wadsworth Longfellow, worked with the public's desires more firmly in mind. Then, too, even Whitman wrote directly to his audience much more than the typical modern poet (if there be such a thing) does, and his great poem, *Leaves of Grass* (1855), is a public celebration of the people.

DECADENCE

The late nineteenth century produced the expected countermovement, in which the characteristic poem is much darker, more decadent, and suspicious of the openness and health of the High Victorians. Under the influence of the darker Romantics and the French Symbolists (who got their own dose of dark Romanticism from Edgar Allan Poe), the late Victorians from the Pre-Raphaelites on demonstrate a tendency toward the sinister and the unhealthy, toward madness and dissipation. Prostitutes, drug addicts, criminals—all those, in short, from the underside of society, from the social strata largely ignored by Tennyson—figure heavily in the work of Dante Gabriel Rossetti and Algernon Charles Swinburne, Ernest Dowson, Lionel Johnson, the early William Butler Yeats, and, of course, Oscar Wilde. Their fascination with dark subjects and dark treatments shows a suspicion of the methods and beliefs of the earlier Victorians analogous to Adams's suspicion of progress. Their work collectively embodies the _fin de siècle_ sense of impending change, the exhaustion of old modes, the existential ennui of a society in decline. The late Victorian poets were not a new beginning but a clear end, a cry for the new, while in America the cry was silence, the absence of any major poetic talents. On both sides of the Atlantic, poetry in English was a gap waiting to be filled, and awaiting of something as yet unknown.

EARLY MODERN MOVEMENTS

The early years of the twentieth century produced three separate groups of poetic innovators: the Georgian poets, the Sitwell group, and the Imagists. Although all three failed to sustain movements, each contributed elements to the large field of modern poetry.

The first two groups were decidedly minor, producing little work that has continued to be held in high esteem by the critical or poetic communities. The Georgians are often dismissed as the old guard that the true modernists struggled to overthrow; yet such an easy dismissal overlooks the radical nature of the movement. As Geoffrey Bullough pointed out in _The Trend of Modern Poetry_ (1934), Georgian poetry, while a throwback to Romanticism, represents a break with the Imperial poetry of the same period, and the established poets of the day looked upon it with some horror. Moreover, while the movement itself died down, some of its work in loosening the reins on traditional verse forms has survived, as one can see in the repeated comparisons of Philip Larkin's work with the Georgian poetry of Edward Thomas. The conversational diction and simplicity of their poetry, as Bullough further notes, has become something of a standard feature in certain strains of modern poetry. Similarly, the work of the group gathered around the Sitwells ultimately came to little, yet there is much in that poetry that foreshadows developments in other, more important poets. The spiritual despair, the often forced gaiety, the combination of wit and bleakness of Sitwellian poetry shows up in many other

writers' work in the century. Ultimately, their work is for the most part ignored or forgotten because they had very little to say; their poetry had much surface but lacked substance.

IMAGISM

Of the three, Imagism is by far the most important school for modern verse at large. The goal of the movement, as the name implies, was to bring to poetry a new emphasis on the image as a structural, rather than an ornamental, element. Growing out of French Symbolism and taking techniques, styles, and forms from Japanese haiku, tanka, and hokku, from Chinese ideograms, and from Classical Greek and Provençal troubador lyrics, Imagism reflects the diverse interests of its founders and their rather dilettantish nature.

While there were a number of very fine practitioners, among them F. S. Flint, D. H. Lawrence, T. E. Hulme, H. D. (Hilda Doolittle), Richard Aldington, William Carlos Williams, Carl Sandburg, and Amy Lowell, it is Ezra Pound who stands as the major spokesman and publicist for the group. Pound, along with Aldington and H. D., formulated the three cardinal rules of the movement in "A Retrospect": direct treatment of the thing discussed; absolute economy of diction; and composition "in the sequence of the musical phrase, not in the sequence of the metronome." At various times others from the group expanded upon or modified those three initial rules, yet they stand as the basis for Imagist technique. In fact, they are descriptive of the movement rather than prescriptive; the Imagist group had been meeting in one form or another for several years when Pound formulated these precepts. Much of the philosophical basis for the school comes from Hulme's study of Henri Bergson's thought. Under Hulme's influence the varied interests of the members jelled into a more or less cohesive body of theory, at least for a short time.

The poetry produced by the group, although by no means uniform, shared certain characteristics. First of all, it was an attempt to put the creation of images at the center of the poetic act. The image is a sudden moment of truth, or, as Pound describes it, "an intellectual and emotional complex in an instant of time." It shares a good deal with other modern moments of revelation, from Gerard Manley Hopkins's "inscape" to James

Joyce's "epiphany." The brevity of the Imagist poem, another defining characteristic particularly of those produced early in the group's history, is a logical extension of the emphasis on the image. As an attempt to eschew rhetorical and narrative forms and to replace them with the "pure" poetic moment, the Imagist poem, existing almost solely for the creation of the image, completes its mission with the completion of that image. A long poem of the type would simply be a series of discrete images whose relation to one another could only be inferred, since explicative transitions would be a violation of precept. The longer poems produced under the leadership of Lowell evidence a loosening of form and a laxity of craftsmanship. The late Imagist poems are not so much transitional, pointing toward some new development, as they are decadent, indicative of the movement's demise.

That Imagism would be short-lived was almost inevitable. The goals and techniques of the movement were antithetical to sustaining even a poem of any considerable duration, let alone a school. The tiny Imagist poem is much too limiting to allow its creator much variety from one poem to the next. The chance to explore themes, ideas, and beliefs simply does not exist, since that sort of argument-oriented poetry is what Imagism sought to replace. Yet even the proponents of Imagism had larger plans than their espoused methods would allow. Pound, for example, even while he was most closely associated with the group, was working on his plan for the *Cantos* (1925-1972). Nevertheless, even if Imagism lacked the qualities to make it a sustained movement, its methods have been adopted in the great majority of poems written in the twentieth century. Imagist techniques appear in Williams's *Paterson* (1946-1958) and in the *Cantos*, but they also appear in the work of such non-Imagists as Allen Tate, Eliot, Sylvia Plath, and Dylan Thomas, and make possible such later developments as Surrealism and the Deep Image poetry of James Wright and Robert Bly.

SYMBOLISM

Imagism, itself a product of diverse influences, is only one of a great many influences on modern poetry. Perhaps the single most important influence has been nineteenth century French Symbolism. Ironically, the source of much Symbolist theory was Poe, whose work was largely ignored by Anglo-American critics. The French, however, saw in his darkly Romantic speculations, in the bleakness and horror of his work, even in his impulse toward dissipation, the vehicle appropriate to poetry on the modern predicament. In his own country he may have been a Gothic oddity; in France he was a prophet. The work produced by his French followers—Jules Laforgue, Tristan Corbière, Charles Baudelaire, Stéphane Mallarmé, Arthur Rimbaud, and Paul Verlaine—incorporated much from Poe: the darkness, the exploration of life's underside, the penchant for urban landscapes, and, most important, the centrality of the symbol.

Certainly symbols have always been used in poetry, and little that the Symbolists accomplished with symbols was entirely new. What was fresh and unique, however, was their insistence on the symbol as the structural *raison d'être* of the poem. No longer relegated to the status of ornament or occasional item, the symbol became for these poets the goal one actively sought to achieve in the poem. Like so many of their modern followers, they were reacting against the Scylla and Charybdis of loose, discursive verse on the one hand, and didactic, allegorical verse on the other. Also like their followers, they mistrusted language, having seen too much bad poetry turned out by following conventional use of "poetic" language. They therefore felt that the achievement of poetry must lie elsewhere than in the play of words. Their solution was to place heavy emphasis on the poetic moment, the symbol. They attempted to separate radically the symbolic from the allegorical use of imagery, and there is about much Symbolist poetry a vagueness that refuses to let the symbol be quite pinned down. In some of the followers of Symbolism, particularly in the work of the English poets of the 1890's, that vagueness drifts off into airy realms too thin for habitation.

Symbolism found its way into Anglo-American modern poetry by so many routes that it is nearly impossible to chronicle them all. Nevertheless, a few of the points of entry require mention. The earliest important mention of Symbolism is in Arthur Symons's famous book of 1899, *The Symbolist Movement in Literature*. Symons, along with Yeats and other poets of the Rhymers' Club, introduced the work of these Frenchmen to English audiences not only through essays and defenses, but also through original English poetry on Symbolist models. Giving as much attention to prose writers as to poets, Symons hailed the new literary wind blowing from Paris as one that did not shrink from neurosis, nightmare, and decadence. Of Mallarmé he says, "All his life he has been haunted by the desire to create, not so much something new in literature, as a literature which should be itself a new art." This sense of newness, of shocking, appalling novelty, was immediately grasped by defenders and vilifiers alike, and Symbolism itself became a symbol. Oscar Wilde could not have set the character of Dorian Gray so well in ten pages of description, at least for his immediate audience, as he did by having Dorian reading, at several key points, J. K. Huysmans's *Á rebours* (1884; *Against the Grain*, 1922). This first wave of enthusiasm, however, was mainly a matter of imitation, and if it largely died out before producing any major works of interest, it was because the writers who experimented in the mode were playing with an exotic toy, not working with an instrument fitted to their own machinery.

The second major attempt at importation, this one aiming for domestication, grew eventually into Imagism. If the work of Symons and Yeats was important because it showed that such a thing as symbolism existed, Imagism's importance lay in the translation of a movement from one century and one place into another movement in another century and another place. Imagism sought to refine the terms of the symbol; Pound, writing of the aims of Imagism, said that symbolic function was one of the possible uses of the image, but that it should never be so important that the poem is lost on a person for whom "a hawk is simply a hawk."

The third major importer of Symbolism into English was T. S. Eliot. He wrote extensively about the Symbolists; he copied their style, even to the point of writing in French in some early poems; he openly acknowledged his debt in direct borrowings from their work; and, most important, he produced the most complete example of a Symbolist poem in English, *The Waste Land* (1922). In the use of urban landscape, the feverish, nightmarish quality of the imagery, the darkness of the vision, the layering of symbols and images within symbols and images, *The Waste Land* demonstrates its creator's overwhelming debt to the Symbolists. The poem's centrality in the modern canon lends weight to the significance of Symbolism for modern Anglo-American poetry. Knowingly or not, all poets who have found themselves affected by Eliot's great work have also been affected by Laforgue and Baudelaire.

THE METAPHYSICAL INFLUENCE

Symbolism was not, however, the only major influence on modern poetry. Another example of Eliot's importance as an arbiter of poetic taste and style is the resurrection of the English Metaphysical poets as models for modern verse. Long ignored by English critics, the Metaphysicals—John Donne, in particular—offer the modern poet another use of a controlling metaphor. If the Symbolists reintroduced the poet to the symbol, Donne and his contemporaries—Andrew Marvell, George Herbert, Henry Vaughan, Richard Crashaw—showed him how to use it in extended forms. The conceit of the Metaphysical poem, like the symbol of the Symbolist poem, is an example of figurative language used not as ornament, but as structural principle. Since the conceit of a Donne poem is used as a way of integrating metaphor with argument, the model served to overcome the limiting element of Imagism and, to a lesser extent, of Symbolism itself. Both the latter movements, since they eschewed argument as a poetic method, shut themselves off from the possibility of sustained use. The Metaphysical conceit (and what is the image of the wasteland if not a conceit, a unifying metaphor?) allows Eliot to adapt Imagist and symbolist techniques to a long, elaborately structured poem.

WHITMAN AND HARDY

Another, very different model for long poems was found in Walt Whitman's *Leaves of Grass*. Whitman's great contribution is in the area of open form. The sometimes chatty, sometimes oratorial, usually freewheeling style of his poetry has done more than anything else to show the path away from iambic verse. His influence is clear on such poets as Williams, Lawrence, Ginsberg and his fellow Beat poets, and Charles Olson and the Black Mountain poets, yet he also often moves through less obvious channels, and virtually any poet who has experimented with open forms owes him a debt. Even a poet as strongly opposed in principle to the looseness of his verse as Pound accorded Whitman grudging respect.

Against this characteristically American model stands the typically British example of Thomas Hardy. Where Whitman's poetic is antitraditional and iconoclastic, open and rhythmic and boisterous, Hardy's is tight-lipped, satisfied to work within established forms, dour and bleak. Yet Hardy's work was not merely traditional; while he worked within standard forms, he often pushed their limits outward, expressing the modern dissatisfaction with form not by rejecting it but by bending it to suit his needs. Very much Victorian, he still anticipates the modern, standing as a threshold figure for such followers as W. H. Auden, Philip Larkin, Roy Fuller, and perhaps the entirety of the British Movement poets of the 1950's.

Both Whitman and Hardy offer alternatives to the mainstream of modernist poetry as embodied by Pound and Eliot, the Fugitive poets, William Empson, and such later poets as Geoffrey Hill. Modern Whitmanesque poetry—such as Olson's *The Maximus Poems* (1960), which also are strongly indebted to the *Cantos*, and Ginsberg's "Howl"—is commonly regarded as avant-garde, that in the Hardy line as reactionary or antimodern. Yet to accept such labels is to misunderstand the nature of modern poetry. These three camps represent not so much three separate attitudes toward art or aesthetics as three attempts at dealing with the world poetically, those attempts being based on regionalism as much as anything else. The poetics of the Eliot-Pound camp are essentially cosmopolitan, the result of ransacking international literary history from the classics and Chinese lyrics to the Provençal poets to the Symbolists. The other two schools are much more closely related to place, to national identity. Auden is not less modern than Williams; he is more British. Moreover, to insist on too clear a dividing line among the camps is to falsify the situation. While the influence of one figure or school of poetry may be more pronounced on some groups or individuals, there is also a general influence on the whole of modern poetry, so that the struggle of a poet such as Larkin to loosen forms may be the result of the undetected (and probably undetectable) influence of Whitman, who has caused a general trend toward openness. On the other hand, if there is a rancor in Ginsberg that is

not present in Whitman, it is perhaps that the later poet has picked up the typically modern ambivalence that is present in Hardy. In short, one should not be too hasty in excluding any potential influence, nor in assessing a poet's "modernity."

AFTER WORLD WAR II

The foregoing discussion, while it has applicability to the entire century, fails to address some of the significant developments since World War II. Poetry after that war underwent a mid-century crisis, during which time it made a number of motions that appeared to indicate rejection of the poetry that had immediately preceded it. The Movement in England, the Beats and Black Mountain poets in America, confessional poetry, and Surrealist poetry were all symptomatic of change, and the critical tendency has been to read that change as sweeping, as a revolution. There is, however, much evidence to suggest just the contrary—that what took place after 1945 was not revolutionary but domestic: a periodic housecleaning occasioned by changes in fashion and perhaps also by changes in the world around the poet.

It is not entirely unfair to say that modern poetry came into being when the dilettantism of Georgian and Sitwellian and Imagist poetry ran into World War I. The utter inability of those movements to deal effectively with a world in which such a cataclysm possibly forced poets to abandon certain precepts that had failed them. It is no mere coincidence, for example, that Imagism flourished in the years immediately preceding the war when, as Paul Fussell notes in his study *The Great War and Modern Memory* (1975), England was blithely, even determinedly ignorant of impending events, or that it faltered and died during the war years. The Imagist poem did not offer sufficient scope for the creation of a work of "a certain magnitude." Eliot's great contribution, as mentioned earlier, lay in grafting Imagist (and symbolist) technique onto forms that allowed greater expansiveness.

Similarly, the tremendous destruction brought about in World War II caused a shift in attitudes and, by extension, in poetic practices. In World War I, the destruction was limited largely to combatants; battle was a distant thing. By the end of World War II, the bombing of population centers, the unveiling of atomic weaponry, and the revelation of genocide had made warfare both more personal and more terrible. The poetics of impersonality and detachment as sponsored by Eliot suddenly seemed outmoded, and the movement in much of modern poetry since that time has been toward a renewed involvement with the self. Eliot's self is an extension of culture, a member of church, state, and critical school, a representative of agencies and institutions. His concern with the self, from "The Love Song of J. Alfred Prufrock" to the *Four Quartets* (1943), is a curiously impersonal involvement. After the war, however, many poets turned their verse inward, examining the self with all its flaws, hungers, and hidden violence.

SURREALISM

Another branch of postwar American and English poetry has been heavily influenced by Surrealism. Whereas the early modernists went directly to the Symbolists, these postwar poets first encountered Symbolism through its later development, Surrealism. The French Surrealism of André Breton had comparatively little impact in England, where only a handful of writers—notably David Gascoyne and Dylan Thomas—employed its techniques with any regularity. It had even less impact in America. Spanish Surrealism, on the other hand, was imported into American poetry through the work of Robert Bly, James Wright, and W. S. Merwin, all prolific translators, and into English poetry in small bits through Charles Tomlinson's association with Octavio Paz. The Deep Image poetry of Bly and Wright, owing much to Federico García Lorca, César Vallejo, and Pablo Neruda, often reads like a Symbolist rendering of deep consciousness. The New York school of Kenneth Koch, Frank O'Hara, and John Ashbery also demonstrates its indebtedness to earlier, continental Surrealists.

RENEWED ROMANTICISM

Earlier native poets have been reevaluated in the postwar period as well. Hardy has become even more important to certain strains of British poetry than he was before the war, while the reappraisal of Whitman and the discovery of Emily Dickinson as a poetic resource has led American poets to a new sense of tradition. If Beat poetry would be impossible without Whitman,

then confessional poetry would also be impossible, or at least radically different, without Dickinson. Her intense concern with self and soul, her death obsession, her striking use of associative imagery, her use of very simple poetic forms for very complex ideas, all show up in the work of Robert Lowell, Sylvia Plath, Anne Sexton, and John Berryman.

As the interest in Dickinson suggests, the renewed emphasis on the self in postwar poetry leads to a new involvement with Romanticism. Often, though, it is with the darker side of Romanticism that poets interact—with Symbolism, with Lawrence and Dickinson—with those elements, in short, that show the self on the edge of disaster or oblivion. There is, of course, the buoyant optimism of Whitman to counteract this trend, yet even his influence often appears darker than the original. The return to favor of Romanticism might be the sole real break with earlier moderns, with modernism, with Eliot's classicism.

Yet even here such a generalization is dangerous. One must remember that Lawrence, Williams, Wallace Stevens, Dylan Thomas, Robert Graves, and even elements in Eliot's work belie the anti-Romantic stance usually accepted as a basis for modernism. Similarly, the more positive attitude toward the Romantics is by no means universal. The Movement poets, for example, adopted a vigorous anti-Romantic position in their dryly ironic verse, while there is much in Romanticism that even those poets who seem closest to it find unappealing. The modern Romantics, like the modern classicists, select only those elements that fit the modern platform they happen to be building.

EASTERN, MYTHIC, AND ARCHETYPAL INFLUENCES

Not all influences on recent poetry are domestic. Like the earlier moderns, the postwar poets have made forays into exotic poetics. Indeed, the period of contemporary poetry might be called the Age of Translation, in which English-language poetry is open to the riches of world poetry as never before. Both Japanese and Chinese poetry have been particularly influential in the postwar years, notably in the work of Kenneth Rexroth and Gary Snyder. In this period there has been a marked trend toward going below the surface of Asian culture to the deep structure of its modes of thought. Snyder, for example, spent several years in a Zen monastery in Kyoto, and while the experience did not turn him away from Western society entirely, it caused him to reexamine more familiar cultural forms in the light of another perspective.

Another distinctive characteristic of modern poetry is its preoccupation with myth and archetype. To be sure, much of the poetry in the Western tradition, from Homer and Ovid to Percy Bysshe Shelley, from Dante to Tennyson, is explicitly concerned with myth, yet the modern sense of the mythic differs from anything that went before. In modern poetry, everyday life is frequently seen as a series of rituals, often acted out unawares, by which humankind expresses its relation to the universal.

In part this distinctively modern awareness of myth and archetype can be attributed to the influence of the new science of anthropology as exemplified in Sir James Frazer's pioneering work *The Golden Bough* (1890-1915). The work of Sigmund Freud and Carl G. Jung early in the twentieth century added to the modern writer's interest in myth. Where Frazer examined mythic patterns as cultural phenomena, Freud and Jung demonstrated the ways in which individuals internalize such patterns. Myth and archetype derive their power, then, from their timeless hold on the individual consciousness.

The result of this thinking was a tremendous explosion of genuinely new literature, of poetry and fiction in which the quotidian acts of ordinary individuals take on meaning beyond their understanding. Among the fruits of this new flowering were the two most important works produced in English in the twentieth century, both too significant for subsequent writers to ignore and too awesome to copy. One was the story of a single day in Dublin in 1904, during which the ramblings of an Irish Jew parallel the wanderings chronicled in Homer's *Odyssey* (c. 800 B.C.E.): James Joyce's *Ulysses* (1922). The other, of course, was the *The Waste Land*. In his essay "*Ulysses*, Order, and Myth," Eliot announced that in place of the traditional narrative method, the modern artist could henceforth use the mythic method, that fiction and poetry would gain power not from their isolated stories, but through the connection of the stories to a universal pattern.

William Butler Yeats, of course, had been working in the field of myth in poetry for a very long time and had been actively creating his own mythology, through the work surrounding *A Vision* (1925), for several years. Lawrence, too, was a mythmaker, both in his poetry and in his fiction. Yet both of these writers' uses of myth constitute dead ends of sorts, for their mythologies are largely private, unusable by others. The mainstream of poetic use of myth in the twentieth century runs, not through the mythmakers, but through myth-followers. From Eliot and Pound to Sylvia Plath and Seamus Heaney, modern poetry has produced a great deal of work that follows mythic patterns.

MORAL AMBIVALENCE

A final defining characteristic of modern poetry is its ambivalence. The modern poet seems, on the whole, constitutionally incapable of wholeheartedly loving or hating the world in which he lives. The foremost example of ambivalence is the work of Yeats, in which he simultaneously strives for release from the world and regret at the possibility of release. Indeed, Yeats carries this double attitude further than anyone else, turning it into an elaborate system. Yeats provides an elaborate image of that ambivalence with his "whirling gyres": The interlocking gyres stand for ideas, beliefs, and qualities which, while completely opposed to one another, nevertheless require each other for completion. In Yeats, one idea is never whole; it must have its opposite idea, for only the interlocking pair are completed, as the tower is incomplete without the winding stair (to use his own symbols).

As a result, Yeats is virtually incapable of rendering a wholehearted judgment in his poetry. He sees both good and bad, the positive and the negative, in all things. In his poems about the Irish Civil War, for example, although he supports Irish independence, he can see the destruction brought about by members of the IRA as well as by the British Royal Irish Constabulary. In "Easter 1916," he celebrates the courage of the insurrectionists, yet at the same time questions their wisdom. Even that questioning is edgy, incomplete; he says that perhaps it was unwise, that perhaps it will set back the cause of Ireland; he refuses either to denounce the uprising or to praise it unreservedly. The most famous example of Yeatsian ambivalence, mirroring the pair of gyres, is a pair of interlocking poems about Byzantium. In "Sailing to Byzantium," the speaker is old and world-weary. He seeks the quietude, the tranquillity of the artificial world represented by Byzantium; he speaks longingly of the work of the city's artisans, of escaping out of the world of flesh into the world of pure beauty. In "Byzantium" he finds himself looking back across the ocean, again longingly, at the world of flesh and mire. Here he is weary of the world of timeless beauty, and the imagery of the poem's desires is of living creatures, particularly of the dolphin that could carry him back to the living world.

The Byzantium poems embody a fundamental feature of modern poetry: The chaos and contingency of the modern world lead the poet to distaste, to a desire for escape, to a retreat into the sheltered world of aesthetics that Edmund Wilson referred to in *Axel's Castle* (1931). Yet contrary to Wilson's contentions, that move is very much an act of engaging the world, every bit as much as Arthur Rimbaud's rejection of poetry (the example that Wilson cites as the alternative) for the life of a gunrunner. The characteristic attitude is not rejection but ambivalence; the poet, while wishing to withdraw from the world, is nevertheless caught in it, is a part of it, can never escape from it. Poetry, therefore, although an attempt to hold the world at arm's length, still remains in contact with it and is constantly a response to, not an escape from, life.

Yeats and Hardy are models for this attitudinal complex, along with the late Victorians—such as Algernon Charles Swinburne, Ernest Dowson, and Dante Gabriel Rossetti—and the French Symbolists. British poetry tends to be dominated by ambivalence more than its American counterpart does; the Beats, for example, seem less ambivalent than the British Movement poets. In general, however, modern poetry may be characterized fairly as the poetry of ambivalence.

NEW CRITICISM

In turn, much of the attitudinal bias of the New Criticism—the influential critical movement spawned by modernism—can be explained on the basis of ambivalence: the emphasis on irony, tension, ambiguity, as keys to poetry; the elevation of the Metaphysical poets and the concomitant devaluation of Romantic and Victorian verse; the blindness to poetry that is open or singleminded. Despite its shortcomings, the New Criticism's great contribution was that it taught readers (and still teaches them) how to read modern poetry. That most of the illustrious practitioners of the New Criticism—Tate, Robert Penn Warren, John Crowe Ransom, William Empson—were also poets of considerable accomplishment should come as no surprise. The New Critics, despite the claims of Cleanth Brooks and others, did not read all kinds of poetry equally well, yet their sensitivity to modern poetry remains unequaled, because they were so attuned to the various forms that ambivalence can take in a poem.

DISJUNCTURE AND DISCONTINUITY

Modern poetry—particularly after *The Waste Land*—is characterized by deliberated discontinuities. Several impulses came together more or less at once to create the disjointed poetics of modern verse. One, of course, was the inheritance of Imagism, the concentration on the intensely poetic moment almost to the exclusion of everything else. More fundamental was the sense of fragmentation in society and in consciousness that many modern writers express, a sense of radical discontinuity with the past. One consequence of this sense of fragmentation was a distrust of language. The ambivalence of modern writers toward the world lead them to suspect received forms, particularly those forms that suggest continuity and wholeness. Such completeness contradicts a writer's experience of the world, in which things are fragmented, discontinuous, chaotic, intractable. To blithely write long, flowing poems in the manner of Tennyson would be to violate one's own experience of the world and one's own consciousness. Other literary forms come under suspicion as well, but the modern poet is particularly wary of sustained, regular forms. Even such artists as Philip Larkin or Yeats, who work in received forms, often take great pains to change them, to make them less regular. The corollary—a suspicion traceable to the Symbolists—is that language itself is unreliable, a debased medium encrusted with connotations from previous usage.

These several forces came together to move the modern poem toward disjuncture and discontinuity. Again, in this respect as in so much else, *The Waste Land* was seminal work. The poem leaps from image to image, throwing unconnected and even antithetical elements violently together to produce a work that, although it draws heavily on earlier literature, is like nothing that had gone before. The links between the five main sections of the poem have particularly troubled readers, since they are not related in any immediately identifiable manner. Still, they do cohere, they do move toward some final point as a group that none of them achieves individually. Their cohesiveness is a function of each section's relation to the whole, rather than, as one might expect, the relations between pairs of successive sections.

THE POEM SEQUENCE

When the disjunctive poetics of modern verse are practiced in works of large scale, as in *The Waste Land*, traditional forms must necessarily be scrapped. In very short lyrics, of course, there is no problem with the connection between sections, but in longer works the sections must stand together in some logical fashion or risk the outrage heaped on Eliot's work when it first appeared. Even so, a poem can go on piling image upon image without respite for just so long before it breaks down, before the reader becomes hopelessly lost in the morass. To circumvent the problems raised by continuity in a disjunctive poetry, the modern writer has turned to the poem sequence. The sequence has been variously defined, but perhaps it is most satisfactory to think of it as a series of poems that are capable of standing alone but that take on greater significance through their mutual interaction.

Thus, a sequence is a long poem made of shorter poems; the modern poem sequence has its opposite number in what Joanne V. Creighton, in her study *Faulkner's Craft of Revision* (1977), calls the "short-story composite." The composite is a book composed of chapters that are themselves stories; the stories can be read separately, as in an ordinary collection, but they also form a unified whole when read together. She cites Ernest Hemingway's *In Our Time* (1924) and William Faulkner's *Go Down, Moses* (1942) as such works, in which the writer has given as much planning and work to the book's larger structure (as in a novel) as he has to the individual parts (as in a normal short-story collection).

The poem sequence is not the exclusive property of the twentieth century, of course. Many earlier examples can be cited, depending on how one judges such matters: Rimbaud's *Une Saison en Enfer* (1873; *A Season in Hell*), Whitman's *Leaves of Grass*, Rossetti's sonnet sequence *The House of Life* (1869), William Morris's *The Earthly Paradise* (1868-1870), perhaps even Dante's *La divina commedia* (c. 1320; *The Divine Comedy*). Yet in almost every case, the premodern sequence attempts to justify its disunity by displaying the unity among its sections, by talking its way through or over the gaps. By contrast, the modern sequence often works through silence, by exploiting the interstices, allowing ambiguity or multiple meanings to slip in through the cracks. The unexplained juxtaposition of elements adds to the possible meanings of the work; the reader must participate in the construction of the sequence.

In the loosest possible sense, any book of poems is a sequence; so, in the twentieth century, sequences come in all denominations. Both Lawrence and Yeats experimented with sequencing fairly informally in their work. Lawrence often collected his poems in a book around a theme or a method of creation, and strung poems together by resonant phrasings, as in the group of poems whose central piece is "The Ship of Death." Yeats, too, carefully arranged the poems in his books, and in his revisions not only changed poems but the order as well. At the other end of the scale stands *The Waste Land*, which is not, strictly speaking, a sequence at all, yet which shares some characteristics of the sequence: fragmentation, separate titles for its sections, length, and scope. Still, it fails to meet one of the criteria: Its separate sections cannot stand alone as poems. One cannot dissect the poem without making hash of it. It looks like a sequence, and indeed it is often listed as one, but it is not. It is a long, fragmentary, truly modern poem. To find a real poem sequence in Eliot, one must look to the end, to *Four Quartets*.

The Waste Land owed its striking discontinuity in large measure to the blue pencil of Ezra Pound. Pound's editorial assistance, as in the case of Hemingway's *In Our Time*, nearly always took the form of radical deletion, and in this poem he cut much transitional and explanatory material, resulting in a formal jumpiness that reinforces the cultural and personal neurasthenia. It is to

Pound's own work, though, that one must look to find an early example of a poem sequence.

Both *Homage to Sextus Propertius* (1934) and *Hugh Selwyn Mauberley* (1920) are early sequences by Pound, and, while not mere exercises, are trial pieces for his major life sequence, the *Cantos*, which even then he had begun. Both are attempts at sustained works made up of smaller units. The *Homage to Sextus Propertius* is a single poem made up of twelve loose translations or renderings of poems by Propertius, each of which had stood alone in the original. The effect, in Pound, is of a series of more or less autonomous pieces that have an affinity for one another, a common language or flavor, a function in part of the latinate diction employed by the poet. His *Hugh Selwyn Mauberley* is a more recognizable sequence, unified by the persona of Mauberley. When read as a whole, the poems take on much greater meaning through their collective resonance. The renderings of Propertius's work are loosely affiliated, are similar to one another; the poems in *Hugh Selwyn Mauberley* are parts of a whole.

It is in the *Cantos* that Pound works most concertedly in the poem sequence. Taking Dante's *The Divine Comedy* as its extremely loose model (Pound once said he was writing a *commedia agnostica*), the poem works its way through ancient and modern history, Eastern and Western thought and art, economics, literature, politics, music, architecture, and personal experience. The *Cantos* comprises a record of a modern poet's experience, an epic-scale work of the man of sensibility in the world.

The unity of the sequence is established through purely internal means: echoes, repetitions, thematic and ideological ties. The apparent obscurity of a given canto is a function of the unity of the poet's mind: The obscure utterance will likely be expanded, explained, revised, rearticulated at some later point in the proceedings. Thus the *Cantos* have a hermetic quality that can make reading a single canto difficult, while rewarding a comprehensive reading of the whole. The publication history suggests that the parts of the *Cantos* can be read singly or in groups, coming out as they did by fits and starts over fifty years, but they prove most rewarding when taken as a total work, when read as the epic they were intended to be. They are the Ur-sequence of modern poetry. Allen Tate said of them that they beg for a ceaseless study at the rate of one a year in depth, the whole to be read through every few weeks to maintain perspective. His comments are suggestive of the demands that twentieth century literature makes upon its readers; works such as *Ulysses* and the *Cantos* are pitched away from the popular audience and toward the professional reader who can give them the kind of constant and loving attention they demand.

The Idea of America

At about the same time that the first thirty cantos were appearing, Hart Crane was writing another sequence that would become a refutation of the wanderlust and classicism of Pound's work and of the wasteland-mentality of Eliot's. *The Bridge* (1930) is a sequence much closer to Whitman's than to Pound's, celebrating America and the American people, very much a home-grown thing. Where Pound is something of a literary Ulysses, traveling the known world for his materials, Crane relies primarily on native sources, native images, native speech, native treatments. Like most poets of his time, he had wrestled with the influence of Eliot and the Symbolists, learning much from them but unwilling to remain in that camp. He found his liberation through Whitman, whose buoyant optimism and sense of universal connectedness countered Eliot's pessimism and exhaustion.

The result of that influence is impressive: If Eliot can connect nothing with nothing, then *The Bridge*, with its emphasis on connections, is the antithesis of Eliotic aesthetics. Crane finds connections everywhere, and the poem's two major symbols, the bridge and the river, are both connectors, uniting distant or separate elements of the country. They are a brilliant pair of symbols, necessary complements. While the river connects one end of the country with another, it also divides it and requires a counter-symbol; the bridge, ridiculous without a river underneath, provides the literally overarching symbol of unification. The poem also strives to unify its disparate elements in ways that neither Eliot's nor Pound's work needs to do. The individual poems in *The Bridge* are much more genuinely separate than the individual cantos, certainly than the sections of *The Waste Land*. They are, for the most part, fully capable of standing alone, poems of unquestionable autonomy. What they lack, when separated from the whole, is the thematic power of Crane's emphasis on unity and wholeness. It is the constant harping on the theme that drives it home for the reader, the continual transformations of the quotidian into the symbolic, the universal. A bridge in New York becomes the symbol of America; a river becomes the Mississippi, which becomes another symbol of the enormous variety and range of experience in the country; a woman becomes Pocahontas, whose presence in the poem leads toward an exploration of American history. Crane shared with his contemporaries Carl Sandburg and John Dos Passos a desire to write works that encompassed the whole of the national experience, which remained open to the promise of America. Dos Passos's novel trilogy, *USA* (1937), has many affinities with *The Bridge* and with William Carlos Williams's *Paterson*.

Two other significant modern poets have sought to capture America in poem sequences, but they have differed from Crane's method in their insistence on the local as the key to the universal. Both Williams's *Paterson* and Charles Olson's *The Maximus Poems* (both of which appeared over a number of years) portray American life by concentrating on individual cities. Neither work shows the kind of boundless enthusiasm and optimism that Crane displays, probably because their very close relationships with the microcosms of Paterson, New Jersey, and Gloucester, Massachusetts, force them to see society with all its warts. Crane's general view, like Whitman's before him, allows him the luxury of not seeing the country close up, of blithely ignoring what does not suit him. Williams, on the other hand, can see all the squalor and pollution of the Passaic River and show them to the reader, but he can also see the falls. His optimism is a greater achievement than Crane's because it is harder won. So too with Olson, who, even while railing against the economic exploitation of nature and what he calls the "perjoracracy" of American society, can still see its possibilities.

While the two works share many similarities, they are also different in many ways. *Paterson* reflects Williams's scientific interest in minutiae, his Imagist background, his passionate attachment to place. The poem focuses almost entirely on the city of Paterson and environs, scarcely bothering to suggest the ways in which it is representative of the larger society. That connection

Williams leaves to the reader to make. He says repeatedly in the poem, "No ideas but in things," and he holds fast to this precept. He makes a collage of newspaper accounts, essays, personal recollection, and direct observation. One of the poem's great innovations, in fact, is Williams's use of unreworked materials, such as newspaper reports, personal letters, and historical accounts. *Paterson* proceeds not by wrenching its materials into poetic form, but by building the poetry around the materials that are evidence of life; it is a genuinely organic work in the most exact sense of its growing out of, and thereby taking its form from, the materials it employs. Williams criticized Eliot for the elitism of his poetry and his criticism; in *Paterson* he demonstrated his commitment to an egalitarian poetry. Unlike Eliot, he does not shy away from the contingency and chaos of life, does not feel obliged to superimpose an artificial order, but instead is content to live with what order he can discover in the world around him. He is closer to Crane and Whitman than to the method of the *Cantos*.

Projective verse

It is Olson who employs Pound's poetics toward a Whitmanian vision of America. Like *Paterson*, *The Maximus Poems* are grounded in a specific place, but they employ the sweeping style, the cross-cultural borrowing, the often declamatory tone of the *Cantos*. Tate says of Pound's work that despite all the allusions, quotations, and foreign sources, the structure and method of the *Cantos* is simply conversational, the talk of literate men over a wide range of subjects. *The Maximus Poems* are also heavily conversational, relying on a listener for all the speaker's pronouncements. They embody a curious paradox: Despite their ostensible epistolary structure (Olson calls the separate poems letters, and even addresses them to various individuals), their principal unit of structure is speech-related.

These poems are the major work exemplifying Olson's theory of "projective verse." In an attempt to break the tyranny of the traditional poetic line and the iambic foot, Olson proposes a system of "composition by field," of thinking in terms larger than the line, of composing by means of, not a formal unit, but a logical one. The line of poetry should reflect the thought it contains and be limited by the breath of the speaker. A line, therefore, is roughly equivalent to an utterance, and should be controlled by it, rather than forcing the thought to conform to the limitations of the line, as in traditional verse. Although few of the other practitioners of projective verse—Robert Duncan, Robert Creeley, Denise Levertov, Edward Dorn—have insisted on a "breath unit" as an essential part of the definition of what they do, Olson does insist on it as the standard for the poetic line, and the result in *The Maximus Poems* is that the letters have a strikingly oral quality. Each poet, Olson believed, must strike his own rhythm in poetry as personal as a signature.

PERSONAL SEQUENCES

Of course, not all sequences have dealt with issues of such enormous scope. When poetry took a confessional turn in the 1950's, so did the poem sequence. Two of the most notable examples of the genre are Robert Lowell's *Life Studies* (1959) and John Berryman's *The Dream Songs* (1969) both of which employ the techniques of sequencing toward highly personal ends. Lowell's career moved from the highly formal poetry he learned under the influence of Ransom at Kenyon College to a looser style. By the time of *Life Studies*, he was able to include a long prose section, "91 Revere Street," something that would have been unthinkable even a few years before. Since each poem deals with a discrete event or mental state or person from a poet's past, little is lost when individual poems are read out of sequence.

By contrast, Berryman's *The Dream Songs* gain greatly by their association with one another. Forming as they do a more or less unified narrative of the life of their protagonist, Henry, the poems develop as they go along, and to excerpt one or a few is to lose much of the flavor of the whole. Alternately riotous and melancholy, boastful and mournful, the songs career through moods and events at a furious pace. Even the voices are unstable. Henry uses a variety of ways of talking about himself, sometimes "I," sometimes "Henry," sometimes even "you," and there is even a voice of a heckler, which may or may not be a separate person, who addresses him as Mr. Bones and who speaks in the parlance of nineteenth century minstrel shows. The poems gain a formal tension in the play between the looseness of the story and the rigid structure; while a given song may use multiple voices, employ jumps in logic or time frame, or tinker with silences and double entendre, it will always contain eighteen lines in three six-line stanzas, a form that the poet says he learned from Yeats. The poems, like Lowell's, chronicle the weaknesses, failures, successes, and torments of their creator, although Berryman's are always masked by the story line.

ENGLISH AND IRISH POEM SEQUENCES

While much of the most interesting work in sequences has been done by American poets, some very fine sequences have come out of England and Ireland, including the work of some recent poets, among them Geoffrey Hill, Ted Hughes, Seamus Heaney, and Charles Tomlinson. Hughes worked with sequences on several occasions, and the most notable product of those experiments was his *Crow* (1970). The book was his first effort at creating a mythology, at overthrowing the tired mythology of Christianity. Where Christ is human, loving, gentle, compassionate, soothing, and bloodless, representing the human desire for order and tranquillity, Crow is lusty, violent, animal, raucous, deceitful, cruel, unsympathetic, and, perhaps worst of all, cacophonous. He represents those qualities of disorder and chaos that humankind tries to control with such myths as Christianity, the side that will not be controlled or denied. Yet Crow is not human; he tries at one point to be, but fails, and the closest he comes is in acquiring language. As an effort at wholesale mythmaking, *Crow* is best read as a complete sequence, since the function of Crow himself is often not fully explained by a single poem.

Hughes furthers the project of sequence-making to greater or lesser extents in other work, including *Gaudette* (1970), *Moon-Whales and Other Moon Poems* (1976), and the very late *The Birthday Letters* (1998). This last is a series of poems written over a period of a quarter century and beginning just a few years after the death of Hughes's wife, poet Sylvia Plath. Hughes's investigation of her genius and pain is raw, honest, careful, and sensitive, opening with his first sighting of her in a photo of newly arrived Fulbright scholars. In "Freedom of Speech" he considers her sixtieth birthday party, if it had happened, and finds everyone concerned—her parents living and dead, her children, even her horse Ariel—smiling and in a sense satisfied, all except Hughes and

Plath themselves. In the last poem, "Red," he notes that while red was her chosen color, blue was her color of life; the adoption of red, while leading her into some of her greatest poetry, also leads her away from life and sanity and toward the death that came, over the years, to seem so inevitable.

Geoffrey Hill, the maker of several sequences, including "Funeral Music," "The Songbook of Sebastian Arrurruz," "Lachrimae," and "An Apology for the Revival of Christian Architecture in England," created a figure similar to Crow in his domination of the poetic landscape in King Offa of the *Mercian Hymns* (1971). Offa is the presiding spirit of the West Midlands, the setting of the work, a figure out of medieval history whose presence explains and unifies the poem as Williams's Paterson and Joyce's Finn do in *Paterson* and *Finnegans Wake* (1939), respectively. Whereas *Crow* takes on the whole of Western experience and culture, Hill satisfies himself with the problems of the England he knows. He is deeply rooted in place, in the sense of history and geography of his England, and the mythology he creates is local, as opposed to the universality of the Crow myth.

In *Mercian Hymns* a series of thirty "prose poems" (although Hill objected to the phrase, he offered nothing in its place) present scenes from past and present English life—especially that of the West Midland region—so juxtaposed that Hill and his grandmother and Offa all appear as figures in the work. Hill drew from literature, history, philosophy, architecture, and anthropology for his materials, weaving them into a tapestry of place. Like Hughes, Hill has continued his work in sequences, most notably in "An Apology for Christian Architecture in England" from *Tenebrae* (1978) and the book-length *The Triumph of Love* (1998).

In these works, so different from each other in numerous ways, Hill investigates the intersection of history, morality, religion, and literature from a perspective of personal outrage. In the 150 small sections of *The Triumph of Love*, he looks back at the barbarity and horrors of the century just ending, considering the role of language, poetry (Donne and Herbert and Dryden and Milton as well as more recent practitioners), the uses of religion, genuine faith, and personal culpability. If in the end he indicts humanity, himself included, for its short-comings, he does so because he believes, he knows, that

we can be better than we are. Redemption, although not likely based on past evidence, is not beyond humanity's reach. He has been compared to Eliot in his concern for the relation of the modern world to traditional society, the function of belief in personal life, the impulse to withdraw from the world; yet he is unlike Eliot in his insistence on locale, as well as in his distrust of his impulse to reform the world. Hill's verse has a built-in heckler, a questioner of motives and achievements. If he owes much to Eliot (and of that there can be no doubt), he also shares many qualities with Hughes, including the recognition of man's animal side and the ferocity of some of his poetry.

Seamus Heaney also sets his poem sequences in a specific place. Throughout his work, Heaney, an Ulster Catholic, is concerned with the relation of his language and the literary forms in which he works to the history of his people and their current troubles. That concern culminates in *North* (1975), in which he explores the history of Irish oppression through poetic excavation. Probing back into literary history, he settles on a modification of Old English poetics, with its heavy alliteration, its pounding rhythms, and its cacophonous vocabulary, as a means of transporting himself out of contemporary Ireland and back to the beginning of the conquests of the Celts by Germanic, Roman, and English armies. He finds an analogous archaeological situation in the excavation of the bog people in Jutland.

The book is made up of two very loosely structured sequences, within which are smaller and more tightly controlled sequences. The first section of the book is the historical exploration and an attempt to turn the intractable forces of history and politics into a workable personal mythology. The section is framed with poems dealing with Antaeus, the earthbound giant of Greek mythology, and indeed all the poems gather their power as well as much of their material from the land. The poems about the bog people and Heaney's reaction to them lie at the very heart of the section, forming a smaller sequence of their own. The poet is also concerned in this first section, through his interest in the bog people, with the Viking occupation of Ireland, and out of that interest grows a small sequence, "Viking Dublin: Trial Pieces." The poem's six sections carry the poet, by means of an ancient whalebone carved as a child's toy, into the Ireland of the Vikings and into those aspects of culture, the poet's culture, that are remnants of that time.

Having made his peace with the past, Heaney turns in part 2 to present social and political conditions. Like the first, this section is a loose thematic sequence, all of the poems building around the same set of subjects: violence, oppression, and suspicion in occupied Ulster. Within the section is the powerful sequence "Singing School." The poem takes its title from Yeats's "Sailing to Byzantium," which hints at his ambivalence toward the conditions in his homeland. Like Yeats, he finds himself torn between the desire to escape the mayhem and violence surrounding him and his need to remain attached to the land. The sequence is composed of six poems recounting Heaney's personal encounters with the forces of oppression, with the highly charged emphasis on personal dialect and language, with the frustration that leads to violence and the fear that violence spawns. "Singing School" is one of the few modern poems to rival Yeats in the authentic presentation of emotional and intellectual responses to social turbulence and personal danger.

One of the most interesting efforts at writing a poem sequence in the mid-century period is the collective poem *Renga* (1971), written by Charles Tomlinson, with Octavio Paz, Jacques Roubaud, and Edoardo Sanguinetti. The *renga* is a traditional Japanese form, a chain poem written collectively, an effort to overcome the ego by blending one's poetry with that of others, sometimes many others. The emphasis is on continuity rather than individual brilliance, and as such is another form of that strain of Eastern thought whose goal is self-effacement. These four Western poets broke with tradition in establishing as the basis of their *renga* a Western form, the sonnet. Each one began a section which was to run for seven sonnets, and each contributed part, a quatrain, a tercet, or a couplet, to each of the first six. The seventh was then to be written by the poet who had begun the series. Sanguinetti declined to write a sonnet at the end of his cycle, declaring that it was complete, so the sonnets total twenty-seven instead of the expected twenty-eight. The multilingual poems, translated into English by Tomlinson, have as their goal the laying aside of ego and personal style for the greater goal of the poem's unity.

The foregoing discussion might give the impression that the poem sequence is the only serious form that po-

etry has taken. Such is not the case, of course. Not all poets have written sequences or have cared to try; a few modern poets have worked successfully in longer, sustained, traditional forms, among them W. H. Auden and Wallace Stevens. Then, too, the short poem has been the most prevalent form in this age. Nevertheless, the sequence is one of modern poetry's great contributions to literature.

Confessional poetry

One of the important divergences from the modernist program in the wake of World War II was the turn toward a more personal poetry, even a painfully personal, confessional poetry. No doubt the shift was motivated in part by politics; a number of those writers who had espoused the impersonal theory of art had also veered dangerously close to totalitarian political thought. Eliot had openly proclaimed himself a reactionary in politics and religion, while Pound, institutionalized at Saint Elizabeth's Hospital, provided an irrefutable link between modernism and fascism. Moreover, the turn toward personal poetry was part of a larger move away from the academic, often obscure verse of Eliot and Pound and toward a more open, more accessible poetry. Among the models for such a move were Whitman and Dickinson, although Whitman's contribution to the proletarianization of poetry was not in confessional but in Beat poetry.

The confessional school was, in its beginnings, a specifically regional movement; indeed, it had deep historical roots in Puritan New England. Puritan literature characteristically revealed the struggle of the soul with belief and with evil; in a world where the Devil was so ominously and constantly present, the soul could never be at rest, and the writings of Edward Taylor and Jonathan Edwards, along with a host of lesser preachers, show the vigilance that the believer must maintain in his war with the powers of darkness. Those highly personal revelations are often public in nature; that is, the purpose for telling of the pits and snares into which one has fallen and out of which one has endeavored to climb is to better equip one's neighbors or one's congregation to fight off the blandishments of the forces of Hell. Yet this is not the only function of such revelations.

In the poetry of Anne Bradstreet, the purpose of such personal revelations is much more private, cathartic; she seems to need release from the pressures and torments of her life, and in writing about them she externalizes them. In the frequency with which her poems deal not with salvation and temptation, but fear of death, anxiety for children's well-being, hope, aspirations for the future, and love for her husband, she displays the privacy of her revelations. These are not pulpit-poems, as so many of Taylor's are, not poems of a person who is first of all a citizen of God's City on the Hill, but rather of a woman, mother, and wife.

Another major model for confessionalism was Emily Dickinson. Her poetry, in its patterns of thought, its death-obsession, its simultaneously domestic and violent imagery, its self-absorption, and its veerings toward the insane and the clairvoyant, exemplifies many of the themes and treatments that show up in confessional poetry. Dickinson's fiercely personal verse concerns itself not with the workings of self-in-society, but with the self-in-its-own-society. In poem 465, "I heard a Fly buzz—when I died," for example, she writes not of death as a universal experience nor of the communal effects of death, but of the personal experience of dying. The poem gains its power from the tension between the commonplace of a buzzing fly and the extraordinary circumstance of a dying person's taking notice of it. Certainly death itself is a commonplace, but Dickinson's attempt to portray the workings of the mind of dying person, or one who is already dead, makes the reader's experience of that death extraordinary. In other poems she makes equally astonishing leaps into madness, despair, delight, grief, solitude, even into closed coffins, and in each of those poems the most remarkable feature is the stark, unmediated sense of reality that she conveys. The states of being in her poems are almost never filtered through the grid of literature; rather, they come directly from her experience, either real or imagined. Like Whitman, she insists on the genuineness of experience and shuns conventions and received forms or modes of expression. Often their very genuineness makes the poems grate on the reader; their cumulative effect can be very nerve-jangling, owing in large measure to her intense rendering of emotion.

It is possible to see the beginnings of contemporary confessional poetry in Pound's *The Pisan Cantos* (1948), which demonstrate a radical departure from the poet's earlier work, focusing much more heavily on personal experience in the nightmare world of his Italian captivity. Yet Pound was never properly speaking a "confessional poet," and perhaps no such thing existed until 1959, when W. D. Snodgrass's *Heart's Needle* and Lowell's *Life Studies* appeared. Lowell has claimed that teaching Snodgrass at the University of Iowa was the greatest single factor in the conversion of his poetry from the intricately formal style of *The Mills of the Kavanaughs* (1951) to the immediacy of *Life Studies*. Certainly it was more than coincidence that the two works appeared in the same year and displayed such similarity in their use of personal material.

Yet there are important differences, as well. Snodgrass, even while looking squarely at the events of his life, incorporating them unglossed into his poetry, maintains a cool irony. *Heart's Needle*, for example, deals directly with his relationship with his daughter in the wake of his divorce. The sequence is filled with moments of melancholy and pathos, rue and self-recrimination. All the while, though, the poet keeps a certain distance from the Snodgrass who is his subject, or attempts to, for the detachment is in constant danger of breaking down. His concentration on the versification, on the syllabics in which he writes, on ironic self-deprecation, on himself as spectator of a scene in which he is also the principal actor, all wrestle with the impulse to bare his feelings. That impulse is most victorious on the edges of poetry: the ends of verses and the ends of sections, at those interstices where the momentum of the conscious poetic necessarily falters. The effect on the reader is a periodic jarring, as the rhythm of the waltz around Snodgrass's true feelings is tripped up by their sudden appearance, by the protruding foot of honest emotion that refuses to be denied. This struggle between alternating sides of the poet's self is paradigmatic of the inner war that manifests itself in all of the chief confessional poets. In Snodgrass, however, it is more gentle, more intellectualized, perhaps, than in any of the others. One rarely has the sense in reading his work that his struggle is of a self-destructive, violent nature, as it is with the others.

The poems of Lowell's confessional mode, similarly, while they may display a greater urgency of self-revelation, are often gentler in tone than those of Plath, Sexton, or Berryman. Still, it is important to remember that not all of Lowell's work is confessional, not even at the time when he was most closely identified with the movement. Two of the sections of *Life Studies* deal with material that cannot be called confessional, and part 1 cannot even be termed personal. Nevertheless, both of those sections show affinities with the work in part 4, "Life Studies," for which the book is most commonly remembered. In the poem about Ford Madox Ford, for example, the laughing, trivializing reminiscence suddenly gives way in the last sentence to "Ford,/ you were a kind man and you died in want." Like Snodgrass's poems, Lowell's often turn on final switchbacks, reclaiming the poet's memory from the trivial, the quotidian, the petty details of scenes and relatives. Those final moments can be quiet, as in the recollection of his father's last words in "Terminal Days at Beverly Farms." Yet those quiet endings thinly veneer a dangerous, even violent reality trying to break through, as the poet, holding a locked razor in "Waking in the Blue," cannot be trusted any more than the wife in "'To Speak of Woe That Is in Marriage'" trusts her drunken husband. The madness and violence of Lowell's poetry contends with the understatement and irony he learned from the Fugitives Tate and Ransom. The controlled diction of his verse gives a greater cutting edge, in its implicit denial, to the wild swings of his mental and emotional life.

Not all of the confessional poets attempted to control those swings as did Lowell and Snodgrass. Berryman, for one, actively exploited the extremes of his emotional states for comic and grotesque effects in *The Dream Songs*, and even invented separate voices to accommodate separate levels of consciousness. Henry speaks of himself in both the third and the first person and goes through periods of wild elation and equally wild despair, through paranoia and delusions of grandeur, and through it all there is the voice of the heckler, the voice of Mr. Bones that undercuts and mocks all other voices. The result is a multilayered narrative in which the various states exist not quite simultaneously but nearly so, on different levels, reflecting the layering of an embattled consciousness. Numerous writers, among them Berryman's first wife, Eileen Simpson, in her book *Poets in Their Youth* (1982), have commented on the wild swings of mood to which Berryman was subject, the turbulence of his personal life, including his alcohol-

ism, his difficulty with his mother, and his extreme, myopic intensity when he was writing. Those various strains find their mythologized way into *The Dream Songs*, and their much more direct way into *Delusions, Etc. of John Berryman*, published shortly before his death in 1972.

Sylvia Plath and Anne Sexton, too, fought their wars much more openly than Lowell, their one-time teacher. Plath in particular dissected her life with a ferocity that, while it is certainly descended from Dickinson's work, is not comparable with any other poet's self-revelation. One of the most disturbing features of the public reception of the work of Berryman, Plath, and Sexton is the morbid fascination with the personal details that their poems reveal. Clearly, Plath fuels such interest; she spares the reader nothing, or virtually nothing, of the pain and despair of her life, yet her poetry is far from the mere raving of a madwoman. She controls, directs, and mythologizes her material rather than remaining its victim. In "Lady Lazarus," from the posthumous *Ariel* (1965), she becomes not simply a woman with suicidal tendencies, but a mythological goddess who dies periodically to rise revivified from the ashes, phoenixlike, to "eat men like air."

In "Daddy" she uses the same material, the pattern of repeated suicide attempts, in the opposite direction. No longer a power-goddess but the victim of abandonment by her father (who died when she was eight), she assumes the role of archetypal victim, a Jewess of the Holocaust, casting her father, whom she comes to associate with all Germans, as her Nazi oppressor. Her great ability to find in the world around her the correlatives of her personal suffering, or perhaps her ability to bring the events and cultural institutions around her into focus through the vehicle of her personal disorder, turns her poetry into a striking, if at times repellent, force. One almost certainly will not feel at ease reading her work; one will almost as certainly be impressed with its power, with the force of her imaginative wrestling with her demons. Such poetic revelation of spiritual turbulence is rarely seen in English literature; perhaps not since Gerard Manley Hopkins has a poet bared psychic anguish so totally.

Each of the celebrated confessional poets has produced very impressive work, although not all of it is of a kind, yet the slackness and self-parodic nature of some of Sexton's and Berryman's later work point to a weakness of the genre: The self can be bared only so often, it seems, before the reader has seen quite enough. The profusion of terrible poetry by followers of these writers has suggested its limitations as well as its attractions. It is very easy to write wretched confessional poetry, since the subject matter is always at hand. It is much more difficult to turn that subject matter into art.

This is reactionary poetry, and like most things reactionary it remains on the fringe; it is extremist. There has been a marked movement in poetry after World War II toward personal, autobiographical poetry. Writers as different as Robert Duncan, Allen Ginsberg, Robert Creeley, Stevie Smith (who, although British, most resembles Dickinson), Thom Gunn, and Jon Silkin all make use of material from their own lives. Very few writers now shy away from autobiographical material as Eliot would have them do, and as writers of the first half of the century often did. Confessional poetry, then, although not of the mainstream itself, however much its apologists, such as M. L. Rosenthal in *The New Poets* (1967), may argue for its centrality, has turned the course of poetry toward the personal.

The work of its main practitioners will probably survive despite, not because of, the confessional nature of the poetry. The ironic self-observation of Snodgrass, the wistful, mournful verse of Lowell, with its tension between the trivial and the painful, the hilarious mythologizing of Berryman's *The Dream Songs*, the power and ferocity of Plath's imagery and phrasing will stand with the work of any group of poets of any age. It is well to remember that much poetry remains important *despite* some major component, be it subject matter, thematic treatment, or political orientation. There is much that modern readers find disagreeable, after all, in Geoffrey Chaucer, John Milton, and William Shakespeare.

BEAT AND MOVEMENT POETRY

Confessional poetry provided, if not the answer for modern poetry after World War II, at least an articulation of the problem. During the 1950's two other literary groups sprang up, one in America and one in Britain, both of which were also concerned with the plight of the individual in an intractable world. Beat and Movement

poetries are violently dissimilar expressions of similar revulsions to the same world situation. Both react against the formalist art of the modernists, against uptight, bourgeois, philistine society, against the repressive political and cultural institutions of the period. The differences between the two lie more in national attitudes and predispositions than in first principles. Moreover, both show affinities with existentialism.

The self underwent a series of shocks beginning with World War II, with its death camps, its blitzkriegs, its atomic bombs. The twentieth century was distinguished by a new scale of violence and terror: the virtual destruction or totalitarian suffocation of vast areas, of whole nations or peoples. In the face of that leveling destruction, the individual was quite lost. Furthermore, the prevailing ideologies of the century did not given the individual much room for maneuver. Both communism and fascism, of course, are anti-individual in their very orientation and quite willing to sacrifice the autonomy of the self for the good of the state. Yet free-enterprise capitalist democracy also partook of its dollop of statism in the modern world, the most outstanding example of which was the McCarthy-era witch-hunts, those exercises designed not so much to ferret out saboteurs and seditionists as to enforce conformity and steamroll deviation from the average. As already mentioned, the impersonal theory of poetry put forth by Eliot and his circle coincided historically as well as theoretically with the rise of totalitarian politics, and it was that entire complex that writers of the 1950's sought to overthrow. To see the argument in purely literary terms is to miss a great deal of the significance of the action.

Both the Beats and the Movement poets, then, wrestled with the problem posed by existentialism; namely, how does the individual maintain his autonomy in the face of an overwhelming, repressive society? Their answers, while divergent, displayed certain similarities that can perhaps be understood in terms of various strains of existentialism. The Movement writers leaned more toward despair and quiet rebellion from within the ranks, while the Beats were open insurrectionists, confronting a hostile world with wild romanticism.

Philip Larkin has written of life at Oxford during the war, showing how, at the very moment when students normally developed their grandest ideas of themselves, the privation, uncertainty, and anxiety of wartime undercut their natural tendencies. He suggested that his own self-effacing poetry and that of his contemporaries were in large measure a by-product of Nazi aerial technology, that the Blitz and the V-2 rockets reduced the range of options available to the undergraduates, and that he never broke out of that range. One has the sense in Larkin's work that he is trapped, that society closes in around the individual before he has a chance to stake out his own territory. That sense is shared in the work of many of his contemporaries, although it takes many different forms.

The generation preceding the Movement, including the Auden circle, was at times highly political. Many writers became involved in the urgent issues of the day; many actively sought roles in the Spanish Civil War. William Empson accompanied Mao Zedong on the Long March. Most, although by no means all, of the writers of the 1930's embraced leftist politics to some degree, and a great many of them, like Auden himself, later either repudiated or quietly slipped away from their earlier beliefs. The Movement writers, even while sometimes claiming kinship with the writers of the 1930's, particularly Empson, shied away from the grand political gesture, as indeed they seemed to suspect all large gestures.

The Movement poets were in some respects a strikingly homogenous group—much more so than the Beats. All of the principals attended one of the two major English universities: Larkin, Kingsley Amis, Robert Conquest, John Wain, Elizabeth Jennings, and John Holloway went to Oxford, while Donald Davie, D. J. Enright, and Thom Gunn were at Cambridge. They were from, or at least they celebrated in their writings, middle-class or working-class backgrounds. For many, education was interrupted by war, and as a result they seemed, in Ted Hughes's analysis, to "have had enough."

The Oxford group, for the most part, emerged from the penumbra of neo-Romanticism. Larkin, for example, recorded his struggle to free himself from the influence of Yeats, and, through Vernon Watkins, of Dylan Thomas. His early poetry is largely a rehash of Yeats's style and imagery, neither of which sounds at all natural coming from Larkin. Not until the privately printed *XX Poems* of 1951 did his true voice begin to assert itself.

Similarly, much of Jennings's early work fairly drips with syrup, wending its way through enchanted woods on the trail of unicorns. Like Larkin, and, for that matter like most of the Oxford writers, she began to find herself only around 1950, although glimmers of her distinctive style had begun to show themselves earlier.

The Cambridge three took a more direct route, one that led straight through their studies under F. R. Leavis. As Blake Morrison points out in *The Movement: English Poetry and Fiction of the 1950's* (1980), all three credit Leavis with shaping their thought and, to a great extent, their poetry. His skeptical rationalism served as a natural springboard to the highly rational, un- or even antimetaphorical poetry of the Movement.

The Movement, then, was a cultural and social phenomenon as well as a literary clique. A great many British writers from about the same time, some of whom turned out to be highly averse to the Movement views, have at one time or another been seen as belonging in some sense or other. The Movement was a reactionary school, looking back to Edward Thomas and the Georgians as well as to the writers of the 1930's for its models, looking away from both the modernism of Eliot and Pound and the Romanticism of such 1940's poets as Thomas, David Gascoyne, and Edith Sitwell. It was anti-Romantic, antimetaphorical, highly rationalistic, and formally very traditional. It stressed colloquial diction and concreteness against both highly wrought "poetic" diction and the airy abstraction of neo-Romanticism and English Surrealism. The tone is often flat, neutral, especially in Larkin, and a chief mode, as one might suspect, is irony. The irony, like the formal precision, is a stay against the isolation and the alienation that lies behind much of this writing.

Nearly everything about the Movement writers points to their alienation as an almost necessary state of young, thinking people of that time. They stood outside the institutions, either looking in the windows or ridiculing those inside, but in either case they were outsiders. Amis's Jim Dixon in *Lucky Jim* (1954) is a textbook case of a Movement hero, an outsider who suddenly finds himself on the inside, who is suddenly confronted with the smallness and tackiness and pomposity and arrogance of the powerful and well-heeled. Typically, he causes disaster wherever he goes.

Larkin lived perhaps closer to the Movement program than any of the others, always isolated, always provincial, always alienated, reeking of spiritual exhaustion and cultural bankruptcy to the point that he could barely bring himself to write at all. (By his own count, he averaged three to five short poems per year.) His poetry has also remained closest to the original line; much of his late work is very similar in spirit and tone, and even technique, to that written in the early 1950's. Its poetic qualities lie in its tight control and its compression rather than in any overtly poetic devices. It crawls rather than leaps, uses reason and intellection rather than surges of spirit. His is a highly Apollonian poetry.

To find the Dionysian poetry of the 1950's, one must leap an ocean and a continent, to San Francisco. If one were to take as a starting point the same basic rejection of values and suspicion of social and cultural institutions that prompted the Movement, and add to it the rejection of values and styles adopted as a makeshift solution by the Movement (and *perhaps* also of the personal, Freudian anguish of the confessional poets), one would be left with approximately the Beat mentality. While the Beats rejected the cozy middle-class complacency of the Eisenhower 1950's, they did so with characteristically American flamboyance, as opposed to the typically British reserve, tightness, and control. The Movement fought by withdrawing; the Beats fought by setting the enemy on his ear.

At its broadest, the Beat generation can be considered to include not only those San Francisco writers (and occasional drop-ins from the East Coast) normally associated with it—Lawrence Ferlinghetti, Gary Snyder, William Everson, Allen Ginsberg, Jack Kerouac, Philip Whalen, Michael McClure, Gregory Corso—but also, as John Clellan Holmes suggests in an essay in Lee Bartlett's *The Beats: Essays in Criticism* (1981), the Black Mountain group of Olson, Duncan, Creeley, Dorn, and Levertov, and perhaps even the New York circle centered on John Ashbery, Kenneth Koch, and Frank O'Hara. Most of these writers share certain attitudes toward literature and toward their audience.

One of the first calls-to-arms was sounded in Olson's 1950 essay "Projective Verse," in which, among other things, he calls for an end to the pedestrian verse line. Olson felt that the tyranny of the accentual-syllabic line,

which had ruled since the Renaissance in English prosody, was strangling creativity. He therefore made his plea for an open-form poetic line, a variable line based on the requirements of phrasing and the poet's own natural voice—and on the devices peculiar to the typewritten poem. What Olson really argues for is the primacy of the poet in the poetry. No longer, he says, should the poet wrench verse around to meet the standards of an exhausted poetics. Rather than emerging from the head only (and this is perhaps the importance of the breath-unit), the poem must emerge from the effort of the whole person. Olson even gives form to his idea in the essay itself. This is no textbook example of essay writing; its form is a large part of its function. The reader knows simply by reading it whether he is one of the chosen, for it is designed to call to the loyal and heap confusion on the enemy; it is intended to perplex the sturdy specimens of traditionalism simply by its language. This exclusionary technique became a hallmark of the entire Beat experience.

Certainly the Beat lifestyle was designed to be offputting to nonhipsters, with its slang, its sexual and drug experimentation, its rootlessness. The poetry itself also challenged its audience, with its free-flowing forms, its often incantatory rhythms, its wild flights of imagination, its sometimes coarse language. These qualities established themselves very early, so that when Robert Lowell, then a rising young poet with a formidable reputation, went to San Francisco to give readings in 1956, he found the audiences bored with his work because they had already become accustomed to hearing verse best typified by the then still unpublished "Howl" of Allen Ginsberg.

If confessionalism looked to New England for its source, then the Beats looked to Camden, New Jersey. There could have been no Beat poetry without Walt Whitman. The movement followed him not only in the openness of its form and in its attitudes but also in its declamatory poetic voice. Ginsberg was particularly indebted to Whitman in the matter of a public poetic voice. Whitman was not the only source, of course, although he was the most important one. Others would include William Blake (whose voice, says Ginsberg, came to him in 1948, reciting poems), D. H. Lawrence, Henry Miller, William Carlos Williams, and Kenneth Rexroth.

These last three were early champions of the fledgling movement as well as models, and Rexroth especially offered intense verbal support. Williams had said that Eliot set back American poetry twenty years or more, that his highly academic, closed poetry flew in the face of the proletarian, egalitarian verse toward which Whitman pointed. When the twenty years (more or less) were up, the new proletarian uprising made itself felt.

In a movement that is overtly social as well as literary, there are always social as well as literary sources. Black culture, especially jazz, Mexican peasant culture for dress and even behavioral models, Zen Buddhism, Hinduism (and Asian culture in general), were among the origins of the exoticism of Beat life. Yet much of what the Beats adopted they turned upside down. There was a demonic quality about their movement, an urge toward self-immolation, toward willful dissipation and disintegration, that was lacking in the originals. While it could be argued that the fiery urge toward dissolution was a by-product of the jazz influence, that the Beats learned self-destruction from Charlie Parker and Billie Holiday, it seems more likely that such an impulse was a fairly natural outgrowth of the rejection of safe, "straight" values. Yet the movement was angelic as well as demonic; "Beat," as Everson reminds the reader, means "Beatific." While Everson may stand closer than any of his compatriots to a traditional Christian mysticism, an ultimate goal of the Beats was a kind of godliness. If they employed the tigers of wrath rather than the horses of instruction, it was nevertheless to arrive at wisdom. It is easy for an outsider to mistake the methods of the Beats for their ends. Certainly there have been many figures both famous and obscure who have used the movement's ideals as a shield for intellectual or moral slovenliness, but just as surely it is a mistake to fail to discern the difference between the pilgrimage and the destination.

Generalizations are dangerous, particularly when dealing with a group of writers so obviously devoted to individualism in life and art, yet there were features common to the generality of Beat poetry. There was a formal openness. The projective verse of Olson and Creeley becomes a wholly subjective form, a totally personal and even unconscious matter in much of Beat writing. Kerouac, who can be considered the discoverer

of the movement, since it was he who named it, hated revision, and his version of revision was to remove and expand sections until they became new works. In many of his novels he wrote in a state of semicontrol, surrealistically allowing his material to take over. In like manner, the poetics of "Howl," for example, work very close to the unconscious. Its rhythmic, pulsating regularities, its incantatory insistence, its word and phrase repetitions insinuate themselves into the reader's (or the auditor's) consciousness, almost without requiring intellectual understanding. It is a poem to be felt as much as to be comprehended. In Gary Snyder's work, crumbled and reassembled syntax creates the effect of compression of thoughts and ideas, of puzzles and conundra stumbled onto in the act of creation. While his poems are considerably more ordered than the prose of William Burroughs's cut-up method, they seem to be springing naturally from the psyche, newly freed from the constraints of rationality.

The formal openness of Beat writing, in fact, is a function of its emphasis on the unconscious, on some aspect of humanity divorced from intellection. The Dionysian impulse is always away from reason, from order, from control, and toward those elements that modern society would have humankind erase or submerge under the great weight of orthodoxy. The use of drugs, of primitive cultures, of Christian mysticism, Oriental meditation, and Hasidic prophecy are all aimed at freeing the kernel of preconscious truth from the centuries-old and miles-deep husk of social conformity and "rational" behavior.

Most of the Beats believed, with Snyder, that if the inner being could be liberated and made to speak for itself, society could be changed. In his essay "Buddha and the Coming Revolution," Snyder quotes the World War I slogan "Forming the new society in the shell of the old," and that slogan can stand as well for the society of one, the primary object of reform for the Beats. Once the individual has learned how to live, the new society can be developed. Only in a society in which people have given up their individuality, where they have willingly immersed their differences in the stagnant waters of conformity, can such a thing as McCarthyism occur. Inevitably, then, the Beats went to the greatest lengths imaginable to assert their individuality. One cannot, after all, write in one's native rhythms unless one knows one's own mind and spirit. The act of writing, then, like living itself, is a political act, and the Beats were as politically visible as any literary group of the twentieth century.

Their work was both important in its own right and tremendously influential. While Ginsberg's *Howl and Other Poems* (1956) and *Kaddish and Other Poems* (1961) and Snyder's *Riprap* (1959), *Myths and Texts* (1960), and *Six Sections from Mountains and Rivers Without End* (1965) are probably the best-known works, there are a host of others. Gregory Corso's *The Mutation of the Spirit* (1964) is clearly a major work, a wrestling with important issues, as is much of Everson's work, including the pre-Beat *The Residual Years* (1968). The sheer mass of good poetry by Everson ensured his continued importance in the movement, although none of it found the audience that Snyder's or Ginsberg's did. Michael McClure, particularly in his drug poems, became a valuable recorder of a phase of experience vital to the movement. It was Ferlinghetti, however, who chronicled the Beat experience and attitude most carefully, and who consciously played the role of Beat poet—sometimes to the point of seemingly losing himself in it. In such books as *A Coney Island of the Mind* (1958) and *The Secret Meaning of Things* (1969), and particularly in such poems as "Autobiography," he captured the essence of Beat life. Perhaps more important, he gave life to the movement through publishing its poets and by overseeing the physical center of the movement in San Francisco's City Lights Bookstore.

WHITHER?

Literature is always an act of becoming, a dialectical process between the mind of a writer and the literary and social-historical forces around him or her. Yet literature at the end of the twentieth century—and to this day—is perhaps uniquely in a state of flux. Its rejection of the past has been so vehement, its condition of upheaval so prolonged, its experimentation so striking that writers and critics alike have come to look upon it as an arrival, as what literature has become. That constant upheaval within modern poetry, however, suggests that such is not the case. Rather, the overthrows and insurrections point to the extremely transitory nature of the modern experi-

ments. In a body of poetry in which versification changed relatively little from Shakespeare to Rossetti, but in which no school of poetics has held sway for much more than a decade since then, the impermanence of modern poetry can hardly be avoided. It may well be that it has arrived at a state of perpetual dislocation, but that is hardly the same as consensus.

The problem lies as much in the modern world as with the writers themselves. When Wallace Stevens says that the modern poem must "find out what will suffice," he implies that the traditional givens of poetry will not suffice, and that they will not because the world has changed. After the myth-analysts and the psychoanalysts of the last one hundred years, after the awful destructions of two world wars, after the rise of modern multinational corporate entities, after the end of traditional society, in the face of post-Cold War terrorists and daily uncertainty, how can poetry be expected to remain where it was? God may or may not be in his Heaven; all is certainly less than right with the world.

So the writing of modern poetry constitutes an incessant quest for form, a struggle to find a form that works in the modern context, that will suffice. The range of attempts can seem utterly baffling, yet it is possible to break them down into several loose categories.

The antimodernist poet recoils from the world, refusing also its chaotic poetics, which he often sees as symptomatic. Instead, antimodernists retreat into traditional forms, writing in regular meters and rhyme schemes, in recognizable stanzaic patterns. Included among the ranks of antemodern poets would be Robert Frost, A. E. Housman, E. A. Robinson, the Georgian poets, the Movement poets, and some of the poetry of the Fugitives, particularly some of the work of John Crowe Ransom and Donald Davidson. Their tradition is primarily English, looking back through Hardy and the Victorians.

By contrast, the modernist poet is, simultaneously, constantly reminded of the literary past and struggling to use it to create a new work of art, to "make it new." This artist's method is probably best described in T. S. Eliot's essay "Tradition and the Individual Talent," in which he says that a new work of art is not merely added to the collection of existing monuments, that a new work both alters and is informed by those already in existence. Eliot is the preeminent modernist poet. Others would include Ezra Pound, Wallace Stevens, Robert Lowell, Geoffrey Hill, Seamus Heaney, Allen Tate, Robert Penn Warren, W. H. Auden and his circle, Sylvia Plath, John Berryman, and W. S. Merwin. The modernist literary inheritance is much more eclectic, and much more continental, than that of the antimodernists, and looks to France, to the Symbolists, for much of its immediate impetus.

Postmodernist poets openly reject the forms and styles of literary tradition in an attempt to create a radically new poetry to engage the world they find. Postmodernists generally choose open forms, employ loose structures, and write out of their own experience. They are much more personal poets than Eliot's modernists, feeling the world move through them, sensing that the necessary forms can be had through self-knowledge rather than through a study of tradition. On the Continent, postmodernists have appeared as Dadaists or Surrealists, and nearly everywhere they are experimentalists. Early types would include Edith Sitwell (sometimes), D. H. Lawrence, William Carlos Williams, Kenneth Rexroth, Louis Zukofsky, David Gascoyne (also sometimes), and Carl Sandburg, while more recent manifestations can be found in the Beats, Charles Olson's Black Mountain group, Ted Hughes, the Liverpool group, and Robert Bly, James Wright, John Ashbery, and their fellow Surrealists.

There is, finally a fourth category, not so much a group as an assortment of leftovers, poets whose work is so individual, whose vision is so much their own, that they defy taxonomic classification. William Butler Yeats is such a poet, certainly, and so too are Hart Crane, Dylan Thomas, Galway Kinnell, and perhaps others already located in one group or another, such as Lawrence, Hill, or Merwin. There are those writers who find themselves confronted with a specific social or political situation that forces their poetry in a direction that it might not otherwise have taken. Such is very likely the case with the Irish poets from Yeats and Louis MacNeice to Seamus Heaney, John Montague, Thomas Kinsella, and Tom Paulin. It may also be that their situation is paradigmatic of modern poetry generally: It is not merely that literature is changing but rather that the context of literature is changing so drastically and so rapidly that writers find themselves in a mad scramble to keep up.

LANGUAGE POETS

Both sides of the Atlantic have experienced developments in this last, largely unclassifiable realm in the "postmodernist" era. Beginning in the late 1970's, America in particular began to see an extreme twist on the postmodernist program in the form of the "Language poets." Growing out of a number of radical poetry journals, most notably $L=A=N=G=U=A=G=E$, from which it takes its name, the movement rejects the author-dominated model of traditional poetry, choosing instead indeterminate forms and incomplete meanings that require the reader to take an active role in creating meaning. The poets and apologists base their approach on a pantheon of radical literary and political thought: deconstruction as practiced especially by Jacques Derrida, the Marxism of the Frankfurt school, the language theories of Jacques Lacan, the experimentalism of Gertrude Stein, the Dadaists, and the poetic practices of such writers as Robert Creeley, Louis Zukofsky, the Objectivists, John Ashbery, and the Russian Futurist Velimir Khlebnikov.

The Language poets use these influences to do battle with what they see as the tyranny of the single-image "voice poem," the poem of individual experience culminating in a dominant image that seeks to explain and justify the poem's existence and control the reader's response. This model of the interaction between active, controlling writer and passive, controlled reader is the point of attack for the Language poets in their prose statements and in their work: Bruce Andrews's *Wobbling* (1981) and *Love Songs* (1982); Charles Bernstein's *Controlling Interests* (1980) and *Islets/Irritations* (1983); Lyn Hejinian's *Writing Is an Aid to Memory* (1978); Ron Silliman's *Tjanting* (1981) and *The Age of Huts* (1986). Their work is often striking in its strangeness, sometimes recalling in its apparent randomness the work of Dada poet Tristan Tzara or various forms of conceptual art. Whether the movement will last or, like Tzara and Dadaism, become a curious byway, an interesting footnote to poetic history, may not be determined for many years.

MARTIAN POETS, WIT AND HUMOR

Pound's dictum to "make it new" has found new and curious adherents in Britain and Ireland since the late

1970's, through a movement and individuals who have sought to bring whimsical observation and satiric scrutiny to the poetic tradition. Craig Raine provided the name of the movement known as the Martian school with the title poem of his collection *A Martian Sends a Postcard Home* (1979). In that poem, the eponymous spaceman observes many of the mundane elements of earth life and makes them alien to the earthling-reader: A car, for instance, becomes a movie with the screen in back so riders can see what they have passed, a telephone is an infant picked up when it cries yet sometimes deliberately awakened by tickling (in dialing a number). This practice of radical re-vision of the world is taken up not only by Raine but also by Christopher Reid and James Fenton, among others. While the Martian poets show a great deal of formal and stylistic variety from one to another, what they share is an emphasis on wit and invention in the treatment of their subjects.

Other writers not specifically in the Martian group who nevertheless rely on wit and humor would include the Ulster poet Paul Muldoon and Wendy Cope. Muldoon's verse is consistently wry and arch; his response to a split national identity (is he British or Irish?), to a history of internecine conflict, is not anger or tragedy but irony. Like Raine, he tests the possibilities of perception and language in *Mules* (1977), *Quoof* (1983), and *Meeting the British* (1987).

Cope investigates the tradition by undermining it. Working in the realm of satire and parody in *Making Cocoa for Kingsley Amis* (1986), she deflates the grandeur of *The Waste Land*, for example, with a series of limericks. Her poems stand as feminist commentaries on a male-dominated tradition of "significance." The nature of her wit is cutting and subversive, and the results are often delightful.

VOICES OF DIVERSITY

One of the major developments in late-century poetry was the development of the voice of the outsider. American minority writers have become increasingly strong. Certainly there have been waves of African American poetry throughout the century, from the Harlem Renaissance between the wars through the Black Arts movement of the 1960's and beyond, from such poets as Langston Hughes, Gwendolyn Brooks and Robert

Hayden to Amiri Baraka, Lucille Clifton, Etheridge Knight, Sonia Sanchez, and Audre Lord. African American poets throughout the century have given voice to people too often silenced by the mainstream culture, while bringing new and dynamic rhythms and forms to American poetry.

Hughes's use of jazz and blues in his work, for instance, together with the marvelous voices of the disenfranchised in poems such as "Madam and the Rentman," "Theme for English B," or "Mother to Son" point the direction for the black poets who follow. While there is a remarkable diversity in the sort of poetry written by those who come later in the century, many subsequent poets—from his near-contemporary Brooks, who died in 2000, to Thylias Moss, whose career began in the last two decades of the century—share with him a great facility with the dramatic monologue, and many of the best remembered African American poems of the century will prove to be those voiced not for the poet, but for characters drawn from the community.

Native American poetry is a somewhat more recent phenomenon on the national scene. Many of the important Native American novelists since 1960 have also written poetry: N. Scott Momaday, Leslie Marmon Silko, James Welch, Louise Erdrich. Often, their work mixes intimate knowledge of tribal life with strong academic influences. Momaday, for instance, draws on his Kiowa ancestry and his experience as a teacher on various reservations in a poetics informed by his graduate studies at Stanford University, where he studied under the formidable Yvor Winters.

Other American Indian poets, such as Simon J. Ortiz and Joy Harjo, are primarily poets. Ortiz is much more heavily grounded than Momaday in his home community, the Acoma Acumeh Pueblo of New Mexico. His concerns with Native American identity, with resistance to assimilation, and with the role of language and poetry in that resistance run through his books, including *Going for the Rain* (1976), *From Sand Creek* (1981), *Woven Stone* (1992), and *After and Before the Lightning* (1994), which records his stay on South Dakota's Rosebud reservation.

The waning century also saw increases in Latino (Alurista, Bernice Zamora, Gloria Anzaldúa) and Asian American (Lawson Fusao Inada, Janice Mirikitani)

Critical Survey of Poetry

voices. Despite the many differences among these writers, they share a concern with both the place of their ethnic group in the larger culture and the dynamics within the group. While Zamora and Anzaldúa, for example, concern themselves with Mexican American struggles in Euro-America, they also critique the macho, sexist culture of the La Raza movement, as represented by Alurista.

The United Kingdom has also seen this increased diversity. A great deal of "British" or "English" poetry—like its fiction—in recent times has come from beyond the customary centers of privilege and power. Gone are the days when poetry was dominated by London, Oxford, and Cambridge, the era of Auden, MacNeice, Spender, and Cecil Day Lewis. As the century came to a close, the poetry scene was increasingly reflecting the provincial, the postcolonial, the racially and sexually diverse nature of contemporary British life.

IRISH POETRY

The final four decades of the twentieth century saw a tremendous flowering of Irish poetry, particularly of poetry from the North. Of that group Heaney is clearly the most prominent feature, although he is joined by Tom Paulin, Paul Muldoon, Derek Mahon, Ciaran Carson, Michael Longley, and Medbh McGuckian as major figures from all points of the political and religious compass. Their work is informed by their experience of the Troubles that began in 1969 and continued throughout the remaining years of the century, although not all of them address the political situation as directly as Heaney. Muldoon's obliqueness often hides his social awareness inside fantastic structures, as in *Madoc: A Mystery* (1990), his epic poem of colonization and cultural domination focusing not on Northern Ireland but on North America. Muldoon asks what might have happened had Robert Southey and Samuel Taylor Coleridge followed through on their project to found a utopian settlement in the United States. The poem follows wild leaps of time, place, person, and philosophical school to conclude that, ultimately, British efforts at colonization do not generally end well.

McGuckian brings a woman's sensibility to the experience in Ulster; she is also one of the few poets to have remained in her native province throughout the Troubles.

In such collections as *The Flower Master* (1982), *Marconi's Cottage* (1992), and *Captain Lavender* (1995) she marries the intensely personal with the political in a verse characterized by sudden juxtapositions and surreal imagery to create a poetry that is intense, fascinating, sometimes forbidding, always intriguing.

The Republic of Ireland also has produced many impressive poets during the same period: Thomas Kinsella, Paul Durcan, John Montague, Paula Meehan, Matthew Sweeney, Eavan Boland. Boland provides an interesting case in her treatment of her status as woman and poet as a postcolonial condition. Her work, particularly in *Outside History* (1990) and *In a Time of Violence* (1994), addresses the customary treatment of women in male Irish poetry and seeks to reclaim the female experience from the mythologizing impulses of that male tradition. That her work has found a very large and enthusiastic audience in America among readers not usually concerned with Irish issues testifies to the timeliness and aptness of her poetry. Her work investigates not merely the power arrangements between the sexes but also the ways in which language and literary practice have served to reify those arrangements. Beyond that diagnosis, however, the great power of Boland's poetry lies in her ability to offer alternatives, to reenvision the dominant myths of the female and invest them with new vigor.

WOMEN'S POETRY

Poetry by women, indeed literature by women, that reexamines male-female relations has been quite prominent in the final decades of the century. The late Angela Carter, for instance, reworked fairy tales and Shakespearean plots to subvert the masculine assumptions of the originals in her fiction. Carol Ann Duffy works similarly in her poetry, which is dominated by the dramatic monologue. If her preferred form is that of Robert Browning, author of "My Last Duchess," the voice she chooses is that of the duchess herself. The title poem of her first volume, *Standing Female Nude* (1985), is a monologue by the model of a Degas-like painter of the female form who takes her existence for granted. Boland also has poems about artists' females—Edgar Degas's washerwomen and Pierre-Auguste Renoir's grape pickers—and arrives at much the same conclusion, although without giving those women voices.

Duffy's nude model is stiff from posing, angry, but spunky and insightful and altogether engaging. Her book *The World's Wife* (1999) is filled with monologues by the wives of famous men in history, myth, and literature: Aesop, Freud, Pilate, Darwin, Faust. These compelling and often hilarious soliloquies remind readers of the extent to which traditional culture has shut out the voice of the woman and either ignored or minimized the contributions of women in the lives of "great men." Because, for so much of the century, British poetry was a men's club, the contributions of writers like Duffy in causing readers to revise their understanding of human nature are immense indeed.

POSTCOLONIAL POETS

It is worth noting that the last two Nobel Prizes in Literature won by English-language poets in the twentieth century went to outlanders: Northern Ireland's Seamus Heaney and St. Lucia's Derek Walcott. Walcott is only one representative of a movement in contemporary poetry: the increasing presence of poets who were either born in or descended from residents of former European colonies in Africa, Asia, and the Caribbean. E. A. Markham, Louise Bennett, James Berry, A. L. Hendricks, Linton Kwesi Johnson, and Edward Kamau Brathwaite from the Caribbean; Fred D'Aguiar, Grace Nichols, Martin Carter, and Jan Carew from Guyana; and Mahmoud Jamal and H. O. Nazareth from India testify to the dynamic poetry scene in the minority communities of England and in the former colonies. Those voices often sound odd to British poetic traditionalists, in the same way that, in the United States, the poetry of Langston Hughes or Amiri Baraka or Gwendolyn Brooks may have initially seemed outside the mainstream even in a country where the example of Whitman has always provided a greater openness.

Walcott is clearly the towering figure among the Caribbean writers—winner not only of the Nobel Prize in 1992 but also of numerous other literary prizes, holder of endowed chairs at American universities, and commander of prime book review space when a new collection appears. While he has been publishing work since the late 1940's, his reputation, if it needed such help, was firmly cemented with the publication of *The Arkansas Testament* (1987) and *Omeros* (1990). The latter is

an epic poem about Caribbean fishermen and their world seen through the filter of Homer's ninth century B.C.E. *Iliad* and *Odyssey* ("Omeros" is a local corruption or variant of "Homer"). In tracing out the passions, rivalries, conquests, and calamities of his characters, Walcott reminds readers that Homer's epics were themselves the tales of fishermen and farmers forced out of their own normal orbits by circumstances larger than themselves, and in so doing he invests his tale, and his people, with a nobility and a grandeur as old as myth.

Poetry has not found itself in such turmoil since Western society careened its way out of the Middle Ages and into the Renaissance. Perhaps when and if society once again settles onto some stable course (and modern weapons technology and multinational economics make that seem unlikely enough), then the course of poetry may also become more uniform. As things stand, though, both society and poetry appear to be headed for a very protracted period of transition. If that is so, then readers of verse will continue to be blessed, or cursed, with the astonishing variety that has characterized modern poetry.

BIBLIOGRAPHY

Acheson, James, and Romana Huk, eds. *Contemporary British Poetry: Essays in Theory and Criticism*. Albany: State University of New York, 1996. Offers a wide-ranging look at the work of feminists and "post feminist" poets, working-class poets, and poets of diverse cultural backgrounds, as well as provocative re-readings of such well-established and influential figures as Donald Davie, Ted Hughes, Geoffrey Hill, and Craig Raine.

Bartlett, Lee, ed. *The Beats: Essays in Criticism*. Jefferson, N. C.: McFarland, 1981. Provides criticism and interpretation of many of the notable Beat poets' works.

Bertram, Vicki, ed. *Kicking Daffodils: Twentieth-Century Women Poets*. Edinburgh, Scotland: Edinburgh University Press, 1997. Eighteen essays demonstrate the need for a thorough reinvestigation of the frameworks within which poetry in general, and women's poetry in particular, is read and critiqued.

Bly, Robert. *Leaping Poetry: An Idea with Poems and Translations*. Boston: Beacon Press, 1975. Part poetry anthology, part critical treatise, this collection presents the idea that great works of art contain leaps within themselves.

Bruns, Gerald L. *Modern Poetry and the Idea of Language*. Rev. ed. Norman, Ill.: Dalkey Archive Press, 2001. Compares two contrasting functions of language: the hermetic, where language is self-contained and self-referencing, and the Orphic, which originates from a belief in the mythical unity of word and being.

Draper, Ronald P. *An Introduction to Twentieth-Century Poetry in English*. New York: St. Martin's Press, 1999. Critical survey of modern poetry, from Thomas Hardy to Seamus Heaney. Considers both the self-conscious revolutionary innovations of modernism and more traditional developments, taking into account the extent to which "English" can no longer be equated solely with England.

Emig, Rainer. *Modernism in Poetry: Motivations, Structures, and Limits*. Boston: Addison Wesley, 1995. Provides a range of criticism and interpretation for such poets as Gerard Manley Hopkins, W. B. Yeats, Ezra Pound, and T. S. Eliot. Includes bibliography and index.

Faas, Ekbert. *Towards a New American Poetics: Essays and Interviews, Olson, Duncan, Synder, Creeley, Bly, Ginsburg*. Santa Barbara, Ca.: Black Sparrow Press, 1979. Examines the nature of poetry authorship through interviews and literary criticism.

Faulkner, Peter. *Modernism*. The Critical Idiom 35. New York: Harper & Row, 1977. Explores the history and criticism of twentieth century literature. Includes bibliography and index.

Fink, Thomas. *"A Different Sense of Power": Problems of Community in Late-Twentieth-Century U.S. Poetry*. Madison, N.J.: Fairleigh Dickinson University Press, 2001. Analyzes the work of social poets who hail from diverse racial and ethnic backgrounds and geographical locations in the United States.

Gregson, Ian. *Contemporary Poetry and Postmodernism: Dialogue and Estrangement*. New York: St. Martin's Press, 1996. Confronts the conflict between "mainstream" poetry and forms of modernist poetry which have had to survive outside the establishment.

Grennan, Eamon. *Facing the Music: Irish Poetry in the Twentieth Century*. Omaha, Neb.: Creighton University Press, 1999. Sympathetic readings give the reader a powerful sense of how Irish poetry in the twentieth century kept pace with the often intractable public and private life of the Irish island, both north and south.

Hamilton, Ian, ed. *The Oxford Companion to Twentieth-Century Poetry in English*. London: Oxford University Press, 1996. Comprehensive guide to modern English-language poetry. The works of 1,500 poets from New Zealand to Zimbabwe are discussed in the context of the literary and cultural movements that spawned them.

Hoffman, Daniel, ed. *Harvard Guide to Contemporary American Writing*. Cambridge, Mass.: Harvard University Press, 1979.

Jeffries, Lesley. *The Language of Twentieth-Century Poetry*. New York: St. Martin's Press, 1993. Explores the thesis that the creativity of poetry in the twentieth century often based its inventiveness on the creativity of everyday language.

Leavis, F. R. *New Bearings in English Poetry*. Reprint. Harmondsworth, England: Penguin, 1972. Examines the literary and poetic situation at the end of World War I, with special attention paid to Gerard Manley Hopkins, T. S. Eliot, and Ezra Pound.

McGuiness, Daniel Matthew. *Holding Patterns: Temporary Poetics in Contemporary Poetry*. Albany: State University of New York, 2001. Arguing that contemporary literary criticism does a disservice to poetry by imposing critical frameworks that many authors of poetry patently reject, McGuiness attempts to provide a criticism sympathetic to each poem's individual poetic.

Melaney, William D. *After Ontology: Literary Theory and Modernist Poetics*. Albany: State University of New York, 2001. Identifies the uniquely postmodern elements in hermeneutics and deconstruction in order to re-read many of the central texts in modernist literature.

Moramarco, Fred, and William Sullivan. *Containing Multitudes: Poetry in the United States since 1950*. New York: Twayne Publishers, 1998. Provides history and criticism of American poetry in the latter half of the twentieth century.

Morrison, Blake. *The Movement: English Poetry and Fiction of the 1950's*. London: Oxford University Press, 1980.

O'Brien, Sean. *The Deregulated Muse*. Newcastle upon Tyne, England: Bloodaxe Books, 1998. Examines cases, causes, methods, influences, quarrels, and achievements in the work of numerous poets from the twentieth century.

Pratt, William C.. ed. *The Fugitive Poets: Modern Southern Poetry in Perspective*. 1965. Rev. ed. Nashville, Ky.: J. S. Sanders, 1991. Chronicles the impact of literary modernism on Southern poets such as Robert Penn Warren, John Crowe Ransom, Donald Davidson, and Allen Tate as their region was taking its "backward glance" before stepping over into the modern world.

_____. *The Imagist Poem*. 1963. Rev. ed. New York: Story Line Press, 2001. Expanded reissue of this cornerstone of modernism. Includes an updated introduction by the editor, and new poems by the movement's greatest poets.

Ray, Paul C. *The Surrealist Movement in England*. Ithaca, N.Y.: Cornell University Press, 1971.

Rosenthal, Macha L., and Sally M. Gall. *The Modern Poem Sequence: The Genius of Modern Poetry*. London: Oxford University Press, 1983. Provides a comprehensive guide to the origins and nature of the lyric sequence.

Silkin, Jon. *The Life of Metrical and Free Verse in Twentieth-Century Poetry*. New York: St. Martin's Press, 1997. Presents a premise that two modes of verse, free and metrical, engage the creative energies of current poetry. The poetic work of Whitman, Hopkins, Eliot, Pound, Lawrence, Dylan Thomas, Bunting, and ten British poets from the post-World War II era illustrate how free and metrical verse create—separately or together—a poetic harmony.

Spender, Stephen. *The Struggle of the Modern*. Berkeley: University of California Press, 1963.

Tate, Allen. *Four Decades of Essays*. 1968. Rev. ed. Wilmington, Del.: ISI Books, 1999. A classic collection of nearly fifty essays by one of the twentieth century's most acclaimed poets and literary critics. Speaks poignantly to the concerns of today's students, teachers, and general literature readers alike and covers the broad sweep of Tate's critical concerns: poetry, poets, fiction, the imagination, language, literature, and culture.

Thomas, Lorenzo. *Extraordinary Measures: Afrocentric Modernism and Twentieth-Century American Poetry*. Tuscaloosa: University of Alabama Press, 2000. Offers a critical reassessment of African American poetry development in the twentieth century within the contexts of modernism and the troubled racial history of the United States.

Thurley, Geoffrey. *The Ironic Harvest: English Poetry in the Twentieth Century*. New York: St. Martin's Press, 1974. Explores irony in twentieth century literary irony. Includes bibliography and index.

Thwaite, Anthony. *Poetry Today: A Critical Guide to British Poetry, 1960-1992*. 2d ed. Reading, Mass.: Addision-Wesley, 1996. Provides a succinct and accessible overview of British poets, movements and themes. The study begins with the poetry of Robert Graves and considers such influential figures as John Betjeman, W. H. Auden, Ted Hughes, and Sylvia Plath, but much of the book focuses on the work of poets who have come into prominence recently, including Wendy Cope, Carol Ann Duffy, Simon Armitage, Glyn Maxwell, Sean O'Brien, and Seamus Heaney.

Wilson, Edmund. *Axel's Castle: A Study in the Imaginative Literature of 1870-1930*. 1931. Reprint. New York: Random House, 1996. A landmark work, this book established Wilson's reputation as one of the twentieth century's foremost literary critics. Traces the development of the French Symbolist movement and its influence on six modern writers: William Butler Yeats, Paul Valery, T. S. Eliot, Marcel Proust, James Joyce, and Gertrude Stein.

Thomas C. Foster

EUROPEAN ORAL AND EPIC TRADITIONS

"Literature," as the word is most often used, means written works: poetry, fiction, prose. The term itself, derived from the Latin word for "letter of the alphabet," enshrines a particular notion of what literature involves—namely texts. The concept of a nonwritten, oral "literature," therefore, might seem a contradiction in terms. Nevertheless, before modern literate culture valued one form of language (written) above the other, before there was even any one word such as "literature" to cover the disparate forms of verbal art often tied to social functions, there existed poems, songs, dramas, and narratives. In contemporary nonliterate societies, there are many examples of flourishing "literary" forms, while even in modern Western society, the most popular verbal artistic modes are "oral" in that they are transmitted without the use of writing. How many people, for example, read the text of a popular hit song, a Broadway play, or a television show?

The fundamental orality of all literature, then, can be seen to reassert itself, even in the most literate of all cultures. Indeed, the audiovisual revolution has helped to broaden the notion of literature; no longer does one limit it to that which can be printed and cataloged in libraries. Consequently, it has become possible to conceive of a traditional oral literature that lies at the roots of modern written Western literature. This overview surveys monumental works of that tradition in the light of research on all kinds of oral literature, explains how and why these works might be called "oral," and draws out the implications of their "oral" character. Finally, some aspects of the influence of oral tradition on later written work will be examined.

DEFINITIONS

"Oral literature" comprises a vast range of verbal products, including modern blues lyrics, African drum songs, ancient Greek epic poetry, urban legends, the latest jokes or limericks, ballads, folk songs, folktales, children's rhymes, and streetcorner games such as the "dozens" (a series of rhyming insult verses that can be extended to any length by improvisation). On one hand, it is quite useful for an investigator to know about all of these genres of oral literature, to take the term at its most inclusive, so that one can learn by comparison exactly what makes each given composition "oral" and therefore different from its written counterpart. On the other hand, some restriction of the term is needed in order to examine in any detail the workings of such literature. This essay, then, focuses on one narrow area of oral literature that has exerted influence of a disproportionate magnitude. While at times referring to African and Asian literature, most of the essay discusses Western literature. Unfortunately, this means excluding such great compositions as the Babylonian *Gilgamesh* (c. 2000 B.C.E.) story, the Iranian *Shāhnāma* (1010 C.E.), and the Sanskrit *Ramāyana* (c. 350 B.C.E.) and *Mahābhārata* (c. fifth century B.C.E.), as well as the hymns of the *Rig Veda* (c. 2500 B.C.E.), all of which have importance for the student of epic poetry in the Western tradition.

This survey will be further limited to poetry thought to be composed, and not merely transmitted, without the aid of writing. This restriction necessarily raises some questions: What of ballads or songs which change as they are transmitted? Is not this a form of composition without writing, even if the original composition were "written"? Such questions might be answered when discussion turns to longer compositions, such as narrative songs, which at times seem to exhibit the same behavior. It will be seen that the interplay of "oral" and "written" comprises a separate problem within the field of oral poetics, and ballad study requires critical notions different from those applied to other oral genres.

Finally, this article makes a further distinction between freely improvised poetry existing within a literate culture alongside written work—for example, the work songs and insult-contest verses that can be heard today—and preliterate compositions, which necessarily transmit large amounts of traditional language, motifs, and themes, and so cannot be called improvised in the same way. These poems, usually lengthy and narrative in nature, demand trained composers using generations-old techniques; at every turn of the poem, one comes across fusions of the individual's creative improvisation with traditional material.

The traditional poems to be discussed are the Greek *Iliad* (c. 800 B.C.E.) and *Odyssey* (c. 800 B.C.E.); the Old

English *Beowulf* (sixth century); the Icelandic *Poetic Edda* (ninth to twelfth centuries); *The Nibelungenlied* (c. 1200), in Middle High German; and the Old French *Chanson de Roland* (c. 1100; *Song of Roland*).

GREECE

Modern Western culture, for which "illiterate" is a pejorative word, takes writing for granted as something both necessary for civilization and good in itself. However, those who set out to read ancient Greek literature must divest themselves of this, among many other modern attitudes, and think themselves back into a culture which, while it valued speech above most things, did not have at all the same regard for the written word. Ancient Greece was an oral culture, and its early literature is oral literature; it is only when one understands the exigencies of oral composition and the expectations of an audience attuned to the oral art that Greek epic and lyric poetry—even history, oratory, and drama—become fully intelligible.

In Plato's dialogue *Phaedros* (c. 388-369 B.C.E.; *Phaedrus*, 1804), Socrates relates the story of the invention of writing; his account provides a good starting point from which to examine Greek attitudes to written art. As Socrates tells it, in the Egyptian region of Naucratis lived the god Thoth, inventor of numbers, geometry, astronomy, and writing. Thoth once asked Thamus, king of the land, to pass on these arts to the citizens, for the good of all. "My discovery will enable the Egyptians to become wiser and better at remembering," said Thoth, when talk came to the new craft of writing. Thamus refused, however, saying, "This will make men forget, seeing that they will neglect memory and remember things not from within themselves but by faith in the exterior signs." Writing, concluded the king, would give Thoth's pupils only the appearance of wisdom; they would lack true teaching (the sort Socrates practiced by dialogue).

Plato's myth of Thoth focuses attention on three important aspects of oral culture: the role of the performer, that of the audience, and the inevitable effects on both brought about by the technological innovation of writing. Even if widespread literacy is not assumed, writing has a powerful impact. In Plato's time, the art probably belonged strictly to an educated elite. In the period surveyed in this essay, the Archaic Age (750-490 B.C.E.),

even fewer Greeks are likely to have known how to use writing in daily life; writing was, after all, a recent invention, having been introduced by Phoenicians in the eighth century B.C.E. The attitude expressed by the Egyptian Thoth is consistent with early Greek notions about the role of writing as an aid rather than an end in itself, and even then, as an aid appropriate only for certain activities. It was certainly useful for inscriptions, to mark tombs or objects to be dedicated at temples, or to record laws—these are, in fact, the first recorded uses of the art of writing in Greece. The two oldest inscriptions, from the eighth century B.C.E., comprise some verses scratched on ceramic ware: "Whoever of all the dancers now sports the most, gets this," says a line on a jug found at Dipylon. A drinking vessel says, "Nestor's cup is good to drink from," then adduces, by means of a favorable contrast, its own capacity for giving wine. Whereas the first mention of a book comes in the late fifth century B.C.E. and the oldest actual surviving manuscript dates to a century later, writing intended to show possession or to memorialize had long been in use. Entertainment and instruction were the province of oral performers, not of written texts.

Thus, *Phaedrus* reflects the status of writing and oral performance in early Greek society. Thoth's conception of writing resembles that of Archaic Age Greeks, who thought in terms of one-way communication directed toward an unspecified audience, including future generations. For example, the Dipylon vase could be passed on, like some modern athletic trophies, annually, without change, its general statement always appropriate to the occasion of a dance contest. The attitude of Thamus, on the other hand, would match archaic modes of thinking about poetry as entertainment: It is an oral performer's attitude.

It is known from twentieth century fieldwork that oral poetry always involves interaction between performer and audience. Even if the audience does not interrupt to make specific requests or suggestions about the poet's tale, the poem is shaped by the context of the performance: the time available, the occasion (whether ritual or secular), and, especially, the poet's perception of what the audience wishes to hear. They may want the "good old stories" or, as Telemachus says in the *Odyssey*, they may desire "the latest song." "Old" and "new" are relative terms; the poet's method of composing remains the same. He relies on his store of memorized traditional material, including both verbatim phrases and large plot structures, to create "new" compositions for each new audience. Every poem is both old—in the sense that each poet's repertoire comes to include only audience-tested material—and new, since the oral poet always competes with others in the craft and with himself as well, attempting to hone and polish his own compositions.

All of these observations are based on scholarship concerning composition techniques of oral poetry as it exists in many parts of the world today (principally Africa, the Balkans, and Asia), but Archaic Greek poetry makes explicit reference to the same techniques. A principal example is the poet's reliance on memory. Archaic Greek poetry consistently invokes the Muses, mythological daughters of Mnēmosunē (memory, or reminding). In Homer, as well as in lyric poetry, the Muses are viewed as the repository of all traditions, precisely because they are immortal goddesses and therefore were eyewitnesses to past events (as Homer says in calling on them to remind him of the catalog of ships in the *Iliad*, book 2). From the Greek standpoint, all poetry is therefore impossible without divine aid in the form of a divinized memory; the poet is automatically a religious figure and his art an act of faith, although the Greeks never make this formulation explicit.

What does the Greek poet remember? The simplest answer is "tradition," taking that word to mean traditional lore about heroes, ancestors, gods, and events, and also traditional expressions—unusual old words and noncurrent word endings (compare the *-th* third-person singular verb ending of English "poetic" language), as well as the traditional adjectives attached to certain nouns. These latter adjective-noun combinations preserve a traditional way of looking at reality, and many are extremely old; for example, Homer often describes "fame" (*kleos*) as "unwithering" (*aphthiton*). Since the same adjective is frequently used of natural phenomena, a Greek audience would be attuned to think of "fame" as somehow growing like a plant. This perception is not the poet's invention, but rather an inherited piece of tradition. Sanskrit, a language related to Greek, preserves in its old poetry the exact equivalent of this phrase, in cognate words (*śravas akṣitam*). Because Sanskrit and Greek speakers had split from a unified group and taken up residence in their respective lands by 2000 B.C.E. at the latest, this agreement in poetic language must go back to the time when both languages had a common dialect and common art; this is an Indo-European poetic tradition, as modern scholars believe. The idea of "undying fame"—what Achilles in the *Iliad* seeks and wins—is preserved because this phrase reflects the very ideology of the poetry itself: Personal heroic reputations are undying because they are recalled and renewed through generations of poets and audiences.

To put this in other terms and to return to the example of Plato's Thoth, one might say that for an oral poet to reject or pit himself against his tradition would be a contradiction in terms. The poet lives by tradition, as it lives through him. The powerful invention of writing, however, begins to erode tradition, offering a competing means of ordering reality, one which purports to be more authoritative. As the work of Albert Lord and others has shown, oral poetic technique begins to die out when a region's poets begin to accept the idea of writing and of "songbooks." Plato's Thamus, then, is absolutely correct in reprimanding the inventor of writing. The unease produced by the introduction of writing into ancient Greece appears in subtle hints near the end of the Archaic Age, when poets such as Xenophanes begin to criticize traditional concepts of the gods and the idea begins to take hold that myth is something subversive, false, or marginal. In contrast, for Homer, at the beginning of the Archaic Age, the word *muthos* is simply an authoritative speech act: a word, tale, or command.

A word should be added about the oral audience. Far from being primitive consumers of art who merely wished to hear the names of famous ancestors, they were doubtless so familiar with oral art in everyday life that a high standard of criticism could evolve among them. The author of the *Hymn to Apollo* (third century B.C.E.), one of the so-called Homeric hymns, commends his poem to the audience in the personal note intruded at the end of the composition and bids the audience to compare his work with that of others which they hear, to spread his fame. A group of listeners valued for the potential favor they might do a poet, preserving his reputation, would always be treated to the height of a performer's art. Such interaction between artist and audience nourished the high art of Homer.

THE ILIAD AND THE ODYSSEY

Any discussion of traditional Western poetry should begin with Homer, because the study of the monumental poems attributed to him has continued throughout the Western literary tradition and first sparked the rediscovery of oral literature's distinctive techniques. From antiquity, there have been questions about the date, composition, and authorship of the two epics. In essence, the Homeric Question (as this collection of uncertainties has come to be called) grows from a lack of knowledge concerning a certain period in Greek history, the Dark Age, which extended from the fall of Mycenaean civilization (c. 1600-1100 B.C.E.) to the eighth century B.C.E., when writing in alphabetic form came to Greece from the Phoenicians and when Greek social institutions assumed their classical shapes.

The Homeric poems can be dated to the eighth century B.C.E. through certain indications of language and content (for example, mention of an oracle at Delphi, of iron, of seated statues). Why not assume, then, that a gifted literate poet of the eighth century, perhaps living in a Greek colony of Asia Minor (as tradition maintained), realized the usefulness of the newly imported alphabet for recording poetry and set himself to write one or two lengthy heroic poems about nearly mythical events of four hundred years before, the siege and fall of Troy? More is currently known, however, about the Mycenaean Age than about the Dark Age. The remains of a great city close to the traditional site of Troy were found at the end of the nineteenth century by Heinrich Schliemann. In 1952, Michael Ventris, a British linguist, finally deciphered the language of the clay tablets found at Mycenaean Age sites on Crete and mainland Greece and discovered that it was an early form of Greek, used to record details of palace administration. These discoveries indicated that Homer's poems contain exact reminiscences of the heroic age they celebrate: a boar's tooth helmet in the *Iliad*, book 10, a body shield in the *Iliad*, book 6, and many other objects that are known to have gone out of use by 1000 B.C.E. are matched by real objects actually dug from Greek earth. Even the long catalog of ships in the *Iliad*, book 2, has been found to contain traces of very old authentic information. Words

found elsewhere only in the newly deciphered Linear B Greek tablets appear in Homer's poetry.

Without a written tradition, one might ask how the memory of such words and objects could be preserved in the four-hundred-year gap between the war at Troy and Homer's own time, if not orally? Linear B writing certainly died out with the downfall of Mycenaean sites around 1100 B.C.E., and, at any rate, it seems never to have been used for literary purposes. On the other hand, if one attempts to explain the *Iliad* and the *Odyssey* as memorized poems, recited verbatim for centuries, there remains the obvious objection that the poems do not present a consistently archaic, Mycenaean picture, but rather a cultural mélange. Even the argument that an eighth century B.C.E. poet could have had access to nonpoetic, oral recollections of distant objects and customs, which he then incorporated into a chronologically haphazard poem, fails to explain the uniqueness of Homeric poetry, for such an argument leaves aside the most important obstacle, the peculiarly mixed Homeric dialect, which linguists affirm could never have been the speech of one poet, time, or place. In other words, the very diction, as well as the content, of the *Iliad* and the *Odyssey* is the product of a long evolution. What does this make of Homer? A series of poets? An editor?

One tradition of Homeric scholarship maintained that the poems were not both the work of one poet, the shadowy Homer, but showed differences of approach and style, leading critics to postulate several authors. With renewed vigor, the scientific nineteenth century German tradition of scholarship, equipped with more exact observations about inconsistencies of plot and language between and within the poems, began to "analyze" the *Iliad* and the *Odyssey* into constituent smaller parts—"lays" or "songs" about separate themes, such as the wrath of Achilles or the return of Odysseus, which had been stitched together to form larger compositions. F. A. Wolf's *Prolegomena ad Homerum* (1795), which proposed a sixth century B.C.E. editing of the shorter lays into longer poems, can be seen as the first of such "analyst" attempts at explaining Homer's legacy. When, however, by the end of the nineteenth century, these critics had still failed to agree on the scheme of subdivision for the poems, the field was left open for fresh interpretations.

In 1928, a young American scholar, Milman Parry, convinced of the essential unity of Homer's poems, demonstrated in detail how it was possible that Homeric poetry could be traditional—the product of evolution—yet the work of one man. Parry investigated the occurrence of "formulas" in the poems, the recurring groups of words "used under the same metrical conditions to express an essential idea," as he defined the term. He pointed out that the use of certain adjectives or "epithets" to modify proper names, such as "much-enduring Odysseus" or "swift-footed Achilles," followed a system that was metrically controlled. Thus, noted Parry, Odysseus would be called "much-enduring, shining Odysseus" (*polutlas dios Odusseus*) when the hexameter line that the poet was composing required an ending of a certain metrical shape; when the poet needed an adjective to modify the name Odysseus in a line one syllable longer at its break, or caesura, he would invariably use "wily" (*polumetis Odusseus*).

Two principles governed the system. First, for each commonly used proper name there was, with fractional exception, one and only one epithet to fit each possible metrical position; this tendency Parry referred to as the "thrift" of the system. Second, the system was extensive, applying to some fifty or more figures in the poems and accounting for the epithets used in a variety of metrical conditions. The important conclusion that Parry drew from the existence of such a thorough system was this: No literate, writing poet could or would have wished to develop it. It could only have evolved through some generations of poets who needed a system to enable rapid composition, in which an epithet would be ready at hand whenever they had to mention a proper name. Parry's investigation of the diction of Vergil and Apollonius Rhodius supported his conclusion. The writing poets used multiple epithets for one and the same metrical position and for proper-name combinations.

In his 1928 work on the traditional epithet, Parry hinted at his next ground-breaking hypothesis but did not make it explicit. Only after an initial trip in 1933 to Yugoslavia, where he studied the singing of contemporary nonliterate epic poets, did Parry suggest that Homer resembled modern "singers of tales," the Yugoslavian *guslars*. Homer was an oral poet, and the formulaic nature of his language confirmed this, for the Serbo-Croatian songs that Parry collected between 1933 and 1935, with the help of his student and coworker Albert B. Lord, were highly formulaic in precisely the same ways. After Parry's accidental death in 1935, Lord continued his teacher's brilliant work, extending his investigations into such matters as traditional motifs and themes in the epic poetry of Greece, Yugoslavia, and medieval England, France, and Germany.

Lord's book *The Singer of Tales* contains valuable observations from his field experience that can be applied to all oral traditional poems. First, Lord pointed out that the performance of poems using the traditional style of formulaic composition differed from singer to singer, from region to region, and even from performance to performance of the same poem by the same singer. It is consequently not possible to speak of any fixed text for any given song in the tradition; put another way, the *Iliad* or the *Odyssey* that one reads now is only one performance of a long line of poems on the same subject. This fluidity of tradition explains why inconsistencies of plot may occur: not because a poet cannot keep details straight, but because there are "formulaic" themes and motifs, offering at each turn various possibilities for elaboration or condensation of traditional material.

A modern oral poet, such as Lord studied, might sing a version of a Serbo-Croatian epic at a coffeehouse during the Muslim Ramadan festival; when asked to sing for a collector of poems, the same poet could expand his version, add other plot details, yet still claim to be telling the same story. Lord found that for these singers and thus, by extension, for other oral poets, "the same poem" usually meant the same basic theme, not word-for-word correspondence. From their boyhood apprenticeships, the *guslars* had soaked up thematic variations, which they developed in a style of semi-improvisation, always with a view toward their audience and its knowledge of hundreds of other performances. One master singer, Avdo Medjedović (whose poems are in the Milman Parry collection), knew fifty-eight epics in 1935. Medjedović dictated to Lord at least two poems that were more than twelve thousand lines in length, thus providing evidence that the *Iliad* and the *Odyssey*—sixteen thousand and twelve thousand lines, respectively—could have been the result of actual performances. In addition, Lord's observation that the songs that Medjedović sang were "finer," in the singer's opinion, when sung to the attentive individual audience that had requested the performance led him to postulate that the same dictation situation was the origin of the Homeric poems.

Lord's hypothesis would account for the perplexing question of the manner in which oral compositions, such as the *Iliad* and the *Odyssey*, finally were handed down as texts. Such a scenario also avoids the pitfalls of postulating an oral poet who becomes a literate poet. As Lord found, such poets gradually lost their ability, and within a generation or two of the introduction of songbooks, the oral art of the singers tended to die out. A true oral poet would, in fact, have no desire to use writing—certainly not as an aid to memory, for which he already possessed an economical nonliterate system; and, in the traditional mode of performance before an audience, there would be no reason to switch modes, to write for an unseen audience. There remains the possibility that Homer, coming at the end of an oral tradition already threatened by literacy in nonpoetic spheres, foresaw the usefulness of the new medium and found a scribe to record his masterpieces. In this way, the poems would be at once "oral" and "written." Lord later noted that, for a literate person living in an area where oral poetry is performed, the traditional oral style is easy to imitate, and thus, there can be "transitional" poetry of a mixed character. Lord was willing to view much of Old English religious poetry, which appears to be formulaic to a degree, as transitional.

The Parry-Lord theory, as it is called, is not the only way to examine oral literature, but it is the most useful for traditional narrative poetry. Lyric, ballads, praise poems, and other genres may require different methodology, as Ruth Finnegan pointed out in *Oral Poetry* (1977). Aside from this, there have been misunderstandings and overextensions of the Parry-Lord type of analysis. The classicist H. T. Wade-Gery said in *The Poet of the Iliad* (1952) of the opposition to the theory of Parry and Lord, "As Darwin seemed to many to have removed the finger of God from the creation of the world and of man, so Milman Parry has seemed to some to have removed the creative poet from the *Iliad* and the *Odyssey*." Lord was the first to admit that his studies of Serbo-Croatian poems were valid only as outlines of broad

principles, not as normative models for oral poetry, but sometimes his strictures went unheeded. Perhaps the most concerted reaction to the theory came immediately after the widespread dissemination of its principles in the 1960's, following the 1960 publication of *The Singer of Tales*.

Later, however, such concern with "creativity" was seen for what it is: a remnant of the Romantic conception of the poet. Neither Homer nor the *Beowulf* poet nor the countless anonymous singers of oral poems were concerned with being "creative" in the modern sense; instead, the oral poet sought fresh variation within a traditional structure of themes and diction. To use the Greek poet Pindar's metaphor (a very old one), "there are many roads of song."

The seminal work of Parry and Lord, then, taught literary critics to view poetry from traditional oral cultures in a new way. Rather than misapplying standards based on written texts to the repetitive elements of oral poetry—whether of word, phrase, scene, or theme—one must focus on just such formulaic elements to see how the individual singer has modified and rearranged the tradition in order to make meaning.

The *Iliad* and the *Odyssey* provide countless examples of such repetition. One does not have to insist on the noun-epithet as the basis of the formulaic analysis of these poems. In fact, the term "formula" and its definition are in dispute, especially in Homeric studies. There is much to be learned from the poet's manipulation of higher-level formulaic elements of a poem: the motif and the theme. The motif, or type-scene, is the recurring use of many of the same details—but not necessarily in the same words—to tell about arming for battle, sending off messengers or a ship, feasting, getting up, going to bed, dueling, and a number of other actions that give weight and texture to long poems.

One such type-scene depicting the sacrifice and consumption of cattle, builds in the *Odyssey* to a central theme. The suitors' continual sacrifice of Odysseus's cattle is both the generating circumstance for Telemachus's decision to rescue his father's house and the reason Odysseus, on returning to the island of Ithaca, must slaughter the suitors. The seemingly inconsequential sacrifice scenes at other points in the poem gain resonance from the centrality of these first and final cattle-kills.

As an example, when Telemachus arrives at Nestor's city of Pylos in book 3, he encounters the old Trojan War veteran performing a huge sacrifice of cattle on the shore; there follows the most detailed use of the type-scene, describing in each particular the gilding of the beasts' horns, the ritual cutting, the cooking, and the feast. Homer expands here on the capsule motif of sacrifice, it seems, precisely because Pylos is meant to form a contrast to the situation on Telemachus's Ithaca, where (with fatal consequences) sacrifice and feasting are conducted in an incorrect manner. Again, sacrifice becomes all-important during the wanderings of Odysseus. The episode of the Cyclops's cave in book 9 presents another "improper" sacrifice which, by repetition of certain key phrases, hauntingly recalls the real purpose of sacrifice—nourishment of men and honor of gods—but refers to the eating of men, raw, by the monster. Finally, the same double allegiance, of reference and resonance, gives added meaning to the sacrifice of the Sun's cattle by Odysseus's disobedient crew, described in book 12: Here, the type-scene of sacrifice once more applies to a wrong sacrifice but foreshadows the "right" (in Greek terms) killing of the suitors, who, like Odysseus's crew, ate what was not theirs.

The type-scene is similar to a musical refrain, except that it never has to be repeated exactly to be effective. The theme, on the other hand, is more like the key signature of a musical piece: It establishes the limits within which the piece is to be "played" against the possible range of all themes. The theme is not bound to any one situation in the plot but, rather, underlies many plot events and can surface in the form of imagery or action or speech. The *Iliad* and the *Odyssey* illustrate the tendency of themes to combine, contract, or expand in narration. In this way, long narratives approach both myth and ritual (sharing common narrative progressions, such as the "return from the dead" theme) as well as the folktale. The latter can be analyzed in terms of "multiforms"—that is, variant tellings of the same essential action, with changes of detail in each version. The theme, too, is multiform—the return of Odysseus from Troy is simply another form of the theme (also narrated in the *Odyssey*, in book 11) of the return from Hades. In the *Odyssey*, this theme is combined with two others, also familiar from folktales: the initiation of a youth and the waiting of a wife (in this case, further combined with a wooing theme, which is found by itself in other Greek poems, such as the "Suitors of Helen" attributed to Hesiod).

The *Iliad* offers an even clearer example of the combination and reduplication of traditional themes. The main plot is centered on the narrative theme of the "withdrawal in anger" of the hero Achilles from battle. Introduced in the first book of the poem, the theme does not find its conclusion until the return of Achilles and the death of Hector. Along the way, it engenders another traditional theme, the "death of a substitute"—clearly a ritual theme as well—in this case, the death of Patroclus, Achilles' alter ego. Important as it is in connection with Achilles, the theme is not confined to him within the poem. Instead, like the type-scene, it is employed to counterpoint Achilles and other characters in the epic.

The theme of withdrawal exists as a narrative possibility whenever a hero retires from the fighting. A striking example occurs when Hector, returning during a lull in the fighting to his home in Troy, encounters Paris, who has been dallying with his abducted bride, the Greek Helen. "It is not good to put anger in your spirit like this," Hector tells Paris on their meeting, as he berates him for leaving the fight. In reality, anger has nothing to do with the withdrawal of Paris; he had been snatched magically back to Troy by Aphrodite when he was about to lose a duel with Menelaus on the plain. Why does Hector mention anger? An earlier generation of critics maintained that Homer here bungled his plot. Now, however, one can explain such words on Hector's part as the working of thematic intrusion: Withdrawal in the tradition, as a theme, usually implies the anger of the hero. Here, the lesser figure Paris only becomes more distinct from the heroic Achilles by the poet's mention of this theme, tied as it is in the main narrative to the anger of Achilles. It is an artful use of traditional material.

Similarly, Homer uses the withdrawal theme to structure another tale-within-a-tale, the story of Meleager, told by Phoenix in book 9 to induce Achilles, his ward, to go back to the fight. The Meleager story mirrors Achilles' own situation: He has retired in anger from a war and cannot be made to return until it is too late. Again, the smaller narrative (like the type-scene of sacrifice in the *Odyssey*) is used to foretell part of the larger story; indeed, Achilles will return to battle too late to save his dearest companion, Patroclus. In this example, one sees the essence not only of narrative themes but also of the importance in an oral culture of the narrative itself: Oral culture needs oral poetry to enforce its morality. The story becomes an exemplum, indicating the best heroic behavior for the young Achilles by reminding him of past heroic deeds and their consequences. Action as well as story is governed by tradition.

Homeric poetry is worth dwelling on because it is preeminently aware of its heritage as oral poetry. In invoking the Muse, the source of all traditional lore concerning the past, the poet acknowledges that what he hears from the goddess is more important than anything he himself might invent. In celebrating Achilles and Odysseus, the *Iliad* and the *Odyssey* make the same acknowledgment: Both heroes are also poets, Achilles singing the deeds of the ancestors as he sits in his hut, Odysseus telling his own adventures to the Phaeacian court.

NON-HOMERIC ORAL POETRY

Although the earliest extant Greek lyric poetry post-dates Homer, one cannot assume that epic poetry was "invented" before lyric; indeed, it is clear from the *Iliad* and the *Odyssey* that Homer knew other genres of poetry. He pictures the social use of genres which were to become familiar from later poets. Wedding songs can be paralleled in the work of Sappho in the late seventh and early sixth century B.C.E.; laments are the first songs in a long oral tradition which is alive today in rural Greece; choral maiden songs were composed later by Alcman and Pindar; and hymns to the gods were later elaborated as long narrative poems such as the Homeric hymns. It must be assumed that these later poems simply continued a tradition of oral poetry as old, if not older, than that of Homeric epic. It may even be that epic verse developed from the simpler meters of lyric poetry, as some scholars suggest (see G. Nagy, *Comparative Studies in Greek and Indic Meter*, 1974). This would explain some of the richness of Homer's poems: They incorporate the varied themes and emotions of the range of concurrent lyric poetry known to the poet Homer, that poetry which closely preserves the folk traditions of the Greek people.

Early Greek lyric poetry shows its oral heritage in several important ways: first, by its directness of style, simple syntax, and use of concrete, often stunning, images (qualities much admired by Ezra Pound and the Imagists in the early twentieth century); second, by its use of formulaic expressions, many of which are also found in Homer ("golden Aphrodite"; "shining children"; "blazing fire"). These devices were meant to be appreciated by an audience of listeners rather than by page-turning readers; therefore, clarity and immediate effect were crucial for the oral composer. Another consequence of this poetry's constant attention to the presence of an audience is its "social" quality. There is no such thing as "confessional" poetry in early Greece. Instead, there are a number of personas, or masks, for the poetic performer, which can also be found to be traditional. A good example occurs in the work of the Boeotian composer, Hesiod.

HESIOD

Hesiodic poetry seems to be contemporary with Homeric epic, with which it shares dactylic hexameter meter and traditional formulaic style, but the two major works attributed to Hesiod are markedly unlike the *Iliad* and the *Odyssey*, particularly in that Hesiod's poetry refers to its own maker. In the opening section of *Theogonia* (c. 700 B.C.E.; *Theogony*, 1728), Hesiod describes his encounter on Mount Helicon with the Muses, while he was pasturing sheep, and he tells of how he received a scepter, a symbol of power, along with the gift of singing about the origins of the gods. This "song" which the Muses taught him (note the oral figure) is then resung by the poet as the substance of the remaining *Theogony*. The origin of all from Chaos and Night, the overthrow of Uranus by Cronus and of Cronus by Zeus, who then orders the cosmos—all of these remind one of portions in the *Iliad* in which a wisdom figure (Nestor, for example, or Phoenix) refers to semidivinized abstract notions in order to explain the workings of the world. Clearly, the *Theogony* is in an old genre; similar explanatory cosmologies are known to have been recited at kingship rituals in the ancient Near East, whence some of Hesiod's own tales also seem to have originated. The innovation in Hesiod's own treatment appears to be his singing of the song in the role of a shepherd (a motif remarkably similar to that in the story of Caedmon, the Old English poet). That this shepherd is a persona, and not necessarily the "real" poet, becomes clear from Hesiod's *Erga kai Emerai* (c. 700 B.C.E.; *Works and Days*, 1618), in which the poet is at one time a farmer and is also a cunning "adviser" to his brother Perses, as well as to local princes. The brother, says Hesiod, wronged him over a dispute about their patrimony. Zeus is also counseled, along with the princes (his earthly representatives), as Hesiod employs the traditional and widespread "Instruction of Princes" genre. An intriguing poem, the *Works and Days* uses the myth of the Five Ages of Man, as well as the stories of Prometheus's invention of fire and of Pandora's box, to point its instruction. Ethics for Hesiod includes "works" as well as a kind of faith, so that the detailed agricultural and ritual admonishments that conclude the poem are organically related to the myth section. Furthermore, it is the persona of the farmer/adviser which unites the two seemingly disparate parts.

Like that of Hesiod, all Greek poetry in the early period instructs and addresses its audience, at times explicitly, at other times by implication, through the exteriorizing of inner emotions. The startling variety of meters and dialects in which Greek lyric is composed cannot conceal the basic similarity in function: The poetry is targeted for limited, local, chosen groups but uses a common Greek store of images and formulas to underline its poetic messages. Inevitably, the poet is viewed as a craftsman—for example, as a maker (*poiētēs* in Greek) of words; his craft is a social institution. The following survey of lyric poetry centers on the ways in which the poets' view of their craft, as reflected in their verses, and their acknowledgment of an audience, point to the oral origins of such poetry.

ARCHILOCHUS

For the soldier-poet Archilochus of Paros (c. 680-c. 640 B.C.E.), poetry is clearly delineated as a craft, one on a level with his other trade: "The servant of Ares I am, and I understand the Muses' lovely gift as well," he writes in one elegiac couplet. Some of Archilochus's poems are set immediately before or after battles—the poet warns about the tactics of an enemy or talks of his bread "won by the spear and eaten while I lean on the spear"—but Archilochus was most noteworthy in the eyes of later antiquity for the attitude he takes toward military life. His persona is that of the dissident warrior; perhaps the audience was meant to think of Achilles. In one

poem, Archilochus bids farewell to the shield that he has thrown away in flight from battle; in other verses, he encourages a watch party to get drunk and pours scorn on a dandified general. Allegiance to the Muse overrules that to the god of war. Archilochus's own martial career as an early colonizer of the northern Aegean island Thasos may have inspired the poems; more likely, this "warrior" is another persona. The poet has a second mask, like Hesiod: He is a dangerous satirist, a practitioner of the art known as *iambus* (from which the term "iambic" derives, although the word originally designated a genre). *Iambus* is the art of blame-poetry, venomous attacks of which are said to have led Archilochus's victims to suicide. Scholars know from other oral cultures that such beliefs in the power of destroying reputation are taken seriously and have real effect. Archilochus practices his invective artfully, attacking in the voice of another, for example, a woman who spurned him, when he makes a character in a dialogue poem say "her bloom has withered" and insinuates that she is less than chaste.

Archilochus's poetry often resembles a conversation which the audience is invited to overhear. Perhaps the best example is his address to his own soul: "Spirit, boiling with incurable woes, get up. Defend yourself, hurl your chest against the foes." It is preeminently Archilochean in combining war images (soul as fighter) with advice ("Do not boast when you win or weep in your house when you lose") and ending with a pragmatic command ("Know what sort of rhythm moves men"). All of his verse convinces and holds an audience through such devices, but rather than being deceived into identifying Archilochus as the first genuinely individual voice in the European lyric tradition (a claim that is often made), one should recognize that his art was the product of a long oral tradition of personal poetry, as conventional as epic poetry in its use of framing techniques, imagery, and personas.

Archilochus, both personal and public composer, warrior as well as poet of the drinking party, provides a good starting point from which to approach two poles of the later Greek tradition, which may be termed the "personal"—represented by Alcaeus and Sappho—and the "social"—as seen here in the Athenian lawgiver Solon's poems and those of the sixth century Theognis of Megara.

ALCAEUS AND SAPPHO

Alcaeus and Sappho both lived on the island of Lesbos in the late seventh and early sixth century. They enormously influenced later European poetry, but because later poets, in their imitations, popularized the images of a jovial, bibulous party poet (Alcaeus) and an intensely personal bluestocking poetess (Sappho), modern critics find it difficult to hear the authentic voices of these consummate lyricists. This is particularly true because later written poetry, as often happens, also adapted Sappho's and Alcaeus's oral-oriented devices and settings, the immediate addresses and allusions to ongoing festivities or rituals among a small circle of friends. Consequently, one comes to their poetry with a false sense of familiarity. What is conventional in the written poems of Horace, for example, should very often be treated as actual utterance in poems by Sappho and Alcaeus: Horace, in Rome of the first century B.C.E., could not have known firsthand the sort of social occasions about which he writes, whereas Sappho and Alcaeus could not have avoided participating in such local institutions as the *kōmos* (festival with procession), the wedding feast, maidens' festivals, or the symposium (men's drinking party). In an oral culture, it makes no sense to compose poems "as if" one were attending such occasions, because the actual occasions demanded poetic accompaniment to be performed on the spot.

Alcaeus explicitly acknowledges an audience at such occasions, while Sappho hints at one, keeping in the foreground her own persona. Still, the assumption that both poets are composing for a present audience must guide interpretation. For Alcaeus and Sappho, the audience can include ancestors; as in Homer, the notion of fame through poetry alone is the overriding incitement to correct behavior. Thus, Alcaeus, in one of his many poems dealing with the local politics of Lesbos, uses an enduring image as he calls on his companions to "bail out" the ship of state, lest it sink, and tells them to "run to harbor" lest they "shame by cowardice the good forebears beneath the ground." Sappho similarly speaks of memory in an address to an unnamed woman, implying that only poetry can give true immortality—a persistent theme of archaic poems, one easily understood in a culture where even the word for fame (*kleos*) means, literally, "that which is heard": "Dead, you will lie, neither

memory nor desire of you will there be," says Sappho, "for you do not have any of the roses of Pieria [the home of the Muses]." To exercise memory, in composing poetry, is to ensure that one is remembered.

In their use of the hymn genre, Alcaeus and Sappho illustrate the ways in which traditional public poetic forms can have personal reference. Alcaeus, who wrote hymns to Apollo, Dionysos, and the Dioscuri, among other deities, calls on the gods to aid in defeating his enemies in the city-state and to bring him back from exile. He combines hymns with symposium poems—the sort of verses designed to muster his group of friends by self-reference, similar to his "ship of state" poems. Sappho, on the other hand, uses the hymn form several times in calling for rescue from love affairs. Her most famous and only completely intact poem beseeches Aphrodite to withdraw her forces; Sappho fills the hymnic framework of the poem with an exquisite flashback description of Aphrodite's previous aid—how she came in a sparrow-drawn chariot and promised to make Sappho's lover reciprocate. Aphrodite is doubly praised in the poem, which attests that her promise was so great in the past as to involve the poet in new love difficulties, prompting the new cry for help.

Aside from their use of traditional, socially fixed oral forms, and their nod to the role of Memory in poetry, Sappho and Alcaeus alike compose poetry to consolidate their audiences—that is, their "friend groups" (the *philoi*, or "beloved," a concept strange to English). In this, they show the tight bond which oral poetry enforces between performer and audience: Sappho's laments for young women who are growing up, moving away, or marrying can be understood as addressed to the remaining group of girls (in a culture where gender segregation was the norm). This applies even to her famous ode which seems to detail with clinical precision the physical effects of jealousy that Sappho feels on seeing a girl she knows next to a man. In reality, this was probably an elaborate praise poem for the *girl*, using traditional metaphors and the device of a "foil," or fictitious rival figure. Alcaeus's most apparently "personal" poems—for example, his exhortations to come drink with him—are also public in that the drinking is understood to take place at a symposium, where serious political talk mixes with philosophical meditation and relaxation.

SOLON

In an oral culture such as that of Archaic Greece, the role of poetry in politics cannot be underestimated; even in the "enlightened" fifth century, rhetoric and poetry swayed Athens to a disproportionate and dangerous degree. Solon (639-559 B.C.E.), the Athenian lawgiver, exemplifies the alloy of poetic and political craft. In one poem, he admits to using the "arrangement of words" (*kosmos*), rather than political speeches, to persuade Athens. This is a sort of sympathetic verbal magic: ordering words begets order in the state. In other poems, he urged the Athenians to remember his reforms. As does Hesiod, Solon frames his poetry as "instruction" to the audience—in this case, the entire city. The instructions often take the mythic form of Hesiodic discourses on abstract concepts which are half divine, such as Justice (*Dikē*). Solon's long poem addressed to the Muses, daughters of Memory, for example, describes in parts the way in which Zeus pursues wrongdoers through their descendants: Like the poet, dependent on Memory, Zeus, too, "does not forget," and it is essential that the audience, also, remember this. Memory, therefore, works on three levels, making this poem a paradigm for the role of poetry in oral society.

THEOGNIS

How do audiences remember? In an oral culture, they must be constantly reminded, and this is where oral art comes to the fore. With the increasing use of writing, such functional poetry as Solon's, meant for performance, was soon being memorialized for future generations. A valuable hint of the procedure survives in the traditional lore about another "political" poet, Theognis of Megara (sixth century B.C.E.), a city near Athens. His poetry, in elegiac couplets, about fourteen hundred lines of which survive, may have been put on deposit in a local temple. An allusion to a "seal" on the poems preventing theft may mean that Theognis actually sealed the verses up with wax on the papyrus roll; it has been suggested that the "seal" may also have a metaphorical significance, indicating that the specific performer-audience relationship which this instructional poetry illustrates between an adviser (Theognis) and his young friend (Kyrnos) will never be duplicated. Because the poet has given Kyrnos immortality ("I have given you wings with which to fly over the sea," as the poet says),

the bond will never slip. As it appears, Theognis uses Kyrnos as a foil in order to counsel his city, Megara, and the poetry, like Solon's, thus embodies the reciprocal relationship characteristic of oral culture: Performers need audiences; Greece remembered Theognis.

CHORAL POETRY

A discussion of the unique combination of public and personal which defines early Greek poetry would not be complete without mention of choral poetry, that elaborate art form which used words, music, and dance to celebrate important community rites. The earliest representative of the form, Alcman, active in Sparta in the seventh century B.C.E., displays the characteristics marking this increasingly important poetry. In his *parthenion* (maiden song), for example, the local mythology of Sparta combines with gnomic utterances ("Do not try to fly to heaven; no one should try to wed Aphrodite") and details of the immediate occasion, such as the praise of the local maidens through extensive comparisons to traditional beauties: stars, sun, moon, horses, goddesses. Only the introduction of strophic structure (the format in which two identical verse units are capped by a third, differing in meter), which might have occurred in the sixth century B.C.E., differentiates Alcman's choral song from those composed in the fifth century flowering of the genre, both in the choruses of Athenian tragedy and in the works of Bacchylides and Pindar.

ENGLAND: *BEOWULF*

"One might say that each song in oral tradition has its original within it and even reflects the origin of the very genre to which it belongs." This observation by Albert Lord, though meant to be general, might apply specifically to *Beowulf*, the earliest full-length Germanic language epic that has survived. Although this poem was probably composed in the eighth century, its historical context is that of the early sixth century on the Continent and in Scandinavia; the story was likely brought to England by the migrating Angles and Saxons. This is *prima facie* evidence for the conservative nature of the poem, a trait often noticed in other oral compositions: The Serbo-Croatian songs that Lord and Parry found were often about battles fought five hundred years previously, such as that at Kosovo Polje in the fourteenth century. *The Nibelungenlied* (c. 1200, *The Lay of the Nibelungs*), *Poem of the Cid* (from the twelfth century) and *Chanson de Roland* (c. 1100, *The Song of Roland*) all share this characteristic.

In the case of *Beowulf*, as clearly as in the Greek epics, the oral origin of the poem is made explicit by the poet's own references to oral poems in the narrative, so that *Beowulf* is conservative in its view of poetry as well as in its historical outlook. As in the *Iliad* and the *Odyssey*, when bards are presented composing poetry, one should not expect exact depiction of the process by which the narrative itself was composed: There is always the possibility that the poet is archaizing, recalling the more glorious poetic as well as heroic past, when oral composers held a higher place in society. Yet the very fact of this "backward look" is important. It is the seal of a poem's traditional content.

The origin of a poem such as *Beowulf* can be viewed within the Old English epic in the important scene starting at line 867. As the Danes return on horseback from the site of Grendel's plunge, a retainer of their king recites the exploit,

> A man proved of old, evoker of stories,
> Who held in his memory multitude on multitude
> Of the sagas of the dead, found now a new song
> In words well-linked: the man began again
> To weave in his subtlety the exploit of Beowulf.

This sort of instant praise-poetry is not, however, simply a direct restatement of the hero's deed. The "evoker of stories" instead praises Beowulf by beginning with the story of Sigemund, who had a similar exploit (killing a dragon), and he ends with a mention of the blameworthy Heremod, an early Danish king, the complete opposite of Beowulf. There is no mention of the way in which he actually praised the maiming of Grendel by the contemporary hero; it could well be that what the old retainer composed in fact made little or no reference to Beowulf. Surprising as this might seem, it would fit with what can be seen in the *Iliad*, in the episode just mentioned above: The present is continually set into its past heroic context in this oral traditional material.

That something like the horseback poem of the retainer could have occurred in early times is suggested by the Roman historian Tacitus's account of Germanic tribesmen, who, he reported, sang the histories of their ancestors before battles and at night in their camps. This urge to turn the past into incentive for the present lies at the root of heroic poetry as well as praise-poetry, the kernel form of the epic. In the song of the retainer, which resembles Greek praise-poetry in its use of a "negative foil" figure (the blamed character), one can see the kernel blossoming into a full-fledged narrative.

As in the analysis of the Greek epics, the notion of type-scene and theme proves useful in establishing connections between *Beowulf* and oral composition. The analysis of the low-level formula—the repeated phrase or word—is less conclusive; *Beowulf* appears to be oral because it appears to have a high percentage of formulas or formula-types (repeated syntactical groupings such as epithet and noun), but the statistical method should not be relied on completely. It has recently been shown that poems known to have been written and signed by Cynewulf, probably in the ninth century, would have to be classified as "oral" if the same counting methods were applied. It could be that both Cynewulf's poems and the epic *Beowulf* are transitional products of the meeting of an oral tradition with a learned, Christianized, literate society. This would explain the seemingly incongruous elements of Christian faith in the heroic poem. Whatever the results of the diction-oriented analysis, the occurrence of traditional type-scenes and themes in *Beowulf* is important in itself and may be taken to show the poem's oral heritage.

Beowulf has its start in an arrangement of type-scenes remarkably like that of the *Odyssey:* A hero sets out by boat, is met on landing, is greeted and entertained, finds important information, and acts on it to the advancement of his own heroic career. In the *Odyssey*, the sequence is repeated, once for Telemachus (like *Beowulf*, a young hero accompanied by a small group) and once for Odysseus (books 5 through 13). Beowulf, however, acts immediately; the poem is consequently much shorter. Odysseus and Telemachus, on the other hand, act only on return to Ithaca, where their reunion and slaying of the suitors forms the grand finale. In this development, conditions of performance must dictate which themes will be doubled and which contracted, how many type-scenes will be inserted, and how large they will be allowed to grow.

The *Beowulf*-poet handles themes with as much dexterity as Homer, although his stock of type-scenes seems smaller. An example is the "taunt of Unferth" scene. The taunt is itself a genre in oral society, as the Homeric epics and modern African examples make clear. Here, the taunt is expanded to contain a thematic narrative remarkably like the theme of the surrounding poem: the underwater exploits of Beowulf. Unferth, a retainer of the Danish king Hrothgar, asks Beowulf on arrival whether he is the man who lost a swimming-match against Breca. Beowulf's reply is an elaborate, suspenseful narrative of a fight with sea-demons—the "correct" version of the story, unlike Unferth's, and a foreshadowing of his defeat of Grendel's mother beneath the lake. Beowulf (like Odysseus) acts the part of the oral poet. Is it not significant, then, that he wins over the final monster, not with Unferth's donated sword Hrunting, but with the "blade of old-time" found in the den of Grendel, which only Beowulf among heroes can lift? His personal weapon, like his personal story, is the one to surpass the competing stories of heroic action; fame, in an oral culture, tunes out the noise of rumor.

As well as containing hints of its own origin, *Beowulf* has one scene that might point to the kind of poetry that ultimately replaced it. The introduction of Grendel into the narrative describes his approach to the hall of the Danes where he had daily heard singing—and the song consists of nothing less than the creation of the world by God. As such, this singing strongly resembles the compositions attributed to Caedmon in a well-known section of Bede's history of the English Church. Caedmon was in the habit of leaving the nightly entertainments at Whitby Abbey because he had never learned songs, Bede reports. One night, guarding the stables, Caedmon dreamed that he was asked to sing the creation of the world; he did so, and the next morning recited the poem to his superiors, who from that time on used him to put stories from religious works into verse. Caedmon clearly was an oral composer; from Bede's viewpoint, his gift was "divine," since he knew no literature. Yet it was through such recruits to Christian tradition that the oral art of the older native singers eventually was lost—the beginning of the end can be seen in the *Beowulf*-poet's knowledge of this theological genre.

POETIC EDDA

The Icelandic compositions dating from about the ninth century C.E., known as the *Edda*, provide more valuable evidence for a quite ancient traditional diction and meter in Germanic poetry. Phrases composed of the same words (with slight sound changes) can be found in the *Edda* and in Old High German and Old English poetry, and must therefore be considered common Germanic. This means that the art of composing such poetry came about before the Germanic dialects had split into separate languages. Furthermore, the preservation in both Old English and Icelandic verse of the same four-stress, alliterative metrical line, composed of two clearly distinguished half lines, argues for a common metrical heritage—this would explain, in part, why similar phrases are preserved in different languages.

What are the implications of these discoveries for the criticism of the poetry? Given that the form of Eddic and other Germanic verse is very old, one is encouraged to look for signs of antiquity both in content and in structural elements—the type-scenes and themes.

The most obvious common inheritances on these higher levels are those of subject matter. Both Eddic poems and *The Nibelungenlied*, for example, focus on historical events of the fifth and sixth centuries C.E.: the deaths of Gunther and Hagen, and the revenge on Attila the Hun. Other Eddic poems (no one composition consists of more than one hundred or so lines) treat episodic, mythological incidents—encounters between Odin or Thor and giants or dwarfs, for example. Here, too, one can see resemblances to other Germanic poems: *Beowulf* is just such an encounter theme, extended to epic proportions in 3,182 lines. It has even been proposed that later, epic-length poems such as *The Nibelungenlied* are no more than collections of short plays that would resemble Eddic poems. The theory, attributed to Karl Lachmann, a nineteenth century German scholar, runs up against the same problems which plague the analysts' division of Homer into separate songs: Where does one make the divisions? Of more importance is the Eddic poems' distinctive viewpoint. Rather than simply narrating an incident from myth or history, the *fornskáld* (Eddic poet) most often used dialogue and allusive speeches in rhetorical settings: arguments, riddle contests, or *flyting* (mutual abuse matches). From such poetry, then, one gets a picture of actual heroic age genres of discourse in a preliterate society. The genre of *flyting*, in fact, helps one to understand the occurrence of episodes, such as Unferth's abuse of Beowulf, in longer compositions. A few examples in this vein will illustrate the ways in which Eddic poetry is conscious of its own role as the repository of the collective memory of the Icelandic people.

First, it is clear from a poem such as "The Words of the All-Wise" that knowledge, in such a preliterate culture, is knowledge of tradition, especially of the traditional formulas—legal, religious, or poetic. The same message is transmitted (subliminally, perhaps) by Homer, who makes his heroes into traditional singers. In the Eddic poem, Alvis ("all-wise"), a dwarf, is questioned by Thor about the names of various things— clouds, sea, wind, and so on. Alvis must answer with the learned lore of poetry; for example, the heavens are called "*Heaven* by men, *The Arch* by gods,/ *Wind-weaver* by vanes,/ by giants *High-earth*, by elves *Fair-roof*,/ By dwarves *The Dripping-Hall*." Thor eventually wins this contest, not by any deficiency in Alvis's answers, but because dawn arrives and Alvis turns to stone. That Alvis's feat was expected of every learned poet in the tradition is evidenced by the so-called *Prose Edda* (c. 1220), a later work by the thirteenth century Icelandic scholar Snorri Sturluson, who wrote the *Skáldskaparmál* or "Poetic Diction" portion specifically for the instruction of a generation of poets whose grasp of the traditional lore was slipping.

The Eddic poems, preserving large amounts of traditional material, including mythological as well as practical advice in the form of gnomic utterances, might be compared with the work of Hesiod. As Hesiod in the *Works and Days* offers gnomic advice for every phase of social life, so the *Hávamál* (ninth and tenth century; *The Sayings of the High One*, 1923) provides guidelines for behavior, stressing (as does Hesiod) reciprocity in friendships, moderation in eating and drinking, and distrust of women. As Hesiod's *Theogony* traces the genesis of gods and men, so the *Words of Vafthrudnir* (ninth and tenth century), another Eddic poem, recounts the origin of the world, of seasons and giants, and even the fate of the gods. This apocalyptic strain in Icelandic poetry takes over completely the *Völuspá* (c. 1000;

Völuspá: The Song of Sibyl, 1968), serving as a reminder to comparatists that poetry and seer craft in traditional preliterate societies are closely related activities: Knowing past lore is the key to the future.

Where words themselves are so important, their bestowal or refusal is crucial if one's heroic deeds are to be considered heroic; the *Edda* is conscious of this fact, as the *Hávamál* proclaims: "Cattle die, kindred die/ Every man is mortal;/ But I know one thing that never dies:/ The glory of the great dead." Not only is word-craft the mark of the wise and the guarantee of heroism; it also brings about social integration, being the means by which an audience is united in pleasure and therefore bonded together in understanding. Again, the *Hávamál* realizes this, in concluding with an audience statement in the form of a wish: "Joy to him who has understood,/ Delight to him who has listened."

THE NIBELUNGENLIED

It is a long distance, chronologically and generically, from the archaic lore of the *Edda* to the courtly life depicted in *The Nibelungenlied*, or "Song of the Nibelungs," a nine-thousand-line composition dating from perhaps 1200. While the Eddic poems exhibit concise diction (sometimes obscure) and dramatic organization, *The Nibelungenlied* has often been criticized for being threadbare, disorganized, and padded in its verse. This may be the effect, partly, of adapting older material to a more modern meter (a longer, three-stress-per-half-line, rhymed verse) and changed social situation, which demanded longer and more "courtly" poetry. Whatever the cause, these surface differences should not stand in the way of an appreciation of the similarities between the Icelandic, Old English, and Middle High German poems. All are rooted primarily in the past.

The Nibelungenlied announces itself as an "old story" of heroic action, feasts, and laments; from the first, one perceives its relationship, thematically, to the "wail after wassail" outlook of *Beowulf*, the *Seafarer* (one of a collection of poems found in the *Exeter Book*, copied about 975 C.E.), and other Old English poems. At least figuratively, the poem characterizes itself as oral by promising that all who wish can hear the story of Kriemhild, Gunther, Siegfried, and Etzel. Other marks of its actual oral heritage are visible in the presence of formulaic language (speech introductions, epithets, and repeated lines) and the picture of a society it presents—one in which traveling entertainers can be given gold for singing praise.

Although often compared to the *Iliad* as a story of heroes resigned to destruction, *The Nibelungenlied* might better be thought of as the thematic equivalent of the *Odyssey*: Both are revenge poems. In this case, it is the revenge of the woman Kriemhild for the murder of her husband Siegfried by Hagen, a vassal of Gunther, Kriemhild's brother. Siegfried's alleged insult to Brunhild, Gunther's wife, brings about a quarrel between sisters-in-law, and Hagen takes it on himself to save the honor of his mistress. Hagen pays for the murder of Siegfried when Kriemhild, later married to a Hun and living far away, invites her relatives to visit her, where she then has them killed by loyal troops of her husband Etzel: The woman-in-waiting theme of the *Odyssey* is melded with the revenge-of-the-returning-hero theme.

On the level of type-scene, as well, *The Nibelungenlied* resembles the *Odyssey*. Here, oral theory might answer the objections of critics who find the continual references to clothes—the wearing and giving of them—to be a flaw in the poem. First, consideration of the heroic status symbolism involved in clothing would lessen such criticism: The *Odyssey* offers the examples of clothes as proper gifts and concerns of heroes. The bestowing of expensive woven goods is a mark of hospitality in epic; in the Greek as well as in the German poem, it marks high points in the action—the solution of conflict, the happy return or arrival of heroes. Thus, this particular custom behind the type-scene has roots in heroic society.

It has been shown above that the sacrifice type-scene became important for Homer's *Odyssey*. In the same way, the refrainlike recurrence of the clothing scenes in *The Nibelungenlied* prepares the way for a reversal of rhythms. The rules of hospitality, always adhered to in the first half of the poem (and marked by the clothing type-scenes), are subverted after the marriage of Kriemhild to the Hun, Etzel. It is not surprising that the poet made use of this repeating device to mark a change in mood; the audience would have been alert to any variations in such traditional scenes. The change is most marked when Hagen crosses the Danube with Gunther and the rest. The crossing itself, which makes clear Hagen's tragic recognition of certain death when he shatters his boat in order to prevent return, is curiously signaled beforehand by some water sprites whom Hagen encounters. He steals the sprites' clothing: the exact opposite of type-scene behavior up to this point. By so doing, Hagen learns his future—as in the *Odyssey*, the abnormal occurrence of the type-scene involves foreshadowing of plot events.

At the Huns' city, the growing gulf between traditional significations of clothing and the new, more menacing meanings is underscored by Hagen again. Seeing his companions dressed in their new clothes (the normal type-scene before a courtly event), Hagen reprimands them: "You want breast-plates, not silken shirts." In the remainder of the poem, the type-scenes of hospitality (of which the clothes scenes are most important) are used with ironic bitterness as negative metaphors for the entire action. "This hospitality to the guests leaves much to be desired," says Hagen as he surveys the slaughter wreaked by his hosts. Even the fiddler, the stock accompanist of hospitable entertainments, is presented here in a negative way: Volker, Hagen's companion, is both musician and warrior, and, in a horrific metaphor, he is said to have "red rosin on his bow." Once again, the metaphors find their fullest resonance precisely because the normal repetitive devices of an oral poem—here, the type-scene—have been subverted in an artful and meaningful manner.

SONG OF ROLAND

Nearly one hundred French *chansons de geste* (songs of heroic action) survive; the earliest among them, the twelfth century *Song of Roland*, is also that with the most-sung theme: the defeat, through treachery, of Count Roland, nephew of Charlemagne, at Roncesvalles in the Pyrenees on August 15, 778, by a Saracen army. The poem is in four thousand ten-syllable lines, arranged in assonating groups of varying length, called *laisses*. Metrically, it is distinct, as are the other chansons, from the romance form that was composed contemporaneously. In content and viewpoint, the chanson is also distinct: While the romance tries to analyze emotions and offers fictional episodes, the chanson commemorates historical actions, from a neutral (or, at least, a third-person omniscient) point of view. As Joseph Duggan has shown, the degree of formulism in the language of the *Song of Roland* marks it as orally composed. The poem perhaps signals the end of a tradition, which must have been flourishing three hundred years before, when the events described by the poem occurred. The new type of poetry—romance—was a literary, written phenomenon, soon to become widespread, and evolving in several centuries into the modern novel. Meanwhile, the older, oral tradition must have been equally widespread in its day. There is evidence of a Spanish equivalent to the *Song of Roland* (the *Cantar de Roncesvalles*); the *Poem of the Cid* (*Cantar de mío Cid*), the great Castilian thirteenth century epic, must have grown out of a deep tradition like that behind the French poem. The transmission from performance by a *jongleur* to written text is still problematic, as is the case with other compositions of the oral style, but once again, the recognition that these poems arise from an oral heritage tends to focus attention away from criticism of the poems as allegory or psychological studies and toward the proper study of oral technique: diction, type-scene, theme, and repetition in all its forms.

The structure of the *Song of Roland* recalls once more the revenge poems. Here the revenge is dual: Charlemagne's punishment of the Saracens who have attacked the rear guard of his army on its return to France, and the later revenge of Ganelon, a Frankish peer who conspired with the Saracens to prompt the attack, in which his enemy Roland was killed. Within the framework of revenge is the description of the battle itself. In turn, this rhythmic unit is structured by smaller units—not the type-scene, but repeated triplets sharing similar diction. As in the *Odyssey* and *The Nibelungenlied*, the repeated units gain resonance as the poem progresses. Thus, in the *Song of Roland*, the use of triplets is common early in the poem for emphasis on any scenes that the poet considers to have important impact, or to be emotionally dense: The agreement between Ganelon and the Saracens, for example, is marked by a triple presentation of gifts to the Frank by the pagans' peers.

The poet can expand the use of triplets to cover wider areas in the poem; one such expansion verbally frames the kernel scene of the composition—that is, the sounding of Roland's ivory horn to summon help from the distant Charlemagne. Three times Oliver asks Roland to sound the horn, and each time Roland, in a slightly varied form, replies that the act would shame him. The hero of an oral poem, it should be noted, is more often than not bound by the very tradition that immortalizes him. Roland cites "what people will say" if he sounds the horn because of the Saracens—like Achilles or Beowulf, he must think of the fame or blame accorded him by later tradition. When the Franks fare badly in the battle, and Roland decides to sound the horn after all, the poet marks the event with a reversal of the triplet structure. This time, Roland speaks first of his resolve, then Oliver answers. Ideological positions are also reversed: Now it is Oliver who cites shame as reason for silence, Roland who seeks help. The device of repetition increases the drama of this tragic reversal; it is clear that Roland's rash arrogance has caused the defeat. When Roland finally sounds the horn, a final triplet echoes the call, describing the repeated, agonized attempt to make the sound, on Roland's part, and the repeated, disbelieving hearing on Charlemagne's. It is a stroke of poetic genius to duplicate the aural image of Roland's despair—the horn call—in an aural device, repetition; this is oral poetry using its traditional techniques to full advantage.

OTHER ISSUES

Although not discussed here, other oral traditions are rich, if not as thoroughly documented in Western literature. A fuller account of the sources and methods of oral traditional narrative poetry is needed. Even if it were to be restricted to Europe, such an account would have to examine Russian poems such as *Slovo o polku Igoreve* (twelfth century; *The Lay of Igor's Host*), and *bylina* poetry; the large field of Romance poetry other than the *Song of Roland* and the *Poem of the Cid*; and nonepic genres such as Greek and Irish praise poetry (Pindar and Bacchylides, bardic verse) and Icelandic skaldic compositions.

Of interest too is the relation between written and oral forms: It is clear that the two modes interact; it is equally certain that there is no one sure marker of oral or written style, since copying goes on from one sort to the other. Yet, while there has been much work done to "prove" that certain works have roots in oral traditionals, the student of modern literature would benefit most from the study of the figure of "speech" in known written literature. Repetition of words, motifs, themes—all of these in written works, such as the novel, are in fact the heritage of a "literature" that was not written but spoken to an audience that responded to such symmetries. What is the true written work—the epistolary novel? How deeply is the idea of speech and hearing ingrained in all literature? These are questions that an interplay of oralist and modern critical methods might have a better chance to solve.

BIBLIOGRAPHY

Acker, Paul. *Revising Oral Theory: Formulaic Composition in Old English and Old Icelandic Verse*. New York: Garland, 1998. Places oral-formulaic analysis within the larger context of folklore and mythology theory, concentrating on Eddic poetry, *Beowulf*, and Old Norse rune poetry.

Duggan, Joseph J. *The Song of Roland: Formulaic Style and Poetic Craft*. Berkeley: University of California Press, 1973. A study of the oral elements in the *Song of Roland*.

Finnegan, R. *Oral Poetry: Its Nature, Significance, and Social Context*. Reprint. Bloomington: Indiana University Press, 1992. A classic study of the anthropological context of oral poetry, largely derived from Finnegan's African fieldwork.

Foley, John Miles. *Traditional Oral Epic: The "Odyssey," "Beowulf," and the Serbo-Croatian Return Song*. Berkeley: University of California Press, 1990. A comparative study of oral techniques in Greek, Anglo-Saxon, and Yugoslavian epics.

_____. *The Singer of Tales in Performance*. Bloomington: Indiana University Press, 1995. Covers the theory of oral-formulaic composition and offers specific analyses of Serbian charms, Homeric hymns, and Old English poetry using the theory.

_____. *Homer's Traditional Art*. Philadelphia: University of Pennsylvania Press, 1999. Addresses the question of how an understanding of oral tradition can illuminate the understanding of the *Iliad* and the *Odyssey* and other ancient poetry.

Haymes, Edward R., and Susann T. Samples. *Heroic Legends of the North: An Introduction to the Nibelung and Dietrich Cycles*. New York: Garland, 1996. Covers the two major cycles of medieval Germanic epic poetry, with special attention to theories of oral composition.

Lord, Albert B. *The Singer of Tales*. 2d ed. Cambridge, Mass.: Harvard University Press, 2000. The classic work on Serbo-Croatian *guslars*, first published in 1960 and based on fieldwork carried out by Lord and Milman Parry, showing what illumination their techniques of oral composition can throw on the composition of the *Iliad* and the *Odyssey*.

_____. *The Singer Resumes the Tale*. Edited by Mary Louise Lord. Ithaca, N.Y.: Cornell University Press, 1995. A collection of Lord's essays, published after his death.

Nagy, Gregory. *The Best of the Achaeans*. Rev. ed. Baltimore, Md.: Johns Hopkins University Press, 1998. An important and controversial study of the construction of heroes and heroism in classical Greek poetry.

Ong, Walter J. *Orality and Literacy: The Technologizing of the Word*. Reprint. New York: Routledge, 1988. A classic explication of oral theory.

Opland, J. *Anglo-Saxon Oral Poetry*. New Haven, Conn.: Yale University Press, 1980. An excellent, thorough examination of the oral and formulaic characteristics of Old English poetry, placed within a comparative context.

_____. "Defining the Characteristics of Oral Style." *Comparative Literature* 45, no. 4 (1993): 361-372. A very useful review essay comparing John Miles Foley's elaboration of oral literary theory with Parry and Lord's original theses.

Parry, Adam, ed. *The Making of Homeric Verse: The Collected Papers of Milman Parry*. Reprint. New York: Oxford University Press, 1993. All of Milman Parry's important works, collected, edited, and in some cases translated by his son.

Zumthor, Paul. *Oral Poetry: An Introduction*. Translated by Kathy Murphy-Judy. Minneapolis: University of Minnesota Press, 1990. A comprehensive introduction to oral poetry, its performance contexts, composition, and evolution.

Richard Peter Martin

FRENCH POETRY TO 1700

ORIGINS

The history of French poetry in the early centuries is in fact the history of French literature as a whole. Prose was not cultivated as a literary medium until the thirteenth century, and for centuries after that the poetic genres continued to predominate. It thus seems appropriate to begin this essay with a brief survey of the history of the French language and of the forces involved in the creation of the nation-state of France.

Before France, there was Gaul. The French language developed out of the popular form of Latin spoken in Gaul under the Roman administration, which went back to Caesar's conquest of the region in the first century B.C.E. and endured until the fifth century C.E. By the time the Western Roman Empire had succumbed to waves of barbarian immigration, this language had already developed a character of its own and could be distinguished from the "purer" Latin of the cleric, scholar, and diplomat (which was to remain the language of learning and international intercourse for many centuries—although it, too, continued to evolve). The barbarian group that assumed political leadership of Gaul in the sixth century was the Franks, and while they gave their name to the territory and the language, they introduced few changes in the latter, which they learned from the Gallo-Roman population. "French" continued to evolve quite rapidly and was the first of the Romance languages to be recorded in writing.

The oldest document in the French language, preserved in a tenth century manuscript, goes back to C.E. 842 and consists of the oaths sworn in ratification of a treaty by Charles the Bald and Louis the German, two grandsons of Charlemagne. From the late ninth or early tenth century there survives a sequence, or liturgical poem, on the martyrdom of Saint Eulalia. It is important to realize that at that time, and for many centuries thereafter, French was not a single language but a group of related dialects, divided along regional lines. By the eleventh century, these dialects could be said to fall into two broad groups, called *langue d'oc* (language of *oc*) and *langue d'oïl*, after the word for "yes" in each. The *langue d'oc*, or Occitan, as it is known to modern linguists, was spoken in the south of France and included Provençal, the dialect of the troubadours. The *langue d'oïl* was a group of northern dialects, used by the authors of the *chansons de geste*. The Parisian dialect, which eventually came to dominate the others, grew in importance from the late twelfth century to the fifteenth, when it became the literary language of the country as a whole.

The first French literature of real importance appeared in the eleventh century. By that time, several institutions that were to play major roles in the development of France—and of French literature—had been established. The most important of these institutions, whose power was enhanced by their alliance, were the Church and the monarchy. A brief survey of their early history seems in order here.

The Church had the deeper roots and was the stronger of the two for many centuries. The Christianization of Roman Gaul had begun as early as the first century C.E., although the new faith encountered persecution there as it did in Rome. (Saint Denis, who gave his name to the basilica where French kings were buried for twelve centuries, was an early martyr, about C.E. 250.) By about the year 400, Christianity was well established, and it was adopted, along with the vernacular, by the Germanic immigrant-invaders of the fifth century. Church organization, modeled on the Roman imperial administration, survived this turbulent period intact and remained a source of stability throughout the Dark Ages that followed.

The baptism of the Frankish chieftain Clovis in 496 created the first link between the Church and what was to become the French monarchy, for Clovis was the founder of the Merovingian Dynasty, which continued to rule the Franks until the mid-eighth century, adding Burgundy and Provence to their realm. The Carolingian Dynasty, which followed, likewise obtained the sanction and support of the Church: Pepin I, its first representative to reign, was anointed at Saint-Denis by the Pope himself, and Charlemagne, Pepin's son, was crowned Holy Roman Emperor in Rome in the year 800. Charlemagne's empire, though short-lived (it fell apart almost immediately after his death), was responsible for a brief revival of classical learning. Indeed, the renewed interest in the classical form of the Latin language at this time helped to preserve Latin as the instrument of scholarship and diplomacy for the rest of the medieval period. Another enduring legacy of the Carolingian Empire was created by the sense of heroic possibility and divine sanction, which was embodied in the figure of Charlemagne himself, who quickly assumed legendary proportions.

The ninth century saw the division of the kingdoms that were to evolve into the states of France and Germany; it also saw violent inroads by the Vikings, Muslims, and Magyars (ancestors of the Hungarians) into Western Europe. During this period of unrest, political control was often reduced to its lowest terms, which meant smaller units of organization based on land tenure and on the capacity for self-defense. When Hugh Capet, founder of the Capetian Dynasty, was anointed by the Archbishop of Reims and succeeded the last Carolingian in 987, the territory under his control amounted to roughly one-fiftieth that of modern France. The centuries to come would see a continuing struggle between kings and nobles as the former sought to increase their lands and influence at the expense of the latter. The alliance between Church and monarchy, already a firmly established historical precedent, would prove a powerful fulcrum in this struggle. The monarchy would triumph, however, only with the help of a "third estate" still to emerge: the bourgeoisie.

THE ELEVENTH CENTURY

French literature, like the literature of ancient Greece, may seem to have sprung up full-blown, for the earliest surviving works—the eleventh century *chansons de geste*—are epics of great power and considerable sophistication. Like the Greek epics, however, they reflect both a period of poetic development (to which they owe their form) and a sense of history—specifically, the sense of looking back to a heroic past. The poetic development is very difficult to trace because of the dearth of evidence; it seems to owe much to the Latin verse forms used in the liturgy of the Church, and it may also reflect the memories of classical (especially Vergilian) epic preserved by the more educated of the clergy, who continued to produce Latin narrative verse throughout the medieval period. The impetus behind the flowering of

the *chanson de geste* seems, however, to have been largely historical and to some extent religious: Its appearance coincides with the beginning of the Crusades and with the consolidation of the feudal system, both eleventh century developments. Heroic songs celebrating the exploits of Charlemagne and his vassals may well have existed in Carolingian times and in the intervening centuries, yet it was in the eleventh century that these songs came into their own, and the glimpses they give of social and political organization correspond to the conditions prevailing during that period.

The heroic songs do not have anything to say (except incidentally) about the life of the peasant class, nor indeed much about the life of women of the noble class. They reflect the point of view and interests of the feudal lords for whose entertainment and edification they were composed. They also reflect to some extent the interests and teachings of the Church, for some were written by clerics, or at least by men of some education—and at this period all education was under the aegis of the Church. As Sidney Painter has demonstrated in his 1940 book, *French Chivalry*, there were conflicts throughout the Middle Ages between the views of the clergy and those of the secular nobility concerning the duties and virtues of a "true knight." Yet within certain bounds, clerical writers on chivalric conduct tended to accommodate Church teachings to the realities of feudal existence, which of necessity were dominated by the interests of the knightly class.

FEUDAL SOCIETY

The feudal system was neither created nor destroyed at a single blow; it evolved out of the confusion of the ninth and tenth centuries, reached its high-water mark in the eleventh, and declined gradually in the face of royal and bourgeois inroads over the course of the next four centuries. Because of its intimate connection with the *chanson de geste* and with the slightly later developments of romance and troubadour poetry, it deserves detailed consideration here.

The feudal social and political structure was based on land tenure and military might. These two factors were interdependent because of the technology of warfare: The knight needed both means and leisure to equip and train himself for combat on horseback in heavy armor. Because the economy was almost exclusively agricultural (until the twelfth century saw the revival of town life), knights depended for their income on the surplus produced by the peasants, serf or free, who tilled their lands. These lands were held as fiefs granted by the king or by one of the greater nobles in return for the knight's service in battle. Many fiefs were also held by the Church, and in early days bishops and powerful prelates were often themselves knights; a prominent literary example is Archbishop Turpin, one of the heroes of the *Chanson de Roland* (c. 1100; *Song of Roland*). The system proved well adapted to an age in which the absence of any strong central authority left the field open for brigandage and made communication and travel difficult. Under these conditions, such control as could be exercised was usually local and based on force or the threat of force. The knight was not seen as a parasite but as a professional soldier who performed the vital service of protecting those who lived on his lands—that is, those who fed and clothed him. The lack of central authority also made him a virtual sovereign, responsible for keeping the peace, enforcing the law, and judging those who broke it within his domain.

From the perspective of the *chansons de geste*, the most important aspect of the feudal system is the network of relationships it fostered among the knights themselves or between the knights and their overlords. The relationship of vassalage, whereby a man vowed his allegiance and loyal service to a more powerful lord in return for a fief, had both Roman and Germanic antecedents. On the fringes of the empire, men were often given land in return for (ongoing) service in the Roman army, and the German chieftains gathered about them groups of loyal retainers, each of whom could in turn call upon the freemen under his authority for help at need. Under the decentralized conditions prevailing after the breakup of Charlemagne's empire, local ties grew stronger, while allegiance to a far-off king grew tenuous. The effective control of much of France reverted to those barons, or lesser nobles, who were themselves the best fighters and could command the most loyal troops.

It is easy to see how important the friendships and rivalries between individuals might become in such a situation. Like Homer's warriors, the knightly heroes of the *chansons de geste* are bound by ties of strong affection and divided by fierce hatreds; each insists on his own prerogatives and is mortally offended by slights to his honor. It is probably no coincidence that Homer's age was also one of decentralized power and of recovery following the collapse of a palace-centered economy. In medieval France as in prehistoric Greece, these conditions gave an unusually wide scope to the ambitions of individual nobles. At the same time, the awareness in each case that a previous age (the Mycenaean for Homer, the Carolingian for the eleventh century poet) had seen achievements on a grander scale focused interest on heroic stories of the past. The historic accuracy of these stories is often questionable and sometimes nonexistent; the historic interest they convey is genuine and significant.

One of the three major cycles, or series of related chansons, deals with the court of Charlemagne and in particular with the prowess of his nephew Roland; the best known, and indeed the earliest, is the *Song of Roland*, which describes his last battle. As in the *Iliad* (c. 800 B.C.E.), the hero of the poem is not the commander in chief but one of his younger retainers, whose strength and daring make him more valuable in battle than men with more lands or larger contingents. The tragic plot of the poem is set in motion by the resentment and hatred of Roland's stepfather, Ganelon, whom Roland nominates for a dangerous embassy. (Roland has himself volunteered for the embassy, but Charlemagne has refused on the grounds that he is too valuable to risk.) Ganelon betrays Roland by urging the Saracens to ambush him in the Pyrenees as he commands the rear guard, covering Charlemagne's retreat from Spain. Overly confident of his own strength, Roland refuses to sound his horn (to summon help) until it is too late; at last, surrounded by dead and dying comrades, he sounds the horn, so that their deaths may be avenged, and dies extending his glove to God in an ultimate act of homage.

In a book-length study, *The Chanson de Roland* (1969), Pierre Le Gentil has shown how complex are the motives of both heroes and villains in the poem, and how subtle are the poet's means of characterization. Because of the directness of the narrative and the relative simplicity of the language, the modern reader may be tempted to dismiss it as "primitive"—from a twentieth century perspective, the absolute antagonism of Christian and "infidel" and the notion of "holy war" do seem both primitive and alien. To appreciate the poem's complexity and coherence, one must try to approach it on its own terms, within its eleventh century feudal context.

An important element of this context which remains to be discussed is the relationship between Christianity and the code of knightly conduct. The Church consistently tried to curb the excesses to which knights were prone, condemning tournaments and private war between Christians as vainglorious and homicidal. Yet war for profit (through plunder and ransom) remained a common occupation of the barons as long as the power of the king and his chief vassals was weak, while tournaments grew in popularity as the possibility of waging local wars waned. The Church did succeed in promulgating two more limited curbs on private warfare: The *Pax Dei*, or "peace of God" (late tenth century), laid a curse on those who plundered churches or the poor or harmed women or clergy, and the *Truga Dei*, or "truce of God" (eleventh century), forbade private war from Wednesday night to Monday morning and during the seasons of Christmas and Easter. Beginning in the twelfth century, ecclesiastical writers also urged the inclusion of a religious ceremony in the dubbing of new knights, to make them aware of belonging to a special "order" bound to uphold the faith (and, of course, the Church) as well as the behests of their secular lords.

The Church's greatest success, however, was in galvanizing the nobility of France for two great series of Crusades—in Spain and in Palestine—against the Islamic world. Although it is clear that the hope of profit was as important a motive in these wars as in local campaigns among rival barons, it would be as wrong to discount the religious motive as to give it sole consideration. Nor should the hope of secular glory—which plays such an important part in the *chansons de geste*—be ignored. The truth is that in this case, religious duty and individual ambition or hopes of profit could be made to coincide. Thus, Roland's love of battle and craving for glory are justifiable when used in the service of God, and spoils taken from Saracens are not considered ill-gotten gains but rewards for upholding a sacred cause. Sidney Painter quotes an especially apt passage from the troubadour Aimeric de Pégulhan: "Without re-

nouncing our rich garments, or station in life, courtesy, and all that pleases and charms, we can obtain honor down here and joy in Paradise." Although considerable opportunism was involved, there is no reason to read such a passage as merely cynical. The *chansons de geste*, no less than the Crusades, undoubtedly reflect, among other motives, a genuinely religious impulse. Like their pagan ancestors, these knights had no trouble reconciling piety and prosperity—or, as in the case of Roland, piety and glory.

EVOLUTION OF THE FEUDAL REGIME

The Crusades were only one factor, although an important one, in the prospects of the feudal class as they evolved over the course of the following centuries. In addition to carving out a Latin Kingdom of Jerusalem (whose first king, or "advocate," Godfrey of Bouillon, became the hero of several late *chansons de geste*), French knights led or took part in a number of foreign campaigns in the second half of the eleventh century which resulted in the creation of new fiefs and kingdoms: William of Normandy's invasion of England in 1066, Norman conquests in Sicily and southern Italy, Burgundian and Champenois inroads in Spain and Portugal. The younger sons of nobles, who had the least to gain by remaining at home, were drawn to these adventures in especially large numbers, and some slackening of feudal warfare at home ensued. During the same period, improvements in agricultural technique and equipment permitted the cultivation and resettlement of great areas within France that had lain fallow since the ninth century. This simultaneous external and internal expansion greatly increased the prosperity of France as a whole, and at first the knightly class was in a position to profit most by it. Alfred de Jeanroy, in *La Poésie lyrique des troubadours* (1934), has suggested that the resulting wealth and leisure were largely responsible for the rapid development of poetry in this period.

A further development of the age, however—the growth of a money economy—was to prove a transitory blessing to the lesser nobility, for it led, in the course of the following centuries, to a centralization of power in the hands of the king and his chief vassals, such as the dukes of Normandy and Burgundy and the counts of

Flanders and Champagne. The growth of towns and the proliferation of trade fairs at first provided nobles with sources of cash in the form of rents and market tolls, but their increasing dependence on such sources of income was eventually to make them vulnerable to royal devaluations of currency (in the fourteenth and fifteenth centuries) and inflation (in the sixteenth century). Meanwhile, the greatest gains were being made by the lords whose dependencies included the largest towns, and within the towns a class was rising that would seriously undermine the financial and even the political position of the nobility. Already by the end of the twelfth century, the king and dukes of France were using armies composed largely of poorer knights, who fought not in return for land tenure but for cash. At the same time, the great lords employed townsmen—bourgeois—as overseers of their estates, while the king, mistrustful of noble ambitions, began to rely increasingly on bourgeois civil servants. Yet the lesser nobility had had a taste of prosperity, and some were not ready to relinquish it, even if it meant abandoning their status as seigneurs and attaching themselves to the army or court of a richer lord. Thus, as Painter puts it, "the nobles of France entered on their metamorphosis into courtiers."

Prevented from waging private war, they increasingly engaged in tournaments for glory and profit, while those who had the leisure and the inclination cultivated the arts of poetry, music, and dance. The *chanson de geste* was not yet past its prime, but it began to face competition. At the richer courts, noble women took a more prominent social role and began to exert a distinct influence on ideals of chivalric conduct. The more powerful of these women, including Eleanor of Aquitaine and her daughter, Countess Marie of Champagne, became patrons of poets working in new lyric and narrative genres that gave a more prominent place to profane love. Originating in the south of France with the troubadours, the new theme soon spread to their northern counterparts, the *trouvères*; meanwhile, the "matter of France" (the Carolingian cycle) was gradually supplanted by the "matter of Britain" (tales of Arthur and his knights) and the "matter of Rome" (tales from classical mythology) as sources of plots for narrative verse. Thus, the *chanson de geste* was finally eclipsed by the *roman* (romance).

THE ROLE OF THE CHURCH

The twelfth and thirteenth centuries saw the high-water mark of the Church's independence and secular power, as well as of its hold on the intellectual life of France. Its independence was the result of a papal effort, begun in the eleventh century, to wrest control of clerical appointments from the nobility and kings of Europe, who had come to consider bishoprics and monastic offices as political plums—a means of rewarding and enriching their favorites. Using the powerful threat of excommunication, popes and their legates had insisted upon the right of monks to elect their abbots and of canons (clergy attached to a cathedral) to elect their bishops. Most Church property was also freed from feudal dues and appropriation. The new abbots and bishops were often men of integrity and considerable learning. In the eleventh and early twelfth centuries, the monastic orders of Cluny and Cîteaux took a leading role in the reform, and their efforts were largely responsible for the surge of church building known today as Romanesque.

During the course of the twelfth century, as towns grew in size and importance, leadership passed to the canons and bishops, and the Gothic phase of church building was focused on the cathedral. Episcopal schools also eclipsed the monasteries as centers of learning and became the seedbeds of what has been called the "twelfth century renaissance." In Chartres and Paris especially, there was a revival of classical learning and a spurt of literary activity in Latin, which remained the language of the schools (as the name of Paris's Latin Quarter recalls). An especially important development was the renewed interest in logic and dialectic as keys to learning. Thanks to contacts with Byzantium and with the Arabs, ancient texts that had been lost to the West were rediscovered, and an interest in Aristotle, the great logician, was stimulated by the commentaries of Islamic scholars. Logic was applied even to the "mistress of the sciences," theology, by Pierre Abélard and his students. Despite the fierce reaction this generated (under the leadership of the stern but charismatic Bernard of Clairvaux), the new schools continued to grow and to attract students from all over Europe; by the thirteenth century, Paris had become the intellectual capital of the West. (The Sorbonne, the first college of the University of Paris to be endowed, was founded in 1257.)

The thirteenth century was also the century of Thomas Aquinas, and it saw the triumph of Scholasticism, a system of philosophy and theology that forged a synthesis of ancient (Aristotelian) and Christian learning. It was chiefly through the cathedral schools and universities that the vernacular literature of France was enriched by contact with the classical legacy of dramatic, lyric, and epic poetry. The tradition of Latin didactic verse, which had been maintained throughout the Middle Ages by such clerics as had any learning, also flowed into the vernacular mainstream at this time, inspiring historical chronicles and other didactic works, at first in verse and then in prose.

LYRIC POETRY: TROUBADOURS AND TROUVÈRES

The first real flowering of lyric—as opposed to narrative or liturgical—poetry in France took place early in the twelfth century, in the southern regions of Aquitaine and Provence. This poetry was written not in the *langue d'oïl*—the language of the *chanson de geste* and the parent stock of modern French—but in the *langue d'oc*, often referred to as Provençal (something of a misnomer, since Provençal was only one of four dialects involved). It deserves more than a passing mention in the history of French poetry, and indeed in that of European poetry as a whole, for its influence on later poets was profound. This is especially true of its major theme—"courtly" love—but the complexity of its form was also admired and emulated for centuries, especially in France.

The South was at this period the most cosmopolitan region of France, thanks to its coastal towns, which carried on a growing trade with Italy, Spain, and the Middle East. The debt of troubadour poetry to Arabic forms of lyric is still a matter of some debate. It seems clear that there was at least some influence, traceable to contacts between the Occitan (southern French) and Islamic cultures in the course of the Spanish Crusades. In particular, the form known as the *zadjal* may have suggested the intricacy of verse forms and the theme of refined love characteristic of the troubadour lyrics. The influence of contemporary Latin verse, especially hymns, has also been demonstrated. Whatever its sources, this sudden flowering owed much to the newfound wealth and leisure of the nobles of Aquitaine and Provence in the early twelfth century; the first known troubadour was in fact the powerful Duke of Aquitaine, Guillaume IX (grandfather of Eleanor), and nearly all troubadours were of the noble class. Indeed, the decline of troubadour poetry—and of the *langue d'oc* as a literary language—may well be linked to the so-called Albigensian Crusade of the early thirteenth century, which in suppressing the Catharist or Albigensian heresy destroyed many of the noble families of southern France.

Troubadour poetry—all of which was written to be sung, either by the *trobador* (poet) himself or by a *jonglar* (French *jongleur*, professional singer)—comprises a number of distinct genres, each with its characteristic form, vocabulary, and themes. Thus, for example, the *planh* laments the death of a noble knight (usually the poet's lord); the *sirventes* explores a political or moral issue (such as prospects for war or peace, or the virtues and vices of different groups—young and old, Italian and German); the *tenson* takes the form of a debate in which opposing views are presented in alternating stanzas. By far the most popular forms, however, were those devoted to the theme of love, such as the *alba* (the lovers' parting at dawn) and the *canso d'amor* (love song). Indeed, even the *tenson* was often devoted to the fine points of courtship. Within an amazingly short time, a highly elaborate system of conventions evolved, and the elaboration was deliberate and self-conscious. It suited both the courtly milieu in which the troubadours moved and their necessarily indirect praise of a passion that was often adulterous.

A key metaphor in this system of conventions was feudal: The knight vowed homage and service to the lady of his heart, as to his liege lord, and (at least in the earlier poems) he often had some hope of recompense—if not in the form of sexual favors, then at least in the form of smiles, looks, kind words, or other "platonic" tokens of affection. A common complaint is that the lady is cruel or haughty and will not respond, although the lover's happiness—indeed, his very existence—depends on her. Sometimes it emerges that she is not unmoved but must feign indifference to protect her reputation or deflect her husband's jealousy, for the nature of this courtly or refined love (*fin' amor*) is such that it is rarely compatible with marriage—an institution more often used to further economic or political ends than to gratify the desires of individual men and women.

Women in particular were rarely consulted about their destined marriage partners, and it is easy to understand their craving, as increased prosperity gave them leisure to imagine such things, for the attentions of men who were attracted not to their houses and lands but to their persons and sensibilities. Although by far the greater number of troubadours were men (there were a few women), noble women seem to have played a considerable part in elaborating the ethic of "courtly" love; at the very least, they must have come to see themselves as worthy of gentle treatment and long courtship, withholding their favors from men who did not approach them with the proper deference.

As Frederick Goldin has indicated in his anthology *Lyrics of the Troubadours and Trouvères* (1973), adherence to the new ethic very soon became a condition of acceptance into the exclusive circles where it prevailed. The result was a new definition of the man of worth. In addition to noble birth and prowess in battle, he was to demonstrate the courtly qualities of fair speech, good manners, and a certain delicacy of feeling; above all, he was to find in love the source and focus of the knightly virtues. One of the fullest expositions of this new code is the *De amore* of André le Chapelain. A Latin prose treatise of the twelfth century, the *De amore* was translated into French in the thirteenth century and later into Italian and German; its author, a northerner (probably a protégé of Marie of Champagne), was one of the men responsible for the diffusion of courtly ideals among writers in the *langue d'oïl*. Needless to say, there were many discrepancies between the ideal and the reality, but the troubadours themselves were the first to acknowledge that, adopting an array of poetic voices—from the resigned "platonic" lover to the coarse womanizer—and playing them off against one another, sometimes within a single poem.

Efforts have sporadically been made to associate the troubadour ethic with the so-called Catharist heresy, the violent suppression of which in 1209 decimated the southern nobility and broke up the courts that had bred and sustained the troubadours. Among the attributes of the poetry that suggest such a connection are its hermetic style (*trobar clus*), which permitted the expression, in a kind of literary code, of ideas and feelings the "vulgar" were not to share, and the quasi-mystical attitude taken by some troubadours toward their ladies. (Women could attain to the highest positions within the Catharist sect and could be counted among "the Perfect," who were considered living saints.) It is difficult, however, to reconcile the often frankly erotic content of troubadour verse with the ascetic practices of the Cathars ("the pure").

The heresy was able to gain ground because, despite the twelfth century reforms, the Church was still a secular power, with all the abuses of its own doctrines that fact entailed. The Cathars, by contrast, preached a return to the austerity, simplicity, and charismatic fervor of early Christianity. The sect earned the respect of the peasants, but most of its adherents were of the noble and bourgeois classes. The Church could not ignore such a powerful challenge to its authority, and when attempts at conversion failed, Pope Innocent III ordered the Cistercians to preach a crusade against the sect. Most of the nobles of northern France took part, spurred by regional antagonisms and hopes of gain as well as by religious promptings. (Many southern nobles were in fact dispossessed of their lands.) The bloodshed was fearful, and the victims included many women and children. In addition, libraries were destroyed, a fact which may account for the dearth of surviving *chansons de geste* in the Occitan dialects.

The troubadour poems survived because they were esteemed and emulated (and thus recopied) in Italy and in the north of France. In this way, they became the antecedents of the *stil nuovo* or "new style" of Dante and his contemporaries, as well as of the lyrics of the French *trouvères* and the German *Minnesänger*. The *trouvères* in particular took over much of the original system of "courtly" images, themes, and forms, although they were less given to the hermetic style. As Frederick Goldin has shown, they also abandoned the troubadour's lively attention to his courtly audience, concentrating instead on the inner experience of the lover and "the possibilities of figurative language"—extended metaphor and simile. Finally, they enriched the repertoire of lyric forms by borrowing from folk song such genres as the *chanson de toile* (sewing song) and by reviving the classical taste for bucolic poetry (thus, the genre called the *pastourelle* portrayed knights wooing shepherdesses).

THE ROMANCE

In the mid-twelfth century, a new genre of narrative verse appeared which absorbed the courtly love ethic and fused it with plot material unknown in the *chanson de geste*. This was the romance. The *chansons de geste* did not disappear but were forced instead to yield first place in popularity to the new genre, which seems to have been inspired by the rediscovery of Roman epic (Vergil, Statius) and Greek romance (in Latin retellings). Another prominent influence was that of Ovid, whose interest in love and in the psychological states of his characters struck a chord in the courtly circles where romance took root. As in the *chansons de geste*, historical accuracy is not a matter of much concern; thus, one of the most famous romances, the twelfth century *Roman d'Alixandre* (from which the twelve-syllable line, or Alexandrine, may take its name) portrays Alexander the Great as a typical twelfth century knight, who holds tournaments and adheres to the chivalric code. Yet despite such contemporary elements, the world of the romances is largely a never-never land, a fabulous past in which magical powers operate and the courtly ideal is incarnated in "perfect knights." This is true not only of the classically inspired romances but also of the Arthurian group, the plots of which, borrowed from Celtic legend, probably entered French literature by way of the Anglo-Norman court of the Plantagenets (where, it should not be forgotten, Eleanor of Aquitaine reigned as queen during the second half of the twelfth century).

In the greatest romances, the flight from reality characteristic of the genre is mitigated by an interest in psychology—especially that of love—and by an exploration of real contradictions within the chivalric ethic. The work of Chrétien de Troyes (1150-1190) is outstanding in these respects. His romance *Érec et Énide* (c. 1164) probes the conflict between the demands of prowess and courtly love: Erec is distracted from knightly pursuits by his love for his young wife, and he tries to right the balance by forcing her to follow him—without speaking—as he goes in search of adventure. *Cligès: Ou, La Fausse Morte* (c. 1164; *Cligès: A Romance*) examines the quandary of a woman who is betrothed to a man she does not love and who has vowed fidelity to another. (Although a magic potion helps her keep her vow and evade her husband, her dilemma—and her husband's fierce jealousy—

are unmistakably real.) *Lancelot: Ou, Le Chevalierà la charrette* (c. 1168; *Lancelot: Or, The Knight of the Cart*), Chrétien's treatment of the Lancelot story, offers the most extreme version of the knight's "love service" to his lady and the frankest endorsement of adultery. It is interesting that Chrétien takes pains in his prologue to explain that his patroness, Marie de Champagne, suggested the story and the theme: It was at her command, he says, that he undertook the work.

Finally, Chrétien's last (and unfinished) romance, *Perceval, ou le conte du Graal* (c. 1180; *Perceval: Or, The Story of the Grail*), undertaken for a later patron, Philip of Flanders, describes the process by which an untutored boy becomes one of Arthur's greatest knights. Despite its fairy-tale quality, the story deals realistically with the pains and pleasures of growing up, as Perceval struggles to assimilate the courtly ethic and reconcile it with his duties as a Christian. (The legend of the Grail quest, which appears in *Perceval* and other early French romances, was reworked by Wolfram von Eschenbach, the German *Minnesänger*—who in turn inspired Richard Wagner's *Parsifal*, 1882—and by English writers in verse and prose, of whom the last and best known was Sir Thomas Malory.)

The romance continued to enjoy unabated popularity for centuries, but as early as the thirteenth century it began to be recast in prose, which would thenceforth eclipse verse as a medium for narrative. One of the last great verse romances, *Le Roman de la rose* (*The Romance of the Rose*), was composed in two sections from 1230 to 1240 (by Guillaume de Lorris) and from 1275 to 1280 (by Jean de Meung). It has been called "the most popular single work of the thirteenth century and perhaps of the whole medieval period" by Geoffrey Brereton in *A Short History of French Literature* (1954). It was also destined to enjoy great influence with the French poets of the sixteenth century. Its popularity seems to have resulted from the success with which it combined the dominant themes and interests of its age: the courtly, the didactic, and the satiric. The first of its two authors was of noble birth, the second bourgeois, and their attitudes toward their subject—the allegorical struggle of a lover to obtain the Rose of his desire—are antipathetic in several ways, yet complementary. Guillaume de Lorris, the greater poet of the two, is a faithful spokesman for the courtly tradition, which he sums up with exquisite grace and psychological subtlety. Jean de Meung, a product of the University of Paris and its Scholastic learning, is a rationalist who looks on love somewhat cynically and indeed seeks to undermine, through satire, the courtly conventions and the supremacy of the class that produced them.

COMIC AND SATIRIC POETRY: THE FABLIAUX AND THE ROMAN DE RENART

Virtually all the works discussed thus far, with the exception of the second part of *The Romance of the Rose*, were written by and for the members of the noble class; similarly, nearly all the characters portrayed in them are noble. The *fabliaux*, short narrative poems written in the meter proper to romance (octosyllabic rhyming couplets), offer a different view of thirteenth century society, one that includes bourgeoisie, peasants, and the lower clergy as well as knights and ladies. Some of the *fabliaux* are known to have been the work of nobles and wellborn clerics, and the genre undoubtedly had a place in courtly circles as a kind of comic foil to romance. Yet it was also used by the *jongleurs* and by the *goliards* (poor students, usually clerics), who tended to live from hand to mouth and were seldom of noble birth.

As the bourgeois class grew and prospered, it, too, sought the entertainment these itinerant singers had to offer, and found it in the down-to-earth *fabliaux*. Although the genre encompasses a wide variety of subjects, *fabliaux* may be distinguished from other short narrative genres, such as the courtly *lai*, pious *miracle*, and polemical *dit*, by their comic tone and ordinary, everyday setting. Although a good number end with a moral, the real focus of interest is usually the tale itself. Sometimes the moral is frankly ironic. In *De Brunain et de Blérain* (thirteenth century), a peasant and his wife give their cow to the local priest, who has assured them that God returns twofold what is offered him; when the cow breaks free and returns home leading the priest's cow, with which it has been tethered, the peasant is overjoyed and believes God has kept his promise. The poet closes with the moral the priest had preached—"He is rich who gives to God, not he who hides and buries [his goods]"—but its religious meaning, discounted by the

story, is replaced by a worldly one: Nothing ventured, nothing gained. Although a satiric vein is often visible in the *fabliaux*, as a group they neither spare nor single out any one class. Covetous priests, arrogant nobles, credulous peasants, and grasping bourgeoisie are all portrayed; the joke may be on any or all of them, depending, presumably, on the sympathies of the poet and of his audience.

The thirteenth century likewise saw the creation of longer and more directly satiric poems inspired by the various serious genres and by indignation at specific social abuses. Thus, the *Bible Guyot* (1205-1218), written by a monk, details the abuses of the clergy, while the mock-epic *Audigier*, in rebuttal of the romances and *chansons de geste*, portrays the nobility as cowardly and coarse. The most successful of all of these attempts, however, was the *Roman de Renart* (c. 1175-1205), which grew from an initial long poem into a vast cycle—indeed, into a veritable genre. Its oldest "branches," as they are called, were probably inspired by medieval Latin versions of the beast fable, a genre ultimately traceable to Aesop's fables (sixth century B.C.E.) but, as the shadowy figure of Aesop himself should indicate, owing much to folktale and thus susceptible to additions and reshapings from popular as well as literary sources.

The various poems of the cycle have in common a wily and unscrupulous hero, Renart the fox—usually known as Reynard in English—whose ability to outwit his "betters" (including not only Ysengrim the wolf and Brun the bear but King Noble the lion) suggested very early, if not from the beginning, a social satire in which the lower orders manage to get the better of their oppressors among the nobility and clergy. It is worth noting that the genre enjoyed its greatest popularity in the northeastern regions of Picardy and Flanders, where the bourgeois class was particularly strong and conscious of its rising economic power. Yet Renart is not a comfortable hero, and in one poem, *Le Couronnement Renart* (coronation of Renart), written about 1250, he actually obtains the crown—only to favor the rich while continuing to oppress the poor. In later branches, as in *The Romance of the Rose*, the stories are increasingly allegorical and didactic, becoming almost encyclopedic in scope; at the same time, political and social criticism is less veiled, and *Renart le Contrefait* (fourteenth century;

the title suggests both "Renart the Misshapen" and "Renart the Dissembler") has been seen as a foreshadowing of the Jacquerie, a fourteenth century peasant uprising.

THE FOURTEENTH AND FIFTEENTH CENTURIES

By the early fourteenth century, a series of strong Capetian monarchs had succeeded in extending the royal domain—the portion of French territory not held as fiefs but administered directly by the king—until it included almost three-fourths of the entire realm. With the help of the Church, which upheld the monarchy's "divine right" to rule, of the legal profession, which consolidated their power on the basis of Roman legal precedent, and of the bourgeoisie, who manned their civil service and whose growing wealth filled their coffers with tax revenues, the Capetians made themselves the most powerful monarchs of Europe. The apex of their fortunes was reached under Philippe le Bel (Philip the Fair, thanks to his good looks), who dared to defy the Pope—and carried the day.

The struggle began in 1296, when Boniface VIII declared that Philip had no right to tax the clergy without papal consent, and ended in 1303, when the aging Pope died, reputedly of shock, after being held under arrest by Philip's agents on charges that included heresy. The King's diplomatic maneuvers next secured the appointment of a French pope, Clement V, who actually transferred the papal court to Avignon in Provence, from which his French successors continued to reign until 1377. A number of important institutions of government were also established or strengthened during this period. Philip was the first French king to convene a meeting of the Estates General, made up of representatives of the country's three "estates," or classes: clergy, nobility, and bourgeoisie (referred to as the "third estate"). The first meeting, in 1302, was designed to align the nation solidly behind Philip in his struggle with the Pope. Later meetings were usually convened to raise general taxes, for which the king had to obtain the consent of feudal lords and independent towns; through its control of taxation, the Estates General wielded considerable power in the fourteenth century and during the Hundred Years' War. Although it lost this power to the monarchy in the late fifteenth century, the precedent had been set for a

governing body that was to include representatives of the nation as a whole. Finally, Philip IV enhanced the authority of the Parlement of Paris (a court of justice, not a parliament in the British sense), to the detriment of the nobility, who lost many of their judicial rights; by the fifteenth century, it had become independent even of the king, over whose legislation it held *de facto* power of judicial review.

At the accession in 1328 of Philip VI, the first king of the Valois line, the monarchy seemed stable and powerful; the kingdom was prosperous, and even the peasantry seem to have been feeling the good effects of two centuries of economic growth. In the course of the next two centuries, however, France was to be ravaged by the long, cruel conflict known as the Hundred Years' War. The steady concentration of power in the hands of the monarchy would be interrupted, to the temporary advantage of the feudal class. At the same time, the self-esteem of the French as a people would be shaken, a deep hatred of the English would be sown among them, and the costs of war, in lives and in resources, would prove staggering.

None of this was apparent until the war was well under way. The source of conflict was the issue of the French royal succession after the Capetian line ran out. After initially acknowledging Philip of Valois (a first cousin of the last Capetian king, Charles IV), Edward III of England decided to press his claim (through his mother, Isabel, Charles IV's sister) to the throne of France. As Duke of Aquitaine and Guyenne—which Eleanor had brought as a dowry to Henry II—Edward Plantagenet was a vassal of the French crown; the encroachments of the French monarchy on feudal privileges made some sort of confrontation between the two kings inevitable. At this date, Anglo-Norman, a dialect of the *langue d'oïl*, was still spoken by the ruling class of England, who shared a common culture with the nobility of France. Edward thus had no trouble picturing himself as king of France; he had everything to gain and relatively little to lose by the attempt. In the event, his success surprised even him. Although France was the richer kingdom, its army—composed of heavily armored knights—proved inferior to the English, whose longbows were able to pierce armor while permitting greater mobility. The battles of Crécy and Poitiers, in

1346 and 1356 respectively, were not only military victories for the English but also severe blows to the prestige and chivalric ideology of the French nobility.

A more serious blow to the French cause was the capture of Philip IV's successor, King John, who had to be ransomed at incredible cost. A striking proof that the chivalric code still had substance at this period is the fact that when one of John's sons, who had been sent to England as hostage pending full payment of his father's ransom, broke his word and escaped, John himself returned voluntarily to London. The Treaty of Calais (1360) gave the French a breathing space, and John's canny successor, Charles V, who renewed the conflict, might have driven the English from France had he lived; he died however, at the age of forty-three, leaving a twelve-year-old son, Charles VI, who went mad in his early twenties and became a puppet of his unscrupulous and ambitious uncles. The latter took advantage of the King's weakness to extend their own power, and a feudal order reemerged in which chronic struggles among the French lords themselves further bled the country.

The vigorous Henry V of England, capitalizing on this state of affairs, allied himself with the dukes of Burgundy and made deep inroads into France between 1415 (the date of the Battle of Agincourt) and 1429, when the tide was finally turned by Joan of Arc, who believed she had been called by God to cast the English out of France. Although she was captured by the Burgundians in 1430 and burned by the English as a witch in 1431, her military victories, and chiefly the coronation of Charles VII, which she brought about, restored French morale. By 1436, Charles was able to reenter Paris, which the English and Burgundians had occupied since 1418. The country was so exhausted by the long struggle that it took until 1450 to expel the English from Normandy and until 1453 to take Guyenne, their last stronghold. (Only Calais, on the Channel opposite Dover, remained in English hands.)

Despite their ultimate victory, the French suffered far more in the war than did their enemies, many of whom were enriched by the spoils they took and whose prestige as a nation waxed as that of France waned. The war was fought almost exclusively on French soil, and the civilian population was subjected to plundering by French

as well as English soldiers. The war likewise interfered with the cultivation of crops and the distribution of food, so that famine was widespread. Still more victims were claimed by the Black Death, or bubonic plague, which reached France in 1348 and 1349, recurring, less severely, in 1361. The disease is believed to have killed about a third of the population of Europe, including half the inhabitants of Paris (fifty thousand people) and thousands more throughout France. The death toll was undoubtedly increased by ignorance of the process of contagion; the same ignorance, in the face of such devastation, fostered the conviction that God had chosen this means to punish his people for their sins. Many believed the end of the world was near. That the plague was no respecter of persons and did not respond to collective acts of penitence struck terror in the believers; the varied responses included fanatical outbreaks of anti-Semitism, attempts to legislate morality, and discontent with the clergy, some of whom avoided ministering to the dying for fear of catching the disease. Although there were upsurges of piety, so that the Church was enriched by bequests, it was seen as having failed to mitigate or even to explain the suffering.

For other reasons as well, the moral authority of the Church declined steadily in the course of the fourteenth century. Corruption was perhaps the greatest single factor: The hierarchy resorted increasingly to simony (the sale of Church pardons, appointments, and dispensations) to satisfy its taste for luxury. At the papal court in Avignon—which Petrarch, writing in the 1340's, called "the Babylon of the West"—cardinals and prelates vied with one another in extravagance of dress; many had private palaces and mistresses. The Avignon "captivity" of the Papacy, which lasted until 1377, was immediately followed by the Great Schism (1378-1417), during which two and even three rival popes simultaneously laid claim to the office. Yet the hold of Catholicism was not easily shaken. It continued to provide the terms in which most men understood their existence and the rituals with which they faced life's crucial moments. Like the idea of chivalry and the prestige of the knightly class, the moral ascendancy of the Church and the prestige of the clergy were undermined by events of the fourteenth and fifteenth centuries, but they did not collapse. Indeed, as Johann Huizinga argued in his important book, *The Waning of the Middle Ages* (1924), the pomp of Church and court and the elaborate distinctions of rank observed by both may well have been alternatives to, or forms of compensation for, the widespread pessimism of the age. It was not an age of reform, and in that respect it was, as Huizinga saw, a prolongation of the Middle Ages.

EVOLUTION OF LITERARY FORMS

The art and poetry of the fourteenth and fifteenth centuries reflect a similar tendency to elaborate old forms and themes rather than to seek new ones. In architecture and sculpture, the "flamboyant" style (so named for the flame-like motif it favored) was an outgrowth of the Gothic. In literature, the romance and even the *chanson de geste* were still in vogue, while the heirs of the *trouvères* continued to celebrate courtly love in intricate lyric measures. Yet new trends were visible as well. Poetry no longer held a monopoly of the literary genres; narratives, including romances and historical chronicles, began increasingly to be written in prose. At the same time, while many poets still wrote works intended to be sung, lyric poetry began to disengage itself from song, as narrative poetry had done at the appearance of the romance. Finally, lyric poetry made room for a certain realism, inspired by the harsh conditions of the age. The supreme poetic achievement of the age is that of François Villon, who combined his contemporaries' attention to form with his own uniquely realistic perspective on the ills—and the sins—of his generation.

In the fourteenth century, the repertoire of lyric forms inherited from the *trouvères* was enriched by the *ballade* (not to be confused with the English ballad), the *rondeau*, and other fixed forms that were to predominate for several centuries. In contrast to the sonnet, a highly versatile form developed in Italy at this period (but which would not enter French literature until the sixteenth century), these forms were both complex and rigid. To borrow a comparison from Geoffrey Brereton,

the composer of the shortest *ballade* has to find fourteen similar rhymes of one sort, six of another, and five of another—besides working in an identical line four times. The sonneteer needs a maximum of only four rhymes of the same sort and he does not have to repeat any of his lines.

It was inevitable that such forms should suggest a certain artificiality, especially in the hands of their less skillful practitioners. Yet some skill in poetry was evidently expected of the average "gentleman," as in Elizabethan England, and a collection of one hundred *ballades* by various hands (none of them professional) attests a fairly high standard of competence.

There were also more or less professional poets attached to the courts of princes; thus, Guillaume de Machault (c. 1300-1377) was chaplain, secretary, and court poet to John, King of Bohemia, while Eustache Deschamps (c. 1346-1406) served at the courts of Charles V and of his son Louis, Duke of Orléans. Jean Froissart was a protégé of Philippa of Hainault, the queen of Edward III of England; he is best known for his prose *Chroniques* (late 1300's; *Chronicles*, 1523-1525) of contemporary history, but he wrote lyric poetry as well. One of the most popular poems of the age, *La Belle Dame sans merci* (1424), was the work of Alain Chartier, secretary to Charles VI and historiographer of Charles VII. Although none of these men was of noble birth, they fully espoused and promoted the chivalric ideology still prevailing in the noble circles in which they moved. The same is true of Christine de Pisan, one of the first professional women of letters, who sought the patronage of various nobles in order to support her three children (she was widowed as a young woman). It is interesting that while these writers made autobiographical allusions in their prose works, most of them clung to conventional courtly themes—the lovers' debate, the allegorical journey—and put relatively little of their personal experience into their poetry.

The same may be said of the most talented of them, who happened also to be the highest-born: Charles, Duke of Orléans (1391-1465), a nephew of Charles VI and father of Louis XII. Taken prisoner at the Battle of Agincourt, he spent twenty-five years in England because his family could not afford the ransom demanded. Thanks to his rank, he was not harshly treated, and he took advantage of his enforced leisure to cultivate his talents as a poet. Although he used the same rigid forms as his contemporaries, his verse is distinguished by an impression of spontaneity—which is the result, however, of a thorough mastery of his medium. With Charles d'Orléans, the medieval taste for allegory finds a culminating expression (his earliest poem is a kind of *The Romance of the Rose* in miniature) and at the same time begins to shift toward true metaphor. It seems fitting that the last great representative of the courtly tradition should have been—like the first, Guillaume IX, the troubadour—a *grand seigneur*, a high-ranking member of the class that tradition had celebrated.

François Villon (1431-1463?), the other great poet of the fifteenth century and one of the greatest of all time, offers a striking contrast in every respect to his noble contemporary, whose court at Blois he seems to have visited. A poor boy, son of an illiterate mother (for whom he wrote a moving prayer to the Virgin), Villon was educated at the University of Paris, thanks to a priest who became his benefactor. He might have made a career in the Church but instead was drawn to the headier, if more dangerous, life of the tavern and the street. He was tried for various crimes, ranging from murder to church robbery, and was certainly guilty of some of them. Banished from Paris in 1458, he wandered about the country and may have belonged—as did two of his friends—to a gang of thieves. Certainly, he saw the miseries of the age at first hand, and he describes them in vivid detail, from the point of view of the poorest classes. Although he used the poetic forms current in his day and made no technical innovations, his subject matter and tone are strikingly new. There were precedents for confessional poetry in the thirteenth century works of Ruteboeuf (a poor student and defrocked cleric), Jean Bodel, and Adam de la Halle; the latter two wrote *congés* (leave-takings) that seem to look ahead to Villon's *Le Grand Testament* (1461; *The Great Testament*). Villon's entire oeuvre, however, is infused with the confessional impulse.

It is especially revealing to compare Villon's entry in a poetic contest sponsored by Charles d'Orléans with Charles's own entry. The theme assigned to all, "I die of thirst beside the fountain," suggested to Charles the unreliability of Fortune, who leads him in good times and in bad, yet the terms of his complaint are general and his tone even, although melancholy. The one specific reference, to "the fire of lovers," even makes it possible to read the poem as a conventional lover's complaint, although this theme is not developed and a broader interpretation seems preferable. To Villon, how-

ever, the paradox of want in the midst of plenty immediately suggests his own precarious existence; as his refrain stresses, he is "bien recuilly, debouté de chascun" ("welcomed and rebuffed by everyone"). It has been suggested that the envoi, or closing stanza, addressed by convention to an unspecified "prince," is in fact an oblique appeal to Charles for support. In any case, the urgency of Villon's tone is unmistakable; he brings a new subject matter to the courtly form, to powerful effect. Of all the poets considered thus far, Villon offers the most immediate and compelling look at his own world. His poems capture the brutality and pessimism of the age that produced the *danse macabre* (a common motif in the visual arts—a procession containing people of all classes, being led away by Death, a grinning skeleton). Yet Villon also sees, and makes his readers see, the humor and the faith that made it possible to survive in that world.

THE SIXTEENTH CENTURY

The sixteenth century in France was dominated by two related movements best known to twentieth century readers as the Renaissance and the Reformation. Both were made up of smaller and disparate movements, yet while it is important to acknowledge the diversity this implies, the labels have stuck because they point to consistent trends amid the diversity. The century *was* characterized by a revival of interest in forms of art and learning stemming from classical models, and it saw the appearance of "reformed" Christian churches whose definitive rejection of Roman Catholicism led to long and bloody struggles. Both movements affected the whole of Europe, and neither began in France. It makes sense to speak of a French *form* of each, however—particularly since the sixteenth century saw the first appearance of strong national feeling among the French. Although this feeling would be seriously threatened by the religious wars of the second half of the century, it would reemerge upon the accession of Henry IV, the first of the line of Bourbon kings.

The Renaissance or "rebirth" of arts and letters had economic underpinnings: It was made possible by a gradual recovery (after the Hundred Years' War), followed by a boom in trade that favored French merchants and artisans because they were in a position to provide the finished goods Europe was seeking. Spain had silver and gold from her New World colonies but wanted cloth, leather, tools, and even food (Spanish agriculture as well lagged behind that of the French). All of these commodities the French had for sale. This was the era in which the modern form of capitalism can be said to have made its appearance, as the merchant class assumed the upper hand in the disposition of the country's wealth: The nobles spent money lavishly, but the bourgeoisie loaned and invested—and earned. Since the reign of Louis XI (1461-1483), who had picked up (or stolen or bought back) the pieces of his realm after the Hundred Years' War, the bourgeoisie had also provided the backbone of the royal administration. The noble class might live extravagantly—indeed, were expected to do so—and win glory in foreign campaigns, but they were chronically in debt and thus dependent on both the bourgeoisie (the moneylenders) and the king (the dispenser of offices and pensions). Meanwhile, a new order of nobility—the *noblesse de robe*, so called because they held judgeships—was being culled from the ranks of the bourgeoisie by kings anxious to reward their faithful officers and to win allies among this newly powerful class. Although social distinctions were carefully maintained between the *noblesse de robe* and *noblesse de sang* (the hereditary nobility), the former imitated the latter as much as they could, and often lived more sumptuously, as did many of the *grands bourgeois*.

Yet despite these far-reaching changes in economic and social organization, French kings continued to rule by "divine right" and to have the final word in most policy decisions, especially those regarding foreign policy. Indeed, thanks to increased control over the debt-ridden nobility and the rising bourgeoisie, the power of the monarchy was more far-reaching than ever before, to the point that the term "absolute" is often applied to the monarchy of this and the following two centuries. The concordat, or agreement with the Pope, of 1516 increased royal power and finances further by making the king the *de facto* head of the Church in France, with authority to name successors to all major ecclesiastical posts. Because of the concordat, French kings were not tempted to use the stirrings of religious reform as an excuse to break with Rome, as did Henry VIII of England. The early years of the century were thus years of relative tolerance, in which religious questioning was but one symptom of the new approach to intellectual inquiry.

A combination of surplus wealth, absolute control of foreign policy, and old chivalric ideas permitted three French kings in succession to invade Italy in the late fifteenth and early sixteenth centuries. Although their territorial gains were short-lived and costly, they brought back with them to France a passion for the way of life they had tasted in Italy and a determination to transplant it to their native soil. They and their officers patronized artists such as Raphael, Michelangelo, and Leonardo da Vinci (the latter died at Francis I's château of Amboise); they built new, airy palaces and decorated them in a style inspired by that of Renaissance Italy, then in its culminating phase. Above all, they collected books and manuscripts and patronized scholars who had rediscovered the learning of the ancient world. Nor was it a simple matter of recovering lost texts and cultivating skills that had waned (such as the knowledge of classical Greek); the old texts were read in a new spirit.

In the first place, an avid intellectual curiosity was fed by new admiration for the powers of the human mind. The work of establishing accurate texts and translations called for critical acumen and self-confidence; instead of resorting to unquestioned authorities, scholars such as Guillaume Budé and Lefèvre d'Étaples produced their own commentaries. They also tended to focus their studies on man rather than on God—but this does not mean that they were irreligious. Although most of them criticized the temporal abuses of the Church, only a few took the further step of rejecting its authority in spiritual matters. While marveling at the purely human virtues they saw in the old pagan authors, they also re-edited the Bible and translated it into French; the study of Hebrew was revived along with that of Greek. Moreover, when the first printing presses appeared in France in the late fifteenth century, the majority of works published were not the classics but missals and other devotional books.

As Lucien Fèbvre emphasized in his influential essays on Renaissance France, printing was from the first a business, requiring considerable capital and hinging on possibilities of profit. The classics were printed later, and in smaller quantities, because they appealed to a smaller public, clustered in a few centers of learning: Paris, the Loire Valley (where the new royal châteaus were rising), Lyons (the great trading center of the age). It is important to realize, however, that the new learning was not confined to the upper classes; in fact, the chivalric ideal, which maintained its hold despite—and perhaps in compensation for—the dwindling power of the nobility, valued social graces and feats of arms above learning, and proportionally fewer nobles than one might expect became scholars.

The Reformation owed as much to the revival of classical learning as it did to the rise of the bourgeoisie. To approach sacred texts in a critical spirit is ultimately to assert the autonomy of the scholar, and of his conscience. John (Jean) Calvin, who became the leader of the reform movement in France, was a student of the Humanist scholar Guillaume Budé; at the Académie, Calvin's seminary in Geneva (established in 1559), his preachers received a thorough training in the classics as well as in theology. The same was true, however, of the preachers recruited by Ignatius Loyola and his Society of Jesus, founded in 1534 to stem the tide of the Reformation; reformers and counterreformers alike turned to the classics as models of clear exposition and—perhaps most important—of effective argument. The struggle between them was a fierce one, and it was not confined to the lecture hall and the pulpit; as nobles, *grands bourgeois*, and even cities took sides, it immediately became a political issue, with bloody consequences.

During the first third of the century, as the ideas of Martin Luther began to circulate in France, Francis I took a tolerant attitude while remaining orthodox himself. (His sister, Marguerite of Angoulême, was still more receptive to the new doctrines, and not only patronized but also protected many of the Huguenot—French Protestant—writers, including the poet Clément Marot.) Francis did not adopt a policy of repression until 1534, when the so-called "affair of the placards" made him fear for his own power. His son, Henry II, pursued this policy in a more fanatic spirit, and great numbers of Protestants were executed as heretics—although martyrdom had the effect of reinforcing Protestant convictions.

The event that led to civil war, however, was the death of Henry II in 1559. His three sons, who succeeded him one after the other, proved unable to control the state, and feudal ambitions, newly fused with religious animosities, erupted in a series of eight wars between 1562 and 1598. Both sides were guilty of fanaticism and atrocities; the most appalling single incident was the massacre of Protestants that began on the feast of Saint Bartholomew in 1572. The struggle was further complicated and intensified by the participation of foreign troops (Spanish and Italian Catholics, English and German Protestants), whose ostensible motive was to aid their coreligionists but who were often used to further the ambitions of foreign monarchs.

With the death of Henry III in 1589, the dynasty of the Valois came to an end and was succeeded by that of the Bourbons, whose first representative, Henry IV, had to renounce his Protestant faith to secure the allegiance of Paris. The bourgeois Parlement, as well as the Estates General (convened in 1592), clearly expressed public resentment of foreign intruders and weariness of religious strife. The Edict of Nantes, which Henry promulgated in 1598, granted freedom of worship to Protestants and Catholics alike, while a treaty with Spain in the same year marked the end of foreign intervention. Henry was not slow to gather the reins of absolute power into his hands, thereby setting the stage for the glories and abuses of the century of Louis XIV.

A CENTURY OF POETS

The sixteenth century saw a great efflorescence in French poetry. Although none of the individual poets had quite the stature of Villon, there were so many of them, and of such high quality, that the term "Renaissance" may be applied without hesitation. It is doubly appropriate because the new poetry was both a reflection of Italian influence at the height of that country's Renaissance and a genuinely French development, infused with confidence in the literary potential of the French language.

The century began with a school of poets known to critics as the *Rhétoriqueurs* because of their fondness for elaborate rhetorical figures. They represent both the end of a phase of development—the obsession with form that had marked the lyric poetry of the fourteenth and fifteenth centuries—and the beginning of the new Renaissance phase. Thus, despite their fondness for old forms, whose complexity they increased wherever possible, and for old themes (allegorical treatments of courtly love), they also took pride in their native language. One of the most talented of them, Jean Lemaire de Belges, even composed a treatise interspersed with poems, whose object was to demonstrate the equality of literary merit between French and Italian. Finally, two of the *Rhétoriqueurs*, Jean Marot and Octovien de Saint-Gelais, had sons who became better poets than their fathers—but who owed to those fathers their early formation as poets.

French Renaissance poetry, like that of the *Rhétoriqueurs*, was superior to all court poetry. Most of its practitioners were not themselves nobles but courtiers, attached to noble patrons who appreciated the arts. The most coveted places were at the royal court, where some of the century's best poets, including Clément Marot and Pierre Ronsard, served in various capacities. (Poetic excellence was not sufficient, however, to ensure permanent favor: Marot fell from grace because of his Huguenot sympathies, and Ronsard because of the death of his royal patron, Charles IX.) Yet there were other milieus in which poetry could flourish. The new passion for learning gave rise to circles or salons among the bourgeoisie, of which the most famous was that of Louise Labé, called "la Belle Cordiére" because both her father and her husband were prosperous rope makers. She was herself a poet of considerable merit, and her circle, in Lyons, attracted other poets of both sexes who drew inspiration from the style of Marot and the Italian Petrarch. The circle of seven poets known as the Pléiade (after the constellation of the Pleiades) took shape at a school in Paris and was made up of students of the Humanist scholar Jean Dorat. Earlier in the century, before the Catholic repression set in, there had been circles united by an interest in religious reform as well as in Humanist learning; the most brilliant of these was the court of Marguerite d'Angoulême, sister of Francis I.

The two most striking characteristics of the new poetry fostered by these circles were its adaptation of Italian and classical forms and its steadily increasing sophistication of style and tone. From Petrarch, the fourteenth century Italian poet, it borrowed the sonnet

sequence, and as Petrarch had celebrated the stages of his idealized love for "Laura," so Maurice Scève explored his for "Délie" (1544) and Joachim du Bellay his for "Olive" (1549). Ancient forms of lyric verse were borrowed—the ode, the epistle, the elegy—and attempts were even made to revive the epic in its classical, Vergilian form. (Classical tragedy was also revived at this period, with considerable success.) A school of so-called neo-Latin verse flourished in Humanist circles, and many of the poets best known for their French verse also composed in Latin.

There was an ongoing debate concerning the relative merits of Latin and French, which prompted the members of the Pléiade to issue a kind of manifesto (composed by du Bellay) called the *La Deffence et illustration de la langue françoyse* (1549; *The Defense and Illustration of the French Language*, 1939). In addition to defending the merits of French as a medium for great poetry, du Bellay recommended that it be further "ennobled" or "elevated" through emulation of the classical genres and by borrowings from Latin vocabulary and syntax. Because of differences in the structures of French and Latin, and notably because Latin (like Greek) is an inflected language, some of these borrowings proved too artificial and were not naturalized into the poetic repertoire of French. In general, however, the emulation of ancient models brought a new sophistication to French lyric, which is perhaps best appreciated by comparing the poetry of the earlier generations of Renaissance poets with that of the Pléiade. This is scarcely to denigrate Marot and his contemporaries, whose style some will prefer *because* it is less polished or more "Gallic" (Marot was, after all, the contemporary of François Rabelais). It is merely to acknowledge a prominent trend, which produced some outstanding results and set the tone for half a century of French verse.

It remains to acknowledge the striking range of theme and mood visible in French Renaissance poetry—a range corresponding to the variety of genres it rediscovered and adapted, but corresponding as well to the range of emotions generated by the events of the century. Thus, side by side with the graceful and often passionate love poetry inspired by Petrarch, one finds the melancholy but stately sonnets of du Bellay's *Regrets* (1558), inspired by classical elegy, and the unfinished epics attempted by Ronsard and Guillaume du Bartas; one also finds Ronsard's eloquent defense of his Catholicism in the *Discours* (1562; discourses) and Agrippa d'Aubigné's fierce blend of satire and indignation (in the Protestant cause this time) in his *Les Tragiques* (1616). Not infrequently, a considerable range is to be found in the work of a single poet. Marot, for example, though best known for his badinage (or light, playful wit), was equally capable of fervent lyricism (as in his translation of the biblical Psalms) and of vehement satire in the vein of d'Aubigné ("L'Enfer," or "Inferno," was inspired by his imprisonment for his Protestant beliefs). For sheer versatility, Ronsard was unequaled; he tried his hand at dozens of genres, and even his failures—such as an attempt to emulate the Pindaric odes—are the result of lapses of taste rather than any lack of poetic vigor. The rediscovery of Greece and Rome had enriched the repertoire of poetic forms and themes, but the passion conveyed was the poets' own— the faith and the anguish, the loves and the ambitions of a turbulent century.

THE SEVENTEENTH CENTURY

In the seventeenth century, the French monarchy, the *ancien régime*, reached its apogee and began its decline. In an important sense, Louis XIV can be held responsible for both of these developments, although it is arguable that he did more to hasten the decline than to gain the summit, which had been the long-sought objective of Cardinal Richelieu and Cardinal Mazarin before him (not to mention Henry IV and Francis I). It was Louis XIV, the "Sun King," who sought to formalize and demonstrate his power in the visible symbol of Versailles—a court whose every grace and virtue (and extravagance and whim) was ultimately an expression of his own will. Clearly, this was in many ways a fiction, and a pernicious one insofar as it blinded Louis himself to important social and economic developments in his realm. It was, however, a fiction of great power, which many seventeenth and eighteenth century rulers tried to emulate and which left its mark on French culture well beyond the Revolution.

Like their predecessors since Philip IV, both Louis XIII and Louis XIV—whose reigns together spanned nearly the entire century—based their power on the em-

ployment of bourgeois ministers while reducing the nobility to the status of dependents of the crown. Because both acceded to the throne in childhood, two of their ministers, the cardinals Richelieu and Mazarin, were virtual rulers of France for long periods. Richelieu was responsible for rebuilding the French military, crushing noble intrigues against Louis XIII, and humbling the Habsburg dynasty in the Thirty Years' War, thereby securing the borders of France. Mazarin pursued Richelieu's policies after the latter's death, and, despite the four-year setback of the Fronde (1648-1652), managed to complete the submission of the nobility and the containment of Habsburg Spain.

The Fronde was in fact the last real attempt of the French nobility to recoup the power they had been steadily losing to the monarchy since the thirteenth century. By allying themselves with the bourgeois Parlement and the Parisian masses, incensed by Mazarin's attempts to tax them, a coalition of princes managed for a time to expel "the Italian," whose foreign birth inspired suspicion and hatred. A quarrel between the rebellious factions, however, which coincided with Louis XIV's coming of age, spelled the end of the uprising. Moreover, the fear and humiliation which the young Louis experienced during the Fronde made him determined never to share his power with the nobility—nor, indeed, with the higher clergy. After Mazarin's death, he served as his own first minister and chose his other ministers from among the lower classes. He refused to convene the Estates General, suppressed what political initiative the Parlement had acquired, and brought even provincial administration under his direct control by the use of agents known as *intendants*.

Considering himself the spiritual as well as the temporal head of the French Church, he took the disastrous step of revoking the Edict of Nantes. This had the practical effect of driving numbers of Huguenots into exile, to the great detriment of French industry. The worst abuse of Louis's reign, however, was his utter disregard of fiscal realities. In planning Versailles and in waging continual war for what he considered the greater glory of France, he stubbornly refused to count costs. When combined with a bureaucratic control of industry and a cruelly unfair system of taxation (which exempted the rich while crushing the peasantry), Louis's prodigality paved the way that was to lead, in another century, to revolution. (A number of tax revolts among the peasants marked the decade of the 1670's.)

Despite its claims to absolutism, the monarchy was not the only institution in seventeenth century France, nor did Louis have a monopoly on the ideas of the age. It was an age in which religion still held great power, not only over the minds of individuals but also over institutions (such as the Sorbonne) and intellectual life—though its premium on philosophical truth would be challenged in the course of the century. If the French Church was largely subordinate to the king in temporal matters, it retained much authority in spiritual matters and could use this authority to political as well as spiritual effect. Thus, the international order of the Jesuits played a role in both the Thirty Years' War and the revocation of the Edict of Nantes.

Louis XIV's confessor was a Jesuit, and the king seems to have been following his advice in suppressing the ideas of Cornelius Jensenius and his French followers. The Jansenists, though Catholics, had ideas on predestination that resembled those of John Calvin. Their adherents included brilliant men of letters such as Jean Racine and Blaise Pascal, whose *Les Provinciales* (1656-1657; *Provincial Letters*) were at once a defense of Jansenist teachings and an attack on the moral "casuistry" of the Jesuits. The Jesuits, and the Pope, focused their attacks on the Jansenists' notion of grace, but there can be little doubt that the moral austerity and integrity of the latter also made them a source of embarrassment to a corrupt Church and a corrupt court. Among the orthodox, too, there were initiatives toward reform, such as the creation of new religious orders and of a secret society, the Compagnie du Saint-Sacrement, whose efforts ranged from charitable works to persecution of Protestants, Jansenists, and freethinkers (Jean-Baptiste Molière criticized its excesses in his *Tartuffe*, 1664).

Religious questions were rendered still more pressing by the growth of skepticism or "libertinism." The work known as Pascal's *Pensées* (1670; English translation, 1688) consists of notes for an ambitious project he never completed: a "Defense of the Christian Religion," addressed to the *mondain*, or "man of the world," who in Pascal's day would have been increasingly likely to doubt or neglect religious teachings. Both the hypocrisy

of the clergy and the luxurious life of the court were factors in this skepticism, but a new factor was philosophical doubt, sown by the growing split between religious and scientific truth. The Copernican theory of the solar system, developed in the sixteenth century, had been reaffirmed by Galileo in 1632. Although the Inquisition forced Galileo to recant, this proved to be a rearguard action, and by 1687, Isaac Newton had laid the foundations for a wholly new science of physics. Pascal himself was a great mathematician as well as religious thinker, contributing to the creation of calculus and probability theory. Pascal's own faith, and the sense of mission that drove him to undertake a defense of Christianity, took on urgency precisely because he glimpsed the vast, indifferent universe science was to reveal and could no longer accept the rationalistic proofs of God's existence offered by the Scholastics. The most influential thinker of the age in France was René Descartes, who was not a solitary genius but the most successful of his contemporaries in formulating the new philosophical problems. His work proved seminal because it provided not a system but a *method* of research, inspired by mathematics and rejecting the testimony of tradition—including religious tradition. Although Descartes himself was a religious man and made room in his theories for a Creator, others went further and denied the existence of God. Those who rejected tradition as the basis of their beliefs were commonly referred to as *libertins* (an epithet that originally meant simply "freethinkers"). An important group of *libertins* gathered about the philosopher Pierre Gassendi, who also espoused the Copernican theory but borrowed his ideas on physics from the ancient "atomists," Democritus and Epicurus. In addition to elaborating new theories, many of these seventeenth century scientists also conducted experiments and shared their results with one another through the creation of *académies*, or scientific societies. *Académies* flourished in Dijon, Rouen, and other provincial cities, as well as in the capital.

Thus, behind the facade of Louis XIV's absolutism, a variety of social, spiritual, and intellectual movements were struggling to define and maintain themselves. In this respect, the history of the eighteenth century was essentially a working out of trends already perceptible in the seventeenth.

AN ECLIPSE OF LYRIC POETRY

Great French poetry was written in the seventeenth century, but almost all of it was dramatic poetry—the tragedies of Jean Racine and of Pierre Corneille, the comedies of Molière. Even the fables of Jean de La Fontaine are narrative and satiric, rather than lyric, poetry. Granted that great lyric genius is rare and owes much to inborn gifts, there is still call to ask why this century should have failed to foster such talents as there were. (The sixteenth and nineteenth centuries offer especially striking contrasts in this regard.) At least a part of the answer lies in the milieus where poetry was produced.

From the beginning, French lyric poetry had flourished chiefly in aristocratic circles, whether the poets were themselves noble or not. This did not change in the seventeenth century; the new element was the overwhelming force of centralization drawing all such circles into the orbit of the king. Hippolyte Taine argued in his history of the *ancien régime* that the creation of a single court as the source of all royal patronage (and the simultaneous reduction of all aristocrats to dependency on the king) had a great effect on both language and thought, which extended throughout the eighteenth as well as the seventeenth century. Because the court was "worldly" but not learned, the more erudite Renaissance borrowings from the ancient world were rejected as pedantic or eccentric; the sophistication that continued to be sought was of a social and not an intellectual order. The exploration of individual emotion, an essential element in most lyricism, was likewise discouraged, as art became preeminently public. Thus, while a certain elaboration of form and refinement of expression might be approved as proper to the exclusivity of court circles, ideas, themes, and syntax were to be clear, logical, accessible.

This ideal of clarity was expressed both at the beginning and near the end of the century by two influential critics, François Malherbe and Nicholas Boileau. Both were poets, but they are best known as the theoreticians of French "classicism," which they did not invent but did much to propagate. Malherbe laid down a set of rules for the composition of verse which forbade hiatus (the juxtaposition of two vowels) and enjambment, while prescribing that rhymes and metrical breaks (caesuras and line ends) should coincide with syntactic breaks. Boileau wrote a treatise on the art of poetry that owed much to Aristotle and Horace, the ancient theoreticians of style, but his work is clearly a product of its own time in its emphasis on reason, which it exalts above the other faculties involved in the creation of poetry.

Although Boileau also upheld the ideal of sublimity and looked to the ancients, as well as to the Bible, for models, his emphasis on logic and his tendency to equate reason with common sense actually had a leveling effect. In Taine's assessment, Boileau and his contemporaries could insist on the transparency of "truth" and "nature" because they shared a language and a perspective shaped by the court, where intense social pressure eliminated both individual and regional ("provincial") idiosyncrasies. It is worth noting that the seventeenth century also saw the creation (by Cardinal Richelieu) of the Académie Française, an officially sanctioned group of writers charged with maintaining the "purity" of the French language.

This is not to say that a dull uniformity of style prevailed in seventeenth century poetry. There were in fact a variety of different trends, yet each reflected to some degree the effects of court pressure. The trend sometimes identified as "Baroque" because of its affinity with that style in the plastic arts is chiefly concerned with appearances and their instability. Jean Rousset's *Anthologie de la poésie baroque française* (1968), which offers a selection of this poetry, arranged by theme, includes sections on metamorphosis, disguise, bubbles, clouds, and water, both as a reflecting or shimmering surface and as a flowing—hence inconstant—element. The influence of Italian poetry, and in particular of Giambattista Marino (who lived in Paris from 1615 to 1622), is visible in these works, but the attention to surfaces is also a characteristic of court life. A curious feature of seventeenth century religious art, which Rousset associates with the Baroque tendency, is a fascination with death and physical decay. This feature is obviously related to the spiritual struggles of the age, but it, too, reveals an obsession with appearances, for the living—including the beautiful and the powerful—may be transformed at any time into corpses. Thus, the spiritual anguish of the age was perhaps increased by the contrast, inherent in court life, between apparent beauty, favor, or power, and its instability.

Some critics, however, deny the existence of a true Baroque style in France and speak instead of *préciosité* and burlesque. These related trends share an exaggerated concern for form, but whereas *préciosité* takes form seriously and makes its observance almost a point of honor, burlesque reveals its ridiculous side. The *précieux* poets flourished in the salons, which emerged as miniature courts in the orbit of the royal court. The most famous and influential of these was that of the Marquise de Rambouillet, whose poor health often prevented her from going out and who, in compensation, assembled about her a circle of literary and social luminaries. During the years of its existence (1620-1665), her salon welcomed Richelieu, Malherbe, Marino, Corneille, and Madame de Sévigné, among others, as well as many of the higher aristocracy.

Though serious works were read and discussed, the salon was primarily a social gathering, where time might be spent in parlor games and above all in polite conversation. Other salons were formed in emulation of the Hôtel de Rambouillet; the most prominent was the bourgeois salon of Mademoiselle de Scudéry, author of multivolume novels in true *précieux* style. Though chosen for its original meaning, "of great price or value," the term *précieux* came to mean a style of writing or behavior that sought consciously to elevate its practitioners. Exotic or abstract words might be substituted for ordinary ones; farfetched or hyperbolic comparisons were sought; medieval poetic forms such as the *ballade* and *rondeau* were revived for the sake of their complexity. Insofar as most salons were organized by women and devoted considerable attention to the refined expression of love, they bear comparison with the courts where troubadour lyrics evolved. Yet the fact that many courtly themes had become clichés forced poets to seek ever more exaggerated treatments of them, while the dependent, courtier status of the people involved offered an implicit contrast to the virtues convention ascribed to them.

The situation invited parody, and indeed some *précieux* poetry verges on self-parody. Writers in the burlesque vein took advantage of this situation, pushing *précieux* tendencies to ridiculous extremes or deflating them with doses of realism. It is interesting to note that the burlesque poets—Paul Scarron, Saint-Amant, Cyrano de Bergerac—tended to occupy more ambiguous or marginal positions in society, while virtually all were *libertins*. Although some of these men frequented the salons, they also gathered in the cabarets and cafés of Paris, where there were no refined standards of etiquette to repress their flights of satiric and obscene humor.

Granted that the centralized court life of the age did not foster lyric poetry, it nevertheless had a positive effect on some other forms of literature, for it encouraged the close study of human character under what might almost be called laboratory conditions. Thus, the genius of La Fontaine, the greatest nondramatic poet of the age, found ample matter in the observation of his fellow courtiers. Like Villon, La Fontaine is remarkable for the range of tone he achieved in a poetic idiom that imposed great formal restrictions. In contrast to Villon, however, La Fontaine is himself absent from his poetry, except as a sharp and sometimes pitiless observer of human foibles. His *Contes et nouvelles en vers* (1665; *Tales and Short Stories in Verse*, 1735) and *Fables choises mises en vers* (1668, 1678, 1694; *Fables Written in Verse*, 1735) have been compared to the great dramatic poetry of his age, which sought to portray universals of human behavior yet in so doing inevitably revealed much about its own time and place.

Thus, La Fontaine's fables manage to give vivid glimpses of contemporary life in the guise of the beast fable. La Fontaine has even been accused (by Jean-Jacques Rousseau, among others) of teaching his readers how to rise in the world by dissembling and well-placed flattery, yet it can more plausibly be argued that his fables unmask the baser motives of courtiers, by attributing these motives to animals and by identifying them in plain words. In fact, the most striking feature of the fables, given La Fontaine's proximity to the court of Louis XIV, is their directness; nor does it come as a surprise to learn that the king was cool toward the poet. It should be noted as well that La Fontaine—who was himself a bourgeois from the provinces—did not limit his purview to the court but peopled his menagerie from all the ranks of seventeenth century society. Although his models were classical, he thus rejoined the French medieval tradition of the *fabliaux* and the *Roman de Renart*, offering a pungent antidote to the artificiality of much court poetry.

BIBLIOGRAPHY

Appelbaum, Stanley, ed. *Invitation to French Poetry: Thirty-nine Works by Poets from Charles d'Orléans to Yves Bonnefoy.* New York: Dover, 1991.

Barzun, Jacques. *An Essay on French Verse: For Readers of English Poetry.* New York: New Directions, 1991.

Castor, Grahame. *Pléiade Poetics: A Study in Sixteenth-Century Thought and Terminology.* Cambridge, England: Cambridge University Press, 1964.

Cave, Terence. *The Cornucopian Text: Problems of Writing in the French Renaissance.* New York: Oxford University Press, 1979.

Dubois, E. T., Elizabeth Ratcliff, and P. J. Yarrow. *Eighteenth Century French Studies: Literature and the Arts.* Newcastle-upon-Tyne, England: Oriel, 1969.

Fox, John. *The Middle Ages.* Vol. 1 in *A Literary History of France.* New York: Barnes & Noble, 1974.

Hollier, Denis, with R. Howard Bloch et al. *A New History of French Literature.* Cambridge, Mass.: Harvard University Press, 1994.

Kelly, Douglas. *The Art of Medieval French Romance.* Madison: University of Wisconsin Press, 1992.

_____. *Internal Difference and Meanings in the "Roman de la rose."* Madison: University of Wisconsin Press, 1995.

_____. *Medieval French Romance.* New York: Twayne, 1993.

_____. *Medieval Imagination: Rhetoric and the Poetry of Courtly Love.* Madison: University of Wisconsin Press, 1978.

McFarlane, I. D. *Renaissance France, 1470-1589.* Vol. 2 in *A Literary History of France.* New York: Barnes & Noble, 1974.

Niklaus, Robert. *The Eighteenth Century, 1715-1789.* Vol. 3 in *A Literary History of France.* New York: Barnes & Noble, 1970.

O'Brien, John, and Malcolm Quainton, eds. *Distant Voices Still Heard: Contemporary Readings of French Renaissance Literature.* Liverpool, England: Liverpool University Press, 2000.

Pensom, Roger. *"Aucassin et Nicolette": The Poetry of Gender and Growing Up in the French Middle Ages.* New York: Peter Lang, 1999.

Price, Glanville. *The French Language: Present and Past.* London: Edward Arnold, 1971.

Sartori, Eva Martin, et al., eds. *The Feminist Encyclopedia of French Literature.* Westport, Conn.: Greenwood, 1999.

Stephens, Sonya. *A History of Women's Writing in France.* New York: Cambridge University Press, 2000.

Yarrow, Philip John. *The Seventeenth Century, 1600-1715.* Vol. 2 in *A Literary History of France.* New York: Barnes & Noble, 1974.

Lillian Doherty

FRENCH POETRY SINCE 1700

It has often been said that the most poetic works of eighteenth century France were written in prose—works such as François de Salignac de la Mothe-Fénelon's *Télémaque* (1699; *The Adventures of Telemachus*, 1720), Jean-Jacques Rousseau's *La Nouvelle Héloïse* (1761; *Eloisa: Or, A Series of Original Letters*, 1761), and especially *Les Rêveries d'un promeneur solitaire* (1782; *The Reveries of a Solitary Walker*, 1783), Bernardin de Saint-Pierre's *Paul et Virginie* (1787; *Paul and Mary*, 1789), and Constanin Volney's *Les Ruines* (1791; the ruins). Here, true poetic feeling and sentiment, as those terms were defined by the Romantics, are indisputably present. Yet the eighteenth century, turned toward reason and progress, was not without poetry of a different sort, and critics who view the period as a mere lacuna in poetry between classicism and Romanticism have not studied the major authors or their influence on the following centuries. There was indeed a great output of poetry, although in many cases quantity substituted for quality.

The eighteenth century was one of the most vibrant periods of French history, yet it has two faces: the face of the salon, the court, the ball, and the masque, preserving the past, and the forward-looking face of the philosophes. In the eighteenth century, France was the idol of culture; European monarchs spoke French and built imitations of Versailles. At the court of Louis XV, although luxury and frivolity flourished, so did such cultural accomplishments as the architecture of Jacques Gabriel, the paintings of François Boucher, Jean-Honoré Fragonard, and Antoine Watteau, and the exquisite cabinets and commodes of Georges Jacob and Jean-Henri Riesener. In Paris, men and women of society gathered in the salons of the Duchesse de Maine, the Marquise de Lambert, Madame de Tencin, and Madame de Geoffrin. It was here that much poetry of the period gained its inspiration; it was inferior to the great seventeenth century masterpieces and somehow displayed in its shallow forms the end of an era.

The more vibrant aspect of the *siècle des lumières*, the Age of Enlightenment, was the activity of the philosophes, the great thinkers and writers who ultimately affected the destiny of France and the modern world with their emphasis on reason and their belief in human progress. At first relatively restrained and committed to popularizing scientific discoveries, as in the works of Pierre Bayle (1647-1706) and Bernard le Bovier de Fontenelle (1657-1757), they began to address more delicate issues. Charles-Louis de Secondat, known by his title of Montesquieu (1689-1755), wrote an anonymous satire of religious and political institutions in his *Les Lettres persanes* (1721; *Persian Letters*, 1722) and produced a scholarly study on law in *De l'esprit des lois* (1748; *The Spirit of Laws*, 1750). The great Voltaire, who so dominated every aspect of the eighteenth century that it is known as the Age of Voltaire, used his clever and ironic pen to satirize virtually everything and everyone, particularly religious intolerance and superstition. Denis Diderot (1713-1784), known especially as the editor of the great résumé of eighteenth century knowledge, *L'Encyclopédie* (1751-1780), was himself a writer of sensibility, already foreshadowing Romanticism, and a man of cold reason bordering on atheism. Finally, Jean-Jacques Rousseau (1712-1778) argued for a return to the simple life, to a new morality and religion based on the heart, and a new type of government under which equality would reign.

Although the philosophes used prose as their principal means of expression, they all began a literary apprenticeship with poetry, and Voltaire expressed many of his important ideas, and all of his tragedies, in verse. Poets touched philosophical ideas, often tangentially, especially in science, nature, and morals, and Voltaire judged each of them by their conformity to his ideas. Poetry, on the whole, kept to classical models, faithful to the precepts of Nicolas Boileau (1636-1711). The great genres—ode, elegy, eclogue, and satire—were the most practiced. Rhythm and rhyme were decorously employed, and allusions to antiquity proliferated. At the beginning of the century, subjects were rarely personal, but after 1750, sentiment and nature themes began to appear. Poems of circumstance were frivolous, sensual, and pagan in inspiration, illustrating the degradation of morals, yet there was a surprising quantity of religious poetry in this age of anticlericalism, Deism, and even outspoken atheism. The century ended with a more lyric poet, André-Marie Chénier, a victim of the very Revolution that he had supported in verse and in action.

Poetry in the eighteenth century, as in the seventeenth, originated in the salons. The elegant Society of the Temple was the meeting place for libertines of the time, and at the turn of the century, a period of literary aridity, Guillaume Amfrye, Abbé de Chaulieu (1639-1720), could be found among the poets of the salons. His works were not published until 1724, but he composed many madrigals and poems of circumstance inspired by the music of Jean-Baptiste Lully. Well versed in the classics, he employed classical allusions and classical verse forms with accuracy, though without poetic feeling. His "Apologie de l'inconstance" (1700; apology for inconstancy) links two centuries and foreshadows future currents. More oriented to the theater, where he enjoyed a moderate success, Antoine Houdar de la Motte (1672-1731) shows greater simplicity and freshness in his style. Though occasionally original, his verse is not brilliant.

The greatest poet of the early eighteenth century is generally acknowledged to be Jean-Baptiste Rousseau (1669-1741), also a member of the libertine Temple group. Jealous of his reputation, he spent the last thirty years of his life in exile after being convicted of calumny. His poetry, much appreciated in his own day though now forgotten, reveals a sensitivity to language and rhythm that anticipates Paul Valéry's preoccupation with language: Rousseau in his *Art poétique* insists on patience, work, and inspiration, much as Valéry was later to do. Rousseau's main sources of inspiration were antiquity and the Bible. Although many poems are imitations of Pindar, Rousseau has original compositions in his *cantates* (love allegories), of which the best is his "Cantate à Circé." His *Odes sacrées* (sacred odes) on biblical themes are his best, but "Ode à la Fortune," "Ode à Adonis," and "Ode à Bacchus" are also excellent, as is his "Paraphrase du Cantique d'Ézéchias," written for a convalescing person, in which the sick man recalls his brush with death in realistic terms.

François-Marie Arouet, known to his contemporaries and to posterity as Voltaire (1694-1778), dominates the history of eighteenth century poetry as he does the entire *siècle des lumières*. His earliest poem, "Sur la reli-

gion naturelle" (on natural religion), was written in 1722; shortly before his death he was still composing epistles (*Épîtres*) to friends and enemies, living and dead, with the same acerbic pen. Voltaire dreamed of creating a great French epic, and early in his career composed *La Ligue: Ou, Henri le Grand* (1723, later published as *La Henriade*, 1728; *Henriade*, 1732). Lacking imaginative life, the poem fails utterly to comprehend the meaning of its subject, the religious wars of the sixteenth century. Voltaire immediately turned to another source of epic inspiration, Jeanne d'Arc, in *La Pucelle d'Orléans* (1755, 1762; *La Pucelle: Or, The Maid of Orleans*, 1785-1786), which he began in 1730 and concluded in 1761 with twenty-one cantos. Although Jeanne, the beloved French heroine for all ages, is presented with sharp sarcasm and irony, the work sold some 300,000 copies and was parodied and burlesqued many times.

Although all of Voltaire's work is satiric, he wrote many poems that are satires proper. *Le Temple du goût* (1733; *The Temple of Taste*, 1734), in prose and verse, is surprisingly conservative in matters of taste and quite perceptive when discussing architecture. Voltaire also assigns a number of writers from the seventeenth and eighteenth centuries to a room in his temple, and he is particularly offensive toward his enemies, dead or alive. The same vein reappears in *Le Pauvre Diable* (1758; the poor Devil), published under the name of the then recently deceased Jean-Joseph Vadé, and likewise a harsh invective against contemporary writers. Voltaire excelled in all the small genres; in fact, it was for them that he was most appreciated by his contemporaries.

Voltaire could also be serious, even reflective. The great Lisbon earthquake in 1755 had shaken his faith in progress and had caused him to reflect more deeply on the role of Providence in human life. Voltaire, though anticlerical, was never atheistic, professing a rather moderate Deism. His "Poème sur le désastre de Lisbonne" (poem on the disaster of Lisbon), is a serious meditation on life and death. "Poème sur la loi naturelle" (poem on the natural law), written in the same year, 1756, stresses the importance of reason in directing man to God, without the need of formal religion.

Although Voltaire believed that his tragedies, all written in Alexandrines, and his epics would assure his future fame, it is rather for his *contes philosophiques* that he is remembered. As a poet, he is the greatest of the eighteenth century after Chénier, which is not to make him great, since Chénier is perhaps the only true poet of that century. Voltaire was an adequate poet, however, and his philosophical works in verse are still read today, though most of his other poetry is forgotten.

In the camp opposed to Voltaire and the philosophes were several didactic and religious poets. Among the best of the religious authors were Jean-Jacques Lefranc, Marquis de Pompignan (1709-1784), and Louis Racine (1692-1763), son of the great Jean Racine, author of seventeenth century classical tragedies. Pompignan is known for his "Ode sur la mort de Jean-Baptiste Rousseau" (ode on the death of Jean-Baptiste Rousseau), but his best works are his *Poésies sacrées* (1734, 1751, 1763; sacred poems), paraphrases of biblical texts, many of which have real literary value. Their lyric accents and ease of versification anticipate the achievements of Alphonse de Lamartine.

Louis Racine, like his father, reveals the influence of Jansenism, though without his father's passion and depth. "La Grâce" (written 1720), a poem in honor of the Holy Spirit, is overtly Jansenist, yet some of its passages anticipate the tone of Lamartine's *Harmonies poétiques et religieuses* (1830). "La Religion," also written in 1720 and widely read at the time, is Racine's most important work. It celebrates God the Father, with many literary exaggerations, such as Christ walking on the waters surrounded by nymphs, receiving the homage of Neptune. Racine's *Odes saintes* (1730-1743; holy odes), the most famous of his twenty-two odes, honor God the Son. Racine's most original ideas are expressed in "Réflexion sur la poésie," his *art poétique*, which insists on the necessity of enthusiasm, harmony, and passion. Unfortunately, he did not incorporate these principles into his work, although his was an erudite mind, formed by the classics and the great Christian thinkers, such as Saint Thomas Aquinas, Saint Augustine, Jacques-Bénigne Bossuet, and Blaise Pascal.

Eighteenth century didactic poetry was not always religious, as in Pompignan and Racine. A great deal of it was directed to nature and science, such as *Les Saisons* (1769; the seasons), by Jean-François, Marquis de Saint-Lambert (1716-1803). Better known for his arti-

cles in *L'Encyclopédie* and his amorous adventures with Madame Du Châtelet and with Madame d'Houdetot, Saint-Lambert wrote this lengthy poem in four cantos in imitation of Hesiod, with observations on the natural phenomena that accompany the changes in the seasons. It was greatly praised by Voltaire because of its philosophical implications. Other contemporaries, such as Diderot and Baron Melchior von Grimm, recognized the exhaustion of this genre, which was to attract inferior poets until the end of the century.

More original in his descriptive poetry was Jacques Delille (1738-1813), a professor of Latin and translator of Vergil's *Georgics* (37-30 B.C.E.) in 1770. Delille's best-known work is *Les Jardins* (1782; *The Gardens*, 1798), a long poem in eight cantos that speaks of the art of gardening and the embellishment of the countryside. Though often monotonous, it does have poetically sensitive passages, especially in its appreciation of autumn, later echoed by Lamartine. Delille's "Les Trois Règnes de la nature" (the three kingdoms of nature), although written in 1809, is entirely in the spirit of the eighteenth century; the work possesses historical value for the richness of its vocabulary, including a number of neologisms. Jean-Antoine Roucher (1745-1794) also represents the rustic tradition with his *Les Mois* (1779; the months), a poem in the tradition of Saint-Lambert's *Les Saisons*. Although Roucher's verse has a certain charm and delicacy, his sensitivity is obscured by an excess of rhetoric. He was guillotined the same day as Chénier and did not live long enough to develop his poetic talent.

Hoping to unite Lucretius and Isaac Newton in his poetry, Ponce-Denis Écouchard Lebrun (1729-1807), known in his time as "Pindare-Lebrun," aimed to replace the mannerism of his age with classical simplicity. Less faithful to his allegiances, he composed poetry in honor of Robespierre during the Revolution and for the glory of Napoleon under the empire. Lebrun projected a great poetic masterpiece, "La Nature: Ou, Le Bonheur philosophique et champêtre" (nature, or philosophic and rustic happiness), but only the section called *Le Génie* (1760; the genius) was completed. In this work, Lebrun anticipates the Romantic conception of genius, but the poem is overburdened with erudite references. Like Voltaire, Lebrun was inspired by the earthquake of Lisbon and in 1755, he composed two pseudoscientific odes on that disaster. His "Ode sur le vaisseau 'Le Vengeur'" (1794; ode on the ship, *Le Vengeur*) is a poem in honor of revolutionary patriotism. Hailed by Diderot as the ideal poet-philosopher, Lebrun occasionally wrote some excellent passages. Inspired by Louis Racine, Lebrun was to become the master of Chénier.

Toward the middle of the eighteenth century, a pre-Romantic spirit, very evident in the prose of Diderot and Rousseau, also appeared in poetry, though it did not fully triumph until Lamartine's *Méditations poétiques* (*Poetical Meditations*, 1839) in 1820. Antoine-Léonard Thomas (1732-1785), author of numerous epistles and odes, none of which has durable value, does, however, show a pre-Lamartinian spirit in his "Ode sur le temps" (ode on time). Certain phrases definitely foreshadow Lamartine's "Le Lac" ("The Lake"), such as "l'océan des âges" and "en vain contre le temps je cherche une barrière." Lamartine evidently knew and admired the poem, which lacks the love element of "The Lake." Thomas evokes the flight of time, the ephemeral life of man on earth, and the hope of eternity—themes that were to become very popular in the nineteenth century.

Even more Romantic and fiercely independent was Nicolas-Joseph-Laurent Gilbert (1751-1780), who attacked the philosophes in satirical works and showed real poetic promise before his untimely death. Although his fate was associated with that of Thomas Chatterton by Alfred de Vigny, Gilbert's death was in fact the result of an accident, and his harsh invectives against his society, such as in *Le Dix-huitième Siècle* (1775; the eighteenth century), were well understood by his contemporaries. In this poem, he condemned the philosophes, inveighing against atheism and immorality accompanied by lack of real art. His "Ode sur le jugement dernier" (1773; ode on the Last Judgment) is pre-Romantic in tone. His most touching work, with a distinctly Romantic feeling for death, "Ode imitée à plusieurs psaumes" ("Ode—Imitated from the Psalms") or "Adieux à la vie" (farewell to life), was written in 1780, shortly before his own death.

Romantic exoticism characterized the works of three poets born in French semitropical islands: Nicolas-Germain Léonard (1744-1793), born on Guadeloupe, and Antoine Bertin (1752-1790) and Évariste-Désiré de Forges de Parny (1753-1814), both born on the Île Bour-

bon, now the Île de la Réunion. The *Idylles* (1766) of Léonard are dreamy and delicate, recalling James Thomson and Oliver Goldsmith in inspiration, though not without a classical influence. Léonard's more descriptive passages anticipate Alfred de Musset and especially Lamartine, who knew and read his works. Bertin, a friend of Parny, is best known for his *Les Amours* (1780), written in the manner of the sixteenth century poet Pierre de Ronsard. They are erotic, lighthearted, and sensual, with overtones of melancholy such as one finds in Watteau's painting *Fêtes galantes*.

The best poet of the three was Parny. He was much appreciated by Voltaire, who—alluding to the Roman elegist Tibullus—called him "mon cher Tibulle"; to posterity, Parny was known by the less flattering diminutive, Tibullinus. A poet of love and sensuality, Parny took as his Elvire a woman named Eléonore, whom he was not permitted to marry. His best love poetry is found in *Poésies érotiques* (1778; erotic poems). He addressed patriotic themes in his "Épître aux insurgents de Boston" (1777). His most original works, however, are his *Chansons madécasses traduites en françois* (1787), which are really poems in prose, although the distinction of inventing the genre usually goes to Aloysius Bertrand. Sensual and even licentious in the manner of the eighteenth century, Parny's poetry is not without the melancholy that was to inspire nineteenth century Romantics.

As the nineteenth century dawned, minor poets already were writing in Romantic accents, yet Romantic poetry did not come into prominence until 1820. A transitional writer, Charles-Hubert Millevoye (1782-1816), began with classical epistles, translations of Vergil, and biblical and historical poems. Yet Millevoye's "Chute des feuilles" (falling leaves), "La Demeure abandonnée" (the abandoned dwelling), "Le Poète mourant" (the dying poet), and "Priez pour moi" (pray for me) are true Romantic poems, distinguished by their melancholy, appreciation of nature, and meditations on death and by their early expression of the cult of the individual.

The eighteenth century, so little known for true poetic inspiration, ended with the voice of a real poet, André-Marie Chénier (1762-1794), whose brother Marie-Joseph (1764-1811) at first eclipsed him in fame. Born in Constantinople of a mother who falsely claimed

Greek ancestry, Chénier was to be haunted throughout his life by the Greek concept of beauty. His early poetry, mostly elegiac, was written in the style of the eighteenth century, yet he gradually attained a masterful simplicity, especially in _Les Bucoliques_ (written 1785-1787, published 1819). Aiming, like Voltaire, to write an epic, he began two, _Hermès_ and _L'Amérique_, neither of which was ever completed, although _L'Amérique_ shows his gift for cosmic vision. In 1794, Chénier wrote _Iambes_, attacking the Jacobine tyranny that would send him to the guillotine the same year.

Chénier was not a Romantic: There is in his verse no cult of the individual, no restless melancholy or evocation of nature and death. If anything, he was a classical poet: His own line, "Sur les pensers nouveaux, faisons des vers antiques" ("On new thoughts, let us make ancient verses"), sums up his aesthetic. Some of his finest poems, such as "L'Aveugle" (the blind man), the story of a meeting of three shepherds with Homer, anticipate the work of Victor Hugo. "La Jeune Tatentine" (the young Tatentine), a classical story of a young woman drowned at sea, is told in sober and clear lines. "La Jeune Captive" (the young captive), inspired by Chénier's meeting with the young Aimée de Coigny in prison, expresses their desire to cling to the young and vibrant life that the revolution was about to snatch from them. Chénier was at least able to attain immortality through his work, for although Romantic poetry was not to follow his style, it did continue his genuine lyrical inspiration. More directly, the Parnassians emulated his sculptural beauty and his love of ancient Greece.

ROMANTICISM

The nineteenth century in France, as in England, Germany, Poland, and Russia, opened under the sign of Romanticism. While this was the Romantic period par excellence, Romantic themes in literature and ideas ebb and flow in alternation with the serenity of classicism. It is the opposition of a Greek temple to a Gothic cathedral, one representing a single, perfect idea repeated endlessly; the other, freedom in original creativity. Authors such as Madame de Staël have romanticized Romanticism, seeing in it the Christian expression of melancholy, the incompleteness of existence, and the somber gray of foggy northern climates. Finally, Romanticism expresses the turbulence of the human spirit as it strives for independence and emancipation from the rules and restraints of classical order and reason.

In France, the Romantic period spanned a century, from the late eighteenth century to the late nineteenth, achieving its fullest expression during the first third of the nineteenth century. Romanticism first appeared in France during the years between 1760 and 1775, largely in prose rather than poetry. It was from England and Germany, however, rather than from Rousseau and Diderot, that the French Romantic movement, especially in poetry, was to take its primary inspiration.

Madame de Staël's _De l'Allemagne_ (1810; _Germany_, 1813) places the roots of Romanticism in Germany, and in the years that followed, French Romantics such as Victor Cousin, Jules Michelet, Charles-Augustin Sainte-Beuve, Hugo, Lamartine, Musset, and others would visit Germany as a hallowed shrine. In France, the most influential German Romantics were Johann Wolfgang von Goethe (1749-1832), whose Werther was the ancestor of René and Adolphe; Friedrich Schiller (1759-1805); and especially the teller of fantastic tales, E. T. A. Hoffmann (1776-1822), whose influence is directly evident in the works of Charles Nodier, Gérard de Nerval, and Théophile Gautier.

For the French Romantics, English inspiration meant William Shakespeare, whom many authors, such as Stendhal in _Racine et Shakspeare_ (1823, 1825; _Racine and Shakespeare_, 1962), were to exalt in place of the French classicists. Voltaire, in the eighteenth century, had already proclaimed Shakespeare's superiority; both poets and dramatists were to discover him in the nineteenth. The sentimental novelists of eighteenth century England, such as Samuel Richardson (1689-1761), not only influenced French Romanticism, but inspired changes in the literature of far-off Russia as well. The two greatest contemporary influences from England were Sir Walter Scott (1771-1832), whose novels of medieval chivalry inspired Vigny, Alexandre Dumas, Honoré de Balzac, Hugo, Prosper Mérimée, and Gautier as well as writers in Italy, Germany, and Russia, and Lord Byron (1788-1824): The Byronic hero became the model for Romantics throughout Europe.

Although literary historians usually date the flowering of French Romanticism from René de Chateaubriand's novels *Atala* (1801; English translation, 1802) and *René* (1802; English translation, 1813) and his treatise *Le Génie du christianisme* (1802; *The Genius of Christianity*, 1802), there was actually a prolonged silence in literary production from the beginning of the French Revolution in 1789 to the exile of Napoleon Bonaparte in 1815. With the exception of Chénier, there was practically nothing of great value in poetry during this period—in fact, not until Lamartine's *Poetical Meditations* in 1820. The intensity of the revolution was no doubt responsible for the early years of this lacuna, although poetry did not have a remarkable history in the eighteenth century. The role of Napoleon (1769-1821) in the history of Romanticism is more problematic. A classicist in taste and philosophy, he launched the most severe and correct of all styles, the Empire style, and he took the ancient Roman Empire as the model of his conquests. No one, however, understood better than he the message of the Revolution: liberty, equality, fraternity, the need for newness, mobility of class structure, patriotism. Although he dreamed of French supremacy in Europe, his "liberation" of Germany and Italy taught the inhabitants of these countries to seek their own roots, and thus he sowed the seeds of nationalism throughout Europe.

French Romanticism, not unlike the Romantic movements in England, Germany, Poland, and Russia, stressed freedom from classical restraints. Since the classical tradition was strongest in France, where the distinction between comedy and tragedy was adhered to with Aristotelian exactness, the call to freedom did not immediately abolish classical forms. Lamartine still wrote in Alexandrines and evoked pagan deities and classical heroes. It was through the emancipation of the theater that poetry was to find new forms of expression, although Hugo's early verse is marked by formal experimentation. Where classicism insists on universal themes, Romanticism stresses the individual: Racine's *Phèdre* (1677; *Phedra*, 1776) dramatizes every woman's jealousy; "The Lake" is Lamartine's personal lament at the loss of love. Classicism made reason the primary law—in the words of Boileau, "aimez donc la raison." Romanticism, echoing Pascal's "raisons du coeur," the reasons of the heart, insisted that emotion had a more powerful role to play.

French Romantic poetry also exalted nature. As Rousseau discovered the mountains of Switzerland, so Lamartine heard the echoes of the Lac du Bourget in the surrounding hills of Burgundy, and Vigny evoked the purple and gold of Mount Nebo in exotic grandeur. Yet nature for the Romantics is more than a setting or, as in the eighteenth century, an object of study. Rather, it reflects the moods of the poet: Chateaubriand's melancholy, for example, becomes the autumn leaves that he hopes will carry him off to the land of happiness and oblivion. Death, too, is a Romantic theme, perhaps best illustrated by Chateaubriand's cult of the tomb. The Romantics, for the most part, share a spiritual orientation, though most of them reject traditional religious forms. Like Rousseau's Savoyard Vicar, they call on the God of the heart, whom they find in nature as well. Hence, they believe in immortality and resurrection, with the possible exception of the stoic Vigny, who stresses the silence of God in response to man's sufferings.

The revolt against classicism further implied a rejection of antiquity and a preference for the Middle Ages. As writers examined their individual memories in meditative introspection, so nations sought their origins in what, until then, had been despised medieval institutions, and buildings. Gothic architecture was again respected. Eugène-Emmanuel Viollet-le-Duc (1814-1879) restored cathedrals and chateaus; medieval manuscripts were collected and studied. Folktales about Renard and *chansons de geste* about Roland were evoked more than Ulysses and Aeneas. Along with medieval themes, exoticism was cultivated. Chateaubriand idealized the New World, the domain of the noble savage; Lamartine and Vigny were inspired by the Holy Land; Eugène Delacroix's somber paintings took on the sunny skies of Algeria after his visit there.

Romanticism, as Madame de Staël observed, is profoundly bathed in melancholy. The French spoke of a pervasive *mal du siècle*, suggesting a mood of restlessness and ennui, a distaste for one's society, a superabundance of life. This state of mind anticipates the dilemma of modern man, overwhelmed by too many options and rejecting traditional and stable values: Romantic melancholy deepens and sours under Charles Baudelaire, and eventually becomes the Absurd of Albert Camus.

Although Chateaubriand was the most profoundly Romantic of all French writers, his works are in prose, albeit with a poetic rhythm and orientation. The great French Romantic poets are Lamartine (1790-1869), Alfred de Vigny (1797-1863), Alfred de Musset (1810-1857), and Victor Hugo (1802-1885). Since Romanticism implies freedom, each one was very different, yet they, like all French writers, gravitated to a salon—in the early 1820's, to Charles Nodier's salon at the Arsenal, and after 1827, to Victor Hugo's *Cénacle*, rue Notre-Dame-des-Champs. Their greatest period of literary productivity was between 1820 and 1850, although Hugo's major poetic works, *Les Châtiments* (1853) and *Les Contemplations* (1856-1857), date from 1853 and 1857, respectively. This was a period of relative conservatism in France: The Restoration of the Bourbons had already taken place in 1815. The Revolution of 1830, however, which brought Louis-Philippe to power, inspired a wave of lyric poetry.

ALPHOSE DE LAMARTINE

The publication of Lamartine's *Poetical Meditations* in 1820 revolutionized French poetry as William Wordsworth and Samuel Taylor Coleridge's *Lyrical Ballads* had revolutionized English poetry in 1798. Immediately, Lamartine became famous, and though he later wrote more profound and scholarly works, it is for his first brief collection that he is remembered in French literature. In it, he immortalizes Elvire, an idealization of Madame Julie Charles, whom he had met at the Lac du Bourget in 1816 and who died shortly afterward. His best-known poem, and one of the most beloved in all of French literature, is "The Lake," in which he evokes the passage of time and the role of memory in keeping alive past happiness. Other poems in the volume treat such Romantic themes as nostalgia for one's childhood and the beauty of the Burgundian countryside. Lamartine continued in the Romantic vein in Nouvelles méditations poétiques (1823, new meditations), La Mort de Socrate (1823, the death of Socrates), and Le Dernier Chant du pèlerinage de Harold (1825, the last song of Harold's pilgrimage), inspired by Byron's Childe Harold.

Harmonies poétiques et religieuses (1830; poetic and religious harmonies) was inspired by a desire to write modern psalms and reveals a deeply religious orientation in the tradition of eighteenth century poets such

as Louis Racine and Thomas. Lamartine had spent the years from 1826 to 1828 in Italy with the French embassy in Florence, and an Italian strain is evident in these volumes. Lamartine writes often of death and immortality, paraphrasing Pascal's comparison of the grandeur of God and the finiteness of man, similar to the disparity between the immensity of nature and the insignificance of man. After 1830, Lamartine became more deeply involved in French politics, and by 1848, he was part of the provisional government in the Second Republic. Hence, his late works are more often explicitly political. Lamartine also dreamed of a vast epic poem that was to be his "Légende des siècles." He realized it in part in two enormous works *Jocelyn* (1836; English translation, 1837) and *La Chute d'un ange* (1838; the fall of an angel). Both are for the most part forgotten today, although *Jocelyn* was immensely successful when it was published. It tells the story of a seminarian, put to flight by the Revolution, who falls in love with another fugitive. Their love cannot be consummated because of his subsequent ordination, yet when she dies, he lovingly buries her, in a scene recalling Chateaubriand's *Atala*.

Lamartine's is lyric poetry in the original sense of the word: poetry that sings. Simple diction, melodic alliteration, repetition, and a gift for memorable formulations make his verse easy to recite and learn by heart. Lamartine's ideas are clear; although he uses symbols and images, they are easily intelligible and they touch the ordinary reader. Lamartine is also noted for his sincerity, both in his personal poetry and in his political verse. M. F. Guyard, however, editor of Lamartine's poems in the Pléiade edition, finds him not exacting enough, too uneven in style, mistaking quantity for quality. Nevertheless, Lamartine introduced into French literature the Romantic and lyrical style, which, after undergoing diverse mutations, profoundly influenced the development of modern literature, not merely in France but virtually worldwide.

ALFRED DE VIGNY

Very different from Lamartine's gentle lyricism is the stoicism and revolt of Alfred de Vigny. Conscious of his ancient family nobility and hostile to the revolution and all that it symbolized, Vigny supported the conservative government of the Restoration and that of Napoleon III. At the same time, his work foreshadows the modern concept of the Absurd, which Albert Camus was to popularize in the mid-twentieth century. A solitary like the existentialists, who see man as thrown into a hostile universe without recourse to divinity or human fellowship, Vigny projected himself in the title figure of his play *Chatterton* (1835): the poet misunderstood by society. In contrast to Lamartine, whose voluminous work touched on many topics, Vigny wrote little and well. He is known especially for *Poèmes antiques et modernes* (1826; ancient and modern poems) and *Les Destinées* (destinies), published posthumously, in 1864.

Although much of Vigny's poetry is declamatory and shows the influence of Chénier, Byron, and Chateaubriand, one of his best works, "Moïse" (1822; Moses), is faithful to its biblical inspiration in its spirit of uncompromising moral solitude. The greatest of the Old Testament prophets, a figure for the poet, is symbolically called by God to the top of the mountain, yet when he complains of his solitude, he receives nothing but silence. In symbolic language, he recalls his mission with pride and distress and seeks only to sleep the sleep of the earth. Later, Vigny was to exalt the fierce and stoic pride of refusal to submit to one's fate in "La Mort du loup" (1838; the death of the wolf), while in "Le Mont des oliviers" (1844; the Mount of Olives), Christ, like Moses, faces a silent and impassive God. Like the Symbolists who followed him, Vigny gradually came to a religion of art.

Essentially a philosophical poet, Vigny builds his poems on a structure of symbols, often weaving a stanza around a single image. In contrast to Lamartine, Vigny's stance is aloof; detached from his creation, the poet expresses his intimate thoughts under the guise of the symbol. Vigny the dramatist is also present in his poetry, where dialogue and gesture reveal the idea to be expressed, as in his account of the wounded she-wolf who does not deign to address her mate's killers, or the dialogue of Christ with his Father. Vigny used the Alexandrine consistently: *Les Destinées* includes eleven poems totaling about two thousand lines, with regular classical rhyme. Vigny has often been accused of living in an ivory tower, but he sought to flee the vulgar crowd in order to bring humanity to a higher level, and he expressed through his own paradoxical nature the eternal conflict of hope and despair.

ALFRED DE MUSSET

Known as the "enfant gâté," the spoiled child of Romanticism, Alfred de Musset exemplifies the suffering Romantic youth full of passion and desire. The volume of his poetry is not great, yet he wrote some of the finest plays of the period, notably *Lorenzaccio* (1834; English translation, 1905). He wrote his best works between the ages of twenty and thirty and spent the final years of his short life in frivolity, forgotten by those who had praised him so highly for his first volume, *Contes d'Espagne et d'Italie* (1829; *Tales of Spain and Italy*, 1905), a collection of charming, lighthearted poems about countries Musset had never visited. Musset, the quintessential Romantic, mocked Romanticism in his witty "Ballade à la lune" ("Ballad to the Moon"), as he mocked contemporary drama in such works as "Une Soirée perdue" ("A Lost Evening").

After Musset's liaison with George Sand—an affair that ended in betrayal and suffering—his poetry took on a new tone; the period after his rupture with Sand (1835-1840) was also his most productive. He is best known for the cycle of poems titled *Les Nuits* (nights), written between 1835 and 1837. Apart from "La Nuit de décembre," in which the poet meets his double at critical moments of his life, the poems of the cycle constitute a dialogue between the poet and his Muse, who calls him forth to poetic creativity. The month determines the image: May, springtime, brings an invitation to love and breathes the perfume of flowers and voluptuousness. August is a more triumphant evocation of the poet's victory over his suffering, though without any definitive result. In "La Nuit d'octobre," the last of the series, the Muse takes on a maternal stance and attempts to cure the poet of his sickness by counseling him to gather the flowers of today's garden, forgetting the past.

Much criticized by contemporaries and later nineteenth century critics for his frivolity and lack of depth, Musset appeals to many twentieth century readers, particularly in his emphasis on the double: The poet engages in dialogue with himself and analyzes his dreams in a strikingly modern manner. Musset's poetry is musical, brilliant, and varied; he employs the Alexandrine and the newer experimental forms with equal facility. Many of his lyrics belong to the genre of the popular song, very much appreciated in the nineteenth century.

His subtle wit places him in the French comic tradition, though not in the overt "esprit gaulois" of François Rabelais and Voltaire. Perhaps Musset's greatest contribution to French Romanticism is a spirit of youth and verve, sensitivity and passion, and a desire to enjoy life and profit from the sufferings it imposes.

VICTOR HUGO

The one figure who unites all French Romantics and towers over them in gigantic proportions is Victor Hugo. Born in the year made famous by Chateaubriand's *René* and *The Genius of Christianity*, Hugo declared, early in life, that he wished to be "Chateaubriand or nothing." Indeed, there is a great similarity between the two: an Olympic vision; a fascination with the *gouffre*, or the abysmal whirlpool, and with the tomb; a sense of the rhythm of words and a facility in manipulating them. Known universally as a thoroughgoing Romantic, Hugo was still publishing lengthy collections in the 1870's and the 1880's, long after Baudelaire had redirected poetry into the path of Symbolism and in the very years in which Stéphane Mallarmé was cloaking it with hermetic obscurity. A prolific novelist and playwright as well as a poet, Hugo proclaimed the Romantic revolution in the theater and opened the path for experimentation in poetry, allowing *rejets* and enjambments, verses of all meters and lengths, and new types of rhyme.

Hugo began to publish poetry in 1822, about the same time as Lamartine and Vigny, and with them, he formed a poetic triumvirate recognized by their contemporaries. Hugo at first seemed the most conservative, yet in 1826, with *Odes et ballades*, and in 1829, with *Les Orientales* (*Eastern Lyrics*, 1879), he launched a wave of medievalism and orientalism that was to dominate early French Romanticism. The second period of Hugo's poetic career, before his exile in 1851, was marked by personal suffering and political involvement. His most important volumes of poetry from this period are *Les Feuilles d'automne* (1831; the leaves of autumn), *Les Chants du crépuscule* (1835; *Songs of Twilight*, 1836), *Les Voix intérieures* (1837; interior voices), and *Les Rayons et les ombres* (1840; the rays and the shadows). The manner of the poems is varied, as is Hugo's wont; there are poems about his love for Juliette Drouet and about his family, as well as French history and the Revolution of 1830. He defines the role of poet as seer and manifests an awareness of the vast panorama of human history.

In 1851, Napoleon III carried out a *coup d'état* and shifted to a conservative rightist position, openly allying himself with the Church and the nobility. Hugo was disillusioned with the leader whom he had previously supported and denounced him with such vehemence that Hugo was obliged to leave France, at first traveling to Belgium and then to the English islands of Jersey and Guernsey. The fruit of his political invective is a volume of poetry titled *Les Châtiments* (1853; chastisements), in which he compares Napoleon I to Napoleon III or Napoleon le Petit. Some of the poems are mere political insults; others are exalted verse, especially the lengthy *Expiation*. While in exile, however, Hugo's wrath cooled, and he began to reflect on more universal topics. His poetic masterpiece, *Les Contemplations* (1856-1857), deals with intimate themes, such as the death of his daughter Léopoldine, the role of the poet, the problem of suffering humanity, and the exaltation of the simple and the poor. The volume expresses Hugo's personal vision of the world and its destiny, mingling Christianity, Illuminism, and eclectic mystical doctrines. It is in this collection of poems that Hugo the visionary emerges: The beggar's cloak becomes a constellation, the sower of plants in the sky, and the harvester's sickle is reflected in the crescent moon as the union of Boaz and Ruth prefigures the birth of Christ.

Hugo continued to work on his vast epic after his return to France in 1870, dreaming of a historical masterpiece that would embrace all time in *La Légende des siècles* (1859-1883; *The Legend of Centuries*, 1867). He also planned it to include God (*Dieu*, 1891) and the Devil (*La Fin de Satan*, 1886). At the same time, in *L'Année terrible* (1872; the terrible year), he recounted the ravages of war and revolution—the bloody birth of the Third Republic in 1870. The heyday of Romanticism was by then long past, yet Hugo remained a living legend. Political deputy and member of the Opposition, spokesman for the Romantic theater, Victor Hugo led as well as wrote. In his vast oevre, he left models for all meters and all topics. Although often trite, he is seldom without wit or sentiment. At times painfully long-winded, he can also compress deep emotion into a few lines, as in a poem about his pilgrimage to his daughter's grave, "Demain, dès l'aube. . . ." Visionary and Olympian, rivaling God in his pride and consumed by sensuality, Hugo was also a poet of delicacy and humility; he has left an indelible mark on French literature.

PARNASSIAN POETS

Romanticism was perhaps the last great literary movement. Others, such as Symbolism and Surrealism, have since appeared, but they have lacked the unity of doctrine and the sweeping appeal of Romanticism. Nevertheless, they have left a profound mark on modern society, itself fragmented and confused.

By 1850, Romantic themes had begun to lose favor. In the novel, realism had already made its appearance: Balzac, in his *La Comédie humaine* (1842-1848; *The Human Comedy*, 1896), showed men as pawns of social forces and victims of their own monomaniacal passions. Romantic emotion was still present, yet it was not the introspective *mal du siècle* of Chateaubriand's *René*. The cult of the individual broadened to a concern for society, particularly in Hugo's poems and novels, where the downtrodden and the unfortunate became heroes rather than the noble savage or the disillusioned noble. In *Le Rouge et le noir* (1830; *The Red and the Black*), Stendhal, too, had chosen for his protagonist a provincial young man who is a far cry from the Byronic heroes of Romantic fiction.

Although the novel was to turn to the middle class for its inspiration, a number of poets turned away from the changing society of the mid-nineteenth century to take refuge in a detached ethereal atmosphere. These Parnassian poets, as they were known, who never constituted a full-fledged literary school with a unified doctrine, edited a journal called *Le Parnasse contemporain* (contemporary Parnassus), named for the home of the Muses. Its first issue, in 1866, contained poems by Gautier, Théodore de Banville, Charles-Marie Leconte de Lisle, Baudelaire, José María de Hérédia, François-Édouard Coppée, Sully Prudhomme, Verlaine, and Mallarmé, several of whom were to gain fame as Symbolists or as talented independent writers. The Parnassians' second volume appeared in 1871; the third volume, issued in 1876, is little more than an anthology, with no unifying theme.

The single doctrine that loosely linked the Parnassian poets was their commitment to art for art's sake.

Reacting against Hugo's metrical freedoms and Romantic introspection, the Parnassians proclaimed the necessity of perfection in form. They wished to remain objective, not revealing their personal emotions or opinions. They sought serenity, equilibrium, and purity in their work, striving for sculptural perfection and a close affiliation with the plastic arts in general. Often finding inspiration in classical sources, they did not abandon the Romantic cult of the Middle Ages or love of the exotic. Although the main representatives of Parnasse are Leconte de Lisle (1818-1894), Banville (1823-1891), Hérédia (1842-1905), and Sully Prudhomme (1839-1907), these poets acknowledged the inspiration of Théophile Gautier (1811-1872) and Gérard de Nerval (1808-1855), whose individualistic voice was claimed by many poetic schools, ranging from the Symbolists to the Surrealists. The Parnassians also greatly admired André Chénier.

THÉOPHILE GAUTIER

Equally Romantic and Parnassian, Gautier was both a poet and a painter in verse. It was the latter quality in particular that attracted the Parnassians, who sought affinities with the plastic arts. Gautier's first volume, *Poésies* (1830), set a new tone in such poems as the calm "Paysage" (countryside). *La Comédie de la mort* (1838; the comedy of death) is Romantic in its cult of death, yet it lacks the fantastic element so characteristic of Romantic verse on this theme. It was with *Émaux et camées* (1852; *Enamels and Cameos*, 1900) that Gautier found his own style. In this enormously influential work, Gautier states his intention to treat a limited number of subjects in a restrained form. He seeks durability rather than movement, noting that he prefers "the statue to the woman." Indifferent to social problems and human suffering, he seeks "plastic poetry." All passes, he writes in his *Art poétique* (1857). Only art will endure: The bust survives the city.

In his "Symphony in White Major" ("Symphonie en blanc majeur"), Gautier seeks to evoke in poetry a fusion of music with the visual arts. He speaks of the swan-maidens (the Valkyries) as impassive statues in icy white, and likens them to a woman whose beauty is self-contained. He carves a poetic statue in solid marble, articulating each part of the body in tones of white, and uses the harmonies of the sounds to create a musical atmosphere. Gautier's combination of Romantic and often ethereal subject matter with poetic forms aspiring to the qualities of sculpture opened new directions in French poetry and, later, through Ezra Pound's Imagism, influenced a generation of poets who did not know the French Symbolists at first hand.

GÉRARD DE NERVAL

Gérard Labrunie, known as Gérard de Nerval, lacked Gautier's sense of aesthetic distance. For Nerval, poetry was exorcism, an attempt to clarify his clouded emotional and mental state. A feminine figure, based on the actress Jenny Colon, with whom he fell in love in 1836, dominates his work. She is named Aurélie or Sylvie and appears in his tales as well as in his poetry. Nerval's eclectic religion of art borrows elements from traditional Christianity as well as from alchemy, the Cabala, and other occult systems; he also places much hope in dreams. For him, "le rêve est une autre vie" (dreams are another life), and the Surrealists were to hail him as their predecessor. Nerval's symbols possess an absolute reality for him: He *becomes* the Prince of Aquitaine evoked in "El Desdichado."

Nerval's principal collection of poems is the sequence of sonnets titled *Les Chimères* (English translation, 1965; also known as *Chimeras*, 1966), published in 1854 with his tales *Les Filles du feu* (*The Daughters of Fire*, 1922). The poems are full of paradox and mystery, like the legendary Chimera; Nerval himself said of them that they "lose their charm if they are explained." Rich in classical allusions loosely woven together, they evoke the unlikely juxtapositions of a dream. The sonnets have the clear, sculptured quality of Gautier's verse mingled with uninhibited fantasy. Nerval's is a private mythology, in which plants and animals have a secret meaning. Translator of Goethe's *Faust* and Hoffmann's tales, Nerval was enamored of German poetry and remained throughout his life under the spell of the Faustian quest for privileged knowledge. Long considered a poet of the second rank—although his admirers included Gautier, Baudelaire, and Marcel Proust—Nerval has been reevaluated by modern critics, who see in him and his "supernaturalism" an important step in the exploration of the subconscious.

LECONTE DE LISLE

If both Gautier and Nerval inspired the Parnassians,

Leconte de Lisle was their uncontested master. After an apprenticeship in political verse, which revealed his attraction to the ideas of Félicité-Robert de Lamennais and Charles Fourier, Leconte de Lisle found his own style in *Poèmes antiques* (1852; ancient poems), *Poèmes barbares* (1862; barbarian poems), *Les Érinnyes* (1873, the Erinyes), *Poèmes tragiques* (1884; tragic poems), and *Derniers poèmes* (1895; last poems). Intransigent in his aestheticism, he made art his religion, not unlike Mallarmé, Valéry, and Proust. Leconte de Lisle's salon became the meeting place of the young poets of his generation, who came to accept his definition of art as the cult of beauty. In his conception, art is reserved for an elite, independent of truth, morality, and utility.

Leconte de Lisle translated the Greek classics in order to gain his livelihood, and his works are permeated by classical figures. In his poems, he often reworks classical myths to convey his message. Like Gautier, Leconte de Lisle resembles a painter or a sculptor, and in classical fashion, exhibits serenity and perfect control of his material. He also draws on oriental myths and Hindu philosophy, the source of his concept of the *néant divin* (divine nothingness). Leconte de Lisle's nature poems are beautiful for their clear and precise evocations. In contrast to Chateaubriand's identification with autumn leaves and misty shores, Leconte de Lisle invites the reader to enter through nature into the *néant divin*, since nothing is real and all is the dream of a dream.

BANVILLE, HÉRÉDIA, AND PRUDHOMME

Among the Parnassians who frequented Leconte de Lisle's salon, the three most important are Banville, Hérédia, and Sully Prudhomme. Banville shows more concern for form than for content, and his early publications, *Les Cariatides* (1842) and *Les Stalactites* (1846), reveal his admiration for Greek art and for a sculptured effect in verse. Inspired by such diverse themes as acrobatic exercises (*Odes funambulesques*, 1857) and the Middle Ages (*Trente-six Ballades joyeuses à la manière de François Villon*, 1873; joyous ballads in the manner of François Villon), Banville worked especially to achieve "rich rhymes."

Hérédia, of Cuban origin, is known for his mastery of the sonnet; his most important collection, *Les Trophées* (1893; *Sonnets from the Trophies*, 1898), contains 118 sonnets evoking past grandeur and exotic countries. Erudite and exact, his gallery of sonnets presents a series of perfect miniatures. Sully Prudhomme, the poet of the "Vase brisé," the broken vase like a broken heart, differs from the other Parnassians in his sensibility, evident in his earlier work, *Stances et poèmes* (1865), *Les Épreuves* (1866; trials), *Les Solitudes* (1869), and *Les Vaines Tendresses* (1875; vain tenderness). His later works, *La Justice* (1878) and *Le Bonheur* (1888; happiness), are oriented toward didactic and philosophical themes.

PROSE POEM

Romanticism, with its call for new forms and experimentation, coupled with Parnassian emphasis on style, provoked a new type of poetry in the mid-nineteenth century. Generally called the *poème en prose*, or prose poem, its origination is credited to Aloysius Bertrand (1807-1841), although Parny, in his *Chansons madécasses* in 1787, had anticipated it by almost a century. Bertrand's *Gaspard de la nuit* was published in 1842, a year after his death. Delicate and exact like a sculpture or a miniature, his work inspired a flurry of interest in the prose poem. Maurice de Guérin (1810-1839) published two prose poems, *La Bacchante* and *Le Centaure*, in 1840, and many critics regard Lamennais's *Paroles d'un croyant* (1834; words of a believer) as a prose poem. This work of mystical socialism expresses religious and political beliefs in vibrant and inspiring terms. It was, however, with Charles Baudelaire, Lautréamont, and Arthur Rimbaud that the prose poem was to become an important literary form. Lautréamont (1846-1870), whose real name was Isidore Ducasse, anticipated the Surrealist revolution in his *Chants de Maldoror*, a prose poem published in 1869.

CHARLES BAUDELAIRE

With Charles Baudelaire (1821-1867), a new generation of poets—and, in fact, modern poetry—was born. At first grouped by literary historians with the Romantics and the Parnassians, Baudelaire was soon linked with the Symbolists, whose work he inspired. His famous poem "Correspondances," included in *Les Fleurs du mal* (1857; *Flowers of Evil*, 1909), expresses in its first stanza the ethos of the entire Synmbolist movement:

> Nature is a temple, in which living pillars
> Sometimes utter a babel of words;
> Man traverses it through forests of symbols,
> That watch him with knowing eyes.

Flowers of Evil, Baudelaire's great volume of poems, admits good and evil, moral, immoral, and amoral, beautiful and ugly, as fit matter for poetry. The greatest modern vice, Baudelaire proclaims, is ennui, and he pictures Satan Trismégiste smoking his pipe as he prepares to swallow the world in one gaping yawn. Baudelaire's ennui is far removed from the romantic *mal du siècle*; it is connected with bourgeois conformity and mediocrity, an absence of true feeling and individual values. It is the same ennui that devours the parish of Georges Bernanos's country priest, and not unlike that which is subjected to a *reductio ad absurdum* in Eugène Ionesco's portraits of contemporary society. Modern society gravitates toward the city, and Baudelaire was one of the first poets of the city in all of its faceless anonymity. He sees the dark and seamy side of Paris—the nightlife, the underworld, the beggars, and the prostitutes—and with true compassion, pities their helplessness.

Baudelaire was constantly torn between two extremes, the desire for spirituality and the pull toward sensuality, and his poetry reveals the torment of guilt and despair. Woman becomes the symbol of this "double postulation": Idealized women, chaste and semidivine, are opposed to the figure of Baudelaire's mulatto mistress, Jeanne Duval, a sensuous Eve whose flowing hair, like the waves of the sea, leads him off into exotic climates and voluptuous paradises, yet whose very sensuality inspires his contempt. The epitome of modern man, Baudelaire seeks the "artificial paradises" of drugs and alcohol, hoping to overcome ennui and disgust and intensify his perceptions.

A brilliant art critic as well as a poet, Baudelaire discovered the talent of Eugéne Delacroix; as a literary critic, he was perhaps the first to grasp the depth of Edgar Allan Poe—indeed, Baudelaire introduced a veritable Poe cult in France, and his translations of Poe greatly influenced Mallarmé. In his slim volume, *Le Spleen de Paris*, or *Petits poèmes en prose* (1869), Baudelaire perfected the new form of the prose poem.

In his prose poems, Baudelaire expresses his hatred

of bourgeois conformism and his faith in art as the path to salvation. Somewhat akin to the Parnassian cult of beauty, this idea was to become the credo of Mallarmé and Verlaine, and it launched a new phase of poetry, not only in France but abroad as well. If Hugo is the greatest Romantic poet, then Baudelaire is the most original and the most modern of the nineteenth century.

SYMBOLISM

Symbolism is more difficult to define than Romanticism or Parnassianism, although it shares elements with both. From the Romantics, the Symbolists inherited an emphasis on subjectivity and the image of the poet as seer, an isolated figure rejected by society. From the Parnassians, the Symbolists took the notions of perfection in art and the importance of language for its own sake. Symbolism is oriented toward the ideal, the vague, the world of dreams and unreality. Closely associated with Impressionism, Symbolism reflects the impression of a moment that changes; it poses the question of the relation of the individual to time. Subtlety, fluidity, harmony—all are Symbolist virtues. To name an object, says Mallarmé, is to deprive it of much of its interest. Opposed to the world of materialism and bourgeois society, the Symbolists sought the Platonic and Hegelian universe of the ideal. Mystical without religious aspirations, the Symbolists nevertheless recognized a world of the spirit. They were also closely allied with music: Verlaine proclaimed, "De la musique avant toute chose" (music before everything else), and his works inspired many composers. Mallarmé's *L'Après-midi d'un faune* (1876; *Afternoon of a Faun*, 1956) is perhaps better known to foreign readers through Claude Debussy's tone poem of the same name.

Unlike Romanticism, which came to France primarily by way of England and Germany, Symbolism was born on French soil. The critic Robert Sabatier (*La Poésie du XIX° siècle*, 2 volumes, 1977) calls the Symbolist movement a "calm revolution." It accompanied the more violent battles of the Franco-Prussian War of 1870, followed by the bloody Commune of 1871. This struggle, shorter but more intense than the Revolution of 1789, eventually subsided into the tumultuous Third Republic. Social agitation was great; workers demanded their rights, protesting against low wages, child labor,

and other evils. At first, it seems a contradiction to place Verlaine's "pure poetry" in *Romances sans paroles* (1874; *Romances Without Words*, 1921) into such an atmosphere; Symbolism, however, was predicated upon a rejection of reality and a quest for perfection.

PAUL VERLAINE AND ARTHUR RIMBAUD

Paul Verlaine (1844-1896), whose verse had appeared in *Le Parnasse contemporain* of 1866, nevertheless epitomizes the quest for suggestion, pure poetry, the vague, and the imprecise. His poetry is pure music, as he himself affirms, written in a minor mode, with an exquisite delicacy markedly opposed to his violent and impulsive character. Friend of the Parnassians, encouraged by Mallarmé and inspired by Rimbaud, Verlaine was well-known and appreciated in literary circles. His first work, *Poèmes saturniens* (1866), was an accomplished performance for a young man of twenty-two, its dreamlike verse always verging on melancholy and grim fantasy. *Fêtes galantes* (1869; *Gallant Parties*, 1912), in the manner of Watteau, recalls Pierrot, Columbine, Harlequin, and the *commedia del l'arte*, though once again with a mood of impending disaster. *La Bonne Chanson* (1870) was written for Verlaine's fiancé, Mathilde Mauthé; the marriage, however, was destined not to survive, just as the dancing figures in *Gallant Parties* disappear with the dawn.

Romances Without Words, the most Verlainean of all Verlaine's works, is a volume in which the symbol alone has reality and all else disappears like the "interminable ennui" of the snow-covered plain. The poet is perfectly identified with the simple aspects of nature, such as rain, snow, or the shadow of the trees, hauntingly evocative in the French musical vowels "l'ombre des arbres." Only the music remains, even the verb disappears, as aptly analyzed by Jacques Borel. Verlaine's later work, including *Sagesse* (1880; wisdom), written after his conversion in prison, and *Jadis et naguère* (1884; formerly and long ago), is good but pales in comparison to his few but exquisite works composed during his sojourn with Rimbaud, who brought him both ecstasy and suffering.

If Verlaine represents the mystery and subtlety of poetry etched in tones of gray, Arthur Rimbaud (1854-1891) is Prometheus, the rebel, the rival of the gods and the thief of their fire. Rimbaud's credo was to become a seer, a *voyant*, by unleashing all of his senses. In 1871, he foreshadowed his spiritual autobiography in "Le Bateau ivre" ("The Drunken Boat"), where he saw himself drunk with adventure and soon bored with life. In the same year, he attempted a Baudelairean *correspondance* with "Voyelles" ("Vowels"), seeing himself as the inventor of the colors of letters. Like Nerval's, Rimbaud's work is enigmatic, full of private symbols.

Rimbaud also produced one of the most important volumes of prose poems ever written. *Les Illuminations* (1886; *Illuminations*, 1932)—the title meaning, according to Paul Verlaine, "colored plates"—was written in 1872, in a burst of poetic inspiration. In this exercise in pure Symbolism, Rimbaud, like the Surrealists, tries to wipe away the former world with another deluge and to create a new world with the innocence of childhood and the pure brightness of the sun. He embraces the dawn like a child caressing a beautiful woman, yet, at the same time, he satirizes contemporary society and its bourgeois mediocrity in the style of Baudelaire. There is a mystical quality also in such prose poems as "Conte" ("A Tale"), "Génie" ("Genie"), and "À une raison" ("To a Reason"), which influenced Paul Claudel.

Rimbaud's rupture with Verlaine provoked *Une Saison en enfer* (1873; *A Season in Hell*, 1932), his farewell to poetry. Here, he mixes traditional verse with the prose poem. More coherent in plan and structure than *Les Illuminations*, it is a kind of spiritual autobiography in which Rimbaud confesses his sadism, cruelty, and inconsistency, especially in his relationship with Verlaine. The critic Enid Starkie (*Arthur Rimbaud*, 1961) sees three principal motifs in the work: sin, God, and life. After believing that he has attained Heaven, Rimbaud discovers that it was really Hell. He had hoped to escape his heritage, but the Christian sense of sin is too strong, and he finds himself "the slave of his baptism." He confesses his Promethean desires, his rivalry with God, and admits that his desire to create the word has ultimately reduced him to silence. Thus, at the age of nineteen, Rimbaud abandoned poetry.

STÉPHANE MALLARMÉ

Stéphane Mallarmé (1842-1898), like Baudelaire and Verlaine, began his career by publishing ten poems in *Le Parnasse contemporain* in 1866. Among them, "Les Fenêtres" ("The Windows") and "Brise marine" ("Sea Breeze") are echoes of Baudelaire's "Les Phares" ("The Beacons"), "Le Voyage" ("The Voyage"), and

"Parfum exotique" ("Exotic Perfume") and the prose poem "Anywhere Out of the World" (original title in English). In fact, the early Mallarmé is hardly distinguishable from Baudelaire, with images of escape, the haunting sound of the sea, and the sick man who always desires another life. It was with *Hérodiade* (1945, 1959; *Herodias*, 1940) and *Afternoon of a Faun* that Mallarmé found his own style. Fame and recognition gradually followed, and he became the center of a salon that included such future writers as Jules Laforgue, Henri de Régnier, Maurice Barrès, Paul Claudel, André Gide, and Paul Valéry.

Mallarmé's style is hermetic, mysterious; in his conception, poetry is addressed to an elite and should speak only in halftones, never revealing the complete message, for to name an object is to rob it of its suggestive magic. Mallarmé's is the poetry of absence, of the inability to realize one's poetic vocation. The azure sky is inaccessible, and the swan is forever imprisoned in the icy lake, haunted by flights that might have been. The faun is perhaps the best image of Mallarmé's poetry; playing sensual music on his flute, the faun evokes the two nymphs that he may or may not have seen, may perhaps have dreamed: "Aimai-je un rêve?" (Did I love a dream?).

Deliberately discouraging the casual reader of his verse, Mallarmé sought to eliminate the beginning and the end of the "plots" of his poems; in his later work, he also introduced dislocations of syntax, so that the words themselves became puzzles to be solved. Images of tombs, of mirrors, of lakes and eyes, sensuous images of women's hair and seductive nymphs grace his poetry. Most of them convey many levels of symbolism, from self-knowledge to artistic creation. The tension between dream and reality, life and death, absence and presence, is at the heart of Mallarmé's work—which, despite its enigmatic quality, has influenced an entire generation of writers, among them Paul Valéry and Marcel Proust, and has provoked numerous exegeses.

"DECADENT" POETS

Ironically, Baudelaire, Rimbaud, Verlaine, and Mallarmé, who represent the best of Symbolism, did not refer to themselves as "Symbolists"; the term was applied to them retrospectively. Around 1885, a group of lesser poets influenced by these masters grouped together to form what they called the Symbolist school. Today, they are known to the world of letters by such various names as decadents, vers-librists, and so on. They wrote in ephemeral journals such as *L'Hydropathe*, *Tout-Paris*, *La Nouvelle Rive Gauche*, and *Lutèce*. They wrote manifestos, such as Jean Moréas's *Manifeste du symbolisme*, published in *Le Figaro* in 1886, and René Ghil's *Traité du verbe*. They produced poems of mixed quality but always inferior to the works of the great masters who preceded them.

Among those who were labeled "decadents," the most noteworthy are Charles Cros (1842-1888), a scientist, inventor, and poet, and Édouard-Joachim, self-styled "Tristan," Corbière (1845-1875), whose *Les Amours jaunes* (yellow loves) was published in 1873. Jules Laforgue (1860-1887), despite the brevity of his life, was perhaps the best known of the group. His principal collections, *Les Complaintes* (1885; complaints) and *L'Imitation de Notre-Dame la lune* (1886; imitation of Our Lady of the Moon), are marked by poetic fantasy and deep sincerity. His later poems are written in free verse, with trivial familiarity, revealing at the same time a preoccupation with death and with the problem of evil. Tormented by the image of Hamlet, Laforgue sought unity through the double. Like Baudelaire, Laforgue observed the monotonous and sad existence of the city; T. S. Eliot acknowledged a considerable debt to Laforgue.

VERHAEREN AND RÉGNIER

The Symbolist tradition continued into the twentieth century. The Flemishborn Émile Verhaeren (1855-1916) was a poet of the modern city. His *Les Campagnes hallucinées* (1893; hallucinatory countrysides) and *Les Villes tentaculaires* (1895; tentacled cities) evoke the city of the future, the labor of workers, and faith in man. In style and inspiration, Verhaeren resembles Walt Whitman. In the five volumes of *Toute la Flandre* (1904-1911; all of Flanders), he praised modern progress in his native country. Quite the opposite is Henri de Régnier (1864-1936), who, after an apprenticeship with Parnasse from which he retained the cult of art and beauty, and a number of Symbolist poems, returned to classicism and the inspiration of the seventeenth and eighteenth centuries. *Les Médailles d'argile* (1900; medals of clay) was written in memory of André Chénier. *La Cité des eaux* (1902; the city of waters), inspired by Michelet, evokes Versailles, which Régnier describes in sculptured motifs.

One can find in his work echoes of Ronsard, Racine, Chénier, and Mallarmé. Even in the 1920's, Régnier continued to write in the same style, and newer modes eclipsed his fame, though his work is excellent in composition and inspiration.

JAMMES AND FORT

A return to a simple and natural style marks the works of Francis Jammes (1868-1938) and Paul Fort (1872-1960). Discovered by Mallarmé, Gide, and Régnier when he was thirty years old, Jammes charmed audiences by the simplicity and sincerity of his work. Profoundly Catholic in his orientation, beginning with *Clairières dans le ciel, 1902-1906* (1906; clearings in the sky), he pleased Claudel. Jammes's religious convictions are especially evident in *Géorgiques chrétiennes* (1911-1912; Christian georgics), in which he extols the family and praises God. Paul Fort's ballads, which at first glance appear to be in prose, feature rhyme, assonance, and other poetic devices. His work is voluminous, and includes plays as well as poetry; in 1890, he created a *Théâtre d'Art* to represent Maurice Maeterlinck's work and Poe's raven. Although Fort's poetry is international, it is also very French; his diction alternates between a simple vocabulary not unlike Francis Jammes's and archaic expressions from the past.

SAINT-POL-ROUX AND CENDRARS

Paul Roux, known as Saint-Pol-Roux (1861-1940), has the distinction of being claimed by Catholics and Surrealists alike. He lived in seclusion for almost forty years, and his work is a strange mixture of mysticism and what he calls poetic *surcréation*. *Les Reposoirs de la procession* (1893-1907; repositories of the procession) illustrates his use of free verse, hallucinatory juxtapositions, and mystical language. Also anticipating Surrealism was Blaise Cendrars (1887-1961), whose travels, ranging from New York to Manchuria in the years before World War I, inspired *Pâques à New York* (1912; Easter in New York) and *La Prose du Transsibérien et de la petite Jehanne de France* (1913; English translation, 1931). The latter includes a dialogue between the author and the legendary Petite Jehanne de France, in which the railroad, in cinematographic fashion, becomes the focus of various images; Cendrars referred to this technique as *simultanéisme*. The original edition was illustrated by Sonia Delaunay and suggests the music of Arthur Honegger's *Pacific 231*. The Swiss-born Cendrars (whose real name was Frédéric Sauser) was also a gifted novelist.

EARLY TWENTIETH CENTURY POETS

The period between 1905 and 1914 was a brilliant one for Paris. The city became, as in the seventeenth and eighteenth centuries, the center of European culture. Impressionists such as Claude Monet and Pierre-Auguste Renoir continued to paint; Paul Cézanne and Henri Matisse had already launched new artistic forms; Pablo Picasso had come to Paris from Spain. Maurice Ravel and Claude Debussy wrote their music for orchestra and ballet; the dance was revolutionized by the appearance of the director Sergey Diaghilev and the Ballets Russes in 1909, with the impetuous and genial dancer Vaslav Nijinsky, and the collaboration of the great Russian composer Igor Stravinsky in *The Fire-Bird* (1910), *Petrouchka* (1911), and *The Rite of Spring* (1913). The theater resumed life again in André-Léonard Antoine's *Théâtre Libre* and Jacques Copeau's *Vieux Colombier* in 1913.

Yet this high degree of culture, calling forth poets and artists from Europe and America, had its dark side. The year 1905 was a year of wars and strikes throughout Europe, especially in Russia, where the shadow of the Revolution was already threatening. European alliances were fragile, and Germany, a victor over France in 1870, was once again a menace. In 1914, World War I broke out. For France, it was a moment of patriotism. The war, however, was long and difficult; soldiers spent months and years in the trenches, and the final victory was marred by great losses, both human and financial. The years immediately following, the 1920's, were years of exuberance and exaltation, of *joie de vivre* and new beginnings. The 1930's, in contrast, were dismal, with the Depression, unemployment, and yet another threat of German rearmament.

It was only natural that poetry should respond in various ways to such circumstances. The great cultural renaissance of the prewar years kept alive the Symbolist quest for beauty in Paul Valéry, Paul Claudel, and André Gide, and Marcel Proust's autobiographical novel in poetic prose, *À la recherche du temps perdu* (1913-1927; *Remembrance of Things Past*). The *renouveau*

catholique (Catholic renewal), which had already attracted Francis Jammes, Ernest Psichari, Jacques Maritain, and others, drew Paul Claudel and Charles Péguy, for it promised stable values in a changing world. At the same time, the unprecedented carnage of the war led to a cult of destruction of all traditional values. Freudian discoveries provoked exploration of dreams, and here the Surrealists found inspiration for their poetry, following the leadership of Guillaume Apollinaire and his nineteenth century predecessors, Lautréamont and Rimbaud. Surrealism touched almost every major French poet during and after the 1920's, and it exercised a considerable international influence as well; no other school of comparable influence is identifiable in twentieth century French poetry.

Part of the *renouveau catholique* at the turn of the twentieth century, though never officially returning to the Church, Charles-Pierre Péguy (1873-1914) turned to poetry for inspiration toward the end of his life. A militant Socialist in his *Cahiers de la quinzaine* (1900-1914; notebooks of the fortnight), Péguy expressed his religious beliefs in the idiosyncratic free verse of *Mystères: Le Mystère de la charité de Jeanne d'Arc* (1910; *The Mystery of the Charity of Joan of Arc*, 1950), *Le Porche du mystère de la deuxième vertu* (1912; the porch of the mystery of the second virtue), and *Le Mystère des saints innocents* (1912; *The Mystery of the Holy Innocents*, 1956). The *Tapisseries* (tapestries), comprising *La Tapisserie de Sainte Geneviève et Jeanne d'Arc* (1912), *La Tapisserie de Notre-Dame* (1913), and the unfinished *Ève* (1913), were written in more traditional meters, as were the interminable and incomplete *Quatrains*. In his verse, Péguy evokes the Middle Ages and the heroism of old France.

Péguy's verse line is often prosaic; a single "line" may take up an entire page or more. He also employs extensive digressions and thematic repetitions. As a result, the texture of his poetry is often forbidding, and he has been most widely read in brief selections that fail to convey the overarching structure of his work. Péguy was to gain fame for his patriotism. Chauvinistic in his conception of France as specially favored by God, Péguy wrote of the glory of dying for one's country in a just war. He joined the army at the outbreak of World War I when he was past forty and was immediately killed in the First

Battle of the Marne. Immortalized as a hero, Péguy was revered even during World War II, when his mix of religion and nationalism was less in vogue. He is still respected today, although in many ways, he stands apart from the mainstream of twentieth century poetry.

An ardent convert to Catholicism and a champion of the Church, Paul Claudel (1868-1955) was a career diplomat as well as a poet. His work took him all over the world, from Asia to the United States and South America, and his poetry reflects this wide experience in its cosmic vision. Claudel himself traced his roots to Rimbaud, in whom he found a liberation of language and of the spirit. Claudel was a playwright as well as poet, and most of his dramatic works are written in symbolic poetry and in his own peculiar rhythmic style. His principal nondramatic poetic works are *Cinq grandes odes* (1910; *Five Great Odes*, 1967) and *Corona benignitatis anni dei* (1915; *Coronal*, 1943). Toward the end of his life, he again returned to poetry in "Paul Claudel interroge . . ." (1948-1955; Paul Claudel questions . . .), a series of invocations of various saints.

Claudel regarded poetry both as a means of *connaissance* and as a means of *co-naissance*, knowledge and birth. His verse is characterized by the primitive structure of dialogue and monologue. To express his sense of time as rhythmic rather than merely sequential, he invented a type of line known as the *verset claudélien*. Recalling the biblical Psalms in both form and inspiration, Claudel's line resembles human breathing or the ebb and flow of the sea, "la dilatation de la houle." Since language for Claudel is essentially oral communication, the poet is the person who *names* an object or an idea; as in Symbolist theory, he becomes a seer and a prophet. In his "Magnificat," one of the *Five Great Odes*, he compares his life-generating paternity in the physical sense to poetic creativity, both of which reflect God's creation of man in his image.

In *Five Great Odes*, Claudel uses his principal images of the Muses, water, and grace to symbolize his poetic creation. Jubilant and triumphant, his work is a vast symphony to the arts and to the divine presence in the world. The fourth ode, "La Muse qui est la grâce" ("The Muse Who Is Grace"), is an *ars poetica* as well as a profession of faith. More accessible than the others, the third ode, "Magnificat," celebrates the birth of Claudel's daughter

Marie and articulates his own spiritual autobiography. Claudel is also much appreciated for his simple works in traditional verse, such as "La Vierge à midi" (the Virgin at noon), deeply religious and more human than the cosmic explosion of his more elaborate creations. It is precisely this cosmic dimension, however, along with his verbal experimentation, that places Claudel in the mainstream of twentieth century poetry, and his original use of images and symbols constitutes a worthy succession to Baudelaire, Rimbaud, and Mallarmé.

Paul-Ambroise Valéry (1871-1945) also was indebted to the Symbolists. Influenced by J. K. Huysmans's *Àrebours* (1884; *Against the Grain*) and by Verlaine and Mallarmé, he began to write poetry in 1889, making the acquaintance of such poets and artists as Mallarmé, Pierre Louÿs, Gide, and Debussy, and later Renoir and Edgar Degas. As Mallarmé's earlier works are close in style to Baudelaire's, so Valéry's first poems, later collected in *Album de vers anciens* (1920; *Album of Early Verse*), resemble Mallarmé's. "La Fileuse" ("The Spinner") evokes Mallarmé's "Sainte" and breathes the Symbolist tradition. In 1892, after a spiritual crisis during which Valéry reflected on the dangers of art and sentiment, he abandoned poetry for twenty years. During this time, he worked, married, and exercised his mind through the study of mathematics, without, however, abandoning his literary and artistic friends.

In 1917, Valéry returned to poetry with *La Jeune Parque* (*The Young Fate*), soon to be followed by *Charmes: Ou, Poèmes* (1922; *Charms*). The style of these works is noticeably different from that of the earlier ones. Serene and controlled, they nevertheless show the influence of Symbolism and the subtleties of Mallarmé. Valéry is a poet who searches for purity of language and action in the here and now. He sees poetry as a sublime vocation, necessitating time and patience, a theme beautifully expressed in the simple "Les Pas" ("Footsteps"), where the poet awaits the Muse as the lover awaits his beloved: The essence of inspiration is the waiting. Valéry's conception of art is perhaps best exemplified in his masterpiece, "Le Cimetière marin" ("The Graveyard by the Sea"). Here, classical serenity blends with realism and idealism to express man's failure to attain absolute perfection and his need to attempt to live.

Not strictly a philosopher, Valéry was, in the fullest

sense of the word, a thinker, and poetry was only one of the forms that his thinking took. His essays and his voluminous notebooks, a lifelong project, have significantly influenced modern French poetry, particularly in arguing the primacy of language—language, that is, regarded not as a means of communication but as a field in which the poet can pursue his autonomous art.

APOLLINAIRE AND SURREALISM

Guillaume Apollinaire (1880-1918) is a poet of the twentieth century in a way that Valéry is not. While Valéry was a product of the *fin de siècle* Symbolist milieu, Apollinaire was energized by the artistic renaissance centered in pre-World War I Paris—the Paris of Picasso. Apollinaire, without a father and without a country, assumed an international and paternal role in the development of a new style of poetry. He saw temporal and spatial relations as essentially different from what they had been in the past. In his verse, he articulates the profound discontinuity and disorientation of modern society, without, however, falling into Baudelairean spleen or the Romantic *mal du siècle*.

Apollinaire introduced striking innovations in form: the removal of all punctuation, the use of free verse with irregular rhyme and rhythm, and the *calligramme*, or picture-poem. His poetry was influenced by his collaboration with the revolutionary painters of his time: Marie Laurencin, Henri Rousseau, Raoul Dufy, Robert Delaunay, and especially Pablo Picasso. Writers who were to be associated with Surrealism, including Philippe Soupault, André Breton, and Tristan Tzara, acknowledged him as their precursor, and Pierre Reverdy and Francis Picabia printed his works in their avant-garde journals.

After 1912, Apollinaire definitely espoused modern art, and the publication of *Alcools* (English translation, 1964) in 1913 was its first poetic manifestation, although *Le Bestiaire* (*Bestiary*, 1978) in 1911 already foreshadows this orientation, with woodcuts by Raoul Dufy. In *Alcools*, the first and last poems, "Zone" and "Vendémiaire" are the most revolutionary in their dislocation of space and time and use of startling images. Many poems in the volume are relatively traditional, including the much appreciated and nostalgic "Le Pont Mirabeau" ("Mirabeau Bridge"). In *Calligrammes* (1918;

English translation, 1980), Apollinaire's picture-poems immediately catch the reader's eye, but the most genuinely innovative poems in the volume are to be found in the first section, "Ondes" ("Waves"), rich with disconcerting juxtapositions and unusual images. In the final poem in *Calligrammes*, "La Jolie Rousse" ("The Pretty Redhead"), Apollinaire bequeaths "vast and strange domains" to anyone willing to take them.

Only a few years before poets and antipoets came to explore these kingdoms, Apollinaire had subtitled his play *Les Mamelles de Tirésias* (1918; *The Breasts of Tiresias*, 1961) a *drame surréaliste*. The Surrealist movement, touching art, poetry, and music, traced its roots to Apollinaire, and even further back to Lautréamont and his *Chants de Maldoror*. Like Romanticism, Surrealism was an international movement, exerting a powerful influence on the development of modern poetry in Greece, Latin America, and other nations and regions with widely diverse poetic traditions.

In part, Surrealism was a reaction to World War I, reflecting a loss of faith in traditional values. At the same time, there was also a feeling of euphoria at the end of the war, a sense of limitless possibilities. There were discoveries to be made in other worlds, especially the world of dreams, opened by the work of Sigmund Freud.

Early Surrealism found a kindred spirit in the Romanian Tristan Tzara (born Sami Roesenstock in 1896), who, in 1916, in Zurich, launched a movement called Dada, which was aimed against all logic, reason, and social organization. In 1918, the Dadaists published a manifesto which expressed their gospel of destruction and celebrated the "fertile wheel of a universal circus in the real powers and fantasy of each individual."

The founding Surrealist group included Philippe Soupault, René Crevel, Robert Desnos, Paul Éluard, Louis Aragon, Benjamin Péret, Max Ernst, and Francis Picabia, all of whom acknowledged André Breton as their master. In their manifesto of 1924, they defined Surrealism as "psychic automation . . . in the absence of any control exercised by reason, and outside of any aesthetic or moral preoccupation." Thus, one of their most important techniques was "automatic writing," in which one wrote whatever occurred to him, without any reflection or concern for sense, grammar, or punctuation.

They also practiced a faithful transcription of dreams, the "other life" so exalted by Nerval.

Many artists became members or associates of the Surrealist group, including the Spaniard Salvador Dalí (born 1904), who was also a poet and an essayist, and who baptized his method "paranoic-critic"; Marcel Duchamp (1887-1968), who brought Surrealist art to the United States; the German Max Ernst (1891-1976), who used collages, among other media of expression, and was interested in depth psychology; and the Belgian René Magritte (1898-1967), whose works evince a metaphysical and disconcerting character. The cinema was also an important vehicle of expression for Surrealism, especially the films of the Spanish director Luis Buñuel, such as *Le Chien andalou* (1928) and *L'Age d'Or* (1930). The Surrealists also produced periodicals, such as *La Révolution surréaliste*. In 1930, the name of this journal was changed to *Le Surréalisme au service de la Révolution*, marking an internal rupture in the Surrealist movement between those who wished to maintain an apolitical stance and those who had embraced Communism.

The most faithful Surrealists were André Breton (1896-1966), Benjamin Péret (1899-1959), Philippe Soupault (born 1897), and, erratically, Robert Desnos (1900-1945). Breton was both the chief theoretician of the movement and its supreme practitioner. His work is difficult to classify by genre, since the Surrealist philosophy is predicated on the breaking down of such categories. *Nadja* (1928) is a sort of poetic novel, emphasizing the role of chance. *Les Vases communicants* (1932) and *L'Amour fou* (1937) resemble Baudelairean poems in prose, with poetic evocations of the city. *Arcane 17* (1945), written in the United States during Breton's lengthy sojourn there during World War II, is a beautiful appreciation of nature and an idealization of woman. The collection is composed of vignettes loosely connected to one another as travel impressions; the work is a lengthy meditation on Nerval's "ma seule étoile est morte" (my only star is dead), into which are woven observations on contemporary life and society.

Robert Desnos was a specialist in the language of dreams. He was a faithful adherent to the Surrealist gospel until 1936, when he proclaimed his own originality. This independence naturally led to a rupture with Breton, but it enriched Desnos, whose poetry showed genuine talent. During his early involvement with Surrealism, he used many *jeux de mots*, as in his and Duchamp's *Rrose Sélavy* (1922). Desnos's most important collections are *Je me vois* (1926; I see myself), *La Liberté ou l'amour* (1927; liberty or love), and *État de veille* (1943; state of waking). During World War II, like Aragon and Éluard, he composed patriotic verse in simple and accessible meters. His other works often take the form of prose poems and of a new type that he invented for the radio, called *poème radiophonique*. A man of varied interests, he was the friend of artists and writers, especially Pablo Picasso and Ernest Hemingway. Poetry for Desnos was essentially the meeting of the unusual and the spontaneous, the natural and the surreal, often mingled with wit and humor. His best love lyric, "Poème à la mystérieuse" ("Poem to the Mysterious Woman"), was written as he lay dying in a concentration camp.

With the exception of Breton, the poets who remained within the Surrealist camp achieved only limited success. It is rather those who received their first inspiration and liberation through Surrealism, and who then followed their own creative instincts, who are among the most representative of modern poetry. Indeed, as noted above, there is hardly a modern French poet who was not touched in some way by Surrealism.

Paul Éluard (1895-1952), born Eugène Grindel, published several early collections under the sign of Surrealism, including *Les Nécessités de la vie* (1921; the necessities of life), *Répétitions* (1922), and *Capitale de la douleur* (1926; *Capital of Pain*, 1973); the latter volume also introduces the orientation toward beauty in expression and the faith in the omnipotence of love that mark Éluard's mature work. In the 1930's, Éluard evolved toward humanitarian idealism, expressed in *La Vie immédiate* (1932; the immediacy of life) and *Les Yeux fertiles* (1936; fertile eyes). Very active in the Resistance, he wrote simple lyric poetry in *Poésie et vérité* (1942; *Poetry and Truth, 1942*, 1949). His last volume, *Poésie ininterrompue* (1946; uninterrupted poetry), expressed his quest for a human community in the face of human solitude. Almost medieval in his idealization of woman in the courtly tradition, Éluard wrote some of the finest love poetry of the twentieth century. He seeks fraternity and solidarity, along with love, to break through human loneliness. Fundamentally positive and optimistic, Éluard assumes a constructive attitude toward life, especially through poetry.

Louis Aragon (1897-1982) evolved in much the same way as Éluard and addressed similar themes, such as love and war, although in a different style. A prolific writer, he was a novelist, a critic, and a journalist as well as a poet. Aragon's style is deceptively casual; his verse has affinities with popular music and medieval ballads, mixed with a certain intellectual cruelty and satire. His most popular poetry was associated with the Resistance; in it, he compares France with his wife, Elsa, the ideal woman of his poetry, whom he celebrates in *Le Crève-coeur* (1941; the heartbreak), *Cantique à Elsa* (1941), and *Les Yeux d'Elsa* (1942; Elsa's eyes). *Je te salue, ma France* (1944; I salute, you, France) and *La Diane française* (1944) reflect his humanitarian and patriotic response to the suffering created by the war. Committed to Communism, he touches on political themes in *Les Beaux Quartiers* (1936; *Residential Quarter*, 1938) and *La Semaine sainte* (1958; *Holy Week*, 1961).

A popular poet, like Aragon, yet with a style unique among modern artists, Jacques Prévert (1900-1977) was a poet, screenwriter, and composer of popular songs. His collaborator, the film director Marcel Carné, described him as the one and only poet of the French cinema. Joseph Kosma set many of his poems to music, including the well-known "Les Feuilles d'automne" ("Autumn Leaves") and "Barbara." Prévert's poetry began to appear after World War II, and his first volume, *Paroles* (1945; words), became a best-seller, unusual for poetry in France. Other popular collections include *Histoires* (1948; stories), *Spectacle* (1951), and *La Pluie et le beau temps* (1955; rain and good weather). Witty and satiric, varied in theme, full of wordplay and understatement, and including traditional verse and prose poems, Prévert's poetry has its roots in the oral tradition. Prévert can be both tender and mocking; he charms the reader with his facile verve and down-to-earth subjects. He is critical of all institutions, and he speaks of nature, birds, and animals with delicate intimacy. Prévert is regarded as the most genuinely popular poet of modern France and the only songwriter who is at the same time a true poet.

Also involved with theater and cinema was Jean Cocteau (1889-1963), whose work has a fantastic qual-ity best expressed by the figure of Orpheus, Cocteau's favorite image. Poet, painter, screenwriter, and novelist, Cocteau himself classified all of his works as poetry. He regarded his films as "poems in action"; the theme of metamorphosis recurs throughout his oeuvre. Among his works more strictly poetic in the traditional sense are *Poésies* (1920), *Vocabulaire* (1922), *Plain-chant* (1923), *Allégories* (1941), and *Le Chiffre sept* (1952; the number seven). Mystery, communication with death, *préciosité*, and a certain obscurity characterize all of his work.

Himself a legend and an influence on Cocteau, Max Jacob (1876-1944) belonged to Apollinaire's circle on rue Ravignan in the period before World War I. Jewish in origin, he became a Catholic in 1915, and his poetry shows a mixture of mysticism and humor. Although Max Jacob was less talented than Apollinaire, his poetry has remained durable: It is a mixture of satire, sarcasm, popular lyricism, and parody, free of all literary affectation. Like so many of his contemporaries, Max Jacob was also an essayist, novelist, and moralist. Among his best collections are *Le Cornet à dés* (1917; the dice box), *Le Laboratoire central* (1921), *Ballades* (1938), and *Derniers poèmes en vers et en prose* (1945). Like Pierre Reverdy, Jacob spent much of his life in the shadow of a monastery, Saint-Benoît-sur-Loire, until his capture and execution by the Germans in 1944. He is especially noted for his mastery of the prose poem and for the narrative, rather than the rhythmic, quality of his poetry.

More influenced by Symbolism (primarily through Jules Laforgue) than by Surrealism, the Uruguayan-born Jules Supervielle (1884-1960) became a link between modern French verse and poetry in Latin America. Popular in style, like the poetry of Prévert and Aragon, his work has strong lyric quality. Supervielle believed in everything and therefore had a strong orientation toward hope, in the manner of Hugo and Péguy. Simplicity, together with a sense of mystery, characterizes his verse: Supervielle is the poet of children and animals. At the same time, he often speaks of death, though without a trace of morbidity. Although he began to write at a very young age, his first success was *Gravitations* (1925). Other important collections include *Le Forçat innocent* (1930; the innocent criminal), *La Fable du monde* (1938; the fable of the world), *Poèmes de la France malheureuse* (1941; poems of unhappy France), and *Oublieuse mémoire* (1949; forgetful memory). He also wrote tales, novels, and plays in a charming poetic style.

In 1928, André Breton hailed Pierre Reverdy (1899-1960) as the greatest poet living at that time. Incapable of sustaining his bonds with the Surrealists, whom he had supported in his journal *Nord-Sud*, or with anyone for that matter, Reverdy spent much of his life in the shadow of the great abbey of Solesmes. He is the most secret and most solitary of the Surrealists, and his poetry reveals the same quality, thus expressing better than his contemporaries the great void that exists in modern society. While most of the Surrealist generation responded to World War II with a burst of patriotic fervor, Reverdy never mentions the war; *Plupart du temps* (1945; most of the time) speaks of lack of comprehension, clouds and shadows, winter, an expected arrival that never occurs, the world in pieces, and similar themes. The critic J-P. Richard, writing on Reverdy, says that a poem for him is a path that goes nowhere yet one that orients the reader to the innermost part of his being. Such is the wartime message of Reverdy.

Reverdy's other principal collections, *Poèmes en prose* (1915), *La Lucarne ovale* (1916), *Sources du vent* (1929; sources of the wind), *Étoiles peintes* (1921; painted stars), and *Main d'œuvre* (1949), are all secret and mysterious, situated in a fragmented universe where walls recede and corridors wind into a labyrinthine abyss. Friend of the cubists, Reverdy gives his poetry a geometric quality, with ovals, circles, and other forms. Bodily shapes are curved, like Mallarmé's swan, in an eternal question mark. Like Verlaine's, Reverdy's poetry has a resonance all its own, with cavernous and metallic sounds and steps that disappear into the distance. Reverdy writes more by negation than by affirmation; as Claudel observed, to give a name (*nom*) is to say no (*non*). Again like Verlaine, Reverdy writes a poetry of absence, yet he somehow seeks for a desired presence. The critic Robert Greene allies Reverdy with the existentialist philosophy of Camus and Jean-Paul Sartre, expressing fundamental human solitude. One senses a mystical quality in Reverdy's work that addresses the dark night of the soul more than the union with the be-loved. Although critics may be tempted to "decode" his work, Reverdy, like Rimbaud, who alone possessed the key to his visions, left only "pure poetry" which is itself the message.

MODERN POETRY

All of modern poetry goes back to Baudelaire, Mallarmé, and Rimbaud. Symbolists, Surrealists, and religious writers alike took their inspiration from a vague doctrine that none of these poets explicitly enunciated. The critic Wallace Fowlie, writing in the 1950's, defined the legacy of Symbolism as a quest for "purity" in poetic expression; in his view, the progressive "spiritualization" of modern art in all of its forms is the principal characteristic of modern-day poetry. Here, "spiritualization" is not meant in a religious sense; rather, it suggests the emancipation of poetry from a mission, from the necessity to signify, to point to a meaning, to deal with personal or social issues. Thus, the modern poet becomes not a prophet—the role played by Victor Hugo and his contemporaries—but rather a magician or a visionary, in the tradition of Rimbaud, an explorer of hidden realms and of the interior kingdom of the subconscious. The modern poet is also in search of the lost paradise of childhood, in the tradition of Baudelaire.

The Surrealists, under the sign of Melusine, defined the poetic vocation as that of the seer and the magician. The poet is not to change society; he is, rather, to illuminate it, to show it visions of another life. The Surrealists insisted on the primacy of language, its independence and its importance in its own right—hence the *jeux de mots*, the startling juxtapositions, the fragmentation of sentences, the popularity of the prose poem, and the abolition of genre distinctions in the practice of what is called simply *écriture*, writing.

Robert Greene, writing at the end of the 1970's, saw a further distinction in contemporary French poetry. He divided contemporary poets into two groups, one associated with the journal *Tel Quel* (the title of which comes from Valéry's essays), increasingly Marxist in its orientation, and the journal *L'Éphémère* (1967-1972), with its successor *L'Argile*, founded in 1973. The *telquelistes* are hermetic writers with links to the analytical and neo-classical tradition of Valéry; they regard the poem as a reflection on itself, with no structure or meaning other than that given it by the reader. Writers who share this orientation also consider themselves as successors to Lautréamont. They ignore all genre distinctions and view all types of writing simply as *écriture*. To this group, Greene assigns Francis Ponge and Marcelin Pleynet, both of whom are regular contributors to *Tel Quel*.

The second group in Greene's schema trace their descent from Rimbaud and Apollinaire. They are Orphic poets who seek adventure: For them, poetry exists to take humanity beyond the everyday to a realm of deeper knowledge. These poets continue the quest of the Surrealists for a reality beyond reality. Like Apollinaire and the Surrealists, they maintain close ties with the world of the plastic arts (Greene feels that the cover of *L'Éphémère*, with an emaciated nude by Alberto Giacometti, is especially significant). Greene sees Reverdy as a predecessor of this second group, which now includes Yves Bonnefoy, René Char, Jacques Dupin, and André du Bouchet.

All modern French writers, whose principal works appeared after 1940 and Germany's occupation of France, are marked by the existentialism articulated by Camus and Sartre. Victims of a senseless war, profoundly humiliated by the Occupation, and psychologically and spiritually shaken by the apparent loss of values, they look for meaning in the fundamental solitude of existence. The fragmentation of society is visible in their fragmented lives; the poetry of such authors as Henri Michaux verges on the absurd, and the linguistic experimentation of Raymond Queneau (1903-1976), whose work knows no genre, expresses a revolution in language and has had a strong influence on modern writing. Other writers, such as Pierre-Jean Jouve (1887-1976), who really belongs to the preceding generation, Patrice de la Tour du Pin (1911-1975), and Pierre Emmanuel (1916-1984) are among the most important representatives of poetry with a religious orientation.

A giant among modern poets, recipient of the Nobel Prize in Literature in 1960, is Alexis Saint-Léger Léger, known as Saint-John Perse (1887-1975). Like Paul Claudel, who became his friend and encouraged his early attempts at poetry, he traveled widely, and his poetry is informed by a cosmic vision. He is a poet of dis-

ciplined but luxuriant sensuality, a great visionary who identifies flesh with spirit in a burst of life, although without the religious dimension that characterizes Claudel. Images of the sea are frequent in Perse's work, as are images of wind, rain, and sky, archetypal images symbolizing the primitive forces of fertility, passion, and vitality. His epic of the Earth and the cosmos is situated in a vast space that has its own time and rhythm.

Perse's first collection, *Éloges* (English translation, 1944), appeared in 1911. In 1924, he published *Anabase* (*Anabasis*, 1930), regarded by many critics as his masterpiece. Among the important volumes that followed are *Exil* (1942; *Exile*, 1949), *Vents* (1946; *Winds*, 1953), *Amers* (1957; *Seamarks*, 1958), and *Chronique* (1960; English translation, 1961). Although all of these works are written in a kind of free verse or are in fact prose poems, Perse is a classical poet in both form and inspiration, for like Valéry, Perse subordinates his sensuous images to a strict and serene discipline. Many of his titles and images are taken from classical Greek culture: *Anabasis* takes its title from the march of Xenephone, while *Seamarks* evokes the setting of an ancient Greek theater. The altar is the sea, and the fragments of humanity around its edges play out in dialogue the conflict between the human and the divine. The sea is also the main actor in *Exile*, written in New Jersey when the poet was in exile from Vichy France; the Atlantic Ocean, which separates him from his homeland, symbolizes the march of a cosmic army. J-P. Richard sees in Perse's work a reflection of the decomposition of Occidental civilization, with an invocation to the primitive forces of life, especially water, to cleanse and reinvigorate the world.

Where Perse's rolling lines present a cosmic flow of images, the works of Henri Michaux (1899-1984) are disconcerting and abrupt in style and content. Some critics regard him as one of the most important and original of modern French poets, yet he is largely undiscovered. Like many of his contemporaries, Michaux abolished the distinction between poetry and prose; his essays, travelogues, and personal journals are all distinctly "poetic." Michaux excels in the small incident rather than in sustained poems, and he shifts grammar as he shifts ideas, for his vision is destructive of syntax. Michaux has described his many experiments with hallucinogens in brilliant poetic prose; he is a poet of magic and ritual, and many of his works are incantations and exorcisms, asserting above all the power of self. Michaux is an artist as well as a poet, and his drawings, equally mysterious and enigmatic, often accompany his poetry. Although it is difficult to distinguish genres in Michaux, *Un Barbare en Asie* (1933; *A Barbarian in Asia*, 1949), *Plume: Précédé de lointain intérieur* (1938), *Ailleurs* (1948; elsewhere), and three long poems in verse, *Paix dans les brisements* (1959; peace in the breakings), "Iniji," and *Vers la complétude* (1967; toward completeness) are among his principal poetic works. These three long poems relate his experiences with drugs; he seeks to represent rather than to explain his hallucinatory visions. Later volumes included *Face à ce qui se dérobe* (1975; facing what unfolds) and *Poteaux d'angle* (1971; corner posts).

The grammatical and linguistic dislocation found in Michaux is even more evident in Francis Ponge (1899-1988). In order to read him, observes Greene, one must change one's idea of what poetry is, for Ponge's work is totally removed from the traditional concept of poetry. Ponge does not attempt to explain, for he believes that the reader holds the key to a poem. Not unlike Samuel Beckett's prose, Ponge's work exemplifies the total loss of self as the center of self-consciousness. He invents words, variously christening his new genre *objeu*, *objet*, and *jeu de mots*, or "metapoem." He reveals an obsessive concern for words, which—frequently in defiance of their etymology—he treats as onomatopoeic or iconic. He employs puns, false starts, repetitions, reversals, and other such means to express the senselessness of the world and his inability to express it. In his view, the contemporary writer is reduced to describing the world by means of a *littérature littérante*.

Ponge has been "discovered" three times: in the 1920's, by the *Nouvelle Revue française*; in 1944, by Sartre; and in the 1960's, by *Tel Quel*. In his work from *Proêmes* (1948) to *Nouveau Recueil* (1967), which includes such significant works as "Le Pré," Ponge assumes the stance of a post-existentialist poet, one who, like René Descartes, sees nature as a clock but goes on to conclude that the wheels of the machinery mean nothing beyond their spinning.

Much younger than Ponge, Marcelin Pleynet (born 1933) expresses his rapidly accelerating disengagement from contemporary culture, which he finds politically repressive and spiritually bankrupt. He began writing during the Algerian War (1954-1962) in a style reminiscent of such disparate writers as Perse, Char, Éluard, and Reverdy. Pleynet's early collections were *Provisoires amants des Nègres, 1957-1959* (1962; provisory lovers of Negroes) and *Paysages en deux* (1963). With *Comme* (1965) and *Stanze* (1973), he achieved an individual style not unlike the metapoetic mode invented by Ponge. In *Comme*, metaphor is not the matter of poetry; it is its sole subject, and form mimes meaning. This change in Pleynet can be attributed in part to the events of May, 1968, when all French institutions came under examination; his stylistic development has also been influenced by a growing admiration for China. Pleynet engages in creative disordering of words to reveal the deep structure of language and mind. His critical works reveal an admiration for Henri Matisse and James Joyce, and he seeks to follow Joyce's example in developing a new *littérature d'engagement*, in which language will play the major role. *Stanze* reveals the diverse influences of Ezra Pound, Lautréamont, Sigmund Freud, Karl Marx, and Mao Zedong in its willful transgression of sexual, political, and syntactic taboos. Although Pleynet's work points to a radically new style of poetry, it is also a work still in the process of evolving and therefore difficult to evaluate with any certainty.

Among the poets designated by Greene as orphic or meaning-oriented, the greatest is René Char (1907-1988). A convinced Surrealist from 1929 to 1934, he wrote *Artine* in 1930, considered the most classically Surrealist work. Breaking from Surrealism because he did not wish to accept the Surrealists' narrow definition of dreams, he nevertheless links Surrealism with present-day writing in the journals *L'Éphémère* and *L'Argile*. His masters include Heraclitus and Georges de La Tour, who embody for him the Greek concept of *energeia*; more immediately, he shares affinities with Martin Heidegger and especially with Camus, who greatly valued his work. He thus manifests a philosophical orientation and, like Camus, an authentic search for human dignity.

Influenced by his Surrealist heritage, Char employs the technique of contradiction—the juxtaposition of semantically incompatible worlds in place of traditional images. This procedure corresponds to his philosophy of poetry as a means whereby the individual self is lost in order to accede to the impersonal fullness of being. It is also an expression of Char's quest for perfection of expression. Char's prose poems are superior to his more traditional verse, where his rhythm is flowing, breathless, and intense. Among his collections are *Commune présence* (1964; common presence), *Le Poème pulvérisé* (1947; the pulverized poem), *Les Matinaux* (1950), and *Dans la pluie giboyeuse* (1968; in the game-stocked rain). A more recent collection, *Aromates chasseurs* (1976; aromatic hunters) uses Orion and the archipelago as a cluster of contradictions and an evocation of the cosmos and outer space. Char maintains throughout his work, much like Nerval, that true life is inaccessible (*ailleurs*) but that one must clutch the bits and pieces within one's grasp and live them authentically.

Two contemporary poets who have worked together on *L'Éphémère* and *L'Argile*, André du Bouchet (1924-2001) and Jacques Dupin (born 1927), are united in their approach to art through the study of Giacometti, yet each uses his own individual manner to resolve the problem of art and consciousness. Du Bouchet studied in the United States and reveals not only American but also English and German influence, especially that of Shakespeare, Joyce, Friedrich Hölderlin, and Paul Celan. Although du Bouchet experiments with language, he declares expressly that language is not the primary object of his work. J-P. Richard, noting in du Bouchet's work a resemblance to Reverdy, adduces the presence of obstacles, nudity of vocabulary, and monochromatic tones typical of du Bouchet's verse. In *Dans la chaleur vacante* (1961; in the vacant heat) and *Où le soleil* (1968; where the sun), du Bouchet shows a Mallarméan preoccupation with consciousness as well as an artistic awareness of the problem of space. It is in the arrangement of his lines, recalling both Mallarmé and Péguy, that this awareness is most evident, for du Bouchet fractures his sentences and leaves blocks of interlinear white, which he considered integral to his poetic expression. More recent works, such as *Qui n'est pas tourné vers nous* (1972; who is not turned toward us), are what he called *poésies critiques*, critical essays of a sort, but the distinction between poetry and criticism is rather tenuous in this highly experimental writer, who maintained that what interested him above all is the human condition.

With *L'Incohérence* (1979; incoherence), *Désaccordée comme par de la neige* (1989; made discordant as if by snow), *Pourquoi si calmes* (1996; why so calm), and *Carnet 2* (1999; notebook 2), du Bouchet continued his varied productivity and concern with the aesthetics of language. The influence of Mallarmé persists all the way to *Carnet 2*, with the use of the single, extended poetic sentence. His is the tendency of modern poetry that attempts to define poetry itself.

Finally, du Bouchet's associate, Jacques Dupin, is also situated in the line of Reverdy and Rimbaud, seeing life and poetry alike as a process of continual creation and destruction. A disciple and protégé of Char, Dupin, in his first volume, *Gravir* (1963; to climb), shows the influence of his mentor, both in his lyrical and lucid passages and in his sibylline utterances. *L'Embrasure* (1969) is more original and questions the very role of language. Finally, *Dehors* (1975; outside) sees *écriture*, the modern appellation for both poetry and prose, as a vehicle for transcendence. Greene sees in Dupin a poet who unites the two principal trends of modern French poetry, suggesting a common ground between the poets preoccupied with language for its own sake and those concerned with meaning, and perhaps indicating the direction that poetry will take in the future. In *Matière du souffle* (1994; stuff of breath), Dupin still attempts to define the poem and the act of poetic creation, essentially making a poem of his own poetic process. Unfortunately, such self-preoccupation has brought poets since Mallarmé to a sense of emptiness that is again reflected in Dupin's *Le Grésil* (1996; sleet).

The need to clarify the enigmas of the world recurs in the poetry of Philippe Jaccottet (born 1925) whose *Cahier de verdure* (1990; green notebook) expresses cautious optimism amid the doubt of earlier poetry. With *Cristal et fumée* (1993; crystal and smoke), the experience of eternity poses questions which lead to a contemplative serenity in *Après beaucoup d'années* (1994; after many years). Expressions in both prose and poetry encourage faith in the transcendent, but doubts return in *La Seconde Semaison* (1996; the second sowing).

The influence of Mallarmé persists with Yves Bonnefoy (born 1923), who has given considerable attention to it in the extensive critical work which supplements his poetry. His poetic productivity, including volumes such as *La Vie errante* (1993; wandering life), *Début et fin de la neige* (1995; beginning and end of the snow), and *L'Arrière-pays* (1972, revised 1998; backcountry), returns to themes of poetic continuity and of mortality. Poetic beauty has aspects that are both permanent and ephemeral. Different aspects of transcendence appear, from the recognition of divine elements in nature to the valorization of dream experiences. Yet problems persist with the inadequacy of language to translate these ideas.

Like many of his contemporaries, Michel Deguy offers pieces in both poetry and prose. His *Aux heures d'affluence* (1993; rush hour) takes a combative, philosophical tone analyzing various problems of the modern world while continuing to deal with fundamental poetic problems of the inadequacy of language and the inevitability of death. *A ce qui n'en finit pas* (1995; to what does not finish) seeks to reconcile oppositions that threaten to fragment life. Amid menaces of disintegration, love may become a unifying force, and along with personal reconciliations may come both poetic unity and solidarity in the world outside it. *L'Énergie du désespoir* (1998; the energy of despair) returns to the poem as both varied expression and unifying utterance of all and nothing.

Bernard Noël (born 1930) returns to the theme of death in both its harsh and elegiac aspects. *La Peau et les mots* (1972; skin and words), *Bruits et langues* (1980; sounds and tongues), *La Chute des temps* (1983; the fall of time), *L'Ombre du double* (1994; shadow of the double), and *Les États du corps* (1999; states of the body) sometimes approach a form of freedom or catharsis amid more negative concerns of a material culture that inform also Noël's writings in art criticism and philosophy.

The hope and despair inspired by modern life reappear in the work of Jude Stéfan (born 1936). *À la vieille Parque* (1989; to the old muse), *Elégiades* (1993; elegies), *Povrésies: Ou, 65 poèmes autant d'années* (1997; poor poetry), and *Epodes: Ou, Poèmes de la désuétude* (1999) employ tones of satire or of bittersweet irony in the face of threats but still posit ideals of both sensual and poetic beauty. Stéfan returns to the poetry of antiquity, of the Renaissance, and of the close of the nineteenth century to recall the concept of poetry as music.

The end of the twentieth century, as women were entering in great numbers into other fields of activity, saw a notable increase of female authors. Andrée Chedid (born 1920) poses central poetic questions with *Textes pour un poème, 1949-1970* (1987; texts for a poem), *Poèmes pour un texte* (1991; poems for a text), and *Par-delà les mots* (1995; beyond words), and with *Territoires du souffle* (1999; realm of breath) moves to an optimism in poetic expression.

BEYOND FRANCE

Female voices are being heard also in Canadian literature in French, where Anne Hébert (born 1916), after having summed up her work with *Œuvre poétique, 1950-1990* (1992; poetic work, 1950-1990) continued with *Poèmes pour la main gauche* (1997; poems for the left hand). Nicole Brossard (born 1943) at the same time published *Vertige de l'avant-scène* (1997; dizziness from center stage), and these represent only a sample of the rising productivity of poetry in Canada.

Meanwhile, the canon of French literature, so long focused on the writers of the mother country, expands to include works from a variety of former colonies. Following the immense attention to the poetry of Léopold Senghor (1906-2001), who, as president of Senegal, enjoyed a unique ability to be heard on the international level, Aimé Césaire of Martinique (born 1913) has found a wide audience for a poetic work ranging from his early *Les Armes miraculeuses* (1946; *Miraculous Weapons*, 1983) to new poems added to his collected works in 1994.

The poets examined here have been selected for the scholarly attention they have inspired. They represent, however, only a very small fraction of the poetry in French that continues to be published. Since 1993, Michael Bishop of Dalhousie University has published an annual article, "L'Année poétique," in *The French Review*. For those who know French, these articles constitute a comprehensive and ongoing listing of new works. Each article is accompanied by a bibliography, and the combined total of these runs to hundreds of individual works.

In some ways the twentieth century resembled the eighteenth in that other literary forms threatened to upstage poetry. The modern novel, with its many forms ranging from popular romance and adventure to more serious intellectual and psychological works, has proliferated. At the same time, new technology has brought films and other electronic forms of publication to be considered on a par with literature. Amid this diversity of forms, however, poetry continues both to be widely written and to cultivate new voices. For the first time since the Renaissance, a significant number of these voices are female. Global communication has brought poets from Canada, Africa, and the Caribbean into the cultural sphere of France. As these many voices are raised, readers will be able to choose from a rich variety of texts for the twenty-first century.

BIBLIOGRAPHY

Blackmore, A. M., and E. H. Blackmore, eds. *Six French Poets of the Nineteenth Century: Lamartine, Hugo, Baudelaire, Verlaine, Rimbaud, Mallarmé.* London: Oxford University Press, 2000. Includes generous selections from the six nineteenth century French poets most often read in the English-speaking world today. Modern translations are printed opposite the original French verse, and the edition contains over a thousand lines of poetry never previously translated into English.

Bonnefoy, Yves. *The Act and the Place of Poetry: Selected Essays.* Chicago: University of Chicago Press, 1989. The first collection of Bonnefoy's criticism to appear in English, this volume offers a selection of his essays, a lecture, and an interview. An introduction by John T. Naughton, professor of Romance languages at Colgate University, touches on many of the essays' concerns.

Breunig, L. C., ed. *The Cubist Poets in Paris: An Anthology.* Lincoln: University of Nebraska Press, 1995. This compilation, a synthesis of the collaboration between cubist art and literature, draws mainly on the works of fifteen Parisian cubist poets of the first two decades of the twentieth century, including Guillaume Apollinaire, Max Jacob, and André Salmon, who, together with Pablo Picasso, formed the nucleus of the French cubist movement.

Burt, E. S. S. *Poetry's Appeal: Nineteenth Century French Lyric and the Political Space.* Stanford, Calif.: Stanford University Press, 1999. In chapters on Chenier, Hugo, Baudelaire, Mallarmé, and Valéry, the book details some of the struggles between the ideological and material sides of poetry with the nineteenth century "remappings" of political space, including memory and the archive, the censorship of material history, and the legibility of founding texts.

Chénieux-Gendron, Jacqueline. *Surrealism.* Translated by Vivian Folkenflik. Reprint. New York: Columbia University Press, 1994. A study of the Surrealist movement in France from its beginnings in 1919 to its dissolution in 1969. Places Surrealism in its historical context, making reference to its interactions with psychology, philosophy, anthropology and politics.

Comeau, Paul T. *Diehards and Innovators: French Romantic Struggle, 1800-1830.* New York: Peter Lang, 1988. Examines the emergence of the French Romantic era and the convergence of politics and literature.

Flores, Angel, ed. *The Anchor Anthology of French Poetry: From Nerval to Valéry in English Translation.* Rev. ed. New York: Doubleday, 2000. First published in 1958, this collection introduced an indispensable corpus of Western poetry to countless Americans. The poetic and cultural tradition forged by the Symbolist poets—Baudelaire, Rimbaud, Verlaine, Apollinaire, and others—reverberated throughout the avant-garde and countercultures of the twentieth century, including modernism, Surrealism, abstract impressionism, and the Beat movement, an influence examined in a new introduction by poet-singer Patti Smith.

Fowlie, Wallace. *Mid-Century French Poets: Selections, Translations, and Critical Notices.* New York: Twayne, 1955.

Greene, Robert W. *Six French Poets of Our Time.* Princeton, N.J.: Princeton University Press, 1979.

Matthews, J. H. *Surrealist Poetry in France.* Syracuse, N.Y.: Syracuse University Press, 1969. History and criticism of the Surrealist movement in France.

Metzidakis, Stamos, ed. *Understanding French Poetry: Essays for a New Millennium.* New York: Garland, 1994. Focusing on the ebbing influence of poetry, this volume provides the theoretical grounding for understanding how and why French verse has become overshadowed by critical and artistic prose. The essays included are mostly original contributions by some of the foremost scholars of French poetry currently writing in the English-speaking world.

Perloff, Marjorie. *The Poetics of Indeterminacy: Rimbaud to Cage*. Evanston, Ill.: Northwestern University Press, 1999. Explores French influences on modernism.

Peyre, Henri. *What Is Romanticism?* Translated by Roda Roberts. Tuscaloosa: University of Alabama Press, 1978. Examines French literature of the eighteenth and nineteenth centuries in the context of the Romantic movement.

_____. *What Is Symbolism?* Translated by Emmett Parker. Tuscaloosa: University of Alabama Press, 1980. Examines nineteenth century French poetry in the context of the Symbolist movement.

Porter, Laurence. *The Crisis of French Symbolism*. Ithaca, N.Y.: Cornell University Press, 1990. Explores the origins and conflicts of nineteenth century French Symbolism.

Prendergrast, Christopher. *Nineteenth Century French Poetry: Introductions to Close Readings*. Cambridge, England: Cambridge University Press, 1990. Essays on eleven different poets from Lamartine to Mallarmé and Laforgue, by eminent scholars representing a wide range of critical and theoretical viewpoints. Each of these essays focuses on the detailed organization of a single poem and opens pathways for further study and discussion.

Sorrell, Martin. *Elles: A Bilingual Anthology of Modern French Poetry by Women*. Exeter, Devonshire: University of Exeter Press, 1995. Introduces English-speaking readers to some of the best French poetry published by women during the last three decades of the twentieth century. Each poet introduces herself with an essay on her conception of poetry and her own position as writer.

Stamelman, Richard Howard. *Lost Beyond Telling: Representations of Death and Absence in Modern French Poetry*. Ithaca, N.Y.: Cornell University Press, 1990. Examines the representations of death and the implications of separation psychology in modern French poetry.

Steele, A. J. *Three Centuries of French Verse, 1511-1819*. Edinburgh University Publications: Language and Literature Texts 4. Edinburgh, Scotland: Edinburgh University Press, 1956.

Thomas, Jean-Jacques, and Steven Winspur. *Poeticized Language: The Foundations of Contemporary French Poetry*. University Park: Pennsylvania State University Press, 1999. Explores the way in which contemporary French poetry places great emphasis on language itself and analyzes the innovations crafted by more than fifty writers. With its eleven chapters and extensive bibliography, this is one of the most comprehensive English-language introductions to French poetry.

Thum, Reinhard H. *The City: Baudelaire, Rimbaud, and Verhaeren*. New York: Peter Lang, 1994. Traces the attempt of three representative poets to explore the uncharted and strangely mysterious realm of the industrialized cityscape as an embodiment of lyric consciousness, as an intimate and enigmatic protection of themselves and their fellow human beings.

Weinberg, Bernard. *The Limits of Symbolism*. Chicago: University of Chicago Press, 1966. Provides criticism and interpretation of thirteen poems, including those by Baudelaire, Rimbaud, Mallarmé, Valéry, and Saint-John Perse.

Irma M. Kashuba,
updated by Dorothy M. Betz

GERMAN POETRY TO 1800

Poetry as a pleasant distraction from life, as a conventional ornament for social occasions, as linguistic play or experiment, even as the sincere expression of heartfelt emotions, belongs to comparatively recent times. In its beginnings, humankind used the magical power of patterned, rhythmic speech to impose meaning and order on the world. Through poetry, humankind hoped to gain mastery of both the natural and the social environment. Certainly this was true of the Germanic tribes: The first writer to mention Germanic poetry, the Roman historian Cornelius Tacitus (c. 55-120 C.E.), expressly refers to the Germanic custom of celebrating gods and heroes in song. Religion (man's relation to God) and history (man's relation to his community in time) were to remain poetry's central domain for centuries to come. Thus, the historical and cultural context can never become a matter of indifference to those who care for poetry. What might appear to later generations as mere background was related strictly to the purpose and theme of poetry in its own day. In ancient times, few deeds were unaccompanied by the poetic word, and fewer still would be remembered were it not for poetry.

Germanic tribes lived on the shores of the North and Baltic seas as early as 2000 B.C.E. Some time after 500 B.C.E., when climatic changes forced most of them to migrate south, they divided into three distinct groups. The North Germanic tribes (Normans, Danes, Jutes) were those that stayed behind; the East Germanic tribes (Goths, Vandals, Burgundians) slowly drifted southward into today's Hungary, Romania, and Bulgaria; and the West Germanic tribes (Saxons, Franks, Angles, Swabians, Alemanni) moved into the middle of Europe, today's Germany, northern France, Belgium, and the Netherlands.

The Germanic tribes had barely settled in their new environment when the Huns, a fierce Mongolian people, swept into Europe around 400 C.E. The impact of the Hunnish invasion was most directly felt by the East Germanic tribes. Pushed forward by the relentlessly advancing Huns, the Germanic tribes fell upon an already tottering Roman civilization, gaining and losing power over the nations in their path with spectacular speed. The Vandals established kingdoms in Italy, Spain, and North Africa; the Goths, in Italy and Spain; the Burgundians, on the Rhine.

ORIGINS TO ELEVENTH CENTURY

Two hundred years later, these tribes had all but disappeared, exhausted and decimated by their heroic exploits, absorbed by the cultures and people they had overrun, yet they disappeared only after leaving behind a lasting record of their remarkable feats. If history demands patterned, poetic order, it certainly demanded it here, in the face of the splendid achievements and the tragic end of the East Germanic tribes. Soon, the scop, the warrior-poet, sang in the lord's hall of heroic courage and loyalty, of betrayal and revenge, of inscrutable fate and man's fortitude when confronted with its cruel decrees. For centuries, this oral poetry informed and stimulated the imagination of the Germanic tribes until, several hundred years later, some accounts were finally given literary form.

Though naturally influenced by the tumultuous events around them, the West Germanic tribes underwent a gradual development. The most notable migratory action was that of the Angles and some of the Saxons, who, after the Roman forces had pulled out of Britain, began to settle there in the fifth and sixth centuries. On the Continent, historical progress took place under the steady ascendancy of the Franks. Clovis I (C.E. 481-511) united all major West Germanic tribes, with the exception of the Continental Saxons, under Frankish leadership. When Clovis converted to Roman Catholicism, Latin culture quickly accompanied Christianity on its missionary journeys. The ensuing political and cultural unification was underscored by a growing linguistic unity among the tribes. Starting among the Alemanni of Germany's southern highlands, a consonant shift spread through the West Germanic tribes, differentiating their language from that of their North Germanic neighbors as well as that of the Angles and Saxons. This language, Old High German, is considered the first distinct forerunner of modern German.

The unity of the West Germanic tribes reached its culmination under the rule of Charlemagne (C.E. 768-814). Charlemagne was not only a brilliant political leader but also a farsighted patron of the arts; from his reign date the earliest extant literary fragments in the vernacular. Baptismal vows, creeds, and prayers give evidence of the importance that church and state placed on the vernacular in their concerted effort to convert the Germanic peoples to Christianity. Nevertheless, cultural life under Charlemagne and his Carolingian successors proceeded mostly in Latin. Of lyric poetry in Old High German, only two fragments of poems have survived. Both are religious in nature, though secular poetry did exist, as is indicated by an ecclesiastical injunction against the writing or sending of *Winileodos* (songs of friendship). The "Wessobrunner Gebet" (c. 780; "Wessobrunn Prayer") contains in twenty-eight lines a fragmentary account of creation, while the "Muspilli" (c. 830), almost four times as long, describes the Day of Judgment.

The most important poetic work of the ninth century, however, is an epic, the religious epic *Der Heliand* (c. 840; *The Heliand*, 1966). In its six thousand lines of dramatic alliterative verse, Christ has been transformed into a magnanimous Germanic lord and his apostles into retainers who, moving with him from castle to castle, believe in his mission with unflinching loyalty. Unfortunately, the epic did not have its deserved impact on German literature, because it was not written in Old High German, but in Old Low German (Old Saxon), a Germanic dialect as yet unassimilated by the developing German language. Thus, it was quickly forgotten and not rediscovered until, in the sixteenth century, the Protestant Reformation searched high and low for a historical tradition.

Charlemagne's liberal cultural policies also encouraged a collection of heroic songs reaching back into the pre-Christian days of the Great Migrations. This collection is said to have been burned by Charlemagne's son, the weak and bigoted Louis the Pious. A glimpse of what such a collection might have contained is provided by a brief fragment, the sixty-eight lines of the *Hildebrandslied* (c. 800; *The Song of Hildebrand*, 1957). It commemorates in a terse and somber style the tragic conflict which pits Hildebrand's loyalty to his liege against his affection for his son, who, with an equally fervent loyalty, has embraced the cause of Hildebrand's sworn enemies. Though the poem breaks off before the issue is decided, it is clear that Hildebrand's ideals of he-

roic conduct will force him to kill his son rather than forsake his lord in battle.

The future of German poetry did not lie with *The Heliand* or with *The Song of Hildebrand*, but with Otfrid von Weissenburg's *Krist* (c. 865; Christ). An Alsatian monk, the first German poet whose name is known, Otfrid incorporated a most promising metrical innovation into his otherwise lackluster disquisitions into the life of Christ. Influenced by the style of Latin church hymns, Otfrid decided to rhyme his poetry. With his work, rhyme—until the ninth century essentially foreign to the alliterative verse of the Germanic tribes—was to establish a hold over German poetry that would not be relinquished until the twentieth century.

Whatever promise Old High German poetry might have held, historical changes brought it to a most ignoble end. Charlemagne's vision of a politically, culturally, and linguistically unified Europe disintegrated in the dynastic feuds of his grandsons. Scarcely thirty years after his death, his empire divided along lines that foreshadowed the borders between the future states of Germany and France. The political split was ratified by a linguistic one: The oaths confirming the Frankish division were no longer sworn in one Frankish language, but in two: Old High German and Romance, the ancestor of modern French.

During the declining years of the Carolingian Empire, the religious unity of Western Europe provided the only force against the centrifugal tendencies of the Germanic tribes. With the growing influence of the Church, Latin inhibited the development of German poetry. This situation became even more serious following the accession of the dukes of Saxony to the throne of what by then had become Germany. With forceful single-mindedness, the Saxon emperors achieved a degree of political and administrative unity which allowed Germany to dominate European politics for more than two centuries. On the other hand, these emperors had neither the time nor the inclination for poetry. Moreover, Saxon—as has been mentioned before—was the only major West Germanic dialect on the Continent that had not yet adopted the consonant shift of Old High German. It was only to be expected that a house of Saxons would have no particular interest or stake in the advance of an Old High German language or literature. The results are certainly striking: Not a single poem in German is extant from a period of some one hundred and fifty years. During these dark ages of neglect, Old High German starved to death. It was only after further linguistic changes, which led to the new language patterns of Middle High German, that German poetry received a second chance.

ELEVENTH TO FOURTEENTH CENTURY

In an effort to weaken tribal independence in their realm, the Saxon emperors had relied increasingly on the prelates of the Church for the administration of the country. Unmarried, the higher clergy would obviously be less likely to form dynastic interests of their own and would be more inclined to give their unreserved loyalty to the man who had invested them with their office. In the course of a century, the Church in Germany had thus been transformed into an effective branch of imperial government. Under the Frankish line of the Salians, which followed that of the Saxons, this practice had finally overtaken Rome itself. Henry III (1039-1056) considered it simply one of his personal responsibilities to install and depose popes as he saw fit. Against this glaring political abuse of the Church, the Burgundian monastery of Cluny started a campaign which struck at the heart of the German Empire. The battle cry of Cluny was that all further lay interference in appointments to high ecclesiastical office should cease. Henry IV (1056-1106), politically dependent on a Church hierarchy willing to do his bidding, had no choice but to defy this religious reform. The confrontation lasted for about fifty years and ended in a devastating defeat of the imperial cause, resulting in a dramatic loss of German power without and German unity within.

The effect of the rigorously ascetic revival on poetry proved, at least immediately, no less intimidating. Heavily dogmatic and didactic poetry dominated the second half of the eleventh century. Yet, it was the very same religious enthusiasm of Cluny that made another spiritual call possible, a spiritual call which was soon to overwhelm Cluny's monastic objectives with a renewed worldliness. Unforeseen adventures arose from the fervent appeal to free the Holy Land from the Saracens, to organize a Crusade. For almost two centuries—the First Crusade began in 1096, the last ended in 1270—the Eu-

ropean imagination was captivated by the ideal and the reality of the Crusades as nothing had captivated it since the Great Migrations half a millennium before. The joys of the world quickly crept back into poetry. Narrative poems were told for the sheer fun of telling tall tales of exotic lands. What these poems still lacked, however, was some organizing principle that would lift their episodic style to the level of a unified theme and ethos. This vacuum was soon to be filled by the new, ideal man of the Crusades, the Christian knight.

Knighthood, or chivalry, could trace its origins most directly to the political and economic conditions during and after the Great Germanic Migrations. At a time of rapid tribal expansion and in the absence of the necessary logistical means for the operation of large-scale armies, the tribal lord stood in need of a highly mobile and well-equipped fighting elite. To maintain this force and to gain its unswerving loyalty, the lord rewarded its members by granting them land, the surplus of which would support them and their military craft befittingly. When not called up to serve his lord, the vassal administered his land. He would also be free to grant land to some of his retainers on similar conditions. In this way, there arose over the centuries a whole pyramid of intricate dependencies—the system of feudalism.

Feudalism, however, had slowly begun to deteriorate. The property which the lord had lent to those who had served him faithfully tended to become hereditary. As tribal expansion within the limits of Western Europe could not go on forever, the lords found themselves increasingly hard put to reward those they needed for the exercise of their power, while at the same time and for the same reason, many young noblemen saw themselves excluded from the lifestyle of their fathers.

In this deepening crisis, the Crusades provided European society with a momentary easing of its social and economic dilemmas. Through the Crusades, the inevitable decline of the feudal system was delayed. Knighthood received a reprieve during which it rose to heights of artistic splendor and ethical idealism that were to dazzle the people of Europe long after knighthood itself had lost its historical relevance.

What was new about the ideal of the Christian knight was that, for the first time, Germanic political and social realities were sanctioned by Christian idealism. The perfect knight was to strike a balance between the primarily Germanic virtues of courage, loyalty, and honor and a more tempered set of Christian values such as moderation, chastity, generosity, and mercy. Self-interest, class-interest, and Christian idealism joined forces, allowing the knight to prove himself, through endless adventures, worthy before God and the world.

France was the first nation in which the ideals of chivalry gained a firm hold on literature and life. In Germany, it was only during the rule of Frederick I (1152-1190) of the Swabian house of the Hohenstaufen that chivalry was accepted as an indigenous element of Germanic culture. An extraordinarily brilliant period of German poetry was soon to follow. In the short span of merely two decades (1190 to 1210), several poetic masterpieces were produced which not even the great works of German Romanticism can be said to have surpassed.

The Nibelungenlied (c. 1200), an epic composed by an unknown Austrian monk, is built on specifically Germanic conceptions in its effort to explore the true values of knighthood. At least two Germanic oral traditions—the Frankish legend of Siegfried and the narrative of the downfall of the Burgundians (or Nibelungs) under the onslaught of the Huns in 437 C.E.—are here combined to create the German national epic. It tells the story of Siegfried, the perfect knight, at the court of the Burgundians and of Kriemhild, his wife, a Burgundian princess, who swears revenge on her kinsmen when she learns that they killed Siegfried—jealous of his unequaled prowess. For thirteen years, she has brooded on the wrong done to her, when Attila offers her his hand in marriage. She accepts and another thirteen years later lures the nobles of her homeland to the court of Attila, where they are slaughtered in a bloodbath which finally engulfs even the vengeful queen. Behind a veneer of courtly decorum and Christian morality, there arises before the listener the most profound image of the heroic age in the German language. A world holds sway in which the joys and sorrows of life are experienced with stark intensity, in which the virtues and vices of men are as bold as the actions they engender, but also a world in which fate, not the deeds of heroes, ultimately determines the course of all events.

More directly indebted to French influence and the newly established ideals of chivalry are the court epics

of Hartmann von Aue (c. 1160-1165 to c. 1210-1220), Wolfram von Eschenbach (c. 1170-c. 1217), and Gottfried von Strassburg (fl. c. 1210). In contrast to the heroic epic, the court epic, or romance (so called because of its origins in the Romance languages), does not restrict itself to the praise of national heroes. Even great men of classical antiquity such as Aeneas and Alexander become heroes of courtly epics. Neither are the fates of nations the concern of romances. Instead, the romance is focused on an individual knight whose valor is tested against the temptations and afflictions of the world. In order to make these tests as representative as possible, a romance will prefer ideal knights in ideal settings to anything that might smack of mere reality.

The most famous and most popular locale of the German romance is the legendary court of King Arthur and his Knights of the Round Table. Hartmann von Aue introduced the Arthurian theme into the German language. His two Arthurian romances, *Erek* (c. 1190; *Erec*, 1982) and *Iwein* (c. 1190-1205; *Iwein: The Knight with the Lion*, 1979), closely follow court epics of the French poet Chrétien de Troyes in their devotion to the typical preoccupation of the French romance: the discussion and exemplification of ethical conflicts arising within the knightly code of values. Erec neglects his duties as a knight for love of his wife; Iwein neglects his wife for love of knightly adventures. In both cases, harmony is reestablished as soon as the knights have learned the lesson of the golden mean.

Yet the discussion of these neatly, dialectically arranged conflicts proved to be more French than German. The two greatest masters of the German court epic moved away from such delicate planning in order to pursue the very limits of all courtly conventions. Wolfram, much less learned than Hartmann, proceeded in his *Parzival* (c. 1200-1210; English translation, 1894) with a decidedly unconventional style and theme. Highly individualistic, often obscure in his use of metaphors, he created a world of daring and immoderate yearnings. The story is that of Parzival's vicissitudes on the way to an understanding of life, suffering, and death. During this journey, King Arthur's Round Table is recognized as little more than a stage on the long and narrow path to perfection. Only by abandoning the security of all previous values—not merely by balancing them in an aesthetically pleasing order—only by a complete change of heart does Parzival finally discover the source of all inner peace in the total submission to the will of God. For Wolfram, perfect knighthood is nothing less than sainthood.

It is hard to believe that two works of such contrasting styles and themes as Wolfram's *Parzival* and Gottfried's *Tristan und Isolde* (c. 1210; *Tristan and Isolde*, 1899) were written in the span of less than a decade. What they obviously have in common is their determination to follow courtly ideals beyond all courtly conventions. Yet where Wolfram was consciously obscure and other-worldly, Gottfried wanted to be consciously lucid and human. *Tristan and Isolde* is also an epic of immoderation: It speaks of the earthly, sensual passion which Tristan and Isolde feel for each other. Tristan is a vassal of King Mark of Cornwall and Isolde is Mark's young wife, yet Tristan and Isolde persist in their love and build an illicit relationship through long adventures of deceit and subterfuge. The willful, often mocking breach of the knightly ideal of chastity was in itself nothing new for courtly poetry. What was new was the total seriousness, the total lack of frivolity with which Gottfried treated this adulterous union as a troubling human predicament.

Lyric poetry, too, experienced an amazing surge of creativity under the auspices of the chivalric ethos. It was poetry devoted primarily to an extremely stylized, extremely idealized form of loving adoration of the fair sex, a love which in German was to be known as *Minne*, the practitioners of which would become known as *Minnesänger*. This lyric poetry reached its most elaborate form in the song of the troubadour, the *canso d'amor* (love song) of southern France. With ever new variations, the poet describes in his song the typical stages through which he courts a lady who is almost always of a higher station than himself and married to another man. Arduous periods of wooing and pleading are often rewarded by shows of the lady's favor. These shows of favor—smiles, acknowledgments, the wearing of the knight's colors (sexual favors are granted only rarely)—are, nevertheless, constantly jeopardized by malevolent friends and cold conventions, frequently by the fickle or obdurate heart of the lady herself. Thus, brief moments of bliss are usually followed by long spells of mournful longing and dejection. Though a poet's love did at times stray from the elevated plane of these platonic feelings, *Minne* was not incompatible with marriage and should not be misunderstood as an actual challenge to the harsh and dreary marriage conventions of the day. More often than not, *Minnelieder* (songs of *Minne*) were barely more than a fashionable parlor game. In spite of the assumed intimacy of the confessional style, little of what is expressed in them should be taken for more than the polite gallantry of a professional singer in his attempt to gain the protection of a powerful lady at court.

Walther von der Vogelweide (c. 1170-c. 1230) gave the conventions of the troubadours their most creative adaptation in the German language. His strong and unabashed zest for life filled his *Minnelieder* with a surprising vitality. It was this zest for life which convinced Walther that *Minne* cannot be bound to social station, that it can be felt toward any woman, and that true nobility of heart is found more often outside rather than inside the nobility of rank. There, too, love seems so much freer to give itself to the beloved. Walther refused to consider a *Minne* that is predicated on the notion of its remaining unfulfilled anything but a false and inhuman emotion.

In a similar vein, Walther's spontaneous appreciation of nature enlivened the many threadbare metaphors inherited from the troubadours. Even the tradition of the troubadour's *sirventes* (poems exploring political and moral questions) assumed in Walther's hands an unusual urgency. Fights between emperor and pope had erupted again; civil war had returned to Germany; and the lyricist of fervent love threw himself into the partisan struggle with political verse of equal ardor. Walther was undoubtedly not only the greatest but also the most versatile poet of the Middle Ages. Love, nature, politics, and religion were themes for his inspiration, creating an unmatched lyric summa of medieval culture on the eve of that culture's collapse.

FOURTEENTH TO SIXTEENTH CENTURY

With the execution of the last of the Hohenstaufens at the hands of his enemies in Italy (1268), the fabric of medieval politics in Germany unraveled rapidly. The election of Rudolph of Habsburg (1273) ushered in an era in which imperial power forsook its claim to European leadership and restricted itself to the politics of dynastic self-aggrandizement. Of even greater importance for the future of medieval culture was the glaring failure of the Crusades in 1270. European nobility in all of its heroic posturing saw itself confronted initially with a serious loss of face and ultimately with an even more serious loss of legitimacy.

While knighthood had weakened itself in seven Crusades, its adventures in the East had helped another class to gather unforeseen strength. As it turned out, the Crusades had opened wider horizons not only for the idealistic imagination of chivalry but also for the decidedly materialistic imagination of the middle class. Trade was flourishing, and so were the cities of Germany. A money economy, originating in Italy, replaced the complex relations of loyalty with the simple cash nexus. Armies of loyal knights gave way to armies of mercenaries; light infantry and gunpowder relegated the heavily armed knight to eventual obsolescence. Even where the knights did manage to redirect their crusading spirit—as did the Knights of the Teutonic Order when they declared the conversion and colonization of Prussia to be a new goal—their efforts could no longer be sustained without the ever more obtrusive money of the burghers. The Middle Ages had entered a period of complex yet obvious transition. The effects of this transition on poetry were equally complex but not nearly as obvious.

The demands of the changing times were felt in the nobility itself. In search of novel themes and renewed vitality, *Minnelieder* strove to combine, rather incongruously, the overwrought ideals of *Minne* with intentionally crude peasant settings. Much of this lyric poetry reads like a deliberate satire of itself. Didactic poems, on the other hand, tried desperately to explain chivalric ideals to a less and less receptive audience. Furthermore, the court epic, sensing the need for a closer grasp of reality, admitted historical events and characters into the never-never land of romance. Soon, the peasant epic evolved to debunk the whole conceited glitter of courtly perfection. *Meier Helmbrecht* (c. 1250; peasant Helmbrecht), the most famous peasant epic in the German language, tells the story of a young man who, seduced by social ambition and the airs of chivalry, joins a band of robber barons. At the end of a short life of tragic

illusions and suffering, he is turned away by his own father and finally hanged by the people of his own village.

Social and economic power shifted from the knightly courts to the towns and its burghers. The rising middle class, however, was slow to realize a class consciousness of its own. The cultural vacuum that arose as a result of this hesitation was not easily filled. Instead of creating values appropriate to its interests and aspirations, the middle class felt that its socioeconomic power titled it at long last to the values of its erstwhile betters. The resulting disparity between the anachronistic idealism of what was believed and the materialism of what was practiced led to a whole culture of satire, a culture castigating itself for its lack of authenticity.

The pretensions of the court epic were lampooned in the mock epic, while the excitement of knightly adventures gave way to stories about the pranks with which clever rogues exploited the vanity of others. The animal fable, derived from Greek and Oriental sources, finally broadened the social critique to include all classes of society. *Reynke de Vos* (1498; *Reynard the Fox*) no longer poked fun at the nobility, but at all the social climbers who, like their archetype, the cunning and unprincipled fox, spare no effort on their way into the antechambers of the king. The international best-seller of late medieval satire was Sebastian Brant's *Das Narrenschiff* (1494; *The Ship of Fools*, 1509), a poem whose author viewed his own times with an utterly jaundiced eye. Brant, who is considered one of Germany's earliest Humanists, was in fact no reformer. He favored no trend or class and offered no prospect of any solution. More than one hundred follies and vices are paraded around and soundly thrashed by an impartially venomous tongue, leaving a vivid picture of the cultural uncertainty that gripped the waning Middle Ages.

The curious inability of the middle class to move beyond the cultural values of a society whose economic and social restrictions it had long left behind is evidenced in the appropriation by sturdy and conscientious burghers of the courtly *Minnelieder*. From a wide variety of *Minnelieder*, which they carefully collected and studied, artisans in the towns culled a system of twelve rigid patterns. These they proceeded to employ, with slavish adherence, for their own songs on moral and didactic themes. *Minnesänger* had turned into *Meistersänger* (master singers), well-intentioned craftsmen who made up for their lack of imagination by a display of pedantic learning and a bizarre ingenuity in the arrangement of their metrical schemes. Inventiveness reached fantastical heights when it was felt that only those singers could be declared *Meistersänger* who had added at least one original "tone" (verse arrangement) to their guild's stock in trade. In his middle-class smugness and with his matter-of-fact imagination, the cobbler Hans Sachs (1494-1576)—one of the last and certainly the most accomplished of the *Meistersänger*—assumed an almost patriarchal stature in German literature. Nine years before his death, he proudly counted among his numerous literary works no fewer than 4,275 *Meistersänge* (master songs) in 275 strophic forms, 13 of which he had invented himself.

The *Volkslied* (folk song)—to the modern sensibility, the most appealing poetic achievement of the fourteenth and fifteenth centuries—occupied a very marginal place in the literary world of its day. It, too, had its origins in the *Minnelied*, but, in contrast to the *Meistersäng*, the *Volkslied* refused to live up to the formality of its courtly predecessor and instead infused the conventional themes of love and longing with the simplicity of experience. In simple rhymes, repetitive images, and catchy refrains, the *Volkslied* deals with typical situations of easily identifiable classes of people: hunters, millers, students, soldiers, and so on. Over the centuries, many of the *Volkslieder* were overlaid with the patina of a garbled text, a naïve nonsense which, if anything, seems to have added to their perennial charm.

Yet in spite of its popularity, the *Volkslied* did not possess the formative power to fill the cultural void that the receding chivalric society had left behind. Other forces had to originate to fashion a new image of world, man, and society. When these forces arrived on the scene, they were not particularly related to poetry, nor were they particularly productive of it. The origins of modern man were accompanied by a tremendous loss of the power of poetry. The culture of knighthood had been an unmistakably poetic one; prose virtually did not exist as a literary form. The new society arose almost in the absence of poetic formulation and evolved a decidedly prosaic culture.

Like the eleventh century, the fourteenth century was marked by a wave of religious fervor. In contrast to the

earlier revival, however, this religious enthusiasm championed no ecclesiastical cause. The secular power of the Church had reached its high point at the end of the thirteenth century when, with almost no transition, it found itself embroiled in every imaginable ecclesiastical and political trouble. The "Babylonian Captivity" of the Papacy in southern France (1309-1377) and the following forty years of schism—in which two, then three popes stood against one another—had driven the religious aspirations of the people upon themselves and into the arms of mysticism. Mysticism, a form of religious individualism which strives for a direct union with God through contemplation, found its most creative expression in the philosophical sermons of Meister Eckhart (died 1327). The imaginative prose style used to explain his difficult and often highly paradoxical thoughts greatly extended the scope of the German language.

At a time when northern Europe developed in mysticism a religious version of individualistic self-reliance, the Italian city-states—for once uninhibited by the presence of either pope or emperor—advanced a strictly secular counterpart. Believing themselves the rightful heirs of classical Rome, the Italians accepted it as their duty to resurrect the classical ideal of a human perfection to be achieved without interference of church or state. Faith in a rebirth (renaissance) of classical antiquity soon spread to other parts of Europe. What the Humanists of the German Renaissance lacked in natural links to the classical spirit, they eagerly compensated for by a meticulous adherence to its letter. Preoccupied with the editing and translating of classical texts, German Humanism quickly degenerated from a rebirth of man to a mere rebirth of philology. It is true that with the image of the *poeta doctus* (poet-scholar), Humanism gave the poet a fresh and lofty mission. As a learned educator, he was no longer to be subservient to anything outside the demands of his chosen profession. At the same time, however, Humanism clipped the wings of German poets by insisting that Humanist poetry could only succeed in the clarity of Latin, not in the murky barbarisms of the German language. The rich harvest of Latin poetry produced by German poets during the Renaissance yielded some impressive fruit. Nevertheless, it has remained a harvest unclaimed, a literature relegated to the limbo of unread and forgotten books.

As admirable as the goals and values of the German Humanists in all of their balanced sanity might have been, no cultural reform is likely to succeed that sets itself up in opposition to the imaginative propensities of the people it wants to educate. Humanism was destined to remain the ideal of a small elite of literati. It was quickly swept away by a reform that did speak to the imagination of the people, Martin Luther's Protestant Reformation.

SIXTEENTH TO EIGHTEENTH CENTURY

When Martin Luther (1483-1546) posted his ninety-five theses against indulgences on a church door in Wittenberg, nobody, least of all Luther, could have predicted the repercussions this act would have for him and his country. Despair about the prevailing corruption of the Church was general, and there was nothing in Luther's theses that had not been said before. Still, the object of his attack was chosen with the instinct of a true rebel.

In the granting of indulgences, the Church had given itself the power to remit some of the punishment a sinner had to expect after death even for those sins that had been forgiven in the sacrament of penance. This remittance of future punishment for past sins was usually tied to some spiritual or material sacrifice on the part of the sinner: fasting, praying, almsgiving, pilgrimages, and so on. In the fifteenth century, a financially strapped Papacy had made monetary "sacrifices" by the sinner—to be paid into the Papacy's always empty coffers—the center of its dealings with indulgences and a regular item in its fiscal planning. Soon, unscrupulous monks roamed the countryside, promising nothing short of salvation to those willing and able to pay for it. The poor, who of all classes were most dependent on the Hereafter for any hope of a happier life, felt excluded from the spiritual benefits of these transactions. The selling of indulgences represented simply too much of what people in Germany had hated for so long: the Church's heavy-handed interference in people's most personal affairs, her greedy exploitation of foreign countries, and her un-Christian preference for the rich. Thus, a devotional practice which had existed in the Church for a long time galvanized the discontented masses of Germany almost overnight.

The initial strength of a movement is rarely a reliable indication of its staying power. What made Luther's reforms survive was that Luther himself, appalled by the widespread anarchy he had caused, directed his reform into the rigid channels of a new ecclesiastical organization. Excommunicated by the pope and under imperial ban, he turned for support to the only authority that could still profit from his cause: the power of Germany's territorial princes. Lured by the promise of the confiscation of Church property, they were only too willing to become Luther's *Notbischöfe* (emergency bishops). When the emperor finally found the time and means to intervene, he saw himself confronted by a well-entrenched state Church. Reluctantly, he accepted its existence in the Peace of Augsburg (1555).

It remains astounding that the sixteenth century, which stirred so many political, social, and religious emotions, produced almost no poetry. It is less surprising that the important contributions that were made came during the first two decades of the Reformation and were the work of Luther himself.

Luther's greatest literary achievement was his extraordinarily successful translation of the Bible. It is hard to think of any book in the German language that has influenced German literature more than has the *Lutherbibel* (1522, 1534). For more than a century, Middle High German had been in transition. The imperial chancery had long attempted to arrive at a uniform German language for its own legal and diplomatic affairs. Yet whatever effort may have gone before, Modern High German came alive only when Luther, through his ingenious use of dialect and idiom, transformed the German of the chanceries into a language that could serve all people for all purposes. Luther's language spread even faster than his Reformation. By the end of his life, more than 100,000 copies of the *Lutherbibel*—an amazing number for those days—were in circulation. For the first time in its history, Germany had a standard written language.

Luther contributed most directly to poetry through his composition of thirty-six hymns, the only lasting poetic creations of the whole of the sixteenth century in Germany. Spiritual songs had certainly existed before, often as converted versions of popular secular songs. What distinguishes Luther's hymns—one has only to think of the rousing "Ein feste Burg ist unser Gott" ("A Mighty Fortress Is Our God")—is that they express not only the communing of an individual with his God, but also the common faith of the whole congregation. Luther's *Geistliche Lieder* (1524; *Spiritual Songs*, 1853) started a tradition of hymnal poetry in Germany which was to remain creative well into the nineteenth century.

It must have seemed clear from the beginning that the Peace of Augsburg had been arranged as little more than a truce between the warring parties. By the early seventeenth century, Catholic and Protestant princes began to arm and organize their hatred in opposing leagues. The bloody Thirty Years' War (1618-1648) started in Prague when the Protestant nobility of Bohemia refused to acknowledge the accession of the Catholic emperor, Ferdinand II, to the throne of Bohemia. With the help of the Catholic League, Ferdinand proved victorious in 1620, and the war appeared to have come to a quick end. Too much, though, rode on the Protestant cause. Alarmed by the Catholics' easy victory and their brutal reprisals, the Protestant princes, under the leadership of Danish King Christian, resolved to try for another outcome. Once again, Ferdinand prevailed in 1626, this time with the help of his celebrated general Albrecht von Wallenstein. The next Protestant willing to try improving Protestant fortunes was Swedish King Gustavus, and under him—not without the financial support of Catholic France—the Protestant cause finally triumphed, though Gustavus himself was killed in the decisive battle in 1632. With the death of Gustavus and the murder of Wallenstein in 1634, it looked as if the war had spent itself, yet as no one seemed satisfied with the resulting stalemate, hostilities were resumed on an even larger scale. France entered the war on the side of the Protestants, while Spain fought for the imperial and Catholic party. In 1635, chastened by seventeen years of grueling war and appalled by its widening dimensions, the Protestant princes arranged a peace with Ferdinand. The task of ridding themselves of their former allies, however, proved to be a lengthy and frustrating affair. None of these friends wanted to leave Germany without having something to show for his pains. War and negotiations dragged on for another thirteen years, until the Peace of Westphalia, in 1648, ratified the total exhaustion and despoiling of Germany.

About half of the German population died as a result of the Thirty Years' War. Agriculture almost ground to a halt as hundreds of villages simply ceased to exist. Trade had been interrupted for too long to be resumed without great delay; neither was there any capital to restart even the most essential industries. The country had been bled white. Only political systems, the most parasitic of all human organizations, increased and multiplied with prodigious fertility. By 1648, Germany had disintegrated into eighteen hundred independent territories, fifteen hundred of them averaging a population of about three hundred people. Even among the remaining territories, barely a handful could be classified as states. The nobility survived the war nearly intact, and the reconstruction of Germany proceeded under its leadership and on its terms, delaying the assertion of a middle-class consciousness for more than a century.

In the context of this momentous national decline, German literature tried belatedly to absorb the Humanism of the Italian Renaissance into the vernacular. For guidance and inspiration, poets and critics turned to France, the country in which such an assimilation of the Italian Renaissance had been accomplished most successfully. What the French poet and aesthetician Joachim du Bellay had done for France with his *La Deffence et illustration de la langue françoyse* (1549; *The Defence and Illustration of the French Language*, 1939), Martin Opitz (1597-1639) wanted to do for his compatriots seventy-five years later.

Opitz's *Das Buch von der deutschen Poeterey* (1624; book on German poetry), a very slim volume by the standards of German scholarship, became the most influential treatise on German poetry for more than a century. Its program was as simple as it was practical. For the Renaissance, poetry was a branch of rhetoric, a rhymed form of oratory whose ultimate aim lay not within itself, but in the pleasing instruction and persuasion of its reader. Since Aristotle's treatment of the subject, rhetoric had always been thought to follow objective, teachable rules. All that needed to be stated more explicitly was simply how German poets could profit from these rules in their efforts to construct more persuasive poems. First, Opitz suggested, rhetorical poetry, like any other argument, needs to be organized rationally, avoiding everything that might startle or confuse. Second, rhetorical poetry ought to be elegant, employing the fitting word while never offending with even the semblance of crudity. Finally, rhetorical poetry must be dignified, a goal to be achieved by borrowing as many lofty metaphors from the ancients as can reasonably be accommodated by the text.

In his poetry—very mediocre stuff—Opitz conformed to the letter of his own law. It is poetry in which virtuosity of form and coldness of feeling stand in direct proportion to each other. As with the classical Sophists, who prided themselves on the fact that they could argue with equal conviction on both sides of any issue, Opitz's poetic persuasiveness comes across as strangely opportunistic, even indifferent to the ostensible purpose for all of his rhetorical posturing: the themes of his poetry. The vanity of all earthly things, the praise of love, the inconstancies of fortune, the sorrows of war, and the longing for peace are all treated with an equally detached expediency.

Soon, however, the frightening insecurities of life, made so obvious by the horrors of the Thirty Years' War, asked more from poetry than Opitz's rationalistic disdain and stoic equanimity. Life could no longer be treated as a mere occasion for the making of good poetry. The resulting seriousness about subject matter also placed greater demands on the rhetorical form, straining it to the breaking point in the service of a poem's passionate pleading. The period characterized by this new strain, this contorted urgency, is called the Baroque (a word of Portuguese origin describing the contorted shape of irregular pearls).

The poet most often identified with German Baroque poetry is Andreas Gryphius (1616-1664). Having experienced the brutalities of war in a traumatic childhood that left him an orphan at an early age, Gryphius became obsessed with the Christian message of man's utterly fallen state. In contrast to Opitz, Gryphius was a man of unshakable conviction, and it was the strength of this conviction which made his rhetoric so Baroque, so forced in its effort to persuade at all costs. At no point did it occur to Gryphius that the direct expression of his personal experiences might be the most appropriate theme for his poetry. The rhetoric of the Renaissance valued the persuasiveness of the representative, not the individualistic or existential. Gryphius, therefore, clothed his fears and pains in the verbal pomp of grandiose metaphors, expanding, recapitulating, polishing his unvarying message in an endless drive for more perfect rhetorical strategies.

If in Gryphius's poetry representative rhetoric and existential message still fused in a creative though distorted vision, by the end of the seventeenth century, the power of rhetoric overwhelmed even the most serious subjects and finally disentangled itself from all of them. Opitz had not been very particular about his themes, but at least the comparative simplicity of his rhetoric had allowed no jarring disparity between elaborate form and superficial content. By the end of the seventeenth century, however, rhetoric resolved to disguise the absence of original themes by a most ornate extravagance in its treatment of traditional ones. This trend toward rhetorical affectation was by no means peculiar to German poetry; Italian and Spanish poets had set the example of virtuosity for its own sake. In Germany, the leading exponent of ultimate refinement and the mastery of all technical skills was Christian Hofmann von Hofmannswaldau (1617-1679).

Hofmannswaldau's cherished subject was the vanity of all earthly joys, particularly the futility of erotic pleasure, yet his painstaking search for the most exquisite epithet, the most luxuriously sensuous metaphor, the most sensational analogy seemed to circumvent rather than to promote his somber faith. The feverish obsession with which Hofmannswaldau dwelled on the erotic pleasures he condemned betrayed him for what he really was: an eroticist with a bad conscience. In this respect, Hofmannswaldau was quite typical of Baroque culture at the end of the seventeenth century. Those espousing this culture no longer were convinced of what it said yet lived under the compulsion to say it ever more vehemently, as if repeating its faltering beliefs might rouse them to their former vigor. Instead, a less troubled generation started to react to the whole phantasmagoric display of the Baroque with swift retribution. At the turn of the eighteenth century, middle-class rationality still prided itself on its own good conscience and felt absolutely no qualms about dismissing the bad conscience that had preceded it.

EIGHTEENTH CENTURY

The politics of Continental Europe in the eighteenth century—until the French Revolution of 1789—were taken up with a series of dynastic struggles that led to several international wars: the War of the Spanish Succession (1701-1714), the War of the Polish Succession (1733-1735), the War of the Austrian Succession (1740-1748), and the War of the Bavarian Succession (1778-1779). The absolute control which royal and princely families exercised over their states transformed any dynastic haggling among the intricately related ruling houses of Europe into an immediate and serious international power struggle. If these prolonged family feuds had a common concern, it was their desire to let no upstart join their illustrious ranks and thus destroy whatever balance of power they had orchestrated. Yet it was the rapid rise of just such an upstart house and nation that provided Germany with its most important political development of the century. Prussia under the rule of the Hohenzollerns was the last state in Europe to emerge as one of its leading powers. Not even a kingdom before 1701, Prussia had become, under the hands of frugal and disciplined rulers, a power that half a century later was able to hold its own against the combined forces of Austria, France, and Russia.

Oddly enough, these dramatic political events did not influence German culture significantly. While the nobility had reserved for itself the theater of international politics, it had, at the same time and by an unspoken agreement, granted the middle class a considerable degree of private security and peace. After the hardships of the Thirty Years' War, the middle class was eager to accept such a bargain, at least until it would be able to rebuild its economic stamina. Thus, the eighteenth century presents the picture of a Germany in which the nobility was responsible for matters of politics and the middle class was responsible for everything else.

In the running of its affairs, the middle class was greatly helped by the spirit of rationalism and empiricism. Rationalism had become the philosophy of the bourgeoisie in France since René Descartes had declared reason, rather than tradition or precedent, as the sole authority in the management of human conduct. Empiricism, an elaboration of rationalism developed in England by John Locke (1632-1704), specified that reason needs to be based on experience and that no rational judgment ought to be made without prolonged observation of the facts. French rationalism and English empiri-

cism combined to inspire the Age of Enlightenment. The middle class, which had nothing to lose by the abolition of a tradition that kept it out of power and had everything to gain from the rational observation of political, social, and economic facts, embraced the Enlightenment as its most sacred mission.

To the poets of the Enlightenment, the contorted rhetoric of the Baroque appeared neither rational nor based on facts. A first reaction against Baroque poetry had occurred in France, where Nicolas Boileau-Despréaux, in his *L'Art poétique* (1674; *The Art of Poetry*, 1683), had insisted on the sober standards of truthfulness, naturalness, and reasonableness in the writing of poetry. In 1730, Johann Christoph Gottsched (1700-1766) presented his countrymen with a German version of Boileau's creed in his *Versuch einer critischen Dichtkunst vor die Deutschen* (1730; attempt at a critical art of poetry for Germans). How quickly, though, attitudes were beginning to change in Germany is evident from the fact that Gottsched and his theories of rational poetry turned into the laughingstock of German poets in less than twenty years.

The reaction against Gottsched was led by two Swiss professors, Johann Jakob Bodmer (1698-1783) and Johann Jakob Breitinger (1701-1776). Both men were admirers of the English scene and favored its literature over that of the French. In typically empiricist fashion, they suggested that it might prove more profitable to deduce a good poetic theory from the study of good poetry, rather than to hope for good poetry to be written in accordance with some preconceived poetic theory. In short, the theory of poetry must follow, not precede, the practice of poetry. Looking at poems without prejudicial expectations, Bodmer and Breitinger discovered that a good poem is, above all, imaginative and that reason played a very secondary role in its creation. The ensuing fight between the two camps ended with the total defeat of Gottsched and of the French influence over German poetry. In the end, what turned the tide in the acrimonious squabbles was the fact that Bodmer and Breitinger could point to a young poet who substantiated and justified all of their claims, while Gottsched, as hard as he tried, could not.

This young, amazingly original poet was Friedrich Gottlieb Klopstock (1724-1803). Klopstock's poetry, with its outbursts of feeling and its flights of the imagination, caught the reading public totally by surprise. Klopstock made it his personal responsibility to restore to poetry the honorable function which it once had exercised within the Germanic tribes: to guide and express man's relation to God, nature, and society. As the prophet of an all-powerful poetry, he naturally felt no inhibition to dismiss what small-minded academicians had laid down as poetic law. Language, Klopstock believed, belongs to poets, and only they can determine its possibilities. In incomplete sentences, in irregular syntax, often in free rhythms, Klopstock stammered in awe before the grandeur of his themes (God, nature, love, patriotism) as much as before the sublime emotions these themes evoked in him.

It was Klopstock's faith in the power of poetry that impelled him to write in the genre in which poetry had exercised its power over society most forcefully: He set out to write an epic. Klopstock's genius, unfortunately, was lyric rather than epic, and his *Der Messias* (1748-1773), which swelled to twenty thousand lines, has remained one of the most monotonous and unreadable epics of all time. The passion which gave Klopstock's shorter poems their distinction could not be sustained over the course of twenty-five years; his emotions turned flat and belabored, exhausting and finally grating on the sensibilities of the reader.

Not even Klopstock's lyric poems withstood the test of time as well as one might have expected. In spite of his emotionalism, Klopstock abided by the basic principles of rhetorical poetry: His feelings did not spontaneously transform themselves into words. In order to create a poetic effect, it was not enough for Klopstock to relate his experience poetically. That experience, however personal, needed to be made representative of all experiences under similar conditions. To arrive at this representative quality, the poet had to generalize the intimacy of what he felt until the feeling became comprehensible, not to say reasonable, to the reader. Klopstock, who was a very emotional poet, almost never lets the reader share in the immediacy of his emotions. Even when Klopstock seems to have been sincerely overwhelmed, one almost always senses the rational scaffolding that supports the poetic expression of his ecstasies.

In the second half of the eighteenth century, faith in human experience as representative and rational received a mighty jolt when it became clear that experiences are neither shared nor accessible to reason. On the contrary, each person's experiences create a unique world—a strictly individualistic world and therefore (as one needs a point of reference outside oneself for rationality) beyond the power of reason.

From these disturbing insights, the philosopher and critic Johann Gottfried von Herder (1744-1803) drew some surprisingly fruitful conclusions for poetry. As language originally was meant to express the emotional responses to experiences, and as these emotional responses are as individualistic and irrational as the experiences which caused them, the most primordial form of language could not have been rational prose but must have been irrational poetry. Poetry is the mother tongue of the human race, because it is in poetry that man's first and only appropriate interpretations of the world occurred.

Most existing poetry, sadly enough for Herder, served as pleasing ornament or rhetorical confirmation of an already charted human environment. This trend needed to be reversed; poetry needed to reassume its primary function. Above all, it had to regain access to basic human experiences within the tradition to which it wanted to speak. Attempts to rejuvenate German poetry in accordance with the standards of Greece, Rome, or France were doomed to fail. Instead, a conscious effort was necessary to enable German poetry to reestablish its ties to the life of the German people. To this end, the poetic language would have to cleanse itself of all artificiality and return to the simplicity and spontaneity exemplified in the creations of folk poetry.

The success of Herder's ideas was not, as has often been claimed, immediate or sweeping. Of the young poets of the time, only one showed himself deeply affected, yet one poet was all Herder needed for his theory to triumph, for this young man was Johann Wolfgang von Goethe (1749-1832).

Goethe met Herder in 1770, and one year later Goethe's poems usually designated as *Sesenheimer Liederbuch* (1775-1789, 1854; *Sesenheim Songs*, 1853) made Herder's program come true. The twenty-two-year-old poet speaks of his love for the pastor's daughter at Sesenheim in tones of boundless joy, as if such love had never existed before and would never exist again. With a relaxed innocence, he trusts the poetic quality of all that is natural and recovers for the language of poetry, without the slightest tinge of embarrassment, love and heart, flowers and kisses, the sun, the moon, the air, and the clouds.

Still, for Herder, the poet was not merely an innocent participant in the world's harmony. As a creator, he also carried grave responsibilities for the state of human affairs. In a series of forceful odes, Goethe explored the challenges of any creative response to earthly existence. Through a study of great prototypes (Prometheus, Mohammed, Ganymede) and their rhythms of life, Goethe felt confirmed in his belief that equal creativity is required for rebellion against and submission to the flow of things in this world. A poet can prefer one of these attitudes to the other only at the expense of constraining his most vital gift, his infinite capacity for experience.

Goethe's career as an administrator at the court of Weimar (1775-1786) demanded a firmer, more realistic response from the poet. In view of man's innumerable limitations, moderation had the last word. Emotional introspection was replaced by objective overview, as the typical rather than the extraordinary in life received Goethe's attention. Only in an occasional lyric sigh for release—as in Germany's most famous poem, the weightless, dreamlike "Über allen Gipfeln ist Ruh" ("Over All the Hilltops It Is Still")—could Goethe admit to himself the strain which his search for order and objectivity had placed upon him.

Emotional release in the midst of order and objectivity became Goethe's great discovery on his journey through Italy (1786-1788). Goethe lived and celebrated this release upon his return to Weimar in his cycle of *Römische Elegien* (1793; *Roman Elegies*). The unashamed eroticism of the classical age is praised here in the strict order of classical meters. Emphasizing the sensual, often outright licentious foundations of antiquity's formal achievements, Goethe freely mocked his compatriots' prudishly ideal conception of classical perfection. Almost a quarter of a century later, Goethe would reaffirm his faith in sensuality as a precondition of great art—this time encouraged by his discovery of Persian poetry—in a similar cycle of poems, his *West-östlicher Divan* (1819, 1827; *West-Eastern Divan*).

Goethe's lyric poetry reached its last peak in the eighteenth century between 1797 and 1798 when, in friendly competition with Friedrich Schiller (1758-1805), Goethe wrote several of his finest ballads. Schiller, the greatest dramatist of the eighteenth century, was a primarily speculative mind, and his poetry rarely achieves the confessional intimacy which so often makes Goethe's poems read like fragments of an autobiography. Schiller philosophized in his poems on the painful antagonism between what is and what ought to be, between the innate freedom of man and the acquired constraints of his conventional mind and heart.

These differences of poetic perspective also distinguish Goethe's and Schiller's ballads. The ballads of Goethe remain close to their popular roots; they focus on the inexplicable omnipresence of demonic powers, as in the well-known "Der Zauberlehrling" ("The Sorcerer's Apprentice"). Schiller's ballads, by contrast, dramatize ethical or philosophical conflicts: The downfall of pride is the theme of "Der Taucher" ("The Diver"); the jealousy of the gods, that of "Der Ring des Polykrates" ("The Ring of Polycrates"); and "Die Bürgschaft" ("The Pledge") proclaims the invincible power of friendship. With their easy combination of dramatic narrative and didactic intent, Schiller's ballads enjoyed an unparalleled popularity throughout the nineteenth century; today, they are often unjustly dismissed.

With an originality which only the twentieth century would appreciate, Schiller's poetry of ideas and Goethe's poetry of experience were fused at the beginning of the nineteenth century by Friedrich Hölderlin (1770-1843). Hölderlin wrestled for a few intense years with such apparent abstractions as freedom, love, fatherland, divinity, and fate in intensely existential, at times opaque poems until the onset of a severe mental illness at the age of thirty-three broke up his creative struggle.

Classical Greece was Hölderlin's model of a harmonious society, and the French Revolution raised his hopes for a reconstitution of such a society even in his own country. Hölderlin wanted to be the prophet of this great advent. To be a worthy prophet, he was ready to bridge the gulf between future and present, ideal and reality, knowing full well that this would mean to be exiled from both, to exist as a lonely wanderer in time, a victim of his own promises. His having been exiled by God and man—expressed in poems such as "Die Heimat" ("Homeland") and "Abendphantasie" ("Evening Fantasy")—Hölderlin considered a great suffering and a great distinction, the suffering and distinction of a heroic fate. Hölderlin's only fear was that he might not be equal to the demands of this calling. His unquestioning faith in the power of poetry he shared with the Romantics of his era, while the humility with which he lived his vocation foreshadowed a much more modern sensibility.

BIBLIOGRAPHY

Bragg, Marvin. *From Gottsched to Goethe: Changes in the Social Function of the Poet and the Poetry.* New York: Peter Lang, 1984. Examines eighteenth century German poetry in the context of literary movements and German society of the day.

Browning, Robert M. *German Poetry in the Age of Enlightenment: From Blockes to Klopstock.* The Penn State Series on German Literature. University Park: Pennsylvania State University Press, 1978. Examines the influence of the Enlightenment on poetry and intellectual life of the eighteenth century.

Cocalis, Susan L., ed. *German Feminist Poems from the Middle Ages to the Present: A Bilingual Anthology.* New York: Feminist Press at the City University of New York, 1986. Introduces and rediscovers German women poets dating back to the thirteenth century.

Frakes, Jerold C. *Brides and Doom: Gender, Property, and Power in Medieval German Women's Epic.* Philadelphia: University of Pennsylvania Press, 1994. Examines gender issues that appear in heroic epics, including *The Nibelungenlied*, that revolve around women. Reviews the conventional scholarship, and discusses property and power, intimate conversations and political strategies, Teuton as Amazon, sovereignty and class, and other topics.

Gentry, Francis G., E. Volkmar, A. Linz, and E. Sander, eds. *German Epic Poetry.* New York: Continuum, 1995. Heroic poetry from the great epics of German literature, including *Jungere Hildebrandslied*, *The Battle of Ravenna*, *Bitterolf and Dietlieb*, and *The Rose Garden*.

Gillespie, Gerard. *German Baroque Poetry.* New York: Twayne Publishers, 1971. Provides history and criti-

cism of German poetry between 1500 and 1700. Includes bibliography.

Hanak, Miroslav John. *A Guide to Romantic Poetry in Germany.* New York: Peter Lang, 1987. Explores the development and influences of Romantic poetry in the eighteenth and nineteenth centuries in Germany.

Haymes, Edward R., and Susann T. Samples. *Heroic Legends of the North: An Introduction to the Nibelung and Dietrich Cycles.* New York: Garland Publishing, 1996. Traces the origins of epic tales in the Dark Ages and follows their spread throughout medieval literature. Surveys the medieval literary versions: the hero, heroic poetry, and the Heroic Age.

Hatto, Arthur T. *Essays on Medieval German and Other Poetry.* Angelica Germanica Series 2. New York: Cambridge University Press, 1983. Provides history and criticism for German poetry between 1050 and 1500. Includes bibliography.

Hutchinson, Peter, ed. *Landmarks in German Poetry.* New York: Peter Lang, 2000. Examines the scope of German poetry, providing critical essays and history.

Kaplowitt, Stephen J. *Ennobling Power of Love in the Medieval German Lyric.* Chapel Hill: University of North Carolina Press, 1986. Examines the influence of medieval civilization on German love poetry.

Mathieu, Gustave, and Guy Stern, eds. *Introduction to German Poetry.* Mineola, N.Y.: Dover Publications, 1991. Includes forty-two works from notable German poets. Complete German text plus expert literal English translations on facing pages. Includes biographical and critical commentary on each poet.

Murdoch, Brian. *The Germanic Hero: Politics and Pragmatism in Early Medieval Poetry.* Rio Grande, Ohio: Hambledon Press, 1996. Describes the literary representations of the early Germanic hero, showing that he was not a sword-wielding barbarian out for glory at any cost, but a dedicated opponent of chaos and champion of social stability who operated within a strict political framework.

Newman, Jane O. *Pastoral Conventions: Poetry, Language, and Thought in Seventeenth Century Nuremburg.* Baltimore, Md.: Johns Hopkins University Press, 1990. Traces the development of the seventeenth century Nuremberg pastoral poetry society Pegnesischer Blumenorden as a historical, interpretive community of theorists and poets, and offers a detailed analysis of their writings, through which are explored issues at the center of scholarly debate about the Renaissance and early modern period.

Schatzberg, Walter. *Scientific Themes in the Popular Literature and the Poetry of the German Enlightenment, 1720-1760*. New York: Peter Lang, 1973. Examines the influence of science on eighteenth century German poetry.

Stahl, Ernest L., ed. *Oxford Book of German Verse, Twelfth to Twentieth Century*. 3d ed. London: Oxford University Press, 1968.

Surles, Robert L. *Roots and Branches: Germanic Epic/ Romanic Legend*. New York: Peter Lang, 1987. Presents history and criticism of German epic poetry.

Thomas, Neil. *The Medieval German Arthuriad: Some Contemporary Revaluations of the Canon*. New York: Peter Lang, 1989. Examines German court epics, depictions of knighthood, and the influence of Arthurian romances on German poetry between the eleventh and sixteenth centuries.

Walsoe-Engel, Ingrid, and Volkman Sander, eds. *German Poetry from the Beginnings to 1750*. New York: Continuum, 1991.

Joachim Scholz

GERMAN POETRY: 1800 TO REUNIFICATION

The French critic Hippolyte Taine (1828-1893) once wrote that between 1780 and 1830, Germany brought forth all the ideas of his age. Although somewhat hyperbolic, Taine's pronouncement should not be taken lightly. These fifty years span the period of Romanticism in German literature, art, and philosophy, and its many innovations in poetry left their mark in a pervasive, if occasionally discontinuous, tradition.

German Romanticism can be said to have an early and a late phase. The early period is identified chiefly with August Wilhelm von Schlegel (1767-1845), his brother Friedrich (1772-1829), Ludwig Tieck (1773-1853), Novalis (Friedrich von Hardenberg, 1772-1801), Friedrich Schelling (1775-1854), and Friedrich Schleiermacher (1768-1834). The early phase was more critical and theoretical than late Romanticism, which counted more poets among its adherents, including Achim von Arnim (1781-1831), Clemens Brentano (1778-1842), and Joseph von Eichendorff (1788-1857).

Walter Benjamin has maintained that the German Romantics confronted their times not primarily on epistemological terms, even though these were in fact significant (for example, the philosophy of Johann G. Fichte, 1762-1814), but instead primarily through the medium of art. Friedrich von Schlegel saw the potential of the new age in the spirit of poetry. His essay "Progressive Universalpoesie" ("Progressive Universal Poetry") addresses a fundamental design of early Romanticism: the universal poeticization of life. Conceptually, Romantic poetry (in the broad sense) embraces all traditional genres of literary and philosophic discourse within its totalizing system. This view radically reformulated the mimetic possibilities of nature and privileged poetic perspective in new, epoch-making ways.

Novalis once wrote:

> Romanticism is nothing other than a qualitative sublimation. . . . By giving the commonplace exceptional significance, the habitual an air of mystery, the familiar the dignity of the unfamiliar, the finite an infinite meaning—in so doing I romanticize.

Viewed against its cultural and sociohistorical context, a basic feature of early Romanticism is its systematic desystematization of what were perceived by the Romantics to be restrictive and rigid norms. Abhorring the profane and mourning the loss of life's poetic qualities, the Romantics were among the first to recognize and react against the modern forces of social and economic alienation. They blamed the rationalization and instrumentalization of Enlightenment ideology for having emptied life of its poetry and in contrast projected the Middle Ages as the last great harmonious historical age.

The revolutionary ideas advanced in philosophy and aesthetics have their parallel in Novalis's collection of poems *Hymnen an die Nacht* (1800; *Hymns to the Night*, 1897, 1948). Novalis suffered greatly at the deaths of his brother and his fiancé in 1797, and in 1799 he composed these six hymns, the poetic manifestation of his encounter with death (a central experience of German Romanticism). *Hymns to the Night*, a combination of ecstatic prose and strophic hymns, asserts that true perception of the world comes only after having acquired complete knowledge of the self. This view, related to Fichte's philosophy, is pivotal, for it locates the human being at the center of comprehending the universe.

The collection recounts both personal and individual experience and, through a quasi-mystical vision, projects the situation onto the dimensions of the historical-eschatological course of humankind. The objectification of Novalis's vision reveals the central transformation of the metaphoric function of light and dark, day and night, whereby night becomes the primal force of the universe. This transvaluation of their respective ranges of meaning takes place through a foregrounding of paradox and oxymora. Evolving ultimately into myth, Novalis's *Hymns to the Night* is a classic example of Romanticism, especially along those lines where its symbolism intersects with that of Christianity.

While Novalis's work is indisputably central to any discussion of early German Romantic poetry, the fact that critics are able today to speak of a "Romantic poetry" is largely a result of other factors. One of them was the publication, in 1805, of *Des Knaben Wunderhorn* (the boy's magic horn), a collection of German folk songs compiled by Achim von Arnim and Clemens Brentano. Interest in folk literature had been generated earlier by the young Johann Wolfgang von Goethe (1749-1832) and Johann Gottfried Herder (1744-1803), who in fact coined the German word *Volkslied* (folk song) in 1775. The work of Arnim and Brentano revived this interest, a task made easier by the current of nationalism running through Germany at the time.

Nearly all writers associated with German Romanticism wrote poetry, but, in the spirit of Schlegel's "Progressive Universal Poetry," these poems generally formed part of a larger text, most often a novel (the privileged genre within Romantic aesthetics). Typically, the heroes of Romantic novels are poets, or at least lead "poetic lives," and they are prone to express their emotional states—whether joy or sorrow, exhilaration or despair—in the relatively spontaneous form of the lyric poem. These factors, then, also help define the contours of Romantic poetry.

Brentano had a great affinity for the folk song and used its features in his own verse. (The folk-song strophe, common to much nineteenth century German verse, is easily recognized by its alternating *abab* masculine/feminine rhyme scheme.) Brentano was a diverse and creative writer with an exceptionally active imagination. Although his poems are sometimes formally inconsistent, the tenor of his work is constant: musical, synesthetic, crafted, rich in texture. "Auf dem Rhein" ("Upon the Rhine") reveals a characteristic fascination for the macabre, manifested (from the Romantic perspective) in the eerie dimensions of the twilight. Appearance and reality become indistinguishable and effect a strikingly modern sense of disorientation. "Sprich aus der Ferne" ("Speak from Afar") uses the refrain as magic incantation. A desire to see all things as related informs this poem's lyric voice: the individual and the universe, the near and the far. The structured dimensions of casual (and causal) reality give way and flow together, presented through synesthesia and oxymora. The poem's closing rhetorical gesture reflects the universalizing tendency of Romanticism.

Eichendorff's poetry displays a longing for unity and simplicity. He uses nature as a medium for understanding human existence and not merely as an object of imitation. Nature becomes a grand hieroglyph, and the

poet's task is to render the most approximate translation. A fundamental Romantic dualism—nature as both demonic and divine—informs his work. The mood evoked by Eichendorff's landscapes often suggests impending danger, perhaps the risk of losing one's way in the dark. One critic has said of Eichendorff—who, unlike his contemporary Brentano, a late convert to Catholicism, was a devout Catholic throughout his life—that he "is not so much the poet of romantic longing as the poet of the *dangers* of romantic longing."

The poetry of Ernst Moritz Arndt (1769-1860), Max von Schenckendorff (1783-1817), and Karl Theodor Körner (1791-1813) represents another dimension of German Romanticism. According to E. L. Stahl,

> The patriotic verse of these soldier-poets expresses the satisfaction of an urge to share in communal life. In the same way conversion to Catholicism fulfils religious Romantic longings, Patriotic activity and traditional religiosity cause the primary Romantic impulse to abate and new attitudes to prevail. The wanderer returns home and settles down to perform his acknowledged civic and domestic tasks. The age of "bürgerlicher Realismus" [Bourgeois Realism] begins with this change in outlook which was imposed on German writers by the social developments and the political events of the post-Napoleonic era.

BIEDERMEIER AND VORMÄRZ

Between 1830 and 1849, two distinct trends appeared within German poetry. The first, known as *Biedermeier*, was an introspective turn in response to the severe social and political repression exercised by Prince Metternich (1773-1859). The second, referred to as *Vormärz*, was an effort to politicize literature in the hope of effecting social and political reform. The public at large still preferred poetry to the popular novel, and in its various forms (verse epic, cycles, and ballads) its purpose was mainly to entertain and (from an ideological point of view) "distract." Tomes of poetry, mostly traditional and derivative, depicted a charming poetic world of tranquil harmony. Against this numerically significant backdrop, the Young Germans, idealists and political activists, advanced their theory of prose. Between 1830 and 1848, social tensions grew and the political spirit turned more radical.

Heinrich Heine (1797-1856) recognized that even the conservative patriotic verse of the Romantic poets could play into the interests of social and political liberals, since as an ideological instrument, poetry was capable of stirring great enthusiasm among the people. Interest in the "political poem" accrued because—viewed pragmatically—it was the most appropriate literary form for subversive agitation and propaganda. Heine derided the hackneyed declarations of freedom and the ponderously didactic reflections often found in the more cumbersome representatives of ostensibly political verse. Concerned with matters of immediate social and political relevance, this poetry was often subjected to the mechanisms of censorship in Metternich's control. (The reports of his spies frequently referred to the danger posed by these political "folk poems," an indication that the liberals had succeeded in part in redefining the readership of poetry as well as the genre's objectives.)

Not all poets wrote within this mainstream of events. Two of note who remained relatively aloof from political affairs are Annette von Droste-Hülshoff (1779-1848) and Eduard Mörike (1804-1875). Although they did not enjoy the recognition they deserved during their lifetimes, their poetry has come to be highly valued for its complexity and its moral intensity.

Droste-Hülshoff, perceptive and intelligent, recognized the changed social conditions of her times, but family ties and the traditions of conservatism and Catholicism, coupled with a deep attachment to the countryside of her home region, Westphalia, exercised a strong authority in her poetry. Westphalia becomes the locus of her search for harmony and order between the individual and nature. In contrast to the Romantic nature imagery of forests and streams, one finds in Droste-Hülshoff for the first time in German literature the poetic treatment of the moors and heaths of her own Westphalia. The realism of her verse lies in its attention to minute detail both in nature and in human nature. The senses of sight and sound play important roles throughout her work. She felt the presence of a demonic undercurrent in all of existence, and thus her poems are often ballads or at least balladesque. The Catholic Church provided a sanctuary for Droste-Hülshoff. She understood her role as author to be a "power by the grace of God." Her confessional poems, such as "Geistliches

Jahr" ("Spiritual Year"), show her coping with the dilemma of sin and the fall from grace.

Mörike is often called the greatest German lyric poet of the nineteenth century. His poetry shares features with that of late Romanticism, and his use of classical forms and themes shows his affinity with classicism. Some consider his work *Biedermeier* because of its introspective and unpretentious nature; still others refer to the "impressionism" of his poetry. All in all, these varying assessments give testimony to the artistic complexity of his work. His poetic technique is marked by a sensitivity for chiaroscuro and for the minutely observed symbolism of the divine within nature.

Mörike sought to reconcile the ideal with the real; his poems are accompanied by a sense of despair, helplessness, and resignation. The landscape of the country idyll provides order and security. Isolated and alienated, Mörike views love and nature in his poems with melancholy. Still, his deep Christian faith seems to have counteracted his melancholy. He always returned to the central problem of death; he preferred a life of the soul, but he failed to find the ultimate harmony he desired. Unlike his contemporary Nikolaus Lenau (1802-1850), Mörike managed to contain his despair at least enough to resist nihilism. Showing the tensions between what Sigmund Freud later described as the pleasure principle and the reality principle, Mörike's poems register important sociohistorical antagonisms of nineteenth century Germany.

Lenau is a figure of several contradictions. At once a great Austrian revolutionary poet and a late Romantic poet of *Weltschmerz*, Lenau suffered the isolation characteristic of the bourgeois intellectual, and his works turn around a central moment of melancholy. His poetry documents both the individual's revolt against the instrumentalization of human beings and the rejection of bourgeois complacency. His early poem "Einsamkeit" ("Loneliness") best illustrates his *Weltschmerz*, bordering on existential dread. In his verse epic *Die Albigenser* (1837; the Albigensia), on the other hand, Lenau acknowledges G. F. W. Hegel's *Weltgeist*. Lenau's reworking of historical material (the fate of the Cathars, against whom Pope Innocent III waged war from 1209 to 1229) reveals his interest in the struggle for economic and political power, an interest not merely antiquarian. The poem begins: "Nicht meint das Lied auf Tote abzulenken" ("Not of the dead shall the song give pause to think").

Probably the most fascinating and enigmatic poet of the nineteenth century, Heinrich Heine is most often identified with his first volume of poetry, *Buch der Lieder* (1827; *Book of Songs*, 1856). With these poems, it became clear that Heine was both the heir and the bane of German Romantic poetry. In the vein of Romantic poets, he could create moods and turn nature into a mirror for subjective feelings, but he no longer shared their belief in the mysterious whole. For Heine, the integrity of the whole is an illusion (even though one that is longed for), and in its place there appears a sense of disintegration, nature as a collage of signs and indicators of his own subjectivity. His Byronic irony draws on both sentiment and sharp criticism. His right hand creates a sentimental mood or atmosphere which his left hand all the while is busy undermining through critical observation, exposing its illusory dimensions, rejecting them as unrealistic. The result of this double labor is the special tension characteristic of Heine's work, the central poignancy behind his poetic voice.

Heine's attraction and aversion to German Romanticism resulted from the fact that by 1830, Romanticism was a greatly inflated commodity. Backward-looking and conservative, it no longer offered appropriate solutions for dealing with the changed conditions. Heine thus distanced himself from its ideological subtext, while on the surface employing to his own advantage its artistic conventions. Thus, the special shape of Heine's wit, a kind of "double take" is evidenced in the poem "Ein Jüngling liebt ein Mädchen" ("A Young Boy Loves a Young Girl"). Here, the final lines reaffirm the validity of feeling after exposing it to mockery. In another poem, "Ich wandle unter Blumen" ("I Amble Among Flowers"), Heine, as the critic Robert M. Browning has observed, "does not so much ridicule feeling, the 'romantic' attitude, as reveal its inappropriateness as a mode of social behavior. Such is the world and we have to accept it." In "Mein Herz, mein Herz ist traurig" ("My Heart, My Heart Does Sorrow"), the antithesis of the pleasant surroundings and the sorrowful observer/narrator suggests at first that the cause for his mood is misfortune in love (although this is not stated explicitly). Instead, the poem is a remarkable example of the more general historical conditions of despair. When contrasted with the expressed death wish of the observer in the final line, the peaceful, serene summer landscape appears as reified and proplike, testifying to Heine's alienation both as lover and vis-à-vis nature. Heine's works thus contain the central ambivalences of his time.

In "My Heart, My Heart Does Sorrow," for example, the ambivalence of the summer idyll is juxtaposed to the ambivalence of the nostalgia expressed for an unattainable restored world. On one hand, Heine indulges his *Weltschmerz*, while, on the other, he exposes it as a pose, as illusionary game playing. The characteristic result is the combination of haunting appeal to sincere emotional states and their frequent reversal through pungent intellectual stimulation. The different tone of Heine's later poetry results from its more explicit politicization. Rejecting aesthetic banality as well as profane content, such as could be found in much of the tendentious poetry of the *Vormärz*, Heine's own political poetry offers successful counterexamples, as in "Die schlesischen Weber" ("The Silesian Weavers").

The political poetry typical of the *Vormärz* virtually disappeared with the failed revolution of 1848. Complacency, disillusionment, and a conservative patriotism prevailed. Derivative didactic poetry predominated, represented by the work of the Munich Circle of poets, the most popular of whom was Emanuel Geibel (1815-1884). The more significant writers and poets of the genre known as Bourgeois Realism relied on the tradition of the *Erlebnislyrik*, or poetry of personal experience, such as that initiated by Goethe and practiced widely by the Romantics. This tradition, as well as that of the *Stimmungsgedicht*, or mood poem, ran its course in the period from 1850 to 1880.

REALISM

It is not customary to speak of lyric poetry in terms of realism, although one can consider it from this point of view, keeping in mind that the term "realism" has a range of meanings. Gottfried Keller's (1819-1890) realism is to be found in the unpretentious experience of his *Erlebnislyrik* and in the restraint of emotion. Friedrich Hebbel (1813-1863) and Conrad Ferdinand Meyer (1825-1898) showed an exacting attention to poetic form and rejected the highly rhetorical declamatory mode of earlier lyric diction. The realism of Theodor Storm (1817-1888) resides in his affinity for the folk song and in the acoustic sensitivity of his poems. Theodor Fontane (1819-1898) used everyday speech and eschewed the predominant bombastic style of the ballad of his day. The realists sought poetic experience in a balance or harmony among the divergent forces acting upon the self and the world around them, forces of alienation and isolation. On the whole, their poems display a preference for simple motifs and rhythms, uncomplicated strophes and lines of verse. Brevity and modesty proved more conducive to a sincere personal tone. Antiquated forms, viewed as rhetorically empty, fell into disrepute. Themes of love and nature, joy and sorrow, longing and remembrance prevailed, with an underlying tone of resignation evident. With some poets, especially Storm and Meyer, one senses an aura of *Spätzeitlichkeit*, the feeling of having been born too late, a condition suggested by the increasing artistic stylization of their poetry. Meyer's symbolic imagery finally broke with the conventions of the *Erlebnisgedicht* (poem of personal experience) more completely than any of his predecessors, and he stands at the threshold of what we commonly acknowledge to be modern poetry.

Hebbel's poetry is pensive and intellectual. He rejected the tendentious poetry of his day, but his own verse sometimes suffers because of its highly intellectualized reflection, especially evident in his later sonnets and epigrams. As a postclassicist, Hebbel was drawn between the reflection and speculation characteristic of Schiller's work and the emotion and immediacy essential to Goethe's. Hebbel's imagery tends to be static, with the intellectual tension and the unnatural syntax of his poems countering the illusion of immediacy. He treats the themes of dream and night, pain and death, in a dialectic fashion. The antithesis of the individual and the universe provides a central tension at the core of his lyric ego. The poetic symbol overcomes the fundamental opposition of self and universe.

With Storm, the poetic symbol loses its comprehensive meaning and evolves into something more psychological and impressionistic, an attribute of a given mood, disposition, or atmosphere. Storm always proceeds from a single experience and then, through precise observa-

tions—particularly acoustic ones—achieves the artistic translation of this moment into compelling figurative language. Aware of the interdependency of form and content, Storm considered the brevity of the lyric poem structurally appropriate to the intense communication of states or moods. After 1848, his often sentimental lyric subjectivity gave way to a preoccupation with external reality in distinct, descriptive language. His nature poems, like those of Droste-Hülshoff, reveal close ties with his own home region, Schleswig-Holstein. Storm's later poems became more acerbic and, as with Meyer, the strong presence of death and isolation within Storm's lyric voice suggests a sense of *Spätzeitlichkeit*.

Meyer's poetry marks a significant historical moment, between the realists' reformulation of the *Erlebnisgedicht* and the Symbolism of Rainer Maria Rilke (1875-1926). Some scholars therefore speak of Meyer's poetry as "anachronistic," while others stress those features of his work which point toward the future and the predominant course of modern poetry into the twentieth century. Meyer dealt continuously and in various ways with the problem of existence. Caught in the historical currents of pessimism and the accompanying sense of the loss of values which afflicted the late nineteenth century, Meyer preached the instructive and redemptive power of poetry. His own poetry evolves toward the poetic figuration of a subjective moment. His collection of poems from 1882 evidences a new kind of language, one intent on uncovering the essence of things through objectification. Even the most personal experience undergoes a transformation that objectifies it as a symbol or an allegorical image. In contrast to the more conventional mode of the *Erlebnisgedicht*, direct speech in Meyer's poetry is rare and generally recedes entirely behind the distance of intellectuality. The formal perfection of his poems is one means of coping with suffering and death, as in, for example, "Eingelegte Ruder" (inlaid rudder) or "Im Spätboot" (in the late boat). In "Zwei Segel" (two sails), the fundamental experience of human love is transformed and objectified in a symbolically rich texture of images.

NATURALISM

The publication of *Moderne Dichtercharaktere* (characters of modern poets) in 1885, an anthology showcasing the revolutionary bravado of the younger generation and its new aesthetic program, introduced Naturalist poetry. Few of the original contributors, however, became significant poets, perhaps because the aesthetics of Naturalism were not compatible with the conventions of lyric poetry. Arno Holz (1863-1929), an avid experimentalist, was the most accomplished poet among the German Naturalist writers. His *Buch der Zeit* (1885; book of this time), a pithy, coarse, and "thoroughly modern" collection of poems, rejected the artifice and pretense of conventional poetic diction. *Phantasus* (1898, enlarged 1916, 1925, 1929, 1961) shows his indebtedness to Walt Whitman's rhythms, his pathos, and his nontraditional use of form.

Although unaffiliated with any literary movement, Detlev von Liliencron (1844-1909) realized in his verse many of the objectives of Naturalist aesthetics. He achieved a Naturalist effect in his combination of simple and precise perceptions, a technique which could just as well be called impressionistic in several instances. (Some critics have remarked that Liliencron's poems are "impressionistic" insofar as they are snapshots of reality as viewed from the surface, evocative glimpses of life, strung together according to the principle of juxtaposition and showing disdain for conventional rules of grammar and syntax.) His poems display spontaneity, rich imagery, and sensitivity to rhythm. The evocative atmosphere of his poems creates a depth which haunts the imagination. *Adjutanternritte* (1883; rides of an adjutant), his first book of poems, proved to be his most lasting; the quality of his later work generally did not live up to its promise.

TURN OF THE TWENTIETH CENTURY

While the Naturalist poem per se remained more a concept than a reality, the abundance of poetry written around the turn of the twentieth century displayed a variety of forms, styles, and graces. There was the neo-Romantic balladry of Agnes Miegel (1879-1964), Börries Freiherr von Münchhausen (1874-1945), and Lulu von Strauss und Torney (1873-1956), generally traditional in form and content and conservative in ideology. There was also a revival of nature poetry in the vein of *Heimatkunst* (provincial art). At the same time, the style known as *Jugendstil*, or Art Nouveau, emerged. With its

penchant for the charming and the ornate, *Jugendstil* was naturally drawn toward poetry. Some of Stefan Zweig's (1881-1942) poems can be considered representative of this style: They deal frequently with death, particularly its paradoxical relation to the centrifugal forces of life. *Jugendstil* experiences nature as a palliative for moroseness, pain, and suffering.

Around the same time, Frank Wedekind (1864-1918) and others were writing much satirical poetry, often with a political thrust, popular above all in the cabarets of large cities such as Berlin and Munich. The work of Christian Morgenstern (1871-1914) was singular in the tenor of his keen, penetrating questions of reality. Then as now, his poems have proved to be enormously popular. The work of Richard Dehmel (1863-1920) met with great success during his own lifetime, but today Dehmel's passionate vitalism is chiefly of historical interest. Erotic and sexual overtones dominate his later poems, and his equation of "poetic power" with "divine power," influenced by Friedrich Nietzsche, reveals a fundamental ideological interest of the time.

Of more lasting significance for modern poetry was Symbolism, which includes the works of Stefan George (1868-1933), Rilke, and Hugo von Hofmannsthal (1874-1929). With George, as Robert M. Browning has said, "modern poetry in the eminent sense begins in Germany." George sought to retrieve the forces of creativity that the forces of materialism had either inhibited or destroyed. Through beauty, he sought to restore magic and majesty to art. Incorporating the tradition of Symbolism from the French poets Charles Baudelaire, Stéphane Mallarmé, and Arthur Rimbaud, George was a language purist, striving for precision and perfection in his highly sculptured works. His aesthetics of *l'art pour l'art* evolved to accommodate a view of the poet as seer and teacher. George identified himself with Dante and with Friedrich Hölderlin (1770-1843) and advocated a kind of pagan beauty and aristocratic conservatism, behind which resided an ideology of heroworship. The manner in which George flaunted his "eccentricity"—from his homosexual Maximin cult and his antiphilistine typographical innovations to the liturgical earnestness with which he read his own verse—repelled and impressed his contemporaries, frequently both. His highly aristocratic view of poetry and his technique of pictorial stylization, whereby the meaning of life can be grasped only as an aesthetic phenomenon, reveal a debt to Nietzsche.

Nearly all of Hugo von Hofmannsthal's poetry was written between 1890 and 1900, between the ages of sixteen and twenty-six. His *Ein Brief* (1901; *Letter to Lord Chandos*, 1952) is a central document for understanding much of the poetry that preceded it. Here, Hofmannsthal confronts the language crisis which plagued him at the time (for a period immediately before and after the fictitious letter, he produced almost nothing). The letter envisions a way out of the dilemma—by seeking a new language, one of ciphers and symbols which allow objects to speak directly. This path was, however, to be Rilke's, not Hofmannsthal's; the latter rejected this kind of aestheticism. One of Hofmannsthal's best-known poems is the "Ballade des äusseren Lebens" (ballad of external life). While the title addresses the external life, it implies an internal—and qualitatively superior—plane of existence, which the poem reveals through an aesthetics of the moment that rescues objects and life from transitoriness and gives meaning to an otherwise meaningless existence. As such, it anticipates the magic exorcism of language as described in the Chandos letter.

The poetry of Rainer Maria Rilke is unrivaled in its aesthetic richness and its capacity to induce new modes of vision. After reading Rilke's poetry, one simply sees the world differently from before. The best example of this transforming power can be found in "Archaischer Torso Apollos," with its thematization of art's redemptive value, as expressed in the final line: "Du musst Dein Leben ändern" ("You must change your life"). This notion of "art's redemptive value" was not new with Rilke, but it is articulated with particular force in his works. It is a notion basic to what one might term the "ideology of art" as it first developed with Romanticism: namely, that art can claim a specific visionary power not common to other forms of human activity and production. Coupled with this fundamental tenet is the assumption that art is not divorced from life, that it has real, affective functions—which is why the lyric voice in Rilke's poem on Apollo, itself a work of art, is compelled to acknowledge its "redemptive effect." Rilke's first volume, *Leben und Lieder* (1894; life and songs), was followed by five more before 1900. Much of the early work reveals that Rilke

was still struggling for a distinctive poetic voice. This he found by the turn of the twentieth century, beginning with *Die frühen Gedichte* (1909; early poems), *Das Buch der Bilder* (1902, 1906; book of pictures), *Das Stundenbuch* (1905; *The Book of Hours*, 1961), and culminating in his *Neue Gedichte* (1907, 1908; *New Poems*, 1964). In *Das Buch der Bilder*, he moved tentatively toward a more objective poetry. From Auguste Rodin, Rilke had learned a new definition of artistic creativity, emphasizing craftsmanship rather than inspiration. In these poems, and later ones, he sought to be as plastic as possible. *The Book of Hours* depicts a Russian monk seeking God and the essence of all things through confession and prayer. Ultimately, this search proves futile, but the prayers are from the very start imbued with an underlying sense of doubt; all of Rilke's overtly religious poetry is informed by a modern skepticism. Rilke then abandoned his search for God and concentrated on creating a type of poem known as the *Dinggedicht*, or "object poem." Instead of a conventional portrayal of the symbolic confluence of the individual and nature, Rilke sought an "objective art." "Der Panther" ("The Panther"), from *New Poems*, was the first text in which Rilke realized this technique to an absolute degree. The poem articulates no sentimentality or "human" sympathy; instead, the affective possibilities of the poem are left entirely to the dimensions of the object itself, the panther.

Rilke's later volumes of poetry, the *Duineser Elegien* (1923; *Duinese Elegies*, 1930, better known as *Duino Elegies*) and *Die Sonette an Orpheus* (1923; *Sonnets to Orpheus*, 1936), written after a decade of silence, celebrate the transmutative power of feeling, a power capable of transforming the material world into spirit. By rendering the physical world "invisible," Rilke hoped to rescue it from the forces of transitoriness, to secure it forever within a dimension beyond space and time. As Browning has commented:

> The world is here to be felt and we are in the world to feel it. We *can* feel it because of our awareness of transiency, i.e., because we know death. Death is therefore Rilke's theme of themes. But for the poet feeling is not enough; the poet must also say. In saying, the rest of humanity is given to understand what is to be felt. In this way, the poet's work extends our consciousness.

EXPRESSIONISM

Rilke's work spans the period of German expressionism, although he should not be identified with it. The strident bravado of the new poetry of expressionism was chiefly concerned with shocking the complacent bourgeoisie. Moralistic pathos and visionary élan exploded the baser constraints on form and material, and the boldness of imagery challenged established perspectives and advocated novel and free modes of perception. Kurt Pinthus (1886-1975), editor of the influential anthology *Menschheitsdämmerung* (1920; twilight of humanity), wrote in 1915 that the new poetry surged forth "out of torment and scream, out of admiration and disdain, analysis and honor . . . toward the essential, toward the essence not only of appearance, but of Being." Expressionist poetry countered the forces which rendered language automatic and void of meaning by introducing innovative syntax and imagery, thus creating novel dimensions within the newly discovered relations of space and time and making manifest a new hermetic reality. Reality was transformed into word and sign, transfigured as cipher. Alienating meter and rhyme effected a grotesque refraction of reality, also an essential feature of expressionist poetry.

The first phase of German expressionism in particular (roughly from 1911 to 1914) discarded the "sensibility wasting in reflection" of much nineteenth century poetry and urged a sensibility animated and absorbed in construction, in presenting simultaneously the "what" and the "how" of perception. Expressionist poetry experimented with the possibilities of metaphor, substituting a fusion of image and idea for the older parallelism of image and idea. Reality and referentiality were thus made problematic. Foreign influence was also a factor. George's translation in 1901 of Baudelaire's *Les Fleurs du Mal* (1857; *Flowers of Evil*, 1909) was an important contribution to the German literary scene. Walt Whitman was introduced to the German public in 1868, but the popular edition of his poems appeared only in 1901, translated by Johannes Schlaf (1862-1941). Translations of François Villon and Rimbaud also appeared. Rimbaud's influence was chiefly in the realm of imagery, and his idea that "the Poet becomes a seer through an extended, immense and consistent disordering of all the senses" compelled Georg Trakl (1887-1914) and others

to break with the concept of purely rational continuity. Filippo Tommaso Marinetti and Italian Futurism also encouraged German poets to experiment with linguistic innovations.

"Weltende" ("End of the World"), by Jakob von Hoddis (1887-1942), is typical of the apocalyptic visions manifest in early expressionist poetry; its discontinuities were intended to reflect the dissolution of civilization. After undergoing psychiatric treatment in 1915, von Hoddis was finally committed to a mental institution in the 1920's. Still, his work struck a central nerve of the time. Writing initially in the fashion of Symbolism, von Hoddis found a distinctive character in his apocalyptic projections. His compression of contemporary thought and emotion into signs and iconic formulas typified the grotesque and cynical expressions of the crisis-consciousness of these years. Similarly, Georg Heym's (1887-1912) "Der Gott der Stadt" ("The God of the City") locates the source of eschatological anxiety in the modern metropolis, where Baal rules as the god of material pleasure. The poem "Morgen" ("Morning"), by Alfred Lichtenstein (1889-1914), is yet another example of the expressionist vision of the world on the brink of destruction, where failure to communicate forebodes the ultimate demise of society.

This basically imagist poetry, which privileged *visionary* experience over *visual* experience (*ex*pressionism versus *im*pressionism), resulted in a diversity of individual poetic dictions. The contours of the early years of German expressionism are marked by a sharp disdain for the bourgeois conventions of poetry and by experimentation with new techniques of montage and imagery. After 1914, as the critic and translator Michael Hamburger has written, "its craft of imagery was vulgarized and, at the same time, its mental climate became predominantly political." Behind the outrage and the utterances—sometimes cynical, sometimes grotesque—one senses the urgent longing for the "New Man."

Despair, fear, and the presentiment of catastrophe are the constant themes of Georg Heym's poetry. Heym experienced life as a prison-house and suffered existential ennui, from which even death promised no escape. Melancholy pervades his eschatological visions; elements of Christian belief are transformed, as with Trakl's poetry, into apocalyptic images. His verse is largely paratactic, and this simple poetic syntax is supported by a predominance of iambic pentameters or rhymed tetrameters. As the poems develop, however, along simple syntactic lines, images are superimposed, one over the other, creating a density and tension that belie the surface simplicity of the discourse.

The poetry of Else Lasker-Schüler (1876-1945) is charged with anxiety, *Weltschmerz*, and ennui. Her poems exhibit a longing for a return to the beliefs of the "fathers" and celebrate mythical origins in transparent and yet enigmatic language. Expressionism with Lasker-Schüler becomes a liberation of the imagination. Her poems exude the sense of security peculiar to dreams.

Georg Trakl viewed in his poems an "all too faithful reproduction of a godless, cursed century." Hyper-accentuated guilt and the experience of horror and degeneration inform his poems. Trakl claimed that his work was an "incomplete attempt" to expiate "guilt," both of the individual and of humankind. Nature objectifies his own inner strife and reveals the lack of harmony within Trakl's poetic world. The recurrence of a few central images in his poems has led one critic to speak of Trakl's oeuvre as "one poem." Trakl's experimentation with drugs heightened his apocalyptic visions. Remembrance, dream, and drug-induced intoxication, along with lines from Maurice Maeterlinck and Rimbaud, produce an evocative poetry, a singular accomplishment of German expressionist writing.

Michael Hamburger maintains that Trakl best understood the nature of the crises that he and his generation faced, exploring how it is that modern men and women relate to death and to evil, whereas Heym (to cite a counter-example) avoided analysis of the crisis by projecting onto the landscapes of his text images of death and evil and suggesting their omnipresence and inexorability. Hamburger also notes that a distinction can be made between Heym's consistently dark view of nature and Trakl's more variable imagery. The effect of the latter's, even if only vague and highly mediated, is to uncover the traces of a paradise that is perhaps not forever lost.

Expressionism was the first literary movement in Germany that made the anticlassicist tendency a mass phenomenon, but the disruption of old realities and old poetic conventions created at the same time a new freedom, or at least the perception that freedom (and nov-

elty) were real possibilities. From then on, every poet had to decide what to do with this potential freedom. Since the time of expressionism, there has been no authoritative norm governing the production and reception of poetry which one could manipulate in order to shock and to draw attention to the work of art ("épater les bourgeois") and to the possibility of new experiences. Expressionism broke with all norms and thereby created an utterly new situation (which, significantly, itself soon became an established and "authoritative" convention).

Ernst Stadler (1883-1914), thoroughly versed in the European literary tradition, experienced the early years of the twentieth century less as an end than as a beginning, seeing in them not the disintegration of modern society but the promise of its transformation. Initially, he had difficulty achieving an individual tone and style. Ultimately, after experimenting with Symbolism, he adopted a dithyrambic voice of political activism—what he called a "new joyous, all-embracing world feeling." His verse espouses an ecstatic devotion to fellow human beings, a longing for freedom, and an acceptance of life's abundance. Rather than viewing the city as the locale of degenerate corruption and destruction, Stadler saw it as a cause for celebration, as the facilitator of ecstatic union.

The early radical poems of Johannes R. Becher (1891-1958) struck out at the bourgeois world in which he grew up. Immoderate and shrill, their forceful imagery "spits in the face" of his immediate milieu and social mores; rhetorical exposition disrupts the traditional form of these poems. With the advent of war, he sent out an urgent appeal for a "new syntax," a "catastrophic syntax" which would raze conventions: Word and deed were coterminous for Becher the political activist. Much later (see the discussion of poetry in the East German Poetry in this volume), his voice lost resonance; his visions largely unfulfilled, Becher wrote that "The poem cannot survive without truth."

The dithyrambic prophecies of human redemption and reconciliation found in the work of Franz Werfel (1890-1945) struck a resonant chord among his generation. As the conscience of his time, Werfel, whose poetry sought to transform feelings into music, represents a significant dimension of expressionism. Werfel celebrates the redemptive value of the poetic word and projects an optimism utterly open to the world, while at the same time humbly acknowledging the presence of God. Art and theology thus blend; political activism yields to a "Christian mission" sustained by verbal dynamism and full-toned musicality. Werfel experienced his poems acoustically and was more concerned with emotive charge than with formal consistency.

Gottfried Benn (1886-1956) drew upon Nietzsche's philosophy of art to form his concept of artistry and perspectivism, whereby form becomes the "primary instance," taking precedence over all contextual considerations. Benn's first volume of poetry, *Morgue und andere Gedichte* (1912; morgue and other poems), used montage and calculated scientific jargon mixed with profane colloquialisms to achieve a shocking alienation. Benn confronted the empty prophecies and shabby progress of his time with the final reality of death. Disease, decay, and death are his themes in the early poems; humans are portrayed as helpless creatures—miserable, pitiful, despicable. The volume *Söhne* (1913; sons), the central theme of which is the characteristically expressionistic father-son conflict, reveals a futuristic aspect (again typical of expressionism) with its projection of a "New Man," an artist who will overcome death in ecstatic vision.

Alfred Lichtenstein (1887-1914) applies the grotesque to expose reality as absurd—a juxtaposition of the ridiculously banal and the sublimely tragic. His lyric voice, marked by alienation and the dislocation of images and motifs, is often compared with that of Jakob von Hoddis. Objects in Lichtenstein's poems are always distorted and displaced, always perceived from bizarre, radical, and unsettling perspectives.

The poetry of August Stramm (1874-1915), characterized by a constructivist style, is not easily accessible. A tremendous diversity is evident within his modest oeuvre, and estimations of his work range from "thoroughly Expressionistic" to "pretense and sham." Striving to reunite meaning and sound, Stramm dispenses with tradition in order to allow the individual word to appear in untrammeled isolation. Such deformation effects an unusual concentration of expression. In allowing the word to exercise its own effect, his poems turn programmatically from empirical reality. The resulting abstraction is charged with the currents of eros and chaos.

THE 1920'S THROUGH 1940'S

Following the strong element of subjectivity evident in the poetry of expressionism, the 1920's ushered in a new responsiveness to the factual and the objective. The human being was of such central interest to the poetry of German expressionism that nature as such found little room there. By the mid-1920's, however, nature was once again a central theme of poetry, often perceived as the only medium through which objectivity and precision of detail could be achieved. As Alfred Döblin proclaimed in 1925: "Art is boring, we want facts, facts." In part, this trend encouraged a revival of nature poetry, in German referred to as *naturmagisch*, focusing on the objective details of nature and celebrating their cosmic relevance. The particular dimensions of this cosmic order vary among poets. For Elisabeth Langgässer (1899-1950), for example, the order is largely determined by Christian ideas, while Günther Eich (1907-1972) concentrates on the parameters of language per se.

Both Langgässer and Eich worked in a circle of poets connected with a poetry journal called *Kolonne* (column), whose contributors included Peter Huchel (1903-1981), Hermann Kasack (1896-1966), and Georg von der Vring (1889-1968). In the works of these *naturmagische* poets, visible nature is considered "wondrous"; their realism is thus "magical" to the extent that their poetic diction is a kind of invocation. Lyric expression is thus an act of revelation as well as of interpretation.

Huchel wrote nature poetry typical of the *Kolonne* group. Nature here appears not as a romantic object of poetic longing, for an elegiac tone is mixed with contemporary metaphors of struggle and warfare. Natural processes are depicted in crystalline, precise language that often reveals their underlying violence. Huchel's nature poetry never simply flees into boundless and timeless space; the poet delivers testimony as an eyewitness.

Günther Eich first began writing poetry in the company of the *Kolonne* group. His early nature poems are both subjective and reflective; one can see in them the first steps toward the dispassionate stance and the extreme brevity which characterize his poems after 1945. Contemplating specific, concrete objects, such as the blue feather in "Die Häherfeder" ("Jay Feather"), Eich searches for the deeper reality behind "signs" and "omens." Still, language—at least the cognitive, rational faculties of the mind—proves unyielding, for the "sly answer" lies somewhere just beyond the dimensions of habituated thought and perception. The sudden surprise initiated by the sign is thus a central moment for Eich's work.

The poetry of Oskar Loerke (1884-1941) gives expression to the complete poetic universe. Balancing intellect and emotion, the static and the fluid, Loerke achieves a consistency and sense of order that extends beyond his own subjectivity. Loerke's concise observations result in a spiritualization of nature.

Wilhelm Lehmann's (1882-1968) poetry deals with nature and myth, the dual constituents of meaning and order in his universe. The individual, subjective ego of the poet recedes behind the objectivity of language, which, through precise concentration on objects, attempts to open vistas to that level of order which transcends the individual. The unreal and the dreamlike are also part of Lehmann's poetic world. There is a certain consistency within or behind Lehmann's poetic landscape, but the imagery is not static; instead, it moves as part of a larger cosmic cycle, as the passing of seasons relates to mythical signs.

Depictions of nature and the presence of myths also determine the imagination of Elisabeth Langgässer, but are used as portals through which to recognize the underlying order of Christianity. This sense of order is not always achieved in her poetry, but where it is absent one at least senses that a struggle has taken place to realize it. During the war, Langgässer held on to the "magical" qualities of reality as a vehicle for hope and for redemption in the Christian sense.

Georg Britting (1891-1964) was the poet of the Bavarian landscape. He stressed the idyllic and the bucolic but experienced nature as magical, disclosing it as a sign of a larger cosmic order. This combination of the sensuous and the intellectual makes Britting's poetry representative of the so-called Magical Realism.

The objectivity of another group of poets, including Kurt Tucholsky (1890-1935) and Erich Kästner (1899-1974), was directed toward social conditions. Their poems read like warnings of imminent catastrophe; their efforts to awaken the public rested on a faith in the social efficacy of the poetic word. In the 1920's, this objective poetry was best represented by the song, the broadsheet, and the ballad. The work of Tucholsky falls into this category, as does that of Kästner and Bertolt Brecht (1898-1956).

The epic quality of Brecht's anti-Aristotelian theater figures in his poetry as well: It is distancing, descriptive, and critical rather than sentimental and empathetic. His poems break with the bourgeois tradition of aestheticism, nature, and confessional poetry. His description of these years as a "bad time for poetry" did not imply a rejection of poetry altogether, but rather only a rejection of the conventional forms and traditional subject matter of poetry, which were no longer adequate to the changed historical circumstances. Brecht thus tried to rejuvenate art, but not (like Rilke) exclusively through formal and aesthetic means, although he was sensitive to the historical necessity of formal experimentation. In his verse, Brecht admits to a longing for the conventional elements of lyric poetry, but since "a talk about trees is almost a crime/because it implies silence about so many horrors," he does not indulge this desire. His vocabulary and poetic diction are strict and sober, marked by clear and unsentimental precision.

Countermovements against the new objective tone are visible in the poetry of Rudolf Alexander Schröder (1878-1962) and Hans Carossa (1878-1956), whose conservative political and aesthetic orientation drew them toward the classical heritage in both form and content. They were more interested in the timeless aspects of poetic diction than in the merely topical. With the advent of National Socialism, their posture became a kind of inner emigration, problematic because, if from the point of view of the individual, political abstinence was a kind of mute contradiction to the Hitler regime, as a whole the totalitarian system was able to disenfranchise their voices, if not actually coopt them altogether. Schröder's work represents a consistent effort to preserve the Western cultural heritage. He had a keenly developed sense for form, which he applied to his humanistic religious poetry. Carossa strived in his verse for harmony and moderation; his artistic perspective was that of a pious humanist, his models Goethe and Stifter. Carossa's conservatism and classicism were manipulated to the advantage of Nazi ideology.

THE NAZI REGIME

Poetry written in accordance with the ideology of National Socialism largely eschewed the principles of precise objectivity. Characterized by the frequent use of archaic words and phrases, it shied away from formal innovation. Josef Weinheber (1892-1945) studied the example of the classics and was concerned primarily with questions of form and aesthetics. He became well known with the volume *Adel und Untergang* (1932, 1934; nobility and decline) and was supported at the time of its publication by the Nazis. Some of his later writings reciprocated this support, and toward the end of the war, suffering from severe depression after having acknowledged his misguided affiliation with National Socialism, he took his own life.

The most significant party-line poet was Erwin Guido Kolbenheyer (1878-1962). The stylistic diversity of his work reveals its fundamental confusion. He greeted the rise of National Socialism as a historical necessity, explaining its emergence through digressions on philosophy, politics, history, economics, biology, religion, and culture. The appeal of his work is utterly totalitarian. Party slogans and verse become indistinguishable in his monumental panegyric to the supremacy of the German spirit in all of its manifestations. As a member of the Prussian Academy of Poets and as the recipient of several distinctions, Kolbenheyer was one of the most forceful poetic voices on the literary scene of the Third Reich. Other party-line poets included Hanns Johst (1890-1978) and Gerhard Schumann (1911-1995).

POSTWAR POETRY AND MODERNISM

The situation for poetry after 1945 was at first ambivalent. On one hand, historical conditions presented German writers with an enormous challenge. On the other hand, the devastation, frustration, and overwhelming loss of orientation made a direct confrontation with the immediate past something to be avoided. Poets inherited a language corrupted in the Nazi era, and they recognized the need to replace it with a new idiom.

Under these circumstances, it is not hard to understand that, initially at least, issues of content mattered more than issues of form. The immediate task of assessing the relation of the present to the past rendered aesthetic considerations secondary. Historically, this phase was probably necessary, because postwar German poetry could become credible once again only after having expunged its affiliation with National Socialism. Gradually, however, aesthetic considerations emerged from the background. A critical factor in this development was the influence of foreign literatures, in particular the force of modernism.

One could therefore consider postwar German poetry along two lines: the political-social, and the linguistic-formal. Progressive experimentation in poetry was impeded by the presence of hackneyed lyric phrases and the failure to confront sociopolitical reality. Formal traditionalism and a social isolation resulting in escapism and indifference toward politics coexisted. It is significant that the most important mode of expression for the immediate postwar years was not poetry but narrative prose, above all the short story. Here, authors pursued the necessary confrontation with contemporary sociopolitical issues, while poetry continued its preoccupation with the vestiges of Surrealism, on the one hand, and the tradition of nature poetry, on the other. These coexisting trends can be visualized as four principal constellations dominating the postwar poetry scene. One of these was a political conscience combined with formal traditionalism. A second resided as well within traditional poetic forms but shied away from political commentary. The other two possibilities were a combination of formal modernism with either a political or an apolitical attitude. While such a scheme is helpful, it should be noted that a distinction between "political poetry" and "poetic escapism" can be misleading. One need only read the works of Hans Magnus Enzensberger (born 1929) to realize that these two descriptions are not mutually exclusive.

Poem after poem of the postwar years revealed that poetry in the service of spiritual and ethical rejuvenation could afford little room for new aesthetic solutions. In this regard, the poetics of Gottfried Benn—namely, the rejection of everything contextual in the attempt to approximate the "absolute poem"—appears as a historically necessary step in the development of postwar German poetry. Theodor Adorno (1903-1969) pronounced that, after Auschwitz, it was no longer possible to write a poem, necessitating a reconsideration of the content, the form, and the function of poetry.

Postwar poetry can be said to have begun not in 1945 but in 1948, for it was in the latter year that the first postwar poems of Benn, Eich, Huchel, and Karl Krolow (1915-1999) appeared, not to mention the first volume by Paul Celan (1920-1970). These poets are all identified with the tradition of hermetic poetry, and they represent the primary avenues through which postwar German poetry drew upon the traditions of modernism. In a sense, then, German postwar modernist poetry represents no really new beginning, but instead the realization, continuation, and extension of established modernist movements. The resonance with which modernism appeared on the postwar German literary scene suggested something radically new; the war obscured lines of development reaching back into the 1930's and earlier.

The overwhelming presence of this obscured tradition was best articulated not by a poet but by a scholar. In 1956, Hugo Friedrich published *The Structure of Modern Poetry*, an attempt to reveal the unity of European-American poetry since the mid-nineteenth century through a study of its genesis and its various typologies. His work dominated scholarly discussions of poetry in Germany for some time. Tracking the development of modern poetry from its origins in Stéphane Mallarmé, Friedrich isolated its more significant features, such as the rejection of old taboos, a preoccupation with darkness, an overwhelming sense of isolation and anxiety, and an insistence on the logic of discontinuity. Friedrich's book has much in common with the spirit of postwar German poetry, for he neglects the sociohistorical constituents of modern poetry and highlights instead its phenomenological-existential dimensions. Gottfried Benn epitomizes this orientation among poets.

Karl Krolow once wrote that metaphor determines "the economy of the single poem." Krolow's imagery reveals the development of his poetry as a whole, as well as the shift in poetics which marked the postwar years. Krolow's first metaphors belong to the category of "traditional nature." Later, he moved to more aggressive, expressionistic, and even surrealistic metaphors. More recently, he focused on decidedly intellectual images, gradually relying less and less on rhyme or regular strophes while developing a laconic style.

Ingeborg Bachmann (1926-1973) published her first volume of poems, *Die gestundete Zeit* (borrowed time), in 1953 and immediately established her reputation as a poet with a keen ability to articulate her doubts about the meaning of history and her anticipation of catastrophe, an anxiety shared by many Western European intellectuals during the Cold War. The specific accomplishment of this volume lies in its suggestive interrelation of societal perplexity and individual despair. Several of her poems combine poetic diction and utopian thought, while others suggest their ultimate irreconcilability. In the tension between "superfluous objects" and words "for the lowest classes," Bachmann exposes as illegitimate the traditional mode of poetic speech and in its place suggests the possibility of a documentary, didactic literature.

The difficulty in understanding the poetry of Paul Celan results less from the allusions embedded in his texts than from his concentration on the expressive possibilities and limits of language. This problem is often the central preoccupation of his poems. The "incontrovertible testimony" of the poet can be achieved only after the utmost exertion, where language is pressed to its limits. Celan's poems are always "under way," in search of a partner in conversation.

By the late 1950's, the tradition of nature poetry had run its course. Already during the mid-1950's, West German poetry was becoming more explicitly political. A fundamental problem thus emerged: that of achieving the aesthetic political poem, of articulating both literary and political progressiveness. The new politicized poetry displayed a certain disenchantment with the state of things, preferred sobriety to ceremony, and, in a sense—because of its basic distrust of any "magical powers" residing in the poetic word—depoeticized poetic diction and renounced the traditional notion of "lyrical" by presenting primarily a cerebral appeal.

The successful articulation of both aesthetic and political progressiveness is perhaps best illustrated in the work of Hans Magnus Enzensberger. Initially, Enzensberger relied on Edgar Allan Poe's "Philosophy of Composition" for the theoretical basis of his work but soon incorporated the philosophy of Theodor Adorno. In the 1950's, Enzensberger conceived experimental poetry and social criticism as mutually dependent. The background of his early poetry is the Cold War, the atomic threat, the rearmament of West Germany, and in particular, the economic recovery of the Konrad Adenauer era, a process which Enzenberger viewed as threatening to the integrity of the individual. In the 1960's, Enzensberger turned increasingly toward political writings. He remains impatient with the cheap (commodified) utopias of would-be reformists. A socialist by choice, a skeptic by nature, and a realist through practice of acute observation, Enzensberger always imbued his poetry with his unmistakable mark. The work of Erich Fried (1921-1988) is likewise politically keen. Fried's poetry achieved recognition in the turbulent decade of the 1960's and is noted for its laconic style, coupled with Brechtian techniques of paradox, antithesis, and dialectic reversal.

MID- TO LATE TWENTIETH CENTURY

A significant experimental phase of West German poetry, one which shared a skepticism of traditional metaphoric expression and poetic diction, was concrete poetry, best represented by Eugen Gomringer (born 1925), Franz Mon (born 1926), and Ernst Jandl (born 1925). The term was introduced by Gomringer in analogy to concrete art, and by it he meant to distinguish a linguistically experimental literature which reflected and thematized its own raw material—that is, language. Applying the principles of functionality, clarity, simplicity, communicability, objectivity, and play, concrete poetry sought to reintegrate literature into social life. Using techniques of reduction and permutation, concrete poetry focused on the presentation of language and linguistic elements and not on the representation of reality beyond language. Ultimately, however, the experimentalism of concrete poetry soon rigidified into rather predictable patterns. Challenging (and entertaining) material continues to be written by Ernst Jandl, whose keen wit and linguistic sensitivity inform the foreground of his work. While focusing on the acoustic and optical valences of language, Jandl at the same time recognizes the social implications of his work, for language as the material of his art is also the material of his thought and speech and, as such, material shared by a significant portion of Western society.

In 1965, Walter Höllerer (born 1922) presented a call for the "long poem," understood as an alternative to the then predominant hermetic poem. This reformulation of poetic diction was carried out by Günter Herburger

(born 1932), Rolf Dieter Brinkmann (1940-1975), and Nicolas Born (1937-1979), among others, who advocated a new subjective realism in the 1970's. For Jürgen Theobaldy (born 1944), a significant representative of the youngest poets, the long poem of the late 1960's gave way to the "new poem" of the 1970's, when several younger poets tried to relocate the self, rearticulating the individual as socially and politically relevant. This renewed emphasis on the self becomes most comprehensible when viewed as a reaction to the agitprop poetry of the late 1960's and the disillusionment of the intellectual Left in the early 1970's.

Poets of this New Subjectivity movement flourished throughout the 1970's, and their concern with personal experience and the intricacies of daily life struck a chord with the public. Theobaldy's "Schnee im Büro" (snow at the office) details the daydreams of an office worker for whom the evenings and vacations with his lover barely compensate for his mundane eight-hour workday, during which he feels "imprisoned" and a mere "number."

More women poets saw publication of their works, and gained prominence and attention to their poetry, which often defied categorization and invigorated the poetic scene. Elisabeth Borchers (born 1926) displays an acute awareness for the nuances of language, and the poems of her *Gedichte* (1976; poems) utilize startlingly ironic imagery such as "solid" ruins, and are infused with her personal experience, as in "Das Begräbnis in Bollschweil" (the funeral in Bollschweil). Here, memory fails the poet to compose a proper eulogy, and the death of a close one leaves behind nothing but "small, slow ghosts" scurrying between the mourners. Hilde Domin (born 1912) similarly includes allusions to her personal life in her poetry, which is also concerned with the play of language, and occasionally conjures up Surrealist images and associations. In "Mauern Sortieren" (sorting walls), in her *Gesammelte Gedichte* (1987; collected poems), a look at "textile patterns" in a mail-order catalog reminds the persona of "patterns of walls," which later form the alliterative "Mauern aus Menschenfleisch" (walls of human flesh) to crescendo in the paradoxical coupling of "Mutter/Mauer" (mother/wall) which lies "zwischen Geschwistern/jeder auf seiner Seite/Berlin" (between siblings/each on his own side/Berlin), bringing the poem to a personal conclusion.

The 1980's saw a surprising return to formal poetry, with rhymes and meters replacing the ubiquitous free verse of the preceding two decades. Poets like Karl Krolow returned to rhymed lines, and Ulla Hahn (born 1946) abandoned her earlier, political poetry in exchange for poems following traditionally forms, and quite surprised her readers. Enzensberger and Jandl returned to traditional reflections on the meaning of being, and even love poetry was read by a serious audience again.

On the other hand, the political issues of the decade, most noticeably environmentalism and the squatter movement in some of the larger cities like Hamburg and Berlin, spawned a flurry of poetic activities, often arising out of the alternative scene. Concerns over America's stationing of short-range nuclear missiles in Germany briefly brought back political passions in poetry. In 1989, the momentous changes in the Soviet Union and in Eastern Europe caught quite a few German poets in the West by surprise. By October 3, 1990, before one year had passed after East Germany allowed the breaching of the Berlin Wall in November, 1989, Germany became reunified again. German poets in the West and the East now had to grapple with the challenges brought forth by the reintegration of two quite different societies.

BIBLIOGRAPHY

Allen, Roy F. *German Expressionist Poetry*. Boston: Twayne, 1979. Comprehensive and readable history and criticism of German expressionism. Includes index and bibliography.

Bloom, Harold, ed. *Modern German Poetry*. New York: Chelsea House, 1989. An excellent anthology of authoritative essays by leading academics in the field. Bloom has done an outstanding service collecting these essays which cover many fields of the subject.

Browning, Robert M. *German Poetry: A Critical Anthology*. New York: Appleton-Century-Crofts, 1962. Despite its age, still a standard work, especially for the poetry of the nineteenth century. Quoted in this essay, Browing offers an attractive, readable summary of German poetry up to the middle of the twentieth century from a decisively humanistic perspective free of the jargon of contemporary literary theory.

Bushell, Anthony. *The Emergence of West German Poetry from the Second World War into the Early Postwar Period*. Frankfurt, Germany: Peter Lang, 1989. Exhaustive study of the roots of early poetry in the Federal Republic of Germany. Nicely shows both continuities and radical breaks within the works of postwar poets. Detailed bibliography.

Hanak, Miroslav John. *A Guide to Romantic Poetry in Germany*. New York: Peter Lang, 1987. A good, concise study of the period. Includes bibliographies and index.

Harper, Anthony, and Ives, Margaret C. *Sappho in the Shadows: Essays on the Work of German Women Poets of the Age of Goethe, 1749-1832*. New York: Peter Lang, 2000. Includes translations of the poems into English, and further bibliographical references. Highlights a freshly emerging aspect of German Romanticism from a mostly feminist perspective.

Prawer, Siegbert S. *German Lyric Poetry: A Critical Analysis of Selected Poems from Klopstock to Rilke*: New York; Barnes and Noble, 1965. Still an authoritative, perceptive study with close critical readings of the poems in the style of New Criticism. Prawer's analysis is refreshingly free of jargon and very accessible, representing a good introduction to the topic. The bibliography refers to mostly older works; the reader should also look at more contemporary studies.

Scrase, David. "Dimensions of Reality: West German Poetry of the Seventies." *World Literature Today*, Autumn, 1981. A definitive survey of the literature of the period.

Rolleston, James. *Narratives of Ecstasy: Romantic Temporality in Modern German Poetry*. Detroit: Wayne State University Press, 1987. A detailed and critically informed discussion of Romanticism and its key ideas in nineteenth and twentieth century German poetry by one of the best contemporary academics in the field. Includes index and bibliography.

Schueler, Heinz Juergen. *The German Verse Epic in the Nineteenth and Twentieth Centuries*. The Hague: Martinus Nijhoff, 1967. An older study that still offers a perceptive reading of the tradition of the epic in German literature, and its use by nineteenth and early twentieth century authors.

Vanchena, Lorie A. *Political Poetry in Periodicals and the Shaping of German National Consciousness in the Nineteenth Century.* New York: Peter Lang, 2000. An innovative approach to the subject, with detailed bibliographical references and index. Shows how some poets were quite ardent German Nation- alists, and illustrates how popular periodicals helped disseminate nationalistic ideas among educated citi- zens. Includes one computer optical disc, which re- quires Windows or Macintosh for running.

Richard Spuler,
updated by R. C. Lutz

GERMAN POETRY SINCE REUNIFICATION

The dramatic events leading to the sudden collapse of the socialist regime of East Germany in 1989 came almost as a complete surprise to many German poets in West Germany. By the late 1980's, most poets in the West had come to accept the separation of Germany into two separate states. In spite of an increasing stream of East German poets who were either forced, like Wolf Biermann (born 1936) in 1976, or allowed, like Uwe Kolb (born 1957) in 1987, to leave East Germany, the socialist regime of the German Democratic Republic (GDR) in the East was considered durable. Western poets were locked in their own debate about the sudden rise of traditional form in poetry, for example, and took scant notice of the massive changes in the East.

A year after the reunification of Germany in 1990, the West's Hans Magnus Enzensberger (born 1929) revisited the effects of this surprise in his collection *Zukunftsmusik* (1991; future music) when he wrote:

> Future Music
>
> That what we can't anticipate
> Will teach itself.
>
> It shines, is uncertain, distant.

Here, the poem acknowledges that great changes may actually catch the human poet unawares. Similarly, the negative ending of the poem that the music of the future "isn't there for us,/ never was there,/ is never there,/ is never," articulates the mood of the post-reunification hangover, with rising Western resentment at the cost of the bailout of the East, and Eastern nostalgia for a time when the state guaranteed employment for all, for example. Enzensberger's conclusion that in spite of all the changes, the future is not "for us," the common people, and echoes popular misgivings surfacing in Germany in the early 1990's.

In the years before reunification, many Western poets looked at their East German counterparts who had stayed in the GDR, with a mixture of disdain and indifference, often regarding East German poetry as backward in form and provincial in theme. Yet relatively unbeknownst to the West, East German poets often found themselves at the vanguard of rising popular unrest. Af-

ter reunification, the "underground" poets of the big cities like East Berlin, Leipzig, and Dresden found themselves in a certain vacuum.

Elke Erb (born 1938) had been an influential, nurturing presence for the initially only loosely associated group of young poets residing in the hip Prenzlauer Berg district of East Berlin. In 1991, she published her collection *Winkelzüge: Oder, Nicht vermutete, aufschluss- reiche Verhältnisse* (shady tricks). These poems, which were actually written just before the fall of the Berlin wall, already foreshadow the poet's uncertainty about the future. "The heroine, led by her history . . . so uncertainly/ that she can identify herself neither in the present/ nor the future" stands at a new path. The old (socialist) directives have vanished, "swallowed up by the Earth," and she has to carve her own way without any external spiritual guidance. Erb's *Poet's Corner 3* (1991) hammers home this point of disillusion with the past coupled with apprehension for the future. Here, her poem "Thema verfehlt" (off the topic) calls upon the ghosts of past communist leaders, who appear "like someone without a home/ someone who holds a sail, not his own,/ into the wind, which is not his own." There is a gathering of restless spirits, whose borrowed ideals have failed them in a world not of their own making, and yet the direction for the future is indeterminable.

For the poets of the East, reunification thus brought a moment of pause after the heady days which had seen the toppling of the repressive regime. Erb's friend and protégé Uwe Kolbe (born 1957) expressed a common nostalgia for the days of struggle and togetherness in his volume *Vineta* (1998). The title poem "Vineta" alludes to a mythical Nordic Atlantis, whose greedy inhabitants caused it to sink forever to the bottom of the Baltic Sea. Ironically, Vineta Street is also the terminus of the subway line running through Prenzlauer Berg, where Kolbe lived and worked before leaving for West Germany in 1987. In his poem, Kolbe reflects:

> Do you still remember, back then, when we knew the
>   name, when we
> knew every name, when the chestnuts were talking to
>   us, burst open
> with their horny shoots

The poet laments the passing of the vitality of the poets' gatherings in the backyards of residential apartment buildings graced by old chestnut trees. In reunified Berlin, modernization increasingly gets rid of these old trees, just as the subversive political journals of the East (samizdat literature) died out for lack of state oppression, which had forced them to be self-published in editions of less than one hundred copies. Some of the famous literary journals to which Kolbe and his associates had contributed poetry survived past 1993, but their character had become more mainstream since the flair of the forbidden had vanished with the advent of freedom of speech after reunification.

Ironically, the opening of the archives of the Stasi, East Germany's secret police, revealed that one of the Prenzlauer Berg poets, Sascha Anderson (born 1953), who later emigrated to West Germany, was one of the Stasi spies himself. Thus, the socialist regime had tried to subvert the opposition, but it had collapsed in spite of these secret machinations.

In the West, poets found themselves less forced to embark on a quest to redefine their position in regard to their art and their audience. There, the continuous strong output by women poets like Elisabeth Borchers (born 1926), Karin Kiwus (born 1942), Ulla Hahn (born 1946), and Ursula Krechel (born 1947) has substantially defined much of German postreunification poetry. Karin Kiwus's *Das chinesische Examen* (1992; the Chinese Examination) focuses on the power of personal memories and the various attitudes towards change. Drawing from the author's cultural exchange with East Asia, Kiwus informs the reader that for a certain kind of Chinese examination, the student has to remember and write down everything he or she is thinking about while sitting in a barren room for a set amount of time. Reminiscent of modernism's fascination with the so-called stream-of-consciousness approach to writing, Kiwus's painter-protagonist Soutine, in "Bonjour Monsieur Soutine," remembers a grizzly scene in his studio:

> And the flayed ox in my studio
> Don't you know that I must rescue
> Its flesh from decay, pouring buckets of
> Blood over it

While flesh and the organic is in danger of decay, statues contain at least the promise of timelessness. Yet timelessness invites stasis, and the world changes around its leftover monuments. "Dieser eine Russe" (this one Russian) is a statue commemorating the Soviet Union's victory over Nazi Germany, such as can be found in the Treptow Park Soviet War Memorial in (East) Berlin. Yet while his expression, literally cast in stone, never changes, history has moved on and has obliterated not only the vanquished Nazis but the victorious Soviets as well. What meaning, the poem inquires, can still be attached to these statues?

Symptomatic of the unexpected lasting power of the traditionalist revival in German poetry since the 1980's, Ulla Hahn, who had begun her career as a radical left-wing poet, continued to surprise her audience with a return to more traditional, formal poetry. In 1993, she published *Liebesgedichte* (love poems), but she reminded her readers that her poems were not the lyric equivalent of easy listening when she wrote that "The poem my lady is not eau de cologne . . . no deodorant for the sweaty smell of fear." Invigorating love poetry with a strong feminist bent, Hahn has developed a devoted readership who welcomed *Epikurs Garden* (1995; the garden of Epicurus).

Feminist rebellion is alive and well in Ursula Krechel's collection *Technik des Erwachens* (1992; techniques of awakening). The poet expresses disgust with societal strictures designed to keep women complacent in traditional roles. "Weisheit" (wisdom) exhorts the reader that "in the margin the woman does not become womaner," ironically using the grammatically incorrect comparison "womaner" to bring home her point of the impossibility of being "more of a woman" if content with a marginal role. Similarly, teachers in the employment of the government, with its conservative rules and regulations, are to be mistrusted regardless of their gender, as "Nachlass" (last will) admonishes:

> I do not believe in the entrails of women teachers
> Girded with principles and ordinances

In Krechel's *Verbeugungen vor der Luft* (1999; obeisances to the air), she combines the political with a more formalist interest in the intricacies of language and sound, almost returning to some of the preoccupations of Germany's "concrete poetry" of the 1970's. She insists that her poems are mere "projections," plays on words, yet also attacks conservatism with cynicism and occasional obscenity. Krechel's poem "Goya, späte Jahre" (Goya, later years) plays fast and lose with history, and insists that artistic work has to go on in spite of political pressures. Her nineteenth century Spaniard Goya shouts, "world, stay outside, I'm painting."

Elisabeth Borchers's *Was ist die Antwort?* (1998; what is the answer?) brought a return of a well-regarded poet who had been silent for a while. Most of her poems are very short, but contain strong moral messages, as in her "Wohnungen" (residences): "Everything returns/ And has reached its end."

There is no escape from history, a point especially relevant as Germany still has to live with its Nazi past. If many of Borchers's poems remain somewhat impersonal and distant, the reader is confronted with an author who generally rejects the autobiographical style in search for a larger truth.

In a career which began in the East and by force moved to the West, Helga Novak (born 1935), who was stripped of her East German citizenship in 1966, saw a steady revival of her poetry in the 1990's. Her collection *Silvatica* (1997), was praised for its use of the metaphor of the hunt to comment on womanhood. Here, Novak returns to the Greek myth of the huntress-goddess Artemis, reviving an interest in classical allusions. Her massive collection of a life's worth of poetry, *Solange noch Liebesbriefe eintreffen* (1999; as long as love letters still come in) met with mixed criticism. Her political poems were criticized for a lack of aesthetic achievement, and her moral focus on the underdog was found lacking in sophistication. Yet her power to evoke emotions with her socially engaged poetry was welcomed by many.

Heinz Czechowski (born 1935) is another poet straddling the East and the West. In *Nachtspur* (1993; night track), he gives voice to his despair of having lost his bearings and calling in life, when he writes in "Damals zuletzt" (back then, for the last time):

> Thus I give up
> To search for my lost identity
> It is sufficient to be here
> And to know that one is still here. . . .

Five years later, in *Mein westfälischer Frieden* (1998; my peace of Westphalia), Czechowski alludes to the peace treaty of Westphalia, which ended the devastating Thirty Years' War in 1648, as an allusion to the peace he has made in his life with his move, in 1995, from his native Dresden in the East to Western Germany. While his voice is still full of sorrow, there is a sense that the poet has forgiven history for having disappointed him. It is a time to make peace and enjoy the beauties of the day.

Reunified Germany's renewed weight in international affairs was echoed by the internationalist poems of Joachim Sartorius (born 1946). A prolific collaborator with international visual artists, Sartorius's poetry celebrates a masculine sensuality that unifies the global sphere. In *Der Tisch wird kalt* (1992; the table turns cold), Sartorius imagines world peace to feel like the first breath after ejaculation: "A final joyous breathing . . . so clear a breath as if it journeyed/ around the whole of the world." In *Vakat* (1993; vacant), Sartorius provides poems to Nan Goldin's pictures of deserted brothel and hotel rooms around the world, reveling in a sex worker's joy that "The evening is young/ Money from beauty/ Jingles in the pockets."

Internationalism takes a different turn in the poetry of Gerhard Falkner (born 1951), who continues to remind Germany that, for example, in spite of winning the soccer world championship in 1990, "there are shadows/ abrupt poems" which function "like supreme tribunals" to remind the reader of the powers of words like "Auschwitz" and the evils of the past that continue to cast a shadow on the joyous present.

Instruments of information technology populate the work of Thomas Kling (born 1957), who has dedicated himself to incorporate the language of the new technology, and issued collections like *nacht.sicht.gerät* (1993; night.vision.apparatus), *morsch* (1996; rotten), and *Fernhandel* (1999; long distant trade). Embracing a technocratic, computerized world, he offers love poems that express age-old sentiments in the language of Silicon Valley.

Refocusing on the human body, yet maintaining an almost clinical distance, has become the trademark stance of celebrated poet Durs Grünbein (born 1962). Growing up in East Germany's Dresden, Grünbein developed his craft by pointing out the absurdities of socialist society. After reunification, he continued to dissect the fabric of comfortable lies attempting to hold together postmodern society. His caustic vision of the loneliness of the Internet age strikes a chord with his urban readership. "Apart from the screen, as you can see/ the image of the screen is a nothing" is his verdict on the empty, self-referential nature of cyberspace, in his poem "Ultra Null" (ultra zero) in *Schädelbasislektion* (1991; skull crash course). His *Nach den Satiren* (1999; after the satires) carries his theme of an impending bio-apocalypse further. His witty satires on the new Berlin, which evokes in the brain "something which cries for destruction," and his somewhat stereotypical denunciation of California's body culture have made Grünbein one of Germany's most widely read living poets.

In the decades after the fall of the Berlin Wall, Germany's poets have embraced a broad variety of styles, themes, and forms in their literary attempt to work through the political, social, and intellectual ramifications of reunification. Their vibrant poetry ranges from a vigorous revitalization of old traditions to a keen awareness of the new self in a newly reconfigured country. The urge to express the impact of the Internet society, to envision integration of East and West, and to give a voice to the female perspective has inspired vivid poetry that continues to connect to an interested, wide-ranging audience.

BIBLIOGRAPHY

Berman, Russell. *Cultural Studies and Modern Germany: History, Representation, Nationhood*. Madison: University of Wisconsin Press, 1994. Poetry is discussed in the light of a general interest in cultural studies, encompassing art and the popular. Spotlights topical intellectual concerns in the reunified Germany. Bibliography and index.

Brockmann, Stephen. *Literature and German Reunification*. Cambridge, England: Cambridge University Press, 1999. An excellent study of the interplay of literature and culture. Ample room is given to discuss poetry and poets' roles in the reunified Germany. One of the best books on the subject in English. Bibliography and index.

Donahue, Neil. *Voice and Void: The Poetry of Gerhard Falkner*. Heidelberg, Germany: Winter Press, 1998. Donahue, Falkner's translator into English, places the poet's work in the context of modernist and postmodernist thought and debate in Germany. The final two chapters link Falkner's work to contemporary German poetry in general, with an interesting comparison to Durs Grünbein.

Eigler, Friederike, and Peter Pfeiffer, eds. *Cultural Transformations in the New Germany: American and German Perspectives*. Columbia, S.C.: Camden House, 1993. Contains an interesting essay by Peter Geist on German poetry immediately after reunification. Other essays focus on the Prenzlauer Berg poets of Berlin. Each essay has its own bibliography. Informative in-depth essays.

Grimm, Reinhold, and Irmgard Hunt, eds. *German Twentieth Century Poetry*. New York: Continuum, 2001. A useful anthology providing well-translated texts. Concise introduction. Includes bibliographical references and indexes.

Rolleston, James, ed. *Contemporary German Poetry*. Special issue of *Studies in Twentieth Century Literature* 21, no. 1 (Winter, 1997). An outstanding choice of essays and newly translated poetry. The best English text on many of Germany's contemporary authors. Each essay comes with notes and bibliographies, even though most secondary material quoted is written in German. An comprehensive overview of the subject that combines detailed analysis with broader studies.

R. C. Lutz

GREEK POETRY IN ANTIQUITY

EARLY GREEK POETRY

The earliest Greek poetry was unlettered, oral, and traditional. For centuries before the appearance of the alphabet in the eighth century B.C.E., Greek poets were creating songs, probably in dactylic hexameter, for entertainment, ritual, and religious purposes. Some of these poems were probably short lyrics and others were longer tales about their heroes and gods. Most, if not all, were probably intended for public performance by individuals or by choruses. Especially in longer, narrative poetry, fixed phrases like epithets and formulas were used as mnemonic devices and compositional tools to tell and retell tales through generations.

While the texts of the earliest surviving Greek poetry, the Homeric epics *Iliad* and *Odyssey*, were probably not written down in definitive form until the sixth century B.C.E., the tales on which they are based may have existed in oral form at least by the late second millennium B.C.E. While the very existence of their author is clouded in a controversy called "the Homeric question," few challenge today "Homer's" debt to a long chain of earlier poets who helped establish tales about a ten-year-long war between the Greeks and the Trojans and the troublesome homecomings of the Greeks after their victory. Homer's *Iliad* deals only with the tenth year of the war and the consequences of the quarrel between the Greek leader Agamemnon and his chief warrior Achilles. The *Odyssey* focuses on the ten-year wanderings of the Greek warrior Odysseus following the war and the troubles he faced when he finally arrived home in Ithaca. Many other tales surrounding these events were part of a tradition called Trojan cycle. Some were concerned with the events leading up to the war or with the nine years of conflict prior to the *Iliad*, others with events following the *Iliad* and with the end of the war. There were also other homecoming tales besides that of Odysseus, and even stories about other wars, such as that known as the Seven Against Thebes, but none of these survives except in fragments.

Also surviving under Homer's name, but probably written by a number of anonymous authors, are the Homeric hymns, a collection of thirty-three songs to individual Greek deities. Thought to have been sung as preludes or introductions, especially for performances of Greek epics, these hymns use the dactylic hexameter and vocabulary of Homer and usually include the traditional parts of a prayer, with an invocation, sanction, and entreaty to the god. A few of these hymns, specifically those to Demeter (2), Apollo (3), Hermes (4), Aphrodite (6), and Dionysus (7), incorporate significant narrative sections telling stories about these deities.

THE ARCHAIC PERIOD

In his two surviving poems *Theogonia* (c. 700 B.C.E.; *Theogony*, 1728) and *Erga kai Emerai* (c. 700 B.C.E.; *Works and Days*, 1618), the poet Hesiod also uses the hexameter and language of Homer but in an often personal, didactic tone. In *Theogony* Hesiod focuses on the birth of the gods and the violent succession of divine rulers from Uranus to Cronus to Zeus. *Works and Days*, usually described as a farming manual, is rather a statement of Hesiod's own philosophy and worldview. In his personal poetic voice he celebrates the justice of Zeus, describes the evils of women, and reflects upon his own divine calling to be a poet. Other well-known myths told by Hesiod in these poems include the stories of the Titan Prometheus and of the first woman, Pandora.

Hesiod's poetry marks a transition in the seventh century B.C.E. from the traditional, oral poetry represented by the surviving Homeric epics to shorter, more individualized verse that often uses this traditional language in novel ways. In most cases, this poetry, like the Homeric epics, continues to be composed for performance rather than for publication. Most of this poetry survives only in short fragments culled from references in later works or found on scraps of Egyptian papyri. These poems are written in a variety of meters, styles, and dialects. Some, like elegy, use the traditional dactylic hexameter, but accompanied by a second line, in dactylic pentameter, to form an elegiac couplet. It is possible that the origin of the word "elegy" is derived from a non-Greek word for flute. This poetry was, in fact, often sung to the accompaniment of such musical instruments. Occasionally the Greeks themselves mistakenly assumed that the word meant "lament," but such poetry is especially associated with commemoration of the dead only in the Greek tombstone inscription tradition. Ancient Greek poems written in a variety of other meters are usually called "lyric," after a stringed-instrument the Greeks called the lyre. A third important type of personal verse used an iambic meter especially for invective or poetry of personal attack. While metrical form and theme are closely associated in Greek poetry, such metrical features are rarely discernible in English translation. All of these varied verse forms, however, share an emphasis on personal self-expression, reflection, and, especially, the use of the first person.

One of the earliest surviving poets of elegiac and iambic was Archilochus of Paros (c. 680-c. 640 B.C.E.). In a famous fragment about losing his shield in battle, Archilochus used Homeric vocabulary to question traditional Greek military values and priorities, which demanded that a warrior return either with his shield or on it. Archilochus argued that saving his life and being able to fight again for his country were more important than the shield, which he lost. Much of Archilochus's poetry seems to have centered on his relationship with a woman named Neobule. When her father Lycambes suddenly broke off Archilochus's engagement to his daughter, the poet turned to violent, abusive invective against both father and daughter, who are said to have committed suicide as a result of Archilochus's attacks. An alternative interpretation of this invective poetry, usually written in a metric form called iambic, is that such poetry is actually ritualistic rather than personal and autobiographical. The relationship between the name Lycambes and iambic argues strongly in favor of such a ritualistic context for Archilochus' poetry.

Greatly influenced by Archilochus' invective iambic poetry was Semonides of Amorgos (fl. late seventh century B.C.E.). His most significant surviving fragment is a strongly misogynistic iambic poem in which various animals are compared to different types of women. Only the industrious woman, compared to a bee, earns the poet's approval.

Sappho and Alcaeus, both of Lesbos, wrote their lyric poetry in the early sixth century B.C.E. Both experimented with metric forms and created meters named after them. Both suffered exile from their homeland due to political upheavals on the island during the reigns of the tyrants Myrsilus and Pittacus. Alcaeus replied to Archil-

ochus by losing his shield in one of his poems. In addition to contemporary politics, the poet wrote drinking songs, love songs, and hymns. He is best known as the possible inventor of the "ship of state" metaphor. Sappho is one of the few female voices in ancient Greece. Her poetry deals occasionally with politics and myth, but especially focuses on apparently autobiographical themes, especially her love for other women. Her only complete poem is probably her "Prayer to Aphrodite," which transforms the public prayer poem into a description of a personal relationship with the goddess.

The lyric poet Alcman worked in Sparta in the late seventh century B.C.E. and wrote hymns to the gods, love poems, and especially songs for choruses of young women. These choral songs, probably sung at festivals and perhaps in competition, may have used a central mythic narrative to make a moral point.

Anacreon of Teos (c. 571–c. 490 B.C.E.) is especially associated with the courts of the tyrants Polycrates of Samos and Hipparchus of Athens, for whom he wrote joyful and reflective lyrics about love, drinking songs, and occasional elegiacs. While his surviving fragments occasionally refer to the political turmoil of his day, Anacreon's poems seem to seek escape from such concerns in the sophisticated pleasures of the aristocratic symposium or drinking party.

One of the few archaic elegists whose work survives substantially in manuscript is Theognis of Megara (fl. 544–541 B.C.E.). Theognis's poetry is addressed to a friend named Cyrnus and includes drinking and love songs. Theognis's emphatic aristocratic bias is revealed in his strong feelings about politics and morality.

The poetry of other early elegists reflects the frequent warfare of the period as Ionian Greeks struggled to resist the great empires of the East and generations of Spartans fought on the Greek mainland against their neighbors the Messinians. Poets like Tyrtaeus of Sparta (fl. seventh century B.C.E.), Callinus of Ephesus (fl. early seventy century B.C.E.) and Mimnermus of Colophon (fl. 632–29 B.C.E.) wrote about war and exhorted their contemporaries to fight on behalf of their cities. Occasionally Mimnermus turned to more personal themes, such as the difficulties of old age.

Archaic Greek poetry was also used for philosophic and political purposes. The pre-Socratic philosopher

Xenophanes of Colophon (fl. late sixth century B.C.E.) wrote in a variety of poetic forms, including epic, elegy, and satirical iambics and hexameters. His surviving fragments challenged many of the assumptions and norms of Greek society, including the anthropomorphism of the Greek gods and the honors awarded to Greek athletes. The Athenian statesman Solon (fl. early sixth century) used poetry to justify the political and economic reforms he instituted as archon in 594-593 B.C.E.

THE CLASSICAL PERIOD

The fifth century B.C.E. saw the finest flowering of poetry in Greece. The tragedies of Aeschylus, Sophocles, and Euripides and the comedies of Aristophanes are the best known and most influential products of this period, associated with the civic life of Athens, which grew to be the center of Greek culture of the time. Practitioners from many places in the Greek-speaking world, however, helped to raise poetry to a high state in the century that saw the defeat of Persia and the downfall of democratic Athens. Pindar's brilliant choral odes celebrating victors in the national games, important philosophical verse, elaborate dithyrambic poetry—all had their roots and flourished outside Athens. Although the achievement of Athenian dramatists came to overshadow the other poetry of the period, a true appreciation of their highly synthetic art form requires a sense of the fifth century poetic "climate"; only then can what is innovative and fresh in the drama of the period be contrasted with that which continues Archaic trends.

POPULAR POETRY AND SKOLIA

The parties, or symposia, at which Greek men gathered regularly to discuss the latest politics, drink, and talk on all topics, from the trivial to the philosophical, often featured informal songs as well. Plato's dialogue *Symposium* (c. 384 B.C.E.) offers a look at the procedures on such occasions: Each member of the party must contribute a performance, poetic or rhetorical. An antiquarian writer of the second century C.E., Athenaeus, preserved about twenty-five examples of various types of songs that might be sung on such occasions. The topics that most occupied the minds of the Athenian leisure class are in kernel form here. It should be remembered that this class gave Athens its preeminent writers and

that, in general, Greek literature was the creation of an elite. The audience for the public poetry of the drama, however, was mixed in a democratic fashion because admission was provided by the city-state; on other occasions, the poetry was performed at free festivals.

What might a fifth century Greek have sung, then, at an evening's entertainment? He might well have chosen a poem by a sixth century lyric poet such as Anacreon or Alcaeus, a poem celebrating the joys of drinking and sporting among friends. For variety, the participants in a symposium, especially those with good voices, might have invented new words for a traditional tune, or they might have had verse-capping contests (like those of Japanese party poetry, *renga*) in which the song would zigzag among the guests. Both of these latter sorts of entertainment seem to have fallen under the heading of *skolia* (crooked songs).

Politics, love, social life, and light philosophy were the most popular subjects of *skolia*. In these occasional poems, several points of interest appear. First, the political allusions, although they may refer to figures of a century earlier, concern the present day: The continuing call for *isonomia* (equal portioning) was a democratic slogan in Athens, so that this *skolion* was no doubt sung among members of the political clubs opposed to aristocrats. Again, the songs reveal glimpses of alternative myths (also a powerful political weapon in Greek culture): Nowhere in the tragedy of the *Iliad*, for example, is it hinted that Achilles will survive death at the hands of the Trojans, but a *skolion* on this theme has a different version. One is reminded that popular Greek culture knew hundreds of myths and bits of lore, many more than have survived, all of which provided an essential background to an understanding by Athenians of Greek tragedy, where some dramatists used alternative versions for the sake of making dramatic points. Thus, the *skolia* serve as reminders of the bulk of fifth century Greek poetry, which has been lost to later generations.

Tragedy also deals with the ethical values of the group, as represented by the *polis* (city-state), and here also, popular poetry can offer insights, providing evidence for a view of life that might have been held by many Athenians in the audience of a dramatic performance. What is a crisis, in ancient Greek terms? Does it resemble anything so terrible as the fates of tragic heroes? One might revise the answer to these questions on reading in a *skolion* that "for a mortal, health is the first best thing; second, fine looks; third, honest wealth; and fourth—to be among friends and be young." These are far from the heroic virtues that many critics take tragedy as teaching.

The friends (*philoi*) mentioned above indicate that in the fifth century, the ethics of an earlier age had not died out. The bulk of extant verse from the Archaic period was meant for performance before friends and directed toward the consolidation of the group which constituted the audience. Such friend groups still determined the course of politics and social life in Greece at a later stage. The fifth century songs continue this emphasis on knowing who one's friends are (although they fail to mention the usual Archaic converse of the statement—that one should hate one's enemies). One poem expresses the wish to open up and look inside the heart of a man in order "to consider, by his guileless mind, whether a man is dear [*philos*]"; other verses call on companions to "drink with me, be young with me, with me love and wear festive crowns; go mad when I'm out of my mind, and be sober when I am."

Finally, a short poem warns, in the manner of earlier didactic poetry: "Friend, a scorpion's under every rock; make sure that he doesn't strike you. All treachery goes with what is hidden." This constant urge to bring out into the light the hidden spaces of the heart—among friends at least—is at the root of Athenian drama, it might be said; tragedy, the highest art form of Greece, is the bringing forth in public (where the friends are those of the city/audience) what is hidden in the souls of enigmatic heroes such as Ajax and Oedipus, so that the public can learn. Although the genres differ widely in scale and occasion, they share a common ideology and a goal of group consolidation.

ELEGIAC POETRY

The historic events of the fifth century B.C.E. brought new demands for such social cohesion as poetry could offer. In the early part of the century, the Greek city-states banded together under the lead of Sparta and Athens to defeat the might of the Persians, first in 490 B.C.E., then in a more protracted struggle ending in 480 or 479 B.C.E. with Greek victories at Salamis and Plataea. This surprising outcome ushered in an era of self-confidence and inspired serious high art that attempted to understand the world system anew: What kind of virtue did Greece have that it could win against such odds? The drama of Aeschylus (525-456 B.C.E.), which attempted to reconcile cosmic problems by pointing to the example of Athens's institutions, is but one indication of this trend. Aeschylus also wrote the only surviving Greek tragedy that deals with a historical rather than a mythic event: His *Persae* (*Persians*), produced in 472 B.C.E., only eight years after the Athenian victory at Salamis, pictures that battle as the inevitable result of the clash between Athenian piety and godless Persian arrogance.

As always in Greece, poetry and politics mixed. Many battles of the Persian War were commemorated shortly after they occurred, as cities paid poets to honor those who had fallen. For this purpose, the type of verse used was an old form called elegiac, dating at least to the seventh century B.C.E. and consisting of couplets in the form of a dactylic hexameter followed by a dactylic pentameter. Elegy had long been used for consolatory or lament poems, but it was also a vehicle for light verse, as examples by Archilochus show, and for instructional poetry, as in the work of Theognis of Megara, in the sixth century B.C.E. The examples of the genre in the fifth century B.C.E. are mainly serious in tone, with a laconic expressiveness that arises from the contrast between the longer first line and the pungent, short second line of the couplet.

Simonides of Ceos (556-468 B.C.E.) is credited with the best epitaphs written for Persian War heroes. A poet with a wide reputation in his time for both choral and elegiac verse, his is the famous inscription for three hundred Spartan dead at Thermopylae: "Friend, to the Spartans report that here, obedient to their words, we repose." Poignant brevity and meaningful understatement are the mark of Simonides' craft; to the memory of the entire Greek force buried at Thermopylae were inscribed his words: "Here, once, fought against three hundred thousand, four thousand from the Peloponnese." For a contingent of sailors who died in the last naval battle of the war, he wrote: "Friend, once we lived in the town that had good harbors—Corinth; now the island of Ajax holds us—Salamis." When read in bulk, this sort of elegiac verse, most often the work of anonymous poets, offers glimpses of Greek feeling on the heroic, on death, and on the afterlife, in an unvarnished manner. Those who died in battle were often given the status of "hero"—a word usually indicating a revered warrior of the distant past. Tragedy looks back to the Trojan War era for its heroes and makes them contemporary with the Athenian fifth century; just so, elegiac verse enshrines contemporary heroes in the tradition of the past, so that there is recompense for their having died—the granting of fame through poetry.

Paradoxically, the complex art form of tragedy is most successful when it attains the elegant simplicity of sentiment and expression characteristic of such epitaphs. Aeschylus and Sophocles are known to have written some elegiac verse, and it perhaps benefited their art. At any rate, this is another instance of the influence of the "poetic climate": A Greek audience, imbued with the spirit of inscriptional verse encountered daily, would be properly primed to appreciate the clarity and seriousness of tragic drama, the convention that left the worst out of view (murder, for example, which was never displayed on stage). Sepulchral verse hardly mentions the fact of dying but renders its significance. Finally, the premise of the epitaphs—that the dead live or are speaking to passersby—illuminates central assumptions that underlie tragedy: One must reenact the hero's sufferings onstage because heroes still "live," at least in annual cult observances. Indeed, so many Greek tragedies actually deal with the death or burial of the hero and so much detail is accorded to the burial site in the plays—as in Aeschylus's *Choēphoroi* (458 B.C.E.; *Libation Bearers*), for example—that it has been suggested that tragedy grew out of the religious act of hero worship, a ritual process which took place at tombs throughout Greece. Thus, the connections between epitaph and tragedy may go deeper than an affinity of tone.

PHILOSOPHY: SIMONIDES, PARMENIDES, AND EMPEDOCLES

Greek tragedy is philosophical poetry; both in the choruses and in the speeches of actors, man's fate, his relation to the gods and to other men in the *polis*, continually occupies the minds of the tragedians. How does one reconcile God and man? What takes precedence, the family or the city? These and other questions force Greek tragedy to become thoughtful, wide-spirited, and therefore universal.

Philosophy in poetic form, however, was by no means confined to tragedy. Both the popular poetry of the symposium and the laconic art of tombstone verse reveal a particular Greek fascination with the large questions of life. Choral poetry (to be discussed below) also traditionally is interwoven with philosophical statements in the form of "gnomes"—pithy moral statements such as that by Alcman (seventh century B.C.E.): "From the gods comes retribution."

Simonides, whose elegiac poetry is mentioned above, was much admired in the fifth century for verse that attempted to deal with ethical questions. His poetry, which explores and expands on common gnomic statements, might well be labeled "philosophical." His poem in praise of the Thessalian aristocrat Scopas seems to have been particularly well known, so much so that Plato, in his philosophical dialogue *Prōtagoras* (fourth century B.C.E.), could represent his master Socrates and other intellectuals as alluding to Simonides' poem as though each knew the verses by heart. "For a man to become truly good, shaped four-square and blameless in foot, hand and mind, is hard," wrote the poet. Like a philosopher, he proceeds to take issue with earlier formulations: He voices disagreement with the saying of the wise man Pittacus, that "It is difficult for a man to be good." It is noteworthy that the professional philosopher Protagoras, in Plato's dialogue, treats Simonides as an equal and begins to argue that the poet was inconsistent in preferring his own statement to that of Pittacus. The correct explanation must be that Simonides intentionally contrasted his verb use (to *become* good) with his predecessor's (to *be* good), for, as the poet goes on to say, "it is hard for one to avoid being *bad* if unfightable chance overcomes him." Only a god can choose to *be* good, while man must evolve from a given lot determined by the divine: He can *become* good, not *be* good. Simonides concludes that the most one can hope for is not to do shameful things willingly—"even the gods do not contest coercion."

The poem is cast in an Archaic fashion, with the poet arguing that one side is to be praised, another blamed, as

Archilochus and Alcman did two centuries earlier when the existence of an oral culture made the meting out of proper reputation the primary task of the poet. Simonides, therefore, finds fault with Pittacus; he praises those who act ethically. Moreover, the entire composition is framed as a praise poem to Simonides' patron, in a centuries-old genre. Finally, the poem treats themes with a long history in Greek lyric and epic: The idea of being good in diverse activities is found in the *Iliad*, and the notion that fate and the gods are "unfightable" (*amēkhanos*) is a key theme from the seventh century on. What, then, is new about Simonides' poem?

Surely to devote an entire poem to gnomic morality, rather than using these statements as asides, is innovative, but also fresh is the fashion in which Simonides attempts to make precise linguistic revisions in the statements of his predecessors. The art of "correct speaking" was actually a discipline practiced by the word-conscious members of the Sophistic movement, the most important intellectual movement in fifth century Greece. The Sophists (some of whom figure in the dialogue of Plato discussing this poem) claimed to be able to teach anything, for a fee, including how to become virtuous. Tragedy, politics, history, and rhetoric were to feel the effects of the Sophists' teachings, but it was primarily poetry which became the battleground of old and new in Greek culture, for, even into the early fifth century, poets laid claim to practice the highest form of wisdom (*sophia*) and to be called wise. With the coming of Sophistic philosophy, poets faced a challenge for the title. Simonides, accepted as *sophos* (wise) by both poets and philosophers, represents the coming trend of intellectualizing poetry; although he clung to established poetic forms, he extended the limits of poetry in attempting to make it do the work of analytical thought.

The fusion of traditional forms with startlingly new content also characterized the work of two fifth century pre-Socratic poets, Parmenides of Elea (writing about 490 B.C.E.) and Empedocles of Acragas (active in mid-century). Both were from the colonies of Magna Graecia (southern Italy and Sicily), and both sought, in different ways, to solve the problem that preoccupied Simonides in the poem on virtue: the conflict between being and becoming. Some critics might object to a consideration of their writings as poetry, because it is clear that the pre-Socratic poets were interested mainly in argument rather than poetic form. Yet they had good precedents if they had wanted to write prose philosophy; that they chose verse is important to understanding fifth century poetry as a whole. It is another indication of the seriousness attached to poetic craft and marks the difference in social structure which in ancient Greece allowed poets to be regarded as serious thinkers. There are further implications in their choice of verse rather than prose. Using epic meter, the two philosophers immediately signaled their connection with the oldest Greek literary tradition (and it must be remembered that Homer, too, was often treated as a philosopher).

Parmenides, in fact, often recalls by his diction several passages in the *Odyssey* (c. 800 B.C.E.) as he describes in his preface to the poem "The Way of Truth" his own journey toward enlightenment. Like Odysseus, he poses as the "knowing man" who is carried through many towns by the influence of a goddess (unnamed here; compare Athena in the *Odyssey*) until he reaches the gates of Night and Day. There the goddess promises that he will learn "the unshaken heart of rounded truth" as well as the untrustworthy opinions of men. For Parmenides, then, the *Odyssey* is a model of plot (featuring, as it does, a return to the land of light and the living) as well as of diction, but the truth, as Parmenides has it, is the opposite of Homer's notion and is, in fact, an enemy of poetry, it seems. Homer takes the world as it appears, describing it in shining epithets; Parmenides considers sense impressions to be inherently false. Working from a premise that "not-being" is unthinkable, the philosopher denies the void, the existence of divisions in nature, and such phenomena as opposites, which imply change (for example, night and day). The possibility which Simonides holds out to man, that of "becoming," is in Parmenides merely another misperception of helpless humans, based on illusion. Here, then, is a final reason for Parmenides' use of poetry as vehicle: Seeing so clearly, he is on the side of the gods; although his thought seems to undercut the possibility of poetry to express truth, his instinct is to use the voice of authority and tradition. After all, the divine oracles of Delphi were always composed in dactylic hexameter.

Empedocles' two poems of several thousand lines each, *Peri physeōs* (fifth century B.C.E., *On Nature*, 1908) and *Katharmoi* (fifth century B.C.E., *Purifications*, 1908), remind one at every turn of Homeric epic, but once again the insistent logical argumentation bears the mark of the fifth century intellect. One example from the more completely preserved nature poem will suffice to point out the gulf between the philosopher and the epic poet. In explaining how he believes respiration works, Empedocles introduces a simile much in Homer's lengthy manner. The blood and air regularly interchange through the pores, pushing one another, he explains,

> just as when a girl plays with a *klepsydria* [water clock] of gleaming brass. When she puts the mouth of the pipe against her shapely hand . . . no liquid enters the vessel, but the bulk of air within holds it back until she uncovers the dense stream.

The close observation of everyday scenes is a virtue of Homeric poetry, one which may have helped later Greek poetry by developing a language for seeing things, but never does Homer go this far or use description thus for its own "scientific" ends.

Yet Empedocles rightly uses poetry for his vehicle of expression. His system, a refinement of Parmenides', explains change and motion within Being as caused by the constant rearrangement of four eternal elements; this, in turn, is effected by the actions of Strife and Love. By employing the key words of the *Iliad* (which is about strife between a soldier and his chief, resolved through the love of the soldier's companion), Empedocles defines the phenomenal world as a grand Homeric struggle.

DITHYRAMBIC POETRY

Parmenides and Empedocles represent one extreme in fifth century poetry—its highly intellectual strain. A Greek audience, for whom the Delphic maxim "nothing in excess" was usually an unattained ideal, could find a counterbalance in another extreme form of poetry—dithyramb. This highly emotive art form, thought to have begun with worship of the revel god Dionysus (patron of poets), remains important for students of Greek literature because, according to Aristotle, the genre gave birth to tragedy. In fact, at the annual Dionysian festivals of Athens, at which tragedy and comedy were performed in the fifth century, dithyrambic competitions still had a

place of honor, and huge choirs strove to win singing prizes. During the course of the century, dithyramb declined as a serious form as its offspring tragedy reached its zenith, so that, near the end of the century, the comic poet Aristophanes could poke fun at the dithyrambists as either effeminate or crazy. He parodied their art in songs such as this one from *Ornithes* (414 B.C.E.; *The Birds*): "Thou author of Aitna, Father/ At whose dire doom do foregather/ All the high hierarchs—Och! wad, thy nod, some giftie/ gi'e me: I don't care what, just a token of your regard." Seeking to compete with the tragedians, the dithyrambists merely produced a stiff and highly mannered art.

Earlier fifth century dithyramb, however, must have retained some of the vigor that had led, in distant times, to the creation of tragic poetry. It had dialogue, used episodes from myth, and, most important, often divided portions between a chorus and a chorus leader. This led to the existence of similar features in tragedy, which was still performed for the Dionysian religious rites in the fifth century. Some idea of the state of dithyrambic art at mid-century can be gained from the poems of Bacchylides, the nephew of Simonides, who excelled in the genre. A poem of his on the Athenian hero Theseus's encounter with Minos of Crete employs an unusual meter, with many short syllables in succession, to create an atmosphere of excitement. One episode in the mythical visit is focused on Minos's challenge to Theseus to prove that he is the son of Poseidon, god of the sea, by diving to recover a sunken ring. Direct speech enlivens the narrative, giving it an epic tone, while newly coined compound adjectives distance the poem from Homeric epic. Perhaps the most original feature of the work is Bacchylides' incorporation of a dramatic audience within the poem in the form of the group of fourteen youths whom Theseus is bringing as a tribute to Minos. They tremble in fear at their leader's dive and shout in joy as he returns from undersea. It is not difficult to see how dithyrambic art that had attained this stage earlier—using a chorus to sing *about* a chorus in myth—could have led to the beginnings of drama. Bacchylides himself, in fact, wrote other dithyrambs entirely in dialogue form, which could easily be acted. The main nontragic element in the poems is not in their outward form but in the particular selection of mythic moment. Rather than centering his compositions on the life-or-death crises of the hero, enlarging the drama by speeches in the mouths of main actors, Bacchylides picks small details in heroic life stories to dramatize. It is miniature art, in contrast to the large-scale Athenian drama, anticipating the Alexandrian Greek art of the *epyllion* (little epic) of the third century B.C.E.

VICTORY ODES

Bacchylides had a nearly contemporary rival, the Boeotian poet Pindar (c. 518-c. 438 B.C.E.), who competed for patronage from great aristocratic families all over Greece by writing dithyrambs, maiden songs, praise poems, and, most important, odes to commemorate the victories of youths at the four national games. Competitions were held in events ranging from boxing to flute playing, and victors, although rewarded only with crowns of leaves, gained instant reputations all over the Greek world. Like much Greek poetry, victory odes were performed at religious occasions, since the games were sacrosanct (even warring states suspended hostilities to attend) and were thought to have been instituted by heroes at sites sacred to particular gods. In Pindar's words, the ode itself was "repayment" for the agony of the athlete in winning. That agony (from the Greek *agon*, meaning "contest") was in Greek terms itself a repayment for the similar trials of the distant hero: Because heroes suffered, carrying out martial or civilizing acts, the athlete, representing the community, did likewise in memory of his predecessors. This complex set of ideas underlies tragedy also, because there are indications that in some city-states, dramas were staged to reenact the sufferings of a god or hero. Like the dithyramb, odes coexisted with tragedy and served a functional purpose on the local level. An athlete could be accompanied home from the games by a poet paid to sing his praises, or spontaneous odes might be performed on the site of the victory itself, at the crowning ceremonies in Olympia, for example. Here again, it is important to note the way in which Greek poetry associates the contemporary in all its homely detail with the heroic past.

A good example is provided by one of the surviving forty-five odes, written for a victor from Pindar's favorite city-state, Aegina. Phylakidas had won the *pan-cratium* event at the Isthmian games in Corinth around 480 B.C.E. In his ode, Pindar combines the three main elements of choral poetry: mention of the specifics of the occasion, myth, and transitional gnomic statements, relating victory to myth. After beginning with an invocation to Theia, divine light, mother of the sun, Pindar immediately shifts his focus to the victor: "In the struggle of the games he has won the glory of his desire." In a fashion characteristic of choral poetry and especially of his own, Pindar then abruptly shifts his attention again, to the lesson which the victor's example illustrates: "Men's valor is judged by their fates, but two things alone look after the sweetest grace of life—if a man fares well and hears his good name spoken. Seek not to become Zeus." The sudden shift to the warning is understandable in the context of the occasion, because success, according to Greek views, tempted the anger and jealousy of the gods. Tragedy continually reinforces the same message by showing the fates of those heroes who sought to become godlike.

After enumerating Phylakidas's past and present victories, the poet proceeds to the victor's homeland, Aegina, and its accomplishments. He praises its wealth of heroes, including the forebears of Achilles. He concludes with a reference to the recent battle of Salamis, where sailors from Aegina had played a large part in gaining the victory. Because Aegina had such heroes in the past, it still produces hero-sailors and hero-athletes, Pindar implies. For the poet, as for Greek poetry in general, the past is continuous with the present and explains it.

HELLENISTIC GREEK POETRY

After the Peloponnesian War and Athens' surrender to Sparta in 404 B.C.E., Greek poetry gradually becomes less public and performative and more scholarly and literary. One exception is comedy, which continued to thrive, especially in Athens, for much of the fourth century and into the third century B.C.E. The only surviving comic writer is the Athenian Menander (c. 342-c. 291 B.C.E.), some of whose work was rediscovered on papyri in modern times. Together with a number of scenes from other plays, his complete *Dyskolos* (*The Curmudgeon*) reveals an emphasis on contemporary, everyday concerns. Unlike the often biting political satire of Aristophanes' Old Comedy, Menander's New Comedy deals with problems with children, spouses, money, and slaves. Like the earlier dramatic tradition, New Comedy is written in a variety of metrical forms, often with musical accompaniment.

The period following the reign of Alexander the Great (336–323 B.C.E.) is marked by a revolution in Greek poetry, which becomes more cosmopolitan, more sophisticated, and more learned as the Greek world expands to include the eastern half of the Mediterranean. The center of this new "Hellenistic" poetry was the Ptolemaic city of Alexandria in Egypt. To this city and its famous library flocked poets from all over the Greek world. Two poets, in particular, define the poetic milieau. Callimachus of Cyrene (c. 305–c. 240 B.C.E.) emphasized short, learned poetry like the aetiological legends he collected in an elegaic poem called *Aetia* ("Causes") while his student and rival Apollonius of Rhodes (fl. third century B.C.E.) used the more traditional epic form in his *Argonautica* about the legendary quest of the Argonauts for the Golden Fleece and the story of the Greek hero Jason and his relationship with the Colchian witch Medea.

Related to the shorter, highly polished poetry of Callimachus are the bucolic or pastoral poems produced by Theocritus of Syracuse (c. 308–c. 260 B.C.E.), Bion of Phlossa (fl. c. 100 B.C.E.), and Moschus of Syracuse (fl. 150 B.C.E.). Probably based upon traditional songs sung by shepherds, usually with flute accompaniment, these more sophisticated Hellenistic poems incorporate singing contests between shepherds, laments, refrains, and stanzaic structures into highly refined, dramatic, and descriptive verse. Occasionally the rural setting is replaced by more urban themes. The iambic mimes of Herodas (fl. third century B.C.E.) share with pastoral poetry an emphasis on the dramatic and the descriptive. Little is known about the author or the context of his work, which may have even been intended for performance, but the surviving seven poems create vivid pictures of various character types, including a bawd, a pimp, a schoolmaster, and a shoemaker.

Another significant use of poetry in the Hellenistic period is for learned, didactic treatises. Aratus of Soli (c. 315–240/239 B.C.E.) produced the *Phaenomena*,

a poem about astronomy which was widely read and imitated for centuries. Nicander of Colophon (fl. second century B.C.E.) used epic hexameters in a variety of poems, including the surviving *Theriaca* (about poisonous snakes and their antidotes) and *Alexipharmaca* (about other poisonous substances and their antidotes).

The Greek lyric tradition, especially the epigram, continued in the Hellenistic period. Some important representatives of the genre in this period are: Asclepiades of Samos (fl. 290 B.C.E.), who introduced the theme of love to the epigram and may have been the first to give Eros (Cupid) wings; Anyte of Tegea (fl. early third century B.C.E.), best known for her tombstone epigrams; Corinna of Tanagra (of uncertain date), whose choral lyrics with a narrative element were probably written for her fellow women; Philodemus of Gadara (c. 110–c. 40/ 35 B.C.E.), an Epicurean philosopher whose highly polished but racy love poems may have influenced the Roman poets Horace and Ovid; and Meleager of Gadara (fl. 100 B.C.E.), a Cynic philosopher noted not only for his lost Menippean satires, in which he mixed prose and poetry, but also for his love epigrams.

The survival of many lyric poems from the Hellenistic period as well as Archaic and Classical periods, is due to Meleager's publication of the first poetic anthology, *Stephanos* (c. 90-80 B.C.E.; *Fifty Poems*, 1890; best known as *Garland*) in which he included outstanding examples from approximately fifty earlier poets, including Archilochus and Anacreon, as well as his own work. Unfortunately, Meleager's *Garland* survives only within anthologies of later date.

THE ROMAN PERIOD AND LATE ANTIQUITY

The Hellenistic Age is usually said to end with the defeat of Anthony and Cleopatra at the Battle of Actium by the Roman Octavian (later, Augustus) in 31 B.C.E. Rome's annexation of Egypt following the death of Cleopatra marked the final stage in the Roman conquest of the eastern Mediterranean in the second and first centuries B.C.E. During the subsequent Roman period, Greek literature in general, and poetry in particular, went into decline.

Several anthologies of Greek lyric and epigram in the tradition of Meleager's *Garland* were made during this period. The most comprehensive of these was probably done by Constantinus Cephalas, a Byzantine official in Constantinople in 917 C.E. Like Meleager's earlier *Garland*, however, Cephalas's anthology survives only in the *Palatine Anthology*, the work of an unknown scholar (or scholars) in the late tenth century C.E. This anthology of approximately thirty-seven hundred epigrams, arranged thematically in fifteen books, includes works from all periods, from the Archaic through the Byzantine. Some of the thematic groupings include *ecphrasis*, or descriptive poems, love poems, dedicatory poems, homosexual love poems, and poems of Christian devotion.

One of the few major pieces of Greek poetry in the Roman period is the *Dionysiaca* of Nonnus of Panopolis in Egypt (fl. fifth century C.E.), an epic in forty-eight books about the god Dionysus, and, especially, his conquest of India.

In 529 C.E., the emperor Justinian ordered the closing of the Academy in Athens. This event effectively marks the end of the ancient Greek world and the beginning of Byzantine history.

BIBLIOGRAPHY

Ford, Andrew. *Homer: The Poetry of the Past*. Ithaca, N.Y.: Cornell University Press, 1992. The Homeric poems are used to define the nature of traditional Greek poetry, especially the Homeric epics, and the role of the oral poet in society. In five chapters, Ford deals, in succession, with the function of traditional poetry as a means to transmit the past, epic poetry as a record of the past known only in full by the Muse, the poet as performer, the relationship between oral song and written text, and a view of ancient poetry as a form of "divine singing." Indexes.

Green, Peter. *Alexander to Actium: The Historical Evolution of the Hellenistic Age*. Berkeley: University of California Press, 1990. Several chapters in this sweeping history of the Greek world—from the death of Alexander the Great in 323 B.C.E. to the victory of Augustus over Anthony and Cleopatra at the Battle of Actium in 31 B.C.E.—deal with Greek poetry. Of particular interest are chapter 11 ("The Poet as Critic"), on Callimachus, Aratus, and Lycophron; chapter 13 ("Armchair Epic"); on Apollonius of Rhodes, and chapter 15 ("Urbanized Pastoralism"), on Theocritus and Herodas. Thirty maps, chronology, four genealogical tables, 217 figures, notes, bibliography, and index.

Hainsworth, John Brian. *The Idea of Epic*. Berkeley: University of California Press, 1991. This genre study surveys the historical progression from the Greek primary, oral epic of Homer through the development of secondary, literary epics, including the Roman historical epic and later medieval and Renaissance forms such as those of Dante and John Milton. Of particular interest to the study of Greek poetry are the initial chapter, on the definition of epic; the second chapter, on heroic poetry, Homer, and other poetry in the Homeric cycle; and the third chapter, on Hellenistic epic, especially the *Argonautica* of Apollonius of Rhodes. Endnotes, general index, and index of passages cited.

Nagy, Gregory. *Poetry as Performance: Homer and Beyond*. Cambridge, Mass.: Harvard University Press, 1996. A prominent scholar of Greek and Homeric poetry traces the development of the Homeric poems from oral performances in the mid-second millennium B.C.E. to the composition of written texts of the *Iliad* and the *Odyssey*. Nagy describes a process that assumes not a single, original text, but rather a "multitext" or series of coexisting oral variants. Includes significant observations on the composition of lyric poetry such as that of Sappho. Preface, bibliography, and index.

Taplin, Oliver, ed. *Literature in the Greek and Roman Worlds: A New Perspective*. Oxford: Oxford University Press, 2000. This collection of seventeen essays by twelve classical scholars is arranged chronologically, beginning with Homer and ending with the culture wars of the second century C.E. and beyond. The authors offer a special focus on audiences and the way that this literature was received by its readers and spectators. Special attention is given to Greek poetry in the essays on Homer, Archaic Greek poetry, Greek literature after the classical period, and Greek literature in the Roman period. Includes eleven maps, forty illustrations, a timeline of chapters, a detailed chronology, a bibliography, and an index.

Toohey, Peter. *Reading Epic: An Introduction to the Ancient Narratives*. London: Routledge, 1992. The first four chapters of this survey of the epic genre in ancient Greece and Rome are of special interest to the study of Greek poetry. In chapter 1, Toohey offers a definition of the genre with special focus on the characteristics of oral epic. In the following three chapters, detailed synopses of the *Iliad* and *Odyssey* of Homer and the *Argonautica* of Apollonius of Rhodes are accompanied by brief discussions of background material. Introduction, bibliography, and index.

Richard Peter Martin and Thomas J. Sienkewicz

GREEK POETRY SINCE 1820

EDITORS' NOTE: This essay uses the system of transliteration recommended by the Modern Greek Studies Association, in which stress marks are eliminated. Essays in the *Critical Survey of Poetry* on individual modern Greek poets use a system of transliteration that comports with the most often cataloged forms of titles and names seen in the Library of Congress. Topics indexed in this essay appear in the index to the *Critical Survey* in the latter form to ensure that all page numbers for any given topic will appear in one location.

In an essay written around 1950, the poet George Seferis defined one of the major obstacles to a contemporary understanding of modern Greek poetry:

> The rarest thing in the world is a foreign author . . . who knows Greek. Even now, according to the general perception of foreigners, and perhaps of our own people, classical Greece, Byzantine Greece, and modern Greece are countries which are unrelated and independent. Thus, everyone is limited in his own area of specialization.

As Seferis argued, in order to appreciate the full scope of modern Greek poetry one must see it as "a living art which belongs to a living tradition"—a tradition that extends from ancient Greece through the centuries of the Byzantine Empire to the renaissance of Greek poetry in the twentieth century.

HISTORICAL OVERVIEW AND THE LANGUAGE PROBLEM

Modern Greek poetry has its roots in a vernacular tradition that is unique among European literatures. Throughout its long history, the Byzantine Empire (300-1453) strongly discouraged the development of a written vernacular. Instead, the fledgling nineteenth century nation-state despots imposed the difficult and exclusive language of purist Greek (*katharevousa*, an artificial derivative of the classical Attic dialect of 500 B.C.E.). The language of the common man, demotic Greek, was officially nonexistent.

With the fall of Constantinople in 1453, Byzantine domination gave way to Turkish rule. In addition, the Turks conquered all Greek territories formerly occupied by the Venetian Empire: Rhodes (1522), Crete (1669), and Corfu (1716). For four hundred years (from 1453 to 1821), Greeks lived under the Ottomans. During these centuries of oppression, the demotic poetry of the Greek folk song expressed the yearnings, joys, and laments of a people who had once defined the principles of Western democracy and freedom.

Throughout the early years of the Greek state—and, with few exceptions, for most of the twentieth century—the purist tongue has been the official language of the nation, the language taught in schools and used for all official communications. Finding little of lasting value in this oligarchical tradition, Greek poets for the most part wrote in demotic, laying the foundation for a regeneration in the poetry of their new republic, which manifested itself in the twentieth century, when Greece earned two Nobel Prizes and became a leader in the art of the "poetic word."

FOUNDATIONS OF DEMOTICISM

The first Greek to grapple with the split identity of the Greek language strictly in terms of poetry was Dionysios Solomos, recognized today as the father of modern Greek poetry. The story of his achievements begins in 1822, when Spyridon Trikoupis, a well-known Greek diplomat, historian, and libertarian, paid the young aristocrat a visit at Solomos's birthplace on Zakynthos, one of the Ionian Islands. Trikoupis's self-assigned mission was to find and promote a Greek poet who would speak out for a liberated Greece in the Greek vernacular. The Greek War of Independence from the Ottoman Empire had begun in 1821. Solomos had recently published a slender volume of poetry in Italian (*Rime improvvisate*, 1822), and Trikoupis knew him to be a man with revolutionary sympathies.

During one of their first meetings, Solomos (who demanded that they speak only of poetry) recited his most recent Italian composition. After an uncomfortable silence, the young poet demanded a response. Trikoupis answered by assuring Solomos that he would certainly secure an undisputed position among the great Italian poets. The diplomat added, however, that "the Greek Parnassus has not yet found its Dante." Dante had released Italian literature from the strictures of Latin and had solidified the written foundations of his native Tuscan (the *lingua vulgaris* which eventually became modern Italian) through his bold and expert style. Five centuries later, Solomos struggled against the use of *katharevousa* to rescue the Greek vernacular from possible extinction as a written form of expression. For centuries, Italy and Greece had dragged along the linguistic chains of their ancestry: the one in classical and church Latin, the other in an imitation of the formal (unspoken) dialect of Plato and Demosthenes. Solomos's early exposure to Dante's victory over Latin proved decisive for the future development of a poetic idiom which, for the first time, reached out to the vast majority of Greeks, who neither understood nor had any hope of understanding *katharevousa*, the language of the few.

At the time of Trikoupis's first visit, there was still a significant language barrier for the young poet; although he spoke Greek, his formal education had taken place in Venice (from 1808 to 1818), where he was trained exclusively in Latin and Italian. Solomos's lessons in the Greek vernacular began immediately following his first interview with Trikoupis. His new tutor taught Solomos the rudiments of his native tongue. Trikoupis must have known that this isolated struggle for written expression in a language that all Greeks might understand would meet with formidable opposition. Most of Solomos's contemporaries, in politics as well as literature, scorned demotic speech with its vulgarities and grammatical irregularities. In his only surviving prose work, *Dialogos* (1824), Solomos stated the problem in Greece with simplicity and exasperation: "Our own learned men want us to write a language that is neither spoken now, nor has ever been spoken in any other period, nor shall ever be spoken in the future."

The most important features of demotic Greek for the evolution of a written poetic idiom were its simplicity and widespread usage among Greek-speaking people, in both Greece and the countries of the Hellenic diaspora. Their long oral tradition provided a wellspring of folk songs and ballads, narrative poems, and early mystical church literature.

In the absence of a poetic mentor in his own time, Solomos turned to whatever he could salvage from the demotic past. For his textbooks in Greek prosody, he studied the two narrative masterpieces of the Cretan Renaissance (1600-1669): *Erofili* (c. 1585), by George Chortatsis, and, in particular, *Erotokritos* (1713; *The Erotocritos*, 1929), by Vitzenzos Kornaros, an epic romance of 10,052 lines. These works, in addition to an immense body of demotic folk songs, provided the linguistic guidelines for Solomos's instinctive sense of metrical balance and line structure. Through his poetic genius, the standard fifteen-syllable line of the demotic folk song gained deeper tones and new dimensions of meaning.

Written in 1823, shortly after his first lessons with Trikoupis, *Imnos is tin Eleftherian* (1823; *The Hymn to Liberty*, 1825), a poem of 158 quatrains and Solomos's first work in modern Greek, received immediate international recognition. Among its early admirers were Victor Hugo, Alphonse de Lamartine, and François-Auguste René de Chateaubriand, while Johann Wolfgang von Goethe hailed the young Greek as "the Byron of the East." The first few quatrains of *The Hymn to Liberty* were soon put to music and, after Solomos's death in 1857, were established as the national anthem of the new republic.

Solomos's major accomplishments, however, began to take shape only after 1824. During these years, many of them spent in Corfu, he completed his most sustained and influential poems: "Sack of Psara," "The Dream," *Lambros* (1834, 1859), "The Poisoned Girl," *I yineka tis Zakynthos* (1927, 1944; *The Woman of Zakynthos*, 1982), "The Nun," *O Kritikos* (1859; the Cretan), and "Porphyras." He completed the third sketch of *I eleftheri poliorkimeni* (1859; the free besieged) in 1848. This poem preoccupied him for nearly twenty years and is considered his finest and most mature work. In the last version of *I eleftheri poliorkimeni* one can detect the outline of Solomos's entire poetic development, from the early patriotic eulogies to the adoration of nature that characterized his middle period to the intense mysticism that infused his later works.

It is characteristic if unfortunate that most of the aforementioned poems are, to greater or lesser degrees, fragmentary or incomplete. Nevertheless, poetically as well as linguistically, Solomos achieved his goals, giving the vernacular of his people a firm base of inspiration and poetic invention for generations to follow.

AN ISOLATED STRUGGLE FOR EXPRESSION

In 1824, one year after the appearance of Solomos's *The Hymn to Liberty*, Andreas Kalvos (1792-1869) published ten poems in a volume titled *I Lira* (lyre) and in 1826 another collection of ten poems under the title *Lyrica* (lyrics). These two thin books represent his only contribution to Greek poetry, but of their generation, these twenty poems had an impact on twentieth century Greek poetry second only to that of Solomos. Kalvos, also from Zakynthos, was born six years before Solomos, in 1792. Kalvos's mother was an aristocrat of the Zantiot landed gentry, while his father was a villager who could not adjust to the aristocratic way of life. When Kalvos was only ten years old, his father took him and his younger brother away from their birthplace and their mother to live in Livorno, Italy. Kalvos never saw his mother again. After his father's death in 1812, Kalvos settled for a short time in Florence, where he worked as a private tutor. There, he met Ugo Foscolo, the eminent Italian-Greek poet and libertarian, who hired Kalvos as his personal secretary.

In 1816, Kalvos dedicated his first poem to Napoleon Bonaparte. What is significant about his first composition is not the dedication or the subject matter, but the poet's decision to write in Greek. Kalvos had no formal knowledge of written or spoken Greek; his everyday means of communication was Italian. As a result, the diction of the poem is strained and uneven, mixing elements of demotic, classical, and purist Greek. Still, the poem embodies a potency of expression that foreshadows Kalvos's later achievements.

By 1820, Kalvos had lived in Zakynthos, Italy, Switzerland, and England, where he parted company with Foscolo. Kalvos then returned to Florence to become a member of the Carbonari, the most radical and progressive political force in Italy at the time. He was so active that the Italian government banished him from the country in the year of his return. Having gone back to Geneva, Switzerland, in 1821, Kalvos immediately involved himself with the movement for Greek independence. There, among the Philhellenes, he attempted to coordinate a revival of classical Greek culture with the movement for Greek independence.

By then twenty-nine years old, Kalvos had spent his most impressionable years among devoted if not fanatic European intellectuals. For these French and English Philhellenes, the independence of Greece symbolized a return to the ancient glory that had spawned Western civilization. While in Europe, Kalvos shared this political fervor. In his poetry, however, Greece was to be transformed into a spiritual landscape of magical and mythical elements.

In 1824, while still residing in Geneva, Kalvos issued *Lirika*. It is noteworthy that these ten poems were accompanied by detailed commentary, footnotes, and a lexicon, all in French. It was important to Kalvos that his audience be international and that his poems communicate universal messages, even though they expressed patriotic sentiments in support of the Greek revolution. His second collection, *Lirika*, was published in 1826 in Paris, where he lived for one year before his first return to Greece after twenty-four years of an active but difficult absence. Kalvos went directly to Nafplion, the first capital of the new state and a hotbed of political activity. He was, however, quickly disillusioned and left after a few days. His abrupt departure from Nafplion marked the end of his involvement with the movement for Greek independence. Embittered by the political infighting that he encountered in Nafplion, he also stopped writing poetry.

For the next twenty-six years, Kalvos lived in Corfu (not far from Solomos), where he taught, wrote philosophical articles, and eventually became a professor at the Ionian Academy. Little else of his life there is known except that his temperament was irascible, and his poetic silence was absolute. In 1852, after having been expelled from the Ionian Academy, Kalvos departed once again, this time for Great Britain, where he spent the last years of his life. In this self-imposed exile, he married an Englishwoman, helped her run a girl's school, and translated religious texts into English for the Anglican Church. Kalvos died in 1869 and was buried in Louth, England.

In his poetry, Kalvos attempted to release his exile's longing for a free fatherland. His idealistic vision of Greece was rooted in the austere mythological world of Pindar. Often Kalvos mentions the Olympian gods—not for ornament but to indicate the living presence of a timeless mythic reality. His twenty odes extol the struggle for liberty, the virtue of a heroic death, and similarly exalted themes characteristic of the Romantic poetry that was flooding Europe throughout the early nineteenth century. Kalvos's distinctive genius emerged not from his subject matter but from his unique mode of expression. He confronted the same problem that challenged Solomos—isolation from the mother tongue—but Kalvos's solution was drastically different.

Whereas other poets of this period tried to unite form and romantic emotion in harmony, Kalvos accentuated their opposition. In contrast to the harmonic, lilting flow of Solomos's poems, Kalvos's odes were classically concise and rigid. He utilized a strict verse form (unrhymed stanzas of four seven-syllable lines and a last line of five syllables) modeled after the Pindaric odes. With severe formal simplicity, Kalvos expressed his intense longing for an end to his own exile.

Although Kalvos had a thorough knowledge of classical Greek, the vernacular was a foreign language to him. His twenty poems are studded with words and phrases borrowed from classical lexicons and old texts. Though the syntax is basically demotic, his inclusion of archaisms and grammatical elements of classical Greek reveal his need to create his own rules out of a language that had many conflicting personalities: classical, Byzantine, purist, demotic. The undercurrent of Kalvos's lyrical genius infuses this awkward, artificial language with poetic substance and vitality.

Though Kalvos was far from prolific, and his devotion to the art of poetry short-lived, his work served as a stepping-stone for many Greek poets of the twentieth century. Odysseus Elytis was one of the first modern Greek poets to discuss the contemporaneity of Kalvos's unusual technique, while George Seferis speculated as to what new peaks of poetic expression Kalvos would have reached if he had continued to write for the duration of his life. Kalvos finally received recognition as a major national poet when his burial place was moved from Great Britain to Zakynthos in 1960, a year that was officially declared as the Year of Kalvos.

Palamas and demoticism revitalized (1880-1920)

Kostis Palamas (1859-1943), a native of the Greek mainland (Missolonghi), is one of the greatest poets in the history of modern Greek literature. With his first publication of poems in 1886, he quickly surpassed his contemporaries and established himself as a central figure in Greek letters. In the poetry he wrote between 1880 and 1920, Palamas embodied the living heritage of Solomos and consolidated what his Ionian predecessor had left unfinished.

Throughout these years, Greek literary life broadened its perspectives beyond the limits of the Romantic school and the aging followers of Solomos. As founder of the New School of Athens, Palamas pioneered new directions in the development of a contemporary demotic poetry. Recognizing man's spiritual and social fragmentation in his own time, Palamas attempted to reconcile the divisive forces of twentieth century history through his poetry and critical studies in Greek and world literature.

While other poets at the turn of the century were able to adopt surface elements of the works of Solomos or the European Romantics, Palamas aspired to integrate the essence of these influences into the main body of his work. One of his greatest desires was to bring the demotic tradition into the mainstream of European art and literature. Palamas achieved his goal by looking in two complementary directions. For linguistic continuity, he turned to Solomos and the evolution of the demotic tradition, which, for Palamas, could be traced back from Solomos through *The Epic of Digenis Akritas* (1100-1150) to the epic narratives of Homer. Palamas's philosophical perspective, which is consistent throughout his work, emerged from a lifelong adoration of Goethe, who stirred Palamas to poetic inspiration and discipline much as Dante had awakened Solomos to his final purpose.

Although Romantics such as Lord Byron and Victor Hugo continued to influence Greek literature toward the end of the nineteenth century, of greater immediacy and impact for Palamas were the French movements, Parnassianism and Symbolism, while in his later years Palamas turned to the lyric mysticism of Rainer Maria Rilke. One could go on for pages listing the poets and thinkers whose works Palamas knew better and more intimately than any of his contemporaries in Greece. This vast accumulation of knowledge is unified by his ability to synthesize and subordinate these influences to the demands of his deep visionary voice.

After having published his first book of poems *Tragoudia tis patridos mou* (songs of my homeland), in 1886, Palamas titled his next volumes *O imnos tis Athinas* (1888; hymn to Athena) and *Ta matia tis psychis mou* (1892; the eyes of my soul), the latter a phrase borrowed from Solomos. This last choice of title indicates how strongly Palamas felt about establishing a bond of continuity between his own efforts and those of his Ionian predecessor. Unlike the epigones of Solomos, Palamas's works were not mere imitations of the father of Greek poetry; instead, Palamas used Solomos's works as stepping-stones to radical innovations in the poetry of his own time.

With *Iamvi ke anapesti* (iambs and anapests) in 1897, Palamas broke from the traditional demotic form of the fifteen-syllable line and, for the first time, introduced Symbolism into Greek poetry. In addition, the stanzaic structure of these poems (three quatrains each, composed of four interchanging anapestic and iambic lines) reveals the unmistakable mark of Kalvos. Indeed, Palamas was the first poet-critic not only to recognize Kalvos publicly as a major Greek poet, but also to acknowledge his poems as a determining influence on his own work.

In 1904, Palamas published *I asalefti zoi* (*Life Immovable*, 1919, 1921), a large collection of poems that included many written a decade earlier. At a critical stage in the evolution of a Greek poetic idiom, these new poems confirmed a world of poetic truth in a lyrical realization of the Greek poet's personal and historical endurance. The volume constituted Palamas's first mature attempt to create a unified metaphysical domain. In reference to these poems, the foremost scholar of Palamas, Thanasis Maskaleris, has maintained that "the whole collection is a song of all life elevated to the harmony and immutability of poetic sublimation."

Finally, it was in his long visionary poem, *O dodekalogos tou giftou* (1907; *The Twelve Words of the Gypsy*, 1964), that Palamas made his most sustained contribution to modern Greek poetry. Published in 1907, thirty-six years before his death in 1943, these twelve cantos of brilliant metrical diversity bring together the wisdom, lyricism, and visionary acuity that Palamas had been striving for in his constant struggle for self-expression and universal transference. The Gypsy-Musician, the protagonist of the poem, records his metamorphosis as a symbol for freedom and art, against the historical background of Byzantine Greece prior to the conquest of Constantinople in 1453. First, through an agonizing process of renunciation, he becomes a Greek patriot who finally embraces a mystical vision that allows him to become a true Hellene—a citizen and teacher, not of one nation, but of all the world. Palamas's preoccupation with the universal emerges with great intensity throughout the poem. Once again, it is the poet's lyric genius that provides this poem with its greatest source of energy and impact. Permeating the poem is a dreamlike flow of time that foreshadows much of modern poetry's conscious disorder and disregard for the classical concept of chronological narrative. *The Twelve Words of the Gypsy* is an epico-lyrical dream narrative, certainly the first of its kind and quality in modern Greek literature.

By the time he died in 1943, Palamas had published eighteen volumes of poetry and nearly 2,500 essays and articles concerning Greek and world literature. Some critics have suggested that Palamas should be remembered primarily for his contribution as an incisive, knowledgeable critic, and not so much for his poetry. Today, however, there is little question among Greek poets and scholars of contemporary literature that his influence as a poet has been paramount. As George Seferis was to observe not long after the death of Palamas: ". . . the work of Palamas is the landscape in which the total realization and resurrection of the Greek poetic idiom take place in life itself."

CONSTANTINE CAVAFY: CONSTRUCTING A NEW STAGE (1904-1935)

By the turn of the century, Athens had evolved into the center of political, cultural, and intellectual life for the Greek people. The climate was often frenetic, sometimes violent. In 1901, the New Testament was published for the first time in demotic. Rioting was the initial response at the University of Athens. Such a translation was considered a sacrilege by the conservative establishment; students' lives were sacrificed, and many were seriously wounded. At this time, demoticism began to stand for much more than simply a radical change in the language; it suggested social and political alternatives as well. Until recently, demotic was the official language of the Greek Communist and Socialist parties, while *katharevousa* was employed by Greek royalists and other right-wing parties.

Another orientation, unassociated with the demotic-purist controversy, was needed in order to awaken Greek poetry to the universal crisis of meaning and art that was preoccupying the masters of twentieth century world poetry. While the demoticists were still singing the praises of the Greek landscape and Greek history in terms of borrowed European models, their contemporaries abroad were weighing the existence and validity of the poetic word itself. The demotic tradition—alone or in combination with European models of Romanticism, Parnassianism, or Symbolism—no longer sufficed as a "center" for Greek poetry. It took a Greek poet who spent practically his entire life outside Greece, in Alexandria, Egypt, to perceive this problem and propel Greek poetry into the mainstream of twentieth century poetry: Constantine Cavafy (1863-1933). Untouched by the constant turmoil and linguistic confusion in mainland Greece, Cavafy created a mythic world that enabled him to see beyond the temporal issues into the heart of the universal. From his vast readings in Hellenic and Alexandrian history, Cavafy pieced together a poetry not of glory or heroic conquests, but of defeats, human frailties, decadence, and the often ironic tragedies behind every conquest and success. As the poet and critic Howard Moss has observed, Cavafy's slim oeuvre embodied "the commonplace life of the streets and the splendor of ancient tales and legends, in which the ordinary man of the first could become the unwitting hero of the second" (*Whatever Is Moving*, 1981).

Cavafy was born in Alexandria, Egypt, in 1863; his family was of a long line of wealthy Alexandrian aristocrats. When the father died in 1869, the Cavafy family inherited the dignity of their lineage but not its fortune. Three years later, at the age of nine, Cavafy began his most extended stay outside Alexandria. Hoping to find better opportunities for her older sons, the mother took Constantine and his brothers to Great Britain. After seven years there, the Cavafy family returned to its beloved city. At the age of sixteen, Cavafy was fluent in English and French and precociously familiar with European history and culture. With the exception of two years of forced exile in Constantinople and four

short trips to Europe and Greece, Cavafy spent the remainder of his uneventful life as a civil servant in Alexandria.

Later in his life, Cavafy referred to the poems he wrote before 1900 as "trash." Most of this verse was clearly a result of both his early exposure to French and English Romanticism and his initial use of *katharevousa*. In contradiction to his blunt rejection of his early work, however, several poems written between 1896 and 1900 indicate another direction in his poetics that eventually led to masterpieces such as "The God Abandons Anthony" and "Alexandrian Kings." During these years, Cavafy wrote five poems that characterized the fruits of this metamorphosis: "Walls," "Candles," "The First Step," "The Horses of Achilles," and "The Funeral of Sarpedon." His early romantic tendencies vanished, to be replaced by a unique, historical sensibility that preferred the stark truths of man's ironic failures and tragic dignity. Between 1900 and 1904, his art came into full flower, with poems such as "Thermopylae," "The City," and, in 1904, "Waiting for the Barbarians," the poem that would place him beside T. S. Eliot, William Butler Yeats, and Ezra Pound. In this same year, he printed a pamphlet of fourteen poems, including the aforementioned, for private distribution to friends and loyal readers. During this period, Cavafy was also writing more lyrical and erotic poems such as "Voices," "Desires," "He Swears," and "One Night."

In his maturity, Cavafy delineated three categories to which all of his completed poems could be individually referred: historical, erotic, and philosophical. Although these boundaries may apply to the form and manifest content of his poems, beneath the surface there is a constant overlap and interaction among these three categories.

What Cavafy called his historical poems had the greatest impact. They all emerge from an ancient city which, in the poet's mind, is of mythic though always human proportions. They are gestures of history that reveal the repetitive conditions of human existence and the humble dignity required to "bid her farewell, the Alexandria that is leaving." In 1911-1912, Cavafy printed three poems that established him as Greece's first poet with a thoroughly modern sensibility: "The God Abandons Anthony," "Philhellene," and "Alexandrian Kings."

In this last poem, Cavafy's ironic bite could not be more incisive or less understated. Of the Alexandrians praising Caesarion, Cavafy observes:

> Him they hailed oftener than his younger brothers,
> him they hailed King of Kings.

> The Alexandrians understood of course that
> these were only theatrics and mere words.

In the service of his irony, Cavafy developed a new poetic idiom that cultivated, for the first time in modern Greek poetry, some of the qualities of prose. The musical cadences of the demotic tradition are absent in these antimelodic poems. Their characteristic rhythm is that of a man speaking in a matter-of-fact voice, objectively recording the tragic and necessary ironies of the human condition.

Although his mode of expression is fundamentally demotic, Cavafy often adds a touch of realism by including colloquial phrases of *katharevousa* that had become just as much a part of everyday speech as demotic. In keeping with his devotion to "Mythic Alexandria," he also gave linguistic authenticity to his narrative poems with his discreet use of the Alexandrian idiom and spelling.

Cavafy's frank, erotic poems express irrepressible memories of sensual longings that excite the senses but torture the mind. Although many of these poems reflect his much-discussed homosexuality, Cavafy's eroticism has a universal relevance. Often, his seemingly distant but detailed recollections of fleeting erotic encounters provide the only redeeming element in the otherwise monotonous flow of time and destiny.

Cavafy's philosophical poems, such as "Thermopylae," are often historical as well: Here, the categories break down. As a whole, this group reflects Cavafy's belief in the ineluctability of fate and in the dignity to be won when man encounters and accepts the dramas of his tragic nature.

The first publicly available edition of Cavafy's collected poems did not appear until 1935, the same year that George Seferis issued his third collection of poems, *Mythistorema* (English translation, 1967). Seferis was thirty-five years old at the time; Cavafy had died two years before, at the age of seventy. Seferis was perhaps the first poet of his generation to recognize and understand Cavafy's essential breakthrough into modern poetry. In the following decades, Cavafy's Alexandrian voice became increasingly influential; today, widely translated, he is recognized as one of the major poets of the twentieth century. Ahead of his time, in almost magical isolation, Cavafy paved the way for a new generation of poets who would make Greek poetry one of the richest literatures in modern Europe.

SIKELIANOS, VARNALIS: MYSTICISM AND SATIRE (1890-1940)

In the early years of the twentieth century, most young Greek poets of the mainland were overwhelmed by a Baudelairean obsession with ennui and self-annihilation. Born on the Ionian island of Leucas, Angelos Sikelianos (1884-1951) was an important exception. Disregarding the melancholy of his contemporaries, Sikelianos celebrated life and death through intensely lyrical realizations of ancient oracular mythology and folk religion. Rooted in the pre-Socratic metaphysics of Ancient Greece, his best poems unveil the confluence of the natural and the supernatural. Sikelianos believed the poet must assume the role of prophet, oracle, and teacher; so strong was this belief that he actively promoted the reestablishment of Delphi as a contemporary center for mystagogues of all persuasions. Here, Sikelianos envisioned the emergence of "the universal soul of the world." Although this vision was never fully realized, it provided him with the spiritual fortitude and poetic resources to create an affirmative alternative to the Greek version of Baudelaire's "generation of the damned."

The pre-Socratic tradition remained archetypal for Sikelianos throughout his life. The teachings of Pythagoras, the Mysteries of Eleusis, Orphism and the cult of Dionysus, and the mantic center at Delphi represented the four main bodies of mystic wisdom that Sikelianos sought to enshrine in his poetry. He perceived this wisdom as the primal undercurrent of the Greek Christian ethos; consequently, Sikelianos had no qualms about including "my Christ, and my Dionysus" in one breath. Similarly, in "The Village Wedding," the poet invokes both the Christian "Word of God" and "Leto giving birth to Apollo. . . ." In the folk rituals of Greek Orthodoxy,

Sikelianos discovered the subconscious continuation of the religious principles he derived from the pre-Socratic world of ancient Greece.

From the rich language of his demotic heritage, Sikelianos assembled his poetic visions. His vocabulary is rooted in the vernacular, particularly in the dialectal variations of his birthplace in the Ionian Islands. In early poems such as "Return" and "The Horses of Achilles," Sikelianos experimented with free-verse alterations of the normal pattern of modern Greek metrics (the fifteen-syllable line). The new rhythms he created served to stress his central motifs of iconoclastic and pantheistic concerns. It is unfortunate that translations cannot capture the forceful and intensely lyrical cadences that flow, unimpeded, through the original Greek of these poems, for it was in his rhapsodies of religious feeling that Sikelianos established himself as a virtuoso of modern Greek poetry.

For the most part, Sikelianos was a traditional poet. By 1920, he had rejected free verse, focusing his attention instead on formal structures of poetic composition: sonnets, fifteen-syllable couplets, and other strict forms of his own devising. Of his short poems, "Songs of Victory I" (a series inspired by the Balkan Wars), "Pan," "Thalero," and "The Mother of Dante" are among his best. By 1917, with the completion of "Mother of God," Sikelianos also had mastered the long poem. "Mother of God" has been praised as the most musical poem written in Greek since the death of Solomos.

Three years prior to the composition of "Mother of God," Sikelianos's beloved sister, Penelope, died. In the poem, Sikelianos gathers symbols of Christianity, matriarchal goddesses, divinities of the natural world, and the spirit of his dead sister to provide a new consciousness of death that might release man from his futile efforts to comprehend death in his own limited terms. The poet's reconciliation with death is a central concern in his poems written between 1927 and 1942.

Sikelianos's output during these years was sporadic, for he began to devote his energies to establishing a Delphic university and Delphic festivals which would feature performances of classical Greek tragedies, exhibitions of folk art, Byzantine music and dancing, even naked athletic contests in the original stadium of ancient Delphi. Though the combined efforts of Sikelianos and his wealthy American wife, Eva Palmer, were originally rewarded with success, the venture was doomed to failure by eventual lack of support and the German occupation of Greece from 1940 to 1945.

From 1935 to 1942, however, Sikelianos made great strides in his poetry. The symbolic texture is tighter and the language more deeply reflective in poems such as "The Sacred Way," "Attic," "Apology of Solon," and "Agraphon." In the last ten years of his life, Sikelianos turned to the composition of lengthy tragedies that were unwieldy and difficult to stage. His zenith as a mystical poet with a tragic vision had already been reached in "Mother of God" and in the shorter poems written during the 1930's and early 1940's.

By the time of his death in 1951, Sikelianos had established an international reputation. In 1946, he had been nominated by the Society of Greek Writers for the Nobel Prize, and a year later he was elected president of this same society. Many of his finest poems had already been translated into Italian, French, and English. In its lyrical spontaneity and its religious identification with nature, his work has been instructive and influential for many Greek poets of subsequent decades.

Another poet whose work remained unscathed by the engulfing despair that characterized Greek poetry in the 1920's was Kostas Varnalis, born in Pirgos, Bulgaria, in 1884. As a student in Bulgaria, Varnalis nurtured an idealized vision of Greece, sustained by his early and intensive studies in the classics. His first poetic compositions were in *katharevousa*, with traditional form, meter, and rhyme. When he arrived in Greece for university studies at the age of nineteen, his romantic conception of Greece soon gave way to a bitter and ironic realism.

From 1913 on, Varnalis chose to write only in demotic, completely rejecting his early purist orientation. Moreover, like Palamas and Sikelianos, he began to accept the influences of the Parnassians and the Symbolists. Adhering to the strict forms of the sonnet and the quatrain, Varnalis reconstructed his dreams of classical glory. Images of ancient Greece abound in poems such as "Alcibiades," "Orestes," and "Aphrodite." In this last poem, however, the satiric mood of his later and more significant work begins to surface. Sarcasm, parody, and invective satire eventually became the vehicles for Varnalis to express his growing disenchantment with modern Greece and the futility of his earlier nostalgic hopes.

By 1920, after a year of studies in the postwar atmosphere of Paris, Varnalis came to embrace dialectical materialism and the Marxist ideology of historical and social change. The tragic outcome of the Balkan Wars and the Asia Minor Catastrophe in 1922 solidified his new political radicalism. Nevertheless, his finest poems lacked the bombast and rhetoric that characterized the emerging wave of leftist writings in the early twentieth century.

While still in Paris, Varnalis had written "The Burning Light," a poem in three parts which combined his early lyricism with poignant satire. Prometheus, Christ, and a contemporary leader of the proletariat are depicted as carriers of the burning light through ages of darkness and repression. Introducing himself, the leader shouts: "for I am the child of Necessity and the mature offspring of Wrath." "The Burning Light," published in 1922, was the first important left-wing poem to be written in Greece.

Varnalis's next major project was "The Enslaved Besieged," an obvious parody of Solomos's major poem, *Eleftheri poliorkimeni* (the free besieged). Divided into four sections, the poem is long and epic in scope. The poet lashes out against an ideology that promoted the mass acceptance of enslavement and Fascism. Varnalis described the essence of the poem as "antiwar and anti-idealistic."

Apart from his original poetry, Varnalis is also widely known in Greece for his brilliant and witty translations of Aristophanes. In addition, Varnalis wrote a great deal of literary criticism informed by his Marxist beliefs. He died in 1969 during the dictatorship of the Colonels (1967-1974).

KARYOTAKIS AND THE DAMNED (1920-1930)

The life and death of Kostas Karyotakis (1896-1928) had two strikingly different consequences for the development of twentieth century Greek poetry. His reputation as a melancholy and dispirited poet along with his dramatic suicide in 1928 inspired a large following of poets who, unlike Sikelianos or Varnalis, remained outside the mainstream of modern Greek poetry. Karyotakis's poetry itself, however, became a strong under-

current in this mainstream, from which emerged the voices of George Seferis (1900-1971), Odysseus Elytis (1911-1996), Yannis Ritsos (1909-1990), and Andreas Embirikos (1901-1974). In contrast to these strongly individual poets, the epigones of Karyotakis were content to repeat clichés of romantic and confessional despair. Indeed, in recent years the term *karyotakismos*, or Karyotakism, has denoted the Greek offspring of Baudelaire's "generation of the damned." Whereas their last echoes were heard in about 1940, the poems of Karyotakis continue to influence even the current generation of leading Greek poets, such as Lefteris Poulios, Yannis Kondos, Vasilis Steriades, and Jenny Mastoraki. It is therefore essential that Karyotakism be clearly distinguished from Karyotakis's poetry which has established itself as a haunting presence on the contemporary scene.

Karyotakis wrote and published three books of poems in his lifetime. The first, *O ponos tou anthropou ke ton pragmaton* (1919; the pain of men and things), maps out the domain of his concerns; at every destination there is fear and oblivion. In his second book, *Nipenthe* (1921), Karyotakis continued his stark explorations of hopeless and self-deceiving lives. Published in 1927, one year before his death, his last book, *Elegia ke satires* (elegies and satires), was both his finest and most unsettling. In its pages were grim and mournful expressions of a voice that found no solace in demotic or classical literature. Arthur Rimbaud, Charles Baudelaire, and Jules Laforgue influenced Karyotakis more than his Hellenic heritage. For Karyotakis, human existence was a limitless void. Beauty existed, but only as a mocking reminder of "the tears, the sweat, and the vast sky's nostalgia, all the bleak wastelands."

In the structured verse of rhymed stanzas, he recreated the emotional abyss that eventually overpowered him. Yet, in this formal style that exemplified the end of French Romanticism in Greek poetry, Karyotakis experimented, taking unusual liberties with diction, imagery, and rhythms, for only by pushing to its limits this already exhausted poetics could he make room for the utter desolation he so effectively expressed.

In place of the self-pity that abounded in the works of his contemporaries, Karyotakis adopted a satirical self-abnegation that would not allow for sentimental flirtations with romantic despair. His unique brand of satire is humiliating and tragic. Most of his images are derived from Greek life in the provinces (which he regarded as a kind of Hell). In this landscape Karyotakis found his characters, bringing to the surface the painstaking routine of their empty lives.

The actual story of this poet's death hauntingly reflects the burden of having been the most profound Greek spokesman of the "generation of the damned." On the night of July 21, 1928, the poet attempted, for several hours, to drown himself in the sea. The next day, having purchased a pistol, he sat in a seaside tavern, The Heavenly Garden, wrote a suicide note, and then, in the shade of a nearby eucalyptus tree, shot himself. Like his poems, the details of his death are satiric and uncomfortably self-conscious. He concluded his suicide note with the following postscript: "I advise all those who swim well not to try death by drowning. . . . At the first opportunity I shall write of my impressions as a drowned man." Although many younger poets were drawn to his work by the dramatic nature of his death, others were deeply disturbed by the poetic impasse that his poems exemplified.

GENERATION OF 1930

GEORGE SEFERIS

In 1931 at the age of thirty-one, George Seferis published a small book of poems titled *Strofi* (*Turning Point*, 1967). In its subject matter and tone, *Turning Point* signaled the first significant turn away from the unrelenting, romantic despair of the previous generation; in spirit and sensibility, these poems were much closer to the tragic dignity of Cavafy. In fact, throughout his life, Seferis considered Cavafy to be his truest and, sometimes, most overwhelming forerunner. Seferis became the primary force in the modernization of Greek poetry for the next twenty-five years.

Seferis (the pen name of Giorgos Stylianon Seferiades) was born on February 29, 1900, in Smyrna, a city of Asia Minor widely known as an intellectual center for Greeks of the Hellenic diaspora. In 1914, the Seferiades family moved to Athens, where the poet completed his secondary education, and from 1918 to 1924, he studied law in Paris. Encouraged by his father, a professor of law, to familiarize himself with all facets of European customs and thought, Seferis spent an additional year (1924-1925) in London, where he first became acquainted with the works of T. S. Eliot. During these formative years abroad, Seferis became increasingly aware of the intellectual and poetical forces that changed the accepted forms of literature soon after World War I. As a young student in Paris, he learned of the Asia Minor Catastrophe and the violent destruction of his beloved birthplace, Smyrna. In his later poetry, this experience helped define one of his central motifs: the constant urge to return to a home that exists only in terms of a frayed and bitter memory.

Seferis returned to Athens in 1926 and immediately entered the diplomatic service, in which he made a lifelong career. From 1936 to 1962, his work took him to Albania, Egypt, South Africa, Italy, Turkey, Lebanon, Syria, Jordan, and Iraq. His last post was as ambassador to Great Britain from 1957 to 1962.

In 1946, Seferis was awarded the coveted Palamas Prize. In 1960, he received an honorary doctorate from Cambridge University, and in 1963, he won the Nobel Prize for Literature. Honorary doctorates soon followed from Oxford, Thessaloniki, and Princeton universities. Finally, an honorary fellowship from the American Academy of Arts and Sciences gave him the opportunity to study, lecture, and write for six months as a poet in residence at Princeton University (1966). From this time onward he lived in retirement in Athens until his death on September 20, 1971.

Although unique in their content and austere tone, the poems of *Turning Point* and those of Seferis's subsequent collection *I sterna* (1932; *The Cistern*, 1967) were thoroughly traditional in form. In particular, Seferis proved himself a contemporary master of the fifteen-syllable line in the longest and most lyrical poem of *Turning Point*, "Erotikos Logos." The influence of both *The Erotocritos* and Solomos is evident in Seferis's melodic and sensitive use of the demotic language. Unlike the narcissistic ego that is heard in the poetry of Karyotakis, Seferis's voice is collective, expressing a personal drama that is elevated to the general character of universal tragedy.

It was not until 1935, however, with the publication of *Mythistorema*, that Seferis was able to inject the poetry of his time with elements that would alter decisively the course of modern Greek poetry. Perhaps the most significant element that Seferis introduced in the poems of this collection was a free-verse form perfectly suited to a simple but intensely lyrical demotic idiom and spelling. Sikelianos had experimented with free verse but only for a short period. Varnalis also had abandoned free verse early in his career, while Karyotakis took few chances in the framework of his European influences. In contrast, from 1935 to the end of his career, Seferis used free verse almost exclusively.

Mythistorema, which can mean either "novel" or "myth" of history, consists of twenty-four parts. The physical and spiritual landscape of this poem is rooted in Greek mythology. In the persona of the poet himself, the characters who travel endlessly in the dry world of *Mythistorema* have been lost in other times as well: the Argonauts, Odysseus, Elpenor, Orestes, Agamemnon, Astyanax. As they search for signs of life and light, their dreamlike anxieties reflect the real anxieties of contemporary man:

> I woke up with this marble head in my hands;
> it exhausts my elbows and I don't know where
> to put it down.

In Seferis's next collection of poems, *Imerologio katastromatos I* (1940; *Logbook I*, 1967), the apprehension of war is accompanied by a sure and tragic awareness of whom its victims will be. There is an atmosphere of anxiety and decay, but also of historical resolve and the courage to endure, a persistent characteristic of Cavafy's finest poems as well. In the last poem of this volume, "The King of Asine," Seferis presents the image of an ancient mask behind which is the void and "the poet a void." Unlike the rootless desperation of Karyotakis, however, the despairing feelings in this poem are mythic in context and therefore more historically enduring and tragic. This mythic aspect persists in all of Seferis's poetry.

Imerologio katastromatos II (*Logbook II*, 1967), completed in 1944, is a poetic summation of Seferis's bitter war experiences. Written in the places of his diplomatic exile during the war, many of these poems are dated with the names of the foreign cities that provided his exiled government with political asylum while the Germans occupied Greece: Transvaal, October, 1941;

Pretoria, 1942; Cairo, August, 1943. The speaker of these poems, who speaks for many, expresses the fragmented identity of the wandering exile. *Logbook I* and *Logbook II* record Seferis's journey through the spiritual netherworld of World War II Europe.

In 1946, Seferis completed a major poem that had been incubating for years. He titled it "Thrush," after the name of a ship sunk by the Germans in the harbor of Poros, the island where Seferis actually wrote the poem. The ship is a symbolic vehicle for the continuation of a voyage that Seferis had begun to chart in *Logbook I*. The tapestry of images and symbols in this poem reflects the influence of T. S. Eliot and especially of Cavafy, with "beds . . . that can haunt you" and "images in the mirror, bodies once alive, their sensuality."

The publication of this four-part work (Seferis's longest poem) in 1946 was followed by a poetic silence that lasted for ten years. A decade later, in 1955, *Emerologio katastromatos III* (*Logbook III*, 1967) appeared—another mythic journey of wandering spirits, inspired by Seferis's close ties to the island of Cyprus. In the best-known poem of this collection, "Helen," myth surfaces as actuality; Seferis addresses Teucer (brother of Ajax in the *Iliad*) as his own brother, and finally asks him: "What is god? What is not? And what is there between them?"

Although several collections of Seferis's poems were issued between 1940 and 1961, after *Logbook III*, no new poems appeared until 1966, with the publication of *Tria krifa piimata* (*Three Secret Poems*, 1969). These relatively short poems are regarded by many critics as Seferis's most esoteric. His central motifs of light and dark, which are heard with a disturbing clarity in "Thrush," are emphasized again in the staccato verse of Seferis's last major composition.

Throughout his life, Seferis also contributed enormously to the growth of modern Greek poetry with his critical writings. *Dokimes* (1962; the collected essays of George Seferis) includes penetrating and contemporary appraisals of *The Erotocritos*, Cavafy, Kalvos, Solomos, the sixteenth century painter El Greco, the Homeric hymns, and an important record of Seferis's discussions with T. S. Eliot. Seferis's other prose works include his only novel, *Six Months on the Acropolis* (written between 1928 and 1930; published twice in Greek: 1974, 1978), and volumes of personal diaries which reveal the painstaking groundwork that preceded each of his published poems. Also significant were his translations into Greek of Rimbaud, Paul Valéry, Paul Éluard, William Butler Yeats, Ezra Pound, Archibald MacLeish, and, in particular, *The Waste Land* (1922) of T. S. Eliot. In one of his essays, Seferis pointed to the three peaks of modern Greek poetry: Solomos, Kalvos, and Cavafy. By consensus, his own name must be added to this list.

ANDREAS EMBIRIKOS

While Seferis linked modern Greek poetry with its rich native heritage, another strong current in modern Greek verse was defined by its radical break with indigenous traditions. Surrealism made its first appearance in Greece in 1935 with the publication of a series of prose poems titled *Ipsikaminos* (blast furnace), by Andreas Embirikos (1901-1975). From 1925 to 1931, Embirikos lived in Paris, closely allying himself with André Breton and his school of Surrealist painters and poets. During these crucial years in the European capital of artistic and literary activity, Embirikos also devoted himself to the study of psychoanalysis.

Born on September 2, 1901, in Braila, Romania, Embirikos was brought to Athens in his infancy. There, he completed his primary and secondary education, going on to study philosophy at the University of Athens. In 1922, he moved to London, where he worked three years for a steamship company owned by his family of international shipbuilders and shipowners. After these years in London, he joined his father in France until 1932, when he returned to Greece. In 1934, Embirikos resigned from the family business and established himself as Greece's first practicing psychoanalyst. He retired in 1951, devoting the rest of his life to writing and photography.

The poems of *Ipsikaminos* were received in Athens with ridicule and critical antagonism. Few were able to understand the often startling but productive method of "automatic writing." In the poem "Light on a Whale," Embirikos begins: "The original form of woman was the braiding of two dinosaurnecks." By juxtaposing images that seemed to bear little or no relationship to each other, the poet was not simply trying to surprise or shock the reader. Rather, his intent was to provide a flow of subliminal motifs drawn from the creative and unifying wellspring of the subconscious.

Embirikos's preoccupation with female sensuality and its mythic origins provided a focal point for his later growth as a poet who could no longer make use of the formless nature of pure Surrealism. In his second collection of poems, *Endohora* (1945; the hinterland), symbols of the Freudian libido appear frequently and with great urgency: "erupting shock of a huge volcano," "the canals' lips," "a very small daughter . . . fondling the day's nipples," "the breasts of youth," "petals of pleasure." These sexual images come to life in mystical exaltations of eroticism that bind humanity to nature in joyful and immortal embraces. A master of both demotic and purist, Embirikos often used puns and other forms of wordplay to bolster the latent meanings of his consistently Freudian interpretation of man and nature in the modern world. *Endohora* consists primarily of poems written in highly structured but idiosyncratic verse forms. This emerging need for form indicated his growing distance from pure Surrealism. Nevertheless, Embirikos always perceived himself as a child of Surrealism.

From the beginning of his lifelong involvement with poetry, Embirikos repudiated the self-annihilating pessimism of Karyotakis. For Embirikos, life always triumphs in love—the spiritual apprehension of the universally erotic. As a result, his poetry also rejected the tragic necessity of guilt voiced by Cavafy and Seferis.

Embirikos was not alone in his discovery of Surrealism. There were other important Greek poets who also used the principles of Surrealism to create poems of intense vision and lyric power. Among the most outstanding of his contemporaries were Nikos Engonopoulos (1910-1985) and Nikos Gatsos (1911-1992), whose only book, *Amorgos* (1943), has been translated four times into English.

ODYSSEUS ELYTIS

In 1935, a new literary periodical titled *Nea grammata*, published under the direction of Andreas Karandonis and George Katsimbalis, began to promote the forthcoming masters of twentieth century Greek poetry. Finding an audience responsive to their work, Cavafy, Sikelianos, Seferis, Gatsos, and Embirikos appeared frequently in its pages. Toward the end of 1935, *Nea grammata* also published the first poems of Odysseus Elytis, who until his death in 1996 reached new heights of poetic expression with each passing decade.

Born on November 2, 1911, in Heraklion, Crete, Elytis (the pen name of Odysseus Alepoudhelis) was truly a child of the Aegean Islands. Even though his family moved to Athens in 1914, Elytis spent his summers on the Aegean Islands between Crete and Lesbos, where his family had originated. It is the natural and historical elements of this brilliant, ancient landscape that later provided the foreground for his most important achievements in poetry. After completing his secondary education in 1928, Elytis decided to study law at the University of Athens in 1930. At about the same time, he began reading the poems of the French Surrealist Paul Éluard, who opened a whole new vista of poetic experience and feeling for the young, impressionable Elytis. In 1935, while still a student at law school, he heard Embirikos's first lecture on Surrealism and its potential significance for modern Greek poetry. During this year, which also saw the first important publication of his poems, Elytis withdrew from law school, having chosen to devote the rest of his life to poetry and art.

Even the advent of World War II could not deter Elytis from pursuing his dream. In 1940, he served as a second lieutenant on the Albanian frontier to help organize Greek resistance against Benito Mussolini's impending invasion of Greek territory. Elytis's experience at the front became the subject of a long elegiac poem, *Azma iroiko ke penthimo yia ton hameno anthipolohago tis Alvanias* (*Heroic and Elegiac Song for the Lost Second Lieutenant of the Albanian Campaign*, 1965), which was first published in 1945. Later, discouraged by the violent repercussions of the war in his own country (the Greek Civil War, 1946-1949), he went to live in Paris (1948-1952). There, he spent much of his time among poets and painters such as Breton, Éluard, Tristan Tzara, René Char, Giuseppe Ungaretti, Henri Matisse, Pablo Picasso, Alberto Giacometti, and Giorgio de Chirico. Many of these artists had also befriended Embirikos, who was to be Elytis's first Greek mentor and a lifelong friend. Since 1952, Elytis has lived primarily in Greece, traveling once to the United States in 1961 and shortly afterwards to the Soviet Union. During this period, he has played a leading role in Greek literary and artistic life as president of the Greek Ballet (1956-1958) and as a governing member of Karolos Koun Art Theater (1955-1956). In addition to writing art criticism, he has

also translated the works of Éluard, Pierre-Jean Jouve, Federico García Lorca, Rimbaud, Vladimir Mayakovsky, and others. Elytis's contribution to modern poetry, increasingly recognized abroad as well as in his native land, was decisively acknowledged with the Nobel Prize in Literature in 1979.

With the publication of his first two books, *Prosanatolizmi* (orientations) in 1939 and *Ílios o pro tos* (sun the first) in 1943, Elytis unveiled a poetry of Surrealistic inspiration brimming with images from his mystical experiences of the Aegean Islands. His early relationship with Surrealism served as a catalyst, allowing him to express the inherently lyric spirit not only of his youth but also of Greece itself. The tone of these poems is highly personal, full of celebration, movement, and metamorphosis. In his poem, "Windows Toward the Fifth Season," for example, Elytis exemplifies his belief in the sensuality of poetic thought: "How beautiful she is! She has taken on the form of that thought/ which feels her when she feels it devoted to her. . . ."

Elytis's major poem, *Heroic and Elegiac Song for the Lost Second Lieutenant of the Albanian Campaign*, depicts in patriotic and lyrical language the Greek defense against Mussolini's invasion of Greece in October of 1940. The Italian invasion is remembered in Greece for its unifying effect on the Greek people. Against seemingly insurmountable odds, the Greeks managed to defeat the Italians quickly, pushing them back into Albania. In the midst of the oppressive years that followed, Elytis felt the need to account for and praise this sudden burst of mass heroism. Divided into twelve cantos, this poem, fertile with images of a living landscape and its magical properties, takes the reader through a verbal metamorphosis from dead body to the living and immortal spirit. By the end of the poem, the lost soldier has been resurrected and deified as "He ascends alone and blazing with light." These twelve songs mark the poet's first important encounter with the tragic elements that distiguish the poems of his maturity.

Though first published in 1960, the poems of *Exi ke mia tipsis yia ton ourano* (*Six and One Remorses for the Sky*, 1974) were written between 1953 and 1958. The dominant voice is somber, finely attuned to the desolating aftermath of both World War II and the Greek Civil

War that immediately ensued. The joyful, unhampered spirit of Elytis's early poems is here tempered by a greater consciousness of "dark forces" and their human price.

Following the composition of this collection, Elytis completed *To axion esti* (1959; *The Axion Esti*, 1974), a work much longer and more intricate than anything he had written before. The title phrase, meaning "worthy it is," is a Greek Orthodox ecclesiastical expression dating back to the early years of the Byzantine Empire. More specifically, the phrase was used for both the title of a Byzantine hymn glorifying the Virgin Mary and the name of a holy icon depicting her. The religious connotations of this expression along with its suggestions of song and image suggest the complex intention of the poem: a spiritual quest of music and imagery leading to a victorious emergence from the "Vast Dark Places." Even the formal structure of the poem is tightly modeled after the structures of Byzantine liturgy and hymnology. In all of its features, this poem illustrates the poet's growing faith in the absolute purity of poetry and its sanctified nature as a means of expression and communication.

The Axion Esti is divided into three sections. In the first, called "Genesis," the persona is born, and grows toward awareness and acceptance of mythic identity. The second section, titled "The Passion," charts the development of a now less innocent but unified consciousness through the experiences of World War II and its tragic aftermath. The last part, "The Gloria," is a long group of hymns that praise and celebrate everything from "the light and man's first prayer carved out of rock" to "a woolen sweater left to the frost."

This ambitious composition is also rich in allusions to Elytis's predecessors in the Hellenic tradition. In the struggles and praises of *The Axion Esti*, there are echoes of Homer, Heraclitus, Byzantine hymnographers, Saint John, Solomos, Andreas Kalvos, and the heroes of the Greek War for Independence, whom the poet sanctifies as saints. Because of its musical construction and contemporary breadth of vision, *The Axion Esti* was soon set to music by Mikis Theodorakis, who, in 1964, orchestrated and conducted the piece with a full choir and orchestra. Since then, the poem has received international recognition.

At about the same time that Elytis finished *The Axion Esti*, he began preparing yet another long poem, *Maria Nefeli* (*Maria Nephele*, 1981), which did not appear in its entirety until 1978. It consists of two parallel monologues spoken respectively by Maria, a symbol for the younger generation, and the Antiphonist, a more ancient, atavistic persona. These voices represent two divergent personalities that nevertheless belong to the poet himself. Though they search along different paths, their goal is the same: "to be slowly united with the grandeur of sunrise and sunset."

The most distinctive characteristic of Elytis's productive commitment to poetry has been his belief that devotion to art, in its purest form, might counterbalance the forces of horror and evil in the modern world. His efforts have often been incorrectly labeled as naïve; even a cursory inspection of a work such as *The Axion Esti* reveals that Elytis is no more a naïve optimist than was T. S. Eliot in his *Four Quartets* (1943): Both works seek metaphysical salvation through a poetic realization of tragedy. To achieve this end, Elytis has created a poetry grounded in a synthesis of complementary realities: contemporary, ancient, mythic, surreal, religious. The concatenation of these realities in his poems is always informed by his unique sensibility.

YANNIS RITSOS

Although Yannis Ritsos belongs to the Generation of 1930, he did not participate in the intellectual exchange and ferment that characterized the early years of *Nea grammata*, around which poets such as Seferis, Elytis, Embirikos, Nikos Gatsos, and George Sarantaris had enthusiastically clustered. Nevertheless, by the 1950's it was clear, especially in Europe, that Ritsos had added an important dimension to the poetry of his times. Born on May 14, 1909, his life story is one of family tragedy, sickness, and political persecution. His constant exposure to the presence of death and suffering has forced him to confront the essential problems of human existence. Poetry for Ritsos has not served as a kind of introspective consolation, but as sustenance essential to the life of his body and spirit. In his work, especially in his later poems, personal experience is transformed into metaphor. His growth as a poet has been characterized by his efforts to learn and create from the wounds of his experience.

Even Ritsos's childhood was scarred by misfortune and loss. His father was a chronic gambler who squandered the family fortune and later suffered a breakdown so severe that he was committed to an asylum in the late 1920's. When Ritsos was twelve years old, his mother and eldest brother died of tuberculosis, the same disease that has tormented the poet himself throughout his life. Afflicted for the first time in 1926, he spent most of the next five years confined to various sanatoriums and clinics. In 1931, Ritsos moved to Athens, where he became involved with Marxist groups. His commitment to Marxism emerged from the overcrowded conditions and mass suffering he witnessed and shared during his years of confinement.

Ritsos's first book of poems, *Trakter* (tractor), appeared in 1934. Traditional in form and belligerent in tone, these early poems reflected his conversion to Marxism. The titles alone provide obvious clues: "To Marx," "To the Soviet Union," "To Christ," "The Intellectual," "The Undecided." Evident throughout is the desperation of Karyotakis and the politically satirical bite of Varnalis, who was Ritsos's first teacher and a lifelong friend. In their poetry, Ritsos and Varnalis had much in common at first. Later, however, Ritsos developed a style indicative of a more profound and introspective orientation.

Ritsos's first major poem, "Epitaphios," divided into twenty songs written in the rhymed couplets of the traditional Greek folk lament, is the dirge of a mother whose son has been killed in a street riot during the calculated and murderous breaking of a strike by government forces in 1936. Issued the same year, the poem elicited such an immediate and empathetic response from the Greek people that the presiding dictator, General Joannes Metaxas, banned the book and ordered that it be burned before the Temple of Zeus in Athens. The title of the poem is taken from the Greek Orthodox liturgy, from the lament of the Virgin Mother kneeling before the dead Christ. Though political on one level, the poem is fundamentally religious, echoing the mourning of a collective psyche.

The years between 1936 and the advent of World War II marked Ritsos's final break from the confinements of traditional form. The four books that were issued during this period all had controlling musical themes: *To tragoudi tis adelfis mou* (1937; the song

of my sister), *Earini symphonia* (1938; spring symphony), *To emvatirio tou okeanou* (1940; the march of the ocean), and *Palia mazurka se rythmo vrohis* (1943; old mazurka to the rhythm of rain). In many of these poems, such as "Rhapsody of Naked Night" and "A Glowworm Illuminates the Night," the poet's synthesis of Surrealism, Impressionism, and Imagistic continuity overshadows the early political rhetoric and pessimism of *Trakter.*

During the Nazi occupation of Greece in World War II, Ritsos played an active role as cultural liaison for the resistance organization EAM-ELAS, whose purpose was to undermine the Nazi regime and reinstate democracy in Greece. Written between 1945 and 1947, "Romiosini," his last long poem of a revolutionary spirit, captured the pain, the longing, and spiritual sacrifice of the war years. Published ten years later and set to music by Theodorakis in 1958, this poem has served as a symbolic reference point for the members and sympathizers of the Greek resistance. With praise and exaltation, Ritsos links the courage and heroism of these rebel forces with the enduring nature of their ancestors, such as Odysseus and the Byzantine folk hero Digenis Akritas.

Because of his active membership in EAM-ELAS, Ritsos was exiled to government detention camps between 1948 and 1953. It was during this bleak period of his life that he turned away from the doctrinaire and theoretical concerns that characterized much of his earlier work. Under the oppressive circumstances of prison life, Ritsos began to write with more urgency than before, often jotting his poems on scraps of paper which he would stuff into bottles or tin cans to be retrieved at a later date. These were primarily short pieces that record his existential struggle for sanity and resolve in the face of constant physical and psychological deprivation. At times cryptic, these poems are consistently subtle and poignant, indicative of the poet's expanded consciousness of human suffering and solitude.

In the next fifteen years following his liberation in 1952, Ritsos wrote prolifically, gaining international acclaim from writers such as Jean-Paul Sartre, Pablo Neruda, Ilya Ehrenburg, and Louis Aragon, who insisted that Ritsos was "the greatest living poet." One of his finest poems of this period is the dramatic monologue *I sonata tou selinofotos* (1956; *The Moonlight Sonata*, 1979). The speaker is a woman dressed in black who yearns to leave her home, which she describes as stifling and decadent—a house that "persists in living with its dead." Yet by the end of the poem, she has chosen to remain. No longer capable of change, this person is trapped by her own fears and memories of a past which is embedded in the house itself. This haunting poem depicts solitude that engenders slow internal decay, leading finally to complete impotence.

Throughout the 1960's, Ritsos concentrated on expanding the poetic dimensions of the dramatic monologue. His efforts were productive, resulting in four consecutive masterpieces of the genre: *Philoktetes* (1965; English translation, 1975), *Orestis* (1966), *Ismene* (1972; English translation, 1977), and "The Return of Iphigenia." In each poem, a character taken from the ancient tragedies of Aeschylus and Euripides is transformed into a lonely spokesman for contemporary reality. Through the dramatic realization of each character's true identity in metaphorical terms, Ritsos reveals the tragic uncertainties of human existence.

In 1967, when the junta of the Colonels seized power, Ritsos was quickly arrested. In exile on the barren landscape of Yiaros and Leros, the poet reached further into himself, distilling short poems in a language that is extremely compressed. Their tone is often reminiscent of Cavafy, who inspired Ritsos to write *Twelve Poems for Cavafy*, published in 1974. These poems, like those from *O tihos mesa ston kathrefti* (the wall in the mirror), also written in 1974, confirmed Ritsos as a master of irony, metaphor, and understatement—all the qualities he admired in Cavafy.

During the military dictatorship from 1967 to 1974, the government banned Ritsos's books, but before and after that period, he received a number of honors: the Grand International Prize for Poetry of the Biennale of Knokkele-Zoute, Belgium, 1972; the Alfred de Vigny Poetry Prize, Paris, 1975; the Etna-Taormina International Poetry Prize, Italy, 1976. The most meaningful honor of all for the poet came, finally, from Greece itself in 1976 when Ritsos was awarded an honorary doctorate from the University of Salonika. In addition, he has frequently been mentioned as a candidate for the Nobel Prize. In keeping with the high and difficult standards of his generation, Ritsos has produced a body of work that is destined to influence contemporary poetry on an international scale.

NIKOS KAZANTZAKIS

Another important poet of the prewar generation was Nikos Kazantzakis (1883-1957), internationally celebrated for novels such as *Vios kai politeia tou Alexe Zormpa* (1946; *Zorba the Greek*, 1952) and *O Cristos xanastaronete* (1954; *The Greek Passion*, 1953; also known as *Christ Recrucified*), who initially made a name for himself in Greece for his poetry and drama. In 1938 he published a modern sequel to Homer's *Odyssey* in the form of a remarkable epic of 33,333 seventeen-syllable iambic verses, *Odysseia*, which took him fifteen years to complete. The nihilistic Odyssean hero encounters in his travels various modes of thought that he explores, but that end in nihilism. Kimon Friar spent many years translating this epic, published in English to much acclaim in 1958 as *The Odyssey: A Modern Sequel*.

TAKIS SINOPOULOS

In the minds of most critics familiar with modern Greek poetry, Takis Sinopoulos (1917-1981) stands firmly beside the more widely known poets such as Cavafy, Seferis, Elytis, and Ritsos. Of these four poets, Sinopoulos often contrasted his work to the poetry of Elytis. For both, the sun is a recurrent image that plays a central and unifying role in their poetry. For Elytis, the sun illuminates reality with its purity, grandeur, and beneficence. The sun of Sinopoulos, on the other hand, is invested with a demoniac power that burns, maims, and transforms the surrealistically bucolic landscapes of Elytis into a ravaged geography of the dead that will not permit the poet to forget.

The devastating qualities of this light, which is Sinopoulos's most prominent leitmotif, are derived in part from his intense involvement as a medical officer serving the government forces during the Greek Civil War of 1944 to 1949. Throughout these years of fratricidal horror, Sinopoulos, who had graduated from medical school in 1944, was confronted by death in a ruthless way. His poems are populated with the dead and their living gestures.

His first book of poems, *Metehmio I* (midpoint I), appeared in 1951. At this time, he had just begun to set up his practice as a physician in the Athens area, attempting to start a new life after his horrifying experiences on the front. The wounds were still fresh, as evidenced in this first book of poems, which begins: "Landscape of death. Sea turned to stone, black cypress trees/ low sea-shore ravaged by salt and light" ("Elpenor"). So pressing was the physician's need to express his rage and his tragic impressions of the war years that he published five more books of poems within the decade: *Asmata I-XI* (1953; cantos I-XI); *I gnorimia me ton Max* (1956; acquaintance with Max); *Metaichmio II* (midpoint II) and *Eleni* (1957); and *I nihta kei antistihi* (1959; night and counterpoint). Many of these poems draw on ancient Greek literature and mythology; as in the works of Seferis and Ritsos, ancient characters emerge frequently, always to express loss and tragic realization.

Another important feature of Sinopoulos's verse is his highly personal and imagistic awareness of his roots in the landscape of his birthplace, Pirgos, in Ilias. The specific nature of this landscape is not so much symbolic as it is a common reference point for the unity and continuity of his most important motifs: time, memory, and human frailty. In his poem "Origin," published in 1962, Sinopoulos concludes: "This is where I was born. This is where I grew up./ So these are what I need for my rage and my pride/ in order to hold and be held./ I have no gods. No fear."

The publication of "Deathfeast" in 1972 solidified Sinopoulos's permanent place beside his already famous contemporaries. This poem—the title piece of a collection—is Sinopoulos's most moving tribute to the comrades and loved ones whom he lost during the war. Scarred, dismembered, and disoriented, these ghosts of his tormented memory approach him. Their names appear as in a Homeric catalog of the dead. In the introduction to his translation of Sinopoulos, *Landscape of Death* (1979), Kimon Friar observes:

The guests who have come unbidden to this deathfeast are not those so grandiloquently summoned by Ángelos Sikelianos in his "Greek Supper for the Dead," to a table spread with silver candelabra, scarlet roses, and crystal cups, but are like those who herd around a fire or a pit of blood and beg for resurrection in the poet's memory.

"Deathfeast" echoes not only Sinopoulos's sense of fragmentation and guilt but that of an entire generation still hounded by its memories of war and devastation.

During the last years of his life, Sinopoulos became one of the first Greek poets to exploit fully a subtle combination of prose and poetry. He had used this technique in *I piisi tis piisis* (1964; the poetry of poetry), a collection of aphorisms that expose the awesome but sustaining nature of his art. More so than in his later works, this small book reveals another, less desperate side of the poet's characteristically dark preoccupations. Like Cavafy, it is only in the strange domain of poetry that Sinopoulos finds his "myth of reality, where things rejoice in the absurd aspect of their existence."

This introduction of prose elements into poetry characterizes much of the work that Sinopoulos completed in the late 1970's, including *To hroniko* (1975; the chronicle), *O hartis* (1977; the chart), and *Nihtologio* (1978; the nightlogue). The consciousness that emerges in these works is dreamlike and, as the poet himself often indicated, cinematic. Although they are written in diary form as recollections of his past, they do not follow chronological sequence. Dream, memory, thought, and feeling mingle freely in these "notes toward a poem" as they do for the poet in reality. In structure and content, *Nihtologio* and *O hartis* reveal the influence of the French poets René Char and Maurice Blanchot. Like Sinopoulos, they too were men with war torn memories who constantly sought the most effective means to express the necessity of poetry in times of destruction and human waste.

Considered by many critics to be Sinopoulos's most mysterious and obscure poem, "The Grey Light" (1980) was also the last work he completed before his death in 1981. Divided into eight short sections, it is an intricately organized web of personal experiences, places, and objects which are linked together to provide a kind of mystical order for the fragmented but meditative reality in which Sinopoulos lived and created. "The Grey Light" is also a final homecoming; it takes Sinopoulos back to "the sky of Pirgos" beneath which "the river sleeps by your side."

The poets who represent the next generation of modern Greek poetry came to regard Sinopoulos as the father of the postwar period. This is confirmed not only by his poetry but also by his personal involvement as a mentor and guide for many of the younger poets who are only now approaching the years of their poetic maturity. During the oppressive years of the Colonels' regime, the doors of his home in suburban Athens were always open to writers and poets who were in need of guidance and support. Aside from his taxing profession as a physician and the constant demands of his poetry, Sinopoulos also found time to write criticism, edit literary publications, translate, and paint. What is most striking about his contribution as a poet is the high degree of excellence that he was able to maintain throughout his work, from his first publication in 1951 to his last, just prior to his death in 1981.

POSTWAR YEARS

The horror of World War II and the civil war that followed was also visible in the work of Sinopoulos's contemporaries—Manolis Anagnostakis (born 1925), Miltos Sahtouris (born 1919), Eleni Vakalo (1921-2001), Nikos Karouzos (1924-1990), Aris Alexandrou (1922-1978), and Ektor Kaknavatos (1920). Along with Sinopoulos, these were foremost among the poets known as the First Postwar Generation. Like Sinopoulos, they were affected by the Symbolist trends of the previous generation, although they wrote largely in free verse and were interested in more experimental forms and diction. Manolis Anagnostakis was a schoolboy during the war years, and came of age toward the end of the German occupation of Greece. He belonged to a leftist group of students in Thessaloniki who established the literary magazine *Ksekinima* (beginning) in 1944 and took part in the leftist resistance. During the Greek Civil War he, along with numerous other freedom fighters, was arrested by the right-wing government and was sentenced to death. Though he was later released, many of his fellow students and comrades in arms were executed. As the Greek critic Dimitrios Tsakonas put it, Anagnostakis was "a dead man who survived the firing squad, or rather a man with multiple rifle wounds made by the bullets that killed others." If Sinopoulos's poetry is the reaction of a young man facing horror and carnage at the front, Anagnostakis's poetry is the more desperate reaction of the adolescent facing horror and carnage at home. His first book of poetry, *Epohes* (the times) was published at the end of World War II in 1945. In it there is no sign of joy at Greece's newfound freedom from the Germans. Instead, his poetry expresses a helplessness and feeling of defeat, the individual falling victim both to the injustice of the powers that be and the evil within himself. In his poem "Epilogue" (translated by Connolly), Anagnostakis writes:

> These verses may well be the last
> The last of the last that will be written
> For the future poets are no longer living
> Those who would have spoken all died young. . . .

Anagnostakis expressed the despair of his generation, which fought for freedom in the resistance only to face persecution after the war. Among the poets of the First Postwar Generation, Anagnostakis paints the most vivid picture of the fatal split within Greek society after World War II. Greek critics have described his poetry as a personal version of wilder and more desperate postwar Karyotakism.

Sahtouris is considered, along with Sinopoulos and Anagnostakis, to be one of the more important poets of the First Postwar Generation. In his first three books of poetry, *I Lismomenin* (1945; the forgotten woman), *Paraloges* (1948; ballads), and *Me to prosopo ston tiho* (1952; with the face against the wall), one can see panic stemming from the chaos of a confused and shattered world. The stylistic trademark that sets Sahtouris apart is his distilled and succinct verse. He continued prewar Surrealism, but in a new direction: The transformation of man, combined with a personal dimension that has strong undertones of sexuality—the private, sensitive person within a murderous society. In the poem "Desolate" (again in a translation by Connolly), he writes:

> . . . crows have dressed in red
> like whores
>
> the church cracked
> under the heavy rain
> saints were to be found
> running in the streets.

Vakalo, the foremost woman poet of the First Postwar Generation, dealt with the terrors of war by turning her back on civilization and focusing on nature, but in stark language that rejects lyricism. European civilization had brought war and destruction. The human beings she evokes are people in their pristine form, stripped of their Europeanness. Vakalo was particularly interested in visual arts and was considered a major art critic, the effects of which can be seen in her poetry. Her attention to the poetics of postmodernism left a mark on the poetry of the next generation of poets, particularly the women poets of the generation of the 1970's.

Karouzos distanced himself from the Surrealist, Symbolist, and political poetry of his generation. His poetry is wild and passionate, containing an uneasy and very original mixture of religious and sexual themes. One of Karouzos's interesting characteristics is the use of elements of purist Greek (*katharevousa*), which gives his poetry a controlled and cerebral dimension even at its most passionate.

The Second Postwar Generation spent their childhood in war and civil war, but came of age in the mid to late 1950's. Some of the notable poets of this generation are Kiki Dimoula (born 1931), Nikos Fokas (born 1927), Vironas Leondaris (born 1932), and Titos Patrikios (born 1928). These poets were interested in keeping and developing the Greek tradition, but after the disruptive years of war were also interested in allying themselves with international poetry movements.

THE 1960'S AND 1970'S

In the late 1960's, politics once more played a crucial role in the development of Greek poetry. The 1950's and early 1960's had been a period of relative calm, as Greece set about rebuilding the infrastructure shattered by World War II and the Civil War. On April 21, 1967, a right-wing military junta seized power in a *coup d'état*. One of the new government's first actions was the enforcement of strict censorship. Some major poets, such as Karouzos, continued publishing, as did Elytis, who avoided the censor by publishing abroad. But the majority of Greek poets, following the example of Seferis and Ritsos, countered the new strictures by refusing to publish their work.

In November, 1969, the Junta government abolished official censorship, replacing it with an equally stringent Press Law, which stipulated that a headline or the title of a book had to correspond exactly to the content. The

first book of poetry representing the generation of the 1970's was consequently titled *Eksi piites* (six poets). The poets were Lefteris Poulios (born 1944), Vasilis Steriades (1947), Katerina Anghelaki-Rooke (1939), Nana Isaïa (1934), Tasos Denegris (1935), and Nasos Vayenas (1945). Other important anthologies followed: *Katathesi '73* (deposition '73) and *Katathesi '74* (deposition '74).

The new generation of poets was the first to attempt a full demystification of ancient Greek myth, recasting it within the parameters of modern reality. The poets were influenced by Western European and American trends, particularly American Beat poets such as Allen Ginsburg and Lawrence Ferlinghetti. While earlier generations of Greek poets had striven to retrieve and re-create the traditions of the Greek past, the new generation juxtaposed these traditions with the increasingly ubiquitous pop culture, weaving classical motifs into modern reality. One of the poems that best demonstrates the clash of old and new (translated here by Karen Van Dyck) is from Jenny Mastoraki's first poetry collection, *Diodia* (tolls):

> Then the Trojan horse said
> no, I refuse to see the Press
> and they said why, and he said
> he knew nothing about the massacre
> after all,
> he always ate lightly in the evening
> and in his younger days
> he had worked a stint
> as a wooden pony on
> a merry-go-round.

Of the generation of the 1970's, Yannis Kondos (born 1943) proved himself master of the short epigram as well as of satire and wry humor, while Lefteris Poulios (born 1944) reflected the alienation and rhetoric of the American Beat generation. Poulios was most closely associated with the Beat movement, although while the American "beatniks" were reacting against the strictures of daily life in American society, Poulios was reacting to the strictures of an increasingly dominant alien culture—American and Western European—which was making ever deeper inroads into modern Greek culture.

While the generation of the 1970's was primarily centered on society and the city, Katerina Anghelaki-Rooke (born 1939) stood out as a nature poet grounded in the physicality of the female body. In the early 1970's she was perceived as the Greek poet with the closest affinity to the contemporary nature poets of northern Europe and the United States. The poetry of Mihalis Ganas (born 1944), on the other hand, focused on themes that centered on the life of provincial Greece, particularly Ioannina, relying on provincial idiom and images.

The Junta fell in 1974, after which freedom of expression was restored. Interestingly, it was the women poets—Vakalo, Kiki Dimoula, Anghelaki-Rooke, Rea Galanaki, Maria Laina, and Mastoraki—who continued experimenting with the elliptical language that had been a product of the censorship period, creating compelling and innovative work.

THE 1980'S AND 1990'S

The generation of the 1980's saw a greater diversity of poetic themes and forms than ever before. Among its foremost poets, Nikos Davettas (born 1960), Thanassis Hatzopoulos (born 1961), Yorgos Houliaras (born 1951), Dyonisos Kapsalis (born 1952), Ilias Lagios (born 1958), Stratis Paskalis (born 1958), Haris Vlavianos (born 1957), and Spiros Vrettos (born 1960) stood out.

In the 1990's, Kiki Dimoula's work gained attention for its linguistic playfulness and specifically Greek themes—particular appealing for readers who are wary of the threat of Greece's losing its cultural and linguistic integrity with the increasing homogenization of Europe. In an era when the Greek language is seen as vulnerable to the onslaught of English—as evidenced by the deep opposition to the proposal in 2001 that English be the second official language in Greece—Dimoula chooses topics viewed by many as privately Greek and untranslatable, in the sense that the poems have a topical meaning for the Greek reader. "Single-Room Symptom" (translated by Connolly) offers an example:

No different in Pylos either
the same disorderly retreat from Syros the year before
twice as bad in Kalamata last year
the train was full and the weeping demanded
we go back to Athens on foot.

An interesting phenomenon of the 1980's and 1990's was the increase in the number of Greek poets living and writing outside Greece, often referred to as the poets of the Greek diaspora. Notable among these are the Australian poet Dimitris Tsaloumas (born 1921) and the American poets Olga Broumas (born 1949) and Eleni Sikelianos (born 1965), the latter the great-granddaughter of Angelos Sikelianos.

BIBLIOGRAPHY

Beaton, Roderick. *Introduction to Modern Greek Literature.* 2d ed. Oxford, England: Clarendon Press, 1994.

Crist, Robert, trans. *Grind the Big Tooth: A Collection of Contemporary Greek Poetry.* Pittsburgh, Pa.: Sterling House, 1998.

Demaras, Konstantinos. *A History of Modern Greek Literature.* Albany: State University of New York Press, 1972.

Ferris, David S. *Silent Urns: Romanticism, Hellenism, Modernity.* Stanford, Calif.: Stanford University Press, 2000.

Friar, Kimon, ed. *Modern Greek Poetry.* New York: Simon and Schuster, 1973.

Hadas, Rachel. *Merrill, Cavafy, Poems, and Dreams.* Ann Arbor: University of Michigan Press, 2000.

Keeley, Edmund. *On Translation: Reflections and Conversations.* Amsterdam: Harwood Academic Publishers, 2000.

Keeley, Edmund, and Peter Bien. *Modern Greek Writers: Solomos, Calvos, Matesis, Palamas, Cavafy, Kazantzakis, Seferis, Elytis.* Princeton, N.J.: Princeton University Press, 1972.

Keeley, Edmund, and Phillip Sherrard. *Six Poets of Modern Greece.* New York: Knopf, 1961.

Lorentzatos, Zesimos. *"The Lost Center" and Other Essays in Greek Poetry.* Translated by Kay Cicellis. Princeton, N.J.: Princeton University Press, 1980.

Mackridge, Peter, ed. *Ancient Greek Myth in Modern Greek Poetry: Essays in Memory of C. A. Trypanis.* Portland, Oreg.: F. Cass, 1996.

Maskaleris, Thanasis. *Kostis Palamas.* New York: Twayne, 1972.

Politis, Linos. *A History of Modern Greek Literature.* Oxford, England: Clarendon Press, 1973.

Seferis, George. *On the Greek Style: Selected Essays in*

Poetry and Hellenism. Translated by Rex Warner and Th. D. Frangopoulos. Athens: Denise Harvey, 1982.

Sherrard, Philip. *The Wound of Greece: Studies in Neo-Hellenism.* New York: St. Martin's Press, 1979.

Van Dyck, Karen. *Kassandra and the Censors: Greek Poetry Since 1967.* Ithaca, N.Y.: Cornell University Press, 1998.

_____, trans. *The Rehearsal of Misunderstanding: Three Collections by Contemporary Greek Women Poets.* Hanover: University Press of New England, 1998.

James Stone,
updated by Peter Constantine and Karen Van Dyck

HUNGARIAN POETRY

THE MEDIEVAL PERIOD

Along the well-worn path the Hungarians (Magyars) took westward during the centuries preceding their entry into the Carpathian Basin in 896 C.E., they shaped a peculiar folk culture and folk poetry. Ethnographers, linguists, and researchers of comparative literature have arrived at this conclusion, even though no written trace of ancient Hungarian literature has survived. The runic alphabet of the seminomadic Hungarians was not used for recording literary texts, but the wealth of ancient poetry is attested by later allusions, although after Christianization in about 1000, both the state and the Church made every effort to eradicate even the memory of the pagan period. The chant of the shaman, an improvised incantation for the purposes of sorcery, prophecy, necromancy, or healing, often combined with music, dance, and a primitive form of drama, thus survived primarily in children's rhymes and other simple ritualistic expressions. The secular counterparts of the shamans, the minstrels (*regősök*), provided the first examples of epic poetry, recounting the origin of the Hungarians. Two of these epics are known (in their later reconstructed forms) as the *Legend of the Miraculous Stag* and the *Lay of the White Steed*. The versification is believed to have been similar to that of other ancient European poetry; it is thought, for example, that the Hungarian minstrels did not use rhyme, relying instead on alliteration.

The culture of medieval Hungary was influenced by both Roman and Byzantine Christianity, but it was most effectively shaped by the various monastic orders (Benedictines, Cistercians, Dominicans, and Franciscans, among others) who settled in the land from the tenth to the thirteenth centuries. Learning remained almost entirely theological until the middle of the fourteenth century, and writing continued even longer in Latin, the language of the Church.

The Latin hymns and laments of Hungarian monk-writers were mostly dedicated to the praise of Hungarian saints, and their subject matter generally derived from the legends associated with these saints. Because only later copies of these creations survived, little is known of their origins or of their authors.

The earliest known poetic text in Hungarian originates from about 1300: The "Ómagyar Mária-siralom" ("Ancient Hungarian Lament of Mary") is an adaptation from the "Planctus Sanctae Mariae" of Geoffroi de Breteuil (died 1196). The original liturgical hymn was transformed into a pious lay song with strong mystical undercurrents. Written in the ancient Hungarian line, consisting of eight syllables, with stress on the first and the fifth, the poetic technique of the "Ancient Hungarian Lament of Mary" is so accomplished that centuries of literary practice must be assumed to have preceded it.

While epic romances and troubadour songs began to flourish in the fourteenth century, the poetry of chivalry left relatively scarce evidence of its existence in Hungary. Its best-known example is the *chanson de geste* woven around the figure of Miklós Toldi, a popular strongman-soldier. Elements of this epic passed into folklore and formed the basis of works several centuries later, including a masterful epic trilogy by János Arany (1817-1882).

By the fifteenth century, secular poetry in the vernacular had made its presence strongly felt in Hungary. The untutored minstrels and rhymesters were joined by clerks and scribes (the *deák*), who supplemented the works of the bards with their own compositions, including "historical" songs as well as love poems and satirical lays. One good example of their work is the narrative song titled *Szabács viadala* (1476; the siege of the Szabács), which recounts an episode of warfare against the invading Ottoman army. Its contradictions continue to intrigue scholars; while its language is bleak and it reads like a school exercise, it exhibits a strikingly modern vocabulary and flawless technique in its use of decasyllabic rhymed couplets.

THE RENAISSANCE AND THE REFORMATION

While indifference toward literacy and the written word continued to be the rule of the period, there arose in Hungary important centers of Renaissance culture during the reign of the Anjou kings (1308-1382) and especially during that of Mátyás (1458-1490). His efforts to establish a strong central authority were well served by the professional men in his employ, recruited from a variety of countries. Besides these learned foreigners, a new crop of Hungarian intellectuals appeared as a result of schooling in the universities of Western Europe.

Outstanding among these was Janus Pannonius (1434-1472), a Ferrara-educated bishop of Pécs, the creator of finely chiseled epigrams, elegies, and panegyrics and the first Hungarian man of letters whose fame transcended the borders of his homeland. His topics included affairs of state, the growing Ottoman peril, the love he felt for his homeland (while missing the culture of Italy), and his disenchantment with the policies of his sovereign. Renaissance luxury and the contemplative atmosphere of court literature were shattered during the stormy period following Mátyás's death, but the tradition of Humanist poetry domesticated by Pannonius and his circle of followers has remained alive in Hungarian literature to this day. The large number of Hungarian poems surviving from the sixteenth century indicates that a considerable body of verse already existed in the Middle Ages, even if most of it is unknown today.

The major impulse for this cultural growth was the Protestant Reformation. The literature of Hungary became a battleground for the various new tenets. Hymns, didactic verses, and rhymed paraphrases of biblical episodes, written in Hungarian, became weapons that assured the rapid acceptance of Protestantism among the people. Of the secular minstrels of the century, the best known and most prolific was Sebestyén Tinódi (died 1556), who was more a storyteller than a poet. His accounts of battles and sieges were accurate, but his verse was monotonous and repetitive, made enjoyable only by musical accompaniment. Free adaptations of Western European poetry abounded during the century, the principal genre being the *széphistória* (named after the Italian *bella istoria*) interwoven with elements of Hungarian folklore, thus reflecting a strong native character.

Representing the finest achievements of Hungarian Renaissance is the poetry of Bálint Balassi (1554-1594), a nobleman whose turbulent life was spent in constant pursuit of love, wealth, and adventure, often under the shadow of political suspicion. His works have something of the flavor of the English Cavalier poets, something of François Villon, with the additional feature of an intimate knowledge of nature. Proficient in eight languages and familiar with the works of the great Human-

ists, Balassi wrote poetry with great dexterity. His cycles of love poems remained unsurpassed for centuries, and the intensity of his Christian verse, in which he disputed with God while seeking solace in Him, foreshadowed the thoroughly personal religious works of later Hungarian poets. The intensity of a soldier's life made itself felt through the discipline of his lines. His most perfectly composed and most frequently quoted poem is a *cantio militaris*, "A végek dicsérete" (1589; "In Praise of the Marches"), an eloquent hymn to life on the marches and to the beauty of nature, ending with a moving grace and farewell. Balassi developed a verse form for himself, a nine-line stanza consisting of six-, six-, and seven-syllable cycles, with an *aab-ccb-ddb* rhyme scheme; named after him, this pattern became a favorite of Hungarian poets.

THE COUNTER-REFORMATION AND BAROQUE

Much of the seventeenth century was characterized by the militant spirit of the Counter-Reformation, resulting in an enormous output of religious poetry, mostly by Roman Catholic writers. The outstanding Hungarian poet of the century, Miklós Zrínyi (1620-1664), a thoroughly baroque man of letters, bore one significant resemblance to Balassi: He also had a firsthand knowledge of combat, and his descriptions of battle scenes, especially in his epic carrying the Latin title *Obsidio Szigetiana* (wr. 1645-1646; *The Peril of Sziget*, 1955), are particularly graphic and authentic. In his narrative, as well as in his prose writings, Zrínyi displayed the explicit and fervent political commitment which was to become an integral part of much Hungarian poetry. Although the influence of Vergil, Ludovico Ariosto, and Torquato Tasso is discernible in *The Siege of Szigetvár*, the presentation of details and the use of atmosphere make it a profoundly original Hungarian creation.

The cultivation of sentimental rococo poetry became a fashionable pastime during the seventeenth century. Even highborn ladies tried their skill at it, most of them producing religious or domestic verse. The epic tradition of Zrínyi was carried forward by an inventive, widely read courtier who stayed away from actual battles. The heroes of István Gyöngyösi (1629-1704) were genuine nobles and ladies; in his numerous epithalamia he revealed their love secrets to his readers in great detail and with obvious relish. He was the typical poet-follower of lords, adjusting his politics and principles to those of the "great family" he served. His works are nothing more than family or society stories, but their accomplishment is undeniable. Gyöngyösi's honest craftsmanship, especially in his descriptions of the countryside, presages the works of the great Romantic and realist poets of the nineteenth century.

With the growth of readership, an eager public appeared for secular as well as religious poetry. For some time, these writings circulated in handwritten copies, but by the 1680's a number of printed songbooks were in popular demand. The vulgarized versions of Renaissance poems in the form of verse-chronicles constituted the bulk of the poetry of the age, with a number of rhymed greetings, soldiers' songs, laments, and dirges also in evidence. The proliferation of love poetry was striking; entire songbooks appeared filled with these often ribald verses, attempting to follow the high standards set by Balassi and Gyöngyösi. Among students, the traditions of goliardic poetry were revived, with sharp expressions of social discontent.

Political and religious intolerance resulted in the outbreak of the *kuruc* wars during the late seventeenth and early eighteenth centuries. Reflecting the makeup of the rebelling armies, many popular songs of this period voiced the complaints of fugitives, outlaws, and impoverished, vagrant students. A large body of (mostly anonymous) poetry was produced during the successive rebellions and campaigns. Written in the simplest folk idiom, suitable for musical adaptation, such songs and laments provide gripping descriptions of the miseries and joys of *kuruc* life. The most famous among them (such as "The Rákóczi Song") later inspired Franz Liszt and Hector Berlioz to compose stirring Romantic music.

EIGHTEENTH CENTURY

From 1711, when the *kuruc* armies of Prince Ferenc Rákóczi II were defeated, to the 1770's, Hungarian literature experienced a period of relative decline. Only the continuing flood of imitative, mannerist rococo verse indicated the survival of poetry. The poets of this period showed a remarkable command of form and diction, and some of them were important in the development of modern poetic techniques. Baron László Amade (1704-

1764), a sophisticated cultivator of *poésie galante*, produced poems worthy of mention. Ferenc Faludi (1704-1779), a Jesuit abbot, also became interested in secular poetry. In spite of its rococo affectations and style, his verse was firmly grounded in reality and took much from Hungarian folk literature. With his earthy realism and his prosodic experimentation, Faludi became one of the early exponents of truly modern poetry.

The Enlightenment reached Eastern Europe by the 1770's and—even though the absolutist Habsburg authorities thwarted any political organization—its effect on the cultural life of Hungary was profound. Intellectual renewal was rapid and irresistible. One of its centers was Vienna, where Hungarian noblemen were educating their sons. French, German, and English-language treatises and literature filtered into Hungary, resulting in the founding of great private collections of books and art, the formation of literary societies, and the publication of periodicals. French (later German) Neoclassicism became the dominant trend in poetry. The earliest prominent figure of Hungarian Enlightenment, György Bessenyei (1747-1811), while known mostly for his essays and his plays, also wrote a number of philosophical poems. Had they appeared in print during his lifetime, they would have been pioneering works.

Much more influential was Ferenc Kazinczy (1759-1831). Although writing relatively few poems, of modest merit, he was for nearly forty years the central figure of Hungarian literary life; he organized, criticized, encouraged, and educated the writers and poets scattered throughout Hungary by maintaining an extensive correspondence from his rural manor. All the good, and many of the bad, poets of the period were indebted to him. While they considered style, presentation, and construction to be of supreme value, attaching secondary importance to the thoughts conveyed, Kazinczy and his circle soon came to the conclusion that, in its uncultivated state, the Hungarian language was inadequate to communicate the timely ideas of literature and the arts. They made reform, refinement, and development of the language a question of primary importance. Proclaiming these aims in their sharply worded epigrams, epistles, and critical essays, they initiated the struggle between "neologists" and "orthologists" which persisted through much of the nineteenth century.

While the early reform generation produced few outstanding poets, one of their contemporaries, Mihály Csokonai Vitéz (1773-1805), exhibited the fruits of his search for new forms of expression. He made use of everything he learned from European literature, transmitting it into his own sphere of experience and producing from the synthesis something original and integrally his own. He was the first Hungarian who attempted (unsuccessfully) to make a living from his literary efforts. Despite the fact that he lived in a state of squalor and acutely felt rejection, many of his poems are marked by a subtle grace and cheerfulness. They range from Rousseauesque philosophical ponderings to drinking songs and village genre pieces. His love cycles written during his many periods of courtship happily blend light passages of rococo fancy with more sober thoughts. Csokonai Vitéz could be compared to the Scottish poet Robert Burns (1759-1796), except that this would overemphasize the populist element of his poetry.

ROMANTICISM

While the Enlightenment gave rise to philosophical and didactic verse, disposed to abstraction and aridity, lyric poetry found another impetus. The reformers and experimenters encouraged originality and aesthetic individuality, in sharp contrast to both Neoclassicism and the earlier baroque orientation. The campaign for national independence revealed a set of common feelings shared by all Hungarians and resulted in anxious efforts to preserve the native tongue and indigenous customs. The intensive exploration of traditional literature, the growing awareness of literary history, and the Romantic influence of Ossianic poetry combined to open the way for unrestrained experimentation. In the area of versification, for example, Western European patterns were adopted by Hungarian poets as if based on stress alone. Consequently, the French Alexandrine was assimilated as a twelve-syllable accented line of two beats, each having six syllables. Four of these lines were arranged into a stanza, at first all lines rhyming, later following the Western example of rhyming couplets. Even more significant was the introduction of a metrical principle that could be based on the length of syllables. Since the Hungarian language makes a clear distinction between long and short syllables, this practice is perfectly suited

to it. Some of the poets introduced the purely metrical, nonrhyming forms of Greek and Roman poetry, while others adapted rhyming verse forms from the West. The flexibility and smoothness resulting from these experiments was unprecedented in Hungarian poetry.

The typical attitudes of Romantic literature—the glorification of history, the preference for a noble and often affected "sublimity," which went hand in hand with a healthy respect for reason—were made more complex in Hungary by an exaggerated emphasis on folk poetry and a contradictory predilection for new techniques of versification. The resulting torrent of poetry during the early decades of the nineteenth century presented a sharp contrast to that of the previous epoch. Lyric ballads, elegies, and epic romances prevailed, in accordance with the requisite extremes of desolation and melancholy on one hand and exhortation and pride on the other. As elsewhere in Eastern Europe, Romantic literature in Hungary contributed to the birth or revival of national consciousness and to the forging of a national identity. With its maturation and with the strengthening of political processes, this literature assisted in democratizing the atmosphere for a national culture. The patriarchal-feudal mode gave way to a semibourgeois one: Writers and poets were able to earn a living from their writings, making noble patronage unnecessary. Publishing became a profitable business; men of letters combined their work with editing and journalism, and they began to be recognized and respected on their own.

One of the architects of the transition to Romanticism was Sándor Kisfaludy (1772-1844), a scion of wealthy landholders, whose two-hundred-verse cycle *A kesergő szerelem* (1801; sorrowful love) combined strong traditional elements with Renaissance, baroque, and rococo influences. The form he created to harmonize with his message, the "Himfy-stanza," composed of eight- and seven-syllable accented lines, came to be one of the favorites of Hungarian poets. Dániel Berzsenyi (1776-1836) did not bring innovations in style or in form, but the emotional intensity with which he proclaimed enduring virtues—moral integrity, courage, love of freedom and justice—accounted for his great popularity during the reform period, when politics and ethics were considered intertwined. His terse and vigorous images and phrases are charged with classical allusions, but his elevated style and antique pose conceal the wounded soul of a modern man. His disillusionment with his morally deficient contemporaries was great; while his intensely disciplined art continued to reflect a remarkable self-control, behind the wisdom of antiquity lay the resignation of a Christian longing for contentment. Although Berzsenyi was disappointed because Hungarian poetry did not develop along his guidelines, his influence on future poets was strong and lasting.

Ferenc Kölcsey (1790-1838) was the most profound thinker among the Hungarian Romantics. A saintly man of uncompromising standards, he embodied the national aspirations of the age. The earlier examples of his relatively small poetic output were clearly influenced by the notion of a *Weltliteratur*, but later he showed a predilection toward a vigorous, striking, though often grave and pessimistic, nationalistic poetry. His best-known poem is "Himnusz" (1823; "Hymn"), a somber invocation to God on behalf of the Hungarian nation, which was put to music and is now the national anthem of Hungary.

Mihály Vörösmarty (1800-1855), the greatest Romantic poet of Hungary, introduced a new element into the literary life of the nation. His works were much more than reflections on the events around him; they expressed well-considered and inspired judgments on the vital questions of the age as dictated by the poet's genius. In "Szózat" (1836; "The Summons") he addressed the world on behalf of his nation: "The sufferings of a thousand years call for life or death." This appeal remains unmatched in its confidence and its effect on the reader's conscience. Familiar with the inherent contradictions in the societies and cultures of his age, Vörösmarty also inquired whether humankind "ever advanced through the medium of books" in his "Gondolatok a könyvtárban" ("Thoughts in the Library"). The ensuing images suggest a pessimistic answer, but the poet appears unable to accept such a dark conclusion: "A new spirit finds its way ahead," he insists in this and in other poems, which shows him to be a true poet of humankind. There is a nagging doubt and a touch of despair in his mature poems, and the defeat of the nationalist revolt by combined Russian-Austrian forces in the Hungarian War of Independence (1848-1849) released the floodgates of his bitter, almost demonic imagery.

In Hungarian literary history, the decade preceding the 1848 Revolution is referred to as the "era of the people and of the nation." Romanticism was very much alive, but by this time some of the best poets found even Romanticism too narrow and infused it with plebeian-democratic ideals expressed in an increasingly realistic manner. The stylistic trend best suited for the purposes of this period was the populist (*népies*) approach. It fused Romantic and realistic elements, steadily (although cautiously) increasing stress on the latter. During the 1840's, a courageous, involved commitment to critical realism became dominant, especially among members of the younger generation. The immediate aims of literature were to rediscover folk poetry, to depict the life of the common people, and to give voice to their aspirations. In a domestication of the universal Romantic philosophy, the concept of the "true man" was adapted to that of the "true Hungarian." The indirect aim of the young writers and poets was the modern expression and interpretation of national character. What they could not foresee was that this national character was to undergo radical transformation during the second half of the nineteenth century.

POPULISM

In the person of Sándor Petőfi (1823-1849), many of these ideals found their consummation. Petőfi was endowed with everything a national poet must have: innate talent, a fiery commitment, the right historical situation, and a sense of manifest destiny. After a brief life (he died in his mid-twenties), he left behind a body of works that, both in quality and in volume, cannot be ignored in any assessment of world literature. (He also shared Lord Byron's fate in that he died a tragic death which made him both a symbol and a myth.) After imitating the folk style so successfully that many of his verses are popularly known as folk songs, he signaled his break with the strict Romantic approach in a spirited parody of the heroic epic, *A helység-kalapácsa* (1844; *The Hammer of the Village*, 1873). His most popular epic, *János Vitéz* (1845; *Janos the Hero*, 1920), also indicated this transition. The tale and its trappings are stock Romanticism, while the treatment and the picture projected are closer to realism.

Political themes became increasingly interwoven with his poetry during the 1840's. Even in his genre-pieces, the setting sun was compared to a bloody ruler, and the clink of wineglasses to the clanging of chains enslaving men. In a letter, he proclaimed his guiding principle: "When the people rule in poetry, they will be close to ruling in politics as well, and this is the task of our century." Not surprisingly, this kind of thinking led him away from a Romantic admiration for the past. Petőfi produced some of the most powerful love poetry of the century, and his descriptive poems (mostly about the plains region between the Danube and Tisza rivers) are imbued with folksy, evocative humor, particularly when presenting the life-style of the Hungarian nobility. He developed a style and a language quite clearly his own, which grew to accommodate the whole spectrum of Hungarian life. As a result of his "democratic style," his readers understood him immediately. While moving away from strict Romanticism, Petőfi found the direct and natural approach his predecessors sought. He moved effortlessly from one type of poetry to another, adopting new techniques at will and solving the most difficult problems of versification with ease and grace.

János Arany was a friend of Petőfi. They agreed on a number of issues and were both committed to making the life of the people the central theme of literature. While Petőfi was a fiery radical, quite conscious of his genius, Arany was an exemplary office-worker who wanted to be "just like everyone else." He first attracted attention by writing the epic poem *Toldi* (1847; English translation, 1914), a thoroughly Romantic historical story with a hero of folk imagination who avenges the outraged feelings of the common people—a natural, simple, untainted soul, unselfish but self-respecting and conscious of his own worth. In Arany's epic, the Hungarian nation is presented as it once was (according to the Romantics): a family community, governed by the rules of justice and nature. The defeat of the Hungarian Revolution and the death of his friend Petőfi injured Arany deeply. In poems that were highly subjective, empirically analytical, and soberly reflective, he tried to bridge the conflict between his ideals and the realities of life in subjugated Hungary. The language of his poetry was something he deliberately created. It was not the straightforward, unambiguous voice of folk poetry, but rather a precise literary speech of carefully chosen words and expressions, bearing the widest variety of meanings and associations. Arany's poems may be immediately comprehensible to the reader, but they are, at the same time, among the most difficult in Hungarian literature to render in a foreign language.

In spite of his considerable lyric output, in which a wide variety of subjective topics were treated, Arany saw himself primarily as an epic poet, and as such, he considered it his task to revive in a contemporary context the common and single-minded national consciousness. This vision explains his predilection to treat a variety of historical subjects in his epics. He avoided the pseudohistorical idealization of the peasant by incorporating into his writings a distinctly un-Romantic view, according to which, even though national character is best preserved by the common people, it may also become primitive because of its isolation, and it should be enriched with values originating in other cultures. Apart from *Toldi*, Arany is best remembered for his ballads, the themes of which were taken from the sad and trying periods of Hungarian history. This outmoded genre, extant only in the villages and marketplaces, was salvaged through Arany's masterful handling of the Hungarian sentence and especially through his use of numerous psychological associations.

The success of Petőfi and Arany resulted in a veritable cult of populist poetry. Petőfi's numerous imitators, not all of them without talent, copied his style and themes with genuine fervor but seldom achieved his level of consistency and brilliance. Thus, the Petőfi cult soon degenerated into absurd virtuosity and buffoonery. Arany's followers were somewhat more successful. Their writings are characterized by literary skill, an effective use of common speech, and a scrupulous concern for details of versification. These poets led long and blameless lives and filled many of the leading positions in the nation's cultural affairs during the late nineteenth century. It was largely as a result of their efforts that the poetic guidelines of Petőfi and Arany, imbued with excessive nationalistic and isolationist tendencies and referred to as populist-nationalism, became the official dogma of Hungarian cultural life. Lyric poetry, its position already weakened by the appearance of new, more subjective prose genres, became even more monotonous and irrelevant to the growing urban and semiurban readership.

The 1880's brought about a flurry of revival in Hungarian poetry, when a few solitary writers, almost completely ignored by the academic establishment, attempted to infuse new vigor into the literary life of Hungary. The name of János Vajda (1827-1897) became synonymous with opposition and stubborn refusal to conform to artificial standards. Largely because of his aggressiveness and lack of objectivity, his antitraditional, pantheistic, and symbol-studded poetry was never even acknowledged, let alone respected by the critics. Seeking visions of glory and greatness in an age when such were outmoded, he spent his declining years in angry meditation, writing more good lines than good poems. Among the younger outcasts, Gyula Reviczky (1855-1889) merits mention for his melancholy, reflective poetry, in which impressionistic and Symbolist elements were first expressed in Hungary. József Kiss (1843-1921) was not an outcast; indeed, for a time he was among the most popular poets of Hungary. As the successful editor of the country's first bourgeois literary weekly, *A hét*, he strongly influenced contemporary taste, and his lyric poems and ballads introduced the life of Hungary's Jews into the mainstream of Hungarian literature.

MODERN POETRY

The turn of the century witnessed the rise of a wealthy liberal middle class in the cities of Hungary. Their desire to gain recognition for their tastes and values alongside traditional Christian-national ones contributed to a spirit of literary secession. Passive and late-blooming as this "secession" was, it achieved a grudging acceptance of relative (as opposed to absolute) values, and by introducing free association into the practice of poetry, it loosened the structure of Hungarian verse. At the same time, a "great generation" of writers and poets appeared on the scene. Their artistic power was too elemental and their appeal too overwhelming to be stopped. Not all of them wanted to change Hungarian society, but most of them agreed in wanting to open all avenues for describing the realities of Hungary as "a country of contradictions."

Among those contributing to the periodical *Nyugat*, one may find some of the brightest names in twentieth century Hungarian poetry. In influence, quality, and complexity, none of them approached Endre Ady (1877-

1919). When he published his first important volume, *Új versek* (1906; *New Verses*, 1969), he embodied the shocking newness of modern European literature, and critics promptly declared him incomprehensible, immoral, unpatriotic, and pathological. Unrelenting, Ady poured forth (besides his numerous newspaper articles) a series of poetry volumes, the titles of which reflect the break he made with traditional poetry: *Vér és arany* (1908; *Blood and Gold*, 1969), *Az Illés szekerén* (1909; *On Elijah's Chariot*, 1969), *Szeretném, ha szeretnének* (1910; *Longing for Love*, 1969), *A minden titkok verseiből* (1910; *Of All Mysteries*, 1969), *Ki látott engem?* (1914; *Who Sees Me?*, 1969), and *A halottak élén* (1918; *Leading the Dead*, 1969). Everything about which he wrote was universal yet at the same time very Hungarian: his enthusiasm to struggle against existing wrongs, his desire for an explainable, "whole" world, his ambivalent attitude toward revolutionary change, and his view of the modern man-woman relationship as a ruthless struggle. He was deeply concerned about the loneliness of his nation in the dangerous modern world and the tragedy this position portends. He was never able to break the bonds of Calvinist determinism, but in his religious poems he presented the most tormented disputes with God and the most complete submission to his will ever witnessed in Hungarian poetry. His technique for creating a strange and mysterious world using the simplest language was supreme. Fusing iambic meter with the stressed rhythm of Hungarian poetry, his uncomplicated sentences evoke a variety of colors and shifting hues.

The most intellectual poet of the first *Nyugat* generation was Mihály Babits (1883-1941), who was willing to experiment with every form, style, and technique. Disdaining the emotional, enthusiastic approach to literature, he emphasized craftsmanship. In the face of significant social issues, however, he revealed that behind the mask of the aesthete, there was a noble, caring soul, devoted to human dignity. Like Babits, Dezső Kosztolányi (1885-1936) is most often referred to as a "bourgeois humanist." Overcoming the strong decadent influence of his youth, he continued to display occasional moments of theatricality. The child who lived in him juggled rhyme and rhythm with great dexterity, sometimes in sheer delight, sometimes ironically. The wonder of all things, the desire to discover every secret, compelled him to blend Impressionism and Symbolism almost spontaneously, in a variety of poetic forms. Later, no longer limited to recording the events of everyday life, he wrote poems concerning the eternal image of human action. His titles became unadorned, his structure well ordered, the stanzas often ending with vigorous Sapphic lines. Thus, he moved away from the bourgeois decadence of the *fin de siècle* and fused the modern immediacy of his poems with traditionally conceived forms.

If Ady represents an energetic and open commitment to social action and Babits represents a bourgeois humanism, passive until forced by desperation into action, then the other *Nyugat* poets may be described as taking positions between these two extremes. Early twentieth century Hungarian poetry was divided between an emphasis on self-expression and a subservience to the eternal demands of art, between the desire to change and the recognition of supreme permanence. The ambience of *Nyugat*, however, was such that the writers of its circle never became sharply polarized.

Gyula Juhász (1883-1937), probably the most "autobiographical" Hungarian poet of the twentieth century, voiced powerfully the distress of the solitary and oppressed individual. His poems, whether evoking images of the physical world or depicting the misery of the peasants, blend the delicate colors of Impressionism, the lethargy of *fin de siècle*, and the most realistic, even radical, tendencies with ease. Frequently recalling the past (especially in his love poems), he used a rich variety of adjectives, thus inducing a mood of melodious sweetness. The poetry of Árpád Tóth (1886-1928) was tired, fragmented, melancholy, expressing a vague desire to break out of the drabness of his world. In a number of other ways, too, he showed an affinity with poets of the West such as Paul Verlaine and Oscar Wilde. Rarely using any Symbolist devices, Tóth's poems were exceptionally rich in word pictures, similies, and metaphors. Lacking in his verse was any sympathy for the masses, as he believed it was in vain to hope to reach other souls in one's isolation. Milán Füst (1888-1967) used the brightest of colors in his relatively few poems, which evoked figures and images from the past. This was no mere return to Romanticism: Füst spent months polishing a single poem, merging the restlessness of Art Nouveau with classical monumentalism and a desire to achieve tranquillity. Füst's poems reveal a shrewdly designed private world in which the struggles with everyday problems of life and artistic destiny can be resolved.

During the politically and materially ruinous period between the two world wars, Hungary experienced a flowering of literary life. *Nyugat* continued to be the most resilient and effective forum for the modern poets of Hungary, in spite of repeated attacks from the Right and the Left alike. The growth of authoritarian nationalism evoked a corresponding wave of humanist opposition, although the latter was often tinged with a sense of hopelessness. The interwar poets broke with the idyllic worldview of the prewar decades, and many of them began seriously to doubt the viability of an "inner man." In order to escape the mannerism of the *fin de siècle*, they reached back to older forms, trying thereby to create order out of chaos. Few poets adhered to avant-garde principles, but their influence was significant. Lajos Kassák (1887-1967) was the first genuine worker who achieved a name for himself in Hungarian literature, largely through his poems exhibiting a bewildering array of Expressionist, Futurist, and decadent influences. His extravagant hopes for humankind were balanced by the firm structure of his verse, which was achieved without relying on rhyme, stress, or regular rhythm. In spite of the personal voice he employed, he did not speak for himself, instead expressing humankind's vehement response to the phenomena of modern technology.

If Ady's task was to initiate a literary revolution, that of Attila József (1905-1937) was to carry on and fulfill its promises. During his tragically short life, marred by poverty and neurosis, this gifted poet absorbed a great variety of influences. From Kosztolányi, he learned to respond to the immediacy of the moment; from Juhász, he gained an intimacy with his country and his fellow men; from Babits, the pursuit of classical values. József's daring use of and dexterity with construction reveal the influence of Kassák, while his interest in the simple forms and rhythm of Hungarian folk songs shows that he was not immune to the sway of modern populism. His poetry, nevertheless, shows a striking originality and uniqueness. True to his time and its influences, József intermingled material phenomena with the subjective stream of his moods, thus presenting an artistic experience which varied and dissolved according to the state of his mind. He demonstrated great facility in his use of traditional forms, achieving particularly striking effects with the sonnet. He may have solved the paramount artistic dilemma of his time, fully experiencing and giving poetic expression to the shattered and shattering twentieth century. He paid a price, however, for this achievement: "My heart is perched on nothing's branch," he wrote during the last year of his life, before he killed himself.

One of József's most original contemporaries was Lőrinc Szabó (1900-1957), who, exhibiting many traits of the bourgeois avant-garde, cannot be placed in any single category. He forged his individualistic style from a blend of strident Expressionism and the influence of the *Neue Sachlichkeit* (New Objectivity), tolerating no affectation. Szabó's poems always have a direct message without recourse to suggestion, invocation, or magic. An early theme of his poetry is the loss of illusions, which he later combined with the ruthlessness of nature and the futility of human struggle. It was only a short step from this to a solipsistic position and a fascination with Eastern philosophy, which may have served the poet well during the years of silence enforced upon him by the cultural policy of post-World War II Hungary.

While the claim is frequently made that the "official" literature of interwar Hungary was conservative and nationalistic, the artists of dissenting views, including those of the noncommunist Left, had considerable access to literary forums such as the periodicals or newspapers. Many of the middle-class poets, from socialist idealists to adherents of Catholicism, were characterized by an intellectual hunger, strong humanist convictions, and an "urbanist" attitude, the latter becoming the collective name under which they were known. Their best-known representatives were Zoltán Jékely (born 1913), a poet of wry, melancholy erudition, and György Rónay (1913-1978), whose modern verse was based on Christian humanism and rational sobriety.

The poetry of Miklós Radnóti (1909-1944) was characterized by the affirmation of order and harmony, respect for reason, and a strong interest in the classics. His early attraction to pastoral themes, emphasizing the joys of life and containing a wholesome eroticism, soon gave way to the realization that fateful social forces were at work in his Hungary. Aware of the terrible inhumanity looming over the horizon, he broke the superficial calm with powerful volumes, such as *Járkálj csak, halál-raítélt!* (1936; *Walk On, Condemned!*, 1980). His poetry blossomed on the verge of his violent death, when, as a prisoner of the Nazis, he penned some of his best lines during his final days. Sándor Weöres (1913-1989) turned away from the objective reality of his surroundings and used his instinctive skill to produce an unbelievably varied poetic output, which emphasized his interest in the sound of words and in the myths and rites of the eternal human condition.

Quite distinct from this group, a large heterogeneous body of writers and poets began to appear during the 1930's, whose special emphasis on rural themes marked them as the new populists. They believed that it was the peasantry who, after a meaningful land reform, would provide the ideology and the energy for a national revival, and that they would also produce a new, dedicated intellectual leadership. They visualized Hungary as forming a bridge between East and West, although most of them had no sympathy for the Soviet system. The rift developing between the new populists and the urbanists proved to be one of the great misfortunes of modern Hungary. Neither group was able to prepare the nation for the changes that were obviously coming after the end of World War II, and neither group was powerful enough to bring about a thorough "moral revolution" which would implement much-needed social reforms.

The outstanding figure of the populists, Gyula Illyés (1902-1983) is generally regarded as one of the foremost Hungarian poets of the twentieth century, as well as a versatile prose writer and playwright. Early in his career, he was strong enough to ignore traditional rules and seemed to delight in a stylized, disciplined "primitiveness." Persuasiveness and originality characterize his best poems, which are heroic in mood and subject, with a touch of melancholy discernible throughout. During the late 1930's, he was the spokesman of the populists, and his radical leftist past made him acceptable to every political group after the end of World War II. His enthusiasm for Soviet-imposed change soon cooled, and in 1956 he wrote *Egy mondat a zsarnokságról* (1956; *One*

Sentence on Tyranny, 1957), which may be called *the* Hungarian poem of the twentieth century. He wrote some of his finest poems in his old age, in verse characterized by musicality, gentle resignation, and introspection.

The end of World War II hardly signifies a milestone in the history of Hungarian literature, although thorough changes were implemented in the makeup of the country's intelligentsia. Hundreds of promising talents were destroyed by the war and its sordid aftermath, and as many or more were silenced later under various pretexts. After a few years of tenuous coalition, which offered genuine opportunities for free cultural development, the message was brought home that in the same manner that "there is no separate solution to Hungary's political problems," there would be no independent Hungarian cultural life, either. The pseudoprinciples of Socialist Realism were enforced in Hungary for only a few years, but their effects proved to be long lasting. Literature was placed completely in the service of daily politics, with bewildering and (in retrospect) amusing results.

Few dramatic changes resulted from the aftermath of the 1956 Revolution. After a handful of writers and poets were imprisoned, and a much greater number thoroughly intimidated, the "new" government declared that it was permissible for an artist to ignore politics. The Writers' Association was disbanded in order to create a "sounder" atmosphere, and the nation's best writers and poets quietly ceased publishing their creations. An eager coterie of political adherents tried to fill the gap, and authorities permitted many blameless and harmless apolitical poets to have their works printed, after years of muzzling them. The 1960's brought amnesties, the renewal of cautious debates, and the admission that there may be more than one kind of Socialist Realism. During the 1970's, with most of the real dissidents safely dead or out of the way, the authorities saw fit to open many avenues for literary experimentation and aesthetic debate, and exceptions to the Marxist hold on the country could be seen to demonstrate the resilience of the people's creative spirit.

POST-COLD WAR POETRY

In post-Cold War Hungary, in which literature and poetry of the prior several decades had functioned as a

moral opposition to the Communist government, there was great expectation of a flowering of literature once the political obstacles were removed and the writer finally could freely explore his or her imagination. Yet critics have found this has not happened, for several reasons. After the fall of the previous system, the dissident writer lost the poetic mission, a point of reference. Many writers also became politicians and had no time to write. Economics played a large role as well, with the cessation of government subsidies, the disintegration of state book-distributing giants, and steep increases in prices of new books. Living under high inflation and suffering from rising unemployment, the public was unable to afford as many books as it once purchased. Also, writers complained that, in the new commercial markets, unless a book promised profit, it would not be published regardless of its merit. The publishers that managed to stay in business tended to be those that published lurid potboilers, criminal and adventure stories, and soft-core pornography. As a reaction to the prohibition of erotic images and thrillers during the communist rule, the Hungarian public often favored such publications over more serious literature.

The literary landscape of the "new" Hungary also found increasing tension between traditional nationalist and religious ideas and those of the modern era. The populists—those who claimed themselves as the cultural arm-bearers of nationalism—started an offensive against cosmopolitan writers, known collectively as "urbanites," for the control of ideology and cultural lifestyle in Hungary. While the roots of this conflict stemmed from a decades-old rivalry between the city and the countryside, the more recent rise of multiparty politics has encouraged rivalry and resentment to increase. Populist authors regard the urbanites as arrogant because of their advantages in education, travel, and knowledge of languages—a gap that will take a generation or more to close. Urban liberals assume that the rural group is burdened by ideology. A glimpse into the populist mentality can be found in contemporary Hungarian poet Ferenc Juhasz's long poem "A szarvassá változott fiú kiáltozása a titkok kapujából" ("The Boy Changed to a Stag Cries Out at the Gate of Secrets"), based on a Transylvanian folktale. The theme "you can't go home again" is evident here, in that the provincial cannot return to the old way of life but also does not fit in with the liberal intellectual world of Budapest.

Sandor Csoori (born 1930), a leading contemporary Hungarian poet, essayist, and scriptwriter, has been called "the genius of discontent" and is considered to be one of the most prominent artistic spokespersons for the Hungarian people in the last decades of the twentieth century. A recipient of the Attila József Prize in Poetry, he also won the prestigious Kossuth Award, Hungary's greatest honor for achievement in artistic and scientific work. He serves as a modern voice for the populist movement, albeit a moderate one, and his poems and other literary works exhibit a never-ending concern over a threatened culture and national identity. For Csoori, the village represents a simpler society, the rudiments of a human community, a rough-hewn harmony beyond the experience of a more complex city. His cynicism is evident in "My Mother, a Black Rose," a tender and sensitive evocation of his mother's daily struggle for existence. Although not well, she still milks the cow, sweeps, and launders. "Unwelcome strangers," a code name for communist functionaries, talk to her "rudely" and, fearful, she tightens "her black shawl as if it were her loneliness." There are "wonderful new machines" around but no one comes to help her. "One night she falls to the ground/ Small, broken, shattered/ A bird will come/ And carry her away in his beak."

Despite the factionalism and political and cultural hurdles facing modern Hungary, it remains a country with an active literary culture. Fortunately, in the 1990's and at the beginning of the twenty-first century, the works of several major contemporary Hungarian poets—Csoori, Gyula Illyés, Ágnes Nemes Nagy, Miklós Radnóti, Gyozo Ferencz, György Petri—have become readily available in translation, widening the narrow conduit between Hungarian and world literatures.

One particular poet who received both critical and public acclaim was Gyorgy Petri, who died of cancer at the age of fifty-six in 2000. Readers appreciated Petri's combination of ideas and the language used to express these ideas. When it was still dangerous, he berated the "socialist regime" and kept the torch of the 1956 revolution burning. With the fall of communism in 1989, he then turned on himself, opposing the fragments of a society that seemed indestructible in its evilness, and he re-

voked memories, half heroic, half satiric, and issued statements on death. His poetic stance was rejection; he used the most ingenious devices to free himself of bile, but it seemed the more he got rid of, the more there was. His poem "Electra" displays his bitterness and is powerful not only because it serves as a powerful allegory of vengefulness in the wake of the abusive communist regime but also because it in part turns the myth around, to highlight universal guilt:

> Take my little sister, cute sensitive Chrysothemis
> to me the poor thing attributes a surfeit of moral
>   passion,
> believing I'm unable to get over
> the issue of our father's twisted death.
> What do I care for that gross geyser of spunk
> who murdered his own daughter!

Reality as equated with sorrowful-history-turning-into-detestable-sociology is not a matter to laugh about or something to play with. Yet, the poet would have liked to have played, if only his fearful honesty and his temperament had let him. Although well known as a love poet, Petri sullied what might be tender verses with obscenity and fierce irony to reflect how living under Hungary's dishonest, brutal communist regime cheapened even the finest feelings. He did not see an easy way to assuage the psychological damage inflicted by the Communists, even in the wake of communism's fall in 1989: "The epoch expired like a monstrous predator./ My favorite toy's been snatched."

BIBLIOGRAPHY

Duczynska, Ilona, and Karl Polányi, eds. *The Plough and the Pen: Writings from Hungary, 1930-1956.* Foreword by W. H. Auden. London: P. Owen, 1963.

Gömöri, George. *Polish and Hungarian Poetry, 1945 to 1956.* Oxford, England: Clarendon Press, 1966.

Gömöri, George, and Charles Newman, eds. *New Writings of East Europe.* Chicago: Quadrangle Books, 1968. English translations.

Grösz, Joseph, and W. Arthur Boggs, eds. and trans. *Hungarian Anthology: A Collection of Poems.* Munich: Griff, 1963. English translations.

Klaniczay, Tibor, ed. *History of Hungarian Literature: Eleventh-Eighteenth Centuries.* Budapest: Corvina

Kiadó, 1964. Collected essays translated into English.

Kolumban, Nicholas, ed. and trans. *The Science of In-Between: An Anthology of Nineteen Contemporary Hungarian Poets*. Introduction by A. M. Dropick. New York: Box Turtle Press, 1999.

_____. *Turmoil in Hungary: An Anthology of Twentieth Century Hungarian Poetry*. Berkeley, Ca.: New Rivers Press, 1982. Offers a broad scope of twentieth century works. Illustrated.

Makkai, Adam, ed. *In Quest of the "Miracle Stag": The Poetry of Hungary, an Anthology of Hungarian Poetry in English Translation from the Thirteenth Century to the Present*. Urbana: University of Illinois Press, 1996.

Nemeskürty, István. *A History of Hungarian Literature*. Budapest: Corvina, 1982. English translation of the Hungarian. Bibliography, index.

Pilinszky, Janos. *Metropolitan Icons: Selected Poems of János Pilinszky in Hungarian and English*. Studies in Slavic Language and Literature 8. Edited and translated by Emery Edward George. Lewiston, N.Y.: E. Mellen Press, 1995.

Reményi, József. *Hungarian Writers and Literature: Modern Novelists, Critics, and Poets*. Introduction by August J. Molnar. New Brunswick, N.J.: Rutgers University Press, 1964.

Szirtes, George, and George Gömöri, eds. *The Colonnade of Teeth: Modern Hungarian Poetry*. Newcastle upon Tyne: Bloodaxe, 1996. Offers a collection of works by modern Hungarian poets, including Miklós Radnoti, Attila József, Gyula Illyés, Ferenc Juhász, Sándor Csoori, and Gyozo Ferencz. The translators' "Notes on the Poems" and "Biographical Notes" are rich supplements.

Tezla, Albert, ed. *Ocean at the Window: Hungarian Prose and Poetry Since 1945*. Minneapolis: University of Minnesota Press, 1980. English translations with bibliography.

András Boros-Kazai,
updated by Sarah Hilbert

INDIAN ENGLISH POETRY

Before Indians could write poetry in English, two related conditions were necessary. First, the English language had to be sufficiently Indianized to be able to express the reality of the Indian situation; second, Indians had to be sufficiently Anglicized to use the English language to express themselves. The first of these two conditions, the Indianization of the English language, began much before the second, the Anglicization of Indians. Hence, though the first Indian poet to write in English was Henry Derozio, in the early nineteenth century, the Indianization of English had begun about three centuries earlier, in 1498, when Vasco da Gama, sailing from Lisbon, landed in Kerala. It was almost another century before the first Englishman came to India, but by the time Father Thomas Stephens arrived in Goa in 1579, a considerable body of Indo-Portuguese words were already being assimilated into English. Such lexical borrowing accelerated with the increasing British presence in India after 1599, when the East India Company was launched. For nearly 150 years after the charter of the East India Company, Englishmen in India wrote only travel books for the public and journals and letters in private. Nevertheless, by the end of the seventeenth century, a number of Indian words had been naturalized into English. The following is a selection from G. Subba Rao's catalog in his book *Indian Words in English* (1969):

> Amuck, Arrack, Bazaar, Bandicoot, Brahmin, Bungalow, Calico, Cash, Cheroot, Chintz, Chit, Compound, Cooly, Dhobi, Divan, Dungaree, Fakir, Ghee, Guru, Gunny, Hakim, Hookah, Imam, Jaggery, Juggernaut, Maharaja, Mongoose, Nabob, Pariah, Pucka, Punch, Pundit, Shampoo, Shawl, Tank, Toddy, Yogi, Zamindar.

Because the functional and pragmatic context of the language changed in India, English began to adapt itself to its new environment. This nativization process continued as the use of English increased, as schools were established to teach it, and as the number of Indians using it increased.

More important than this large-scale lexical borrowing was the fact that, by the end of the eighteenth century, Englishmen in India had started to write poetry on local Indian subjects, whereas earlier, they had written only travelogues, journals, and letters. Of these Englishmen in India, the most important was Sir William Jones (1746-1794), one of the first British Indian (or Anglo-Indian) poets. An accomplished linguist and translator, his familiarity with Indian traditions is reflected in his eight hymns to the various Indian deities. These poems are strictly Indian in both style and theme; in writing them, Jones demonstrated for future Indian poets that the English language could be a fit vehicle for Indian subject matter. Hence, by the beginning of the nineteenth century, the prospective Indian English poet not only inherited an English whose expressive range had been enlarged by a substantial lexical borrowing of Indian words, but also an English which, as British Indian poets such as Jones had shown, was richly amenable to Indian subject matter.

The second precondition, the Anglicization of Indians, began when the British became a powerful colonial power in India. This happened more than 150 years after the East India Company was chartered. In 1757, the British won the historic Battle of Plassey, which gave them control of Bengal. In 1772, they assumed the *Diwani*, or revenue administration, of Bengal, and in 1790, they took over the administration of criminal justice. Not until the British had changed from traders to administrators did the large-scale Anglicization of India begin. This Anglicization around the turn of the eighteenth century was marked by several crucial events. First, in 1780, India's first newspaper, *Hickly's Bengal Gazette*, was published in English. Second, in 1817, Raja Rammohan Roy, a prominent social reformer, helped found the Hindu College of Calcutta, which later, as Presidency College, became the premier educational institution of Bengal. Third, and most important, by 1835, the British government had laid the foundations of the modern Indian educational system, with its decision to promote European science and literatures among Indians through the medium of the English language. The result was that English became in India, as in other British colonies, a passport to privilege and prestige.

A study of the social and cultural contexts of Indian English poetry reveals several important insights into its origin. First, Indian English poetry began in Bengal, the province in which the British first gained a foothold. In addition, Indian English poetry was an urban phenomenon centered in Calcutta. In fact, for the first fifty years, Indian English poetry was confined entirely to Bengalis who were residents of Calcutta. Then, gradually, it moved to other urban centers, such as Madras and Bombay; even today, Indian English poetry is largely urban. Finally, because English was an elite language in India, Indian English poets belonged to the upper class. Thus, in its early years, most of the practitioners of Indian English poetry came from a handful of prominent Calcutta families.

CRITICAL APPROACHES

There are basically three ways of approaching Indian English poetry: as an extension of English poetry, as a part of Commonwealth poetry, or as a part of Indian poetry. The first approach is largely outdated today, while the second, though still current, has gradually yielded to the third.

When Indians first began to write poetry in English, they were outnumbered by Eurasians and Englishmen who also wrote poetry on Indian subjects. Hence, poetry by Indians was not distinguished from poetry by non-Indians. Indeed, both types were published by the same publishers, the Indian subsidiaries of British publishers such as Longman or Heinemann, or by the English newspapers and magazines of India, which were usually owned and edited by Eurasians or Englishmen. Most Indian English poets were educated by Englishmen in Anglophone schools; like other English poets, they studied English literature. Because India was a part of the British Empire, Indian English poets did not have a strong national identity, and their early efforts were considered to be a tributary of the mainstream of English literature. Anglo-Indian literature was the term used to denote their poetry, the implication being that this was English literature with Indian themes. The term referred primarily to the literature produced by Englishmen and Eurasians in India, though it also included work by "native" Indians. The first scholarly work on Anglo-Indian literature was Edward Farley Oaten's *A Sketch of Anglo-Indian Literature* (1908), a condensed version of which was included in the *Cambridge History of English Literature* (1907-1914), edited by A. C. Ward. Oaten's primary concern was with English writers such as Jones, Sir Edwin Arnold, and Rudyard Kipling, and Oaten made only passing reference to Indian writers in English. With India's independence from Britain and the withdrawal of the British from India, Anglo-Indian literature, defined as literature written by Englishmen in India, more or less came to an end. On the other hand, literature by Indians in English increased, gradually evolving an indigenous tradition for itself. Consequently, Oaten's approach became untenable in dealing satisfactorily with Indian English literature. Nevertheless, it continues to have a few adherents—among them George Sampson, who, in *The Concise Cambridge History of English Literature* (1970), contends that Indian English literature is a tributary of mainstream English literature.

Another approach, initiated by scholars in England in the early 1960's, is to consider Indian English literature as a part of Commonwealth literature or the literature of former British colonies and dominions such as Canada, Australia, the West Indies, and countries in Africa, South Asia, and Southeast Asia. *The Journal of Commonwealth Literature*, based at the University of Leeds, has done much to foster such an approach. Later, academics in the United States attempted to see Indian English poetry as a part of a global literature in English. The journal *WLWE: World Literatures Written in English* represents this approach. These approaches are fairly useful when the focus is large and the scholar is located in the United States or the United Kingdom, but they share the problem that the literatures of the various nationalities have little in common and often belong to different traditions: for example, Nigerian English literature and Australian literature. Nor does such an approach serve very well when one literature, such as Indian English poetry, is studied in depth. It then becomes clear that labels such as "Commonwealth literature" or "world literature in English" simply help to provide a forum for these literatures in Western academia and that detailed study is still pursued by nationality.

The most widely accepted approach to Indian English poetry is to regard it as a part of Indian literature. This approach might seem the obvious one, but it took nearly a century to gain wide acceptance and is not without its problems. In the first place, there is no such thing as Indian literature per se: Indian literature is constituted of literatures in the several Indian languages, including Hindi, Tamil, Bengali, and Manathi. Most of these literatures, however, have their roots in the Sanskrit tradition of Indian literature which flourished from roughly 1500 B.C.E. to 1500 C.E. After the latter date, the regional literatures in the various Indian languages emerged. Hence, it is possible to argue that a unified tradition in Indian literatures does exist. Once that is granted, the task of the critic is to place Indian English literature into such a framework. Considering that English is not traditionally an Indian language, that is not easy, although at the time that Indian English literature began to emerge, there was a renewed efflorescence in the other regional languages of India as well. Moreover, the "renaissance" of regional literatures occurred under a stimulus similar to the one that caused the emergence of Indian English literature— namely, the impact on India of British rule, Western knowledge, and the English language. It is reasonable, then, to regard Indian English poetry as a limb of the larger body of Indian poetry, a creation of the same sensibility that has produced other regional language poetry in India since the nineteenth century.

This approach was first propounded by Indian critics during the 1930's and 1940's, the most influential among them being K. R. Srinivasa Iyengar, whose *Indo-Anglian Literature* (1943) was the first book-length discussion of Indian English literature. Iyengar used the term "Indo-Anglian" to distinguish this literature from Anglo-Indian literature and to suggest that it was a part of Indian literature. In his introduction to *Indian Writing in English* (1982), Iyengar mentions that the phrase "Indo-Anglian" was used "as early as 1883 to describe a volume printed in Calcutta containing 'Specimen Compositions from Native Students.'" Probably, "Indo-Anglian" was merely an inversion of "Anglo-Indian," used to distinguish the poetry written by Indians from that of the Englishman. Alongside the term "Indo-Anglian," "Indo-English" was also used by critics who did not like the former. Both terms were used until the early 1970's, after which Indo-English gradually acquired greater acceptance. The term "Indian English" was used from the 1960's as synonymous with "Indo-English." Nowadays, it is being used increasingly in preference to other terms.

A BRIEF SURVEY

Henry Louis Vivian Derozio (1807-1831) is generally credited with being the first Indian English poet. His father was of Portuguese descent and his mother an Anglo-Indian. Derozio was Indian not only by birth but also by self-definition. This was especially remarkable because Derozio, a Christian, was reared among Eurasians and Englishmen, and many of his Hindu Bengali contemporaries strove hard to identify themselves with the British. Derozio's love for India is revealed in several of his poems. In his short life of twenty-three years, Derozio had a remarkable career as a journalist, a teacher at Hindu College, a leading intellectual of his day, and a poet. He has often been compared to John Keats.

Derozio wrote short poems for several magazines and newspapers of his day, but only one volume of his poems, *The Fakeer of Jungheera* (1828), appeared during his lifetime. A selection of his poems, published in 1923 by Oxford University Press, has subsequently been reprinted. As a poet, Derozio showed great promise, though he did not live to fulfill it. His poems reveal the great influence of the English Romantic poets, particularly Lord Byron and Sir Walter Scott. Derozio's sonnets and short poems, such as "To India My Native Land" and "The Harp of India," are his most accomplished works. His ambitious long poem *The Fakeer of Jungheera* is an interesting attempt to fuse the Byronic romance with the realities of the Indian situation. Despite the fact that Derozio's output was uneven and meager, he is counted as one of the major Indian English poets for both historical and artistic reasons.

NINETEENTH CENTURY: 1830-1880

A contemporary of Derozio, the Indian English poet Kasiprasad Ghose (1809-1873), published *The Shair and Other Poems* in 1830. Ghose has the distinction of being the first Hindu Bengali Indian to write English verse. He continued Derozio's efforts to deal with Indian subjects in his poems. An interesting example is his semicomic poem "To a Dead Crow," in which Ghose uses the unglamorous, common Indian crow as a subject. The persona Ghose created for himself was that of the *Shair*, or the poet in the Indian Persian tradition, indicating that although he wrote in English, his stance was that of an Indian poet.

Michael Madhusudan Dutt (1824-1873), whose long narrative poem *The Captive Ladie* (1849) was published about twenty years after Ghose's book, is an interesting figure in Indian English poetry. Dutt is remembered today not as an English poet but as the first and one of the greatest modern Bengali poets. After his failure at English verse, he turned to Bengali, his mother tongue. Dutt's case is frequently cited by those critics who believe that Indians cannot write good English poetry and should write only in their mother tongue. Since Dutt, there have been several other poets who began to write in English but turned to their native languages after being dissatisfied with their efforts in English. Dutt is also interesting because, though he acquired fame as a Bengali poet, he was extremely Anglicized. He not only converted to Christianity but also married an Englishwoman and qualified for the bar in England.

Another family of the Dutt name brought out *The Dutt Family Album* in 1870, featuring about two hundred pieces by Govin Chunder Dutt (1828-1884), his two brothers, and a nephew. Earlier, the whole family had converted to Christianity and, in 1869, had left India to live in England and other parts of Europe. The volume sheds light on the literary atmosphere prevailing in the aristocratic Dutt family, which was to produce another generation of poets in Govin's daughters Aru and Toru Dutt. Another notable poet of this time was Ram Sharma, born Nobo Kissen Ghose (1837-1918), who published three volumes of verse between 1873 and 1903. Sharma, who practiced Yoga for several years, tried to bring an Indian religious dimension to Indian English poetry. In this period, Indian English poetry moved out of Bengal for the first time with the publication of the Bombay poet B. M. Malabari's *Indian Muse in English Garb* (1876). Soon Cowasji Nowrosi Versuvala's *Counting the Muse* (1879) and A. M. Kunte's *The Risi* (1879) were published in Bombay and Poona, respectively. Though still an upper-class hobby, Indian English poetry was slowly spreading to metropolitan centers outside Bengal.

The poetry of the first fifty years of Indian English poetry (1825-1875) is generally considered imitative and derivative by critics. Certainly, the poems from this period which are usually anthologized do not show signs of very great talent. A judgment on the quality of these poets, however, must not be passed hastily, because most of their books are out of print and hence not easily available for critical scrutiny.

There is almost complete critical consensus that the talent of Toru Dutt (1856-1877) was an original one among Indian English poets. Like Derozio, she died young, and like Emily Brontë, her life has been the object of as much interest as her poetry. Toru Dutt left for Europe with her family when she was thirteen and attended a French school in Nice with her elder sister, Aru. The Dutts then moved to Cambridge, England, where Toru participated in the intellectual life of the university. Though converted to Christianity and very Anglicized, the Dutts felt alienated in England, and they returned to Calcutta four years after they had left, when Toru was seventeen. In 1874, soon after their return, Aru died. Earlier, when Toru was nine, her elder brother Abju had died. One year after her sister's death, Toru published *A Sheaf Gleaned in French Fields* (1875), which also featured eight pieces by Aru. These poems, "renderings" from the French, were enthusiastically received in India and England and soon went into three editions, the third published by Kegan Paul, London, with a foreword by Arthur Symons. In that same year, 1875, Toru took up the study of Sanskrit, and ten months later she was proficient enough in it to think of producing "A Sheaf" gleaned from Sanskrit fields. This volume was published in 1882, after her death, as *Ancient Ballads and Legends of Hindustan*, with a foreword by Edmund Gosse. Meanwhile, she had written one French novel and left incomplete an English novel, both of which were published after her death. Weakened by tuberculosis, she died in 1877 at the age of twenty-one.

The most significant aspect of Dutt's literary career was her return to her Indian heritage after her sojourn in the West. In *Ancient Ballads and Legends of Hindustan*, she converted popular myths from the *Rāmāyaṇa* (c. 500 B.C.E.), the *Mahābhārata* (c. 400 B.C.E.-c. 200 C.E.), and the *Purāṇas* into English verse. In this, she pioneered a way for several later Indian English writers who had similar problems regarding their literary identity. Dutt's English versions, except in a few instances, are without condescension to the original and without authorial intrusions. In addition to longer "ballads" and "legends" from Sanskrit mythology, Dutt wrote short lyrics, odes, and sonnets. The best of these, probably her best single poem, is "Our Casuarina Tree." This poem, reminiscent in both form and content of Keats's odes, is about the beautiful Casuarina tree in the poet's garden at Baugmaree. The tree, by the end of the poem, becomes a symbol not only of the poet's joyous childhood but also, through an extension in time and space, of the poet's longing for permanence and eternity. The poem is a masterpiece of craftsmanship, a fine blending of thought, emotion, and form. Though her output as a poet was not particularly prolific, *A Sheaf Gleaned in French Fields* and *Ancient Ballads and Legends of Hindustan* show sufficient accomplishment to entitle Dutt to her place in the pantheon of Indian English poets.

TURN OF THE CENTURY: 1880's-1920's

Sri Aurobindo (Aurobindo Ghose, 1872-1950) probably has the best claim to be regarded as the greatest Indian English poet. In a poetic career of more than fifty-five years, his output and range were truly staggering. Sri Aurobindo wrote lyrics, sonnets, long narrative poems, poetic drama, and epics. He was fluent in a variety of conventional meters, such as iambic pentameter and hexameter, and he also experimented with quantitative meter and mantric poetry. His reputation rests most securely on the posthumously published *Savitri* (1954), an epic of some twenty-four thousand lines. In *Savitri*, Sri Aurobindo used the story of Savitri's conquest of death in the *Mahābhārata*—a story that has influenced Indians for centuries as an exposition of perfect womanhood—and expanded it to create his epic. In this epic, Savitri realizes her divine potential as a human being and, like Christ, defeats death; after her conquest of death, she returns to earth as a symbol of what humanity can achieve. A mystic and a seer, Sri Aurobindo claimed merely to have described his own, palpable experience in writing the poem. In his "Letters on *Savitri*," which are attached to the authoritative edition of the poem, Sri Aurobindo says that the work was written under the highest possible poetic inspiration, which he called "over-mind poetry," a state in which there was no effort on his part and in which he was merely the scribe of a "vision" which descended, perfect and complete, upon him. *Savitri*, one of the longest poems in the English language (it is roughly twice the length of John Milton's *Paradise Lost*,

1667, 1674), is the most discussed poem in Indian English literature. It took about fifty years to finish—from the germ of the idea to the final written product—and a complete reading demands a long time; nevertheless, year after year it continues to attract and challenge critics, students, and readers.

As *Savitri* is the most discussed Indian English poetic work, Sri Aurobindo is the most discussed of the Indian English poets. His was a multifaceted personality—he was a seer, mystic, Vedantist, poet, philosopher, revolutionary political activist, literary critic, and thinker. Like many other major Indian English poets, he was born into an upper-class Anglicized family and was educated in England. Finding himself completely Westernized, he strove to find his roots, to realize himself, after returning to India. Remarkably successful in this, he is considered one of the greatest thinkers of modern India. As a poet, he was extremely well-versed in the European tradition of literature as well as the Indian tradition. Sri Aurobindo was fully conscious of what he was doing as a poet; he had a comprehensible theory of poetry and a clear view of what he sought to accomplish, both formally and thematically. His appraisal of the nature of poetry is clearly formulated in *The Future Poetry* (1953), and it is with this knowledge that his later, more difficult poetry is to be approached. Sri Aurobindo's poetry is easily available in the centenary edition of his *Complete Works* (1972).

If Sri Aurobindo is the greatest Indian English poet, Sarojini Naidu (1879-1949) is certainly the most popular, accessible, and moving—in a sense, the best Indian English poet. Naidu's poems are all songs, meant more to be heard than read. She is a lyric poet whose work shows a mastery of rhyme and meter. Her typical poem is short, usually consisting of fewer than twenty lines, although she did write some long sequences of short poems. The chief quality of her poetry is melody—the sound and sense combine to produce emotion, as in music. Within this musical, lyric paradigm, Naidu is extremely versatile. Like Rabindranath Tagore, she was a truly all-Indian poet, drawing upon the poetic traditions of several Indian languages and inspired by different regions of India and by different religious traditions.

The most remarkable feature of Naidu's poetry is its complete authenticity as Indian poetry. She achieves an

Indian quality of both form and content without the slightest self-consciousness. She uses both the rhythms and the conventions of Indian folk songs as inspiration for much of her poetry. The range includes songs of professions ("Palinquin Bearers," "Wandering Singers," "Indian Weavers"), love songs ("Indian Love-Song," "Love-Song from the North," "A Rajput Love-Song"), lullabies ("Cradle-Song," "Slumber-Song for Sunalini"), seasonal songs ("The Call of Spring," "Harvest-Song," "The Coming of Spring"), and devotional songs ("Lakshmi, the Lotus-Born," "Hymn to Indra, Lord of Rain," "Songs of Kanhaya"). Naidu's imagery, too, is strikingly Indian, transferred into English from conventions in Indian poetry. In "A Rajput Love-Song," for example, she says, "O Love! were you the *keora's* soul that haunts my silken raiment?" and "O Love! were you the scented fan that lies upon my pillow?" Both of these images are stylized and sophisticated, not naïve or simplistic. Naidu also uses discourse-types from Indian folk songs: Some of her songs are monologues, others duets, and still others are communal songs in several separate voices and in chorus. Naidu uses several Indian words as well as quotations from Indian languages to enhance the Indian flavor of her poems. These words and quotations, however, are harmonized completely in the poem and not used indiscriminately. All in all, Naidu's attempts to locate herself in an Indian tradition of poetry were highly successful.

During Naidu's lifetime, four volumes of her poems were published, *The Golden Threshold* (1905), *The Bird of Time* (1912), *The Broken Wing* (1917), and *The Sceptered Flute* (1943), a collection of the first three books. *The Feather of the Dawn* (1961) was published by her daughter after Naidu's death. Naidu's poetry shows no major change or development from her first to her last book; although the tone becomes more somber, the metric felicity is the same. Naidu was chiefly a love poet, and her poetry explores the many facets of love as outlined in the Sanskrit tradition of love poetry: love in union, love in longing, love in separation; the pain of love, the joy of love, the sin of love, the desire of love; earthly love, divine love. Toward the end of her career, she became increasingly a *bhakti*, or devotional, poet, expressing in poem sequences her transcendent love for the Almighty. Although her work is unpopular with a number of recent Indian English poets, Naidu remains the most critically acclaimed Indian English poet after Sri Aurobindo.

Aside from Sri Aurobindo and Naidu, the period from the 1880's to the 1920's produced two other major poets. Chief among these is Rabindranath Tagore (1861-1941). Strictly speaking, Tagore is not considered an Indian English poet. He wrote only one long poem, *The Child* (1931), directly in English, writing all of his other works in Bengali, translating some later into English. Nevertheless, it was Tagore's 1912 English rendering of his famous Bengali poem *Gitanjali* (1910) that won for him the Nobel Prize in 1913. After that, Tagore "translated" several of his works into English, deviating considerably from the originals in the process. These renderings into English pose a unique, theoretical problem for the student of Indian English poetry: Should these works be regarded as originals or as translations? This problem has not been solved satisfactorily, but the consensus is that they are translations. Tagore, as the greatest Bengali writer, obviously belongs rightfully to Bengali; his influence on Indian English poets, however, is so great that he cannot simply be ignored in that area of study. The least that can be said is that Tagore is another example of a bilingual poet, a phenomenon not at all uncommon in the traditionally multilingual society of India.

Another important poet of this period is Sri Aurobindo's elder brother Manmohan Ghose (1869-1924). Some of Ghose's early poems appeared in *Primavera* (1890) while he was still in England. During his lifetime, only one volume of his verse, *Love Songs and Elegies* (1898), appeared, but when he died, he left in manuscript several volumes of poetry—short poems; two incomplete epics, *Perseus, the Conqueror* and *Adam Unparadised*; and one long, incomplete poetic drama, *Nollo and Damayanti*. After his death, his longtime English friend Laurence Binyon published some of these lyrics as *Songs of Life and Death* (1926), prefaced by a memoir of Ghose. Recently, Calcutta University published Ghose's complete poems in five volumes, under the supervision of his daughters. Ghose's life was tragic. Returning to India after a completely English upbringing, he found himself out of place—in his own words, "de-nationalized." His wife's health had deteriorated, and she died after being paralyzed for years. Finally, the poet himself went blind. The most common criticism of his poetry is that it is totally un-Indian in form and content. This is largely true, though he did try to write his long poetic drama, *Nollo and Damayanti*, on an Indian theme. Ghose came close to being an English poet despite being Indian, but at that, too, he was doomed to fail. Today, despite his metric virtuosity, neither do his poems appeal to Indian readers nor has he found a place in the canon of English poetry. Ghose, at best, is uneasily an Indian English poet. His example, unfortunately, has not deterred other Indians from completely Westernizing themselves.

TWENTIETH CENTURY: 1920'S-1950'S

The period from the 1920's to the 1950's was marked by a great efflorescence of Indian English poetry. It produced literally scores of poets, each with several volumes of verse to his or her credit. For the first time, a large mass of Indian English poetry was created, no longer confined to the upper class. Unfortunately, though this period produced a large quantity of poetry, it has been neglected by critics, primarily because the modernist poets of the 1950's were so united in their aversion to their predecessors.

Though this period produced a large quantity of poetry, it is the most neglected and underrated period in Indian English poetry. The chief reason for this is the severe reaction against this poetry by the post-1950's poets. Indeed, contemporary Indian English poets have been so united in this aversion that most recent anthologies totally omit the poets who came to maturity in the preceding generation. Although it is common in literature for the present generation to react against the previous generation, this reaction has reached allergic proportions in contemporary Indian English poetry. Much of the poetry of the period from the 1920's to the 1950's is becoming scarce—many of the publishers of that era are now defunct, and no serious attempt has been made to preserve these texts. Few libraries outside India possess texts from this period, and even in India, they are scattered in different places. Consequently, the poets of this period have received very little critical attention.

The best-known poet of this period is Harindranath Chattopadhyaya (born 1898). Starting with his *Feast of Youth* (1918), he regularly published volumes of verse and poetic drama into the 1960's. He is easily one of the most prolific poets in Indian English poetry. The range of his content is very diverse, covering a whole spectrum of ideologies from extreme Aurobindonian idealism to revolutionary Marxist materialism. His formal range, however, is limited; he usually writes rhymed, metric verse which, though competent, is sometimes predictable and cloying.

Most of the other poets of this period can be divided into three groups: the Aurobindonian and religious poets, the lyric and Romantic poets in the tradition of Naidu and Tagore, and the poets whose work reflects a transition from this Romanticism to the modernity of the post-1950's poets.

This period produced several poets who were inspired by Sri Aurobindo; they are sometimes called the Pondicherry school, because they lived in the Aurobindo ashram in Pondicherry and were disciples of Sri Aurobindo. The most famous of them are K. D. Sethna (born 1904) and Dilip Kuman Roy (born 1898). Others, also inspired by Aurobindo, are Nirodbaran, Nolini Kanta Gupta, Prithri Singh Nahar, Anilbaran, Punjalal, Romen, and Themis. Some of their poetry has seemed obscure to readers because of its mysticism. Other religious and devotional poets are Ananda Acharya, T. L. Vaswani (1879-1966), and Jiddu Krishnamurti (born 1895).

The largest number of poets in this period practiced the lyric, Romantic mode of Naidu and Tagore. It is perhaps because of these two poets that the impact of European modernism on Indian English literature was considerably delayed. Many of these neo-Romantics were professors of English in India; examples are P. Seshadri (1887-1942), N. V. Thadani, Shyam Sunder Lal Chordia, Govinda Krishna Chettur (1898-1936), Armando Menezes (born 1902), Hymayun Kabir, V. N. Bhushan (1909-1951), and P. R. Kaikini. There are many more, and their total output is massive. Their poetry has long been out of fashion, seeming effusive and quaint, but certainly not all of it can be dismissed outright, as has often been the case.

Several poets of this period effected the transition from Romanticism to the modernism of the post-1950's poets. These transitional poets introduced concrete, commonplace imagery, irony, the language of common speech, and a personal, psychological dimension to Indian English poetry. Probably the earliest "new" poet of Indian English was Shahid Shurawardy, whose *Essays in Verse* (1937) was avowedly influenced by T. S. Eliot and other modernists. Though some of his poetry seems to be merely self-conscious muttering and vague, allusive cerebration, Shurawardy certainly brought a new tone to Indian English poetry. His work, however, was lost to most Indians after he migrated to Pakistan after the partition of India in 1947. Another poet who struck a new, realistic note was Manjeri Iswaran (1910-1968). Bharati Sarabhai created a sensation in English literary circles with her poetic drama *The Well of the People* (1943), in which she used several of Eliot's techniques. Joseph Furtado (1872-1947) was another talented poet of this period who experimented considerably with language. Though he was predominantly a lyric poet, he brought an element of realism and rustic humor to Indian English poetry. His chief contribution was his use of Indian English pidgin and code-mixed varieties in poems such as "Lakshmi" and "The Old Irani." In these poems, Furtado not only anticipated contemporary poets such as Nissim Ezekiel, who exploit pidgin in their poetry, but also helped to bring the language of Indian English poetry closer to the language of the bilingual speech community in which English is actually used in India. What is interesting is that Furtado's use of pidgin, unlike Ezekiel's, is not parodic or condescending; whereas for Ezekiel, the joke is at the expense of an Indian variety of English, for Furtado, the comedy derives from authentic characterization.

A REVOLUTION IN TASTE

During the 1950's, the dominant tone in Indian English poetry shifted from Romanticism to irony. The revolution in taste did not occur overnight, but once established, its impact was swift and sweeping. What had been minority voices suddenly became the majority: A whole generation rejected its immediate past. This rejection is nicely voiced in Nissim Ezekiel's first book, *A Time to Change and Other Poems* (1951).

The new poets were a vocal group and did not hesitate to denigrate openly their predecessors. P. Lal, for example, attacked Sri Aurobindo at length, though Lal retracted his strictures a few years later; dividing readers into those who could appreciate Sri Aurobindo and those who could not, Lal firmly placed himself and the poets of his generation in the latter category. This debunking of poetic ancestors continued. In an influential article titled "The New Poetry," published in *The Journal of Commonwealth Literature* (July, 1968), the poet Adil Jussawala required fewer than three pages to dismiss Indian English poets from Derozio to Naidu, claiming that the best Indian English poetry was being written by poets of his generation. Eight years later, R. Parthasarathy, another contemporary poet, introducing his now widely used anthology *Ten Twentieth Century Indian Poets* (1976), reiterated Jussawala's claims.

Many other poets of this generation echoed the notion that theirs was the only Indian English poetry worthy of the name. However, these "new" poets soon divided into two main factions, those who practiced the dominant ironic mode and those who preferred a more traditional lyricism and Romanticism.

Besides Ezekiel, some of the poets who practice the ironic, clipped mode are Parthasarathy, A. K. Ramanujan, Gieve Patel, Shiv K. Kumar, Arun Kolatkar, and Jayanta Mahapatra. A typical poem in this mode involves an alienated speaker observing a typically Indian situation with detachment. Examples are numerous: In Keki Daruwala's "Routine," a policeman cynically regards yet another violent mob that he has to disperse; in Ezekiel's "Background, Casually," the poet assesses ironically his own lack of identity; in Kolatkar's *Jejuri* (1974, 1976), a place of pilgrimage is seen through the eyes of a detached and nonconformist visitor; Mahapatra's "The Whorehouse in Calcutta Street" shows a detached, self-critical observer recording his impressions of a brothel; in "Homecoming," Parthasarathy records his homecoming experience with self-critical irony; in "Naryal Purnima," Patel sits apart, commenting on a religious tradition from which he is alienated; in "Obituary," Ramanujan views the death of his father with ironic detachment. The same paradigm repeats itself. The situation is Indian; the observer is a self-critical, detached outsider. The poets use this mode to write both about themselves and, as in Mahapatra and Daruwala, about the external world. Often, as in Kamala Das, the early poems of A. K. Mehrotra, or in Pritish Nandy, the irony turns to anger. Most of these poets write free verse in a language that is as precise and close to "standard" English as possible. Exceptions, such as Ezekiel's poems in Indian English, are usually parodies.

There were, however, some poets who chose to write in the lyric and Romantic strain. The chief practitioners of this mode include V. K. Gokak, Keshav Malik, Karan Singh, Shankar Mokashi-Penekar, and, in their later works, Lal and Nandy.

INDIAN WOMEN POETS: NEW SUBJECTS, NEW SENSIBILITIES

In the final years of colonial rule and even in the first decade after Independence, there were far fewer women poets in India than men. In the 1960's, Kamala Das (born 1934) established her reputation by writing striking, confessional poems exploring female sexuality and arguing for women's sexual rights. However, it was not until the middle 1970's that works by women poets began appearing in significant numbers. *The Bird's Bright Ring: A Long Poem*, by Meena Alexander (born 1951), was published in 1976, and her collection *Without Place*, in 1978. In 1979, the Goan Eunice de Souza (born 1940) published her first volume, *Fix*. The telling portraits of de Souza's fellow Catholics made this book not only the writer's most controversial but probably the most distinctive of her many fine works. *Fix* is also important in that it was published by Newground, a cooperative started by three poets, including Melanie Silgardo (born 1956), another of the many outstanding women writers who came to the attention of readers late in the 1970's.

It should be noted that controversial ideas and radical views were also expressed by women writing in the regional languages, such as the Bengali poet and social worker Maitraye Devi (born 1914), who voiced her concern for peasants and for tribal people, and Amrita Pritam (born 1919), whose poems in Punjabi focus on the mistreatment of women after her native area of India became part of Pakistan. Pritam herself settled in India, and her experiences help to explain why there are so many more women writers in India than in Muslim Pakistan. However, in *We Sinful Women: Contemporary Urdu Feminist Poetry* (1991), seven Urdu women poets protest the ongoing repression of their gender by the religious and civil authorities of Pakistan. This collection

was recognized throughout the world as an important expression of feminist feeling within the Muslim world. Wisely, the editor of this collection, Rukhsana Ahmad, had made wide circulation of the volume possible by translating all of the poems into English and printing her versions beside the Urdu originals.

Although not all of the women writers who have emerged since the 1960's are preoccupied with sexuality, feminism, or social justice, they are far more concerned with such issues than with that of language, which loomed so large in the minds of the first postcolonial generation of writers. It now seems to be generally accepted that English is no longer to be regarded as the language of an oppressor, but instead is seen as a convenience, as a common means of expression, which can be adapted to reflect everyday life on the Indian subcontinent and which will probably ensure a much wider distribution of one's work than publication in a regional language. On the other hand, those who choose to write in one or another of the regional languages are no longer faced with almost insurmountable difficulties in finding a translator. As Vinay Dharwadker comments in his preface to *The Oxford Anthology of Modern Indian Poetry* (1994), there are now a great many excellent translators actively seeking new materials for new audiences throughout the world. Whether they write in regional languages or in English, Indian poets of both genders can now aspire to international distribution.

WRITERS AND THE WIDER WORLD

If Partition displaced some writers, many more left their native areas as international travel became less costly and as opportunities for them to study and to teach abroad multiplied. Since the new multiculturalism among Western readers was creating a rapidly expanding market for works by Indian writers, whether written in English or translated into English, it was only natural that those writers would go west to meet this new and highly appreciative public, some of them to visit or to stay for a time, some of them to remain permanently.

These new developments made the old nationalistic objections to writing in English seem irrelevant; now the question was whether or not the writers of the diaspora should even be classified as Indian writers. The English-language Muslim poet Agha Shahid Ali, for example, was born in Delhi in 1949, grew up in Kashmir, and returned to Delhi for his education before moving permanently to the United States in 1976. One might expect exile to be the theme of Ali's poems. However, he draws upon his own experiences primarily as a basis for his definition of the human condition. Wherever people live, Ali suggests, they are subject to change, and as a result they will suffer from a sense of loss and of longing for what is past.

Displacement and loss are also major themes in the poetry of Dom Moraes (Dominic Frank Moraes, born 1938). Born in Bombay, educated there and at Jesus College, Oxford, Moraes was a great success in England, both personally and professionally, from the time his first book of poems, *A Beginning* (1957), written when he was only nineteen, won the 1958 Hawthornden Prize. However, he did not feel at home there or in his native Bombay, where he finally settled after a journalistic career that took him all over the world. Like Ali, Moraes believes that one always feels like an exile, even if technically one is "at home." Keki N. Daruwalla (born 1937) would agree. Although he was born and educated in India and made his home in New Delhi, Daruwalla does not feel any sense of stability. Again and again he points out in his poetry that no place on earth is exempt from change. What bothers him about history, which Daruwalla defines as no more than a record of changes, is that it records public events rather than private tragedies. In such poems as "Hawk" and "A City Falls," Daruwalla stresses his conviction that what transpires in the life of an individual, caught in cataclysmic change, is more significant than what happens to a city or even to a society.

In his revised edition of *Modern Indian Poetry in English* (1987), Bruce King credits Vikram Seth (born 1952) with altering the Western world's attitude toward Indian poetry in English, which up to that point had been classified more as a hobby for a few readers than as part of mainstream English literature. Seth's volume *The Humble Administrator's Garden* (1985) so delighted the London reading public, King explains, that critics began talking about including the title poem in future anthologies of English poetry. Their approval was due as much to Seth's evident rejection of the excesses of modernism in favor of a more polished style as to his captivating

wit. Seth was soon just as popular in New York as he had become in London, and with the publication of his novel in rhymed verse titled *The Golden Gate: A Novel in Verse* (1986), he gained an international reputation. Seth is a typical representative of the new cosmopolitanism among Indian writers. He was born in Calcutta and eventually made his home in New Delhi. However, Seth was educated at Oxford, at Nanjing University in China, and at Stanford University in California, where for several years he also was an editor for the Stanford University Press. Tibet was the setting of Seth's award-winning travel book, *From Heaven Lake: Travels Through Sinkiang and Tibet* (1983). Perhaps it was not surprising that his verse novel, which is set in San Francisco, drew criticism in India for not being "Indian" enough. These critics were happier with Seth's story of an Indian family, the best-selling novel *A Suitable Boy* (1993).

Wherever they live and whatever their subject matter, however, it is evident that Indian poets remain conscious of their roots. For example, Sujata Bhatt (born 1956), who was born in Ahmedabad of a family originally from Gujarat, was educated in the United States and eventually made her home in Germany. However, not only does she translate Gujarati poetry into English, but she also uses Gujarati words and even whole lines of Gujarati in her own poems. It has been pointed out that good intentions do not necessarily make for good poetry. Often Bhatt's bilingual experiments do not work. Nevertheless, her attempts to express the multicultural experience must be noted, and some of her poems, especially those in *Brunizem* (1988) are very good indeed.

At the end of the twentieth century, Indian poetry written in English, as well as regional poetry translated into English, was at last attaining the recognition it deserved. Critics were enthusiastic about the new generation of Indian writers; publishers in Great Britain and in the United States were anxious to bring out their works; and readers throughout the world were becoming familiar with poets hitherto unknown to them. In this case, at least, change was all for the better.

BIBLIOGRAPHY

De Souza, Eunice. *Talking Poems: Conversations with Poets*. New Delhi: Oxford University Press, 1999. Interviews with ten important Indian poets, conducted by a writer and editor who is herself a major poet.

_____, ed. *Nine Indian Women Poets: An Anthology.* Delhi: Oxford University Press, 1997. Two generations of post-Independence Indian writers, selected because their poetry is of consistently high quality, are represented in this volume. Contains biographical notes, critical commentaries, and an index of first lines.

Dharwadker, Vinay, and A. K. Ramanujan, eds. *The Oxford Anthology of Modern Indian Poetry.* Delhi: Oxford University Press, 1994. Dharwadker's introduction, focusing on translation, and his lengthy "Afterword: Modern Indian Poetry and Its Contexts" are both invaluable. Annotations to the poems, biographical notes on both poets and translators, and a comprehensive index.

King, Bruce. *Modern Indian Poetry in English.* Rev. ed. New Delhi: Oxford University Press, 2001. This important critical work, which first appeared in 1987, now has a second section covering the final decade of the twentieth century. Chronology, useful appendices, and index.

Mehrotra, Arvind Krishna, ed. *The Oxford India Anthology of Twelve Modern Indian Poets.* Delhi: Oxford University Press, 1992. Includes a good general introduction, as well as biographical-critical essays on each writer. Bibliography and indices.

Naik, M. K. *Dimensions of Indian English Literature.* New Delhi: Sterling, 1984. Four of the essays in this volume deal with poetry. The discussions of A. K. Ramanujan, Arun Kolatkar, and Nissim Ezekiel are all insightful. Also recommended is "The Achievement of Indian English Poetry." Index.

Verma, K. D. *The Indian Imagination: Critical Essays on Indian Writing in English.* New York: St. Martin's Press, 2000. In addition to an introductory discussion of "Structure of Consciousness, Literary History and Critical Theory," contains chapters on Sri Aurobindo and Nissim Ezekiel. Notes and an index.

Makarand Paranjape,
updated by Rosemary M. Canfield Reisman

ITALIAN POETRY TO 1800

Poetry and literature in the Italian vernacular, the common language that sprang from the ashes of Latin, arose in Italy around the beginning of the thirteenth century and soon displayed itself in literary works of major importance, such as Dante's *La divina commedia* (c. 1320; *The Divine Comedy*, 1802), Petrarch's *Canzoniere* (manuscript 1374, pb. 1470; *Rhymes*, 1976), and Giovanni Boccaccio's *Decameron: O, Prencipe Galetto* (1349-1351; *The Decameron*, 1620). This linguistic success is so extraordinary that one wonders how it was possible that such a literary phenomenon could take place in a language whose written tradition is so recent. The spoken language, however, had a long history, which is represented by the development of Latin into several vernaculars. The heritage and cultured structures of Italian have roots that are deep and extensive, developing from the culture and literature of the medieval period, the time from the fall of the Western Roman Empire to the beginning of the thirteenth century.

FROM LATIN TO ITALIAN

During that long period of time, Italy developed a literature that, on one hand, was no longer in Latin but, on the other, was not yet in Italian. This language maintained the appearance of Latin but was quite different from classic Latin; it was the Latin used by the Church and by educated people, a language that, after the fall of the Roman Empire, spread throughout Europe as the cultured language and remained as the official language of science until the modern age. Medieval literature, however, was not developed extensively, and its quality, from an artistic point of view, was rather limited.

During the Middle Ages, the Church had become the major source of knowledge and culture, and it had inherited from Rome its characteristic of universality. The major documents of medieval Christian thought profoundly shaped the values of the new vernacular literature; particularly influential were the works of the Scholastic philosophers, among whom towers Saint Thomas Aquinas and in which one can find the vital roots of Dante's *The Divine Comedy*.

Italian vernacular poetry began in the thirteenth century with the simultaneous flowering of written literature in several of Italy's competing dialects. In the twelfth century, it had appeared that the Sicilian dialect was going to acquire the status of a national language; Sicily, at the time of the Emperor Frederick II (1194-1250), had become an important center of cultural life and art. This Sicilian superiority was ephemeral, however, vanishing after the death of the emperor. It was instead the Florentine tongue that, for several reasons, became the national language. The Florentine dialect prevailed primarily because, during the period of assertion of the vernacular, some of the greatest masterpieces of Italian literature were written in that dialect.

EARLY VERNACULAR WORKS

The earliest extant poetic compositions in the vernacular are religious works intended for doctrinal instruction; typical examples of this genre are Bonavesin della Riva's *Libro delle tre scritture* (c. 1300; book of the three scriptures) and Fra Giacomino da Verona's *De Jerusalem celesti* (c. 1230) and *De Babilonia civitate infernali* (c. 1230). In the field of specifically religious poetry, which contains a clear and pure effusion of spiritual feelings, there is the *Laudes creaturarum* (c. 1225) by Saint Francis of Assisi and the oeuvre of Jacopone da Todi, which includes 102 laudes. Though the majority of these religious poems narrate the deep mystical experience of the author, there are also several that are of a moral and satiric nature.

Of greater importance from an artistic and cultural point of view is the development in Italy of a lyric poetry of Provençal origin, which reflected a courtly concept of love that was conceived as an homage to "the lady" according to the principles dictated by the codes and rules of feudal society. The courtly content of this poetry and the very elaborate style rarely offered the possibility of expressing truly sincere and deep feelings. The poetry created by this style gave more importance to the artifice of the form than to the originality of the inspiration and was therefore characterized by a certain coldness.

The poetic genre had some success in northern Italy as a result of the troubadours, who traveled from court to court from Provence into northern Italy. The most consistent achievement of this lyric style, however, took place in Sicily at the court of Frederick II, where it assumed the status of a school. Among its most celebrated poets were Frederick himself and his sons, Enzo and Manfredi. In addition, there were resident courtiers such as Jacopo da Lentini and Giacomino Pugliese. The aesthetic value of the poetry of the Sicilian school is minimal; there, the worst traits of Provençal poetry were accentuated. Nevertheless, the historical significance of the Sicilian school is great: It constituted the first attempt to use the vernacular with a clear artistic intention. At this historical moment, as earlier mentioned, Sicilian could have become the national language. Historical events, however, prevented that. Frederick II died in 1250, and with his demise the power of his court soon disappeared and the cultural and literary effort which he so strongly supported collapsed.

DOLCE STIL NUOVO

The poetry of the Sicilian school had, nevertheless, already found a fruitful development in Tuscany, where its poetic themes were enriched with political and religious elements—particularly in the works of Guittone d'Arezzo and in the amorous poetry of Chiaro Davanzati. Furthermore, the Sicilian experience was instrumental in suggesting a new development, a new conception of love poetry that was proposed by the advocates of the *dolce stil nuovo* (sweet new style). In this new style, feelings are based on a bourgeois experience—the culture of the communes—not on a feudal one as was the case with Provençal poetry. Supported by a mystical consciousness, the new poetry exemplified a greater sincerity of expression and was supported by deeper sensitivity and more ardent feelings. Guido Guinizzelli's lyric poem "A cor gentile ripara sempre amore" ("Love Seeks Its Dwelling Always in a Gentle Heart") established what could be considered the schematic structure of the new school. Originating in Bologna, this innovative way of creating verses reached Florence, where Guido Cavalcanti further developed it in his poem "Donna mi prega" ("A Lady Asks Me"). Cino da Pistoia brought to the *dolce stil nuovo* a new psychological concept of love, substantively humane, with a potential that Dante was to explore in his work *La vita nuova* (*The New Life*), written shortly after 1292. *The New Life* narrates the spiritual unfolding of his pure love for

Beatrice, a girl whom he met early in his life and who died young in 1290, leaving the poet grief-stricken. Under the influence of the *stilnovisti*, Dante cultivated his love for Beatrice as a pure—almost religious—feeling through which he might be led to spiritual perfection. This concept would be developed extensively in his masterpiece, *The Divine Comedy*.

DANTE

Dante Alighieri was born in Florence in 1265 into a Guelph family that claimed ancient noble origins. He received his early education from the Franciscan friars of Santa Croce Church in his native town and, from the poetry of the Sicilian school that had spread into central Italy, he learned to write verses in the vernacular. Like many other citizens of Florence in his social condition, Dante participated in the tumultuous political life of the commune. As a consequence of these activities, he was exiled when the Black faction of the Guelph party, which was supported by Pope Boniface VIII, won political dominance over the White faction, to which Dante belonged. The Blacks banished the leaders of the Whites from Florence and its territory. Military attempts to regain power organized by the White faction failed. Dante resigned himself to the life of an exile and stayed at several courts in northern Italy, finally settling down in Ravenna at the court of Guido da Polenta. In Ravenna, he devoted his attention to completing his sacred epic, *The Divine Comedy*. He died in Ravenna in 1321.

It is significant that Dante composed his masterpiece in exile. After a long period of tumultuous events, the moment for deliberation had come. On the one hand, the recent past appeared to him as a forest of mistakes; on the other hand, he could visualize the possibility of a transcending order, embracing Heaven and Earth. Dante believed that the misled and corrupt humanity of his time could organize itself into a new order which could reach the goal of temporal and eternal happiness. This empire would be universal and divinely ordained, and the emperor would be independent in his temporal power, his authority granted directly to him by God and not by the Pope. Other motives that certainly influenced the composition of the poem were Dante's love for Beatrice and the desire to glorify her, his desire for justice, and his need to express his aesthetic insight and creative imagination.

In *The Divine Comedy*, Dante describes being lost in "una foresta oscura," a dark forest which represents the confusion of life. As a result of his experience, he acquires a consciousness of the sad condition of his spirit. He wants to free himself from this anguished state, but with human resources alone the soul cannot save itself. If a man with a soul in distress shows good intentions, however, he deserves the help of God; the Holy Virgin, representing "Divine Mercy," comes to his aid. She calls on Lucia (Saint Lucy), the "Enlightened Grace," who, in turn, goes to Beatrice, the symbol of knowledge in divine matters. Beatrice—who is also the human woman loved by Dante—descends into Limbo and begs Vergil, who represents "right reason," to bring help to Dante. Reason tells Dante that he cannot go suddenly from a sinful life to one of perfection; he must first face the dreadful consequence of sin by visiting Hell. He must then continue to Purgatory to make amends for his sins. Only then, after having reached the condition of natural perfection (the Terrestrial Paradise), will Dante be able to go to the Celestial Paradise and therefore reach the supreme reward, undergoing the beatific Vision of God. In this last part of Dante's mythical voyage, Vergil, "right reason," will not be a sufficient guide, and Dante will visit Paradise with the help of Beatrice.

The Divine Comedy is an epic poem of one hundred cantos. These cantos are collected into three parts, each of which is dedicated to one of the kingdoms of the life beyond: *Inferno, Purgatorio* (*Purgatory*), and *Paradiso* (*Paradise*). The *Inferno* is described in strong and vivid terms: the terrible heat and fires of the underworld, the agonies of the suffering, the terrors of the devils. In *Purgatory*, where the passions are appeased, there predominates a condition of melancholy generated by the recollection of the flawed past life and the interminable waiting for the state of eternal beatitude. In *Paradise*, Dante acknowledges the impossibility of conveying absolute happiness and holiness in earthly terms.

Although *The Divine Comedy* is Dante's masterpiece, he left other notable works as well. In addition to the poems that are included in *The New Life*, pervaded by mystical love, he composed a collection of *canzoniere* (lyric poetry) that documents the further artistic development that the poet had to undergo in order to reach the richness of motive that characterizes *The Divine Comedy*.

Dante's achievements mark a moment of great cultural change in the history of Italy. On the one hand, he summarizes the thought, life, and aspirations of the Middle Ages; on the other hand, he opens the door to a modern conception of life and culture. If Dante's gaze is fixed toward Heaven, he is not blind to temporal happenings, and he observes the Earth in all of its aspects and details. He does not ignore the mystery of the human soul. Rather, as exemplified in one of the cantos of *The Divine Comedy*, he embraces the courage of Ulysses, who ventured to discover new worlds. Thus, Dante anticipates the questing spirit of the Renaissance.

PETRARCH

The political ideas of Petrarch, the other major poet of the thirteenth century and one of the major figures of Italian literature, present a historical ambience quite different from that of Dante. Politically, Petrarch is far removed from the conception of a universal empire. His interest is clearly concentrated on Italy seen as a country geographically and ethnically different from any other country beyond the mountain chain of the Alps. Culturally, Petrarch departs from the medieval worldview; for him, the classical world acquires a new interest. Thus, Petrarch could be considered a precursor of Humanism.

From a psychological point of view, Petrarch does not possess the self-assurance that is typical of Dante. He appears to be more introspective, with a tendency toward self-analysis which may have accounted for his uncertainty and unhappiness—elements that constitute the essence of his poetry. The conflict between his religious desires and his worldly attitudes is never fully resolved. There is no serenity or dramatic resolution for him, only the constant melancholy that is characteristic of the modern spirit.

Petrarch was born Francesco Petrarca in Arezzo on July 20, 1304, the son of Pietro di Parenzo (commonly known as Ser Petracco), a Florentine notary who belonged to the White political faction and was exiled in 1302, the same year in which Dante was exiled. In 1312, the family moved to near Avignon, in France, where

Petrarch's father had found employment with the papal court. Petrarch studied law at the universities of Montpellier and Bologna, but his interest was oriented more toward literature than law. In 1327, in the Church of Santa Chiara in Avignon, he first saw Laura, the woman who was the major source of inspiration for his poetry. Petrarch served several lords in Italy, especially those of Colonna, a powerful Roman family that contributed several popes to the Church. Petrarch traveled through the many regions of Italy as well as in France, Flanders, and Germany. Later, he returned to Provence and retired to Vaucluse, a small town not far from Avignon. He spent his time writing a long epic poem in Latin, *Africa* (1396; English translation, 1977), his most extended work in that language. The poem was inspired by Vergil's *Aeneid* (c. 29-19 B.C.E.) and was written in hexameter and subdivided into nine cantos. Petrarch felt this epic to be his major contribution to the literature of his time. It was successful during his lifetime, and in 1340 Petrarch was rewarded with the title of poet laureate by the Senate in Rome. During this period, he continued his activities as a diplomat at the service of various courts in Italy. He also continued with his literary endeavors, which included collecting ancient texts by Latin authors. Later, he went to live in the territories of the Republic of Venice and died in 1374 in Arquà, a small town near Padua, where he had gone into seclusion.

The true poetic glory of Petrarch, however, derives almost exclusively from the lyrics he wrote in the vulgar tongue, *Rerum vulgarium fragmenta*, or *Canzoniere*. Though he dismissed these lyrics as *nugellae* (little things), he refined and edited them throughout most of his life. *Canzoniere* comprises 366 poems, most of them sonnets recounting the melancholy story of his love for Laura, a love that did not cease even with Laura's death, which occurred in 1340 during the plague. Well acquainted with the love poetry of the Provençal troubadours, the Sicilian school, and the *stilnovisti*, Petrarch derived from these traditions elements that became vital and inseparable parts of his own poetic world. Nevertheless, the imprint, the essence of *Canzoniere*, stems from his passion for Laura, the focus of an intense conflict between the seductions of the world and the enduring values of spiritual love.

The work is divided into two parts, usually designated "In vita di madonna Laura" (in the lifetime of Laura) and "In morte di madonna Laura" (after the death of Laura). In the first part, Petrarch's love has great impulses, prostrations, enthusiasms, and a gloomy bitterness. The poet blesses the moment of his falling in love and swears eternal fidelity to his feelings for Laura. Only rarely does sensuality appear in his verses, but at the same time the poet does not attempt to transform his feelings into a mystical thought that will raise him—through his love of the woman—to love of God. In the second part, those poems written after Laura's death, there is at first an expression of grief, the torture of separation, the tormenting thought that Laura's beautiful face, the "dolce sguardo," the endearing glance, are gone forever. Then, the image of Laura begins to live a new life in the soul of the faithful lover; she is no longer a temptress. Instead, Laura becomes a maternal figure and the consoler of Petrarch's sufferings. Also, with this new vision, Petrarch believes that his love, even if spiritualized, is still love for a human creature and therefore a distraction from the love for the Creator. Petrarch's *Canzoniere* has been among the most influential poetic works not only of Italian literature but also of world literature. With a psychological acuity that anticipates the modern discovery of the self, Petrarch describes refined and sophisticated feelings, spellbinding in their perplexity but at the same time never completely detached from a lived human experience.

GIOVANNI BOCCACCIO

The third of the great Italian writers of this period is Giovanni Boccaccio (1313-1375), whose fame is founded on *Decameron: O, Prencipe Galetto* (1349-1351; *The Decameron*, 1620), commonly called the *Decameron*. A literary work in prose, it is a collection of one hundred short stories related to one another by a frame story.

Of limited artistic value, Boccaccio's poetry is nevertheless of historical interest. For the most part, it is allegorical, reflecting Dante's model and the general pattern of the medieval literary tradition. His most significant early works include *Il filostrato* (c. 1335; *The Filostrato*, 1873), a lyric composition somewhat biographical in style, which was followed by *Teseida* (1340-1341; *The Book of Theseus*, 1974), an epic poem imitating the style of Vergil's *Aeneid* and Statius's *Thebais* (c. 92 C.E.; English translation, 1766). There is also *Caccia di Diana* (1334; Diana's hunt), a mythological poem describing the life at the court of Naples where Boccaccio spent some time during his youth. Other works written before the *Decameron* are *Il ninfale d'Ameto* (1341-1342; also known as *Commedia delle ninfe*), an idyllic poem of popular love, and *L'amorosa visione* (1343-1344; English translation, 1986), an allegorical poem inspired by Dante's *The Divine Comedy*.

ITALIAN RENAISSANCE

Between the end of the fourteenth century and the beginning of the fifteenth century, there appeared in Italy the first signs of a profound change in Western culture. The typical representative of this period, which would be later called the Renaissance, sought above all the full and balanced development and enjoyment of his human potential. Transcendence was not explicitly denied but was simply neglected. The Renaissance man did not feel the need of divine grace to achieve these goals, and the ideal of the ascetic, who runs away from the world so that the spirit will thrive, was completely foreign to him—indeed, almost incomprehensible.

At the beginning of this period, there was a great interest in the studies of classical languages and literature. This interest in classical culture and the new critical sense with which these cultures were analyzed bred a large cultural movement called Humanism. In the infancy of the new movement, in the first part of the fourteenth century, there was little interest in the vernacular, since the aspirations of men of letters were oriented toward classical languages. Among the Humanists who distinguished themselves as poets in this first part of the century, Giovanni Pontano entrusted all of his creative literary efforts to the Latin language; his works include an astrological poem, *Urania* (1505), an epic poem, *Lepidina* (1505), and three books of elegies, *De amore coniugalis* (1480-1484; conjugal love), which are dedicated to his wife.

LORENZO DE' MEDICI

At this historical moment, Tuscany no longer held predominance in the national literature but nevertheless was, along with Florence, a very active cultural center because of the patronage of Cosimo de' Medici and of his grandson Lorenzo the Magnificent. Lorenzo has a place in the history of Florence and Italy because of his great abilities as a politician and administrator and his munificent and intelligent patronage of the arts; in addition, he distinguished himself as a man of letters.

In Lorenzo's oeuvre one finds the influence of the most contrasting poetic currents of his time. His *L'altercazione* (after 1473) reveals the influence of the Platonist Center founded in Florence by the renowned Humanist Marsilio Ficino. In *Selve* (1515), Lorenzo narrates an allegorical love story which, as in Petrarch's *Trionfi* (wr. 1356-1374, pb. 1470; *Tryumphes*, 1565, as *Triumphs*, 1962), goes through several stages—jealousy, hope, despair—to conclude finally in the contemplation of the eternal beauty, God. In his *Rime* (1680), dedicated to Lucrezia Donati, he was inspired by the *stilnovisti*, whose philosophical ideas were close to Platonism. Also deserving of special consideration are *Nencia da Barberino* (c. 1474), a short lyric poem in which the peasant Vallera gives vent to his passionate love for the beautiful shepherdess Nencia, and *Canto trionfale di Bacco e Arianna* (c. 1490), a work in which Lorenzo becomes the interpreter of the soul and spirit of the Renaissance with the accomplished skill of a highly developed artist.

POLIZIANO (POLITIAN)

The most eminent poet of his century, Angelo Ambrogini (Poliziano), who later assumed the appellation Politian, was born in 1454 in the Tuscan town of Montepulciano. Although born into a family of humble condition, Poliziano was able to educate himself at the school of noted Humanists in Florence. He also attracted the attention of Lorenzo the Magnificent, who took him into his house as the tutor of his children.

Poliziano was a brilliant Humanist and wrote verses both in Latin and in Greek. Some of his poems in classical languages have remarkable taste and artistic value, but his reputation as a poet is based on his vernacular poetry, especially on *Stanze cominciate per la giostra del magnifico Giuliano de' Medici* (1518; English translation, 1979), commonly referred to as *Stanze, Orfeo* (1480; English translation, 1879), and *Rime* (wr. 1498, pb. 1814). *Stanze* is an incomplete lyric poem, of which

Poliziano wrote only the first book and part of the second. This work was supposed to celebrate the joust won in Florence in 1475 by Lorenzo's brother Giuliano, who was later killed during Pazzi's conspiracy in 1478.

The poem describes how Giuliano, a handsome and vigorous young man, is living an intense and happy life in close contact with nature, spending most of his time riding and hunting and giving little attention to love and sentiment. Cupid is offended by this young man's attitude and plans to take revenge by making Giuliano fall in love with a beautiful nymph, Simonetta. In the second book of the poem, Venus and Cupid send Giuliano a dream that instills in him the desire for warlike glory, which is necessary in order that he be deserving of Simonetta's love. He prepares to organize a joust, and it is at this point that the poem is interrupted.

The poem interprets with admirable grace that moment in which the sentimentally immature young man, who is completely involved with the exterior world, withdraws into himself and achieves for the first time a new awareness, noticing the rise of unsuspected love feelings.

Poliziano wrote *Orfeo*, his second major literary work, during his stay at the Gonzagas' court in Mantua. The tone of this composition is dramatic, but it lacks a true conflict of passions. The poem places instead a greater importance on the lyric and elegiac motives, but they seldom reach the expressive intensity of *Stanze*. Of more significant artistic value, from the lyric point of view, is *Rime*, a collection of love poems that also includes the famous "I' mi trovai fanciulle un bel mattino" ("I Went A-Roaming, Maidens, One Bright Day"). This poem ends with an invitation to capture the fleeting moment and to "gather ye therefore roses . . . ere their perfume pass away"—a topos which was to become one of the most pervasive in Renaissance poetry throughout Europe.

JACOPO SANNAZZARO

The same accents are found in the poetry of the Neapolitan author Jacopo Sannazzaro (1458-1530), who, lacking the depth of inspiration, the vitality, and the human understanding of Poliziano, succeeds nevertheless in reaching a respectable artistic sophistication. Sannazzaro's reputation rests on *Arcadia* (*Arcadia and Piscatorial Eclogues*, 1966), a pastoral poem published in 1504. To his contemporaries, the *Arcadia* appeared to be a unique combination of all the various motives of pastoral poetry, deriving its inspiration from classical poets such as Vergil, Ovid, and Theocritus.

LUIGI PULCI

Another author of the fifteenth century, Luigi Pulci (1432-1484), profited from the enlightened patronage of Lorenzo the Magnificent. Pulci tried several forms of traditional poetry without great success, achieving fame only when he turned to an epic poem, *Morgante*, which he started almost as a joke. Instead, it introduced a genre that acquired a large popularity in Italy. The poem took up the subject matter of the *Chanson de Roland* (c. 1100; *Song of Roland*) and the legend of Charlemagne—a theme that had found an unusual popularity among the simple people in Italy and had created a rich florescence of epic poems, none of which had arrived at any reputable artistic level. These epic poems had gradually taken a very definite structure, a structure that was monotonously repeated. The plot usually revealed the treacheries and evil deeds of the members of the House of Maganza, which had expelled from France the members of the House of Chiaromonte and called the Saracens to fight against Charlemagne, the leader of the Chiaromonte. These same adventures, usually narrated by storytellers in the streets, reappear in Pulci's *Morgante*. Pulci, however, succeeds in bringing the story to a level that is artistically moving and epic in scope.

Pulci ended his poem at the twenty-third canto, and his work was published as it was, incomplete, with the title *Morgante* (1481). Later, urged by a friend to complete it, the poet added another five cantos which tell of the defeat at Roncesvalles, where the rear guard of Charlemagne's army, returning from Spain and being led by the Paladin Roland, is destroyed by the Saracens. Thus completed, the epic poem was titled the *Morgante maggiore* (1483).

MATTEO MARIA BOIARDO

This new literary genre was continued by Matteo Maria Boiardo, who freed it from the popular tradition that still existed in Pulci's work and initiated with refined artistic awareness the poetic theme of the old chivalry, or Romantic epic. His major work, the *Orlando innamorato* (1483, 1495; English translation, 1823), a grandiose enterprise originally planned to include 120 cantos divided into four parts (though interrupted after the second part), merges the two major themes of chivalric poetry: the events narrating the story of Charlemagne, from which Boiardo obtained his major characters and the plot of the Christian world fighting the Saracens, and the Arthurian legend, from which he deducted the individualistic spirit of love and adventure as well as the fair land aspect.

Love and adventure are evident in the *Morgante maggiore*, but both seem somewhat incidental to the story, lacking the well-organized and well-planned structure found in this new poem. In the *Orlando innamorato*, love and adventure are closely connected, and it is indeed love that drives the restless knights to undertake the most unusual and risky endeavors. Boiardo is also credited with having created numerous characters with well-defined personalities; in turn, these characters were taken up by Ludovico Ariosto in *Orlando furioso* (1516, 1521, 1532; English translation, 1591), in which special attention is given to the character of Angelica, a girl of charming beauty but capricious personality, who is willing to use devious means to achieve her ends.

Several parts of Boiardo's *Orlando innamorato* have a high poetic value, but the poem is not considered a true masterpiece: It lacks a unifying spirit that would give life to all parts of the story. There is, however, in Boiardo's poem an interesting taste for the primitive, from which stems a grandiosity that is not handicapped by exceptional or complicated psychological depth. One also perceives in his stories a fascinating and uncontrolled indulgence in the simple and powerful passions of love, vengeance, and a desire to conquer that is clearly an asset to his work and poetic conception. This raw energy, however, cannot be sustained throughout the poem. Little by little, the rich vein of inspiration exhausts itself, and the episodes of the story monotonously repeat themselves until the reader's interest in the adventure weakens and disappears. The spirit of the Renaissance, so deeply different from the one of the Middle Ages, demanded an entirely new vision of the world of the *chanson de geste*, and it was Ariosto who met this demand.

LUDOVICO ARIOSTO

Ludovico Ariosto (1474-1533) was born in Reggio Emilia. His father was in the service of the lords of that region, the Este family, and Ludovico inherited the position when his father died. He worked at first for the Cardinal Ippolito d'Este and then for the Cardinal's brother, the duke Alfonso d'Este, who had his court in the city of Ferrara. Often, however, the poet had to leave his favored city, sent by his patrons on missions to various parts of the Duchy and Italy. Later in life, he was able to live in a house that he bought on the outskirts of Ferrara, where he could dedicate himself completely to writing, the greatest passion in his life.

In his youth, under the Humanistic influence, Ariosto wrote only in Latin. To his early period belongs the *Carmina* (1502), an elegant collection of poems which imitates Catullus and Tibullus. After 1503, however, the poet rarely wrote in Latin; his lyric poetry was composed primarily in the vulgar tongue.

Ariosto began writing his masterpiece *Orlando furioso* around the year 1503 and published a first edition of sixteen cantos in 1516. After extensive revision, he published a second edition in 1521. Finally, yet another version, with several cantos added, was published in 1532. This careful revision produced a poem that for its excellent style could be compared to Petrarch's *Canzoniere*. Moreover, the form in which the poem is written, the ottava rima, gave such musicality to Ariosto's verses that it was called the "golden octave."

Orlando furioso is a continuation of the *Orlando innamorato*; Ariosto's poem more or less begins where Boiardo concluded his story. In spite of the fact that the *Orlando furioso* has an extraordinary number of episodes, its plot is based solidly and clearly upon a few fundamental events. The multiplicity of the facts narrated does not create confusion or boredom but unfold in harmonious and orderly ways. All the characters, who may at times appear scattered, are intermittently collected at a specific point, be it the palace of the sorcerer Atlante or under the walls of Paris, walls from which they subsequently depart in search of new, wonderful adventures.

The spirit of the poem should be sought in the vision of life as a changing scene, a continuously changing spectacle, a vision that Ariosto had obtained from the

Renaissance conception at its highest and most balanced stage of development. According to this conception, life should be observed with a certain detachment, without bitterness and without moralizing.

LATE SIXTEENTH CENTURY

In the second part of the sixteenth century, the great magnificence of the Renaissance faded, perhaps because of the natural exhaustion of the intense fervor of life, both elegant and merry, that had charmed the Italian courts. Politically, the change was particularly severe. The Spanish domination of Italy drastically changed life in the courts of several states. From a literary point of view, artistic production was tightly controlled and dominated by the rules and suggestions of several learned societies, especially the Accademia della Crusca (academy of the chaff), founded in 1583 with the intention of purifying the literary language.

There was, however, in the late sixteenth century an interesting ferment of new ideas. The theoretical elements implicit in the Renaissance conception of life became explicit only during this period. They were expressed in organized philosophical thought by thinkers such as Giordano Bruno (1548-1600), Bernardino Telesio (1509-1588), and Tommaso Campanella (1568-1639), a prolific author whose masterpiece is *La città del sole* (1623; *City of the Sun*, 1880). Inspired by Plato's philosophy, Campanella describes in *City of the Sun* a utopian, egalitarian society ruled by a priest-philosopher.

An important influence on Italian literary development after the Renaissance was exercised by the sweeping religious movement known as the Counter-Reformation. This Catholic movement tried to contain the spread of the Protestant revolution while renewing the life of the Catholic Church. In this period, literature followed the natural consequence of the exhaustion of the Renaissance, and the Counter-Reformation ideals succeeded from time to time in animating literary production with renewed religious spirit. Included among these works is the oeuvre of Torquato Tasso, who closed the Renaissance that Petrarch had opened.

TORQUATO TASSO

Torquato Tasso was born in Sorrento, near Naples, in 1544. His father, Bernardo, was an accomplished man of letters and had written a lyric poem, the *Amadigi* (1560), which had been somewhat successful. Bernardo Tasso was the secretary to the prince of Salerno, Ferrante di San Severino, and when the prince was forced to leave his state and go into exile for political reasons, Bernardo, accompanied by his son, followed his patron. This exile brought the Tassos to the courts of several Italian princes, and young Torquato pursued his studies in different universities, finally graduating from the University of Padua with a degree in literature. He was soon admitted to the retinue of Cardinal Luigi d'Este, to whom he had dedicated his pastoral drama *Aminta* (1581; English translation, 1591), a work that showed artistic maturity and that expressed in lovely forms the serenity of Tasso's spirit at that time in his life. Distinguished by this serenity and by its lighthearted sensuality, *Aminta* is the culmination of the Renaissance pastoral tradition.

Aminta was followed by *Gerusalemme liberata* (1581; *Jerusalem Delivered*, 1600), Tasso's major work. This period was not only the most prolific for the poet but also the happiest in his life. After 1575, the year in which *Jerusalem Delivered* was read publicly to the duke of Ferrara and his court, Tasso's mental health began to deteriorate. His sensitive mind was racked by doubts about the critical and religious soundness of his poem. He also became very suspicious of his friends and benefactors, and after some irrational episodes, the duke of Ferrara was compelled to confine Tasso to an asylum, where he remained for seven years. When he was released in 1586, the poet went to live at the court of the Gonzagas in Mantua, but only for a short time. He soon returned to his wanderings: Naples, Florence, back to Mantua, and Rome, where Pope Clement VIII planned to crown him with laurel. Tasso, however, could not manage to extend his life to the day of the coronation. Exhausted, he found shelter in the convent of Sant' Onofrio of the Giannicolo and there he died, on April 25, 1595.

Tasso had begun to work on his masterpiece, *Jerusalem Delivered*, with a greater concern than had characterized his earlier works. At the end of the sixteenth century, it was not conceivable that a poet would be starting to work on what was considered the most noble of the literary genre, the *poema epico* (the romantic poem), so much discussed by the supercilious academicians, yet without an adequate critical preparation. Tasso, therefore, expressed his ideas about the romantic poem in a short treatise, *Discorsi dell'arte poetica* (1587). The poet believed that the purpose of literature was more to entertain than to instruct and that in the romantic poem one should strive for credibility. For this reason, the poet should turn to history; tales of marvels and miracles should be religious in inspiration, it being undesirable for Christian people to believe in the prodigies of pagan divinities. Finally, Tasso asserted that the poet should seek greatness and nobility in the characters and the events, excluding ridiculous, comical, and vulgar facts and creatures.

During his youth, Tasso had conceived a romantic poem on the Crusades and had written the first book of a work titled "Il Goffredo." Later he undertook the project again and, working intensively, completed it in twenty cantos of ottava rima in 1575, publishing it in the final form in 1581 with the title *Gerusalemme liberata*.

In this literary composition, the poetic world of Tasso manifests itself in all of its richness and depth. At first it appears that, from an artistic point of view, one is confronted again by the world of the Renaissance with major elements including glory, expectation, anticipation, anxiety, heroic efforts, idyllic visions, pleasure, power, and melancholy. Moralistic and religious elements are present only in rhetorical and artificial forms, and there are only a few passages of sincerely felt spirituality and mysticism. If one observes the essence and the structure of the poem with greater care, however, one realizes that in those Renaissance motives there is hidden a new spirit, a new feeling that, without dissolving them, without transforming anything, gives to these realities a new expression, a new and deeper significance. Desire, expectation, enthusiasm, and heroic efforts are no longer an end in themselves, a pure expression of exuberant energies; they need now an ideal that will support and fulfill them. Force, power, has lost its barbaric beauty and opens itself to human feelings. Melancholy is not regret for the fleeting, transitory aspect of happiness, but rather an anxious desire for a more spiritual happiness and fulfillment, a fulfillment that Tasso's religiosity circumscribes. In this correct merging and balancing of the two opposing and contrasting forces—the love for the world and the attraction toward spirituality—Tasso supersedes his mentor, Petrarch.

After Tasso completed *Jerusalem Delivered*, his instability worsened. He began a new version of his epic, titled *Gerusalemme Conquistata* (1593; *Jerusalem Conquered*, 1907), an artistic failure on which he expended enormous labors. He also wrote a tragedy, *Il re Torrismondo* (1587), inspired by Sophocles' *Oidipous Tyrannos* (c. 429 B.C.E.; *Oedipus Tyrannus*, 1715), as well as a poem of religious inspiration, *Le sette giornate del mondo creato*, published posthumously in 1607. None of these works could duplicate the intensity and the artistic fervor of his masterpiece.

Another work deserving of recognition and written in the same period is the pastoral tragicomedy *Il pastor fido* (pb. 1590; *The Faithful Shepherd*, 1602; translation by John Fletcher), by Battista Guarini (1538-1612), a poet from Ferrara who was for several years at the court in his own town and then in Florence and Urbino. More than for its dramatic qualities or artistic prominence of the protagonist, *The Faithful Shepherd* is famous for its musicality of expression, which brings Guarini's characters closer to those of the melodrama, a genre that had tremendous success in the seventeenth and eighteenth centuries.

The melodrama, as an artistic form, was created at the end of the sixteenth century by the Camerata dei Bardi, a group of literati and musicians who gathered at the Bardi's palace in Florence. Their intention was to effect a closer relationship between music and poetry, following the example of classical Greek authors. The first melodrama (or *favola per musica*) produced was *Dafne* (1600), written by Ottavio Rinuccini (1562-1621) with music by Jacopo Corsi and Jacopo Peri. In 1600, Rinuccini wrote *Euridice*, also with music by Peri, for the marriage of the king of France, Henry IV, and Marie de Médicis. A few years later, in 1608, he wrote the libretto for the opera *Arianna* (1608), by Monteverdi, which was performed at the court of the duke of mantua.

Considerable success was enjoyed in the sixteenth century by lyric poetry which imitated Petrarch (*petrarchismo*), and among the numerous poets who wrote verses in this style, several are notable: Luigi Tansillo (1510-1568), Annibal Caro (1507-1566), Giovanni Della Casa (1503-1555), and Galeazzo di Tarsia (1520-1553), who is perhaps the best in this group. In addition, two women poets achieved artistic renown in this period: Vittoria Colonna (1492-1547), a member of the Roman aristocracy and a good friend of Michelangelo (1475-1564), the great sculptor and painter (who also wrote noteworthy poetry), and Gaspara Stampa (1523-1554), from Padua, whose powerful and passionate verses are regarded by many modern readers as among the finest in European literature of her time.

SEVENTEENTH CENTURY MANNERISM

Poetry in seventeenth century Italy was characterized by a phenomenon that is usually identified as *secentismo* or *Marinismo*, from the name of the poet Giambattista Marino, who, more than anyone, was responsible for the vogue of this new poetic style throughout Europe. This new poetry gave an extraordinary importance to form, partly in consequence of slavish imitation of classical authors, a practice that gradually gave the impression that form was something detached from content. Artists used style as a means of attracting the attention of the reader. In order to generate a sense of wonder and amazement, poets tended to emphasize oddity, a characteristic that typified the literary production of the seventeenth century.

The most daring and applauded representative of this style was Marino himself, who was born in Naples in 1569. After a restless and adventurous youth, Marino, who had distinguished himself as a gifted and brilliant writer of verses, spent some time at the pontifical court in Rome and then was a guest in Turin at the court of Duke Carlo Emanuele I of Savoy, where he found glory and honor. Soon, however, he fell out of favor and was imprisoned. As soon as Marino was free, he left Italy for France, where he resided for many years in Paris, honored and admired at the court of Marie de Médicis. His reputation, especially after the publication of his major work the *L'Adone* (1623), was immense. When Marino returned to Italy, he was received with great celebration in Rome and Naples. He died in Naples shortly after his return in 1625.

Marino's lyric poems, which present various subjects, are collected in a book titled *La lira* (1615). Other compositions are *La galeria* (1619), a group of iconographic poems, *La sampogna* (1620), a pastoral idyll,

and the sacred epic *La strage degli innocenti* (1632; *The Slaughter of the Innocents*, 1675), which enjoyed widespread and popular success.

L'Adone is by far Marino's most important work. It embodies both the strengths and the shortcomings of his art, and it stands as the most representative expression of the spirit of its epoch. *L'Adone* is a mythological poem, conceived at first as a short idyllic poem and then enlarged, with extraordinary richness of digressions and episodes, to reach the impressive size of five thousand verses. These five thousand verses were then subdivided into twenty long cantos which center on the love of Venus and Adonis.

Although *secentismo* was predominant in this period, a number of other poets wrote according to the principles of more orthodox forms, those classical writers who opposed the group represented by Marino and his followers. They cannot, however, be separated from the previous group, because they, too, followed the same abstract conception that form and style are completely separate from content.

Among these poets, the best known is Gabriello Chiabrera (1552-1638), who lived at the courts of the Medici in Florence, the Gonzagas in Mantua, and the Savoias in Turin, and who was rewarded for his services and his art with honors and generous stipends. Chiabrera acquired his reputation through his *canzonette*, the pastoral poem "Alcippo," and his several odes imitating Horace, Anacreon, and particularly Pindar. His fame did not reach the heights of Marino's, but it was more constant, even if his artistic achievement was by far inferior.

Another poet who was also inspired by the classic tradition was Fulvio Testi (1593-1646), a courtier of the Estes in Ferrara. His artistic model was the lyric poetry of Horace, from which he drew erotic inspiration and moralistic reflections. Testi's poems have survived not because of their artistic achievement, but rather for their political significance: denouncing the political dominance of Spain over Italy during that historical period.

Among the minor poets of this century one could mention Francesco Redi (1626-1698), a poet who gained some reputation for a dithyrambic poem, *Bacco in Toscana* (1685; *Bacchus in Tuscany: A Dithyrambic Poem*, 1825), written in praise of the wines of his region.

To the creation of a new literary genre—the mock heroic or heroicomic—the poet Alessandro Tassoni (1565-1635) contributed *La secchia rapita* (1622, 1630; *The Rape of the Bucket*, 1825). A poem written in ottava rima, subdivided into twelve cantos, it narrates in epic style the struggle between the towns of Modena and Bologna over the possession of a bucket, which is a caricature of some of the trivial aspects of the life of his times. The poem is fragmentary and, with the exception of some shorter parts, is of rather limited importance.

Among the writers of dramatic poetry in this century was Federico Della Valle (1565-1628), author of several tragedies of substantial value. The *Reina di Scotia* (wr. 1590-1600, pb. 1628) projects the powerful figure of Mary Stuart, human in her grief and elevated in her dignity as queen. A second tragedy that had a good success is *Judit* (wr. 1590-1600, pb. 1627), in which the Jewish heroine hides in her heart the austere and dreadful duty that she must carry out against the savage figure of Holofernes, a primitive man dominated by his instincts. The pair tower over a background of Oriental splendor. Both of these works are of remarkable artistic quality; they are superb as dramatic works and could be considered comparable to some of the best tragedies of Vittorio Alfieri, who is, perhaps, the most outstanding Italian tragedian.

EIGHTEENTH CENTURY NEOCLASSICISM

Toward the end of the seventeenth century, fourteen scholars and men of letters in the circle of Christina, queen of Sweden—who, after her abdication and conversion to Catholicism, resided in Rome—founded a literary academy, the Accademia dell'Arcadia, whose purpose was to exterminate the bad taste of *secentismo* and to return to Italian poetry the qualities of natural candor, simplicity, and classical purity. The members of the Accademia dell'Arcadia took names that were supposed to be of pastoral inspiration, and branches of the academy were soon established in every major Italian town.

The simplicity which the Accademia dell'Arcadia was planning to set against the despised mannerisms of *secentismo* was itself, however, a purely literary convention, and new affectations substituted for the old: Poetry remained imprisoned by the entanglements of rhetoric. Nevertheless, there were some positive aspects to this new literary movement. The Accademia dell'Arcadia represented a return to the pure classicism of the sixteenth century, and classical poets, both Greek and Latin, were once again the object of the attention that had been usurped by the dazzling Mannerist poets of the seventeenth century. Style and structure meant the reassumption of a composed and dignified form in poetry. The ideal of beauty was no longer confined to the expression of the unusual or the surprising, and poets were once again under the influence of the logic that had already guided men of letters during the sixteenth century, a logic that elaborated on the concepts of Aristotle's *Poetics* (334-323 B.C.E.).

The only true poet produced by the Accademia dell'Arcadia was Pietro Metastasio, whose works constitute the fullest poetic expression of the Italian society of his time. Metastasio was born Pietro Trapassi in Rome in 1698. At a very young age, he showed an exceptional ability in improvising verses. This dexterity attracted the attention of G. V. Gravina, who was one of the founders of the Accademia dell'Arcadia. Gravina was convinced that the renovation of poetry had to take place through the restoration of the concept of classical art. He thought that the young Trapassi, properly educated, could achieve what he, Gravina—who was a theoretician, not a poet— would never be able to do. Gravina then took the young poet to live with him, changed his last name to the Greek-sounding Metastasio, and saw that he was instructed in the philosophy of René Descartes and in Latin and Greek literature and language. Gravina never imagined that with that kind of education his pupil could have brought to the maximum height a dramatic genre that any true follower of Aristotle's poetic theories should have considered at least spurious.

At the death of his mentor, Metastasio almost abandoned his art, but a dramatic sketch, *Gli orti esperidi*, which he had written in 1721 for a festivity at the court of Naples, opened the gates to his fortune as a dramatist and a poet. Diva "La Romanina" (Marianna Bulgarelli) took a liking to the young Metastasio; she saw that he was educated in the art of music and introduced him to the melodramatic genre. In 1724, Metastasio completed his first melodrama, the *Didone abbandonata* (*Dido Forsaken*, 1952), which was received with great favor and was followed by *Catone in Utica* (1727-1728; *Cato in Utica*, 1767) and *Semiramide* (1729; *Semiramis Recognized*, 1767), all of them works of unusual mastery.

During the second part of the seventeenth century, the poetic aspect of the melodrama had been completely overwhelmed by musical and choreographic dramas. Early in the 1700's, Apostolo Zeno, a learned Venetian who was the official poet at the court of Vienna, attempted a reform of the melodrama and tried to make the plots less absurd in order to bring them closer to historical truth. Zeno was not a gifted poet, and he believed that what he himself had not been able to accomplish could be done by Metastasio, who was an extremely talented writer of verse. Zeno, therefore, recommended Metastasio as his successor at the Viennese court, where, free from financial concerns, the latter would be able to continue his artistic pursuits. After some hesitation, Metastasio went to Vienna in 1730. The decade that followed was the most prolific in the career of the poet. Besides *oratori* and other short dramatic compositions, Metastasio wrote eleven melodramas, among them some of his best: the *Olimpiade* (1733; *The Olympiad*, 1767), *Demofoonte* (1733; *Demofoone*, 1767), *La clemenza di Tito* (1734; *The Mercy of Titus*, 1767), *Temistocle* (1736; *Themostocles*, 1767), and *Attilio regolo* (1750; *Atilius Regulus*, 1767). Though his poetic inspiration weakened, his reputation remained unchanged for the rest of his life, and when he died in 1782, he was honored and remembered as the Italian Sophocles.

In spite of the dramatic and serious subjects with which Metastasio's melodramas dealt, it could be said that in reality they are lacking in the heroic and dramatic spirit that they presuppose; the protagonist on whom the action is centered never acquires the warm personality of a real character, because Metastasio has for these heroes an admiration that he has learned through books rather than an attraction that grows from an innermost conviction of feeling. The elegiac elements of his plays have instead a singular poetic consistency and find their most complete realization in the *ariette* (usually two stanzas that are supposed to be sung). In these brief compositions of crystalline clarity, the poet is free from any obstacle of heroic travesty, and he finds the way to convey the best expression of the Arcadian spirit.

The Enlightenment

In the second part of the eighteenth century, a crisis began in Europe that would eventually find its resolution in the French Revolution. In only a few years, this revolution would cause a deep transformation in people's ways of thinking, of living, and of expressing themselves, through the demolition of all the surviving forms of the Renaissance and of the period that followed. A new philosophy developed which had its precedents in the works of the Frenchman René Descartes, the German Gottfried Wilhelm Leibniz, and the Englishman John Locke—a philosophy that placed man in the center of his universe. Man was regarded as the supreme judge of reality, capable of subjecting any question to strictly rational analysis.

This movement was known as the Enlightenment; its spirit was epitomized by the Frenchman who created *L'Encyclopédie* (1751-1780), a rational and scientific dictionary of all the sciences and arts. This encyclopedia was published in France under the direction of Denis Diderot (1713-1784) and Jean d'Alembert (1717-1783), with the precise design of divulging new ideas and illustrating through the light of reason all the theoretical, moral, artistic, economic, and practical problems with which man could be confronted. The representative members of this movement, even if they moved intellectually in different directions and carried different points of view, were other intellectuals and artists such as Charles-Louis de Secondat, Montesquieu (1689-1755), Voltaire (1694-1778), and Jean-Jacques Rousseau (1712-1778). This movement, which affected all the ways of life and thought of European society, had a significant effect on literature as well.

In Italy, the highest poetic expression of the moral and spiritual renewal proposed by the Enlightenment was the work of Giuseppe Parini. Parini was born into a humble family in Bosisio, a small rural town near Milan, in 1729. He appeared to be a very intelligent boy and was brought to Milan to study. In Parini's time, for a bright but poor youngster who wanted to acquire an education, the best course was to undertake a religious career. Parini entered a seminary and became a priest. He was very interested in literature and published, when still very young, a collection of poems. As was then fashionable for a poet, he became a member of the

Accademia dell'Arcadia. From 1754 to 1762, he was a tutor in the house of the Duke Serbelloni. He left his job and was for several months in severe financial difficulties. The publication of the first part of what is considered his major work, *Il giorno* (1763-1801; *The Day: Morning, Midday, Evening, Night*, 1927), a satiric poem in which he criticizes the sterile life of the aristocracy, brought him to the attention of the public and also of Count Firmian, who was the minister of Maria Theresa in Milan. Firmian was glad that Parini, with his writings, was calling upon the aristocracy to assume more responsibility in their position in society. Firmian made Parini director of the *Gazzetta di Milano* for a year, and in 1769, Firmian appointed Parini as professor of literature at the Scuole Palatine.

When Napoleonic troops occupied Milan in 1796, Parini was called to be part of the new government; mistrusting any demagogic excess, he refused the offer and retired to private life. When the Austrians returned to Milan in 1799, he greeted them with joy. He died, on August 15, 1799.

Parini wrote several odes that reflect the credo of the Enlightenment and are of didactic and moralistic inspiration. Some of his poems expressing deep moral emotions include *La caduta* (1766), *A Silvia* (1795), and *Alla Musa* (1795). Others such as *Il pericolo* (1787), *Il dono* (1790), and *Il messaggio* (1793), are written in flattery of women; they are sparkling in their courtly, gallant fashion and full of aesthetic admiration for feminine beauty.

Parini's moral spirit and his conception of poetry are more fully expressed in *The Day*, the satiric and didactic poem in which he describes the futile day of a young lord of the Milanese aristocracy. The same Arcadian touches that are present in the *odi* are also part of the structure of *The Day*. A masterpiece that foretells the French Revolution, it nevertheless reflects Parini's excessive dependence on the conventions of his time. Proceeding with a slow documentary style, it is encumbered with too many details, and it has not aged well.

The renewal of Italian moral consciousness in the eighteenth century had its first suggestive poetic expression in the works of Parini, but it was the work of Vittori Alfieri that unambiguously announced the political renewal of the country.

Vittorio Alfieri was born in Asti in 1749, into a family of the Piedmontese aristocracy. His father died when he was only a year old, and his mother soon remarried. As a child, Alfieri was withdrawn, dominated by a melancholy unusual in one so young. In 1758, he entered the Royal Military Academy of Turin, from which he was graduated after eight years of *ineducazione* (ineducation) with the rank of *portainsegna* (lieutenant) in the regiment of his own town. Military life did not attract him, since he was intolerant of any discipline. He was very fond of traveling, and between 1766 and 1772 he made three trips, the first within Italy, the other two through Europe, visiting all the major countries from Spain to Russia. When he returned to Turin, he allowed himself to luxuriate in a life of idleness and passion for horses. Even this rootless life, however, left him restless and dissatisfied, as reflected in the pages of his diary. Actually, his continuous discontent, his furious search without any apparent goal or purpose, was in reality caused by the clash of spiritual energies as he looked for a way of expressing his talents.

This expression he finally found in 1744 while assisting a sick friend. Alfieri scribbled down the sketch of a tragedy, *Cleopatra* (1795; English translation, 1876), which after going through a process of painstaking revision, was staged with success at the Carignano Theater in Turin. This success did not make Alfieri vainly proud, but it made him conscious of his literary and moral mission and of the tremendous effort that he had to make in order to become worthy of his success. Until that moment, his education had been rather modest and fragmented, and he decided therefore to put aside horses, friends, and other pleasures and immerse himself in the study of letters. To improve his knowledge of the literary language, he went to live in Tuscany, and, to be more free in his pursuit, he renounced his aristocratic rights in favor of his sister and kept for himself a life annuity that would allow him to live comfortably. His tragedies were written one after the other, interspersed with other literary works, and all of them were pervaded by the burning ideal of freedom. Alfieri was supported in his effort, which he thought was an artistic as well as a political mission, by a great love: his love for the Countess Maria Luisa Stolberg of Albany, whom he met in Florence. In 1785, Alfieri went to live in France with Stolberg, whose husband, Charles Eduard Stuart, had died. There he had the opportunity to witness the outbreak of the French Revolution, which he greeted with a panegyric poem, *Parigi sbastigliata* (1789). He also had welcomed the American Revolution with a collection of five poems, *L'America libera* (1781-1783; *America the Free: Five Odes*, 1975). When the French Revolution degenerated into anarchy and terror, Alfieri left Paris and returned to Florence with Stolberg, living a quiet life while concentrating on his studies. He died in 1803.

During the last years of his life, Alfieri wrote an autobiography in which he presented an interesting artistic version of his life and of the evolution of his personality. The same autobiographical spirit is present in his *Rime de Vittorio Alfieri* (1933), which often is an analysis of his feelings and of his moods.

Alfieri's vocation as a tragedian was dictated by his desire to contribute to the Italian culture in a literary field that was not developed as it had been in France and other countries. The poet, in planning the structure of his tragedies, considered both the classical tragedy and the French tragedy as it had been developed by Corneille and Racine. He maintained in his work the three dramatic unities of time, place, and action which had been imposed by the Renaissance interpreters of Aristotle's *Poetics*, as well as the division of each play into five acts. He did not continue the tradition of chorus and messengers, and he excluded the confidants that, in the French tragedy, through complicated introductory scenes, informed the public about the preceding action. Alfieri also minimized the love scenes and limited the number of characters so that he could concentrate the action on one or, at most, two of them. In Alfieri's tragedies, there is no description of the development of passion and spiritual tension. When the scene opens, these emotions have already reached the limits of human tolerance, and the tragic consequence cannot be avoided.

Because of these structures, the tragedies of Alfieri appear to be very close to the classical example and definitely classical in the precise clarity of his psychological implications as well as the precise separation between good and evil and the monolithic representation of the protagonist in his moral and spiritual composition. It is apparent, however, that all of these characters of unusual and solitary stature do not belong to the mea-

sured correctness of the neoclassical art at the end of the eighteenth century. Instead they predict the burgeoning Romantic movement, which established a drastically changed and renewed physiognomy of European art. This unusual aspect of Alfieri's tragedies is even more evident in those plays in which the protagonists have complex personalities full of contradictions and whose actions are projected on an anxious background which is threatened by obscure forces. Most representative of these dark plays are *Oreste* (1784; *Orestes*, 1876), *Rosmunda* (1784; English translation, 1876), *Agamennone* (1784; *Agamemnon*, 1876), *Saul* (1788; English translation, 1876), and *Mirra* (1789; *Myrrha*, 1876), which also represent some of his best works. Other tragedies that are likewise considered among the most successful in Alfieri's oeuvre are *Virginia* (1784; English translation, 1876), *Filippo* (1784; Philip II, 1876), *Merope* (1784; English translation, 1876), *Agide* (1788; *Agis*, 1876), *Bruto primo* (1788; *The First Brutus*, 1876), *Bruto secondo* (1788; *The Second Brutus*, 1876), and *Don Garzia* (1788; *Don Garcia*, 1876).

TRANSITION TO ROMANTICISM

Both Romantic and neoclassical elements are present in the poetry of Vincenzo Monti, a poet who in many respects concludes the literary activities of the eighteenth century and opens those of the nineteenth century and Romanticism. Monti was born in Fusignano, near Ferrara, in 1754. As a young man he received an education strongly based on classical culture and, since he had the unusual ability to write poetry, he captured the attention of Cardinal Scipione Borghese, who brought him to Rome to the papal court in 1778. There, Monti was soon involved with the dramatic political events of his times. At first he condemned the horrors and the excesses of the French Revolution in his poetic work *In morte di Ugo Bassville* (1793; *The Penance of Hugo: A Vision on the French Revolution*, 1805), commonly known as *Basvilliana*; subsequently, as a result of Napoleon's successful military campaign in Italy, he became a supporter of the new hero and wrote several panegyric poems in his honor. With the end of the Napoleonic Empire and the return of Austrian influence in Italy, Monti returned his support to the old master with new poems and other writings. He died in Milan in 1828.

Among Monti's best-known work of his Roman period is "Presopopea di Pericle," which celebrates the finding of an ancient bust of the famous Athenian statesman. In *Al Signor di Montgolfier* (1784), he honors, according to the fashion of the Enlightenment, the greatness of the human mind. *The Penance of Hugo* is his best-known political work, and during the Napoleonic period, Monti's most noted works were *Il prometeo*, *Il bardo della Selva Nera* (1806), and *La spada di Federico II* (1806). This latter poem celebrates the victory of Napoleon over Prussia and has strong Romantic characteristics. After the fall of Napoleon, Monti celebrated the Austrian return with *Il ritorno di Astrea* (1816).

Unusually powerful and emotionally direct is his canzone "Per il giorno onomastico della sua donna" (for his lady's name day). Later in life, Monti resumed work on an earlier poem, "Feroniade," which was left unfinished; in it, he narrates the activities surrounding the draining and reclamation of the Pontine Marshes. This theme was dear to the hearts of the followers of the Enlightenment. Monti was not quite capable of creating the vital and complex structure of an extended or more engaging poem, although he had exceptional technical abilities in the composition of verses and therefore was greatly successful in his translations. Particularly masterful were his translations from classical languages, of which his translation of Homer's the *Iliad* (c. 800 B.C.E.) is considered his masterpiece.

ROMANTICISM

Monti's oeuvre is characteristic of the period during which the ground was being prepared for Romanticism. At this time, art, literature, and public life in Italy were inspired by classical culture to a degree unprecedented even in the Renaissance. For the most part, this was a rather superficial and gaudy phenomenon fostered by the caesarism of the Napoleonic age and, perhaps, by an instinctive reaction of the Latin world against the surging German Romanticism. Thus, Italian neoclassicism, as this movement was called, bore the seeds of a Romantic sensibility. There was in Romanticism a torment and restlessness, an unsatisfied aspiration toward a perfected beauty—an unreachable region symbolized for the Romantics by classical Greece. This myth of Greece, present in all the best-known national literary

compositions of the early nineteenth century, was the Romantic aspect of neoclassicism.

Monti is the most representative poet of this period, for his poetry is by nature oriented toward external forms. The new Romantic sensibility, preoccupied with the content of artistic reality, is not well assimilated in his art. This assimilation was to be the task of the poets who followed him, from Ugo Foscolo to Giacomo Leopardi, from Giosuè Carducci to Gabriele D'Annunzio. In D'Annunzio's poetry, the myth of the ancient world is no longer a serene and somehow superficial vision, but rather an island dreamed of and lost, a land of perfect beauty sought without hope.

BIBLIOGRAPHY

Bernardo, Aldo S., and Anthony L. Pellegrini, eds. *Dante, Petrarch, Boccacio: Studies in the Italian Trecento in Honor of Charles S. Singleton*. Medieval and Renaissance Text and Studies 22. Binghamton, N.Y.: Center for Medieval and Early Renaissance Studies, State University of New York, 1983. Scholarly papers.

Everson, Jane E. *The Italian Romance Epic in the Age of Humanism: The Matter of Italy and the World of Rome*. London: Oxford University Press, 2001. Demonstrates how the romance, or chivalric epic, owed its appeal to a successful fusion of traditional, medieval tales of Charlemagne and Arthur with the newer cultural themes developed by the revival in classical antiquity that constitutes the key to Renaissance culture.

Gardner, Edward Garrett. *Dukes and Poets in Ferrara: A Study in the Poetry, Religion, and Politics of the Fifteenth and Sixteenth Centuries*. Reprint. St. Clair Shores, Mich.: Scholarly Press, 1972.

Haar, James. *Essays on Italian Poetry and Music in the Renaissance, 1350-1600*. Berkeley: University of California Press, 1987.

Holmes, Olivia. *Assembling the Lyric Self: Authorship from Troubador Song to Italian Poetry Book*. Minneapolis: University of Minnesota Press, 2000.

Looney, Dennis. *Compromising the Classics: Romance Epic Narrative in the Italian Renaissance*. Detroit: Wayne State University, 1996. Examines the evolution of narrative poetics in three of the canonical poems of the Italian Renaissance, the romance-epics of

Matteo Maria Boiardo, Ludovico Ariosto, and Torquato Tasso. Combining cultural criticism with literary analysis, this volume focuses on how these poets renovated the popular genre of romance into a new kind of narrative through their imitation of classical epic, as well as through their imitation of pastoral, satire, history, and to a lesser extent, comedy and tragedy.

O'Grady, Deirdre. *Alexander Pope and Eighteenth Century Italian Poetry.* New York: Peter Lang Publishers, 1986.

Rebay, Luciano, ed. *Introduction to Italian Poetry.* Mineola, N.Y.: Dover, 1991. Highlights thirty-four hymns, sonnets, madrigals, heroic epics (in selection), and lyrics by Dante, Petrarch, Boccaccio, Ariosto, Tasso, d'Annunzio, and fifteen others. Full Italian texts with expert literal translations on facing pages, plus biographical and critical commentary on each poet.

Stortoni, Laura A., and Mary P. Lillie, eds. *Women Poets of the Italian Renaissance: Courtly Ladies and Courtesans.* New York: Italica, 1997. Presents the rich flowering of Renaissance women's poetry: from the love lyrics of famous courtly ladies of Venice and Rome to the deeply moral and spiritual poets of the age.

Talbot, George. *Lord Charlemont's History of Italian Poetry from Dante to Metastasio: A Critical Edition from the Autograph Manuscript, Vol. 1.* Mellen Critical Editions and Translations 4. Lewiston, N.Y.: Edwin Mellen Press, 2000. Presents a history of early Italian poetry by Lord Charlemont. Part I commences with the sonnets of fourteenth century poet Petrarch with an introduction by his lordship on the translations, but no prefatory remarks by the editor. Part II showcases seventeen fifteenth and sixteenth century successors and imitators of Petrarch including Lorenzo de' Medici, Veronica Gambara, Giovanni della Casa, Annibal Caro, and Luigi Tansillo. Includes a reproduction of a facsimile page from Charlemont's autograph manuscript.

Patrizio Rossi

ITALIAN POETRY SINCE 1800

At the time of Italy's unification in 1861, Alessandro Manzoni was the only living member of the great triad of early nineteenth century writers (composed of Manzoni, Ugo Foscolo, and Giacomo Leopardi), and he had written little poetry after the completion of his masterpiece, the novel *I promessi sposi* (1840-1842). Also surviving were a trio of late Romantic poets, Aleardo Aleardi (1812-1878), Giovanni Prati (1814-1884), and Giacomo Zanella (1820-1888). The first was a patriotic poet; the second, although he was famous for his long Byronic poem of contemporary Venetian life, *Edmenegarda* (1841), had abandoned Romanticism and turned classicist; and Zanella, who has withstood the test of time somewhat better than the other two, was a priest interested in reconciling science and religion. His masterpiece, "Sopra una conchiglia fossile nel mio studio" ("On a Fossil Shell in My Study"), often compared to Henry Wadsworth Longfellow's "The Chambered Nautilus," is an imaginative history of Earth and a reflection on the higher destiny which awaits humanity.

The unification of Italy robbed her writers of one of their main inspirations; without a direct political mission, Italian literature lost some momentum during the last third of the century, fragmenting into various movements. Some writers wished to cling to a dying Romanticism, some returned to the classical past, and some looked ahead to realism. Those who championed realism, called *Verismo* in Italy, were chiefly novelists and dramatists.

Scapigliatura movement

In the 1860's, there flourished a movement in Milan called the *scapigliatura*, from the disheveled or Bohemian appearance of its members, who reacted against the traditional forms of late Romanticism in their desire to achieve a spontaneous artistic expression. They looked toward such non-Italian poets as Gérard de Nerval, Charles Baudelaire, Henri Murger, Paul Verlaine, Arthur Rimbaud, and Heinrich Heine, and their work exhibited overtones of decadence ("art for art's sake"), realism, and Satanism. At their worst, they substituted allegory and symbol for genuine thought and feeling.

Emilio Praga (1839-1875), a painter as well as a poet, wrote in the style of Baudelaire and died of alcoholism. The nostalgic motifs of his poetry are couched in pessimism and sensuality and can hardly be classified as examples of realistic writing. Arrigo Boito (1842-1918), offspring of an Italian father and a Polish mother, who ranks second after Giuseppe Verdi among Italian composers of the late nineteenth century, wrote poetry that sadly and sternly evokes the past, but his best lyric work, such as the legend of *Re orso* (king bear), has today been forgotten. Giovanni Camerana (1845-1905), also a painter, who committed suicide at the age of sixty, wrote landscape poetry with a painter's eye for color and form.

Peripheral to the *scapigliati* were Vittorio Betteloni (1840-1910), who was drawn to realism—a translator of Lord Byron and Johann Wolfgang von Goethe and a forerunner of the crepuscular movement—and his friend Olindo Guerrini (pseudonym of Lorenzo Stecchetti, 1845-1916), known for his peculiar brand of realism that approached pornography and for his satirical view of politicians.

While the *scapigliatura* movement failed to produce any great work of poetry, it created a commotion of new ideas from which other rebellious movements arose. Indeed, it could be argued that the decadent aspect of the poetry of Giovanni Pascoli and Gabriele D'Annunzio represents a continuation of the precepts of the *scapigliati*.

Giosuè Carducci and his followers

At that time, there arose a giant of a poet who would command and receive such respect from the Italian people as is rare in modern times, and who would receive the first Nobel Prize awarded to an Italian (1906). The Tuscan Giosuè Carducci (1835-1907)—rebellious, republican, and anticlerical—presented a drastic contrast to Abbe Zanella, who had fought for the Catholic ideal of a confederated Italy under the authority of a liberal pope. Carducci instead wrote "Inno a Satana" ("Hymn to Satan"); although Carducci's Satan is a progressive "avenging force of Reason" rather than a prince of darkness, Carducci continued for many years to harbor a grudge in response to what he deemed Pope Pius IX's betrayal of Italy in the secular interests of the Vatican.

Carducci was hostile toward Romanticism for its emotionalism and its deficiencies in formal expression. He equated Romanticism with the Middle Ages. Classicism for him was the glistening and gladdening sun, while Romanticism was the infecund ghost of the moon (whose "stupid round face" Carducci said he hated), the haunter of ruins and cemeteries. Although his father admired Manzoni and had encouraged the young Carducci to read him, the poet was instead attracted to Homer and Vergil and the pre-Manzonian and pre-Romantic classicists (as well as these aspects in the poetry of Ugo Foscolo).

Carducci tried to subdue Romantic impulses by successfully adapting Greek and Latin quantitative meter to Italian verse, an achievement that his Italian predecessors (including Gabriello Chiabrera, 1552-1638; Leon Battista Alberti, 1404-1472; and Tommaso Campanella, 1568-1639) had attempted but had not attained. To the critics, his use of unrhymed Alcaics, sapphics, hexameters, and asclepiads seemed like nothing less than an insult to the Italian language. Carducci had foreseen this reaction and ironically called his three-volume collection *Odi barbare* (1877, 1882, 1889; *The Barbarian Odes of Giosuè Carducci*, 1939), not because the odes offended Italian readers but because Horace and Vergil would have been offended to hear their language corrupted in Italian. In his unbounded admiration for the sculptural lines of ancient Latin poetry, Carducci sometimes indulged a fascination with mere sound. His poetry is not often tender, but it is always cast in a mold of majestic form.

It is precisely Carducci's more tender poems, however, with their highly controlled emotionality, that are most alive for modern readers. His "Alla stazione in una mattinata d'autunno" ("To the Station on an Autumn Morning") is an impressive love poem reflecting the mood of his passion for Carolina Piva ("Lidia"); in the poem "Pianto antico" ("Ancient Lament"), while observing the greenness of a flowering pomegranate tree, he is reminded that his infant son, who once stretched out "his little hand" toward that very tree, is now dead.

Significantly, the poets whom Carducci chose to translate into Italian were Hellenistic Germans of the earlier part of the century, Friedrich Gottlieb Klopstock, August Platen, and Heine. Also revealing of his tastes are his eulogies for figures such as Giuseppe Garibaldi, the redeemer of Italy; Queen Margherita, the accomplished consort of King Umberto I; Homer; Vergil; Dante, whom he could appreciate but not love; Victor Hugo, to whom he writes: "Sing to the new progeny, O divine old man,/ time-honored song of the Latin people;/ sing to the expectant world: Justice and Liberty"; and even Jaufre Rudel and Martin Luther. A great orator, Carducci was often asked to make public addresses on literary figures of the past; at Pietole, he spoke on Vergil, at Arqua on Petrarch, at Certaldo on Giovanni Boccaccio, at Recanati on Leopardi. In Bologna on June 4, 1882, two days after the death of Garibaldi, Carducci delivered an extemporaneous tribute that has hardly been surpassed in any time or place. Carducci's heavy glorification of the past ("I stand on the mount of centuries"), however, became a suffocating burden from which his successors felt the need to free themselves.

As dogmatic as he was, Carducci was capable of changing his opinions and evolving with the times. The poet who wrote of ancient Rome, "No more she triumphs since a Galilean/ with russet hair, the Capitol ascending,/ thrust on her back a cross," gradually accepted a vigorous and loving morality touched with the divine, and even came to appreciate the historic mission of the Church. Indeed, the author of a savage poetic invective against Pope Pius IX mellowed to such an extent that he poetically invited "Citizen Mastai" (Count Giovanni Maria Mastai-Feretti, later Pope Pius IX) to drink a toast to liberty.

Though foremost a classicist, Carducci came to appreciate modern literature, both foreign and Italian. His "Colloqui con gli alberti" (conversations with the trees) even recalls one of Abbe Zanella's poems that Carducci admired, "Egoismo e carita" (selfishness and charity). In pre-Risorgimento days, Carducci was a staunch republican, but he slowly came to agree with Camillo Bensodi Cavour that Italy was not ready for democratic government, and he endorsed a kingdom under the House of Savoy. This decision led to a deep friendship with Queen Margherita, who in fact purchased his personal library a few years before his death to prevent it from being scattered.

OTHER NEOCLASSICISTS

There were other Italian Neoclassicists at that time, many of whom were devoted followers of Carducci and many, like Carducci himself, who were professors in the new lay university system. This group gave rise to the term "professorial poetry," characterized by its solemn tone and pedagogical intent. Carducci's lifelong friend Giuseppe Chiarini (1833-1908), with whom he had founded the literary society of the Amici Pedanti in 1856, is known for his *Lacrymae* (1879; tears), a collection of simple verses on the premature death of his son, Dante. Other *carducciani*, such as Enrico Panzacchi (1840-1904), Giovanni Marradi (pseudonym of G. Labronio, 1852-1922), Severino Ferrari (1856-1905), and Guido Mazzoni (1859-1943), were evokers of historical landscapes or poets of personal fantasies uninterested in realism. Another poet of rebellious spirit, but one antagonistic to Carducci, was the Sicilian Mario Rapisardi (1844-1912), professor and translator of Lucretius and Catullus and singer of the fatal unhappiness of man and of the assault of science on long-accepted dogma. The same concern for the problem of human destiny is found in the poetry of Arturo Graf (1848-1913), the son of a Bavarian father and an Italian mother and, like Rapisardi, a professor.

GIOVANNI PASCOLI

Toward the end of the century, Carducci's position as unofficial poet laureate was assumed by his former student Giovanni Pascoli (1855-1912), who, like Carducci, was a professor and was interested only in the genre of poetry. As a humanist he even surpassed Carducci, writing the finest Latin poetry since the age of Poliziano (1454-1494). By his emphasis on everday objects and activities, he shifted the focus of Italian poetry from the bourgeois to the petite bourgeoisie. As an outgrowth of his appreciation for the language of the common people, he incorporated many common and dialectal words into his Italian, and his example led to a more hospitable atmosphere for the ultimate acceptance of dialectal words into the standard language. His use and sometimes abuse of the onomatopoeic resources of language (for example, the *tellterelltellteretelltell* of sparrows, the *siccecce siccecce* of stonechats) was widely imitated. Because of his great love for little things, his poetry has

been loosely termed "religious," yet, in his conception, religion was hardly more than a cause around which men could rally in order to become closer to one another.

In his youth, Pascoli was for a brief time partial to Socialism, and in his maturity he lived always without material pretensions. Yet the long years of prosperous peace that followed the unification of Italy were materialistic years during which social and religious concerns played a minor role, and Pascoli's message of simplicity and appreciation for small things had to be tempered somewhat. It was to Italy's classical past and to its more recent patriotic and historical themes that he turned in his last years. His treatment of the classical world, however, was peculiarly his own; his classical heroes are not remote ideals but rather real people with the problems of all men. Thus, Alexander the Great is portrayed not as a conqueror but as a man who laments that there are no more worlds to conquer. Pascoli also acted as spokesman for the hopes and dreams of the Italian people for an empire in Africa. When the Italians were repulsed by the Ethiopians at Adua in 1896, Pascoli mourned the defeat in a poem, and when Italians wished to annex Libya in 1912, he wrote a treatise in agreement with their imperialistic ideals.

Pascoli presented his ideas about poetry in an essay called "Il fanciullino" (1897; the little boy), where he argues that the true poet sees things as a child sees them, spontaneously finding the analogies necessary to express his wonder. Pascoli, himself a child at heart, found fault with literary Italian, cramped by classical tradition and a limited poetic vocabulary, and he led a campaign for a "svecchiamento del lessico" (an updating of the poetic lexicon). About the same time, Edmondo De Amicis (1846-1908), who also esteemed the childlike sense of wonder that is so often stifled in adulthood, was finding similar fault with literary Italian. In *L'idioma gentile* (1905; the noble language), he recommended that aspiring poets study the specialized vocabularies of the peasant trades; the aesthetician Benedetto Croce (1866-1952), who valued ideas above the words that dress them, asked in rebuttal if young Italians should become cooks in order to become poets. Croce, like other critics then as well as now, attacked Pascoli for his informality, sentimentality, and emotionalism, and was especially offended when Pascoli allowed his mother to address him in "La voce" ("The Voice") by his childhood (and dialectal) nickname, Zvanì. However uncontestable these charges seem, Italian (rather than British or American) critics today generally view Pascoli as the primary forerunner of most twentieth century Italian poetry.

GABRIELE D'ANNUNZIO

Pascoli's younger friend and admirer, Gabriele D'Annunzio (1863-1938), the third and last surviving member of the triad, was born "of pure Sabelian race" at Pescara, halfway down the Adriatic coast of Italy. A figure of European stature who occupies a significant place in the political and social, as well as literary, history of Italy, D'Annunzio was the most versatile of the triad, for when he realized that poetry no longer counted as the highest art, he applied himself to the novel and to drama. The crass sensuality of his novels and the exaggerated rhetoric of his plays, however, caused them to be forgotten in due time, while his poetry has proved to be of more lasting value. Because he attempted such a phenomenally wide range of stylistic and metrical possibilities in his poetry, D'Annunzio's legacy to subsequent generations has been great. To separate the enduring from the ephemeral in his vast output (a complete edition of his works, published by Mondadori from 1927 to 1936, comprises forty-nine volumes) has been an ongoing challenge to critics since Croce, Giuseppe Antonio Borgese, and Alfredo Gargiulo.

At the age of sixteen, D'Annunzio published an ode on the birthday of King Umberto I, written in the sapphic meter of Carducci. His first book of poems, *Primo vere* (1879, 1880; early spring), written while he was still at school, and his second, *Canto novo* (1882, 1896; new song), are imitative of Carducci and Olindo Guerrini and exhibit most of the characteristics for which he would become known—classical allusions *ad nauseam*, graphic description, linguistic and metrical dexterity, and an overwhelming joie de vivre. Another trait which became associated with him is his excessive use of the imperative mood, expressive of his sense of superiority and suggesting a master-novice relationship with his readers. The poems *Elegie romane* (1892) and *Poema paradisiaco—Odi navali* (1893) mark his attempt to free himself from the compulsion of the senses

by means of human pity and sympathy—an attempt inspired by Leo Tolstoy and Fyodor Dostoevski.

D'Annunzio was also inspired by his mistress, Eleonora Duse; during the years of their affair (1894-1903), he produced his best works. His most ambitious undertaking bore the impressive title, *Laudi del cielo del mare della terra e degli eroi* (1899); he intended to expand this work into a series of seven books—each named for one of the seven Pleiades—but he never completed the project. The first book, *Maia* (1903), subtitled "Laus vitae" (praise of life), contrasts the myths of Hellas with the dogmas of Christianity in an ideal journey undertaken by the poet through Greece, celebrating joy in the perception of the natural beauty inherent in art, poetry, and legend. *Maia* takes up the theme of Carducci's *Barbarian Odes* and ends, in fact, with a tribute to Carducci. *Elettra* (1904), the second book of the proposed seven, offers an epic glorification of Garibaldi's efforts to liberate and unite Italy and sings the praises of other national heroes, of Victor Hugo, and of Friedrich Nietzsche. *Alcyone* (1904; English translation, 1977), the third book, renews the Mediterranean tradition of the pastoral genre with its consummate simplicity and contains many of D'Annunzio's best-known poems; this volume is generally considered to represent the height of his poetic achievement.

Influenced by the French Parnassians and Symbolists, the English Pre-Raphaelites, and the German rhetoric of Richard Wagner and Nietzsche, D'Annunzio evolved a cult of decadence centered on the relationship between beauty and decay. Not at all Christian, although always respectful to the clergy, D'Annunzio cultivated a fascination for Saint Francis of Assisi and went about his retreat, "Il Vittoriale," in a dressing gown reminiscent of the Franciscan habit. The title of his poetic masterpiece, *Le laudi*, is from the *laudes* of the saint, and *Alcyone* includes pantheistic addresses that are paraphrased from the refrain of the "cantico delle creature." *Elettra* includes the poem "Assisi," in which D'Annunzio evokes Saint Francis from the very landscape, observing the "tortuous windings of desire" first in the "fresh breath of the evening prayer" and then in the "flesh of Francis/ inflamed by the demon of the flesh,/ bleeding on the roses' thorns." Daring to add outrageous detail to Christian myth, his boundless ego empowers him to transfer the turmoil of his own erotic fury to the landscape of Assisi and even to the saintly Francis himself, transforming his fantasy to the likes of a fertility rite. The same morbid mixture of carnality with Catholic myth and ritual is evident in D'Annunzio's mystery play, written in French, *Le Martyre de Saint Sebastien* (pr., pb. 1911), which was condemned as blasphemous by the bishop of Paris.

As a result of his Fascist connections and his sympathy for Benito Mussolini (which, however, has been exaggerated by his detractors), D'Annunzio's fame faded rapidly after World War II. In the 1960's, glimmerings of a D'Annunzio revival began to appear: Some of his plays reopened; in 1976, Luchino Visconti made a film from the poet's novel *L'innocente* (1892; *The Intruder*, 1898); critics began to write about him again, and today tourists flock to his last home, "Il Vittoriale," on Lago di Garda, to savor its historical implications. Two of D'Annunzio's more successful followers were women, Sibilla Aleramo (1876-1960) and Vittoria Aganoor Pompili (1857-1910). The suffocating influence of D'Annunzio's rhetoric, though less pervasive than Carducci's, did much to suppress genuine poetry and to push it to the sidelines of Italian literature, whence it had slowly to begin its way to recovery.

SIBILLA ALERAMO

The gifted and alluring Sibilla Aleramo (pseudonym of Rina Faccio) grew up in the Marches, where her Northern Italian father had been forced to take a position and where she made a bad marriage. Her free verse, often egocentric and cloyingly sensual, reaches lofty heights only when she describes the vanity of temporary carnal gratification. Her claim as Italy's foremost woman writer in the first century of the country's existence rests on the success of her novel, *Una donna* (1906; *A Woman at Bay*, 1908), in defense of women's rights. Among her lovers were the poets Vincenzo Cardarelli (1887-1959), Dino Campana (1885-1932), Clemente Rèbora (1885-1957), Giovanni Papini (1881-1956), and Giovanni Cena (1870-1917); she is sometimes compared to George Sand, whose correspondence with Alfred de Musset she translated into Italian. Although at earlier and later stages of her life she embraced Socialism, in her poverty she was obliged to use her literary talents on behalf of Mussolini. With hindsight, she expressed her envy of D'Annunzio, who died before the Fascist debacle.

REGIONAL AND DIALECTIC POETRY

Traditional Italian poetry before the unification of Italy, as Ruth Phelps has noted, often lacks the "feeling of place" so evident in English poetry. Pascoli was the first of many modern Italian poets to convey this "English" love for a particular corner of the world. Salvatore Quasimodo (1901-1968), in his book of essays *Il falso e vero verde* (1954), notes that Italian poets who are engaged most intensely by a world gathered up in a narrow landscape are often from the South, the tragic and much maligned South that has inspired even Northern poets to reflect upon its destiny. Quasimodo himself wrote a "Lamento per il sud" ("Lament for the South") in which he noted that "the South is tired of hauling the dead/ on the banks of malarial marshes,/ is tired of solitudes, of chains,/ is tired of the curses/ in its mouth," and elsewhere in his poems he frequently alludes to his childhood in Sicily. The heat of the Sicilian midday sun is a major force in the amatory poetry of Giuseppe Villaroel (1889-1965), and Lucio Piccolo (1903-1969) sought to preserve the Baroque Sicily of agave plants, sirocco nights, and colored wagons in his poetry. The savage terrain of isolated Basilicata has inspired such native poets as Rocco Scotellaro (1923-1953), who wrote of "Backbones of mountains/ touched by the light winter sun," and Leonardo Sinisgalli (1908-1981), who celebrated this "Land of huge mamas, of fathers dark/ and radiant as skeletons, overrun by roosters/ and dogs."

Libero de Libero (1906-1981) conveys his deep attachment to the land of his native Ciociaria (between Rome and Naples) in his allusive and elliptical poetry written in the hermetic tradition. Ada Negri (1870-1945), in *Canti dell'isola* (1924; songs of the island), paints the transcending beauty of the dream island of Capri. Diego Valeri (1887-1976) celebrated Venice, his city of adoption, in both poetry and prose. Umberto Saba (1883-1957) loved Trieste and mentions his native city, "beautiful between the rocky mountains and the luminous sea," as one of the personal treasures denied him by the "vile Fascist and greedy German." Andrea Zanzotto (born 1921) writes of his bucolic Pieve de Soligo among the foothills of the Dolomites (especially in *Dietro il paesaggio*, 1951; beside the landscape) and assails real-estate developers poised for ecological rape. Pier Paolo Pasolini (1922-1975) tenderly sprinkles Friulian place-names throughout his poetry.

Eugenio Montale (1896-1981), who spent most of the first thirty years of his life in Genoa, painted the Ligurian landscape in terms of *petrosita*, *scabrezza*, and *aridita* (stoniness, roughness, aridity), and Camillo Sbarbaro (1888-1967), who also wrote lovingly of Liguria, is in fact mentioned in Montale's "Caffè a Rapallo" ("Cafe at Rapallo") as part of the beachside landscape. Other poets who used Ligurian themes in their poetry or drew upon the Ligurian Riviera for local color and veristic imagery include Ceccardo Roccatagliata Ceccardi (1872-1919), Mario Novaro (1868-1944), and Giovanni Boine (1887-1917), who turned his eyes yearningly back to his native town on the Ligurian coast from a sanatorium in the Swiss Alps.

Closely linked to poetry celebrating a particular region is that which employs a dialect in the face of pressure to employ the standard language. When Italy became a united nation in 1861, only slightly more than 2.5 percent of the population could speak Italian in addition to their native dialect. Although the Italian dialects all share the same Latin origin as the national language, and in fact share a vast quantity of lexical and grammatical features, there are also bewildering dissimiliarities that can make mastery of standard Italian a difficult task. As a result of the prescriptivist stance of linguistic arbiters since the time of Pietro Bembo (1470-1547), who argued for the purity of the Tuscan variety of Italian to the exclusion of borrowings from other dialects, the Italian language that the nation inherited in 1861 was a rigid medium of expression whose parameters would not be broadened until Giovanni Pascoli undertook the task—a half century before television and radio would do the job more efficiently.

Coinciding with the rise of *Verismo* during the second half of the nineteenth century, an impressive number of talented poets chose to write occasionally or exclusively in their native dialects, and they have given to Italian literature a curious offshoot that is neglected in many surveys of Italian poetry. Although poets have been writing in their local dialects since the literary

emergence of those dialects in medieval Italy, and although such preunification poets as the Sicilian Giovanni Meli (1740-1815), the Milanese Carlo Porta (1775-1821), and the Roman Giuseppe Gioachino Belli (1791-1863) enjoyed local followings, it was not until there was a united Italy that dialectal literature won a wider audience, and it was not until the emergence of Salvatore Di Giacomo (1860-1934) that Italian critics began to take dialectal literature seriously.

The Neapolitan Di Giacomo, who ranks as one of Italy's greatest lyric poets, employed a dialect that is musical, refined, and polished, not at all like street talk, though he frequently depicts street scenes in his poetry. Since Di Giacomo believed that his fame would rest on his scholarly studies (thirty-four volumes) treating the history and sociology of Naples, he wrote those works and some of his *novelle* in Italian, reserving his use of dialect for his poetry. He began writing during the vogue of *Verismo* and folklore studies, but his treatment of subject matter is sentimentalized and subjectivized to such an extent that the effect it achieves is quite different from that of *Verismo*. His poetry is dreamy and melancholy, sentimental but not mawkish, as in the sonnets of *O munasterio* (1887; the monastery), about a jilted sailor who becomes a monk and still longs for the freedom of the outside world, for green things growing, and for the water of the bay in the moonlight. Simple and innocent, Di Giacomo displays a childlike enchantment with the stars and moon. At times, too, he is fascinated by macabre elements. In his ghastly dream of a winter night, "Suonno 'e na notte 'e vierno," he sees before him all the women he has loved; when he fails to recognize one of them, who is veiled, she invites him to embrace her, and he realizes that she is Death.

Two poets of the same period, both writing in the dialect of modern Rome (*romanesco*), were also widely read and appreciated: Cesare Pascarella (1858-1940) and Carlo Alberto Salustri (1871-1950), called Trilussa. Pascarella wrote his *Sonetti* (1900; sonnets) in a medium close enough to standard Italian as to be understood easily (the glossary that accompanies the collection contains a mere forty words). The twenty-five sonnets of his *Villa Gloria* (1886) recount the ill-fated attempt by a group of patriots to wrest Rome from the Papacy (1867), and *Scoperta dell' America* (1894; the discovery of

America), consisting of fifty sonnets, portrays Columbus, Ferdinand and Isabella, the Spanish sailors, and the American Indians all speaking the Roman dialect with humorous effects as they reenact the drama of discovering America.

Trilussa employed the *romanesco* dialect in its aspects of low-life (*gergo furfantino*) to construct fables in a variety of metrical forms. His art is witty, cynical, melancholy, epigrammatic, and not without a religious vein (as in "Sermone 1914," an antiwar poem). His cynicism is sometimes excessive, as in "L'omo inutile" (the superfluous man), about a six-month-old fetus under alcohol in a vat in a museum who claims that he is happier watching the people in the museum than dying as an adult in somebody's war; more often, his fables are simply delightful, as in "La carita" (charity), in which the president of an association for mistreated animals refuses to spare a dime to a beggar, claiming that only animals qualify for his sympathy, whereupon the beggar renews his appeal by displaying a headful of lice. Trilussa is probably best known for his political fables, which concern the freedom lost as a result of the Fascist *ventennio*.

Having produced Di Giacomo and a host of other poets during its centuries as the largest city in Italy (a distinction it retained for several decades even after the Risorgimento), Naples has been the most prolific source of dialectal literature. Next to Di Giacomo is his contemporary and competitor for recognition, the *verista* Ferdinando Russo (1866-1927), whose poetry portraying Neapolitan life is more dramatic and less tragic than that of Di Giacomo. His poems, like those of Di Giacomo, often deal with unrequited or impossible love. Other Neapolitan poets, less accomplished than Di Giacomo or Russo, clung to the melic tradition and contributed to the repertory of Neapolitan *canzonette*.

After Naples, the area around Venice has produced the richest vein of dialectal poetry. The Venetian Giacomo Noventa (1898-1960), who, with Alberto Carocci and Franco Fortini, in 1936 founded the Florentine review *Riforma letteraria* (which was closed down by the Fascists three years later), was an aristocratic popular poet who embraced liberal, Socialist, and Catholic views. The Veronese poet Berto Barbarani (1872-1945) wrote of the humble people and of his own loves and sorrows,

depicting children with the warmth and sympathy of someone who has not had any of his own. Writing in the dialect of Trieste, Virgilio Giotti (1885-1957), abjuring historical and folkloric themes, elaborated a crepuscular inwardness, while Biagio Marin (1891-1985) is essentially a religious poet. In Friulian, Pietro Zorutti (1792-1867), author of humorous and sometimes sentimental sonnets and impressive epigrams, wrote his *Strolic furlan* (1847; Friulian almanac), a title echoed in the name of a poetry magazine, *Stroligut di cà da l'aga* (little almanac from this side of the water), published by a modern Friulian, Pier Paolo Pasolini. Pasolini founded the Academiuta di Lenga Furlana at Casarsa, an institution that was active from 1946 to 1950, and compiled, in collaboration with the *romanesco* poet Mario Dell'Arco, an anthology of contemporary dialectal poetry from the entire Italian peninsula, *Poesia dialettale del Novecento* (1952; dialect poetry of the twentieth century). To the socialistic Pasolini, the dialect of his mother's native Friuli represented a sacred language spoken by the blessed poor, and he began his career as a poet describing the Alpine enclave, which for him represented an idyll of sexual (in his case, homosexual) freedom as opposed to the sexual corruption offered by the cities. Ironically, however, it was in Friuli that Pasolini's homosexual activities with local youths first led to blackmail and to lawsuits.

The Milanese dialect was represented by Delio Tessa (1886-1939), whose work embodies an invigorated crepuscularism, and the Ligurian dialect by Edoardo Firpo (1889-1957), whose poetry evokes the harsh Ligurian earth and the rigorous lives of those close to it. Nearer to the historical seat of the national language in Tuscany is the Pisan dialect, used by Renato Fucini (1843-1921) in his sonnets, which present vignettes of everyday life.

Writing in the harsh and little-known dialect of Basilicata is Albino Pierro (1916-1995), whose printed poems are characteristically accompanied by translations in Italian, as in *Nd'u piccicarelle di Tursi/Nel precipizio di Tursi* (1967; on the cliff of Tursi). Coming to poetry not from literary study but from inner need, he writes of the mystery of life and death, of the ancient landscape of the Italian South. From neighboring Calabria came the philosophizing poet Vincenzo Padula (1819-1893), who occasionally wrote in his Calabrian dialect.

Sebastiano Satta (1867-1914) is regarded as the national bard of Sardinia, even if his best poetry was written in Italian. His work is often shallow and his diction stilted, but at moments in *Canti barbaricini* (1910), he evokes a primitive epic grandeur.

CREPUSCOLARI, FUTURISTI, AND VOCIANI

In the twentieth century, Italian poetry escaped the provincialism that had dominated it for some time. Even the great figures Carducci and D'Annunzio came to represent a limiting classicism and an overblown rhetorical nationalism. To be sure, such figures exercised an influence on poets following them, but on the whole, the turn of the century saw a reaction against them. Of the triad, only Pascoli can be said to have anticipated contemporary poetry. The reaction took three forms: the style of the *crepuscolari* (crepuscular poets), that of the *futuristi* (Futurists), and the poetics of the writers associated with the magazine *La voce*, the *vociani*.

The crepuscular poets never constituted a school as such. Their name, which means "twilight," was derived from an article by Giuseppe Antonio Borgese (1881-1952) assessing the poetry of the turn of the century. In Borgese's view, the triad's achievements were so great that the younger generation of poets, men such as Sergio Corazzini (1886-1907), Guido Gozzano (1883-1916), Corrado Govoni (1884-1965), and Aldo Palazzeschi (pseudonym of Aldo Giurlani, 1885-1974), could hardly hope to express themselves in new ways; theirs could be only a waning poetry. Borgese found these men to be filled with world-weariness and an unnaturally early awareness of death; the language of their works he thought Pascolian in its simplicity, its emulation of ordinary linguistic rhythms, and its concern for "small things." Though none of these poets was to become great, they established the Pascolian vocabulary and concern for ordinary cadences later employed by the great Italian modernists.

The poets identified by Borgese as *crepuscolari* wrote for only a short time. Either they died young, as did Corazzini, or they turned to other literary forms, as did Palazzeschi. Nevertheless, some of these writers should be given serious attention. In the poetry of Gozzano, for example, the danger of the crepuscular style, a self-indulgent melancholy, is balanced by a mor-

dant irony, an irony especially incisive when directed against the foibles of the poet-self. In his fine poem "Totò Merumeni," Gozzano elaborates on a Prufrockian caricature. Totò, a fallen aristocratic type with "culture up to his ears," struggles, but without too much anguish, to comprehend his circumstances. He is a man with sensibilities but without will: "He's the *good man*, that fool of/ Nietzsche's. . . ." Totò incarnates an overripe culture and the malaise of a spirit without direction because its greatness is past. A chilly objectivity prevents any sentimentality. One line that could otherwise have been excessive states the theme of the poem: "One by one Life took all of its promises back."

The weakness of the crepuscular style, and the reason for its short vogue, is evident in Govoni's "La trombettina" ("The Little Trumpet"). This poem opens clearly and interestingly with a direct statement that all the magic that is left from a fair is in a trumpet carried across a field by a girl. The poet goes on to add: "But within its forced note/ are all the clowns, white ones and red ones,/ the band . . ." and so on. These added lines are not necessary and reduce the powerfully imagistic opening to pretty description that sinks to easy nostalgia. Even though the poet provides a surprising reversal of tone as an ending—finding "the wondrousness of spring" in the "flicker of a firefly"—he does not balance the sentimentality of the larger part of the poem. In fact, the ending substitutes another kind of sentimentality.

It was not the crepuscular poets who succeeded in reentering the European world. In 1909, publishing in the Parisian newspaper *Le Figaro*, Filippo Tommaso Marinetti (1876-1944) issued the *Manifeste du futurisme*. The Futurist movement, which embraced sculpture and painting as well as poetry, took one side of the Nietzschean philosophy of will and elevated it to a religion. Marinetti praised courage and boldness, unabashed egotism, and the purifying air of war. The machine age transcended all previous ages: Noise, speed, and mastery were its central values. Men such as Marinetti, Ardengo Soffici (1879-1964), Govoni, Papini, Palazzeschi, and even Giuseppe Ungaretti (1888-1970) wrote under the Futurist banner.

Marinetti's call for the destruction of culture, though absurd in one way, was, in another way, prophetic, for

World War I, which many of the Futurists foresaw and welcomed, threw European culture into a whirlwind of self-questioning. By the end of the war, it appeared as if Carducci had been forgotten. Ironically, the Futurist advocacy of war and its identification with fascism assured its fate: The reaction against the war meant that most writers turned their backs on Futurism as well.

Marinetti's "words in freedom," a poetic style in which syntax is interrupted or destroyed in order to achieve unusual juxtapositions of words, and in which words are stretched and given new, or absurd, meanings, became an element in a new poetic style emerging in Italy in the 1920's and focusing on the magazine *La voce*. Arturo Onofri (1885-1928) and Ungaretti were the major exponents of this style.

La voce saw its first number in December of 1908 under the editorship of Giuseppe Prezzolini (1882-1982). A center of social, political, and literary debate for eight years, the magazine became progressively more literary until, in December of 1914, under the editorship of Giuseppe De Robertis (1888-1963), it became completely literary. The writers published in *La voce* came from every side of the political spectrum. Even Benito Mussolini and the dialectal poet Di Giacomo published in the magazine, but the writers who came to be known as *vociani* were men such as Sbarbaro, Papini (who had collaborated with Prezzolini on the magazine *Leonardo*), Rèbora, Piero Jahier (1884-1966), Palazzeschi, Cardarelli, Saba, and Campana.

Like Soffici, Palazzeschi, and Papini, Jahier had been a Futurist. For him, social issues were crucial in poetry, and in this belief he was typical of the *vociani*. His social concerns might have been colored, however, by his strict Protestant upbringing. Jahier's poetry was an antecedent of Ungaretti's, for it was fragmented, analogical, and aimed at an almost mystical apprehension of reality beyond any rational order.

Onofri had seen a crepuscular and Futurist phase, but his mature voice is identified with his *La voce* years. Following the French Symbolists, he insisted that the poem was a reality unto itself that had to be taken on its own terms. As Onofri's poetry developed, it became progressively more mystical, and his aesthetics reflected the influence of German Idealism, for he sought a union of the creative ego with the cosmos.

De Robertis, the editor of *La voce* from December, 1914 to December, 1915, saw the magazine through its most significant phase. With Ungaretti, De Robertis played an important part in the revaluation of Giacomo Leopardi, establishing the nineteenth century poet as perhaps the dominant native influence on Italian poetry in the first half of the twentieth century. The critic Silvio Ramat further asserts that this period in the history of *La voce* represented the beginnings of the hermetic school, the most important movement in twentieth century Italian poetry.

Campana, often called one of the *vociani*, must be treated separately, for he defies categorization. His association with the magazine was by default, for Soffici, to whom Campana had entrusted the manuscript of *Canti orfici* (1914; *Orphic Songs*, 1968), lost it; Campana thus had to publish his work himself. When Soffici read it, he praised it highly and was instrumental in arranging for a second edition.

Campana was influenced by the American poet Walt Whitman. A restless traveler, pathologically lonely and eventually mad, Campana wrote impassioned poetry. Imitating Whitman, he wrote in free verse, with erratic syntax and disquieting imagery. His sole work, *Orphic Songs*, lyrically depicts travels, women, loneliness. His writing is reminiscent of Vincent van Gogh's expressive power—as, for example, when he describes Genoa, making it any modern city: "And The City is aware/ And lights up/ And the flame titillates and swallows up/ The magnificent residues of the sun. . . ."

Campana's poetry is spontaneous, filled with brilliant insight, but sometimes without sustaining integument. True to their name, these poems seem, at their best, inspired in a demoniac fashion, and it is that quality that keeps them safe from pathos. Ironically, it might have been Campana's madness that preserved his work from melancholy. His life, however, was not thus preserved, for soon after the publication of his poems he was committed to a mental hospital at Castel Pulci near Florence, where he remained until his death in 1932.

UNGARETTI, MONTALE, QUÁSIMODO, SABA

Giuseppe Ungaretti is the central figure of twentieth century Italian poetry. Next to him are Eugenio Montale and Umberto Saba, and in the succeeding generation, Salvatore Quasimodo. Only Ungaretti, Montale has said, could benefit from the air of freedom around the time of World War I. Though Saba was writing at that time also, his poetry remained derivative of Pascoli until he encountered Ungaretti.

Ungaretti was born in Alexandria, Egypt. His education was French, which probably accounts for the decidedly Symbolist influence on his poetry. His style brings together Symbolist, Futurist, and Leopardian techniques. The use of fragmented lines, analogy, nonmetrical but rhythmic cadences, and mysterium characterizes his early writing, the works of World War I: *Il porto sepolto* (1916; the buried port) and *Allegria di naufragi* (1919; the joy of shipwrecks).

In describing his verse, Ungaretti spoke of a poetics of the word, suggesting that words have a plethora of significations which it is the task of poetry to unearth. Ungaretti's spare style was a consequence of this belief. "I flood myself with light/ of the immense." So goes the poem "Mattina" ("Morning"); such a poem is evocative, incantatory. Even in those poems based on a narrative, Ungaretti removed all spare words—anything that served a merely decorative or metrical function—in order to get at the significant elements only. Such a narrative poem is "In memoria" ("In Memoriam"), about the suicide of his friend Mohammed Sheab. On its surface, the poem appears to be simply a whittled-down account of a tragic event, but when the reader takes into account the role of the poetic speaker, his condition as a soldier at the Italian Front during World War I, and the fact that the poem stands as a successful song, such lines as "And he could not/ set free/ the song/ of his abandon" or "And only I perhaps/ still know/ he lived," it becomes clear that the apparent simplicity and directness of the poem conceal depths of meaning. This poem is not, in any simple sense, an effort to memorialize its subject through art; indeed, the poem suggests that the precariousness of things and of people is the very precondition of song.

After his first collections, Ungaretti turned to an intensive study of traditional Italian lyrics: Petrarch, Tasso, Leopardi. From the highly condensed line and music of his first works, he turned to traditional metrics as an inspiration, seeking, he said, "true Italian

song." Without abandoning the lean quality of his early verse, Ungaretti managed in volumes such as *Sentimento del tempo* (1933; the feeling of time) and *La terra promessa* (1950; the promised land) to infuse his work with the music of the hendecasyllabic line. At the same time, his syntax became more complex, and he introduced subtle allusions to the classics. These features of his poems provoked resistance among some critics and inspired the label "hermetic"—that is, requiring secret knowledge.

For Ungaretti, poetry and experience are in dialogue with each other (he called poetry "seemly biography"), so that a more complex poetry reflects a deepening experience. In fact, poetry is the vehicle by which experience is deepened, or, to put it in a more Ungarettian fashion, restored to its purity. Such an understanding of the role of poetry reveals how central language is to Ungaretti's worldview. For most human beings, caught up in a fragmented or clichéd language, experience is alienated from them at the very moment of its occurrence; though the poet might not come closer to the moment of experience, in recollection through poetry, he can uncover the truth of experience. Others, like Ungaretti, move from atheism to faith, suffer the loss of an only son, and confront old age, but they cannot capture the truth of these experiences as Ungaretti was able to do in his poetry.

Ungaretti's dialogue with tradition is an extension of his dialogue with experience. The essentials of experience do not change—love, death, memory—and the truth of these is held in the collective memory of tradition. The poet cannot work alone, but must return to the past creatively as a source. In one of his last poems, titled "Per sempre" ("For Ever") and written, perhaps, in memory of his wife, Ungaretti captured something of the sense of this twofold dialogue: "With no impatience I shall dream,/ Bend to the work/ That has no end...."

Ungaretti gained an international reputation, lectured widely, and influenced almost every major modern poetic movement in Italy. He, along with Montale, Quasimodo, and others, was also active as a translator, helping to lead Italy out of cultural provincialism.

While contemporary Italian poetry begins with Ungaretti, its greatest figure may be Eugenio Montale, though the bulk of Montale's work makes up only four modest collections: *Ossi di seppia* (1925; partial translation, *The Bones of the Cuttlefish*, 1983; full translation, *Cuttlefish Bones*, 1992), *Le occasioni* (1939; *The Occasions*, 1987), *La bufera e altro* (1956; *The Storm and Other Poems*, 1978), and *Satura* (1962; English translation, 1969).

Montale's earliest poems are in the crepuscular mood, showing especially the influence of Gozzano as well as of Pascoli, but D'Annunzio is also present. Though Montale is not really a regional poet, his reflection of Sbarbaro, a fellow Ligurian, gives his poetry a regional feel. Unlike Sbarbaro's landscapes, however, Montale's settings verge on metaphysical realities, providing images emblematic of man's condition.

Not completely a pessimist, Montale nevertheless wraps whatever sense of extraordinary reality is attained in his poems in a language of desolation and spiritual fragmentation. In the poem "I limoni" ("The Lemon Trees"), for example—which many critics treat as thematically central to Montale's first collection, *The Bones of the Cuttlefish*—there are several suggestions of a breakthrough into a heightened reality: "Here by a miracle is hushed/ the war of diverted passions,/ here even to us poor falls our share of riches,/ and it is the scent of the lemon trees. . . ." These openings, however, are quickly obscured: "But the illusion wanes and time returns us/ to our clamorous cities. . . ." In Ungaretti, the desolate landscape of modern existence is likewise seen as resulting from the reality of time, but for him there is also a way beyond depersonalized time; in Montale, the landscape is bleaker, the music more muted.

Montale's greatness lies in his ability to evoke cosmic order in the midst of ordinary things and events. A thunderstorm holds back ultimate reality, for example, in "Arsenio," a poem many critics take to be a self-portrait. Montale commented that at the time of the writing of this poem, he was under the influence of Henri Bergson, the French philosopher: "Miracle was as evident for me as necessity." For Montale, however, there was never a complete breakthrough to extraordinary reality; thus, Arsenio, after contemplating the possibility that the sound of castanets holds the key to a heightened reality, is suddenly swept along in a thunderstorm: "Everything about you is washing with overflow, the loose awnings/ flap in the wind, and immense rustling skirts/ along the earth, and down collapse with strident sounds/ the paper lanterns. . . ."

Montale's later poetry, beginning with *The Occasions*, became more difficult, more hermetic: "I wanted a fruit that could contain its motives without revealing them, or better, without flaunting them." He was after an extreme concentration of meaning, an obscurity he considered good. The title of *The Occasions* suggests the difficulty of these poems; in them, one is immersed in occasions without introduction and must make one's way in the midst of objects suggestively arranged, but without any obvious relationships among them. Montale's is often a poetry of things imbued with meanings and memories.

For Montale, the central drama of existence is a striving for harmony with the self and the cosmos. Neither of these is finally achieved in life, but the poems themselves stand as a testament that Montale will not sink into cynicism or complete pessimism; although the poems do not offer ultimate consolation, they do limn a heightened experience. Thus, there is a kind of faith in beauty underlying these works, not aestheticism but an aesthetic stoicism: "The life that seemed/ so vast is briefer than your handkerchief."

Umberto Saba lived and wrote during a period of tremendous poetic innovation in Italy, yet his own work remained close to the lyric tradition of Petrarch and Leopardi. To be sure, his poetry reveals the influence of his contemporaries (he himself acknowledges the influence of Ungaretti on his style), but the great body of his work cannot be categorized as belonging to any of the schools of twentieth century Italian poetry. Even though he is said to be a major force in the development of neorealism after World War II, he never shared any of the political themes of this school. Saba's poetry is fundamentally autobiographical. His recurring subjects are ordinary things, animals, and the people close to him—his mother, his father, and, above all, his wife.

Saba was born in Trieste, a city to which he remained passionately attached throughout his life. His mother was Jewish, and it was her religious identity that the poet chose for himself. His father deserted the family when Saba was a young boy. When he met his father years later, at the age of twenty, Saba says it was then that he discovered the origin of his poetic spirit. The images of

Trieste found in his poetry were connected in his imagination with his wet nurse, a woman Saba loved; his emotional allegiance to her caused his mother some jealousy and pain. Saba suffered often during his adult life thinking of the pain he had given his mother, and it was probably only with his marriage that he found some sense of peace with himself.

Saba's major opus, the *Il canzoniere* (1961, revised 1965; songbook), bears the title of Petrarch's great work—no doubt in homage to it. Written between 1900 and 1954 and having appeared in several editions before the 1961 collection, these poems are addressed to Saba's daughter Linuccia in an ironically offhand, self-deprecating way. The book is an autobiography in verse, and critics have often commented that the poet becomes self-indulent and technically lax in some of the poems, but, taken as a whole, the work has a greatness that is undeniable. Indeed, Saba's *Il canzoniere* is one of those rare masterpieces that combine unswerving artistic vision with great popular appeal.

A Pascolian, Saba balances potentially sentimental themes, such as the love he has for his wife, with a muted and ironic language. In "A mia moglie" ("To My Wife"), he develops a series of similes between his wife and barnyard animals. These images never become cute, and by the end of the poem, they ring with surprisingly passionate power: ". . . as in all the females/ of the peaceful animals,/ close to God;/ and in no other woman." Saba was a master of classical meters and forms. His career as a poet was traditional in the sense that he apprenticed himself to his craft, learning more and more difficult forms. This painstaking craftsmanship in the service of emotional authenticity made for great poetry. Though he valued simplicity, Saba was in no way simple.

Salvatore Quasimodo, born in Modica, Sicily, stands with Ungaretti, Montale, and Saba as one of the great poets of modern Italy. His winning of the Nobel Prize for Literature in 1959 aroused a great deal of critical debate, for many had expected the older Ungaretti or Montale to win. Quasimodo, furthermore, won the Nobel Prize based upon his later work, such as *Giorno dopo giorno* (1947; day after day), which he wrote after his turn away from hermeticism to a more socially and politically engaged poetry. For those critics who considered his early work superior, the Nobel Prize seemed a mistake. There is no doubt today, however, that Quasimodo is held in the highest critical esteem.

Educated as an engineer, though he discovered his love of poetry early in life, it was not until his late twenties that Quasimodo sought publication. His first poems were published in *Solaria*, a magazine whose internationalism, intellectualism, and political nonalignment were considered anti-Fascist. In 1930, the same year as his first publications, his collection *Acque e terre* (1930; waters and land) appeared, immediately establishing Quasimodo as a major new voice. These first poems were obscure, subdued, mysterious—hermetic in the manner of Montale and Ungaretti. Though his early work revealed a strong sense of landscape, Quasimodo's main concerns—like Montale's—were spiritual. His was a voice of human loneliness and anguish. In "Ed èsubito sera" ("And It Is Suddenly Evening"), this mood is beautifully, if epigrammatically, conveyed: "Each alone on the heart of the earth,/ impaled upon a ray of sun:/ and suddenly it's evening."

Quasimodo often evokes classical music, as in "Vento a Tindari" ("Wind at Tindari"): "Tindari, I know you mild/ among broad hills, above the waters/ of the god's soft islands. . . ." In the Italian, the cadences of classical Greek structure the line and add to the evocative power of the landscape. Like Ungaretti, Quasimodo sought a promised land which poetry somehow prefigured. In this case, it is Sicily sung in such a way that it becomes a mysticized realm. Just as Quasimodo practiced what Ungaretti called the "excavation of the word," so, too, he uncovered classical resonances in the scenes of his native island.

Quasimodo, along with many other Southern writers, lived in the North because of the deplorable condition into which the South had sunk, but in his writing he remained a southerner, even ascribing to men of the South a capacity for creative invention because of their destitution. It was during his first stay in the North that Quasimodo encountered an important influence, Monsignor Rampolla del Tindaro, who encouraged him to study the classics. After teaching himself Greek and Latin, Quasimodo went on to the study of poetry and philosophy in the classical languages. In 1940, he published a powerful, controversial volume of translations,

Lirici greci (1940; Greek lyrics), establishing himself as a major translator of the classics.

During World War II, Quasimodo went through a critical change. The involuted, obscure poetry of the 1930's came to seem to him a manifestation of self-indulgence, and he turned to a more socially engaged poetry. In this new poetry, he sought to communicate with a wider audience and to bear witness to the absurdity of the contemporary situation. In poems such as "Auschwitz," he called for a rejection of inhumanities: "Upon the plains, where love and lamentation/ rotted . . . , a no/ to death. . . ." His project, which he shared with many other artists of this century, was the remaking of man. The cry which closes "Uomo del mio tempo" ("Man of My Time") is as old as Greek tragedy, expressing, perhaps, man's only real hope: "Forget, O sons, the clouds of blood/ risen from the earth, forget the fathers:/ their tombs sink down in ashes,/ black birds, the wind, cover their heart."

ERMETISMO

There are many ways of understanding the phenomenon called *ermetismo*, or hermeticism. Essentially an extension of Symbolism into Italy, the movement nevertheless developed distinctively Italian features. The term "hermetic" was first used in a 1936 article by the Crocean critic Francesco Flora (1891-1962), who deplored the lack of clarity in the poetry of Ungaretti and his fellow spirits. Flora criticized Ungaretti in particular for practicing an art that was French, an "analogical art"; like the French Symbolists, Ungaretti employed metaphor and ellipsis to bring out an inherent richness in words that went beyond any logical order. Flora's analysis, however, failed to acknowledge the native Italian influences that also shaped Ungaretti's art, particularly the "poetics of memory" elaborated in Leopardi's *Zibaldone* (1898-1900; notebook of thoughts).

Ungaretti, Montale, and later Quasimodo were the most important poets associated with hermeticism; other poets identified with this school were Mario Luzi (born 1914), Vittorio Sereni (1913-1983), Alfonso Gatto (1909-1976), and Sinisgalli. Sandro Penna (1906-1977) is also counted in this group, but the character of his poetry—like that of Saba's, to which it is sometimes compared—defies categorization.

Sinisgalli, a Lucanian poet, wrote of his region but also of urban life; his poetry is characterized by a remarkable precision that reflects his study of mathematics. As a poet, Sinisgalli moved from revelation to revelation. In his later poetry, leaving behind the mannerisms of hermeticism, he became more epigrammatic, simpler and more direct. As he says of the poet in "Alla figura del poeta": "Like a rabbit in a hutch, every morning he finds—under his paws, before his eyes, near his nose—his portion of syllables and signs."

Of the other hermetic poets, Luzi is perhaps the most significant, for he emerged, after the war, as a major spokesman in defense of hermetic poetry, which was coming under attack at that time by the emerging neorealists. The war had an effect on Luzi himself, however, and by the 1950's his style had broadened considerably from that of his earlier poetry. Luzi's work is allusive, refined, complex. He said of poetry: "The great adventure of modern poetry consists . . . in its attempt to reconstruct through language that unity lost by the ideal, practical, expressive world."

Gatto and Sereni both began in the analogical style of hermeticism, and both changed direction as a result of the war. Gatto's earlier poetry—impressionistic, filled with landscapes—was highly melodic, perhaps reflecting his Neapolitan heritage (Gatto was born in Salerno). Sereni explored the historical and ideological questions raised by the war.

RELIGIOUS POETRY

The patriotism that produced the Risorgimento and the prosperity that followed it were not conducive to the writing of lofty religious poetry. An exception is the poetry of the Calabrian Antonino Anile (1869-1943), a Neoclassicist and follower of Carducci as well as a university professor of anatomy who saw no irreconcilable conflict between science and faith. Always deeply religious, his poems portray the beauty of nature as a manifestation of God.

Many of the *vociani* wrote what might be called religious poetry. Giovanni Papini (1881-1956) converted to Catholicism after the trauma of World War I and wrote his famous *La storia di Cristo* (1921; *The Life of Christ*, 1923), a work neither theological nor scientific but charged with love and hope. From 1921 until his death, he was constantly concerned with deepening his faith, as in "Domande al Signore" ("Requests of the Lord"), where he asks for simplicity, humility, a serene smile, the cleansing of his "turbid soul that reeks of the sewer," and the burning of his heart "so that, in pursuing pain, it would find/ Your irrefutable will."

The Milanese Clemente Rèbora, another of the *vociani*, started to write poetry as an atheist. The victim of shell shock in World War I, he was discharged in 1915, and the experience forced him to do more than ask the usual existential questions about war. In 1929, he retired to a monastery, was ordained a priest in 1936, and abjured the writing of poetry until 1955, when he wrote "Curriculum vitae," an autobiographical meditation on his spiritual pilgrimage.

The response of *vociani* such as Rèbora, Onofri, and Jahier to the rhetoric of the nineteenth century was a moral indignation. Rèbora became traditionally religious, Onofri became a mystic, and Jahier expressed himself in philosophical terms. Jahier, unlike Rèbora, saw war as the symptom of a corrupt capitalistic society and as such saw it as God's way of destroying that corruption. Onofri, on the other hand, embarked upon a mystical quest that produced poems less successful than his earlier attempts.

The spiritual crisis that Ungaretti underwent after 1928 led to his return to Catholicism and ultimately is reflected in the most important part of his collection *Sentimento del tempo*. In the central poem of the section, titled "La pietà" ("Pity"), the poet expresses serious doubts about the power of his poetry and seems to waver between two poles: the solipsism of a poetry pursued in a world without God, and the certitude of a renewal of faith. Though Ungaretti expresses a tone of greater harmony in his later works, the struggle persists. Ungaretti remained the paradoxical agnostic believer; every introduction of a Christian value or image in his verse is balanced by a pagan or a humanistic counterweight.

Always insistent that he belonged to no school, Carlo Betocchi (1899-1986) cultivated his own style and his own sympathetic outlook toward objects of ordinary life. Although his post-World War II poetry is more somber, all experiences are interpreted as proof of his love for God and humanity. A land surveyor and construction engineer, Betocchi was instrumental in the or-

ganization of *Il frontespizio*, a Florentine review for Catholic poets (1929), of which he and Papini were coeditors.

Quasimodo was probably the most conventionally religious of the first-rank poets of this era. His work translating the New Testament and his knowledge of the Old Testament are echoed allusively in all of his poetry, and religious references are not always treated hermetically. His poem "Man of My Time" takes on the directness of a sermon: Man, with his "exact science bent on extermination," is "without love, without Christ," and the poet then includes a scriptural quotation: "The blood smells as on the day/ when one brother said to the other brother: 'Let us go out to the fields.'" His great antiwar poem "Alle fronde dei salici" ("On the Branches of the Willows"), in which the poet asks, "And how could we have sung/ with the alien foot upon our heart?" and in which lyres hung on willow branches swaying in the sad wind form a counterpart to the "black howl" of a mother who meets her son crucified on a telegraph pole, was inspired by the Psalm 137, in which the children of Israel, who have hung their harps "upon the willows in the midst thereof," ask "How shall we sing the Lord's song in a strange land?" The most important lesson that Quasimodo learned from his faith was the acceptance of suffering, an acceptance that gives his mature poetry great moral authority.

The poet-priest David Maria Turoldo (1916-1992), of Friulian origin, published his first book of poetry, *Io non ho mani* (1948; I have no hands), in the painful years after World War II, establishing himself as a lover of all living things, even of the earth itself. His imagery is sensuous and uninhibited ("And while the kisses of others/ stopped at the mouth,/ I ate You at every dawn"). Although he inveighs against the destructiveness of the Western world, he can praise even the cities and the machines of the world, for they are man's handiwork and are not in themselves profane.

LA RONDA AND THE RONDISTI

The review *La ronda*, founded by Vincenzo Cardarelli and published in Rome between 1919 and 1923, represented an attempt to encourage a renewal of Italian letters after World War I. The *rondisti* wished to restore good writing in poetry and prose by a return to classical tradition, well-constructed syntax, clear style, and a literary vocabulary. The creation of literature was once again to be viewed as a craft with as few infractions of the rules as possible. In their task of reeducating Italians in the art of writing, they chose as their model Leopardi, ultimately emphasizing his prose over his poetry. They failed for the most part to achieve these goals, for the world was changing, and although they rejected fascism, the academicism that gradually developed from their aims came dangerously close to suiting the needs of fascism.

Only in the work of Cardarelli did the *rondisti* produce a significant contribution to poetry. Cardarelli, whose critical work revealed a particular distaste for Pascoli and a virtually idolatrous regard for sixteenth century literature, wrote of the seasons as emblems for the cycle of human life, of landscapes in the harsh light of a sun that often obliterates hopes and dreams. Some of the other writers associated with *La ronda*, such as Emilio Cecchi (1884-1966) and Riccardo Bacchelli (born 1891), were influential in propounding the vision of art as an autonomous sphere, a notion that became an important aspect of hermeticism. Initially Ungaretti, from 1919 to 1920, was involved with the *rondisti*, but he split with them because he felt they wanted prose poems instead of creations approaching song.

Like the *rondisti*, Ada Negri (1870-1945), who was the first woman member of the Italian Academy, held traditional views about poetry. In her poems, she exalts the virtue of the working classes and, in those written after her marriage to a wealthy Piedmontese industrialist, the joys of motherhood. After a period of disillusionment, she wrote *Il libro di Mara* (1919), a powerful love poem that has been likened to the lyrics of Sappho and the Song of Solomon.

POETRY OF THE RESISTANCE

It is an understatement to say that for the Italian people, the experience of World War II was traumatic and that they emerged from it with changed values. The fact that virtually all postwar literary movements are introduced with the prefix *neo-* (for example, neorealism, neoexperimentalism) is but a single example of the rupture caused by the war. A great polemic arose after the war over charges that Italian poets had done little or nothing to stop the rise of fascism. One result of the charges was that previously hermetic poets such as Quasimodo, Sereni, and Luzi underwent profound changes of attitude; another was that poetry reflecting on the mission of the Resistance movement came to be highly esteemed. In an attempt to unify poets, some critics have amplified the meaning of "Resistance" poetry to include any antiwar poetry of the period. Thus, the very fine *Antologia poetica della resistenza italiana*, edited by Elio Accrocca and Valerio Volponi and published in 1955, includes poets such as Ungaretti, who initially admired Mussolini and only later became disillusioned, and Sereni, who was imprisoned by the Americans in North Africa.

Italian poets sympathetic to the Resistance poured forth torrents of verse to commemorate the heroism of the fallen, and torrents of deeply felt invective, such as Saba's refrain, "All this the vile Fascist/ and the greedy German took from me," or Palazzeschi's cry, "Death to the Germans." Italians of Jewish descent were especially vocal: Saba, Natalia Ginzburg, and Franco Fortini, who wrote, speaking of Italy, "Now it is not enough just to die/ for that empty ancient name." The death of Corrado Govoni's son at the Fosse Adreatine (the massacre in Rome by the Germans of 335 partisans on March 24, 1944, about which Libero De Libero also wrote movingly) inspired an elegy, *Aladino: Lamento su mio figlio morto* (1946; Aladino: lament for my dead son), reminiscent in breadth and length of Alfred, Lord Tennyson's *In Memoriam* (1850).

Especially significant among the Resistance poets are Cesare Pavese (1908-1950), Pasolini, and Gatto. Pavese, one of those who attacked the hermeticists for their failure to speak out against fascism, was arrested for anti-Fascist activities in 1935 and then imprisoned. He was profoundly affected by the deaths of his friends Giaime Pintor and Leone Ginzburg, killed in their partisan undertakings, but his feelings about the period were given fuller development in his novels than in his poetry. Pasolini was just as deeply affected by the death of his younger brother Guido at the beginning of 1945, and it is Guido's tale that Pasolini tells in "Il testamento Coran" (the Koran testament), later incorporated into *La meglio gioventì* (1954; the finest youth). For Pasolini, who was drafted into the Italian army in

September, 1943, but who deserted after a mere week, the Resistance was "a style all light, memorable/ awareness of sun."

Like Pavese and Pasolini, Gatto was a Communist. Seeds of his moral dilemma were evident in his *Amore della vita* (1944), and in 1944 and 1945 his verses circulated secretly; in 1949, they were assembled in *Il Capo sulla neve* (the head on the snow).

Because he failed to join the Fascist Party, Montale was investigated by the Questura of Florence in 1937 and in the following year was discharged from his employment at the Gabinetto Vieusseux, at that time the largest lending library in Europe. Hitler's visit to Florence in the spring of 1938 is recalled in Montale's "Primavera hitleriana" ("Hitlerian Spring"), in which the poet observes the cries of "alala" and the swastikas (the Italian term for which means "hooked crosses") with consternation and irony. Some readers, however, felt that in his later poetry, Montale did not make that consternation explicit enough.

Quasimodo, who was active in the Resistance and was imprisoned by Mussolini for a time at Bergamo, felt impelled after the war to reconsider his role as a poet. His conversation was no longer with a vague and generalized humanity but with men specifically. He emerged from his poetic seclusion and became committed to helping man remake himself. His Resistance poems are contained in *Giorno dopo giorno*, in which there abound references to this change in self-perception, to the difference between his previous and his present poetic mission ("I can no more return to my elysium"), and denunciations in savage terms of man's inhumanity to man ("You are still the one with the stone and the sling,/ man of my time"). In his poem "Auschwitz," he tells the soldier that he will find the smoke-immolated victims within him, but adds as an afterthought, "or are you, too, but ash/ of Auschwitz, medal of silence?"

THE HERMETIC-REALIST DEBATE

The passions released by the ordeal of World War II and the bitter civil strife of the Resistance could not help but spill over into literary debate, and this was especially the case in Italy, where poetry aligned itself with schools in which political ideology was explicitly or implicitly supported. Because of their passive resistance, the her-

metic poets came under attack from the Left; the attack was initiated in an article published in *La rinascita* in 1944 and went on for several years, finally wasting itself in mere verbal exercise. In the meantime, the political realities of Italy had changed considerably, for the Italians, along with other Europeans, entered a period of economic well-being.

Several of Italy's most significant writers participated in the debate. More significant, however, these were the years in which neorealism emerged as the most vital form of Italian artistic expression, and though neorealism is associated to a large extent with the novel and the cinema, this movement also had its poetic exponents.

Pavese anticipated the neorealist art of the postwar period in *Lavorare stanca* (1936; *Hard Labor*, 1976). These poems are generally expressions of unromanticized landscapes filled with people from daily life. Though they have lyrical moments, they are informed by a pervasive bitterness. In "Instinct," Pavese speaks of dogs copulating and then refracts the attitudes of various emblematic persons through this act in such a way as to humble human pretenses: "Anything can happen out in the/ open. Even a woman, shy when face to face with a man,/ stands there. . . ."

Of all the exponents of neorealism, it is Pasolini who stands out as the central figure. Born in Bologna but at heart a Friulian, Pasolini was the quintessential *homme engagé*. A filmmaker, novelist, and political essayist as well as a poet, he showed not only a love for the great classics and for the hermetic style of Ungaretti, but also a devotion to leftist apologetics and Roman Catholicism. Pasolini was lionized and rejected by almost every group with which he came in contact. His poetry cannot be said to follow any specific style, but it is clear that his interests are in an art of social relevance. His volume *Le ceneri di Gramsci* (1957; the ashes of Gramsci) was in part an act of homage to Antonio Gramsci, the head of the Italian Communist Party who was imprisoned under Mussolini but who managed to send out letters and journal entries expressing his vision of society and art.

In the title poem "Le cenari di Gramsci" ("Gramsci's Ashes"), Pasolini combines historical reflections on the years before World War II with personal confession: "I live in the non-will/ of the dead postwar years: loving/ the world I hate. . . ." It may be that there is no resolution for the conflict between the artist's absorption in art and the artist's moral duty to communicate with his fellow man; in Pasolini, one finds a man living this contradiction.

A simpler case of neorealism is evident in Rocco Scotellaro, whose poetry is of a regional character. Scotellaro was born in Basilicata in 1923; a Socialist, he became mayor of his town but died at an early age in 1953. His poetry expresses his understanding of the peasantry, from which he himself came; his lyrics depict the life of his region and its ancient, even atavistic, character.

Franco Fortini (pseudonymn of Franco Lattes, born 1917) began as a hermetic poet but turned to a poetry of social engagement. A prominent Marxist critic, Fortini, a Jew, went through a period of disillusionment during the war. Despite his Marxist orientation, his poetry maintains classical references and style; he writes, as Ramat puts it, in the Petrarchan-Leopardian tradition.

Although neorealism was dominant in the years after World War II, several prewar poets, among them Luzi and Sereni, continued in the postwar era to write in the hermetic style. In the 1950's, a number of younger poets associated with Luzi came to be regarded as neohermetic; two principal figures of this group are Andrea Zanzotto (born 1921) and Luciano Erba (born 1922). What distinguished them from the hermetics of the 1930's was a greater concern for language per se—an attempt to regain a poetically significant language in a world in which language itself has been technologized.

Zanzotto's poetry, beginning with *Dietro il paesaggio* (1951; behind the landscape), poems written between 1940 and 1948, shares with hermeticism a surface difficulty, a highly condensed but personal symbolism suggesting the need to penetrate appearances in order to apprehend the real. In his later poetry, access to the real is permitted only by linguistic experimentation, for the language of everyday usage has been enslaved for superficial, purely utilitarian ends. Shattering syntax, struggling to unearth what he calls a "nether language," Zanzotto has much in common with that of the avant-garde experimentalists. At its most radical, Zanzotto's poetry virtually eschews content, suggesting the fragmentation, asymmetry, and nonnaturalism of much modern music.

Erba's development was the reverse of that of many later poets, for he began as a socially committed poet and then moved to neohermeticism, one of a group of Lombard poets who sought to move beyond the heroics of neorealism to the expression of disillusionment. In many ways, there is a Pascolian streak in the poetry of Erba, for he develops a poetry of "small things" in order to focus on the insignificant lives of modern humanity. Erba's poetry has a clarity of line that gives the people portrayed in his work a vividness belying their ordinariness. This quality is exemplified in "Tabula rasa?": "Do you see me going along as usual/ in the districts without memory?/ I have a cream tie, an old burden/ of desires. . . ."

Another important postwar poet is the Sicilian Bartolo Cattafi (1922-1979). A recurring motif in Cattafi's poetry is the figure of a traveler or nomad set in a precisely and vividly described landscape. Cattafi strives to build blocks of words, to create poems that are thinglike assemblages of images: "Ex nihilo God/ from tatters scraps/ carrion trash me."

AVANT-GARDE AND LATER POETS

Other changes in poetry in the 1950's all centered on the role of language. The avant-garde focused on the absurdity of any rational philosophy—even worldviews as diverse as those of Benedetto Croce and Antonio Gramsci—in the modern world. The poets of this avant-garde, such as Antonio Porta (born 1935), Alfredo Giuliani (born 1924), Nanni Balestrini (born 1935), Edoardo Sanguineti (born 1930), and Elio Pagliarani (born 1927), are reminiscent of Surrealism in their insistence that art must reflect the schizophrenia of modern society. They also employ the open form of American poets such as Charles Olson and William Carlos Williams. Influenced by literary theory, often to a crippling degree, the avant-garde poets reflect the ideas of the New Novel in France (in their insistence on an art of things) and of semiotics (in fact, Umberto Eco, a noted semiotician, is usually considered a poet of this group).

As the twentieth century came to a close, Italian poetry was characterized by a bewildering diversity, in marked contrast to the time-honored Italian tendency to form schools. In part, this fragmentation seemed to be the result of the failure of the protests that swept Europe in 1968 to effect genuine social change. Italian poetry after the Cold War embraces computer poets and experimentalists who tear language apart and attempt to rebuild it in new forms, but also more traditional poets who continue to ply their trade.

BIBLIOGRAPHY

Ballerini, Luigi, Paolo Barlera, and Paul Vangelisti, eds. *The Promised Land: Italian Poetry After 1975*. Los Angeles: Sun & Moon Press, 1997.

Bedani, Gino, Remo Catani, and Monica Slowikowska, eds. *The Italian Lyric Tradition: Essays in Honor of F. J. Jones*. Cardiff: University of Wales Press, 1993.

Blum, Cinzia Sartini, and Lara Trubowitz, eds and trans. *Contemporary Italian Women Poets: A Bilingual Anthology*. New York: Italica Press, 2001.

Cary, Joseph. *Three Modern Italian Poets: Saba, Ungaretti, Mondale*. 2d ed. Chicago: University of Chicago Press, 1993. Focuses on the work of Umberto Saba, Giuseppe Ungaretti, and Eugenio Montale. Cary's careful readings of these noted figures facilitates a better understanding of their poetry. Cary also presents striking biographical portraits and a discussion of the first half of twentieth century Italy, a most difficult period in its literary and cultural development.

Donadoni, Eugenio. *History of Italian Literature*. Vol. 2. Translated by Richard Monges. New York: New York University Press, 1969.

Elliot, Alistair, ed. and trans. *Italian Landscape Poems*. Chester Springs, Pa.: Dufour Editions, 1993. Explores attitudes toward the Italian landscape through poems or excerpts from poems from the Middle Ages into the twentieth century. The originals are printed opposite the translations.

Golino, Carlo Luigi. *Contemporary Italian Poetry*. Berkeley: University of California Press, 1962. Lengthy introduction explores Hermeticism, Futurism, and postwar neorealistic poetry movements.

Picchione, John, and Lawrence R. Smith, eds. *Twentieth-Century Italian Poetry: An Anthology*. Toronto: University of Toronto Press, 1994.

Ridinger, Gayle, and Gian Paolo Renello, eds. *Italian Poetry, 1955-1990*. Boston: Dante University of America Press, 1996. This anthology of the work of three generations of Italian poets presents the poems in Italian followed by their English translations. Each poet's section begins with a short biography and includes a bibliography listing all the poet's published work.

Serrao, Achille, Justin Vitiello, and Luigi Bonaffini. *Via Terra: An Anthology of Contemporary Italian Poetry*. Brooklyn, N.Y.: Legas, 1999.

Tusiani, Joseph. *From Marino to Marinetti: An Anthology of Forty Italian Poets*. New York: Baroque Press, 1974.

Wilkins, Ernest H. *A History of Italian Literature*. Cambridge: Harvard University Press, 1974.

Jack Shreve and Robert Colucci

JAPANESE POETRY TO 1800

The history of Japanese poetry begins indisputably with the eighth century anthology titled *Manyōshū* (mid-eighth century; *The Collections of Ten Thousand Leaves*; also as *The Ten Thousand Leaves*, pb. 1981, and as *The Manyoshu*, 1940) although the earlier historical chronicles *Kojiki* (c. 712 C.E.; *Records of Ancient Matters*, 1883) and *Nihon shoki* (c. 720; *Nihongi: Chronicles of Japan from the Earliest Times to A.D. 697*, 1896), as well as a few stone inscriptions, also preserve scattered early poems and sacred songs. The significance of the *Manyōshū* collection is manifold. As the most literal translation of its title, "collection of myriad leaves," suggests, it is a work of imposing bulk; containing more than 4,500 poems, it is by virtue of its age and size simply not to be ignored. Another interpretation of its title, "collection of (or for) myriad generations," hints at the importance accorded poetry in eighth century Japan.

THE MANYŌSHŪ

The *Manyōshū* was assembled at a stage of Japanese cultural development roughly comparable to that of northern and western Europe at the close of the Dark Ages. In both cases, literacy was confined to very small groups, elite islands of advanced culture in a sea of what was by comparison barbarism. In the European case, literacy was a legacy of the Roman conquests, held in trust by the Church until an ebbing in the tide of barbarian invasion allowed it to infiltrate secular courts. Literacy was in a sense indigenous, a skill that, from the viewpoint of the early Middle Ages, had been known (although not widely practiced) from time immemorial. The written word came to Japan, however, as the central monument of a flourishing, contemporary foreign civilization, embodied in the energetic culture of the Sui (581-618) and Tang (618-907) Dynasties. Chinese culture and the idea of literacy did not come with a conquering army but rather, it appears, by choice. The future imperial court, having consolidated its sway over competing tribal or regional groups, began in perhaps the fifth century to maintain what seems to have been fairly regular intercourse with China by way of the land route up the Korean peninsula. It was at this time, most agree, that written records began to be kept in Japan, but

they were in Chinese, the work of Chinese and Korean scribes imported by the court.

The rich sophistication of Chinese culture in comparison with that of Japan, Korea, and Vietnam must have been almost absurdly evident to the first generations of Japanese who set themselves the task of learning Chinese and its complex writing system, through which medium the entirety of more than a thousand years of literary culture was suddenly visible in an undigested mass. In addition to the native Chinese classics, there was a huge body of Buddhist texts in Chinese to contemplate. By the end of the seventh century, however, the emerging Japanese state, headed by an aristocratic court, had accomplished much by way of assimilating the new culture. Governmental forms and court rites were modeled on Tang examples, and alongside the native animist religion, Shintō, Chinese Buddhism was officially established and encouraged, for the power of Tang in China—where Buddhism was enjoying a short-lived ascendancy—was thought to rest in part on the magical efficacy of Buddhist ritual. Under such circumstances, where political power was legitimized by Chinese precedent and the spiritual realm was increasingly dominated by a complex Indian faith that the Japanese could approach only in Chinese, the dominance of Chinese in the field of letters is no surprise. The true cause for wonder is that the *Manyōshū* testifies to a vigorous parallel tradition of sophisticated literary activity in Japanese—a tradition that was a century and more old by the time the collection was compiled.

The poetry of the *Manyōshū* dates largely from the first half of the eighth century, but a significant portion of it was composed in the preceding century, and a small number of verses seem to be authentic survivals, if perhaps retouched by later hands, from even earlier. The poetry of the *Manyōshū* and the history of the *Kojiki* are written with Chinese characters, but because the Chinese ideographs are used for their phonetic values, these texts may be read as pure Japanese. However absorbed they may have been, therefore, in making Chinese culture their own, the Japanese were occupied as well with the difficult task of adapting the new tool of writing to record in their own language what they most valued in the native tradition, at a very early time in comparison with other East Asian societies.

The *Manyōshū* and the *Kojiki* thus may be viewed as evidence of a persistent Japanese determination to maintain a significant degree of independence from foreign cultural influence, but their existence also ironically underlines the power of Chinese example, for poetry and historiography occupied the vital center of the Chinese literary canon as it reached the Japanese. These works can thus also be thought of as part of a broader enterprise on the part of the Japanese aristocracy to equip itself with all the trappings of a modern Asian state in the age of the Tang. That the *Manyōshū* exists at all is symbolic of the ambitions of the imperial court, an assertion of cultural equality with China, the emulation of which was not simply a matter of fashion but a conscious policy designed to enhance the power and dignity of the state.

It would be a mistake, however, to dismiss the *Manyōshū* as nothing more than an exercise in imitation, for it contains some of the most technically sophisticated, imaginative, and emotionally satisfying poetry in the entire Japanese canon. It does show a great deal of Chinese influence, as in its "songs of the East" and "songs of the border guards," the inclusion of which may echo one of the supposed functions of the *Shijing* (traditionally fifth century B.C.E.; *The Book of Songs*, 1937), the oldest Chinese anthology of verse—namely, the gathering of intelligence about the temper of the people of the realm. More broadly, *Manyōshū* poetry in general is strongly colored by Chinese poetic practice, and some individual verses can be shown to have been based on specific Chinese sources. Nevertheless, this is genuinely Japanese poetry in its language and special emphases. The *Manyōshū* is also an anthology that can give considerable pleasure to modern readers, for its poets possess, to a surprising degree, individuality of voice.

Manyōshū poet Kakinomoto Hitomaro (fl. 680-700) is usually accorded primacy of place as the earliest master of poetry in Japanese. He wrote in both of the dominant verse forms of the period, the *tanka*, or short poem, and *chōka*, or long poem. The *tanka* was short indeed, fixed at a length of thirty-one syllables which were distributed in five lines or, more properly, in units of five, seven, five, seven, and seven syllables. This would be-

come the standard form of Japanese poetry in succeeding centuries—so dominant, in fact, that another name for it would be *waka*, simply "Japanese verse," as opposed to *kanshi*, Japanese poetry written in the Chinese language. The *chōka*, despite its name, was long only in comparison with the *tanka*; the longest example in the *Manyōshū* occupies only four pages in an English translation with generous margins, hardly an extended composition by the standards of other literary cultures. The *chōka* was of indeterminate length, a formally simple sequence of alternating five- and seven-syllable phrases ending in a couplet of seven-syllable lines. The *chōka* was usually followed by one or more verses in standard *tanka* form that were called *hanka* (envois or responses). Hitomaro originated neither of these forms, but his consummate mastery of both helped to establish them at the core of the Japanese poetic tradition.

Rhyme schemes and metrical feet play no part in the formal apparatus of Hitomaro's poetry, for they are simply meaningless in Japanese. Rhyme is more or less trivial, because every syllable in Japanese ends in a vowel or *n*, and there are only five vowels in the language, meaning that rhyme occurs randomly and frequently without poetic intercession. All syllables in Japanese are stressed so nearly equally that metric patterns based on alternation of stress are impossible. Nor does assonance or alliteration play any role in the formal rules of composition, again because of the simplicity of the sound system. Thus the prominence of syllable count in Japanese poetic structure: It is virtually all that is left by way of effects based on sound alone. Why units of five and seven syllables have proved so congenial to Japanese poets is unknown, but Hitomaro's importance lies in part in his success in demonstrating the ample sufficiency of this simple scheme, which has prevailed until the present alongside blank-verse forms introduced in the nineteenth century. In Hitomaro's verse, these small building blocks are built into phrases and sentences of great length and complexity; some entire *chōka* can be construed as consisting grammatically of single extended sentences with a complicated structure of parallel independent and dependent clauses rolling forward in rhythmic cadence to a final predication in the concluding couplet. Hitomaro showed the way for later poets, developing in both the expansive *chōka* and the terse *tanka* an armory of techniques to bridge the natural pauses at the end of metric units with the momentum of syntax or imagistic association.

Little is known of Hitomaro's life, but it appears that he may have functioned at least quasi-officially as a poet laureate, for many of his poems were occasioned by events important in the life of the court or nation—elegies on the death or interment of royal personages, for example, and celebrations of more auspicious events. These public poems are suffused with a sense of the awesome, even divine dignity of the sovereign and his or her (women could still occupy the throne in Hitomaro's day) immediate family. This sense of immanent divinity extended to the land itself. Place-names, for example, figure prominently in Hitomaro's poetry, recalling other *Manyōshū* poems that are actually attributed to emperors themselves, rulers of generations even earlier than that of Hitomaro, whose compositions seem sometimes to be little more than ritual incantations of the names of the mountains and plains of Yamato, the region south of modern Kyoto from which the imperial clan ruled early Japan. Hitomaro reinforced this invocation of place-names, originally no doubt a way of claiming hegemony by "naming" the bounds and features of the realm, through the use of *makurakotoba* (pillow words), which were either epithets traditionally coupled with certain place-names (or other parts of speech) or similar attributive phrases coined by Hitomaro himself on traditional models. Thus, epithets such as "Izumo of the eight-fold clouds," "Yamato which fills the skies," and "Sanuki of gemlike seagrass" make the earthly landscape glow with hints of the heavenly connections of high places and the mysteries of the depths. Such poems have as their purpose the exaltation of imperial rule, but they succeed as art because of Hitomaro's mastery of language and a particular gift for personalizing verse on even the most public occasions by relating them to the individualized human emotions they evoke in their participants.

The elegance and grandeur of Hitomaro's public commemorations are complemented in a body of highly personal verse of great emotional power, the most impressive of which is a sequence of *chōka* laments honoring his love for his wife (or wives—his biography is unclear) at partings in this life and at the final, awful parting of death. These poems share with his public

verse a nice manipulation of *makurakotoba* epithets (such as "seagrass-lithe and bending girl"), which serve here not to add mythic significance to the landscape, but rather to relate the emotional substance of the poem to the phenomena of the natural world, a technique that gives this poetry a universality that transcends its intimate particularity.

The balance of majesty and individuality in Hitomaro's poetry moves both his public and nominally private verse toward a tonal middle ground precisely suited to poems composed for public recitation—which, authorities agree, was probably their original mode of presentation. Hitomaro was not, however, the last bard of a preliterate tradition, despite his use of the *makurakotoba* technique, which is obviously related to similar phenomena in indisputably oral traditions. The public recitation of poetry would continue to be a formal part of court life for centuries, making that aspect of his practice doubtful proof that Hitomaro was a late survivor of a diminished breed of oral poets. There is, moreover, substantial evidence of Chinese influence in Hitomaro's choice of imagery and subject matter and in the strong parallelism that structures his longer pieces. Finally, there is in his verse an idealization of a simpler past close to nature that can best be called pastoralism, clearly the product of a poet who still had access to the oral past but could speak in a complex and sophisticated voice trained in the methods and attitudes of a foreign, written literature.

Poets of the generation immediately following Hitomaro's wrote in an idiom even more clearly shaped by contact with Chinese poetry. Yamanoe Okura (c. 660-733), for example, is represented in the *Manyōshū* by a group of *chōka* on such subjects as poverty, destitution, and old age that can be read almost as a translated pastiche of Chinese poetic statements on the same themes, although his masterly use of Japanese has made them an admired (if rarely emulated) part of the native canon. Ōtomo Tabito (665-731), a close associate of Okura, left a series of *tanka* on the virtues of rice wine in which his adopted persona, that of the talented literary bureaucrat languishing in an enforced retirement, is as Chinese as anything by Okura, though Tabito's poetry is in a Japanese quite free of Chinese linguistic influence and in a form quintessentially Japanese. Both men were members of what was probably one of the earliest generations thoroughly at home in the world of Chinese letters, and their poetry may be read both as an homage to Chinese verse and as an intelligent experiment with expanding the range of Japanese poetic expression. They represent an extreme, however, for few later poets went as far as they did toward a Sinification of Japanese poetry, perhaps because the pessimism and intellectuality of their verse was believed to be simply too Chinese, too much a violation of the sunnier precedents of Japanese poetry.

Tabito's son, Ōtomo Yakamochi (718-785), may safely be called the most important and influential of the final generation of *Manyōshū* poets, both because of the quality of his verse and because he appears to have taken the leading role in the compilation of the anthology itself. Yakamochi's poetry marks him genuinely as a transitional figure. He is among the last masters of the *chōka*, which seems to have fallen from fashion rather soon after the *Manyōshū* was put together; at the same time, his work foreshadows what would become the dominant traditions of Japanese poetry for centuries to come.

There is a strong element of nostalgia in Yakamochi's poetry, most especially a longing for a glorious martial past, because the Ōtomo were a warrior clan. Later poets would not focus on this particular past—too redolent of violence for courtly tastes—preferring a more generalized evocation of antique timelessness; still, the stance toward the present, which is somehow drab, pedestrian, and ephemeral, is much the same as Yakamochi's, and quite different from Hitomaro's pastoralism. In Yakamochi's time, too, poetry moves indoors, or at least into the urban nobleman's garden; gone are the grand vistas of mountain and plain, replaced by the singularities of garden plantings viewed close up over a balcony rail. Here Yakamochi was following one strand of Chinese verse, but he was also writing poetry germane to his time and place, since his was the first poetic generation to know the distinctive qualities of settled urban life; until 710, when a permanent capital city modeled on the Chinese metropolis was laid out on the site of modern Nara, the capital of Japan was wherever the emperor's court happened to be, and the court was mobile, for in accordance with Shintō belief, death rendered the sovereign's palace irremediably unclean, unfit for the sacral duties of the throne.

KOKINSHŪ

The next great landmark in Japanese poetry after the *Manyōshū* is another anthology, the *Kokinshū* (905; *Kokinshu: A Collection of Poems Ancient and Modern*, 1984), which is dated to 1905 by its introduction. Universally known by the abbreviated title *Kokinshū*, this collection marks the maturation of a tradition that has become known in English as court poetry. It is significant that it is once again an anthology that Japanese literary historiography singles out as important rather than, say, the achievements of a single poet or innovative poetic school, and doubly significant that this collection should bear the title it does—together these facts attest a conception of poetry as a collective cultural endeavor to which tradition and precedent are as important as innovation. Important also is the fact that the *Kokinshū* was an imperially commissioned collection, the first in a series of twenty-one that would appear at irregular intervals until 1433, and thus an early symbolic declaration of how important a part of court life poetry was and would be thereafter.

The scope and variety of the poetry of the *Kokinshū* are much constricted in comparison with the *Manyōshū*. The collection is smaller—it contains only some eleven hundred poems—and the overwhelming majority of the verses in it are *tanka*. There is little doubt, moreover, that this was a highly selective anthology. The *Kokinshū* was not meant as a representative sampler of the best of Japanese poetry, but rather, it appears, as a normative guide to what its compilers thought poetry should be. Principal among the compilers was Ki no Tsurayuki (884-946), whose introduction to the collection, the earliest extant piece of literary criticism in Japanese, would stand for centuries as the definitive statement of the proper concerns of the poet. Tsurayuki's most famous dictum is his metaphoric definition of Japanese poetry, which "takes as its seed the heart of man, and flourishes in the countless leaves of words." Emotion and its direct expression, he is saying, are what poetry is all about; in short, lyricism is at the core of Japanese poetry, and from Tsurayuki forward it would not be displaced. The classical Japanese canon would simply never admit the more expansive and multidimensional allegories, ballads, epics, and poetical discourses on religion, philosophy, and even politics that constitute so much of the high classical tradition of Western verse.

The *Kokinshū* is for the most part arranged topically, grouping together in the first books of the collection, for example, poems with seasonal subjects, season by season. Within each of these books, the poems are arranged roughly according to the order in which their dominant natural images occur as the seasons progress, so that in the first spring book, the flowering plum precedes the cherry. Love poems are arranged in like manner, to echo in the aggregate the pattern of a love affair, from initial infatuation through tentative courtship and passion to the inevitable abandonment. Not all topics allow this kind of mimetic organization—the books of celebratory poems, poems on parting, and poems based on wordplay are instances—but nowhere do Tsurayuki and his colleagues seem to have in mind the usual literary-historical objectives of Western anthologizers, grouping poems by author or in some way chronologically, to show stylistic changes over time.

The *Kokinshū*, it appears, was assembled not as a work of scholarship or preservation, but rather for the use of practicing poets, to whose needs its finely tuned topical organization was ideally suited. Despite Tsurayuki's insistence that poetry be an expression in "the leaves of words" of the movements of the heart, all the evidence—fiction, diaries, annotations to private and official anthologies—argues that poets in the age of the *Kokinshū* composed for specific occasions, not when seized by a lyric impulse. In this context, the *Kokinshū* and subsequent anthologies look very much like handbooks that were assembled as authoritative guides to the sort of poetry sanctioned by tradition and contemporary taste as appropriate to any number of clearly defined circumstances. As works such as the eleventh century novel *Genji monogatari* (c. 1004; *The Tale of Genji*, 1925-1933) illustrate so well, court poetry was a social art practiced either in full public view—at poetry contests, on flower-viewing expeditions, at banquets—or, if in private, as a form of communication between friends or lovers; any courtier or lady of the court with pretensions to social grace had to be ready to produce passable verse whenever called upon. The *Kokinshū* and other anthologies were organized to allow quick consultation for an appropriate model or for a poem that could be alluded to in one's own composition.

Within the narrowed confines of the poetry of the *Kokinshū*, there is still much to be admired, for its special province, the human heart, is after all not an easily exhausted subject. Poetry of love and courtship is not surprisingly one of the long suits of the collection. Particularly engaging is the work of such ninth century poets as Ariwara no Narihira (825-880), a courtier who quickly became a model of the ideal courtly lover, and the court lady Ono no Komachi (834-880), whose passionate verse threatened to escape the bounds of seemly reserve that most other poets were at pains to observe. Narihira's is a poetry of great wit and elegance, but it is colored also by a much-admired Buddhist awareness of the inconstancy of the temporal world and the deceptiveness of the emotions. Komachi, on the other hand, is a very subjective poet whose immersion in her own sometimes violent emotional states cost her admirers in a world that valued the pose, at least, of detachment more than direct cries from the heart. She and Narihira stand at the head of a long line of poets, male and female, whose *Kokinshū* verses established love poetry as one of the honored genres of court poetry.

By the time the *Kokinshū* was compiled, Buddhism had become a powerful force in shaping the Japanese poetic sensibility, which it entered indirectly through the influence of Chinese verse and directly as it became more and more a part of Japanese life. It did not, however, result in the development of an explicitly religious or devotional poetry. Rather, it provided a fundamental point of view for the poet in its insistence upon a radical conception of phenomenal reality as a slippery, everchanging flux given an illusory substance and stability by fallible human perception and rationalization. Impermanence and the unreliability of subjective observation are seldom spoken of explicitly in *Kokinshū* verse, which like all premodern Japanese poetry shies away from abstract nouns and overt philosophizing, but an acceptance of them as fundamental truths underlies much of the literature of the time.

There is a dark quality of resignation in the Buddhist conception of human experience that seems to be at odds with the more life-affirming, unreflective vision of man and his world that characterizes Shintō animism, but in fact court poetry frequently manages a resolution of the conflict by finding a paradoxical comfort in the wholly reliable way the natural world eternally reaffirms the truth of universal flux; nature continues to be invested with meaning, but the meaning changes. Viewed in this way, nature is a rich repository of metaphor directly relevant to the human condition, which is why natural imagery comes to play such a large role in the lyric poetry of the Japanese court, particularly imagery that underlines change as a constant in nature and in human affairs. The beauty of spring blossoms is less interesting to the poet than the fact that they will fall or that fallible human eyes mistake them for a late spring snow.

Several techniques peculiar to Japanese poetry were exploited to their fullest for the first time by *Kokinshū* poets. The first is the *kakekotoba*, or pivot word, which takes advantage of both the special features of Japanese syntax and the existence in the language of a large number of homophones in what amounts to a highly refined form of wordplay. In the phrase *ko no me no haru ni*, for example, the word *haru* carries two distinct meanings. As a verb, it means "to swell," and with *ko no me*, "tree buds," and the subject-marking particle *no*, it produces the phrase, "tree buds swell." As a noun, however, *haru* means "spring," the season, and with the locative *ni* it makes an adverb of time, "in spring." Here, *haru* is therefore a *kakekotoba*, a word that "pivots" between two overlapping phrases that together mean something like, "in spring, when tree buds swell." The effect in Japanese is far less contrived than it would be in English, as in a phrase such as "in the grass spring blossoms forth," where "spring" and "blossoms" could be called pivot words of an awkward sort. In the Japanese example, as in the English, the *kakekotoba* consists of two superimposed homophones of different meaning and grammatical function. In other cases, the meaning of the pivot word is unchanged, but its syntactic function is different in the two phrases it links. In practiced hands, the *kakekotoba* technique—whose compact "punch" can almost never be translated adequately—is an effective method not only of adding a few precious syllables of meaning to the *tanka*, but also of greatly enriching the texture of a poem by involving the reader (or listener) in unraveling its overlapping meanings and functions.

A second device frequently exploited by *Kokinshū* poets is the *jokotoba* or *joshi*, a "preface" of one or more lines that forms part of the poem proper but is not directly related to its primary statement, to which it is most often linked by a pivot word. The *jokotoba* preface is similar to the *makurakotoba* epithet, but it is more complex, usually longer, rarely conventional, and more likely to be used consciously by the poet to establish a metaphoric relationship between two otherwise unrelated images. The *jokotoba* virtually disappears in translation, where it becomes simply a simile or metaphor, but it is a distinctive feature of classical *tanka* in Japanese.

A third technique polished in the *Kokinshū* and often used in conjunction with both *jokotoba* and *kakekotoba* to enrich the *tanka* is *engo* (related words). The *engo* technique is a refinement of diction in which the poet chooses his words in such a way that they both carry the intended meaning of the poem and at the same time relate to one other semantically or by sound alone in ways quite unrelated to the primary content of the poem. "Giving her a frosty glance, he leaves; from crimsoned lips fall raging storms of words" will have to serve as an English illustration of the principle of *engo*. The Japanese classical poet would recognize two parallel statements here—a surface description of an angry lovers' parting and an embedded evocation of late autumn in the sequence of related words: frosty-leaves-crimsoned-fall-raging-storms. Once again, the English example is labored because the technique is alien, but the conception is not inappropriate, since autumn in Japanese poetry is the season to reflect on the transience of life and love. In its native environment, when the *engo* technique is used in conjunction with other devices, the result is poetry of great complexity that can carry two or more serious messages simultaneously—no small feat in the compass of thirty-one syllables.

These techniques clearly functioned to allow far more to be said in the scant confines of a *tanka* than would otherwise have been the case, and it is probably no accident that they came into use at a time when the conventions of the form were becoming ever more clearly defined and restrictive. As previously noted, certain sorts of discourse and subject matter were felt to be more properly the province of Chinese poetry than Japanese, but diction itself was regulated as well. Loan words from Chinese, for example, were out of bounds to the *tanka* poet, even though by the time of the *Kokinshū* they had begun to enter everyday language in considerable numbers; no doubt they were prohibited in part because of their phonetic inelegance, but there may well have been an element of linguistic chauvinism at work as well. In any case, from the *Kokinshū* forward, poetic language would necessarily move further and further from the spoken language, which continued quite naturally to assimilate a great deal of Chinese vocabulary.

Perhaps even more important, the poetic consensus seems to have been that entire categories of imagery and native Japanese vocabulary were simply unpoetical. Bodily functions, for example, are almost entirely absent from classical Japanese poetry, even as metaphor— no poet would seriously "drink in" the beauty of a landscape or even "breathe" the fragrance of a blossom, much less "hunger" for a lover's "touch." Given the strong Buddhist influence in poetry of the classical period, it is perhaps a little surprising that even birth and death and any words clearly associated with them have no place, except by the most oblique sort of reference. This particular taboo probably had something to do with the preoccupation of Shintō ritual with cleanliness and purification, but more generally, it appears that there was an unspoken agreement among poets that poetic language simply did not admit of reference to the grosser stuff of human existence, not out of prudery but rather in the spirit of what is best called courtliness, a set of attitudes that valued above all else stylization, refinement, restraint, cultivation, and a disdain for the pedestrian and coarse in all aspects of behavior.

SHINKOKINHŪ

The courtly pose could and did sometimes result in a facile and shallow poetry in a world where versification was widely practiced as a social art, but it is a tribute to the high seriousness of purpose of the court poets that it did not produce, on the whole, a mannered and precious body of poetry. In the centuries following the appearance of the *Kokinshū*, the ever-growing canon of court verse took on the status almost of secular scripture, a collaborative text to be elaborated by each succeeding generation of poets. The culmination of this process is

aptly symbolized in another great anthology, the *Shinkokinshū* (new *Kokinshū*), which appeared as the eighth in the series of imperial collections about 1206. The title was more than a token homage to the *Kokinshū*: It was a declaration affirming the primacy of tradition in the world of court poetry. The intervening anthologies had all, in a general way, taken the *Kokinshū* as their model of organization, but the *Shinkokinshū* makes constant reference to the earlier collection in ways alternately explicit and extremely subtle.

To explain the complex relationship between the "new *Kokinshū*" and its antecedent requires an acquaintance with the poetic technique known as *honkadori*— literally, "taking from a source verse," or incorporating into a new verse recognizable elements of an older poem in the canon. *Honkadori* is nothing more than a specialized variety of allusion requiring a clear quotation from an earlier poem, but that does not begin to explain its significance, for in many ways it is a key to understanding how poetry developed after the *Kokinshū*.

First, *honkadori* gave the poet another escape route from the confines of the classical *tanka*. The canon of "quotable" poetry was relatively manageable, being limited to the imperial anthologies and a small number of widely circulated private collections and prose works, such as *The Tale of Genji*, that contained poetry; this meant that in the elite subculture of the court, a poet could be confident of having an audience that would recognize his allusions. A poem utilizing a *honkadori* allusion, therefore, expanded in the minds of its readers or listeners to include the entirety of the excerpted source poem. Thus, for example, a *Shinkokinshū* verse describing the desolation of a deserted village in autumn gains significant depth because the village, identified by name, is described with words borrowed from a pair of *Kokinshū* love poems, set in the same place, which dwelt on the sorrows of parting.

Beyond their effects within individual poems, *honkadori* allusions had a second important role to play in court poetry—namely, their function in tying new poems into an expanding canon that was not merely an accumulation of successively newer strata of poetry, but a complex fabric of allusion, cross-reference, and echo that worked continuously to revivify old poems while at the same time adding depth and the authority of tradition to new ones. The process was supported by the remarkable conservatism of poetic language, which came to be defined as the language of the *Kokinshū*. Because the language of the new poems was essentially of the same age as that of the source poems, it was possible to weave words and phrases from poems centuries old into original compositions with virtually no seams showing. The difficulty of composing poetry in antique language was mitigated for the poets of the *Shinkokinshū* and later periods by their intense absorption in the poetic canon, whose language became a natural mode of expression, neither dead nor artificial.

The loyalty of the compilers of the *Shinkokinshū* to the idea of precedent in poetry is most strikingly revealed at a number of places in the collection where entire sequences of poems, a dozen or more at a time, are selected and arranged so that they allude individually and collectively to precisely parallel sequences in the *Kokinshū*. Such feats of creative editorship required not only erudition and artistic sensitivity, but also painstaking care on the part of the poets who assembled the anthology, a group led by Fujiwara Teika (1162-1241) under the active, involved sponsorship of the retired poet-emperor Gotoba (1180-1239). At a distance of eight centuries, it is possible only to speculate about what motivated such labors. One cause may have been simply the sheer intellectual and aesthetic pleasure of this complex interplay of old and new, a pleasure denied the modern reader but no doubt quite unaffected among poets to whom the *Kokinshū* was an old friend and who were thoroughly accustomed to the effects of *honkadori*. Their purpose may have been also in part didactic, insofar as the elaborate juxtaposition of modern poems to their *Kokinshū* analogues illustrated what was meant by the contemporary injunction to "old words, new heart" in the writing of poetry—that is, to compositions that obeyed the iron rules of diction but were informed by contemporary sensibilities that saved them from a sterile antiquarianism.

The "new heart" of *Shinkokinshū* poetry is often defined with reference to an elusive aesthetic concept known as *yūgen*, whose definitions include allusiveness, evocativeness, "dark mystery," "mysterious vagueness," "mysterious depth," and even, simply, "elegance." A poem embodying *yūgen* points to a world beyond words whose outlines a true artist can evoke in the inner eye of his audience. *Yūgen* is in a way a specialized instance of the more general Buddhist philosophical preoccupation with the problematic relationship between perception and reality. The primary concern of the poet remained the authentic expression of emotion, but the true poet was moved by what a refined sensibility could see behind superficial reality—not by beauty, but by its transience, not by love, but by the inevitability of its loss. The characteristic mood of the *Shinkokinshū* is therefore emphatically not a sunny one but rather thoughtful and somber. That it is so clearly defined is remarkable, for this is a poetry that leaves much unspoken, the truths with which it concerns itself being of a sort that cannot be explained directly in the limited vocabulary of the court poet, from which all of the immense Chinese philosophical lexicon was banned. *Shinkokinshū* poets relied instead on highly concrete language and objective description devised to evoke in the reader, without intermediation, the same subtle vision that inspired the poetic act in the first place.

The tendency of *Shinkokinshū* poetry to reveal its "heart," its real meaning, not in its words but rather in the spaces between them, as it were, or in the history behind them, bespeaks a highly sophisticated understanding that "poetry" is not merely words on a page but the result of a very complex interactive process involving poet, ideas, words, and the reader. That this understanding was not subliminal but fully conscious is borne out by the evidence of modern Japanese scholarship.

As noted above, the *Shinkokinshū* closely follows the lead of the *Kokinshū* in its organization. Like the *Kokinshū*, the *Shinkokinshū* arranges poems so that they mimic natural progressions in the real world, be they those of the seasons or that of a love affair. Konishi Jin'ichi and other scholars have discovered that such sequences in the later collection were also ordered, however, in accordance with certain rules quite independent of the natural progressions they follow. Specifically, each poem in a sequence seems to have been chosen not only to forward the movement in question but also with a clear awareness of how it "fit" with the poems before and after it. Each successive, overlapping pair of verses must therefore be in harmony, sharing a common or closely similar tone, image, or point of view. A sequence of early-spring poems might thus begin with a verse containing the image of scattered patches of snow in a garden where flowering plums have begun to bloom; the next verse might then mention water trickling out from under melting snow, to be followed in its turn by one describing a swollen hillside freshet; the scene might then shift to a mountain village still snowbound but wreathed in wisps of springlike haze.

The reader supplies continuity to such a series by sensing, perhaps not always even consciously, that there is a logic operating in multiple dimensions here which makes for a natural movement from poem to poem. The location, for example, gradually shifts upward in space from garden to hillside (linked by the common image or implied image of melting snow) to mountain village, while at the same time the successive scenes are rendered from an increasingly distant point of view. The mood changes from the domesticity of a garden to the daunting isolation of the mountains, but the changes come slowly and naturally, thanks to the intervening verses. The sequence in effect reverses the natural progress of spring by beginning with blossoms and ending with a snowbound village, but the geographical shift up into the mountains explains the retrogression, which itself has the secondary effect of reaffirming the larger framework of early spring, always a time of false starts and late snows.

How aware any given reader might have been of this complex manipulation of images and associations is problematic, but it seems quite undeniable that the compilers themselves were fully conscious of the effects they created. Nothing else can really account for what is otherwise a puzzling randomness in the order of the verses when they are considered from the point of view of age or authorship, or for the inclusion of a surprising number of verses that by any standard are not the best the age produced, but that turn out to be precisely what is needed to effect transitions between pairs of clearly superior poems which carry associations that would otherwise clash or at least not dovetail neatly.

HAIKU AND RENGA

While the *Shinkokinshū* marks a high point in the classical poetic tradition, it by no means marks its end, which in a sense has come only in the past century with

the decay of the custom of rote memorization of the poetic canon (or at least large parts of it)—a custom that was integral both to the appreciation and to the practice of court poetry. Indeed, until the first decades of the twentieth century, *tanka* in the court style, still subject to the ancient rules of diction and style, were a natural part of the repertoire of the literary-minded elite, and they are still far more a part of the popular conception of what poetry is than any specific poetic form of comparable age in the West.

This survival is all the more remarkable in view of the fact that the classical tradition itself engendered an entirely new world of poetic practice as early as the fifteenth century, culminating in the *haiku*, the only form of Japanese poetry generally known in the West and the only serious challenge in Japanese literary history to the preeminence of *tanka*. The seventeen-syllable *haiku* is a direct descendant of a form of poetry known as *renga* (linked verse), which in its origins was both an elaboration of and a challenge to the attitudes that shaped the poetry of the *Shinkokinshū* and the late classical age.

Renga developed originally as a pastime among court poets, a formalization of poetic games that included "verse-capping," in which contestants had to supply the second half—the seven/seven-syllable "lower verse"—of either a well-known *tanka* or an opponent's original composition, and *utaawase* poetry competitions, in which teams of poets publicly composed poems on a series of set themes. The term *renga* refers specifically to a sequence of alternating five/seven/five- and seven/seven-syllable units, each verse except the first being written in response to the verse preceding it. Each pair of verses, written by two different poets, was expected to be able to stand alone as a coherent *tanka*, even though every second pair necessarily inverted the upper and lower verses of the standard *tanka* form. The resulting chain, usually of thirty-six or one hundred links, was in effect a single poetic composition by multiple authors (most commonly three) who took turns supplying each successive verse. There was, however, no requirement that the *renga* sequence be restricted to a single theme. In fact, as it developed, one of the requirements of *renga* was that the subject matter of the verses in a sequence be varied to include as many of the traditional topics— seasons, love, grievance, and so on—as possible. There was therefore no overall unity to a *renga* chain, only the serial unity within each overlapping pair of verses. That late-classical poetics favored concrete imagery and objectivity aided the *renga* poet, because verses with those qualities were subject to multiple interpretations. A verse centering on the image "dew at daybreak," for example, could function nicely as a companion to a spring poem before it, and equally well as a lead-in to a verse describing a lover stealing away after a nighttime tryst.

Renga began as a light entertainment but soon began to be taken seriously as a poetic form of great potential. By the fifteenth century, two varieties of *renga* were being practiced, a light or comic form labeled *mushin* (frivolous, or lacking heart) and a serious form called *ushin*. In the hands of its most accomplished practitioners, such as the poet-priest Sōgi (1421-1502), serious *ushin renga* became what some regard as the supreme achievement of Japanese classical poetry. *Renga* was not, however, a form of poetry whose practice or appreciation could ever be widespread, since it required skills and erudition not to be found outside a small population of dedicated practitioners. As an outgrowth of classical *tanka*, serious *renga* conformed to all the rules of the court tradition within its constituent verses; in addition, it developed a detailed, elaborate set of conventions governing the poetics of the sequence as a whole.

A typical *renga* chain shares a number of characteristics with the carefully constructed *Shinkokinshū* sequences described above, but there are also major differences. In both cases, adjacent verses are linked on any of several levels—imagery, subject, point of view, and so on; *renga* sequences also often contain very complex links formed on the basis of *honkadori* in which a source poem called to mind by an allusion in one verse supplies materials that inspire the next. Both kinds of sequence depend for their coherence on manipulation not only of poetic materials but also of the actual experience of reading or hearing each verse as it is added to the chain, for it is the totality of all the associations a verse evokes in the mind's eye with which the compiler or poet works in building links from verse to verse.

The *renga* chain differs fundamentally from *Shinkokinshū* precedents, however, in two vital ways. First, it is an original composition, not compiled from existing materials; second, there is no external framework corresponding to the progression of a season or a love affair as is seen in the *Shinkokinshū*. The formal rules of *renga* composition no doubt developed as a strategy for averting the shapelessness that these characteristics made likely. The rules sometimes seem to have been needlessly minute and almost arbitrary in their specifications—as of exactly which verses in a sequence could and must contain the word "moon"—but their effect was to establish a tension between imagination and tight control that in the best surviving sequences results in a very pleasing rhythm of excitement and relaxation as the poets deal, verse by verse, with the difficulty of submitting inspiration and free association to discipline.

The sheer difficulty of serious *renga* made it the province of a small elite of professional poets, often Buddhist priests or laymen who adopted a priestly lifestyle in order to free themselves of ordinary social concerns. *Renga* poets were no longer courtiers for whom poetry was a polite art, but full-time artists who subsisted either on inherited means or the largesse of patrons. The imperial court itself, for so long the locus of poetic activity, had ceased to be an institution of any but symbolic political significance by the time *renga* became an important poetic mode. Patronage had therefore passed into the hands of a new class, the military leaders who gradually assumed control of the country as power slipped away from the court, beginning as early as the twelfth century. The old court culture enjoyed a brief resuscitation under the hereditary military dictators or shoguns of the Ashikaga clan, whose power base was the old imperial capital of Kyoto, but by the first decades of the fifteenth century, real power began to pass into the hands of local magnates known as *daimyō* or "great names," petty warlords who maintained their own courts and, as their means permitted and their tastes inclined them, extended patronage to poets and other artists. The stable, refined world that had nurtured the genteel ideal of the courtly poet, however, was gone forever. It is little wonder that the *renga* poets, men of immense learning and sensitivity surrounded by people who in an earlier age would have been thought unimaginably coarse, produced a poetry whose predominant moods were melancholy and nostalgia.

SIXTEENTH AND SEVENTEENTH CENTURIES

The sixteenth century brought change and upheaval on a scale that had not been seen since the earliest years of imperial expansion and the importation of Chinese culture nearly a thousand years before. Civil war touched all corners of the country, its destructiveness magnified by the use of firearms, which were introduced by Portuguese traders when they reached Japan in the middle of the century. Except in this one respect, the West would not have a profound effect upon Japan for another three centuries, but until Japan was officially cut off almost completely from foreign contacts in the seventeenth century, a small but steady stream of Portuguese, Spanish, Dutch, and English missionaries and traders destroyed forever the complacent Japanese view of civilization as something coterminous with the self-contained Chinese cultural sphere. The nearly total collapse of the old order—one famous story has a sixteenth century emperor peddling samples of his calligraphy to make ends meet—raised men to power who had only the most tenuous of connections with the courtly values of the past, and it was inevitable that when peace finally came again at the end of the century, the art of poetry would emerge no less profoundly changed than any other sphere of Japanese life.

The year 1600 (or, by some reckonings, 1603) marks the beginning of a dynamic new era known to Japanese historians either as the Tokugawa period, after the dynasty of shoguns founded by Tokugawa Ieyasu, or the Edo period, after the city that was the seat of Tokugawa rule, modern Tokyo. Through a combination of political negotiation and brute force, Ieyasu brought the civil wars to an end after more than a century, and peace was soon followed by unprecedented prosperity. The democratization of formerly elite kinds of artistic endeavor that this new prosperity fostered would prove to be the most dramatic cultural development of the new era.

The activities of Matsunaga Teitoku (1571-1653) illustrate how profoundly poetry in particular was affected by these changes in the larger cultural environment. Teitoku was trained in the ancient traditions of classical *tanka*, which by his day were treated as a hermetic body of secret lore by the remaining court poets in Kyoto. He shared with his teachers the Confucian attitude that the practice of literature was an essential ele-

ment in the cultivation of moral rectitude, but he saw that literature could never be accessible to the greater mass of the population, among whom literacy was spreading rapidly, if it continued to be treated as the private property of a hereditary poetic priesthood. He therefore undertook a career as a popularizer, giving public lectures on the classics in direct defiance of his mentors and—most important for the development of Japanese poetry—promoting a new style of linked verse that met what he believed were the needs of the time for a form of literature that could be practiced by the educated common man but that at the same time was not vulgar. Teitoku's chosen vehicle of literary instruction was *haikai*, more formally *haikai no renga*, or "comic *renga*," a descendant of the *mushin* mode in linked verse.

Before Teitoku, *haikai* was most decidedly a comic poetry of dubious morals. Its humor came in part from wordplay, parody, scatology, and other obvious comic effects, but also in considerable measure from the deliberate violation of the rules of serious *renga*, particularly those regarding diction—there was humor, for example, in the mere presence of as innocent a word as "nose" in a verse that otherwise followed thousand-year-old conventions of decorum. Teitoku lamented the unabashed vulgarity of *haikai* but recognized certain virtues in it. The proficient *haikai* poet still honored, if in a backhanded way, the principle that poetry was a matter of precedent and convention, without which much of the humor of *haikai* was meaningless, and *haikai* also admitted the use of colloquial language, which meant that it could become a poetry accessible to people who lacked a thoroughgoing education in the classical idiom.

Teitoku did not single-handedly make *haikai* the characteristic verse form of the Edo period, but his tireless promotion of it, aided by the beginnings of a printing industry, was certainly important in its spread. His attitude was condescending and didactic, but he attracted a great number of literary disciples from classes previously uninvolved in literary activity, particularly the middle and lower ranks of the samurai military caste and newly wealthy urban merchants. There quickly arose, however, a reaction against the uneasy compromise between vulgarity and traditional belletrism that characterized *haikai* of Teitoku's school. It is significant that the reaction came not, as might be supposed, from poets who protested against Teitoku's vulgarization of the high classical tradition, but rather from those who believed he was destroying the straightforward, comic irreverence of *haikai* by trying to turn it into an ersatz "serious" poetry for the masses.

The fight against what they considered to be the pretentious stuffiness of the Teitoku school was led by a group known as the Danrin school of *haikai*, disciples of Nishiyama Sōin (1605-1682), a traditional *renga* poet turned *haikai* partisan. Danrin *haikai* was a short-lived phenomenon, defeated by its excesses in combat with the Teitoku school in the first public literary feud Japan had seen. The Danrin poets steadfastly refused to credit the Teitoku school's insistence that *haikai*, if only it would accept the discipline of serious *renga* while changing with the times to allow everyday language and subject matter, could become a form of poetry with real depth and dignity.

There is an element suggestive of Dadaism in Danrin-school reactions against the Teitoku-school attitude toward *haikai*, best illustrated, perhaps, by the brief poetic career of Ihara Saikaku (1642-1693), better known as a fiction writer who was the first to chronicle the new, vigorous life of the urban middle classes. Saikaku's claim to fame as a poet comes from his practice of the extemporaneous solo composition of *haikai* sequences in public. His first great success came in 1675, when he produced a thousand verses at a single sitting. He finally retired from competition—actually, there was no competition—in 1684, after composing a record 23,500 linked verses in the space of a day and night, a tour de force that earned for him the sobriquet Niman'ō, "Old Man Twenty Thousand." (No record of the poems survives, since Saikaku produced them orally faster than a scribe could follow.)

MATSUO BASHŌ

Haikai survived and flourished, despite the guerrilla tactics of Sōin's Danrin-school followers and the excesses of Teitoku didacticism, thanks largely to the artistry of Matsuo Bashō (1644-1694), who is probably the only poet of the premodern period whose name is known to practically every Japanese today and whose poetry, rightly or wrongly, has come in the minds of Western readers to represent Japanese poetry in general. Bashō's early training in *haikai* was in the Teitoku school, favored in the conservative rural samurai milieu of his youth. After moving to Edo to pursue a career as a poet and teacher in 1672, however, he came under the influence of the Danrin poets, who found the openness of the shogun capital, still something of a boomtown, more congenial than the tradition-bound atmosphere of Kyoto.

Bashō did not join in the Teitoku-Danrin conflict; instead, he borrowed elements of both styles to produce his own, distinctive poetry in what came to be known as *shōfū*, the Bashō manner. In Teitoku *haikai*, Bashō found a commitment to discipline, polish, and technical skill essential to any real poetry. From the Danrin school, Bashō learned the importance of direct observation and objective description of the world of the senses, unmediated by artificial ideas of what was and was not "poetic." To this synthesis, he added a certain philosophical depth derived from his study of Chinese poetry and Zen Buddhism. His poetry, quickly disseminated in printed form, struck such a responsive chord that even by the time of his death, Bashō had become a national institution; some two thousand poets all over Japan claimed personal discipleship.

Interestingly, the immense popularity of Bashō's poetry played no small part in the demise of the *haikai* form, for the haunting beauty and technical sparkle of his individual verses overshadowed their role in linked-verse sequences. Bashō himself almost always composed in a group linked-verse setting, and much of his critical writing concerns itself with the paramount importance of keeping the linking process foremost in mind when writing *haikai*. Poetic practice and the spread of publishing, however, were at work even in his day to put greater emphasis on the individual units of the *haikai* chain, particularly the *hokku*, the first verse in a sequence. The *hokku* was of great importance in *haikai*, as it had always been in *renga*. First, it was the only verse in a sequence that was specifically required to have reference to anything outside the other poems in the chain—the rules dictated that it specify as clearly as possible the setting, circumstances, and season in which the poets were gathered. Further, the *hokku* was by tradition the responsibility of the most accomplished poet present, who was by convention, if not in actuality, treated as an honored guest. The *hokku*, therefore, could be and often was composed beforehand; its distinctive status encouraged its author to take special pains.

The great majority of the verses by which Bashō's poetry came to be known in Japan were originally composed as *hokku*, whose distinctive qualities and special status made them attractive candidates for inclusion in published handbooks of *haikai* practice. Furthermore, one important means by which Bashō's work was disseminated was his published travel diaries, which recorded a number of poetic pilgrimages he took late in life, visiting sites important in the classical tradition. Bashō was by that time a literary celebrity, and so at nearly every stop on these journeys he was put up by local poets, in return for whose hospitality he participated in *haikai* sessions. As a guest, he invariably had responsibility for the *hokku*, and naturally enough it was his *hokku* that he chose to preserve in his diaries, for they alone were uniquely tied to the places he visited.

These circumstances conspired to help make the seventeen-syllable *hokku* an independent verse form, called *haiku*, which is nothing more than a *hokku* composed with no thought of its being part of a *haikai* sequence. Linked verse in the modern *haikai* style continued to be practiced, but poets after Bashō tended increasingly to concentrate on single *haiku*, which proved to be highly satisfying vehicles for poetic expression, insofar as they partook of the special qualities of the *hokku*—the polish that was possible in a verse that need not be an impromptu public performance, for example, and the way in which it took much of its inspiration from the immediate surroundings of the poet.

EIGHTEENTH CENTURY

Bashō was followed by a legion of notable *haikai* (or *haiku*—the terms were for some time interchangeable) poets, among whom might be singled out Takarai (or Enomoto) Kikaku (1661-1707), who added the kaleidoscope of city life to the poet's palette, restoring something of the earthiness that Bashō's otherworldliness had temporarily banished from *haikai*; Kikaku's poetry was not, however, any less touched with meaning than that of Bashō. Another poet deserving special note is Yosa Buson (1716-1783), whose verse is very elegant and at

the same time sentimental. It is difficult to generalize about *haiku*. One of its chief virtues, fostered by Bashō's insistence on combining craftsmanship with authenticity of observation and emotional content, is that it allowed the expression of greater individuality than any poetic form that had preceded it, save perhaps the *chōka* a thousand years earlier.

The revolution that the *haiku* brought to Japanese poetry by disencumbering it of the most stifling aspects of classicism is characteristic of the diverse, iconoclastic creativity of Edo-period culture—a culture that flourished in spite of its near-total isolation from the currents of social and economic change that were reshaping other traditional cultures elsewhere in the world. Some of the important innovations of Edo literary culture lie beyond the scope of this essay, but the eighteenth century was not lacking in significant developments. Even the *tanka*, so long the embodiment of traditionalism, began to change as *haiku* poets redefined the purposes of poetry; *tanka* admitted colloquial language and prosaic subject matter and generated its own lively comic derivative, the *kyōka* (mad verse), which was wildly popular in the 1780's among a slightly jaded coterie of avant-garde intellectuals in Edo. Nativist scholars such as Kamo Mabuchi (1697-1769) and Motoori Norinaga (1730-1801) experimented with revivals of *chōka* and *tanka* in the style of the *Manyōshū* with a decidedly chauvinistic, anti-Chinese coloration. At the same time, however, the intense involvement of many eighteenth century intellectuals in the study of Chinese literature also produced much verse written in Chinese, some of it of remarkable quality. Together, these trends foreshadowed the explosion of creativity in all fields of literature that would occur when Japan once more opened its doors to outside influence in the nineteenth century.

BIBLIOGRAPHY

Brower, Robert, and Earl Miner. *Japanese Court Poetry.* Stanford, Calif.: Stanford University Press, 1961. Still the standard history of the development of the standard thirty-one-syllable *waka*, from its beginnings through the medieval period.

Carter, Steven D. *Waiting for the Wind: Thirty-six Poets of Japan's Late Medieval Age.* Translations from the Asian Classics Series. Reprint. New York: Columbia

University Press, 1994. Presents more than four hundred poems by a range of poets from Japan's late medieval age (1250-1500), along with biographical sketches and critical evaluations of each.

Keene, Donald. *Seeds of the Heart*. New York: Henry Holt, 1993. The definitive account of the development of Japanese literature from the beginnings through the late sixteenth century. A good deal of space is dedicated to the development of Japanese poetry in all forms.

_____. *World Within Walls*. New York: Holt, Rinehart and Winston, 1976. A continuation of Keene's history of Japanese literature until 1867. Provides useful analyses of poets and poetry in all styles.

Miner, Earl. *Japanese Linked Poetry*. Princeton, N.J.: Princeton University Press, 1979. A detailed history of medieval linked-verse, or *renga*, with copious translations.

Ooka, Makoto. *The Poetry and Poetics of Ancient Japan*. Translated by Thomas Fitzsimmons. Santa Fe, N.Mex.: Katydid Books, 1997. Explores the great library of poetry anthologies compiled by the Imperial order. Re-creates in detail the social, political, and cultural realities surrounding the development of Japanese poetry from ancient until modern times.

Sato, Hiroaki. *One Hundred Frogs: From Renga, to Haiku, to English*. New York: Weatherhill, 1983. Provides definitions, history, the forms, and the rules of these poems, with many useful insights into the techniques of translating Japanese poems, and adds many examples of poems and translations.

Shirane, Haruo. *Traces of Dreams*. Stanford, Calif.: Stanford University Press, 1998. A history of the development of *haiku*, concentrating on the career and accomplishments of Matsuo Bashō.

Yasuda, Kenneth. *Japanese Haiku: Its Essential Nature History and Possibilities in English*. New York: Charles E. Tuttle, 1991. Provides theory and criticism of the *haiku*.

Robert W. Leutner,
updated by J. Thomas Rimer

JAPANESE POETRY SINCE 1800

At the beginning of the nineteenth century, the long and powerful tradition of Japanese poetry continued to make possible the production of accomplished and moving poems in the great forms that had developed during various periods in the past: the thirty-one-syllable *waka* (also known as *tanka*, the name by which the form is familiar to many Western readers), the seventeen-syllable *haiku*, and the more philosophical medium of *kanshi*, or poetry in Chinese, which permitted both greater length and the kind of philosophical abstraction that had long been deemed unsuitable for the shorter forms of classical Japanese verse. These traditions might well have ossified but for the spread of literacy and learning and the inspiration of Chinese poetry available from the continent, which made it possible to achieve new variations within old forms. For example, Kobayashi Yatarō, known as Issa (1763-1827), a farmer from the mountainous countryside, had been able to create a style of *haiku* that could capture both the joys and the anguish of the plebeian world in which he lived, while Ōkuma Kotomichi (1798-1868) extended the boundaries of *waka* to include an interest in human personality and psychology that gave his poems a strikingly modern flavor. Rai Sanyō (1780-1832), writing in Chinese, dealt with extremely diverse subject matter—including the presence of the Dutch in Nagasaki—in his lengthy and sometimes polemical poetry. The traditions of Japanese poetry, then, were by no means moribund.

On the other hand, Japan's self-imposed seclusion from other nations, dating from the early 1600's, had denied her poets the opportunity to gain any real perspective on their own traditions, as they had always done before, through an exposure to literary traditions from other cultures. Thus, in the closing decades of the nineteenth century, when young Japanese finally were permitted to go abroad, an awakening interest among them in European literature brought about a profound change in the development of the Japanese poetic sensibility. Native traditions were continued, although much expanded in range of subject matter and vocabulary permitted, but a whole new form of poetry, based on Western models and usually referred to as *shintaishi* ("new style verse" or "free-style verse"), developed into the standard vehicle for modern Japanese poetry. Both the traditional forms and the new forms grew and developed in response to the profound interest taken by Japanese poets in Western verse, which led to their attempts to understand, translate, and make use of those forms themselves.

FIRST EXPERIMENTS

Before it became possible to write effective poetry in the new forms, a period of experimentation was required. These experiments were undertaken by a variety of gifted poets and usually involved their attempts to translate Western poems into Japanese (a language itself moving quickly, under the influence of Western example, toward a closer alignment between the written and spoken forms than had ever before seemed possible). Their various enthusiasms assured that, by the first decade of the twentieth century, there would be examples in good modern Japanese of some of the finest examples of European and American poetry from all periods. These translated poems, in turn, inspired an efflorescence of high poetic accomplishment in the Japanese language that continues unabated today.

The first significant contribution to the acculturation of Japanese poetry appeared in 1882, when three Tokyo University professors, two of whom had studied in the United States, produced a series of fourteen translations and five poems of their own based on Western models. This small collection, the *Shintaishisho* (selection of new style verse), included a number of poems quite popular with nineteenth century English and American readers, including Alfred, Lord Tennyson's "The Charge of the Light Brigade," Thomas Gray's "Elegy Written in a Country Churchyard," Henry Wadsworth Longfellow's "A Psalm of Life," and Tennyson's "The Captain," as well as a few bits and pieces of William Shakespeare, including Hamlet's famous soliloquy, "To be or not to be." In presenting these works in translation, the authors stressed their conviction that such poems could well serve as models for the future, since both *waka* and *haiku* were too short to express any sustained mood or argument and too bound by traditional vocabulary and subject matter. This small collection remained very influential with young writers, and the interest it generated was reinforced by the publication, in 1889, of *Omokage* (vestiges). This collection of translations included selections from the German Romantic poets, Johann Wolfgang von Goethe, Heinrich Heine, Nikolaus Lenau, and E. T. A. Hoffmann; the volume also included selections from Shakespeare by way of the German translation of Friedrich von Schlegel and from Lord Byron by way of Heine's German version. The translations were prepared by Mori Ōgai (1862-1922), one of the foremost novelists of early modern Japan, who had lived in Germany from 1884 to 1888 and had learned to appreciate the great German poets in the original. He prepared his translations with a group of colleagues, sometimes attempting a literal rendering, sometimes developing forms that captured the content but strove to achieve a more natural expression in Japanese. These widely read translations brought Japan closer to a truly modern poetry, but the most influential models were those provided by Ueda Bin (1874-1916) in his 1905 collection *Kaichōon* (the sound of the tide), which brought the first adequate versions of Symbolist poetry to Japan. Through these elegant and still widely appreciated translations, Japanese readers were first able to read important poems by Charles Baudelaire, Paul Verlaine, Stéphane Mallarmé, Gabriele D'Annunzio, Christina and Dante Gabriel Rossetti, and Émile Verhaeren. Response to these poems suggested a certain congruence between European Symbolist values, with their suggestion of an unspoken and mysterious beauty, and the traditional values of Japanese poetry, with its emphasis on such qualities as the hidden depths of beauty captured in the courtly ideal of *yūgen*. Indeed, for several decades, the influence of French poetry was to remain paramount in Japan, and it was very much under the French influence that the first great collection of modern Japanese poetry, Hagiwara Sakutarō's *Tsuki ni hoeru* (*Howling at the Moon*, 1969), appeared in 1917.

TURN OF THE CENTURY: CHANGES IN TRADITIONAL FORMS

The same influences that were to create the new forms in Japanese poetry also helped bring about enormous changes in the traditional forms. In fact, four of the most important poets of the modern period continued to write in the traditional modes, using the possibili-

ties of personal involvement and fresh vocabulary that had opened up to them by the turn of the century. The first of these was the poet Masaoka Shiki (1867-1902), who wrote both *haiku* and *waka* and did much to introduce the element of real and observed life into these forms. For Masaoka, the composition of poetry involved going out into nature to record what the poet himself could observe, and his principle of *shasei*, or "sketching from life," brought new vigor and reality to traditional forms that had tended to be restricted to a fixed vocabulary and a narrow range of emotional attitudes. Yosano Akiko (1878-1942), a poet whose vibrancy recalls the women writers of the early classical period such as the *waka* poet Ono no Komachi (834-880), instead plumbed the depths of her own emotional responses to life in order to produce *waka* full of emotional force and sensual consciousness. In a somewhat similar vein, Ishikawa Takuboku (1886-1912) wrote *waka* that told unsparingly of himself, his moods, and his defeats. Toward the end of his short career, Takuboku also began to introduce an element of political consciousness into his poetry that gave him another important role in the development of the modern poetic consciousness (see below).

Saitō Mokichi (1882-1953) began his career as a doctor and studied neuropsychiatry in Vienna, yet he continued to make use of the *waka* form to record his intimate feelings and responses to the emotional complexities of his experiences. In the work of all of these writers, poetry became in a highly significant way an extension of their own personalities, permitting new possibilities for the *waka* and *haiku* forms. Thus, the democratization of poetry that began with Matsuo Bashō (1644-1694) and the Tokugawa (1579-1632) *haiku* has continued into the contemporary scene, where collections by dozens of poets provide for the continuity of a now comfortable tradition, which, while no longer at the cutting edge of modern poetry, still serves an honorable purpose in Japanese letters.

Other poets experimented with the older forms in order to make them as spare and flexible as possible. Several of the finest *haiku* poets of the period withdrew from conventional society and dedicated themselves to the service of Buddhism and the pilgrimage ideal. Their poetry thus shows powerful ties with the past wedded to complex contemporary sensibility. Ozaki Hōsai (1885-

1926) was an insurance executive who after a period of instability abandoned his employment to serve as a Buddhist sexton in a small temple, where he wrote most of his remarkable free-style *haiku*. Taneda Santōka (1882-1940) led a dissolute life until becoming a mendicant monk; in the style of his great predecessor, Ryōkan (1758-1831), Taneda walked through the countryside, seeking salvation and writing down his trenchant and striking responses to the lonely life that he led. Ogiwara Seisensui (1884-1976) also did much to develop the style of free-form *haiku* and so make the tradition more available to modern writers and readers as a mechanism for expressing genuine contemporary concerns. Indeed, the work of these three men revealed the enormous range of which the venerable seventeen-syllable form was capable.

Kanshi also remained a possibility for those Japanese writers in the late nineteenth and early twentieth centuries who had been educated in classical Chinese, although, by the turn of the century, German, English, and French had replaced Chinese as the most important foreign languages to be studied in Japan, and as a result interest and skill in composing traditional Chinese verse waned. Perhaps the finest *kanshi* poet in the early years of the twentieth century, and indeed perhaps the greatest in the history of Chinese poetry written in Japan, was the novelist Natsume Sōseki (1867-1916), one of the pivotal figures in modern Japanese culture. Educated in English literature and the author of the most sophisticated psychological novels of his time, Sōseki nevertheless summoned up his classical training to write down his private thoughts in a series of Chinese poems that tell more about his aspirations, disappointments, and spiritual life than most of his other, more accessible works. By Sōseki's time, very few Japanese were capable of reading, let alone appreciating, such poetry; perhaps it was precisely Sōseki's realization that he was writing in what was destined even in his time to become a kind of private code that made it possible for him to be so open about himself in this most ancient form.

EARLY TWENTIETH CENTURY: JAPAN AND
THE EUROPEAN AVANT-GARDE

Japanese free-style verse came of age with the publication of Hagiwara's *Howling at the Moon*, a short book of poems which, despite its debts to European Symbolism, revealed a mastery of colloquial language in the service of an authentic rendering of Hagiwara's inner world—troubled, ironic, and highly colored. Hagiwara himself had never been abroad ("I thought I'd like to go to France," he wrote in one of his poems; "France is too far away"). *Howling at the Moon* and the collections that followed contained poems filled with images that served as objective correlatives to elements in Hagiwara's own neurotic sensibility. Some of these are drawn from nature ("blurred bamboo roots spreading"), some from his own imagination. The most famous poem in *Howling at the Moon* begins: "At the bottom of the ground a face emerging,/ a lonely invalid's face emerging."

Reading Hagiwara's poetry while living in Europe, Nishiwaki Junsaburō (1894-1982) realized that it might be possible after all to write poetry in Japanese rather than in English or French. Nishiwaki, who once described himself as a "beggar for Europe," had decided that to participate in the creation of modern poetry, he would have to leave his homeland in order to shake off the weight of old traditions. Nishiwaki met Ezra Pound and T. S. Eliot (he was later to become the definitive translator of Eliot's works into Japanese) and began to publish in little magazines in London, but his encounter with Hagiwara's revolutionary volume of poems brought him back to Japan and the beginnings of a genuine avant-garde movement there. Nishiwaki had become interested in Surrealism while in Europe and found a means to adapt for his own work that method of piercing through everyday reality ("like looking at a hole in a hedge into eternity," he wrote). Nishiwaki's difficult verse, filled with references to Blaise Pascal, Rainer Maria Rilke, Pablo Picasso, and other figures of European culture, represents the high tide of Japanese poetry in the international style. Nishiwaki's high accomplishments seem to owe relatively little to the Japanese tradition and set him apart from his more conservative contemporaries in somewhat the same way that Pound's work constituted a break with the conservative traditions of English poetry. Both are eclectic, highly committed, and utterly individual, and both, in a special way, represent the literary ideals of the period in which they lived. Translations of a wide variety of Nishiwaki's best work can be found in Hosea Hirata's *The Poetry and*

Poetics of Nishiwaki Junzaburō: Modernism in Translation (1993).

Other poets traveled to Europe but remained more within the developing traditions of modern Japanese poetry. Takamura Kōtarō (1883-1956) went to France, where he studied sculpture with Auguste Rodin, and returned to become one of the major lyric voices of his day. His poems were modern in style and spirit, but not aggressively so, and his best-known poems deal with the growing madness and death of his wife Chieko, who haunts the pages of these remarkable lyrics like the ghost in a traditional No play. Extensive translations can be found in Hiroaki Sato, *A Brief History of Imbecility: Poetry and Prose of Takamura Kōtarō* (1992). Others, such as Kitahara Hakushū (1885-1942), Kaneko Mitsuharu (1895-1975), and Miyoshi Tatsuji (1900-1964), added other elements from European and American poetry to the expanding vocabulary of techniques available to modern Japanese poets and left behind important collections that are still widely appreciated.

While it may be correct to say that European models suggested possibilities for modern Japanese poetry, it would be wrong indeed to hold that the poetry produced was merely derivative. The work of Nishiwaki and the others described above is, as is clear even when read in translation, distinctly individual. In terms of authenticity of voice, no modern Japanese poet is more appreciated than Miyazawa Kenji, or Kenji Miyazawa (1896-1933), as he is known in the West. Miyazawa was a devout Buddhist. After training at an agricultural college, he taught poor farmers in Iwate Prefecture, far to the north of Tokyo, how to better their lives. Miyazawa was little read during his lifetime, but later he became a powerful presence in modern Japanese poetry, even a cult figure. His remarkable verse, which owes more to Buddhist sutras than it does to European models, develops its metaphysical stance with an almost hallucinatory force. Miyazawa's work first became known to English-speaking readers through a series of translations by the American poet Gary Snyder, included in his collection *The Back Country* (1968), followed by a much more extensive translation by Hiroaki Sato, *A Future of Ice* (1989). As a result, Miyazawa's utterly individual voice is widely appreciated in translation. The best of his work is a rich and dazzling mixture of language and imagery that stretches modern Japanese to its limits and reveals possibilities of the congruence of sound and meaning unexplored in Japanese poetry before or since.

WAR AND POSTWAR YEARS

The rich and sophisticated mix of poetry produced in the 1920's and early 1930's came to an end with the dark days leading up to World War II. Some poets, such as Hagiwara, retreated to the use of traditional forms; some, such as Takamura, wrote patriotic poetry. Cut off from European developments and beleaguered at home by a repressive government and the difficulties of everyday living, Japanese poets seemed to turn inward. It was not until the end of the war that new trends could develop. When they did, it was perhaps not surprising that, in the wake of the war and the destruction that it had caused, younger poets came to distrust their own cultural past, which in their view had permitted a complicity with Japanese war aims. For them, the Japanese past seemed tainted, and beginning in the 1950's, poets looked again to Europe for their inspiration. In a sense, then, the war could be looked upon as an interruption in the internationalization of Japanese literature that had begun by the 1920's. In the postwar period, however, the break with the past became more definite and often assumed political significance.

Two trends in particular characterized the immediate postwar years. Following the example of Nishiwaki, who remained an immensely powerful figure in literary circles, a number of younger poets drew on European poetry in their effort to create a new tradition for themselves out of the ruins of the past. Considering that time of despair, it is perhaps not so surprising that in 1947, Ayukawa Nobuo (1920-1986) and his colleagues formed a group they called Arechi (the wasteland), suggesting both the impact of Eliot and their own sense of destruction and hopelessness. Others, such as Yoshioka Minoru (born 1919), continued to develop highly idiosyncratic symbolism and poetic forms that call to mind the commitment to the expanding mechanisms of language first undertaken by Nishiwaki. In the work of writers such as these, the legacy of European experimentation was still predominant.

A second trend placed a number of poets in the role of social critics who used the insights of the lyric mode to deepen and intensify their critique of postwar society. In this position, they had a powerful predecessor in the figure of Takuboku, who toward the end of his life had become increasingly wary of what he took to be reactionary trends in the development of the Japanese government and had begun to write poems that expressed his interest in socialism, even anarchism. Among the postwar poets who wanted to put society and its concerns back into the scope of their poetic vision, some were humanists horrified by the war, by the way in which human character had been degraded by destruction on the battlefield, and by the destruction caused by the atomic bomb. A few were Marxists. Little of this poetry has been studied or translated by Western scholars, but the work of early figures such as Oguma Hideo (1901-1940) certainly deserves proper study. Poets such as Ando Tsuguo (born 1919), most of whose work has been written in the postwar period, perhaps capture best this need of a generation to look back in an attempt to understand—emotionally, intellectually, and politically—what has happened to them. A reader who encounters their work in English may find it difficult to appreciate. A wider understanding of, say, Bertolt Brecht's poetry in England and the United States has now made it possible to write ironically in English on political issues, but the lyric thrust of the Japanese tradition applied to the war brings an overloading of images that may remain difficult for a reader from the Western tradition to encompass. Still, a search for authenticity in the early postwar period doubtless required this kind of linguistic travail, and the best of the works produced have a somber power that cannot be denied.

As the United States became involved in the Cold War and the Korean War as well, Japanese intellectuals began to react to what seemed to them a usurpation of their own sovereignty by the collusion of the Japanese and American authorities. Thus, there was a strain of contemporary Japanese poetry that, paralleling political movements, was largely reactive, particularly against the American involvement in Vietnam. Some of this political poetry had a satiric bite that was undeniably as effective as it was bitter.

A still later generation of poets, those who now have pride of place in Japanese literary circles, were born too late to have any direct experience of the war. These writers reached their maturity at a time when powerful changes had been wrought upon the fabric of Japanese society, where the processes of democratization and equalization of social class begun by the American occupation after World War II had altered the language as well as the society. Accordingly, Japanese poetry has tended to become increasingly colloquial, emphasizing the interior life of the poet, oppressed by the flatness, emptiness, and arbitrariness of modern life. As in English and American poetry, the grand gesture has been reduced to the ironic shrug, the powerful spiritual insight transformed into a wry and temporary awakening of sensibility. With the commercialization of communication, poets have found themselves more popular, and more vulnerable, than ever before. The work of Tamura Ryūichi (1923-1998), who owes something of his development to the Arechi school, has moments of a certain somber grandeur, but Tanikawa Shuntarō (born 1931) writes of the small disappointments and pleasures of his private world in a fashion that recalls the horizons, if not the style, of John Updike. His poetry is extremely popular in Japan and widely translated; the authenticity of his stance, which accurately reflects the spiritual condition of men and women in so many countries of the world, seems unquestioned.

Other writers among the postwar poets have attempted to strike out against this lassitude—some highly sophisticated, such as Anzai Hitoshi (born 1919), whose work is characterized by brilliant language and a suggestive and ironic treatment of the Japanese past, and others, aggressively plainspoken, such as Ishigaki Rin (born 1920), who uses her experience as a working woman as the basis for moving and often wryly humorous verses.

LATE TWENTIETH CENTURY

In more recent decades, it has become more difficult to make any definitive generalizations about poetic practice, as the quantity and diversity of poetry published, both in traditional and contemporary forms, remain enormous. It is perhaps too early for the reputations of younger writers to be settled in the minds of the multitude of readers attracted to poetry. In the midst of such continuing vitality, the increasing prominence of women poets, among them Tada Chimako (born 1932), Shinkawa Kazue (born 1929), and Yoshihara Sachiko (born 1932) is an important and welcome development. A range of new themes have also become possible, as the high reputation of Takahashi Mutsuo (born 1937), a poet dealing extensively with homosexuality, makes evident.

Tanka (*waka*), the thirty-one-syllable form that goes back more than one thousand years, is still being composed. Certain poets have declared themselves as avant-garde poets in the genre and are anxious to set aside much of the traditional vocabulary in order to work towards what they consider a more unsentimental style. In any case, the form can still remain widely attractive. Indeed Tawara Machi (born 1962) achieved an international best-seller in her fresh and often piquant collection of *tanka* titled *Salada kinenbi* (1987; *Salad Anniversary*, 1989).

Haiku, the seventeen-syllable form, also continues to attract a wide variety of poets, both professional and amateur. The kinds of expanded subject matter and fresh uses of the form which helped set the trends for more recent generations can be found in the seminal work of Saitō Sanki (1900-1962), with some of his best translated in *The Kobe Hotel* (1993).

Modern forms of verse, not surprisingly, retain pride of place as a privileged means of poetic expression. At least three larger trends might be noted here. The first involves the continued influence of French poetry and poetics in Japan. In those terms, such French poets as Baudelaire, Arthur Rimbaud, Paul Éluard, Mallarmé, André Breton, and Paul Valéry remain important; indeed, many contemporary Japanese poets who work and teach in university circles have done academic research on the French school and incorporate many of those principles into their own poetics. The resulting poetry is the most international in style of that composed in Japan at the end of the twentieth and beginning of the twent-first centuries. More often than not, poems are produced which are about words or the nature of language itself. Such work is particularly difficult to translate, since the subject matter itself involves the nature of the Japanese language. Some poets, such as the popular and highly respected Ooka Shōhei, (born 1931) can sometimes link their work to the classical language of the traditional *tanka*, while the use of patterns and sounds is important in the work of such prominent "intellectual" poets as Hiraide Takashi (born 1950) and Asabuki Ryōji (born 1952).

In contradistinction to these kinds of verse, which overtly aim at the status of high art, a more popular kind of verse has also emerged, also often international in atmosphere, but one which makes use of elements in popular culture, such as the rhythms of jazz, and seeks to move poetry closer to a living oral culture. These poets in particular have revived the custom of poetry readings, long a feature in classical times, and come closer to expressing in their work an overt expression of political and social concerns. The best known poet working in this vein, and arguably the best known Japanese poet outside of the country is Shiraishi Kazuko (born 1931), whose wit, feminist point of view, and antiestablishment stance have won her many friends and admirers around the world.

A third trend is the emergence of important longer poems and poetry sequences. Such efforts go back to the prewar generation of Nishiwaki Junzaburō, mentioned above, but more and more of these extended efforts have captured and sustained public interest. Here, three widely appreciated poets might be noted. Gōzō Yoshimatsu (born 1939), who at one point studied in the United States, has expressed his admiration for Rimbaud. For many of his readers, he seems uniquely successful in capturing a certain sense of the emptiness and vacuum he finds in contemporary Japanese life. His poetry has sometimes been characterized as a series of voyages away from that felt sense of futility. Soh Sakon (born 1919) belongs to an earlier generation but began writing poetry after World War II, inspired by his reading of Rimbaud and Valéry. His book-length poem *Moeru haha* (mother burning), published in 1967, now a classic of modern Japanese poetry, deals with the death of his mother in a 1942 fire bombing. Hara Shirō (born 1924), like other contemporary Japanese poets, is widely traveled and has been especially attracted to France. His highly regarded 1985 book-length poem *Ishi no fu* (*Ode to Stone*, 1990), uses as its links a series of stones, which serve as narrators from a variety of cultures and historical periods. These sections are interspersed with a continuing focus on a famous stone bridge in the southern city of Nagasaki, the town were Hara was raised.

Whatever the experimental nature of the language employed by all these poets, the very length of their work puts a necessary emphasis on larger themes, rather than merely a focus on the words themselves. This scale of verbal architecture creates a larger and more unified scale impossible to achieve in the shorter forms of poetry written in the Japanese classical and modern traditions.

Poetry has always been a highly respected form of artistic practice in Japan, and that pattern persists today. Most Japanese with a high school diploma can make an educated stab at writing *haiku*, perhaps even *waka*, and the relative evenness of vowel and consonant patterns in the Japanese language makes the composition of free verse relatively easy in a technical sense. Poetry magazines abound, and many accomplished writers compose for a circle of friends rather than for a national audience; indeed, some critics would maintain that this personal interchange between poets and their friends, so much a part of the Japanese poetic tradition since its beginnings in the *Manyōshū* (mid-eighth century; *The Collections of Ten Thousand Leaves*; also as *The Ten Thousand Leaves*, pb. 1981, and as *The Manyoshu*, 1940) and the *Kokinshū* (905; *Kokinshu: A Collection of Poems Ancient and Modern*, 1984), helps explain why so many achieve some real sense of craft and why the best of the poets have become supreme manipulators of the language. The popularity and acceptance of poetry in Japanese life may debase it on the lower end of the scale, where businessmen without sensibility scribble down *haiku*, the imagery of which is worn clear of genuine meaning. Yet on the other end of that scale, those who write and rewrite for their poetic colleagues have achieved a level of accomplishment that is remarkably high.

Translation of any language is slippery enough, and good translations of poetry are particularly difficult to achieve; certainly, the barrier of the difficult Japanese language prevents most Western readers from discovering one of the most active poetic traditions in the world today. It may well be, however, that in the generation to come, the increasing number of good translations of contemporary Japanese poetry will create and sustain the same kind of excitement among readers and writers of poetry in English that European artists felt one hundred years ago when they first saw woodblock prints imported from Japan.

BIBLIOGRAPHY

Heinrich, Amy. *Fragments of Rainbows: The Life and Poetry of Saitō Mokichi, 1882-1953*. New York: Columbia University Press, 1983. A useful account of developments in the use of classical forms in the modern period, centering on the work of Saitō Mokichi.

Keene, Donald. *Dawn to the West*. Vol. 2. New York: Holt, Rinehart and Winston, 1984. The development of modern poetry in all forms is documented in useful detail.

Kirkup, James, comp. and trans. *A Book of Tanka: An Anthology of Tanka from the Earliest Times to the Present Day*. Portland, Oreg.: University of Salzburg, 1996.

Koriyama, Naoshi, and Edward Lueders, eds. and trans. *Like Underground Water: Poetry of Mid-Twentieth Century Japan*. Port Townsend, Wash.: Copper Canyon Press, 1995.

Morton, Leith. *An Anthology of Contemporary Japanese Poetry*. New York: Garland, 1993.

Ooka, Makoto, and Thomas Fitzsimmons, eds. *A Play of Mirrors: Eight Major Poets of Modern Japan*, Rochester, Mich.: Katydid Books, 1987.

Sato, Hiroaki, and Burton Watson, eds. and trans. *From the Country of Eight Islands: An Anthology of Japanese Poetry*. Seattle: University of Washington Press, 1981.

Solt, John. *Shredding the Tapestry of Meaning*. Cambridge, Mass.: Harvard University Press, 1999. An account of the rise of avant-garde poetry in Japan, centering on the career and work of Kitasono Katsue.

Ueda, Makoto. *Modern Japanese Poets and the Nature of Literature*. Stanford, Calif.: Stanford University Press, 1983. Vibrant summaries of the work and thought of a series of major modern Japanese poets.

_____. *Modern Japanese Tanka: An Anthology*. New York: Columbia University Press, 1996.

_____, comp. and trans. *Modern Japanese Haiku: An Anthology*. Toronto: University of Toronto Press, 1976.

J. Thomas Rimer, updated by Rimer

LATIN AMERICAN POETRY

The panorama of Latin American poetry spans five hundred years, from the sixteenth to the twenty-first centuries.

FROM ENCOUNTER TO THE COLONIAL ERA

The first "Renaissance" in the New World (1492-1556) was the era of discovery, exploration, conquest, and colonization under the reign of the Spanish monarchs Ferdinand and Isabela and later Carlos V. The origins of Latin American literature are found in the chronicles of these events, narrated by Spanish soldiers or missionaries. The era of colonization during the reign of Philip II (1556-1598) was a second Renaissance and the period of the Counter-Reformation. During this time, Alonso de Ercilla y Zúñiga (1533-1594) wrote the first epic poem, *La Araucana* (1569-1589). The native saga narrated the wars between the Spanish conquistadors and the Araucano Indians of Chile. This is the first truly poetic literary work with an American theme.

During the period of the Austrian Habsburg kings (1598-1701), this Renaissance was gradually replaced by the Baroque era. While the Golden Age of Spanish letters was declining in the Old World, Sor Juana Inés de la Cruz (1648-1695) reigned supreme as the queen of colonial letters. She was the major poet during the colonial era. The autodidactic nun, who wrote plays and prose as well as poetry, was known as the tenth muse, *la décima musa*. Her poetic masterpiece, the autobiographical "Primero sueño," combines Baroque elements with a mastery of Spanish and classical languages and her unique style. Her shorter poems capture popular Mexican culture, with its lyrical verse phrasing and native themes. Some of her most famous sonnets are "Este que ves, engaño colorido" (what you see [is] dark deception), "¿En perseguirme, mundo, qué interesas?" (in pursuing me, world, what interests you?), "Détente, sombra de mi bien esquivo" (stop, shadow of my elusive love), and "Esta tarde, mi bien, cuando te hablaba" (this afternoon, love, when I spoke to you). Her most recognized *redondillas* (or "roundelays," stanzas of four octosyllabic lines rhyming *abba*) are "Este amoroso tormento" (this tormented love) and "Hombres necios, que acusáis" (stupid men, you accuse). Her charm and brilliance won her many wealthy and royal patrons. While she initially accepted their admiration, she died a recluse after rejecting her literary career and denouncing her precocious fame and vain pursuits.

During the Wars of Independence (1808-1826), Neoclassicism and other French influences dominated literary production. Andrés Bello (1781-1865) is better known for his prose, but he was also a prolific verse writer who followed the European Neoclassical movement. He wrote the poems "Alocución a la poesía" and "La agricultura en la zona tórida" with American themes and European style. José María de Hérédia (1803-1839) was a Cuban exiled in Mexico and the United States who wrote about the beauty of the countries that adopted him. Romanticism characterized his poems about Niagara Falls, "Niágara," Aztec ruins, "En el Teocalli de Cholula," and other wonders such as a storm in "En una tempestad." His ode "Himno a un desterrado" relates his experience as an exile in adopted nations.

Gertrudis Gómez de Avellaneda (1814-1873) left Cuba to write in Spain because of the greater freedom she could enjoy there as a female poet. Romanticism influenced her poems about love, God, and her homeland, such as "Noche de insomnio y el alba" (night of insomnia and dawn), "Al partir" (upon leaving), and "Amor y orgullo" (love and pride).

José Hernández (1834-1886) wrote about the Argentinean gauchos in *El Gaucho Martín Fierro* (1872; *The Gaucho Martin Fierro*, 1935) and *La vuelta de Martín Fierro* (1879; *The Return of Martin Fierro*, 1935). His Romantic verses followed the structures and lyrical rhythms of popular songs that romanticized the gauchos as a dying breed in the wake of industrialization.

MODERNISMO

By 1875, the roots of a poetic movement had grown into a new poetic era. The Latin American *Modernistas* were innovators and critics of the conservative thematic and stylistic structures that persisted from the colonial period. In Latin American society, global industrialization, capitalism, North American cultural and economic imperialism, and Spain's loss of all its colonies had a significant impact on artistic development.

A definitive moment in the progress of the movement resulted from José Martí's publication of *Ismaelillo* in 1882. The poet and hero, who died fighting for Cuban independence (1853-1895), published *Versos libres* that same year, a collection that followed *Versos sencillos*, published in 1881. All three collections characterized the existential angst of the era as they experimented with new lyrical forms and themes. Martí approached language as a sculptor approaches clay and molded words into new forms. His innovations have allowed him to be considered the first great visionary Latin American poet as he sought to define *Nuestra América*, a Latin American identity struggling for artistic as well as political and economic independence. Throughout the movement, the anguish, emptiness, and uncertainty of modernity provided a unifying thread for poets seeking innovation.

The Mexican modernist Manuel Gutierrez Nájera (1859-1895), was a journalist renowned for his prose writings in his own time. He founded *La Revista Azul*, a literary review that promoted *Modernismo* throughout Latin America. His contemporary Rubén Darío (1867-1916), however, defined the *Modernista* poetic. Darío's poetry was a reaction to the decadence of Romanticism in which he sought a unique voice while reinvigorating the Spanish language. He led a movement that borrowed themes popularized by the European Romantics and stylistic models of the French Parnassian movement. Darío not only was an instigator and initiator of the vindication of his language, but also served as a bridge to the second stage of *Modernismo*. His *Azul* (1888; blue), *Cantos de vida y esperanza, Los cisnes, y otros poemas* (1905; songs of life and hope, the swans, and other poems), and *Poema de otoño y otros poemas* (1910; poem of autumn and other poems) represent Darío's dynamic style, respect for beauty, search for harmonious words, and celebration of pleasure. Despite the decadence of his later poetry collections, Darío maintained confidence in the saving power of art and its use to protest against social and historical injustices and resolve existential enigmas. The *Modernistas* defended humanism in the face of economic progress and international imperialism, which devaluated art. They elevated art as an end in itself.

Leopoldo Lugones (1874-1938) was the major Argentinean *Modernista* poet. His poems "Delectación morosa," "Emoción aldeana," and "Divagación lunar"

lament ephemeral beauty captured and immortalized by perfectly placed words. Alfonsina Storni (1892-1938) was influenced by postmodernist tendencies. Her intense verse experimented with Symbolism and other twentieth century innovations. Her vivid sensual poems include "Tú me quieres blanca," "Epitafio para mi tumba," "Voy a dormir," "Hombre pequeñito," and "Fiera de amor." The Uruguayan Delmira Agustini (1886-1914) wrote intensely emotional and erotic poems that highlighted the dualities of human nature. Pleasure and pain, good and evil, love and death create and maintain verbal tension. These opposites struggle for dominance in poems such as "La musa," "Explosión," and "El vampiro."

All of these individual elements come together in these poets' faith in the artistic power of the word. This autonomous aesthetic power opposed the *fin de siglo* (turn of the century) angst resulting from industrialism, positivism, and competing ideologies. While reflecting on their predecessors, the *Modernistas* created original verse with unique usage of sometimes archaic or exotic words. The language was sometimes luxurious and sensual, adapting classical and baroque usage, from elements of the Parnassians to those of the Pre-Raphaelites to the Art Nouveau and European Symbolist movements and tendencies of decadent Romanticism. The symbolic impact of words characterized the movement as a whole. This all-encompassing factor defines the movement and its existential nature. This poetry is the living expression of an era of spiritual crises, personal and societal anguish, and uncertainty about the future of art as well as humanity's direction as it embarked upon the twentieth century.

POSTMODERNISM AND THE VANGUARD

No exact date marks the transition from Latin American Modernism to postmodernism or to a vanguard movement. A combination of historical and societal factors influenced the artistic development of individual Latin American countries. In the first two decades of the twentieth century, World War I and the Mexican Revolution interrupted artistic and literary exchange between the Old World models and the New World innovators. The urban bourgeoisie, who were patrons of the arts, were displaced. The United States had gradually replaced the European masters in science and industry as well as politics, and its dominance permeated all levels of Latin American society.

Altazor (wr. 1919, pb. 1931), by Chilean Vicente Huidobro (1893-1948), marks a break with the past. Huidobro originated stylistic practices never seen before in Latin American poetry. In *creacionismo*, his personal version of creationism, he sought to create a poem the way nature made a tree. His words, invested with autonomous linguistic and symbolic significance, reinvent themselves by creating a world apart from other words. They are antilyrical, intellectual, and disconnected from emotional and spiritual experience. Nevertheless, Huidobro's world, created by his unique use of words, was a human creation because in it the poet experiences alienation and existential angst. Huidobro's poems "Arte poética," "Depart," and "Marino" voice his despair in isolation.

Huidobro had a significant influence on younger poets, particularly in his development of a school of thought that centered on the theory of *Ultraísmo*, which attempted to construct alternative linguistic choices to those offered by the external world. *Ultraísmo* synthesized Latin American with Spanish and European tendencies. Among those influenced by *Ultraísmo* were Jorge Luis Borges (1899-1986), and in fact Borges became its main proponent. While his short stories have repeatedly caused him to be nominated for the Nobel Prize in Literature, his poetry reveals a linguistic expertise and lyrical genius unparalleled by his contemporaries. He believed that lyricism and metaphysics united to justify the means of the poetic process. This fusion provides the genesis of his most representative poems, "Everything and Nothing," "Everness," "Laberinto," "Dreamtigers," and "Borges y yo."

The Peruvian César Vallejo (1892-1938) developed a unique and distinctive poetic voice. His *Los heraldos negros* (1918; *The Black Heralds*, 1990), *Trilce* (1922; English translation, 1973), and *Poemas humanos* (1939; *Human Poems*, 1968) demonstrate the impossibility of mutual communication and comprehension, the absurdity of the human condition, and the inevitability of death.

In 1945, Gabriela Mistral (1889-1957) was the first Latin American writer to receive the Nobel Prize in Literature. Her verses echo the folksongs and traditional ballads of her native Chile, the Caribbean, and Mexico. They naturally blend native dialects with Castilian in a lyrical fusion. Some of her best poems include "Sonetos a la muerte," "Todos íbamos a ser reinas," "Pan," and "Cosas."

Mistral's countryman Pablo Neruda (1904-1973) also won the Nobel Prize in Literature, in 1971. During his formative years he was influenced by *Modernismo*, experimenting with various styles while serving as an international diplomat. The last stage of his poetry was marked by didacticism and political themes, and he was exiled for his activity in the Communist Party. Neruda sought to create a forum for "impure" poetry that encompassed all experience. His *Canto general* (1950) voiced his solidarity with humanity in his political and poetic conversion. *Odas elementales* (1954; *The Elemental Odes*, 1961) continued his mission of solidarity with the humblest members of creation. Other landmark collections include *Los versos del capitán* (1952; *The Captain's Verses*, 1972) and *Cien sonetos de amor* (1959; *One Hundred Love Sonnets*, 1986). Neruda believed that America and clarity should be one and the same.

The Mexican literary generation known as the *Taller* was led by Octavio Paz (1914-1998). He was awarded the Nobel Prize in Literature in 1990 for his brilliant prose and poetry that defined the Mexican culture and connected its isolation and universality to other cultures. His landmark analysis of poetic theory is proposed in *El arco y la lira* (1956; *The Bow and the Lyre*, 1973). The poetic evolution of linguistic progression considered "signs in rotation" culminated in *Piedra de sol* (1957; *Sun Stone*, 1963) and synthesized all twentieth century poetic theories into a highly original yet distinctly Mexican work. Representative poems include "Himno entre ruinas," "Viento entero," and "La poesía."

The Chilean poet Nicanor Parra (born 1914) developed a unique yet popular style. He called his poems *antipoemas* for their super-realism, sarcasm, self-criticism, and humor. Parra's poetry speaks to the masses and rejects pretension, as the poet revitalizes language and innovates with words in action. His masterwork, *Poemas y antipoemas* (1954; *Poems and Antipoems*, 1967), epitomizes antirhetorical and antimetaphorical free verse. "Soliloquio del individuo" and "Recuerdos de juventud" are representative.

The work of Sara de Ibáñez (1910-1981) represents the antithesis of fellow Uruguayan Delmira Agustini.

Her intellectual and metaphysical themes and neoclassical style allude to the poetry of Sor Juana Inés de la Cruz and Golden Age masters such as Spain's Luis de Góngora y Argote. Love and death are analyzed in "Isla en la tierra," "Isla en la luz," "Liras," and "Soliloquios del Soldado."

The "impure" poetry of Ernesto Cardenal (born 1925) unites political ugliness and the beauty of the imagination. It is characterized by *exteriorismo*, a technique that incorporates propaganda, sound bites, advertisements, and fragments of popular culture into poetry that seeks to convert and enlighten. The aesthetic value of these poems is not overshadowed by their political and spiritual message. Representative collections include *La hora O* (1960), *Salmos* (1967; *The Psalms of Struggle and Liberation*, 1971), *Oración por Marilyn Monroe y otros poemas* (1965; *Marilyn Monroe and Other Poems*, 1975), and *Cántico cósmico* (1989; *The Music of the Spheres*, 1990; *Cosmic Canticle*, 1993).

Rosario Castellanos (1925-1974) is best known for her novels and essays about social injustice in her native Chiapas. Because she focused on the status of women within the Mayan culture, as well as within Mexican society as a whole, she was considered a feminist. Her poetry and prose are concerned with the human condition, not only with the plight of women. Her most representative poems are "Autorretrato," "Entrevista de Prensa," and "Se habla de Gabriel."

Thematically and stylistically more militant and radical, Rosario Ferré (born 1938) writes overtly feminist poetry utilizing elements of symbolism and irony. Her poems include "Pretalamio," "Negativo," "La prisionera," and "Epitalamio." As editor of a literary journal, Ferré introduced feminist criticism to Latin American literature.

Movements on a smaller national scale characterize present-day poetry. They are characterized by experimental, politically and socially conscious efforts. The twenty-first century heralds the work of *los nuevos*, the new poets whose work is linked to national as well as international issues.

Individual postvanguard poets do not identify with particular ideologies. The poetry of Argentineans Mario Benedetti (born 1920) and Juan Gelman (born 1930) deals with personal exile as well as the universal experience of exile. Since the 1980's, women have emerged with empowered poetry that serves as liberation from oppression. Poets including Alejandra Pizarnik (born 1936), Rosario Murillo (born 1951), Giaconda Belli (born 1948), Claribel Alegría (born 1924), Juana de Ibarbourou (1895-1979), and Ana Istarú (born 1960) have given voice to the silent struggles of women striving to realize their potential in a male-dominated society.

Poetry written during the last twenty years of the twentieth century focused on oppression and exile. The focus upon the withdrawal from history as a condition for the poetry of Octavio Paz has shifted to the poet belonging in the historical moment so that poetry has a public place and common concern. Contemporary Latin American poetry has become the process of naming the word and rewriting history in a lived world. The making of that world is the creative act that celebrates the word.

BIBLIOGRAPHY

Agosín, Marjorie. *These Are Not Sweet Girls: Latin American Women Poets*. Fredonia, N.Y.: White Pine Press, 1994. Agosín is a prolific and influential poet as well as a distinguished professor and literary critic. This volume from the Secret Weavers series focuses on the poetic production of Hispanic women since the advent of feminism as expressed through their work, written predominantly during the last thirty years of the twentieth centurty. Agosín edited the collection and translated the poems in this bilingual volume.

Gauggel, Karl H. *El cisne modernista: Sus orígenes y supervivencia*. New York: Peter Lang, 1997. This study examines an icon of Latin American *Modernismo*: the swan, and its multitude of connotations. Gauggel examines its manifestations in the work of Darío, Lugones, Herrea y Reissig, and Jaimes Freyre, among other poets. He explores their roots in the Renaissance and the Spanish Golden Age, as well as neoclassical poets. Gauggel illustrates how poetic traditions were maintained by Sor Juana Inés de la Cruz and other New World poets. This is a fascinating literary adventure spanning several centuries of literary history. In Spanish.

Gonzalez, Mike, and David Treece. *The Gathering of Voices: The Twentieth Century Poetry of Latin Amer-*

ica. New York: Verso, 1992. This study addresses a wide range of topics. The contradictions of Latin American *Modernismo* are explored, including its elements of shock and despair that distinguished it from its predecessors. The roots of the Vanguard movement are examined, and the enduring poetry of Neruda is discussed in detail. Special topics are discussed, such as Brazilian *Modernismo* and the Guerrilla Poets of Cuba. The work concludes with studies of Postmodernism in Brazil and Spanish-language poets in exile. The collaboration between Gonzalez and Treece offers a wide variety of topics and approaches to over a century of poetry.

Green, Roland Arthur. *Unrequited Conquests: Love and Empire in the Colonial Americas.* Chicago: University of Chicago Press, 1999. This volume offers insight into Spanish colonialism, European imperialism, and their influences upon literature. Colonial love poetry is analyzed within its sociopolitical and historical contexts. Chapters are devoted to Sor Juana's fascinating life and works. This illustrated volume provides an extensive list of bibliographical references.

Jiménez, José Olivio, ed. *Antología crítica de la poesía modernista hispano-Americana.* Madrid: Ediciones Hiperión, 1985. This critical anthology discusses the corpus of the most prominent *Modernista* poets. Jiménez is recognized as an authority on Latin American poetry. While Darío's poetry is the primary work, Martí, Lugones, Herrera y Reissig, and Agustini are highlighted. Jiménez lays the groundwork for a thorough understanding of *Modernismo* with a substantial introduction and detailed presentations of each poet. In Spanish.

_____. *Antología de la poesía hispanoamericana contemporánea, 1914-1970.* Madrid: Alianza Editorial, 1984. This anthology continues where Jiménez left off by describing the decadence of *Modernismo* and the origins of several vanguard movements. The first movement was initiated by Vicente Huidobro, and the second stage was characterized by Neruda. Jiménez also discusses several postvanguard developments in the evolution of Latin American poetry. This collection is one of the most complete anthologies of postmodernist poetry. In Spanish.

Ortega, Julio, ed. *Antología de la poesía latinoamericana del siglo XXI: El turno y la transición.* México: Siglo Veintiuno Editores, 1997. Ortega gathers together some of the newest voices in Latin American poetry, including writers who bridge the gap between the postmodernist era and the present. These poets carry on the poetic tradition while breaking with their predecessors stylistically and thematically. Ortega admits that the endurance of their poetry will be tested by time and circumstance. In Spanish.

Rowe, William. *Poets of Contemporary Latin America: History and Inner Life.* New York: Oxford University Press, 2000. This study discusses contemporary Latin American poets who bridge the centuries, including Nicanor Parra, Carmen Ollé, and Ernesto Cardenal. Williams explores two major influences on late twentieth century and early twenty-first century poetry: the avant-garde movement and politically motivated poetic writing. He examines these roots from contextual and historical perspectives.

Smith, Verity. *Encyclopedia of Latin American Literature.* Chicago: Fitzroy Dearborn, 1996. This reference of nearly one thousand pages contains essays of at least fifteen hundred words on major poets, novelists, dramatists, other writers, movements, concepts, and other topics relating to South American, Central American, and Caribbean (including Spanish, French, and English) literatures. Overview essays cover literatures of individual countries, eras, and themes (such as science fiction, children's literature, and indigenous literatures), as well as the literatures of the major U.S. Latino communities: Cuban, Mexican, and Puerto Rican.

Sonntag Blay, Iliana L. *Twentieth-Century Poetry from Spanish America: An Index to Spanish Language Poetry and Bilingual Anthologies.* Lanham, Md.: Scarecrow Press, 1998. Three indexes provide access to more than twelve thousand Latin American poems from seventy-two anthologies: an author index, a title index, and an index of first lines. An important reference for serious scholars.

Spooner, David. *The Poem and the Insect: Aspects of Twentieth Century Hispanic Culture.* San Francisco: International Scholars Publications, 1999. This study examines the historical and literary contexts of poetic work spanning several continents, from Spain to South and Central America, then to Mexico and the United States. Spooner first discusses the work of Federico García Lorca, Antonio Machado, Pedro Salinas, and other Spanish poets. He connects the Old World to the New with analyses of Pablo Neruda and Octavio Paz. Spooner also discusses the innovative work of less well known poets, including Delmira Agustini. He offers some original ideas about some familiar poems.

Tapscott, Stephen. *Twentieth-Century Latin American Poetry: A Bilingual Anthology.* Austin: University of Texas Press, 1996. This is the first bilingual collection of the most important Latin American poets. Portuguese as well as Spanish poems are translated, and the selections cover the full range of the century, from the *Modernistas* to the postmoderns, the vanguardists, and contemporary political and experimental poetry. Tapscott provides background material and introductions to eighty-five poets in a well-organized volume with excellent translations.

Unruh, Vicky. *Latin American Vanguards: The Art of Contentious Encounters.* Berkley: University of Cal-ifornia Press, 1994. This study focuses on the context and the character in the vanguard movements throughout Latin America. Unruh believes that the *Vanguardia* was a form of activity rather than a set of poems with similar characteristics. She demonstrates how the vanguard movement emphasized action in art and how vanguard poetry served as creative action. This perspective sheds new light on the poets' lives as well as their creative acts.

Yurkievich, Saúl. *Suma crítica.* Mexico City: Fondo de Cultura Económica, 1997. Yurkievich is one of the most highly regarded critics of Latin American literature. His analyses have provoked critical response and thoughtful discussion since the 1980's. He delves into the work of the *Modernistas*, including Darío, Lugones, López Velarde, and Gabriela Mistral. His analyses of *vanguardista* poetry address the work of Huidobro, Vallejo, and Neruda. He then demonstrates how the poetry of Borges and Paz goes beyond the limits of the vanguard movement. Yurkievich is a consistently brilliant literary critic. In Spanish.

Carole A. Champagne

LATIN POETRY

Extant Latin poetry dates from 240 B.C.E., when the Greek Livius Andronicus made his first Latin translations of Greek dramas, but there is ample evidence of a poetic tradition in Rome prior to this date. Most literary histories of Rome terminate their surveys with the close of the second century C.E., yet a strong Latin poetic tradition continued in Europe well into the seventeenth century. Further, even if one were to limit the chronological range of Latin poetry to the period between 240 B.C.E. and 1700 C.E., or, yet more narrowly, between 240 B.C.E. and 200 C.E., the diversity of style and language within the field is striking. The term "Latin" implies a common language, yet Latin itself changed greatly over its active literary life. Just as the English language evolved between the time of Geoffrey Chaucer and William Shakespeare and, again, between that of Shakespeare and W. B. Yeats, so does the Latin of the earliest poets differ markedly from that of the great first century B.C. poet, Vergil, and Vergil's Latin from Latin poetry of the Renaissance.

Latin poetry is at times termed "Roman." The word "Roman" links the poetry with the city that controlled the Mediterranean world between the second century B.C.E. and the fourth century C.E., yet remarkably few Latin poets were native Romans. Many were from other areas of Italy—areas that did not receive full-citizen status until the first century B.C.E.; others came from scattered parts of the Roman Empire, including Spain and North Africa. Like the empire in which it evolved, then, Latin poetry was diverse and cosmopolitan, and its development cannot be separated from the political and social history of Rome and its empire.

To allow discussion of such a complex poetic tradition in a manageable way, the history of Latin poetry is here divided into seven chronological periods: its origins to 264 B.C.E.; early Republican poetry, from 264 to 100 B.C.E.; late Republican poetry, from 100 to 27 B.C.E.; Augustan Age poetry, from 27 B.C.E. to 14 C.E.; Silver Age poetry, from 14 to 138 C.E.; Latin poetry in late antiquity, from 138 to 476 C.E.; and medieval and Neo-Latin poetry, from 476 to 1700 C.E. Discussion of each period includes a historical overview that focuses on events of major significance in the evolution of Latin poetry, an outline of contemporary literary trends, and a survey of several important poets of the period in the context of these historical and literary perspectives.

ORIGINS TO 264 B.C.E.

Compared to societies in the eastern Mediterranean, Rome was a late bloomer. At the peak of Egyptian civilization, the ancestors of the Romans apparently had not yet inhabited central Italy. In the seventh century B.C.E., by which time Greece had already produced Homer, Hesiod, and Sappho, the inhabitants of Latium were still primitive herdsmen and farmers. The social organization was patriarchal. The basic unit was the *familia*, which included not only the immediate but also the extended family, as well as slaves and other members of the household, over which the *paterfamilias*—that is, the oldest living male—held absolute authority.

Roman society's agricultural and familial orientation was reflected in its religious life, which revolved around a host of divinities: Jupiter and Mars, who controlled fertility; the Lares and Penates, who were the personal gods of each household; Vesta, who was the goddess of the hearth; and a host of others. Civic worship paralleled private cults, and the city of Rome had its own Lares and Penates as well as virgin priestesses of Vesta who oversaw the state hearth. To a great extent, the traditional relationship of a Roman to his state was considered to parallel that of a member of the *familia* to his *paterfamilias*, and a Roman was expected to exhibit the same *pietas*, or sense of piety and respect, toward the state that he demonstrated toward his own father. In addition to *pietas*, other traditional Roman virtues were distinctly agricultural in character and included industry, obedience, and seriousness. All of these qualities played an important thematic role in Roman literature from its inception.

Beyond the *familia*, the basic social units were the *pagi*, villages or cantons, which were only loosely united into several population groups (Latins, Sabines, Umbrians, and Lucanians, among others) partially based upon dialects such as Latin, Oscan, or Umbrian. There was little unity among these groups and frequent warfare.

A significant change occurred in central Italy around 650 B.C.E., when Latium was invaded by the Etruscans, a mysterious people who had inhabited Tuscany in north-central Italy for at least several centuries. The provenance of the Etruscans lies outside the scope of this essay, but their influence upon the Latins politically, socially, and culturally cannot be underestimated. It was the urban-oriented and highly civilized Etruscans, many scholars believe, who caused the tribal Italians to settle in cities, and through whom the Italians were first exposed to Greek civilization.

In matters of religion, the Etruscans brought the Latins a more formal set of rituals, especially pertaining to augury. Under Etruscan influence, the taking of auspices by special priests called *augures* became customary prior to many public and private acts. Further, Roman temples and cult statues came to be based upon Etruscan models. Such features of Roman religion became important themes in Latin literature, which, throughout its development, was continuously affected by changes in Roman religious beliefs and practices.

The founding of the city of Rome, traditionally dated to 735 B.C.E., is shrouded by diverse myths and legends, but archaeological evidence suggests that the site was inhabited early in the first millennium B.C.E., principally by Latin tribes, although there is a possibility that the city was founded under Etruscan influence.

Etruscan rule for at least part of Rome's early history is well supported by ancient evidence. Of the seven legendary kings of Rome, two, Tarquinius Priscus (commonly known as Tarquin the First) and Tarquinius Superbus (commonly known as Tarquin the Proud), were Etruscan in origin. Traditionally, the expulsion of the latter from Rome in 510 B.C.E. marked the end of Etruscan rule of the city and the founding of the Roman Republic.

Very early in their urban history, the Romans developed a two-tiered social structure. The small, privileged class of patricians were large landowners who controlled and protected numerous tenants and laborers under a patron-client relationship. In the early Republic, only members of patrician families could hold important political offices, such as the consulship, or become members of the Roman Senate. The mass of people were called the *plebs* or plebeians, and much of the history of the early Roman Republic is marked by the struggle of the plebeian class to wrest itself from the political and economic stranglehold of the patricians. De-

spite periodic compromises, this class conflict was never resolved during the lifetime of the Roman Republic. To a large extent, literature, as it developed especially in the Republican period, was composed by and for the patrician class. Plebeians usually achieved only limited literacy in this period and generally lacked the leisure time to read and to create literary texts.

In addition to class conflict, the early years of the Republic are marked by a series of wars between Rome and her neighbors and by the gradual absorption of the Italian Peninsula into the Roman sphere of influence. The Latin peoples were brought into a voluntary military federation called the Latin League, which gradually evolved into a Roman dependency: Keeping the name *socii* (allies), the Latins retained their local self-government and local citizenship but were forced to yield all foreign policy decisions to Rome. The invasion of north Italy by a Celtic tribe of Gauls and their brief capture of Rome in 390 B.C.E. were traumatic events which left a permanent mark on the Roman psyche. Threat of foreign seizure thenceforth became a frequent political rallying point for the Roman people. The fourth century B.C.E. was also marked by the gradual conquest of Etruscan cities by Rome, beginning with the Roman capture of Veii in 396 B.C.E. The same century witnessed a series of conflicts called the Samnite Wars, fought against Italian tribes in the southern peninsula, which led ultimately to Roman control of all Italy south of the Po Valley. This territorial expansion by Rome during the fourth century B.C.E. was the beginning of a remarkable military growth leading to Roman rule of the entire Mediterranean basin by the end of the millennium.

Such rapid expansion was not without its ramifications on Rome itself. The city may have absorbed Italy politically, but at least two centuries passed before her allies became completely Romanized; the intervening period was marked by revolts by various *socii*. Further, Rome's growth brought her suddenly into contact with two more advanced civilizations, the Etruscans in the north and the Greeks in the south. Such contacts transformed Roman society profoundly, not the least in the area of poetic expression.

Writing appears to have been introduced to Latium by the Etruscans, since it was the Etruscan alphabet rather than its Greek parent which was adapted to the

Latin language. The earliest surviving inscriptions can be dated to about 500 B.C.E., and there are no extant literary pieces prior to about 240 B.C.E. The written Latin of the period from 500 to 240 B.C.E. is primarily legal and religious in character. Extant examples of primitive Latin include such legal documents as the *Leges regiae* (*The Laws of the Kings*) and the famous Twelve Tables, both of which survive in late prose adaptations but which were probably originally composed in verse. A priestly literature developed around formalized Roman ritual, and fragments of texts listing the order of ceremonies and lists of feasts (*fasti*) survive. Other extant documents include epitaphs (such as the famous inscriptions on the Scipios) and a few fragments from political and dedicatory monuments.

The Romans themselves maintained a tradition of oral literature but unfortunately lacked a Latin Homer or Hesiod to transform their oral compositions into written texts. Because none of this oral Latin poetry survives, many modern scholars deny the existence of any Latin poetry prior to 240 B.C.E. Such a view is extreme. Like other primitive cultures, the early Latins probably possessed some native forms of oral poetic expression. While these oral forms did not survive Rome's transformation from an oral to a literate culture and the exposure of Rome to Etruscan and Greek literary traditions, these native Latin forms were nevertheless remembered by later Romans and left their mark on written Latin literature.

The earliest Latin verse was composed in a metrical system that was probably accentual, like native English verse, rather than quantitative, like the system that later Latin poets adapted from Greek models. These later poets named the native form *versus saturnius* (Saturnian verse), referring to the mythical golden age of the god Saturn. A few examples of this verse survive, but the texts are so corrupt that it is impossible to reconstruct the actual metrical system with certainty. The ancient evidence suggests that Saturnian verse was used for a variety of literary purposes: religious verses, such as the extant *Carmen Arvale* (*Song of the Arval Brothers*, a hymn to Mars); popular forms, such as lullabies and aphorisms; *carmina triumphalia*, greetings to triumphant generals; epitaphs; dirges; and perhaps even epic songs about heroes of the past.

Two native literary forms warrant special mention because of their influence on later Latin poetic genres: *versus fescennini* (Fescennine verses) and *satura*. The Fescennine verses were probably connected originally with agricultural festivals but came to be used also at such celebrations as weddings and military triumphs. Significant features of this form include banter or repartee, which is often cited as a primitive stage in native Italian drama, and ribaldry or invective, thought to have been originally apotropaic in character and to have been influential in the development of later forms of Latin ribaldry, such as the harsh invectives of Catullus and Martial and the biting satires of Juvenal.

Another native genre was the *satura*, although there is a possibility that the form was actually imported from the Etruscans. The name *satura* may have derived from a Latin word referring to a dish with a variety of foods; ancient references suggest that the *satura* was essentially a medley, a performance in various forms, materials, and moods, including a mixture of singing, dancing, music, and spoken parts. Like the Fescennine verses, the *satura* may have been an early form of Roman drama and was certainly an important stage in the development of Latin satire.

Thus, prior to the Greek-influenced tradition of Latin literature beginning in 240 B.C.E., there was a poetic tradition in Latin that was ancient, indigenous, and oral. Though little survives of this literature, it is clear that it exhibited native Roman characteristics which affected later Latin poetry. Roman *gravitas* was offset by a basic respect for verse and an instinctive awareness of the role of poetry in the sacred and festive occasions of public life. Later Latin literature could not have developed if the Roman character were completely unfamiliar with and unresponsive to such forms of literary expression.

EARLY REPUBLICAN POETRY (264-100 B.C.E.)

This period marks not only the first Roman expansion outside Italy and the beginnings of the Roman Empire, but also the first extant Latin literature. Politically, the period was dominated by Rome's struggle with the city of Carthage, a Punic city on the coast of present-day Tunisia, in a series of three wars usually called the Punic Wars. This conflict, which saw military encounters in Italy, Africa, Spain, and the eastern Mediterranean, led ultimately to the destruction of Carthage in 146 B.C.E. and the recognition of Rome as the political and military power in the Mediterranean. During this period, too, Rome acquired her first provinces—in Sicily, Cisalpine Gaul, Spain, Narbonese Gaul (modern Marseilles), Africa, Greece, and Asia Minor—and first encountered the complex difficulties of foreign occupation and provincial administration. By the end of the second century B.C.E., the demands of empire had made Rome critically dependent upon her far-flung armies and upon politically ambitious generals.

During this period, Rome's political situation continued to be affected by problems of class conflict and social change. In the fifth and fourth centuries B.C.E., the plebeians had wrested several political concessions from the patrician class, including recognition of the legislative rights of the *concilium plebis* (the plebeian assembly) and the veto of the *tribuni plebis* (tribunes of the plebeians). The same period also witnessed the granting, to a few wealthy plebeian families, of political privileges once exclusively patrician, such as admission to the Senate and election to the consulship. The latter changes resulted not so much in increased power for the plebeian class as in a new alliance of wealthy plebeians with patricians, who together came to be called *nobiles* (nobles). During the third and second centuries B.C.E., it was this political group, as members of the Senate, which controlled the city and its growing empire. At the same time, the majority of plebeians, in effect, lost political ground; as the citizen population of Rome was dispersed with the expansion of the franchise, fewer and fewer plebeian citizens could make the long journey to Rome to cast their votes, and the plebeian assemblies were increasingly composed, not of small independent farmers as formerly, but of poor urban masses, including dispossessed peasants and freedmen. Systematic bribery of the urban plebeian population, via such methods as free food distribution and public entertainment, was already common in the second century B.C.E. and demonstrated the widening social and political gap between nobles and plebeians, between Roman citizens and the disenfranchised Italian and provincial populations.

Futile attempts to remedy some of the worst social inequalities were made by the Gracchi brothers, Tiberius and Gaius, toward the end of the second century B.C.E., but the Gracchis' plans for land reform and political enfranchisement of the Italians met with effective opposition by the nobility.

To a large degree, Roman society was unprepared for the dramatic changes brought by the growth of her empire. The necessity for standing armies created both political problems and social difficulties. The need for farmland for retiring veterans, especially in the first century B.C.E., led to widespread land confiscations. No longer were Italian farms worked on a small scale by a single family. The tendency was toward *latifundia*, large estates owned by wealthy absentee landholders and worked by slave labor. The growth of the slave population in Italy was in direct proportion to the growth of the empire, since war captives were the primary source of slaves. A slave-based economy gave Roman nobility more leisure to pursue other interests, such as literature, but it also led to another social problem, slave revolts, which increased in the first century B.C.E.

Empire also brought great wealth into the city, by way of military plunder, taxation, and economic opportunities in the provinces. Many a Roman governor made a quick fortune in the year he spent in his province. The largest fortunes, however, were made not by the nobility, who traditionally despised commerce, but by a growing merchant class, called *equites* (knights), who were not part of the governing nobility. Traditional Roman virtues (such as industry and frugality) were put to a severe test by the city's new wealth, as is evidenced by the need for sumptuary laws in the city as early as the late third century B.C.E.

In addition to wealth, the empire affected Roman society in another basic way by exposing it to foreign and, often, more sophisticated cultures. Although the introduction of exotic religious cults was strictly regulated and officially discouraged, the popularity of rituals such as that of the Eastern goddess Cybele demonstrates the futility of this regulation. The transformation of Roman society from its rustic Latin origins into an urban cosmopolitan center was inevitable.

More than any other conquered people, it was the Greeks who profoundly changed the traditional Roman way of life. Actually, Rome had long been exposed to Greek civilization, especially through commercial contact with the Greek cities of southern Italy and Sicily, called collectively Magna Graecia, but Roman society remained generally unaffected by these early Greek contacts. Roman subjection of the Greek cities on Italian soil, such as Tarentum and Rhegium in the early third century B.C.E., and the founding of Roman provinces in Sicily in 227 B.C.E. and in Greece itself in 197 B.C.E. made inevitable the Hellenization of Roman society. Greek works of art and Greek literary texts began flowing into the capital. Especially in the third century B.C.E., Greek war captives began to educate their masters in Greek ways and customs, and many Romans started to adopt Greek ways. Bilingualism in Greek and Latin became a political and cultural necessity. A famous statement by the Roman poet Horace in his *Epistles* (c. 20-15 B.C.E.) summarizes well the relationship of Greece to Rome: "Captive Greece took its rough victor captive and brought the arts to rustic Latium." In reality, the initial Roman reaction to Hellenism was a combination of admiration and distrust, best demonstrated by the attitudes of two second century B.C.E. statesmen, Marcus Porcius Cato (commonly known as Cato the Censor or Cato the Elder, 234-149 B.C.E.) and Publius Cornelius Scipio Aemilianus (184-129 B.C.E.). Cato the Censor spent most of his career advocating traditional Roman values and education and condemning Greek voluptuousness and duplicity. By contrast, Scipio Aemilianus—the conqueror of Carthage and adopted son of Scipio Africanus, the defeater of Hannibal—was a staunch Hellenophile and the leader of an intellectual group that included some of the outstanding Greeks and Romans of his day. Members of this "Scipionic circle" included the Greek historian Polybius, the Stoic Greek philosopher Panaetius, the Latin dramatist Terence, and the Latin satirist Lucilius. Later enthusiastic Hellenists included the Gracchi brothers. The resolution of this conflict was presaged by Cato the Censor himself, who toward the end of his life took up the study of Greek.

The third and second centuries B.C.E. were also marked by dissemination of Greek philosophical ideas in Rome. The three popular Hellenistic schools—the Platonists, the Epicureans, and the Stoics—all sent representatives to Rome and all had their Roman advocates, but of the three, Stoicism, with its emphasis on virtue and endurance, proved to be most appealing to the Roman character. Except for a few attempts at philosophic

poetry, the period was largely given to the assimilation of Greek philosophy; there were no noteworthy Roman attempts at philosophy, in either prose or poetry, until the first century B.C.E. By the time of Augustus, Greek philosophy had become completely assimilated, and it is nearly impossible to read a passage in Latin literature that does not reveal the influence of Greek philosophy in some form.

The earliest extant Latin literature is datable to the period just after the First Punic War, and it is perhaps not coincidental that the first known Latin author, Lucius Livius Andronicus, was a war captive from the Greek city of Tarentum in southern Italy. Indeed, all the Latin poets of the period came from conquered territory, and it is only in prose that a few native Roman authors are known. This early period of Latin literature was marked by the assimilation of Greek literary themes and genres into the Latin language and by the blending of these Greek types with the native Roman literary temperament and forms of expression. Indeed, while these earliest poetic attempts were mostly Latin translations or adaptations of Greek works, within one generation after Livius Andronicus, Latin authors were putting a distinctively Roman imprint on the foreign literary forms which they had assimilated and Latin literature was launched on a life of its own. It is unfortunate that this early Latin literature, with a few exceptions, survives only in fragments; it was apparently read and admired by Romans for many generations, but its influence on later authors is difficult to gauge from its fragmentary state.

The earliest Roman prose appears at the time of the Punic Wars, and Greek influence is demonstrated by the fact that the first Romans to write history, Fabius Pictor and Lucius Cincius Alimentus, wrote in Greek. The first Roman to write history in Latin was Cato the Censor, whose seven books of *Origines* (origins) covered the history of Rome to 149 B.C.E. and were a landmark in Latin prose. Cato the Censor also demonstrated his skill in prose composition in several didactic works, including the extant *De agri cultura* (c. 160 B.C.E.; *On Agriculture*), and in his speeches, some of which he published. Roman oratory, a native field of expression, was encouraged by Rome's political system and eventually fused with the Greek rhetorical tradition. The periodic prose of Cicero in the first century B.C.E. was the result.

The history of Latin poetry begins with a Latin translation of Homer's *Odyssey* (c. 800 B.C.E.) by the Tarentine Greek, Lucius Livius Andronicus (commonly known as Livius, c. 284-204 B.C.E.). Livius's *Odyssey*, in Saturnian verse, apparently originated as a school text and was quickly followed by adaptations of Greek comedies and tragedies which were actually produced in Rome and in which Livius introduced Greek meters into Latin. Greek quantitative meters were quite different from the apparently accentual, native Saturnine verse, and many Latin words would not fit the Greek quantitative patterns. Yet, within a generation, Greek meters had replaced the Saturnian as the normal poetic medium in Latin. Livius, who is often justly called the "father of Latin literature," also composed some lyrics, about which little is now known.

Gnaeus Naevius (c. 270-201 B.C.E.), an Italian from Campania, continued Livius's adaptations of Greek literature into Latin, but with a bit more originality in that he sometimes replaced Greek stories with Roman ones. This is true in drama, where he not only adapted Greek comedies to Latin but also composed *fabulae praetextae*, plays on historical Latin themes. It is also true in epic, where he produced the first original epic in Saturnian verse, *Bellum Punicum* (*The Punic War*). Thus began the nationalistic vein which became a near constant in later Latin literature. Naevius's career also shows another, more unfortunate link between poetry and politics in Rome: the personal risks with which the Latin political poet often was confronted. Naevius, who died in exile for offending in verse the powerful Metelli family, was but the first of many Latin poets to suffer political oppression.

While the history of Roman drama generally lies outside the scope of this essay, it should be mentioned that the trends begun by Livius Andronicus and Naevius were continued by several generations of playwrights, including the extant comic authors Titus Maccius Plautus (commonly known as Plautus, c. 254-184 B.C.E.) and Publius Terentius Afer (commonly known as Terence, c. 195-159 B.C.E.), as well as the tragedians Marcus Pacuvius (commonly known as Pacuvius, c. 220-130 B.C.E.) and Lucius Accius (commonly known as Accius, c. 170-86 B.C.E.). Like their dramatic predecessors, none of these authors was from Latium, and all continued to produce adaptations of Greek originals or, more rarely, *fabulae praetextae*.

Drama in Rome was also important as a means of transmitting Greek culture to the plebeian class. While the other literary forms of the period were, for the most part, directed toward the educated, leisured classes, drama was intended for public performance, especially at religious and civic festivals, and hence introduced less educated Romans to the new, Hellenized Latin literature. The popular, oral literary forms also continued in this period. Although evidence is limited, these forms, too, probably became Hellenized, with Saturnian verse gradually giving way to Greek meters.

Another dramatist of the period warrants special mention here because of his prolific nondramatic output. Quintus Ennius (commonly known as Ennius, 239-169 B.C.E.) was from Calabria in southern Italy. In addition to at least twenty known tragedies (including one *fabula praetexta* titled *Rape of the Sabines*) and a few comedies, Ennius produced a major epic, *Annales*, in eighteen books covering the history of Rome from Aeneas to Ennius's own day. Ennius's epic, which survives only in fragments, apparently owed much to the annalistic tradition in Rome, to the Greek epic genre, and to his precursor Naevius. One of Ennius's most significant contributions to the Latin epic was his use of dactylic hexameter, the traditional Greek epic meter, rather than Saturnian verse, which was never again used in a Latin epic. Besides the *Annales*, Ennius tried his hand at elegiac verse, as well as at several lost didactic works with philosophic themes: *Epicharmus*, a poem about the famous Sicilian Pythagorean, and *Euhemerus*, a work, perhaps in verse, on the well-known Greek rationalist.

Ennius also wrote four books of satire. In the native Latin tradition of satiric medleys, these books were a miscellany of themes and meters. Gaius Lucilius (c. 180-103 B.C.E.), a Campanian and a member of the Scipionic circle, followed Ennius in writing thirty books of satires, also in mixed meters and themes, including political commentary and travel journals. Because the satires of Ennius and Lucilius represent a native Latin genre and inevitably influenced later writers such as Horace and Juvenal, their loss creates a most unfortunate lacuna in the history of Latin poetry.

The literature that arose in Rome in the mid-third century B.C.E. may have been stimulated primarily by outside influence, but it began a literary development which led directly to Vergil and Horace and which continued for more than fifteen hundred years. Rome's debt to Livius Andronicus, Naevius, Ennius, and Lucilius is immeasurable.

LATE REPUBLICAN POETRY (100-31 B.C.E.)

The final decades of the Roman Republic were a tumultuous period politically and socially and an exciting period intellectually. It is indicative of the age that some of its most politically active figures, such as Caesar and Cicero, found the time to write, both in prose and in verse. While most of the surviving texts of the period are historical or political prose, the late Republic was not an age exclusively of politics or prose. There is evidence of a poetic movement, although most of the contemporary poetry has now been lost. It is generally impossible to separate the politics from the literature of the period, but such a blending of purposes was never really a literary flaw in Roman eyes. In the late Republic flourished some of Rome's most versatile authors, who were prominent politicians as well as writers skilled in both prose and verse. By the next generation, authors tended to limit their attention to either prose or poetry.

The period from 100 to 31 B.C.E. was a time of nearly constant warfare, both on the borders of the empire and, more seriously, within Italy itself. The political events of this period not only led to basic changes in Roman political and social structures but also became a subject for later Roman poetry (such as Lucan's *Bellus civile*, better known as *Pharsalia*). The basic problem was the inability of Republican institutions to satisfy the political ambitions of rival military men. The 80's B.C.E. witnessed a bitter power struggle between two generals, Gaius Marius, a native of north Italy and victor of the Jurgurthan War, and Lucius Cornelius Sulla, a member of an old noble family and hero of the war against Mithradates in the East. The forces of both sides exercised such horrible reprisals against each other that the old noble families were severely decimated. After Marius's death in 85 B.C.E., the conservative Sulla ruled Rome as dictator from 82 to 79 B.C.E. and attempted to revive the Republican constitution by means of a pro-

gram of aristocratic reforms, including restrictions on the powers of the tribunes and enlargement of the Senate by admission of individuals of equestrian rank and of Italian background.

Sulla's reforms were unsuccessful, however, and his confidence in the Republic was unwarranted. The political chaos of the 80's B.C.E. was only a foreshadowing of worse turmoil later in the century. Within a generation of Sulla's death, several ambitious generals once again were contending for power. Both Gnaeus Pompeius Magnus (commonly known as Pompey) and Gaius Julius Caesar used their military careers—Pompey's in Spain and in the eastern Mediterranean, Caesar's in Gaul—to further their own political ambitions. By 49 B.C.E., Pompey and Caesar had thrown the Republic into a fatal civil war. Most of the old aristocratic families supported Pompey as champion of the Republic, but their cause was lost at the sea battle of Pharsalus in 48 B.C.E. Unlike Sulla, Caesar followed his victory with clemency toward his opponents, but his acceptance of an unprecedented dictatorship for life incited his assassination by desperate Republicans led by Cassius and Brutus in 44 B.C.E.

Caesar's death precipitated a period of even more violent unrest. Marcus Antonius, Caesar's trusted lieutenant, and Gaius Julius Caesar Octavianus (commonly known as Octavian), Caesar's grandnephew and adopted son, overcame mutual distrust only long enough to defeat Caesar's assassins, at Philippi in 42 B.C.E., before they turned on each other. The following decade was marked by another wave of proscriptions (including the death of the great orator Cicero), by confiscation of the property of political enemies, by civil war throughout the empire, and even by foreign incursions on the borders, especially by the feared Parthians in the East. The entire empire was in danger of disintegration.

For a time, it appeared that the empire would be divided between Octavian, who controlled the West, including Italy, and Antony, who ruled the East and had allied himself with Cleopatra, the Ptolemaic ruler of Egypt. Octavian's propaganda, however, making much of Antony's "orientalization" and of his liaison with Cleopatra, succeeded in swaying popular opinion, and in 31 B.C.E., Octavian defeated his rival in a sea battle at Actium.

Octavian's victory placed him in unquestioned control of the empire. For all practical purposes, the Republic was defunct, although Republican institutions, such as the Senate, were allowed to continue. Octavian, who took the name Caesar Augustus (the Revered Caesar) after Actium, may have avoided *rex*, the Latin word for "king," and preferred the title *imperator* (general), but he was monarch in all but name. Augustus's political settlement introduced a period of peace and tranquillity which contrasted starkly with the terrors of the Republic's final decades.

By the first century B.C.E., the social changes caused by the expansion of the Roman Empire and Rome's contacts with the Greeks had become nearly complete. Rome, no longer the society of farmers with traditional values that she had been in the third century B.C.E., was wealthy and cosmopolitan. Roman society had also become more Italian in background and Greek in culture.

Indeed, probably the most significant social development in the first century B.C.E. was the social unification of Italy. Bound politically to Rome since the fourth century B.C.E., the Italian tribes were thoroughly Latinized by the first century B.C.E., when their demand for political enfranchisement, climaxed by the so-called "Italian Wars" of 91-83 B.C.E., was a vivid indication of their assimilation into Roman political society. Italians in this period came to play visible roles in Roman politics and letters. Sulla's reorganization of the Senate increased the number of Italian senators. Marius and Cicero both hailed from the same north Italian town. Sallust the historian was from Sabine country, and Catullus was a native of Verona, in what was then called Transpadane Gaul. It took the Italian Wars to force the Roman ruling class to recognize the fact, but by the first century B.C.E. the distinction between Roman and Italian was a fine one. In fact, Latin was, by this time, rapidly replacing the local Italian dialects and was beginning to become the language of trade throughout the western Mediterranean.

At the same time, Greek language and literature had achieved a permanent place in Roman society and were considered an essential part of a good education. Indeed, it became fashionable for Romans to travel to Greece to complete their education. Both Cicero and Caesar, for example, studied rhetoric at Rhodes. The effect of Greek philosophic training on nearly every important figure of the period—including that of Stoicism on Cato the Younger and of Epicureanism on Caesar and Lucretius—is also evident.

Another important change in Roman life was the liberation of Roman women, who traditionally had no legal or political rights and were absolutely bound to a male guardian. About the time of the Punic Wars, the status of women began to change, and they won increasing freedom to own property, to become educated, and to move about in society. While women never gained the right of suffrage in Rome, they did manage a great amount of indirect political influence. For example, Cornelia, the daughter of Scipio Africanus and mother of the Gracchi brothers, was the leader of an intellectual salon in the mid-second century B.C.E., while in the first century B.C.E., Clodia, the sister of the politician Publius Clodius, became the powerful leader of a notorious social circle and was perhaps the inspiration for Catullus's Lesbia.

At the same time, marriages became a tool of political alliance, and women were divorced and married as the political wind changed. Pompey's marriage to Caesar's daughter Julia was originally a sign of *amicitia*, or "friendship," between the two leaders. Apparently, this marriage was an unexpected success, and Julia's untimely death is usually cited as a major cause of the rift between her father and her husband. Antony's divorce from Octavian's sister Octavia, in order to marry Cleopatra, led to the Battle of Actium. Nevertheless, while women obviously played significant roles in the political and social life of he first century B.C.E., it would be at least another generation before a first female voice entered Latin literature.

Wealth and education led to more sophisticated and ostentatious social intercourse. The wealthy nobility led lives of luxury, with fancy city residences and huge country villas. Their farms and wealth were overseen by others, and they could devote themselves to politics, partying, and literature. The uncertain political situation and the fear of confiscation or even proscription fostered a life-style of gay abandon and recklessness. Traditional Roman *gravitas* (seriousness) gave way to a sophisticated sense of *urbanitas* (urbanity) and *humanitas* (culture), evident in both the life and the literature of the period.

The succession of proscriptions and wars during the century meant the loss of nearly an entire generation of young Romans. That Roman letters flourished as much as they did during this period is a testament to the tenacity of the Roman people. One of the most pathetic images of this determination is that of the elderly scholar Marcus Terentius Varro (commonly known as Varro, 116-27 B.C.E.) pursuing his studies in Rome even though his villa and books had been confiscated by Antony.

The literature of the late Republic was directed almost exclusively toward the educated classes and is for the most part intensely political. It was an age of political and historical prose written by men intimately involved in the politics of the day. It was also an age of verse. While only the poetry of Titus Lucretius Carus (commonly known as Lucretius, c. 98-55 B.C.E.) and of Gaius Valerius Catullus (commonly known as Catullus, c. 85-c. 54 B.C.E.) survives from this period, nearly all the contemporary prose authors, including Marcus Tullius Cicero (commonly known as Cicero, 106-43 B.C.E.) and Gaius Julius Caesar (commonly known as Caesar, 102-44 B.C.E.), also composed in verse.

By far the most famous prose writer of the period was Cicero, whose rhetorical talents early fostered political ambitions. Although he did attain the coveted consulship in 63 B.C.E., Cicero's career was generally overshadowed by the conflict between Pompey and Caesar, and in his later years he was left to direct his energies toward philosophy and letters. Cicero's extant corpus is extensive and includes fifty-seven public speeches, several books of epistolary correspondence, and several treatises on politics, rhetoric, and philosophy. Cicero is particularly admired for his periodic prose and was a pioneer in adapting the Latin language to Greek philosophic concepts.

Cicero was also a poet in his own right. He translated several Hellenistic Greek poems into Latin, wrote a short poem in hexameters on the general Marius, and even composed an autobiographical epic titled *De consulatu suo* (*On His Consulship*). While his poetic output survives only in fragments, Cicero did make a lasting imprint on Latin poetry as the probable editor of the poet Lucretius.

By contrast to Cicero's elaborate sentence structures, the prose of Caesar is concise and direct. His extant

works are political commentaries, *Comentarii de bello Gallico* (52-51 B.C.E.; *On the Gallic War*) and *Comentarii de bello civili* (45 B.C.E.; *On the Civil War*). He also wrote speeches, letters, treatises on grammar and astronomy, a tragedy, and even love poems, all of which have been lost. That the most significant and active statesman of his day found the time for such a diverse literary output is an indication of the high degree of culture which Roman society had achieved.

Other historical texts of the period also demonstrate the pervasiveness of contemporary politics in Roman letters. Gaius Sallustius Crispus (commonly known as Sallust, 86-35 B.C.E.) served Caesar in Africa during the Civil War and spent his remaining years enjoying a luxurious estate in Rome and writing history. Abandoning the annalistic method favored by earlier Latin historians, Sallust wrote several thematic histories, two of which are extant, *Bellum Catilinae* (*The Catilinarian War*) and *Bellum Jurgurthum* (*The Jurgurthian War*). In both works, Sallust demonstrates his Caesarian and anti-Republican biases. Another historian of the period, Cornelius Nepos (c. 100-25 B.C.E.), wrote a universal history as well as a collection of Greek and Roman biographies, some of which survive. While Nepos appears to have avoided political bias by emphasizing Greek or noncontemporary subjects, even here politics intrudes with Nepos's juxtaposition of Cato the Younger to great generals of the past. Like Cicero and Caesar, Nepos composed some poetry and received the dedication of Catullus's book of poems.

The scholar Varro perhaps best shows the bond between prose and poetry in the first century B.C.E. A prolific writer and scholar in the Alexandrian tradition, Varro is known to have composed numerous antiquarian and technical works, including the extant *De lingua Latina* (*On the Latin Language*) and *De re rustica* (*On Agriculture*), and he is believed to have been an early editor of the plays of Plautus. As a poet, Varro was best known in antiquity for 150 books of *Saturae Menippeae* (Menippean satires). Unlike the early satires of Ennius and Lucilius, which were in verse, Varro's apparently were modeled on the philosophic dialogues of the third century B.C.E. Greek Cynic Menippus and were a mixture of verse and prose. Varro thus introduced into Latin a special satiric form, the prose-poetry medley, which would be explored by Seneca and Petronius and eventually carried into the medieval Latin tradition.

Only two poetic works survive from the late Republic: Lucretius's epic poem *De rerum natura* (c. 60 B.C.E.; *On the Nature of Things*) and Catullus's *Carmina* (*Poems*). Both works show strong Hellenistic influence. Lucretius composed his didactic epic based upon the philosophy of the late fourth century B.C.E. Greek Epicurus, while Catullus wrote a collection of short, mostly erotic poems in mixed meters according to Alexandrian poetic standards. There were many other poets of the period whose works do not survive. Indeed, Catullus was part of a poetic movement in Rome calling itself the Neoterics or *novi poetae* (new poets), who modeled their works on the Alexandrian standards of brevity, obscurity, and skill. Besides Catullus, other known *novi poetae* included Varro of Atax, Gaius Helvius Cinna (commonly known as Cinna), and Gaius Licinius Calvus. Without the knowledge that these poets flourished in the first century B.C.E., one might be tempted to consider Lucretius and Catullus anomalies of their age.

In a sense, both Lucretius and Catullus sought escape from their intensely political and dangerous age through their poetry. Lucretius appears to have isolated himself from politics and to have absorbed himself in Epicureanism, a much misunderstood philosophy which taught that the true goal of life was a pleasure achieved through *ataraxia* (nondisturbedness). A true Epicurean would not lead a life of luxury and debauchery, but rather would sever himself from the hectic world and lead a life of simplicity in the country. Epicureanism did not always appeal to the Roman mentality as much as other Greek philosophies, such as Stoicism, but it did seem to offer some attraction in the chaotic first century B.C.E. Caesar had a reputation as an Epicurean, and Cicero is said to have edited Lucretius's *On the Nature of Things*.

Unlike Lucretius, Catullus apparently did not avoid a political career but attempted unsuccessfully to make his fortune as a member of the provincial staff of a governor named Memmius, who may have been the same person to whom Lucretius addressed his epic. Catullus responded to his age not by losing himself in philosophy but by abandoning himself to his art and to his love for a woman called "Lesbia" in his poems. His poetry is intensely personal, sometimes obscene, often containing bitter invective. While such contemporary figures as Caesar and Nepos are named in Catullus's poems, they are mentioned only in passing. Catullus's focus is not on the momentous events taking place in the outside world but on the intensely personal world of his own feelings. Like Lucretius, Catullus was an escapist, and it is sometimes difficult to remember that both Lucretius and Catullus were contemporaries of Cicero and Caesar. Yet, despite their differences, the poetry and prose of the first century B.C.E. complement each other and together paint a vivid picture of a very turbulent age.

AUGUSTAN AGE POETRY (31 B.C.E.-14 C.E.)

Latin literature was approaching maturity in the first century B.C.E. just as the Republic was collapsing. The reign of Augustus (27 B.C.E.-14 C.E.) introduced a period of prolonged peace, a new political order, and the cresting of Latin literature. During this short period flourished such outstanding Latin authors as Livy in history, Vergil in the epic, and Horace in satire and lyric poetry.

The new literature was a mirror of a new age. Relief after the horrors of civil war and pride in the reestablished Roman state under Augustus permeate the age and its literature. These feelings of relief and pride were justified: It is a tribute to Augustus's military, political, and administrative skills that Rome did not merely survive the chaos of the first century B.C.E. but entered the next century with relatively settled territorial boundaries and a revised system of government which worked, with minor modifications, for several hundred years.

A major principle of the new Augustan order was continuity. Far from eliminating Republican institutions and practices, Augustus maintained and encouraged them. The population of the Senate, severely diminished by a generation of civil wars, was buttressed by an influx of members from Italy and from the equestrian rank. Augustus's own powers were consistently defined in Republican terms; he was, at different times, *imperator* (general), consul, tribune, and *pontifex maximus* (chief priest). Thus, he sought to establish the notion that the Republic had been restored, not destroyed, under his rule.

A second Augustan principle was security. Augustus's defeat of Antony at Actium introduced a period of unprecedented peace within the boundaries of the empire. It would be nearly one hundred years before this Pax Romana (Roman Peace) was broken by a serious internal conflict. The problem of control of the armies was temporarily solved by making Augustus commander in chief and by fostering military allegiance to the emperor alone. During Augustus's reign, the empire made major territorial additions, especially along its northern boundaries, which provided more secure and natural limits.

As a result of this sudden political security in the Mediterranean, the empire entered a period of unprecedented prosperity. Agriculture and commerce flourished, especially in the provinces, and foreign trade increaed significantly. Roman traders were making contacts in areas as far away as Britain, Scandinavia, India, and Mongolia. Urban life expanded and improved not only in Rome itself but also in other centers of population and trade. It was not long before municipal centers, constructed upon the Roman model with forums, public baths, and theaters, could be found throughout the empire. For several centuries, the Roman Empire had expanded rapidly; Augustus ushered in a long-overdue period of assimilation.

Augustan policy included a program of social legislation. Deeply concerned about a population decline among old Roman families and committed to restoring ancient Roman virtues, Augustus enacted a series of marriage laws which discouraged celibacy, adultery, and childlessness. While not very effective in countering either the population decline or the lax morals and high living to which wealthy Romans had become accustomed, Augustus's marriage laws reflected an interest in the past and its virtues which can be seen also in the literature of the period, especially in Vergil and Livy.

Indeed, the relationship between literature and public policy was particularly close in the Augustan Age. Augustus was a master of propaganda, as his earlier conflict with Antony demonstrated, and he was vividly conscious of the power of literature to sway public opinion. As a result, he encouraged a system of literary patronage which was based on the ancient patron-client relationship and which had been applied to letters as early as the late Republic (as in the relationship of Memmius to Lucretius and, perhaps, Catullus) or even the early Republic (as in the links between Scipio and the poets

Terence and Lucilius). Under the emperors, such a patronage system became a political and literary necessity. Augustus needed to control the literary output of Rome, and authors needed powerful patrons to protect them from official disfavor.

Augustus's circle included a number of patrons and clients. Marcus Valerius Messalla, one of Augustus's generals, was the patron of Albius Tibullus (commonly known as Tibullus, 48?-19 B.C.E.). Another member of his circle was his niece, the poet Sulpicia (fl. 25-20 B.C.E.), the only feminine voice in ancient Latin literature. Gaius Asinius Pollio (76 B.C.E.-5 C.E.), a general, a historian, and a poet in his own right, "discovered" Publius Vergilius Maro (commonly known as Vergil, 70-19 B.C.E.), who later came under the influence of Gaius Maecenas, Augustus's wealthy adviser. Maecenas was also the patron of the poets Quintus Horatius Flaccus (commonly known as Horace, 65-8 B.C.E.) and Sextus Propertius (c. 57-48 to c. 16-2 B.C.E.), and probably did more than any other individual in the Augustan Age to encourage letters. The emperor himself also showed personal interest in the works of Vergil, Horace, and Livy.

On the other hand, the dangers for a poet in an absolute monarchy were very real, as was proved by the careers of two Augustan poets, Gaius Cornelius Gallus (commonly known as Gallus, 69-26 B.C.E.) and Publius Ovidius Naso (commonly known as Ovid, 43 B.C.E.-17 C.E.), both of whom suffered for their indiscretions against Augustus. Gallus, the probable inventor of the Latin love elegy, was a lieutenant of Augustus in Egypt but was forced to commit suicide because of his administrative incompetence and also, it was hinted, because of his scandalous poetry. Although the cause of Ovid's exile to Tomis in 8 C.E. is also uncertain, it is widely believed that he was banished for his poetry. His *Ars amatoria* (c. 2 B.C.E.; *Art of Love*, 1612) is sometimes cited as the decisive indiscretion, flaunting Augustus's program of moral restoration.

As in the late Republic, Augustan authors wrote primarily for a very limited circle of educated and cultured Romans. There is ample evidence of public recitations and performances, often in the presence of the emperor. Authors of the period thus knew their primary audience intimately. At the same time, however, these writers experienced immediate success and popularity outside the court circle. That lower-class Romans knew these writers and their works is evidenced by graffiti in the ill-fated city of Pompeii, destroyed by an eruption of Vesuvius in 79 C.E.; the walls of Pompeii show quotations from Vergil, Ovid, and even Tibullus. Apparently, the writings of the Augustan Age quickly became standard texts, read by all literate Romans.

The consequence of this patronage system was a curious mixture of censorship, freedom of expression, nationalistic themes, and sophisticated literature. Encouraged to express certain themes and avoid others, writers were permitted free rein within these limits. Both patron and writer agreed that the duty of art was both aesthetic and utilitarian. According to Horace's *Ars poetica* (c. 17 B.C.E.; *The Art of Poetry*), a poet had to express himself *utile et dulce*, "usefully and sweetly." If one were able to create a refined piece of literature that was also intensely nationalistic, this was seen to improve rather than to detract from its literary quality. As a result of such restrictions, the literature of the Augustan Age may lack some of the vibrancy and excitement of the Republican period, but it achieves instead a refinement and polish that blend poetic expression and nationalistic sentiment in perfect proportion. For example, the *Satires* (35 B.C.E., 30 B.C.E.; English translation, 1567) of Horace are devoid of the biting political commentaries which were apparently commonplace in Horace's predecessor Lucilius, but what Horace lacks in what the modern would call "satire," he compensates for with the polish and good humor that he applies to the traditional Roman concept of satire as a medley.

While the late Republic was an age of great prose and poetry, the Augustan Age was, with the brilliant exception of Livy, an age of only outstanding poetry. Certainly, the political climate was not conducive to great oratory such as Cicero's, and history, especially contemporary history, was a delicate subject. Pollio's history of the civil wars conspicuously ended with Philippi, and even the 142 volumes of *Ab urbe condita libri* (c. 26 B.C.E.-15 C.E.; *The History of Rome*, 1600), by Titus Livius, commonly known as Livy, 59 B.C.E.-17 C.E.) were published serially over a span of forty years; Livy did not reach the dreaded civil wars until late in Augustus's reign. The only other major prose text to survive from the period is *De architectura* (*On Architecture*), a practical treatise by Marcus Vitruvius Pollio (commonly known as Vitruvius).

As in the earlier periods of Latin literature, nearly all the writers of the Augustan Age, both in prose and in poetry, were of Italian background. In fact, Tibullus is one of the few Latin writers who was actually born in Latium. By the time of Augustus, Latin literature had become, without question, a literature not merely of Rome, its literary center, but of all Italy.

In addition to the well-known poets of this period, especially Vergil, Horace, and Ovid, there were a great many other contemporary authors whose works are mostly lost. Works by two minor poets of the period survive, the *Cynegetica* of Grattius, a didactic poem on hunting, and the *Astronomica* of Manilius, a similar work on the stars. Both of these poems are modeled on the *Georgics* (37-29 B.C.E.) of Vergil and follow a didactic tradition that can be traced back to Alexandria.

Several characteristics dominate the poetry of the Augustan Age. High poetic standards and careful composition were carried to an extreme. Vergil was a particularly slow craftsman and was so cautious that he requested on his deathbed that the unfinished *Aeneid* be burned. Horace, too, sought perfection of form, especially in his *Odes* (23 B.C.E., 13 B.C.E.).

A second important characteristic of the period was genre innovation. Poets showed a definite inclination toward genres which had not yet been perfected in Latin: Vergil's *Eclogues* (43-37 B.C.E.) imitated the bucolic *Idylls* of the Hellenistic Greek poet Theocritus and represent the center of a great European pastoral tradition, while his *Georgics* combined the Hellenistic type of didactic poetry with Roman love of the countryside. Horace's *Epodes* (c. 30 B.C.E.) and *Odes* were conscious and successful attempts to introduce into Latin the many meters of Greek lyric. Horace's *Epistles* (c. 20-15 B.C.E.) and Ovid's *Heroides* (before 8 C.E.) and *Epistulae ex Ponto* (after 8 C.E.; *Letters from the Black Sea*, 1639) were all poetic variations on the prose letter or sermon. Ovid was also innovative with his *Fasti* (before 8 C.E.; English translation, 1859), a poetic calendar of Roman religious events, and his *Metamorphoses* (c. 8 C.E.; English translation, 1567), a thematic rather than heroic epic based upon tales in which there is a change of form or shape. Finally, poets of this period, especially Tibullus, Propertius, and Ovid, created a new poetic genre, the Latin love elegy, which applied the Greek elegiac couplet to the theme of love.

Epicureanism is a third characteristic of much Augustan poetry. Vergil was taught by an Epicurean named Siro, and this philosophy permeates his work, especially the *Georgics*. The goal of pleasure in a secluded villa is a constant Epicurean theme of Horace, and Tibullus linked the same Epicurean principle with passion for Delia, his mistress, to create an ideal existence, a golden age.

Finally, Augustan poetry is distinguished by a nationalism combining patriotic feeling for Rome's past and for Augustus's settlements with a love of the Italian countryside. This combination can be seen in the *Eclogues*, where Vergil's allusions to the confiscation of his own farm are contrasted with his relief in the new peace instituted by Augustus. The *Georgics*, too, are filled not only with love of Italy but also with praise of Augustus as the savior of the countryside from the ravages of war. The *Aeneid* (c. 29-19 B.C.E.), the great national epic of Rome, uses the story of the Trojan Aeneas, his mission to settle in Italy, and his love for the Carthaginian Dido to praise the old Roman virtues of duty and *pietas* and to herald Rome's future greatness. With the figure of Aeneas, a hero of Greek mythology who settles in Italy, Vergil not only praises the Roman past but also symbolically unites Greek with Roman culture. Vergil's conscious imitation of Homer's *Iliad* (c. 800 B.C.E.) and *Odyssey* (c. 800 B.C.E.) in the *Aeneid* heralds a pride in Latin poetry that had finally reached a level of equality with its Greek models.

Nationalism can also be seen in Horace, especially in the *Odes*, where Augustus is frequently praised, and in Ovid, whose *Metamorphoses* climaxes with the apotheosis of Julius Caesar. In general, nationalism is not a dominant theme in the love elegy, which tends to avoid the outside world of politics in favor of the internal world of love and poetry, although Propertius, especially in his last book of *Elegies* (after 16 B.C.E.; English translation, 1854), sought to transform the genre, abandoning the love theme in favor of etiological stories praising the ancient city of Rome.

Augustan poetry, then, was the perfect combination of all the best features of Latin literature: the native Latin genius and character, Hellenistic literature and thought, and careful craftsmanship. The literature of this period, together with that of the last decades of the Roman Republic, represents the greatest literary achievements in Latin, and, for this reason, the approximately eighty-year period lasting from the mid-70's B.C.E. until the death of Augustus in 14 C.E., from the poetry of Lucretius to the works of Ovid, is often justly called Rome's Golden Age of literature.

SILVER AGE POETRY (C.E. 14-138)

The period usually referred to as the Silver Age of Latin literature is bracketed by the accession of Tiberius in 14 C.E. and the death of Hadrian in 138 C.E., and covers the reigns of thirteen very different emperors. The feeling of security created during the reign of Augustus did not last long after his death, in large part because the problems of succession had not yet been satisfactorily solved. While Augustus's four immediate successors, Tiberius, Caligula, Claudius, and Nero, were all his descendants or those of his third wife, Livia, none of the Julio-Claudian emperors, as they are called, felt completely secure on the throne. Their reigns were marked by fear of political intrigue, widespread use of imperial informants, and summary executions, usually of men of senatorial rank. Two of the emperors themselves died violently.

The political nadir of the period was the year 69 C.E., the infamous Year of the Four Emperors, which witnessed a complete breakdown in imperial control and the violent deaths of three emperors in succession. The fourth, Vespasian, restored a measure of stability and established a new "Flavian" dynasty with his succession by his two sons. His second son, Domitian, however, abused his power and was assassinated in 96 C.E. The last emperors of this period, Nerva, Trajan, and Hadrian, all avoided succession difficulties by the ancient Roman custom of *adoptio* (adoption), whereby each ruler chose his successor on the basis not of heredity but of ability. This system of succession established a series of "five good emperors" which lasted nearly a century.

The government became more openly monarchical after Augustus's rule, and the nominal powers of the Senate were gradually eroded. Although the body continued to meet, it did so increasingly to listen to the emperor's decrees rather than to enact its own legislation. The "swan song" of senatorial power occurred with the death of Domitian, when the Senate freely selected Nerva as emperor. Similarly, plebeian powers became extinct. The popular assemblies last met under the reign of Nerva. Nostalgia for the Republic and its freedoms became a theme for some writers and leading men of the period, but sporadic plots to replace despots with more enlightened rulers, especially in the reigns of Nero and Domitian, were aborted. The imperial system was too well established by this time for true Republican government to be restored.

By the reign of Hadrian, the Roman Empire had reached its farthest extent, with the addition of Britain under Claudius and Dacia (modern-day Romania) and Armenia under Trajan. A noteworthy trend of the period was the expansion of the Roman franchise outside Italy, beginning with Spain under Vespasian. Indeed, Spain's complete assimilation into the empire is demonstrated by the fact that the province produced not only the first non-Italian emperor, Trajan, but also most of the major writers of the period, including the two Senecas, Lucan, Quintilian, and Martial.

In general, the first century C.E. was a time of peace and prosperity within the borders of the empire, of increasing urbanization throughout the provinces, and of a growing interest in education. The growth in the number of schools and libraries, both in Italy and in the provinces, was considerable during this period, and this educational trend was perhaps the distinguishing characteristic of the age.

To be sure, Roman society had always been interested in education. In its earliest period, Roman education focused primarily on domestic and agricultural concerns and on traditional values such as discipline. With the introduction of Greek culture on a large scale, during the Punic Wars, education by Greek masters became commonplace. Gradually, there developed a three-tiered system, similar to the grammar-high-school-university sequence, in which a Roman youth was first taught his letters and introduced to classical texts by a *litterator*; then advanced to a *grammaticus*, who taught more than mere grammar, emphasizing oral and written exercises designed to increase the student's logical and compositional skills; and finally worked under a *rhetor*, who

prepared his pupils for public life by instruction in deliberative and forensic skills. The surviving *Controversiae* (English translation, 1900) and *Suasoriae* (*Declamations*, 1974) of Lucius Annaeus Seneca (commonly known as Seneca the Elder, c. 55 B.C.E.-39 C.E.), are good examples of the kind of rhetorical exercises such students would pursue. Even after the fall of the Republic, the study of law and especially of oratory was the goal of most Roman education. Both Ovid and Propertius were educated to be lawyers, and, although they eventually abandoned the law for poetry, the effect of rhetorical studies on their poetry is evident in their language and forms of expression.

This educational system was privately financed and administered until the second century C.E., when there was a noticeable growth of governmental involvement in education. Vespasian fixed an annual salary for rhetoricians; Trajan financed the public education of five thousand poor boys; Hadrian introduced retirement pay for teachers and founded schools throughout the provinces. By the reign of Antoninus Pius (C.E. 138-161), there is evidence that every municipality in the empire had its own educational staff.

Men of letters no longer had to rely for a livelihood solely on the whim of rich patrons, on public recitals, or on wealthy students. A formalized system of education, well on its way to being established in the second century C.E., meant a more secure position for scholars and a very favorable literary climate. An example of this system at work is found in the career of Spaniard Marcus Fabius Quintilianus (commonly known as Quintilian, c. 35-after 96 C.E.), whom Vespasian salaried as a professor of rhetoric and whose extant *Institutio oratoria* (c. 95 C.E.; English translation, 1921) is a valuable record, not only of contemporary rhetorical education but also of literary criticism.

Many writers of the Silver Age also held prominent political positions. Seneca the Younger was tutor and adviser to Nero between 49 and 62 C.E.; the poet Silius Italicus was an informer under Nero, the last Neronian consul in 65 C.E., and proconsul in Asia under Vespasian; Pliny the Younger served in various offices under Nero, Domitian, and Nerva, and as governor of the province of Bithynia under Trajan, with whom he maintained a correspondence which is still extant. The two great historians of the period, Tacitus and Suetonius, both held significant political offices under Trajan, the former as governor of Asia and the latter as master of imperial correspondence.

The Silver Age also held its dangers for writers. Seneca the Younger spent eight years of exile under Claudius, and both he and his nephew, the poet Lucan, were forced to commit suicide under Nero. Both men probably suffered more for their political positions, but their literary creations certainly did not help their causes. The satirist Juvenal is also said to have endured a period of banishment during the reign of Domitian, allegedly because of his lampoons.

The nationalistic themes of the Golden Age receded into the background in the Silver Age, which emphasized instead individualistic feelings. Writers such as Seneca and Pliny in prose and Persius, Juvenal, and Martial in poetry were generally more interested in presenting their personal views than in praising Rome. As a rule, poets forsook nationalistic themes for the safety of the distant past and mythology. Tiberius Catius Asconius Silius Italicus (c. 25-100 C.E.) wrote an epic, *Punica*, about the second Punic war, and Publius Papinius Statius (commonly known as Statius, c. 45-96 C.E.) composed the *Thebaid* (c. 91 C.E.; English translation, 1928), about the War of the Seven against Thebes. Gaius Valerius Flaccus (commonly known as Valerius Flaccus, fl. first century C.E.) wrote an *Argonautica* (English translation, 1863) on the adventures of Jason and the Argonauts. Only Marcus Annaeus Lucanus (commonly known as Lucan, 39-65 C.E.) dared a riskier political epic in his *Pharsalia*, which took as its subject the defeat of Pompey by Caesar. The Republican sympathies that Lucan projected in this epic were undoubtedly a factor in the poet's forced suicide under Nero.

Stoicism also became a very important theme in the literature and thought of the period. The list of Stoic writers of the Silver Age is impressive: Persius, Lucan, and Juvenal in poetry; Seneca, the elder Pliny, and Tacitus in prose. It was not long after this period that the Stoic Marcus Aurelius became emperor.

The men who were emperors from 14 C.E. to 138 C.E. were, as a rule, well educated and often writers and poets themselves. Tiberius was a friend of Messalla, Tibullus's patron, and wrote some poetry of his own. Both Tiberius

and Claudius are said to have composed memoirs, and Claudius's brother Germanicus (15 B.C.E.-19 C.E.) was a talented and prolific writer of Greek comedies, elegiac epigrams in both Latin and Greek, and astronomical didactic poems. The emperor Nero, Germanicus's grandson, also professed vainly to write poetry and produced a variety of short verse, tragic monologues, and an epic on the city of Troy. Vespasian was well educated in Greek literature, could quote Homer fluently, and wrote his own memoirs; both of his sons were poets. Domitian supported public poetic competitions and was a friend of the poet Statius. Trajan encouraged the important writers of his day, including Pliny and the Greek authors Dio Chrysostom and Plutarch, and founded the largest library in Rome, the Basilica Ulpia. Hadrian, a Hellenophile who also wrote some Latin verse, probably did more than any of his predecessors to encourage art and letters, and his reign coincided with a revival of Greek literature in the second century C.E., including such authors as Plutarch and Lucian.

The literature of the Silver Age, very much the product of this educated environment, displays a consciousness that Latin literature had already reached a pinnacle of literary expression in the Golden Age. The influence of rhetoric and of Augustan literature was very strong. Rhetorical training made the Silver Age author emphasize artificiality, cleverness, literary convention, and, to a certain extent, encyclopedic learning. At the same time, imitation of the classics of the Golden Age became a common feature. "Vergilianism" is strong in such Silver Age poets as Persius, Lucan, Silius, and Statius. Poetic expressions and vocabulary also invaded Silver Age prose; the poetic *senium*, for example, replaced the prose *senectum* as the word for "old age" in Seneca.

Two major prose authors of the period were also active in poetic fields. Besides extensive extant philosophical, epistolary, and dramatic writings, Lucius Annaeus Seneca (commonly known as Seneca, c. 4 B.C.E.-65 C.E.), sometimes called "the Younger" to distinguish him from his learned uncle "the Elder," composed elegiac and lyric poems, some of which survive in the *Latin Anthology*. Also often attributed to Seneca is *Apocolocyntosis divi Claudii* (c. 54 C.E.; *The Deification of Claudius*, 1614), a biting satire on the deification of the late emperor. This work was written partly in prose and partly in verse, in the tradition of Menippean satire employed earlier by the Republican satirist Lucilius. Another example of the prose-poetry medley is the partly extant *Satyricon* (c. 60 C.E.; *The Satyricon*, 1694) of Petronius. Both the *Apocolocyntosis* and the *Satyricon* serve as a reminder that the modern divisions of prose and poetry were not always fixed in the ancient world.

Another major prose author of the Silver Age who also wrote poetry was Gaius Plinius Caecilius Secundus (c. 61-c. 113 C.E.), called Pliny the Younger to distinguish him from his uncle and adopted father, Pliny the Elder, a natural historian. Pliny is known today mostly for his extensive correspondence in nine books, but he also composed elegiac, lyric, and epic poems, and even a Greek tragedy, all lost. Pliny was also part of an important literary circle that included the poets Silius Italicus and Martial and the prose authors Frontinus, Tacitus, and Suetonius.

The African historian and rhetorician Lucius Annaeus Florus (commonly known as Florus, fl. 100-130 C.E.) may also have been a poet, since several poems in a variety of meters survive under his name. Florus is best remembered for his extant *Epitome bellorum omnium annorum DCC* (*Epitome of Roman History*, 1852), a summary of Livy's histories. He may also have been the author of the *Perviligium Veneris* (vigil of Venus), a short religious poem in trochaic tetrameter that is often considered one of the loveliest Latin poems.

The most popular poetic forms of the period were satire and epic. In addition to the Menippean satires of Seneca and Petronius noted above, the Silver Age produced two outstanding verse satirists: the Stoic Aulus Persius Flaccus (commonly known as Persius, 34-62 C.E.) and Decimus Junius Juvenalis (commonly known as Juvenal, c. 60-c. 130 C.E.). Like their great predecessor Horace, Persius and Juvenal wrote their satires in hexameters. While the poems of the severe Persius and the bitter Juvenal are quite different in tone, both project the strong moralistic message traditionally characteristic of Roman satire.

The Spanish epigrammatist Marcus Valerius Martialis (commonly known as Martial, c. 38-41 to c. 130 C.E.) may also be listed with the satirists Persius and Juvenal. Although technically he wrote not satires but epigrams, short poems in mixed meters, Martial presents in his poems a critical picture of Roman society which the modern world, at least, would call satiric. In his career, Martial may have intersected with the great figures of the Silver Age. Critics speculate that in his youth, he may have been a member of the literary circle of his fellow Spaniards Seneca and Lucan; in later life, he was a friend of Pliny and, perhaps, Juvenal. Martial's poetry not only shows the influence of the Roman satiric and Greek epigrammatic traditions but also owes a debt to earlier Roman poets, especially to Catullus and Ovid.

The epic poets of the Silver Age can be divided into two groups: those, such as Valerius Flaccus and Silius Italicus, who wrote only in this genre, and those such as Lucan and Statius, whose poetic output was more diverse. In addition to his extant *Pharsalia*, Lucan produced a variety of works now lost, including the following in verse: *Adlocutio ad Pollam* (address to Polla), *Iliacon* (Troy), *Catachthonion*, about a descent into the underworld, and *Silvae*, a collection of miscellaneous poems. Lucan's *Epistulae ex Campania* (letters from Campania), in prose, has also been lost. The Neapolitan poet Statius, a younger contemporary of Lucan, also produced a large collection of *Silvae*, in addition to his epics.

Two other poets are usually dated to the early Silver Age and further demonstrate the diverse poetic output of the period: Titus Calpurnius Siculus (commonly known as Calpurnius Siculus, fl. 50-60 C.E.), whose eleven extant *Eclogues* modeled on the Vergilian type were probably written during the reign of Nero; and Phaedrus (c. 15 B.C.E.-c. 55 C.E.), a freed Thracian slave from the imperial household who published verse fables in the Aesopian tradition during the reigns of Tiberius and Caligula.

Despite an often oppressive political environment, then, the poets of the Silver Age, generally well educated and well versed in earlier Latin literature, continued the prolific and polished output begun in the Golden Age of the late Republic and of Augustus. The traditional label Silver Age suggests an inferiority to the Golden Age of which even Silver Age poets themselves were aware, but, despite their conscious imitation of their great predecessors, there is much life, ingenuity, and originality in their poetry. Juvenal and Martial, for example, are usually ranked with Horace as Rome's greatest satirists, and Lucan and Statius display poetic skill that has been much admired and influential in later periods. The Latin poetry of the Silver Age, then, is an eloquent testimony to the vigor and intelligence of Roman life and letters in the first and early second centuries C.E.

LATE ANTIQUITY (138-476)

After the reign of Hadrian, Latin poetry came to a virtual standstill until the early fourth century C.E. Once again, the history of Latin literature was strongly influenced by developments in the field of Greek letters, for this long poetic silence in Latin can be attributed, at least in part, to a renaissance in Greek prose literature which was carried into Latin.

The revival of Greek letters that began under Hadrian continued to flourish through the third century C.E. and produced several important Greek prose works: the histories of Appian (c. 95-c. 165) and of Cassius Dio Cosseianus (commonly known as Dio Cassius, c. 150-c. 235 C.E.); the essays of Aelius Aristides (c. 117-c. 181); the satires of Lucian (c. 120-c. 180); the works of the Neoplatonic philosopher Plotinus (c. 205-270), and even the Stoic writings of the emperor Marcus Aurellius (121-180). This Greek Second Sophistic movement, as it is called, developed a style emphasizing rhetorical features and imitation of Attic Greek texts from the fourth century B.C.E.

The Second Sophistic's counterpart in Latin was *elocutio novella* (new speech), inspired by the African *rhetor* Marcus Cornelius Fronto (commonly known as Fronto, c. 100-c. 166). One of Marcus Aurelius's tutors, and later an epistolary correspondent with the emperor, Fronto wrote speeches and letters using vocabulary and expressions from early Republican writers and from contemporary spoken Latin. Where writers of the Silver Age had imitated those of the Golden, Fronto and his followers sought their stylistic models in the Latin of Plautus. Consequently, works employing the *elocutio novella* are often characterized by archaisms.

The *Metamorphoses* (c. 180-190; *The Golden Ass*, 1566), a prose novel by Lucius Apuleius (commonly known as Apuleius, c. 125-after 170), exhibits a striking blend of archaisms, linguistic innovations, and rhetorical figures of speech. Apuleius was, like Fronto, a *rhetor* from

north Africa and was a prolific writer. In addition to the extant *Metamorphoses*, Apuleius produced works in a variety of genres, including speeches, hymns, and miscellaneous light verse in a volume called "Ludicra," all lost. The antiquarian tendency of the age is also evident in the extant *Noctes Atticae* (c. 180 C.E.; *Attic Nights*, 1927) of Aulus Gellius (commonly known as Gellius, born c. 125-128), a friend of Fronto. *Attic Nights* is a compilation of extracts from Greek and Latin writers and discusses matters of archaic language, literature, and history, among other things.

The emphasis of *elocutio novella* on colloquial Latin also points to significant linguistic trends in late antiquity: the gradual transformation of the Latin language from its classical, "Ciceronian" models into more colloquial forms, and the eventual dissolution of Latin into the several Romance languages. Developments in second century Latin prose thus reflected a permanent change in Latin forms of expression. Latin poetry, when revitalized in the fourth century, already showed the effects of these linguistic changes.

The only Latin poet to emerge between the Silver Age and the fourth century C.E. was Marcus Aurelius Olympius Nemesianus (c. 253-after 283; commonly known as Nemesianus), a Carthaginian whose extant *Cynegetica* (c. 283; *The Chase*, 1934) is a didactic poem on hunting strongly influenced by Vergil and Calpurnius Siculus. Nemesianus also wrote two other didactic poems, "Halieutica," on fishing, and "Nautica," probably on fowling, which are now lost.

The chaotic political situation of the late second century and the third century was certainly another factor affecting poetic output in this period. The series of "five good emperors" chosen by adoption rather than heredity was unfortunately broken by the succession of Marcus Aurelius's incompetent son, Commodus (180-193), whose inevitable assassination led to four rival imperial candidates, a brief civil war (193-197), and the accession of the military man Lucius Septimius Severus (193-211).

A major development during the reign of the Severian family (193-235) was the final extension of Roman citizenship, first to the eastern provinces by Septimius Severus and then to all free men in the empire by his son Caracalla (211-217). After five hundred years of empire, all free Roman subjects were finally granted Roman citizenship, and there was no longer a distinction between Roman and non-Roman within the empire. By this period, emperors themselves also came from all over the empire: The second century had seen the Spanish emperors Trajan and Marcus Aurelius; the third century produced Septimius Severus from North Africa; and later centuries brought Aurelian (270-275), Diocletian (284-305), and Constantine (308-337) from Illyria (modern Yugoslavia). This "internationalism" was paralleled in Latin literature, which embraced several Spanish writers in the Silver Age, North Africans in the second and third centuries, and Gallic writers in the fourth and fifth centuries.

In general, the third century C.E. was a period of military anarchy. Not only were there the internal problems of disrupted succession, with twenty-five emperors in the one-hundred-year period between Commodus and Diocletian, but there were also critical problems on the frontiers. Incursions by fierce Germanic tribes, including the Goths, Allamanni, and Franks, led to the temporary loss of the Danube and Rhine frontiers and the invasions of Gaul and even northern Italy. In the east, the important province of Syria was lost for a time.

These military difficulties caused major social and economic difficulties. Travel became severely limited; commerce was disrupted; urban life deteriorated as city populations shrank, municipal governments decayed, and cities walled themselves against invasions. Society became more rustic, more oriented toward the farmland, as large landholders usurped political and legal authority on their *latifundia* and their workers, formerly free *coloni*, became bound serfs with no freedom of movement. The medieval feudal system was thus already developing in the fourth century.

Through the military and administrative abilities of several good emperors, such as Claudius Gothicus (260-270), Aurelian, Diocletian, and Constantine, the boundaries of the empire were restored in the late third century and were preserved essentially intact for another century. Diocletian, recognizing the difficulties of governing an immense area with increasingly insecure borders, divided the empire into two administrative halves, the Greek-speaking East and the Latin-speaking West. This division became permanent in the fourth century. Under

Constantine, the East, by then more stable than the West, became the site of the empire's new capital city, Constantinople (modern Istanbul), where the successors of Constantine continued to rule their Byzantine Greek empire for another thousand years. This division of the empire also led to a diminishing influence of Greek letters on the Latin West.

By the late fourth century, the city of Rome was no longer the capital city of even the Western Empire, the ruler of which sat in Milan for military purposes. The Roman senate continued to meet, but as a mere town council with a *praefectus urbi* (city prefect) instead of a consul as presiding officer. It is indicative, however, of the resilience of Roman political institutions that Constantine established a senate and consuls in his new capital.

The Western Empire was not as long-lived as its eastern counterpart. The early fifth century witnessed the loss of Britain and the permanent occupation of Gaul, Spain, and North Africa by Germanic tribes. The city of Rome itself was sacked in 410 by Alaric the Goth, and in 476 the last Roman emperor in the West, Romulus Augustulus, was deposed by the German Odoacer.

The causes of the fall of the Roman Empire in the West are complex, but it is significant that in the midst of the great political and social changes that occurred from the third through the fifth century, Rome maintained her status as the intellectual and literary center of the Latin-speaking world. Nearly all the writers of late antiquity had some contact with this city, which remained a magnet for scholars. Roman education, both in Rome and in the provinces, also continued to display a high level of quality and accessibility. The educational advances begun in the Silver Age were upheld in late antiquity. Both Diocletian and Constantine, for example, retained the financial privileges conferred on teachers by their imperial predecessors. Several emperors, including Septimius Severus, Constantine, and Gratian (367-383), were well educated, and Severus's Syrian wife, Julia Domna, even sat at the head of the important literary salon which included the Greek philosopher Flavius Philostratus (commonly known as Philostratus, c. 170-245). The African *rhetor* and Christian writer Caecilius Firmianus Lactantius (commonly known as Lactantius, 240-320) held a teaching post under Diocletian and was tutor to the emperor's son Crispus. A significant number of the poets of late antiquity were *rhetores* by profession.

Another important development of this period, with profound consequences for Latin letters, was the growth of Christianity, which began in the East in the first century, as a religion especially of the non-Latin-speaking lower classes. Christianity suffered several centuries of persecution before it was officially tolerated by Constantine in 313, and several more centuries passed before Christianity had completely displaced the ancient "pagan" religions.

A major problem for early Christian writers was the role in Christian life and letters of the Latin literary tradition in which they themselves had been educated. Some Christians wished to dismiss the entire tradition as morally and religiously unwholesome; others argued strongly for the value of the "pagan" Latin literature in a Christian education.

Fortunately, these Latin classics managed to survive until Christianity, no longer threatened by the pagan world, became the conservator of classical culture, especially through the scribal efforts of medieval monks. Preservation of classical texts began to be particularly critical in the fourth and fifth centuries, as papyrus, long used as a writing material, became less accessible and scribes began using parchment. This change in material also meant a change in text format, with the transition from the scroll to the quarto. Because of these changes, if an ancient text was not copied onto parchment in this period, it generally did not survive.

Christians in late antiquity not only helped preserve these ancient texts but also continued the Latin literary tradition with their own poetic and prose creations. The Latin literature of late antiquity reflects the initial tensions between the classical and Christian worlds as well as their eventual reconciliation. The literary transition from "pagan" to "Christian," however, was not sudden, and the criteria for calling a fifth or sixth century Latin author "ancient" or "medieval" are often arbitrary.

Symbolic of these changes in Latin literature on the threshold of the medieval period are two Christian works: the *Vulgate*, a Latin translation of the Bible by Eusebius Hieronymus (c. 348-420), better known as Saint Jerome, and *De civitate Dei* (c. 413-426; *The City of God*), by Aurelius Augustinus (known as Saint Au-

gustine, 354-430). These two works had a profound effect upon contemporary and later Latin literature and, in a sense, mark the end of a literary era, the transition from "pagan" to Christian Latin literature. Jerome's *Vulgate* included translations of Hebrew poetic passages, such as the Psalms and the Song of Solomon, which established basic vocabulary and forms of expression for later Latin poetry. Besides *The City of God*, Augustine wrote some verse, including *Psalmus contra partem Donati* (393-396; *Against the Donatists*). This work, also known as the *Abecedarium*, was the first Latin poem based upon rhythm rather than on the quantitative system derived from Greek, and was thus another harbinger of the changes Latin poetry would undergo in the medieval period.

Contemporary with the *Vulgate* and *The City of God* is the *Saturnalia* (fifth century) of Ambrosius Theodosius Macrobius (commonly known as Macrobius, fl. 400), a work which demonstrates the tenacity of classical religion and culture. Named after a major Roman religious holiday and modeled on the Platonic symposium, the *Saturnalia* discusses a broad range of topics, mostly antiquarian. As participants in his *Saturnalia*, Macrobius chose several contemporary literary figures, the most important of which was Quintus Aurelius Symmachus (commonly known as Symmachus, c. 340-402), a famous orator of his day, a staunch defender of pagan culture, and a significant figure in the preservation of Livy's *Histories*. Marius Servius Honoratus (commonly known as Servius, fourth century), another character in the *Saturnalia*, was a commentator on Vergil. A third, Avianus, wrote a collection of animal fables in elegiac verse (c. 400), which were extracted from Phaedrus and became particularly influential in the medieval period.

Macrobius's literary circle was quite learned and was committed to the preservation of the literature of the past. Commentaries and epitomes of classical writers were common in this period. Macrobius himself, a Neoplatonist, wrote a commentary on Cicero's *Somnium Scipionis* (51; *Dream of Scipio*). The great fourth century commentator Allius Donatus, who worked on Terence, was also a teacher of Saint Jerome. There was even a versified epitome of Livy, now lost, by the fourth century author Festus Ruf(i)us Avienus, who also composed several epitomes of ancient geographical and astronomical poems, some of which are extant. In the field of history, Ammianus Marcellinus (c. 325-392), a Greek from Antioch, wrote a history of the years 96-378, more than half of which survives. Marcellinus was also a member of the circle of Macrobius and Symmachus. That a Greek-speaker from the East would choose to write a history of Rome in Latin in the fourth century is an eloquent statement of the empire's persistent cosmopolitanism and of the continued vigor of Roman culture and letters in this period.

Nor was Marcellinus an anomaly of his age. The late fourth century also produced the poet Claudius Claudianus (c. 370-405), or Claudian, an Egyptian who may have originally written in Greek but who produced a diverse poetic corpus in Latin, including public panegyrics, marriage songs, invectives, historical epics in the Vergilian style, and the Ovidian epyllion *De raptu Proserpinae* (rape of Proserpina). Claudian's work, filled with contemporary allusions to the court of Honorius (393-423), demonstrates once again the Roman tendency to forge politics into poetry, a tendency that had been with Latin poetry from its inception. Also significant are Claudian's literary debts to a long list of ancient authors, including Vergil, Ovid, Catullus, Lucretius, and Juvenal. Though he was nominally Christian, Claudian's poetry is generally "pagan" in theme, as the mythic title *De raptu Proserpinae* suggests.

Another member of Symmachus's circle was Decimus Magnus Ausŏnius (c. 310-394). A Christian *rhetor* from Bordeaux, Ausŏnius became tutor to the future emperor Gratian, under whom he held several important political posts. He wrote epistles, mostly in verse, including exchanges with Symmachus; epigrams, mostly elegiac, in both Greek and Latin; and several miscellaneous poems in hexameter. Christianity is not a prominent theme in Ausŏnius's poetry. In his most famous poem, *Mosella* (fourth century; *The Moselle*, 1915), a description of the German river Moselle, Ausŏnius exhibits a fondness for the countryside and for travel, a theme which is indigenously Latin and which had previously appeared in such earlier works as Lucilius's and Horace's travel satires.

Rutilius Claudius Namatianus (commonly known as Rutilius Namatianus) a pagan from Gaul who served under Honorius, followed Ausŏnius's example and produced an elegiac travel poem, *De reditu suo* (fifth century; *The Home-Coming*, 1907). This poem, the beginning of which survives, describes an actual journey by Rutilius Namatianus from Rome to his home in Gaul in about 417 and includes some striking praise of the former capital by a Gallic poet.

Ausŏnius also shared a correspondence with his student, Meropius Pontius Paulinus (commonly known as Paulinus of Nola, c. 353-431), another Gaul, who later became bishop of Nola in Italy. Paulinus of Nola was one of the earliest composers of Christian lyric poetry. His works include eulogies on the saints and martyrs, the first Christian wedding hymn, the first Christian consolation for the dead, and *Eucharisticon*, an autobiographical piece in hexameters.

The Spaniard Aurelius Prudentius Clemens (commonly known as Prudentius, 348-405) was another composer of Christian poetry. In addition to twelve lyric poems or hymns called *Cathemerinon* (Christian day), Prudentius produced the first Christian allegorical poem, *Psychomachia* (*The Soul's Conflict*), and several didactic Christian poems, *Hamartigenia* (*Birth of Evil*), *Contra Symmachum* (*Against Symmachus*), and *Apotheosis*, a work on the Trinity. An effort to transform classical, "pagan" literary forms into truly Christian poetic expressions is especially evident in Prudentius's works.

Two other Christians who attempted to use poetry for didactic purposes were Commodianus (fl. third or fourth century) and Gaius Vetteius Aquilinus Juvencus (commonly known as Juvencus, fl. early fourth century). Commodianus, who may be the first recorded Christian poet, produced a work titled *Instructiones* (*The Instructions in Favour of Christian Discipline*, 1870), eighty acrostic satires of pagan gods, drunkards, and so forth. Commodianus also wrote the *Carmen apologeticum* (poem of apologetics), which was intended as an explanation of Christianity for the unlearned. Juvencus, a Spaniard, wrote verse paraphrases of the Old and New Testaments and the *Evangeliorum librum* (c. 330; book of evangelists), an epic poem in hexameter on the New Testament, composed in Vergilian style.

An important poetic form that appears early in the Christian Latin tradition is the hymn. Hilarius of Poitiers (commonly known as Saint Hilary, c. 317-367), known primarily for his theological treatises, may have been the first author of Christian hymns. Aurelius Ambrosius (commonly known as Saint Ambrose, c. 339-397) was, like Hilary, a doctor of the Western Church and was also an early composer of religious hymns, in addition to his treatises and letters. These early hymns began an extensive tradition in the Middle Ages.

Other Christian writers followed Ausŏnius, producing poetry that was not intensively Christian. Sidonius Apollinaris (c. 431-479) was born in Lyons and was the son-in-law of the emperor Avitus (455-456). His extant poetry comprises twenty-four pieces on miscellaneous subjects and in various meters, including two epithalamia. All of Sidonius Apollinaris's poetry predates his accession to the episcopacy at Clermont, after which he wrote only epistles. Magnus Felix Ennodius (commonly known as Ennodius, 473-521), born in Arles and later bishop of Pavia, wrote extensively in both prose and verse but avoided Christian themes. In addition to letters and several rhetorical discourses in the fashion of the elder Seneca, Ennodius wrote numerous pieces in verse, including marriage poems, epigrams, travel poems, panegyrics, and hymns.

De nuptiis Mercurii et Philologiae (*On the Marriage of Mercury and Philology*), by Martianus Capella (fl. late fourth to early fifth centuries) is a fitting climax to the Latin poetry of late antiquity, at once looking back to the classical age and forward to the medieval period. Written in the form of a Menippean satire in prose and verse, the work of the North African Capella shows the influence of the classical satirist Varro and also has many linguistic parallels to Apuleius. *On the Marriage of Mercury and Philology*, which makes no reference to Christianity, is an allegorical introduction to the seven liberal arts of a traditional Roman education and became very important in the medieval system of learning. Capella's book thus marks the final success of the ancient classical literary tradition in an increasingly Christian environment.

MEDIEVAL POETRY (476-1700)

The dissolution of the Roman Empire in the West did not mean the end either of Roman political and social institutions or of the Latin literary tradition. Roman emperors may have been replaced by Germanic kings, but the new rulers and their subjects continued to consider themselves the legitimate successors of the Romans. In 800, Charlemagne, King of the Franks, accepted the title "Roman Emperor" and thus established the concept of a "Holy Roman Empire," which continued into the nineteenth century. Roman law, especially through codifications in late antiquity by emperors Theodosius II (408-450) and Justinian (527-565), maintained a continuous influence in the West and became the basis both of ecclesiastical "canon law" and of the legal codes of most of modern Europe.

Despite the growth of vernacular languages, Latin continued to be used as a medium of communication in the Church, in the universities, and in educated circles through the eighteenth century. While the period 500 to 1000 is often called the European Dark Ages, Roman culture and learning never really ceased. While literacy did decrease drastically among the general population, old Latin texts continued to be read and copied and new texts composed, especially in the monasteries.

The works of several sixth century authors demonstrate that learning did not die with the Western Roman Empire. Ancius Manlius Severinus Boethius (commonly known as Boethius, c. 480-524), a highly educated member of an old Roman family, was one of the last in the West to know Greek until the Renaissance. From the death of Boethius in 524 until the fourteenth century, the Latin and Greek literary traditions maintained little contact. Boethius's most important work, *De consolatione philosophiae* (523; *The Consolation of Philosophy*), a Menippean satire in prose and mixed meters, was written in prison while Boethius awaited execution for treason under the Ostrogothic king Theodoric (493-526). *The Consolation of Philosophy*, which discusses the problem of evil in a world governed by a just deity, had considerable influence upon the later medieval period. Menippean structure and philosophic content demonstrate the author's debts to the classical past. It was especially through the influence of Boethius, as well as through Capella's *On the Marriage of Mercury and Philology*, that the prose-verse medley became a major genre in later European literatures, especially in the Renaissance, and continued to be used, even in didactic and scientific works, as late as the seventeenth century.

While not a poet, Flavius Magnus Aurelius Cassiodorus Senator (commonly known as Cassiodorus, c. 490-583), another native Roman and a friend of Boethius, is significant as the founder of an early monastery with a *scriptorium* for the copying of texts. Cassiodorus, who served in several royal offices from 507 to 537, produced a variety of prose works, including *Variae epistolae* (537), his official correspondence; a history of the Goths; speeches; and religious works.

Venantius Honorius Clementianus Fortunatus (commonly known as Fortunatus, c. 540-603), who was born at Trieste and eventually became Bishop of Poitiers, wrote several prose works, eleven books of miscellaneous poetry, and a long hexameter work, *De virtutibus S. Martini* (sixth century; on the virtues of Saint Martin). The themes of Fortunatus's miscellaneous poems show the influence of the Latin poets of late antiquity and include marriage songs, travel poems, and hymns. His verse demonstrates a peculiar combination of religious fervor, epicurean tastes, and mythological allusions, in marked contrast to the unlettered asceticism with which the medieval period is often erroneously associated.

A revival of learning in the reign of Charlemagne (768-814) is further evidence of the continuity of learning in the medieval period. This Carolingian Revival, as it is usually called, witnessed a major innovation in paleography, the transition from magiscule to minuscule writing. The period also saw a rejuvenation of Latin poetry under such writers as the English prelate Alcuin (c. 732-804), who wrote occasional, nonreligious verse, as well as a long hexameter poem on the history of York, and the German theologian Gottschalk of Orbais (died c. 867-870), who wrote some verse in addition to the heretical religious writings for which he was imprisoned. Perhaps the most brilliant poet of the Carolingian period, however, was Walahfrid Strabo (809-849), Abbot of Reichenau and tutor to Charlemagne's son, Charles the Bald. Besides the prose *Glossa ordinaria* (ninth century), which is a collection of scholarly notes on the Bible, Walahfrid Strabo wrote a collection of poems, including some impressive Sapphics about his abbey, and a didactic work in verse, *De cultura hortorum* (ninth century; *Hortulus*, 1924), with a famous dedicatory poem reminiscent of Catullus.

One of the earliest "wandering scholars" was Sedulius Scottus (commonly known as Sedulius, fl. 848-874), who went from his native Ireland to Liège and wrote much miscellaneous verse, including *Carmen Paschale* (ninth century; *The Easter Song*, 1922). Such wandering scholars, later known as goliards, are responsible for a great anonymous tradition of medieval verse, religious, moralistic, satiric, and erotic in nature, of which the best example survives in a manuscript from Benediktbeuern in Germany. This collection of medieval secular verse, known as *Carmina burana*, is perhaps best known through the musical adaptation of Carl Orff (1895-1982).

The ninth or tenth century epic *Waltharius* (*Walter of Aquitaine*, 1930), by Ekkehard I, a monk of the monastery of Saint Gall in Switzerland, stands out, in its epic form, from the rest of medieval Latin poetry, which is generally didactic or miscellaneous in nature. This work, is stylistically indebted to the epic tradition of Vergil and Ovid but is thematically original, since its hero lived in the time of the European invasions.

A few poets of the late medieval period warrant mention for their varied and learned compositions. Hrosvitha of Gandersheim (c. 935-1000), a German nun, was one of the few women poets of the Middle Ages. Besides several prose plays written in the style of Terence, Hrosvitha's corpus includes religious narrative poems about Christian legends and a verse chronicle, *Carmen de gestis Oddonis* (tenth century; *Song About the Deeds of Otto the Great*, 1936), a work in which the resurgence of nationalism in Latin poetry begins to appear. Alanus de Insulis, or Alain of Lille (c. 1128-1202), wrote theological treatises and allegorical poetry. An example of Alain's didactic and moral verse is *Anticlaudianus* (twelfth century; English translation, 1935), an allegory on creation and the perfection of the human soul by God. *Vita Merlini* (twelfth century C.E.; *The Life of Merlin*, 1925), in hexameter, by Geoffrey of Monmouth (died c. 1155), was part of a mythic tradition that later greatly influenced the Arthurian legend.

RENAISSANCE

The last stage of a living Latin poetic tradition was the result of the Humanistic revival known as the Renaissance, which began in Italy in the midfourteenth century and spread to northern Europe in the fifteenth and sixteenth centuries. Renaissance writers, exhibiting a renewed interest in ancient culture and literature, sought to uncover and preserve as many Greco-Roman texts as possible, and to use these texts as literary models.

Much Renaissance literature was written in the vernacular languages, but a significant number of works were written in Latin. Desiderius Erasmus (c. 1466-1536), for example, wrote his great prose satire *Encomium moriae* (1509; *In Praise of Folly*, 1549) in Latin. The Latin poets of the Renaissance, often called Neo-Latin writers, flourished from about 1350 until about 1700, producing an astonishing variety of poetic types based upon classical models. The most popular genres were epigrams, love poems, elegies, odes, didactic poetry, epithalamia, and eclogues.

The list of Italian Neo-Latin poets is impressive. The Florentine Francesco Petrarca (commonly known as Petrarch, 1304-1374) wrote twelve *Eclogues* of a Vergilian type and an epic poem, *Africa* (1396; English translation, 1977), about Scipio Africanus, which Petrarch modeled on the *Aeneid* and considered more important than his famous vernacular sonnets. Petrarch's friend Giovanni Boccaccio (1313-1375), best known for the Italian *Decameron* (1348-1353; English translation, 1620) in prose, later composed *Bucolicum carmen* (1351-1366; *Bucolic Song*, 1913), which, like Petrarch's poems, was filled with allegories and contemporary allusions.

The Neapolitan Giovanni Giovano Pontano (1423-1503) wrote Latin poetry in a considerable range, from love poems to an astrological poem, *Urania* (fifteenth century). Pontano's colleague, Jacopo Sannazzaro (1458-1530), known in Latin as Actius Ayncerus, wrote much religious pastoral verse, such as *De partu Virginis* (1526; on the birth of the Virgin), and some secular poetry, such as *Piscatoriae* (1526; *Piscatorial Eclogues*, 1958).

A later Florentine Neo-Latinist, Angelo Poliziano (commonly known as Poliziano and also known as Politian, 1454-1494), wrote not only in Latin but also in Italian and Greek. His Latin output consists of a few elegies, odes, and epigrams which became models for later epigrammatists.

Poliziano's interest in Greek reflected an important Renaissance trend. While the poetic literature of the Middle Ages was the direct offspring of Christianity and of the Latin poetic tradition, the Renaissance saw a rediscovery of Greek literature, encouraged by the exodus of Greek scholars and texts from the disintegrating Byzantine Empire. One such Greek expatriate was the poet Michael Tarchaniota Marullus (died 1500), whose Latin love lyrics and poems of exile were long admired and imitated in France and Germany.

Two German Neo-Latin poets were Konradus Celtis (1459-1508), who composed odes, love poems, and epigrams, and Petrus Lotichius (1528-1560), who wrote love elegies in the fashion of Ovid and Catullus.

Neo-Latin output in France was early offset by a preference for the vernacular, represented by *La Deffence et illustration de la langue françoyse* (1549; *The Defence and Illustration of the French Language*, 1939) by Joachim du Bellay (1522-1560), but most of the members of the Pléiade, du Bellay's literary group, including du Bellay himself, produced Latin verse. Du Bellay's *Poemata* (poems) of 1558 included epigrams and love poems. J. A. de Baïf (1532-1589) published a volume of Latin poems titled *Carmina* (songs) in 1577. Perhaps the most unusual Latin poem of the Pléiade is by Rémy Belleau (1528-1577), *Dictamen metrificum de bello huguenotico* (sixteenth century), a macaronic poem on the Huguenotic wars. Despite the swift dominance of the vernacular in French poetry, Latin poetry continued to be written by French poets as late as the mid-nineteenth century, notably by Charles Baudelaire.

There was also a significant group of British Neo-Latin poets, the most outstanding of whom was a Scot, George Buchanan (1506-1582), tutor to Mary Queen of Scots. Buchanan was closely associated in his youth with the Pléiade and produced a variety of poetic works in Latin, including an influential version of the Psalms, plays, *De Sphaera* (a defense of Ptolemy), and occasional verse, such as an epithalamium for Mary's marriage to the Dauphin in 1558. Several other British Neo-Latin poets are the great English epic poet John Milton (1608-1674), the Welshman Henry Vaughan (1622-1695), the religious poet Richard Crashaw (c. 1612-1649), and the Metaphysical poet Abraham Cowley (1618-1667).

After 1700, the gradual displacement of Latin as the language of the educated and the rise of vernacular poetry meant the end of a living Latin poetic tradition. Where Latin poetry continues to be written today, it is done more as a sophisticated exercise and display of skill than as a true poetic statement. Today the Latin poetic tradition is most important for its influence on the Western literary tradition. There is no field of modern poetry and virtually no poet untouched either directly or indirectly by Latin poetry. No better expression exists of the debt of modern poetry to Latin literature than that of the great Italian poet Dante Alighieri (commonly known as Dante, 1265-1321), who was positioned at the virtual beginning of the vernacular poetic tradition in the West. While Dante did write in Latin, including letters and the treatise *De monarchia* (c. 1313; *On World Government*) in prose and *Eclogae Latinae* (*Latin Eclogues*) in verse, his major work, *La divina commedia* (c. 1320; *The Divine Comedy*), is in the vernacular. In the first part of this monumental epic, *Inferno*, modeled on Aeneas's descent to the underworld in book 6 of the *Aeneid*, Dante replaces Aeneas's prophetic guide, the Sibyl, with Vergil himself, and praises his classical guide with the following immortal tribute:

> Tu se, lo mio maestro e, 1 mio autore
> tu se' solo colui, da cu' io tolsi lo bello stile
> che m'he fatto onore.
>
> (You are my master and my author.
> You alone are the one from whom I took
> the beautiful style which has rendered me
> honor.)

Dante's debt to Vergil is the West's debt to the Latin poetic tradition.

BIBLIOGRAPHY

Adams, J. N., and R. G. Mayer, eds. *Aspects of the Language of Latin Poetry.* New York: Oxford University Press, 1999.

Albrecht, Michael von. *Roman Epic: An Interpretive Introduction.* Boston: E. J. Brill, 1999.

Brock, R., and A. J. Woodman, eds. *Roman Comedy, Augustan Poetry, Historiography.* Leeds, England: F. Cairns, 1995.

Cairns, Francis, and Malcolm Heath, eds. *Greek Poetry, Drama, Prose, Roman Poetry.* Leeds, England: F. Cairns, 1998.

Conrad, Carl W. *From Epic to Lyric: A Study in the History of Traditional Word-Order in Greek and Latin Poetry.* New York: Garland, 1990.

Conte, Gian Biagio. *Latin Literature: A History.* Translated by Joseph B. Solodow. Baltimore, Md.: Johns Hopkins University Press, 1999.

Copley, Frank O. *Latin Literature: From the Beginnings to the Close of the Second Century A.D.* Ann Arbor: University of Michigan Press, 1969.

Courtney, Edward. *The Poems of Petronius.* Atlanta, Ga.: Scholars Press, 1991.

Curtius, Ernst Robert. *European Literature and the Latin Middle Ages.* Translated by Willard R. Trask. New York: Pantheon Books, 1953.

Dalby, Andrew. *Empire of Pleasures: Luxury and Indulgence in the Roman World.* New York: Routledge, 2000.

Duff, J. W. *A Literary History of Rome from the Origins to the Close of the Golden Age.* New York: Barnes and Noble, 1963.

_____. *A Literary History of Rome in the Silver Age, from Tiberius to Hadrian.* New York: Barnes and Noble, 1964.

Edmunds, Lowell. *Intertextuality and the Reading of Roman Poetry.* Baltimore, Md.: Johns Hopkins University Press, 2001.

Edwards, Mark W. *Sound, Sense, and Rhythm: Listening to Greek and Latin Poetry.* Princeton, N.J.: Princeton University Press, 2002.

Francese, Christopher. *Parthenius of Nicaea and Roman Poetry.* New York: Peter Lang, 2001.

Galinsky, Karl, ed. *The Interpretation of Roman Poetry: Empiricism or Hermeneutics?* New York: Peter Lang, 1992.

Grant, Michael. *Roman Literature.* Cambridge, England: Cambridge University Press, 1954.

Hadas, Moses. *A History of Latin Literature.* New York: Columbia University Press, 1952.

Harrison, S. J., ed. *Homage to Horace: A Bimillenary Celebration.* New York: Oxford University Press, 1995.

Highet, Gilbert. *The Classical Tradition.* Oxford, England: Clarendon Press, 1949.

Hinds, Stephen. *Allusions and Intertext: Dynamics of Appropriation in Roman Poetry.* New York: Cambridge University Press, 1998.

Hornsby, Roger A. *Reading Latin Poetry.* Norman: University of Oklahoma Press, 1969.

McFarlane, I. D. *Renaissance Latin Poetry.* Totowa, N.J.: Barnes and Noble, 1980.

Martindale, Charles. *Redeeming the Text: Latin Poetry and the Hermeneutics of Reception.* New York: Cambridge University Press, 1993.

Murphy, Carol A., Ryan T. Moore, and Daniel G. Thiem, eds. *Embers of the Ancient Flame: Latin Love Poetry from Catullus, Horace, and Ovid.* Wauconda, Ill.: Bolchazy-Carducci, 2001.

O'Daly, Gerard J. P. *The Poetry of Boethius.* Chapel Hill: University of North Carolina Press, 1991.

Otis, Brooks. *Virgil: A Study in Civilized Poetry.* Norman: Oklahoma University Press, 1995.

Powell, Anton, ed. *Roman Poetry and Propaganda in the Age of Augustus.* London: Bristol Classical Press, 1992.

Rose, H. J. *A Handbook of Latin Literature: From the Earliest Times to the Death of St. Augustine.* Wauconda, Ill.: Bolchazy-Carducci, 1996.

Smith, R. A. *Poetic Allusion and Poetic Embrace in Ovid and Virgil.* Ann Arbor: University of Michigan Press, 1997.

Thomas, Richard F. *Virgil and the Augustan Reception.* New York: Cambridge University Press, 2001.

Waddell, Helen. *Medieval Latin Lyrics.* Baltimore, Md.: Penguin, 1968.

Watson, Lindsay. *Arae: The Curse Poetry of Antiquity.* Leeds, England: Cairns, 1991.

Wheelock, Frederick M. M. *Latin Literature: A Book of Readings from Cicero, Livy, Ovid, Pliny, the Vulgate, Bede, Caedmon, Medieval Poetry.* Prospect Heights, Ill.: Waveland Press, 1993.

White, Peter. *Promised Verse: Poets in the Society of Augustan Rome.* Cambridge, Mass.: Harvard University Press, 1993.

Williams, Gareth D. *The Curse of Exile: A Study of Ovid's "Ibis."* Cambridge, England: Cambridge University Press, 1996.

Wills, Jeffry. *Repetition in Latin Poetry: Figures of Allusion.* New York: Oxford University Press, 1996.

Ziolkowski, Theodore. *Virgil and the Moderns.* Princeton, N.J.: Princeton University Press, 1993.

Thomas J. Sienkewicz

LATINO POETRY

In the 1960's and 1970's, poets and other writers of Mexican, Puerto Rican, and Cuban descent formed three discrete groups in literary response to various social, historical, and cultural impulses in the United States at that time. The Civil Rights movement inspired literary Chicanos and Puerto Ricans (especially the Nuyoricans, as Puerto Ricans in New York were known) to write about their experiences in their own voices, which frequently were excluded from mainstream publications. The Cuban American poets of this period wrote primarily in Spanish and in response to the historical circumstance of their exile from Cuba. Chicanos, Puerto Ricans, and Cuban Americans still comprise the largest groups of Latino poets in the United States, although the field has grown to include writers of other backgrounds.

LITERARY MAGAZINES AND ANTHOLOGIES

The literary magazines and small press publications of the burgeoning Chicano, Nuyorican, and Cuban American literary culture are an essential source of information on the initial development of Latino poetry. Among the magazines of varying regional or national renown, significance, and circulation were the Chicano periodicals *De Colores* (Albuquerque, New Mexico), *El Grito* and *Grito del Sol* (Berkeley, California), and *Tejidos* (Austin, Texas); the Puerto Rican diaspora magazine *The Rican* (Chicago); and the Cuban American review *Areíto* (New York). Some of these small journals were edited by leading poets, such as *Maize* (San Diego), by Alurista, and *Mango* (San Jose), by Lorna Dee Cervantes. These and numerous other journals, whether interdisciplinary or purely literary in focus (and many of them highly ephemeral), provided a necessary publishing outlet for the alternative voices erupting throughout the United States during the 1960's and 1970's. These publications grew to afford a rich historical record of a momentous turning point in American literature.

No serious study of the origins and development of Latino literature of any genre can be undertaken without considering *Revista Chicano-Riqueña* (1973-1985) and its continuation, *The Americas Review* (1986-1999). A long-running literary magazine founded by the scholar Nicolás Kanellos, the journal focused on creative writing, with interviews, literary essays, scholarly articles, book reviews, and visual art complementing each issue. Beginning with the premier issue, the work of most of the major Chicano, Nuyorican, and, as coverage quickly expanded, other Latino poets appeared in the pages of these magazines, in many cases marking the first appearance of a writer on the literary radar. Tino Villanueva, Alurista, Lorna Dee Cervantes, Victor Hernández Cruz, Gary Soto, Ricardo Sánchez, Tato Laviera, Sandra María Esteves, Jimmy Santiago Baca, and Pat Mora—to indicate only a few—figure among the Chicano and Nuyorican poets featured. In addition, the magazines published the poetry of writers better known for different genres, such as Rolando Hinojosa, Carlos Morton, Miguel Piñero, and Tomás Rivera. Many of these poets and other writers helped shape and influence the journal by doubling as contributing editors or editorial board members. Special or monographic issues focused on particular topics within U.S. Hispanic literature. The celebrated *Woman of Her Word: Hispanic Women Write*, edited by Chicana poet Evangelina Vigil (volume 11, nos. 3/4, 1983) anthologizes the finest Latina writing of that time. Several issues emphasize the Latino writers active in various regions of the United States, including Chicago (volume 5, no. 1, 1977), Wisconsin (volume 13, no. 2, 1985), Houston (volume 16, no. 1, 1988), and the Pacific Northwest (volume 23, nos. 3/4, 1995). The tenth and twentieth anniversary anthologies (1982 and 1992) provide a selection of the major poetical works published in the *Revista* and the *Review* during those decades. *The Americas Review* ceased publication in 1999, but Kanellos's singular mission to promote and publish Hispanic literature of the United States would continue through the ongoing publications of Arte Público Press (founded in 1979) and the activities of the Recovering the U.S. Hispanic Literary Heritage project (established in 1992).

The Bilingual Review/La Revista Bilingüe (founded in 1974) is another long-standing periodical fundamental to the study of Latino literature. Primarily an academic journal of scholarly articles, book reviews, and interviews relating to bilingualism and to U.S. Hispanic literature, *Bilingual Review* has not published the same volume of creative writing as did *Revista Chicano-Riqueña* and *Americas Review*, despite a stated focus as a literary magazine. Even so, poetry appears in almost every issue (Gustavo Pérez Firmat, Martín Espada, and Judith Ortiz Cofer are among the poets represented) and is the subject of some of the research and interviews. More significant to the study of Latino poetry is Bilingual Press/Editorial Bilingüe, the press established by the journal in 1976. The extensive poetry backlist includes not only Chicanos of early distinction (Alurista, Alma Luz Villanueva, Tino Villanueva, and Bernice Zamora), but also Latinos of later periods (Marjorie Agosín, Elías Miguel Muñoz, Virgil Suárez, and Gina Valdés, for instance). Several anthologies published or distributed by the press, along with monographic issues of *Bilingual Review*, contain representative Latino poetry in a variety of specialized categories. These include poets in New York (*Los paraguas amarillos: Los poetas latinos en New York*, 1983), poetry for or about young adults (*Cool Salsa: Bilingual Poems on Growing Up Latino in the United States*, 1994), and women poets (*Floricanto Sí! A Collection of Latina Poetry*, 1998). Such collections afford easy and important access to the vast and ever-flourishing numbers of Hispanic poets who have not gained the national prominence of the proportionately few better-publicized writers.

Anthologies, like literary magazines, are an invaluable primary source of Chicano, Nuyorican, and Cuban American poetry. Early anthologies like Luis Valdez and Stan Steiner's *Aztlan: An Anthology of Mexican American Literature* (1972) and Alurista's *Festival de Flor y Canto: An Anthology of Chicano Literature* (1976) indicate that Chicano literature, including poetry, was already under critical consideration by the early 1970's. (Virginia Ramos Foster annotates more than twenty-five such compilations from that decade in the Mexican American literature chapter of *Sourcebook of Hispanic Culture in the United States*, 1982, edited by David William Foster.)

Several early anthologies of Puerto Rican and Nuyorican literature share the distinction of bringing together island and mainland writers, in seeming recognition of the ongoing aesthetic and literary historical connections between "the two islands," Puerto Rico and Manhattan. (This concern exists to the present day for some scholars and compilers.) These compilations include Alfredo Matilla and Iván Silén's *The Puerto Rican Poets/Los poetas puertorriqueños* (1972), María Teresa Babín and Stan Steiner's *Borinquen: An Anthology of Puerto Rican Literature* (1974), and Julio Marzán's *Inventing a Word: An Anthology of Twentieth-Century Puerto Rican Poetry* (1980). More recently, Roberto Santiago has taken the same composite approach to Puerto Rican literature in *Boricuas: Influential Puerto Rican Writers—An Anthology* (1995). On the other hand, Miguel Algarín and Miguel Piñero's landmark *Nuyorican Poetry: An Anthology of Puerto Rican Words and Feelings* (1975) documents exclusively the initial period of creativity and so is the best starting point for any retrospective study of Nuyorican poetry.

The first Cuban American literature anthologies also emphasize the connections between writing in the United States and the homeland, Cuba. For example, several poets who write in Spanish in exile appear in Orlando Rodríguez Sardiñas's *La última poesía cubana: Antología reunida, 1959-1973* (1973; the latest Cuban poetry: an anthology) and exile poets are the exclusive focus of Angel Aparicio Laurencio's *Cinco poetisas cubanas, 1935-1969* (1970; five Cuban women poets); both collections were published in the United States. By the same token, an early critical dictionary, *Bibliografía crítica de la poesía cubana (exilio: 1959-1971)* (1972; critical bibliography of Cuban exile poetry), by exile writer Matías Montes Huidobro with Yara González, confirms that virtually all the poetry books of the decade under discussion were written in Spanish. The poetry in Silvia Burunat and Ofelia García's *Veinte años de literatura cubanoamericana: Antología 1962-1982* (1988; Twenty years of Cuban American literature: an anthology) illustrates the tendency throughout two decades of exile and immigration to explore issues of identity within the context of the nascent Cuban American experience (and, in the 1970's as in the preceding decade, in Spanish). Ultimately, the study of the Chicano, Nuyorican, or Cuban American poetry in the foregoing and similar anthologies affords a synopsis both of individual poets and of each discrete group, at specific moments as well as over time.

EARLY CHICANO POETRY

Many of the poets featured in the early Chicano anthologies or in other publications continued to publish or to appear in later anthologies, suggesting their ongoing significance in Chicano literary history even as others emerged. These include Alurista, Angela de Hoyos, José Montoya, Luis Omar Salinas, Raúl Salinas, and Tino Villanueva. Rodolfo Gonzales's *I Am Joaquín/Yo soy Joaquín* (1967) and the poetry of Ricardo Sánchez are especially representative of this early period. The bilingual *I Am Joaquín/Yo soy Joaquín*, by Denver-based activist and writer Gonzales, may be the single best-known Chicano poem of any period. It has been widely read, reproduced, and distributed by newspapers and magazines, students and teachers, performers, labor organizers, and Chicano organizations and organizers in every possible educational, cultural, political, and social milieu. *I Am Joaquín* is as much a historical commentary as a modern epic poem, and intentionally so. An early popular edition (Bantam Pathfinder, 1972) even supplemented the poem with paintings depicting historical events and a chronology of Mexican and Mexican American history. Also, as Gonzales himself states in the informative fact list that prefaces the poem, "*I Am Joaquín* was the first work of poetry to be published by Chicanos for Chicanos and is the forerunner of the Chicano cultural renaissance." Gonzales combines the poetic sensibilities of Walt Whitman's "Song of Myself" and Ginsberg's "Howl" (1956) as Joaquín, a Chicano Everyman, explores himself and the history of the Chicano people—from the pre-Columbian and colonial periods, through independence and revolution up to the present day:

> I am Joaquín,
> lost in a world of confusion,
> . . . .
> and destroyed by modern society.

Repetition, enumeration, and parallelism dominate the poem's short lines and long stanzas. The liberal use of displaced lines and capitalized words emphasizes key concepts, such as "MY OWN PEOPLE," "THE GROUND WAS MINE," and, in the prophetic and self-affirming final lines of the poem, "I SHALL ENDURE!/ I WILL ENDURE!"

The late Ricardo Sánchez also began writing in social protest. The lines that frame "In Exile" (from Sánchez's first book, *Canto y grito mi liberación*, 1971; I sing and shout my liberation) exemplify several of the salient characteristics of his poetry: the typographic hodgepodge and free verse, the sensation of getting out as much as possible in a single breath, and the vociferous sense of both self and people.

> it is by way of definition that i
> now write this short introduction of myself,
> . . . .
> and
> i write of my people, LA RAZA!

Elsewhere in this collection as in all his subsequent books, Sánchez frequently writes in Spanish or a mixture of Spanish and English, he experiments with word formation ("soul/stream"; *piensasentimientos*, or "mind-feelings"; *mentealmacuerpo*, or mindsoulbody), he inserts expository or poetic prose texts, and he articulates his aesthetic and political visions. The enthusiasm and immediacy of his Beat-inflected voice readily draw the reader into the experience. Even the titles of Sánchez's books and poems emphasize this aesthetic of spontaneity: "This of Being the Soul/Voice for My Own Conscienceness Is Too Much (Petersburg, Virginny)," *Hechizospells: Poetry/Stories/Vignettes/Articles/Notes on the Human Condition of Chicanos and Pícaros, Words and Hopes Within Soulmind* (1976) and *Eagle-Visioned/ Feathered Adobes: Manito Sojourns and Pachuco Ramblings October 4th to 24th, 1981* (1990). Sánchez's poetry has enjoyed wide circulation in both small and university presses, and has even been published in a private edition (*Amerikan Journeys = Jornadas americanas*, 1994, in Iowa City by publisher and longtime Sánchez associate Rob Lewis). The publication of *Chicano Timespace: The Poetry and Politics of Ricardo Sánchez* (2001), a scholarly monograph by Miguel R. López, establishes in no uncertain terms Sánchez's position in the canon of Chicano—and, by extension, Latino and American—poetry.

NUYORICAN POETRY: 1970'S

The beginnings of Nuyorican poetry were equally strident. The anthology edited by Miguel Algarín and

Miguel Piñero, *Nuyorican Poetry: An Anthology of Puerto Rican Words and Feelings* (1975), introduced a wide audience to the recent poetry that was coming out of the experience of being Puerto Rican in New York City. Even the title of the anthology captures the emotive lyricism that underlies the use of an ethnic-specific lexicon ("Puerto Rican words") to document a group experience ("[Puerto Rican] feelings") in poetry inspired by a place ("Nuyorican poetry"). Several of the featured writers went on to distinguish themselves in poetry beyond the anthology, including Sandra María Esteves, José Angel Figueroa, Pedro Pietri, and the compilers themselves. (Two poets active in the early 1970's, Victor Hernández Cruz and Tato Laviera, are not in the Nuyorican anthology.) The late Piñero, known more for the play *Short Eyes* (pr. 1974) than for his poetry, made a significant contribution nonetheless. The selections in the anthology exemplify his savage irreverence. In "The Book of Genesis According to Saint Miguelito," for instance, Piñero derides the God who created ghettos, slums, lead-based paint, hepatitis, capitalism, and overpopulation. A later work, the much-anthologized "A Lower East Side Poem" (*La Bodega Sold Dreams*, 1980), covers similar ground as the poet contemplates dying among the pimping, shooting, drug dealing, and other unsavory activities of the neighborhood. The perverse but catchy refrain "then scatter my ashes thru/ the Lower East Side" affirms both Piñero's allegiance to his barrio roots and the musical rhythms that inspire many Nuyorican poets.

While social reality is a thematic interest and protest a dominant tone throughout *Nuyorican Poetry*, Algarín and Piñero clearly were committed to promoting diverse voices. The "dusmic" poetry of the third and final section of the book, for example, proposes the possibility of finding love, positive energy, and balance. Esteves's "Blanket Weaver" exemplifies this impulse: "weave us a song of many threads/ that will dance with the colors of our people/ and cover us with the warmth of peace." (Some of Esteves's later poems, such as those in *Bluestown Mockingbird Mambo* (1990), indicate a similarly broad array of preoccupations and interests; these include a touching elegy for the artist Jorge Soto, numerous love poems, and strong but poetic statements against brutal regimes in Guatemala and South Africa.) Also,

Algarín's introduction to the anthology, "Nuyorican Language," constitutes an indispensable discussion of the poet and poetry in the Nuyorican context, in both theory and practice. Algarín, in fact, is located squarely in the mainstream of contemporary poetry and poetics. He has translated into English the poetry of Pablo Neruda, he has written extensively on poetics, and he has taken his literature classes from Rutgers University to the Passaic River and Paterson Falls to enhance his students' study of William Carlos Williams's *Paterson* (1946-1958). The Nuyorican Poets Café, a cultural-arts venue Algarín founded in 1974, has broadened considerably the scope of its poetry and performance activities.

One of many remarkable books to come out of the Nuyorican movement is Pedro Pietri's *Puerto Rican Obituary* (1973), published by the progressive Monthly Review Press. In the title poem (which had achieved underground cult status long before its initial publication), the generic Puerto Ricans Juan, Miguel, Milagros, Olga, and Manuel trudge repeatedly through the daily routines in "Spanish Harlem" that only bring them closer to death and, ultimately, burial on Long Island. In the final analysis, only the afterlife and Puerto Rico offer respite from the poverty and discrimination suffered in New York: "PUERTO RICO IS A BEAUTIFUL PLACE/ PUERTORRIQUENOS ARE A BEAUTIFUL RACE." Pietri is at his best with the antiestablishment rhetoric with which he parodies religious and civic mainstays like the Lord's Prayer and the Pledge of Allegiance, as in "The Broken English Dream," in which he pledges allegiance "to the flag/ of the united states/ of installment plans." The contrast between New York and Puerto Rico—and between English and Spanish—underscores the irony of the political status of Puerto Ricans vis-à-vis the racial discrimination and linguistic choices awaiting them as they pursue the elusive American Dream.

CUBAN AMERICAN POETRY: 1960'S-1970'S

Spanish, not English, was the language of record for Cuban exile poets and Cuban American poets during the 1960's and 1970's, so language choice per se was not a conscious issue of either form or content, as it was for many Chicano and Nuyorican writers at that time. In fact, in contrast to the Nuyorican example, Cuban poetry in the United States of this early period often was seen as part of Cuban literature or Cuban exile literature else-where, not as a nascent branch of American ethnic liter-ature. (Naomi Lindstrom analyzes this problem in the chapter on Cuban American and mainland Puerto Rican literature in *Sourcebook of Hispanic Culture in the United States*, 1982, edited by David William Foster.) Even so, a number of individual poems anthologized by Silvia Burunat and Ofelia García in *Veinte años de literatura cubanoamerica: Antología, 1962-1982* (1988; twenty years of Cuban American literature) illustrate the tendency to explore issues of identity within the context of Cuban exile in the United States.

Uva Clavijo often defines her exile, as she does here in "Declaración" (declaration), in highly specific spatio-temporal terms:

> I, Uva A. Clavijo,
>
> . . . .
>
> declare, today, the last Monday in September,
> that as soon as I can I will leave everything
> and return to Cuba.

The enumeration of what she is prepared to give up—a house in the suburbs, credit, a successful husband and beautiful family, perfect English (in short, all the trap-pings of the American Dream)—presents a striking con-trast to the specificity and simplicity of this declaration. In "Al cumplir veinte años de exilio" (upon completing twenty years of exile), Clavijo commemorates that anni-versary as any other, pondering the growth and develop-ment of a Spanish-speaking, Cuban self formed "before confronting/ an immigration official/ for the first time." By the same token, Clavijo frames "Miami 1980" with very precise markers that pinpoint her loneliness and isolation: "Here, Miami, nineteen/ eighty, and my lone-liness. . . .// And my astonishing loneliness." The sim-plicity of Clavijo's expressive and emotional needs in these poems might explain why she favors relatively short lines. In the Miami poem, for example, three espe-cially significant lines succinctly capture the essence of the poem and the poet: "and hatred," "in the distance," and "loneliness."

For some Cuban American poets, the confrontation with New York is not unlike that of the Nuyoricans. In "Caminando por las calles de Manhattan" (walking through the streets of Manhattan), Alberto Romero meets with drug addicts, prostitutes, go-go dancers, and other marginal characters who people the streets of New York. Yet a sense of order and belonging pervades his search for God amid this riffraff:

> in the Jews of Astoria, in the Italians
> of Flatbush . . .
> in the Dominicans of 110th Street, in the South
>   Americans
> of Queens, in the Cuban refugees.

Place influences identity for Lourdes Casal, too, who is "too much a Habanera to be a New Yorker,/ too much a New Yorker to be, . . ./ anything else" ("Para Ana Veldford"). Despite some suggestive parallels with the Puerto Rican and Chicano experiences, however, the early Cuban American poetry written in Spanish was in-accessible to a broad readership of Latino literature. Moreover, the language factor has precluded the inclu-sion of these poets in English-language college text-books like *The Prentice Hall Anthology of Latino Liter-ature* (2002, edited by Eduardo del Rio).

CHICANO, PUERTO RICAN, AND CUBAN AMERICAN POETRY: 1980'S-1990'S

By the 1980's and 1990's, the diverse body of Latino literature by Chicano, Puerto Rican, and Cuban writers in the United States was receiving considerable critical, popular, and pedagogical attention. As current compil-ers are quick to point out, Latino poets—including those trained in graduate writing programs—were being rec-ognized more widely through national fellowships, prizes, and other honors and awards. They, like other American writers, were publishing in mainstream liter-ary magazines like *The American Poetry Review*, *The Kenyon Review*, *Parnassus*, and *Poetry*. U.S. Latino lit-erature in English was being included in general anthol-ogies of American literature and in American literature curricula in North American colleges and universities.

Gary Soto, Lorna Dee Cervantes, and Jimmy Santi-ago Baca are some of the Chicano poets of broad ac-claim and distribution at the beginning of the twenty-first century. Soto is not only one of the most prolific La-tino poets but also probably the best known outside the confines of Chicano and Latino poetry. His sense of hu-mor, the accessibility of his poetic language, and his sensitive portrayal of youth also have contributed to his success as a writer for young adults and children. (For many years Soto was virtually the only Chicano writing for the important young-adult market.) Like Soto, Chicana writer Pat Mora is a prolific poet and children's author. She counts several books of poetry among her works in various genres, including *Chants* (1984), *Borders* (1986), *Communion* (1991), *Agua Santa = Holy Water* (1995), and *Aunt Carmen's Book of Practical Saints* (1997). From her perspective as a woman and a Latina, Mora writes eloquently about diverse topics, including marriage, family life, and children; traditional and modern Latino and Mexican Indian culture; the Catholic devotion of saints; women; and the southwestern desert. In "Curandera" (folk healer) from *Chants*, for example, Mora interweaves several of these interests. When the villagers go to the healer for treatment, "She listens to their stories, and she listens/ to the desert, always to the desert." In many other poems, Mora similarly portrays the nurturing qualities of the southwestern desert, as in "Mi Madre" (my mother), also from *Chants*, "I say teach me. . . ./ She: the desert/ She: strong mother." Like the traditional healer and the desert-mother, the many women who populate Mora's poems (the grandmothers, mothers, daughters, and granddaughters, the famous and the humble alike) tend to be strong, wise, and nurturing. That is not to say these women are uncritical, though. Extending the desert-woman metaphor in "Desert Women" (in *Borders*), Mora writes: "Don't be deceived./ When we bloom, we stun."

The 1975 publication of Algarín and Piñero's anthology *Nuyorican Poetry* helped pave the way for a later compilation of Puerto Rican writing, Faythe Turner's *Puerto Rican Writers at Home in the USA: An Anthology* (1991). Turner includes poets of both generations and recognizes the significant expansion of the Puerto Rican literary diaspora outside of New York. The newer generation includes poets Martín Espada, Judith Ortiz Cofer, Rosario Morales, and Aurora Levins Morales. Espada's poetry is informed variously by his own Puerto Rican heritage, experiences in the Latino enclaves of the United States, and radical causes in the United States and Latin America. Ortiz Cofer's *The Latin Deli: Prose and Poetry* (1993) invites the reader to negotiate a challenging but engaging combination of stories, essays, and

poems that "tell the lives of barrio women." Similarly experimental in composition is Morales and Levins Morales's *Getting Home Alive* (1986), a mother-daughter collaboration of mixed genre (including poetry, poetic prose, and memoir), further distinguished by the intermingling of texts written by either mother or daughter. Significantly, the last piece, "Ending Poem," is itself a collaborative product (as indicated by the distinct typefaces):

> I am what I am.
> *A child of the Americas.*
> A light-skinned mestiza of the Caribbean.
> *A child of many diaspora, born into this continent at a crossroads.*

These Caribbean women are not exclusively African or Taíno or European: "We are new . . ./ *And we are whole.*" And their measured celebration of multiculturalism contrasts markedly with the earlier antipoetic angst of the Nuyorican experience.

Unlike their predecessors, the new Cuban American poets write in English and as part of American, not Cuban, literature. Dionisio D. Martínez, for example, appears in the 1996 edition of *The Norton Anthology of Poetry*. In *Little Havana Blues: A Cuban-American Literature Anthology* (1996), Delia Poey and Virgil Suárez have identified a corpus of sixteen recent poets, several of whom appear in many other groupings of canonical Latino or Cuban American poetry (among them Carolina Hospital, Ricardo Pau-Llosa, Pablo Medina, and Gustavo Pérez Firmat). The poetry of scholar and writer Pérez Firmat offers a good example of the new Cuban American poetry. As he explains in his memoir, *Next Year in Cuba: A Cubano's Coming-of-Age in America* (1995): "Born in Cuba but made in the U.S.A., I can no longer imagine living outside American culture and the English language." Much of Pérez Firmat's English-language and bilingual poetry in *Carolina Cuban* (pb. in *Triple Crown: Chicano, Puerto Rican, and Cuban-American Poetry*, 1987) and *Bilingual Blues: Poems, 1981-1994* (1995) supports this notion. For example, he calls the Spanish-language preface to *Carolina Cuban* "Vo(I)ces," in deceptively simple recognition of an anglophone self (*I*) located in between Spanish (*voces*) and English (*voices*). In the verse dedication to the same collection he ponders the paradox of writing in a language to which he does not "belong," at the same time belonging "nowhere else,/ if not here/ in English." Pérez Firmat explores the equivalence of language and place further in "Home," in which home is as much a linguistic as a geographic construct: "[L]et him have a tongue,/ a story, a geography." Bilingual wordplay at the service of identity is Pérez Firmat's forte, as in "Son-Sequence": "Son as plural being./ Son as rumba beat./ Son as progeny." Suggestively, the confluence in this poem of language (*son*, "they are," from the Spanish verb of being *ser*), culture (the Cuban *son*, a musical form), and ancestry (the English *son* or offspring) acknowledges some of the time-honored preoccupations of many Latino poets.

END OF THE TWENTIETH CENTURY

In the 1980's and 1990's, the changing demographic patterns of Spanish-speaking immigrants combined with an ever-increasing interest in multicultural literature in both the marketplace and the classroom to bring broader recognition for Latino literature. Anthologies with a pan-Latino approach not only have brought together Chicano, Puerto Rican, and Cuban American writers but also have introduced new writers from other Latino backgrounds. Certainly Julia Alvarez, a Dominican born in New York City, is the most prominent of these writers (if for her fiction more than her poetry). As in her fiction, though, she has examined various problems of language and identity in her poetry (*The Other Side/El otro lado* [1995], *Homecoming: New and Collected Poems* [1996], and *Seven Trees* [1998]). Of special interest in Alvarez's poetry and poetics is the interplay of identity, form, and the poetic tradition as she proposes new ways to approach set forms (the sonnet, the villanelle, and the sestina) that reflect her identity as a woman poet, a bilingual poet, and a Latina poet.

The example of Alvarez underscores some significant developments in the field of Latino poetry since the publication of foundational works like *I Am Joaquín* and *Puerto Rican Obituary*. Latina poets, of course, receive more attention now than ever before. In addition, however, Latinas are included in the context of women poets in general. Similarly, anthologies and research have brought together Latinos and other poets on the basis of broad multicultural considerations. Some Latino poets

also write for a young adult or children's audience. Other configurations have incorporated Latino poetry into American diaspora literature, Jewish letters, border writing, or gay and lesbian literature. Perhaps the most sweeping trend is the approach championed by the research activities of the Recovering the U.S. Hispanic Literary Heritage project: the inclusion of all Hispanic literature written in the United States, of all periods and in Spanish as well as in English. The project's anthology *Herencia: The Anthology of Hispanic Literature of the United States* (2002, edited by Nicolás Kanellos) reflects this objective. In fact, in this body of literature, Latino literature written in English is incorporated within the broader parameters of U.S. Hispanic literature.

BIBLIOGRAPHY

Cruz, Victor Hernández, Leroy V. Quintana, and Virgil Suarez, eds. *Paper Dance: Fifty-five Latino Poets*. New York: Persea, 1995. Notable for the inclusion of bicultural poets from numerous backgrounds, primarily Chicano and Mexican, Dominican, Cuban, and Puerto Rican, but also Colombian, Ecuadorian, and Guatemalan.

González, Ray, ed. *After Aztlan: Latino Poets of the Nineties*. Boston: Godine, 1992. Prolific anthology editor González collects thirty-four "poets coming into their own in the eighties and nineties," mostly Chicanos but also the leading Puerto Rican poets (Martín Espada, Victor Hernández Cruz, and Judith Ortiz Cofer).

Kanellos, Nicolás, ed. *Herencia: The Anthology of Hispanic Literature of the United States*. New York: Oxford University Press, 2002. This multigenre anthology, which begins with the Spanish American colonial period, has an indispensable introduction and biobibliographical synopses of each of the more than 150 authors or anonymous works. Reflects the current status of the Recovering the U.S. Hispanic Literary Heritage project and of Kanellos's own contributions to the field.

Lomelí, Francisco, ed. *Handbook of Hispanic Cultures in the United States: Literature and Art*. Houston: Arte Público and Instituto de Cooperación Iberoamericana, 1993. An essential source with discrete essays (and extensive bibliographies) by experts on

Puerto Rican, Cuban American, and Chicano literature; Hispanic aesthetic concepts; Latina writers; literary language; and Hispanic exile in the United States. The first of a four-volume set; the other three cover history, sociology, and anthropology.

Milligan, Bryce, Mary Guerrero Milligan, and Angela de Hoyos, eds. *¡Floricanto Sí! A Collection of Latina Poetry*. New York: Penguin, 1998. Brings together forty-seven both established and previously unknown or emerging Latina poets, including a few who write primarily in Spanish. These San Antonio-based writer-publishers had featured some twenty-five of the same writers in a previous compilation, *Daughters of the Fifth Sun: A Collection of Latina Fiction and Poetry* (1995). The insightful introductions to both collections elucidate aesthetic, thematic, critical, and bibliographic issues of Latina poetry and poetics in the 1990's.

Poey, Delia, and Virgil Suárez, eds. *Little Havana Blues: A Cuban-American Literature Anthology*. Houston: Arte Público, 1996. Features sixteen poets (mainly second-generation Cuban Americans) writing principally in English and from within the boundaries of American literature, as distinct from their literary forebears. A brief but informative introduction to the multigenre anthology outlines historical, chronological, aesthetic, and thematic considerations.

Revista Chicano-Riqueña (1973-1985), continued by *The Americas Review* (1986-1999). These reviews published poetry (among other genres), scholarly articles and book reviews, interviews, and visual art. The foundational journal of Latino literature in both breadth and depth of coverage.

Sánchez González, Lisa. *Boricua Literature: A Literary History of the Puerto Rican Diaspora*. New York: New York University Press, 2001. Although this study focuses on narrative genres rather than on poetry, it illuminates the literary historical, cultural, and intellectual framework within which Nuyorican poetry has flourished.

Catharine E. Wall
(including original translations)

MACEDONIAN POETRY

Like the Slovenes, the Macedonians have had to travel a rocky historical path. After their early state was subjugated in the eleventh century by the Byzantines and, later, by the Turks, they did not enjoy independence until 1945. During those long centuries, however, they were able to maintain their identity, both ethnically and culturally; when conditions became favorable at the end of World War II, they began to produce their own literature.

Despite this long history of oppression, Macedonian culture can trace its heritage back to the earliest Slavic writings, which appeared in the ninth century in the language of the Macedonian Slavs around Salonika. Centering on the lively activity of Macedonian missionaries, led by Klement Ohridski and Naum Ohridski and their disciples, early Macedonian literature was exclusively related to the Church. Indeed, for many centuries, the only Macedonian literature that was not directly connected with the Church was oral folk literature, which was as abundant in Macedonia as in other South Slavic lands. Much of this literature was in poetic form. Unfortunately, because of its oral nature, not much has been preserved. Today, folklorists are making concerted efforts to record and document what remains of this tradition, and at least some of the folk literature that can still be heard has been handed down for generations.

EIGHTEENTH AND NINETEENTH CENTURIES

The first known verses in Macedonian were written by Kiril Pejčinoviḱ-Tetoec (c. 1770-1845). The beginning of known Macedonian poetry coincided with the revival of national awareness and the struggle against the Turks and the Greek clergy, who had tried strenuously to suppress the Macedonian language and the development of Macedonian literature. The next generation of writers included several poets: Jordan Hadži Konstantinov-Džinot (1820-1882), Dimitrije Miladinov (1810-1862), Konstantin Miladinov (1830-1862), Rajko Žinzifov (1839-1877), and Grigor Prličev (1830-1893). The Miladinov brothers were especially active in their efforts to introduce Macedonian in schools and in collecting and publishing folk poetry. For their nationalistic activity, they both died in a prison in Constantinople.

Žinzifov, a talented poet and an erudite scholar (he was graduated from Moscow University), was also instrumental in collecting and translating folk poetry, and his own poetry is not without merit. The most talented of these writers was Grigor Prličev. As a student of Greek, he wrote in Greek the epic poems *Serdar* (1860; *The Sirdar*, 1973) and *Skender beg* (1861; Skender Bey), which he later translated into Macedonian. He also translated Homer's *Iliad* (c. 800 B.C.E.) and *Odyssey* (c. 800 B.C.E.) into his native language. The poetry of all of these poets, being so closely connected with the struggle of their people for independence, has more historical than artistic value. By writing in their own language, they helped to preserve it in literature after centuries of suppression. They also drew heavily from folk poetry, bringing that cultural treasure into focus and perhaps saving it from oblivion.

TWENTIETH CENTURY

In the creation of Yugoslavia at the end of World War I (the new nation of the Southern Slavs was not known by that name until 1929), the Macedonians were denied their nationality once again. Their writers were again forced to live and write outside their native land, for writing and publishing in Macedonian were not allowed. Among these émigré writers, three stand out: Kosta Racin (1908-1943), Venko Markovski (born 1915), and Kole Nedelkovski (1912-1943). By far the most important of the three, Racin was the first to publish a collection of poems in Macedonian, *Beli mugri* (1939; white dawns). Here, Racin depicts the plight of his countrymen, who were often forced to go for long periods to other countries, especially the United States, to look for work.

The recognition of Macedonian nationality within Yugoslavia at the end of World War II triggered a burst of cultural and literary activity. A single dialect was chosen to serve as the basis for Macedonia's literary language, and books began to be published in great numbers. More important, several writers and poets of unmistakable talent emerged, laying the foundation of contemporary literature and poetry. Among these, three stand out: Slavko Janevski (1920-2000), Blaźe Koneski

(1921-1993), and Aco Šopov (1923-1983). Janevski's poetry, whether about his war experiences or about his intimate concerns, is characterized by a picturesque quality, originality, boldness, and even a touch of black humor. In form, he is just as bold, imaginative, and innovative. The author of the first Macedonian novel, he is active in other genres, although poetry still seems to be his main interest. Blaže Koneski, an academician who has done pioneering work in the field of the Macedonian language, writes direct, intimate, and meditative poetry. Macedonian motifs—mythical, folkloric, and contemporary—are frequently found in his somewhat traditional and subdued poems. Koneski is a master of controlled pathos and understatement. Aco Šopov published the first Macedonian book of poetry after World War II and thus started, along with Janevski and Koneski, the process of establishing the right of Macedonian poetry to exist. A subtle lyricist, a sensitive observer, and a poet of intense personal experience, Šopov enriched Macedonian poetry at the very beginning of the new period, thus creating models for the younger poets. He was also one of the first to liberate Macedonian poetry from nonaesthetic criteria in the late 1940's.

After these three poets, the road was open for a large number of remarkably capable poets. Mateja Matevski (born 1929) and Gané Todorovski (born 1929) were the leaders in the second generation of contemporary Macedonian poets. Matevski contributed to the transformation of declarative, descriptive, and confessional Macedonian poetry into a meditative and abstract approach bordering at times on the surreal. Influenced by French poets, he paid great attention to form, attempting to strike a balance between an abundance of impressions and an economy of expression. Todorovski's poetry shows a peculiar sensitivity and strong linguistic ability.

Radovan Pavlovski (born 1936) and Bogomil Gjuzel (born 1939) belong to the third wave of modern Macedonian poets. Pavlovski is a poet of extraordinary imagistic invention and an almost animistic approach to the natural world. His images seem to rise out of the unconscious with echoes of folklore and rural life. The sense of nostalgia, of loss, that one experiences in reading his verse recalls the spirit of anonymous folk poetry, yet Pavlovski gives his expression a thoroughly modern and sophisticated tone. Gjuzel is a more contemplative poet, but with equally close ties to his native soil. In his work, one can see the beginnings of a conscious effort to organize the Macedonian experience and sensibility. His poems impress the reader by their formal excellence and the evocative and sensuous quality of his language.

BIBLIOGRAPHY

Barac, Antun. *A History of Yugoslav Literature.* Ann Arbor. Mich.: The Joint Committee on Eastern Europe Publication Series, 1973. A standard history of all Yugoslav literatures and poetry, including a brief discussion of Macedonian poetry, by a leading literary scholar. Although somewhat outdated, it still provides reliable information, especially of the older periods

Padron, Justo Jorge. "Contemporary Poetry in Macedonia." *Equivalences*, no. 17 (1989): 7-21. Interesting views on Macedonian poetry by a Spanish poet and publisher, thus offering an outsider's perspective.

Reid, Graham W. "Difference of Soil and Climate: Poetry in Macedonia." *Macedonian Review* 2 (1972): 230-235. A long-standing translator of Macedonian poetry, Reid provides a brief overview of contemporary Macedonian poetry, stressing the influence of soil and climate on its poets.

Szporer, Michael. Introduction to *Stremež* 30, nos. 4/5 (1986): 223-239. The editor of an important anthology of Macedonian poetry, Szporer writes down his views and impressions of this poetry, seeing different waves of poetic generations, and including women poets and younger poets hitherto inadequately represented.

Urošević, Vlada. "Macedonian Poetry Between Yesterday and Today." *Concerning Poetry* 17, no. 2 (1984): 157-163. An essay by a leading Macedonian poet, discussing the sources of Macedonian poetry, its present achievements, and favorable outlook for the future.

Vasa D. Mihailovich

NATIVE AMERICAN POETRY

The first humans to inhabit the North American continent are believe to have arrived by crossing the land bridge over the Bering Strait, between ten and perhaps as early as fifty thousand years ago. During the long development of many highly elaborated cultures in the Western Hemisphere, a rich body of literature was produced, the earliest of which manifested itself as spoken, or oral, literature. Of that oral literature, some minute portion has been recorded in written texts and, more recently, in film and audiotape. Within contemporary traditional Indian communities, oral poetry is still being composed and performed.

ORAL TRADITIONS OF THE SOUTH AMERICAN INDIAN

The categories of verbal arts among peoples with oral cultures are not always the same as genres in written literatures. The English category of "verse," for example, has no counterpart in many North American Indian literatures. Speakers of indigenous languages may say, "We have no poetry in our language," meaning that spoken, metered verbal artifacts are not composed; the same languages may, however, have a highly developed song tradition, which will be recognized as comparable to the European concept of lyric. For example, the O'odham (Papago) of southern Arizona maintain that "poetry" as it is defined in English does not exist in their language, but they have many songs. Moreover, songs belong to a special category of verbal production; they are composed in a unique language used only for songs, and special composition processes and performance requirements go along with the production of songs. The following Papago song illustrates some of these characteristics:

> In the great night my heart will go out.
> Towards me the darkness comes rattling,
> In the great night my heart will go out.

The words and music were not consciously composed by the song's "owner" but were received in a dream from a person who had died. "Song dreaming" is a feature of traditional Papago literary composition. The function of the song, as part of a ritual intended to heal the sick and prevent death, is also characteristic of many oral poetic traditions.

LYRIC POETRY

In *Native American Literature* (1985), Andrew Wiget identified two major types of American Indian poetry: lyric poetry and ritual poetry. Lyric poetry, while it may have ritual or religious subject matter, is personal, expressive, and often highly emotional. Although composers and their audiences would be likely to divide songs into very different categories, non-Indian readers of translated lyrics may recognize familiar classifications such as love songs, elegies for grief, or lyrics of exultation and boastfulness. An elegy translated from Tlingit, a language spoken in coastal British Columbia, is by a woman whose brothers were drowned; it alludes to the place and manner of their death as she expresses the grieving emotions of sorrow, denial, and despair: "Your reef has beaten me, Kagwantan's children./ But take pity on me."

Not all lyrics are tied so closely to personal experience or emotion. Like other peoples, Native Americans have a large store of songs identified with various functions of daily living. Some recognizable categories are work songs, such as corn-grinding songs or rowing songs (which accompany the carrying out of repetitious tasks), lullabies, hunting songs, and gambling and game songs, such as the many songs still being composed to accompany the widespread hand game. Numerous traditional corn-grinding songs, some very old, are part of the literatures of the agricultural peoples of the Southwest. This corn-grinding song from the pueblo of Laguna, New Mexico, has characteristic forms and devices:

> I-o-ho, wonder-water,
> I-o-ho, wonder water,
> Life anew to him who drinks!
> Look where southwest clouds are bringing rain;
> Look where southeast clouds are bringing rain!

Like many others, this song contains vocables; these untranslatable syllables or phrases may be remnants of archaic languages, they may be part of the special poetic language reserved for songs, or they may simply be rhythmic units incorporated into the total structure of the song. Rain, water, and clouds appear repeatedly in all the songs and stories from this arid region. Directional signals are important for the continual expression of the people's relationship to the center of their universe; the balancing of southeast and southwest integrates the life of the community with the four cardinal directions.

RITUAL POETRY

Ritual poetry, in relation to lyric poems, is more communal and less personal in expression, composition, and performance. While the actual texts of ritual poems may appear quite short, often elements are intended to be repeated many times. In other cases, individual passages or poems may be part of much larger performance productions, great ceremonies lasting as long as eight or nine days, which could be considered whole poems or dramatic productions in themselves.

Wiget subdivides ritual poetry into integrative, restorative, and transformational modes. Integrative rituals function as rites of passage, assisting the individual to pass safely from one stage of life, or identity, to another. Thus there are ceremonies for birth and naming, for puberty and initiation into adulthood, for death and dying. Among the integrative songs Wiget also includes healing songs intended to enable the sick or dying individual to make safe passage back to the community.

One of the most widely known healing songs is a lyric that forms part of the Navajo Night Chant. The Night Chant is a major ceremony of healing for the Navajo people; when performed in full it lasts ten days and nights and involves many ceremonial observances such as face and body painting, ingestion of medicines, dry painting of sacred pictures, and feasting and dancing. The poem is sung as part of the ceremonial activities of the third day; the words allude to a particular place, which is said to be the House of Dawn, and also to sacred or holy beings that are part of the spiritual reality of the Navajo people.

The Night Chant ceremony of which the song is a part is performed to cure and reintegrate the individual into a healthy, viable community. The title of N. Scott Momaday's Pulitzer Prize-winning novel, *House Made of Dawn* (1968), comes from this poem; the novel depicts the struggle of an alienated young man to heal himself of deep psychological distress and reintegrate himself into his Pueblo community. In the novel, the poem

appears as sung by one of the characters; it becomes part of Abel's healing.

The words of this song, as translated by Washington Matthews, express fundamental Navajo ideas regarding the ideal relationship of the individual to the universe:

> Happily, with abundant dark clouds, may I walk.
> . . . .
> May it be beautiful all around me.
> In beauty it is finished.

The English word "beauty" is used to translate a Navajo term that encompasses concepts of balance, harmony, and movement through time. Balance is expressed in the alternation and repetition of parallel figures and tropes: Dawn and evening light, clouds and showers, plants and pollen are paired and joined in the poem. The rhetorical pairing and doubling of pairs corresponds to the Navajo conceptualization of the universe: All entities are seen as gendered (hence the poem makes reference to "male rain" and "female rain"), and quaternary patterning in doubled pairs reflects the fundamental cognitive ordering principle. Four directions, four colors, four sacred mountains at the four corners of the world, four sacred plants, and countless other sets of four recur in all forms of Navajo discourse. The magnificent culmination of the poem expresses the sense of motion, centering, and balancing of four in the repositioning of the speaker at the center of a world of beauty: The four significant directions are before, behind, below, and above, and then comes the inclusive "all around."

Restorative poetry is a type Wiget defines as forming part of communal ceremonies devoted to redefining the origins and continuity of the community within the natural world. Such ceremonies characteristically incorporate references to myths of creation and origin; sometimes they are called "world-renewal" ceremonies. Like important rituals in other cultures, ceremonial observances in Native American traditions have some resemblance to dramatic performances. An early attempt to transcribe, describe, and translate such a ceremony of renewal is Alice Fletcher's work in the 1800's with the Hako ceremony of the Pawnee, which honors Mother Corn:

> Loud, loud the young eagles cry, cry, seeing their
>   mother come;

Flies she to them slantwise, flies;
Then over the nest she hangs, there hovering, stays her
     flight;
Thanks, thanks as we look we give.

. . . .

Then over the nest she drops; there, folding her wings,
     she rests,
Rests safely within her nest.

The translation reflects both Fletcher's nineteenth century conception of appropriate poetic diction and her attempt to replicate the rhythms she thought she heard in the original Pawnee. The poem displays the acute observation of natural phenomena characteristic of much Native American literature; it vividly renders the sight of the mother eagle approaching the nest, circling and seeming to hover, and finally settling upon it. In addition, the poem reflects a particular moment in the ceremony. Fletcher's notes explain to the reader that these texts are part of rites involving feathers, meant to represent nest building and the relationship of parent and child in the founding myth.

Wiget finds transformational ritual and poetry in the Ghost Dance religion and its songs and rites. Such rituals, he maintains, attempt to negotiate passage between the death of some fundamental element in the culture and the origin or birth of a new order. They differ from world-renewal rites, which replicate an original mythic creation of the universe, by introducing the idea of a new reality not referable to the old, original order. Certain syncretic religious forms, such as the Yaqui Easter ceremonies (which incorporate Catholic and traditional motifs) or the North American peyote rite (which combines Mexican, Plains Indian, and Methodist elements) might also be included under this rubric.

Certain features recur characteristically in lyric and ritual poems of Native American cultures. Repetition is obvious and logical as a mnemonic device. The visual and verbal compression of many written translations of lyric texts, mistaken by the early twentieth century Imagist movement as a protomodernist, Native American form of literary Imagism, belies the effect of these texts' performance, for verses are customarily repeated, sometimes as many as thirty-six times. Striking visual imagery based on close observation of the natural world pervades the poems, but translated poems can be difficult to grasp or may mislead the English-speaking reader unfamiliar with their references to occasions of composition or reception or to places with which particular stories are associated. Thus, a song received from an animal or another being in a dream may be spoken in the persona of that creature, as are these lines from a hunting song:

> I ate the thornapple leaves
> And the leaves made me dizzy.
> I drank thornapple flowers
> And the drink made me stagger
> The hunter, Bow-remaining,
> He overtook and killed me,
> Cut and threw my horns away.

Not only are the sung words understood as spoken by the deer, but the whole song forms part of a ceremony designed to assure a successful hunt by inducing the deer to sacrifice itself to the hunters. Part of the ceremony involves eating a mind-altering drug, *datura*, which the translator here calls "thornapple leaves." This song would be sung by a dancer who assumes the persona of the deer in the ceremony; the language refers simultaneously to the behavior of an actual deer, to the singer's dream, and to the circumstances of the rite.

WRITTEN TRANSCRIPTIONS OF ORAL POETRY

The collection of written texts of Native American oral poetry begins with the preservation of some few of the great codices of the Mayas and the Aztecs of Mexico and Central America; many of these works were transported as curiosities to collections in Europe, and translations into European languages have been attempted from time to time. Serious attempts to transcribe and translate North American oral literatures began in the 1830's, when Henry Rowe Schoolcraft transcribed the legends and myths told to him by his wife and members of her Ojibwa family.

Somewhat later in the century, after the Civil War, a major movement to record Native American languages and preserve records of native cultures was launched under the sponsorship of major museums, folklore societies, and, especially, the United States government through the Bureau of American Ethnology. The impetus for the project in "salvage ethnography" was a perception that American Indian cultures were inexorably disappearing, and it was important to preserve as much of their remains as possible before the expected end came. The preservationist motive led to collecting of texts primarily for purposes of linguistic study and ethnographic information, rather than as aesthetic objects in their own right. Nevertheless, some of the finest examples of literary translation come from this period; the translations of Washington Matthews from Navajo and the studies of the musician Frances Densmore are particularly noteworthy. Such poems as were translated were published as parts of government reports, bulletins of learned societies, or articles in scholarly journals. From these sources were mined the selections presented in the earliest anthologies of traditional American Indian poetry.

A very early compendium of American Indian literature and song texts is Natalie Curtis's *The Indians' Book* (1907, 1968). Curtis intended her book to permit Indians to speak for themselves as much as possible; she took pains to use graphics by Indian artists, as well as to include musical notation to encourage performance of the songs. Her translation method remains the model for translating such texts today: Her fourfold presentation of each text included a transcription from the original language, a separate transcription with musical notation, an interlinear ("non-grammatical") literal translation, and a more "literary" poem text. Curtis's collection was followed by *The Path on the Rainbow* (1918), edited by George W. Cronyn and reissued as *American Indian Poetry* (1962). Unlike Curtis, Cronyn did not himself collect the texts he printed from their Indian owners, but reprinted excerpts from the ethnological collections then being published in abundance. He was not particularly knowledgeable about Indian culture or literature, and he sometimes changed texts he did not understand into something more conformable to his idea of the poetic. He also included non-Indian poems written by contemporaries who had been inspired by the modernist characteristics they perceived in Native American poems. Nevertheless, *The Path on the Rainbow* was the first collection to bring the literary accomplishments of Native American oral poets to the attention of the larger reading public.

Following Curtis and Cronyn, two anthologists working in the 1940's brought out responsibly edited general collections of Native American poetry and prose. Margot Astrov's *The Winged Serpent* (1946), reprinted as *American Indian Prose and Poetry* (1962), included some contextual notes to the texts and fragments she reprinted, as well as a reliable bibliography and helpful introduction. Astrov was the first to reprint the "House Made of Dawn" song from the Night Chant, and it was probably in her collection that Momaday found the poem he placed at the heart of his novel. In 1951, A. Grove Day published *The Sky Clears: Poetry of the American Indians*. Grove Day's book also reprints poems from ethnological and other publications but incorporates them into an extensive discussion of the literary, cultural, and historical backgrounds that form the context for the lyrics; the book is not so much anthology as it is a scholarly introduction incorporating many texts as examples. This collection has the most comprehensive bibliography of sources for translated poem texts. A later collection of American Indian poetry is John Bierhorst's *The Sacred Path: Spells, Prayers, and Power Songs of the American Indians* (1983).

From the beginnings of such studies, translators, editors, and scholars have been in general agreement that lyric texts from Native American cultures correspond to poetry in English, whereas narrative texts are basically prose productions. In the 1960's, two linguistics specialists challenged this view by offering conceptualizations of Native American narratives as essentially poetic in nature. Dennis Tedlock and Dell Hymes, using different approaches and materials, initiated discussion of an aesthetic and linguistic discourse that they call ethnopoetics.

Tedlock, a field researcher, collected and translated texts from a number of poet-storytellers. The basis for his theory of ethnopoetics, and the illustrative translations, came out of his work with Zuñi storytellers in New Mexico. Tedlock's theory of poetry holds that phonetic components of language, such as pitch, pause, and stress, define the poetic line. He identifies patterning of these elements in Zuñi narratives and asserts that these tales must actually be regarded as narrative poems comparable to ballads or epics in other traditions. The explanation and examples of his theory are worked out in the introduction and texts he compiled in *Finding the Center: Narrative Poetry of the Zuñi Indians* (1972). The texts themselves are printed in Zuñi and English, with typographical cues such as capitals, superscripts, subscripts, and italics to indicate performance elements of pause, pitch, and stress.

Hymes's ethnopoetics theory derives from work with written texts. Hymes worked with texts collected by linguists working with peoples of the Northwest (Oregon, Washington, and British Columbia), notably the collections of Melville Jacobs. The ethnopoetic theory he developed from these works sees poetic patterning in rhetorical configurations of repetition, parallel, and chiasmus at the level of word, phrase, line, and plot element. This analysis led to reconfiguring printed versions of the stories to look less like prose and more like poetry, with parallel elements set off by line divisions and indentation. Many narrative texts that Hymes restructured in this way came to have an apparently dramatic structure, which he sometimes indicates by notations of act and scene divisions. Hymes did not publish an anthology of texts but printed examples of ethnopoetic renderings of stories in his major work *"In Vain I Tried to Tell You": Essays in Native American Ethnopoetics* (1981).

MODERN WRITTEN POETRY

By contrast with the long and rich history of oral poetry, written poetry by Native Americans is of relatively recent date. Two nineteenth century poets are noted by A. LaVonne Brown Ruoff in her introductory book, *American Indian Literatures* (1990): John Rollin Ridge and Emily Pauline Johnson. These two poets wrote conventional nineteenth century verse; they were followed in the first half of the twentieth century by writers such as Alexander Posey, who primarily produced fiction, satire, humor, or nonfiction and who wrote little if any poetry. After World War II, in the 1950's and 1960's, a Native American Renaissance in literature began to take place; it continued in the 1970's and 1980's with a virtual explosion of poetry by young Native American writers.

Nora Marks Dauenhauer occupies a unique place among late twentieth century Native American poets. A fluent speaker of Tlingit, Dauenhauer is one of few poets who translate from the classical Native American languages. She undertook a massive project to publish significant works on Tlingit oral literature by the few remaining performers of that literature. She has written and edited many works on Tlingit language and literature, including *Haa Shuká, Our Ancestors: Tlingit Oral Narratives* (1987); *Haa Tuwunáagu Yís, for Healing Our Spirit: Tlingit Oratory* (1990), featuring a dual-language presentation that makes use of a free-verse format to suggest speech performance; *Haa kusteeyí, Our Culture: Tlingit Life Stories* (1994), Dauenhauer's own poetry reflects an interest in formal experimentation as well as preoccupations of traditional Native American life; "Tlingit Concrete Poem," for example, uses the conventions of concrete poetry as well as mixing Tlingit and English in a visual pun. Her major collections include *The Droning Shaman* (1990) and *Live Woven with Song* (2000).

Dauenhauer is only one of a number of poets of the Pacific Northwest. Another notable poet is Duane Niatum, who has published several collections, including *Songs for the Harvester of Dreams* (1981) and *The Crooked Beak of Love* (2000). Niatum also edited the most representative collection of contemporary American Indian poetry, *Harper's Anthology of Twentieth-Century Native American Poetry* (1986), which remained in print through 1999.

Although most widely noted as a writer of prose, fiction, and nonfiction, Kiowa writer N. Scott Momaday began his career as a poet. His major collection *The Gourd Dancer* (1976) shows a variety of influences: the post-Symbolist poetics that intrigued his mentor and friend Yvor Winters; American Romanticism and anti-Romanticism of the nineteenth century, especially in the work of Emily Dickinson, whom Momaday admires greatly; and oral traditions of both Native American and Euroamerican culture. His poetry finds a place in the meditative-contemplative tradition of Western literature. His complex and highly wrought poem "Before an Old Painting of the Crucifixion" displays characteristics typical of much of Momaday's work: a speaker, positioned before some visible object or vista, who silently contemplates the enigma of phenomena as they appear before him. Momaday's philosophical position in such poems resembles that of Wallace Stevens: Both poets assert the absolute cleavage between knowing mind and intractable external reality, and both affirm the power of the imagination to create coherence and significance beyond the nihilism of the mind-world abyss. Explicitly in interviews, and by implication in his writings, Momaday has expressed admiration for what he sees as the Native American sense of continuity and familiarity with nature; unlike the Romantic Western vision, Momaday says, American Indian philosophy does not see an unbridgeable chasm between mind and matter. His second novel, *The Ancient Child* (1990), an uneven work that contains some of his poetry published elsewhere, explores the possibility of undoing the split and restoring the old continuity with the natural world.

The Keresan-speaking pueblos of Laguna and Acoma in New Mexico, and their environs, have been home to four of the most productive younger Native American poets. Leslie Marmon Silko, Simon J. Ortiz, Paula Gunn Allen, and Carol Lee Sanchez all have family or childhood roots in the area. Silko's best-known work, her novel *Ceremony* (1977), appeared a few years after her poetry collection *Laguna Woman* (1974); some of the poems from that volume as well as new works were incorporated into the later mixed-genre book *Storyteller* (1981). Although her theoretical emphasis is on narrative forms and she has spoken extensively on the process of storytelling and its function in maintaining identity and community, Silko's poems often tend to be brief first-person lyrics relying on natural imagery to convey deep personal emotion. An exception is "Storytelling," which captures in its free-verse rhythms the give-and-take of storytelling in the communal situation as well as the sense of ancient myth that stands behind and lends coherence to chaotic present reality.

Simon J. Ortiz, from the pueblo of Acoma, is unusual in living close to the landscape that inspires him and has informed his sense of generations of continuity with the land. His poetry is often sacramental in its reverence for the mysterious power of the particular place and in its outrage at desecrations perpetrated by materialism and commercialism; yet he reaches out, as in the collection titled *From Sand Creek* (1981), to embrace a vision of Indian (as distinct from tribal) identity and common purpose. Both this collection and his *After and Before the Lightning* (1994) interweave prose narrative and poetry, the latter to relate his experiences during a winter on the Rosebud Indian Reservation.

Paula Gunn Allen and her cousin Carol Lee Sanchez maintain their continuity with land and landscape in imagination from the perspective of urban academia. Allen is outspoken in an ongoing project of reclaiming feminist thought from what she sees as middle-class Anglo values; in poems such as "Madonna of the Hills" she sets out to recover and celebrate the strength of women and to subvert facile judgments of victimization and superficial categories of beauty. Allen has also published fiction and criticism; her major collections of poetry include *Skins and Bones: Poems, 1979-1987* (1988) and *Life Is a Fatal Disease: Collected Poems, 1962-1995* (1997).

The poems of Sanchez's *Conversations from the Nightmare* (1975), *She) Poems* (1995), and *From Spirit to Matter: New and Selected Poems, 1969-1996* (1997) make highly experimental use of traditional Pueblo and Indian material; "Open Dream Sequence" expresses the nightmare distortions of surrealist art, while "Tribal Chant" explores the question of dual identity in a synthesis of Spanish and English. Like Momaday, Wendy Rose, and Joy Harjo, Sanchez is a visual artist as well as a poet.

Louise Erdrich and Gerald Vizenor, Ojibwa poets, both have roots in the woodlands area of the Great Lakes, though Erdrich belongs to the displaced Turtle Mountain Chippewa of North Dakota. Widely recognized for her series of North Dakota novels as well as collaborations with her husband, Michael Dorris, Erdrich has also collected her poems in *Jacklight* (1984) and *Baptism of Desire* (1990). Both collections expand her exploration in her fiction of the clashes and dissonances brought about by membership and loyalty to both Euroamerican and Native American traditions. The two books contain retellings of oral tales featuring the folk hero Potchikoo. The poignant poem series "The Butcher's Wife" in *Jacklight* explores the delicacy of feeling and violent passions of ordinary, unremarkable people. In *Baptism of Desire* Erdrich celebrates in a series of poems based on popular hagiographies the Catholic folk beliefs that provide much of the comedy of her novels; other poems in this collection express her continuing fascination with various occult symbol systems. Since the publication of *Baptism of Desire*, Erdrich has focused on essays and novels. Critics note her interest in exploring the tension between Christian and Anishinaabe belief systems, no doubt due to her own experiences as a person of mixed heritage.

Gerald Vizenor is one of the most prolific of American Indian authors, producing journalism, fiction, criticism, screenplays, and autobiography as well as poetry. He has lived in Asia for extended periods, first in Japan with the armed forces and then as a visiting professor in the People's Republic of China, and has incorporated into his work an appreciation for Asian literatures, particularly the very short Japanese form of *haiku*. *Seventeen Chirps* (1964, 1968) and *Slight Abrasions* (1966) are collections of Vizenor's haiku; appreciation of the imagistic compression of haiku also informs Vizenor's reworking in *Summer in the Spring* (1981) of Frances Densmore's translations of Chippewa lyrics. In 1984, much of Vizenor's poetry was collected in *Matsushima: Pine Islands*.

Joy Harjo, Carter Revard, and Linda Hogan are joined by a common heritage in Oklahoma, the old Indian Territory. Harjo, a distant relation of Creek writer Alexander Posey, is a musician as well as a painter and poet. Her poetry seeks an organic synthesis of visual and sound effects in what is often a dreamlike sense of metamorphosis and dissolution of cognitive boundaries. "Rainy Dawn," from her major collection *In Mad Love and War* (1990), is one of several prose vignettes in the volume; like many of her poems, it is dedicated to a family member. Later, she wrote two more collections of poetry—*The Woman Who Fell From the Sky* (1994) and *A Map to the Next World* (2000). Harjo, like many other poets, has combined her poetry with performing arts. She performs her work and plays saxophone with her band, Poetic Justice, which was originally envisioned as a musical vehicle to enhance her poetry but has become something more. In one of her recent poems she says, "All acts of kindness are lights in the war for justice." This sums up her theme dealing with politics. Her poetry goes beyond strictly Native American concerns; she explores the common American experience of immigration.

Both Harjo and Hogan, who is from a Chickasaw family, confront difficult social and political questions in their work. Harjo's elegy "For Anna Mae Pictou Aquash . . . ," dedicated to a young Native American woman apparently murdered by the Federal Bureau of Investigation, bears witness to ongoing persecution of those who work on behalf of the dispossessed. Hogan's poems frequently take up themes of poverty, deprivation, and injustice. In *Daughters I Love You* (1981), reprinted in *Eclipse* (1983), she offers a series of meditations on the evil and destruction of the nuclear culture. Her fourth collection of poetry, *Seeing Through the Sun* (1985), is more diverse, as she deals with mixed-blood heritage, human strengths and weaknesses, use of the land, urban life, feminism, and environmentalism. She attempts to synthesize all life in these poems—herself and others, humans and their environment. In 1988 she produced another volume of poems, *Savings*, that deals with the flight of many Native Americans to the cities, where they led frustrated and desperate lives. Her 1993 collection, called *The Book of Medicines* (1993), focuses on Hogan's belief that women need to be the primary caretakers of the environment. The poems act as therapeutic prayers to enable humans to clean up and restore their planet. Both Hogan and Harjo offer social criticism through the first-person lyric.

Osage poet Carter Revard, like Momaday, has won academic as well as literary honors. A professor and former Rhodes scholar, he has published fiction, autobiography, and criticism as well as poetry. Also like Momaday a compelling storyteller and enthusiastic raconteur, Revard is often at his best, as in "My Right Hand Don't Leave Me No More," when celebrating memories of his rambunctious, energetic family. Growing up in the Dust Bowl Oklahoma of the Great Depression, Revard chronicles his experiences from a childhood of poverty to his status as a respected scholar of medieval literature, using both forms and allusions ranging from Anglo-Saxon alliterative verse to tribal chants in such collections as *An Eagle Nation* (1993) and *Winning the Dust Bowl* (2001).

Wendy Rose and Maurice Kenny express the distinctive sensibility of urban experience. Rose's tribal background is Hopi and Miwok, but her life has been lived in the urban centers of the West Coast. Trained as an anthropologist, she has written from both sides of the studier-and-studied divide of Western scholarship; her poem "Academic Squaw" (from the collection *Academic Squaw: Reports to the World from the Ivory Tower*, 1977) is an acerbic look at the academic world from the point of view of the object of study. One of Rose's most noted collections is *The Halfbreed Chronicles and Other Poems* (1985); the title section contains a series of poems in which the personas of circus freaks, concentration camp survivors, and other victims offer stinging critiques of Western culture. Rose also produced *Lost Copper* (1986), in which her poems, or songs as some called them, reaffirmed her connection with the earth. In 1993 she issued *Going to War with All My Relations: New and Selected Poems*, and in 1994 *Bone Dance: New and Selected Poems, 1965-1993*, a major collection of selections from her previous collections as well as new poems. One critic said her poetry is able to "enhance our awareness of the human complexity of our social and moral dilemmas."

Rose's sometime collaborator Maurice Kenny is Mohawk and an award-winning poet, fiction writer, playwright, editor, and longtime resident of New York City. Kenny has been a publisher, directing the Strawberry Press; his poetry reflects some of the main currents in experimental literature in the mid-twentieth century, especially an affinity with the Beat generation. The opening lines from his "Wild Strawberry" carry resonances of Allen Ginsberg: "And I rode the Greyhound bus down to Brooklyn/ where I sit now eating woody strawberries/ grown on the backs of Mexican farmers." Kenny's work comprises both short and long poems. A book-length poem, *Tekonwatonti, Molly Brant, 1735-1795: Poems of War* (1992) chronicles the experiences of the sister of Mohawk leader Joseph Brant during the French and Indian War, who led her people in cooperation with the British, believing it the best way to preserve their Mohawk land and way of life. Kenny's many collections include *The Mama Poems* (1984) and *Between Two Rivers: Selected Poems, 1956-1984* (1987). A compilation of Kenny's major poems and prose was collected in 1995 in *On Second Thought*, edited by Joseph Bruchac.

Bruchac, with an Abenaki Indian, Slovak, and English heritage, was raised in the Adirondack foothills in New York. He is not only a well-known editor and chronicler of Native American literature but also a poet, a children's author, and a teller of traditional Native American tales. Like other poets, he has written and performed songs with his own musical group, the Dawn

Land Singers. Collections of his poems include *Flow* (1975), *The Good Message of Handsome Lake* (1979), *Near the Mountains* (1987), and *No Borders* (1999). In an attempt to understand poets and their poetry, Bruchac interviewed Native American poets and put the results together in *Survival This Way* (1987). He edited *Returning the Gift* (1994), a book that contains poetry and prose from the first Native American National Writers' Festival, and *Smoke Rising: The Native North American Literary Companion* (1995), an anthology of works by thirty-five Native American writers.

Ofelia Zepeda, professor of linguistics, was born and raised near the Tohono O'odham (Papago) and Pima reservations in Arizona. She not only is the foremost authority in Tohono O'odham, having created the first grammar for the language, but also teaches many Native Americans strategies for preserving their vanishing languages. She has published several bilingual collections of her own poetry in English and Tohono O'odham, the most important of which is *Ocean Power* (1995), dealing with the importance of the desert climate to people who live in the arid Southwest. In this collection she reflects on her life, the natural environment of the Arizona-Mexico border region, the seasons, the meeting of old and new, the past and the present, the human and natural worlds. The closing poems take as their subject the sea, and the Tohono O'odham's past relationship with the sea. Much of the poetry is in the Tohono O'odham language, with English translations provided. Zepeda has also edited poetry collections, such as *When It Rains*, a collection of Papago and Pima poetry.

Perhaps one of the most visible Native American writers to mainstream audiences is a Spokane/Cœur d'Alene Indian, Sherman Alexie, who grew up on an Indian reservation in Washington State. Soon after he was graduated from college, Alexie published two of his poetry collections: *The Business of Fancydancing* (1992) and *I Would Steal Horses* (1992). He shares with other contemporary Native American poets a love of performing his work, so he occasionally does readings and stand-up performances with musician Jim Boyd, a Colville Indian. Alexie is known for his humor as well as his performance ability. He and Boyd recorded an album, *Reservation Blues*, which contains songs from a novel of the same name that Alexie published in 1995.

In June, 1998, Alexie competed in his first World Heavyweight Poetry Bout, in which he defeated world champion Jimmy Santiago Baca. Because of his poetry, novels, and screenwriting skills, in 1999 *The New Yorker* recognized Alexie as one of the top writers of the twentieth century. His collection of mixed poetry and prose *One Stick Song* (2000) reveals many of his skills: his ability to handle multiple perspectives and complex psychological subject matter, his sense of humor, his facility with vivid scene setting, and a sweet sarcasm. Alexie gives voice to the feelings of many Native Americans combatting negative perceptions of them, and the emotions here range from dark humor to anger to grief. His formula "Poetry = anger × imagination" is expressed throughout this collection and reflects the experiences and emotions of many Native Americans at the beginning of the twenty-first century.

WHAT IS "NATIVE AMERICAN"?

Native Americans or American Indians (the terms themselves are misleading) are no monolithic group: Although contemporary Native American poets are close-knit as friends, colleagues, and collaborators, they do not form a distinctive school of poetry. Their formal allegiances are largely to experimental modes, though the first-person free-verse lyric tends to predominate, even in such apparently public modes as satire. Two major motifs can be identified as characteristic: on one hand, an abiding sense of continuity with the land (as distinguished from landscape), and on the other, a pervasive social consciousness stemming from the historical and personal experience of injustice. Ties to land, and meaning derived from survival within a given natural environment, are explicit in the works of poets such as Nora Dauenhauer, Simon Ortiz, and Leslie Silko; even urban poets such as Maurice Kenny and Wendy Rose look to severance from land as the precipitating injustice in their critique of contemporary civilization. Furthermore, in one way or another each of these poets is engaged with the difficulties and delights of being at once an inheritor of ancient cultural riches and a mediator between worlds of affluence and deprivation. Each is committed to tribal and Indian heritage and sees that heritage as a source of strength not only for Native American people but also for the world.

BIBLIOGRAPHY

Fast, Robin Riley. *The Heart as a Drum: Continuance and Resistance in American Indian Poetry.* Ann Arbor: University of Michigan Press, 1999. The author, who also has written on traditional American poets such as Emily Dickinson, has covered topics here on audience, community, "Talking Indian," telling stories, and "Toward a Native Poetics of Contested Spaces."

Harjo, Joy. *The Spiral of Memory: Interviews.* Ann Arbor: University of Michigan Press, 1995. Harjo, wrote the well-received *The Woman Who Fell from the Sky* (1994), has a unique poetic voice that speaks of her experiences as Native American, woman, and Westerner in today's society. This book is a collection of her discussions over the years covering her art, her origins, and the confrontation of Anglo and Native American civilizations.

Lincoln, Kenneth. *Sing with the Heart of a Bear: Fusions of Native and American Poetry, 1890-1999.* Berkeley: University of California Press, 1999. Lincoln examines contemporary poetry by way of ethnicity and gender. He tries to explain American as well as Native American literature, spirituality, and culture.

Niatum, Duane, ed. *Harper's Anthology of Twentieth Century Native American Poetry.* San Francisco, Calif.: Harpers, 1988. Not as new as some of the others on the list, this book still remains a good collection. Thirty-one poets are included, representing those who have written since 1900. Considered a definitive anthology.

Rosen, Kenneth. *Voices of the Rainbow: Contemporary Poetry by Native Americans.* New York: Arcade Publishing, 1993. Rosen has collected two hundred poems by twenty-one Native Americans, representing many tribes: Laguna, Sioux, Cheyenne, Pueblo, Chippewa, Oneida, Seneca/Seminole, Mohawk, and Blackfoot.

Rothberg, Jerome, ed. *Shaking the Pumpkin: Traditional Poetry of the Indian North Americas.* Albuquerque: University of New Mexico Press, 1991. The author, who also has written on ethnopoetics, has edited a large collection here of more than four hundred pages. Authors include Leslie Marmon Silke.

Smelcer, John, ed. *Durable Breath: Contemporary Native American Poetry.* Anchorage, Alaska: Salmon Run Publishing, 1994. The author has collected a good balance between an ancient vision and the modern world, using a wide range of authors. Central themes include loss and gain, and images of home.

Swann, Brian, ed. *Native American Songs and Poems: An Anthology.* New York: Dover Publications, 1997. A good cross-section of Native American songs and poetry. The poems range from lullabies to works by contemporary modern authors, both male and female.

Wilson, Norma. *The Nature of Native American Poetry.* Albuquerque: University of New Mexico Press, 2000. A collection of appealing and accessible essays that introduce and celebrate the poetry of modern Native American writers. Wilson draws from contemporary criticism, tribal history and folklore, interviews with writers, and the poetry itself. She places Native American poetry in a global and historical context.

Helen Jaskoski, updated by Gary Zacharias and Christina J. Moose

POLISH POETRY

THE MIDDLE AGES

Poland's acceptance of Christianity in its Western form in 966 resulted in the long-lasting domination of Latin as the language of written communication. It was three centuries later that Polish emerged as the language of literature. Paradoxically, the first known poem in Polish is, at the same time, the most accomplished literary product of the whole medieval period. "Bogurodzica" (Mother of God), an anonymous religious hymn from the thirteenth century preserved in a fifteenth century manuscript, consists of two stanzas with a highly complex parallel construction and sophisticated verse structure. Such a masterly piece could not have been created in a cultural vacuum; some tradition of oral poetry in Polish must have existed around that time, although nothing except "Bogurodzica" has been preserved in a written form.

Throughout the fourteenth and fifteenth centuries, Polish literature was characterized by the prevalence of religious poetry. The increasing participation of laymen in religious life brought about the growth of popular devotional literature in the vernacular. Its lyric genre breaks down thematically into Lenten and Easter songs, Christmas carols, hymns to the Virgin Mary, and so on. While being, for the most part, adaptations from Latin, some of these poems manage to strike an original note. "Żale Matki Boskiej pod Krzyżem" (the lament of the Mother of God at the foot of the Cross), a first-person monologue, is distinguished by its individualized point of view and emotional intensity. The epic genre was poorly represented in Polish literature of this period. "Legenda o św. Aleksym" (legend of Saint Alexis), for example, is a typical verse hagiography, drawing upon foreign sources and rather primitive in its form.

Polish secular poetry of the Middle Ages is less homogeneous. What has been preserved is a mosaic of poems written for various purposes and with various results. Some of them are merely mnemonic devices, while others are didactic or satiric; there are some shy attempts at erotic poetry as well. Perhaps the most interesting secular poem of the period is the fifteenth century "Rozmowa mistrza ze śmiercia" (conversation of a master with death); one of numerous variations upon the medieval theme of *memento mori*, it stands out by virtue of its vivid imagery and macabre humor.

In its versification, Polish medieval poetry was apparently based on a system of "relative syllabism," with lines equal to clauses and approximative rhymes. Judgments concerning the verse forms of this period, however, remain highly conjectural.

THE RENAISSANCE

Western European Humanism made its way into Poland as early as the second half of the fifteenth century, but it was only a hundred years later that the "Golden Age" of the Polish Renaissance came into full swing. Meanwhile, a few poets emerged who represent the period of transition. The first Polish poet whose biography is at least partly known is Biernat of Lublin (c. 1465-after 1529). *Raj duszny* (1513; paradise of the soul), his translation of a Latin prayer book, was thought until quite recently to be the first Polish book ever printed. His major poetic work, however, was *Zywot Ezopa Fryga* (the life of Aesop the Frygian), published probably in 1522, the first part of which is a rhymed biography of the legendary Aesop, and the second part of which presents a collection of fables supposedly "told" by him. The work expresses the philosophy of plebeian Humanism, but its style, versification, and humor are still of a distinctly medieval kind.

Another transitional figure, although much closer to the Renaissance mentality, was Mikolaj Rej (1505-1569), called, perhaps with some exaggeration, the father of Polish literature. A country squire with almost no formal education, he wrote prolifically all of his life and wrote exclusively in Polish. He therefore was not typical of the Renaissance epoch, which demanded from a writer equal fluency in Polish and Latin. Rej's stubborn defense of the vernacular was, however, also a result of the more general phenomenon of the awakening of national consciousness in the beginnings of the Renaissance. He was quite original in his appreciation of specifically Polish traits and ways of life. His poetry is mostly didactic, descriptive, or satiric, and it ranges from enormous versified treatises or dialogues to brief epigrams. As a poet, Rej undeniably lacks subtlety and artistic balance; his strengths are his passion for the particulars of life and his straightforward stylistic manner.

After all the shortcomings of his predecessors, the work of Jan Kochanowski (1530-1584) appears as a shining example of artistic perfection. He was a rare genius, not to be matched by any other poet of the Slavic world for the next two centuries. Kochanowski's work represents the Polish Renaissance in its most mature and refined form. A thoroughly educated Humanist, he was indebted to the classical heritage as well as to contemporary poetry of Italy and France, but he was able to give his writing a national specificity and personal tone. The bulk of his work is written in Polish, which he himself raised to the rank of a proficient literary language. His Polish output includes the collections *Fraszki* (1584; trifles), *Pieśni* (1586; songs), and *Treny* (1580; *Laments*, 1928), a masterly poetic adaptation of the Psalms, *Psalterz Dawidów* (1578), several epic poems, and a classical tragedy in verse, *Odprawa posłów greckich* (1578; *The Dismissal of the Grecian Envoys*, 1928). If the Anacreontic *Fraszki* and Horatian *Pieśni* present Kochanowski as a classical, well-balanced mind that enjoys the *aurea mediocritas* of everyday life, his *Laments* has a radically different tone. Written after the death of his young daughter, this sequence of funeral elegies presents a wide range of changing feelings, from utter despair and doubt to reconciliation with God. The poet's usually lucid and sedate style acquires an almost Baroque complexity and tension.

Kochanowski's general influence on the subsequent phases of Polish poetry was enormous. Perhaps his most durable legacy was his contribution to the development of Polish versification. The radical change he carried out consisted of replacing the remnants of "relative syllabism" with a strictly syllabic system, with exact rhyme, stabilized caesura, and paroxytonic cadence. This rigor allowed him freedom to employ enjambments and thus make intonation and syntax independent of the verse structure. He was also able to introduce a bewildering variety of verse formats and stanza patterns. Despite the nineteenth century success of the more melodious "syllabotonism," Kochanowski's syllabism remains one of the active verse systems of Polish poetry, and only since the beginnings of the twentieth century has it

been rivaled seriously by "tonism" and free-verse systems.

A peculiar feature of Polish literary history is that its "classical" periods never last long. As early as the second half of the sixteenth century—that is, at the zenith of the Renaissance—new literary phenomena were foreshadowing the arrival of the Baroque. Oddly enough, Mikolaj Sep Szarzyński (1550-1581) was a full-fledged Baroque poet. His only collection, *Rytmy abo wiersze polskie* (published posthumously in 1601; Polish rhythms or verses), has been rediscovered and appreciated in recent decades, after centuries of oblivion. Szarzyński was a poet with a small output but endowed with extraordinary creative force. In particular, a handful of his metaphysical sonnets, which reveal his spiritual torment and religious crisis by means of tortuous syntax, violent enjambments, and oxymoronic imagery, bear comparison with the best of John Donne and George Herbert.

Compared with Kochanowski's perfection and Szarzyński's intensity, other poets of the Polish Renaissance seem definitely minor figures. Yet some of them are not without significance. Sebastian Grabowiecki (1540-1607) was an author of quite refined devotional lyricism. Sebastian Fabian Klonowicz (1545-1602) wrote lengthy descriptive poems that abound with picturesque details. Szymon Szymonowicz (1558-1629) is best remembered as the author of the half-bucolic, half-realistic *Sielanki* (1614; idylls), a highly valuable contribution to the pastoral genre.

The Baroque

After a brief, though brilliant, Golden Age in the Renaissance, Polish culture, prompted by the rapid progress of the Counter-Reformation, entered the prolonged era of the Baroque. In poetry, the new Baroque style soon evolved into two different manners, sociologically distinguished by the cultural horizons of royal or aristocratic court life, on the one hand, and those of the petty gentry's manor life, on the other. While the former, more cosmopolitan, manner strongly resembled the Western European Baroque of Giambattista Marino and Luis de Góngora y Argote, the latter style, often called the Sarmatian Baroque, was much more local and conservative. Apart from these two trends within the vernacular, the tradition of classical poetry written in Latin was still cultivated. Maciej Kazimierz Sarbiewski (1595-1640), who has been dubbed the "Polish Horace," achieved pan-European fame under the name of Casimire as an author of Latin odes as well as of the influential treatise *De perfecta poesi* (early seventeenth century).

Polish Marinism had its most illustrious representative in Jan Andrzej Morsztyn (1613-1693), who could also be compared with the English Cavalier poets. A courtier and statesman, in his opinions he was close to French libertinism, and his poetry shunned any didactic purpose. While considering writing a kind of entertainment, he nevertheless focused on the poetic analysis of the paradoxes of worldly happiness. The paradoxes of love are illustrated in Morsztyn's poetry by a wide variety of striking conceits, in which there is as much frivolity as metaphysical fear. The complex interplay of symmetries, oppositions, and contrasts makes many of his brief poems masterpieces of construction. Beside Morsztyn, the Polish "line of wit" was represented by, among others, his relative Zbigniew Morsztyn (1624-1698), author of erotic poetry as well as devotional "emblems," and Daniel Naborowski (1573-1640), author of dazzling poems close in style to Italian *concettismo*.

While the court poets excelled in brief lyric or epigrammatic forms, the powerful current of the Sarmatian Baroque was more diversified in this respect. Its choice of genres and styles ranged from pure, songlike lyrics to enormous epic poems. The lyric branch is best represented by Szymon Zimorowic (1608-1629), whose only book, *Roksolanki* (1654; Ruthenian girls), was published posthumously by his brother, Józef Bartlomiej Zimorowic (1597-1673), himself an interesting poet in the same vein. *Roksolanki* is an ingeniously composed sequence of songs or lyric monologues of country girls and boys, stylistically alluding to folk poetry and sounding the psychological mysteries of love with subtle simplicity. Kasper Miaskowski (1550-1622), on the other hand, was perhaps the most gifted representative of early Baroque poetry of nature; his *Zbiór rytmów* (1612; collected rhythms) added metaphysical depth to the traditional style of pastoral poetry.

What dominated, however, in the middle and late phases of Polish Baroque poetry was moralism, didacticism, satire, and a taste for historical epic. The historical epic was introduced in 1618 with a splendid adaptation of Torquato Tasso's *Gerusalemme liberata* (1581; *Jerusalem Delivered*, 1600) by Jan Kochanowski's nephew, Piotr Kochanowski. The poet who supremely exemplified all of these trends was Waclaw Potocki (1621-1696), a petty nobleman who, in the seclusion of his country manor, wrote an immense amount of verse, including the epic *Wojna chocimska* (1670, 1850; the war of Khotim) and the collections *Moralia* (1688) and *Ogród fraszek* (1907; a garden of trifles). Samuel Twardowski (1600-1661) was another poet of this type. In addition to writing yet another historical epic, the posthumously published *Wojna domowa* (1681; a civil war), he achieved some originality in his mythological tale in verse, *Dafnis drzewem bobkowym* (1638; Daphne transformed into a laurel tree), and in the poetic romance *Nadobna Paskwalina* (1655; the lovely Pasqualina). Krzysztof Opaliński (1609-1655), a magnate and statesman, was the most prominent representative of the satiric bent in Baroque poetry. Finally, Wespazjan Kochowski (1633-1700) was the central figure of the late Baroque; his collection of lyric poems and epigrams, *Nieprózujace próznowanie* (1674; unleisurely leisure), surpasses the average production of those years in its technical finesse, and his long poem in biblical prose, *Psalmodia polska* (1695; a Polish psalmody), is an early expression of messianic Polish historiosophy, full of powerful images and striking metaphors.

The so-called "Saxonian Night," covering the first sixty years of the eighteenth century, marked a general decline in Polish culture. Polish poetry of this period, still dominated by the Sarmatian Baroque, was becoming monotonous in its shallow bigotry and its reliance on worn-out conceits. The last great triumph of Baroque imagery and style—although a much belated one—occurred around 1768, when the gentry uprising called the Confederacy of Bar triggered an outburst of anonymous poetic creativity. Some of the songs written at that time are gems of religious and patriotic lyricism.

THE ENLIGHTENMENT

In the mid-1760's, new tendencies began to dominate the Polish cultural scene. Under the reign of the last Polish king, Stanisław August Poniatowski (1732-

1798), the ideology of the Enlightenment rapidly gained ground, coinciding with a renewed interest in Western (especially French) cultural novelties. In poetry, the last decades of the eighteenth century were marked by another brief resurgence of neoclassicism. The purification of language (after the damage done by Baroque writers with their habit of interpolating Latinisms into their already ornate style) went hand in hand with a return to discipline and clarity in writing. Classical genres, including descriptive poems, mock epics, odes, epistles, satires, fables, and epigrams, were revived during this period.

Among the circle of poets close to the royal court and supporting the King's reformist policies, the most outstanding was undoubtedly Bishop Ignacy Krasicki (1735-1801). An extraordinarily gifted satirist, he made a stir in 1778 by publishing anonymously his *Monachomachia albo wojna mnichów* (monomachia, or the war of the monks), a mock epic in ottava rima ridiculing the obscurantism and indulgence of monks. As a satiric poet, he reached his climax in *Satyry* (satires published between 1779 and 1784), a series of penetrating ironic observations of contemporary morals which succeeded in being didactic without an intrusive rhetoric. Another of his masterpieces is the collection *Bajki i przypowieści* (1779; fables and parables), later complemented by *Bajki nowe* (1802; new fables). Under Krasicki's pen, the old genre of the animal fable acquired a new form, close to epigram and characterized by conciseness. Krasicki's great virtues as a poet are his ironic wit and stylistic precision. Despite his apparently optimistic didacticism, his humor is often bitter and disillusioned: He understood humanity too well to be fooled by wishful thinking.

A poet of almost equal stature was Stanisław Trembecki (1735-1812), another favorite of the enlightened monarch. A libertine and courtier, he wrote with equal ease political odes to the King and obscene, erotic poems. Trembecki's highest achievements, however, are his Rococo Anacreontics and his descriptive poem *Sofjówka* (Sophie's garden), which first appeared in a periodical in 1806 and was published in book form in 1822. Trembecki also excelled in poetic fables, as a rule more extensive and elaborate than the epigrammatic fables of Krasicki. In contrast to the latter's clarity and moderation, Trembecki's style is expressive and colorful, always striving for emotional extremes; he remained as close to the Baroque as a poet of the Enlightenment could afford to be.

Generally, though, the stylistic options of the Polish Enlightenment were contained between a strict classicism and a pre-Romantic sentimentalism. The former is exemplified by the work of Bishop Adam Stanisław Naruszewicz (1733-1796); its belated extension can be seen in the conservative and rigid stance of the so-called "Pseudoclassicists," including Kajetan Koźmian (1771-1856) and Ludwik Osiński (1775-1838), during the first decades of the nineteenth century. The trend of sentimentalism, on the other hand, surfaced in lyric songs and eclogues by Dionizy Kniaźnin (1750-1807) and Franciszek Karpiński (1741-1825), who at their best were able to produce fine examples of simplicity and emotional directness. Another link between the Enlightenment and Romanticism can be discerned in the poetic work of the versatile writer Julian Ursyn Niemcewicz (1757-1841): He was the first to popularize the genre of the ballad through both his translations and his original poetry.

ROMANTICISM

In Polish literary history, Romanticism is not simply another period. Its growth coincided with political events which made literature, and particularly Romantic poetry, the most powerful means of shaping the national mentality. One of the most conspicuous features of Polish Romanticism, however, is the enormous disparity between a few literary giants and all other poets of the period, as regards both their artistic innovation and their spiritual leadership. It is significant that the specifically Polish notion of the *wieszcz* (a "bard," but also a prophet) has been applied only to Adam Mickiewicz, Juliusz Słowacki, and Zygmunt Krasiński; twentieth century opinion has added Cyprian Kamil Norwid as the last of the great four. It is also significant that all four poets achieved their prominence in exile; their works, of unprecedented value to the spiritual life of the oppressed Polish nation, were written mostly in Paris.

Since 1795, the date of the final partition of Poland—when the Polish nation ceased to exist as an even nominally sovereign state and was divided among Russia, Prussia, and Austro-Hungary—the rhythm of Polish literary life has been defined, first and foremost, by the chronology of political events. Thus, the period of domination of great Romantic poetry is framed by the dates of two abortive insurrections against czarist Russia, in 1831 and 1863. The starting point of Polish Romanticism in a broader sense, however, is 1822, the year that saw publication of the first collection of poems by Adam Mickiewicz (1798-1855).

Mickiewicz entered Polish literature as a young student at the University of Wilno and soon became the central figure within the rapidly emerging Romantic movement. His early work was still strongly influenced by the heritage of the Enlightenment; "Oda do młodości" ("Ode to Youth"), for example, is a peculiar combination of classical rhetoric and the new *Sturm und Drang* ideology. Well-read in Johann Wolfgang von Goethe, Friedrich Schiller, and Lord Byron, Mickiewicz developed his own Romantic style. His first volume, *Ballady i romanse* (1822; ballads and romances), was an audacious manifesto of a specifically Polish version of early Romanticism, in which references to native folklore provide ample means to introduce elements of fantasy and the supernatural and to express the "living truths" of emotions and sentiments. Mickiewicz's debut was hailed as a literary revolution by his own generation, but was despised by the "old ones," the rationalistic classicists. The ensuing strife between the Romantics and the classicists was fueled by Mickiewicz's subsequent publications during the 1820's. Two tales in verse, *Grażyna* (1823; English translation, 1940) and *Konrad Wallenrod* (1828; English translation, 1883, 1925), parts 2 and 4 of the poetic drama *Dziady* (1823; *Forefathers' Eve*, 1925), and the brilliant sequence of *Sonety krymskie* (1826; *Sonnets from the Crimea*, 1917) all offer an entirely new set of stylistic devices and ideological proposals. The stress falls upon the Romantic notions of frenetic love, the tragic loneliness of the hero, and the value of individual sacrifice. While the diction of these works admits anticlassical regionalisms, colloquialisms, and exoticisms, the poet retains what he achieved in his classical training: conciseness, precision, and an infallible exactness in his choice of words and construction of metaphors.

Mickiewicz's leading role becomes apparent when contrasted with the emergence of other early Romantics.

Antoni Malczewski (1793-1826) left behind only one work, though a highly valuable one: the Byronic tale in verse, *Maria* (1826). Józef Bogdan Zaleski (1802-1866) was an author of serene, songlike lyrics alluding to the forms of folk poetry. Seweryn Goszczyński (1801-1876) appeared as an extreme example of political radicalism, which he professed particularly in the tale in verse, *Zamek kaniowski* (1828; Kaniów Castle).

None of these poets achieved a position comparable to that of Mickiewicz. After the 1831 defeat of the November Insurrection, Mickiewicz became the uncrowned prince of Polish poets, many of whom settled in Paris as political refugees. He had already initiated, in *Konrad Wallenrod* and in some of the lyric poems of the late 1820's, a new thematic current in Romantic poetry: the theme of patriotic struggle and heroic sacrifice. After the shattering of the nation's hopes in 1831, Mickiewicz's patriotism acquired new, historiosophical and metaphysical dimensions, while in his poetic art he constantly sought new forms of expression. Part 3 of *Dziady* (1832; *Forefathers' Eve*, 1944-1946) offered a new vision of Poland's national destiny as well as a new step in the development of Romantic drama; the work is a masterpiece of innovative construction, style, and verse. Only two years later, Mickiewicz published a completely different book, yet another masterpiece, his greatest: *Pan Tadeusz: Czyli, Ostatni Zajazd na litwie historia Szlachecka zr. 1811 i 1812 we dwunastu ksiegach wierszem* (1834; *Pan Tadeusz: Or, The Last Foray in Lithuania, a Tale of Gentlefolk in 1811 and 1812, in Twelve Books in Verse*, 1917), a Homeric epos on the poet's homeland, the Polish-Lithuanian province at the time of Napoleonic wars, in which nostalgia and sorrow mix with warm humor and discreet irony. Thanks to both the subtlety of its narration (the interplay of the narrator's identification with and distance from the reality presented) and its stylistic richness, *Pan Tadeusz* remains to this day the crowning achievement of Polish epic poetry. After its publication, Mickiewicz, more and more absorbed in mystical soul-searching and political activity, lapsed into silence as a poet, interrupted only by a brief sequence of the so-called Lausanne poems (written in 1839), purely lyric in character and strikingly innovative in their use of indirect symbolic language.

Mickiewicz's authority as *the* poet of the Polish nation was never seriously challenged in his lifetime; his main rival, another exile, Juliusz Słowacki (1809-1849), was not appreciated by his contemporaries as he deserved to be, though his fame eclipsed Mickiewicz's for a time only a half century after the death of both men. Słowacki's voluminous output includes various genres, from lyric poems through poetic dramas to tales in verse and visionary epics. His plays are an extremely important contribution to Polish Romantic poetry as well as to the theater. Written mostly in verse, they experiment with both versification and dramatic construction; their settings are variously realistic, historical, fairy-tale-like or legendary, dreamlike or symbolic. In his poems, Słowacki was able to move freely from epic description to lyric digression and from complex stanza patterns to biblical prose. His long poem in ottava rima, *Beniowski* (1841), is a magnificent example of the genre of "poem of digressions" and of Romantic irony, close in its style to Byron's *Don Juan* (1819-1824) and Alexander Pushkin's *Evgeni Onegin* (1825-1833; *Eugene Onegin*, 1881). The most impressive product of the last, "mystical" period in Słowacki's short life was an immense (even though unfinished) poem, also in ottava rima, titled *Król-Duch* (1847; king-spirit), a mythological vision of Polish destiny shown through consecutive reincarnations of the nation's spirit. Słowacki's significance lies not only in his matchless technical virtuosity, but also—and more important—in the fact that in his last phase, he was an early forerunner of Symbolism. Significantly, his fame grew rapidly in the 1890's and 1900's. His dazzling imagery and stylistic fireworks are in exact opposition to Mickiewicz's sparing and concrete manner; in fact, with all of his uniqueness taken into account, Słowacki can be considered the most typically Romantic of all Polish Romantic poets.

General critical opinion concerning the other two poets of the nineteenth century "great four" has dramatically changed in the twentieth century. Zygmunt Krasiński (1812-1859), for some time praised for his poetic genius, today is appreciated mostly as an author of fascinating letters and two political plays, the first of which, *Nie-boska komedia* (1835; *The Undivine Comedy*, 1924), written in 1833, is a prophetic analysis of revolution. With a perspicacious and sophisticated mind, Krasiński nevertheless lacked both Mickiewicz's poetic force and Słowacki's craftsmanship. His long poems *Przedświt* (1843; dawning) and *Psalmy przyszłości* (1845; psalms of the future), though interesting as expressions of his conservative historiosophy, have dated badly.

The posthumous career of the work of Cyprian Kamil Norwid (1821-1883) presents a stark contrast with Krasiński's diminishing popularity. Forgotten and isolated in his lifetime and discovered only several decades after his death, today he is considered the spiritual and artistic harbinger of modern Polish poetry. One generation younger than Mickiewicz, Norwid developed his art both under the influence of and as a polemic against Polish Romanticism. He replaced the prevalent Romantic attitude of nationalistic messianism with his original version of humanistic universalism: a concept of modern man as the heir to the great civilizations of the past. From this point of view, Norwid tried to analyze the most essential problems of history, politics, and culture. Although he employed a wide variety of genres and forms, he was certainly most successful in his brief lyric poems, distinguished by their highly intellectual content. In particular, his collection of one hundred such poems titled *Vade-mecum* (written before 1866) offers an astonishingly modern model of poetry. The poems included are semantically dense, ambiguous, and often obscure; they replace an easy melodiousness with irregular verse in which rhythm and intonation adjust to the flow of thoughts. Norwid's poems can be analyzed as a constant dialogue with an implied reader who is forced to assume a much more active part in deciphering the poem's meanings than is usually required in Romantic poetry.

In contrast to the achievement of the four great émigrés, the so-called "domestic" offshoot of Polish Romantic poetry was of rather inferior quality. Among the multitude of poets who wrote at that time, only a few names rise above the average. Kornel Ujejski (1823-1897) reached a large readership with his poems of patriotic lamentation. Ryszard Berwiński (1819-1879) was a bard of social revolution and an ironic observer of contemporary society. The strongest suit of Teofil Lenartowicz (1822-1893) was a lyric poetry imbued with stylistic references to folklore.

THE POST-ROMANTIC AND NEO-ROMANTIC PERIODS

The 1863 defeat of the January Uprising, another insurrection against the czarist oppressors, generated a distrust in Romantic ideology and particularly in Romantic poetry: the ensuing epoch of Positivism was definitely an antipoetic age. In literature, there was a general shift toward realistic and Naturalistic fiction and drama. Only a few names of relative significance emerged in the field of poetry during this period. Adam Asnyk (1838-1897) owed his popularity to the post-Romantic conventions through which he expressed his anti-Romantic convictions. Maria Konopnicka (1842-1910) wrote in accordance with Positivism as far as its reformist tendency was concerned; her poetry of social criticism and defense of the oppressed is characterized by its skillful use of elements of folklore and its introduction of a speaker from the lower classes.

In the last decade of the nineteenth century, the "prosaic" epoch of Positivism gave way to another era of poetry. This new trend, variously called Young Poland, modernism, or Neo-Romanticism, was strongly influenced by Western-European Symbolism and the philosophy of Friedrich Nietzsche and Arthur Schopenhauer, but it also gave vent to specifically Polish doubts and perplexities. The Positivist program of social reform had evidently failed; it had been unable to find any cure for Poland's political enslavement. Thus, the end of the century marked the apogee of an ideological crisis: Literature was polarized between Naturalistic "objectivism" in fiction and prosaic drama, and Symbolist or Expressionist "subjectivism" in poetic drama and lyricism.

Perhaps the most typical representative of the "decadent" mood of the end of the century was Kazimierz Przerwa Tetmajer (1865-1940), who in his lyric poems published in the 1890's set up an emotional pattern for the whole generation of Young Poland—a norm of sensitivity consisting of pessimism, individualism, distrust of any dogma, and a despondency that easily turned into a cult of sensual pleasure. Other poets of this period underwent a more complicated development. Jan Kasprowicz (1860-1926), for example, started with Naturalistic depictions of peasants' poverty and after intermediary stages of Symbolism and Expressionism ended as a serene poet of reconciliation with God and with the world. What is most interesting in his work is his progress from a Promethean rebellion to a final Franciscan acceptance of Being; from the technical point of view, his late poems are an important contribution to "tonism," a system of verse based on an equal number of stresses rather than syllables.

Stanisław Wyspiański (1869-1907), best known as a dramatist, was perhaps the most Romantic of all poets of Young Poland: He revived the genre of poetic drama and enriched it with Symbolist imagery. His visionary plays refer to both Polish history and contemporary events, mingling mythological or legendary figures with historical or present-day characters. Tadeusz Miciński (1873-1918), also an innovative (though less popular) playwright, wrote lyric poetry which anticipated Expressionism; his only collection, *W mroku gwiazd* (in the darkness of stars), was published in 1902. Leopold Staff (1878-1957) lived long enough to participate in three consecutive literary epochs; within Young Poland, he represented the trend of Nietzscheanism, a trend opposing "decadence" and favoring classical lucidity. In contrast to the majority of his poetic generation, he was aware of changing attitudes, and his model of poetry appealed to the tastes of the next generations. Indeed, his popularity has never diminished, and the last volume that he published, *Wiklina* (1954; osiers), amazingly modern in its style and versification, is undoubtedly his highest achievement.

The epoch of Young Poland abounded with poets, and its lyric style soon degenerated into worn-out conventions. Some of the second-rate poets, however, are a cut above the average. Antoni Lange (1861-1929) stands out as a Parnassist with exceptional technical abilities. Maria Komornicka (1876-1948) was also able to free herself from the prevailing stereotypes to create her individual, intensely Nietzschean verse; mental illness ended her writing career in 1907, although she lived for many years after that date.

The greatest poet of Young Poland, however, emerged—quite paradoxically—when the epoch was already in decline. Bołeslaw Leśmian (1878-1937) published his first book in 1912, and his next two books appeared in 1920 and 1936. In other words, chronologically he belongs to the literary epoch that succeeded Young Poland. Nevertheless, he must be considered a belated Symbolist, and only the striking originality of his language obscures this genetic link. Leśmian's poetic style is utterly consistent with his philosophy. An enthusiast of Henri Bergson, he saw the world as a field of incessant conflict between inert Matter and the creative force of Spirit; the conflict cannot be resolved, and thus the world is always in the course of becoming. The task of poetry is to express this instability: Its rhythm should become the equivalent of the world's élan vital, and its imagery should fix the reflection of reality's metamorphoses. The poet himself should assume the cognitive stance of primeval man, whose act of perception creates, as it were, the world perceived. Accordingly, Leśmian's poetry is distinguished by his astonishing variety of complex rhythms, his figures of speech that emphasize the mutual transformations of elements of reality, his frequent use of myth and folklore, and his invention of new words (forming nouns out of verbs and verbs out of nouns, for example) in order to capture the flux of experience.

INDEPENDENT POLAND (1918-1939) AND THE WAR YEARS (1939-1945)

The twenty years of independent Poland can be visualized as a gradual turn from light to darkness, from initial optimism and hope to final catastrophe. This change found its reflection in the evolution of poetry. The first decade of the interwar period was characterized by an explosion of new, mostly avant-garde programs and a multitude of poetic groups, periodicals, even cabarets. Many of these initiatives were ephemeral, but some of them developed into influential "schools" and trends. As far as popularity was concerned, there was only one poetic school that managed to hold sway over public opinion for two decades, if not longer. Five poets who emerged as a group called Skamander—Julian Tuwim (1894-1953), Antoni Słonimski (1895-1976), Jan Lechoń (1899-1956), Jarosław Iwaszkiewicz (1894-1980), and Kazimierz Wierzyński (1894-1969)—owed their popularity to the fact that their poetry was original and innovative while also comprehensible.

Skamander's only program consisted of rejecting traditional concepts of poetry's "duties" and enjoying artistic freedom; accordingly, the group abandoned all Neo-Romantic conventions and turned to contemporary reality and a refreshingly direct style. In fact, each

of the five poets possessed a different personality, and the differences among them were to increase as their works progressed. Tuwim, perhaps the most talented of them all, was a master of verbal magic with an explosive lyric force. Słonimski's poetry was rationalistic, discursive, and rhetorical. Lechoń, obsessed with Polish history, made an interesting use of the Romantic tradition. Iwaszkiewicz, after his brief fascination with Expressionism, chose aestheticism as his principal attitude. As for Wierzyński, his most impressive achievement is his postwar poetry written in exile and much modernized in form. Within the circle of Skamander's influence, some other poets followed their individual paths. Władysław Broniewski (1897-1962), a pro-Communist poet, managed to combine his radical ideology with close ties to the Polish Romantic tradition. In her metaphorically concise poems, Maria Pawlikowska-Jarnorzewska (1894-1945) achieved a modern formulation of and a feminine perspective on the theme of love. Jerzy Liebert (1904-1931) was an original poet of religious experience.

While Skamander was dominating the poetic scene, more radical programs of new poetry were propounded by numerous avant-garde groups. The Polish Futurists, including Bruno Jasieński (1901-1939) and Aleksandr Wat (1900-1967), did not win a great following, but they prepared the ground for the program of the so-called Krakow Vanguard, the most outstanding representatives of which were Tadeusz Peiper (1891-1969) and Julian Przyboś (1901-1970). In contrast to the Futurists' anarchism, the Krakow Vanguard advocated constructivism and rigor based on metaphor and syntax. Their precise and consistent program had a great impact on the evolution of Polish poetry in the next decades, although as early as the 1930's it was quite clear that their poetry was unable to cope with the problems of twentieth century history. Among other avant-garde poets, Adam Ważyk (1905-1982) is worth mentioning as a representative of Surrealism, although his style changed radically in subsequent decades.

The 1930's, marked by intense economic, political, and ideological crisis, brought about the so-called Second Vanguard—a new generation of poets who prophesied the approaching global catastrophe. Konstanty Ildefons Gałczyński (1905-1953), who later was to become one of the most popular Polish poets, did it by use of the grotesque and mockery. Józef Czechowicz (1903-1939), initially a highly accomplished poet of idyllic provincial landscapes, in his later poems expressed his fears using his own avant-garde technique of metaphorical condensation. Czesław Miłosz (born 1911), the greatest living Polish poet and the winner of the 1980 Nobel Prize for Literature, underwent a complicated evolution, from his prewar catastrophism to metaphysical lyricism.

The atrocities of World War II confirmed the predictions and premonitions of catastrophist poetry, and the theme of "apocalypse come true" was central in the work of a new generation of poets, most of whom died young during the Nazi Occupation as underground fighters or soldiers in the Warsaw Uprising. Such was the fate of Krzysztof Kamil Baczyński (1921-1944), who left behind a brilliant collection of lyric poems, visionary and Symbolist in style.

POSTWAR POLAND

After World War II and the imposition of Communist rule on Poland, many poets worked in exile. Despite censorship, a great deal of émigré literature found its way into the country, and its popularity was remarkable, to mention only the examples of Miłosz, Wierzyński, and Wat. Those poets who remained in Poland or were repatriated faced a situation of more or less limited freedom of speech. In spite of that, postwar Polish poetry scored many artistic successes. The immediate postwar years brought about the debut of Tadeusz Różewicz (born 1921), who propounded a new, ascetic style devoid of metaphors and sparing in imagery. After a general decline of literature during the years of Stalinism, one of the first harbingers of the approaching "thaw" in cultural policy was the publication in 1955 of Adam Ważyk's "Poemat dla doroslych" ("Poem for Adults").

The year 1956 marked the beginning of a genuine eruption of new names, trends, and poetic programs. The poetry of the late 1950's and 1960's was characterized by the coexistence of a strong current of ironic moral reflection, as found in the works of Zbigniew Herbert (born 1924), Wisława Szymborska (born 1923), and Wiktor Woroszylski (born 1927), and an equally powerful trend of linguistic experimentation, as exemplified by Miron Białoszewski (born 1922), Tymoteusz Karpowicz (born 1921), and Witold Wirpsza (born 1918).

At the same time, poets such as Stanisław Grochowiak (1934-1976), Jerzy Harasymowicz (born 1933), and Tadeusz Nowak (born 1930) build their private worlds of imagination and fantasy. The school of neoclassicism and the "poetry of culture" is represented by, among others, Jarosław Marek Rymkiewicz (born 1934).

In the early 1970's, another generation of Polish poets came to the fore, combining the "moralistic" and "linguistic" tendencies in order to find a new language for antitotalitarian protest. Ryszard Krynicki (born 1943), Ewa Lipska (born 1945), Adam Zagajewski (born 1945), and Julian Kornhauser (born 1946) are strong representatives of this trend. All trends in Polish poetry since World War II followed the vicissitudes of the socialist governments and looming presence of neighboring Communist U.S.S.R. Writers recognized by the state were guaranteed publication and a comfortable life style. They also, however, agreed to write only what was acceptable to government censors. The underground writers were heard only as loudly as any current leadership concerned itself with silencing them. Whether the objects of aggressive government crackdown or the minor concern of a government generally ignoring them, these writers were still reacting to government. They were not perceived as leaders in reform.

Most of the poetry created during these years was not considered truly "Polish" in character. It was all a reaction to an imposed and generally unpopular political structure. This structure fell apart in the 1980's. The decade began with the strong suppression of intellectual and artistic works. Thousands of journalists were suspended or forced to resign, publishers and writers' organizations were closed and disbanded, authors and other intellectuals were being arrested. The government relaxed its censorship by the mid-1980's and underground publishing started to flourish. In 1988, Soviet president Mikhail Gorbachev declared that the U.S.S.R. would no long directly influence Polish politics. This statement effectively removed the yoke of censorship in Poland and the target or theme of writers for the past forty-five years.

END OF THE TWENTIETH CENTURY

There seems little cohesion or uniformity in approach of the poets born after 1950. If there is a common thread, it seems to be a focus in the individual, the inner-world, the self. This is in direct opposition to the committed poetry of the previous decades that spoke to and for the people. These newer voices include Marcin Baran, Krzysztof Koehler, Zbigniew Machej, Jacek Podsiadlo, Marcin Sendecki, Jerzy Sosnowski, Marcin Swietlicki, and Robert Tekiel.

The whole world then focused its attention on Polish poetry in 1996 when Wisława Szymborska was awarded the Nobel Prize in Literature. The choice seemed surprising at first; then more people read her poetry and discovered her wit, wisdom, irony, commitment to human issues, and complete mastery of the Polish poetic language. She well represented to the world a rich, deep, and still very dynamic poetic tradition.

BIBLIOGRAPHY

Barańczak, Stanisław, and Clare Cavanagh, eds. and trans. *Polish Poetry of the Last Two Decades of Communist Rule: Spoiling Cannibals' Fun.* Foreword by Helen Vendler. Evanston, Ill.: Northwestern University Press, 1991.

Carpenter, Bogdana, ed. *Monumenta Polonica: The First Four Centuries of Polish Poetry, a Bilingual Anthology.* Ann Arbor, Mich.: Michigan Slavic Publications, 1989.

Czerniawski, Adam, ed. *The Mature Laurel: Essays on Modern Polish Poetry.* Chester Springs, Pa.: Dufour, 1991. Contains essays on poets, analyses of individual poems, and overview articles on history and theory. Appropriate for introductory readers of Polish poetry and scholars alike.

Eile, Stanisław. *Literature and Nationalism in Partitioned Poland, 1795-1918.* New York: St. Martin's Press, 2000. Published in association with the School of Slavonic and East European Studies at the University of London.

Eile, Stanisław, and Ursula Phillips, eds. *New Perspectives in Twentieth-Century Polish Literature: Flight from Martyrology.* Houndsmill, Basingstoke, Hampshire, England: Macmillan, 1992. Includes bibliographical references and index.

Gömöri, George. *Magnetic Poles: Essays on Modern Polish and Comparative Literature.* London: Polish Cultural Foundation, 2000.

Krzyżanowski, Julian. *A History of Polish Literature.* Translated from the Polish by Doris Ronowicz. Warsaw, Poland: PWN-Polish Scientific Publishers, 1978.

Levine, Madeline G. *Contemporary Polish Poetry, 1925-1975.* Boston: Twayne Publishers, 1981. Part of Twayne's World Authors Series.

Miłosz, Czesław. *The History of Polish Literature.* 2d ed. Berkeley: University of California Press, 1983.

Tighe, Carl. *The Politics of Literature: Poland, 1945-1989.* Cardiff: University of Wales Press, 1999.

Pirie, Donald, ed. and trans. *Young Poets of a New Poland: An Anthology.* London: Forest Books/UNESCO, 1993. Includes the work of twenty-three poets born between 1950 and 1969.

Stanisław Barańczak

RUSSIAN POETRY

For Russians, Aleksandr Solzhenitsyn says, "Poetry is born from the torment of the soul." Only a part of the multicultural, multilingual Soviet Union, Russia is still a vast land, bordered on the north and south by the Baltic and the Black Seas, on the west by the Carpathian Mountains, and on the east by the mighty Volga River. In the thousand-year history of Russian literature, no natural barrier has preserved the Russian people from the agony of invasion, and Russian poetry has become unbreakably forged to their historical suffering.

THE POETRY OF RUSSIA'S YOUTH

The earliest ancestors of the modern Russians, the agricultural East Slavs, settled the inland plateau of the thirteen-hundred-mile Dnieper River and were preyed upon during the ninth century by the Varangians, piratical Scandinavian merchants who founded petty principalities around Kiev. Under Grand Prince Vladimir of Kiev, their loose confederation was converted to Byzantine Christianity in 988 C.E., an immense religio-cultural invasion which consolidated its position in Russia by introducing the Old Church Slavonic alphabet based on the spoken dialect, importing Byzantine Greek forms as literary models, and assimilating native pagan elements into religious ritual. Although Old Church Slavonic served as the chief vehicle of Russian literature from the eleventh to the eighteenth centuries, it choked off exposure to the classical Humanistic heritage of the West and rigidly identified Church with State fortifying the autocracy of Russian rulers.

Russia's earliest poetic form was the vernacular and formulaic *bylina* (plural *byliny*; literally, things-that-have-been). These oral epics celebrated mythological figures and, more frequently, human heroes in groupings that resembled the Arthurian cycles. In the Kievan *byliny* cycle centered on Grand Prince Vladimir, the hero Ilya becomes "a symbol of the self-consciousness of the people," according to Felix J. Oinas in *Heroic Epic and Saga* (1978). Novgorod, a northern city belonging to the Hanseatic League, had a *byliny* cycle whose central figure was Aleksandr Nevsky, prince and saint, who repelled the Livonian and Teutonic knights. The Galician-Volhynian *byliny* cycle records the strife between this area and its western neighbors in the thirteenth and fourteenth centuries. As Oinas remarks, the *byliny* of patriarchal Russia "captivated and thrilled people of all walks of life until the nineteenth century," inspiring later poets with traditional Russian ideals.

During the twelfth century, the disintegration of feudal Russia set the bitter groundwork for the Mongol invasion of 1237 to 1240 and the imposition of the "Tartar yoke." *Slovo o polku Igoreve* (c. 1187; *The Lay of Igor's Host*) is Russia's first written poetic achievement, a stirring blend of the aristocratic warrior spirit and a call to self-sacrifice in defense of the Land of Rus. The poem poignantly and accurately predicts the great defeat to come: "O, how the Russian land moans, remembering her early years and princes!/ . . . in discord their pennons flutter apart." Based on the Novgorod Prince Igor's unsuccessful attempt in 1185 to dislodge Turkish Polovtsian usurpers from the lands near the Don, and startlingly modern in its complex imagery, allusion, and symbolism, *The Lay of Igor's Host* has sometimes been considered an imposture since its discovery in the early 1790's. Alexander Pushkin claimed, however, that not enough poetry existed in the eighteenth century for anyone then to have written it, and more recent scholars concur.

Until 1480, the Mongol tribute was paid by a Russia brutally severed from the West and struggling to unite itself sufficiently to cast off the hated Tartar yoke. Little national strength was left for poetry. Looking back from 1827, the religious philosopher Pyotr Chaadayev observed, "At first, brutal barbarism, then crude superstition, then fierce and humiliating bondage whose spirit was passed on to our own sovereigns—such is the history of our youth."

FROM DARK AGE TO GOLDEN

Kiev was destroyed in Russia's literary Dark Age under the Tartars, and Russian culture was dominated by the Grand Duchy of Moscow, whose ruler Dmitri won a victory over the Tartars at Kulikovo, memorialized in the fifteenth century Cossack epic *Zadónščina* (beyond the river Don). Ivan II at last drove the Tartars from a unified Russia in 1480, less than a generation after the Turkish conquest of Constantinople, and Moscow became the "third Rome." Imperial power was inseparable from Orthodox belief, and Ivan II, wed to a Byzantine princess, regarded himself as the sole genuine defender of the Orthodox faith. His grandson and namesake, Ivan IV, popularly known in the West as Ivan the Terrible (more accurately, the Awesome), a talented political polemicist, practiced heinous excesses in the name of personal absolutism. After Ivan murdered his oldest son, his line died out, and for the next generation civil disorder was exacerbated by crop failures, famine, and plague. Finally, in 1613, delegates from all the Russias elected Mikhail, the first of the Romanov czars.

During the post-Ivan "Time of Troubles," literature in Russia was confined to Old Church Slavonic, though the people clung to folktales and Russianized Western romances. Under the first Romanovs, every Western form of literature except theology began to be translated and widely promulgated with the advent of Russian printing in 1564. In 1678, Simeon Polotsky, tutor to Czar Alexei's children, introduced a syllabic verse system, solemn and even pompous, that dominated Russian poetry for a century.

Westernization accelerated under Peter the Great, who during his reign from 1682 to 1725 reformed every aspect of Russian civilization. The Czar personally directed this mammoth invasion of Western thought, but he enforced its adoption by ruthless, even barbaric means. Peter's unprecedented debasement of the Church removed schools and literature from religious control, and from 1708, all nonreligious texts were published in a simplified Russian alphabet rather than in Old Church Slavonic. West Russian syllabic verse, originally panegyric or didactic, became fashionable among Peter's courtiers as an instrument of amatory and pastoral poetry, in imitation of French and German models.

Peter's reformations were implemented at enormous cultural cost. The secularization of literature contributed to the dangerous rift opening between the general population and Peter's sophisticated nobility, who largely abandoned the language and the folklore of the exploited populace.

In the thirty-seven years of political upheaval which followed Peter's death in 1725, the first four great men of Russian literature imposed French classical standards on Peter's simplified Russian language. All men imported Western literary forms and theories while employing at the same time traditional Russian materials.

Prince Antioch Kantemir (1708-1744) is widely considered the first Russian writer to "blend life and poetry in his works." Kantemir served as Russian ambassador to London and Paris, and as a confirmed neoclassicist concurred with Nicolas Boileau that the highest of literary forms were the ode and the satire, which he used to attack reactionary Russian political and social elements. Kantemir's language is realistic, but his satires are framed in the imported syllabic verse dependent on fixed accents, a form of versification unnatural to the Russian language. Kantemir's less talented and non-noble contemporary, Vasily Trediakovsky (1703-1769), freed Russian poetry from these unnatural constraints by introducing a syllabo-tonic system based on equal bisyllabic metrical feet, a rhythm found in the Russian popular ballad.

Mikhail Lomonosov (1711-1765), a peasant poet, achieved scientific fame abroad and returned to found the University of Moscow in 1756. Lomonosov's *Pismo o pravilakh rossiyskogo stikhotvorstva* (1739; letter concerning the rules of Russian prosody) set stylistic criteria for poetry: a "Noble Style," employing Old Church Slavonic elements, used for heroic poetry and tragedy; a "Middle Style," for ordinary drama; and a colloquial "Low Style," for correspondence, farce, and everyday usage. Lomonosov's syllabo-tonic odes exhibit conventional patriotic themes, but as Marc Slonim has noted, Lomonosov's meditations are "still living poetry." With Lomonosov, the aristocratic poet Aleksandr Sumarokov (1718-1777) established the principles of Boileau and Voltaire as paramount in Russian letters.

Russia's most famous empress, Catherine the Great, who ruled from 1762 to 1796, ranked herself with Peter the Great and consciously patterned her dazzling reign upon his. After the abortive Cossack uprising (1773-1775) under Emelian Pugachev and the sobering example of the French Revolution in 1789, Catherine tempered enlightenment with political conservatism. She extended education into the middle class and encouraged a fivefold increase in published translations from the major European languages. She also imported many foreign artists and sponsored secular music. Catherine, who wrote widely herself, indelibly marked Russian literature by naming Gavrila Derzhavin (1743-1816) as her poet laureate.

Nikolai Gogol called Derzhavin "the poet of greatness" who dominated Russian literature for more than thirty years. Alexander Pushkin (1799-1837), however, accused Derzhavin of thinking "in Tartar," a pungent assessment of Derzhavin's sacrifice of Russian syntax in favor of voicing his deistic and epicurean love of the sublime. Derzhavin's stylistic duality presaged the dismemberment of the Russian classical order; he pioneered Russian civic poetry, which burgeoned in the nineteenth century with Kondraty Rylevyev and Nikolai Nekrasov, and he left a sensually concrete language to the flamboyant oratorical poets of the twentieth century, his legacy as well to his immediate followers, who taught Pushkin.

The harsh fate of the prose writer Aleksandr Radishchev (1749-1802), however, indicates that Catherine did not practice what her humanistic love of letters preached. On calling for the Empress to amend Russian social sins, especially serfdom, Radishchev was exiled to Siberia and later committed suicide. Despite heavy risks in a censored land, Radishchev, whom Pushkin called the "foe of slavery," was widely read by youthful poets well into the nineteenth century.

By 1800, historical research in Russia was uncovering folk literature, and young Russian poets were intensely discussing the unification of aesthetic principle with cultural heritage. Though rapidly Westernized under Peter and then Catherine, Russian literature now was straitjacketed by state, not Church censorship, and the democratic ideals that emanated from the West were difficult to implement in Russian poetry. Into this complex literary milieu loomed the shadow of yet another invader: Napoleon Bonaparte.

Prior to the disastrous Napoleonic invasion in 1812, the country had passed through the lunatic reign of Catherine's son, Paul I, who despised revolutionary ideas and attempted to beat them out of his people. After Paul was strangled in 1801 with the scarf of a palace guards officer, Paul's son Alexander I, whom Napoleon called "the cunning Byzantine," liberalized government, education, and literature, and writers began to hope for emancipation from the state.

Just as the novelist and historian Nikolai Karamzin had begun to use sentimentalism in prose, launching the pre-Romantic movement in Russian literature between 1791 and 1802, the poet and translator Vasily Zhukovsky (1783-1852) sounded the first poetic notes of the Golden Age. Zhukovsky believed that "translators of prose are the slaves of their original text, whereas the translators of the poets are the rivals of the poets themselves." Zhukovsky thus established a tradition that has ensured the excellence of Russia's poetic translations, such as the Russian *Iliad* of Zhukovsky's contemporary, Nikolai Gnedich (1784-1833), described by Slonim as "probably the best in the world." Zhukovsky's original poetry is highly subjective. He identified poetry with his virtue, and his lyric melancholy caused one of his contemporaries to observe, "Happiness would break his lyre's most beautiful string!" Later, under the influence of German Romantics such as Friedrich von Schlegel, Zhukovsky celebrated human sentiment in melodic diction and transitory impressions which introduced the enchantment of Romantic idealism to Russian verse. The young Pushkin praised Zhukovsky's captivating sweetness, and twentieth century Symbolists such as Aleksandr Blok revered Zhukovsky as their predecessor.

At the same time, however, bureaucratic Russian conservatives were furiously striving to preserve the Noble Style in Russian poetry and stamp out all vestiges of "that vile and foul word—Revolution!" As Slonim has noted, "A literary problem was, as is always the case in Russia, assuming the character of an ideological clash." Complicating the literary scene, the profound strain of Classicism so eloquently displayed in Gnedich's *Iliad* dominated the poetry of Konstantin Batiushkov (1787-1855), who called himself "The bard of earthly happiness." Batiushkov was a modernist in form and diction, but he reveled in the mere joy of being, claiming that perfect happiness is attainable only by youth, physically capable of experiencing the heights of ecstasy. Batiushkov's delicate Latinate sweetness inflamed the youthful Pushkin, who rejoiced at his mingling of classical themes with sensual delights.

Pushkin's early poetic mentors, Zhukovsky and Batiushkov, soon fell from Russia's literary firmament— Zhukovsky abandoning poetry for the court of Alexander I, and Batiushkov, his closest friend, dying mad after serving as a Russian officer between 1812 and 1815. This period was marked by an internal struggle between Russia's conservatives, allied against the "infernal sophistication of French enlightenment," and the liberals, who believed that the victory against Napoleon had been won by the Russian people, not their leaders.

Growing up during this crisis, Alexander Pushkin became, as Thaïs Lindstrom says, the Russians' "comrade in life . . . whose stanzas, recited with universal familiarity and pleasure, crystallize Russian life in the language of the people." Pushkin took pride in both his ancient Russian aristocratic family and his descent from "Peter the Great's negro," the Abyssianian engineer General Abram Hannibal. Pushkin's earliest poems date from 1811, and while he was still attending the new lyceum in Tsarskoe Selo, the established poets Zhukovsky and Batiushkov came to consider him their poetic equal. Pushkin steeped himself in Russian and French literature, and at his lyceum graduation in 1817 he swept into the glittering debauchery of St. Petersburg, savoring wine, women, gambling, and dueling.

Because Alexander I had outgrown his youthful liberalism even before 1812, the Russian Army, sadly not for the last time, had been greeted by brutal government police as it returned victorious from the West in 1815. After the Czar had become hypnotized by "exalted prophetesses," the uneducated General Arakcheyev, whom Pushkin called a "brutal and treacherous hangman of freedom," dominated Russia for a period characterized, in Alexander Herzen's words, by "servility, coercion, injustice everywhere . . . serfdom solid as a rock, military despotism, silence and whips. . . ."

Russia's youth, many of whom had been exposed to Western revolutionary ideals during the Napoleonic Wars, responded with what Slonim describes as "a revolt of words in a country where silence was compulsory." In 1817, a group of young Imperial Guards officers formed a secret "Union of Salvation," the "True Sons of the Fatherland." Their efforts culminated eight years later, on December 14, 1825, in the ill-fated Decembrist uprising. "Even if we fail," wrote the poet Kondraty Ryleyev, "our failure will serve as a lesson for others."

Remembering the Decembrists, Herzen recalled, "The cannons on Senate Place awakened a whole generation." Pushkin and his contemporaries were secretly familiar with the long historical poems of Ryleyev (1795-1826), who sacrificed family and life to the Decembrist cause. Ryleyev cited the democratic ideals of the Cossacks and the ancient Slavs, writing, "I know that death awaits those who are the first to fight the despots, yet self sacrifice is the price of freedom."

Such youthful idealism permeates *Ruslan i Lyudmila* (1820; *Ruslan and Liudmila*, 1936), Pushkin's first long poem, a romantic epic written under the sign of Byron. It captivated an immense audience, and Pushkin received a portrait of Zhukovsky inscribed, "To a victorious pupil from a vanquished master." Alexander I was less enthused about Pushkin's revolutionary epigrams, however, and the poet was exiled to the South for four years, a period inspiring his Caucasian verse tales. In these works, Pushkin moved from the stereotyped Byronic hero to a three-dimensional protagonist, the conception of which formed the nucleus of his monumental "novel in verse" *Evgeny Onegin* (1825-1833; *Eugene Onegin*, 1881), begun in 1823.

After an unfortunate love affair that resulted in his expulsion from the Russian Civil Service, Pushkin spent a period under house arrest at his mother's estate, Mikhailovskoe. During this time he fell under the spell of William Shakespeare, after whose chronicle plays Pushkin patterned his *Boris Godunov* (1831; English translation, 1918), a towering attempt to banish French classicism from Russian literature. Lindstrom believes that *Boris Godunov* "recognizes and stresses the power of a faceless, formless mass of common people to alter the course of history."

Even Pushkin, a most uncommon man, found himself restricted severely by the Russian government. His poems had been found in the Decembrists' possession, and though he was allowed to live in Moscow again in 1826, censors reviewed all of his work before publication and secret police constantly monitored his words and actions. He continued work on *Eugene Onegin*, completing it in 1873. Regarded as his masterpiece, it is widely considered to be the greatest single work in Russian poetry, and generations of Russians have memorized passages from it.

Pushkin became infatuated with sixteen-year-old Natalie Goncharova and married her in 1831, after which he was constantly short of money. Their opulent

St. Petersburg lifestyle detracted seriously from his writing, but Pushkin still produced remarkable lyric poetry and prose novellas in his last period, as well as the great dramatic poem, *Medniy vsadnik* (1841; *The Bronze Horseman*, 1936), in which he accurately predicted Russia's eventual enslavement by totalitarianism. He died in a duel involving his lovely but vapid wife.

Pushkin's works, which Russians claim to be untranslatable, have influenced all the Russian arts—music, ballet, sculpture, and painting. Pushkin left Russian literature its modern language, a profound fusion of popular idiom and elegant expression that sublimely weds sound to meaning. He bequeathed to world literature one of its most magnificent apologiae for the dignity of man, making poetry a living instrument of humanistic values. Gogol called him "an astounding and perhaps a unique phenomenon of the Russian spirit," embodying "what the Russian may become two hundred years hence." Pushkin's most fitting memorial, however, appears in his own rendition of Horace's "Exegi monumentum":

> I shall long be loved by the people
> Because I awakened their goodness with my lyre
> And in my cruel country celebrated freedom
> And appealed for mercy for the downtrodden.

For the multitude of other brilliant writers of Russia's Golden Age, Pushkin's creativity was, in Gogol's metaphor, "a fire tossed out of the sky, from which lesser poets of his day, like candles, become alight." Evgeny Baratynsky (1800-1844), an intellectual and classicist, lacked Pushkin's *sprezzatura*, that attribute of genius which makes the most difficult achievement appear effortless. A poet with a strong metaphysical bent, Baratynsky decried the decay of human vitality that accompanies industrialism. Nikolai Yazykov (1803-1846) contributed intoxicating rhythms to traditional Russian poetic recitation. Alexei Koltsov (1809-1842) based his Burnsian lyrics on Russian folk life, while more progressive poets of the 1830's, notably Aleksandr Poleshayev (1805-1848) and Prince Aleksandr Odoyevsky (1802-1839), rejected Pushkin's classicism completely and stressed the emotional impact of poetry. Odoyevsky, who died as a private soldier in the Caucasus, is chiefly remembered because Mikhail Lermontov, the most widely recognized heir to Pushkin, wrote an elegy for Odoyevsky that is often cited as the most beautiful in the Russian language.

A Eugene Onegin with a touch of the demon, Lermontov (1814-1841) was demoted and exiled in 1837 for circulating manuscript copies of a poem on Pushkin's death, attacking "base lovers of corruption" who dared to "strangle freedom, genius, glory, and hide within the shelter of the law." Lermontov had an unhappy early life. His mother had died young, and he was separated from his father by his wealthy grandmother, an unhealthy situation reflected in several of his poems. A precociously talented child, Lermontov matured into an unappealing young man who admired Lord Byron deeply, seeing in the English poet a reflection of his own passionate revolt and *Weltschmerz*. Lermontov nevertheless realized their essential difference: "No. I am not Byron; like him I am a persecuted wanderer, but mine is a Russian soul."

While attending Moscow University, Lermontov was influenced deeply by secretly obtained works of the revolutionary Decembrist Ryleyev. At that time, Lermontov wrote an uncanny prediction of Russia's future: "The dark day of Russia will come when the crown of the Czars will fall, when the mob, oblivious of its former allegiance, will spread death and blood far and wide." Such musings continued to obsess him even after he joined the Imperial Guard Hussars in 1832, though he abandoned himself to the dissipation of St. Petersburg. Just as eagerly, he welcomed his exhausting, dangerous Caucasian exile, where he began his most successful novel, *Geroy nashego vremeni* (1840; *A Hero of Our Time*, 1854). Lermontov's patriotic historical epics, influenced by the contemporary popularity of *byliny* collections, and his romantic monologue "Mtsyri" ("The Novice"), the tale of a religious novice who prefers freedom to the futile safety of the monastery, were all written in the Caucasus.

Almost all of Lermontov's important poetry was produced in the last four years of his life. He was pardoned in 1839 and became a celebrity in St. Petersburg. The novelist Ivan Turgenev remarked, "There was something fatal and tragic about Lermontov . . . grim and evil force, passion, pensiveness, and disdain." Lermontov's fury at the vacuousness of society appears in biting satire, as in "Smert Poeta" ("The Death of a Poet"), where, Coriolanus-like, he spurns the mob, and the powerful "New Year's Night," where he contrasts his early vision, "the creation of my dream, with eyes full of an azure fire," with his present disillusionment. Again he was exiled, and after a brief fling in the capital he wrote as he left for the South, "unwashed Russia, land of slaves, of slaveholders, of blue uniforms and of the people whom they rule." Not long after, Lermontov dueled with a fellow officer over a woman and was killed at the first shot.

Like Pushkin, Lermontov shed his romantic postures early and adopted a vivid realism. Lermontov's style, unlike Pushkin's chiseled classicism, resembles "verbal masses molten into indistinguishable concrete," according to D. S. Mirsky, who sees Lermontov's "Valerik," "a letter in verse," as "a link between *The Bronze Horseman* and the military scenes of *War and Peace*." Nicholas I is said to have commented on Lermontov's end, "A dog's death befits a dog," but later critics rank Lermontov as one of Russia's greatest poets. Lermontov gloried in his "proud enmity against God," as "the Cain of Russian letters," and a melancholy rebellion lies at the heart of his finest works. He wrote, "There are words whose sense is obscure or trivial—yet one cannot listen to them without tremor," a quality of poetic expression used by the Symbolists at the turn of the century.

Perhaps Lermontov's greatest work is his long narrative poem *Demon* (1841; *The Demon*, 1875), composed between 1829 and 1839; his appeal to his countrymen lies above all in his "strange love" for Russia, as seen in "My Native Land," a peculiarly Russian response to "the cold silence of her steppes, her poor villages, the songs and dances of her peasants." For outsiders, the enigmatic life and abrupt death of this talented and tormented young poet seem to sum up the brief glory and the eloquent sunset of Russia's poetry in the first half of its Golden Age.

Although the glow of Pushkin's literary gold, subtly blending Romantic and classic elements, lingered through the 1840's, prose realism soon became the literary ideal in the harsh atmosphere inflicted on Russia by Nicholas I, determined to stamp out revolutionary liberalism at home. Discipline worthy of Ivan the Terrible was imposed on the Russian Army, whose common soldiers served twenty-five-year terms. The Czar's secret police dominated the country's political life, while "censors were unleashed on Russian literature like a pack of bloodhounds," according to one contemporary. Paradoxically, in the thirty years of Nicholas's rule, writers and philosophers flourished. Herzen wrote, "We devoted ourselves to science, philosophy, love, military art, mysticism, in order to forget the monstrous shallowness about us."

Pyotr Chaadayev, the religious philosopher who was the first Russian dissident to be forcibly confined in a madhouse, claimed in 1837, "There is something in our [Russian] blood that repels all true progress," and he defined the opposing positions in Russian thought which have persisted until the present. Slavophiles determined to expel all foreign ideologies and Westernizers such as Chaadayev, seeking Russia's salvation in imported liberalism, clashed in an atmosphere of ferocious governmental repression in a land that was ninety percent illiterate. Vissarion Belinsky (1811-1848), poor and desperately ill, became Russia's first and most influential literary critic, still cited today in the Soviet Union as "a great teacher." Belinsky called literature "the vital spring from which all human sentiments percolate into society," and he insisted that "he who deprives art of its rights to serve social interests debases the reader instead of elevating him."

Belinsky's fellow believer in Western ideals, Alexander Herzen, looked to Russia's "naturalness of peasant life" and "our remarkable ability to assimilate foreign ideas" for his country's rebirth. From his exile in Europe, Herzen propagandized against the czarist government, while Belinsky defended the "Russian Natural school" of literature, whose chief concern was social problems and whose leading representative was Nikolai Gogol. Herzen and Belinsky initiated "Russian Socialism," while Mikhail Bakunin, later Karl Marx's opponent in the First International promulgated revolutionary anarchism.

As Ivan Turgenev, Fyodor Dostoevski, and Leo Tolstoy were shaping their immense contributions to the world's great fiction, creating amazingly diverse panoramas characterized by acute political, social, and psychological analysis, Russian poetry developed along two distinct paths. One group espoused *l'art pour l'art* as an escape from everyday Russian reality, submerging themselves in stylistic simplicity, folk emotionalism, and Belinsky's dictum that poetry was "thinking in images." In contrast, civic realism in poetry found its voice in the works of Nikolai Nekrasov (1821-1878).

Nekrasov's father had turned him out of the house because of his obsessive desire to become a man of letters. "Famished every day for three years," he managed to become the foremost publisher of Russia's new realistic school of fiction. A contemporary remarked that if the ceiling collapsed on a soirée given by Nekrasov's mistress, "Most of Russian literature would have perished."

Nekrasov chose to "sing of your suffering, O my people" in intensely emotional language and innovative metrical usage. His most important work was a satiric epic, *Komúna Rusí žit' chorošó?* (1870-1874, 1879; *Who Can Be Happy and Free in Russia?*, 1917), which traces the wanderings of seven peasants through "wretched and abundant, oppressed and powerful, weak and mighty Mother Russia." His "Reflections Before a Mansion Doorway" observes unequivocally, "Where the people are, the moan is."

Because of Nekrasov's message and his immense popularity, the government allowed only one edition of his works during his life. He felt the disparity between his peasant sympathies and his wealthy position keenly, and he was large enough in spirit to recognize and encourage his talented contemporary Fyodor Tyutchev (1803-1873), who pursued pure art. Though Tyutchev was overshadowed during his lifetime by Nekrasov, the Symbolists of the Silver Age claimed Tyutchev as their spiritual ancestor.

Tyutchev was Tolstoy's favorite poet, and like the great novelist, Tyutchev was a fervent Slavophile who, despite his noble rank, wrote, "I love poetry and my country above all else in this world." While a diplomat in Germany, he was profoundly affected by the pessimistic philosophy of Arthur Schopenhauer, and Tyutchev's poetry shows the influence of a dualistic universe in which a Manichaean chaos and the "all-engulfing, all-pacifying abyss of the cosmos" dominate man's existence. For Tyutchev, a Schopenhauerean affinity between love and death was inherent in man's nature, a confirmation for Dostoevski, too, of dark tendencies he

recognized in his own writing. Tyutchev's four hundred short poems range from a perverse joy in destruction to a sublime desire to be "diffused in the slumbering Universe." His oratorical fervor continued the tradition established by Derzhavin of public poetic performance, and Tyutchev was the "last great master of the High Style," in which Old Church Slavonic rhetoric is supreme. Marc Slonim calls Tyutchev, after Pushkin, Lermontov, and Nekrasov, "the fourth great leader of Russian poetry . . . the profound interpreter of cosmic mysteries."

TOWARD THE SILVER AGE

Except for Count Aleksei Konstantinovich Tolstoy (1817-1875), a popular neo-Romantic poet in the German vein who opposed civic poetry bitterly and sought to reestablish the old norms of art, the 1860's and 1870's were dominated in Russia by fine poetic translations, not native Russian poetry. The costly Crimean War (1854-1856), a shocking waste of Russian lives brought about by the neglect and shortcomings of Russian leadership, had drained the nation's spirit. Russian prestige suffered a mortal blow through the ill-advised conduct of this war, and Alexander II and his government reluctantly faced the necessity of domestic reform. After taking the throne in 1855, Alexander freed the forty million Russian serfs in 1861, two years before Abraham Lincoln's Emancipation Proclamation, but taxes and land payments created tensions that resulted in many peasant uprisings throughout 1862. "The plague of Russian life" had ended, though, and the *zemstvos*, new self-governing bodies, relieved enough of the pressure on Russia's lower classes to maintain the status quo until 1905.

After 1865, Alexander's policies became more conservative. He was stalked and at last assassinated in 1881, ironically on the same day he had granted the *zemstvos* a larger voice in government, as the liberal intelligentsia had urged. Alexander III, his son, threw all reform proposals to the bitter winds from Siberia, increasing police powers, tightening the noose of censorship, and persecuting religious minorities, especially the Jews. His creation of a police state at home, coupled with his expensive and unsuccessful foreign ventures in Europe and Central Asia, made his reign a dismal time for literature. The last vestiges of the Golden Age had faded, and the Silver Age was waiting to be born.

In the 1880's, drought and poor agricultural practices resulted in massive famines and epidemics throughout Russia. Capitalism was fortifying a formidable industrial expansion, but the lives of ordinary Russians became increasingly miserable. Political theorists envisioned a necessary alliance of the peasantry, the workers and the intelligentsia, and a new form of Russian populism began to become part of the country's cultural atmosphere, tinged by more ideas from the West, the doctrines of Karl Marx.

The precise date of the beginning of modernism in Russian literature is uncertain. Some critics date the period from the publication in 1893 of Dmitri Merezhkovsky's lecture *O prichinakh upadka: o novykh techeniyakh sovremennoy russkoy lityeratury* (on the origins of the decline of Russian literature and on new currents in it), a theoretical work which announces the principles of Russian Symbolism. Others believe modernism began later, with the turn of the century or even with the 1905 Revolution, which Merezhkovsky and his wife, the poet Zinaida Gippius, supported. The Bolshevik Revolution of 1917, however, concluded the modernist period in Russia, just as it decisively ended the Russian monarchy forever.

In the 1890's, young Russian artists began to look inward, reassessing their values and redefining the function of the artist and his art. They became absorbed in the creative individualism evident in translations of the works of Friedrich Nietzsche, Stefan George, the English Pre-Raphaelites, and the French Symbolists, especially Charles Baudelaire. Merezhkovsky and others protested against the radical intellectuals who had been dominating Russia's literary life and pronounced a new cultural dogma involving Western-style humanism, Russian tradition, mysticism, intuition, mystery, and myth—a spiritual obbligato to the strange goings-on of Grigory Rasputin at the Imperial Court.

At first, the new writers were dismissed as decadents, but their successors became the spokesmen for a remarkable explosion of Russian art and literature, a conscious transmutation of Pushkin's Age of Gold known today as the Silver Age of Russian letters. More Russian philosophical works appeared between 1890 and 1910 than during the part of the nineteenth century up to that point, and an abundance of small literary magazines provided an outlet for poetry and criticism. Until 1903, the Russian literary scene was dominated by the decadents' reaction against realism. They were led by Valery Bryusov (1873-1924), sometimes called the Peter the Great of Russian literature.

After translating Maurice Maeterlinck and Paul Verlaine at the age of fourteen, Bryusov "sought a new body for the new art" in synaesthesia, "the subtle ties between the shape and the scent of a flower." The keynote of the landmark anthology *Russkiye simvolisty* (1894) is the slogan, "The personality of the artist is the essence of art." In 1903, Bryusov and his mesmerized followers founded *Vesy* (first published in January, 1904), which became the most important Russian decadent literary periodical and preached such Baudelairean themes as erotic nihilism and Arthur Rimbaud's *dérèglement des sens* (disorder of the senses).

Konstantin Balmont (1867-1943), the other great decadent, a public performer as Bryusov was not, became "the Poet" of turn-of-the-twentieth-century Russia. Balmont drew a large and mostly youthful following at his public recitations. He was a spontaneous poet whose first poetic credo, "Words are chameleons," developed into Nietzschean vehemence by 1903: "I want daggerlike words and lethal moans of death. . . . Who equals my might in song? No one—no one!"

"Moans of death" erupted throughout Russia with the disastrous Russo-Japanese War (1904-1905), followed by the 1905 Revolution, which started on "Bloody Sunday," January 22. The following October, after months of turmoil, Nicholas II granted some civil liberties and the democratic election of a duma (legislative assembly). The Czar's manifesto split the revolutionaries into three major camps: the Octobrists, satisfied with the Czar's action; the Constitutional Democrats, liberals who wanted far more power invested in the Duma; and the Social Democrats, who had organized a soviet (workers' council) at St. Petersburg and attempted to force additional reform by strike. The Czar put them down, trying to stamp out the revolutionaries and limiting the power of the Duma in late 1905. Counterrevolutionary forces in the Second and Third Dumas (1906-1912) prevented any advancement of liberalism prior to World War I.

After 1903, the decadent movement in literature had an older faction and a younger one, the original decadents being more occupied with social and political themes and the new Symbolists turning to the neo-Romantic inspiration of Lermontov and Tyutchev. Most critics agree, however, that no stated doctrinal differences distinguished the two groups in the prewar period, and that they lived harmoniously with each other in Moscow and St. Petersburg.

A startling manifestation of the decadent movement appears in the work of the Satanist poet-novelist Sologub (the pen name of Fyodor Teternikov, 1863-1927). He regarded modern humanity as a horde of living dead, and he believed a poet inhabited a shadowy limbo, where, sorcerer-like, he had to make himself the only credible god in a universe as evil as its creator. His nihilism is somewhat restrained in his lyrics, which he compares in his poem "Amphora" to a fine vase carried so carefully that no drop of the venom it contains is spilled. In his later years, he abandoned poetry for a perverse fictional vision of man's debasement.

An antidote to Sologub's horrid view of humankind was offered by the metaphysical *Weltbild* drawn from the cult of Dostoevski at the end of the nineteenth century. The diverse works of Merezhkovsky and of Vladimir Solovyov (1853-1900) depart from decadent nihilism and seek individual concepts of "Godmanhood," an absolute achieved through Sophia, the incarnation of Divine Wisdom, the archetypal Eternal Feminine. The German Neoplatonic idealism that had fostered the creativity of Lermontov and Tyutchev influenced many of the Symbolist disciples of Solovyov, who accepted the notion of the poet's intermediation between God and Man, conveying to ordinary mortals his experience of the ideals of Truth and Beauty reflected in the principle of Sophia. Vladimir Solovyov himself accepted Christ's incarnation as proof of man's redemption. He believed that despite all of history's evils, man will at last attain divinity, and his concept of the Divine Sophia appeared frequently in his own verse, although he occasionally treated the symbol lightly, as in his long poem *Tri svidaniya* (1898; three encounters). Solovyov hoped for the reunion of all Christian denominations, and during his last years he preached salvation through collective effort. Solovyov's teachings indelibly marked the entire religious movement connected with Russian Symbolism.

Each of the Symbolist triumvirate, Vyacheslav Ivanov, Andrey Bely, and Aleksandr Blok, owed a profound spiritual and artistic debt to Solovyov's definition of poetry as the "incantatory magic of rhythmic speech, mediating between man and the world of divine things." Ivanov (1866-1949) considered all of human culture the path to God, and he believed that artistic intuition grasped symbols in the ordinary world that reflect the "real" reality of God. Hence the artist, having been given greater gifts, has the responsibility to lead men to the Divine Presence. Andrey Bely (the pen name of Boris Bugayev, 1880-1934), whose strong enthusiasms bordered on the pathological, incorporated Solovyov's doctrine of Divine Wisdom in his lyrics *Zoloto v lazuri* (1904; god in azure), but within a few years he had become the leading Russian disciple of Rudolph Steiner's anthroposophy. An important novelist as well as a poet, Bely embodied the mixture of mysticism, diabolism, and obsession with the special fate of Russia that was so characteristic of his time.

Despite the considerable achievements of Ivanov and Bely, Aleksandr Blok (1880-1921) was the culminating figure of the Silver Age. His lyrics place him with Pushkin and Lermontov, and his ideals remain a rare blend of ecstasy and despair. The young Blok experienced a supernatural vision of a "beautiful lady from Beyond," the Solovyovian Sophia, who inspired more than 240 of his lyrics. In "Gorod" ("The City"), however, set in St. Petersburg's "artificial paradises," disillusionment shattered Blok's Romantic dreams, and in "Nezna Komka" ("The Stranger"), one of his most powerful poems, his ideal woman appeared as an expensive prostitute. Such blasphemous irony caused Blok's break with the Moscow Symbolists. After 1906, Blok continued to suffer from his irreconcilable inner conflict; he wrote, "I see too many things clearly, soberly," and he hurled himself into intense experiences, trying to reconcile art and morality at the same time that he was frantically avoiding confrontation with himself. By 1909, he had become infatuated with his "beloved fatal country," and his lyric cycle "On the Battle of Kulikova Field" celebrates the fourteenth century victory of the Russians over the Tartars. Just prior to August, 1914, Blok predicted in poetry Russia's "road of the steppe and of shoreless grief," and following the 1917 Bolshevik Revolution, in a Rilkean "dictated" composition, Blok produced his masterpiece, *Dvenadtsat* (1918; *The Twelve*, 1920), a poetic vision of a revolution that would cleanse Russia and redeem its soul from its long agony. By 1921, however, representatives of every segment of Blok's postrevolutionary world, from Communist officials to his old intellectual friends, had ridiculed *The Twelve*, and Blok died convinced that "Vile, rotten Mother Russia has devoured me."

Innokenty Annensky (1856-1909), the Russian poet who links the decadents and the Symbolists, devoted fifteen years to translating the works of Euripides. Not surprisingly, his own themes were beauty, suffering, and death, the absolutes of a futile human existence which could only be ennobled through art and love. Annensky's finely honed meters and rhythmic effects influenced both the Symbolists and the Acmeists, the next major poetic group in Russia.

ACMEIST POETS

The Symbolists' nebulous Westernized ideals did not prevail for long against the literary realism being promoted by Maxim Gorky in the relatively stable bourgeois climate of Russia between 1910 and 1914. Acmeism was born in 1912, a movement primarily based in St. Petersburg and resembling the controlled, concrete Imagism of Ezra Pound and T. S. Eliot. The three major Acmeist poets, Nikolay Gumilyov, Anna Akhmatova, and Osip Mandelstam, despite significant differences in style and message, concurred that "we want to admire a rose because it is beautiful, and not because it is a symbol of mystical purity."

Gumilyov (1886-1921), leader of the Acmeists, had a "bravura personality" that blossomed in physical danger and exotic landscapes. In his 1912 article, "Acmeism and the Heritage of Symbolism," he stressed the Greek meaning of "acme": "the point of highest achievement," and Théophile Gauiter's rule, "The more dispassionate the material . . . the more beautiful will the work come out."

Often likened to Rudyard Kipling's, Gumilyov's virile style could not have differed more strikingly from that of his wife for eight years, Anna Akhmatova (1889-1966). Akhmatova's earliest poetry, mostly small lyrics which sang of the woman's inevitably unhappy role in

love, was extremely popular immediately upon publication, and her work has since completely overshadowed Gumilyov's. Even today Russian readers memorize Akhmatova's poetry, and she remains Russia's foremost woman poet, unforgettably uniting passion and asceticism. Periodically suppressed by the Soviets, Akhmatova's work has endured; among her greatest works is the cycle *Rekviem* (1963; *Requiem*, 1964), her lament for the victims of Joseph Stalin's purges.

INFLUENCE OF THE POLITICAL STATE

Russia's human losses in the twentieth century defy comprehension. The agony of World War I, closely followed by the February Democratic Revolution and the October Bolshevik Revolution, both in 1917, combined with the ravages of the Civil War, cost millions of lives. Later, the famines, the collectivization of agriculture, and the purges of the 1930's established a dark backdrop for the staggering losses, estimated at twenty to twenty-five million lives, which the Soviet Union sustained during World War II.

The Bolshevik Revolution and the consequent establishment of the Soviet state have enormously affected Russian literature, although seldom in Russia's history, if ever, has literature enjoyed the freedom of expression provided by Western democracies. In the Soviet era, works of prose and poetry have often been surreptitiously circulated in samizdat (editions) and clandestinely shipped abroad, to become tamizdat (literally, three-published) works in less restricted societies. The cost of the human devastation suffered by Russians in their century, however, is reflected in the estimates of those lost in Stalin's prison system, the Gulag Archipelago, where hundreds of writers perished among countless numbers of their countrymen.

In response to the phenomenon of Soviet Communism, too, literature of the period after the 1917 Revolution evidences two major tendencies. Those writers who remain within the Soviet Union and function within its intellectual and artistic borders often turn to apolitical themes or those acceptable to their government, in both cases revealing glimpses both accurate and distorted of life within their country; commentators such as Ronald Hingley observe that the distortions sometimes provide the truest insights. Writers who dissent from official Soviet positions eventually export either their works or themselves, and from exile their writings occasionally find their way back to their native land, to circulate at considerable risk among readers of Russian samizdat.

Indeed, the tyranny of the Soviet state has produced three distinct "waves" of emigration. The first emigration, the largest of the three, took place during the decade following the 1917 Revolution. Among the many Russian poets who emigrated at this time, perhaps the foremost were Marina Tsvetayeva, who later returned to the Soviet Union, and Vladislav Khodasevich, who died in exile. The fate of Khodasevich (1886-1939) is particularly representative. Little read in the West, Khodasevich, like many émigrés, has suffered from what the critic and translator Simon Karlinsky calls the "Western self-censorship"—the conviction, inherited from the thirties, that a Russian writer who resides outside the Soviet Union cannot be of any interest to a Western reader. The second emigration, following World War II, brought to the West fewer writers of note, but the third wave, beginning in the 1970's and continuing to the present, has carried with it a host of brilliant writers, including Aleksandr Solzhenitsyn, Andrei Sinyavsky, and the poet Joseph Brodsky (1940-1996).

Among the poets who have remained in the Soviet Union, the finest invariably have suffered persecution at the hands of the state. No loss to the world of poetry seems crueller than the death of Akhmatova's friend and fellow Acmeist Osip Mandelstam (1891-1938), who perished in a Far Eastern transit prison, bound for the mines of Kolyma beyond the Arctic Circle. Nadezhada Mandelstam retrospectively described her husband's spirit as endlessly *zhizneradostny*, which approximates the English phrase, "rejoicing in life." Mandelstam never bowed to political pressures; he was an admirer of classicism in the oratorical style of Derzhavin and Tyutchev, a Jew more aware of Russian tradition than the Russians themselves were. "I am nobody's contemporary," he wrote, because as an inveterate Westernizer he yearned for world culture. His solemn and exquisitely crafted poems were his conscious effort to achieve "pure" poetry, often employing little-known historical detail and a "sprung" rhythm somewhat resembling Gerard Manley Hopkins's metrical experiments. Like Akhmatova, Mandelstam was forbidden to publish un-

der Stalin, and his mental and physical health collapsed under torture. What sustained him so long as his frail constitution could endure was his concept of poetry as a moral obligation to his countrymen: "The people need poetry that will be their own secret/ to keep them safe forever. . . ."

FUTURIST POETS

The Acmeists' contemporaries, the Futurists, opposed literary and artistic tradition with a zeal that owed a considerable debt to Nietzsche. In 1912, their manifesto, "Poshchechina obshchestvennomu vkusu" ("A Slap in the Face of the Public Taste"), presented Russian readers with an extreme literary case of shocking the bourgeois. One of its authors, Vladimir Mayakovsky (1893-1930), described himself in his important poem *Oblako v shtanakh* (1915; *A Cloud in Pants*, 1965), as "the loud-mouthed Zarathustra of our day," and his associate Velimir Khlebnikov (1895-1922), a linguistically experimental poet, rejected all emotional emphasis derived from previous ages from his powerful poems. Russia, he insisted, had "amplified the voice of the West as though transmitting the screams of a monster," and he explored new symbolic uses of language to rouse the world from its petrification. Aleksei Kruchonykh (1886-1968) provided Futurism with its most famous poem, "Dyr bul shchyl" (1913), written in words that have "no definite meaning," that is, in *zaum* (transrational language) which he and Khlebnikov pioneered. *Zaum* is akin to abstractionism in art in that it is intended to have a direct evocative power without a specific, definable referent, and was one of the most avant-garde innovations in Russian poetry. Kruchonykh wrote quite a number of usually short poems in *zaum* and published them in primitive-looking handmade manuscript booklets. The *zaum* "opera" *Pobeda nad solntsem* (pr. 1913;*Victory Over the Sun*, 1971), that in St. Petersburg rivaled the premier of Igor Stravinsky's *Rite of Spring* in Paris of the same year, was one of the signal Russian avant-garde events of the age. Although the Moscow group of Futurists was most prominent and inventive, the St. Petersburg group included Vasilisk (Vasily) Gnedov (1890-1978), who became famous as the author of "Poema kontsa" (1913, "Poem of the End"). This proto-minimalist poem consisted of a blank space on a page where a text was supposed to be. Gnedov performed it with a silent gesture to much acclaim. Just after the Bolshevik Revolution, the Futurists dominated Soviet cultural life briefly, mainly through the achievements of the dynamic Mayakovsky, who, like Nietzsche, called forcefully for the destruction of the old world and the invention of a new one to supercede it.

The Russian Formalist critic Viktor Shklovsky, Mayakovsky's contemporary, claims that Mayakovsky's chief accomplishment was the broadening of verse semantics, building an oratorical language which changed the very syntax of the Russian language. Mayakovsky's ego and his anarchic inclination feasted on the Bolshevik Revolution, but in "Homeward" (composed in 1925) he wrote, "From poetry's skies I plunge into Communism." In 1930, openly critical of Soviet bureaucracy, Mayakovsky committed suicide, which he described as "my final performance." The Soviet Union has enshrined Mayakovsky with their supreme poets, praising his declaration of the artist's obligation to the state. Mayakovsky's savage individuality is said to have stamped as diverse poets as Joseph Brodsky now in exile, and the Soviet poets Yevgeny Yevtushenko and Andrei Voznesensky.

FOLKLORE AND RUSSIAN HERITAGE

Diametrically opposed to Mayakovsky's idiosyncratic poetic style is that of Sergei Esenin (1896-1925), a "peasant poet" who harked back to Russia's traditional past, its rich folklore, and its Orthodox religion. Esenin, a poet from the people, founded the Imaginist school of poetry between 1914 and 1919. His personal excesses led to a self-image he described in *Ispoved 'khuligana* (1921; *Confessions of a Hooligan*, 1973), and his unhappy marriages, first to the American dancer Isadora Duncan and then to Tolstoy's granddaughter Sofya, contributed to his final breakdown. He attempted to write political poetry on contemporary topics, but near the end of his life his work was filled with nostalgia for the past and sadness at the fate of his home village, and his later poems made him the voice of many of his countrymen in their disenchantment with Soviet policies. After his suicide in 1925, Esenin's work was out of favor with the Soviet government, but he has since been fully rehabilitated.

Something of Mayakovsky's originality and force and something of Esenin's tender devotion to his Rus-

sian heritage meet in Russia's *inneres Mädchen*, as Rainer Maria Rilke called Marina Tsvetayeva (1892-1941), Akhmatova's friend and only rival as Russia's most famous woman poet. At eighteen, Tsvetayeva described her poetry as "torn from me like droplets from a fountain . . . their themes made up of youth and death." She emigrated to Paris in 1921, outraged at events in Russia, but she and her family returned in 1939 on the eve of war. After her husband, a Soviet secret agent, was shot by the government as a traitor and one of her children was sent to a labor camp, Tsvetayeva hanged herself in 1941.

As a daughter of the Russian intelligentsia, she wrote for this audience. Her intricate romanticism, like Rilke's, verged on the mystical, and she shared with him, as his long 1926 poem to her reveals, an awareness of "the other world" and the possibility of a new myth that would lead humankind to a better future. Akhmatova hailed Tsvetayeva's creative vitality in one of her last poems, a tender memory of "A fresh, dark elder branch/ Like a letter from Marina." Tsvetayeva, like Boris Pasternak, was one of the outstanding idealists in Russian poetry. Her impressionistic technique and elliptic imagery show evidence of Pasternak's influence, and she once remarked that he was the only poet among her contemporaries whom she considered her peer.

Boris Pasternak (1890-1960), child of a gifted musician and a famous painter, synthesized the classical tradition in Russian verse, the musical qualities of the Symbolists, and the near-telegraphic style of the mature Tsvetayeva. Pasternak wrote poetry early, at first attracted and soon repelled by the flamboyant Mayakovsky. Pasternak found his own voice in *Sestra moyazhizn* (1922; *My Sister, Life*, 1959) a collection which immediately established him as one of the leading poets of his generation.

In his autobiographical sketch *Okhrannaya gramota* (1931; *A Safe-Conduct*, 1949), Pasternak wrote, "Focused on a reality which feeling has displaced, art is a record of this displacement." A sense of the artist's isolation pervades Pasternak's life and work. As Max Hayward has suggested, Pasternak believed it essential "by responding submissively to high and lonely destiny . . . to contribute in some vital way to the life of the times." Already during World War I, Pasternak had pondered his "contribution," later to become his novel *Doktor Zhivago* (1957; *Doctor Zhivago*, 1958), the record of the Russian intelligentsia caught in the savagery of those revolutionary times. For writing the novel, Pasternak was expelled from the Soviet Writers' Union and forbidden to accept the 1958 Nobel Prize for Literature. The novel closes upon "The Poems of Doctor Zhivago," in which Pasternak reaffirms the Christian sanctity of his poetic mission: "If Thou be willing, Abba, Father,/ Remove this cup from me."

ABSURDIST POETS

It was not until the 1980's that the Russian reading public became fully aware of the work of a small group of absurdist poets from the 1920's and 1930's who named themselves Oberiu (Association for Real Art), the existence of which was declared in a 1928 manifesto. The leading figures in the group were Daniil Kharms (Yuvachov, 1905-1942), Aleksandr Vvedensky (1904-1941) and Nikolai Zabolotsky (1903-1958), the primary drafter of the manifesto. Zabolotsky was able to publish one book of poems, *Stolbtsy* (1929, *Columns*), but the other two were able to publish only a few individual poems and stories for children. Their work, which included plays and, in the case of Kharms, short prose sketches that have since become famous, involves totally unexpected, illogical, and sometimes tautological twists of action, imagery, and thought, such as "The sun shines in disarray,/ and the flowers fly in their beds" (Vvedensky) and "This is This./ That is That./ This is not That./ This is not not This./ The rest is either this or not this./ All is either that or not that" (Kharms). They reveal a philosophical depth beneath an absurd, often nightmarish surface. The group ran afoul of the Stalinist regime and Kharms and Vvedensky both died in prison. Today their work is perceived as a major literary movement and the last gasp of the pre-revolutionary Russian literary avant-garde. It is extremely popular now among young intellectuals.

POST-STALIN ERA

The cooperation between the Western Allies and the Soviet Union during World War II dissolved in Cold War tension during the 1950's, but after Stalin's death in 1953 a degree of artistic freedom was temporarily achieved by Russian writers. An amnesty decree a month after Stalin's death led to the release of prisoners who had survived the rigors of the Gulag, and the Writers' Union restored the membership of Anna Akhmatova in 1954. By 1955, the "thaw" had occasioned the posthumous rehabilitation of many writers who had died in the camps and prisons; this revisionist movement reached its peak with Nikita Khrushchev's famous speech at the Twentieth Party Congress in February, 1956, denouncing Stalin. Despite the suppression of *Doctor Zhivago*, the thaw lasted long enough to permit the publication of Aleksandr Solzhenitsyn's novel *Odin den Ivana Denisovicha* (1962; *One Day in the Life of Ivan Denisovich*, 1963), but soon thereafter Brezhnev ousted Khrushchev from power. After Brezhnev's accession in 1964, literature in the Soviet Union was subject to rigid Stalinist controls, and, one after another, the most talented Russian writers have emigrated to the West or have been forcibly exiled.

Nevertheless, there exists within the Soviet Union an immense thirst for poetry, attested by the immense popularity of such poets as Yevgeny Yevtushenko (born 1933) and Andrei Voznesensky (born 1933). Both rose to prominence in the early 1960's as spokesmen for liberal forces during that time of the thaw. Yevtushenko, as the first poet to enunciate the shift in mood in his country, gained considerable acclaim at home and abroad for his revelation of Soviet anti-Semitism in "Babii Yar" (1961) and the effects of Stalinism as a social force in "Nasledniki Stalina" (1962; "The Heirs of Stalin"). Yevtushenko has used his travels abroad in several volumes of his works, such as the poetic drama *Pod kozhey statuey sbobody* (1972; under the skin of the Statue of Liberty). Certain of his more personal poems are reminiscent of Esenin's candor and nostalgia, but Yevtushenko's "novella in verse," *Golub' v Sant'iago* (1978; *A Dove in Santiago*, 1982), a tale of a tormented young art student in Chile at the time of the Augusto Pinochet coup, reflects the tragedy of a talented individual who is caught between his politics and his art.

Like Yevtushenko, Voznesensky writes and publishes prolifically in the Soviet Union, having survived the artistic restrictions imposed first by Khrushchev in 1963, closing the thaw, and subsequently by Brezhnev and his successors. Voznesensky's histrionic style of poetic delivery, modeled on Mayakovsky's made him popular with large and youthful audiences, while American critics have praised his imagery and originality. One of his translators, W. H. Auden, has cited the broad range of Voznesensky's subject matter as evidence of his imaginative power. Although Voznesensky has been the object of articles in the Soviet press accusing him of intelligibility and "supermodernism," he continues to be widely published in the Soviet Union.

POEMS "TO REMEMBER"

The increasing stream of samizdat and tamizdat poetry emerging from the Soviet Union, on the other hand, bears the self-imposed charge: "to remember"—to memorialize the victims of Stalin's Gulag, and to speak out against the punishment of dissenters in labor camps and psychiatric hospitals. Poets who dissent against the government of the U.S.S.R. must choose between writing "for the desk drawer," exile, or death, as the fate of Yuri Galanskov (1939-1972) demonstrates. In 1956, when the Hungarian revolt was suppressed by the Soviets, Galanskov gathered a samizdat collection of protest poems. After he set forth his "Human Manifesto," "calling to Truth and Rebellion . . . a serf no more," Galanskov was held in a Soviet special psychiatric hospital; he later died in a labor camp for his role in the Human Rights Movement within the Soviet Union. The themes of samizdat and tamizdat poetry reflect the mediocrity of everyday Soviet life, the horrors of war, and the martyrdom of earlier poets such as Tsvetayeva, who perished under Stalin. Occasionally, too, this clandestinely exported poetry is quietly illuminated by the folk values of Old Russia, as in Gelb Garbovsky's "To the Neva": "I will come back, no matter what, even if, when I do return, I'm dying."

The most famous poet-exile was Joseph Brodsky (1940-1996), who felt himself to be a poet by the grace of God and therefore for whom no other social role was necessary. A native of Leningrad, in the late 1950's he became associated with the circle of young poets around Anna Akhmatova and was recognized by her as a significant new talent. Though his poems were apolitical, his independence of mind caused him to be arrested in 1964 for "parasitism," that is, not having a legally approved job, and he was sentenced to five years of internal exile

in the north. Released in a year, he was ultimately forced into exile in the United States, where he spent most of the rest of his life teaching, writing, and reciting his poetry, which he did with a unique intensity and melodiousness. In 1987 he won the Nobel Prize for Literature, and in 1991 he became the United States poet laureate, the first non-native to be so honored. Although he did not complete high school, his poetry is characterized by the erudition of someone steeped in classical learning and world culture. It has a philosophical depth and complexity of imagery comparable to his favorite English metaphysical poets and modernists such as T. S. Eliot and W. H. Auden. His verse forms are basically traditional, but within them he created an unusual degree of lyrical tension. His typical themes are loneliness and suffering, death and salvation, often ventriloquized through some famous historical or mythological figure in a moment of realization or crisis. Though he had the opportunity in the late twentieth century to visit and even return to Russia, he chose not to do so, but instead to die in exile and to be buried in Venice.

Parallel to the public existence of poetry in the post-Stalin period represented on one hand by Yevtushenko and Voznesensky, and on the other by Galanskov and Brodsky, there was a more private, underground development that occurred in formal and informal poetry circles. Formal circles centered around officially sponsored clubs and seminars in which senior poets mentored younger aspiring poets. This was in part a subtle way for the authorities to keep an eye on the younger generation, but in the better groups, for example, those led by Mikhail Svetlov (1903-1964) and Kirill Kovaldzhi (born 1930), some talented poets did find useful mentoring and occasional outlets to publication. More important were the informal groups of the underground. One of the earliest of these, the Nebyvalisty (Unprecedentists, 1939-1940) headed by Nikolai Glazkov (1919-1979), who coined the term samizdat, actually began before the war at the Moscow Pedagogical Institute as a continuation of Futurism. Though the group soon dissolved, Glazkov (and for their part Kruchonykh and Pasternak) we able to serve as personal mentors to several generations of younger poets. SMOG (The Youngest Society of Geniuses), also in Moscow but in the early 1960's, like the Nebyvalisty, was not noted for the innovativeness of their poetry, but rather for their unrestrained behavior. It did include one lyric genius in the mold of Yesenin, Leonid Gubanov (1946-1983). On the other hand, the Lianozovo school, which centered around the suburban Moscow barracks apartment of Evgeny Kropivnitsky (1893-1979), fostered poets of genuine originality and innovation. Among them were Vsevolod Nekrasov (born Kholin, 1920-1999), Genrikh Sapgir (1928-1999), and even the scandalous Eduard Limonov (born 1943), all of whom emerged as major literary figures in the *glasnost* period. In Leningrad in the late 1950's, the Philological school, which included among its members the now prominent poets Vladimir Ufliand (born 1937), Lev Losev (born 1937), Aleksandr Kondratov (1937-1993), and Mikhail Yeryomin (born 1936) was one of the first such underground groups. A monumental contribution to an awareness of this period, especially in Leningrad, is Konstantin Kuzminsky's nine-volume *Blue Lagoon Anthology of Modern Russian Poetry* (1980-1986).

BARD POETRY

Along with the poetry underground there developed another trend that had its roots in popular and folk song, namely, the guitar poetry of the so-called "bards." These poets chose to set their texts to melodies with simple guitar accompaniment and sing them in private gatherings and around campfires. The recognized founder of this trend was Bulat Okudzhava (1924-1997), who began to compose such songs immediately after World War II. With the advent of readily available tape recorders in the 1960's, Okudzhava's songs became well known and popular throughout the Soviet Union, despite the lack of official recordings. Other important figures in this genre were Aleksandr Galich (1918-1977), whose songs developed a social protest edge that resulted in his being exiled abroad, and Vladimir Vysotsky (1938-1980), whose broad-ranging themes and personae made him immensely popular with all levels of Russian society, a popularity that only increased after his untimely death from heart failure. What distinguishes the work of the bards from popular song is the high quality of the poetic text itself, which can usually stand on its own as fine poetry, regardless of its musical aspects.

With Mikhail Gorbachev's accession to power in 1985 and his introduction of a policy of *glasnost*, official

censorship began to be reduced. By 1989 it was virtually eliminated, producing an ever-increasing wave of poetry publications. Initially, much of this was past work that finally emerged from the underground to reach the general reading public. Soon new voices and new work by older generations began to flood the public sphere, creating an impression of postmodern Babel. Where earlier there had been only a handful of published poets worth reading, there now were dozens, if not hundreds, with a range of orientations and styles. Parallel with this was a sharp decline in popular interest in poetry. What had been a narrow and exciting passageway to freer speech was made to face competition from a deluge of popular entertainment and the unfettered news media. Yet at the same time it has been a time of major flowering for poetry. Attempts to categorize the new poetry into trends such as metametaphorism and conceptualism are useful to some extent, but do not do justice either to the richness and complexity of the current situation or to such unique major figures as Gennady Aygi (born 1934), Viktor Sosnora (born 1936), Aleksandr Kushner (born 1936), Ry Nikonova (born 1942), Lev Rubinstein (born 1947), Ivan Zhdanov (born 1948), Olga Sedakova (born 1949), Nina Iskrenko (1951-1995), Timur Kibirov (born 1955), and Vitaly Kalpidi (born 1957), to name just a few. Moreover, with the freedom to travel, publish, and distribute books, the separation among Russian poets living throughout Russia and those living abroad has been eliminated. The landscape of modern Russian poetry more and more resembles that in the West.

BIBLIOGRAPHY

Bristol, Evelyn. *A History of Russian Poetry*. New York: Oxford University Press, 1991. A recent, solid history of Russian poetry from its beginnings to the 1970's.

Brown, Edward J. *Russian Literature Since the Revolution*. Rev. ed. Cambridge, Mass.: Harvard University Press, 1982. Among the best histories of Russian literature of the Soviet period.

Cornwell, Neil, ed. *A Reference Guide to Russian Literature*. Chicago: Fitzroy Dearborn, 1998. Provides extensive articles on key authors and key works.

High, John, et al., eds. *Crossing Centuries: The New Generation in Russian Poetry*. Jersey City, N.J.: Talisman House, 2000. A large gathering of recent Russian poetry in translation, including feminist and gay poetry.

Johnson, Kent, and Stephen M. Ashby, eds. *Third Wave: The New Russian Poetry*. Ann Arbor: University of Michigan Press, 1992. Among the best anthologies of Russian poetry in translation, from the 1980's.

Mirsky, D. S. *A History of Russian Literature from its Beginnings to 1900*. Reprint. Evanston, Ill.: Northwestern University Press, 1999. Still valuable as a classic history.

Scherr, Barry P. *Russian Poetry: Meter, Rhythm, and Rhyme*. Berkeley: University of California Press, 1986. One of the best treatments of the principles of Russian versification.

Slonim, Marc. *The Epic of Russian Literature, from Its Origins Through Tolstoy*. New York: Oxford University Press, 1950.

_____. *Modern Russian Literature, from Chekhov to the Present*. New York: Oxford University Press, 1953. Both of Slonim's books provide a thorough history of Russian literature through World War II.

Smith, Gerald S. *Songs to Seven Strings: Russian Guitar Poetry and Soviet "Mass Song."* Bloomington: Indiana University Press, 1984. The main general source in English for information on the "bards."

_____, ed. *Contemporary Russian Poetry: A Bilingual Anthology*. Bloomington: Indiana University Press, 1993. A somewhat conservative but broad selection of important poets with parallel Russian and English texts.

Terras, Victor. *A History of Russian Literature*. New Have, Conn.: Yale University Press, 1991. A magisterial overview by a distinguished senior scholar.

Yevtushenko, Yevgeny, et al., eds. *Twentieth Century Russian Poetry: Silver and Steel, an Anthology*. New York: Anchor Books, 1994. A large, sometimes quirky and inaccurate, but useful anthology of translations.

Mitzi M. Brunsdale,
updated by Gerald Janecek

SCANDINAVIAN POETRY

The oldest evidence of lyric writing in the Nordic countries can be dated back to the introduction of the runic alphabet in the third century. Thousands of runic inscriptions—first carved in wood and on tools and later in stone as memorials—are preserved in Denmark, Norway, and especially Sweden; more than two thousand inscriptions dating from the eleventh century are known to exist in Sweden alone. These inscriptions, characteristically concise and laconic, provide invaluable insights into both personal destinies and events of national scope. Frequently, the inscriptions employ a stylized language using alliteration and poetic circumlocutions called *kenningar*. At times, these messages, which may consist of several hundred runic signs, incorporate phrases known from the common Germanic literary tradition and regular stanzas known from the far more sophisticated—and better preserved—West Nordic Old Norse poetry.

EDDIC POETRY

In order to form a better understanding of Old Norse poetry, one must turn to this early Norwegian-Icelandic literature, divided into Eddic poetry and skaldic poetry. The anonymous Eddic poems have been preserved primarily in the Codex Regius manuscript from the latter part of the thirteenth century, the so-called *Elder* or *Poetic Edda* (English translations 1923, 1928, 1962, 1997). A number of these texts are also quoted in Snorri Sturluson's (1179-1241) book on Nordic mythology and poetry, written about 1220—the so-called *Younger* or *Prose Edda* (English translations, 1916, 1954, 1987). The written tradition does not go further back, but it is evident that many Eddic poems were for several centuries transmitted via the oral tradition. They take their topics from both Old Norse mythology and Germanic heroic legends, employing three metrical measures: *fornyrthislag* (epic measure), *málaháttr* (speech measure), and *ljothaháttr* (chant measure). All of these measures are based on old Germanic alliterative long line, and all of them tend to be stanzaic.

Codex Regius opens with *Völuspá* (*Völuspá: The Song of the Sybil*, 1968), a prophecy about the Creation as well as the end of the world and the rise of a new world order. While this mythical vision is cultic, forming a Nordic parallel to the biblical Genesis and Revelation, the following poem, *Hávamál* (*The Sayings of the High One*, 1923), is an expression of worldly wisdom. The first stanza advocates caution and distrustfulness through the sayings of the god Odin, who expresses the essence of Viking philosophy in the following lines: "Cattle die,/ kinsmen die,/ one dies oneself also;/ but fame [reputation] alone/ will never die/ for him who gains good fame."

Among the gods of the Eddic poems, Odin is the most distinguished, but, as in the Homeric poems, the frailties of the gods are also exposed. In *Hárbarthsljóth* (*The Lay of Hárbarthr*), Odin is thus played off, with coarse humor, against the god Thor, and Thor becomes the main character in *Thrymskvitha* (*The Lay of Thrymr*), the most popular of all Eddic poems. It tells of the god's recovering his hammer from the giant Thymr, a high point of Old Norse poetry with its pithy portraits and agile narrative. No direct Germanic counterpart to the Eddic mythological poetry is known to exist. The heroic poems in Codex Regius, on the other hand, have parallels in the British *Widsith* (c. seventh century) and *Beowulf* (c. 1000) and the German *Hildebrandslied* (c. 800). The basic concept of this heroic poetry, as well as that of its mythological counterpart, is epic and dramatic. The worldview is tragic-heroic, and human action is governed by the dictates of honor and revenge. The major portion of the Eddic heroic poetry is connected with the Germanic hero Sigurthr (Siegfried) and the specifically Nordic Helgi Hundingsbani, who is made a half brother to Sigurthr. In a number of poems, partly linked together and supplemented by prose sections, Sigurthr's youth, the avenging of his father, his dragon slaying, his winning of the hoard, his flame-wall ride to release the sleeping Brynhildr, and finally his death are related. The characters confront one another in terse, stylized dialogues, and a light of tragic pathos and timeless idealism is cast upon their lives of strong wills and emotions.

SKALDIC POETRY

The skaldic poems, on the other hand, generally have a more current atmosphere and are linked to certain situations in the named authors' own time. Certain poets, skalds, were even employed as official chroniclers at the courts in order to celebrate the kings and their deeds. This historical function of skaldic poetry explains why it is frequently quoted in the sagas, especially the kings' sagas of the thirteenth century; in fact, a considerable portion of this literature has survived only as such quotations. Skaldic poetry (a selection of which appears in English in *The Skalds*, 1945, 1968) is a unique Nordic genre. Like Eddic poetry, it is alliterative, but it follows far stricter metrical rules. The use of *kenningar* as ornamentation is likewise much more widespread and creates an immensely concentrated imagery difficult to interpret in its sophisticated appeal to the intellect rather than to the emotions.

The first-known skald was the ninth century Norwegian Bragi Boddason (Bragi the Old). In his writing, the metrics and diction of skaldic poetry are already fully developed. A culmination is reached by Eyvindr Skáldaspillir (c. 920-990), the last of the Norwegian court poets, with his memorial poem *Hákonarmál* (c. 960; *The Lay of Hákon*, 1936), which describes how Odin sends two of his Valkyries to the battlefield to fetch King Hákon to Valhalla. Gradually, the genre became exclusively Icelandic. Egill Skallagrímsson (c. 910-990), the most important poet in Old Norse literature, introduces an important formal feature, the end rhyme, in *Höfuthlausn* (948; *The Death Song of Egil the Son of Grim*, 1921), a poem that Egill composed to save his life when he was captured by his mortal enemy. Particularly renowned is Egill's lament *Sonatorrek* (961; *The Loss of My Sons*, 1924), the title of which alludes to Egill's loss of two sons, one by drowning, the other by sickness. Primarily, however, the work presents the poet's lament concerning his own helplessness and loneliness and a critical description of his relationship to the gods and to poetry itself. Here, for the first time in Nordic literature, one recognizes a distinctly subjective and independent artistic personality.

SACRED MEDIEVAL POETRY

With the final victory of Christianity in all the Nordic countries around 1100, the Latin alphabet was introduced, establishing a Church culture and didactic genres such as the sermon and the legend of saints, which, be-

sides bodies of laws and chronicles, dominate the prose of the Middle Ages. A unique position was occupied by the Icelandic sagas, and it was Iceland that dominated the religious poetry of the period, as if the forms of the Eddic and skaldic poems were adapted to praise Christian martyrs and saintly kings. The most exquisite of these sacred poems written in the Old Norse tradition is the anonymous *Sólarljóth* (c. 1200; *The Lay of the Sun*, 1950). The meter is the *ljothaháttr*, or chant measure, and occurs also in *The Sayings of the High One*. Both works are didactic, with concrete illustrations of the ways of evil, and they advise how to avoid eternal damnation. Yet *The Lay of the Sun* concludes in apocalyptic visions reminiscent of *Völuspá*, placing the former in the European context of Catholic visionary literature such as Dante's *La divina commedia* (c. 1320; *The Divine Comedy*). The most encompassing religious medieval poem in the vernacular, however, is the Icelandic *Lilja* (c. 1350; *The Lily*, 1870), a panorama of the entire history of the world from a Christian perspective, from Creation to Last Judgment; it comprises one hundred stanzas and is attributed to the monk Eysteinn Ásgrímsson (died 1361).

A distinct group within the sacred medieval poetry is formed by the so-called *Mariaviser* (songs to Mary), the most typical examples of which were written by the Dane Per Raer Lille (c. 1450-1500). In his poems, the biblical imagery from the Song of Songs is merged with the courtly ideals of the troubadour poetry. The Virgin Mary is praised with romantic chivalrousness as the quintessence of everything worth worshiping.

MEDIEVAL BALLADS AND FOLK LITERATURE

During the late Middle Ages, from about 1350 to 1500, the literary dominance of the West Nordic countries—especially Iceland—sharply decreased, accompanied by the artistic decline of the most distinguished genre of this country, the saga. Shortly after 1200, the anonymous folk ballad, originating in France, emerged to become the most prominent genre of the period, especially in Denmark and Sweden.

Scandinavian ballads are traditionally classified according to their contents. "Knightly ballads," by far the largest group, depict the milieu and characters of the medieval aristocracy and usually focus on erotic conflicts. The "magic ballads" deal with supernatural beings and events—revenants, transformations, and runic spells—and are based partly on folk belief, partly on internationally known motifs. Characteristic of Norwegian tradition are a number of later "troll ballads" from the fourteenth and fifteenth centuries, based on Old Norse folklore but often rendered with elements of burlesque irony. Whereas the rare traces of Christianity seem only secondary in these ballads, the "religious ballads" are clearly of Catholic origin. Very few of them exist in Scandinavia. In Sweden, they center on Saint Stephen; in Norway, on Saint Olav. Unique is the Norwegian *Draumkvede* (*The Dream Ballad*, 1946), an offshoot of European visionary literature. Characteristic of Danish balladry are the numerous "historical ballads," frequently centered on characters known from national history. Some of the historical ballads have been dated to the eleventh century, whereas the seemingly older "heroic ballads," whose subjects find counterparts in Old Norse and Germanic legends, are relatively late, dating from the fourteenth century. The heroic ballads are less formulaic and less tightly structured than the knightly ballads, for example, as are the "novelistic ballads," another late type, a Scandinavian offshoot of the courtly Continental poetry such as that about Charlemagne, Tristan and Isolde, and Paris and Helen. The novelistic ballads were especially popular in the Faeroe Islands, where some of the versions reach a length of more than two hundred stanzas, embroidering the original plot. A final group of ballads, the "jocular ballads," frequently with a racy erotic point, does not share the formal or metrical uniformity of the other ballad categories. The age of these ballads is difficult to determine, and they seem to have their origin in the lower social strata from the close of the Middle Ages.

A main function of the ballad was to accompany the chain dances. When the Middle Ages drew to a close, this type of dance went out of fashion—except in the Faeroe Islands—and the ballad survived only as a means of vocal entertainment. The ballad was not a creation of ambitious troubadours following strict aesthetic rules but rather an art form with a functional purpose—thus the simplicity and flexibility of ballad forms and meters: couplets and quatrains, as in the British ballad, with a refrain. The stanzas are end-rhymed, but assonance is ac-

ceptable. The milieu of the ballad is that of the country gentry; the ideals, those of feudal society. Character delineation is formulaic: "so fair a maid," "my handsome lad," and so on. The psychology of the characters is not individualized or analyzed but projected with great artistic finesse through dialogue and action. Feelings are described in set phrases—"proud Adelus" or "with truth and modesty"—and the characters are presented in a limited number of situations, each of which is described identically: "There was brave Sir Nilus/ from home he rode away;/ he betrothed proud Hillelil,/ she was so fair a maid."

The ballad texts were created by individuals but were transmitted orally from one generation to another as part of a living, centuries-long tradition. The ballads, therefore, should not be regarded as historical relics; likewise, they cannot be read as valid mirrors of the period in which they were sung. They are not merely statements but also highly sophisticated interpretations of the human condition. It is this existential perspective that, in the last resort, gives the Nordic ballads their timeless value.

Of a totally different character is the rich Finnish literature of medieval origin, which was not recorded until the period of nationalistic Romanticism. In 1835, Elias Lönnrot (1802-1884) published the nonstrophic epic poem *Kalevala* (English translation, 1889, 1963, 1989), containing songs dealing with heroic mythological persons and themes. In 1840, he also issued the extensive collection of lyric folk poetry *Kanteletar* (English translation, 1888, 1992), which, together with *Kalevala*, constitutes the major national work in Finnish literature.

FOURTEENTH THROUGH SIXTEENTH CENTURIES

During the fourteenth century, a more epic type of poetry—probably developed from the folk ballad—emerged in Iceland, the *rímur*, which gradually turned into entire lengthy cycles, frequently versifications of earlier prose works such as Continental chivalric novels. The chivalric novel in verse was introduced in the other Nordic countries in the early fourteenth century with the three *Eufemia visur* (Eufemia lays), reworkings from French originals. A further step toward pure prose was taken with the Danish and Swedish rhyming chronicles from the fourteenth and fifteenth centuries, which relate the national history of the two royal houses but nevertheless are continuations of a Continental, particularly German, genre.

This connection became disrupted through the Lutheran Reformation of about 1530, which in its militant phase of consolidation focused on strictly didactic literature: Bible translations and prayer books. In Denmark, the Reformation was characterized by fierce polemics, pamphlets, and primitive, versified anti-Catholic satires after German models. In Finland, however, a stronger Humanistic tradition prevailed, whose major figure was the bishop Mikael Agricola (c. 1510-1557), who translated parts of the Psalms of David. A hymnbook was published by Jacobus Finno (c. 1540-1588) in 1583; of its approximately one hundred hymns, ten are his own and the rest are translations. The hymn became the predominant lyric genre of the sixteenth century. Significant was the publication in Denmark in 1569 of a hymnbook by Hans Thomissøn (1532-1573), which achieved official recognition. Not until Hans Christensen Sthen (1544-1610), however, did an original Danish, and Nordic, hymn writer come forth, who in his poems succeeded in combining the meters and tone of the popular song with a specifically Christian message.

SEVENTEENTH CENTURY

Strong theological orthodoxy suppressed free artistic expression during the sixteenth century. Not until the end of that century and the first half of the seventeenth century were the ideas of Humanism and the Renaissance fully accepted, encouraging the creation of a literature in the vernacular based on classical traditions of genre, style, and meter. Limitations on subject matter were abandoned, literature became increasingly secularized, and individual authors were free to be as subjective as they wished. They were encouraged to experiment with language and expression, and gradually a literature emerged for which figures of speech were as important as ideas, a characteristic feature of the concluding literary trend of the seventeenth century, the Baroque.

The most ambitious genre, the religious epic, was, via a French model, introduced in Denmark by Anders Arrebo (1587-1637) with his *Hexaemeron* (published posthumously in 1661), a didactic poem describing the six days of the Creation and employing details from Nordic nature and folk life. The style is stately and rhetorical and does not match in vivacity the second large epic of the century, by the Swede Georg Stiernhielm (1598-1672). Written in hexameter, the topic for the latter epic, *Hercules* (1658), is classical, incorporating the motif of Hercules at the crossroads between two ways of life, that of pleasure and that of virtue.

The first original Swedish lyric poet, with his roots in the popular-song tradition, was Lars Wivallius (1605-1669). His reputation is based on a number of short, subjective poems in which the poet, writing in prison, succeeds in expressing his deeply felt, stirring concepts of freedom. Wivallius's vivid appreciation of nature, coined in graceful stanzas, was new in Swedish literature. In his poetry, private complaints give way to a broad stream of images of the changing seasons, of the occupations of farmers and shepherds, and of the joy to be found in nature.

A similarly Bohemian character was Lasse Lucidor (1638-1674), whose songs and hymns point to the intense and antithetical stylistic ideals of Baroque literature. His works are concerned with the horror of death and sin, of Satan's power and God's wrath. In *It samtaal emellan Döden och en säker menniskia* (a conversation between Death and a confident man), a dialogue related to the medieval motif of the Dance of Death, Lucidor tells in tightly structured stanzas how the arrogant pleasure seeker gradually is driven to despair but in his moment of death invokes Divine Grace.

The culmination of the Swedish Baroque is the monumental burial poem by Gunno Dahlstierna (1661-1709), *Kunga skald* (1697; the king's poet), a lamentation in response to the death of King Charles XI, brimming with allegorical figures, sweeping historical overviews, and a detailed description of a voyage around the world. A brighter aspect of Baroque literature is represented by Johan Runius (1679-1713), the most eminent Swedish writer of occasional poetry. Despite personal disappointments, Runius emerged as a poet as naïvely pious as he was unrestrainedly merry, juxtaposing religious emotion and comic effects.

The poetry of both Dahlstierna and Runius has a strong pastoral element, already present in the writing of Wivallius—an element that finds a noteworthy representative in Denmark in Anders Bording (1619-1677).

Most of his work consists of occasional poetry, but more valuable are his pastoral verses composed in a simple yet elegant syntax. The pastoral genre finds another Danish representative in the clergyman Thomas Kingo (1634-1703), whose graceful poem *Chrysillis* consists of a glowing declaration of love for his wife, framed by descriptions of idyllic nature.

In Kingo's hymns, Danish—and Nordic—Baroque reached its culmination. His devotional work in two parts, *Aandelige siunge-koor* (1674-1681); spiritual chorus), was intended to oust foreign, especially German, hymnbooks. The fundamental feeling evinced by the work is fear of the power of sin and the fickleness of this world, expressed through powerful antithetical constructions in the speculative poems "Far, verden, farvel" (fare, world, farewell) and "Sorrig og glæde" (sorrow and joy). The battle within the soul and the troublesome path toward God are portrayed with intense insight. Kingo was rewarded for his achievements by being appointed as a bishop, and in 1689, he published a collection of hymns, *Vinter-Parten* (the winter part), intended to be the official Danish hymnal. Easter hymns are the highlight of the volume, evoking the Passion with unsurpassed intensity and lifelikeness and peaking in a grand celebration of the Resurrection.

Another characteristic Baroque genre was the topographic description. Arrebo's epic of the Creation was an early example of topographic interest, and Kingo himself wrote a number of topographic works, but the artistic summit of this genre was reached with the Norwegian clergyman Petter Dass's (1647-1707) ambitious presentation of the geography, fauna, and folk life of northern Norway, *Nordlands trompet* (1739; *The Trumpet of Nordland*, 1954). Based on Dass's own journeys and on oral and written sources, it is a realistic and humorous portrayal of everyday life in the seventeenth century.

EIGHTEENTH CENTURY

In a European perspective, the Nordic literatures of the Renaissance and the Baroque—with the sole exception of the Danish hymn writer Kingo—appear strikingly poor. Not until the beginning of the eighteenth century, when French classicism reached Scandinavia combined with the philosophical ideas of the Enlighten-

ment, did a modern literature of lasting value emerge, centered on the Dano-Norwegian writer Ludvig Holberg (1684-1754) and the Swede Olaf von Dalin (1708-1763). Characteristically, Holberg's merits lie within drama, while Dalin, through his weekly periodical *Den swänska Argus* (1732-1734; the Swedish Argus), virtually established modern Swedish prose.

In counterbalance to the Enlightenment, however, a lyric and sentimental undercurrent—often connected with pietistic religiosity—runs throughout the literature of the eighteenth century up to the pre-Romantic period of about 1770. It was in this pietistic milieu that the emotional and fervent hymns of the Danish clergyman Hans Adolph Brorson (1694-1764) emerged. In 1739, he collected a number of hymn translations as well as his own poems in a volume titled *Troens Rare Klenodie* (the rare jewel of faith), all of which are based on the contrast between earthly and heavenly existence. Humankind is seen as corrupt, and conversion is portrayed in scenes of rebirth through prayer and grace. Brorson's texts were intended primarily for household devotion. Many are composed in complex meters, following the contemporary rococo aria, and employ ingenious rhyme patterns, encore effects, and dialogue verse—features that are present to an even greater extent in Brorson's final collection, *Svane-Sang* (1765; swan song).

Light and graceful stanzas and melodious rhythms can also be found in the writing of Ambrosius Stub (1705-1758)—in his hymns as well as in his drinking songs and occasional poetry. His masterpiece, and the first poem in Danish literature to be based on a direct observation of nature, is *Den kiedsom Vinter gik sin Gang* (the tiresome winter went its course). It depicts, with a multitude of delicate details, a walk on a spring day, but the scenery is personalized, and the poem turns into a symbol of the course of life. One senses in each stanza the Divine Creator guiding everything for the best.

Related in its theme but executed with more ingenious rhetoric is the wedding poem *En Maji Dag* (1758; a May day), by the Norwegian Christian Braunmann Tullin (1728-1765). The poem is a glorification of the countryside as an idyllic antithesis to corrupt city life, and, as in Stub's poem, the attention is shifted from nature to its Creator—a clear reflection of Deistic theology, with its notion of God as the Creator of the best of all possible worlds. At the poem's conclusion, the newly married couple appear dressed as rococo shepherds. Tullin was inspired by the nature scenes of Alexander Pope and James Thomson and by Jean-Jacques Rousseau's attacks on modern civilization. Tullin's final work, *Skabningens Ypperlighed* (1764; on the excellency of Creation), on the other hand, is a didactic and religious poem, the sense of infinity and high-flown style of which were influenced by Edward Young's renowned poem *Night Thoughts* (1742-1744).

The deliberate refinement of literary language and the aesthetic taste in general, which the poetry of the Norwegians Brorson, Stub, and Tullin exemplifies, can also be found in Swedish literature. A pietistic tone first colored the poetry of the Finno-Swedish writer Jacob Frese (1690-1729), but the clear emergence of a more subjective and emotional writing took place later in the thin volume *Den sörgande turtur-dufwan* (1743; the grieving turtledove), by Hedvig Charlotta Nordenflycht (1718-1763). The collection consists of lamentations by the young widow, rendered in a soft-spoken melodious aria form, and points toward the 1750's, a decade stylistically dominated by a combination of French classicism and elegant rococo and influenced by the Rousseauistic longing for primitive nature and unrestrained emotional life.

Leading authors besides Nordenflycht were Gustaf Fredrik Gyllenborg and the Finnish-born Gustaf Philip Creutz. Gyllenborg (1731-1808) established himself as a moralist and satirist, fiercely attacking church and society. Creutz (1731-1785) is the author of the most valuable lyric work of the period, the elegantly written *Atis och Camilla* (1762; Atis and Camilla). A love story with a pastoral setting, it analyzes the awakening youthful passion in which the gods of antiquity constantly intervene.

The last third of the eighteenth century in Sweden was dominated by King Gustav III and his brilliant, French-oriented court. The prose of this period is mainly nonfictional and of only minor interest; poetry, drama, and opera are the predominant genres. It is among the lyric poets that one finds the greatest Swedish writer of the century, the Bohemian Carl Michael Bellman (1740-1795). The writings of Bellman—he was himself a celebrated singer and musician—have their point of departure in the drinking song, its tempo and wit, but with an undertone of tragic compassion. Another characteristic element is Bellman's penchant for imitation and parody—particularly of figures from the Old Testament in songs such as "Gubben Noah" (Old Man Noah) and "Joachim uti Babylon" (Joachim in Babylon).

Bellman's major works are the two song cycles, *Fredmans epistlar* (1790; Fredman's epistles) and *Fredmans sånger* (1791; Fredman's songs; selections in English translation appeared in 1939 and later). They consist of songs about Fredman and his friends—drunkards, Bohemians, and prostitutes from the Stockholm tavern milieu—interspersed with impressionistic passages concerning the city and its surroundings. But despite all of its realistic elements, the milieu of these texts is basically mythic, depicting a group of good-humored sybarites, not distinctly individualized, living in joy and sorrow in a tragicomic universe created as a divine jest. The pleasures of the moment appear as the only and highest goal, but transitoriness and death are the somber backdrop for the turbulent events. Bellman's stanzas are technically brilliant in their language, rhyme, and rhythm; nothing is improvised, and each detail is carefully rendered. Performing his own songs, Bellman used partly popular tunes of the times and partly his own compositions, achieving an unsurpassed unity of text and music.

A stricter representative of the French classicist ideas of the Enlightenment is Johan Henrik Kellgren (1751-1795), who embraced the radical philosophy of Voltaire. After writing some portentous odes—some celebrating an Epicurean outlook, some displaying stoic resignation—Kellgren found his personal style in *Sinnenas förening* (1778; the union of senses) and *Mina löjen* (1778; my ridicules), philosophical poems written in flowing, conversational stanzas; the latter contains strong satirical attacks on the clergy, scholars, and writers but also a considerable amount of self-directed irony in the author's portrait of himself. A more serious counterpart to *Mina löjen* is *Våra villor* (1780; our illusions), a didactic poem about the question of truth and illusion, which was a burning problem for Kellgren as a skeptical representative of the Enlightenment. In his later years, Kellgren was influenced by pre-Romanticism. *Den nya skapelsen* (1790; the new creation) is a dithyrambic glorification of Eros and fantasy. The beloved becomes the archetype of beauty that vitalizes and inspires all nature, which until now has seemed dead to the poet. Kellgren continued his fight for spiritual liberty and reason with numerous biting aphorisms and two great comic poems: *Dumboms lefverne* (1791; life of Mr. Simpleton), a suite of pointed satirical texts defending common sense against a large variety of follies, and *Ljusets fiender* (1792; enemies of the light), an allegorical paean to the French Revolution.

Philosophically more moderate than Kellgren is Karl Gustaf af Leopold (1756-1829), whose best-known poems, particularly from the 1790's, are long, speculative texts bearing titles such as *Försynen* (1793; providence) and *Predikaren* (1794; the sermonizer) and composed in a perfected, classical ode style that lends to the poet's philosophy of resignation a striking, personal touch. Contemporary satire together with a detailed realism finds a convincing representative in Anna Maria Lenngren (1754-1817), whose writings were not published until 1819, in *Skaldeförsök* (poetic attempts). In her works from the 1790's, Lenngren succeeds in combining French classicism with the more concrete realism of a later era. In the satires *Porträtterna* (1796; the portraits) and *Fröken Juliana* (1796; Miss Juliana), the pretentiousness and folly of the Swedish nobility are displayed with burlesque vigor. Lenngren's criticism is also aimed at the other social classes, and occasionally it develops into stirring and compassionate tragicomic portraits of drab destinies in an insensitive society.

The only significant and aggressive representative of an opposite trend is Thomas Thorild (1759-1808). *Passionerna* (1785; the passions), a didactic poem about divine power and harmony and a hymn to nature, invokes Ossian, William Shakespeare, and Friedrich Gottlieb Klopstock, the heroes of pre-Romanticism. The tone is passionate, the style high-flown and abrupt. Thorild's subsequent writings are uneven, but in his unrhymed, free verses he is able to express both the unique greatness and the passionate sufferings of the lonely genius, thus anticipating the hero worship of the nineteenth century.

Pointing directly toward Romanticism is the poem by Frans Mikael Franzén (1772-1847) titled *Människans anlete* (1793; the human face). It is a bright, multi-colored lyric picture of the sixth day of Creation, when the splendor of newborn nature pales when confronted with man, who mirrors God himself. The Christian viewpoint is further emphasized in *Det nya Eden* (1795; the new paradise), in which Franzén, through an almost chaotic stream of images and visions, conjures up a paradisaical dream of the ascension of the soul.

In Denmark, the ideals of the Enlightenment and rationalism were expounded by a group of writers centered on the Norwegian poet and playwright Johan Herman Wessel (1742-1785), but completely without the force and talent found in Swedish literature. On the other hand, the highly emotional pre-Romanticism based on English and German models has its greatest Scandinavian representative in Johannes Ewald (1743-1781). Through the German poet Klopstock, who lived in Denmark from 1751 to 1770, Ewald became acquainted not only with Shakespeare and Ossian but also with Old Norse mythology. Less successful as a playwright, Ewald must be regarded as the greatest Danish lyric poet before the Romantic era. His greatness emerges in the ode *Rungsteds Lyksaligheder* (1775; the joys of Rungsted). Taking its point of departure in concrete descriptions of the locality, the poem rises to an enthusiastic glorification of God, of whom nature is not merely a reflection but an integral part.

Ewald also displayed a great talent as a writer of occasional poetry. Through a combination of sensitivity and strict adherence to structure, he was able to elevate this genre above similar contributions of the period. Particularly successful are his death poems, which focus on the pain and sorrow of the bereaved, as well as a number of poems to friends and benefactors. Ewald's last, pietistically inspired poetry is predominantly confessional. He describes man's—and his own—condition until he has placed his destiny in God's hands in *Til Sielen: En Ode* (1780; ode to the soul). The fallen soul is symbolized by the disobedient young eagle, which has fallen from its nest to the depths and helplessly strives toward the light until its mother comes to its rescue. It is in his individualism, his sensitive self-consciousness, that Ewald points beyond his own time. He focuses directly on the self, emphasizing the importance of the subjective experience in man's encounter with God Almighty. This experience is expressed with overwhelming poetic force that is kept in tight rein by strict artistic discipline.

Another link between rationalism and Romanticism is seen in the works of Jens Baggesen (1764-1826). The spirit of the eighteenth century is embodied in a number of ironic and satiric epic poems published as *Comiske Fortællinger* (1785; humorous tales). In his principal work, the travelogue *Labyrinten* (1792-1793; the labyrinth), Baggesen, using Laurence Sterne and Jean-Jacques Rousseau as his models, is primarily concerned with his emotional reactions to the places and people he encounters. Baggesen also wrote a number of intimate love poems: Platonic yet sensuous in their view of love, occasionally marred by sentimentalism, these love poems belong to the Romantic era. Baggesen is a tragic figure in Scandinavian literature. Vacillating between two epochs, he was never fully accepted at home, and his attempt to establish a career in Germany was unsuccessful.

ROMANTICISM AND POETIC REALISM

The Romantic movement, which originated in Germany, was introduced in Scandinavia in 1803 through Adam Oehlenschläger's (1779-1850) *Digte* (poems). The first decades of the nineteenth century in Denmark and Sweden were dominated by the so-called universal Romanticism, which set forth the pantheistic theories of the divine spirit's manifestation in nature and history, to be realized through the intuition of the poetic genius.

Adam Oehlenschläger's *Digte* and the succeeding collection in two volumes, *Poetiske Skrifter* (1805; poetic works) contain all the elements of Romanticism: mixed genres including lyric poetry and ballads in changing meters, epic cycles, and prose and drama, culminating in the fairy-tale play *Aladdin* (1805; English translations, 1857, 1968), a symbolic glorification of the power of the genius over chaos and evil. *Poetiske Skrifter* also contains a saga imitation which points to further development of Oehlenschläger's writings, and of Danish literature in general, toward a national and patriotic Romanticism with motifs drawn from Nordic mythology and history. In the works of Oehlenschläger, this school is represented in the collection *Nordiske Digte* (1807; Nordic poems) and in a large number of plays,

culminating in the masterful epic cycle *Helge* (1814). Superbly executed in a multitude of meters, it concludes with a verse drama that elevates the entire work to a tragic vision of man as a plaything of merciless fate.

Oehlenschläger was the forerunner of a whole generation of poets. The clergyman N. F. S. Grundtvig (1783-1872), in his *Nordens Mythologi* (1808; Nordic mythology), as well as in his collection of lyric dialogues *Optrin af Kiempelivets Undergang i Nord* (1809-1811; scenes from the decline of heroism in the North), interprets Old Norse mythology as a universal drama, a reflection of the continuous battle between spirit and matter. An existential crisis in 1810 led Grundtvig to convert to Christianity, and he began producing not only didactic and occasional poetry but also religious poems and hymns. In 1837, the first volume of his *Sang-Værk til den danske Kirke* (collection of songs for the Danish church) appeared; the entire five-volume work was completely published by 1880. Approximately half of these more than fourteen hundred biblical poems and hymns are reworkings of foreign models such as the Caedmon, Luther, the Psalms of David, and so on. Grundtvig's own poems are connected either with the liturgical year, especially Easter and Pentecost (such as the magnificent "I al sin Glands nu straaler Solen"—in all its splendor the sun shines) or with the sacraments of baptism and the Eucharist. The fundamental contrast is not between sin and grace but between life and death, isolation and the fellowship of love with God and man. From this contrast stems the affirmation of life and the defiance of death in Grundtvig's universe. Although many of his hymns are linguistically unpolished, his best texts are characterized by concrete observations employing imagery inspired by the Bible and Old Norse mythology.

Grundtvig's most important fellow writer on the national front was B. S. Ingemann (1789-1862). Following Sir Walter Scott, Ingemann wrote several historical novels which, together with his poetry cycle *Holger Danske* (1837; Holger the Dane), belong to the heyday of Danish national Romanticism. Purely religious is his *Morgen- og Aftensange* (1839; morning and evening songs), whose naïve nature scenes express not only a child's feeling of insecurity with God but also a cosmic sense of infinity.

In Swedish literature, a similar development can be followed from a metaphysically oriented philosophical system toward a plainer, historical literature. The major mouthpiece for the early universal Romanticism was the monthly journal *Phosphoros* (1810-1813), which was dominated by contributions from P. D. A. Atterbom (1790-1855). His poetry cycle *Blommorna* (1812; the flowers), rather than spontaneous nature impressions, is a series of lyric meditations on transitoriness and immortality, symbolizing various human temperaments and ways of existence. More significant are the two fairytale plays *Fågel Blå* (1814; bluebird) and *Lycksalighetens ö* (1824-1827; the island of bliss). The latter, in two parts, although not intended for performance, is a dramatic dialogue, sustained by a richness of lyric episodes, which develop into a complex philosophical work related to Johann Wolfgang Goethe's *Faust* (1790, 1808, 1833) and Oehlenschläger's *Aladdin*.

Pure poetry, on the other hand, is the natural means of expression for Erik Johan Stagnelius (1793-1823). He early acquired the style and meters of German Romanticism, the melodiousness, coloring, and evocative imagery of which he was to carry further than any other Scandinavian writer without ever becoming vague or rambling. Stagnelius's extraordinarily musical poetry is concrete and precise both visually and sensuously, conveying an artistic experience difficult to interpret fully. His major collection, *Liljor i Saron* (1821; lilies of Sharon), is based on two themes: erotic fantasies and the tragic concept of man's continuous suffering as the beloved remains unattainable forever. The tension between these themes runs throughout his oeuvre: He wrote a series of short poems that portray the sensual bliss of love in a pastoral setting, while other works express contempt for this world and a clear religious and ascetic mood. On the basis of his deeply rooted Christianity as well as his speculative Platonism and his belief in a spiritual fellowship, Stagnelius constructs a rich world of symbols in an almost inaccessible but nevertheless evocative language. After the publication of *Liljor i Saron*, Stagnelius abandoned the ideas that had sustained this highly wrought work, and, during the last years of his life, he experimented with various genres. In dramatic scenes colored by Gothic Romanticism, he portrayed negative, almost demoniac, aspects of earthly eroticism; he also wrote his most accomplished dramatic poem, *Bacchanterna* (1822; the Bacchants), which, in subject and style, shows the influence of Greek tragedy.

The strong interest in the Nordic past which early became a dominating force in Danish Romanticism was paralleled in Sweden by a preoccupation with national history. This so-called Gothic movement was partly caused by the anger at the loss of Finland to Russia in the war of 1808-1809. The leading figure of the movement was Erik Gustaf Geijer (1783-1847). In the poem *Manhem* (1811), Geijer presents the program in the rhetorical language of Gustavian classicism, yet using the favorite stanza of Romanticism, ottava rima. In *Den siste kämpen* (1811; the last warrior), he describes in passionate monologues the demise of pagan religion and life in Scandinavia. *Odalbonden* (1811; the freeholder) and *Vikingen* (1811; the viking), on the other hand, are somewhat stereotyped and idealized portrait poems, although rendered in a lucid and clear language and brilliantly varied rhythms, which have made them perfect for recitation.

The greatest poet of Swedish Romanticism, connected with the Gothic movement but impossible to categorize, is Esaias Tegnér (1782-1846). Inspired by the loss of Finland, he wrote a long patriotic epic poem, *Svea* (1811), the main part of which is a eulogy of the nation's forefathers. For most of the poem, Tegnér uses the traditional Alexandrine meter, but he concludes with a dithyrambic section, an ecstatic vision of battle and victory in varied meters with an eruptive, pre-Romantic coloring. The poem *Jätten* (1813; the giant), a monumental symbolic picture of the evil forces in life, is based on an Old Norse motif, while *Sång till Solen* (1813; song to the sun) is colored by Platonic Romanticism in its broad perspective of cosmic desolation, yet allows for a possible reconciliation of good and evil. During the 1820's, Tegnér began to suffer mental depression. During this period, he created the hexametrical religious idyll *Nattvardsbarnen* (1820; the child communicants), the Byronic verse epic *Axel* (1822), and his famous Frithiofs saga (1825; *Frithiof's Saga*, 1833). It is composed as an epic cycle, inspired by Oehlenschläger's *Helge*, and represents the culmination of national Romanticism in Sweden. The characters possess psychological credibility, and both the dramatic tension of the narrative and the vigor of its style give the cycle a timeless vitality.

At the close of the 1820's, the Romantic flight from external reality was being replaced by a down-to-earth bourgeois idyllic literature. Traditional love poetry flourished, but the ecstatic, Romantic worship of Eros as a divine force was much more subdued, as in the writings of the Danish poets Christian Winther (1796-1876) and Emil Aarestrup (1800-1856); here, however, an influence from the more complex and disharmonic authors Lord Byron and Heinrich Heine is also noticeable. The essence of Winther's elegant and firm mastery of meter and style can be found in his long epic poem with a medieval setting and adventurous episodes of love and hatred, *Hjortens Flugt* (1855; the flight of the hart), while the strength of Aarestrup lies in short, pointed erotic scenes.

A clear break with this aestheticism is represented by the ironic heroic epic *Adam Homo* (1842-1849; English translation, 1980), by the Dane Frederik Paludan-Müller (1809-1876). It tells of how its opportunistic hero rises from the parsonage of his childhood to the top of society, relating along the way his first erotic encounters in Copenhagen and his engagement to Alma, whom he abandons for the sake of his career. Adam has become corrupt and is in danger of losing his soul, but the unselfish love of Alma, whom he sees again on his deathbed, saves him from perdition. The conclusion takes the form of an apocalyptic poem, a Danish counterpart to Dante's *The Divine Comedy* and Goethe's *Faust*, equaling these great works in artistic quality.

The epic poems that Paludan-Müller wrote after *Adam Homo* took their motifs largely from either the Bible or Greek mythology, pointing to the fact that Old Norse topics by the mid-nineteenth century had played out their role not only in Danish but also in Scandinavian Romanticism. An exception is the epic poem *Kung Fjalar* (1844; *King Fjalar*, 1912), by the Finnish writer Johan Ludvig Runeberg (1804-1877). The destiny of the title character, a fictitious saga king, mirrors the clash between human will and the power of the gods. Also unique in their time were Runeberg's hexameter idylls, such as *Älgskyttarne* (1832; the elk hunters), while his two-part heroic cycle of poems, *Fännrik Ståls sägner* (1848-1860; *The Songs of Ensign Stål*, 1925, 1938), is yet another expression of national Romanticism, an idealization of Finnish feats during the 1808-1809 war against Russia.

An extreme example of the spiritualism found in universal Romanticism is present in the works of the Swede C. J. L. Almqvist (1793-1866). From 1833 to 1851, he published *Törnrosens bok* (the book of the briar rose), a diverse mixture of novels and tales, plays and essays, lyric and epic poems. His novel *Det går an* (1839; *Sara Videbeck*, 1919, also as *Why Not!*, 1994), a discussion of marriage as an institution, bears the first signs of realistic description and factual treatment of everyday life that were to influence Swedish literature increasingly during the 1840's.

The poetry of the period, however, remained strongly idealistic. On the threshold to the epoch of realism and naturalism stands Carl Snoilsky (1841-1903). His collection *Dikter* (1869; poems), dominated by his impressions from travels to southern Europe, employs melodious rhythms and colorful scenes. Snoilsky focuses on contemporary life, and his endorsement of political freedom, in the form of a glorification of Italy's struggle for independence, is interwoven with the poet's strong affirmation of life. At the end of the 1870's, his poetry became more socially involved; a number of portraits and scenes, primarily from Swedish history, deal with the adversities and the poverty of the lower class, while others tackle then-current social issues. Similar motifs also appear in Viktor Rydberg's (1828-1895) essentially philosophical poetry, published in the two collections *Dikter* (1882; poems) and *Nya dikter* (1891; new poems). Here, Christian ethics and speculative idealism clash with a vivid interest in the current social changes resulting from the industrialization of Swedish society. The discussion of materialism, modern natural science, and naturalism is, however, frequently placed in a historical or mythological setting and executed in a rhetorical, declamatory style.

While Denmark and Sweden, and to some degree Finland, turned during the 1830's and 1840's toward greater realism in literature, the Romantic movement did not reach Iceland and Norway until these decades. Both countries had come under Danish rule in 1387, and contact with European cultural life was not very extensive until the 1830's. The leading spokesmen for Icelandic Romanticism were the two poets Bjarni Thorarensen

(1786-1841) and Jónas Hallgrímsson (1807-1845); the latter's lucid poems about the nature and history of Iceland made him the national poet. Both were deeply inspired by their country's medieval literature, the sagas and the Eddic poems.

The year 1814 brought political and economic independence to Norway, but until the mid-nineteenth century, intellectual life was predominantly determined by the political events of the period. In literature, the short stories of Mauritz Hansen (1794-1842) and the plays of H. A. Bjerregaard (1792-1842), from the 1820's and 1830's, characterized by imitation of pre-Romanticism, were widely popular. Not until the works of Henrik Wergeland (1808-1845) and Johan Sebastian Welhaven (1807-1873) did the newer Norwegian literature become original. The theory of an animated universe and of a world of spirit and power permeates Wergeland's major work, the dramatic poem *Skabelsen, mennesket og Messias* (1830; creation, man and Messiah). In crude and often verbosely rendered scenes from world history, the poem depicts the battle between earthly and divine spirits, between suppression and freedom. Wergeland rejected any kind of retrospective Romanticism; in his view, it is the task of the writer to look ahead, to be the teacher of his people and a leader of ideas. This sense of mission became increasingly important to Wergeland, who was an active participant in Norwegian political life. *Digte* (1833; poems) glorifies liberty in a style more lucid and plainer than Wergeland's previous work. This trend toward a more concise form became more pronounced in the volume *Poesier* (1838; poems), which introduced a lyric phase that continued until Wergeland's death.

Unlike Wergeland, his opponent Welhaven stressed solidarity with Danish culture. A fierce debate raged between the two poets throughout the 1830's. Welhaven's main contribution was the collection of polemical sonnets *Norges daemring* (1834; Norway's dawn), but his most valuable poetry, published in *Digte* (1839; poems), takes its motifs from a personal love experience and from Norway's nature and folk life. The essential element in Welhaven's nature poetry is not its descriptive detail but the sense of totality which is created by its rich tapestry of sound. Whereas Wergeland brought to Norwegian poetry linguistic imagination and a wealth of im-

agery, Welhaven emphasized musicality and sophisticated versification.

The atmosphere of the 1850's and 1860's was the worst conceivable for poetry. It was a time of practical interests, of economic and industrial development. The old Romantics sought in idyllic fantasy an alternative to the era of industrialization or actively rebelled against the new spirit of the times. The younger ones—in Norway as well as in the other Nordic countries—had to wait for the emergence of the new ideas of realism and naturalism.

REALISM AND NATURALISM

The definite breakthrough of the theories of realism and naturalism in Scandinavia during the 1870's, entailing radical biblical and social criticism, can primarily be attributed to the Danish critic Georg Brandes (1842-1927). The most popular genres of this new school were the drama and the novel. Only Denmark and Iceland possessed significant lyric poets; most of them, however, were also accomplished prose writers. In the early poetry of the Dane Jens Peter Jacobsen (1847-1885), such as the cycle *Gurresange* (1869; Gurre songs), medieval motifs are treated in a Romance-like mode. Jacobsen is fully original in his purely speculative poetry, such as the death poem "Saa standsed'—" (thus ended—) and in his so-called arabesques, a series of free images of a penetrating spiritual content shrouded in ornamental language and illuminated by intense sense impressions. Jacobsen was by nature a dreamer, and the struggle between dream and reality is a principal motif both in his novels and in his entire lyric production (which was not published until 1886), titled *Digte og Udkast* (poems and sketches).

The best known of the early poems by the other outstanding Danish lyrical writer of the period, Holger Drachmann (1846-1908), is the melodramatic "Engelske Socialister" (English socialists) in the volume *Digte* (1872; poems). It was the revolution in Brandes's message that inspired Drachmann in this and the next collection, *Dæmpede Melodier* (1875; muted melodies), both based on social questions and the struggle between the reactionary old and the victorious new. Besides politically radical lyric poems, one finds Bohemian songs in which Drachmann appears as a sailor, a peasant, or a vagabond without bourgeois inhibitions. One also encounters enchanting, intimate verses in which bright nights and the sea are images of freedom and of the poetic spirit, pointing beyond naturalism. The collections *Ungdom i Digt og Sang* (1879; youth in poem and song) and *Gamle Guder og nye* (1881; old gods and new) mark a turning point in Drachmann's development. In them, he praises domesticity instead of free love and returns to a patriotic, bourgeois poetry heralding such ideals as the sanctity of mother, child and home. By the late 1880's, however, these ideals were again replaced by a revolutionary spirit, as in the volume *Sangenes Bog* (1889; book of songs). Nevertheless, the playful tone, caused by a new love experience, is mixed with pain. Behind the hectic happiness lurks anxiety about approaching old age. Drachmann considered freedom and beauty the main ideas of his creative work. An incorrigible dreamer, he lived outside of his time, but his significance for later Danish poetry is extraordinary, owing to the greatness of his exceptional artistic personality and the infinite wealth of rhythms and moods in his poetry.

A development away from propagandistic naturalism is also a major feature of Icelandic poetry of the period. The first collection of poems by Thorsteinn Erlingsson (1858-1914), *Thyrnar* (thorns), was not published until 1897. Besides bitter political and social satires, it contains a number of rather traditional patriotic poems and sensitive, melancholy love poetry, exquisite in form and language. Lyric beauty and social satire are combined in Erlingsson's major work, *Eithurinn* (1913; the oath), a cycle of narrative poems composed on a tragic love theme.

Hannes Hafstein's (1861-1922) poems did not appear in book form until 1893, in *Ýmisleg ljóthmæli* (various poems). As in the poetry of Drachmann and Heinrich Heine, Hafstein's artistic models, nature and love motifs dominate, with no trace of naturalistic determinism but marked, rather, by optimism and virility.

The only significant Swedish lyric poet of the period, which is otherwise totally dominated by the towering figure of August Strindberg (1849-1912), is Ola Hansson (1860-1925). In his youth, he wrote pale social propaganda poems, but in his second collection, *Notturno* (1885), he created a nature poetry influenced by the Dane J. P. Jacobsen, based on exact observation and permeated by a soft and musical tone. Later, Hansson embraced Friedrich Nietzsche's doctrine of the "superman"—a notion which was to exert a tremendous influence on Nordic literature.

In Norway, the same epoch was dominated by the playwrights Henrik Ibsen (1828-1906) and Bjørnstjerne Bjørnson (1832-1910), the latter also an acknowledged author of lyric poetry. In the monologue romance "Bergliot," from the volume *Digte og sange* (1870; *Poems and Songs*, 1915), his portrayal of Bergliot's mourning of her murdered husband and son penetrates deeply the psyche of a saga character; equally imposing is the epic poem *Arnljot Gelline* (1870; English translation, 1917). Bjørnson published only the one poetry collection from 1870, which was expanded in later volumes. His lyricism took the form of poetry only under great pressure caused by specific situations. The style is elevated, influenced by Grundtvig, particularly in texts in the saga mold or when linked to historical situations.

The only other significant poetry of the time was written by Arne Garborg (1851-1924). After a number of naturalistic novels, his two poetry cycles *Haugtussa* (1895; the mound elf) and *I Helheim* (1901; in hell) mark a transition toward the main literary trends around 1900, neo-Romanticism and Symbolism. *Haugtussa* portrays, in musically expressive strophes, the visionary peasant girl Veslemøy and her struggle against the dark powers. The supernatural element is also a theme and starting point for the sequel *I Helheim*, in which Veslemøy is led in a dream vision through the realm of the dead, where everybody receives his or her deserved fate, modeled on Dante's *Inferno* and the medieval dream ballad.

TURN OF THE TWENTIETH CENTURY

The new movement of the 1890's rejected the ethical demand for truth that characterized naturalism and favored instead an aesthetic demand for beauty. Heroic deeds were admired at the expense of the practical, and against anti-religious rationalism there arose a new metaphysical and mystically colored religiosity. Nature and history became the favorite sources of inspiration, and lyric poetry, which had been almost totally neglected, flourished again in all five Nordic countries.

In Sweden, the new aesthetic program was expressed in Verner von Heidenstam's (1859-1940) first collection, *Vallfart och vandringsår* (1888; pilgrimage and wander years), a glorification of the carefree life of the Orient. In Heidenstam's historical novels and stories, a humanistic view underlies the descriptions of heroic, national events, and that view blossoms in Heidenstam's last work, *Nya dikter* (1915; new poems). In short, well-formed strophes, he confesses to a transfigured, fervent belief in life and a melancholy resignation to death. The Romantic has become a classicist, like his models Goethe and the aforementioned Finnish writer Runeberg. In 1916, Heidenstam was honored with the Nobel Prize in Literature.

A greater lyric talent, indeed one of Sweden's greatest poets, is Gustaf Fröding (1860-1911). His humorous, witty pictures of peasant life in his native Värmland as portrayed in his first collection *Guitarr och dragharmonika* (1891; *Guitar and Concertina*, 1925) were entirely new to Swedish poetry and were received enthusiastically, whereas his melancholy, wistful poems were overlooked. In several of these poems, one senses that the author feels kinship with the disreputable and unhappy characters; Fröding's feeling of ineffectuality and failure pervades all of his poetry. Scenes from Värmland, many of them written in the local dialect, form the first part of the next volume, *Nya dikter* (1894; new poems). Here, too, Fröding portrays folk figures from the countryside, but his poems, in spite of their apparent objectivity, also have a personal flavor, which comes clearly to the fore in his nature poetry conveying subjective moods of *Weltschmerz*.

In 1894, Fröding was plunged into a severe emotional crisis characterized by crippling anxieties and hallucinations, which form the transition to the dream moods and visions of his most significant book, *Stänk och flikar* (1896; splashes and rags). The new elements in this volume are the boldly erotic poems, shattering self-accusations, and gripping personal confessions. In the poem "Sagan om Gral" (the story of the Grail), Fröding attempts to present a mystical unity of the universe, in the symbol of the Grail. This motif, which he drew from Richard Wagner's operas, appears more clearly in *Gralstänk* (1898; sprinklings from the Grail). During the last years of his life, Fröding returned to realistic poems about the life and people in his home region. In these poems, one finds an astonishing variety of expression: humorous portraits of folk types, philosophical speculations and meditations, and, not least, subjective, impassioned nature poetry distinguished by its musical virtuosity.

Erik Axel Karlfeldt (1864-1931) also drew inspiration from his home province; his writing expresses a longing for a vanished idyll. He achieved his first real success with *Fridolins visor* (1898; Fridolin's songs), followed three years later by *Fridolins lustgård* (1901; Fridolin's garden of delight). In these two volumes, one encounters not only dancing and happiness but also disharmony and melancholy, which gives depth to Karlfeldt's Fridolin poems. He transforms old rural notions of natural events into animated natural mysticism and uses legends, folk piety, and superstition to create a rich world of symbols. During World War I, Karlfeldt wrote the volume *Flora och Bellona* (1918; Flora and Bellona), which contains his reactions to the social and political movements of the new century, especially his attacks on both communism and capitalism. In his last work, *Hösthorn* (1927; Autumn horn), Karlfeldt returned to Fridolin's world. The mood is still one of resignation, but it is mingled with humility and gratitude for life, together with a clear acceptance of Christianity. Especially significant are Karlfeldt's artistic mastery of form and his melodious language. In Karlfeldt's poetry, Swedish neo-Romanticism finds its perfect conclusion. In 1931, he was posthumously awarded the Nobel Prize.

Unlike their Swedish and Icelandic counterparts, the young poets in Denmark did not turn to the national past or peasant life but to the soul. The primary figures, Johannes Jørgensen and Sophus Claussen, had begun their careers in the 1880's and introduced a new epoch in Danish literature influenced by J. P. Jacobsen, Drachmann, Nietzsche, and the French poets Charles Baudelaire and Paul Verlaine.

Johannes Jørgensen (1866-1956) became the leading exponent and theoretician of Danish Symbolism. His spiritual struggle with naturalism led in *Bekendelse* (1894; confession) to a religious breakthrough; the title poem closes with the cry: "Eternity! I am in your hands." The early texts still bear traces of pantheism, but in the concluding poem, "Confiteor," Christianity is victorious. In the collections appearing just after the turn of the twentieth century, Jørgensen achieved a more concentrated form of expression and a simpler, image-free style, and in *Der er en Brønd, som rinder* (1920; the well that flows), his poetic art reached its zenith. Like that of the French Symbolist Verlaine, Jørgensen's poetry consists of simple meters and rhythmic forms in which ideas are conveyed solely by means of the intensity of the described feelings. After his conversion to Catholicism in 1896, Jørgensen achieved a place as an international author with travelogues and biographies of saints, but the hallmark of his writing is his unique lyricism, expressed in a plain, songlike style evocative of intimate moods.

The greatness of Sophus Claussen (1865-1931) as a poet was established with the two collections *Pilefløjter* (1899; willow pipes) and *Djævlerier* (1904; diableries). They are broadly expressive, from the darkly macabre to the exuberant and enchanting. Claussen studied the French Symbolists and was the first Danish poet to follow their aesthetics consistently. Nevertheless, *Pilefløjter* was primarily influenced by Heine and the Danish Romantic Emil Aarestrup. The volume closes with the symbolic travel sketch "Røg" (smoke), the major poem of this period. Claussen lets his thoughts and moods drift like changing clouds of smoke, which become symbols of his encounter with reality. *Djævlerier* displays Italian and French motifs. With Baudelaire as his model, Claussen was inspired to an artistic Satanism whose central erotic theme is woman as vampire. The volume treats larger sets of problems, however, paying particular attention to the plights and prospects of the artist.

In *Danske vers* (1912; Danish verses), Claussen focuses on his home province. Side by side with pantheistic hymns in praise of nature, there is again a preponderance of erotic poems, more profound and bold than before. In his last significant collection, *Heroica* (1925), Claussen reconciles contradictory aspects within himself: exuberance and passion versus mildness and friendliness. His writing is a defense of fantasy and beauty against the closed horizons of naturalism and materialism. Like the other Symbolists, he wants to express the inexpressible and to form all words and emotions into images of a truth that we can only intuit.

The most outstanding representatives in Norway of the neo-Romantic movement as a national art form were Hans E. Kinck (1865-1926) and Knut Hamsun (1859-1952), both prose writers of the highest quality. The lyric poet who best expressed the *spiritual* breakthrough and who came to typify the *fin de siècle* mood in Norwegian poetry was the pietistically reared Sigbjørn Obstfelder (1866-1900). His writing has its point of departure in his notion that he "seems to have come to the wrong planet" and conveys his longing for the eternal truth underlying the world of material appearances. His speculative poetry, *Digte* (1893; *Poems*, 1920), unrhymed prose poems often of extraordinary beauty, is, with its evocative form and mystical attitude, a characteristic example of the Symbolism of the 1890's, signifying a decisive break with naturalism.

In Finland, the lyric revival was much more extensive than in Norway. The young neo-Romantics found their motifs not only in Finnish history and folklore but also in distant countries, antiquity, mythology, and the Bible. The most talented writer and the most productive of the generation—also writing plays and novels—was Eino Leino (1878-1926). A hike through eastern Finland in 1897 left a strong imprint on his poetry. In 1903, the first part of *Helkavirsiä* (*Whitsongs*, 1978) was published, followed in 1916 by the second part, a bold attempt to give the old *Kalevala* motifs a modern historical and symbolic interpretation in stylized language. Both a national and a purely cosmic view of life is expressed here, influenced by Theosophical ideas of reincarnation. The climax in Leino's lyric period is reached with the two collections *Talvi-yö* (1905; winter night) and *Halla* (1908; frost). The first contains a suite of erotic and sensuous texts with Oriental settings; the latter is dominated by depressive and melancholy moods. Leino's later works were first inspired by the Finnish Civil War of 1918 between socialist and nonsocialist forces, then by a faith in universal human values which made the poet turn to myth and history. Leino brought about a radical renewal of Finnish poetry. His pantheistic religion and universal humanism originated in Scandinavian and German literature, but his country's mythology and folklore supplied the most valuable impulses.

The second important neo-Romantic poet, Otto Manninen (1872-1950) was a striking contrast to Leino—very sophisticated and not easily accessible. In his lifetime, he was not much read, but his poetry has become increasingly appreciated. Manninen created his own style by extracting from language the greatest possible degree of expressiveness and precision. His writing is never sentimental or tedious; he succeeds in balancing intellect and emotion. In the volumes *Säkeitä, I-II* (1905-1910; verses), *Virrantyven* (1925; still waters), and *Matkamies* (1938; the traveler), there are several poems representing traditional poetic genres: patriotic and historical poems, satires and humoresques. Manninen's best works are his subjective lyrics, which, without illusion and with occasional irony, revolve around the dominating forces of life, love and death, praising love's omnipotence even when love is hopeless.

A lyric revival also took place within Finno-Swedish literature around 1900. The two greatest poetic talents, though essentially different, were Bertel Gripenberg (1878-1947) and Arvid Mörne (1876-1946). In his first poems, Gripenberg praises the wonders of love and youth, but beginning with the collection *Svarta sonetter* (1908; black sonnets), his vitality became increasingly imbued with a tragic tinge. Feelings of defeat are most exquisitely expressed in *Aftnar i Tavastland* (1911; evenings in Tavastland); death is regarded as a welcome rest, a merciful end to a wasted life. Mörne manifested himself as a political writer with socialist sympathies in the collection *Ny tid* (1903; a new time). The volume *Döda år* (1910; dead years), however, can be read as an expression of his disappointment with the outcome of his political commitment. Mörne turned for solace to Finnish nature, which for him combined freedom and sanity with loneliness and fierceness. The language in his nature poetry is sensitive and varied, stringent and exact, thereby pointing to the lapidary, reflective poetry which is his greatest achievement—increasingly bitter in tone, marked by his isolation and his feeling of not being understood.

In 1904, Iceland's struggle for independence was crowned with the establishment of home rule. The new nationalism brought a renewed interest in the old traditions: The languishing medieval *rímur* poetry enjoyed a revival, and a generation of conservative peasant writers came forward. The period's foremost poets, Stephan G. Stephansson (1853-1927) and Einar Benediktsson (1864-1940), are two of Iceland's greatest writers.

Stephansson emigrated to the United States at the age of nineteen and later became a farmer in Alberta, Canada. Much of his most valuable poetry, written in Icelandic, is published in six collections, titled *Andvökur* (1909-1938; wakeful nights). Here, he praises his adopted country, drawing a series of magnificent pictures of the prairie and pioneer life and also of Iceland, to whose cultural heritage he is inextricably linked. As Stephansson grew older, he increasingly included incidents from the Eddic poems, sagas, and legends, and he interpreted these incidents in such a way that they took on a symbolic and universal significance. He always had his own time in mind, however, and he criticized violence and oppression sharply. He was a glowing pacifist, vehemently denouncing modern warfare.

Politically, Benediktsson belongs to the wing opposite from Stephansson. He published and edited the first Icelandic daily, *Dagskrá* (1896-1898), in which he introduced European Symbolism—demanding of the young writers a reverence not only for beauty, infinity, and eternity but also for national greatness and history. As a poet, Benediktsson gradually created his own universe and style—exclusive and hence not readily accessible. In his poetry, published in such volumes as *Hrannir* (1913; waves) and *Hvammar* (1930; grass hollows), he is able to capture in one short text the essential elements in the atmosphere of great cities, to describe with great suggestive power factories and gigantic machines. Cosmopolitan as he was, Benediktsson was nevertheless fundamentally nationalistic, delighted to be writing on Icelandic subjects. In all of his poems, he wrestles with the desperate problems of human existence: the ultimate meaning and goal of life. He is obsessed with a boundless pantheistic longing to perceive and understand the mysteries of the universe.

BEFORE WORLD WAR I

The period from 1900 to the beginning of World War I was marked by many conflicting trends. Still, one can speak of a general reaction in Nordic literature by young poets against the predominance of Symbolism and neo-Romanticism. The new poetry reacted primarily against the preoccupation with the self; it opened new thematic areas, such as the realities of industrial revolution and city life, and experimented with language.

In Sweden, many of the younger authors began as neo-Romantics. The most significant among them had lost their faith in evolution but maintained their belief in determinism. The influence of the 1890's can be recognized in a mood of disillusionment and refined skepticism, as in the pessimistic poetry of Bo Bergman (1869-1967). His first collection bears the characteristic title *Marionetterna* (1903; the marionettes), corresponding to the author's conception of life as a fatalistic game. It contains satiric texts, influenced by Heine, and melancholy scenes from Stockholm, as well as tender love poems and melodious songs.

Nietzsche's views and the cult of beauty in the 1890's found an outstanding representative in Vilhelm Ekelund (1880-1949). His early poetry captures moods of anxious loneliness and impressions of nature, but in the volume *Melodier i skymning* (1902; melodies in twilight), his nature poems have lost their descriptive character and have become the expression of emotional states; in lyric ecstasy, the poet seeks to unite nature and eternity, which gives peace to his restless soul. Influenced by German classicism, Ekelund found in Greek antiquity a way out of his Romantic melancholy and his Symbolist dreamworld. This attempt led to a new intellectual and ethically oriented poetry in the volumes *Elegier* (1903; elegies) and *In candidum* (1905). Ekelund's inclination toward verbal conciseness and personal coloration of words developed over the years—for example, in *Concordia animi* (1942)—into a cryptic style that can be interpreted only with difficulty. Nevertheless, Ekelund exerted a great influence on the modernistic movements in Swedish and Finno-Swedish literature.

In Norway, drama moved into the background, whereas prose, with such major writers as Olav Duun (1876-1939) and Sigrid Undset (1882-1949), and poetry were dominant, reestablishing a link to the poetry of the 1890's. In the major work of Olav Aukrust (1883-1929), *Himmelvarden* (1916; cairn of heaven), religious, ethical, and national themes are in the forefront. There is no epic substance in the single poems; rather, they bear witness to the struggle of good and evil powers in the soul of the poet himself. Through powerful symbols, modeled on visionary medieval poetry, Aukrust depicts the battle between Christ and Satan, a battle that ends with divine victory and the salvation of the soul.

A completely opposite point of departure characterizes the impressionistic poems of Herman Wildenwey (1886-1959), praising summer, wine, and women. He seeks not the abstruse, but the cheerful and light, which are expressed in the charming rhythms and exquisite musicality of his language. The writing of Olaf Bull (1883-1933) lacks, to be sure, Wildenwey's elegance and carefree quality, but it offers far greater visual and symbol-creating power. Bull called himself a nomad, "shrouded in my coat, my home," and his life became the restless existence of a Bohemian in Oslo, Copenhagen, and Paris; it was in Paris that he discovered his source of inspiration, Henri Bergson's philosophy and the literature of Symbolism. Homelessness and spiritual unrest were the decisive, tragic experiences of his life; in vain he longed to exchange oppressive loneliness for a sense of fellowship, to leave the world of dreams behind him in favor of reality. This painful longing manifests itself in *Nye digte* (1913; new poems) but also sets the serious undertone of Bull's erotic poems in the collection *Oinos og Eros* (1930; Oinos and Eros), permeated by Bull's brooding spirit—in elegies about the brevity of life or in despairing accusations against God. Life and pain are fulfilled only in death and, as expressed in the volumes *Stjernerne* (1924; the stars) and *Metope* (1927), reality, created by observing objects, is transformed into a longing for eternity and ecstatic fantasy.

The lyric, introspective poetry of the 1890's was followed in Denmark around 1900 by a new realistic and rationalistic wave, differentiated from the naturalism of the 1870's and 1880's by a decidedly materialistic approach and occasionally by socialist ideas. The poetry of Johannes Jørgensen expressed the longing and yearning for eternity of a spiritual man; now the central writer was Johannes V. Jensen (1873-1950), who, influenced by the imperialistic writing of Rudyard Kipling, portrayed characters striving to realize an extroverted, pragmatic view of life. The predominant genre was the novel. Only in the works of Johannes V. Jensen, one of the literary pathfinders in twentieth century Denmark and honored in 1944 with the Nobel Prize, do we find a well-developed and highly disciplined poetic sense. It is expressed both in his evocative lyric prose and in his poetry, collected in five volumes (1906-1937). The first collection, *Digte* (1906; poems), which contains all of his youthful poems, is a milestone in the development of modern Danish lyric poetry. The most significant as well as the most characteristic texts are the prose poems—linked in their imagery to modern technology and the metropolis. Here, Jensen expresses his firm belief in the joy of the present moment and his untrammeled longing for the distant and the past. After 1920, the traditional closed-verse form and the alliterative poem in the Old Norse style predominated. In classic calm and harmony, Jensen praises children, Danish nature, and woman as wife and mother. Whether Jensen employs the most elevated expression or the most intimate whisper, he succeeds as no other Danish poet in melding precise observation, vision, and reflection into a perfect artistic entity.

BETWEEN THE WORLD WARS

Although prose predominated in Sweden from 1900 to the 1930's, a younger generation of important poets stepped forward during and immediately after World War I. A long artistic development led Birger Sjöberg (1885-1929) to his first success, *Fridas bok* (1922; Frida's book). These graceful songs derive from his numerous imitations of Swedish poets Bellman and Fröding. The elegant form of the 1922 poems, set to music by Sjöberg himself, are in sharp contrast to the sentimental contents attributed to the half-educated singer of these songs. His love for the office girl Frida is expressed in images and words that naïvely exaggerate his admiration and parody his jealousy. However, the idyll of the volume is an illusion, although the large audience did not recognize it. In contrast, Sjöberg's next collection, *Kriser och kransar* (1926; crises and wreaths), surprised and shocked the public; he suddenly showed an entirely new face, tormented by anguish and suffering. The motifs are the same as before; only the perspective has changed. Using symbols that are not always easy to grasp, Sjöberg deals with the futility of existence and the impenetrability of death. Death is present not only as a threat but also as a liberator that opens religious perspectives. Attempting to clarify and solve this mystery, Sjöberg uses bold juxtapositions, personifications of abstract concepts, and a mixture of pure naturalism with

the most tender lyricism. With his first book, Sjöberg renewed the Swedish song tradition; with his last, he introduced modernism into Swedish literature.

The central figure of the 1920's, Pär Lagerkvist (1891-1974), emerged as a lyricist in 1916 with a volume titled *Ångest* (anguish). The fear of death that had filled him as a child, the shattering experience of World War I, and a deep personal crisis had released in him a boundless feeling of anxiety. In Lagerkvist's work, everything is loneliness, eternity is empty, and God is silent. Lagerkvist's originality lies neither in his symbolic language nor in his vocabulary, but in his use of classically simple language to voice spontaneous, desperate moods, making him the first Swedish expressionist. Lagerkvist's longing to reconcile himself with life succeeded after the war and is expressed both in his prose works and in two poetry collections with the significant titles *Den lyckliges väg* (1921; the path of the happy one) and *Hjärtats sånger* (1926; songs of the heart). These poems, frequently using traditionally rhymed verse forms, express how Lagerkvist's experience of love changed his life and conquered the darkness of his youthful works. The international crises of the 1930's sharpened his will to fight for the humanistic cultural heritage mirrored especially in his prose, which in the following decades won for him international fame—and, in 1951, the Nobel Prize. His prose expresses his continuous search for truth, a search which also permeates his poetry collection *Aftonland* (1953; *Evening-Land*, 1975).

World War I and the following world crises proved that the old values were bankrupt. A sense of disillusionment, of the transitoriness of existence, and a strong apocalyptic atmosphere prevailed. Many authors expressed a feeling of homelessness, brooding over the meaning of life or seeking in new value systems a replacement for what they had lost. The most significant Swedish poets of this trend were Nils Ferlin, Karin Boye, and Hjalmar Gullberg.

The poetry of Hjalmar Gullberg (1898-1961) is distinguished by its formal virtuosity, ranging from elegant, sharp epigrammatic verse through melodious songs to classical cantatas. A religious admixture is present in his early works, and in the collection *Att övervinna världen* (1937; to overcome the world), he shapes a tendency toward mysticism into purely Christian symbols. In the 1940's, Gullberg found himself in a creative crisis, which he did not overcome until 1952, when he published *Dödsmask och lustgård* (death mask and garden of pleasure). Influenced by foreign and Swedish modernistic poetry, he changed his imagery and abandoned his view of the poet as a prophet called by God. Gullberg's last collection, *Ögon, läppar* (1959; eyes, lips), synthesizes a formbound style and free associative verse. The texts contain variations on and summaries of previous themes: the vocation of the artist, the personal struggle with Christianity, suffering, and death.

The period's pessimism is aptly represented by Nils Ferlin (1898-1961). His life and writing is an incarnation of the myth of the Bohemian artist and is related to the writing of Bellman. His occupation as a revue and cabaret writer, which inspired his use of the refrain and his surprising rhymes, can be deduced from his first collection, *En döddansares visor* (1930; ballads of a dancer of death). A satirical note is added in *Goggles* (1938), in which another characteristic trait emerges: his deep sympathy with the misfits of society, often expressed through biblical imagery.

A similar restlessness is present in the writing and life of Karin Boye (1900-1941), a life that ended in suicide. With religious earnestness and passionate tenacity, constantly driven to new horizons, she tested all the various messages of salvation of her time. She rebelled against the ecstatic Christianity of her youth; with the help of the heroic philosophy of Nietzsche, she sought to perfect her personality and to affirm even the darker side of life. This striving characterizes her poems during the 1920's, which are strongly influenced by Ekelund in their prophetic attitude, free rhythm, and choice of words. In *För trädets skull* (1935; for the sake of the tree), Boye attempted to unify her divided nature in verses alternating between moods of affirmation and despair.

Influenced by D. H. Lawrence, a group of Swedish authors called the Primitivists emerged toward the end of the 1920's. In 1929, they published an anthology of modernistic poetry titled *Fem unga* (five young ones), in which they differentiated themselves from earlier Swedish modernists by their worship of instinctual drives and by their strong interest in exotic themes and primitive peoples. Closest to this program was Artur Lundkvist

(1906-1991). Motifs from the big cities and life in the countryside characterize his collections *Glöd* (1928; glow) and *Naket liv* (1929; naked life), which display an ecstatic intoxication with life as well as confidence in the instincts of human beings. In Lundkvist's later volumes of prose poems from the 1930's, Romantic sensuousness yields to gloom. He is now seeking the world of myths, and in dark and suggestive visions, along the lines of French Symbolism, he tries to give expression to the unconscious life of the soul. In *Liv som gräs* (1954; life as grass) and *Vindrosor, moteld* (1955; wind roses, counterfire), however, he again turns toward an almost propagandistic reverence for sensuality. The poems are filled with Lundkvist's faith in the power of the primitive and the ability of poetry to change life. They represent a revolutionary criticism of sterile civilization as well as a search for fellowship. Around 1980 Lundkvist published a series of prose poems and finally, in 1984, a gripping account of his visions while lying in a coma after a heart attack, *Färdas i drömmen och föreställningen* (*Journeys in Dream and Imagination*, 1991).

A more genuine poetic talent is Harry Martinson (1904-1978). In all of his works, including several novels, the human being stands at the center. This humanism is particularly noticeable in the poem cycle *Passad* (1945; trade winds), in which he creates a sweeping picture of the fundamental division of Western culture. Here, Ulysses is contrasted with Robinson Crusoe—that is, the humanist and poet is compared with the empiricist and scientist. The trade wind becomes a symbol of the goodwill that can find the way to unity, a way that leads to humankind itself. In the volumes *Cikada* (1953) and *Vagnen* (1960; the car), Martinson continues his protest against violence. In a series of artless nature poems and resigned meditations, he gives vent to his disgust with the modern world. In *Tuvor* (1973; tussocks), he protests the exploitation and destruction of nature; on a larger scale is the verse epic *Aniara: En revy om människan i tid och rum* (1956; *Aniara: A Review of Man in Time and Space*, 1963), a vision of humankind on its way out of this world into eternity. The spaceship "Aniara" is a symbol of human civilization; during its voyage through space, the course of humankind's cultures and religions is recapitulated and the songs of the earth become holy myths, until finally all is silent. The work is one of the central poetic accomplishments of the twentieth century, a pioneering effort that gained international attention, not the least as an opera set to music by Karl-Birger Blomdahl.

The most prolific modernist of interwar Sweden was Gunnar Ekelöf (1907-1968). He never embraced the gospel of primitivism, and in the collection *Sent på jorden* (1932; late arrival on Earth, 1967), he broke radically with traditional form and syntax. In *Dedikation* (1934; dedication), the revolt against the common conception of reality has changed to a belief in the task of the poet as a seer and redeemer. The volume is permeated with sumptuous imagery and a suggestive, lyric rhythm, linking it to Swedish Romanticism and French Surrealism. In *Non serviam* (1945) and *Om hösten* (1951; in autumn), Ekelöf regards the self as a battlefield for contesting spiritual forces. He seeks the unity behind the conflicting elements of this world and elevates the border between life and death to a mystical experience of the dissolution of the self in the universe. *Strountes* (1955; nonsense) consists of a series of fragmentary, bagatelle-like poems, in which Ekelöf employs satire, parody, and word play to reflect on the nature of language and the emptiness of existence. *En Mölna-elegi* (1960; *A Mölna Elegy*, 1984) analyzes the fantasies of the self at the moment when the present is combined with the past in a free-flowing chain of associations— reminiscences, recollections, and visions—which lead to purification in a consuming song of fire.

Interested in Persian poetry since his student days, Ekelöf took several trips in the 1950's and 1960's to the Near East, the inspiration for the trilogy that concluded his career, beginning with *Dīwān över fursten av Emgión* (1965; Diwan over the prince of Emgión). Ekelöf was a learned poet. Like T. S. Eliot and Ezra Pound, he used cultural history as material, as a constantly active reality. The two primary sources of his style are music and mysticism. He was the first Swedish poet to attempt to carry the vocabulary of music directly over to the language of literature. His poems are never structurally complete, nor are they definite expressions of thoughts and feelings; rather, they are attempts to reconcile his never-ending battle with the problems of the self, reality, and death. Ekelöf is the most difficult and the greatest modern poet in the Nordic countries.

After World War I, a modernist breakthrough occurred in Finno-Swedish literature—a modernism that remained something of an underground movement during the 1920's and was not manifest in the other Nordic countries. One must turn to the Anglo-American poets Eliot and Pound to find corresponding trends. The first and perhaps greatest of these modernist writers, Edith Södergran (1892-1923), made her debut in 1916 with *Dikter* (poems). Characteristic of this volume is a series of brief pictures of nature, but the landscape is a dream landscape in which the natural and spiritual are blended completely. Södergran's next collections were influenced by Nietzsche's philosophy of the superman, which mobilized her vitality and strength of will. Hymns to the beauty and richness of life alternate in these works. This exertion of strength led in 1920 to a crisis in which Södergran's materialistic worldview collapsed. She sought religious stability and finally found her way, through Rudolf Steiner's Anthroposophy, to the Christ of the Gospels, where she experienced peace. Against this background, her last, profound, and transfigured poems of the posthumous collection *Landet som icke är* (1925; the land which is not) constitute a personal preparation for death.

A striking aesthetic radicalism is represented by Elmer Diktonius (1896-1961), who, in his collections from the 1920's, rejected any aesthetic view of art. In *Stark men mörk* (1930; strong but dark), he experimented with a number of Dadaistic effects and simultaneously assumed a humanistic attitude in the face of threatening political catastrophies. In addition, social criticism is present in a number of his proletarian poems, together with a new positive attitude toward nature, influenced by Walt Whitman. In *Jordisk ömhet* (1938; earthly tenderness), the previously very aggressive poet unreservedly accepts the brighter aspects of life, employing biblical motifs and shaping his poems with broad, vigorous strokes, fascinated by the tiny miracles of nature which symbolize the eternal cycle of life and death. Diktonius's exuberant joy in life is sustained throughout his work, as the title of his last book, *Novembervår* (1952; November spring), indicates.

The most singular and radical of the modernists was Gunnar Björling (1887-1960). As he attempted to capture life's boundlessness, he began to realize the limited possibilities of language. He therefore constructed his own syntax, in which parts of sentences and suffixes were dropped. The method is fully developed in *Korset och löftet* (1925; the Cross and the promise), expressing in Björling's own words, "a universal Dada-individualism," which culminates in *Kiri-ra!* (1930). After the publication of *Solgrönt* (1933; sun green), nature became an increasingly important source of inspiration as Björling reacted against intellectualism, and his early nihilistic tendencies were replaced by mystical calmness. In the 1940's, Björling published seven collections and, beginning in the early 1950's, one volume each year. A representative selection of these, *Du jord du dag* (you earth you day), was published in 1957. His poetry became increasingly laconic; his point of departure was the realization that words will never be able to render a complete picture of experience, a realization that is raised in his verse to a metaphysical level.

The poetry of Rabbe Enckell (1903-1974), one of the main theoreticians of Finno-Swedish modernism, differs from that of the other poets of the group in that it is neither visionary nor prophetic, neither violent nor ecstatic, but rather consists of delicate analyses of his feelings. Enckell mastered the art of the miniature in *Vårens cistern* (1931; spring's cistern) and *Tonbrädet* (1935; the sounding board). The latter volume displays a fascination with classical motifs, and simultaneously Enckell began to write a series of Greek-inspired verse dramas that illuminate the often tragic relationship between human beings and fate. Throughout the 1950's and up to the date of his last collection, *Flyende spegel* (1974; fleeing mirror), Enckell published a number of volumes in which he employed additional classical motifs in small lyrical portraits or in dialogues—meditative, refined poetry that complements the visionary, provocative, and philosophical elements of Finno-Swedish modernism with moderation and strong self-criticism.

The most remarkable of the poets writing in Finnish during the interwar period were Uuno Kailas, Aaro Hellaakoski, and P. Mustapää. The early collections of Kailas (1901-1933) bear witness to his knowledge of Charles Baudelaire and expressionistic German poetry in their use of free verse and exotic imagery. Kailas employs Christian symbols, though he seldom speaks of the relationship of humankind to divinity; for him, the world is governed by blind fate. *Silmästä silmään* (1926; eye to eye) marks a transition in Kailas's art from free verse to more traditional forms and shows his progressive introversion. The tension he felt was primarily ethical, a Christian dualism between spirit and matter, ideal and reality.

An ethical element also dominates the writing of Hellaakoski (1893-1952) but in a much less speculative way. In his debut work, *Runoja* (1916; poems), Hellaakoski portrays the poet's struggle to acquire an artistic means of expression. The important part played by the creative will is demonstrated in *Me kaksi* (1920; we two), as a dialogue between reason and heart. *Jääpeili* (1928; ice mirror), the only work of the 1920's that can be considered parallel to those by the Finno-Swedish modernists, is epoch-making because of its innovative meters and varied content. Hellaakoski's modernism was based on his interest in pictorial arts, especially cubism, and the influence of the French Surrealist poet Guillaume Apollinaire. The collection *Uusi runo* (1943; new poetry) initiated a period of brilliant creativity, culminating in *Sarjoja* (1952; series), which placed Hellaakoski among Finland's greatest postwar poets; its long, meditative verses are reminiscent of Rainer Maria Rilke's *Duineser Elegien* (1923; *Duino Elegies*, 1930) and T. S. Eliot's *Four Quartets* (1943).

In the work of P. Mustapää (the pseudonym of Martti Haavio, 1899-1973), Hellaakoski's influence is evident in the rejection of traditional formal patterns and the refusal to adopt the fashions of the 1920's. As an internationally renowned folklorist, Mustapää was well acquainted not only with the *Kalevala* tradition but also with newer ballads and broadsides, whose style he slightly parodied to create a naïve mode of expression. Not until after World War II, however, did Mustapää, in volumes such as *Linnustaja* (1952; the fowler) and *Tuuli Airistolta* (1969; the wind blows from Airisto), create the rhythmic and metaphoric effects that so clearly point to new literary developments. The poems are rhythmically light and rather singable, filled with highly sensuous imagery reminiscent of Ezra Pound.

The only great lyricist in Norway during the 1930's, Arnulf Øverland (1889-1968), certainly belongs to the generation of Wildenwey and Bull, but the decisive influences on his work were from a different era. For no other Norwegian author did World War I, and even more the postwar period, signify such a sharp separation of past from present. His youthful poetry from 1911 to 1915 did not arouse particular attention. Death and isolation were very significant themes, and it was clear that Øverland was picking up where the poetry of the 1890's left off. Beginning with the volume *Brød og vin* (1919; bread and wine), he occupied himself with his own time; the poetry of the self gave way to bloody scenes from the battlefield hospitals, the aesthetic egocentric had become a moralist and an indignant satirist. In the 1920's, Øverland adopted a socialist, even communist, point of view. His collection of profound intellectual poetry, *Berget det blå* (1927; blue mountain), portrays in biblical terms the slavery of humankind and the migration to the promised land of social solidarity. With the outbreak of World War II, Øverland changed his attitude again. Abandoning his communist and anti-Christian activism, he worked to unite the Norwegian people. His poems of resistance—lyrics of peace—circulated secretly during the German occupation and were not printed until 1945, in the volume *Vi overlever alt* (we shall live through all). Øverland's last collections contain more complicated, metaphoric, intellectual poetry. *Den rykende tande* (1960; the smoldering wick) is in part a stocktaking of reality, seen with the clear vision of age. Old truths are shown in new light, with altered contours. Øverland's lyric accomplishment has often been compared with that of Heinrich Heine; Øverland himself never concealed that the German poet was his immediate model. Like Heine, he was no formal experimenter, no artistic innovator; his poetry, nevertheless, presents a wealth of nuances and simple greatness.

Radical socialism remained a trademark in the writing of the playwright, novelist, and poet Nordahl Grieg (1902-1943). In the volume *Norge i våre hjerter* (1929; Norway in our hearts), however, Grieg's radicalism was entirely overlooked by the public; only the declamatory, patriotic effects were noticed, which made Grieg more popular than any other Norwegian poet. After a two-year stay in Moscow, from 1932 to 1934, Grieg returned as a determined communist, and his criticism of capitalist society became increasingly sharper. During World War II, he served as a pilot in the British Royal Air Force and was shot down over Berlin, enhancing his reputation

beyond what his talent really merits. His greatest artistic accomplishment during the war was his war poems, collected in a volume titled *Friheten* (1943; all that is mine demand, 1944). Here Grieg took the basic theme of *Norge i våre hjerter* and carried it further in poems that are among the most valuable that have been written about war and the homeland.

Immediately after World War I, there emerged in Denmark a new generation of lyric poets affirming the glory of existence. As the creator of a new poetic mentality, the central figure is doubtless Emil Bønnelycke (1893-1953), with his glowing enthusiasm for the technology of the modern metropolis. As a poet, however, Tom Kristensen (1893-1974) is the most significant. He learned much from Bønnelycke, whose poetry served as the model for the Copenhagen scenery and language in Kristensen's early collections. *Fribytterdrømme* (1920; pirate dreams) and *Mirakler* (1922; miracles). With a purely artistic attitude toward existence as the point of departure, Kristensen sought to re-create metropolitan life in a new poetic form. He transformed external reality into a festive orgy of screaming colors. This occurs not only when he loses himself in exotic fantasies, but also when he describes the brutal beauty of a fight in a billiard hall in a proletarian part of Copenhagen. Just as the colors are appreciated for their own sake, so is the sound of the words exploited in a purely aesthetic manner, intensified in the poem "Itokih" almost to Dadaism. In the volume *Paafuglefjeren* (1922; the peacock feather), Kristensen employs material from a trip to China and Japan; he breaks with the expressionistic style and finds a controlled lyricism, saturated with color, which approaches impressionism. The external harmony, however, only increases the tension in the homeless soul of the poet. This restlessness grows in Kristensen's novels from the 1920's and 1930's into despair and a longing for self-destruction which makes him the most important Danish representative of the "lost generation."

As in Norway, the major Danish authors of the interwar period were prose writers either dealing with social and political issues or analyzing human destiny on an existential level. The period was also a high point in Danish drama, with Kjeld Abell (1901-1961) and Kaj Munk (1898-1944); from completely different political standpoints, they defended the humanistic values of Western civilization. Nevertheless, as a result of the great success of the expressionistic writers Bønnelycke and Kristensen, a new generation of poets stepped forth, attempting in various way to find their footing in a changed world. Paul la Cour's (1902-1956) two main collections from the 1930's, *Dette er vort liv* (1936; this is our life) and *Alt kræver jeg* (1938; I demand all), are dominated by feelings of guilt about the fate of Europe as the poet discerns the power of his own ruthless instincts. Simultaneously, there is a growing belief in the necessity of change. The result of la Cour's search beyond the intellect is presented in his major work, *Fragmenter af en Dagbog* (1948; fragments of a diary), a mix of philosophical teaching, poetics, and poetry describing the meeting of the rational and irrational forces in art.

Jens August Schade (1903-1978), in his turn, captures the tension between the infinite and finite in numerous collections of Surrealistic poetry, already fully developed in his first book, *Den levende violin* (1926; the living violin). All of the later volumes, from *Hjerte-Bogen* (1930; the heart book) on, are characterized by daring and disrespectful love poems, erotic nature poetry, and cosmic fantasies. They are permeated by Schade's all-embracing sexual message—the closest Danish literature has ever come to the primitivism of D. H. Lawrence.

The most artistically convincing expression of the restlessness and the nihilism of the period, besides the poetry of Tom Kristensen, is found in the novels and poems of Nis Petersen (1897-1943). He made his debut as a lyricist with the collection *Nattens Pibere* (1926; *whistlers in the night*, 1983), in which these moods are apparent. His later volumes, such as *En drift vers* (1933; a drove of verse), convey a similar atmosphere of doubt and despair but change from the rhetorical style influenced by Kipling and Wilde to plain verse of great beauty. Icelandic poetry, which around 1900 had been largely traditional and Romantic, moved after 1920 toward greater realism, stylistic flexibility, and receptiveness to foreign influences. A cult of the self, the present, and sexuality emerged, together with a greater political awareness. The first poems by Stefán Sigurthsson (1887-1933), collected in *Söngvar förumannsins* (1918;

the wanderer's song), became a literary event. More personal than any encountered before in Iceland, they are revelations of all aspects of the poet's emotional life. Sigurthsson's next book, *Othur einyrkjans* (1921; the song of the lonesome crofter), is colored by his life as a farmer. The poems are more earthy and objective, and the range of themes greater, as the poet turns to folklore and fairy tales for inspiration. A eulogy of Catholicism, to which Sigurthsson converted in 1923, is found in *Heilög kirkja* (1924; holy church), reminiscent of the sacred poetry of medieval Icelandic writers, masterful in metrical excellence and lyric sensitivity, which also characterizes his later collections of religious poetry.

Davíth Stefánsson (1895-1964) is more typical of the changing times—an exaggerated worship of life contrasted, in his debut poems of *Svartar fjathrir* (1919; black feathers), with a destructive world war and presented with a self-conscious air of libertinism. A trip to Italy provided new motifs for Stefánsson's later collections: Colorful descriptions of the social misery he observed abroad dramatically contrast with the splendor of historic monuments. In 1947, *Ný kvæthabók* (a new book of poems) appeared, containing his reactions to the war and expressing his disillusionment at the rearmament of the superpowers. The variety of his motifs and forms, his straightforward language, and the fact that his emotional life is the subject of many of his poems make Stefánsson one of the greatest renewers of Icelandic poetry.

This renewal was furthered by Tómas Guthmundsson (1901-83), who consistently has combined neo-Romantic language with everyday speech. He appeared in 1933 as a mature artist with *Fagra veröld* (fair world), in which the busy life of the Icelandic capital, Reykjavík, becomes an important theme, the poet discovering there a new dimension of beauty. In both *Fagra veröld* and the next volume, *Stjörnur vorsins* (1940; stars of spring), his worship of beauty takes on a mystical dimension. *Fljótith helga* (1950; the holy river) was written during and after World War II and contains a number of polemical poems against Nazism. His most powerful works, however, are those in which he confronts the transitoriness of life, clothing his sense of resignation in linguistic and rhythmic splendor.

The nature poetry of Jóhannes úr Kötlum (pseudonym of Jóhannes B. Jónasson, 1899-1972) follows the national, Romantic tradition of Einar Benediktsson. Less poetic, but far more convincing, are his satires on corrupt capitalistic society and his preaching of a new social order in *Samt mun ég vaka* (1935; yet I will stay awake), marking his conversion to communism. *Hart erí heimi* (1939; world is in chaos) is largely concerned with the anti-democratic signs of the times and the threat of war. His poetry from the 1950's and 1960's is written in a similar pacifist mode, but whereas the style of Kötlum's earlier works is characterized by rich lyricism, in his later works, it became fragmented and rhetorical, mirroring the revolutionary author's bitterness in response to postwar developments.

POSTWAR DEVELOPMENTS

Following the brutality and destructiveness of World War II, the quest for a meaningful metaphysical and existential basis of life became a driving force in Nordic literature. Anxiety and a feeling of powerlessness became the central experience. The social function of literature was negated; any private experience of the world was considered narrow and devoid of value. Every line of a poem was supposed to express a universal feeling. To capture the all-embracing nature of consciousness, the poets of the 1940's employ a rich metaphorical language; thus, the poetic image, inspired by Eliot, Pound, and Stéphane Mallarmé, assumed a dominant position. The literature is not easily accessible, since it reflects a splintered and complex reality that can be rendered only in a fragmented syntax.

Although Sweden adopted a neutral posture during World War II, the war's brutality influenced a whole generation of writers and became their central problem; one could no longer rely on national, religious, or even humanistic values. The work of Erik Lindegren (1910-1968) is in many ways typical. In addition to the disillusioning experience of the time, there is a Romantic attitude, an imaginative component reminiscent of French Surrealism and the Welsh poet Dylan Thomas. Lindegren's poetry is set in an abstract universe. He seeks above all to express an inner psychological reality in ecstatic rhetoric in his volume *Mannen utan väg* (1942; *The Man Without a Way*, 1969), the unsurpassed masterpiece of the 1940's. It consists of forty unrhymed, symmetrical poems, almost every line of which is saturated with dissonant imagery. This work had a great influence on younger writers, but none of them went as far as Lindegren. In his later collections, however, he turned again to more traditional forms. Even his pessimism abated gradually, especially in *Sviter* (1947; suites).

If Lindegren was the era's inspiring stylistic innovator, Karl Vennberg (1910-1995) was its critic and theoretician. His poetry is deliberately anti-Romantic and is linked to the concrete worldview of the natural sciences. He is a didactic poet who constantly occupies himself with the problems of intellectual life. His pessimism finds its most bitter expression in *Tideräkning* (1945; reckoning of time), turning against all forms of faith and all solutions. In a series of ironic and scornful verses, Vennberg emphasizes that all teachings of salvation are merely the expression of selfish interests. Nevertheless, Vennberg could not maintain his distrust. The next collection, *Fiskefärd* (1949; fishing trip), displays an almost idyllic mood of intimacy and warmth, which yields in the religious poems to a hope for salvation. Yet this cheerful tone is only an intermezzo. In the 1950's, Vennberg became involved in politics as an advocate of a neutral position between the two superpowers—a view entirely in accord with his own poetics. Personal feelings are given more space, and a feeling of resignation predominates. After a period of silence Vennberg returned to poetry in the 1970's and in 1987 published his last collection, *Längtan till Egypten* (longing for Egypt), an exquisitely executed farewell to life permeated with resignation as well as a longing for an unknown god.

A tone of sarcasm and desperation similar to that in Vennberg's early poetry characterizes the volume *Skriket och tystnaden* (1946; the scream and the silence), by Werner Aspenström (1918-1997). Vennberg's dry, conversational tone, however, was replaced by tighter form and more precise expression. This tendency, developed into a more intimate tone and a simpler style, influenced by legend and fairy tale, can be found in *Snölegend* (1949; snow legend) and *Litania* (1952). Aspenström's extraordinary linguistic precision remained intact throughout the 1960's and indeed reached new heights of virtuosity in the collections Ordbok (1976; dictionary),

Enskilt och allmänt (1991; private and public), and *Ty* (1994; for).

The lyric poetry of the 1950's in Sweden was based on the poetics of the 1940's. The influence of Lindegren, in particular, is noteworthy. Symbols—either sophisticated or naïve—continued to play an important role, but the tone was less gloomy. Typical subjects were nature and love, portrayed in poetic and playful language. Accordingly, Pound succeeded Eliot as an important source of inspiration. The catastrophic atmosphere of the 1940's is still evident in the first collection of Lars Forssell (born 1928), *Ryttaren* (1949; the rider), containing compact and hermetic poems about the transitoriness of life and the inevitability of death. Here, and even more in *Narren* (1952; the jester), Forssell's preference for employing masks and roles and for allowing various personas to act as his spokespersons is evident. This technique was to form the basis of his transition to successful dramatist. He published two translations of Pound's poems, and his own poetry is indeed related to Pound's cryptic work. In the mid-1960's, however, Forssell turned to the cabaretlike song with *Röster* (1964; voices) and a few years later to political poetry. This trend reached its zenith with *Oktoberdikter* (1971; October poems) and *Forsök* (1972; attempt), texts dealing with the Bolshevik revolution and the U.S. bombing of Hanoi, respectively. Subsequently, Forssell focused on more personal themes, and his collection *Förtroenden* (2000; confidences) is permeated with a tragic awareness of his own aging in a world of suffering and misery.

Among the most successful poetry collections of the 1950's are the slim and rather exclusive volumes by Tomas Tranströmer (born 1931). In *17 dikter* (1954; seventeen poems), he works primarily with impressions of nature around Stockholm, using many concrete details; the basic experience, however, is that of a cosmic power, a universal coherence, which occasionally takes on a religious dimension. Tranströmer becomes more concrete in *Klanger och spår* (1966; sounds and tracks), which deals with current political topics. In *Mörkerseende* (1970; *Night Vision*, 1971), however, he deals less with ideological issues than with moral questions concerning the individual; his vague political commitment is transformed into a discussion of society's responsibilities toward the human being. He deals with the same theme in *Östersjöar* (1974; *Baltics*, 1975), a volume that embraces both spiritual reflections and historical and political perspectives on the Baltic Sea. Now an earlier mood of pessimism recedes in favor of a more optimistic viewpoint which in *Sanningsbarriären* (1978; *Truth Barriers*, 1980) turns into a clear affirmation of a supernatural world. With the volume *Samlade dikter, 1954-1996* (2001; collected poems, 1954-1996) Tranströmer has confirmed his position as one of the most prolific writers of twentieth-century Scandinavian literature.

Tranströmer, whose poems are characterized through an almost explosive metaphoric vitality, belongs to the Symbolist school and has been criticized for his uncommitted attitude. Sandro Key-Åberg (1922-1991), on the other hand, definitely wishes to provoke the reader into opposing brutal reality. Throughout his works, a dominant theme is the pain of the fleeting moment—in the midst of life, we are embraced by death. This romantically shaded pessimism culminates in *Bittergök* (1954; bitter fool). In his later poetry collections, such as *En stordikt till dej* (1968; a great poem for you), Key-Åberg, without abandoning this dark vision, makes a passionate appeal to people's sense of responsibility.

Much of the prose after World War II in Danish literature is a direct continuation of the realistic traditions of the 1930's. It is in poetry that innovative and provocative ideas come forth. Some poets, such as Piet Hein (1905-1996), follow tradition, writing simple, rhymed verse. In Hein's twenty volumes of *Gruk*, 1-20 (1940-1963; as Kumbel Kumbell; *Grooks*, 1-6, 1966-1978), he is exceptionally skilful with the epigrammatic play of words and ideas.

The absence of cultural consensus after the war was to be reflected in literary style, and a recognition of the crisis permeates the writing of the most significant Danish poet of the 1940's, Ole Sarvig (1921-1981). In his cycle in six volumes appearing between 1943 and 1952, he renders in a modernistic and imagistic language, related to abstract painting, a grandiose portrayal of modern man in crisis at a cultural and historical turning point. The driving force of his poems is the search for resolution to this crisis. The central poems of *Grønne Digte* (1943; green poems) form a coherent metaphysics of history. The tone is often surprisingly harmonious, standing in absolute contrast to the mood of crisis in the volume *Jeghuset* (1944; the house of self), a crisis that is overcome in *Menneske* (1948; man). The decisive themes of the latter are the experience of God and of love between man and woman. The retrospective cycle *Forstadsdigte* (1974; suburban poems) marks a return to the theme of Sarvig's early work, the experience of Christ and love. This theme also permeates his brilliant prose works and reaches the zenith in his last book, a collection of hymns, *Salmer og begyndelser til 1980'erne* (1981; hymns and beginnings to the 1980's), establishing his position in Danish literature as its most outstanding representative of a metaphysical outlook.

Sarvig saw love and grace as a liberation from chaos. For Thorkild Bjørnvig (born 1918), faith in poetry is the liberator. In his first collection, *Stjærnen bag Gavlen* (1947; the star behind the gable), Eros is the dominant theme. Bjørnvig depicts the metamorphosis of young love, expounding on his belief that everything is governed by the law of transformation. *Anubis* (1955) employs the same theme, but in it, Bjørnvig's diction has matured and taken on greater musicality and substance. In the 1970's, he turned to contemporary issues, and ecological problems dominate the volumes *Delfinen* (1975; the dolphin) and *Abeguder* (1981; ape gods). *Siv vand og måne* (1993; rush water and moon) marks a return to Bjørnvig's main themes: the glorification of art and love as humanity's redeeming forces and of nature as the point of departure for cosmic experiences.

Erik Knudsen (born 1922) began as a typical representative of the 1940's with the volume *Blomsten og sværdet* (1949; the flower and the sword), in which he expressed his deep anxiety and called for human fellowship. In his later collections from *Sensation og Stilhed* (1958; sensation and silence) and *Journal* (1963) to *Ord fra Humlebæk* (1986; words from Humlebaek), Knudsen presented his socialist ideas and his criticism of Western society and culture. He maintained this stance in a number of successful television plays. Knudsen has always used language as a tool for agitation. The volume *Vietnam* (1973), for example, was directed against American involvement in Asia and against capitalism in general.

In Norway, there was also a sudden shift to poetry after the war. Yet, while modernism had gained a foot-

hold in Denmark in the work of Ole Sarvig and Swedish writers had established contact with modern world literature through the metaphysical poetry of the 1940's, similar trends were barely present in Norway, and there was little experimentation. On the other hand, there had been trends toward renewal already in the 1930's. Like the Danish poets Bønnelycke and, earlier, Johannes V. Jensen, Rolf Jacobsen (1907-1994) attempted to incorporate all of modern civilization, technology, and urban life into a cluster of poetic themes in his collections *Jord og jern* (1933; earth and iron) and *Vrimmel* (1935; tumult). In later collections from *Stillheten efterpå* (1965; the silence afterward) and *Headlines* (1969) to his last work, *Nattåpent* (1985; open twenty-four hours), however, Jacobsen expresses in somber language a strong disgust with the results of the machine age. His field of associations became increasingly more complicated; he creates bold images which he permits to work without interpretation, his writing therefore emerging as a sophisticated Norwegian parallel to Pound's Imagism.

Pound, together with Eliot and William Butler Yeats, were the major models for Claes Gill (1910-1973). In his epoch-making collections *Fragment av et magisk liv* (1939; fragments of a magic life) and *Ord i jærn* (1942; words of iron), Gill not only breaks with traditional metrics but also frees himself from traditional syntax. The metaphors flow in free succession, guided only by his often paradoxical associations.

For a long time, Gill and Jacobsen were isolated phenomena. Not until 1947 did Tarjei Vesaas (1897-1970) publish his volume of poems *Leiken og lynet* (games and lightning), marking the beginning of postwar Norwegian modernism. Vesaas's style developed under the influence of Edith Södergran's poems in his three collections published in the period from 1949 to 1956, followed in 1970 by his last volume, *Liv ved straumen* (life by the river). By eliminating everything superfluous and leaving only words and metaphors that bear associations, Vesaas created in his best poems a uniquely suggestive tension. The central motifs are the same as in his novels: the metaphysical evil of the time, the powers within and outside the uprooted person of the twentieth century, and the fear of catastrophe.

In 1949, Paal Brekke (born 1923) published a translation into Norwegian of Eliot's *The Waste Land*

(1922) together with his own collection *Skyggefektning* (shadow fencing), in which he attempted to explain the contemporary world picture. The volume is characterized not only by free rhythms but also by bold syntactical tension and, above all, a sparse modernistic vocabulary. Brekke's intellectualism, schooled by Eliot and Pound and influenced by Finno-Swedish and modern Swedish literature, was rejected by the public. After the negative reception of *Skyggefektning*, Brekke turned to prose. In 1957, however, he published another volume of poetry, *Løft min krone, vind fra intet* (lift my crown, wind out of nothingness), which is thematically linked to the first collection but marked by an even stronger inner tension; its poems show that chaos and fragmentation increasingly dominate. *Det skjeve smil i rosa* (1965; the wry smile in pink) is permeated by the poet's feeling of anguish. The volume is a nightmare with elements of so-called concrete poetry, dealing with the surrogates of modern consumer society and the indifference of human beings who wallow in commercialism and sexuality in the face of possible extinction. Moralist sentiments also dominate the prose poems in *Granatmannen kommer* (1968; the grenade man is coming). Inspired by the newspaper headlines about murder, war, and sex as a substitute for that love in which only poets believe, Brekke employs a collagelike form to demonstrate the power of evil. In later collections, such as *Aftenen er stille* (1972; the evening is quiet), *Flimmer. Og strek* (1980; shimmering. and lines), and *Men barnet i meg spør* (1992; but the child in me asks), Brekke—in a more subdued, ironic manner—focuses on alienation and isolation in contemporary Norwegian welfare society.

For Finland, World War II was a total catastrophe. The Winter War against Russia lasted from 1939 to 1940 and was resumed from 1941 to 1944 with the support of Germany, which did not prevent Finland's defeat. During the war years, almost all literary activity ceased, and modernistic poetry did not gain a foothold in Finland until the 1950's. The poets now concentrated on ridding language of clichés and rhetoric in order to release rhythm and images and to make the diction more colloquial.

The lyric breakthrough occurred with the collection *Tämä matka* (1956; this journey), by Eeva-Liisa Manner

(1921-1995), a severe critique of over-intellectualized modern civilization, which leads humanity to a state of isolation and alienation. The poet sees a way out of desolation in the pantheistic experience of the unity of all things. This insight gradually leads her to a meditative attitude colored by ancient Chinese philosophy. The sources of Manner's next collection, *Orfiset laulu* (1960; Orphic songs), a journey into the land of myth and the subconscious, include the Revelation of Saint John, medieval troubadour poetry, and astrology. In the 1960's, Manner showed a new awareness of social reality, as in *Kirjoitettu kivi* (1966; the written stone), and, as a result, her style became more proselike and colloquial. The volume *Kuolleet vedet* (1977; dead waters), however, marked a return to the mystical perspectives of Manner's early poetry, focusing on contemporary human estrangement from nature.

Paavo Haavikko (born 1931), the second modernistic Finnish poet of stature in the 1950's, consolidated his position through linguistic virtuosity, surprising juxtapositions of metaphors, and intense rhythmic expressions. No one has written of the insecurity and relativism of human life more convincingly than Haavikko in his collections from the early 1950's. A social and political approach becomes clearer in the volume *Synnyinmaa* (1955; the fatherland), which anticipates the critical attitudes of the 1960's, as well as Haavikko's own later poetry, such as *Neljätoista hallisijaa* (1970; fourteen rulers), the unifying element of which is the poet's criticism of fascist ideology. On the other hand, in *Kaksikymmentä ja yksi* (1974; twenty and one), Haavikko's inspiration is the old *Kalevala* poem, and he alternates between modernistic language and the technique of folk poetry. In the 1980's Haavikko began to cross the border between literary genres. Thus *Rauta-aika* (1982; *The Age of Iron*, 1982) is an interpretation of the *Kalevala* poem, accompanied by *Kullervon tarina* (1982; *Kullervo's Story*, 1989). In addition, Haavikko has written historical works, novels, and dramas. Not only is the multiplicity of genres and the diversity of his subject matter extraordinary, his oeuvre in general marks the most radical rupture with tradition in modern Finnish literature.

A similar position in Finno-Swedish literature is occupied by Bo Carpelan (born 1926), who is the first poet to go beyond the prewar traditions. In his early collections from the 1940's, Carpelan employs elements from Swedish poetry of that decade: denseness, heavy imagery, and philosophical pessimism. *Objekt för ord* (1954; objects for words) clearly marks a change in Carpelan's position. He begins to express more openness and confidence—reality regains its concreteness. Carpelan abandons the private sphere at the same time that his language becomes more concise, developing into a rare formal mastery in the volumes *Källan* (1973; the source) and *I de mörka rummen, i de ljusa* (1976; in the dark rooms, in the bright ones). The selection of poems in *Dikter från trettio år* (1980; poems from thirty years) can be considered the summation of a remarkable career. Later volumes primarily pay tribute to a number of writers to whom Carpelan felt related; in *År som löv* (1989; *Years Like Leaves*, 1993), he glorifies the great German poet Friedrich Hölderlin.

After World War II, Icelandic writers became less insular. Although some of them produced conventional epics, others began experimenting with style and language. Despite the political optimism of 1944 resulting from Iceland's proclamation of total independence from Denmark, a pessimistic note is sounded among the young writers, inspired by the Swedish poetry of the 1940's and approaching an almost nihilistic feeling of despair, voiced in unconventional free verse and impenetrable imagery.

Steinn Steinarr (1908-1958) led the experimentation with abstract styles. His short, simple, and unrhymed poems express a radical skepticism based on a feeling of isolation and loneliness and on the realization of the absurdity of human existence, as pronounced in the programmatic titles *Sporí sandi* (1940; tracks in the sand) and *Ferth án fyrirheits* (1942; journey without promise). These volumes were influenced by American poet Carl Sandburg, abstract painting, and Swedish modernism. These models also led Steinarr to a number of typographical experiments, resulting in his most avant-garde work, the cycle of poems *Tímmin og vatnith* (1948; *Time and Water*, 1972).

Iceland's most important postwar lyricist, Hannes Pétursson (born 1931), wrote traditional verse before he began to employ a more experimental method; the shift in style reflecting his growing sense of alienation, a feeling of universal transitoriness. In the volumes *Í*

sumardölum (1959; in the summer valleys) and *Stund og stathir* (1962; time and places), the poet clearly states that his feeling of helplessness can be overcome only when he recaptures what is closest and most precious to him: the beauty of Iceland and his childhood memories. His book *Úr hugskoti* (1976; recollections), a collection of occasional poetry and essays, demonstrates how Pétursson's work has moved from the traditional to the innovative and back to the traditional, a movement back to a formal concern which finds an exquisite expression in the much later volumes *36 ljóth* (1983; thirty-six poems) and *Eldhylur* (1993).

Nordic literature became increasingly marked by a demand for political commitment, which reached its climax in the 1960's. In addition, the modern welfare state and growing materialism became the targets of sharp attacks, which were also aimed at the ivory-tower attitude, defended by some writers as the only means of artistic survival. One group of writers emerged whose work was experimental, dealing with the function of language from a philosophical point of view. This eventually developed into the so-called concrete literature, which looks on language as a social and political system. Another group chose stylistic simplicity, a neo-realistic approach called the New Simplicity, which first appeared in Sweden around 1960.

It is poetry's role in the communication process that has constantly been stressed by the most significant spokesman of the New Simplicity, Göran Palm (born 1931). His first collection, *Hundens besök* (1961; the dog's visit), contains deliberately simple, often aphoristic poems, which primarily convey basic elements of reality; but in addition, it treats of human isolation in a world determined by social gulfs. In *Världen ser dig* (1964; the world sees you), Palm demands that the poet abandon the traditional, aesthetic role and concentrate on establishing communication. Around 1965, Palm turned to the essay and published a number of "debate books," but in 1971, he returned to poetry with the volume *Varför har nätterna inga namn?* (why do the nights have no name?), which, although a thematic continuation of *Världen ser dig*, transfers responsibility from the poet to the politically awakened human being. After many years of silence as a poet Palm returned with *Sverige en vintersaga* (1984-1997; Sweden: a winter's tale), a three-volume epic poem about his home country filled with sarcasm, polemics, and humor reminiscent of Heinrich Heine.

Björn Håkansson (born 1937) is also paradigmatic of the 1960's. The volume *Mot centrum* (1963; toward the center) is an exercise in the methods of the New Simplicity, employing colloquial language from advertisements and newspapers. Håkansson meets the challenge of a politically involved literature with several collections, such as *Fronter i tredje världskriget* (1975; fronts in World War III), nondogmatic formulations of his political creed. In *Tjänstemannens son* (1978; the son of a civil servant), Håkansson violently protests a welfare-state bureaucracy that denies the individual's moral responsibility. Much more direct in his political message is Göran Sonnevi (born 1939). A basic element in his poetry is his concept of the "structures," representing the principles that deprive life of its spontaneity. Language is one of these structures, and its power over our thoughts is analyzed in *Inngrep—modeller* (1965; interventions—models). Sonnevi's emergence as a political writer was marked by the separately published poem "Om kriget i Vietnam" (about the war in Vietnam), from 1965. His revolutionary activism is apparent in the titles of works such as *Det måste gå* (1970; it has to work), which places Sonnevi beside Danish author Ivan Malinovski as one of the most convincing political writers of postwar literature. *Det omöjliga* (1975; the impossible) and its sequel, *Språk; verktyg; eld* (1979; language; tools; fire), are Sonnevi's most significant collections from the 1970's. *Oavslutade dikter* (1987; unfinished poems) as well as *Klangernas bok* (1998; the book of sounds) demonstrate a much increased thematic and formal sophistication. A visionary, even metaphysical aspect has been added; the previous expansion of the universe is now accompanied by an expansion of the soul that is triggered by various encounters with death. Sonnevi must be regarded as one of the great Swedish poets of the twentieth century.

Preoccupation with the function of language led not only to a literature critical of society but also to a so-called concrete poetry, in which words are employed as concrete, malleable material, freed of meaning and intention. The letters are arranged in patterns, and the words are exploited as sounds. A pioneer of this is Carl Fredrik Reuterswärd (born 1934). In his collection *På samma gång* (1961; at the same time), the latter gives up syntax completely and arranges single words in a lyric verbal tapestry. Where Reuterswärd writes with the intention of provoking the reader, Bengt Emil Johnson (born 1936) attempts above all to communicate his artistic experiences. For that reason, he let his collection *Gubbdrunkning* (1965; old man's drowning) be accompanied by a phonograph record, in order to convey more vitally the printed word. With the poems in *Skuggsång* (1973; shadow song) Johnson emerges as an accessible nature poet, a direction he continues to exploit throughout the 1980's with an increased focusation on existential themes as convincingly demonstrated in the pessimistic volumes *Lika* (1991; equal) and *Över Oxbrobäcken* (1996; over Oxbro stream), in which nature is seen as incomprehensible and death perhaps as the only comprehensible truth.

The linguistic trend is continued by Tobias Berggren (born 1940), who clearly attempts to release language from the mental associations that bind one to old patterns. In *Den främmande tryggheten* (1971; the strange security) he, like Sonnevi, speculates about the possibility of creating a new language capable of bringing about change—thereby combining a political and a Romantic attitude. The abstract, occasionally dry statements of this volume have completely disappeared in *Namn och grus* (1973; names and gravel), a major work of modern Swedish poetry in which the author's presence is intense. A journey through an inferno toward the light occurs in the volume *Resor i din tystnad* (1976; journeys in your silence), containing poems of extraordinary visionary beauty, a trait even more characteristic of the collections *Bergsmusik* (1978; mountain music) and *Threnos* (1981). The volume *Fält och legender* (1997; spheres and legends) both marks a return to the earlier discussion of the cognitive function of language and a metaphysical expansion of the poet's universe.

Similarly eclectic is the work of Gunnar Harding (born 1940), who in the preface to his collection *Poesi 1967-73* (1973; poetry 1967-1973) mentions jazz, painting, and French Surrealism as important influences. In addition, Harding stresses that his poetry is clearly visual, a characteristic which in his earlier work is linked to language, but which gradually becomes associated with typography. In later volumes, *Gasljus* (1983; gaslight) and *Stjärndykare* (1987; star divers), a search for an all-encompassing unity, which extinguishes any boundary between the private and public spheres, is noticeable. This trend reaches its zenith with *Salongstycken* (2001; parlor pieces), a collection of highly sophisticated, poetic speculations on topics such as art, infinity, love, and death.

Lars Norén (born 1944) also found inspiration in French Surrealism. His early writing culminates in the hectic, visionary collection *Stupor: Nobody Knows You When You're Down and Out* (1968), the last volume in a series of autobiographical works since 1965; the background is the poet's hospitalization for schizophrenia. In these volumes, Norén deliberately re-creates the passive impulses, voices, and images that had penetrated the mental emptiness resulting from his psychic paralysis. In his later poetry, Norén attempts to avoid the private sphere, thereby turning his writing in a more conventional direction, but this change is also an indication that the previous chaos has been overcome. The longing for purity that permeates Norén's works of the 1960's was realized, with strong religious overtones, in the volumes *Order* (1978) and *Hjärta i hjärta* (1980; heart in heart), whose linguistic brilliance is unequaled in Norén's generation. In the 1980's Norén emerged as one of Scandinavia's most prolific playwrights, a position he maintained throughout the 1990's.

Like Norén, the prose writer and lyricist Lars Gustafsson (born 1936) cannot be placed in a specific literary category. His poetry collections from *Ballongfararna* (1962; the balloon travelers) to *Varma rum och kalla* (1972; *Warm Rooms and Cold*, 1975) contain primarily variations on the themes of his novels: the relationship between fiction and reality, art and life, past and future. Gustafsson's superb handling of language is evidenced by the volume of formally brilliant poetry, *Sonetter* (1977; sonnets). Feelings of angst and transitoriness run as a leitmotif through Gustafsson's later collections, such as *Fyra poeter* (1988; four poets) and *Variationer över ett tema av Silferstolpe* (1996; variations on a theme by Silferstolpe), confirming his position in Swedish literature as an accomplished classicist who succeeds in establishing total correspondence between form and content.

During the early 1970's a political radicalization took place in Sweden just as in the other Nordic countries. It was accompanied by a militant women's movement and, in literature, by a growing feminism. This trend was anticipated by Sonja Åkesson (1926-1977), whose autobiographical collection *Husfrid* (1962; domestic peace) deflates various romantic myths about relations between man and woman. Elisabet Hermodsson (born 1927) wrote *Disa Nilsons visor* (1974; the ballads of Disa Nilson) as a corrective to the more romantic collection of Birger Söberg, *Fridas bok* from 1922. Disa is much more spontaneous and self-assured, and a related motif inspired the poems in *Gör dig synlig* (1980; make yourself visible): how women have tended to see themselves through the eyes of men rather than defining themselves. Hermodsson's collection from 1985, *Stenar skärvor skikt av jord* (stones, shards, layers of soil), on the other hand, focuses entirely on ecological concerns.

The same distance to feminist themes is found in the poetry of Katarina Frostensson (born 1953). Her early collections, *Imellan* (1978; between), *Den andra* (1982; the other), and *I det gula* (1985; in the yellow) express in a series of rather fragmentary texts her strong criticism of linguistic abuse in contemporary society; in *Stränderna* (1989; seashores), this criticism develops into a general distrust in language as it fails to convey the mutability of today's world. More accessible are the texts in *Joner* (1991; ions), echoing well-known medieval ballads, folk songs, and church hymns.

This approach of borrowing from many different sources and styles is characteristic of the eclectic, postmodern approach to literature. The most accomplished representative of contemporary Swedish postmodernism is the novelist, filmmaker, playwright, and poet Stig Larsson (born 1955), whose concept of reality initially is strictly defined by the fictional universe. In *Minuterna före blicken* (1981; the minutes before the look) and *Händ!* (1988; happen!), he even strips away any semantic content and simply records his observations without using imagery and other stylistic means. In his later poetry collections, such as *Uttal* (1992; pronunciation), Larsson expresses his inability to shape experience and impression in words, and his inability to shape reality artistically, which to him pertains to a general problem haunting humankind: how to orient oneself in time and space, how to create one's own identity. Nevertheless, in *Natta de mina* (1997; putting the family to bed), the writing process appears to be the only means to rope in and hold on to reality and thus offer a way out of this existential predicament. Amid strong subjectivity, a belief in possible values surfaces time and again, a belief paralleled with religious faith. This volume is both a crucial source for a more thorough understanding of Larsson's own authorship and a remarkable Scandinavian contribution to the discourse on the relationship between utterance and meaning, writing and cognition.

A metaphysical orientation, as exemplified in Larsson's latest works is characteristic of contemporary Swedish poetry. In Christina Falkenland's (born 1967) collection *Blodbok* (1995; book of blood), a woman's relation in love to a man is paralleled to her relation to God; Lotta Olsson (born 1973), in her twenty-two sonnets in *Skuggor och speglingar* (1994; shadows and reflections), depicts Persephone on her way to Hades to become the consort of the God of Death, and Kristian Lundberg (born 1966), in his collection of poems *Är och blir* (1996; being and becoming), employs a rather exalted, hymnic tone to express his struggling relationship with God.

The relationship between fiction and reality as dealt with in Swedish literature by Stig Larsson and, before him, for instance, by Lars Gustafsson, is also discussed in the works of Stein Mehren (born 1935), who, together with Olav H. Hauge and Georg Johannessen, is among the most gifted Norwegian poets of the 1960's. The relationship between words and experience, the recognition of the environment and the self, take on an imposing form in Mehren's collection *Aurora det niende mørke* (1969; Aurora the ninth darkness). The internal structure is a journey through language, various styles and forms of expression that mirror one another. Mehren's dominant position among modernist poets in Norway is confirmed by *Vintersolhverv* (1979; winter solstice), which expresses the author's opinion that poetry is the only medium through which one can take hold of reality—an opinion which is particularly evident in Mehren's novels from the 1970's. His later poetry collections *Corona: Formørkelsen og dens lys* (1986; Corona: the eclipse and

its light) and *Det andre lyset* (1989; the other light) have become increasingly philosophical, dealing with pairs of opposites: light and darkness, presence and absence, love and isolation.

Olav H. Hauge (1908-1974) published his first work, a collection of introspective poetry titled *Glør i oska* (embers in the ashes), in 1946, but until the 1960's was recognized for his volume *På ørnetuva* (1961; on eagle mound), which is marked by a laconic style influenced by Ezra Pound and Japanese haiku. Hauge's symbolic use of nature almost disappears in *Dropar i austavind* (1966; drops in the eastern wind). Here, the objects stand alone and speak for themselves, and in the collection *Spør vinden* (1971; ask the wind), the harsh environment of the fjords and mountains finds an almost aphoristic expression. His *Dikt i samling* (1985; collected poems) confirms Hauge's position as one of the foremost modernists in postwar Norwegian poetry.

The work of Georg Johannesen (born 1931) reveals a more outward-directed tendency, behind which one senses a moral, ideological worldview. He possesses a rich, metaphor-filled creative talent and has written poetry of great complexity. Johannesen senses that traditional modernistic language does not capture reality. The simple title of his first collection, *Dikt 1959* (1959; poems 1959), reflects his demand for a poetry without superfluous decoration, as exemplified in the two volumes *Ars moriendi* (1965; the art of dying well) and *Nye dikt* (1966; new poems). Here, as well as in Johannesen's works from the following decades, primarily essays and novels, the main purpose is to analyze critically contemporary society.

Simultaneously with Johannesen's neorealistic poetry, the New Simplicity and concrete poetry gained a foothold in Norway. One of the most talented representatives of these new trends is Jan Erik Vold (born 1939). He is aware of his time and often excessively sensitive to its prevailing moods and various forms of artistic expression. He made his debut in 1965 with *Mellom speil og speil* (between mirror and mirror), which includes a number of figurative texts about the search for a reality that is nonexistent—the world consists of mirrors, of emptiness and deception. *Mor Godhjertas glade versjon. Ja* (1968; Mother Goodheart's happy version: yes), like Mehren's *Aurora*, is a labyrinthine journey through language and fantasy, from a convoluted linguistic system to a recognizable reality of the self. A deep mistrust of words, on the other hand, prevails in *Kykelipi* (1969; cock-a-diddle-dee) and increases in the volume *Spor, snø* (1970; tracks, snow), in which Vold attempts to recreate an atmosphere of emptiness and inconsistency in short poems inspired by Japanese haiku. This manifestation of the New Simplicity is offset by the linguistic virtuosity and burlesque imagination that pervades *Sirkel, sirkel* (1979; circle, circle), a volume based on impressions from a trip around the world, but is resumed in the collections *Sorgen. Sangen. Veien* (1987; the sorrow. the song. the road) and *Elg* (1989; moose), focusing on basic aspects and details of everyday life.

Vold was a leading figure in the group of writers who contributed to *Profil* (established in 1943), a journal originally attacking the psychological and aestheticizing trends in Norwegian postwar literature and, since the 1970's, the mouthpiece for Marxist literary theory. The central poet of this group is Tor Obrestad (born 1938), who, in *Den norske løve* (1970; the Norwegian lion) and *Stå saman* (1974; stand together), conveys a direct, revolutionary message aimed at both the United States and the North Atlantic Treaty Organization and at social domestic questions. Here, as well as in *Vinterdikt* (1979; winter poems), political propaganda frequently overwhelms aesthetic form. In *Misteltein* (1988; mistletoe), on the other hand, Obrestad reaches back to Old Norse myths for inspiration.

A number of other writers in the *Profil* group, on the other hand, joined Vold in refusing to enter the political fight. The first poetry collection by Einar Økland (born 1940), *Ein gul dag* (1963; a yellow day), although somewhat private in theme, is pointed toward the simplicity and the commonplace that dominated the second half of the 1960's. The volume *Bronsehesten* (1975; the bronze horse) is completely devoid of ideological commitment; underlying the description of an apparently trite reality is an analysis of language, or rather poetry, as the only, if problematic, means of communication.

Norwegian poetry of the 1970's was not as significant as the prose written during that decade. Nevertheless, a number of lyricists emerged who contributed to the antidogmatic trend that distinguished the decade. Tove Lie (born 1942) consistently follows a symbolic,

antimodernistic mode, expressed in the volumes *Lotus* (1972) and *Vi sprang ut av ild* (1979; we jumped from the fire). Árvid Torgeir Lie (born 1938) moved from nature poetry to political propaganda with his collection *Skrive og tenke* (1971; write and think), but his later volumes, such as *Sju svingar opp* (1976; seven sharp curves), employ increasingly subtle means of expression. More uncompromising is the straightforward, forceful poetry of Stig Holmås (born 1946) in the collections *Vi er mange* (1970; we are many) and *Tenke på i morgen* (1972; think of tomorrow), works that also display a redeeming sense of humor, being both sarcastic and compassionate. Paal-Helge Haugen (born 1945) shows a strong affinity for contemporary American poetry, some of which he has translated into Norwegian. He made his lyrical debut with *På botnen av ein mørk sommar* (1967; at the bottom of a dark summer), a fine example of the Swedish school of New Simplicity, with its simple and striking imagery taken from everyday life. In later volumes, such as *Fram i lyset, tydeleg* (1978; forward into the light, distinctly), this trend continues—with, however, an increased focus on ideological issues. The beginning social awareness of a boy and the ensuing personal conflicts form the theme of *Steingjerde* (1979; *Stone Fences*, 1986); the collection of experimenting prose poems, *I dette hus* (1984; in this house), deals primarily with the relationship between nature and culture; and *Det overvintra lyset* (1985; hibernated light) highlights, in a prehistoric setting, the contrast of love and war. *Meditasjoner over Georges de la Tour* (1990; meditations on Georges de la Tour) offers subdued reflections inspired by the French painter of the title, focusing, like the Mehren's later poems, on themes of darkness and light.

Norwegian literature of the 1980's and 1990's is dominated by a number of gifted playwrights such as Peder W. Cappelen (1931-1992) and Cecilie Løveid (born 1951) and prose writers such as Bjørg Vik (born 1935), Herbjørg Wassmo (born 1942), Kjartan Fløgstad (born 1944), and Jan Kjaerstad (born 1953). However, several of them began as poets, Løveid with *Most* (1972; juice), a love story in poetry and prose, Wassmo with *Vingeslag* (1976; beating wings) and *Flotid* (1977; high tide), and Fløgstad with *Valfart* (1968; pilgrimage), conveying sensitive experiences of nature and city life.

Løveid has continued to experiment with mixing genres. Thus, *Sug* (1979; *Sea Swell*, 1986), combines prose and poetry to depict the protagonist's struggle for self-realization. It is in Løveid's generation in particular that one finds the most interesting lyrical poets of today: young women writers, such as Inger Elisabeth Hansen (born 1950), Eva Jensen (born 1955) and Cindy Haug (born 1956), focusing in a nondogmatic fashion on the themes of love and power, not so much on attempts at exerting power over others than at gaining control over one's own selfhood. The younger generation's Eirik Lodén (born 1976) and Alexander Rubio (born 1974), both representatives of a new, form-oriented trend, deliberately see themselves as parts of a classical tradition. Lodén, in *Preludium* (1993; prelude), with his strict use of rhyme and rhythm, is clearly inspired by the formal mastery of John Keats, William Blake, and William Wordsworth, whereas Rubio, in *Nylonroser* (1993; nylon roses), patterns his beauty-seeking poetry on works by Edgar Allan Poe and Comte de Lautréamont, allowing, in his compassionate love poetry (and quite in line with a significant trend in contemporary Scandinavian literature), a distinct religious tone be heard.

In Finland, the poetry of the 1960's developed toward a clear political commitment that eventually found expression in realistic, everyday poetry. The writings of Pentti Saarikoski (1937-1983) reflect the entire literary development of this and the following decade. Disorder and the threat of chaos are characteristic and crucial themes in the volume *Kuljen missä kuljen* (1965; I walk where I walk). Saarikoski's aversion to absolute views and ideological authoritarianism leads to resignation and to a number of miniature poems about happy and unhappy love in *En soisi sen päättyván* (1968; I wish it would not end). The private sphere becomes a major motif in the 1970's. In *Alue* (1973; territory), Saarikoski writes about his family, his farm, and its surroundings. This development is reflected linguistically in a change from aphoristic to more lyric diction. The tension between Saarikoski's skepticism—which in the collection *Tanssilattia vuorella* (1977; the dancing floor on the mountain) leads him to depict the contemporary world as a fossilized labyrinth—and his need to experience faith and life as meaningful make him the most agile of the postwar Finnish writers and perhaps the one with the

widest scope, a characteristic confirmed by the posthumous collection *Hämärän tanssit* (1983; *Dancers of the Obscure*, 1987).

The work of Väinö Kirstinä (born 1936), the second major Finnish lyric poet of the 1960's, is linguistically far more advanced than Saarikoski's. He made his debut in 1961 with *Lakeus* (the plain), which reverts to the imagery of the 1950's. In *Puhetta* (1963; talk), Kirstinä does a complete reversal, employing correct and incorrect quotations, far-fetched associations, and excerpts from the Helsinki telephone directory in Dadaist word series and sound combinations—expressions of the poet's determination not to stagnate in rigid attitudes. During the 1970's, Kirstinä seemed to have found a solution to his search in depictions of the secluded, idyllic life in nature, portrayed with desperate humor in *Talo maalla* (1969; a house in the country), a humor that emerges with increasing clarity as the poet's only weapon against a world so absurd that everyone must laugh in order to remain sane. Oriented toward French culture, Kirstinä has become increasingly influenced by the Surrealism of, for instance, André Breton. Thus his pessimistic visions of the dead end of human civilization have increasingly been permeated with dreamlike sequences, as in *Säännöstelty euthanasia* (1973; rationed euthanasia) and *Yötä, päivää* (1986; night, day), although executed with a certain macabre linguistic and metaphoric beauty.

A stronger political emphasis is found in the works of Jyrki Pellinen (born 1940). The prose poems in *Niin päinvastoin kuin kukaan* (1965; so on the contrary than nobody) are primarily labyrinthine incursions into the world of words, whereas the concise poems in *Tässä yhteiskunnassa on paha nukkua* (1966; you cannot sleep well in this society) are more traditional, with refined nature scenes and romantic melancholy. In his collections from the 1970's, Pellinen moved toward surreal romanticism and mysticism. This trend, which added to the diversified quality of his writing, led to the cyclic poem *Kertosäkeiden laulu* (1976; the song of refrains), which is a prolonged search for the self, a dialogue with the poet's mirror image. In later collections, such as *Huulilla kylmä tuuli* (1990; a cold wind on the lips), Pellinen increasingly deals with the creative act, the writing process itself, and thus contributes to a general trend toward metapoetry that is particularly evident in contemporary Danish literature.

The protest literature of the 1970's is represented in the writing of Kari Aronpuro (born 1940), who openly satirizes a number of political and social situations inside and outside Finland. More rewarding but less accessible are Aronpuro's collections from the following decade, *Merkillistä menoa* (1983; remarkable progress) and *Kirjaimet tulevat* (1986; the letters are coming), displaying his intellectual curiosity and obsession with cultural studies. Finnish protest literature reached its culmination in the work of Matti Rossi (born 1934), whose first collection, *Näytelmän henkilöt* (1965; the characters of the play), contains the most artistically varied poems on the Vietnam War in Finnish literature; it was followed by additional volumes of political poetry, *Tilaisuus* (1967; the opportunity) and *Agitprop* (1972). In his poetry of the 1980's Rossi, like the aforementioned Paavo Haavikko, turns to the *Kalevala* epic for further inspiration.

The wave of debate literature reached its crest around 1975. From then on, the young poets became occupied with a more intimate atmosphere, a care for detail and a predominant interest in nature, partly motivated by opposition to the materialism of the modern welfare state. Thus, when Tommy Tabermann (born 1947) in 1970 published his first volume, *Ruusuja Rosa Luxemburgille* (roses for Rosa Luxemburg), critics looking for dogmatic political verse were greatly disappointed. They found sensitive and romantic poetry about nature and young love, themes that Tabermann also treats with successful variation in *Kaipaus* (1976; yearning) and *Anna mina kumoan vielä tämän maljan* (1977; grant that I may still drink up this cup). Jarkko Laine (born 1947) uses the features of Western popular mass culture to attack the culture of the welfare society. The tone of his collections *Muovinen Buddha* (1967; the plastic Buddha) and *Viidenpennin Hamlet* (1976; five-penny Hamlet) is critical but balanced by a strong element of humor and the use of puns. In the following decades, Laine becomes a major Finnish representative of a neoromantic, nonpolitical trend in Scandinavian literature. A very talented nature poet, Risto Rasa (born 1954), concentrates in a seemingly naïve fashion on the little things and the ways of nature, which he considers essential compo-

nents of human life, in his collection *Kulkurivarpunen* (1973; the vagabond sparrow).

This romantic trend was continued in the 1980's by Jukka Kemppinen (born 1944) but counterbalanced by writers such as Tiina Kaila (born 1951) and Kersti Simonsuuri (born 1945). Kemppinen adds a religious tone to his poems in *Linnusta länteen* (1985; west of the bird) and *Kiertävä kivi on kuolut* (1986; a rolling stone is dead), the latter volume also including prose poems, in which he depicts nature as a reflection of God. A totally different topic dominates the volume *Riitamaa* (1989; disputed land), a commemoration—with frequent references to the battlefields of World War I—of the fiftieth anniversary of Finland's Winter War against Soviet Russia. Kaila writes in the same intellectual tradition as the aforementioned Aaronpuro. Thus her debut collection, *Keskustelu hämärässä* (1975; Dialogue in the twilight), contains a sophisticated dialogue with the writer Franz Kafka about the absurdity of existence, whereas in the cosmological texts of the later volumes, *Kala on meren kuva* (1983; the fish is the image of the sea) and *Valon nälkä* (1986; light hunger), a strong pantheistic religiosity dominates, focusing on the unity of the small detail and the infinite universe. Simonsuuri's poetry—from *Murattikaide* (1980; the ivy balustrade) to *Enkelten pysäkki* (1990; angel's bus stop)—has its foundation in European intellectual history and avoids reference to social issues or the period's feminist discourse.

Contemporary Finno-Swedish literature is more accessible than during previous decades. The writers of today desire to embrace all social, political, and psychological realities, as demonstrated by Claes Andersson (born 1937). In *Bli, tilsammans* (1971; become, together), he interweaves debate poems and poems of love and personal happiness, alternating subjectivity and external issues. By the end of the 1970's, Andersson's poetry had turned away from social and political questions, and in *Trädens sånger* (1979; the trees's songs) he approaches a pantheistic view of nature if not outright mysticism. While strictly personal matters relating to parents, family life, and cohabitation are analyzed in *Under* (1984; miracles) and *Huden där den är som tunnast* (1991; the skin where it is thinnest), the scope is widened in *Mina bästa dagar* (1987, my best days), a pessimistic vision of terror and world destruction.

A similar somber tone permeates Andersson's collection from 1997 *En lycklig mänska* (a happy human being), in which death hits the apparent idyll like lighting. However, in contrast to life's transitoriness, love and music (the poet himself is an accomplished pianist) stand out as dynamic and positive forces portrayed with such exquisite artistry that the volume confirms Andersson's position as the leading Finno-Swedish poet of his generation. On the other hand, the conflicts in love, married life, and work form the subjects of the prose poems by Märta Tikkanen (born 1935) in *Århundradets kärlekssaga* (1978; *The Love Story of the Century*, 1984), combining, as do her various prose works, warmth and pithiness in their penetrating portraits. The same combination is found in the volume *Mörkret som ger glädjen ljus* (1981; the darkness that gives happiness depth), which deals with her child's emotional illness.

A focus on provincial life, another example of the romantic trend toward the end of the twentieth century, is present in the poems of Lars Huldén (born 1926), a selection of which was published in 1976 as *Långdansen* (the long dance), followed by subtle contemplations on the changing seasons and the aging process in *Jag blir gammal, kära du* (1981; darling, I am growing old). Influenced by the dialect and folklore of his home region, Huldén depicts life, with liberating and unique humor, as a series of coincidences. The concept that death as well as redemption is part of this life becomes the point of departure for *Psalmer för trolösa kristna* (1991; hymns for faithless Christians).

With Huldèn Finno-Swedish literature distanced itself from the ideological concerns of former decades. In this respect Huldén can be seen as a forerunner of poets such as Kjell Westö (born 1961), Diana Bredenberg (born 1963) and Agneta Enckell (born 1957). Whereas Westö (also an accomplished prose writer) in *Epitaf over Mr. Nacht* (1988; epitaph on Mr. Nacht) draws on features from pop music and excels in wordplays and melodramatic role-playing, Bredenberg analyzes her own emotions and attitudes in *Hinna* (1989; membrane) and *Sekvens* (1991; sequence), in the latter volume also expressing an ecological concern about nature's destruction. Enckell employs the technique of the comic strip in *Rum: Berättelser* (1987; rooms: narratives), which is partly a symbolic journey through the underworld realm

of the dead, revisited in *Falla (Eurydike)* (1991; the fall [Eurydice]). However, in this volume the poems are also about sexuality as well as the writing of poetry—a metapoetic topic found among contemporary writers in the other Scandinavian countries as well.

In the 1960's, there was in Iceland a considerable upsurge of leftist literature, turning in particular against foreign political and economic influences. This critical tone was especially prevalent in prose, while poetry only gradually became politically committed and experimental. Nature is, as it always has been, a major motif in modern Icelandic poetry. One of the most talented contemporary poets, Thorsteinn frá Hamri (pseudonym of Thorsteinn Jonsson, born 1938), has been able to join new and old both linguistically and philosophically in a flexible and rhythmic language. Thus, in his poems against the Vietnam War, political radicalism is combined with nationalistic pathos. Hamri's preoccupation with Iceland's history, literature, and folklore resulted in a number of optimistic and well-balanced collections during the 1960's, such as *Lífandi manna land* (1963; land of the living). His growing awareness that the hermetic style of modernism had established a barrier to communication led in 1972 to the strongly pessimistic poems of *Vethrahjalmur* (sun rings), which constitute a dream about the possibilities of human fellowship, further explored in collections from the following decades, including *Ljóth og myndir* (1988; poems and pictures) and *Sæfarinn sofandi* (1992; the sleeping seafarer).

A more direct political consciousness is found in the work of Pétur Gunnarsson (born 1947), a typical representative of the postwar generation who stepped forward around 1975 and spoke for a political activism that appears most convincing when combined with a linguistic renewal. Gunnarsson's collection *Splunkunýr dagur* (1973; a brand-new day) is, indeed, based on the optimistic realization that the world is ever in flux, that life is a continuous process. After this collection, Gunnarsson wrote primarily prose fiction. Sigurthur Pálsson (born 1948) displays verve and freshness in common with Gunnarsson, and both employ obviously autobiographical material. In *Ljóth vega salt* (1975; poems on the seesaw), Pálsson presents a number of half-nostalgic, half-mocking scenes from his childhood in the countryside, his school years, and various jobs. He is not, however, narcissistic; rather, the description of his youth becomes the point of departure for his emotional and intellectual movement toward a new, far more complicated reality in later collections such as *Ljóth vega gerth* (1982; poems on the road building), *Ljóthlínudans* (1993; poems—tightrope walking), and *Einhver í dyrunum* (2000; somebody in the door).

The trend toward the more private sphere as well as a focus on the artistic and cognitive function of language is continued by a number of outstanding contemporary poets. Linda Vilhjálmsdóttir (born 1958) made her highly acclaimed debut in 1990 with *Bláthráthur* (hanging by a thread), a collection of highly introspective poetry as well as exquisite nature descriptions also to be found in her following works, such as *Klakabörnin* (1992; the children of ice). A more pronounced feminist orientation can be found in the poetry collections of Kristin Ómarsdóttir (born 1962), such as *Therna á gömlu veitingahúsi* (1993; waitress in an old tavern), characterized by sophisticated linguistic experimentation and significantly less dogmatic than in the literature of the 1960's and 1970's. An even more pronounced playfulness with language and image concealing an in-depth exploration of personal, existential issues is found in the work of Bragi Ólafsson (born 1962), particularly his collections *Ansjósur* (1991; anchovies) and *Ytri höfnin* (1993; the outer port)—here often combined with historical features.

A historical perspective is also found in the poetry of Sjón (pseudonym of Sigurjón Birgir Sigurthsson, born 1962). His first three collections were reprinted in the volume *Drengurinn meth röntgenaugun* (1986; the boy with the X-ray eyes), containing texts that combine the surreal with aspects of Icelandic experience and literary heritage. A similar combination can be found in the volume *Ég man ekki eitthvath í skýin* (1991; I remember something in the clouds). Likewise remarkable is the poetry of Ísak Hartharson (born 1956) with highly acclaimed collections such as *Slý* (1985; slime) and *Hvítur ísbjörn* (1995; white polar bear), and Sigfús Bjartmarsson (born 1954). In volumes such as *Hlýja skugganna* (1985; the heat of the shadows) and *Án fjathra* (1989; without feathers), Bjartmarsson emerges as the Icelandic poet who demonstrates the most advanced command of language and imagery at the beginning of the new

millennium. His choice of foreign countries and cultures as topics is exceptional and innovative, primarily in *Zombí* (1992), a geographical expansion that is still rather unusual in Icelandic poetry.

The lyrical blossoming of Danish literature during the 1960's is largely attributable to Klaus Rifbjerg (born 1931), the most productive and versatile Danish postwar author, whose more than one hundred titles include not only poetry but also prose, drama, film scripts, and reviews. Rifbjerg's breakthrough collection, *Konfrontation* (1960; confrontation), presents conflicts drawn from everyday experience, whereas an ecstatic element appears in his long poem *Camouflage* (1961), an attempt to conquer reality through a journey into the unconscious, back to myths and memories. The technique is strictly associative. Rifbjerg plays with words, using them in surprising combinations and fragmented syntax. This method of confrontation is modified in his later poetry but appears again in *Mytologi* (1970; mythology). These poems are based on a direct encounter of classical myth with modern conditions. Another reaction against the lyric style introduced in *Konfrontation* is *Amagerdigte* (1965; Amager poems). Here Rifbjerg's style is sober and matter-of-fact, inspired by the Swedish New Simplicity. The volume *Ved stranden* (1976; at the beach) resumes the uninhibited flight of fancy characteristic of the earlier works but in a more serene tone and with a new, original attitude of confrontation with nature, which is continued in the volumes *Det svävende trä* (1984; the floating tree) and *Septembersang* (1988; September song). In Rifbjerg's later volumes, from *Bjerget i himlen* (1991; the mountain in heaven) to *Terrains vague* (1998), he returns to the spunky tone of his earliest collections, blended with personal observations about human folly and the poet's own aging process. These are works that confirm Rifbjerg's position in Danish literature not only as the most productive but also one of the most accomplished post-World War II lyrical poets.

In 1960, Jess Ørnsbo (born 1932) made his debut with *Digte* (poems), imbued with a sense of social involvement which is new to modernism. The point of departure is a worker's district in Copenhagen, but the locale is subordinated in a series of confrontations with the malice of modern urban existence. Ørnsbo's baroque metaphors are developed further in *Myter* (1964; myths), an attempt to expand the choice of motifs to include the subconscious. The decisive themes are alienation, aggression, and death, described with piercing verbal effects. In *Mobiliseringer* (1978; mobilizations), Ørnsbo's social criticism is given political overtones in a bitter diagnosis of a society in the process of dissolution. This indignation reaches new heights in his later collections *Hjertets søle* (1984; slush of the heart) and *Tidebog* (1997; book of hours).

For Ivan Malinowski (1926-1989) the technique of confrontation also is a basic principle, a formal expression of his experience of the senselessness of existence. In *Romerske bassiner* (1963; Roman basins), a collection of catalog-like prose poems, objects are juxtaposed in an attempt to paint a pathological picture of modern civilization, while *Poetomatic* (1965) alternates between nihilism and hope in a series of pithy, concentrated aphorisms. Malinowski's socialist position emerges more clearly in *Leve som var der en fremtid og et håb* (1968; living as if there were a future and hope), in which there rises, above the zero point of absurdity, an imperishable will to live, leading the poet to a socialist political involvement. This theme is developed further in *Kritik af tavsheden* (1974; *Critique of Silence*, 1977) which, in addition, deals with the indoctrinating function of language. In Malinowski's most important collections from the 1980's, *Vinterens hjerte* (1980; the heart of winter) and *Vinden i verden* (1988; the wind in the world), he resumes his criticism of capitalism, but the social questions are now placed in the much larger context of nature and universe, distinctly expressing the longing for harmony and totality that has been the driving force behind his work.

Jørgen Sonne (born 1925), on the other hand, alludes constantly in his poems to distant times and foreign cultures. His first three collections, from 1950 to 1952, are still marked by the postwar period's spiritual crisis and search for meaning. These works can be seen as talented introductions to *Krese* (1963; cycles), one of the most mature works of the 1960's. The latter is an attempt to regain the primitive quality and richness of childhood feelings through intellectual introspection, an attempt to recognize the coherence of all things, which is also the theme of *Huset* (1976; the house). Here, Sonne com-

bines observations, reflections, and visions in a long associative journey into fantasy, memory, and history, using a strictly imagistic technique. The poems in *Nærvær: Suite på rejsen* (1980; presence: suite on the journey), on the other hand, are based on concrete travel experiences; *Nul* (1987; zero) is an attempt to conjure moods of universal harmony. Here, and particularly in later volumes, such as *Have* (1992; garden), Sonne approaches a succinct, even aphoristic mode of expression.

The associative technique is developed to full mastery in the debut poems of Jørgen Gustava Brandt (born 1929), *Korn i Pelegs mark* (1949; grain in Peleg's field), in which the poet constantly refers to the Old Testament, to Oriental mysticism, and to the poetry of Dylan Thomas. The formally skillful but somewhat impersonal collections of the 1950's are succeeded in 1960 by *Fragment af imorgen* (fragment of tomorrow). Narcissism is replaced by a perception that harmonizes the inner and outer worlds. Brandt's poems are often formed of tireless descriptions of an object, the details of which create the poetic image. The poems in *Ateliers* (1967) are characterized by myths and religious symbols. In *Her omkring* (1974; around here), Brandt uses such symbols to express his longing for a mystical rest in existence. A similar reflective mood, but now accompanied by a direct religious confession, dominates Brandt's numerous succeeding collections, such as *Giv dagen dit lys* (1986; give the day your light), with a subtitle meaning "church hymns," and *Ansigt til ansigt* (1996; face to face).

In Denmark, as in Sweden, there also arose around 1965 a tendency toward the concrete, in which words, functioning as signs, have intrinsic value. In poetry, it is present in Malinowski's *Romerske bassiner*, in Benny Andersen's easily accessible writing, and, to an even greater extent, in the esoteric works of Per Højholt (born 1928). *Den indre bowlerhat* (1964; the inner bowler hat), by Andersen (born 1929), employs a witty, elegant form, in which the ambiguities of language create surprising and unexpected connections, seen in the light of social attitudes. Andersen cultivates the portrait poem, in which he depicts the alienated human being, generally by means of a monologue, as in his best-selling work, *Svantes viser* (1972; Svante's songs), for which Andersen wrote the music as well. After publishing collections of poems dealing with private or political issues, Andersen returned in *Under begge øjne* (1978; under both eyes) to purely existential questions, which are also dealt with in the volumes *Andre sider* (1987; other sides) and *Skynd dig langsomt* (1998; hurry slowly), both concluding with the acknowledgment that close human contact is the only way to achieve lasting happiness.

The perception of language as a means of cognition is the dominant idea in the work of Højholt. He experiments with different types of language: quotations, technical jargon, neologisms, and clichés. Paper and type are used as artistic materials, a cultivation of formal elements which in *Punkter* (1971; points) transforms the language into mere signs and closed symbols. In a series of small, numbered collections with the common title *Praksis* (1977-1996; praxis), Højholt continues his linguistic experimentations.

The high point of this tendency is reached in *Det* (1969; it), by Inger Christensen (born 1935). This work is composed strictly symmetrically and exhibits a flowing verbal creativity in rhymed strophes, prose, and song lyrics. Between language and experience an infinite chasm exists; only the self associates words with objects and makes possible a movement from chaos to order, a movement which is mirrored in the text. The interaction between the creator and the created continued to fascinate Christensen. After a decade of silence, she returned with *Brev i april* (1979; letters in April) and *Alfabet* (1981; alphabet), both highly sophisticated linguistic experiments, the latter concluding with a pessimistic apocalyptic scene. Yet, since words are needed to describe annihilation, there is still something of substance left, and on this basis Christensen builds a vision of love, femininity, and nature. Again, after a long interval during which she published several prose works, she returned in 1991 with the collection *Sommerfugledalen* (the butterfly valley), an exquisite sonnet cycle that confirms Christensen's position as one of Denmark's most accomplished contemporary poets.

This position she shares with Henrik Nordbrandt (born 1945), who, however, is much more accessible, expressing a neoromantic current in contemporary Danish literature. Whereas nature—Nordbrandt's favorite setting until 1998, when he moved to Spain, has been Asia Minor—and seasonal changes permeate the earlier vol-

umes, love becomes increasingly important in the collections *Glas* (1976; glass) and *Guds hus* (1977; *God's House*, 1979). Both contain sensitive and philosophical poetry of great diversity. The metaphysical element found in the latter volume increases in Nordbrandt's books of the 1980's, of which *84 digte* (1984; 84 poems) must be considered a principal work of the decade, with its reflections on life and art as well as on the paradox that only through absence can the presence manifest itself. *Glemmesteder* (1991; places of oblivion) is characterized by accomplished formal experimentation, whereas a less polished existential approach is taken with *Ormene ved himlens port* (1995; the worms at heaven's gate), written on the occasion of a friend's death. In *Drømmebroer* (1998; bridges of dreams), for the first time, a Danish setting predominates.

Social and political engagement, absent from Nordbrandt's oeuvre, dominates the early collections of Marianne Larsen (born 1951), such as *Billedtekster* (1974; captions) and *Det må siges enkelt* (1976; it must be said simply). In a lucid and powerful manner, she covers issues of sexual politics, class struggle, and imperialism. A recurring theme is the inability of humans to express themselves, which is especially typical of oppressed and socially powerless groups. In later collections, Larsen tried to reconcile the private self with the outer world and found consolation and joy in everyday occurrences. *I en venten hvid som sne* (1996; in a waiting white as snow) and *Lille dansk sindsjournal* (1998; small Danish mind journal) analyze the poet's creative process and mildly satirize Denmark's welfare society.

Søren Ulrik Thomsen (born 1956)—from his first poetry collection, *City Slang* (1981), followed by additional four volumes, from which *Nye digte* (1987; new poems) and *Hjemfalden* (1991; become liable) stand out for their intellectual and formal sophistication—rejected any ideological function of literature. For Thomsen, art—poetry—can be created only when it relates to death, to the unknown and the mysterious. Thomsen's *Mit lys brænder* (1984; my light burns), in which he stresses the importance of artistic form as the only way of capturing the elusive, had an enormous impact on the young, individualistic Danish poets of the 1980's and 1990's.

Klaus Høeck (born 1938) wrote the 608-page collection, *Hjem* (1985; home) in an attempt at encompassing the Creator, and the cult-like frontrunner Michael Strunge (1958-1986) recorded in *Skrigerne!* (1980; the screamers) with extreme sensitivity his collision with the world of the media, technology, and pop culture. After a collection of exquisite love poetry, *Væbnet med vinger* (1984; armed with wings), Strunge was afflicted by angst and severe depressions, analyzed in *Verdenssøn* (1985; son of the world), which led to his suicide the following year.

The more contemplative line drawn by Nordbrandt is followed up by Bo Green Jensen (born 1955), whose poetry cycle in seven volumes, *Rosens veje* (1980-1986; the roads of the rose), is an attempt to establish coherence in a fragmented postmodern world. Niels Frank (born 1963) produced the collection *Genfortryllelsen* (1988; the reenchantment), which describes a journey through loneliness to the regenerative sphere of love. Also Pia Tafdrup (born 1952), since her debut in 1981 with *Når der går hul på en engel* (when an angel is punctured), has tried used images of exquisite sensual beauty to establish coherence and unity, in her case, among erotic experiences, impressions of nature, and an awareness of the necessity to capture all aspects of life. The metaphysical orientation, so characteristic of Tafdrup's generation, finds expression in her ninth collection, *Dronningeporten* (1998; the queen's gate), an attempt to interpret the microcosm as well as the macrocosm of human existence.

These contemporary Danish poets, together with their colleagues in the other Nordic countries, exemplify how Scandinavian poetry is in a constant process of new departures and change. They hold forth the promise that the talent and versatility found in today's Scandinavian literature will also characterize future artistic developments.

BIBLIOGRAPHY

Naess, Harald S., ed. *A History of Norwegian Literature*. Vol. 1 in *A History of Scandinavian Literatures*, edited by Sven H. Rossel. Lincoln: University of Nebraska Press, 1993.

Neijman, Daisy, ed. *A History of Icelandic Literature*. Vol. 1 in *A History of Scandinavian Literatures*, edited by Sven H. Rossel. Lincoln: University of Nebraska Press, 2002.

Rossel, Sven H., ed. *A History of Danish Literature*. Vol. 1 in *A History of Scandinavian Literatures*, edited by Sven H. Rossel. Lincoln: University of Nebraska Press, 1992.

Schoolfield, George C., ed. *A History of Finland's Literature*. Vol. 1 in *A History of Scandinavian Literatures*, edited by Sven H. Rossel. Lincoln: University of Nebraska Press, 1998.

Stecher-Hansen, Marianne, ed. *Twentieth-Century Danish Writers*. Woodbridge, Conn.: The Gale Group, 1999. In *Dictionary of Literary Biography* 214. A generously illustrated reference work with reliable biographical and bibliographical information.

Warme, Lars G., ed. *A History of Swedish Literature*. Vol. 1 in *A History of Scandinavian Literatures*, edited by Sven H. Rossel. Lincoln: University of Nebraska Press, 1996. All five volumes listed above present Scandinavian literature from the beginning until the dates of publication. They are provided with indexes and extensive bibliographies focusing on secondary sources in English.

Zuck, Virpi, ed. *Dictionary of Scandinavian Literature*. Westport, Conn.: Greenwood Press, 1990. A reference work with brief presentations and precise characteristics. With bibliography and index.

Sven H. Rossel, updated by Rossel

SERBIAN POETRY

Like all other South Slavic literatures, Serbian literature began after the Serbs were converted to Christianity around 873, having migrated from somewhere in Eastern Europe, from the sixth century on, to their present territory on the Balkan Peninsula. A special alphabet had to be devised for that purpose. There is no doubt that the Serbs had brought along their oral poetry and that they composed poems in praise of the newly adopted religion, but manuscripts from before the twelfth century were not preserved. There were also folk poems imitative of *chansons de geste*, which were sung by the singers accompanying the crusaders of the First Crusade (1096-1097) passing through the Serbian lands along the southern Adriatic Coast (Duclea). These poems were preserved in a manuscript titled "Kraljevstvo Slovena" (twelfth century; the kingdom of the Slavs) by Dukljanin of Bar.

EARLY POETRY

Among the earliest extant Serbian poems are church songs commissioned and often composed by Saint Sava (1175-1235), the founder of the Serbian Orthodox Church and of Serbian literature. These poems were patterned after Byzantine church songs, but there were also original Slavic songs among them. As the Serbian state grew in size and strength, more poetry was written, mostly in the form of *pohvale* (encomiums) to national and church leaders. In addition, in the famous biographies of Serbian kings and archbishops, as well as in historical writings, there are passages so strikingly lyrical and rhetorical that some scholars now treat them as poems. "Slovo ljubve" (c. fifteenth century; a song of love), by Stephan Lazarević, and "Pohvala Knezu Lazaru" (1402; the encomium to Prince Lazar) are good examples of this kind of poetic literature. "Slovo ljubve" is written in a rather intricate form of acrostic, indicating that the poet drew upon a sophisticated literary tradition.

With the advance of the Ottoman army into the Balkans and the gradual loss of Serbian independence, beginning with the Battle of Kosovo (1389) and ending with the fall of the last piece of Serbian territory (1459), Serbian literature entered a period of eclipse that would last almost until the eighteenth century. During this period, written literature was very difficult to maintain. Books were written exclusively by monks in secluded monasteries, aided by numerous intellectuals and writers from other countries who were fleeing the Turks. Among these writers, Dimitrije Kantakuzin (c. 1410-1474) and Pajsije (1550?-1647) stand out with their spiritually suffused poems.

FOLK LITERATURE

The demise of written literature was more than offset by abundant folk literature in oral form—lyric and epic poetry, folktales, fairy tales, proverbs, riddles, and so on—and this folk tradition exercised a powerful influence on Serbian poets down to the present day. Indeed, when Vuk Stefanović Karadžić (1787-1864) collected, classified, and published a rich variety of Serbian folk literature in the first half of the nineteenth century, it was praised by such writers as Johann Gottfried Herder, the Brothers Grimm, Johann Wolfgang von Goethe, Sir Walter Scott, Prosper Mérimée, Alexander Pushkin, and Adam Mickiewicz, and it inspired them to translate many poems and stories.

Serbian folk poetry consists of both lyric and epic poems. Lyric, or "women's poems," as Karadžić termed them, depict every phase of life: worship, work, play, customs, friendship, and, above all, love. Many poems have mythological elements, some of them showing kinship with the folk literature of other peoples in Europe and Asia, hinting at a common ancestry. These lyric poems are in various meters and verse forms and are often accompanied by a tune to be sung by a woman or an ensemble of women. As the poems were passed on from generation to generation, their linguistic form changed accordingly. They were recorded by Karadžić in a language that differs little from present-day Serbo-Croatian, indicating that they were probably the first literary works to be composed in the vernacular.

The epic poems of the folk tradition are on a much higher artistic level. For the most part, they deal with historical events, though often they transform history into legend. Divided chronologically into cycles, they follow the rise and fall of the medieval Serbian Empire, its glory and the subsequent misery under the Ottoman rule. Two cycles stand out: the cycle about the feats of the Nemanjić Dynasty from the twelfth to the fifteenth centuries, culminating in the tragic but glorious defeat at Kosovo, and the cycle of poems about the legendary hero of the Serbs, Kraljević Marko (Prince Marko). Like the lyric folk poetry, these epics reflect the national philosophy of the Serbs, their understanding of life as a constant struggle between good and evil, and their willingness to choose death rather than succumb to the forces of evil. It is the ethical value of these poems that sets them above others of a similar kind. Their artistic value is also considerable. Almost all of them are composed in a decasyllabic meter (resembling a trochaic pentameter), with a regular caesura after the fourth syllable. They are concise and straight-forward, overflowing with formulaic patterns, striking metaphors, and images, and told in a highly poetic language. They were sung by a male singer called a *gouslar* (a few of these skilled oral poets are still active today), accompanied by a one-string bow instrument, the *gousle*. Since these poems have been handed down orally for generations, their original authors will never be known. For that reason, among others, Serbian folk poetry is revered as a national treasure.

SERBIAN DIASPORA

The long occupation by the Turks, lasting in one form or another from the end of the fourteenth to the beginning of the twentieth century, forced many Serbs to migrate north, into Austro-Hungarian territories north of the Sava River and in the Danube region called Voyvodina, where they were well received in the hope of stemming the Ottoman tide. They brought along their religion and cultural heritage, which they endeavored to advance under the auspices of the enlightened absolutist rulers of the Austrian Empire. When Austrian rule seemed to threaten the national identity of the Serbs, they turned toward the Russians for help. As a result, at the end of the seventeenth and into the eighteenth century, a new, hybrid language came into use, the so-called Russo-Slavic, employed by most Serbian poets of the time. Outstanding among these were Gavrilo Stefanović Venclović (died 1746?) and Zaharije Orfelin (1726-1785). It is significant that they strongly advocated the use of a language comprehensible to the people and themselves wrote poems in a vernacular.

By the end of the eighteenth century, after a prolonged exposure to Western influence, Serbian poets wrote more and more in the spirit of the Enlightenment. The Russo-Slavic language gave way to a more comprehensible Slavo-Serbian, only to be supplanted by a full-fledged vernacular about the middle of the nineteenth century. Serbian poets displayed an ever-increasing erudition and familiarity with contemporary currents in world poetry, abandoning the provincial outlook of a confined culture. Their poetry became philosophical and contemplative, couched in higher, solemn, dignified tones. In line with Enlightenment trends, Serbian poetry at this period was highly didactic; it also reflected the influence of neoclassicism, as exemplified by the leading poet of the period, Lukijan Mušicki (1777-1837).

NATIONALISM AND ROMANTICISM

A reawakening of national awareness among the Voyvodina Serbs was spurred by uprisings in Serbia proper against the centuries-old Turkish rule. This patriotic enthusiasm, coupled with the revolutionary reform of the written language carried out by Karadžić in the first half of the nineteenth century on the principle "Write as you speak," led to a nationwide renaissance. It first manifested itself during the transitional period leading toward Romanticism.

The leading proponent of this trend was Jovan Sterija Popović (1806-1856), a playwright and a novelist as well as a poet. His only collection of poetry, *Davorje* (1854; laments), showing a mixture of classicist, didactic, and Romantic features, laments the transience of life. Other transitional poets with an increasing inclination toward Romanticism were Sima Milutinović Sarajlija (1791-1847), Petar Petrović Njegoš (1813-1851), and Branko Radičević (1824-1853). Milutinović is more significant for his influence on other writers, especially Njegoš, than for his own works, but the few poems Milutinović wrote are distinguished by their pure lyricism and their unaffected celebration of earthly love. Both he and Njegoš drew heavily from folk poetry, which, owing to Karadzić's work, the rise of Romanticism, and the successful national revival, became the primary source of poetic inspiration. Njegoš wrote all of his works, including his plays, in verse. His short poems reveal a predilection for meditation, a willingness to try new forms, and a language close to that of the people, while his long epic poem, *Luča mikrokozma* (1845; the ray of microcosm), which resembles John Milton's *Paradise Lost* (1667, 1674), offers in poetic form the author's philosophical views on the origin of life and on the moral order of the universe. With this poem and the epic play in verse, *Gorski vijenac* (1847; *The Mountain Wreath*, 1930), Njegoš established himself as the greatest Serbian poet. Branko Radičević was the first to employ successfully in lyric poetry the vernacular as advocated by Karadžić. His ebullience and his celebration of simple, earthly joys would have been inexpressible in the era of neoclassicism.

The Romantic spirit reached its zenith with a group of poets all of whom owed their inspiration, in one way or another, to Milutinović, Njegoš, and Radičević. Again, it was the poets from Voyvodina who set the tone, but, unlike those of the earlier generation, they fused the patriarchal heroism of Serbia proper and Montenegro with the fervor of the Voyvodina Serbs acquired during the Revolution of 1848, thus uniting the literatures of the north and the south. The verse of Djura Jakšić (1832-1878) illustrates more clearly than that of any other poet this revolutionary fervor. In his highly emotional patriotic poems, his fighting spirit and his indignation against all enemies of his people are combined with a yearning for freedom as promised by the revolutions in Europe around the middle of the nineteenth century. His unabashed love poems and his avowed taste for earthly pleasures make him one of the most emotional of Serbian poets. Jovan Jovanović Zmaj (1833-1904), on the other hand, dealt with similar feelings in a much more subdued manner. A physician by profession, he was capable of greater understanding of human nature and of inexhaustible love for his fellow human beings. Often struck by tragedy in personal life, he gave his sorrows a highly poetic expression in *Djulići* (1864; rosebuds) and *Djulići uveoci* (1882; rosebuds withered). His sincere patriotism was matched by his boundless love for children. Other Romantic poets were Jovan Ilić (1823-1901) and Laza Kostić (1841-1910). While Ilić was a popular, down-to-earth poet of love and passion, of freedom and faith in the Serbian people, Kostić was a poet of lofty

flights of the imagination. Combining metaphysical speculation with forceful love lyrics, Kostić was a bold innovator in metrics, thoroughly acquainted with other literatures (he translated William Shakespeare), especially with European Romanticism, and he developed a unique style of his own that often ignored traditional forms.

Romanticism in Serbian literature manifested itself best in lyric poetry. Thus, it was no wonder that poetry took a backseat when realistic tendencies began to assert themselves in the last third of the nineteenth century. Of all the poets in this period, only Vojislav Ilić (1862-1894) reached the level of his predecessors, and in some ways he surpassed them. The son of Jovan Ilić, Vojislav discarded early the Romantic spirit in which he had been reared and instead combined classical themes with a realistic depiction of nature and human relationships. His ability to create lasting images was complemented by the musicality of his verses and by his sensitive impressions of life around him. Vojislav Ilić's potential was cut short by untimely death, but not before he had effected in Serbian poetry a turn that most new poets would soon follow.

EARLY TWENTIETH CENTURY

That turn manifested itself at the end of the century, when three powerful poets—Aleksa Šantić (1868-1924), Jovan Dučić (1874?-1943), and Milan Rakić (1876-1938)—brought completely new tones to Serbian poetry. While Šantič was, to a large degree, still related to the preceding generation in his emotional inclinations and closeness to the native soil, he nevertheless showed in his love poems and poems on social themes a new awareness of problems besetting his fellowman. His pure, sincere, and highly emotional lyrics were often set to music and are still very popular among common readers.

It was with Dučić and Rakić, however, that the new turn in Serbian poetry received its full impetus. Both educated in the West, they were inculcated with the *fin de siècle* spirit of the Symbolists and the Parnassians. Dučić used his erudition, refined taste, and aristocratic spirit to modernize Serbian poetry and free it from provincial confines. All traditional modes of expression were transformed into his peculiar idiom, primarily through new sensitivity, formalistic excellence, clarity, precision, elegance, musicality, and picturesque images. Though he paid lip service to the decadence fashionable at the time, he was too much a poet of Mediterranean *joie de vivre* and of faith in life's ultimate meaning to allow his pessimism to become a driving force.

Not so with Milan Rakić, who was unable to alleviate his constant pessimistic outlook on life, especially in matters of love and the meaning of life. His few poems, collected in a single volume, *Pesme* (1903; poems), reveal a deep-seated decadence and a firm belief that life inevitably brings decay and misery. This intellectual awareness of man's futility in trying to mitigate pain and misery was not a mere pose, and it is Rakić's conviction and sincerity that, together with artistic excellence, render his poems highly poignant and aesthetically satisfying.

Other poets of the first two decades of the twentieth century worth noting are Vladislav Petković Dis (1880-1917), Sima Pandurović (1883-1960), Milutin Bojić (1892-1917), and Veljko Petrović (1884-1967). They all wrote in the shadow of Dučić and Rakić, yet they all contributed to the broadening of horizons in Serbian poetry of their time.

INTERWAR PERIOD

Amid titanic struggles and profound changes in Serbia during and after World War I, Serbian poets changed with the times, bringing on yet another decisive break with the past, not only in poetry but also in other forms of literature. The entire period between the two world wars was marked by these fundamental changes. At first, a new generation of poets raised its voice against the horrors of war and clamored, often in vain, for humaneness and greater understanding. Dušan Vasiljev (1900-1924), Miloš Crnjanski (1893-1977), and Rastko Petrović (1898-1949), the leaders among the modernist poets, reflected the influence of the German expressionists. Toward the end of the 1920's, a group of poets, led by Dušan Matić (1898-1980), Marko Ristić (1902-1982), Oskar Davičo (1909-1989), and Aleksandar Vučo (1897-1985), introduced a form of Surrealism, to which they gave a peculiarly Serbian twist. In the 1930's, a socially conscious poetry developed, dwelling on the pervasive social turbulence besetting the world in

the decade prior to World War II. This pronounced politicization resulted in great commotion but not in great literature. During the war, the muses fell silent, as is often the case, nor were they articulate in the immediate postwar years, a period marked by profound political and social changes. It was only at the beginning of the 1950's that Serbian poetry experienced another renewal.

LATER TWENTIETH CENTURY

To be sure, several major prewar poets continued to write after 1945. Some added relatively little to their opus, while others reached their full potential only after the war. Miloš Crnjanski published only one significant poetic work after the war, the long poem *Lament nad Beogradom* (1962; lament over Belgrade), continuing where he left off almost four decades earlier. If this late work was not innovative, however, it did add a reflective quality to the essentially elegiac movement of Crnjanski's poetry. Stanislav Vinaver (1891-1955), another prewar modernist, also published only one collection after the war, *Evropska noć* (1952; the European night), in which he confirmed his reputation as an interesting experimenter with language. Desanka Maksimović (1898-1993) wrote some of her best poetry after the war. Combining patriotic feelings with traditional lyricism and the apotheosis of nature, her poems in *Tražim pomilovanje* (1965; I seek mercy) are among the best in contemporary Serbian poetry.

Oskar Davičo also reached his full stature only after the war. In numerous collections, he exhibited his revolutionary spirit and his mastery of imagery and language. Unable or unwilling to compromise, he always went to the heart of the matter, carrying on polemics, attacking, changing positions, and often preaching. Above all, his strong sensual imagination, manifested in unexpected metaphors and paradoxical twists of language, makes Davičo one of the most gifted of contemporary poets. Two other Surrealists wrote significant poetry after the war, Dušan Matić and Milan Dedinac (1902-1966). Matić influenced many younger poets with his contemplative, controlled poetry, which often has the fragmentary quality of journal entries. He was interested primarily in the essence of appearances, and his range is wide and rich in imaginative possibilities. The case of Dedinac is much simpler. After the turbulent Surrealist era, he combined, in his mature years, the old avant-garde spirit with an almost traditional lyricism.

In the first generation of postwar poets, Vasko Popa (1922-1991) and Miodrag Pavlović (born 1928) played a very important and influential role. All the complex problems of tradition, and the manner in which this tradition is to be absorbed, can be seen through the two distinct approaches these poets have taken. The aim of both poets, broadly speaking, is to rediscover the authentic native poetic tradition, to make its imagination contemporary, and, at the same time, to make available the processes and laws of that discovery.

Vasko Popa is generally considered to be the best contemporary Serbian poet. His intensely original poetry is the result of a close attention to the metaphorical and mythical overtones that one finds buried in idiomatic language: For Popa, the archetypal animistic imagination survives in contemporary idioms. Informed by Surrealism and folklore, his cycles of poems construct intricate and precise systems of symbols that are never merely arbitrary, however baffling they may appear at first glance. His poems, even when they refer to historical events, have a timeless quality. With each new cycle, it becomes apparent that his entire opus partakes of one vast and original vision of man and the universe.

Miodrag Pavlović began his career with preoccupations similar to those of Popa, but Pavlović's verse has gradually assumed a more historical orientation and a classical sense of form. Exploring the historical continuum which leads back to Byzantium and the ancient Slavs, Pavlović's method, in contrast to that of Popa, is highly intellectual. Pavlović is searching for the philosophical and religious legacy of Serbian culture. To understand the need for and the complexity of that search, one must remember that historically the development of Serbian culture has been interrupted by several "dark ages." Pavlović's search is not a matter of literary antiquarianism (for very little of the actual material of Serbian culture remains) but of an imaginative search for origins. At the same time, it cannot be denied that Pavlović taps the most ancient currents of Serbian poetry.

Ivan V. Lalić (1931-1996) also sought a living tradition, and he shared the intellectual and classical sensibility of Pavlović. What distinguishes his poetry from the latter's is his sensuousness, his lyric precision and im-

mediacy, which render the poet visible in his poems. Lalić's historical vision always has at its center a contemporary individual, as a victim or simply as a witness. His genuine mastery of form and the beauty of his language must also be emphasized.

Similar characteristics can be seen in some other Serbian poets of the same generation. The poetry of Jovan Hristić (born 1933)—meditative, philosophical, and with an austere, almost classical rhetoric—has a cool elegance. Milorad Pavić (born 1932) is closer to Popa, in that Pavić, too, has based his poetry on language, specifically the predominantly religious texts of seventeenth and eighteenth century Serbian literature. He approaches these texts with the eye of a Surrealist who dreams of being a myth maker. His poems have the appearance of metaphorical tapestries. Ljubomir Simović (born 1935) is much more an instinctive poet, guided by an intimate, often confessional lyric sense. His poems combine simplicity of language with expressionistic imagery and a kind of Breughelian earthiness. The lyricism of Božidar Timotijević (1932-2000) is more traditional and subdued. The poet is always in the foreground, and it is his own life that is being explored. What is remarkable about all of these poets turned toward the various aspects of native tradition is that they are often the ones who are, from the point of view of prosody and imagery, the most experimental.

Stevan Raičković (born 1928) represents the neo-Romantic wing in contemporary Serbian poetry. His books express his basic themes: nature as a source of perfection, and yearning for silence and solitude. Raičković's anxiety over man's disappearing ties with nature leads him at times into deep pessimism. Simplicity, directness, and a genuine lyric gift are his main traits. One of the most talented postwar Serbian poets, Branko Miljković (1934-1961), committed suicide and thus gave rise to a considerable legend. Influenced by French and Russian Symbolists as well as by the intellectual Surrealism of Yves Bonnefoy, Miljković's poetry abounds in epigrammatic utterances, unexpected metaphoric constructions, and philosophical questioning, resulting in a poetry of heightened lyricism. Each one of his poems has the intensity of a farewell note.

Miljković influenced many young poets. Borislav Radović (born 1935) owes a debt to him and to Dušan

Matić. Radović is probably the most hermetic poet of his generation. Beneath the prosiness of his lines, there is a powerful lyric pressure, and his poems open areas of language and style that are entirely new for Serbian poetry. Matija Bećković (born 1939) stands somewhat by himself. His socially conscious poetry, his original and deliberate selection of antipoetic images, and his sense of humor establish his kinship with other Eastern European poets such as Miroslav Holub and Tadeusz Róż-ewicz. The Villonesque emotional climate of Bećković's poems has had a great influence on younger Serbian poets and foreshadows an interesting new development in Serbian poetry.

Among the younger poets, there are many who are worth mentioning, especially Dragan Jovanovic Danilov (born 1960) and Milan Orlić (born 1962). Serbian poetry at the beginning of the twenty-first century continued in a state of growth, quantitatively if not qualitatively. There has never been a period in Serbian history that has witnessed such a proliferation of talent and poetic output. More important, young poets are completely open to the world, follow the development of poetry everywhere, are susceptible to cross-cultural influences, and regard themselves as true members of the world poetic community. At the same time, they are constantly searching for their roots and examining their poetic tradition, sometimes making discoveries in the most unexpected places. The language of present-day Serbian poetry has reached an unprecedented stage of development. There is also a tendency among young poets to close themselves hermetically and guard their isolation fiercely.

BIBLIOGRAPHY

Barac, Antun. *A History of Yugoslav Literature*. Ann Arbor, Mich.: Joint Committee on Eastern Europe Publication Series, 1973. A standard history of all Yugoslav literatures and poetry, including Serbian, by a leading literary scholar. Although somewhat outdated, it still provides reliable information, especially of the older periods.

Debeljak, Aleš. "Visions of Despair and Hope Against Hope: Poetry in Yugoslavia in the Eighties." *World Literature Today* 68, no. 3 (1992): 191-194. Debeljak looks at poetry from the former Yugoslavia, including Serbian, on the eve of tumultuous events and changes in Yugoslavia in the 1990's. Poetry of the 1980's in some ways foreshadowed those events, giving vent to despair and forlorn hope.

Dragić Kijuk, Predrag R. Introduction to *Medieval and Renaissance Serbian Poetry*. Belgrade: Relations, 1987. This anthology provides an extremely valuable and lengthy introduction by Dragić Kijuk, an eminent authority on the subject, about all aspects of this significant period in Serbian poetry.

Holton, Milne, and Vasa D. Mihailovich. *Serbian Poetry from the Beginnings to the Present*. New Haven, Conn.: Yale Center for International and Area Studies, 1988. In this unique anthology, extensive introductions to the periods and individual poets offer not only a comprehensive overview of Serbian poetry but also succinct portraits of key poets.

Mikić, Radivoje. "On Significant Features of Modern Lyrical Speech." *Serbian Literary Quarterly*, nos. 1/2 (1995): 349-360. The author endeavors to define and analyze the neo-Symbolist tendencies in contemporary Serbian poetry.

Petrov, Aleksandar. "In the Stream of Time: Contemporary Serbian Poetry." *Literary Quarterly* 1, no. 2 (1965): 58-69. A sophisticated analysis of modern Serbian poetry by a leading contemporary Serbian literary critic and historian. Petrov addresses the modernistic tendencies of Serbian poetry, highlighting its greatest achievements.

Vasa D. Mihailovich

SLOVAK POETRY

Slovakia is the least known among the West Slavic group of nations: Poland, Bohemia, and Slovakia. That is also true of its poetry. The reasons for both are mainly historical. The Slovak nation dates its beginnings to the ninth century Great Moravian Empire that, in its flourishing under Svätopluk, included the territory of the former Czechoslovakia, southern Poland, parts of Austria, and most of Hungary. Attempts to Christianize this territory go back to the eighth century missions from the West, but it was in 863 that the apostles of the Slavs, Saints Cyril and Methodius, arrived from Constantinople with the Old Church Slavonic liturgy. In the tenth century, the Great Moravian Empire, after a period of decline, was defeated by the Magyars, and Slovakia became a part of the Kingdom of Hungary. Slovakia remained under Hungarian rule until 1918, when the new state of Czechoslovakia was established.

Slovak literature in general, and Slovak poetry in particular, reflect this tragic history. The lack of independence for more than a millennium forced Slovak poets, historians, and scientists to use other languages: Latin, Hungarian, German, and biblical Czech. While such literary works are usually mentioned in Slovak literary history, they are also claimed by others. There was, then, a long period when Slovak poets wrote their poetry predominantly in foreign languages: the Multilingual Period (tenth through sixteenth centuries). The Revival Period (1790-1863) saw a great flourishing of Slovak literature, especially of poetry. In the Period of Struggle (1863-1918), this revived literature met the challenge of Magyarization, the campaign by Hungarian authorities to stamp out the Slovak nationalist aspirations and to suppress the Slovak language. Large-scale emigration to America was one consequence of this harsh policy. The Modern Period (1918 to present) has been shaped by the increasing influence of foreign literary trends, by the ideological influence of the former Soviet Union, and by the resurgence of Catholic poetry.

MULTILINGUAL PERIOD (900-1790)

Slovak poetry did appear sporadically even in the multilingual context. Of crucial importance to Slovak poetry is the rich heritage of folk songs, some of which are of ancient origin. Also extant are a number of religious and historical songs; the latter describe military events resulting from Tatar (1241) and Turkish (sixteenth and seventeenth century) invasions of Slovakia. Descriptions of sackings of castles and fortresses predominate, as in *Muráó* (song about Murán castle) and *Modrý kameó* (song about Modrý Kameň castle), but there is also a more sophisticated poetry, based on the chivalrous epic, as in the ballad *Siládi a Hadmázi* (Siládi and Hadmázi), a tale of battle against the Turks. Most of these historical compositions are anonymous.

Of more importance are the religious songs. The popularity of this genre is attested by the approximately 150 editions of *Vithara sanctorum* (1636; the lyre of saintliness), a Protestant hymnal compiled by Juraj Tranovský (1591-1637). Among translations, this hymnal included Slovak songs still sung in Slovakia today. *Cithara sanctorum* was also tremendously influential as a manual of versification and therefore played an important role in the development of Slovak poetry. The establishment of the Jesuit University in Trnava further strengthened the use of Slovak for literary purposes; there Benedikt Szöllösi-Rybnický compiled a collection of songs, *Cantus catholici* (1655; Catholic hymnal), with more than two hundred songs in Slovak.

The Jesuit University of Trnava was not the first Slovak university; that honor goes to the Academia Istropolitana, founded in Bratislava in 1467, a center of Humanistic studies influenced by Western European Humanism. Slovaks who studied there published in Latin, but in Trnava, Slovak was encouraged and a number of historical, philosophical, and grammatical works appeared, supporting the national cause. Whether Protestant or Catholic, the poetry of the Baroque period was largely the work of priests. Indeed, a poet without a priestly vocation was a rarity; one such poet was Peter Benický (1603-1664), author of *Slovenské verše* (1652; Slovak poems).

A poet close to Benický and probably influenced by him was the Franciscan Hugolín Gavlovič (1712-1787), author of *Valaská šola* (1755; the shepherd's school), the most significant work of the Multilingual Period. A poem of some seventeen thousand lines, *Valaská škola* is divided into twenty-two cantos of fifty-nine "ideas" each, in three rhymed quatrains. The work is a compendium of genres: satire, fable, folk poetry, exemplum, and even social poetry.

A great disadvantage the poets of the period had to face was the absence of codified Slovak. Thus, some variety of Slovakized Czech was often used. Moreover, it was biblical Czech, derived from the standard Czech translation of the Bible, not the living, contemporary Czech language, which the Slovak poets used. In Slovakia, a variety of Slovak dialects vied for poets' attention. Of the three main dialect groups, Western, Central, and Eastern, Antonín Bernolák (1762-1813) championed the Western dialect in his pioneering *Grammatica slavica* (1790; Slovak grammar). It was not the best choice, but nevertheless Bernolák's work provided a basis for the systematic literary use of Slovak as an alternative to the artificial Slovakized Czech.

THE REVIVAL PERIOD (1790-1863)

Bernolák's Slovak was only a beginning, and there was quite a struggle ahead for the literary use of the Slovak language. Those who used Czech advanced the argument of unity to anyone suggesting the use of Slovak for literary purposes, while others would use Slovak, but not of Bernolák's variety—that is, they preferred another dialect. Thus, Jozef Ignác Bajza (1755-1836) published *Slovenské dvojnásobné epigramatá* (1794; Slovak double epigrams) in his own Slovak, using hexameter and pentameter in the first attempt to adapt classical prosody to Slovak poetry. Bajza's work was mercilessly criticized by Bernolák, and Bernolák's approach prevailed. An entire Bernolák movement appeared, first acting through the Learned Society, founded in 1792 and comprising some five hundred influential members throughout Slovakia. It is the Bernolák movement that must be credited with saving Slovakia from total assimilation. Bernolák also authored the monumental *Slovak-Czech-Latin-German-Hungarian Dictionary* (1825-1827), which runs to six volumes and more than five thousand pages.

After the generation of Bernolák and his followers, who prepared the soil with dictionaries and grammars, a generation of talented poets appeared. Pavel Jozef Šafárik

(1795-1861), the founder of Slavic studies, wrote a collection of poems, *Tatranská múza s lýrou slovanskou*

An equally important poet of this period was Ján Hollý (1785-1849), author of historical epics and beautiful nature lyrics. His epic trilogy, *Svatopluk* (1833), *Cyrilometodiada* (1835), and *Sláv* (1839), is a triumph of classicism, a happy marriage of history, legend, myth, and religion.

The poems of Kollár and Hollý were used to build up national consciousness. The new generation of revivalists found their inspiration in poetry. The Romantic movement in Slovak poetry coincided with the revival movement: Both were nurtured by Slovak classicism, with its Pan-Slavic ideal. Literary magazines and almanacs (such as *Hronka*, *Tatranka*, *Plody*) appeared to help the movement along.

The greatest figure of the revival movement was Ludovít Štúr (1815-1856). In 1843, he definitively solved the language problem by suggesting the Central Slovak dialect for the literary language. His suggestion was soon accepted, and today's Slovak is a modified form of Štúr's. Štúr published the first Slovak political newspaper, *Slovak National Newspaper*, with a literary supplement, *Orol Tatránski* (the eagle of Tatras). There, as well as in the almanac *Nitra*, Štúr's generation published the best poetry yet to appear in Slovakia. The remarkable group of poets associated with Štúr included Samo Chalúpka, Janko Král, Andrej Sládkovič, and Ján Botto. Štúr himself published a book of poetry, *Spevy a piesne* (1853; lyrics and songs).

Janko Král (1822-1876), more than any other Slovak poet, was the embodiment of Romanticism. His poetry, marked by strong balladic and folk elements, celebrates the outsider, the Romantic hero, and bristles with imagery derived from dreams and fairy tales, as in *Zakliata panna vo Váhu a divný Janko* (1844; the enchanted maiden in the river Váh and strange Janko). In the revolutionary year 1848, Král rushed to fight and, like Štúr and others, languished in disappointment over the failure of the revolution. The haunting, prophetic, and enchanting quality of Král's poetry is entirely his own.

Of the four great poets associated with Štúr, Andrej Sládkovič (1820-1872) has the distinction of having written the most beautiful and memorable poetry—poems that generations of students have memorized and loved. His *Marína* (1846) is a personification of the beauty of Slovakia and its language, as well as a deeply felt tribute to his beloved. His *Detvan* (1846), which tells of the freeing of a poor mountain boy from a certain punishment, is a parable of national liberation. Stylistically, Sládkovič's poetry is very original, and it exercised a significant influence on the next generation of poets.

Samo Chalúpka (1812-1883) and Ján Botto (1829-1881) are also numbered among the four great poets of the Štúr generation. Chalúpka, in *Spevy* (1868; songs), consciously revised the classical tradition of such heroic epics as Hollý's *Svatopluk*. Chalúpka's hero is anonymous or collective. Botto returned to the Jánošík epic with his *Smrt Jánošíková* (1862; the death of Jánošík), a work that is at once legendary, fantastic, exaggerated, and tragic. There is both grandeur and pathos here, as well as deeply satisfying beauty.

The beginning of the 1860's marked the end of Slovak Romanticism, although Slovakia's nationalistic ambitions had not been satisfied. A new period of reaction and national oppression was about to begin, coinciding with the advent of realistic conventions in prose and Symbolism in poetry.

THE PERIOD OF STRUGGLE (1863-1918)

In 1867, the political situation in Hungary (the northern part of which was Slovakia) radically changed for the worse: Minorities were held in disfavor, and Slovak nationalist aspirations were deemed treasonous.

The two leading poets of this period, particularly of the last two decades of the century, were Svetozár Hurban-Vajanský (1847-1916) and Pavol Orságh-Hviezdoslav (1849-1921). Vajanský, the author of *Tatry a more* (1879; the Tatras and the sea) and two other collections, was a journalist, novelist, and critic, as well as a poet. His first book of poems was a breakthrough and gained for him a wide readership, but his attempt to write a novel in verse was abandoned in favor of prose writing. Vajanský, though very interesting, is overshadowed by Hviezdoslav. Hviezdoslav's best-known work is *Krvavé sonety* (1914; bloody sonnets), but this collection alone does not permit a fair assessment of his lifework. Indeed his oeuvre, which includes lyric and epic poetry as well as drama, is of such variety and richness that it has no equal in Slovak literature. Among his epics, *Hájniková žena* (1844-1886; gamekeeper's wife) should be mentioned, and among his dramas, *Herod i Herodias* (1909).

Ludmila Podjavorinská (1872-1951) was the first significant female Slovak poet. She painstakingly documents the clash of Romantic and realistic worldviews in works such as *Po bále* (1903; after the ball), while her *Balady* (1930) takes up allegorical, symbolic, and tragic themes close in spirit to the Romantic school.

Podjavorinská in one way and Hviezdoslav in another seem to be poets of transition, ushering in the new poetic sensibility in Slovak literature known as *Moderna*. The main representative of this movement was Ivan Krasko (1876-1958), author of two slender collections: *Nox et solitudo* (1909) and *Verše* (1912). Another *Moderna* poet of note was Vladimír Roy (1885-1936), who, influenced by the power of Krasko's art, took the modernizing tendency even further, into the Modern Period.

THE MODERN PERIOD

Out of the ashes of the Austro-Hungarian Empire at the end of the World War I, a new state appeared: Czechoslovakia. Slovak national life was strengthened, despite the fact that the new government continued the nineteenth century fiction of a Czechoslovak nation, instead of two distinct nations of Czechs and Slovaks. Thus, the Slovak nationalist movement persisted and in 1939 a Slovak Republic was proclaimed under Nazi pressure and with a pro-Nazi government lasting until 1945, when the Czechoslovak Republic was reestablished. The communists took over the government through a coup in 1948, and only after the fall of communism in 1989 did the country manage to free itself of totalitarianism and become a democracy. In 1993 the Czech and Slovak Federation separated, and two states emerged: the Czech Republic and the Slovak Republic. This was an amicable divorce, arranged by the political elite.

Institutionally, Slovak culture received a tremendous boost with the reopening in 1919 of Matica Slovenská, a central cultural institution. Slovak schools were organized, from the elementary level to Comenius University, founded in 1919 in Bratislava with the help of

Czech professors. Thus the obligatory instruction in Hungarian ended, and Slovak poetry ceased to be the sole repository of Slovak cultural, national, and linguistic aspirations.

Enthusiasm, a sense of a new beginning, a desire to catch up with the rest of Europe—such was the prevailing mood of the period between the wars. Slovak poets became aware of a variety of foreign literary movements from which they borrowed eclectically without committing themselves wholly to a single program. The only exception is Surrealism. From the mid-1930's to the mid-1940's, this movement united poets, artists, and critics in a spontaneous manifestation of creative and aesthetic unity reminiscent of the efforts of the revivalist generation of Štúr. The older, more conservative, but at the same time best forum for Slovak literature during this period was the literary magazine *Slovenské pohľady* (Slovak views), founded in the nineteenth century (1846), Europe's oldest continuously published literary magazine.

Ján Smrek (1898-1982), the most popular and widely read Slovak poet of the twentieth century, began his career with an eclectic style influenced by French Symbolism and, to a lesser degree, Hungarian poetry. Soon, however, he formed his own vision: Sensuality, healthy eroticism, and the celebration of love and tenderness are his main characteristics, as in his *Básnik a žena* (1934; the poet and a woman). To these he added in later years melancholy reminiscences and the nostalgic celebration of women. The career of this Dionysian poet was complemented by that of the Apollonian poet Emil Boleslav Lukáč (1900-1979). While in Smrek's works, from *Básnik a žena* to the nostalgic *Obraz sveta* (1953; image of the world), the reader encounters the world of the senses—of the individual appreciating the happiness, beauty, and love of women—in Lukáč one finds the opposite. Lukáč was tormented by his philosophical musings, from his first collection, *Spoved* (1922; confession), to his highly personal *O láske neláskavej* (1928; on unkind love) to his late *Óda na poslednú a prvú* (1967; ode to the last and the first of Eumenides).

The third and perhaps the most eminent of this generation was Valentín Beniak (1894-1973). From his first collection, *Tiahnime dalej oblaky* (1928; clouds, let's move on), to his magisterial epic trilogy *Žofia* (1941;

Sophia), *Popolec* (1942; ashes), and *Igric* (1944; the minstrel), he experimented with language, style, and imagery, presenting a haunting, hallucinatory, and obsessively hypnotic vision of the world both distant and immediate, the world of war and love, of tormenting hopes and soul-searching. This fine Catholic poet was joined by an entire Catholic *Moderna* movement, including Pavol Gašparovic Hlbina (1908-1977) and Rudolf Dilong (1905-1986), a prolific and gifted author of mystical poetry who blended Fransiscan religiosity with Surrealist imagery, as in *Mladý svadobník* (1936; young member of the wedding party). They had many followers, particularly Mikuláš Šrinc (1914-1986) and Ján Silan (1914-1984).

The first important Surrealist work in Slovak poetry was *Utaté ruky* (1935; severed hands), by Rudolf Fábry (1915-1982). The most talented of the Slovak Surrealists proved to be Stefan Žáry (born 1918), whose *Pečat plných amfór* (1944; the seal of full amphoras) expresses the tragedy of uprooted modern humanity at the mercy of wars and ideologies and suffering from lack of love. Vladimír Reisel (born 1919), Pavol Horov (1914-1975), and others also published fine Surrealist poetry, giving the movement a strong foundation. This potential could have resulted in a richer harvest had it not been for the official disbanding of the movement following the communist takeover after 1948.

The proletarian school of Slovak poets was influenced by the Czech poet Jiří Wolker (1900-1924) as much as by the socialist ideals and the Russian Revolution of 1917. The most talented of the group of the so-called *DAV* poets (named after their magazine) was Ladislav Novomeský (1904-1976), as his *Svätý za dedinou* (1935; a patron saint behind the village) shows.

Ludo Ondrejov (1901-1962) brought into his poems the untamed world of folk poetry, especially in his *Pijanské piesne* (1941; drinking songs). Folk poetry also influenced such poets as Andrej Plávka (1907-1982) and Ján Kostra (1910-1975).

The decade of the 1960's was a time of experimentation and of a departure from the sterile dictates of the Socialist Realism imported from the Soviet Union. A strong group of "concretist" poets, gathered under the leadership of Miroslav Válek (1927-1991), included such poets as Ján Ondruš (born 1932), Ján Stacho, and

Lubomír Feldek (born 1936), all of whom turned away from Socialist Realism toward the heritage of the Western avant-garde and modernism. Válek's collection of his four early collections, *Štyri knihy nepokoja* (1971; four books of unease) documents his search for an original voice, as well as the initial schematic beginnings to which he returns in his last period.

Beginning in the late 1950's, Milan Rúfus (born 1928), the strongest Slovak voice of the second half of the twentieth century, began to be noticed. His most important work, collected in *Básne* (1972, revised 1975; poems), represents a different path from the one taken by the concretists. Rúfus is purposefully antimodern in the sense that it is not the avant-garde that inspires him, but rather his rural background, his family and the Bible with its imagery. Rúfus has successfully integrated his religiosity in his work and managed to find a form acceptable to the authorities. After the fall of communism, the religious component of his work becane even more pronounced.

Before the end of the century another movement of poets of different orientations appeared, the "lonely runners": Ivan Laucík (born 1944), Peter Repka (born 1944), and particularly Ivan Štrpka (born 1944). Their roots are in the 1960's and in the protest against stale schematic poetry. A poet of Dionysian character who experimented with language and celebrated the Western Slovak region of Záhorie with panache and genius as a counterpart to the "lonely runners" is Štefan Moravcík (born 1943). Moravcík chose the world of senses, of eroticism, and above all the world of nature over the world of the decaying order of the 1980's, beginning

with his first collection, *Slávnosti baránkov* (1969; the feast of the lambs). His Záhorie is a refuge as well as a fount of inspiration for his playful linguistic experimentation. This tendency to excess continues with Ivan Kolenic (born 1965), whose stress on hedonism and intimate relationships is actually an attempt to build an autarchic world of the senses uncontaminated by ideology, as demonstrated in his *Prinesené búrkou* (1986; brought by the storm). Thus, the Modern Period demonstrates that Slovak poetry, which long served as a repository of a subjugated people's hopes and dreams, remains a vital force as the twenty-first century begins.

BIBLIOGRAPHY

Cincura, Andrew, comp. *An Anthology of Slovak Literature*. Riverside, Calif.: University Hardcovers, 1976.

Kirschbaum, J. M. *Slovak Language and Literature*. Cleveland, Ohio: University of Manitoba, Dept. of Slavic Studies, 1975.

Kramoris, Ivan Joseph, ed. *An Anthology of Slovak Poetry: A Selection of Lyric and Narrative Poems and Folk Ballads in Slovak and English*. Scranton, Ohio: Orbana Press, 1947.

Manning, Clarence A., ed. *An Anthology of Czechoslovak Poetry*. New York: Columbia University Press, 1929.

Petro, Peter. *A History of Slovak Literature*. Toronto: McGill-Queens University Press, 1995.

Selver, Paul, ed. and trans. *A Century of Czech and Slovak Poetry*. London: New Europe Publishing, 1946.

Peter Petro

SLOVENIAN POETRY

The Slovenes, a small Slavic nation at the northwestern edge of the former Yugoslavia, have had a very unhappy history. One of the first among the Slavic peoples to have their own independent state (in the eighth century), they were the first to lose it (to Germanic tribes in the ninth century). They remained under German or Austrian domination until 1918—a period of almost a thousand years. It is not surprising that under such conditions Slovenian culture could not develop properly; indeed, it is a miracle that it survived. Like their South Slavic brethren, the Slovenes began their literature during their conversion to Christianity, in the ninth century, but the work among them of the disciples of the missionaries Cyril and Methodius was of such short duration that it left no lasting literary documents. Indeed, until the Reformation, very little Slovenian literature was preserved. Among the few pieces that have survived are church and ritual songs, troubadour lyrics, and folk poems, all of which are anonymous; most of them are translations, preserved only because they were interspersed in German texts.

EARLY POETRY

The Reformation in the sixteenth century produced some poetry, mostly connected with the Church. Indeed, for many centuries, the clergy alone sustained Slovenian culture. It was not until 1689 that the first Slovenian secular poem, by Jozef Zizenčeli, was recorded. It was only in the second half of the eighteenth century, under the enlightened absolutist rulers of Austria, that Slovenian literature began to develop. The poetry contained in three almanacs, the so-called *Pisanice* (1779-1781), marked the first noteworthy attempt at genuine poetry in Slovenian. Although much of this poetry was highly derivative, it was written by Slovenes in their own language, which had been suppressed for centuries.

The first poet to write in the native tongue was Valentin Vodnik (1758-1819), usually considered to be the founder of Slovenian poetry. After unsure beginnings in *Pisanice*, he published two books of poetry, *Pesmi za pokušino* (1806; poetic attempts) and *Pesmi za brambovce* (1809; poems to the defenders). Vodnik discarded foreign models and took Slovenian folk poetry as the basis for his language, meter, and even subject matter. He greeted Napoleon's creation of Illyria, in which the western Southern Slavs were united for the first time since their common arrival in the Balkans. Enthusiastic about the opportunities for education and liberation of his people promised at the beginning of the nineteenth century, he encouraged his mostly peasant nation to work and fight for its betterment. After Napoleon's demise, Vodnik lost his position and soon died, but not before he had laid the foundations for Slovenian poetry, inspiring his followers to use the people's language. He also was a forerunner of the Slovenian Romantic movement, which would have been unthinkable without his contribution.

NINETEENTH CENTURY

Slovenia produced its greatest poet in France Prešeren (1800-1849), interestingly enough at about the same time time as other Slavic literatures produced their greatest—Aleksandr Pushkin in Russia, Adam Bernard Mickiewicz in Poland, and Petar Petrovič Njegoš in Montenegro, for example. The son of a peasant, Prešeren broke with many traditions: Instead of entering the priesthood, he studied law in Vienna; instead of writing religious and didactic literature, he expressed his own thoughts and feelings, particularly about love; instead of limiting himself to the narrow confines of a small nation, he employed classical, Renaissance, Romantic, and even Oriental forms and metrics and endeavored to write poetry at the world level. His *Sonetni venec* (1834; the wreath of sonnets) shows a remarkable maturity for a young poet from a hitherto unknown nation. Although it deals primarily with his unhappy love affair and resulting suffering, it also declares, in an astonishingly developed Slovenian language, his love for, and faith in, his nation. It is this combination of the personal, the national, and the universal that lends Prešeren's poetry its power and poignancy. The epic poem *Krst pri Savici* (1836; the baptism on the Savica) underscores his preoccupation with the fate of his people, represented by a pagan leader who resists conversion to Christianity until his love for his betrothed leads him to it. It is generally thought that this epic signifies the poet's own defeat at the hands of many enemies (the foreign-dominated clergy and the narrow-minded, middle-class cultural officials). Prešeren's last book, *Poezije* (1847; poems), voices the pessimism that marked the last years of his life. The unity of form and subject matter in this work, the genuineness of the poet's feelings, the purity of his language, and the clarity of his ideas combine to distinguish this masterpiece, a work unequaled in Slovenian literature before or since.

Prešeren's achievements opened the gate for a number of excellent poets during the Romantic era. At the head of this group was Fran Levstik (1831-1887). Although not a poet of Prešeren's stature, he wrote sincere poetry about his personal misfortunes in love and in life generally, for he was often misunderstood and persecuted by conservative critics. Josip Stritar (1836-1923), also a son of a peasant family, fortunately did not have to spend most of his energy fighting the powers that be. Of a more practical nature, he spent his life educating his people and traveling in Europe. His main contribution lies in the field of literary education through critical writings. His predominantly pessimistic poetry is augmented by high artistry. Another Romantic poet, Simon Jenko (1835-1869), also wrote love poetry, severely criticized by the conservatives for its alleged eroticism. In addition, he wrote patriotic poems, one of which, "Naprej zastava slave" (onward, the banner of glory), became the Slovenian national anthem. Jenko's poetry is characterized by pure lyricism, youthful enthusiasm, kinship with folk lyrics, and closeness to nature, although his later verse is dominated by a melancholy realization of the transience of life. The last noteworthy Slovenian Romantic, Simon Gregorčič (1844-1906), followed more or less in the footsteps of others. He, too, sang of love and of the harsh lot of his people. Forced into the priesthood, he felt confined and unable to express himself freely except in his poetry, for which he was heavily criticized. The immediacy, freshness, and warmth of his poetry make him a very popular poet to this day.

By the closing decades of the nineteenth century, Romanticism in Slovenian literature had run its course, and a more realistic literature took its place, along with similar movements in the Serbian and Croatian literatures and under similar influences—French and Russian. Like the poetry of those other Slavic literatures, Slovenian poetry did not fare well in this period, with the exception of one poet worthy of note, Anton Aškerc (1856-1912). Another priest, author of numerous books of ballads and romances, of lyric and epic poems, Aškerc reflected in his poetry the changing spirit of the times. Instead of voicing private concerns in an overly subjective manner, as the previous generation had done, he raised his voice in support of social changes. Instead of sentimentality and passive pessimism, he called for a struggle against the enemies of his people, not necessarily always foreigners. In order to bolster his pleas and arguments, he borrowed motifs from Slovenian history as well as from that of other nations. He was and remains a very popular poet.

MODERNISM

At the turn of the century, Slovenian poetry, like that of other Slavic literatures, was transformed by a strong modernistic movement led by several strong personalities. The first of these, and perhaps the greatest writer in Slovenian literature, was Ivan Cankar (1876-1918). A great fiction writer and playwright, he made his debut with a book of poems, *Erotika* (1899; erotica). There is in these poems little of the fiery activism in the service of social justice that he would later espouse, yet they are indicative of his future development. They shocked the establishment by their boldness and directness, if not by their artistic quality. Another modernist, Dragotin Kette (1876-1899), died too young to develop fully his poetic talent. In his only book of poetry, *Poezije* (1900; poems), he revealed himself as a genuine lyricist of an openhearted, direct, and cheerful disposition. His sonnets are proof of his knowledge of world literature and of his artistic promise. Josip Murn Aleksandrov (1879-1901) also died young (of the same disease and in the same room as Kette) and consequently never achieved his full potential. He began as a poet of the countryside idyll, but the premonition of death colored his outlook with premature melancholy. Most of his poems are impressionistic sketches that captivate the reader with their directness and genuine feeling. By far the greatest modernist poet was Oton Župančič (1878-1949). He was born in a village but, through schooling and traveling, developed into a cosmopolitan intellectual and managed to be at home in both the city and the country. During his career of almost five decades, he assumed a wide variety of literary attitudes: The freewheeling modernist became a contemplative aesthete who measured every word and thought. His first book, *Čaša opojnosti* (1899; a cup of bliss), is marked by restlessness, decadent sensualism, and unbridled individualism, while his last, *Zimzelen pod snegom* (1945; evergreen under the snow), expresses his love and concern for his homeland during the struggle against the enemy in World War II. Between these two poles lies a steadily improving artistry that eventually made him the second-best Slovenian poet, after Prešeren.

Srečko Kosovel (1904-1926) is considered the best Slovenian poet of the interwar period. Like so many of his fellow writers, he died too young to achieve his full potential, but he succeeded in writing a number of powerful expressionistic poems in which he combined a total experience of life with a premonition of death, not only his own but also that of the European intellectual. Alojz Gradnik (1882-1967) was similarly preoccupied with death, but he also wrote about the power of love, about the love of his country, and about the meaning of life. Gradnik stands high among Slovenian poets of all time.

LATE TWENTIETH CENTURY

The traumatic experiences of World War II and the ensuing years of difficult reconstruction left little room for the development of poetry, particularly because the older poets who had survived the war were not heard from again. It was left to the new generation to revive poetry, although not necessarily to continue prewar traditions. In a relatively short time, a number of new poets arrived on the scene. Of these, Matej Bor (pseudonymn of Vladimir Pavšič, born 1911) won fame with his war poetry, in which he proved himself to be the most engaged of contemporary Slovenian poets. He shows a similar attitude in later poems about heroes and the dangers of the atomic age. Edvard Kocbek (1904-1981) wrote sparingly, but his poems reveal a completely contemporary spirit which draws him closer to young poets such as Tomaž Šalamun (born 1941) than to older figures such as Bor. Kocbek's well-crafted poems, quiet in tone, cast an ironic eye on the world. His is not the irony

of a man who feels superior to what he sees, but rather that of a man who is an endless victim, tied to the very thing he abhors.

Of the younger poets, Ciril Zlobec, Dane Zajc, Cene Vipotnik, and Gregor Strniša signal a decisive change. Zlobec (born 1924) began as a neo-Romantic, exploring the traditional themes of love and loss of childhood. Later, he turned to the problems of contemporary society and the individual. Zajc (born 1929) similarly shows a strong individualistic attitude unhindered by the burden of war trauma. In that sense, his poetry breaks with that of revolutionary Romanticism. Instead, one finds in his poetry Symbolist tendencies, and his subject matter is the loneliness and the resulting negation of man. Vipotnik (born 1914), who made his debut rather late, was first influenced by the war but has moved in his recent works toward a more private, lyric poetry with love as its main focus. Gregor Strniša (1930-1987), a unique and highly articulate poet, has developed an original and easily recognizable style. His reaction to the fear and alienation of modern man is expressed through elaborate historical allegories and dream sequences, cyclically arranged. Each cycle revolves around a central metaphor, the dialectic of which is then explored with economy and precision of expression. There is a desire here to mythologize, not too far removed in spirit from that of Serbian poet Vasko Popa.

Other significant poets writing in the 1980's and 1990's were Tone Pavček (born 1928), Kajetan Kovič (born 1931), Veno Taufer (born 1933), and Tomaž Šalamun. In some respects, these were the most experimental poets writing in the former Yugoslavia. While Croatian and Serbian poets were often torn between their native tradition and the need "to make it new," these Slovenian poets seem to have completely committed themselves to discovering a modern style. Taufer and Šalamun are by far the most radical experimenters, and Taufer appears to be the more calculating of the two. The strategies of his poems reveal a close knowledge of modern art and literature. Šalamun's poems, on the other hand, have an associative quality that gives the impression of automatic writing. What ties them together and gives them their inevitability is his keen sense of the organism of the poem with all of its verbal and lyric connotations. Consequently, the apparent chaos of Šalamun's poems is a ruse, a freeing agent, for his poems never fail to drive their meaning home. Šalamun and Taufer, with their creative freedom and adventurousness, initiated a new beginning for Slovenian poetry.

BIBLIOGRAPHY

Barac, Antun. *A History of Yugoslav Literature.* Ann Arbor, Mich.: Joint Committee on Eastern Europe Publication Series, 1973. A standard history of all Yugoslav literatures and poetry, including Slovenian, by a leading literary scholar. Although somewhat outdated, it still provides reliable information, especially of the older periods.

Biggins, Michael. "Slovenian Poetic Tradition and Edvard Kocbek." *Litterae Slovenicae* 33, no. 2 (1995): 9-18. Biggins looks at the Slovenian poetic traditions as embodied in the poetry of the greatest contemporary Slovenian poet Edvard Kocbek.

Cesar, Ivan. "In the Beginning Was a Sign: Contemporary Slovene Poetry." *Slovene Studies* 7, nos. 1/2 (1985): 13-22. An expert survey of contemporary Slovene poetry.

Debeljak, Aleš. "Visions of Despair and Hope Against Hope: Poetry in Yugoslavia in the Eighties." *World Literature Today* 68, no. 3 (1992): 191-194. Debeljak looks at Yugoslav poetry, including Slovenian, on the eve of tumultuous events and changes in Yugoslavia in the 1990's. Poetry of the 1980's in some ways foreshadowed those events, giving vent to despair and forlorn hope.

Kalan, Filip. *The Problems of Slovene Poetry Today.* Ljubljana: Slovenian Writers' Association, 1965. A frank discussion of Slovenian poetry in the second half of the twentieth century, evaluating its achievements and pointing out the problems it had to face.

Ožbalt, Irma M. "Slovene Poetry in English: Challenges and Problems." *Acta Neophilologica* 27 (1994): 67-74. Ožbalt discusses the state of the translation of Slovene poetry into English and achievements and problems connected with it.

Vasa D. Mihailovich

SPANISH POETRY TO 1400

The development of Spanish poetry through the fourteenth century is a facet of what Ramón Menéndez Pidal, the preeminent Spanish medievalist, called *frutos tardios* (late fruits). Extant manuscripts from this period are few in number, and their condition is generally poor, but their literary quality is very high. Although this essay will focus on poetry written in Spanish, it is important to note that, during this rich period in the cultural history of Spain, significant poetry was written in other languages as well—notably the Arabic-Hebraic *jarchas*, the Galician *cantigas de amigo*, and Catalan lyric verse. Just as many consider modern Spain a quilt of five distinct national patterns (Galacian, Basque, Catalan, Andalusian, and Castilian), so medieval Spain was a mosaic of regional political entities—Asturian, Galician, Leonese, Castilian, Navarrese, Aragonese, and Catalonian, to name a few—as well as racial and religious patterns: Christian, Jewish, and Muslim.

EIGHTH THROUGH TENTH CENTURIES

The Moorish invasion of 711 and the virtual conquest of the Iberian Peninsula by the year 718 left the Hispano-Visigothic kingdom in disarray. Many of the conquered Visigoths were absorbed into Islamic culture (they became known as *mozarabes*), while others retreated into the protective mountain ranges of the northern Cantabrian coastline. From the latter came the Reconquest, a seven-century-long effort to recapture the Peninsula. Isolated pockets of resistance to Moorish domination grew into kingdoms with competing priorities and interests involving territory, preeminence of power, and collection of taxes as well as the cultural variables, such as language and literature, that made each of them distinct. Intriguingly, Galicia, Castile, León, Navarre, Aragon, and Catalonia all developed separate linguistic traditions, but only Galicia, Castile, and Catalonia produced literatures that have survived. While much medieval knowledge was hoarded and hidden to benefit a specific interest, language and literature were much more democratic; every bard, *juglar*, or *jongleur* needed to keep his material fresh, and the subsequent give-and-take of poetic style and vocabulary crossed from one language to another and from one culture to another. Medieval Spanish poetry is the product of these many influences.

The development of the Spanish language followed a path distinct from that of other languages of the Iberian Peninsula. With a tendency toward simplification of sounds and forms, Castilian standardized its grammar and vocabulary very early, making possible, for example, the reading of eleventh and twelfth century documents by an untrained twentieth century eye. (By comparison, the fourteenth century English of Geoffrey Chaucer's *The Canterbury Tales* is resistant to the untrained modern reader.) The early formation of Spanish clearly had an effect on Spanish literature, as did the pioneer environment of its origin. Artificial attempts have been made to differentiate Castilian from Spanish. In the purest of senses, Castilian can be distinguished as a dialect with its marked peculiarities, but it exerted its dominion over an entire peninsula and subsequently, the New World, thereby becoming the language of Spain.

ELEVENTH CENTURY: BEGINNINGS

The extraordinary and controversial beginning of Spanish verse must be assigned to the *kharjas*. Written in Arabic and Hebrew script—hence the controversy concerning their "Spanishness"—these refrains served as transitional passages between longer classical Arab stanzas known as *muwassahas*. When one transliterates *kharjas* into Roman characters and adds the missing vowels, the resulting text is clearly an archaic form of Spanish. Thus, according to Alan Deyermond, the refrain

> tnt' m'ry tnt' m'ry hbyb tnt' m'ry
> 'nfrmyrwn wlyws gyds(?) ydwln tn m'ly

becomes

> Tant' amare, tant' amare habib, tant' amare
> enfermiron welyos nidios e dolen tan male.
> (My love is so great, my love is so great
> Lover, my love is so great
> My healthy eyes have sickened
> And hurt so badly)

In a 1948 article that constituted the first systematic study of the *kharjas*, S. M. Stern demonstrated that a Spanish vocabulary lies hidden in the Arabic and Hebrew script of these refrains. Stern's discovery revolutionized critical understanding of the origins of Spanish verse—and, indeed, of European lyric verse. Dámaso Alonso, the distincguished Spanish poet and critic, refers to these verses as the "early spring" of the European lyric, for they predate by a century the earliest poems written in Provence.

The content of the *kharjas* is almost invariably love-oriented. Like the example quoted above, many of these refrains express the pain of separation, the sense of hurt as a result of a lover's absence or infidelity; others employ "love" as a metaphor for the relationship between a poet and his patron. Since these verses were written as transitional passages between longer texts and rarely can stand on their own as expressions of a complete sentiment, their acceptance as the earliest form of the European lyric has been questioned. On the other hand, their beauty and compactness of expression reflect the existence of a tradition of popular song or cultured verse, or both, in the Spanish eleventh century.

TWELFTH CENTURY: TEXTUAL DESERT

Study of Spanish poetry in the twelfth century is hampered by a scarcity of texts. Despite the lack of texts, however, it is clear that lyric traditions were well established by the twelfth century. This is confirmed not only by the *kharjas* but also by two other verse forms which appeared in this century: the Galician-Portuguese *cantigas* and the Castilian *villancicos*. The *cantigas*, which have survived in three *cancioneros* (songbooks), of the fifteenth century, fall into three categories: a woman's lament for her lover (*cantigas de amigo*); a man's lament (*cantigas de amor*); and invective verse (*cantigas d'escarnho*). The similarity of content (lament for a lover) and speaker (a woman) between the *cantigas de amigo* and the *kharjas* suggests a connection, though none has been established.

Villancicos, multiverse refrains, repeated before and after every stanza, were not written down until the fifteenth century but are generally considered to date from the twelfth century. Their similarity to the *kharjas* is striking: They share a similar structure (refrain), content (lament for a lover), and speaker (a woman).

THIRTEENTH CENTURY: POETS AND MONKS

Thirteenth century Spanish poetry is notable for the genesis of native epic verse; unfortunately, scholars of the thirteenth century Spanish epic have barely five thousand lines of text with which to work, in comparison to the million lines of verse available to French medieval scholars. Adducing plot summaries in later chronicles, some critics postulate the existence of lost epics, while others suggest that many poems of epic nature were never written down because of their oral means of transmission. In any case, Spanish scholarship has been left with four national epic poems: *Cantar de mío Cid* (early thirteenth century; *Poem of the Cid*), *Las mocedades de Rodrigo* (fourteenth century), and *Cantar de Roncesvalles* (thirteenth century; *Song of Roland*), composed in traditional epic meter (assonant lines of fourteen to sixteen syllables), and *Poema de Fernán Gonzalez* (c. 1260), composed in *cuaderna vía*, a syllabic meter distinguished by its rigidity of form.

The single most important epic composition of the thirteenth century was *Poem of the Cid*. Like the other epics of its period, *Poem of the Cid* is the subject of ongoing critical debate concerning the nature of its composition. The so-called traditionalist critics argue that the Spanish epic originated in popular culture, in the songs of traveling entertainers or *juglares*. The most popular of these traditional songs, so the theory goes, were set down in manuscript and preserved for future generations. In contrast, the so-called individualist critics believe that the great epics of medieval Spain were the work of individual poets, shaped by individual genius. Finally, the oralist critics argue that the epics of this period were transmitted exclusively by oral performance and were not committed to writing until a later date.

A manuscript of *Poem of the Cid* does exist, yet a gap in the transcription of the date, "MCC VII," has convinced the traditionalists that the date of composition was actually 1307. On the other hand, the individualists see the gap as typical of scribal transcription and build an argument for a date of 1207. Traditionalists argue that Per Abad, the name appearing at the end of the manuscript, refers to a copyist, while the individualists suggest that he was the actual author of the epic. In *The Making of the "Poema de mío Cid"* (1983), a book C. C. Smith calls "bold," Smith affirms that his work

> . . . is the first in which the following proposition is argued: that the *Poema de mío Cid*, composed in or shortly before 1207, was the first epic to be composed in Castilian; that it was in consequence an innovatory and experimental work, in ways apparent in the surviving text; and that it did not depend on any precedents or existing tradition of epic verse in Castilian or other Peninsular language or dialect.

Smith goes on to assert that Per Abad was the actual author of the poem, not merely the copyist. Regardless of the exact method of composition of *Poem of the Cid*, however, it seems reasonable to assume that *juglares* sang verse narratives of this type, commemorating historical events and following a general, though loose, metric pattern.

Composed in traditional Spanish epic meter, *Poem of the Cid* is the story of a nobleman who is banished from the kingdom of Castile, survives the rigors of exile by defeating Moorish forces and fending off Christian encroachments on his territories, and finally achieves renown by conquering the Caliphate of Valencia. The work is divided into three *cantares*, or "tales," which highlight the rise and fall of the Cid's fortunes.

A powerful noble, the Cid is banished when King Alfonso VI of Castile heeds the insidious rumors of the Cid's enemies. Feudal relationships in the poem are not clear, and the reader is left with the impression that the two hundred men who join the Cid in exile do so of their own free will. The Cid leaves his wife, Jimena, and his two daughters, Sol and Blanca, in the monastery of San Pedro de Cardeña for safekeeping.

The second division of the poem, the *Cantar de Bodas*, relates the Cid's triumph in his struggle to survive. Fighting Moor and Christian alike, he multiplies his fortune and his prestige. With the conquest of Valencia and the betrothal of his daughters to the sons of the Count de Carrión, a match specifically arranged by the King of Castile, it appears that the Cid's achievements are complete.

In a masterful juxtaposition of villainy and nobility, however, the third division of the poem, the *Cantar de Corpes*, plays havoc with the Cid's world prior to a resolution in the final verses. The engagement of the Cid's daughters to future counts is an extraordinary achievement, given his status as a middle-line noble, yet the *Cantar de Corpes* reveals the cowardice, egotism, and greed of the de Carrión brothers. The brothers, known as the Infantes, decide that their wives are not worthy of them; but they do not want to lose their dowries. Convincing the Cid that it is time to return to Carrión, the Infantes, once well away from Valencia, take their wives into a secluded glade, beat and strip them, and leave them to die. Fortunately, a retainer, disobeying the Infantes' orders to stay away from the area, rescues them.

The conclusion of the poem celebrates the triumph of civilizing order over brutality justified by birth. Instead of pursuing and punishing the Infantes, the Cid appeals to Alfonso VI, who by this time has come to consider the Cid an equal, to summon a convocation of nobles to judge his accusations against the Infantes. In the trial, the arrogant brothers are stripped of honor: First, the Cid demands that his swords be returned by the Infantes, then the dowry of his daughters; finally, the Cid accuses the brothers of *menos-valer*, or "less worthiness." The Infantes, enraged at this affront, call for a duel and subsequently lose to the Cid's champions. As the crowning glory to the Cid's success and the triumph of judicial process, emissaries from Navarre and Aragon appear, requesting the hands of the Cid's daughters for their kings.

Poem of the Cid is a monument to the individual whose dedication to right values is ultimately rewarded and whose salient qualities are protection of his family, generosity to all, religious devotion, and loyalty to the established order. The Cid's concern for his family is presented early in the poem as he leaves them in the care of the monks at San Pedro de Cardeña, promising to reward them richly. Parting causes such anguish in him that the poet observes that "parten unos d'otros como la uña de la carne" (they part like a fingernail pulling away from the skin).

The oldest manuscript of the poem signed by the enigmatic Per Abad, is missing the first folio and two others within the work. The meter, as has been noted, is traditional to Spanish epics: mono-rhymic assonance lines divided into half by a caesura and normally totaling fourteen syllables, though the irregularity of the meter, as shown in the third line of the following passage, is a puzzle to critics.

> Dezidle al Campeador, que en buen hora nasco,
> que destas siet sedmanas adobes con sos vassallos,
> vengam a Toledo, estol do de plazdo
> Por amor de mío Cid esta cort yo fago.
> (Say to the Campeador he who was born in good hour
> to be ready with his vassals seven weeks from now
> and come to Toledo; that is the term I set for him
> Out of love for My Cid I call this court together.)

The verse of *Poem of the Cid* is characterized by the oral qualities of the *mester de juglaría* (minstrel's meter, the meter of the *juglares*). It is instructive to compare this form with the *mester de clerecía* (clergy's meter), an almost exclusively thirteenth century verse form. While the *mester de juglaría* allows, along with its oral formulas, considerable freedom, resulting in verse with a tentative, experimental flavor, the *mester de clerecía* is highly formalized. The term *mester de clerecía* is often used interchangeably with the name of the meter in which verse so designated was generally written, *cuaderna vía*. A rigidly structured syllabic verse form, *cuaderna vía* is composed of four-line stanzas; each line must be fourteen syllables long, with a caesura exactly in the middle and a full rhyme of *aaaa*. The demanding rigidity of the form is evident in the following example, as presented by Germán Bleiberg (1915-1990), from the *Libro de Alexandre* (c. 1240; book of Alexander):

> Mester traigo fermoso, non es de juglaría
> mester es sin pecado ca es de clerecía
> fablar curso rimado por la cuaderna vía,
> a sílabas contadas que es de gran maestría
> (A beautiful skill I bring, it is not of the singers:
> a skill without sin since it comes from churchmen.
> To follow a rhymed course using the four verse way
> by counted syllables that requires great mastery.)

Another example of the *mester de clerecía* is a work in the hagiographic tradition, the *Vida de Santa Marîa Egipcíaca* (thirteenth century; life of Saint Maria the Egyptian), but curiously enough, it is not composed in *cuaderna vía*. The poem is a rendition of the legend of an Egyptian prostitute who, after a lifetime of dissipation, converts to Christianity when two angels deny her entrance to the temple at Jerusalem. While artistically the poem does not represent a significant advance, the clear expression of the craft of the *mester de clerecía* makes worthwhile reading. The author was able to adapt a Latin source to Spanish in a learned yet popular style; numerous learned words are integrated into the text without disturbing the poet's rapport with his audience.

The first major poet to use *cuaderna vía* as a distinguishing characteristic of his work was Gonzalo de Berceo (c. 1190-after 1250), a secular priest. Born around the end of the twelfth century, his name probably reflects his birthplace, the village of Berceo in the province of La Rioja. Information about his death is equally sketchy, and internal evidence in his poetry suggests that he died after 1250.

Gonzalo de Berceo's work can be categorized into three groups: hagiographic poems commemorating the Spanish saints Millán, Domingo, and Oria; devotional poems dedicated to the Virgin Mary; and doctrinal works related to apocalyptic material and the symbolism of the Mass; in addition, three hymns are attributed to him. His best-known works, however, are his poems about the Virgin Mary, particularly the *Milagros de Nuestra Señora* (c. 1252; the miracles of Our Lady).

The relationship between man and the Virgin Mary in the *Milagros de Nuestra Señora* could be described as maternal vassalage. The theme of the work is not obscure; those who show devotion and loyalty to the Virgin Mary will be rewarded, saved from peril or death, and even have their souls rescued from Hell.

The poem relates twenty-five miracles performed by the Virgin Mary, adapted from a Latin manuscript collection. The opening lines describe an allegorical *locus amoenus*. After calling on his "amigos e vasallos de Dios" ("friends and vassals of God") to listen, he writes:

> Yo maestro Gonçalvo de Verçeo nomnado
> Idendo en romeria caeçi en un prado
> Verde e bien sençido, de flores bien poblado,
> Logar cobdiçieduero pora omne cansado.
> (I, master Gonzalo of Berceo by name
> While out walking I lay down in a field
> Green and lush, with abundant flowers
> A comforting place for a tired man.)

The story of the second miracle presents a good example of Berceo's art. Presented in a simple, straightforward progression of events, the narrative deals with a monk who demonstrated his devotion to the Virgin Mary by kneeling in front of her statue and reciting an "Ave Maria" every time he passed. A demon, "a vicar of Beelzebub," corrupted him with lust at night, and the monk began to wander, though every time he passed the statue of the Virgin, he would kneel and pray. One night, after an escapade, he fell into a river and drowned.

At this point, the story becomes a metaphysical dispute between devils and angels for the wayward monk's soul. The Virgin Mary intervenes, citing his devotion to her statue, but she is challenged by the chief devil, who reminds her that dogma decrees that whatever state of grace exists at death determines a man's life after death. The Virgin refuses to argue and calls upon Jesus to resolve the problem; the solution is the revival of the monk, who dies much later after a long life of devotion to the Virgin.

Stylistically, Berceo's verse is measured, consistent, and reminiscent of several traits of the *mester de juglaría:* direct address, enjambment, and popular vocabulary. Indeed, the poem's diction is remarkably non-Latinate, even though the topic is religious; for example, Berceo uses the word *beneito*, a vulgarized form of *benedictino*, for the term "Benedictine."

Berceo's authorship has also been claimed for the *Libro de Alexandre*, a poem of 2,675 lines composed in *cuaderna vía* around 1240. The importance of the *Libro de Alexandre* cannot be dismissed; it is the longest epic poem of the thirteenth century, in addition to being the only survivor of Spanish verse epics about antiquity. Its artistic merit is substantial as well. In his 1934 edition, Raymond S. Willis notes that

> . . . the poem is not an artless assemblage, but a well contrived and coherent whole. The poetic gift and charm of its author, even though distorted by our present corrupt manuscripts, can be discerned as considerable. And, finally, this epic is a symposium of much of the erudition of the period and a mirror of contemporary life, thought, and language.

The *Libro de Alexandre* is a pageant of figures of antiquity across an epic stage. The poem begins with the birth and childhood of Alexander, with Aristotle playing a major role as adviser, councillor, and teacher. When his father, Philip, dies, Alexander's succession is challenged in Athens and Thebes, and, immediately after his coronation, he is forced to put down rebellions in those cities.

The core of the story is the conflict between Alexander and another great figure of antiquity, his rival Darius of Persia. Alexander's success in Macedonia and Greece moves him to challenge the persistent Persian threat, and he crosses the Hellespont to invade Asia Minor. The ensuing battles cast Alexander more and more in the role of a demigod. He creates the Twelve Peers, cuts the Gordian Knot, defeats Darius twice, captures Persepolis, and presides at Darius's funeral. The steady encroachment of the pathos of power on Alexander's character is developed in this central part of the epic, preparing the reader or listener for the conclusion.

Alexander cannot stop his conquests. Even though the pressure to return home is ever-growing, he alternately harangues and leads his men to defeat the Hyrcanians and the Scythians and to conquer the subcontinent of India. The element of fantasy also grows in the narrative: Alexander is visited by the Amazons; there is a detailed description of the wonders of the Orient (such as the flight of a griffon); and Alexander descends into the sea in a submarine-like vessel.

Only metaphysical forces, Nature and Satan, can play a causative role in Alexander's death. The world has surrendered to him, but at the moment of his greatest achievement, he is poisoned by a trusted lieutenant, Jobas.

The interweaving of the fantastic, the allegorical, and the moral threads in the frame of the Alexander lore that had accumulated over the previous thousand years makes the *Libro de Alexandre* a notable monument in medieval Spanish verse for the modern scholar; indeed, its merits were recognized in its own day, for it is now accepted that the author of the *Poema de Fernán González* closely imitated the *Libro de Alexandre*.

The *Poema de Fernán González* (poem of Fernán González), written around 1260, is the second great epic of the thirteenth century. Though its topic is local—the deeds of a Castilian nobleman—and thus characteristic of the *mester de juglaría*, the poem is clearly a product of the *mester de clerecía* tradition. The meter is *cuaderna vía*, and the details of the story reveal a dependence on Latin historical sources, the poems of Berceo, and the *Libro de Alexandre*, all of which leads modern scholars to believe that a cleric was the author. Another clue to authorship, reinforcing the attribution to a churchman, is a mythical-biblical pattern that J. P. Keller, in his article, "The Structure of the *Poema de Fernán González*," classifies as "rise, treachery, and fall," though ultimately the hero achieves a state of prominence. Fernán González is present as a divinely chosen figure in the mold of biblical heroes.

The poem consists of three parts. The first sets the overall dimensions of the three significant episodes in Spanish history until that time: the Visigothic Empire, the Arab invasion, and the beginning of the Reconquest. The second and third parts reflect the rise of Castile: The small, frontier region gains prominence with the victories over the Moors won by its heroic leader, Fernán González, who subsequently is seated in the *cortes* (parliament) of the kingdom of León. Ambushed and imprisoned by Leonese jealous of his success, he escapes to lead the Castilians to independence from León and supremacy over the kingdom of Navarre.

In contrast to the pragmatic religious devotion of the Cid, Fernán González is carefully characterized as a God-chosen leader who reciprocates with Christ-like behavior. He prays continuously, has dreams in which spirits visit, and hears voices of saints during battle that tell him how to direct his troops, and he encourages his men with the promise that those who die on the battlefield will rejoice with him in paradise.

The anonymous *Libro de Apolonio* (book of Apolonio, c. 1240) and the *Castigos y ejemplos de Catón* (the punishments and examples of Catón, c. 1280) are two other significant verse compositions. The first descends from the tradition of late classical Greek romance, full of plot mechanisms turning on storms, pirates, separations, misfortunes, and, finally, a happy ending in which virtue and trust in God are rewarded. The second is notable for its popularity in the sixteenth century but is distinct from other poems of the *cuaderna vía* style. It has no story line and is more similar to wisdom literature than to the hagiography and classical and historical epics typical of the *mester de clerecía*.

FOURTEENTH CENTURY: DIVERSIFICATION

In his classic study, *European Literature and the Latin Middle Ages* (1953), Ernst Curtius describes the impact of the *Libro de buen amor* (c. 1330; book of good love), the most poetically and artistically diverse composition of the Spanish Middle Ages:

> Then about 1330 Juan Ruiz (1283?-1350?) makes a bold innovation with his *Libro de buen amor*. He imports Ovid's eroticism and its medieval derivatives. To a free rendition of the *Ars amandi* . . . he added a recasting of the extremely popular medieval comedy *Pamphilus de amore*, which in turn goes back to an elegy of Ovid's (*Amores* I, 8). . . . There are critics who rank the *Libro de buen amor*, the *Celestina*, and *Don Quijote* together as the three peaks of Spanish literature.

Curtius's description, though, is only the half of it. As a peak, the *Libro de buen amor* has yet to be scaled. Its structural diversity, thematic multiplicity, and rich characterization make it one of the most intriguing works of European literature.

The author, like the work itself, is a mystery. Little is known about Juan Ruiz, the archpriest of Hita, a small town north of Madrid. This lack of biographical data has given rise to the notion that perhaps "Juan Ruiz" was not the actual author but rather a persona through which the author represented himself.

In the poem, there are tidbits of biographical information about Juan Ruiz, such as a plea for mercy in response to an unjust incarceration and constant reminders that he has not been a very successful lover. Critics have sought to extrapolate information about the author from his work. They have concluded, for example, that he was almost certainly a priest, since he reveals great familiarity with ecclesiastical terminology; indeed, it is likely that he was an archpriest—that is, a priest with administrative responsibility over several dioceses. His education, however, was not confined to scripture and religious literature: He paraphrased the *Pamphilus de amore* (twelfth century), a medieval Latin love farce, and composed his verse in a variety of meters.

The *Libro de buen amor* is a tour de force. Opening with an invocation to God or the Virgin Mary, the poet pleads for help in his present trouble, which seems to be an imprisonment. A sermon, based on the scripture "I will give understanding" (Psalms 31:8), states the purpose of the work, ostensibly to instruct the audience in the forms of "bad" (that is, sexual) love in order that they might avoid it and practice "good" love—that is, the love of God. This is followed by a series of *loores* (praises) extolling the virtue and power of the Virgin Mary. Scattered throughout are fables, illustrating a moral through tales of animals characterized as humans, and *fabliaux*, often of a ribald nature. The poet then begins his autobiography and follows it with a *cazurro* verse, a coarse, often humorous love story—though in this case, Juan Ruiz flirts with sacrilege as he compares forlorn lovers with the Crucifixion of Christ. A panegyric arguing that love changes men completely leads into a vision, an allegorical narrative of the poet's three-time failure at seduction.

After his failures, a debate ensues between the poet and Don Amor (Sir Love) concerning the joys and dangers of love; this is followed by invective verse condemning love. A scriptural parody, based on sexual allusions in the canonical hours, is concluded by an Ovidian *ars amandi*.

The source of the longest verse narrative in the *Libro de buen amor* is the *Pamphilus de amore*, a popular twelfth century Latin comedy. Notable is the poet's introduction of the character Trotaconventos, an old go-between destined to become a type in Spanish literature. Her intervention into his love life does not provide satisfactory results, and the poet, in a counsel, warns women about the wickedness of love and suggests that men not use negative epithets for their go-betweens. He finishes the section with an enumeration of the various comments gentlemen have been known to make.

The *cantigas de serrana* are bawdy verses telling how mountain women jump unsuspecting travelers, such as the poet; these verses are followed by a collection of devotional poems concerning the Passion of Christ. Another baffling shift in tone follows, as the poet introduces a satirical mock-epic contest between Don Carnal (Lord Flesh) and Doña Cuaresma (Lady Lent), terminating in the triumphal procession of Don Carnal's forces.

A "book of hours" with allegorized seasons of the year prepares the reader for an extended reappearance of Trotaconventos, the procuress, who attempts (unsuc-

cessfully) to woo a nun for the poet. Her rhetorical portrait of the nun provides an intriguing insight into the concept of beauty in the Spanish Middle Ages. When Trotaconventos dies, the poet delivers an impassioned lament and subsequently writes her epitaph.

Juan Ruiz's irreverence resurfaces in a mock sermon on the virtues of little women, and the poem concludes with a summation in which the poet suggests how his work should be understood. A postscript follows with a collection of *cantares de ciegos* (beggars' songs), a complaint, and goliardic verses attacking the Church.

The metric patterns in the *Libro de buen amor* reveal a conscious manipulation of verse length to combat monotony and to enhance the content. While most of the narrative sections of the poem are in *cuaderna vía*, the poet often shifts between lines of fourteen and sixteen syllables. The rhyme is virtually perfect. The lyric sections of the poem present a dazzling array of verse forms, ranging from the *zéjel* (a Moorish composition with stanzas and a refrain) to the *pie quebrado*, in which four-syllable lines and eight-syllable lines are used in a single stanza.

The diversification of Spanish verse in the fourteenth century continued with the appearance of lyric poetry. Setting aside the disputed nature of the *kharjas*, Rafael Lapesa, the noted Spanish critic and linguist, suggests that lyric verse of a learned nature did not appear until 1300, with the composition of the *Razón de amor*. This earliest extant lyric poem survives in a confusing manuscript in which the first part narrates the visitation of a young man in a *locus amoenus* by a young woman who has prepared a glass of wine and another of water for them. Their lyric conversation is reminiscent of the *cantigas de amor* and *cantigas de amigo*, in which the lovers complain about love. Suddenly, the young woman leaves, and a white dove appears, spilling the vessel of water into the wine. The rest of the poem, called the "Denuestos del agua y del vino," is of the debate genre: The personified wine and water argue their respective strengths and defects; for water, wine is too sentimental; for wine, the water is too coldly rational. In *A Literary History of Spain: The Middle Ages* (1971), Alan Deyermond accurately sums up the *Razón de amor* as "the best and most puzzling" of poems. The dramatic change midway through the poem has generated considerable critical debate, some scholars arguing that the work is in fact a single poem while others contend that it comprises two distinct poems rudely joined.

It is appropriate that a survey of Spanish verse through the fourteenth century should end on the note with which it began: the dichotomy between popular and learned verse. The early contrast between the *mester de juglaría* and the *mester de clerecía* repeats itself at the end of the Middle Ages. There are, on the one hand, the predecessors of the popular *romanceros* (collections devoted exclusively to romances or ballads), and, on the other, the philosophical verse of Rabbi Sem Tob and the early Spanish Humanism reflected in Pero López de Ayala.

The diversity of medieval Spanish literature is exemplified by the *Proverbios morales* (fourteenth century) of Rabbi Sem Tov (or Santob), born in Carrión de los Condes around 1290. The distinguished Spanish historian Claudio Sánchez Albornoz referred to Sem Tob as the first Spanish intellectual.

The *Proverbios morales* entries are almost exclusively composed in Alexandrine verse and—oddly, for a medieval composition—contain virtually no exempla relating the content to everyday life. The poet is a philosopher, observing life through the prism of classical and Hebraic thought, never losing sight of the reality of being a Jew in an ever-hostile environment. His poetry is a celebration of learning and knowledge, tempered with the reservations of a skeptic.

Spanish Humanism begins with Pedro López de Ayala, courtier, knight, and man of letters. As an adult, he lived through the cataclysms of fourteenth century Spain: the plague, the Trastámaran usurpation of the Castilian throne, international wars, and the Great Schism of the Roman Catholic Church. As a man of letters, he translated or was connected with the translations into Spanish of works by Livy, Boethius, Gregory the Great, and Giovanni Boccaccio. His great poetic work, the *Rimado de palaçio* (fourteenth century), stands alongside his chronicle of the reign of Peter I of Castile as a significant contribution to Spanish literature.

The *Rimado de palacio*, an extensive poem of 8,200 lines composed over several years, provides a serious counterpoint to the frivolity of Juan Ruiz's *Libro de buen amor*. The poem is divided into three sections. The first is a scathing satire of the secular and ecclesiastical society of the day. The second part is composed of lyric *loores* and prayers to the virgins of Monserrat, Guadalupe, and Rocamador and to other religious icons, invoking their favors. It is believed that this portion was written during an imprisonment, while the third and final part was set down in the last years of Ayala's life. This last section is a compendium of religious and ethical reflections based on the Book of Job and Saint Gregory's *Moralia* (c. C.E. 6).

In contrast to the learned verse of Ayala and Sem Tob, the late fourteenth century saw the first appearance of the *romanceros*, or romances. It is generally accepted that the composition of these popular ballads began as the longer epic poems (their probable source) were forgotten or lost their relevance. The romances are written in the same sixteen-syllable assonant line that characterizes Spanish epic verse and are generally categorized as historical (based on a recent event), literary (derived from a previous chronicle or epic), or adventurous (a miscellaneous grouping of diverse themes such as love, revenge, mystery, or simply adventure).

The quilt of Spanish culture is at once a social, political, religious, and literary phenomenon. The interplay between learned and popular, Galician and Castilian, Moor, Jew, and Christian created a poetic tradition as multifaceted as any found in Western Europe, a tradition enriched and deepened by its diversity.

BIBLIOGRAPHY

Barnstone, Willis, ed. *Spanish Poetry from Its Beginning Through the Nineteenth Century: An Anthology.* New York: Oxford University Press, 1970.

Cohen, John M., ed. *Penguin Book of Spanish Verse.* New York: Penguin Books, 1988. Explores nine centuries of Spanish verse poetry. Bilingual.

Crow, John Armstrong, ed. *An Anthology of Spanish Poetry: From the Beginnings to the Present Day, Including Both Spain and Spanish America.* Baton Rouge: Louisiana State University Press, 1979.

Curtius, Ernst. *European Literature and the Latin Middle Ages.* New York: Pantheon Books, 1953. This classic discussion of the dominant language of letters in Europe through the Middle Ages traces the development and trends in Latin literature and in Spain as well.

De Chasca, Edmunc. *The Poem of the Cid*. Boston: Twayne, 1976. Excellent basic introduction to the poem and its history.

Deyermond, Alan. *Epic Poetry and the Clergy: Studies on the "Modedades de Rodrigo."* London: Támesis Books, 1968.

_____. *The Middle Ages*. In *A Literary History of Spain*. New York: Barnes & Noble, 1971.

_____, ed. *Medieval and Renaissance Spanish Literature: Selected Essays of Keith Whinnom*. Exeter, England: University of Exeter Press, 1994.

_____, ed. *Medieval Hispanic Studies Presented to Rita Hamilton*. London: Támesis Books, 1976.

_____, ed. *Mio Cid Studies*. London: Támesis Books, 1977.

Florit, Eugenio. *Introduction to Spanish Poetry*. Mineola, N.Y.: Dover Publications, 1991. Offers works ranging from the twelfth century *Poema de mío Cid* to twentieth century poets. Full Spanish texts with expert literal English translations on facing pages. Also contains a wealth of biographical information and critical commentary.

Keller, John Esten. *Pious Brief Narrative in Medieval Castilian and Galician Verse: From Berceo to Alfonso X*. Lexington: University Press of Kentucky, 1978.

Montgomery, Thomas. *Medieval Spanish Epic: Mythic Roots and Ritual Language*. University Park: Pennsylvania State University Press, 1998.

Pattison, D. G. *From Legend to Chronicle: The Treatment of Epic Material in Alphonsine Historiography*. Oxford, England: Society for the Study of Mediaeval Languages and Literature, 1983.

Powell, Brian. *Epic and Chronicle: The "Poema de Mio Cid" and the "Crónica de Veinte Reyes."* London: Modern Humanities Research Association, 1983.

Schippers, Arie. *Spanish Hebrew Literature and the Arab Literary Tradition: Arabic Themes in Hebrew Andalusian Poetry*. New York: Brill Academic, 1993.

Smith, Colin C. *The Making of the "Poema de mío Cid."* New York: Cambridge University Press, 1983. The well-known scholar and editor of the Collins English-Spanish dictionaries traces the development of the Spanish epic. Bibliography, index.

_____, ed. *Spanish Ballads*. 2d ed. London: Bristol Classical Press, 1996. Originally published in 1964, this collection is accompanied by a useful introduction and notes by Smith.

Vaquero, Mercedes, and Alan Deyermond, eds. *Studies on Medieval Spanish Literature in Honor of Charles F. Fraker*. Madison: Hispanic Seminary of Medieval Studies, 1995.

Willis, Raymond S. *El "Libro de Alexandre": Texts of the Paris and Madrid Manuscripts with an Introduction*. Princeton, N.J.: Princeton University Press, 1934.

John Richard Law

SPANISH POETRY SINCE 1400

During the fifteenth century, Spain's mercurial transformation into a world power was the direct result of having achieved national unification (1492)—a reality that took more than seven centuries of armed conflict between the various Christian principalities scattered throughout the northern half of the Iberian Peninsula and the powerful Moslem caliphates that dominated virtually all of Spain for several centuries following the Moors' initial invasion in 711. As Spain found herself emerging into a modern state whose strong central government was busy removing the last medieval vestiges from its newly created empire (thus ushering in an era of unsurpassed economic prosperity), so, too, in the field of art and literature, a new awareness of the ancient Greek and Latin masters was taking root.

FIFTEENTH AND SIXTEENTH CENTURIES

The two men most responsible for introducing Spain to a new spirit of Humanism via Greek, Latin, and Italian literary traditions were Juan Boscán (c. 1490-1542) and Garcilaso de la Vega (1501-1536).

Whereas 1492 marked the political birth of modern Spain, the year 1543 may be said to have marked Spain's cultural rebirth into the Humanistic tradition that had been eclipsed until its rediscovery a century earlier by the great fifteenth century Italian poets. With the publication of *Las obras de Boscán y algunas de Garcilasso de la Vega repartidas en quatro libros* (1543; the works of Boscán and some of Garcilaso de la Vega), a wholly new poetic vision was introduced into Spanish literature. To appreciate the magnitude of change that Boscán and Garcilaso brought to sixteenth century Spanish poetry, both in its form and in its content, one must recall the tradition from which their revolutionary poetics were born.

Not until the fifteenth century did the Spanish literary lyric first appear as an independent written work of art. Prior to that time, Castilian verse was dominated, for the most part, by the fourteenth century romance (ballad) and the thirteenth century *villancico*. While traveling troubadours sang of the joys and woes associated with courtly love, a clerical tradition also developed which focused on more spiritual themes, such as the many miracles of the Blessed Virgin. In 1445, the first important collection of Castilian verse was published, the *Cancionero de Baena* (songbook of Baena). Here were recorded numerous *canciones de amor* (love songs) which echoed the earlier ballads in both theme and form.

Two exceptions to these traditions were the Marquis of Santillana and Juan de Mena. They transcended the traditional compositions that were recorded in the *Cancionero general* (1511; general songbook), a collection of fifteenth century verse filled with *villancicos* and ballads that reflected the love songs of the earlier troubadour tradition. Santillana is credited with the first sonnets written in a language other than Italian, while Mena's allegorical and philosophical poems are sprinkled with frequent classical allusions and a Latinized vocabulary.

The poetic revolution that was to characterize sixteenth century Spain, however, did not truly begin until 1526, when the Spanish poet Juan Boscán met with the Venetian ambassador to the court of Charles V, Andreas Navagero. It was at this time that Boscán was first introduced to the new Italianate forms with their classical focus on man and nature. Although it would be another seventeen years before Navagero's revolutionary seeds would bear Spanish fruit, the poetic manifesto contained within *Las obras de Boscán y algunas de Garcilasso de la Vega repartidas en quatro libros* heralded a radical change in the exterior form of poetic expression and promised a vibrantly new vision of humankind.

Boscán found that the Italian hendecasyllable created a cadence much less emphatic than that of the traditional Castilian octosyllable, allowing the poet to express subtleties of rhythm and rhyme previously unattainable. The flexibility afforded by this new meter complemented the new aesthetic sensibility that Boscán and Garcilaso brought to Castilian verse. For example, in Boscán's *Canzoniere* (songbook), which consists of ninety love sonnets and ten *canzones* (songs), the theme of human love is explored in all its splendor. Unchecked by reason, it is a passion fraught with pain and suffering; when properly expressed, this same love brings peace and joy to the human spirit.

Garcilaso, too, reflects this newfound faith in man's ultimate worth and goodness. Innovative in form (he introduced into Spanish verse, among other meters, the five-line stanza known as the *lira*), his poetry evokes a landscape whose sensuously bucolic images and mythological allusions have forever changed the course of Spanish poetry. Indeed, Garcilaso might be considered the cornerstone on which modern Spanish verse has been built.

Following Garcilaso's lead, two schools of Castilian poets developed—one centered in Salamanca, and the other in Seville. Whereas the Salamancan group (known as El Broncense), headed by Francisco Sánchez, was known for moralistic and philosophical perspectives exemplified in the work of its most renowned poet, Luis de León, the Sevillan poets, whose outstanding figure was Fernando de Herrera, were known for their sensuous musicality and erudite knowledge of classical mythology. Both groups put unwavering faith in Aristotelian poetics: Art was to imitate nature, not the ephemeral happenings associated with the senses but the ideals and principles that lay hidden beneath the surface. Masters such as Horace, Vergil, and Petrarch served as models for the expression of universal themes.

Distinct from the schools of Salamanca and Seville but of equal quality was a specialized tradition, that of mystical verse. The Carmelite monk Saint John of the Cross (1542-1591) represents the zenith of this uniquely Spanish poetic expression. In his masterpiece, *Cántico espiritual* (c. 1577-1586; *A Spiritual Canticle of the Soul*, 1864, 1909), based on the Bible's Song of Solomon, he expressed with erotic intensity the soul's passionate quest for God. One can detect in the sensuous pastoral imagery produced by Saint John of the Cross the presence of Garcilaso's eclogues: Even the most religious of poets found himself enveloped within the growing Humanism of the Renaissance spirit.

The Renaissance not only reawakened an interest in classical mythology but also engendered a renewed sense of national identity. Unlike its neighbors to the west, Spain did not produce an epic comparable to Portugal's *Os Lusíadas* (1572; *The Lusiads*, 1655), by Luís de Camões. One of her native sons, however, did record the heroic events involving the conquest of Chile. Alonso de Ercilla's *La Araucana* (1569-1590; English translation, 1945) sings the praises of both the conqueror and the vanquished. His vivid account of the heroic deeds accomplished by his Spanish comrades and the valiant defense of the proud Araucanian people places Ercilla y Zúñiga's poem alongside the other great epics of Western civilization.

SEVENTEENTH CENTURY

During the seventeenth century, as Spain's political and economic prowess began to show the first signs of vulnerability, the stylistic innovations first introduced into Spanish literature by Boscán and Garcilaso were embellished and brought to their ultimate poetic fruition—to the point of excess. The simplicity and clarity of the Renaissance gradually gave way to the complexity and obscurity of the Baroque.

Encouraged by literary academies and an ever-increasing number of literary competitions, poets began to create newer and more unusual images, to experiment with traditional word order, and to search for subtler allusions. In particular, two main currents came to dominate seventeenth century poetic expression: *culteranismo* and *conceptismo*. the former is characterized by its emphasis on ornate and complex images, its revolutionary syntax, and its obscure mythological allusions; the latter is characterized by its intellectual and philosophical sophistication. The many puns and double entendres which one encounters in this poetry reveal the *conceptistas'* fundamental cynicism and disillusionment with life. For the *culteranistas*, beauty was to be found in the most complex of metaphors, whereas for the *conceptistas* truth was to be expressed in satire and wit.

Of the many poets associated with these two literary tendencies, four overshadow the others because of the quality and depth of their work. The driving force behind the *culterano* style of poetry was Luis de Góngora y Argote (1561-1627); his very name has become synonymous with intricately complex metaphors and tantalizingly obscure images. Góngora's influence on seventeenth century Spanish verse was monumental; like Garcilaso de la Vega a century earlier, Góngora was imitated by virtually all of his fellow poets, even those who were most vocal in their criticism of his stylistic intricacies.

Although the term Gongorism is frequently used today to describe a type of poetry characterized by excessive ornamentation and artificially complex syntax, Góngora himself was not guilty of such literary failings. The negative connotations associated with his name more accurately describe the many less gifted poets who attempted to emulate the master's unique gift for expressing beauty in startling metaphors that both dazzled and amazed the sensitive reader. His ability to juxtapose vibrant, concrete images in a world of poetic illusion makes his verse the high point of the Spanish Baroque.

In his two masterpieces, *Fábula de Polifemo y Galatea* (wr. 1613, pb. 1627; *Fable of Polyphemus and Galatea*, 1961) and *Soledades* (wr. 1613, pb. 1627; *The Solitudes*, 1964)—a projected series of four poems only one of which, written in 1613, was completed—Góngora contrasted human mutability with nature's lasting beauty and grandeur. His fable about Polyphemus and Galatea is based on a story found in Ovid's *Metamorphoses* (c. 8 C.E.), which recounts the love affair between Acis and Galatea. Acis is eventually killed by the jealous Cyclops, Polyphemus, but, through the intercession of the gods, the slain Acis is transformed into a stream. Góngora's version, although true to the original, is much more a celebration of nature's inherent dynamism and beauty than is Ovid's.

Góngora intended to write four *Solitudes* but died before completing his second. The first one describes a love-smitten youth, who, as he travels through the countryside, comes upon a pastoral wedding celebration. In the fragmentary second poem of the series, the young man is seen visiting with a seafaring family. Although their plot is a simple one, *The Solitudes* are rich in subtle allusions and bewildering syntax, which, once properly contemplated, lead the reader to a greater sense of nature's overpowering majesty.

If Góngora is remembered today because of the sheer perfection of his poetic technique, Lope de Vega Carpio (1562-1635) is remembered for his prodigious creative output. The great lyrical playwright of Spain's Golden Age, he also managed to compose more than sixteen hundred sonnets, several literary epics, ballads, and several volumes of miscellaneous verse. Lope de Vega Carpio's poetry is not as polished as Góngora's re-fined verse, but what it lacks in erudition and technical skill, it more than adequately possesses in spontaneity and flowing grace.

Still further removed from the ornate images of *culteranismo* was the epigrammatic style of Francisco de Quevedo y Villegas (1580-1645). Indeed, Quevedo was one of Góngora's most caustic critics. Unlike his rival, who tried to capture in words the beauty and dynamism of nature, Quevedo was fascinated by humanity's ugliness and corruption. Rejecting the sensuous style of the *culteranistas*, he preferred a more austere and elliptical mode of expression, filled with tersely worded puns, that reflected his cynical view of life. The satirical observations and witty wordplay that characterize his poetry exemplify the mode of poetic expression known as *conceptismo*. Quevedo's stoicism led him to employ poetry as an effective way to teach his fellow man about the ugly reality of life. If there is one principal theme running through Quevedo's poetry, it is *disengaño* (disillusionment): a total disenchantment with the things of this world.

Ironically, the poet who encompassed most fully the complexity and obscurity of seventeenth century Spanish verse did not live in Spain, but in New Spain (Mexico). Her name was Sor Juana Inés de la Cruz (1651-1695). In a society that favored men, Sor Juana was regarded as one of the New World's finest examples of seventeenth century Humanism. She explored the wonders of science, the mysteries of philosophy, and the marvels of art and literature. Nevertheless, she saw the highest achievements of Renaissance Humanism as ultimately futile. In her major poem, "Primer sueño" (first dream), she expressed, in true *culterano* style, the human mind's inability to grasp life's purpose by means of purely intellectual or aesthetic activity. Ultimately, for Sor Juana, the things of this world led to disillusionment. What began in the sixteenth century as a optimistic quest for truth and beauty, ended, at the close of the seventeenth century, with man's faith in himself deeply shaken if not shattered.

EIGHTEENTH CENTURY

As the eighteenth century approached, Spanish poetry, like the other major literary genres of the time, was in a state of decline. Poets, for the most part, attempted to imitate dominant styles of the seventeenth century. Just as political decline ultimately led to a change of royal families (the House of Bourbon inherited the Spanish throne in 1700), so, too, the decadence to which Spanish literature had fallen led to serious attempts at literary reform. For example, in 1713, the Royal Academy was founded with the responsibility of protecting and guiding the Spanish language, and was commissioned to produce an authoritative dictionary and grammar.

In 1732, there appeared a journal titled *Diario de los literatos de España* (diary of the writers of Spain), which, until its demise in 1742, attempted to review and to evaluate the literary merit of all the books being printed in Spain at that time. In one of its last editions, it published a work titled *Sátira contra los malos escritores de este siglo* (satire against the poor writers of this century), which condemned the Baroque excesses associated with the poetry of the day. The inclusion of French terms in this critical diatribe suggests a knowledge of the French neoclassical critic, Nicolas Boileau-Despréaux.

The most significant evidence of literary reform, however, appeared in 1737 with the publication of Ignacio de Luzán's *La poética o reglas de la poesía* (poetics or rules of poetry). In it are criticized the inordinate use of artificially contrived metaphors, unnecessarily complex syntax, and unusually difficult puns characteristic of many contemporary poets. Rejecting the sophisticated cynicism of Gabriel Alvarez de Toledo (1662-1714) and the bitterly satirical language of Diego de Torres Villarroel (1694-1770), Luzán advocated a clear and concise language. Literature, besides pleasing and entertaining the reader, should instruct him. Above all, a literary work should exhibit good taste. Exaggeration, either in form or in content, was to be avoided, since order and symmetry best reflected the natural harmony existing within the universe.

Luzán's poetics, like those of his French counterpart, Boileau, were an attempt to return to the clear and measured writing which had characterized the ancient Greek and Latin poets. Whereas France looked more toward classical antiquity for its models, Spain rediscovered her own classical writers such as Garcilaso de la Vega and Luis de León.

The neoclassical reformation championed by Luzán did not begin to bear fruit until the second half of the eighteenth century. Of the many poets who followed the dictates of neoclassical good taste, Nicolás Fernández de Moratín (1737-1780) was the most respected and influential. Known primarily for his innovative ideas and techniques in the field of drama, Moratín was a key figure in the popularization of Luzán's poetic theory. Moratín formed a group of writers known as the Tertulia de la fonda de San Sebastián, among whom were such leading literary figures as José Cadalso and Tomás de Iriarte. From their literary soirées came some of the most important critical essays in support of the neoclassical style of writing.

Perhaps the most appropriate genre for expressing the Neoclassical ideal of instructing while entertaining was the fable. At any rate, the second half of the eighteenth century saw the publication of two collections of fables, the second of which was a direct defense of Luzán's poetics. From 1781 to 1784, Félix María de Samaniego (1745-1801) published his *Fábulas morales* (moral fables), in which he imitated both classical and modern fabulists. In 1782, Tomás de Iriarte published his highly original *Fábulas literarias* (literary fables), in which he expressed his ideas on literature. In his fables focusing on poetry, he satirized those poets who disregarded the neoclassical call for clarity, order, and balance.

The eighteenth century neoclassical emphasis on order and sobriety clearly reflected the spirit of the times. The political and civil reforms instituted by the newly installed House of Bourbon established an atmosphere of well-being throughout the country. In particular, the highly progressive reign of Charles III (1759-1788), whose economic and social reforms helped instill within the Spanish people a newfound feeling of prosperity and stability based on intelligent planning and careful implementation of programs, supported the neoclassicists' demand for clear and orderly writing. Poetry, it was thought, like all meaningful elements of society, should not only amuse and distract but also provide the utilitarian function of instructing its citizenry. To the neoclassicists' chagrin, however, Charles III's well-ordered society soon found itself beset once again by turmoil and confusion. As the eighteenth century came to a close, the winds of change began to blow from within and without the Spanish borders, giving birth to a new literary mentality.

NINETEENTH CENTURY

The first two decades of the nineteenth century saw the total collapse of Spain's traditional political system, which is perhaps best described as a form of enlightened despotism. There followed an onslaught of radical political and social changes that combined to undermine the many years of apparent prosperity and stability associated with eighteenth century Bourbon Spain.

In 1807, heeding the unwise advice of his prime minister, Manuel de Godoy, Bourbon monarch Charles IV allowed Napoleon's forces to enter Spain (Napoleon's ostensible target was Portugal). Six years of foreign rule and a brutalizing civilian-led revolution followed Napoleon's entry into Spain. Once having ousted the foreign monarch (Joseph Bonaparte) and having restored the legitimate Bourbon heir (Ferdinand VII) to the Spanish throne, Spain experienced even greater political turmoil. Ferdinand ruled with the absolutism of his predecessors but lacked their vision and dedication. The liberal revolutionary groups that had fought so valiantly for restoration felt betrayed by their conservative monarch. After six years of absolutist rule, a *coup d'état* in 1820 ushered in three years of liberal reforms. With France's help, Ferdinand managed to regain his throne and ruled uncompromisingly until his death in 1833. After his death, although the pendulum was to swing in favor of the liberals, Spain suffered no less than three civil wars (the Carlist Wars) over royal succession. What was once a well-organized and well-integrated society soon found itself polarized into opposing camps: *afrancesados* (French supporters) versus those in favor of restoration, absolutists versus constitutionalists, conservatives versus liberals. The resulting chaos found its intellectual and aesthetic expression in the Romantic movement, which reflected both in its form and in its content the turbulent reality of early nineteenth century Spain.

In the field of Spanish poetry, two men in particular foreshadowed the literary revolution of the nineteenth century. Manuel José Quintana (1772-1857) and Juan Nicasio Gallego (1777-1853), although trained in the rigors of neoclassicism, infused new vigor into their verse by unabashedly singing the praises of their homeland. Quintana, in his "A España" ("Ode to Spain"), and Gallego, in his "Al dos de Mayo" (to the second of May), took the first steps in the transition from a poetics dominated by reason to one that was primarily an expression of deep emotion.

Not until Ferdinand VII's death, however, did Spanish poetry begin to free itself in earnest from the artificial bonds imposed upon it by the neoclassical demand for moderation in the name of good taste. With Isabel II's accession to the throne in 1833, many of the liberals who were formerly living in exile in England, France, and Germany returned to Spain, bringing with them a radically uninhibited style of poetry.

Nineteenth century Romanticism was unquestionably a love affair with freedom. It was a direct response to and rejection of the literary norms of the day. Like most reactions, however, it frequently defined itself in terms of what it rejected. Since eighteenth century neoclassicism produced a poetry refined by reason, Romanticism strived to express a poetry unshackled by reason's tyranny. In its place, the Romantics exalted human feelings, emotions, instincts, intuition, and imagination—all of those qualities that had waited so long to be liberated. The freedom of the Romantics, therefore, was a freedom *from* the established rules of society, be they political, social, or aesthetic. Like Ferdinand VII's political tyranny, which ultimately coerced the majority of liberals to search for a means of escape via self-imposed exile, so, too, reason's tyranny over free poetic expression ultimately led the young Romantics to seek refuge by escaping into private worlds, unencumbered by the demands and responsibilities that society exacts from its members.

Although the Romantic movement, which dominated the first half of the nineteenth century in Spain, produced many fine poets, three are of major literary importance: Ángel de Saavedra (better known by his title, Duque de Rivas, 1791-1865), José de Espronceda (1803-1842), and José Zorrilla (1817-1893). These three men revolutionized both the form and content of nineteenth century Spanish poetry.

Ángel de Saavedra, in his *Romances históricos* (1841; historical ballads), turned the focus of Spanish verse from the ancient Greek and Latin myths to Spain's own heroic past. Rejecting the artificial syntax and latinized vocabulary of previous generations, he captured his country's customs in a lively language that complemented its exciting history.

Accompanying their interest in Spain's glorious past was the Romantics' fondness for expressing intimately personal feelings. One of Spain's greatest lyric poets, José de Espronceda expressed more vividly than most his deepest emotions. One notes immediately, both in his disregard for traditional forms and in his rebellious themes and motifs, his unbounded love of freedom and spontaneity. Five poems in particular manifest his almost adolescent contempt for any form of coercion. In his "Canción del pirata" ("Song of the Pirate"), "Canto del cosaco" (cossack's song), "El mendigo" ("The Beggar"), "El reo de muerte" ("The Condemned to Die"), and "El Verdugo" ("The Headsman"), he expressed a deep desire to be freed from society's dominion over the individual. In his later work, "A Jarifa en una orgía" ("To Harifa, in an Orgy"), one of the most pessimistic poems ever composed in the Spanish language, he views death as the only path to freedom.

From José Zorrilla, known today principally for his dramatic reworking of Tirso de Molina's *El burlador de Sevilla* (1630; *The Trickster of Seville*, 1923), titled *Don Juan Tenorio* (1844; English translation, 1944), Spain received not only some of its most beautiful lyric poetry but also a series of legends that recorded many of the memorable deeds associated with Spain's colorful and turbulent past.

As the political turmoil of the first half of the nineteenth century gradually subsided and Spanish society once again began to experience relative stability, poetic expression showed signs of losing much of its revolutionary fervor. During the latter half of the nineteenth century, poetry became less lyrical as it attempted to involve itself with philosophical, political, and social questions being discussed in the novel, the recently rediscovered genre whose popularity was rapidly increasing. In an effort to be more relevant, poets such as Ramón de Campoamor (1817-1901) and Gaspar Núñez de Arce (1832-1903) began to focus on philosophical and social issues.

Two notable exceptions to that trend were the Andalusian poet Gustavo Adolfo Bécquer (1836-1870) and the Galician poet Rosalía de Castro (1837-1885). In many ways, their delicate lyricism bridged the high-spirited and spontaneous verse of Romanticism with the subtler subjectivism associated with Symbolism and the measured plasticity of Parnassianism.

In particular, Bécquer might be considered the culmination of the Romantic movement, inasmuch as his *Rimas* (1871; *Poems*, 1891; better known as *The Rhymes*, 1898) expressed the most intimate of feelings. In a sense, Bécquer's verse is Romanticism come of age. Whereas Espronceda's *raison d'être* as a poet lay in his puerile attempt to escape the harsher realities of life by vicariously experiencing, through his verse, the imagined lives of such exotic personalities as a gun-toting pirate, an arrogant beggar, and a defiant prisoner, Bécquer drew from the springs of his own soul to express a precise, melodic language that ultimately transcended words—Beauty, Love, Poetic Creation. With delicate nuances of light and color, sound and rhythm, he created some of the most beautiful images in Spanish poetry.

TWENTIETH CENTURY: 1898-1936

European Romanticism during the latter part of the nineteenth century had been dominated by Bécquer. During his reign, Romanticism attained a particularly Spanish style. Current European literary trends, including French liberalism, had influenced Spanish Romantic poets. Bécquer's style eventually gave way to *costumbrismo*, the depiction of customs and manners, and realism replaced Romanticism as prose began to become the dominant form. Realism characterized Spanish prose fiction during the early twentieth century.

The literary movements of the *fin de siglo* passage from the nineteenth to the twentieth century were marked by political, philosophical, and artistic turbulence. In 1898 Spain lost its last colonies. Since the seventeenth century, Spain's expansionism had been in decline. The *generación del 98*, or Generation of '98, rose as both a literary and a philosophical movement of writers who referred to 1898 as a turning point in Spanish society. They searched for causes of its decline and ways to regain their nation's past glories. Together, the Generation of '98 and the *generación del 27*, or Generation of '27, created a kind of Silver Age that approached the literary and artistic excellence of the masters of the Spanish Golden Age. This era of literary brilliance and prolific creative activity reigned until 1936, stifled by the onset of the Spanish Civil War.

Literary influences shifted from *costumbrismo* and realism to *Modernismo*, similar to French Symbolism, and artistic and musical impressionism. A group of young writers at the turn of the century proclaimed a moral and cultural rebirth for their defeated homeland. Through studying the simplicity and austerity of Castilian life, these writers found the essence of Spain. They sought to portray it through a direct and compact style. The literary association rejected most European literary and aesthetic trends, but embraced political liberalism.

The Basque poet and prose writer Miguel de Unamuno y Jugo (1864-1936) anticipated the essential themes of existentialism. Unamuno believed that the personal aspects of history were eternal because they sustain the temporal events of public history. This concept of *intrahistoria* permeates his poems. Their symbolic elements acquire universal relevance as they relate to the Spanish experience between 1898 and 1936. After a spiritual crisis reflected in *En torno al casticismo* (1902), Unamuno sought to identify a popular protagonist. This "intrahistorical" way of life defined the Spanish spirit for his literary as well as spiritual generation.

Azorín (José Martínez Ruiz, 1873-1967) coined the phrase *generación del 98*. In his overriding goal to define the eternal qualities of Spanish life, he depicted the Castilian people and countryside with impressionistic sensitivity that captured the beauty of ordinary life. His poetry acquired an original musicality rooted in folk songs. His poetry's lyrical quality results from an adept application of rhyme and meter. Azorín is best known for his novels, but he promoted the works of poets whose idealism rebelled against bourgeois styles and themes.

Antonio Machado (1875-1939) founded modern Spanish poetry by blending profound meditations on time and place and concern for the nation's future with symbolism. His original voice paved the way for the poets of the Generation of '27 to experiment with rhyme and meter in order to express their particular voice. His poems are lucid meditations that evoke a harsh yet sharply defined Spanish landscape. *Campos de Castilla* (1912; *The*

Castilian Camp, 1982) was inspired by his wife. The transition from lyricism to reflection is evident in the 1924 publication of *Nuevas canciones* (new songs), which followed *Soledades, galerías, y otros poemas* (1907; *Solitudes, Galleries, and Other Poems*, 1987). Together, they paint the Castilian landscape with clarity and sonority. He also wrote plays and translated French literature with his brother, the poet Manuel Machado (1874-1947). Tragedy marked his later works: Machado's wife died after five years of marriage from a sudden illness. Antonio died in 1939 while fleeing from the Spanish Civil War with his brother and mother, all exiled loyalists and victims of the national tragedy.

Juan Ramón Jiménez (1881-1958) wrote symbolic poetry. Over time, he developed an abstract and complex lyricism. He expanded the limits of language to convey truth through nature's images. A later stage of his work evidences his images whittled away to their essence. In *Platero y yo* (*Platero and I*, 1956), published to popular acclaim in 1914, a young poet is followed by a donkey during his reveries and idyllic journeys. Other works demonstrate the transformation and maturity of his style and structure. *Eternidades* in 1918 and *Belleza* in 1923 contemplated the changing face of beauty. He did not publish new works until the outbreak of the Spanish Civil War, when General Francisco Franco sent him to the United States as a cultural attaché. He taught at the University of Maryland and University of Puerto Rico until his wife's death in 1956, soon after he had won the Nobel Prize. His last major work, *Dios deseando y deseante* (1964), identifies with a universal consciousness that seeks beauty in nature.

The Generation of '98 initiated a cultural revival, an ongoing literary movement that gained momentum as it was energized by the new wave of writers after 1927 until the outbreak of civil war in 1936. As literary revisionists, they were responsible for the renewal of Spanish themes and traditions as they exposed their nation to European modernity.

The transition to the twentieth century inevitably led to European cultural influences, despite Iberian isolationism. José Ortega y Gasset (1883-1955) criticized the "Europeanization" of Spain with a landmark essay, *La deshumanización del arte* (1925), which criticizes literary realism. According to Ortega y Gasset, the Industrial

Revolution of the early nineteenth century led to the confusion of life with art so that art represented reality. Through the method of dehumanization, the narrative and descriptive elements of literature are removed and devalued. This approached the avant-garde European movements such as Futurism, creating a marginal literature that gained popularity during the first decades of the twentieth century. Spanish translations of works by James Joyce, Maxim Gorky, André Gide, and Marcel Proust were popular.

The tercentenary of the death of the Golden Age master poet Góngora began a new poetic age. Literary as well as artistic genius coincided in Madrid during the second decade of the new era. The surrealist Catalonian artist Salvador Dalí (1904-1989) lived and worked with Zaragozan Luis Buñuel (1900-1983) and Federico García Lorca in the Student Residence (Residencia de Estudiantes) in Madrid. The intellectual atmosphere was fed by the creative geniuses of several more residents in this neighborhood. The group of poets known as the Generation of '27 was founded in this creative community. Not since the seventeenth century's Golden Age had such a preeminent group of poets come together. Jorge Guillén (1893-1984), Federico García Lorca (1898-1936), Pedro Salinas (1891-1951), Rafael Alberti (1902-1999), Vicente Aleixandre (1898-1984), Dámaso Alonso (1898-1990), Luis Cernuda (1902-1963), and Gerardo Diego (1896-1987) were among the major poets.

Several literary movements characterized this generation. The European avant-garde and cinematographic realism inspired them stylistically. French Symbolism and Eastern European Dadaism influenced their approaches to art and its role in society. The concept of art for art's sake gained acceptance. As a result, art was dehumanized. The role of the symbol or metaphor was not transcendent, but ephemeral. The metaphor was elevated to serve a central temporal function in poetry. This symbolic impact had political implications. During the first phase of the movement, from 1920 to 1927, the poets distinguished themselves from their predecessors with their new poetic vision. During the second phase, from 1927 to 1936, their poems were politically motivated. The creation of the Second Republic and weakening of the bourgeoisie inspired them politically to envision a societal and aesthetic revolution in which art was the patrimony of the people.

The most emblematic poet and dramatist with enduring international prominence is Federico García Lorca. From 1919 until his death, García Lorca devoted himself to creative activity in the Residencia de Estudiantes area of Madrid. *Flamenco andaluz* and the Gypsy culture influenced his poetry. His publication of *Romancero gitano, 1924-1927* (1928; *The Gypsy Ballads of García Lorca*, 1951, 1953) gained for him international fame. A few years later he visited New York and related the similarities between the spirituals of Harlem and the *cante jondo*, or deep song of the Gypsy culture. The collections *Poema del cante jondo* (1931; *Poem of the Gypsy Seguidilla*, 1967) and *Poeta en Nueva York* (1940; *Poet in New York*, 1940, 1955) resulted from his American experience. He established the theater company *La Barraca*, which toured throughout Spain. At the outbreak of the Spanish Civil War, Franquista soldiers tortured and murdered García Lorca soon after assassinating his brother-in-law, the mayor of Granada. His poems and plays were burned and banned until the end of Franco's reign.

The Spanish Civil War destroyed many of these poets' utopian dreams as well as their lives. García Lorca's assassination by the Franquistas came to symbolize the destruction of the creative hopes of the nation. Alberti, Cernuda, Salinas, Guillén, Rosa Chacel, and María Zambrano were forced into exile. The nation torn apart by Franco's brutal and intolerant Fascist regime was gradually regenerated after almost fifty years of *franquismo*. Despite the domestic tragedies, the nation's banished intellectuals were extraordinarily prolific in exile.

Vicente Aleixandre, winner of the Nobel Prize in 1977, was the lone member of the Generation of '27 to remain in Spain during *franquismo*. He served as mentor and spiritual guide for the succeeding postwar generation. In 1933, he won Spain's national prize for literature. His greatest work, which led to his nomination for the Nobel Prize, was *Sombra del paraíso* (1944; *Shadow of Paradise*, 1987). Aleixandre's imagery of human pain and horror contrasts with that of the immutable power and harsh reality of nature. Loss, sorrow, and despair characterize this stage of poetic production. Without overtly political imagery, the Spanish Civil War experience was acutely portrayed. Aleixandre's later works revealed elements of Surrealism. This technique enabled him to escape from the desolation of a paradise lost and envision a peaceful and whole Spain.

Dámaso Alonso developed the concept of "poetry for the people." He communicated with the reader by abandoning the ivory tower and humanizing his poetry. Alonso utilized free verse, lexical variation, and rationalism that countered the trend toward Surrealist poetry. His major works include *Poemas puros: Poemillas de la ciudad* (1921) influenced by the work of Jiménez and Machado, and *Hijos de la ira* (1944), an intellectual inquiry into the role of man in society and his relationship to God. In his final work, *Duda de amor sobre el Ser Supremo* (1985), Alonso reflects upon his imminent death and the eternal nature of the soul.

The poetry of Pedro Salinas can be divided into three stages. His early work includes *Presagios* (1923), influenced by Jiménez. *Fábula y signo* (1931) begins the reference to the "beloved" in order to continue a quest toward attaining higher goals through his poetic voice. His second phase is characterized by love poetry: *La voz a tí debida* (1933; *My Voice Because of You*, 1976) and *Razón de amor* (1936), in which love is reinvented. The concept of "I" and "you" is redefined by the interplay of words. For Salinas, to love was to live within each other. During the third stage of his poetic evolution, Salinas was concerned with the role of the poet and the philosophical search for permanence through art. In *El contemplado* (1946; *The Sea of San Juan: A Contemplation*, 1950), he contemplated the sea through a series of philosophical reflections. In *Todo más claro y otros poemas* (1949), Salinas conducted a dialogue with nature and, in "Cero," contemplated the horrors of human nature.

Jorge Guillén wrote a series of poetry five sections collected over thirty years as *Cántico: Fe de vida* (1928, 1936, 1945, 1950; *Canticle*, 1997). The series reflects his faith in a life centered in nature. *Clamor: Tiempo de historia* (1957-1963; includes *Maremágnum*, 1957; *Que van a dar en el mar*, 1960; and *A la altura de las circunstancias*, 1963), translated in 1997 as *Clamor*, reflects on human history and the fall of humanity into chaos. *Homenaje* (1967; *Homage*, 1997) reflects on the generous nature of art to forgive and eventually conquer human frailties.

The poetry of Luis Cernuda serves as a biography of his lifelong spiritual journey. In *Perfil del aire* (1927) he follows the model of Bécquer as he expresses internal and external realities. *Un río, un amor* (1929) displays Surrealist characteristics, and here he laments the absence of love. The pessimistic tone of *Donde habite el olvido* (1934) reflects the predominant theme, the death of love. Cernuda's *Invocaciones* (1935) seeks to evade reality; here the poet's pessimism leads him to fall into the depths of despair.

Gerardo Diego developed his own style of creationist poetry. Creationist techniques dominate in *Imagen* (1922). He won the Premio Nacional de Literatura after publishing *Versos humanos* (1925; human verses). In honor of his poetic icon Góngora, Diego published *Antología poética en honor de Góngora* (1927). Góngora's influence is evident in Diego's postwar work *Alondra de verdad* (1941; lark of truth). These later sonnets paid homage to their Golden Age models as they followed traditional patterns of rhyme and meter rather than the creationist forms and syntax of Diego's early poems.

MIDDLE AND LATE TWENTIETH CENTURY

Miguel Hernández (1910-1942) represents the transition from the Generation of '27 to the succeeding generation. His poetry was influenced by the Golden Age genius Góngora. Henández blended formal structure with surreal imagery. He befriended García Lorca, Aleixandre, and the Chilean poet Pablo Neruda, among others. After serving with the losing army of the Republicanos during the Spanish Civil War, Hernández fled to Portugal. He was captured and imprisoned until his death. When offered his freedom only if he would be exiled forever from Spain, Hernández refused. His most original poetry, written while in prison, reveals unwavering compassion and faith in the human spirit. It was published posthumously as *Cancionero y romancero de ausencias* (1958; *Songbook of Absences*, 1972).

Writers within Spain during *franquismo* either went along with Franco's political policies or devoted their creative energy to resistance. Luis Rosales (1910-1992) and Leopoldo Panero (1909-1962) wrote insular poetry with aesthetic objectives. Blas de Otero (1916-1979), Gabriel Celaya (1911-1991), and José Hierro (born 1922) were influenced by Social Realism.

Salvador Espriu (1910-1992) was stylistically influenced by the avant-garde in his prose poems characterized by nationalist themes. The group of *Novísimos* (very recent ones) experimented with avant-garde poetry and developed a particular style. This regional literary and philosophical movement was led by José María Castellet, a Catalonian critic. The *Novísimo* phenomenon represents the politicized literary milieu of the postwar generation. Major poets were Catalonian Socialists who considered Barcelona the center of avant-garde creativity. The Editorial Seix Barral supported their efforts by publishing and distributing their poetry and prose.

Spain lacks a literary tradition for women writers. Some twentieth century women poets and prose writers have distinguished themselves, despite the success of their male counterparts. The philosopher, essayist, and poet María Zambrano (1904-1991) and novelist and poet Rosa Chacel (1898-1994) have distinguished themselves among their male literary peers with many national honors.

The women writers during the Republic include Rosa Chacel and Mercè Rodoreda (born 1908). Women who wrote during *franquismo* include Carmen Laforet (born 1921), Ana María Matute (born 1926), Elena Quiroga (1921-1995), and Carmen Martín Gaite (born 1925). In her essay "Hipótesis sobre una escritura diferente" (hypothesis about a different writing), Marta Traba finds a textual difference between the works of male and female writers. She finds that feminine poetics link images rather than endow them with symbolic value. Their poetry is more concerned with explanations rather than with interpretations of the universe. Feminine text depends on the impetus of detail to convey meaning. Another feminist critic, Carme Riera, finds stylistic and thematic tendencies in feminine writing. The interplay between subject and object, syntactic repetition, greater lexical variance, and thematic commonalities is addressed by female poets.

Since 1979, the definitive end of the Franco era, poetry production has been more identified with cultural and linguistic groups than by nationalist interests. Catalonia, Galicia, and the Basque provinces have created poetry with regional rather than centralized national identities.

BIBLIOGRAPHY

Barnstone, Willis, ed. *Spanish Poetry from Its Beginning Through the Nineteenth Century: An Anthology.* New York: Oxford University Press, 1970.

Bellver, Catherine G. *Absence and Presence: Spanish Women Poets of the Twenties and Thirties.* Lewisburg, PA: Bucknell University Press, 2001. The reception of major women poets of Spain is examined from a feminist perspective. The work and literary status of Concha Méndez, Josefina de la Torre, Rosa Chacel, Carmen Conde, Ernestina de Champourcin, Blanca Andréu, and others are analyzed within their social and historical contexts.

Benegas, Noni, and Jesús Munarriz, eds. *Ellas tienen la palabra/Women of Words: Dos decadas de poesia española/Two Decades of Spanish Poetry.* New York: Lectorum Publications, 1998.

Bergmann, Emilie L., ed. *Art Inscribed: Essays on Ekphrasis in Spanish Golden Age Poetry.* Cambridge, Mass.: Harvard University Press, 1979.

Bloom, Harold, ed. *Modern Spanish and Latin American Poetry.* New York: Chelsea House, 1990.

Brown, Gerald Griffiths. *The Twentieth Century.* In *A Literary History of Spain.* New York: Barnes & Noble, 1972.

Cardona-Hine, Alvaro, ed. *Spring Has Come: Spanish Lyrical Poetry from the Songbooks of the Renaissance.* Albuquerque, N.Mex.: La Alameda Press, 2000.

Crow, John Armstrong, ed. *An Anthology of Spanish Poetry: From the Beginnings to the Present Day, Including Both Spain and Spanish America.* Baton Rouge: Louisiana State University Press, 1979.

Davis, Elizabeth B. *Myth and Identity in the Epic of Imperial Spain.* Columbia: University of Missouri Press, 2000. Davis discusses the cultural role of the epic poem during the era of Spanish Imperialism. The political implications of the genre as well as the transition into the Baroque literary styles and cultural values are explored.

Debicki, Andrew P. *Modernity and Beyond: A History of Contemporary Spanish Poetry.* Lexington: University Press of Kentucky, 1994. The first English-language history and analysis of modern Spanish verse. Debicki relates Spanish poetry to European Symbolists and postmodernists. Poetic movements are comprehensible in the European literary context.

Ferran, Jaime, and Daniel P. Testa, eds. *Spanish Writers of 1936: Crisis and Commitment in the Poetry of the Thirties and Forties, an Anthology of Literary Studies and Essays.* London: Tamesis, 1973.

Flores, Ángel, ed. *Poesia Española: A Dual-Language Anthology, Sixteenth-Twentieth Centuries.* New York: Dover, 1998.

Florit, Eugenio, ed. *Introduction to Spanish Poetry.* New York: Dover, 1991.

García Herrera, José Luis. *Los Nuevos poetas.* Barcelona: Seuba Ediciones, 1994. This literary critic discusses several contemporary Spanish writers. He analyzes the poetry of emerging women writers such as Isabel Abanto, Carmen Albert, Ada Soriano, and Ilia Galán. He also addresses the works of Jordi Doce, Álvaro Fierro, and Ramón Sandoval, among others.

Glendinning, Nigel. *The Eighteenth Century.* In *A Literary History of Spain.* New York: Barnes & Noble, 1972.

Harris, Dereck. *Metal Butterflies and Poisonous Lights: The Language of Surrealism in Lorca, Alberti, Cernuda, and Aleixandre.* Anstruther, Fife, Scotland, U.K.: La Sirena, 1998. This critical study examines how elements of the Surrealist movement in the arts influenced each poet and how its peculiar characteristics are manifested in particular poems. Harris demonstrates his understanding of Surrealism as he explains its origins and development.

Jiménez-Fajardo, Salvador, and John C. Wilcox, eds. *After the War: Essays on Recent Spanish Poetry.* Boulder, Colo.: Society of Spanish and Spanish-American Studies, 1988.

Jones, R. O. *The Golden Age: Prose and Poetry, the Sixteenth and Seventeenth Centuries.* In *A Literary History of Spain.* New York: Barnes & Noble, 1971.

Mayhew, Jonathan. *The Poetics of Self-Consciousness: Twentieth-Century Spanish Poetry.* Lewisburg, Pa.: Bucknell University Press, 1994.

Navarrete, Ignacio Enrique. *Orphans of Petrarch: Poetry and Theory in the Spanish Renaissance.* Berkeley: University of California Press, 1994.

Paulino Ayuso, José. *Antología de la poesía española del siglo XX.* Madrid: Editorial Castalia, 1996. This overview of twentieth century Spanish poetry is thorough yet concise. Movements are organized for easy reference. Poets are presented with bibliographical information and analyses of major works. This first volume focuses on poetic production from 1900 to 1939.

Persin, Margaret H. *Getting the Picture: The Ekphrastic Principle in Twentieth-Century Spanish Poetry.* Lewisburg, Pa.: Bucknell University Press, 1997.

Pritchett, Kay. *Four Postmodern Poets of Spain.* Fayetteville: University of Arkansas Press, 1991. The critic and translator analyzes the poetry of Pere Gimferrer, Manuel Vásquez Montalbán, Guillermo Carnero, and Antonio Colinas. Pritchett draws comparisons between the contemporary poets, all born after the Spanish Civil War. Her criticism places their works within a socio-historical framework.

Ramos-Garcia, Luis A., Dave Oliphant, and Miguel Casado, eds. *A Bilingual Anthology of Spanish Poetry: The Generation of 1970.* New York: Edwin Mellen Press, 1997.

Robertson, Sandra Carey. *Lorca, Alberti, and the Theatre of Popular Poetry.* New York: Peter Lang, 1991. Robertson analyzes the roots of these prominent poets in folklore and the popular culture. She demonstrates the link between poetry and theater through textual analysis. Bibliographical references are included.

Shaughnessy, Lorna. *The Developing Poetic Philosophy of Pedro Salinas: A Study in Twentieth Century Spanish Poetry.* New York: Edwin Mellen Press, 1995.

Shaw, Donald Leslie. *The Nineteenth Century.* In *A Literary History of Spain.* New York: Barnes & Noble, 1972.

Terry, Arthur. *Seventeenth-Century Spanish Poetry: The Power of Artifice.* New York: Cambridge University Press, 1993.

Turnbull, Eleanor L., ed. *Ten Centuries of Spanish Poetry: An Anthology in English Verse with Original*

Texts, from the Eleventh Century to the Generation of 1898. Baltimore, Md.: Johns Hopkins University Press, 1969.

Wardropper, Bruce W., ed. *Spanish Poetry of the Golden Age*. New York: Appleton-Century-Crofts, 1971.

Wilcox, John. *Women Poets of Spain, 1860-1990: Toward a Gynocentric Vision*. Urbana: University of Illinois Press, 1997. This study focuses on often-overlooked women poets who have contributed to literary movements as well as developed original poetic voices. Poets include Rosalía de Castro, Francisca Aguirre, Carmen Conde, and Clara Janés. Contemporary poets include Amparo Amorós, Ana Rosetti, and Blanca Andréu. This critical analysis begins with Romanticism and covers the most accomplished women poets of the twentieth century.

Richard Keenan,
updated by Carole A. Champagne

TIBETAN POETRY

Tibetans refer to their country as the "Land of Snows," and this name accurately conveys the remoteness, mystery, and beauty of the land which contains the world's highest mountain, Everest (or "Goddess Mother of the Snows" in Tibetan), and which continues to be, even in the twentieth century, nearly inaccessible in its geographic and political isolation. Tibet is currently an autonomous region of the People's Republic of China, comprising an area of approximately 500,000 square miles. By contrast, historical Tibet—the region over which the cultural, religious, and frequently political influence of Tibet extended—encompassed roughly double that area and included all the highland plateaus between the Himalayan mountain range in the south and the Altyn Tagh and Kunlun ranges in the north.

The Tibetan Empire was established prior to the seventh century C.E., and recorded Tibetan history begins with the reign of Srong-brtsan sgam-po, who ruled Tibet from 620 to 649. Through its military campaigns, Tibet came into contact with a number of civilizations which had an immediate and profound influence on Tibetan culture. The religions and cultures of Iran, Gilgit, Kashmir, Turfan, Khotan, China, and, perhaps most important, the Buddhist kingdoms of northern India, all had an impact on the development of Tibetan civilization.

Tibetans attribute the invention of their alphabet to Thonmi Sambhota, a minister of Srong-brtsan sgam-po. The King first sent a group of Tibetans to India to study Indian alphabets to develop an alphabet suited to the Tibetan language, but this group met with failure. Srong-brtsan sgam-po then sent Thonmi to India. Thonmi's success is attested by the epithet "Sam-bho-ta" ("Excellent Tibetan"), given him by his Indian teachers, and by the attribution to his authorship of eight books, only two of which are extant, on the subject of Tibetan grammar and scripts.

The Tibetan language, part of the Sino-Tibetan language family, is a monosyllabic language with no inflection of verbs or nouns. The alphabet which Thonmi devised for Tibetan includes thirty consonants and four vowels and is written from left to right. Thonmi adapted his alphabet from a Kashmiri model and fashioned two styles of script: The *dbu-can* (literally, "having a head") script is most frequently used in printed books, while the cursive script, *dbu-med* (literally, "without a head"), is used in documents, letters, and some books. Later, a more stylized cursive called *khyug-yig* (literally, "running script"), was developed and used for correspondence as well as for official documents.

The format of Tibetan books also followed an Indian model, the *pothi*: Tibetan books were printed on oblong pages and kept unbound between two wooden covers, which were frequently decorated with carvings or with polychrome paintings. Tibetan manuscripts were frequently adorned with illuminations of the Buddha or of various religious teachers, done in gouache; these manuscripts were often written in an ink made of ground gold or silver. Tibetan printed books were produced by means of hand-carved printing blocks or, less frequently, metal plates. Because an individual block or plate was required for each page of a work, the expense of producing a Tibetan book was considerable, and vast warehouses were required for the storage of printing blocks. The religious nature of Tibetan literature, however, transformed the labor and expense of book printing into an act of religious devotion. The colophons of Tibetan books customarily record the names of carvers, artists, editors, and patrons whose dedicated labor and financial support made the production of such books possible and gained spiritual merit for the participating individuals.

The actual printing of Tibetan books was supervised by the monasteries which owned the appropriate printing blocks, and it was customary for books to be printed only on demand. The customer generally was responsible for providing the necessary paper and was naturally expected to compensate the monastery for the labor involved in printing and, just as important, checking the finished edition for completeness and legibility. The paper of Tibetan books is frequently toxic, a result of the use of poisonous plants, notably several species of daphne, in its production, and of the practice of adding arsenic to the paper to discourage its destruction by insects. Extant catalogs (*kar-chag*) of many monastic printing houses are of enormous value in the study of Tibetan literary history. Manuscripts, particularly those with ornamental writing and illuminations, were produced up to the present century and were particularly favored by wealthy, if only marginally literate, patrons. Such manuscripts were most frequently copies of various editions of well-known Buddhist works, such as the *Prajnyaparamita* (perfection of wisdom), and were usually consigned to the altar of a wealthy individual to serve as an object of veneration, to be read only when a visiting monk was commissioned to read or chant the text.

Religion and Tibetan Literature

Although Tibet enjoys a rich tradition of folk literature, the bulk of Tibetan literature is religious, representing the country's two major religions, Buddhism and Bonpo, the latter a pre-Buddhist Tibetan religion incorporating some elements of indigenous folk beliefs as well as influences from the religions of other countries, such as Iran. A significant amount of Buddhist literature consists of translations from the Indian Buddhist canon. The Tibetan *bKa'-'gyur* (also known as *Kanjur*), which is considered to contain the actual teachings of the Buddha, consists of 108 volumes, while the *bsTan-'gyur* (also known as *Tanjur*), which contains the orthodox textual exegesis of the *bKa'-'gyur*, contains 225 volumes.

The indigenous religious literature of Tibet is immeasurably vast and rich, including works which deal not only with religion and philosophy but also with history, medicine, science, grammar, astrology, divination, and the techniques of crafts, such as painting and the casting of bronze images. The collected works (*gsung-'bum*) of many important Tibetan religious figures are, in fact, encyclopedic in their contents and contain, in addition to learned discourses on the topics mentioned, a wealth of information in the form of correspondence and private biographical writings.

Tibetan literature abounds with a variety of minor religious genres that parallel those of medieval Europe, such as the hagiography, the pilgrimage guide, the exemplum, and the mystical visionary account. The *'das-log* genre, which deals specifically with visionary accounts of the journey to the underworld, is particularly rich in its correspondences, not only to similar visionary literature in the writings of medieval Christian saints but also to similar themes in many epic and folk traditions throughout the world.

The influence of earlier literary and oral traditions is often evident in Tibetan literature, particularly in the hagiographic literature. In addition to containing motifs and themes which clearly derive from a folk tradition, such works sometimes alternate passages of prose and verse, in which religious teachings are presented in the form of didactic poetry. The *Hundred-Thousand Songs* of the Tibetan poet and saint Milarepa (1040-1123) is the best-known example of such a work.

The provenance of many early Tibetan religious works, particularly those of the Buddhist *rNying-ma* (old ones) school and many works in the Bonpo tradition, is obscure. An entire genre called *gTer-ma* (treasure) is purported to be the work of various historical (and sometimes mythical) religious personages and to have been unearthed by later religious masters called *gTer-bston* (revealers of treasure). The *Bar-do thos-sgrol* (book which grants liberation in the place between death and rebirth merely by its hearing, commonly called *The Tibetan Book of the Dead* in Western translations) is such a work and is attributed to the eighth century Indian Tantric master Padmasambhava, who is venerated as one of the two major founders of Tibetan Buddhism.

The Tibetan Book of the Dead is perhaps the best-known Tibetan work in the West, although it is far from representative of the many genres and schools of Tibetan literature. The book contains teachings which guide the deceased person through the transitory illusions that appear after death. These illusions serve to confirm the individual's belief in the existence of his individual ego, binding him to the cycle of death, rebirth, and suffering, which, in the Buddhist view, prevents one's entry into the state of Nirvana. In *The Tibetan Book of the Dead*, poetic prayers alternate with admonitions and instructions in prose, both couched in an archaic style. Despite the book's title, which seems to guarantee its efficacy if it is simply read to the deceased, most Tibetan religious teachers insist that its contents must be internalized over years of serious study, so that one's responses to the illusions of *The Tibetan Book of the Dead* are both spontaneous and deliberate.

Since *The Tibetan Book of the Dead* contains several references to deities which may be of Bonpo origin, it is frequently supposed that much early Tibetan Buddhist literature, particularly of the rNying-ma sect, is suffused with non-Buddhist (that is, Bonpo, animist, or even shamanistic) ideas. This view does little justice to the seriousness with which the Tibetans translated Indian Buddhist works and ignores the system through which teams of highly educated monks proofread editions of religious works prior to their publication. Although Buddhist teachers were willing to accommodate the indigenous Tibetan deities, who were converted to the status of "Protectors of the [Buddhist] Religion" by Padmasambhava and other religious masters, the correct doctrinal content of Buddhist literary works was scrupulously maintained. Thus, the view that Tibetan Buddhism represents an unorthodox version of Buddhism (often labeled "Lamaism") is inaccurate and misleading.

It is evident that many of the similarities of Bonpo and Buddhist literature derive from a Bonpo imitation of the script, style, and genres of Buddhist literature brought to Tibet from India. Although the Bonpo religion had a rich tradition of its own, the existence of a Bonpo literature before the advent of Buddhism in Tibet is doubtful. The Bonpo possess several of their own specialized scripts, but the majority of these scripts clearly derive from the cursive Tibetan alphabet. The language of these texts is exceedingly complex, partly because of the custom of writing in an abbreviated form (in which several letters of certain words may be omitted) and partly because the vocabulary of Bonpo writings contains words of Zhang-zhung, rather than Tibetan, origin. Zhang-zhung was an area that lay to the west of Tibet in the Himalaya Mountains; it was at one time an independent country with its own language, and it was there that gShen-rab, the founder of the Bonpo religion, is believed to have lived. When the area was incorporated into the Tibetan state in the late eighth century, the language and script of the Tibetan Empire were adopted. The writings of the Bonpo religion, which flourished in Zhang-zhung, were thus translated into Tibetan and naturally followed the stylistic pattern of Buddhist writings. The Bonpo possess an extensive literature, including their own versions of the *bKa'-'gyur* and *bsTan-'gyur.*

The first period of Buddhist development in Tibet, initiated by its establishment as the state religion in 779, lasted until the reign of Glang-dar-ma, who ruled Tibet from 838 to 842 and who restored Bonpo as the official state religion. This period signaled the decline of Tibet as an imperial power in Inner Asia and witnessed the persecution of Buddhists and the return to a state of feudal anarchy. The establishment of the state of Gu-ge in western Tibet in the late ninth century marked a return to both political stability and Buddhism. This period is known as the "second introduction" of Buddhism to Tibet, and the vital link with Indian Buddhist teachers and monasteries played a central role. Countless Tibetans made the rigorous and expensive journey to India to learn Buddhist doctrine directly from eminent Indian Buddhist masters, and upon their return to Tibet, many of these individuals naturally attracted their own disciples. The groups that formed in this manner developed their own particular literatures and liturgies. Each was Buddhist, but each had a peculiar identity shaped by the characteristics of its founder.

In this fashion, a number of Buddhist schools developed in Tibet: The bKa'-rgyud-pa school was founded by Mar-pa (1012-1096); the Sa-skya-pa school was founded by 'Khon-dkon-mchog rGyal-po in 1073; and so on. Several of these schools played a major role in both the internal and the external politics of Tibet. In the thirteenth century, the Sa-skya-pa school had a central role in Tibet's relations with the Mongol Empire, and in 1642, the control of secular power in the Tibetan state was transferred to a religious leader, the Dalai Lama (a Mongolian epithet meaning "Religious Teacher [whose knowledge is as vast as the] Ocean"). Thereafter, ecclesiastical rule (often, and inexactly, called a "theocracy") was to continue in Tibet until the Fourteenth Dalai Lama's flight from Tibet to India during the Chinese annexation of Tibet in 1959.

PRE-BUDDHIST FOLK LITERATURE

Both the Tibetan Buddhists and the Bonpo distinguish the period preceding the Tibetan imperial period as the time in which the *mi-chos* (religion of man) flourished, in contrast to the later period in which Buddhism and Bonpo, which share the common label of *lha-chos* (divine religion), came to Tibet. The literature of this period consisted mainly of two genres: the *lde'u*, or riddle and the *sgrung* (sometimes called *sgrung-gtam*), a narrative legend or fable.

These early works dealt chiefly with creation legends and traditional codes of behavior. The *lde'u* are essentially proverbs which carry a moral message, while the *sgrung* are tales composed by storytellers and based on the earliest myths and legends of the Tibetan people. The language of these works is frequently complex, and the abundance of often obscure metaphors increases the difficulty of understanding such texts. Nevertheless, these texts are of great interest, since they represent an archaic body of writings which obviously had a basis in an oral tradition.

Some of the most striking examples of such literature are found in the ancient literary fragments unearthed at Tun-huang, an oasis city in the western part of the Chinese province of Kansu. Here, an ancient library was sealed up in the early part of the eleventh century C.E., escaping discovery until the early part of the twentieth century. A collection of approximately eight hundred manuscripts was obtained from this site by the famous explorer Sir Marc Aurel Stein, and a selection of these manuscripts is available in English translation with extensive introductions and notes in F. W. Thomas's *Ancient Folk-Literature from North-Eastern Tibet* (1957).

The collection edited by Thomas includes writings in both prose and verse, the latter generally favoring dactylic meter. These texts include several tales of a mythical nature. One tale tells of humankind's fall from an earlier golden age to an "Age of Debts and Taxes," which was brought on by the return to the sky of a lineage of divine kings. Another tale repeats the theme of the decline of a golden age, during which all creatures lived in harmony, and the subsequent dark age, brought on by the influences of evil demons and ill luck, during which the horse became separated from its wild relative, the *kiang* (a species of wild ass) and fell under the subjugation of man. Other texts contain long lists of proverbs or manuals devoted to the methods of *mo* divination. These writings display a vigorous style with frequent repetitions and parallelism, derivative of earlier oral sources, and extensive onomatopoeia. The overall tone of these works is decidedly pessimistic, and the theme of social decline which pervades them is reminiscent of similar complaints found in the authors of classical antiquity in the West.

THE GE-SAR EPIC

The Ge-sar epic is the most important epic cycle in Inner Asia, and versions of it are found in all the major areas of Tibet and Mongolia, as well as in areas occupied by various Turkic tribes and in areas bordering the Himalayas, such as Sikkim and Hunza. The epic alternates brief prose passages with longer poetic sections, which are sung by an epic bard in a variety of melodies; each melody implies a particular mood or tone and is selected by the bard to suit each poetic passage. The first written version of the Ge-sar epic dates from approximately the fifteenth century, but the earlier existence of the epic cycle is attested by references in eleventh century texts, and it is certain that portions of the epic existed in the oral literature of Inner Asia for centuries before that date.

Ge-sar's name derives from the Byzantine word for emperor, *kaisar*, a cognate of the Latin *caesar* and the German *Kaiser*, and early texts connect his name with the place-name Phrom (Rome, meaning, in this context, Byzantium). Despite this unexplained connection with Byzantium, the hero of the Tibetan epic is identified as the ruler of a land called Gling, a kingdom which once existed in an area of Tibet that later became part of the provinces of Kham and Amdo. It has been pointed out by Rolf A. Stein in *Tibetan Civilization* (1972), however, that the term *Gling* is to be considered an abbreviation for the phrase *'dzam-bu-gling*, a Tibetan term referring to the world continent of Jambudvipa; thus, the epithet *Gling* may be taken to mean that Ge-sar is the ruler of the entire world, not merely of a particular Tibetan kingdom.

There are many versions of the Ge-sar epic in Tibet, with many episodes devoted to his conquest of various countries, including China, Iran, Kashmir, and the Nakhi region of Yunnan. Several versions of the epic even include an episode in which Ge-sar descends to Hell and conquers the Lord of the Underworld; this episode is of particular interest to the comparative study of the epic in Asia and the West, since a majority of epics, including *The Epic of Gilgamesh* (c. 2000 B.C.E.), Homer's *Odyssey* (c. 800 B.C.E.), and several versions of the romances of Alexander the Great, feature an underworld journey. The Ge-sar epic invariably begins in a heavenly realm. There, a group of gods decide that it is necessary to send a divine leader to humankind, and they convince one of their number to be born as a man. After a miraculous birth and several attempts on his life by his uncle, the child who is to become Ge-sar retreats with his mother to a desert. By the use of magically produced illusions, Ge-sar convinces the tribal leaders—particularly his uncle—to take part in a horse race that will determine the leadership of the empire. Ge-sar naturally triumphs and goes on to lead his people to victory over all the countries of the world.

The religion of the Ge-sar epic belongs to the *mi-chos* tradition, although the epic has exerted an influence on later Bonpo and Buddhist works. The Ge-sar epic is still sung by epic bards and may take days or weeks to complete. The propagation of the Ge-sar epic is generally not encouraged by Tibetan Buddhist schools, although some versions of the epic have been recast in the Buddhist mold and maintain that Ge-sar was sent to Earth to protect the Buddhist religion from its enemies. Ge-sar is nevertheless an important popular hero in Tibet, and, like many folk heroes such as King Arthur in Britain and Frederick I in Germany, is connected with an apocalyptic *cultus* which maintains that Ge-sar will one day lead his people in a final battle against the evil forces of the world.

TIBETAN FOLK POETRY

Several distinct genres of folk poetry and songs exist in Tibet and are still performed at special times of the year, such as at the time of planting or harvesting crops, at the celebration of the new year, and at marriages and other special occasions. Popular songs and poems are generally termed *glu* or *glu-bzhas* and are distinguished from poems found in religious writings, which are most often called *mgur* or *dbyangs*.

Gral-glu (row songs) are chanted by groups of singers arranged in rows; their texts consist maintly of sayings whose recitation brings good luck, and they are therefore most frequently sung at weddings or at new year's festivals. *Chang-glu* (beer songs) are poems composed during drinking parties, while *sgor-bzhas* (circle songs) are sung by groups of men and women who hold hands in a circle and move to the left and right as they chant. *Bzhas-chen* (great songs) are long poems chanted at harvest celebrations.

POETRY IN INDIGENOUS BUDDHIST LITERATURE

When Tibetan Buddhists engaged in an organized and meticulous campaign of translating the corpus of Indian Buddhist literature, the sophisticated metrical patterns of Indian literature became the models for Tibetan Buddhist poetry; the Tantric songs, called *doha*, of Indian Buddhist mystic poets such as Kanha and Saraha also exerted an influence on Tibetan poetry. The dactyl, which had been the dominant meter in the early Tibetan poetry of the Tunhuang documents, was supplanted by the trochee, which became the dominant form not only in most religious poetry but also in many varieties of secular songs.

Poems containing maxims and proverbs, which have been found in the earliest Tibetan documents excavated at Tun-huang, also found popularity in the writings of Tibetan Buddhist authors. The *Subhasitaratnanidhi*, composed by the eminent Tibetan master Sa-skya Pandita (1182-1251), is an excellent example. The work contains more than 450 four-line poems of an aphoristic nature; its popularity was so great that it was widely circulated in Mongolia as well as in Tibet.

Tibetan exegeses of Tantric Buddhist texts often contain verses which exactly duplicate the Indian *doha*. In a treatise dealing with the *Cakrasamvaratantra*, the Tibetan Sa-skya-pa master Sa-chen Kun-dga'-snying-po relates the legendary biography of the Indian teacher Kanha, a renowned master of the *doha*, by interweaving the narrative of his hagiography with Tibetan *doha* verses composed by Kun-dga'-snying-po. The alternation of prose and verse is a characteristic of much Tibetan literature; perhaps the finest example of this alternating structure of prose and verse is found in the *Biography* and *Hundred-Thousand Songs* composed by the Tibetan poet and Buddhist saint Milarepa.

MILAREPA

Milarepa's *Biography* and *Hundred-Thousand Songs* (here, "hundred-thousand" is to be construed as meaning "many" and is not to be taken literally) are perhaps the most widely read books among literate Tibetan laymen and monks alike. Although Milarepa is venerated as one of the founders of the bKa'-rgyud-pa school in Tibet, his works are read by members of all Tibetan religious schools, and literary references to his writings are to be found in the literature of all Tibetan Buddhist sects. The best-known editions of the *Biography* and *Hundred-Thousand Songs* are those compiled by gTsang-smyon He-ru-ka (literally, the mad yogin of gTsang) in 1488, but other editions are known to exist; an especially important edition of the *Hundred-Thousand Songs*, compiled by Rang-byung rDo-rje (1284-1339), the Third Black Hat Karmapa, contains nearly twice as much material as is found in the gTsang-smyon version and was reprinted in 1978.

Milarepa's *Biography* begins with the story of the hero's childhood; in the manner of many Inner Asian folktales and epics, such as the Ge-sar epic and the *Secret History of the Mongols*, the death of Milarepa's father precipitates a period of degradation and poverty for his family which must be avenged by the son. Milarepa's aunt and uncle, who are named as custodians of the father's legacy, treat Mi-la, his mother, and his sister as virtual slaves, and the mother urges Mi-la to learn black magic in order to effect vengeance. Mi-la travels to study with several sorcerers, and his personal qualities of perseverance and obedience become evident. After acquiring the necessary magical powers, Mi-la avenges the greed of his aunt and uncle by sending a powerful magical assault on their eldest son's wedding feast, destroying his relatives' property and killing all of their guests. His mother is momentarily satisfied but soon informs her son that the villagers are planning to punish her for this destruction. Mi-la responds by sending a hailstorm to devastate the village's crops and thus complete his campaign of vengeance.

Far from resulting in satisfaction, these deeds trouble Milarepa's conscience and lead to an awareness of the Karmic consequences that will follow Mi-la for countless future lives. Mi-la then decides to follow the Buddhist path of salvation with the same dedication he showed in his previous studies of black magic. He eventually encounters his religious teacher (*bla-ma* or lama), Mar-pa, whose rigorous and often brutal treatment of Mi-la fills the next section of the *Biography*. Milarepa's determination is rewarded when Mar-pa initiates him as his foremost disciple, and the final third of the *Biography* is an account of Milarepa's experiences as a Buddhist master who leads his own disciples toward the path of enlightenment.

The *Biography* and the *Hundred-Thousand Songs* both consist of prose passages interwoven with Milarepa's religious poems, fashioned after the mystic poems of the Indian *doha* tradition. Milarepa's works achieve a unique beauty, combining the clarity of Buddhist teachings with a distinctly Tibetan appreciation for the beauty of nature (generally perceived as an illusion in conventional Buddhist literature) and for the customs, occupations, and tastes of the Tibetan people. For this reason, Mi-la occupies a central position in Tibetan literature and especially Tibetan poetry; his influence and popularity have been both pervasive and constant in the history of Tibetan literature, art, and drama.

THE SIXTH DALAI LAMA

The "Love Songs" of the Sixth Dalai Lama, Rin-chen-blo-bzang-rig-'dzin-tshangs-dbyangs-rgya-mtsho (1683-1706), are a collection of four-line poems which resemble the most common form of the Tibetan folk poem, the *gtang-thung bzhad* (short song). This collection contains approximately sixty songs, written in a deceptively simple language. The Sixth Dalai Lama was reputed to be a libertine who frequently left the cloister of his palace, the Potala, in disguise to visit a variety of lovers in Lhasa and to enjoy the local taverns. Such behavior was contrary to the vows of all Buddhist monks, and the Dalai Lama's reputation became the pretext for an invasion of Lhasa by the Khoshot Mongols, who sought to gain control of Tibet. The Dalai Lama was replaced by a monk chosen by the Khoshot leader Lha-bzang and died in captivity.

Despite the seemingly unorthodox behavior of the Sixth Dalai Lama, Tibetans refused to recognize the Khoshot pretender and even today consider Tshangs-dbyangs- rgya-mtsho to have been the legitimate Dalai Lama. It has been suggested that his poetry is, in fact, metaphorical and that the poems should be viewed within the context of Tantric Buddhism rather than as evidence of actual romantic adventures. The question of whether the Sixth Dalai Lama remained true to his monastic vows, however, remains secondary to the beauty of his poems, which may be appreciated for their imagery and language in any case. Several of his poems are remarkably similar to a medieval European form, the aubade, in which lovers are parted by the calls of a town watchman which signal the coming of a new day.

MODERN SECULAR POETRY

In addition to the *gtang-thung bzhad*, which is the most frequent model for secular poetry, a poetic form favored by educated Tibetans in the past several centuries is the *ka-bzhas*. This poetic form derives its name from the letter *ka*, the first letter of the Tibetan alphabet, and uses the thirty consonants of the Tibetan alphabet as the initial letters, in alphabetical order, of a thirty-line poem. The *ka-bzhas* is often employed in love poems and is also used as an elegant form for correspondence.

BIBLIOGRAPHY

Bosson, James E. *A Treasury of Aphoristic Jewels: The Subhasitaratnanidhi of Sa Skya Pandita in Tibetan and Mongolian.* Uralic and Altaic Series 92. Bloomington: Indiana University Press, 1969.

Cabezon, Jose I., and Roger R. Jackson. *Tibetan Literature: Studies in Genre.* Ithaca, N.Y.: Snow Lion Publications, 1995. Survey of poetry, novels, biographies, histories, and other writings that span thirteen hundred years.

Chang, Garma C. C., trans. *The Hundred-Thousand Songs of Milarepa.* Abridged ed. New York: Harper & Row, 1977.

Chang, Kun. "On Tibetan Poetry." *Central Asiatic Journal* 2 (1956): 129-139.

David-Neel, Alexandra, and the Lama Yongden. *The Superhuman Life of Gesar of Ling.* Reprint. New York: Arno Press, 1978.

Duncan, Marion A. *Love Songs and Proverbs of Tibet.* London: Mitre Press, 1961.

Evans-Wentz, W. Y. *Tibet's Great Yogi Milarepa.* 2d ed. London: Oxford University Press, 1969. A biographical history of Jetsün-Milarepa. Edited with introduction and annotations by Evans-Wentz.

_____, ed. *The Tibetan Book of the Dead.* New York: Causeway Books, 1973. Details the after-death experiences on the Bardo plane, according to Lama Kazi Dawa-Samdup's English rendering. Includes bibliographical references and index.

Freemantle, Francesca, and Chogyam Trungpa, eds. *The Tibetan Book of the Dead.* The Clear Light Series. London: Shambhala, 1975. Details the great liberation in the Bardo by Guru Rinpoche according to Karma Lingpa. A new translation from the Tibetan with commentary by Francesca Fremantle and Chögyam Trungpa.

He-ru-ka, Gtsan-smyon. *The Life of Milarepa.* 1977. 2d ed. Translated by Lobsang P. Lhalungpa. Boulder, Colo.: Prajña Press, 1982.

Hodgeson, Brian H. *Essays on the Language, Literature, and Religion of Nepal and Tibet.* Columbia, Mo.: South Asia Books, 1991.

Roerich, George N. "The Epic of King Kesar of Ling." *Journal of the Asiatic Society of Bengal* 8 (1942): 277-311.

Stein, Rolf A. *Tibetan Civilization.* Rev. ed. Translated by J. E. Stapleton Driver. Stanford, Calif.: Stanford University Press, 1972. Includes original drawings by Lobsang Tendzin and a bibliography.

Thomas, F. W. *Ancient Folk-Literature from North-Eastern Tibet.* Berlin: Akademie-Verlag, 1957. Presents introduction, texts, translations, and notes.

Tucci, Giuseppe. *Tibetan Folk Songs from Gyantse and Western Tibet.* 1949. 2d rev. and enlarged ed. Ascona, Switzerland: Artibus Asiae Publishers, 1966. Includes two appendices by Namkhai Norbu and biographical footnotes.

Van Tuyl, Charles D. "The Tshe Rin Ma Account: An Old Document Incorporated in the Mi la ras pa'i Mgur 'bum?" *Zentralasiatische Studien* 9 (1975): 23-36.

Zeitlin, Ida. *Gessar Khan: The Legend of Tibet.* 1927. Reprint. Jullundur, India: Asian Publishers, 1978. Chiefly based on the German version of the Mongolian text, edited by Isaac Jakob Schmidt and published in St. Petersburg, Russia, 1839, under the title *Die Thaten Bogda Gesser Chans.* Illustrated by Theodore Nadejen.

Paul A. Draghi

RESEARCH TOOLS

AWARDS FOR POETRY AND POETS

THE ACADEMY OF AMERICAN POETS FELLOWSHIP

The Academy of American Poets awards American poets with Fellowships for "distinguished poetic achievement." No awards were given between 1938 and 1945, or in 1949 and 1950.

1937: Edwin Markham

1946: Edgar Lee Masters

1947: Ridgely Torrence

1948: Percy MacKaye

1950: E. E. Cummings

1952: Padraic Colum

1953: Robert Frost

1954: Louise Townsend Nicholl and Oliver St. John Gogarty

1955: Rolfe Humphries

1956: William Carlos Williams

1957: Conrad Aiken

1958: Robinson Jeffers

1959: Louise Bogan

1960: Jesse Stuart

1961: Horace Gregory

1962: John Crowe Ransom

1963: Ezra Pound and Allen Tate

1964: Elizabeth Bishop

1965: Marianne Moore

1966: Archibald MacLeish and John Berryman

1967: Mark Van Doren

1968: Stanley Kunitz

1969: Richard Eberhart

1970: Howard Nemerov

1971: James Wright

1972: W. D. Snodgrass

1973: W. S. Merwin

1974: Léonie Adams

1975: Robert Hayden

1976: J. V. Cunningham

1977: Louis Coxe

1978: Josephine Miles

1979: May Swenson and Mark Strand

1980: Mona Van Duyn

1981: Richard Hugo

1982: John Frederick Nims and John Ashbery

1983: James Schuyler and Philip Booth

1984: Richmond Lattimore and Robert Francis

1985: Amy Clampitt and Maxine Kumin

1986: Irving Feldman and Howard Moss

1987: Josephine Jacobsen and Alfred Corn

1988: Donald Justice

1989: Richard Howard

1990: William Meredith

1991: J. D. McClatchy

1992: Adrienne Rich

1993: Gerald Stern

1994: David Ferry

1995: Denise Levertov

1996: Jay Wright

1997: John Haines

1998: Charles Simic

1999: Gwendolyn Brooks

2000: Lyn Hejinian

2001: Ellen Bryant Voigt

THE BOLLINGEN PRIZE IN POETRY

Administered by the Yale University Library, this award is given to an American poet. Awarded every two years since 1963.

1949: Ezra Pound

1950: Wallace Stevens

1951: John Crowe Ransom

1952: Marianne Moore

1953: Archibald MacLeish and William Carlos Williams
1954: W. H. Auden
1955: Léonie Adams and Louise Bogan
1956: Conrad Aiken
1957: Allen Tate
1958: E. E. Cummings
1959: Theodore Roethke
1960: Delmore Schwartz
1961: Yvor Winters
1962: John Hall Wheelock and Richard Eberhart
1963: Robert Frost
1965: Horace Gregory
1967: Robert Penn Warren
1969: John Berryman and Karl Shapiro
1971: Richard Wilbur and Mona Van Duyn

1973: James Merrill
1975: A. R. Ammons
1977: David Ignatow
1979: W. S. Merwin
1981: Howard Nemerov and May Swenson
1983: Anthony Hecht and John Hollander
1985: John Ashbery and Fred Chappell
1987: Stanley Kunitz
1989: Edgar Bowers
1991: Laura Riding Jackson and Donald Justice
1993: Mark Strand
1995: Kenneth Koch
1997: Gary Snyder
1999: Robert Creeley
2001: Louise Glück

THE T. S. ELIOT PRIZE

Administered by the Poetry Book Society, this annual award is given to the best new poetry collection published in the United Kingdom or the Republic of Ireland.

1993: Ciaran Carson—*First Language*
1994: Paul Muldoon—*The Annals of Chile*
1995: Mark Doty—*My Alexandria*
1996: Les Murray—*Subhuman Redneck Poems*
1997: Don Paterson—*God's Gift to Women*

1998: Ted Hughes—*Birthday Letters*
1999: Hugo Williams—*Billy's Rain*
2000: Michael Longley—*The Weather in Japan*
2001: Anne Carson—*The Beauty of the Husband*

THE FROST MEDAL

Awarded by the Poetry Society of America (PSA) to a poet for "distinguished lifetime service to American poetry." Awarded annually since 1984.

1930: Jessie Rittenhouse
1941: Robert Frost
1942: Edgar Lee Masters
1943: Edna St. Vincent Millay
1947: Gustav Davidson
1951: Wallace Stevens
1952: Carl Sandburg
1955: Leonora Speyer
1967: Marianne Moore
1971: Melville Cane
1974: John Hall Wheelock

1976: A. M. Sullivan
1984: Jack Stadler
1985: Robert Penn Warren
1986: Allen Ginsberg and Richard Eberhart
1987: Robert Creeley and Sterling Brown
1988: Carolyn Kizer
1989: Gwendolyn Brooks
1990: Denise Levertov and James Laughlin
1991: Donald Hall
1992: Adrienne Rich and David Ignatow
1993: William Stafford

1994: A. R. Ammons
1995: John Ashbery
1996: Richard Wilbur
1997: Josephine Jacobsen

1998: Stanley Kunitz
1999: Barbara Guest
2000: Anthony Hecht
2001: Sonia Sanchez

THE JAMES LAUGHLIN AWARD

The Academy of American Poets gives this annual award to a poet for the publication of an outstanding second poetry collection. Originally known as the Lamont Poetry Selection, the name was changed in 1995 to honor poet and publisher James Laughlin.

1954: Constance Carrier—*The Middle Voice*
1955: Donald Hall—*Exiles and Marriages*
1956: Philip Booth—*Letter from a Distant Land*
1957: Daniel Berrigan, S. J.—*Time Without Number*
1958: Ned O'Gorman—*The Night of the Hammer*
1959: Donald Justice—*The Summer Anniversaries*
1960: Robert Mezey—*The Lovemaker*
1961: X. J. Kennedy—*Nude Descending a Staircase*
1962: Edward Field—*Stand Up, Friend, with Me*
1963: no award
1964: Adrien Stoutenberg—*Heroes, Advise Us*
1965: Henri Coulette—*The War of the Secret Agents*
1966: Kenneth O. Hanson—*The Distance Anywhere*
1967: James Scully—*The Marches*
1968: Jane Cooper—*The Weather of Six Mornings*
1969: Marvin Bell—*A Probable Volume of Dreams*
1970: William Harmon—*Treasury Holiday*
1971: Stephen Dobyns—*Concurring Beasts*
1972: Peter Everwine—*Collecting the Animals*
1973: Marilyn Hacker—*Presentation Piece*
1974: John Balaban—*After Our War*
1975: Lisel Mueller—*The Private Life*
1976: Larry Levis—*The Afterlife*
1977: Gerald Stern—*Lucky Life*
1978: Ai—*Killing Floor*
1979: Frederick Seidel—*Sunrise*

1980: Michael Van Walleghen—*More Trouble with the Obvious*
1981: Carolyn Forché—*The Country Between Us*
1982: Margaret Gibson—*Long Walks in the Afternoon*
1983: Sharon Olds—*The Dead and the Living*
1984: Philip Schultz—*Deep Within the Ravine*
1985: Cornelius Eady—*Victims of the Latest Dance Craze*
1986: Jane Shore—*The Minute Hand*
1987: Garrett Kaoru Hongo—*The River of Heaven*
1988: Mary Jo Salter—*Unfinished Painting*
1989: Minnie Bruce Pratt—*Crime Against Nature*
1990: Li-Young Lee—*The City in Which I Love You*
1991: Susan Wood—*Campo Santo*
1992: Kathryn Stripling Byer—*Wildwood Flower*
1993: Rosanna Warren—*Stained Glass*
1994: Brigit Pegeen Kelly—*Song*
1995: Ralph Angel—*Neither World*
1996: David Rivard—*Wise Poison*
1997: Tony Hoagland—*Donkey Gospel*
1998: Sandra Alcosser—*Except by Nature*
1999: Tory Dent—*HIV, Mon Amour*
2000: Liz Waldner—*A Point Is That Which Has No Point*
2001: Peter Johnson—*Miracles and Mortifications*

THE LENORE MARSHALL POETRY PRIZE

Awarded by The Nation *and the Academy of American Poets annually to a poet for the publication in the United States of an outstanding poetry collection.*

1975: Cid Corman—*O/I*
1976: Denise Levertov—*The Freeing of the Dust*

1977: Philip Levine—*The Names of the Lost*
1978: Allen Tate—*Collected Poems, 1919-1976*

1979: Hayden Carruth—*Brothers, I Loved You All*

1980: Stanley Kunitz—*The Poems of Stanley Kunitz, 1928-1978*

1981: Sterling A. Brown—*The Collected Poems of Sterling A. Brown*

1982: John Logan—*The Bridge of Chance: Poems, 1974-1980*

1983: George Starbuck—*The Argot Merchant Disaster*

1984: Josephine Miles—*Collected Poems, 1930-1983*

1985: John Ashbery—*A Wave*

1986: Howard Moss—*New Selected Poems*

1987: Donald Hall—*The Happy Man*

1988: Josephine Jacobsen—*The Sisters: New and Selected Poems*

1989: Thomas McGrath—*Selected Poems, 1938-1988*

1990: Michael Ryan—*God Hunger*

1991: John Haines—*New Poems, 1980-1988*

1992: Adrienne Rich—*An Atlas of the Difficult World*

1993: Thom Gunn—*The Man with Night Sweats*

1994: W. S. Merwin—*Travels*

1995: Marilyn Hacker—*Winter Numbers*

1996: Charles Wright—*Chickamauga*

1997: Robert Pinsky—*The Figured Wheel: New and Collected Poems, 1966-1996*

1998: Mark Jarman—*Questions for Ecclesiastes*

1999: Wanda Coleman—*Bathwater Wine*

2000: David Ferry—*Of No Country I Know: New and Selected Poems and Translations*

2001: Fanny Howe—*Selected Poems*

THE NATIONAL BOOK AWARD FOR POETRY

Awarded by the National Book Foundation to a United States poet for the publication of the "best book of poetry" during the year. Not awarded from 1984-1990.

1950: William Carlos Williams—*Paterson: Book III and Selected Poems*

1951: Wallace Stevens—*The Auroras of Autumn*

1952: Marianne Moore—*Collected Poems*

1953: Archibald MacLeish—*Collected Poems, 1917-1952*

1954: Conrad Aiken—*Collected Poems*

1955: Wallace Stevens—*The Collected Poems of Wallace Stevens*

1956: W. H. Auden—*The Shield of Achilles*

1957: Richard Wilbur—*Things of the World*

1958: Robert Penn Warren—*Promises: Poems, 1954-1956*

1959: Theodore Roethke—*Words for the Wind*

1960: Robert Lowell—*Life Studies*

1961: Randall Jarrell—*The Woman at the Washington Zoo*

1962: Alan Dugan—*Poems*

1963: William Stafford—*Traveling Through the Dark*

1964: John Crowe Ransom—*Selected Poems*

1965: Theodore Roethke—*The Far Field*

1966: James Dickey—*Buckdancer's Choice: Poems*

1967: James Merrill—*Nights and Days*

1968: Robert Bly—*The Light Around the Body*

1969: John Berryman—*His Toy, His Dream, His Rest*

1970: Elizabeth Bishop—*The Complete Poems*

1971: Mona Van Duyn—*To See, to Take*

1972: Frank O'Hara—*The Collected Poems of Frank O'Hara* and Howard Moss— *Selected Poems*

1973: A. R. Ammons—*Collected Poems, 1951-1971*

1974: Allen Ginsberg—*The Fall of America: Poems of These States* and Adrienne Rich—*Driving into the Wreck: Poems, 1971-1972*

1975: Marilyn Hacker—*Presentation Piece*

1976: John Ashbery—*Self-Portrait in a Convex Mirror*

1977: Richard Eberhart—*Collected Poems, 1930-1976*

1978: Howard Nemerov—*The Collected Poems of Howard Nemerov*

1979: James Merrill—*Mirabell: Book of Numbers*

1980: Philip Levine—*Ashes*

1981: Lisel Mueller—*The Need to Hold Still*

1982: William Bronk—*Life Supports: New and Collected Poems*

1983: Galway Kinnell—*Selected Poems* and Charles Wright—*Country Music: Selected Early Poems*

1991: Philip Levine—*What Work Is*
1992: Mary Oliver—*New and Selected Poems*
1993: A. R. Ammons—*Garbage*
1994: James Tate—*A Worshipful Company of Fletchers*
1995: Stanley Kunitz—*Passing Through: The Later Poems*
1996: Hayden Carruth—*Scrambled Eggs and Whiskey*

1997: William Meredith—*Effort at Speech: New and Selected Poems*
1998: Gerald Stern—*This Time: New and Selected Poems*
1999: Ai—*Vice: New and Selected Poems*
2000: Lucille Clifton—*Blessing the Boats: New and Selected Poems, 1988-2000*
2001: Alan Dugan—*Poems Seven: New and Complete Poetry*

THE NOBEL PRIZE IN LITERATURE

Awarded annually since 1901, this award is given to an author for an entire body of literary work. The list below includes only the poets who have been so honored.

1906: Giosuè Carducci
1907: Rudyard Kipling
1913: Rabindranath Tagore
1923: William Butler Yeats
1945: Gabriela Mistral
1948: T. S. Eliot
1956: Juan Ramón Jiménez
1959: Salvatore Quasimodo
1960: Saint-John Perse
1963: George Seferis
1966: Nelly Sachs
1969: Samuel Beckett

1971: Pablo Neruda
1974: Harry Martinson
1975: Eugenio Montale
1977: Vicente Aleixandre
1979: Odysseus Elytis
1980: Czesław Miłosz
1984: Jaroslav Seifert
1987: Joseph Brodsky
1990: Octavio Paz
1992: Derek Walcott
1995: Seamus Heaney
1996: Wisława Szymborska

THE POET LAUREATE CONSULTANT IN POETRY

An appointment is given through the Library of Congress to a poet who then serves as the United States' official poet, or "poet laureate."

1937-1941: Joseph Auslander
1943-1944: Allen Tate
1944-1945: Robert Penn Warren
1945-1946: Louise Bogan
1946-1947: Karl Shapiro
1947-1948: Robert Lowell
1948-1949: Léonie Adams
1949-1950: Elizabeth Bishop
1950-1952: Conrad Aiken
1952: William Carlos Williams (did not serve)
1956-1958: Randall Jarrell
1958-1959: Robert Frost

1959-1961: Richard Eberhart
1961-1963: Louis Untermeyer
1963-1964: Howard Nemerov
1964-1965: Reed Whittemore
1965-1966: Stephen Spender
1966-1968: James Dickey
1968-1970: William Jay Smith
1970-1971: William Stafford
1971-1973: Josephine Jacobsen
1973-1974: Daniel Hoffman
1974-1976: Stanley Kunitz
1976-1978: Robert Hayden

1978-1980: William Meredith

1981-1982: Maxine Kumin

1982-1984: Anthony Hecht

1984-1985: Robert Fitzgerald (limited by health) and
Reed Whittemore (interim consultant)

1985-1986: Gwendolyn Brooks

1986-1987: Robert Penn Warren (first poet to be
designated Poet Laureate Consultant in Poetry)

1987-1988: Richard Wilbur

1988-1990: Howard Nemerov

1990-1991: Mark Strand

1991-1992: Joseph Brodsky

1992-1993: Mona Van Duyn

1993-1995: Rita Dove

1995-1997: Robert Hass

1997-2000: Robert Pinsky

1999-2000: Rita Dove, Louise Glück and W. S. Merwin
(special bicentennial consultants)

2000-2001: Stanley Kunitz

2001-2002: Billy Collins

THE PULITZER PRIZE FOR POETRY

Awarded by Columbia University's Graduate School of Journalism to honor an American poet who has published a distinguished collection of poetry.

1918: Sara Teasdale—*Love Songs*

1919: Margaret Widdemer—*Old Road to Paradise* and
Carl Sandburg—*Corn Huskers*

1920: no award

1921: no award

1922: Edwin Arlington Robinson—*Collected Poems*

1923: Edna St. Vincent Millay—*The Ballad of the
Harp-Weaver and Other Poems*

1924: Robert Frost—*New Hampshire: A Poem with
Notes and Grace Notes*

1925: Edwin Arlington Robinson—*The Man Who Died
Twice*

1926: Amy Lowell—*What's O'Clock*

1927: Leonora Speyer—*Fiddler's Farewell*

1928: Edwin Arlington Robinson—*Tristram*

1929: Stephen Vincent Benét—*John Brown's Body*

1930: Conrad Aiken—*Selected Poems*

1931: Robert Frost—*Collected Poems*

1932: George Dillon—*The Flowering Stone*

1933: Archibald MacLeish—*Conquistador*

1934: Robert Hillyer—*Collected Verse*

1935: Audrey Wurdemann—*Bright Ambush*

1936: Robert P. Tristram Coffin—*Strange Holiness*

1937: Robert Frost—*A Further Range*

1938: Marya Zaturenska—*Cold Morning Sky*

1939: John Gould Fletcher—*Selected Poems*

1940: Mark Van Doren—*Selected Poems*

1941: Leonard Bacon—*Sunderland Capture*

1942: William Rose Benet—*The Dust Which Is God*

1943: Robert Frost—*A Witness Tree*

1944: Stephen Vincent Benét—*Western Star*

1945: Karl Shapiro—*V-Letter and Other Poems*

1946: no award

1947: Robert Lowell—*Lord Weary's Castle*

1948: W. H. Auden—*The Age of Anxiety*

1949: Peter Viereck—*Terror and Decorum*

1950: Gwendolyn Brooks—*Annie Allen*

1951: Carl Sandburg—*Complete Poems*

1952: Marianne Moore—*Collected Poems*

1953: Archibald MacLeish—*Collected Poems,
1917-1952*

1954: Theodore Roethke—*The Waking*

1955: Wallace Stevens—*Collected Poems*

1956: Elizabeth Bishop—*Poems: North and South*

1957: Richard Wilbur—*Things of This World*

1958: Robert Penn Warren—*Promises: Poems,
1954-1956*

1959: Stanley Kunitz—*Selected Poems, 1928-1958*

1960: W. D. Snodgrass—*Heart's Needle*

1961: Phyllis McGinley—*Times Three: Selected Verse
from Three Decades*

1962: Alan Dugan—*Poems*

1963: William Carlos Williams—*Pictures from
Breughel*

1964: Louis Simpson—*At the End of the Open Road*

1965: John Berryman—*Seventy-seven Dream Songs*

1966: Richard Eberhart—*Selected Poems*

1967: Anne Sexton—*Live or Die*

1968: Anthony Hecht—*The Hard Hours*
1969: George Oppen—*Of Being Numerous*
1970: Richard Howard—*Untitled Subjects*
1971: W. S. Merwin—*The Carrier of Ladders*
1972: James Wright—*Collected Poems*
1973: Maxine Kumin—*Up Country*
1974: Robert Lowell—*The Dolphin*
1975: Gary Snyder—*Turtle Island*
1976: John Ashbery—*Self-Portrait in a Convex Mirror*
1977: James Merrill—*Divine Comedies*
1978: Howard Nemerov—*Collected Poems*
1979: Robert Penn Warren—*Now and Then*
1980: Donald Justice—*Selected Poems*
1981: James Schuyler—*The Morning of the Poem*
1982: Sylvia Plath—*The Collected Poems*
1983: Galway Kinnell—*Selected Poems*
1984: Mary Oliver—*American Primitive*
1985: Carolyn Kizer—*Yin*
1986: Henry Taylor—*The Flying Change*

1987: Rita Dove—*Thomas and Beulah*
1988: William Meredith—*Partial Accounts: New and Selected Poems*
1989: Richard Wilbur—*New and Collected Poems*
1990: Charles Simic—*The World Doesn't End*
1991: Mona Van Duyn—*Near Changes*
1992: James Tate—*Selected Poems*
1993: Louise Glück—*The Wild Iris*
1994: Yusef Komunyakaa—*Neon Vernacular: New and Selected Poems*
1995: Philip Levine—*The Simple Truth*
1996: Jorie Graham—*The Dream of the Unified Field*
1997: Lisel Mueller—*Alive Together: New and Selected Poems*
1998: Charles Wright—*Black Zodiac*
1999: Mark Strand—*Blizzard of One*
2000: C. K. Williams—*Repair*
2001: Stephen Dunn—*Different Hours*
2002: Carl Dennis—*Practical Gods*

THE SHELLEY MEMORIAL AWARD

Awarded by the Poetry Society of America to an American poet on the basis of "genius and need."

1929: Conrad Aiken
1930: Lizette Woodworth Reese
1931: Archibald MacLeish
1932: no award
1933: Lola Ridge and Frances Frost
1934: Lola Ridge and Marya Zaturenska
1935: Josephine Miles
1936: Charlotte Wilder and Ben Belitt
1937: Lincoln Fitzell
1938: Robert Francis and Harry Brown
1939: Herbert Bruncken and Winfield T. Scott
1940: Marianne Moore
1941: Ridgely Torrence
1942: Robert Penn Warren
1943: Edgar Lee Masters
1944: E. E. Cummings
1945: Karl Shapiro
1946: Rolfe Humphries
1947: Janet Lewis

1948: John Berryman
1949: Louis Kent
1950: Jeremy Ingalls
1951: Richard Eberhardt
1952: Elizabeth Bishop
1953: Kenneth Patchen
1954: Leonie Adams
1955: Robert Fitzgerald
1956: George Abbe
1957: Kenneth Rexroth
1958: Rose Garcia Villa
1959: Delmore Schwartz
1960: Robinson Jeffers
1961: Theodore Roethke
1962: Eric Barker
1963: William Stafford
1964: Ruth Stone
1965: David Ignatow
1966: Anne Sexton

1967: May Swenson
1968: Anne Stanford
1969: X. J. Kennedy and Mary Oliver
1970: Adrienne Rich and Louise Townsend Nicholl
1971: Galway Kinnel
1972: John Ashbery and Richard Wilbur
1973: W. S. Merwin
1974: Edward Field
1975: Gwendolyn Brooks
1976: Muriel Rukeyser
1977: Jane Cooper and William Everson
1978: Hayden Carruth
1979: Julia Randall
1980: Robert Creeley
1981: Alan Dugan
1982: Jon Anderson and Leo Connellan
1983: Denise Levertov and Robert Duncan

1984: Etheridge Knight
1986: Gary Snyder
1987: Mona Van Duyn
1988: Dennis Schmitz
1989: no award
1990: Thomas McGrath and Theodore Weiss
1991: Shirley Kaufman
1992: Lucille Clifton
1993: Josephine Jacobsen
1994: Kenneth Koch and Cathy Song
1995: Stanley Kunitz
1996: Robert Pinsky and Anne Waldman
1997: Frank Bidart
1998: Eleanor Ross Taylor
1999: Tom Sleigh
2000: Jean Valentine
2001: Alice Notley and Michael Palmer

THE WALLACE STEVENS AWARD

Awarded by the Academy of American Poets to a poet for "outstanding and proven mastery of the art of poetry."

1994: W. S. Merwin
1995: James Tate
1996: Adrienne Rich
1997: Anthony Hecht

1998: A. R. Ammons
1999: Jackson MacLow
2000: Frank Bidart
2001: John Ashbery

THE WALT WHITMAN AWARD

Awarded by the Academy of American Poets to a poet for the publication of a distinguished first collection of poetry.

1975: Reg Saner—*Climbing into the Roots*
1976: Laura Gilpin—*The Hocus-Pocus of the Universe*
1977: Lauren Shakely—*Guilty Bystander*
1978: Karen Snow—*Wonders*
1979: David Bottoms—*Shooting Rats at the Bibb County*
1980: Jared Carter—*Work, for the Night Is Coming*
1981: Alberto Ríos—*Whispering to Fool the Wind*
1982: Anthony Petrosky—*Jurgis Petraskas*
1983: Christopher Gilbert—*Across the Mutual Landscape*

1984: Eric Pankey—*For the New Year*
1985: Christianne Balk—*Bindweed*
1986: Chris Llewellyn—*Fragments from the Fire*
1987: Judith Baumel—*The Weight of Numbers*
1988: April Bernard—*Blackbird Bye Bye*
1989: Martha Hollander—*The Game of Statues*
1990: Elaine Terranova—*The Cult of the Right Hand*
1991: Greg Glazner—*From the Iron Chair*
1992: Stephen Yenser—*The Fire in All Things*
1993: Alison Hawthorne Deming—*Science and Other Poems*

1994: Jan Richman—*Because the Brain Can Be Talked into Anything*
1995: Nicole Cooley—*Resurrection*
1996: Joshua Clover—*Madonna anno domini*
1997: Barbara Ras—*Bite Every Sorrow*

1998: Jan Heller Levi—*Once I Gazed at You in Wonder*
1999: Judy Jordan—*Carolina Ghost Woods*
2000: Ben Doyle—*Radio, Radio*
2001: John Canaday—*The Invisible World*

EXPLICATING POETRY

Explicating poetry—the process of analyzing a poem and its constituent parts, from meter and rhythm to rhyme and imagery, or what the French have called *explication du texte*—begins with a process of distinguishing the poem's factual and technical elements from the reader's emotional ones. Readers respond to poems in a variety of ways that may initially have little to do with the poetry itself but that result from the events in their own lives, their expectations of art, and their philosophical, theological, and psychological orientations. Every serious reader hopes to find poems that can blend with the elements of his or her personal background in such a way that for a moment or a lifetime his or her relationship to life and the cosmos becomes more meaningful. This is the ultimate goal of poetry, and when it happens—when meaning, rhythm, and sound fuse with the reader's emotions to create a unified experience—it can only be called the magic of poetry, for something has happened between reader and poet which is inexplicable in rational terms.

When a poem creates such an emotional and intellectual response in a reader, then it is at least a partial success. To be considered excellent, however, a poem must also be able to pass a critical analysis to determine whether it is mechanically superior. Although twentieth century criticism tended to judge poetic works solely on their individual content and treated them as independent of historical influences, such a technique often makes a full explication difficult. The best modern readers realize that good poetry analysis observes all aspects of a poem: its technical success, its historical importance and intellectual force, its effect on the reader's emotions, and often its embeddedness in a particular set of cultural or ethnic experiences.

Students of poetry will find it useful to begin an explication by analyzing the elements that poets have at their disposal as they create their art: dramatic situation, point of view, imagery, metaphor, symbol, meter, form, and allusion. The outline headed "Checklist for Explicating a Poem" (see box) will help guide the reader through the necessary steps to a detailed explication.

Although explication is not a science, and a variety of observations may be equally valid, these step-by-step procedures can be applied systematically to make the reading of most poems a richer experience for the reader. To illustrate, these steps are applied below to a difficult poem by Edwin Arlington Robinson.

"Luke Havergal"

Go to the western gate, Luke Havergal,
There where the vines cling crimson on the wall,
And in the twilight wait for what will come.
The leaves will whisper there of her, and some, 4
Like flying words, will strike you as they fall;
But go, and if you listen, she will call.
Go to the western gate, Luke Havergal—
Luke Havergal. 8

No, there is not a dawn in eastern skies
To rift the fiery night that's in your eyes;
But there, where western glooms are gathering,
The dark will end the dark, if anything: 12
God slays Himself with every leaf that flies,
And hell is more than half of paradise.
No, there is not a dawn in eastern skies—
In eastern skies. 16

Out of a grave I come to tell you this,
Out of a grave I come to quench the kiss
That flames upon your forehead with a glow
That blinds you to the way that you must go. 20
Yes, there is yet one way to where she is,
Bitter, but one that faith may never miss.
Out of a grave I come to tell you this—
To tell you this. 24

There is the western gate, Luke Havergal
There are the crimson leaves upon the wall.
Go, for the winds are tearing them away,—
Nor think to riddle the dead words they say, 28
Nor any more to feel them as they fall;
But go, and if you trust her she will call.
There is the western gate, Luke Havergal—
Luke Havergal.

E. A. Robinson, 1897

Checklist for Explicating a Poem

I. THE INITIAL READINGS
A. Before reading the poem, the reader should:
1. Notice its form and length.
2. Consider the title, determining, if possible, whether it might function as an allusion, symbol, or poetic image.
3. Notice the date of composition or publication, and identify the general era of the poet.
B. The poem should be read intuitively and emotionally and be allowed to "happen" as much as possible.
C. In order to establish the rhythmic flow, the poem should be reread. A note should be made as to where the irregular spots (if any) are located.

II. EXPLICATING THE POEM
A. *Dramatic situation.* Studying the poem line by line helps the reader to discover the dramatic situation. All elements of the dramatic situation are interrelated and should be viewed as reflecting and affecting one another. The dramatic situation serves a particular function in the poem, adding realism, surrealism, or absurdity; drawing attention to certain parts of the poem; and changing to reinforce other aspects of the poem. All points should be considered. The following questions are particularly helpful to ask in determining dramatic situation:
1. What, if any, is the narrative action in the poem?
2. How many personas appear in the poem? What part do they take in the action?
3. What is the relationship between characters?
4. What is the setting (time and location) of the poem?
B. *Point of view.* An understanding of the poem's point of view is a major step toward comprehending the poet's intended meaning. The reader should ask:
1. Who is the speaker? Is he or she addressing someone else or the reader?
2. Is the narrator able to understand or see everything happening to him or her, or does the reader know things that the narrator does not?
3. Is the narrator reliable?
4. Do point of view and dramatic situation seem consistent? If not, the inconsistencies may provide clues to the poem's meaning.
C. *Images and metaphors.* Images and metaphors are often the most intricately crafted vehicles of the poem for relaying the poet's message. Realizing that the images and metaphors work in harmony with the dramatic situation and point of view will help the reader to see the poem as a whole, rather than as disassociated elements.
1. The reader should identify the concrete images (that is, those that are formed from objects that can be touched, smelled, seen, felt, or tasted). Is the image projected by the poet consistent with the physical object?
2. If the image is abstract, or so different from natural imagery that it cannot be associated with a real object, then what are the properties of the image?
3. To what extent is the reader asked to form his or her own images?

4. Is any image repeated in the poem? If so, how has it been changed? Is there a controlling image?
5. Are any images compared to each other? Do they reinforce one another?
6. Is there any difference between the way the reader perceives the image and the way the narrator sees it?
7. What seems to be the narrator's or persona's attitude toward the image?
D. *Words.* Every substantial word in a poem may have more than one intended meaning, as used by the author. Because of this, the reader should look up many of these words in the dictionary and:
1. Note all definitions that have the slightest connection with the poem.
2. Note any changes in syntactical patterns in the poem.
3. In particular, note those words that could possibly function as symbols or allusions, and refer to any appropriate sources for further information.
E. *Meter, rhyme, structure, and tone.* In scanning the poem, all elements of prosody should be noted by the reader. These elements are often used by a poet to manipulate the reader's emotions, and therefore they should be examined closely to arrive at the poet's specific intention.
1. Does the basic meter follow a traditional pattern such as those found in nursery rhymes or folk songs?
2. Are there any variations in the base meter? Such changes or substitutions are important thematically and should be identified.
3. Are the rhyme schemes traditional or innovative, and what might their form mean to the poem?
4. What devices has the poet used to create sound patterns (such as assonance and alliteration)?
5. Is the stanza form a traditional or innovative one?
6. If the poem is composed of verse paragraphs rather than stanzas, how do they affect the progression of the poem?
7. After examining the above elements, is the resultant tone of the poem casual or formal, pleasant, harsh, emotional, authoritative?
F. *Historical context.* The reader should attempt to place the poem into historical context, checking on events at the time of composition. Archaic language, expressions, images, or symbols should also be looked up.
G. *Themes and motifs.* By seeing the poem as a composite of emotion, intellect, craftsmanship, and tradition, the reader should be able to determine the themes and motifs (smaller recurring ideas) presented in the work. He or she should ask the following questions to help pinpoint these main ideas:
1. Is the poet trying to advocate social, moral, or religious change?
2. Does the poet seem sure of his or her position?
3. Does the poem appeal primarily to the emotions, to the intellect, or to both?
4. Is the poem relying on any particular devices for effect (such as imagery, allusion, paradox, hyperbole, or irony)?

STEP I-A: *Before reading*

1. "Luke Havergal" is a strophic poem composed of four equally lengthened stanzas. Each stanza is long enough to contain a narrative, and involves description or situation, or a problem and resolution.

2. The title raises several possibilities: Luke Havergal could be a specific person; Luke Havergal could represent a type of person; the name might have symbolic or allusive qualities. Thus, "Luke" may refer to: Luke of the Bible; "Luke-warm": meaning indifferent or showing little or no zeal. "Havergal" could be a play on words. "Haver" is a Scotch and Northern English word meaning to talk foolishly. It is clear from the rhyme words that the "gal" of Havergal is pronounced as if it had two "l's," but it is spelled with one "l" for no apparent reason unless it is to play on the word "gal," meaning girl. Because it is pronounced "gall," meaning something bitter or severe, a sore or state of irritation, or an impudent self-assurance, this must also be considered as a possibility. Finally, the "haver" of "Havergal" might be a perversion of "have a."

3. Published in 1897, the poem probably does not contain archaic language unless it is deliberately used. The period of writing is known as the Victorian Age. Historical events which may have influenced the poem may be checked for later.

STEP I-B: *The poem should be read*

STEP I-C: *Rereading the poem*

The frequent use of internal caesuras in stanzas one and two contrast with the lack of caesuras in stanzas three and four. There are end-stopped lines and much repetition. The poem reads smoothly except for line twenty-eight and the feminine ending on lines eleven and twelve.

STEP II-A: *Dramatic situation*

In line one of "Luke Havergal" an unidentified speaker is addressing Luke. Because the speaker calls him by his full name there is a sense that the speaker has assumed a superior (or at least a formal) attitude toward Luke and that the talk which they are having is not a casual conversation.

In addition to knowing something about the relationship in line one, the reader is led to think, because of the words "go to the western gate," that the personas must be near some sort of enclosed house or city. Perhaps Luke and the speaker are at some "other" gate, since the western gate is specifically pointed out.

Line two suggests that the situation at the western gate is different from that elsewhere—there "vines cling crimson on the wall," hinting at some possibilities about the dramatic situation. (Because flowers and colors are always promising symbols, they must be carefully considered later.)

The vines in line two could provide valuable information about the dramatic situation, except that in line two the clues are ambiguous. Are the vines perennial? If so, their crimson color suggests that the season is late summer or autumn. Crimson might also be their natural color when in full bloom. Further, are they grape vines (grapes carry numerous connotations and symbolic values), and are the vines desirable? All of this in line two is ambiguous. The only certainty is that there is a wall—a barrier which closes something in and something out.

In line three, the speaker again commands Luke to go and wait. Since Luke is to wait in the twilight, it is probably now daylight. All Luke must do is be passive because whatever is to come will happen without any action on his part.

In line four, the speaker begins to tell Luke what will happen at the western gate, and the reader now knows that Luke is waiting for something with feminine characteristics, possibly a woman. This line also mentions that the vines have leaves, implying that crimson denotes their waning stage.

In line five, the speaker continues to describe what will happen at the western gate: The leaves will whisper about "her," and, as they fall, some of them will strike Luke "like flying words." The reader, however, must question whether Luke will actually be "struck" by the leaves, or whether the leaves are being personified or being used as an image or symbol. In line six, the speaker stops his prophecy and tells Luke to leave. If Luke listens, "she" will call, but if he does not, it is unclear what will happen. The reader might ask the questions, to whom is "she" calling, and from where?

In summarizing the dramatic situation in stanza one, one can say that the speaker is addressing Luke, but it is not yet possible to determine whether he or she is present or whether Luke is thinking to himself (interior monologue). The time is before twilight; the place is near a wall with a gate. Luke is directed to go to the gate and listen for a female voice to call.

From reading the first line in the second stanza, it is apparent that Luke has posed some kind of question, probably concerned with what will be found at the western gate. The answer given is clearly not a direct answer to whatever question was asked, especially as the directions "east" and "west" are probably symbolic. The reader can expect, however, that the silent persona's response will affect the poem's progress.

Stanza three discloses who the speaker is and what his relationship is to Luke. After the mysterious discourse in stanza two, Luke has probably asked "Who are you?" The equally mysterious reply in stanza three raises the issue of whether the voice speaking is a person or a spirit or whether it is Luke's imagination or conscience.

Because the voice says that it comes out of the grave, the reader cannot know who or what it is. It may be a person, a ghost, or only Luke's imagination or conscience. Obviously the answer will affect the dramatic situation.

In line eighteen the reader learns that the speaker is on a particular mission: "to quench the kiss," and the reader can assume that when the mission is complete he or she will return to the grave. This information is sudden and shocking, and because of this sharp jolt, the reader tends to believe the speaker and credit him or her with supernatural knowledge.

In stanza four it becomes apparent that Luke and the speaker have not been stationary during the course of the poem because the western gate is now visible; the speaker can see the leaves upon the wall (line twenty-six).

The wind is blowing (line twenty-seven), creating a sense of urgency, because if all the leaves are blown away they cannot whisper about "her." The speaker gives Luke final instructions and the poem ends with the speaker again pointing toward the place where Luke will find the female persona.

In summary, one can say that the dramatic situation establishes a set of mysterious circumstances which are not explained or resolved on the dramatic level. Luke has been told to go to the western gate by someone who

identifies himself or herself as having come from the grave in order to quench Luke's desire, which seems to be connected with the estranged woman who is, perhaps, dead. The dramatic situation does not tell whether the commanding voice is an emissary from the woman, or from the devil, or is merely Luke's conscience; nor does it suggest that something evil will happen to Luke at the western gate, although other elements in the poem make the reader afraid for him.

The poet, then, is using the dramatic situation to draw the reader into questions which will be answered by other means; at this point, the poem is mysterious, obscure, ambiguous, and deliberately misleading.

STEP II-B: *Point of view*

There are a number of questions which immediately come to mind about the point of view. Is the speaker an evil seducer, or is he or she a friend telling Luke about death? Why is the poem told from his or her point of view?

From a generalized study, readers know that the first-person singular point of view takes the reader deep into the mind of the narrator in order to show what he or she knows or to show a personal reaction to an event.

In "Luke Havergal," the narrator gives the following details about himself and the situation: a sense of direction (lines one and nine); the general type and color of the vegetation, but not enough to make a detailed analysis of it (line two); a pantheistic view of nature (line four); a feeling of communication with the leaves and "her" (lines five and six); a philosophic view of the universe (stanza two); the power to "quench the kiss," a sense of mission, and a home—the grave (line eighteen); special vision (line twenty); a sense of destiny (lines twenty-one and twenty-two); and a sense of time and eternity (lines twenty-seven through twenty-nine).

Apparently, the narrator can speak with confidence about the western gate, and can look objectively at Luke to see the kiss upon his forehead. Such a vantage point suggests that the speaker might represent some aspect of death. He also knows the "one way to where she is," leaving it reasonable to infer that "she" is dead.

There is another possibility in regard to the role of the speaker. He might be part of Luke himself—the voice of his thoughts, of his unconscious mind—or of part of his past. This role might possibly be combined with that of some sort of Spirit of Death.

The poem, then, is an internal dialogue in which Luke is attempting to cope with "she," who is probably dead and who might well have been his lover, though neither is certain. He speaks to another persona, which is probably Luke's own spirit which has been deadened by the loss of his lover.

Once it is suggested that Luke is a man who is at the depth of despair, the dramatic situation becomes very important because of the possibility that Luke may be driving himself toward self-destruction.

The dramatic situation, therefore, may not be as it originally seemed; perhaps there is only one person, not two. Luke's psychological condition permits him to look at himself as another person, and this other self is pushing Luke toward the western gate, a place which the reader senses is evil.

If the voice is Luke's, then much of the mystery is clarified. Luke would have known what the western gate looked like, whereas a stranger would have needed supernatural powers to know it; furthermore, Luke had probably heard the leaves whispering before, and in his derangement he could believe that someone would call to him if he would only listen.

Establishing point of view has cleared up most of the inconsistencies in this poem's dramatic situation, but there is still confusion about the grave and the kiss. It is easy to make the grave symbolically consistent with point of view, but the reader should look for other possibilities before settling on this explanation.

In stanzas one and two there is no problem; the dramatic situation is simple and point of view can be reconciled since there is no evidence to prove that another person is present. If, however, the voice is that of Luke's other self, then why has it come from the grave, and where did the kiss come from? At this point, it is not possible to account for these inconsistencies, but by noting them now, the reader can be on the alert for the answers later. Quite possibly accounting for the inconsistencies will provide the key for the explication.

STEP II-C: *Images and metaphors*

Finding images in poems is usually not a difficult task, although seeing their relation to the theme often is.

"Luke Havergal" is imagistically difficult because the images are introduced, then reused as the theme develops.

In stanza one the reader is allowed to form his own image of the setting and mood at the western gate; most readers will probably imagine some sort of mysterious or supernatural situation which is related to death or the dead. The colors, the sound of the words, and the particular images (vines, wall, whispering leaves) establish the relationship between the living and the dead as the controlling image of the entire poem.

Within the controlling death-in-life image, the metaphors and conceits are more difficult to handle. Vines clinging crimson on the wall (line two) and waiting in the twilight for something to come (line three) are images requiring no particular treatment at this point, but in lines four and five the reader is forced to contend directly with whispering leaves which are like flying words, and there are several metaphorical possibilities for this image.

First, there is the common image of leaves rustling in a breeze, and in a mysterious or enchanted atmosphere it would be very easy to imagine that they are whispering. Such a whisper, however, would ordinarily require a moderate breeze, as a fierce wind would overpower the rustling sound of leaves; but there is more ambiguity in the image: "The leaves will whisper there for her, and some,/ Like flying words, will strike you as they fall."

Because of the syntactical ambiguity of "some,/ Like flying words, will strike," one cannot be sure how close or literal is the similarity or identity of "leaves" and "words." The reader cannot be completely sure whether it is leaves or words or both that will strike Luke, or whether the sight of falling leaves might be forcing him to recall words he has heard in the past. There is a distinct metaphoric connection between leaves and words, however, and these in some way strike Luke, perhaps suggesting that the words are those of an argument (an argument in the past between Luke and "her" before her death) or perhaps meant to suggest random words which somehow recall "her" but do not actually say anything specific.

In stanza two, the poet forces the reader to acknowledge the light and dark images, but they are as obscure as the falling leaves in stanza one. The dawn which the reader is asked to visualize (line nine) is clear, but it is immediately contrasted with "the fiery night that's in your eyes"; Luke's smoldering, almost diabolic eyes are imagistically opposed to the dawn.

Line eleven returns to the western gate, or at least to the "west," where twilight is falling. The "western glooms" become imagistic as the twilight falls and depicts Luke's despair. Twilight is not "falling," but dark is "gathering" around him, and glooms not only denotes darkness, but also connotes Luke's emotional state.

The paradox in line twelve, "The dark will end the dark," beckons the reader to explore it imagistically, but it is not easy to understand how darkness relieves darkness, unless one of the two "darknesses" is symbolic of death or of Luke's gloom. With this beckoning image, the poet has created emphasis on the line and teases with images which may really be symbols or paradoxes. The same thing is true for lines thirteen and fourteen, which tempt the reader to imagine how "God slays Himself" with leaves, and how "hell is more than half of paradise."

The beginning of stanza three does not demand an image so much as it serves to tell where the narrator comes from, and to present the narrator's method for quenching the kiss. Line nineteen however, presents an image which is as forceful as it is ambiguous. The kiss, which may be the kiss of the estranged woman, or "the kiss of death," or both, flames with a glow, which is also paradoxical. The paradox, however, forms an image which conveys the intensity of Luke's passion.

Stanza four returns to the imagery of stanza one, but now the whispering leaves take on a metaphorical extension. If the leaves are whispering words from the dead, and if the leaves are "her" words, then once the wind tears all the leaves away, there will no longer be any medium for communication between the living and the dead. This adds a sense of urgency for Luke to go to the western gate and do there what must be done.

In summary, the images in "Luke Havergal" do more than set the mood; they also serve an important thematic function because of their ambiguities and paradoxical qualities.

STEP II-D: *Words*

Because the poem is not too old, the reader will find that most of the words have not changed much. It is still important, however, for the reader to look up words as they may have several diverse meanings. Even more important to consider in individual words or phrases, however, is the possibility that they might be symbolic or allusive.

"Luke Havergal" is probably not as symbolic as it at first appears, although poems which use paradox and allusion are often very symbolic. Clearly the western gate is symbolic, but to what degree is questionable. No doubt it represents the last light in Luke's life, and once he passes beyond it he moves into another type of existence. The west and the twilight are points of embarkation; the sun is setting in the west, but even though the sun sets, there will not be a dawn in the east to dispel Luke's dark gloom. Traditionally the dark, which is gathering in the west, is symbolic of death (the west is also traditionally associated with death), and only the dark will end Luke's gloom in life, if anything at all can do it.

There is one important allusion in the poem, which comes in stanza three; the kiss which the speaker is going to quench may be the "kiss of death," the force which can destroy Luke.

In both concept and language, stanza three is reminiscent of the dagger scene and killing of Duncan (Act II, Scene 1) in William Shakespeare's *Macbeth* (1606). Just before the murder, Macbeth has visions of the dagger:

> Art thou not, fatal vision, sensible
> To feeling as to sight? or art thou but
> A dagger of the mind, a false creation,
> Proceeding from the heat-oppressed brain?
> I see thee yet, in form as palpable
> As this which now I draw.
> Thou marshall'st me the way that I was going;

And a few lines later (Act II, Scene 2) Lady Macbeth says:

> That which hath made them drunk hath made me bold;
> What hath quench'd them hath given me fire.

The reversal in point of view in "Luke Havergal" gives the poem added depth, which is especially enhanced by the comparison with Macbeth. The line, "That blinds you to the way that you must go" is almost a word-forword equivalent of "Thou marshall'st me the way that I was going," except that in "Luke Havergal" whoever is with Luke is talking, while Macbeth himself is talking to the dagger.

The result of the allusion is that it is almost possible to imagine that it is the dagger that is talking to Luke, and the whole story of Macbeth becomes relevant to the poem because the reader suspects that Luke's end will be similar to Macbeth's.

The words of Lady Macbeth strengthen the allusion's power and suggest a male-female relationship which is leading Luke to his death, especially since, in the resolution of *Macbeth*, Lady Macbeth goes crazy and whispers to the spirits.

If the reader accepts the allusion as a part of the poem, the imagery is enhanced by the vivid descriptions in *Macbeth*. Most critics and writers agree that if a careful reader finds something that fits consistently into a poem, then it is "there" for all readers who see the same thing, whether the poet consciously put it there or not. Robinson undoubtedly read and knew Shakespeare, but it does not matter whether he deliberately alluded to *Macbeth* if the reader can show that it is important to the poem.

There is a basic problem with allusion and symbol which every explicator must resolve for himself: Did the poet intend a symbol or an allusion to be taken in the way that a particular reader has interpreted it? The New Critics answered this question by coining the term "intentional fallacy," meaning that the poet's *intention* is ultimately unimportant when considering the finished poem. It is possible that stanza three was not intended to allude to *Macbeth*, and it was simply by accident that Robinson used language similar to Shakespeare's. Perhaps Robinson never read *Macbeth*, or perhaps he read it once and those lines remained in his subconscious. In either case, the reader must decide whether the allusion is important to the meaning of the poem.

STEP II-E: *Meter, rhyme, structure, and tone*

Because "Luke Havergal" is a poem that depends so heavily upon all the elements of prosody, it should be scanned carefully. Here is an example of scansion using the second stanza of the poem:

No, there/ is not/ a dawn/ in eas/tern skies

To rift/ the fie/ry night/ that's in/ your eyes;

But there,/ where wes/tern glooms/ are gath/ering,

The dark/ will end/ the dark,/ if an/ything:

God slays/ Himself/ with eve/ry leaf/ that flies,

And hell/ is more/ than half/ of par/adise.

No, there/ is not/ a dawn/ in east/ern skies—

In eas/tern skies.

The basic meter of the poem is iambic pentameter, with frequent substitutions, but every line except the last in each stanza contains ten syllables.

The stanza form in "Luke Havergal" is very intricate and delicate. It is only because of the structure that the heavy *a* rhyme (*aabbaaaa*) does not become monotonous; yet it is because of the *a* rhyme that the structure works so well.

The pattern for the first stanza works as follows:

Line	Rhyme	Function
1	a	Sets up ideas and images for the stanza.
2	a	Describes or complements line one.
3	b	Lines three-four-five constitute the central part of the mood and the fears. The return to the *a* rhyme unifies lines one-five.
4	b	
5	a	
6	a	Reflects on what has been said in one-five; it serves to make the reader stop, and it adds a mysterious suggestion.
7	a	Continues the deceleration and reflection.
8	a	The repetition and dimeter line stop the stanza completely, and the effect is to prepare for a shift in thought, just as Luke's mind jumps from thought to thought.

Stanza two works in a similar manner, except for lines thirteen and fourteen, which tie the stanza together as a couplet. Thus, thirteen and fourteen both unify and reflect, while fifteen and sixteen in the final couplet continue to reflect while slowing down.

Line	Rhyme	Function
9 & 10	a	Opening couplet.
11 & 12	b	Couplet in 11-12 contains the central idea and image.
13 & 14	a	Couplet in 13-14 reflects on that in 11-12, but the autonomy of this third couplet is especially strong. Whereas in stanza one only line five reflects on the beginning of the stanza to create unity, this entire couplet is now strongly associated with the first, with the effect of nearly equating Luke with God.
15 & 16	a	Final couplet reflects on the first and completes the stanza.

Stanza three works in the same manner as stanza two, while stanza four follows the pattern of stanza one.

Each stanza is autonomous and does not need the others for continuation or progression in plot; each stanza appears to represent a different thought as Luke's mind jumps about.

The overall structure focuses on stanza three, which is crucial to the theme. Stanzas one and two clearly present the problem: Luke knows that if he goes he will find "her," and the worst that can happen is that the darkness will remain. With stanza three, however, there is a break in point of view as the narrator calls attention to himself.

With stanza four there is a return to the beginning, reinforced by the repetition of rhyme words; the difference between stanzas four and one is that the reader has felt the impact of stanza three; structurally, whatever resolution there is will evolve out of the third stanza, or because of it.

The stanza form of "Luke Havergal" achieves tremendous unity and emphasis; the central image or idea presented in the *b* lines is reinforced in the remainder of the stanza by a tight-knit rhyme structure. There are several types of rhymes being used in the poem, all of which follow the traditional functions of their type. Stanza one contains full masculine end rhyme, with a

full masculine internal rhyme in line two (*There where*). Lines two and three contain alliteration (*c* in line two, *t* in line three) also binding the lines more tightly.

With "go" occurring near the end of stanza one and "No" appearing as the first word in stanza two, this rhyme becomes important in forming associations between lines. Lines nine, ten, fifteen, sixteen, and eighteen form full masculine end rhyme, with line fourteen "paradise" assonating with a full rhyme. Lines eleven and twelve are half falling rhymes; these lines also contain a full internal rhyme ("there," "where") and alliteration (*g* and *w* in line eleven). "Dark" in line twelve is an exact internal rhyme. The *l* and *s* in "slays" and "flies" (line fourteen) create an effect similar to assonance; there is also an *h* alliteration in line fifteen.

In stanza three, the plosive consonants *c* and *q* make an alliterative sound in line eighteen, binding "come" and "quench" together; there is also an *f* alliteration in line nineteen. All the end rhymes are full masculine in stanza three except line twenty-one, which assonates. Stanza four contains full masculine end rhyme, with one internal rhyme ("they say") in line twenty-eight, one alliteration in line twenty-nine, and consonance ("will call") in line thirty.

In addition to its function in developing the stanza, rhyme in "Luke Havergal" has important influence on sound, and in associating particular words and lines.

In lines one and two of "Luke Havergal," there are a number of plosive consonants and long vowels, in addition to the internal rhyme and *c* alliteration. The cadence of these lines is slow, and they reverberate with "cling" and "crimson." The tone of these lines is haunting (which is consistent with the situation), and the rhythm and sound of the poem as a whole suggest an incantation; the speaker's voice is seductive and evil, which is important to the theme, because if Luke goes to the gate he may be persuaded to die, which is what the voice demands.

Through its seductive sound, the poem seems to be having the same effect on the reader that it does on Luke; that is, the reader feels, as Luke does, that there is an urgency in going to the gate before all the leaves are blown away, and that by hearing "her" call, his discomfort will be relieved. The reader, unable to see the evil forces at work in the last stanza, sympathizes with Luke, and thinks that the voice is benevolent.

Whereas sound can be heard and analyzed, tone is a composite of a number of things which the reader can feel only after coming to know the poem. The poet's attitude or tone may be noncommittal or it may be dogmatic (as in allegory); sometimes the tone will affect the theme, while at other times it comes as an aside to the theme.

Poems that attempt to initiate reform frequently have a more readily discernible tone than poems which make observations without judging too harshly, although this is not always true. "Luke Havergal" is, among other things, about how the presence of evil leads toward death, but the poet has not directly included his feelings about that theme. If there is an attitude, it is the poet's acceptance of the inevitability of death and the pain which accompanies it for the living.

Perhaps the poet is angry at how effectively death can seduce life; it is obvious that Robinson wants the poem to haunt and torment the reader, and in doing so make him conscious of the hold death has on humanity.

Luke must meet death part way; he must first go to the gate before he can hear the dead words, which makes him partly responsible for death's hold over him. The tone of "Luke Havergal" is haunting and provocative.

STEP II-F: *Historical context*

Finished in December, 1895, "Luke Havergal" was in Robinson's estimation a Symbolist poem. It is essential, then, that the explicator learn something about the Symbolist movement. If his explication is not in accord with the philosophy of the period, the reader must account for the discrepancy.

In a study of other Robinson poems, there are themes parallel to that of "Luke Havergal." One, for example, is that of the alienated self. If Robinson believes in the alienated self, then it is possible that the voice speaking in "Luke Havergal" is Luke's own, but in an alienated state. This view may add credence to an argument that the speaker is Luke's past or subconscious, though it by no means proves it. Although parallelisms may be good support for the explication, the reader must be careful not to misconstrue them.

STEP II-G: *Themes and motifs, or correlating the parts*

Once the poem has been placed in context, the prosodic devices analyzed, and the function of the poetical techniques understood, they should be correlated, and any discrepancies should be studied for possible errors in explication. By this time every line should be understood, so that stating what the poem is about is merely a matter of explaining the common points of all the area, supporting it with specific items from the poem, secondary sources, other poems, other critics, and history. The reader may use the specific questions given in the outline to help detail the major themes.

BIBLIOGRAPHY

Beacham, Walton. *The Meaning of Poetry: A Guide to Eplication.* Boston: Allyn and Bacon, 1974.

Bloom, Harold. *A Map of Misreading.* New York: Oxford University Press, 1980.

Burton, S. H. *The Criticism of Poetry.* 2d ed. London: Longman, 1974.

Burton, S. H., and C. J. H. Chacksfield. *African Poetry in English: An Introduction to Practical Criticism.* London: Macmillan, 1979.

Carroll, Paul. *The Poem in Its Skin.* Chicago: Follett, 1968.

Coleman, Kathleen. *Guide to French Poetry Explication.* New York: G. K. Hall, 1993.

Cox, C. B., and A. E. Dyson. *The Practical Criticism of Poetry: A Textbook.* London: Edward Arnold, 1965.

English Institute. *Explication as Criticism.* New York: Columbia University Press, 1963.

Hayden, John O. *Inside Poetry Out: An Introduction to Poetry.* Chicago: Nelson-Hall, 1983.

Hirsch, Edward. *How to Read a Poem and Fall in Love with Poetry.* New York: Harcourt Brace, 1999.

Jones, R. T. *Studying Poetry: An Introduction.* London: Edward Arnold, 1986.

Kohl, Herbert R. *A Grain of Poetry: How to Read Contemporary Poems and Make Them a Part of Your Life.* New York: HarperFlamingo, 1999.

Kuntz, Joseph Marshall, and Nancy Martinez. *Poetry Explication: A Checklist of Interpretation Since 1925 of British and American Poems Past and Present.* 3d ed. Boston: G. K. Hall, 1980.

Lennard, John. *The Poetry Handbook: A Guide to Reading Poetry for Pleasure and Practical Criticism.* New York: Oxford University Press, 1996.

Martínez, Nancy C., and Joseph G. R. Martínez. *Guide to British Poetry Explication*. 4 vols. Boston: G. K. Hall, 1991-1995.

Preminger, Alex, et al., eds. *The New Princeton Encyclopedia of Poetry and Poetics*. 3d rev. ed. Princeton, N.J.: Princeton University Press, 1993.

Raffel, Burton. *How to Read a Poem*. New York: New American Library, 1984.

Ruppert, James, and John R. Leo. *Guide to American Poetry Explication*. 2 vols. Boston: G. K. Hall, 1989.

Statman, Mark. *Listener in the Snow: The Practice and Teaching of Poetry*. New York: Teachers & Writers Collaborative, 2000.

Werlich, Egon. *Poetry Analysis: Great English Poems Interpreted*. Dortmund, Germany: Lensing, 1967.

Wimsatt, William K., ed. *Explication as Criticism: Selected Papers from the English Institute, 1941-1952*. New York: Columbia University Press, 1963.

The World's Best Poetry: Supplement X, Poems Explicated: Explanation and Interpretation. Great Neck, N.Y.: Roth Publishing, 1998.

Walton Beacham

LANGUAGE AND LINGUISTICS

Although the development and history of world languages is as much the province of anthropologists, archaeologists, and scientists as it is of those studying literatures and their cultures, the ways in which language is used is of particular interest to those studying poetry. Poetry itself—despite its diverse variations—is, at base, always an endeavor to make use of language's full range of expressive devices—not only the denotations or literal meanings of words but also their sounds, rhythms, connotations, allusions, etymologies, and even visual appearance on a page—to their full emotive effect. An understanding of the history and evolution of world languages—the province of linguists—can therefore contribute significantly to both the writing and the reading of poetry.

THE NATURE OF LANGUAGE

Most humans past the infant stage have a spoken language and use it regularly for understanding and speaking, although a sizable percentage of the world's population is still illiterate and cannot read or write. Language is such a natural part of life that people tend to overlook it until they are presented with some special problem, as when they lose their sight or hearing, have a stroke, or are required to learn a foreign language. People may also study their own language, but seldom do they stand aside and view language for what it is: a complex human phenomenon with a history reaching back to humankind's beginnings. A study of the development of one language will often reveal intertwinings with other languages. Sometimes such knowledge enables linguists to construct family groups; just as often, the divergences among languages or language families are so great that separate typological variations are established.

True language is characterized by its systematic nature, its arbitrariness of vocabulary and structure, its vocality, and its basis in symbolism. Most linguists believe that language and thought are separate entities. Although language may be necessary to give foundation to thought, it is not, in itself, thinking. Many psychologists, however, contend that language *is* thought. An examination of language on the basis of these assertions reveals that each language is a purely arbitrary code or set of rules. There is no intrinsic necessity for any word to sound like what it means. Language is essentially speech, and symbolism is somehow the philosophical undergirding of the whole linguistic process. The French author Madame de Staël (1766-1817) once wrote, in describing her native language, that language is even more: "It is not only a means of communicating thoughts, feeling and acts, but an instrument that one loves to play upon, and that stimulates the mental faculties much as music does for some people and strong drink for others."

ORIGINS OF LANGUAGE

How did language originate? First, the evidence for the origin of language is so deeply buried in the obscurity of the past that it is unlikely that we shall ever be able to do more than speculate about the matter. If we had direct knowledge of humankind's immediate ancestors, we should be able to develop some evolutionary theory and be able to say, among other things, how speech production and changes in the brain are related. Some linguists maintain that language ability is innate, but this assertion, true though it may be, rests on the assumption of a monogenetic theory of humankind's origin. Few scholars today are content with the notion that the human race began with Adam and Eve.

According to the Bible, Adam is responsible for human speech. Genesis reports:

> And out of the ground the Lord God formed every beast of the field, and every fowl of the air, and brought them unto Adam to see what he would call them; and whatsoever Adam called every creature, that was the name thereof. And Adam gave names to all cattle, and to the fowl of the air, and to every beast of the field.

If the story of Adam and Eve is taken literally, one might conclude that their language was the original one. Unfortunately, not even the Bible identifies it. Some people have claimed that Hebrew was the first language and that all the other languages of the world are derived from it; Hebrew, however, bears no discernible relationship to any language outside the Hamito-Semitic group. Besides, any so-called original language would have changed so drastically in the intervening millennia before the onset of writing that it would not bear any resemblance to ancient Hebrew. Whatever the "original" language was—and there is every reason to believe that many languages sprang up independently over a very long span of time—it could not sound at all like any language that has been documented.

Many theories of the origin of language have been advanced, but three have been mentioned in textbooks more frequently than others. One, the "bow-wow" or echoic theory, insists that the earliest forms of language were exclusively onomatopoeic—that is, imitative of the sounds of animals and nature, despite the fact that the so-called primitive languages are not largely composed of onomatopoeic words. Furthermore, some measure of conventionalization must take place before echoisms become real "words"; individual young children do not call a dog a "bow-wow" until they hear an older child or adult use the term. Another theory, called the "pooh-pooh" or interjectional theory, maintains that language must have begun with primitive grunts and groans—that is, very loose and disjointed utterances. Many have held that such a theory fits animals better than humans; indeed, this kind of exclamatory speech probably separates humans quite clearly from the animals. Still another theory, dubbed the "ding-dong" theory, claims that language arose as a response to natural stimuli. None of these theories has any strong substantiation. Some linguists have suggested that speech and song may have once been the same. The presence of tones and pitch accent in many older languages lends some plausibility to the idea; it is likely that language, gestures, and song, as forms of communication, were all intertwined at the earliest stages.

Is it a hopeless task to try to discover the origin of language? It has been suggested that prehumans may have gradually developed a kind of grammar by occasionally fitting together unstructured vocal signals in patterns that were repeated and then eventually understood, accepted, and passed on. This process is called compounding, and some forms of it are found in present-day gibbon calls.

HISTORY OF LANGUAGE STUDY

In the history of language study, a number of signposts can be erected to mark the path. The simplest outline consists of two major parts: a prescientific and a scientific period.

The earliest formal grammar of any language is a detailed analysis of classical Sanskrit, written by the Indian scholar Pānini in the fourth century B.C.E. He called it the *Sutras* (instructions), and in it, he codified the rules for the use of proper Sanskrit. It is still an authoritative work. Independently of Pānini, the ancient Greeks established many grammatical concepts that strongly influenced linguistic thinking for hundreds of years. Plato, although by today's standards severely misguided in many respects, offered a number of useful insights into language, among them the basic division of the sentence into subject and predicate, the recognition of word stress, and the twofold classification of sounds into consonants and vowels. Following him in the third century B.C.E., Aristotle defined the various parts of speech.

In the next century, Dionysius Thrax produced a grammar that not only improved understanding of the sound system of Greek but also classified even more clearly the basic parts of speech and commented at length on such properties of language as gender, number, case, mood, voice, tense, and person. At no time, though, did the Hindu and Greek scholars break away from a focus on their own language to make a comparison with other languages. This fault was also largely one of the Romans, who merely adapted Greek scholarship to their own needs. If they did any comparing of languages, it was not of the languages in the Roman world, but only of Latin as a "corrupt" descendant of Greek. In sum, the Romans introduced no new concepts; they were, instead, content to synthesize or reorganize their legacy from ancient Greece. Only two grammarians come to mind from the fourth and fifth centuries of the Roman Empire: Priscian and Donatus, whose works served for centuries as basic texts for the teaching of Latin.

The scientific period of language study began with a British Sanskrit scholar Sir William Jones, who headed a society organized in Calcutta for the exploration of Asia. In 1786, he delivered a paper in which he stated:

"the Sanskrit language [is] more perfect than the Greek, more copious than the Latin, and more exquisitely refined than either; yet [bears] to both of them a stronger affinity . . . than could possibly have been produced by accident; so strong, indeed, that no philologer could examine them all three without believing them to have sprung from some common source, which, perhaps, no longer exists.

He went on to say that Germanic and Celtic probably had the same origin. His revolutionary assertion that Sanskrit and most of the languages of Europe had descended from a single language no longer spoken and never recorded first produced considerable scholarly opposition but shortly thereafter set the stage for comparative analysis. He insisted that a close examination of the "inner structures" of this family of languages would reveal heretofore unsuspected relationships.

Franz Bopp, a German born in 1791 and a student of Asian languages, including Sanskrit, was the founder of comparative grammar. In his epochmaking book *Über das Conjugationssystem der Sanskritsprache in Vergleichung mit jenem der griechischen, lateinischen, persischen und germanischen Sprache* (1816), he demonstrated what Jones and Friedrich von Schlegel and other researchers had only surmised. A young Danish contemporary named Rasmus Rask corroborated his results and established that Armenian and Lithuanian belong to the same language group, the Indo-European. The tool to establish these relationships was the "comparative method," one of the greatest achievements of nineteenth century linguistics. In applying this method, linguists searched in the various languages under investigation for cognates—words with similar spelling, similar sound, and similar meaning. They then set up sound correspondences among the cognates, much like looking for the lowest common denominator in a mathematical construction, from which the original linguistic forms could be constructed.

The German linguist Jakob Grimm (one of the Grimm brothers of fairytale fame) took Rask's work one step further and, in a four-volume work published between 1819 and 1822, showed conclusively the systematic correspondences and differences between Sanskrit, Greek, and Latin, on one hand, and the Germanic languages, on the other hand. The formulation of this system of sound changes came to be known as Grimm's law, or the First Sound Shift, and the changes involved can be diagrammed as follows:

Proto-Indo-European: *bh dh gh b d g p t k*
Proto-Germanic: *b d g p t k f θ h*

Where the Indo-European, as transmitted through Latin or Greek, had a *p* sound (as in *piscis* and *pēd*), the German-based English word has an *f* ("fish" and "foot"); the Latinate *trēs* becomes the English "three." In addition to the changes described above, another important change took place in the Germanic languages. If the *f θ h* resulting from the change of *p t k* stood after an unaccented vowel but before another vowel, they became voiced fricatives, later voiced stops, as in the pair *seethe: sodden*. This change also affected *s*, yielding *z*, which later became *r* (Rhotacism) and explains, for example, the alternations in *was: were*. It was described by Karl Verner, a Danish linguist, and is known appropriately as Verner's law. There are one or two other "laws" that explain apparent exceptions to Grimm's law, illustrating the basic regularity of Grimm's formulations. At the very end of the nineteenth century, the Neo-Grammarians, led by Karl Brugmann, insisted that all exceptions could be explained—that, in fact, "phonetic laws are natural laws and have no exceptions." Even those studying the natural sciences do not make such a strong assertion, but the war cry of the Neo-Grammarians did inspire scholars to search for regularity in language.

The German language itself underwent a profound change beginning probably in the far south of the German-speaking lands sometime during the fifth century, causing a restructuring of the sounds of all of the southern and many of the midland dialects. These became known, for geographical reasons, as High German, while those dialects in the north came to be known as Low German. Six consonants in various positions were affected, but the most consistently shifted sounds were the Indo-European *b* which in English became *p* and in German *pf*, and the *d* to *t* and *ts*. For example, the Latin *decim* became the English "ten" and the German *zehn*.

In the course of the nineteenth century, all such changes were recognized, and scholars were enabled to identify and diagram the reflex languages of Indo-European into five subgroups known as *satem* languages and four known as *centum* languages. This division is significant both geographically, because the *satem* languages are located clearly to the east of where the original home of the Indo-Europeans probably was, and linguistically, because the *satem* languages have, among other characteristics, *s* sounds where the *centum* languages have *k* sounds (the word *centum* is pronounced with an initial hard *c*). The very words *satem* and *centum*, meaning "hundred" in Avestan (an Indo-Iranian language) and Latin, respectively, illustrate the sound divergence.

The *Satum* Languages

Indo-Iranian	Earliest attested form, Sanskrit; modern languages include Hindi, Bengali, and Persian.
Albanian	Spoken by a small number of people in that country.
Armenian	Spoken by a small number of people in Armenia, an area once part of the Soviet Union.
Slavic	Divided into East Slavic (Great Russian, the standard language; Little Russian or Ukrainian, spoken in present-day Ukraine; White Russian, spoken in the region adjacent to and partly in the present Poland); West Slavic (Czech, Slovak, Polish); South Slavic (Slovenian and Serbo-Croatian, spoken in present-day Slovenia, Croatia, and parts of the former Yugoslavia; Bulgarian).
Baltic	Lithuanian and Lettic, spoken in present-day Lithuania.

INDO-EUROPEAN LANGUAGES

Where was the original home of the Indo-Europeans? This is a question that has not been answered to everybody's satisfaction and remains a matter of debate, but evidence points to present-day Lithuania. For one thing, the Lithuanians have resided in a single area since Neolithic times (2500-2000 B.C.E.) and speak a language of great complexity. Furthermore, Lithuania is situated on the dividing line between *centum* and *satem* languages. One would also assume that the original home was somewhere close to the area where the reflex languages are to be found today and not, for example, in Africa, Australia, or North or South America. For historical and archaeological reasons, scholars have ruled out the British Isles and the peninsulas of southern Europe. Last, there are indications that the Indo-Europeans entered India from the northwest, for there is no evidence of their early acquaintanceship with the Ganges River, but only with the Indus (hence "Indo-"). Certain common words for weather conditions, geography, and flora and fauna argue in favor of a European homeland.

Scholars have classified the Indo-European languages as a family apart from certain other languages on the basis of two principal features: their common word stock and their inflectional structure. This type of classification, called genetic, is one of three. Another, called geographical, is usually employed initially. For example, if nothing whatsoever was known about American Indian languages, one might divide them into North American and South American, Eastern North American and Western North American,

The *Centum* Languages

Greek (Hellenic)	Attic, Ionic, and Doric, formerly spoken throughout the eastern areas around the Mediterranean; modern Greek.
Italic	Latin; modern Italian, French, Spanish, Portuguese, Catalan, Sardinian, Romanian, and Rhaeto-Romanic.
Celtic	modern Welsh, Cornish, Breton, Irish, and Scots Gaelic.
Germanic (Teutonic)	East Germanic (Gothic, now extinct); North Germanic (Danish, Norwegian, Swedish, Icelandic); West Germanic (Low German: English, Dutch, Frisian, Plattdeutsch; High German: standard German).
In addition	several extinct Indo-European languages, such as Tocharian and the Anatolian languages, especially Hittite.

and perhaps some other geographical categories. A third variety of classification, called typological, is possible only when a good deal is known about the structure of a language. The four main types of languages arrived at through such classification are *inflectional*, meaning that such syntactic distinctions as gender, number, case, tense, and so forth, are usually communicated by altering the form of a word, as in English when -*s* added to a noun indicates plurality but, when added to a verb, singularity; *agglutinative*, meaning that suffixes are piled onto word bases in a definite order and without change in phonetic shape (for example, Turkish *evlerimden*, "house-s-my-from"); *isolating*, meaning that invariable word forms, mostly monosyllabic, are employed in variable word order (for example, Chinese *wǒ* meaning, according to its position in the utterance, "I," "me," "to me," or "my"); and *incorporating* or *polysynthetic*, meaning that a sentence, with its various syntactic features, may be "incorporated" as a single word (for example, Eskimo /a: wlisa-utissʔar-siniarpu-na/, "I am looking for something suitable for a fish-line").

OTHER LANGUAGES

Although the Indo-European languages have been studied in more detail than other language families, it is possible to classify and describe many of the remaining language families of the world, the total comprising more than twenty-seven hundred separate languages. In Europe and Asia, relatively few languages are spoken by very large numbers of people; elsewhere, many distinct languages are spoken by small communities. In Europe, all languages are Indo-European except for Finnish, Estonian, Hungarian, and Basque. The last-named is something of a mystery; it appears to predate Indo-European by such a long period that it could conceivably be descended from a prehistoric language. The first three belong to the same family, the Finno-Urgic. Sometimes Turkish is added to the group, and the four are called the Ural-Altaic family. All are agglutinative.

The most extensive language family in eastern Asia is the Sino-Tibetan. It consists of two branches, the Tibeto-Burman and Chinese. Mandarin is the language of the northern half of China, although there are three different varieties—northern, southwestern, and south-

ern. In the south, there is a range of mutually unintelligible dialects. All are isolating in structure.

In other parts of Asia are found the Kadai family, consisting of Thai, Laotian, and the Shan languages of Burma, and, in southern Asia, the Munda languages and Vietnamese. The latter has a considerable number of speakers.

Japanese and Korean are separate families, even though cultural relationships between the two countries have produced some borrowing over the years. Japanese is essentially agglutinative.

On the continent of Africa, the linguistic family of prime importance is the Hamito-Semitic family. Hebrew, Arabic, and some of the languages of Ethiopia make up the Semitic side. There are four Hamitic languages: Egyptian, Berber, Cushitic, and Chad. All exhibit some inflectional characteristics. In addition to these languages, Hausa, an important trade language, is used throughout the northern part of the continent. In central and southern Africa, the Niger-Congo language family is dominant. The largest subgroup of this family is Bantu, which includes Swahili in central and eastern Africa, Kikuyu in Kenya, and Zulu in the south. Most appear to be either agglutinative or polysynthetic.

The Malayo-Polynesian languages are spoken as original tongues all the way from Madagascar to the Malay Peninsula, the East Indies, and, across the Pacific, to Hawaii. Many seem to be isolating with traces of earlier inflections.

The indigenous languages of the Americas are all polysynthetic. Until recently, these languages were classified geographically. Many of the North American languages have been investigated, and linguists group them into distinct families, such as Algonquian, Athabaskan, Natchez-Muskogean, Uto-Aztecan, Penutian, and Hokan.

MODERN LINGUISTICS

In addition to the distinction between prescientific and scientific periods of language study, other divisions can help to clarify the various approaches to this vast topic. For example, the entire period from earliest times until the late nineteenth century was largely historical, comparative at best, but scarcely truly scientific in terms of rigor. Beginning with the Neo-Grammarians Brugmann and Delbrück, the stage was set for what may be called a period of general or descriptive linguistics. Languages were examined not only diachronically—that is, historically—but also synchronically, where a segment or feature of language was scrutinized without regard to an earlier stage. The most important names associated with this descriptive school are those of N. S. Trubetzkoy and Roman Jakobson. Strongly influenced by the theories of the Swiss linguist Ferdinand de Saussure, they examined each detail of language as a part of a system. In other words, they were ultimately more interested in the *system* and the way it hung together than in each individual detail. These scholars were members of the European school of linguistic thought which had its origin in Jakobson's "Prague Circle." Across the Atlantic, their most important counterpart was Leonard Bloomfield, who, in 1933, published his classic linguistics text, *Language*. Like his contemporary, Edward Sapir, Bloomfield began as a comparativist in Germanic linguistics, then studied American Indian languages, and finally became an expert in the general principles of language. Bloomfield's theory of structuralism has been criticized for its resemblance to the psychological theory of behaviorism, which restricts itself to the observable and rejects the concept of mind.

Since the 1930's, a steady procession of American linguists have studied and reported on the sounds and grammatical features of many different languages, in some sense all derivative from the foundation laid by the phonemicists beginning with Saussure and Bloomfield. Kenneth Pike's tagmemics, in part an attempt to present language behavior empirically through a description at each level of grammatical form, evolved directly out of descriptive linguistics. In 1957, Noam Chomsky launched transformational-generative grammar, concerned at first only with syntax, but later also with phonology. Today there is considerable tension between structuralists and transformational-generative grammarians, concerning not only syntactic analysis but also the representation of sounds. For some, stratificational grammar provides a connection, through strata or levels of description, among descriptive, tagmemic, and computational analyses.

THE TECHNICAL SIDE OF LANGUAGE

A language is made up of its sound system, grammar, and vocabulary. Sound systems and grammar may

differ considerably from language family to language family, but there is a workable range in the extent and type of sounds and grammatical functions. The inventory of significant sounds in a given language, called phonemes, extends from about twenty to about sixty. English has forty-six, including phonemes of pitch, stress, and juncture. If the grammatical facts of a complicated language can be written out on one or two sheets of paper, the grammar of English can be laid out on the back of an envelope. In short, some languages are simpler phonologically or grammatically than others, but none is so complicated in either respect that every child cannot learn his or her language in about the same time.

The study of the sounds of which speech is made up became scientific in method by the end of the nineteenth century, when Paul Passy founded the International Phonetic Association. Down to the present day, articulatory phonetics has borne a close relationship to physiology in the description of the sounds of speech according to the organs producing them and the position of these organs in relation to surrounding structures.

By the mid-1920's, phoneticians realized that the unit of description of the phonology of a language had to be a concept rather than some physical entity. The term phoneme was chosen; it designates a minimally significant sound unit, an abstraction around which cluster all the phonetic realizations of that generalized sound. Thus, the English phoneme /p/ represents all recognizably similar pronunciations of [p], with more or less or no aspiration depending upon position within a word or the speech habits of a given speaker. In other words, it designates a class of sounds distinct from others in the language. It carries no meaning as such, but it serves to distinguish one sound from another and, together with other phonemes, produces morphemic, or meaning, differences. Thus /p/, /i/, and /n/ are separate phonemes, but, taken together, make up a morpheme—the word *pin*—which is distinct, by virtue of a single phoneme, from, say, /bin/, "bin," or /tin/ "tin." Sometimes, morphemes show relations between words, as when -*s* is added to a noun to indicate plurality or possession or to a verb to indicate singularity.

The sound system and grammar of a language are thus closely related. Grammar, at least for Indo-European languages and many others, can be defined as consisting of a morphology and syntax, where, expressed simply, the former refers to the words and their endings and the latter to the order of words. Accompanying the words are, however, other features of language which can alter meaning. It matters, for example, whether the stress occurs on the first or second syllable of the word *pervert* or *permit*. If the stress falls on the first syllable, the word is a noun; if on the second, it is a verb. It matters whether the last few sounds of an utterance convey an upturn or a downturn and trail-off, for a question or a statement may result. It matters also what the pitch level is and whether juncture is present. These features, too, are phonemic.

In order to function in a language, one must have control of close to one hundred percent of the phonology and seventy-five percent or more of the grammar, but a mere one percent of the vocabulary will enable the speaker to function in many situations. For a speaker of a language the size of English, a vocabulary of six thousand words will suffice. Possessing a vocabulary implies an unconscious knowledge of the semantic relationship to the phonology and grammar of the language. One theory of the word regards the word as a compound formed of two components: a physical element, the sequence of sounds of speech; and a semantic element, the amount of meaning expressed by the segment of speech. The first is called the formant, the second the morpheme. The word "cook" /kuk/ is one morpheme expressed by one formant—the formant consisting of one syllable, a sequence of three phonemes. In the plural of "cook," -*s* is a formant which is not even a syllable. In fact, a formant is not even necessarily a phoneme, but can be the use of one form instead of another, as in "her" instead of "she." There is no reason that the same formant, such as -*s*, cannot express more than one morpheme: "cooks" (noun) versus "cook's" versus "cooks" (verb). The same morpheme can also be expressed by more than one formant; there are, for example, many different formants for the plural, such as basis/bases, curriculum/curricula, datum/data, ox/oxen, child/children, man/men, woman/women, cherub/cherubim, monsignore/monsignori.

The distinction in morphology made above between words and their endings needs further amplification. An examination of a stanza from Lewis Carroll's "Jabber-wocky" illustrates the manner in which the poet uses formants with no evident meaning to the average speaker:

> 'Twas brilling, and the slithy toves
> Did gyre and gimble in the wabe;
> All mimsy were the borogoves,
> And the mome raths outgrabe.

Alice herself remarks that the words fill her head with ideas, but she does not know what they are. The fact of the matter is that there is a rightness about the way the poem sounds because the endings, the structural morphemes, are correctly placed. When the message is of primary importance and the speaker knows the language only imperfectly, the structural morphemes may be incorrect or missing and a string of pure message morphemes may be the result: Her give man bag money.

Message morphemes have their own peculiar properties, limiting their use to certain contexts, regardless of the accuracy of the combined structural morphemes. To illustrate this principle, Noam Chomsky composed the sentence "Colorless green ideas sleep furiously." The subject is "colorless green ideas"; the predicate, "sleep furiously." This sentence has the same structure as any sentence of the shape: adjective/adjective/noun/intransitive verb/adverb. Yet there is something semantically troubling. How can one describe something green as colorless? Can ideas be green? How can an intransitive verb which describes such a passive activity be *furiously* involved in an action?

Chomsky's example was designed to combine structural familiarity with semantic impossibility. It is possible to devise similar sentences which, though semantically improbable, could conceivably be used by an actual speaker. The sentence "Virtue swims home every night" attributes to an abstract noun an action performed by animate beings, and poses other difficulties as well (in what setting can one swim home?), yet such strange semantic violations, given a meaningful context, are the stuff of poetry.

Indeed, semantic change actually occurs with a measure of frequency in the history of a language. It is usually of two types. Words that are rather specific in meaning sometimes become generalized; for example, Latin *molīna* (gristmill), originally meant "mill" but expanded to cover "sawmill," "steel mill," even "diploma mill."

Many words in English of very broad meanings, such as "do," "make," "go," and "things," derive from words of more specific notions. At the same time, the opposite often happens. Words that once were very general in meaning have become specific. Examples include *deer*, which formerly meant merely "animal" (compare German *Tier*), and *hound*, "dog," now a particular kind of dog. Sometimes, words undergo melioration, as in the change in *knight*, meaning originally a "servant," to "king's servant," or pejoration, as in the change in *knave*, meaning "boy" (compare German *Knabe*), to "rascal."

Perhaps the most significant force for change in language is analogy. It is occasioned by mental associations arising because of similarity or contrast of meaning and may affect the meaning or the form of words or even create new words. Most verbs in English are regular and form their preterit and past participles by the addition of *-ed* (or *-t*), as "dream, dreamed, dreamt," and not by vowel change, as in "drink, drank, drunk." New words taken into the language, as well as some of the irregular ones already in use, will usually become regular. It is by no means unusual to hear a child utilize analogy in forming the past of, say, "teach" or "see" as "teached" and "see'd" instead of "taught" and "saw." Since most English nouns form their plural by the addition of *-s*, it is to be expected that unfamiliar words or words with little-used, learned plural forms will be pluralized in the same way: for example, "memorandums" (or "memos") for *memoranda*, "stadiums" for *stadia*, "gymnasiums" for *gymnasia*, "prima donnas" for *prime donne*, and "formulas" for *formulae*. Sometimes a resemblance in the form of a word may suggest a relationship which causes a further assimilation in form. This process is known as folk etymology and often occurs when an unfamiliar or foreign word or phrase is altered to give it a more meaningful form. There are many examples: "Crayfish" comes from Old French *crevisse* (crab), but *-visse* meant nothing and thus was changed to the phonetically similar *-fish*; a hangnail is not a (finger)nail that hangs, but one that hurts (from Old English *ang*); the second element of "titmouse" has nothing to do with a mouse, but comes from Middle English *mose*, the name for several species of birds.

There are many other processes in language by which changes are brought about. Among them are several of great importance.

Assimilation causes a sound to change in conformance with a neighboring sound, as in the plural of "kit" with [-s] (/kits/), as opposed to the plural of "limb" with [-z] (/limz/), or in the preterit and participial forms of regular verbs: "grazed" [greyzd], but "choked" [čowkt].

Dissimilation is the opposite process, whereby neighboring sounds are made unlike, as in "pilgrim" from Latin *peregrīnus*, where the first *r* dissimilates.

Conversion is the change of one part of speech or form class into another, as the change from noun to verb: The nouns "bridge," "color," and "shoulder" are converted to verbs in "to bridge a gap," "to color a book," and "to shoulder a load."

A *back formation* occurs when a word is mistakenly assumed to be the base form from which a new word is formed, as in "edit" from "editor," "beg" from "beggar," "peddle" from "pedlar."

Euphemisms are words and expressions with new, better-sounding connotations—for example, to "pass away" or "breathe one's last" or "cross the river" for "to die"; "lingerie" or "intimate wear" for "underwear"; "acute indigestion" for "bellyache."

Slang consists of informal, often ephemeral expressions and coinages, such as "turkey" for "stupid person," "blow away" for "to kill," and "kook," meaning "odd or eccentric person," from "cuckoo."

Some words are *blends*: "flash" + "blush" = "flush"; "slight" (slim) + "tender" = "slender"; "twist" + "whirl" = "twirl"; "breakfast" + "lunch" = "brunch."

All three constituents of language change over a long period of time—sounds, structure, and vocabulary—but each language or dialect retains its distinctiveness. The most durable and unchanging aspect of language is writing, of which there are two major varieties: picture writing, also called ideographic writing, and alphabetic writing. The former kind of writing began as actual pictures and developed gradually into ideograms linked directly to the objects or concepts and having no connection with the sounds of the language. The latter variety began as symbols for syllables, until each symbol was taken to represent a single spoken sound. Although alphabetic writing is much more widespread and easier to learn and use, ideographic writing has the advantage of maintaining cultural unity among speakers of dialects and languages not mutually intelligible. An alphabetic writing system can, over time, act as a conservative influence on the spoken language as well as provide valuable etymological clues. Ideographic writing can be, and often is, seen as art capable of conveying messages separate from speech. Both systems are vehicles for the transmission of history and literature without which civilization would falter and perish.

THE SOCIAL SIDE OF LANGUAGE

The social side of language is inextricably linked to behavior. It is concerned with the use of language to create attitudes and responses toward language, objects, and people. For example, certain overt behaviors toward language and its users can create unusual political pressures. The insistence by the Québecois on French as the primary, if not sole, language of their province of Canada has led to near secession and to bitter interprovincial feelings. The creation of modern Hebrew has helped to create and sustain the state of Israel. The Irish are striving to make Irish the first language of that part of the British Isles. The Flemish urge full status for their variety of Dutch in the Brussels area. American black people sometimes advocate clearer recognition of black English. Frisians, Bretons, Basques, Catalans, and Provençals are all insisting upon greater acceptance of their mother tongues.

Within a language or dialect, there can be specialized vocabulary and pronunciation not generally understood. The term "dialect" is commonly taken to mean a regional variety of language or one spoken by the undereducated, but, strictly speaking, it is differentiated from language as such largely as that which people actually speak. Some dialects differ so substantially from standard, national tongues that, to all intents and purposes, they are languages in their own right. The term "vernacular" is similar in that it designates everyday speech as opposed to learned discourse. "Lingo" designates, somewhat contemptuously, any dialect or language not readily comprehended. "Jargon" is specialized or professional language, often of a technical nature; in this context, the term "cant," as in "thieves' cant," is virtually synonymous with "jargon." Closely related to these two terms is the term "argot," referring to the idiom of a closely knit group, as in "criminal argot." Finally, "slang," discussed above, refers to the colorful, innova-

tive, often short-lived popular vocabulary drawn from many levels of language use, both specialized and nonspecialized.

Words, like music, can produce moods. They can raise one's spirits or lower them. They can stir up discontent or soothe human anger. They can inspire and console, ingratiate and manipulate, mislead and ridicule. They can create enough hatred to destroy but also enough trust to overcome obstacles. While a mood may originate in physical well-being or physical discomfort and pain, language can express that mood, intensify it, or deny it. Language can be informative (emotionally neutral), biased (emotionally charged), or propagandistic (informatively neutral).

Language is informative when it states indisputable facts or asks questions dealing with such facts, even though those facts are very broad and general. One can also inform with misstatements, half-truths, or outright lies. It does not matter whether the statement is actually true or false, only that the question can be posed.

Language often reflects bias by distorting facts. Frequently, the substitution of a single derogatory term is sufficient to load the atmosphere. Admittedly, some words are favorably charged for some people, unfavorably for others. Much depends on the context, word and sentence stress, gestures, and former relationship.

Language can be propagandistic when the speaker desires to promote some activity or cause. The load which propaganda carries is directly proportional to the receiver's enthusiasm, bias, or readiness to be deceived. Almost invariably, propaganda terms arise out of the specialized language of religion, art, commerce, education, finance, government, and so forth. Propaganda is a kind of name-calling, using words from a stock of esoteric and exclusive terms. Not many people are thoroughly familiar with the exact meanings of words such as "totalitarian," "Fascist," "proletarian," and "bourgeois," but they think they know whether these words are good or bad, words of approval or disapproval. The effect is to call forth emotions as strong as those prompted by invectives.

The language of advertising achieves its effectiveness by conveniently combining information, bias, and propaganda. A good advertisement must gain immediate attention, make the reader or listener receptive to the message, ensure its retention, create a desire, and cause the person to buy the product without setting up resistance. Advertising must, moreover, link the product to "pleasant" or "healthy" things. In advertising circles, there is no widespread agreement as to which is more important: the avoidance of all associations that can create resistance or the creation of desire for a particular object. Even if the latter is regarded as the prime objective, it is still important to avoid resistance. The most powerful tools of the advertiser are exaggeration and cliché. The words generally used in ads deal with the basic component and qualities of a product, while the qualifiers are hackneyed and overblown: lather (rich, creamy, full-bodied); toothpaste (fights cavities three ways, ten ways, tastes zesty); cleanser (all-purpose, powerful, one-step); coffee (full of flavor buds, brewed to perfection, marvelous bouquet). The danger of advertising is evident when its pathology carries over into other areas of life. Every culture must be on guard against the effect of advertising on the health of its citizenry and the shaping of its national image. Even foreign policy can be the victim of advertising that stresses youth over maturity, beauty of body over soundness of mind, physical health over mental serenity, the power of sex appeal over everything else.

Language has also been closely examined by groups aiming to rid it of prejudice. Such struggles have always occurred: Language naturally reflects the attitudes of dominant groups, and with shifts and clashes in cultures and attitudes toward those cultures come shifts in the use of language. In recent decades, for example, feminists have had a significant affect on vocabulary, parts of speech, and even the structure of languages that differentiate along gender lines. Women and men concerned that the symbols of perception—words—give both meaning and value to the objects they define have succeeded in changing language to be more gender-neutral and more inclusive: For example, words with the affix -*man* to an occupation (thereby suggesting that only men are capable of assuming such roles) have been changed: "chairman" to "chairperson" or simply "chair" is a classic example; the use of "he" to refer generically to a doctor or another professional has now become taboo; gender is eliminated altogether in modern uses of "humankind" or "humanity" (for "mankind"). Similarly, racially and ethnically prejudicial uses of grammar, once found acceptable, are no longer tolerated. English speakers no longer refer to the colors beige or pink with the term "flesh-colored," for example. Entire books on the topic of "bias-free usage" have been published and pored over by editors, journalists, and writers, who have helped proliferate a relatively new, inclusive, and egalitarian social sensibility simply through the use of language.

Likewise, political movements and activist groups often appropriate language to call attention to their cause or push forward an agenda—in the process often changing the uses and connotations of words permanently and adding significantly to a language's vocabulary. The term "Mexicano," used pejoratively by Anglos in the Southwest during the 1950's, was appropriated by the Mexican American community and became the militant and later culturally positive self-identifier "Chicano" in the 1960's and 1970's. The term "Negro" was used in the United States prior to the 1970's to refer to African Americans; although many members of the dominant white society considered the term race-neutral at that time, members of the black community recognized its prejudicial etymology and felt its abuse, and they proactively succeeded in circumscribing or eliminating it, replacing it with "African American" in a refusal to be subjugated by a European name that set them apart on the basis of color.

Even technology has permanently entered the language and shaped it: radio, television, space travel, and most recently personal computers, the Internet, and mobile communications devices have contributed entire new vocabularies as well as completely new meanings to old words. Real-time communications and world trade have also effectively shrunk the globe, inevitably broadcasting the world's dominant languages, particularly English, to all parts of the world, where the language becomes incorporated into other languages and even replaces other languages for purposes of business or science.

APPLICATIONS OF LANGUAGE STUDY AND LINGUISTICS

Almost everybody is intimately acquainted with at least one language. Everybody can produce the sounds and sound combinations of his or her language and understand the meanings of the sounds produced by other speakers. Everybody knows which sounds and sound combinations are allowable and which do not fit the language. Sentences that are grammatically or semantically unacceptable or strange are easily recognized. Despite this intuitive or unconscious knowledge of one's language, the average native speaker cannot comment authoritatively on the sound system or the structure of his or her language. Furthermore, there are no books containing the complete language of English or Arabic or Mandarin Chinese in which all possible sentences and sound combinations are listed. Instead, people must rely largely on dictionaries for a list of words and on grammars and linguistic texts for a statement of rules dealing with sounds, morphology, and syntax. To study one's language as an object or phenomenon is to raise one's consciousness of how language functions.

Some people have a professional need to know a lot *about* a language as opposed to simply being able to use it. Some of the more obvious examples include language teachers, speech correctionists, advertising writers, communications engineers, and computer programmers. Others, such as the anthropologist or the historian, who often work with documents, employ their knowledge as an ancillary tool. The missionary may have to learn about some very esoteric language for which there is no grammar book and perhaps even no writing. The psychologist studies language as a part of human behavior. The philosopher is often primarily interested in the "logical" side of language. Students of foreign languages can benefit greatly from linguistic knowledge; they can often learn more efficiently and make helpful comparisons of sounds and structures between their own and the target language.

Translation and interpretation are two activities requiring considerable knowledge about language. Strictly speaking, the terms are not interchangeable; translation refers to the activity of rendering, in writing, one language text into another, whereas interpretation is oral translation. Translation is of two kinds, scientific and literary, and can be accomplished by people or machines. In general, machine translation has been a disappointment because of the grave difficulties involved in programming the many complexities of natural language.

Interpretation is also of two kinds: legal and diplomatic. Whereas the legal interpreter requires a precise knowledge of the terminology of the court and must tread a thin line between literal and free interpretation, the diplomatic interpreter has the even more difficult task of adding, or subtracting, as circumstances dictate, allusions, innuendos, insinuations, and implications. Interpretation is accomplished in two ways: simultaneously with the speaker, or consecutively after a given segment of speech.

LINGUISTICS AND LITERATURE

One of the important questions before linguistics is: Does linguistics aid in the study and appreciation of literature? Many would automatically assume that the answer is an unqualified yes, since the material of which literature is made is language. There are others, however, who find linguistic techniques of analysis too mechanical and lacking in the very feeling that literature tries to communicate. Probably most thoughtful people would agree that linguistics can make a contribution in tandem with more traditional analytical approaches, but that alone it cannot yet, if ever, disclose the intrinsic qualities of great literary works.

By one definition at least, literature consists of texts constructed according to certain phonological, morphological, and syntactic restrictions where the result is the creation of excellence of form and expression. For poetry in the Western tradition, for example, the restriction most frequently imposed is that of rhythm based on stress or vowel quantity. In other cultures, syntactic and semantic prescriptions can produce the same effect.

For both poetic and prose texts, the discovery and description of the author's style are essential to analysis. In contrast to the methods of traditional literary criticism, linguistics offers the possibility of quantitative stylistic analysis. Computer-aided analysis yields textual statistics based on an examination of various features of phonology and grammar. The results will often place an author within a literary period, confirm his region or dialect, explain the foreign-vocabulary influences, describe syllabication in terms of vowel and consonant count, list euphemisms and metaphors, and delineate sentence structure with regard to subordinating elements, to mention some of the possibilities. All of these applications are based on the taxemes of selection employed by an individual author.

Of all literary endeavors, literary translation seems to stand in the closest possible relationship to linguistics. The translator must perform his task within the framework of an awareness, be it conscious or intuitive, of the phonology, syntax, and morphology of both the source language and the target language. Like the linguist, he should also be acquainted in at least a rudimentary fashion with the society that has produced the text he is attempting to translate. His work involves much more than the mechanical or one-to-one exchange of word for word, phrase for phrase, or even concept for concept. The practice of translation makes possible the scope and breadth of knowledge encompassed in the ideal of liberal arts, and without translation relatively few scholars could claim knowledge and understanding of many of the world's great thinkers and literary artists.

BIBLIOGRAPHY

Akmajian, Adrian, Ann K. Farmer, Robert M. Harnish, and Richard Demers. *Linguistics: An Introduction to Language and Communication*. Cambridge, Mass.: MIT Press, 2001. Divided into two sections: The first part deals with the structural and interpretive parts of language while the second part is cognitively oriented and includes chapters on pragmatics, psychology of language, language acquisition, and language and the brain.

Beekes, Robert S. P. *Comparative Indo-European Linguistics: An Introduction*. Philadelphia: John Benjamins Publishing, 1996. Examines the history of Indo-European languages and explores comparative grammar and linguistics.

Cavalli-Sforza, L. L. *Genes, Peoples, and Languages*. Berkeley: University of California Press, 2001. Cavalli-Sforza was among the first to ask whether the genes of modern populations contain a historical record of the human species. This collection comprises five lectures that serve as a summation of the author's work over several decades, the goal of which has been nothing less than tracking the past hundred thousand years of human evolution.

Chomsky, Noam. *Language and Thought*. Wakefield, R.I.: Moyer Bell, 1993. Presents an analysis of human language and its influence on other disciplines.

Lycan, William G. *Philosophy of Language: A Contemporary Introduction*. London: Routledge, 2000. Introduces the nonspecialist to the main issues and theories in twentieth century philosophy of language, focusing specifically on linguistic phenomena.

Pinker, Stephen. *The Language Instinct: How the Mind Creates Language*. New York: Perennial Classics, 2000. Explores how humans learn to talk, how the study of language can provide insight into the way genes interact with experience to create behavior and thought, and how the arbitrary sounds we call language evoke emotion and meaning.

Ruhlen, Merritt. *The Origin of Language: Tracing the Evolution of the Mother Tongue*. New York: John Wiley & Sons, 1996. Provides an accessible examination of nearly one hundred thousand years of human history and prehistory to uncover the roots of the language from which all modern tongues derive.

Trudgill, Peter. *Sociolinguistics: An Introduction to Language and Society*. 4th ed. New York: Penguin Books, 2001. Examines how the way in which humans talk is deeply influenced by class, sex, and ethnic background and explores the implications of language for social and educational policy.

Vygotsky, Lev S. *Thought and Language*. Edited by Alex Kozulin. Rev. ed. Cambridge, Mass.: MIT Press, 1986. A classic foundational work of cognitive science. Vygotsky analyzes the relationship between words and consciousness, arguing that speech is social in its origins and that only as children develop does it become internalized verbal thought. Revised edition offers an introductory essay by Kozulin that offers new insight into the author's life, intellectual milieu, and research methods.

Yule, George. *The Study of Language*. 2d ed. Cambridge, England: Cambridge University Press, 1996. Revised edition includes a new chapter on pragmatics, and an expanded chapter on semantics; incorporates many changes that reflect developments in language study at the end of the twentieth century.

Donald D. Hook

POETICAL TERMS

Accentual meter: One of four base meters used in English (accentual, accentual-syllabic, syllabic, and quantitative), accentual meter is the system in which the occurrence of a syllable marked by a stress determines the basic unit, regardless of the number of unstressed syllables. In other words, it is the stresses that determine the metrical base. An example from modern poetry is "Blue Moles" by Sylvia Plath, the first line of which scans: "They're out of the dark's ragbag, these two." Because there are five stressed syllables in this accentually based poem, the reader can expect that many of the other lines will also contain five stresses. (See also *Scansion*)

Accentual-syllabic meter: By far the most common base meter for English poetry, accentual-syllabic meter measures the pattern of stressed syllables relative to the unstressed ones. In the first line of William Shakespeare's Sonnet 130, "My mistress' eyes are nothing like the sun," there is a pattern of alternating unstressed with stressed syllables, although there is a substitution of an unstressed syllable for a stressed syllable at the word "like." In the accentual-syllabic system, stressed and unstressed syllables are grouped together into feet.

Allegory: A literary mode in which a second level of meaning—wherein characters, events, and settings represent abstractions—is encoded within the surface narrative. The allegorical mode may dominate the entire work, in which case the encoded message is the work's primary excuse for being, or it may be an element in a work otherwise interesting and meaningful for its surface story alone.

Alliteration: When consonant repetition is focused at the beginning of syllables, the repetition is called alliteration, as in: "Large *m*annered *m*otions of his *m*ythy *m*ind." Alliteration is used when the poet wishes to focus on the details of a sequence of words and to show relationships between words within a line. Because a reader cannot easily skim over an alliterative line, it is conspicuous and demands emphasis.

Allusion: When a reference is made to a historical or literary event whose story or outcome adds dimension to the poem, then poetical allusion occurs. "Fire and Ice" by Robert Frost, for example, alludes to the biblical account of the flood and the prophecy that the next destruction will come by fire, not water. Without recognizing the allusion and understanding the biblical reference to Noah and the surrounding associations of hate and desire, the reader cannot fully appreciate the poem.

Anacrusis: The opposite of truncation, anacrusis occurs when an extra unstressed syllable is added to the beginning or end of a line, as in the line: "their shoul/ders held the sky/suspended." This line is described as iambic tetrameter with terminal anacrusis. Anacrusis is used to change a rising meter to falling, and vice versa, in order to change the reader's emotional response to the subject.

Anapest: One of six standard rhythmic units in English poetry, the anapestic foot associates two unstressed syllables with one stressed syllable, as in the line, "With the sift/ed, harmon/ious pause." The anapestic foot is one of the three most common in English poetry and is used to create a highly rhythmical, usually emotional, line.

Anaphora: Anaphora occurs when successive phrases or lines begin with the same word or words. Timothy Steele's "Sapphics Against Anger" uses anaphora in the repetition of the phrase "May I."

Approximate rhyme: The two categories of approximate rhyme are assonance and half rhyme (or slant rhyme). Assonance occurs when words with identical vowel sounds but different consonants are associated. "Stars," "arms," and "park" all contain identical *a* (and *ar*) sounds, but because the consonants are different the words are not full rhymes. Half rhyme or slant rhymes contain identical consonants but different vowels, as in "fall" and "well." "Table" and "bauble" constitute half rhymes; "law," "cough," and "fawn" assonate.

Archetype: The term "archetype" entered literary criticism from the psychology of Carl G. Jung, who defined archetypes as "primordial images" from the "collective unconscious" of humankind. Jung believed that works of art derive much of their power from the unconscious appeal of these images to ancestral memories. In his extremely influential *Anatomy of Criticism* (1957), Northrop Frye gave another sense of the term wide currency, defining the archetype as "a symbol, usually an image, which recurs often enough in literature to be recognizable as an element of one's literary experience as a whole."

Assonance: See *Approximate rhyme*

Aubade: An aubade is a type of poem welcoming or decrying the arrival of the dawn. Often the dawn symbolizes the separation of two lovers. An example is William Empson's "Aubade."

Ballad: The ballad stanza, a type of quatrain, may alternate its rhyme scheme as *abab* or *abcb*. If all four lines contain four feet each (tetrameter), the stanza is called a "long ballad"; if one or more of the lines contain only three feet (trimeter), it is called a "short ballad." Ballad stanzas, which are highly mnemonic, originated with verse adapted to singing. For this reason, the poetic ballad is well suited for presenting stories. Popular ballads are songs or verse which tell tales, usually impersonal, and they usually impart folk wisdom. Supernatural events, courage, and love are frequent themes, but any experience which appeals to people is acceptable material. A famous use of the ballad form is *The Rime of the Ancient Mariner* (1798), by Samuel Taylor Coleridge.

Ballade: The French "ballade," a popular and sophisticated form, is commonly (but not necessarily) composed of an eight-line stanza rhyming *ababbcbc*. Early ballades usually contained three stanzas and an envoy, commonly addressed to a nobleman, priest, or the poet's patron, but no consistent syllable count. Another common characteristic of the ballade is a refrain that occurs at the end of each stanza.

Base meter (or metrical base): Poems in English and in most European languages which are not free verse are written in one of four base meters (accentual, accentual-syllabic, syllabic, or quantitative), measured by the number, pattern, or duration of the syllables within a line or stanza. Rhythm in verse occurs because of meter, and the use of meter depends upon the type of base into which it is placed.

Blank verse: Although many variations can occur in the meter of blank verse, its base meter is iambic pentameter. Blank verse lines are unrhymed, and are usually arranged in stichic form (that is, not in stanzas). Most of Shakespeare's plays are written in blank verse; in poetry it is often used for subject matter that requires much narration or reflection. In both poetry and drama, blank verse elevates emotion and gives a dramatic sense of importance. Although the base meter of blank verse is iambic pentameter, the form is very flexible, and substitution, enjambment, feminine rhyme, and extra syllables can relax the rigidity of the base. The flexibility of blank verse gives the poet an opportunity to use a formal structure without seeming unnecessarily decorous. T. S. Eliot's "Burnt Norton" is a modern blank-verse poem.

Cadence: The rhythmic speed or tempo with which a line is read is its cadence. All language has cadence, but when the cadence of words is forced into some pattern, it then becomes meter, thus distinguishing poetry from prose. A prose poem may possess strong cadence, combined with poetic uses of imagery, symbolism, and other poetic devices.

Caesura: When the poet imposes a pause or break in the poem, with or without punctuation marks, a caesura has occurred. The comma, question mark, colon, and dash are the most common signals for pausing, and these are properly termed "caesuras"; pauses may also be achieved through syntax, lines, meter, rhyme, and the sound of words. The type of punctuation determines the length of the pause. Periods and question marks demand full stops; colons take almost a full stop; semicolons take a long pause; commas a short pause. The end of a line usually demands some pause even if there is no punctuation.

Cinquain: Any five-line stanza, including the madsong and the limerick, is a cinquain. Cinquains are most often composed of a ballad stanza with an extra line added to the middle.

Classicism: A literary stance or value system consciously based on the example of classical Greek and Roman literature. While the term is applied to an enormous diversity of artists in many different periods and in many different national literatures, "classicism" generally denotes a cluster of values including formal discipline, restrained expression, reverence for tradition, and an objective rather than a subjective orientation. As a literary tendency, classicism is often opposed to Romanticism, although many writers combine classical and romantic elements.

Conceit: One of several types of metaphor, the term "conceit" is used for comparisons which are highly intellectualized. A conceit may therefore be said to be an extended, elaborate, or complex metaphor. The term is frequently applied to the work of the Metaphysical poets, notably John Donne.

Connotation: Words convey meaning through their sound, through their formal, denotative definitions, through their use in context, and through connotation. When a word takes on an additional meaning other than its denotative one, it achieves connotation. The word "mercenary," for example, simply means a soldier who is paid to fight in an army not of his own region, but connotatively a mercenary is an unprincipled scoundrel who kills for money and pleasure, not for honor and patriotism. Connotation is one of the most important devices for achieving irony, and readers may be fooled into believing a poem has one meaning because they have missed connotations which reverse the poem's apparent theme.

Consonance: When the final consonants of stressed syllables agree but the preceding vowels are different, consonance occurs. "Chair/star" is an example of consonance, since both words end with *r* preceded by different vowels. Terminal consonance creates half or slant rhyme (see *Approximate rhyme*). Consonance differs from alliteration in that the final consonants are repeated rather than the initial consonants. In the twentieth century consonance became one of the principal rhyming devices, used to achieve formality without seeming stilted or old-fashioned.

Consonants: Consonants (all letters except the vowels, *a, e, i, o, u,* and sometimes *y*) are among the most important sound-producing devices in poetry. There are five basic effects that certain consonants will produce: resonance, harshness, plosiveness, exhaustiveness, and liquidity. Resonance, exhaustiveness, and liquidity tend to give words—and consequently the whole line if several of these consonants are used—a soft effect. Plosiveness and harshness, on the other hand, tend to create tension. Resonance is the property of long duration produced by nasals, such as *n* and *m*, and by voiced fricating consonants such as *z, v,* and the voiced *th,* as in "them." Exhaustiveness is created by the voiceless fricating consonants and consonant combinations, such as *h, f,* and the voiceless *th* and *s.* Liquidity results from using the liquids and semivowels *l, r, w,* and *y,* as in the word "silken." Plosiveness occurs when certain consonants

create a stoppage of breath before releasing it, especially *b, p, t, d, g, k, ch,* and *j.*

Controlling image/controlling metaphor: Just as a poem may include as structural devices form, theme, action, or dramatic situation, it may also use imagery for structure. When an image runs throughout a poem, giving unity to lesser images or ideas, it is called a "controlling image." Usually the poet establishes a single idea and then expands and complicates it; in Edward Taylor's "Huswifery," for example, the image of the spinning wheel is expanded into images of weaving until the reader begins to see life as a tapestry. Robert Frost's "The Silken Tent" is a fine example of a controlling image and extended metaphor.

Couplet: Any two succeeding lines that rhyme form a couplet. Because the couplet has been used in so many different ways, and because of its long tradition in English poetry, various names and functions have been given to types of couplets. One of the most common is the decasyllabic (ten-syllable) couplet. When there is an end-stop on the second line of a couplet, it is said to be "closed"; an enjambed couplet is "open." An end-stopped decasyllabic couplet is called a "heroic couplet," because the form has often been used to sing the praise of heroes. The heroic couplet was widely used by the neoclassical poets of the eighteenth century. Because it is so stately and sometimes pompous, the heroic couplet invites satire, and many poems have been written in "mock heroic verse," such as Alexander Pope's *The Rape of the Lock* (1712). Another commonly used couplet is the octasyllabic (eight-syllable) couplet, formed from two lines of iambic tetrameter, as in "L'Allegro" by John Milton: "Come, and trip as we go/On the light fantastic toe." The light, sing-song tone of the octasyllabic couplet also invited satire, and in the seventeenth century Samuel Butler wrote one of the most famous of all satires, *Hudibras,* in this couplet. When a couplet is used to break another rhyme scheme, it generally produces a summing-up effect and has an air of profundity. Shakespeare found this characteristic particularly useful when he needed to give his newly invented Shakespearean sonnet a final note of authority and purpose.

Dactyl: The dactyl, formed of a stress followed by two unstressed syllables ($\prime \cup \cup$), is fairly common in isolated words, but when this pattern is included in a line of poetry, it tends to break down and rearrange itself into components of other types of feet. Isolated, the word "meaningless" is a dactyl, but in the line "Polite/meaning/less words," the last syllable becomes attached to the stressed "words" and creates a split foot, forming a trochee and an iamb. Nevertheless, a few dactylic poems do exist. "After the/pangs of a /desperate/lover," is a dactyllic line.

Deconstruction: An extremely influential contemporary school of criticism based on the works of the French philosopher Jacques Derrida. Deconstruction treats literary works as unconscious reflections of the reigning myths of Western culture. The primary myth is that there is a meaningful world that language signifies or represents. The deconstructionist critic is most often concerned with showing how a literary text tacitly subverts the very assumptions or myths on which it ostensibly rests.

Denotation: The explicit formal definition of a word, exclusive of its implications and emotional associations (see *Connotation*), is its denotation or denotative meaning.

Depressed foot: Occasionally, two syllables occur in a pattern in such a way as to be taken as one syllable without actually being an elision, thus creating a depressed foot. In the line: "To each the boul/ders (that have)/fallen/to each" the base meter consists of five iambic feet, but in the third foot there is an extra syllable which disrupts the meter but does not break it, so that "that have" functions as the second half of the iambic foot.

Diction: John Dryden defined diction concisely as the poet's "choice of words." In Dryden's time, and for most of the history of English verse, the diction of poetry was elevated, sharply distinct from everyday speech. Since the early twentieth century, however, the diction of poetry has ranged from the banal and the conversational to the highly formal, and from obscenity and slang to technical vocabulary, sometimes in the same poem. The diction of a poem often reveals its persona's values and attitudes.

Dieresis: Caesuras which come after the foot (see *Split foot* for a discussion of caesuras which break feet), called "dieresis" (although the technical name is seldom used), can be used to create long pauses in the line, and they are often used to prepare the line for enjambment.

Dramatic dialogue: When two or more personas speak to each other in a poem or a play, they engage in dramatic dialogue. Unlike a dramatic monologue, both characters speak, and in the best dramatic dialogues, their conversation leads to a final resolution in which both characters and the reader come to the same realization at the same time.

Dramatic irony: See *Irony*

Dramatic monologue: In dramatic monologue, the narrator addresses a silent persona who never speaks but whose presence greatly influences what the narrator tells the reader. The principal reason for writing in dramatic monologue form is to control the speech of the major persona through the implied reaction of the silent one. The effect is one of continuing change and often surprise. In Robert Browning's "My Last Duchess," for example, the duke believes that he is in control of the situation, when in fact he has provided the emissary with terrible insights about the way he treated his former duchess. The emissary, who is the silent persona, has asked questions which the duke has answered; in doing so he has given away secrets. Dramatic monologue is somewhat like hearing one side of a telephone conversation in which the reader learns much about both participants.

Duration: The measure of quantitative meter is the duration or length of the syllables. Duration can alter the tone and the relative stress of a line and influence meaning as much as the foot can.

Elegy: The elegy and pastoral elegy are distinguishable by their subject matter rather than their form. The elegy is usually a long, rhymed, strophic poem whose subject is meditation upon death or a lamentable theme, while the pastoral elegy uses the natural setting of a pastoral scene to sing of death or love. Within the pastoral setting the simplicity of the characters and the scene lends a peaceful air despite the grief the narrator feels.

Elision: The two types of elision are synaeresis and syncope; they occur when a poet who is attempting to maintain a regular base meter joins two vowels into a single vowel or omits a vowel altogether. In the line "Of man's first disobedience, and the fruit" the "ie" in "disobedience" is pronounced as a "y" ("ye") so that the word reads dis/o/bed/yence, thereby making a five-syllable word into a four-syllable word. This process of forming one vowel out of two is synaeresis. When a vowel is dropped altogether, rather than combining two into one, it is called "syncope," as when "natural" becomes "nat'ral" and "hastening" becomes "hast'ning." Less frequent uses of elision are to change the sound of a word, to spell words as they are pronounced, and to indicate dialect.

Emphasis: Through a number of techniques, such as *caesura*, the line, relative stress, counterpointing, and substitution, poets are able to alter the usual emphasis or meaning of words. Whenever the meter of a poem is intentionally altered through one of these techniques, certain words or an entire line will be highlighted or emphasized for the purpose of calling attention to the most important parts of the poem.

End rhyme: See *Rhyme*

End-stop: When a punctuated pause occurs at the end of a line, the line is said to be "end-stopped." The function of end-stops is to show the relationship between lines and to create emphasis on particular words or lines. End-stopping in rhymed poems creates more emphasis on the rhyme words, which already carry a great deal of emphasis by virtue of their rhymes. Enjambment is the opposite of end-stopping.

Enjambment: When a line is not end-stopped—that is, when it carries over to the following line—the line is said to be "enjambed," as in John Milton's: "Avenge, O Lord, thy slaughtered saints, whose bones/Lie scattered on the Alpine mountains cold." Enjambment is used to change the natural emphasis of the line, to strengthen or weaken the effect of rhyme, or to alter meter.

Envoy: Generally, an envoy (or envoi) is any short poem or stanza addressed to the reader as a beginning or end to a longer work. Specifically, the envoy is the final stanza of a sestina or a ballade in which all the rhyme words are repeated or echoed.

Epic: Although this term usually refers to a long narrative poem that presents the exploits of a central figure of high position, the term is also used to designate a long novel that has the style or structure usually associated with an epic. In this sense, for example, Herman Melville's *Moby Dick* (1851) and James Joyce's *Ulysses* (1922) may be called epic.

Extended metaphor: When metaphors are added to one another so that they run in a series, they are collec-

tively called an "extended metaphor." Robert Frost's poem "The Silken Tent" uses an extended metaphor; it compares the "she" of the poem to the freedom and bondage of a silken tent. (See also *Controlling image/ controlling metaphor*)

Eye rhyme: Words that appear to be identical because of their spelling but that sound different are known as "eye rhymes." "Bough/enough/cough" and "ballet/pallet" are examples. Because of changes in pronunciation, many older poems appear to use eye rhymes but do not. For example, "wind" (meaning moving air) once rhymed with "find." Eye rhymes which are intentional and do not result from a change in pronunciation may be used to create a disconcerting effect.

Fabliau: A fabliau is a bawdy medieval verse, such as many found in Geoffrey Chaucer's *Canterbury Tales*.

Falling rhyme: Rhyme in which the correspondence of sound comes only in the final unstressed syllable, which is preceded by another unstressed syllable, is known as a "falling rhyme." T. S. Eliot rhymes "me-tíc-u-loùs" with "ri-díc-u-loùs" and creates a falling rhyme. (See also *Feminine rhyme*; *Masculine rhyme*)

Falling rhythm: A line in which feet move from stressed to unstressed syllables (trochaic or dactyllic) is said to "fall," as in this line from "The Naming of Parts": "Glístens/líke cór/al in/áll of the/néighboring/gárdens." Because English and other Germanic-based languages naturally rise, imposing a falling rhythm on a rising base meter creates counterpointing.

Feminine rhyme: Feminine rhyme occurs when (1) a line's final accented syllable is followed by a single unaccented syllable and (2) the accented syllables rhyme, while the unaccented syllables are phonetically identical, as with "flíck-er/sníck-er" and "fín-gers/ma-lín-gers." Feminine rhymes are often used for lightness in tone and delicacy in movement.

Feminist criticism: A criticism advocating equal rights for women in a political, economic, social, psychological, personal, and aesthetic sense. On the thematic level, the feminist reader should identify with female characters and their concerns. The object is to provide a critique of phallocentric assumptions and an analysis of patriarchal ideologies inscribed in a literature that is male-centered and male-dominated. On the ideological level, feminist critics see gender, as well as the stereotypes that go along with it, as a cultural construct. They strive to define a particularly feminine content and to extend the canon so that it might include works by lesbians, feminists, and women writers in general.

First person: This point of view is particularly useful in short lyrical poems, which tend to be highly subjective, taking the reader deep into the narrator's thoughts. First-person poems normally, though not necessarily, signal the use of the first person through the pronoun "I," allowing the reader direct access to the narrator's thoughts or providing a character who can convey a personal reaction to an event. (See also *Third person*)

Foot/feet: The natural speech pattern in English and other Germanic-based languages is to group syllables together in family units. In English, the most common of these rhythmic units is composed of one unstressed syllable attached to one stressed syllable (an iamb). When these family groups are forced into a line of poetry, they are called "feet" in the accentual-syllabic metrical system. In the line "My mis/tress' eyes/are noth/ing like/the sun" there are four iambic feet (◡′) and one pyrrhic foot (◡◡), but in the line "There where/the vines/cling crim/son on/the wall" there are three substitutions for the iamb—in the first, third, and fourth feet. The six basic feet in English poetry are the iamb (◡′), trochee (′◡), anapest (◡◡′), dactyl (′◡◡), spondee (′′), and pyrrhus (◡◡).

Form: The form of a poem is determined by its arrangement of lines on the page, its base meter, its rhyme scheme, and occasionally its subject matter. Poems which are arranged into stanzas are called "strophic," and because the strophic tradition is so old a large number of commonly used stanzas have evolved particular uses and characteristics. Poems which run from beginning to end without a break are called stichic. The form of "pattern poetry" is determined by its visual appearance rather than by lines and stanzas, while the definition of free verse is that it has no discernable form. Some poem types, such as the sestina, sonnet, and ode, are written in particular forms and frequently are restricted to particular subject matter.

Formalist criticism: There were two particularly influential formalist schools of criticism in the twentieth century: the Russian Formalists and the American New Critics. The Russian Formalists were concerned with the conventional devices used in literature to defamiliarize

that which habit has made familiar. The New Critics believed that literary criticism is a description and evaluation of its object and that the primary concern of the critic is with the work's unity. Both schools of criticism, at their most extreme, treated literary works as artifacts or constructs divorced from their biographical and social contexts.

Found poetry: Found poetry is created from language which is "found" in print in nonliterary settings—on menus, tombstones, fire extinguishers, even on shampoo bottles. Any language which is already constructed, but especially language which appears on artifacts that characterize society, such as cereal boxes, provides the material from which the found poem is created. The rules for writing a found poem vary, but generally the found language is used intact or altered only slightly.

Free verse: A poem that does not conform to any traditional convention, such as meter, rhyme, or form, and that does not establish any pattern within itself, is said to be a free verse poem. There is, however, great dispute over whether "free" verse actually exists. Eliot said that by definition poetry must establish some kind of pattern, and Frost said that "writing free verse is like playing tennis with the net down." However, some would agree with Carl Sandburg, who insisted that "you can play a better game with the net down." Free verse depends more on cadence than on meter.

Ghazal: The ghazal is a poetic form based on a type of Persian poetry. A ghazal is composed of couplets, often unrhymed, that function as individual images or observations but that also interrelate in sometimes subtle ways.

Gnomic verse: Gnomic verse typically includes many proverbs or maxims.

Haiku: Haiku is a Japanese form which appeared in the sixteenth century and is still practiced in Japan. A haiku consists of three lines of five, seven, and five syllables each; in Japanese there are other conventions regarding content which are not observed in Western haiku. The traditional haiku took virtually all of its images from nature, using the natural world as a metaphor for the spiritual.

Half rhyme: See *Approximate rhyme*
Heroic couplet: See *Couplet*

Historical criticism: In contrast to formalist criticism, which treats literary works to a great extent as self-contained artifacts, historical criticism emphasizes the historical context of literature; these approaches, however, need not be mutually exclusive. Ernst Robert Curtius's *European Literature and the Latin Middle Ages* (1940) is a prominent example of historical criticism.

Hymn stanza: See *Ballad*

Hyperbole: When the poet deliberately overstates in order to heighten the reader's awareness, he is using hyperbole. As with irony, hyperbole works because the reader can perceive the difference between the importance of the dramatic situation and the manner in which it is described.

Iamb: The basic foot of English speech, the iamb associates one unstressed syllable with one stressed (‿ˊ). The line "So long/as men/can breathe/or eyes/can see" is composed of five iambs. In the line "A cold/coming/we had/of it," a trochaic foot (a trochee) has been substituted for the expected iamb in the second foot, thus emphasizing that this is a "coming" rather than a "going," an important distinction in T. S. Eliot's "The Journey of the Magi."

Iambic pentameter: Iambic pentameter is a very common type of poetic line in English. It consists of five iambic feet together in a line (a foot is a two-syllable grouping). The following two lines by Thomas Wyatt are in iambic pentameter: "I find no peace and all my war is done,/I fear and hope, I burn and freeze like ice." (See also *Foot/feet*; *iamb*)

Identical rhyme: Identical rhyme occurs when the entire final stressed syllables contain exactly the same sounds, such as "break/brake," or "bear" (noun), "bear" (verb), "bare" (adjective), "bare" (verb).

Imagery: Imagery is traditionally defined as the verbal simulation of sensory perception. Like so many critical terms, "imagery" betrays a visual bias: it suggests that a poetic image is necessarily visual, a picture in words. In fact, however, imagery calls on all five senses, although the visual is predominant in many poets. In its simplest form, an image re-creates a physical sensation in a clear, literal manner, as in Robert Lowell's lines, "A sweetish smell of shavings, wax and oil/blows through the redone bedroom newly aged" ("Marriage"). Imagery becomes more complex when the poet employs metaphor and other figures of speech to re-create experience, as in Seamus Heaney's lines, "Right along the lough shore/A smoke of flies/Drifts thick in the sunset" ("At Ardboe Point"), substituting a fresh metaphor ("A smoke of flies") for a trite one (a cloud of flies) to help the reader visualize the scene more clearly.

Interior monologue: A first-person representation of a persona's or character's thoughts or feelings. It differs from a dramatic monologue in that it deals with thoughts rather than spoken words or conversation.

Internal rhyme: See *Rhyme*

Irony: Irony is among the three or four most important concepts in modern literary criticism. Although the term originated in classical Greece and has been in the vocabulary of criticism since that time, only in the nineteenth and twentieth centuries has it assumed central importance. The term is used in many different contexts with an extraordinary range of meanings, eluding precise definition. In its narrowest sense, irony is a figure of speech in which the speaker's real meaning is different from (and often exactly opposite to) the apparent meaning. In Andrew Marvell's lines, "The Grave's a fine and private place,/But none I think do there embrace" ("To His Coy Mistress"), the speaker's literal meaning—in praise of the grave—is quite different from his real meaning. This kind of irony, the easiest to define, is often called "verbal irony." Another kind of irony is found in narrative and dramatic poetry. In the *Iliad* (c. 800 B.C.E.), for example, the reader is made privy to the counsels of the gods, which greatly affect the course of action in the epic, while the human characters are kept in ignorance. This discrepancy between the knowledge of the reader and that of the character (or characters) is called "dramatic irony." Beyond these narrow, well-defined varieties of irony are many wider applications.

Limerick: The limerick is a comic five-line poem rhyming *aabba* in which the third and fourth lines are shorter (usually five syllables each) than the first, second, and last lines, which are usually eight syllables each. The limerick's anapestic base makes the verse sound silly; modern limericks are almost invariably associated with bizarre indecency or with ethnic or anticlerical jokes.

Line: A line has been defined as a poetical unit characterized by the presence of meter, and lines are categorized according to the number of feet (see *Foot/feet*) they contain. A pentameter line, for example, contains five feet. This definition does not apply to a great deal of modern poetry, however, which is written in free verse. Ultimately, then, a line must be defined as a typographical unit on the page that performs various functions in different kinds of poetry.

Lyric poetry: The two ancient roots of poetry are the narrative and lyric traditions. Narrative poetry, such as the *Iliad*, relates long stories, often historical, which preserve information, characters, and values of a culture. Lyric poetry developed when music was accompanied by words, and although the "lyrics" were later separated from the music, the characteristics of lyric poetry have been shaped by the constraints of music. Lyric poems are short, adaptable to metrical variation, and usually personal compared with the cultural functions of narrative poetry. Lyric poetry sings of the self, exploring deeply personal feelings about life.

Mad-song: The mad-song—verse uttered by the presumably insane—usually expresses a happy, harmless, inventive sort of insanity. The typical rhyme scheme of the mad-song is *abccb*, and the unrhymed first line helps to set a tone of oddity and unpredictability, since it controverts the expectation that there will be a rhyme for it. The standard mad-song has short lines that help suggest benign madness, since "simple" people are associated with uncomplicated sentence patterns.

Marxist criticism: Based on the nineteenth century writings of Karl Marx and Friedrich Engels, Marxist criticism views literature as a product of ideological forces determined by the dominant class. However, many Marxists believe that literature operates according to its own autonomous standards of production and reception: It is both a product of ideology and able to determine ideology. As such, literature may overcome the dominant paradigms of its age and play a revolutionary role in society.

Masculine rhyme: Masculine rhyme occurs when rhyme exists in the stressed syllables. "Men/then" constitute masculine rhyme, but so do "af-ter-noons/ spoons." Masculine rhyme is generally considered more forceful than feminine rhyme, and while it has a variety of uses, it generally gives authority and assurance to the line, especially when the final syllables are of short duration.

Metaphor: Metaphor, like irony, is one of a handful of key concepts in modern literary criticism. Like irony, the term "metaphor" is used in such a wide variety of contexts that a precise, all-encompassing definition is impossible. In its narrowest sense, metaphor is a figure of speech in which two strikingly different things are identified with each other, as in "the waves were soldiers moving" (Wallace Stevens). A metaphor contains a "tenor" and a "vehicle." The tenor is the subject of the metaphor, and the vehicle is the imagery by which the subject is presented. In D. H. Lawrence's lines, "Reach me a gentian, give me a torch/let me guide myself with the blue, forked torch of this flower" ("Bavarian Gentians"), the tenor is the gentian and the vehicle is the torch. This relatively restricted definition of metaphor by no means covers the usage of the word in modern criticism. Some critics argue that metaphorical perception underlies all figures of speech. Others dispute the distinction between literal and metaphorical description, saying that language is essentially metaphorical. The term "metaphor" has become widely used to identify analogies of all kinds in literature, painting, film, and even music.

Meter: Meter is the pattern of language when it is forced into a line of poetry. All language has rhythm; when that rhythm is organized and regulated in the line so as to affect the meaning and emotional response to the words, then the rhythm has been refined into meter. Because the lines of most poems maintain a similar meter throughout, poems are said to have a base meter. The meter is determined by the number of syllables in a line and by the relationship between them.

Metonymy: When an object which is closely related to an idea comes to stand for the idea itself, such as saying "the crown" to mean the king, "metonymy" is being used. The use of a part of an object to stand for the entire object, such as using "heart" to mean a person, is called "synecdoche." Metonymy and synecdoche are used to emphasize a particular part of the whole or one particular aspect of it.

Mnemonic verse: Poetry in which rhythmic patterns aid memorization but are not crucial to meaning is called "mnemonic verse." Ancient bards were able to re-member long poems partly through the use of stock phrases and other mnemonic devices.

Mock-heroic: See *Couplet.*

Modernism: An international movement in the arts that began in the early years of the twentieth century. Although the term is used to describe artists of widely varying persuasions, modernism in general was characterized by its international idiom, by its interest in cultures distant in space or time, by its emphasis on formal experimentation, and by its sense of dislocation and radical change.

Multiculturalism: The tendency to recognize the perspectives of works by authors (particularly women and non-European writers) who, until the latter part of the twentieth century, were excluded from the canon of Western art and literature. In order to promote multiculturalism, publishers and educators have revised textbooks and school curricula to incorporate material by and about women, minorities, non-Western cultures, gays, and lesbians.

Myth: Anonymous traditional stories dealing with basic human concepts and antinomies. Claude Lévi-Strauss says that myth is that part of language where the "formula *tradutore, tradittore* reaches its lowest truth value. . . . Its substance does not lie in its style, its original music, or its syntax, but in the story which it tells."

Myth criticism: Northrop Frye says that in myth, "we see the structural principles of literature isolated." Myth criticism is concerned with these basic principles of literature; it is not to be confused with mythological criticism, which is primarily concerned with finding mythological parallels in the surface action of a narrative.

Narrator: The terms "narrator," "persona," and "speaker" are roughly synonymous. They all refer to who is doing the talking—or observing or thinking—in a poem. Lyric poetry most often consists of the poet expressing his or her own personal feelings directly. Other poems, however, may involve the poet adopting the point of view of another person entirely. In some poems—notably in a dramatic monologue—it is relatively easy to determine that the narrative is being related by a fictional (or perhaps historical) character, but in others it may be more difficult to identify the "I."

New Criticism. See *Formalist criticism.*

Occasional verse: Broadly defined, occasional verse includes any poem written for a specific occasion, such as a wedding, a birthday, a death, or a public event. Edmund Spenser's *Epithalamion* (1595), which was written for his marriage, and John Milton's "Lycidas," which commemorated the death of his schoolmate Edward King, are examples of occasional verse, as are W. H. Auden's "September 1, 1939" and Frank O'Hara's "The Day Lady Died."

Octave: An octave is a poem in eight lines. Octaves may have many different variations of meter, such as ottava rima.

Ode: The ode is a lyric poem which treats a unified subject with elevated emotion, usually ending with a satisfactory resolution. There is no set form for the ode, but it must be long enough to build intense emotional response. Often the ode will address itself to some omnipotent source and will take on a spiritual hue. When explicating an ode, readers should look for the relationship between the narrator and some transcendental power to which the narrator must submit in order to find contentment. Modern poets have used the ode to treat subjects which are not religious in the theological sense but which have become innate beliefs of society.

Ottava rima: Ottava rima is an eight-line stanza of iambic pentameter, rhyming *abababcc.* Probably the most famous English poem written in ottava rima is Lord Byron's *Don Juan* (1819-1824), and because the poem was so successful as a spoof, the form has come to be associated with poetic high jinks. However, the stanza has also been used brilliantly for just the opposite effect, to reflect seriousness and meditation.

Oxymoron: Closely related to paradox, an oxymoron occurs when two paradoxical words are placed in juxtaposition, such as "wise fool" or "devilish angel."

Pantoum: A French form of four quatrains in which entire lines are repeated in a strict pattern of 1234, 2546, 5768, 7183. Peter Meinke's "Atomic Pantoum" is an example.

Paradox: A paradox is a statement that contains an inherent contradiction. It may be a statement that at first seems true but is in reality contradictory. It may also be a statement that appears contradictory but is actually true or that contains an element of truth that reconciles the contradiction.

Pentameter: A type of rhythmic pattern in which each line consists of five poetic feet. (See also *Accentual-syllabic meter*; *Foot/feet*; *Iamb*; *Iambic pentameter*; *Line*)

Periphrasis: Periphrasis is the use of a wordy phrase to describe something that could be described simply in one word.

Persona: See *Narrator*

Phenomenological criticism: Although best known as a European school of criticism practiced by Georges Poulet and others, this so-called criticism of consciousness is also propounded in America by such critics as J. Hillis Miller. The focus is less on individual works and genres than it is on literature as an act; the work is not seen as an object, but rather as part of a strand of latent impulses in the work of a single author or an epoch.

Point of view: Point of view may be simply defined as the eyes and other senses through which readers experience the situation of a poem. As with fiction, poems may be related in the first person, second person (unusual), or third person. (The presence of the words "I" or "we" indicates singular or plural first-person narration.) Point of view may be limited or omniscient. A limited point of view means that the narrator can see only what the poet wants him or her to see, while from an omniscient point of view the narrator can know everything, including the thoughts and motives of others.

Postcolonialism: Postcolonial literature emerged in the mid-twentieth century when colonies in Asia, Africa, and the Caribbean began gaining their independence from the European nations that had long controlled them. Postcolonial authors, such as Salman Rushdie, V. S. Naipaul, and Derek Walcott, tend to focus on both the freedom and the conflict inherent in living in a postcolonial state.

Postmodernism: A ubiquitous but elusive term in contempory criticism, "postmodernism" is loosely applied to the various artistic movements that followed the era of so-called high modernism, represented by such giants as writer James Joyce and painter and scuptor Pablo Picasso. In critical discussions of contemporary fiction, the term "postmodernism" is frequently applied to the works of writers such as Thomas Pynchon, John Barth, and Donald Barthelme, who exhibit a self-conscious awareness of their modernist predecessors as

well as a reflexive treatment of fictional form. Such reflexive treatments can extend to poetry as well.

Prose poem: The distinguishing feature of the prose poem is its typography: It appears like prose on the page, with no line breaks. There are no formal characteristics by which a prose poem can be distinguished from a piece of prose. Many prose poems employ rhythmic repetition and other poetic devices not normally found in prose, but others use such devices sparingly if at all. Prose poems range in length from a few lines to three or four pages; most prose poems occupy a page or less.

Psychological criticism: While much modern literary criticism reflects to some degree the impact of Sigmund Freud, Carl Jung, Jacques Lacan, and other psychological theorists, the term "psychological criticism" suggests a strong emphasis on a causal relation between the writer's psychological state, variously interpreted, and his or her works. A notable example of psychological criticism is Norman Fruman's *Coleridge, the Damaged Archangel* (1971).

Pun: A pun occurs when words which have similar pronunciations have entirely different meanings. By use of a pun the speaker establishes a connection between two meanings or contexts that the reader would not ordinarily make. The result may be a surprise recognition of an unusual or striking connection, or, more often, a humorously accidental connection.

Pyrrhus: When two unstressed syllables comprise a foot, it is called a pyrrhus or a pyrrhic foot, as in the line "Appéar/and dís/appéar/in the/blue depth/of the sky," in which foot four is a pyrrhus.

Quatrain: Any four-line stanza is a quatrain; aside from the couplet, it is the most common stanza type. The quatrain's popularity among both sophisticated and unsophisticated readers suggests that there is something inherently pleasing about the form. For many readers, poetry and quatrains are almost synonymous. Balance and antithesis, contrast and comparison not possible in other stanza types are indigenous to the quatrain.

Realism: A literary technique in which the primary convention is to render an illusion of fidelity to external reality. Realism is often identified as the primary method of the novel form: It focuses on surface details, maintains a fidelity to the everyday experiences of middle-class society, and strives for a one-to-one relationship between the fiction and the action imitated. The realist movement in the late nineteenth century coincides with the full development of the novel form.

Regular meter: A line of poetry that contains only the same type of foot is said to be regular. Only the dullest of poems maintains a regular meter throughout, however; skillful poets create interest and emphasis through substitution.

Relative stress: When more emphasis is placed on one syllable in a pattern than on another, that syllable is said to be "stressed." Once the dominant stress in the line has been determined, every other syllable can be assigned a stress factor relative to the dominant syllable. The stress factor is created by several aspects of prosody: the position of the syllable in the line, the position of the syllable in its word, the surrounding syllables, the type of vowels and consonants which constitute the syllable, and the syllable's relation to the foot, base meter, and caesura. Since every syllable will have a different stress factor, there could be as many values as there are syllables, although most prosodists scan poems using primary, secondary, and unstressed notations. In the line "I am there like the dead, or the beast" the anapestic base meter will not permit "I" to take a full stress, but it is a more forceful syllable than the unstressed ones, so it is assigned a secondary stress. Relative to "dead" and "beast," it takes less pressure; relative to the articles in the line, it takes much more.

Resolution: Generally, a resolution is any natural conclusion to a poem, especially to a short lyric poem which establishes some sort of dilemma or conflict that the narrator must solve. Specifically, the resolution is the octave stanza of a Petrarchan sonnet or the couplet of a Shakespearean sonnet in which the first part of the poem presents a situation which must find balance in the resolution.

Rhyme: Rhyme is a correspondence of sound between syllables within a line or between lines whose proximity to each other allows the sounds to be sustained. Rhyme may be classified in a number of ways: according to the sound relationship between rhyming words, the position of the rhyming words in the line, and the number and position of the syllables in the rhyming words. Sound classifications include full rhyme and approximate rhyme. Full rhyme is defined as words that have the same vowel sound, followed by the same con-

sonants in their last stressed syllables, and in which all succeeding syllables are phonetically identical. "Hat/cat" and "laughter/after" are full rhymes. Categories of approximate rhyme are assonance, slant rhyme, alliteration, eye rhyme, and identical rhyme.

Rhyme classified by its position in the line includes end, internal, and initial rhyme. End rhyme occurs when the last words of lines rhyme. Internal rhyme occurs when two words within the same line or within various lines recall the same sound, as in "Wet, below the snow line, smelling of vegetation" in which "below" and "snow" rhyme. Initial rhyme occurs when the first syllables of two or more lines rhyme. (See also *Masculine rhyme*; *Feminine rhyme*)

Rhyme scheme: Poems that establish a pattern of rhyme have a "rhyme scheme," designated by lowercase (and often italicized) letters. The letters stand for the pattern of rhyming sounds of the last word in each line. For example, the following A. E. Housman quatrain has an *abab* rhyme scheme.

> Into my heart an air that kills
> From yon far country blows:
> What are those blue remembered hills,
> What spires, what farms are those?

As another example, the rhyme scheme of the poetic form known as ottava rima is *abababcc*. Traditional stanza forms are categorized by their rhyme scheme and base meter.

Rime royal: The only standard seven-line stanza in English prosody is rime royal, composed of iambic pentameter lines rhyming *ababbccc*. Shakespeare's *The Rape of Lucrece* (1594) is written in this form. The only variation permitted is to make the last line hexameter.

Romanticism: A widespread cultural movement in the late eighteenth and early nineteenth centuries, the influence of which is still felt. As a general literary tendency, Romanticism is frequently contrasted with classicism or neoclassicism. Although there were many varieties of Romanticism indigenous to various national literatures, the term generally suggests an assertion of the preeminence of the imagination. Other values associated with various schools of Romanticism include primitivism, an interest in folklore, a reverence for nature, and a fascination with the demoniac and the macabre.

Rondeau: One of three standard French forms assimilated by English prosody, the rondeau generally contains thirteen lines divided into three groups. A common stanzaic grouping rhymes *aabba, aabR, aabbaR,* where the *a* and *b* lines are tetrameter and the *R* (refrain) lines are dimeter. The rondel, another French form, contains fourteen lines of trimeter with alternating rhyme (*ababab bababab*) and is divided into two stanzas. The rondeau and rondel forms are always light and playful.

Rondel: See *Rondeau*

Scansion: Scanning is the process of assigning relative stresses and meter to a line of poetry, usually for the purpose of determining where variations, and thus emphasis, in the base meter occur. Scansion can help explain how a poem generates tension and offer clues as to the key words. E. E. Cummings's "singing each morning out of each night" could be scanned in two ways: (1) singing/each morn/ing out/of each night or (2) sing/ing each/morning/out of/each night. Scansion will not only affect the way the line is read aloud but will also influence the meaning of the line.

Secondary stress: See *Relative stress*

Seguidilla: Like the Japanese haiku, the Spanish seguidilla is a mood or imagistic poem whose success hinges on the reader's emotional recognition or spiritual insight. Although there is no agreement as to what form the English seguidilla should take, most of the successful ones are either four or seven lines with an alternating rhyme scheme of *ababcbc.* Lines 1, 3, and 6 are trimeter; lines 2, 4, 5, and 7 dimeter.

Semiotics: The science of signs and sign systems in communication. Literary critic Roman Jakobson says that semiotics deals with the principles that underlie the structure of signs, their use in language of all kinds, and the specific nature of various sign systems.

Sestet: A sestet is a six-line stanza. A Petrarchan or Italian sonnet is composed of an octave followed by a sestet, as in John Milton's Sonnet XIX and William Wordsworth's "The World Is Too Much with Us."

Sestina: A sestina is composed of six six-line stanzas followed by a three-line envoy. The words ending the lines in the first stanza are repeated in different order at the ends of lines in the following stanzas as well as in the the middle and end of each line of the envoy. Elizabeth Bishop's "Sestina" is a good example.

Shakespearean sonnet: See *Sonnet*

Simile: Loosely defined, a simile is a type of metaphor that signals a comparison by the use of the words "like" or "as." Shakespeare's line "My mistress' eyes are nothing like the sun" is a simile that establishes a comparison between the woman's eyes and the sun.

Slant rhyme: See *Approximate rhyme*

Sonnet: The most important and widely used of traditional poem types, the sonnet is almost always composed of fourteen lines of iambic pentameter with some form of alternating rhyme, and it contains a turning point that divides the poem into two parts. The two major sonnet types are the "Petrarchan" (or "Italian") sonnet and the "Shakespearian" sonnet. The original sonnet form, the Petrarchan (adopted from the poetry of Petrarch), presents a problem or situation in the first eight lines, the "octave," then resolves it in the last six, the "sestet." The octave is composed of two quatrains (*abbaabba*), the second of which complicates the first and gradually defines and heightens the problem. The sestet then diminishes the problem slowly until a satisfying resolution is achieved.

During the fifteenth century, the Italian sonnet became an integral part of the courtship ritual, and most sonnets during that time consisted of a young man's description of his perfect lover. Because so many unpoetic young men had generated a nation full of bad sonnets by the end of the century, the form became an object of ridicule, and the English sonnet developed as a reaction against all the bad verse being turned out in the Italian tradition. When Shakespeare wrote "My mistress' eyes are nothing like the sun," he was deliberately negating the Petrarchan conceit, rejoicing in the fact that his loved one was much more interesting and unpredictable than nature. Shakespeare also altered the sonnet's formal balance. Instead of an octave, the Shakespearean sonnet has three quatrains of alternating rhyme and is resolved in a final couplet. During the sixteenth century, long stories were told in sonnet form, one sonnet after the next, to produce "sonnet sequences." Although most sonnets contain fourteen lines, some contain as few as ten (the curtal sonnet) or as many as seventeen.

Speaker: See *Narrator*

Split foot: A split foot occurs when the natural division of a word is altered as a result of being forced into a metrical base. For example, the words "point/ed," "lad/der," and "stick/ing" have a natural falling rhythm, but in the line "My long/two-point/ed lad/der's stick/ing through/a tree" the syllables are rearranged so as to turn the falling rhythm into a rising meter. The result of splitting feet is to create an uncertainty and delicate imbalance in the line.

Spondee: When two relatively stressed syllables occur together in a foot, the unit is called a "spondee" or "spondaic foot," as in the line "Appear/and dis/appear/in the/blue depth/of the sky."

Sprung rhythm: If accentual meter is taken to its extreme, one can never predict the patterns of succeeding stresses: It is possible only to predict a prescribed number of stresses per line. This unpredictability characterizes sprung rhythm, first described near the end of the nineteenth century by Gerard Manley Hopkins. In sprung rhythm "any two stresses may either follow one another running, or be divided by one, two, or three slack syllables."

Stanza: When a certain number of lines are meant to be taken as a unit, that unit is called a "stanza." Although a stanza is traditionally considered a unit that contains rhyme and recurs predictably throughout a poem, the term is also sometimes applied to nonrhyming and even irregular units. Poems that are divided into fairly regular and patterned stanzas are called "strophic"; poems that appear as a single unit, whether rhymed or unrhymed, or that have no predictable stanzas, are called "stichic." Both strophic and stichic units represent logical divisions within the poem, and the difference between them lies in the formality and strength of the interwoven unit. Stanza breaks are commonly indicated by a line of space.

Stichic verse: See *Stanza*

Stress: See *Relative stress*

Strophic verse: See *Stanza*

Structuralism: As a movement of thought, structuralism is based on the idea of intrinsic, self-sufficient structures that do not require reference to external elements. A structure is a system of transformations that involves the interplay of laws inherent in the system itself. The study of language is the primary model for contemporary structuralism. The structuralist literary critic attempts to define structural principles that operate intertextually throughout the whole of literature as well as principles that operate in genres and in individual works. The most accessible survey of structuralism and literature is Jonathan Culler's *Structuralist Poetics* (1975).

Substitution: Substitution, one of the most common and effective methods by which the poet can emphasize a foot, occurs when one type of foot is replaced by another within a base meter. For example, in the line "Thy life/a long/dead calm/of fixed/repose," a spondaic foot (´´) has been substituted for an iambic foot (˘´). Before substitution is possible, the reader's expectations must have been established by a base meter so that a change in those expectations will have an effect. (See also *Foot/feet; iamb; spondee*)

Syllabic meter: The system of meter which measures only the number of syllables per line, without regard to stressed and unstressed syllables, is called syllabic meter.

Symbol: Loosely defined, a symbol is any sign that a number of people agree stands for something else. Poetic symbols cannot be rigidly defined; a symbol often evokes a cluster of meanings rather than a single specific meaning. For example, the rose, which suggests fragile beauty, gentleness, softness, and sweet aroma, has come to symbolize love, eternal beauty, or virginity. The tide traditionally symbolizes, among other things, time and eternity. Modern poets may use personal symbols; these take on significance in the context of the poem or of a poet's body of work, particularly if they are reinforced throughout. For example, through constant reinforcement, swans in William Butler Yeats's poetry come to mean as much to the reader as they do to the narrator.

Synaeresis: See *Elision*

Synecdoche: See *Metonymy*

Tenor: See *Metaphor*

Tercet: A tercet is any form of a rhyming triplet. Examples are *aaa bbb*, as used in Thomas Hardy's "Convergence of the Twain"; *aba cdc*, in which *b* and *d* do not rhyme; *aba bcb*, also known as terza rima.

Terza rima: Terza rima is a three-line stanzaic form in which the middle line of one stanza rhymes with the first line of the following stanza, and whose rhyme scheme is *aba bcb cdc*, and so on. Since the rhyme scheme of one stanza can be completed only by adding the next stanza, terza rima tends to propel itself forward, and as a result of this strong forward motion it is well suited to long narration.

Theme: Loosely defined as "what a poem means," theme more specifically refers to recurring elements. The term is sometimes used interchangeably with "motif." A motif is any recurring pattern of images, symbols, ideas, or language and is usually restricted to the internal workings of the poem. Thus, one might say that there is an animal motif in William Butler Yeats's poem "Sailing to Byzantium." Theme, however, is usually more general and philosophical, so that the theme of "Sailing to Byzantium" might be interpreted as the failure of human attempts to isolate oneself within the world of art.

Third person: Third-person narration exists when a poem's narrator, or speaker, has not been part of the events described and is not probing his or her own relationship to them; rather, the speaker is describing what happened without the use of the word "I" (which would indicate first-person narration). A poet may use a third-person point of view, either limited or omniscient, to establish a distance between the reader and the subject, to give credibility to a large expanse of narration, or to allow the poem to include a number of characters who can be commented on by the narrator.

Tone: Strictly defined, tone is the expression of a poet's attitude toward the subject and persona of the poem as well as about him- or herself, society, and the poem's readers. If the ultimate aim of art is to express and control emotions and attitudes, then tone is one of the most important elements of poetry. Tone is created through the denotative and connotative meanings of words and through the sound of language (principally, rhyme, consonants, and diction). Adjectives such as "satirical," "compassionate," "empathetic," "ironic," and "sarcastic" are used to describe tone.

Trochee: One of the most common feet in English poetry, the trochee associates one stressed syllable with one unstressed syllable (´‿), as in the line: "Double/ double toil and/trouble." Trochaic lines are frequently substituted in an iambic base meter in order to create counterpointing. (See also *Foot/feet*; *iamb*)

Truncation: Truncation occurs when the last, unstressed syllable of a falling line is omitted, as in the line: "Tyger,/tyger/burning/bright," where the "ly" has been dropped from bright."

Vehicle: See *Metaphor*

Verse: The term "verse" has two or three different applications. It is a generic term for poetry, as in *The Oxford Book of English Verse* (1939). Verse also refers in a narrower sense to poetry that is humorous or superficial, as in "light verse" or "greeting-card verse." Finally, "verse" is sometimes used to mean stanza or line.

Verse drama: Drama which is written in poetic rather than ordinary language and which is characterized and delivered by the line is called "verse drama." Verse drama flourished during the eighteenth century, when the couplet became a standard literary form.

Verse paragraph: A division created within a stichic poem (see *Stanza*) by logic or syntax, rather than by form, is called a "verse paragraph." These are important for determining the movement of a poem and the logical association between ideas.

Villanelle: The villanelle, like the *rondeau* and the rondel, is a French verse form that has been assimilated by English prosody. It is usually composed of nineteen lines divided into five tercets and a quatrain, rhyming *aba*, *bba*, *aba*, *aba*, *abaa*. The third line is repeated in the ninth and fifteenth lines. Dylan Thomas's "Do Not Go Gentle into That Good Night" is a modern English example of a villanelle.

CHRONOLOGICAL LIST OF POETS

EDITOR'S NOTE: *Poets covered in volumes 1-7 of the* Critical Survey of Poetry, Second Revised Edition *are listed by year of birth and, within the same year, alphabetically by name.*

ANCIENT WORLD

9th cent. B.C.E.	Homer
7th cent. B.C.E.	Theognis
700 B.C.E.	Hesiod
680 B.C.E.	Archilochus
630 B.C.E.	Sappho
571 B.C.E.	Anacreon
518 B.C.E.	Pindar
308 B.C.E.	Theocritus
305 B.C.E.	Callimachus
3d cent. B.C.E.	Leonidas of Tarentum
295-260 B.C.E.	Apollonius Rhodius
98 B.C.E.	Lucretius
85 B.C.E.	Catullus
70 B.C.E.	Vergil
65 B.C.E.	Horace
57-48 B.C.E.	Propertius, Sextus
43 B.C.E.	Ovid
34 C.E.	Persius
39 C.E.	Lucan
45 C.E.	Statius
210 C.E.	Ruan Ji
365 C.E.	Tao Qian

SEVENTH-TWELFTH CENTURIES

7th cent.	Caedmon
701	Li Bo
701	Wang Wei
712	Du Fu
9th cent.	Cynewulf
941	Firdusi
1048(?)	Omar Khayyám
1075	Judah ha-Levi
1084	Li Qingzhao
1150	Marie de France
1160-1165	Hartmann von Aue
1170	Vogelweide, Walther von der
1170	Wolfram von Eschenbach

1200	Layamon
1200	Saʿdi

THIRTEENTH-FOURTEENTH CENTURIES

1207	Rūmī, Jalāl al-dīn
1215	Guillaume de Lorris
1240	Jean de Meung
1259	Cavalcanti, Guido
1265	Dante
1304	Petrarch
1320	Hafiz
1330	Gower, John
1332	Langland, William
1343	Chaucer, Geoffrey
1365	Christine de Pizan
1370(?)	Lydgate, John
14th cent.	Pearl-Poet, The
1385	Chartier, Alain
1391	Charles d'Orléans

FIFTEENTH CENTURY

1425	Henryson, Robert
1431	Villon, François
1454	Poliziano
1460	Dunbar, William
1460	Skelton, John
1470	Bembo, Pietro
1474	Ariosto, Ludovico
1475	Michelangelo
1478	Fracastoro, Girolamo
1497	Heywood, John

SIXTEENTH CENTURY

1501	Garcilaso de la Vega
1503	Wyatt, Sir Thomas
1517	Surrey, Henry Howard, earl of
1523	Stampa, Gaspara
1524	Camões, Luís de

1524	Ronsard, Pierre de
1527	León, Luis de
1536	Sackville, Thomas
1539	Gascoigne, George
1542	John of the Cross, Saint
1544	Tasso, Torquato
1545	Breton, Nicholas
1552	Ralegh, Sir Walter
1552	Spenser, Edmund
1554	Greville, Fulke
1554	Sidney, Sir Philip
1555	Malherbe, François
1558	Greene, Robert
1558(?)	Lodge, Thomas
1559	Chapman, George
1561	Góngora y Argote, Luis de
1561	Southwell, Robert
1562	Constable, Henry
1562(?)	Daniel, Samuel
1562	Vega Carpio, Lope de
1563	Drayton, Michael
1563	Sidney, Sir Robert
1564	Marlowe, Christopher
1564	Shakespeare, William
1567	Campion, Thomas
1567	Nashe, Thomas
1569	Davies, Sir John
1569	Marino, Giambattista
1572	Dekker, Thomas
1572	Donne, John
1573	Jonson, Ben
1585	Drummond of Hawthornden, William
1591	Herrick, Robert
1592	King, Henry
1592	Quarles, Francis
1593	Herbert, George
1595	Carew, Thomas
1600	Calderón de la Barca, Pedro

SEVENTEENTH CENTURY

1606	Davenant, Sir William
1606	Waller, Edmund
1608	Fanshawe, Sir Richard
1608	Milton, John
1609	Suckling, Sir John

1612(?)	Bradstreet, Anne
1612	Butler, Samuel
1612	Crashaw, Richard
1618	Cowley, Abraham
1618	Lovelace, Richard
1621	La Fontaine, Jean de
1621	Marvell, Andrew
1622	Vaughan, Henry
1623	Newcastle, Duchess of
1630	Cotton, Charles
1631	Dryden, John
1635	Etherege, Sir George
1637	Traherne, Thomas
1639	Sedley, Sir Charles
1640	Behn, Aphra
1644	Matsuo Bashō
1645	Taylor, Edward
1647	Rochester, John Wilmot, earl of
1648	Sor Juana Inés de la Cruz
1653	Oldham, John
1661	Finch, Anne, Countess of Winchelsea
1664	Prior, Matthew
1667	Swift, Jonathan
1670	Congreve, William
1672	Addison, Joseph
1674	Watts, Isaac
1683	Young, Edward
1685	Gay, John
1688	Pope, Alexander
1700	Thomson, James

EIGHTEENTH CENTURY

1709	Johnson, Samuel
1716	Gray, Thomas
1721	Collins, William
1722	Smart, Christopher
1730	Goldsmith, Oliver
1731	Cowper, William
1749	Goethe, Johann Wolfgang von
1752	Chatterton, Thomas
1752	Freneau, Philip
1753(?)	Wheatley, Phillis
1754	Crabbe, George
1757	Blake, William
1759	Burns, Robert

1759	Schiller, Friedrich		1809	Słowacki, Juliusz
1762	Bowles, William Lisle		1809	Tennyson, Alfred, Lord
1763	Issa		1810	Musset, Alfred de
1770	Hölderlin, Friedrich		1811	Gautier, Théophile
1770	Wordsworth, William		1811	Hallam, Arthur Henry
1771	Scott, Sir Walter		1812	Browning, Robert
1772	Coleridge, Samuel Taylor		1812	Lear, Edward
1772	Novalis		1813	Very, Jones
1774	Southey, Robert		1814	Lermontov, Mikhail
1775	Lamb, Charles		1817	Arany, János
1775	Landor, Walter Savage		1817	Thoreau, Henry David
1778	Foscolo, Ugo		1818	Brontë, Emily
1784	Hunt, Leigh		1819	Clough, Arthur Hugh
1785	Manzoni, Alessandro		1819	Lowell, James Russell
1788	Byron, George Gordon, Lord		1819	Melville, Herman
1788	Eichendorff, Joseph von		1819	Whitman, Walt
1790	Lamartine, Alphonse de		1821	Baudelaire, Charles
1792	Shelley, Percy Bysshe		1821	Tuckerman, Frederick Goddard
1793	Clare, John		1822	Arnold, Matthew
1794	Bryant, William Cullen		1823	Patmore, Coventry
1795	Darley, George		1823	Petőfi, Sándor
1795	Keats, John		1824	Allingham, William
1797	Heine, Heinrich		1828	Meredith, George
1797	Vigny, Alfred de		1828	Rossetti, Dante Gabriel
1798	Leopardi, Giacomo		1830	Dickinson, Emily
1798	Mickiewicz, Adam		1830	Gezelle, Guido
1798	Solomòs, Dionysios		1830	Rossetti, Christina
1799	Hood, Thomas		1832	Carroll, Lewis
1799	Pushkin, Alexander		1834	Morris, William
1800	Vörösmarty, Mihály		1834	Thomson, James
			1835	Carducci, Giosuè
			1836	Bécquer, Gustavo Adolfo
NINETEENTH CENTURY			1837	Castro, Rosalía de
1802	Hugo, Victor		1837	Swinburne, Algernon Charles
1803	Beddoes, Thomas Lovell		1840	Hardy, Thomas
1803	Emerson, Ralph Waldo		1842	Lanier, Sidney
1803	Mangan, James Clarence		1842	Mallarmé, Stéphane
1806	Browning, Elizabeth Barrett		1844	Bridges, Robert
1807	Longfellow, Henry Wadsworth		1844	Hopkins, Gerard Manley
1807	Whittier, John Greenleaf		1844	Verlaine, Paul
1808	Nerval, Gérard de		1849	Riley, James Whitcomb
1809	FitzGerald, Edward		1850	Stevenson, Robert Louis
1809	Giusti, Giuseppe		1854	Rimbaud, Arthur
1809	Holmes, Oliver Wendell		1854	Wilde, Oscar
1809	Poe, Edgar Allan		1855	Pascoli, Giovanni

1855	Verhaeren, Émile	1881	Colum, Padraic
1856	Annensky, Innokenty	1881	Guest, Edgar A.
1856	Reese, Lizette Woodworth	1881	Jiménez, Juan Ramón
1859	Housman, A. E.	1881	Neihardt, John G.
1860	Laforgue, Jules	1881	Zweig, Stefan
1861	Tagore, Rabindranath	1882	Joyce, James
1863	Cavafy, Constantine P.	1882	Pratt, E. J.
1863	D'Annunzio, Gabriele	1883	Babits, Mihály
1863	Holz, Arno	1883	Gibran, Kahlil
1864	Unamuno y Jugo, Miguel de	1883	Kazantzakis, Nikos
1865	Kipling, Rudyard	1883	Saba, Umberto
1865	Yeats, William Butler	1883	Williams, William Carlos
1867	Æ (George William Russell)	1884	Teasdale, Sara
1867	Darío, Rubén	1885	Lawrence, D. H.
1868	Claudel, Paul	1885	Pound, Ezra
1868	George, Stefan	1885	Untermeyer, Louis
1868	Masters, Edgar Lee	1886	Benn, Gottfried
1869	Robinson, Edwin Arlington	1886	H. D.
1870	Belloc, Hilaire	1886	Khodasevich, Vladislav
1871	Crane, Stephen	1886	Sassoon, Siegfried
1871	Dučič, Jovan	1887	Arp, Hans
1871	González Martínez, Enrique	1887	Brooke, Rupert
1871	Morgenstern, Christian	1887	Jeffers, Robinson
1871	Valéry, Paul	1887	Moore, Marianne
1872	Dunbar, Paul Laurence	1887	Perse, Saint-John
1873	de la Mare, Walter	1887	Sitwell, Edith
1873	Péguy, Charles-Pierre	1887	Trakl, Georg
1874	Frost, Robert	1888	Eliot, T. S.
1874	Hofmannsthal, Hugo von	1888	Pessoa, Fernando
1874	Kraus, Karl	1888	Ransom, John Crowe
1874	Lowell, Amy	1888	Ungaretti, Giuseppe
1874	Service, Robert W.	1889	Aiken, Conrad
1874	Stein, Gertrude	1889	Akhmatova, Anna
1875	Machado, Antonio	1889	Cocteau, Jean
1875	Rilke, Rainer Maria	1889	McKay, Claude
1877	Ady, Endre	1889	Mistral, Gabriela
1878	Masefield, John	1889	Reverdy, Pierre
1878	Sandburg, Carl	1889	Reyes, Alfonso
1878	Thomas, Edward	1890	Gurney, Ivor
1878	Yosano Akiko	1890	Pasternak, Boris
1879	Lindsay, Vachel	1890	Rosenberg, Isaac
1879	Stevens, Wallace	1891	Mandelstam, Osip
1880	Apollinaire, Guillaume	1891	Sachs, Nelly
1880	Blok, Aleksandr	1891	Salinas, Pedro
1881	Bynner, Witter	1892	Aldington, Richard

1892	Bishop, John Peale	**TWENTIETH CENTURY: 1900'S**	
1892	MacDiarmid, Hugh	1901	Ausländer, Rose
1892	MacLeish, Archibald	1901	Brown, Sterling
1892	Millay, Edna St. Vincent	1901	Manger, Itzik
1892	Södergran, Edith	1901	Quasimodo, Salvatore
1892	Tsvetayeva, Marina	1901	Seifert, Jaroslav
1892	Vallejo, César	1902	Alberti, Rafael
1893	Foix, J. V.	1902	Cernuda, Luis
1893	Guillén, Jorge	1902	Drummond de Andrade, Carlos
1893	Mayakovsky, Vladimir	1902	Fearing, Kenneth
1893	Owen, Wilfred	1902	Hıkmet, Nazım
1893	Parker, Dorothy	1902	Hughes, Langston
1894	Cummings, E. E.	1902	Illyés, Gyula
1894	Reznikoff, Charles	1902	Nash, Ogden
1894	Toomer, Jean	1902	Smith, Stevie
1894	Van Doren, Mark	1903	Cullen, Countée
1895	Éluard, Paul	1903	Follain, Jean
1895	Esenin, Sergei	1903	Niedecker, Lorine
1895	Graves, Robert	1903	Rakosi, Carl
1895	Słonimski, Antoni	1904	Birney, Earle
1896	Blunden, Edmund	1904	Day Lewis, Cecil
1896	Breton, André	1904	Eberhart, Richard
1896	Clarke, Austin	1904	Kavanagh, Patrick
1896	Miyazawa, Kenji	1904	Martinson, Harry
1896	Montale, Eugenio	1904	Neruda, Pablo
1896	Tzara, Tristan	1904	Zukofsky, Louis
1897	Aragon, Louis	1905	Hein, Piet
1897	Bogan, Louise	1905	Kunitz, Stanley
1897	Wheelwright, John	1905	McGinley, Phyllis
1898	Aleixandre, Vicente	1905	Rexroth, Kenneth
1898	Benét, Stephen Vincent	1905	Ważyk, Adam
1898	Brecht, Bertolt	1905	Warren, Robert Penn
1898	Cowley, Malcolm	1906	Beckett, Samuel
1898	García Lorca, Federico	1906	Betjeman, John
1898	Tolson, Melvin B.	1906	Empson, William
1899	Adams, Léonie	1906	Senghor, Léopold
1899	Crane, Hart	1906	Still, James
1899	Lewis, Janet	1907	Auden, W. H.
1899	Michaux, Henri	1907	Char, René
1899	Ponge, Francis	1907	Ekelöf, Gunnar
1899	Tate, Allen	1907	Hope, A. D.
1900	Bunting, Basil	1907	Kirstein, Lincoln
1900	Prévert, Jacques	1907	MacNeice, Louis
1900	Seferis, George	1908	Jacobsen, Josephine
1900	Winters, Yvor	1908	Oppen, George

1908	Pavese, Cesare
1908	Pentzíkis, Nikos
1908	Roethke, Theodore
1909	Barnard, Mary
1909	Radnóti, Miklós
1909	Ritsos, Yannis
1909	Rolfe, Edwin
1909	Spender, Stephen

TWENTIETH CENTURY: 1910'S

1910	Olson, Charles
1910	Scott, Winfield Townley
1911	Belitt, Ben
1911	Bishop, Elizabeth
1911	Cunningham, J. V.
1911	Elytis, Odysseus
1911	Miłosz, Czesław
1911	Miles, Josephine
1911	Patchen, Kenneth
1912	Durrell, Lawrence
1912	Everson, William
1912	Fuller, Roy
1912	Prince, F. T.
1912	Sarton, May
1913	Césaire, Aimé
1913	Hayden, Robert
1913	Nims, John Frederick
1913	Rukeyser, Muriel
1913	Schwartz, Delmore
1913	Shapiro, Karl
1914	Berryman, John
1914	Ignatow, David
1914	Jarrell, Randall
1914	Kees, Weldon
1914	Parra, Nicanor
1914	Paz, Octavio
1914	Randall, Dudley
1914	Reed, Henry
1914	Stafford, William
1914	Thomas, Dylan
1914	Villa, José García
1915	Merton, Thomas
1916	Ciardi, John
1916	McGrath, Thomas
1916	Otero, Blas de

1916	Viereck, Peter
1917	Bobrowski, Johannes
1917	Brooks, Gwendolyn
1917	Lowell, Robert
1918	Smith, William Jay
1919	Duncan, Robert
1919	Ferlinghetti, Lawrence
1919	Meredith, William
1919	Swenson, May
1919	Whittemore, Reed

TWENTIETH CENTURY: 1920'S

1920	Bukowski, Charles
1920	Celan, Paul
1920	Clampitt, Amy
1920	Nemerov, Howard
1921	Carruth, Hayden
1921	Ponsot, Marie
1921	Różewicz, Tadeusz
1921	Van Duyn, Mona
1921	Wilbur, Richard
1922	Davie, Donald
1922	Larkin, Philip
1922	Moss, Howard
1922	Pasolini, Pier Paolo
1922	Popa, Vasko
1923	Abse, Dannie
1923	Bonnefoy, Yves
1923	Dickey, James
1923	Dugan, Alan
1923	Hecht, Anthony
1923	Hoffman, Daniel
1923	Holub, Miroslav
1923	Hugo, Richard
1923	Levertov, Denise
1923	Logan, John
1923	Schuyler, James
1923	Simpson, Louis
1923	Szymborska, Wisława
1923	Xie Lingyun
1924	Alegría, Claribel
1924	Amichai, Yehuda
1924	Beer, Patricia
1924	Bowers, Edgar
1924	Corman, Cid

1924	Field, Edward	1929	Hollander, John
1924	Herbert, Zbigniew	1929	Howard, Richard
1924	Miller, Vassar	1929	Kennedy, X. J.
1924	Mueller, Lisel	1929	Montague, John
1924	Stryk, Lucien	1929	Rich, Adrienne
1925	Booth, Philip	1929	Sorrentino, Gilbert
1925	Cardenal, Ernesto		
1925	Gomringer, Eugen		TWENTIETH CENTURY: 1930'S
1925	Justice, Donald	1930	Brathwaite, Edward Kamau
1925	Kizer, Carolyn	1930	Corso, Gregory
1925	Koch, Kenneth	1930	Hughes, Ted
1925	Kumin, Maxine	1930	Oppenheimer, Joel
1925	Menashe, Samuel	1930	Pagis, Dan
1925	Stern, Gerald	1930	Silkin, Jon
1926	Ammons, A. R.	1930	Snyder, Gary
1926	Bachmann, Ingeborg	1930	Walcott, Derek
1926	Blackburn, Paul	1930	Williams, Miller
1926	Bly, Robert	1931	Bernhard, Thomas
1926	Creeley, Robert	1931	Haavikko, Paavo
1926	Ginsberg, Allen	1931	Knight, Etheridge
1926	Merrill, James	1931	Tranströmer, Tomas
1926	Middleton, Christopher	1932	Hill, Geoffrey
1926	O'Hara, Frank	1932	MacBeth, George
1926	Snodgrass, W. D.	1932	McClure, Michael
1926	Wagoner, David	1932	Meinke, Peter
1927	Ashbery, John	1932	Pastan, Linda
1927	Coulette, Henri	1932	Plath, Sylvia
1927	Kinnell, Galway	1932	Updike, John
1927	Merwin, W. S.	1933	Kunze, Reiner
1927	Tomlinson, Charles	1933	Voznesensky, Andrei
1927	Wright, James	1933	Yevtushenko, Yevgeny
1928	Angelou, Maya	1934	Baraka, Amiri
1928	Davison, Peter	1934	Berry, Wendell
1928	Hall, Donald	1934	Di Prima, Diane
1928	Kinsella, Thomas	1934	Flint, Roland
1928	Levine, Philip	1934	Hollo, Anselm
1928	Macdonald, Cynthia	1934	Lorde, Audre
1928	Pavlović, Miodrag	1934	McDonald, Walt
1928	Sexton, Anne	1934	Momaday, N. Scott
1928	Sissman, L. E.	1934	Sanchez, Sonia
1929	Cassity, Turner	1934	Strand, Mark
1929	Dana, Robert	1934	Zimmer, Paul
1929	Dorn, Edward	1935	Applewhite, James
1929	Enzensberger, Hans Magnus	1935	Awoonor, Kofi
1929	Gunn, Thom	1935	Johnson, Ronald

1935	Kelly, Robert		1943	Giovanni, Nikki
1935	Oliver, Mary		1943	Glück, Louise
1935	Slavitt, David		1943	McPherson, Sandra
1935	Wright, Charles		1943	Ondaatje, Michael
1935	Wright, Jay		1943	Tate, James
1936	Biermann, Wolf		1943	Voigt, Ellen Bryant
1936	Clifton, Lucille		1944	Boland, Eavan
1936	Jordan, June		1944	Lifshin, Lyn
1936	Piercy, Marge		1944	Shomer, Enid
1936	Williams, C. K.		1944	Walker, Alice
1937	Bell, Marvin		1945	Dubie, Norman
1937	Harrison, Jim		1945	Muske, Carol
1937	Harrison, Tony		1945	Wallace, Ronald
1937	Howe, Susan		1945	Zagajewski, Adam
1937	Wakoski, Diane		1946	Levis, Larry
1938	Carver, Raymond		1947	Hogan, Linda
1938	Galvin, Brendan		1947	Kenyon, Jane
1938	Harper, Michael S.		1947	Komunyakaa, Yusef
1938	Murray, Les A.		1947	Orr, Gregory
1938	Oates, Joyce Carol		1947	Peacock, Molly
1938	Simic, Charles		1947	Shore, Jane
1939	Atwood, Margaret		1948	Ehrhart, W. D.
1939	Bidart, Frank		1948	Goldbarth, Albert
1939	Breytenbach, Breyten		1948	Silko, Leslie Marmon
1939	Dacey, Philip		1948	Steele, Timothy
1939	Heaney, Seamus		1948	Wormser, Baron
1939	Plumly, Stanley		1949	Cruz, Victor Hernández
1939	Young, Al		1949	Fenton, James
			1949	St. John, David
TWENTIETH CENTURY: 1940'S			1949	Weigl, Bruce
1940	Brodsky, Joseph			
1940	Heyen, William		**TWENTIETH CENTURY: 1950'S**	
1940	Pinsky, Robert		1950	Alvarez, Julia
1941	Collins, Billy		1950	Forché, Carolyn
1941	Derricotte, Toi		1950	Gioia, Dana
1941	Hass, Robert		1950	Hirsch, Edward
1941	Ortiz, Simon J.		1950	Twichell, Chase
1942	Hacker, Marilyn		1951	Becker, Robin
1942	Madhubuti, Haki R.		1951	Graham, Jorie
1942	Matthews, William		1951	Harjo, Joy
1942	Olds, Sharon		1951	Hongo, Garrett Kaoru
1942	Smith, Dave		1951	Muldoon, Paul
1942	Taylor, Henry		1952	Baca, Jimmy Santiago
1943	Balaban, John		1952	Dove, Rita
1943	Gallagher, Tess		1952	Fulton, Alice

1952	Mura, David		1953	Wojahn, David
1952	Nye, Naomi Shihab		1954	Baker, David
1952	Seth, Vikram		1954	Cervantes, Lorna Dee
1952	Shapiro, Alan		1954	Eady, Cornelius
1952	Soto, Gary		1954	Erdrich, Louise
1953	Collier, Michael		1955	Chin, Marilyn
1953	Doty, Mark		1955	Song, Cathy
1953	Hirshfield, Jane		1957	Espada, Martín
1953	Schnackenberg, Gjertrud		1957	Lee, Li-Young

BIBLIOGRAPHY

CONTENTS

ABOUT THIS BIBLIOGRAPHY

Organization. This bibliography contains three main sections. The first, "General Reference Sources," lists books that treat poetry of all or several languages and countries. The section "English-Language Poetry" includes sources primarily relevant to poetry written in English; it is subdivided into general and country-specific materials, sometimes further grouped by type (biographical, indexes, etc.). The section headed "Foreign-Language Poetry" contains sources primarily relevant to poetry in languages other than English; it is also further subdivided into "General Reference Sources" and then language- or region-specific sources, and again, where appropriate, further subdivided by type of source. Materials that treat bilingual poetry written by U.S. writers are placed in the section on the United States. Sources treating poetry of multilingual geographical areas, such as the Caribbean, Africa, and Latin America, are listed in more than one section, as appropriate. Section headings also indicate, by means of "see also" cross-references, when more than one section is likely to contain relevant sources.

Selection. Preference has been given to books in English that focus on poetry and provide substantial biographical, historical, or bibliographical information. In categories for which such sources are unavailable or limited, general literary reference sources have also been included. Anthologies and other collections of primary works have been excluded unless they also contain critical or historical essays. For fuller listings of more specific resources by language, region, ethnicity, or period, readers are referred to the bibliographies appearing at the ends of the overview essays appearing in volume 8 of this *Critical Survey of Poetry*.

Maura Ives

GENERAL REFERENCE SOURCES

BIOGRAPHICAL SOURCES

Colby, Vineta, ed. *World Authors, 1975-1980.* Wilson Authors Series. New York: H. W. Wilson, 1985.

_____. *World Authors, 1980-1985.* Wilson Authors Series. New York: H. W. Wilson, 1991.

_____. *World Authors, 1980-1985.* Wilson Authors Series. New York: H. W. Wilson, 1995.

Dictionary of Literary Biography. 254 vols. Detroit: Gale Research, 1978. Biographical and critical overviews, with bibliographies of primary and secondary works.

International Who's Who in Poetry and Poets' Encyclopaedia. Cambridge, England: International Biographical Centre, 1993.

Magill, Frank N., ed. *Cyclopedia of World Authors.* 3d Rev. ed. 5 vols. Pasadena, Calif.: Salem Press, 1997. Most of the authors included are from English-speaking countries.

Seymour-Smith, Martin, and Andrew C. Kimmens, eds. *World Authors, 1900-1950.* Wilson Authors Series. 4 vols. New York: H. W. Wilson, 1996.

Thompson, Clifford, ed. *World Authors, 1990-1995.* Wilson Authors Series. New York: H. W. Wilson, 1999.

Wakeman, John, ed. *World Authors, 1950-1970.* New York: H. W. Wilson, 1975.

_____. *World Authors, 1970-1975.* Wilson Authors Series. New York: H. W. Wilson, 1991.

Willhardt, Mark, and Alan Michael Parker, eds. *Who's Who in Twentieth Century World Poetry.* New York: Routledge, 2000.

CRITICISM

Classical and Medieval Literature Criticism. Detroit: Gale Research, 1988- . 46 volumes as of 2001; ongoing.

Contemporary Literary Criticism. Detroit: Gale Research, 1973- . 146 volumes as of 2001; ongoing.

Draper, James P., ed. *World Literature Criticism 1500 to the Present: A Selection of Major Authors from Gale's Literary Criticism Series.* 6 vols. Detroit: Gale Research, 1992.

Jason, Philip K., ed. *Masterplots II: Poetry Series, Revised Edition*. 8 vols. Pasadena, Calif.: Salem Press, 2002.

Literature Criticism from 1400 to 1800. Detroit: Gale Research, 1984- . 71 volumes as of 2001; ongoing.

Magill, Frank N., ed. *Magill's Bibliography of Literary Criticism*. 4 vols. Englewood Cliffs, N.J.: Salem Press, 1979.

MLA International Bibliography. New York: Modern Language Association of America, 1922- . Essential index to scholarship on language and literatures. Electronic version available; ongoing.

Nineteenth-Century Literature Criticism. Detroit: Gale Research, 1981- . 105 volumes as of 2001; ongoing.

Twentieth-Century Literary Criticism. Detroit: Gale Research, 1978- ; ongoing.

Vedder, Polly, ed. *World Literature Criticism Supplement: A Selection of Major Authors from Gale's Literary Criticism Series*. 2 vols. Detroit: Gale, 1997.

Young, Robyn V., ed. *Poetry Criticism: Excerpts from Criticism of the Works of the Most Significant and Widely Studied Poets of World Literature*. 29 vols. Detroit: Gale Research, 1991.

POETRY DICTIONARIES AND HANDBOOKS

Carey, Gary, and Mary Ellen Snodgrass. *A Multicultural Dictionary of Literary Terms*. Jefferson, N.C.: McFarland, 1999.

Deutsch, Babette. *Poetry Handbook: A Dictionary of Terms*. 4th ed. New York: Funk & Wagnalls, 1974. A classic guide to poetry terms.

Drury, John. *The Poetry Dictionary*. Cincinnati, Ohio: Story Press, 1995.

Kinzie, Mary. *A Poet's Guide to Poetry*. Chicago: University of Chicago Press, 1999.

Lennard, John. *The Poetry Handbook: A Guide to Reading Poetry for Pleasure and Practical Criticism*. New York: Oxford University Press, 1996.

Matterson, Stephen, and Darryl Jones. *Studying Poetry*. New York: Oxford University Press, 2000.

Packard, William. *The Poet's Dictionary: A Handbook of Prosody and Poetic Devices*. New York: Harper & Row, 1989.

Preminger, Alex, et al., eds. *The New Princeton Encyclopedia of Poetry and Poetics*. 3d rev. ed. Princeton, N.J.: Princeton University Press, 1993.

Shipley, Joseph Twadell, ed. *Dictionary of World Literary Terms, Forms, Technique, Criticism*. Rev. ed. Boston: Writer, 1970.

INDEXES OF PRIMARY WORKS

Frankovich, Nicholas, ed. *The Columbia Granger's Index to Poetry in Anthologies*. 11th ed. New York: Columbia University Press, 1997. Coverage through January 31, 1997.

_____. *The Columbia Granger's Index to Poetry in Collected and Selected Works*. New York: Columbia University Press, 1997.

Guy, Patricia. *A Women's Poetry Index*. Phoenix, Ariz.: Oryx Press, 1985. Covers poetry in anthologies.

Hazen, Edith P., ed. *Columbia Granger's Index to Poetry*. 10th ed. New York: Columbia University Press, 1994. Indexes English language poems and foreign language poems that have been translated into English.

Hoffman, Herbert H., and Rita Ludwig Hoffman, comps. *International Index to Recorded Poetry*. New York: H. W. Wilson, 1983.

Kline, Victoria. *Last Lines: An Index to the Last Lines of Poetry*. 2 vols. Vol. 1, *Last Line Index, Title Index*; Vol. 2, *Author Index, Keyword Index*. New York: Facts on File, 1991. Coverage through 1987.

Marcan, Peter. *Poetry Themes: A Bibliographical Index to Subject Anthologies and Related Criticisms in the English Language, 1875-1975*. Hamden, Conn.: Linnet Books, 1977.

Poem Finder. Great Neck, N.Y.: Roth Publishing, 2000. Searchable by keyword, author, and subject.

POETICS, POETIC FORMS, AND GENRES

Attridge, Derek. *Poetic Rhythm: An Introduction*. New York: Cambridge University Press, 1995.

Brogan, T. V. F. *Verseform: A Comparative Bibliography*. Baltimore: Johns Hopkins University Press, 1989.

Fussell, Paul. *Poetic Meter and Poetic Form*. Rev. ed. New York: McGraw-Hill, 1979.

Jackson, Guida M. *Traditional Epics: A Literary Companion*. New York: Oxford University Press, 1995.

Hollander, John. *Rhyme's Reason.* 3d ed. New Haven: Yale University Press, 2001.

Padgett, Ron, ed. *The Teachers and Writers Handbook of Poetic Forms.* 2d ed. New York: Teachers & Writers Collaborative, 2000.

Pinsky, Robert. *The Sounds of Poetry: A Brief Guide.* New York: Farrar, Straus and Giroux, 1998.

Preminger, Alex, and T. V. F. Brogan, ed. *New Princeton Encyclopedia of Poetry and Poetics.* 3d ed. Princeton, N.J.: Princeton University Press, 1993.

Spiller, Michael R. G. *The Sonnet Sequence: A Study of Its Strategies.* Studies in Literary Themes and Genres 13. New York: Twayne, 1997.

Turco, Lewis. *The New Book of Forms: A Handbook of Poetics.* Hanover: University Press of New England, 1986.

Williams, Miller. *Patterns of Poetry: An Encyclopedia of Forms.* Baton Rouge: Louisiana State University Press, 1986.

ENGLISH-LANGUAGE POETRY

GENERAL REFERENCE SOURCES
Biographical sources

Bold, Alan. *Longman Dictionary of Poets: The Lives and Works of 1001 Poets in the English Language.* Harlow, Essex: Longman, 1985.

Riggs, Thomas, ed. *Contemporary Poets.* Contemporary Writers Series. 7th ed. Detroit: St. James Press, 2001.

Criticism

Alexander, Harriet Semmes, comp. *American and British Poetry: A Guide to the Criticism, 1925-1978.* Manchester, England: Manchester University Press, 1984.

_____. *American and British Poetry: A Guide to the Criticism, 1979-1990.* 2 vols. Athens, Ohio: Swallow Press, 1995.

Annual Bibliography of English Language and Literature. 1921- . Annual bibliography of scholarship on literature in English. Online version available.

Childs, Peter. *The Twentieth Century in Poetry: A Critical Survey.* New York: Routledge, 1999.

Cline, Gloria Stark, and Jeffrey A. Baker. *An Index to Criticism of British and American Poetry.* Metuchen, N.J.: Scarecrow, 1973.

Coleman, Arthur. *Epic and Romance Criticism: A Checklist of Interpretations, 1940-1972.* New York: Watermill Publishers, 1973.

Donow, Herbert S., comp. *The Sonnet in England and America: A Bibliography of Criticism.* Westport, Conn.: Greenwood, 1982.

Jason, Philip K., ed. *Masterplots II: Poetry Series, Revised Edition.* 8 vols. Pasadena, Calif.: Salem Press, 2002.

Kuntz, Joseph M., and Nancy C. Martinez. *Poetry Explication: A Checklist of Interpretation Since 1925 of British and American Poems Past and Present.* 3d ed. Boston: Hall, 1980.

Roberts, Neil, ed. *A Companion to Twentieth-Century Poetry.* Malden, Mass.: Blackwell Publishers, 2001.

Walcutt, Charles Child, and J. Edwin Whitesell, eds. *The Explicator Cyclopedia.* 2 vols. Vol. 1, *Modern Poetry*; Vol. 2, *Traditional Poetry: Medieval to Late Victorian.* Chicago: Quadrangle Books, 1968.

The Year's Work in English Studies. 1921- . Annual survey of scholarship on literatures in English.

Dictionaries, histories, handbooks

Draper, Ronald P. *An Introduction to Twentieth-Century Poetry in English.* New York: St. Martin's Press, 1999.

Gingerich, Martin E. *Contemporary Poetry in America and England, 1950-1975: A Guide to Information Sources.* American Literature, English Literature, and World Literatures in English: An Information Guide Series 41. Detroit: Gale, 1983.

Hamilton, Ian, ed. *The Oxford Companion to Twentieth-Century Poetry in English.* New York: Oxford University Press, 1994.

Perkins, David. *A History of Modern Poetry: From the 1890's to the High Modernist Mode.* Vol. 1 in *A His-*

tory of Modern Poetry. Cambridge: Belknap-Harvard University Press, 1976.

_____. *A History of Modern Poetry: Modernism and After.* Vol. 2 in *A History of Modern Poetry.* 2 vols. Cambridge: Belknap-Harvard University Press, 1987.

Indexes of primary works

Poetry Index Annual: A Title, Author, First Line, Keyword, and Subject Index to Poetry in Anthologies. Great Neck, N.Y.: Poetry Index, 1982-   .

Poetics

Brogan, T. V. F. *English Versification, 1570-1980: A Reference Guide with a Global Appendix.* Baltimore: Johns Hopkins University Press, 1981.

Malof, Joseph. *A Manual of English Meters.* Bloomington: Indiana University Press, 1970.

Shapiro, Karl, and Robert Beum. *A Prosody Handbook.* New York: Harper, 1965.

Post colonial anglophone poetry

(see also Australia; Irish poetry in English; Scottish poetry in English; Welsh poetry in English)

Benson, Eugene, and L. W. Connolly. *Encyclopedia of Post-Colonial Literatures in English.* 2 vols. London: Routledge, 1994.

Lawson, Alan, et al. *Post-Colonial Literatures in English: General, Theoretical, and Comparative, 1970-1993.* A Reference Publication in Literature. New York: G. K. Hall, 1997.

Mohanram, Radhika, and Gita Rajan, eds. *English Postcoloniality: Literatures from Around the World.* Contributions to the Study of World Literature 66. Westport, Conn.: Greenwood Press, 1996.

Ramazani, Jahan. *The Hybrid Muse: Postcolonial Poetry in English.* Chicago: University of Chicago Press, 2001.

Williams, Mark. *Post-Colonial Literatures in English: Southeast Asia, New Zealand, and the Pacific, 1970-1992.* Reference Publications in Literature. New York: G. K. Hall, 1996.

Women writers

Davis, Gwenn, and Beverly A. Joyce, comps. *Poetry by Women to 1900: A Bibliography of American and British Writers.* Toronto: University of Toronto Press, 1991.

Mark, Alison, and Deryn Rees-Jones. *Contemporary Women's Poetry: Reading, Writing, Practice.* New York: St. Martin's Press, 2000.

AFRICA AND THE CARIBBEAN

(see also in the foreign-language section: AFRICAN LANGUAGES; CARIBBEAN; FRANCOPHONE; SPANISH AND PORTUGUESE*)*

General

Lindfors, Bernth, and Reinhard Sander, eds. *Twentieth-Century Caribbean and Black African Writers: First Series.* Dictionary of Literary Biography 117. Detroit: Gale Research, 1992.

_____. *Twentieth-Century Caribbean and Black African Writers: Second Series.* Dictionary of Literary Biography 125. Detroit: Gale Research, 1993.

_____. *Twentieth-Century Caribbean and Black African Writers: Third Series.* Dictionary of Literary Biography 157. Detroit: Gale Research, 1996.

Africa

Fraser, Robert. *West African Poetry: A Critical History.* Cambridge, England: Cambridge University Press, 1986.

Killam, Douglas, and Ruth Rowe, eds. *The Companion to African Literatures.* Bloomington: Indiana University Press, 2000.

Lindfors, Bernth. *Black African Literature in English: A Guide to Information Sources.* American Literature, English Literature, and World Literatures in English: An Information Guide Series 23. Detroit: Gale, 1979.

_____. *Black African Literature in English, 1977-1981 Supplement.* New York: Africana, 1986.

_____. *Black African Literature in English, 1982-1986.* New York: Zell, 1989.

_____. *Black African Literature in English, 1987-1991.* Bibliographical Research in African Literature 3. London: Zell, 1995.

Ojaide, Tanure. *Poetic Imagination in Black Africa: Essays on African Poetry.* Durham, N.C.: Carolina Academic Press, 1996. Includes Anglophone, Francophone, and Lusophone literatures.

Parekh, Pushpa Naidu, and Siga Fatima Jagne. *Postcolonial African Writers: A Bio-Bibliographical Critical Sourcebook.* Westport, Conn.: Greenwood Press, 1998.

Scanlon, Paul A., ed. *South African Writers*. Dictionary of Literary Biography 225. Detroit: Gale Group, 2000.

Caribbean and West Indian

Allis, Jeannette B. *West Indian Literature: An Index to Criticism, 1930-1975*. Reference Publication in Latin American Studies. Boston: Hall, 1981.

Arnold, A. James, ed. *A History of Literature in the Caribbean*. 3 vols. Philadelphia: J. Benjamins, 1994.

Bloom, Harold, ed. *Caribbean Women Writers*. Women Writers of English and Their Work. Philadelphia: Chelsea House, 1997.

Breiner, Laurence A. *An Introduction to West Indian Poetry*. Cambridge, England: Cambridge University Press, 1998.

Dance, Daryl Cumber, ed. *Fifty Caribbean Writers: A Bio-Bibliographical Critical Sourcebook*. New York: Greenwood Press, 1986.

Dawes, Kwame, ed. *Talk Yuh Talk: Interviews with Anglophone Caribbean Poets*. Charlottesville: University Press of Virginia, 2001.

Fenwick, M. J. *Writers of the Caribbean and Central America: A Bibliography*. Garland Reference Library of the Humanities 1244. New York: Garland, 1992.

Herdeck, Donald E., ed. *Caribbean Writers: A Bio-Bibliographical-Critical Encyclopedia*. Washington, D.C.: Three Continents Press, 1979.

Hughes, Roger, comp. *Caribbean Writing: A Checklist*. London: Commonwealth Institute Library Services, 1986.

Jordan, Alma, and Barbara Comissiong. *The English-Speaking Caribbean: A Bibliography of Bibliographies*. Reference Publication in Latin American Studies. Boston: Hall, 1984.

AUSTRALIA

Aboriginal poetry

Healy, John Joseph. *Literature and the Aborigine in Australia, 1770-1975*. New York: St. Martin's Press, 1978.

Schurmann-Zeggel, Heinz. *Black Australian Literature: A Bibliography of Fiction, Poetry, Drama, Oral Traditions and Non-Fiction, including Critical Commentary, 1900-1991*. New York: Peter Lang, 1997.

Shoemaker, Adam. *Black Words, White Page*. UQP Studies in Australian Literature. St. Lucia: University of Queensland Press, 1989.

Bibliography

Hergenhan, Laurie, and Martin Duwell, eds. *The ALS Guide to Australian Writers: A Bibliography*. UQP Studies in Australian Literature. Queensland: University of Queensland Press, 1992.

Webby, Elizabeth. *Early Australian Poetry: An Annotated Bibliography of Original Poems Published in Australian Newspapers, Magazines, and Almanacks Before 1850*. Sydney: Hale, 1982.

Biographical sources

Samuels, Selina, ed. *Australian Literature, 1788-1914*. Dictionary of Literary Biography 230. Detroit: Gale Group, 2001.

Who's Who of Australian Writers. 2d ed. Clayton: National Centre for Australian Studies, 1995.

Dictionaries, histories, handbooks

Andrews, B. G., and William H. Wilde. *Australian Literature to 1900: A Guide to Information Sources*. American Literature, English Literature, and World Literatures in English: An Information Guide Series 22. Detroit: Gale, 1980.

Elliott, Brian Robinson. *The Landscape of Australian Poetry*. Melbourne: Cheshire, 1967.

Gray, Robert, and Geoffrey Lehmann, eds. *Australian Poetry in the Twentieth Century*. Port Melbourne: William Heinemann Australia, 1991.

Green, H. M. *A History of Australian Literature: Pure and Applied, A Critical Review of All Forms of Literature Produced in Australia from the First Books Published After the Arrival of the First Fleet Until 1950*. Revised by Dorothy Green. 2 vols. London: Angus & Robertson, 1984.

Hergenhan, Laurie. *The Penguin New Literary History of Australia*. Victoria: Penguin, 1988.

Hooton, Joy, and Harry Heseltine. *Annals of Australian Literature*. 2d ed. Melbourne: Oxford University Press, 1992.

Jaffa, Herbert C. *Modern Australian Poetry, 1920-1970: A Guide to Information Sources*. American Literature, English Literature, and World Literatures in English: An Information Guide Series 24. Detroit: Gale, 1979.

Lever, Richard, James Wieland, and Scott Findlay. *Post-colonial Literatures in English: Australia, 1970-1992*. A Reference Publication in Literature. New York: G. K. Hall, 1996.

Lock, Fred, and Alan Lawson. *Australian Literature: A Reference Guide*. 2d ed. Australian Bibliographies. New York: Oxford University Press, 1980.

Wilde, W. H., Joy Hooton, and Barry Andrews. *The Oxford Companion to Australian Literature*. 2d ed. New York: Oxford University Press, 1994.

Women writers

Adelaide, Debra. *Bibliography of Australian Women's Literature, 1795-1990: A Listing of Fiction, Poetry, Drama, and Non-Fiction Published in Monograph Form Arranged Alphabetically by Author*. Port Melbourne: Thorpe with National Centre for Australian Studies, 1991.

Hampton, Susan, and Kate Llewellyn, eds. *The Penguin Book of Australian Women Poets*. Victoria: Penguin Ringwood, 1986.

CANADA

(*see also in the foreign-language section:* FRANCOPHONE)

Biographical sources

Lecker, Robert, Jack David, and Ellen Quiqley, eds. *Canadian Writers and Their Works: Poetry Series*. Downsview, Ont.: ECW Press, 1983.

McLeod, Donald, ed. *Canadian Writers and Their Works Cumulated Index Volume: Poetry Series*. Toronto, Ont.: ECW Press, 1993.

New, W. H., ed. *Canadian Writers Before 1890*. Dictionary of Literary Biography 99. Detroit: Gale Research, 1990.

_____. *Canadian Writers, 1890-1920*. Dictionary of Literary Biography 92. Detroit: Gale Research, 1990.

_____. *Canadian Writers, 1920-1959: First Series*. Dictionary of Literary Biography 68. Detroit: Gale Research, 1988.

_____. *Canadian Writers, 1920-1959: Second Series*. Dictionary of Literary Biography 88. Detroit: Gale Research, 1989.

_____. *Canadian Writers Since 1960: First Series*. Dictionary of Literary Biography 53. Detroit: Gale Research, 1986.

_____. *Canadian Writers Since 1960: Second Series*. Dictionary of Literary Biography 60. Detroit: Gale Research, 1987.

Criticism

Platnick, Phyllis. *Canadian Poetry: Index to Criticisms, 1970-1979*. Ontario: Canadian Library Association, 1985.

Dictionaries, histories, handbooks

Marshall, Tom. *Harsh and Lovely Land: The Major Canadian Poets and the Making of a Canadian Tradition*. Vancouver: University of British Columbia Press, 1979.

Stevens, Peter. *Modern English-Canadian Poetry: A Guide to Information Sources*. American Literature, English Literature, and World Literatures in English: An Information Guide Series 15. Detroit: Gale, 1978.

Indexes of primary works

Fee, Margery, ed. *Canadian Poetry in Selected English-Language Anthologies: An Index and Guide*. Halifax, N.S.: Dalhousie University, University Libraries, School of Library Service, 1985.

McQuarrie, Jane, Anne Mercer, and Gordon Ripley, eds. *Index to Canadian Poetry in English*. Toronto: Reference Press, 1984.

INDIA AND SOUTH ASIA

King, Bruce. *Modern Indian Poetry in English*. New York: Oxford University Press, 1987.

Naik, M. K. *A History of Indian English Literature*. New Delhi: Sahitya Akademi, 1989.

Rama, Atma. *Indian Poetry and Fiction in English*. New Delhi: Bahri Publications, 1991.

Singh, Amritjit, Rajiav Verma, and Irene M. Johsi. *Indian Literature in English, 1827-1979: A Guide to Information Sources*. American Literature, English Literature, and World Literatures in English: An Information Guide Series 36. Detroit: Gale, 1981.

Sinha, R. P. N. *Indo-Anglican Poetry: Its Birth and Growth*. New Delhi: Reliance Publishing House, 1987.

IRISH POETRY IN ENGLISH

(*see also in the foreign-language section:* CELTIC LANGUAGES)

Biographical sources

Sherry, Vincent B., Jr., ed. *Poets of Great Britain and*

Ireland, 1945-1960. Dictionary of Literary Biography 27. Detroit: Gale Research, 1984.

_____. *Poets of Great Britain and Ireland Since 1960*. Dictionary of Literary Biography 40. Detroit: Gale Research, 1985.

Dictionaries, histories, handbooks

Hogan, Robert, ed. *Dictionary of Irish Literature*. Rev. ed. 2 vols. Westport, Conn.: Greenwood Press, 1996.

Schirmer, Gregory A. *Out of What Began: A History of Irish Poetry in English*. Ithaca, N.Y.: Cornell University Press, 1998.

Women writers

Colman, Anne Ulry. *Dictionary of Nineteenth-Century Irish Women Poets*. Galway: Kenny's Bookshop, 1996.

McBreen, Joan, ed. *The White Page = an Bhileog bh´an: Twentieth-Century Irish Women Poets*. Cliffs of Moher, Co. Clare: Salmon, 1999.

Weekes, Ann Owens. *Unveiling Treasures: The Attic Guide to the Published Works of Irish Women Literary Writers: Drama, Fiction, Poetry*. Dublin: Attic Press, 1993.

NEW ZEALAND

Sturm, Terry, ed. *The Oxford History of New Zealand Literature in English*. Auckland: Oxford University Press, 1991.

Thomson, John. *New Zealand Literature to 1977: A Guide to Information Sources*. American Literature, English Literature, and World Literatures in English: An Information Guide Series 30. Detroit: Gale, 1980.

SCOTTISH POETRY IN ENGLISH

(see also in the foreign-language section: CELTIC LANGUAGES*)*

Glen, Duncan. *The Poetry of the Scots: An Introduction and Bibliographical Guide to Poetry in Gaelic, Scots, Latin and English*. Edinburgh: Edinburgh University Press, 1991.

Scottish Poetry Index: An Index to Poetry and Poetry-Related Material in Scottish Literary Magazines, 1952-   . Edinburgh: Scottish Poetry Library, 1994-2000.

ENGLAND

(see also IRISH POETRY IN ENGLISH; SCOTTISH POETRY IN ENGLISH; WELSH POETRY IN ENGLISH*)*

Bibliographies

Case, Arthur E. *A Bibliography of English Poetical Miscellanies, 1521-1750*. London: Oxford University Press for the Bibliographical Society, 1935.

Dyson, A. E., ed. *English Poetry: Select Bibliographical Guides*. London: Oxford University Press, 1971.

Criticism

Guide to British Poetry Explication. 4 vols. Boston: G. K. Hall, 1991. Individual volumes cover Old English/medieval, the Renaissance, Restoration and Romantic poetry, and Victorian through twentieth century.

Dictionaries, histories, handbooks

Courthope, W. J. *A History of English Poetry*. New York: Macmillan, 1895-1910.

Garrett, John. *British Poetry Since the Sixteenth Century: A Student's Guide*. Totowa, N.J.: Barnes & Noble Books, 1987.

Mell, Donald Charles, Jr. *English Poetry, 1660-1800: A Guide to Information Sources*. American Literature, English Literature, and World Literatures in English: An Information Guide Series 40. Detroit: Gale Research, 1982.

Smith, Eric. *A Dictionary of Classical Reference in English Poetry*. Totowa, N.J.: Barnes & Noble, 1984.

Woodring, Carl, and James Shapiro, eds. *The Columbia History of British Poetry*. New York: Columbia University Press, 1993.

Old and Middle English

Aertsen, Hank, and Rolf H. Bremmer, eds. *Companion to Old English Poetry*. Amsterdam: VU University Press, 1994.

Beale, Walter H. *Old and Middle English Poetry to 1500: A Guide to Information Sources*. American Literature, English Literature, and World Literatures in English: An Information Guide Series 7. Detroit: Gale Research, 1976.

Brown, Carleton, and Rossell Hope Robbins. *The Index of Middle English Verse*. New York: Columbia University Press for the Index Society, 1943.

Jost, Jean E. *Ten Middle English Arthurian Romances: A Reference Guide*. Boston: G. K. Hall, 1986.

Martinez, Nancy C., and Joseph G. R. Martinez. *Old English-Medieval*. Vol. 1 in *Guide to British Poetry Explication*. Boston: G. K. Hall, 1991.

O'Keeffe, Katherine O'Brien, ed. *Old English Shorter Poems: Basic Readings*. Garland Reference Library of the Humanities 1432. New York: Garland, 1994.

Pearsall, Derek. *Old English and Middle English Poetry*. Vol. 1 in *The Routledge History of English Poetry*. London: Routledge, 1977.

Renaissance to 1660

Frank, Joseph. *Hobbled Pegasus: A Descriptive Bibliography of Minor English Poetry, 1641-1660*. Albuquerque: University of New Mexico Press, 1968.

Gutierrez, Nancy A. *English Historical Poetry, 1476-1603: A Bibliography*. Garland Reference Library of the Humanities 410. New York: Garland, 1983.

Hester, M. Thomas, ed. *Seventeenth-Century British Nondramatic Poets: First Series*. Dictionary of Literary Biography 121. Detroit: Gale Research, 1992.

_____. *Seventeenth-Century British Nondramatic Poets: Second Series*. Dictionary of Literary Biography 126. Detroit: Gale Research, 1993.

_____. *Seventeenth-Century British Nondramatic Poets: Third Series*. Dictionary of Literary Biography 131. Detroit: Gale Research, 1993.

Martinez, Nancy C., and Joseph G. R. Martinez. *Renaissance*. Vol. 2 in *Guide to British Poetry Explication*. Boston: G. K. Hall, 1991.

Ringler, William A., Jr. *Bibliography and Index of English Verse Printed 1476-1558*. New York: Mansell, 1988.

Ringler, William A., Michael Rudick, and Susan J. Ringler. *Bibliography and Index of English Verse in Manuscript, 1501-1558*. New York: Mansell, 1992.

Rivers, Isabel. *Classical and Christian Ideas in English Renaissance Poetry: A Student's Guide*. 2d ed. New York: Routledge, 1994.

Restoration (1660) through eighteenth century

Foxon, D. F. *English Verse 1701-1750: A Catalogue of Separately Printed Poems with Notes on Contemporary Collected Editions*. 2 vols. Cambridge, England: Cambridge University Press, 1975.

Jackson, J. R. de J. *Annals of English Verse, 1770-1835: A Preliminary Survey of the Volumes Published*. Garland Reference Library of the Humanities 535. New York: Garland, 1985.

Martinez, Nancy C., Joseph G. R. Martinez, and Erland Anderson. *Restoration-Romantic*. Vol. 3 in *Guide to British Poetry Explication*. Boston: G. K. Hall, 1991.

Nokes, David, and Janet Barron. *An Annotated Critical Bibliography of Augustan Poetry*. Annotated Critical Bibliographies. New York: St. Martin's, 1989.

Rothstein, Eric. *Restoration and Eighteenth-Century Poetry, 1660-1780*. Vol. 3 in *The Routledge History of English Poetry*. Boston: Routledge & Kegan Paul, 1981.

Sitter, John, ed. *The Cambridge Companion to Eighteenth-Century Poetry*. New York: Cambridge University Press, 2001.

_____. *Eighteenth-Century British Poets: First Series*. Dictionary of Literary Biography 95. Detroit: Gale Research, 1990.

_____. *Eighteenth-Century British Poets: Second Series*. Dictionary of Literary Biography 109. Detroit: Gale Research, 1991.

Nineteenth century

Bristow, Joseph, ed. *The Cambridge Companion to Victorian Poetry*. New York: Cambridge University Press, 2000.

Faverty, Frederic E., ed. *The Victorian Poets: A Guide to Research*. 2d ed. Cambridge: Harvard University Press, 1968.

Fredeman, William E., and Ira B. Nadel, eds. *Victorian Poets Before 1850*. Dictionary of Literary Biography 32. Detroit: Gale Research, 1984.

_____. *Victorian Poets After 1850*. Dictionary of Literary Biography 35. Detroit: Gale Research, 1985.

Greenfield, John R., ed. *British Romantic Poets, 1789-1832: First series*. Dictionary of Literary Biography 93. Detroit: Gale Research, 1990.

_____, ed. *British Romantic Poets, 1789-1832: Second Series*. Dictionary of Literary Biography 96. Detroit: Gale Research, 1990.

Jackson, J. R. de J. *Poetry of the Romantic Period*. Vol. 4 in *The Routledge History of English Poetry*. Boston: Routledge & Kegan Paul, 1980.

Jordan, Frank, ed. *The English Romantic Poets: A Review of Research and Criticism*. 4th ed. New York: MLA, 1985.

Martinez, Nancy C., Joseph G. R. Martinez, and Erland Anderson. *Victorian-Contemporary*. Vol. 4 in *Guide to British Poetry Explication*. Boston: G. K. Hall, 1991.

Reilly, Catherine W. *Late Victorian Poetry, 1880-1899: An Annotated Biobibliography*. New York: Mansell, 1994.

_____. *Mid-Victorian Poetry, 1860-1879: An Annotated Biobibliography*. New York: Mansell, 2000.

Reiman, Donald H. *English Romantic Poetry, 1800-1835: A Guide to Information Sources*. American Literature, English Literature, and World Literature in English: An Information Guide Series 27. Detroit: Gale, 1979.

Richards, Bernard Arthur. *English Poetry of the Victorian Period, 1830-1890*. 2d ed. New York: Longman, 2001.

Roberts, Adam. *Romantic and Victorian Long Poems: A Guide*. Brookfield, Vt.: Ashgate, 1999.

Twentieth century and contemporary

Anderson, Emily Ann. *English Poetry, 1900-1950: A Guide to Information Sources*. American Literature, English Literature, and World Literatures in English: An Information Guide Series 33. Detroit: Gale Research, 1982.

Davie, Donald. *Under Briggflatts: A History of Poetry in Great Britain, 1960-1988*. Chicago: University of Chicago Press, 1989.

Lehmann, John. *The English Poets of the First World War*. New York: Thames and Hudson, 1982.

Martinez, Nancy C., Joseph G. R. Martinez, and Erland Anderson. *Victorian-Contemporary*. Vol. 4 in *Guide to British Poetry Explication*. Boston: G. K. Hall, 1991.

Persoon, James. *Modern British Poetry, 1900-1939*. Twayne's Critical History of Poetry Studies. New York: Twayne, 1999.

Quinn, Patrick, ed. *British Poets of the Great War: Brooke, Rosenberg, Thomas: A Documentary Volume*. Dictionary of Literary Biography 216. Detroit: Gale Group, 2000.

Reilly, Catherine W. *English Poetry of the Second World War: A Biobibliography*. Boston: G. K. Hall, 1986.

Schmidt, Michael. *A Reader's Guide to Fifty Modern British Poets*. New York: Barnes & Noble, 1979.

Sherry, Vincent B., Jr., ed. *Poets of Great Britain and Ireland, 1945-1960*. Dictionary of Literary Biography 27. Detroit: Gale Research, 1984.

_____. *Poets of Great Britain and Ireland, Since 1960*. Dictionary of Literary Biography 40. Detroit: Gale Research, 1985.

Shields, Ellen F. *Contemporary English Poetry: An Annotated Bibliography of Criticism to 1980*. Garland Reference Library of the Humanities 460. New York: Garland, 1984.

Stanford, Donald E., ed. *British Poets, 1880-1914*. Dictionary of Literary Biography 19. Detroit: Gale Research, 1983.

_____. *British Poets, 1914-1945*. Dictionary of Literary Biography 20. Detroit: Gale Research, 1983.

Thwaite, Anthony. *Poetry Today: A Critical Guide to British Poetry, 1960-1992*. New York: Longman with the British Council, 1996.

Women writers

Jackson, J. R. de J. *Romantic Poetry by Women: A Bibliography, 1770-1835*. Oxford: Clarendon-Oxford University Press, 1993.

Thesing, William B., ed. *Late Nineteenth- and Early Twentieth-Century British Women Poets*. Dictionary of Literary Biography 240. Detroit: Gale Group, 2001.

_____. *Victorian Women Poets*. Dictionary of Literary Biography 199. Detroit: Gale Research, 1999.

UNITED STATES

Criticism

Guide to American Poetry Explication. Reference Publication in Literature. 2 vols. Boston: G. K. Hall, 1989. See individual volumes for specific periods.

Dictionaries, histories, handbooks

Kamp, Jim, ed. *Reference Guide to American Literature*. 3d ed. Detroit: St. James Press, 1994.

Parini, Jay, ed. *The Columbia History of American Poetry*. New York: Columbia University Press, 1993.

Perkins, George, Barbara Perkins, and Phillip Leininger, eds. *Benét's Reader's Encyclopedia of American Literature*. New York: HarperCollins, 1991. Also covers Canadian and Latin American literature; includes a substantial overview entry devoted to poetry.

Shucard, Alan. *American Poetry: The Puritans Through Walt Whitman.* Twayne's Critical History of Poetry Series. Boston: Twayne, 1988.

Waggoner, Hyatt H. *American Poets from the Puritans to the Present.* Rev. ed. Baton Rouge: Louisiana University Press, 1984.

Indexes of primary works

Annual Index to Poetry in Periodicals. Great Neck, N.Y.: Poetry Index Press, 1985-1988.

American Poetry Index: An Author, Title, and Subject Guide to Poetry by Americans in Single-Author Collections. Great Neck, N.Y.: Granger, 1983-1988.

Caskey, Jefferson D., comp. *Index to Poetry in Popular Periodicals, 1955-1959.* Westport, Conn.: Greenwood, 1984.

Index of American Periodical Verse. Lanham, Md.: Scarecrow, 1971.

Index to Poetry in Periodicals, 1925-1992: An Index of Poets and Poems Published in American Magazines and Newspapers. Great Neck, N.Y.: Granger, 1984.

Index to Poetry in Periodicals, 1920-1924: An Index of Poets and Poems Published in American Magazines and Newspapers. Great Neck, N.Y.: Granger, 1983.

Index to Poetry in Periodicals: American Poetic Renaissance, 1915-1919: An Index of Poets and Poems Published in American Magazines and Newspapers. Great Neck, N.Y.: Granger, 1981.

Colonial to 1800

Lemay, J. A. Leo. *A Calendar of American Poetry in the Colonial Newspapers and Magazines and in the Major English Magazines Through 1765.* Worcester, Mass.: American Antiquarian Society, 1972.

Scheick, William J., and JoElla Doggett. *Seventeenth-Century American Poetry: A Reference Guide.* Reference Guides in Literature 14. Boston: G. K. Hall, 1977.

Wegelin, Oscar. *Early American Poetry: A Compilation of the Titles of Volumes of Verse and Broadsides by Writers Born or Residing in North America, North of the Mexican Border [1650-1820].* 2d ed. 2 vols. New York: Smith, 1930.

Nineteenth century

Haralson, Eric L., ed. *Encyclopedia of American Poetry: The Nineteenth Century.* Chicago: Fitzroy Dearborn, 1998.

Jason, Philip K. *Nineteenth Century American Poetry: An Annotated Bibliography.* Pasadena, Calif.: Salem Press, 1989.

Lee, A. Robert, ed. *Nineteenth-Century American Poetry.* Critical Studies Series. Totowa, N.J.: Barnes & Noble, 1985.

Ruppert, James. *Colonial and Nineteenth Century.* Vol. 1 in *Guide to American Poetry Explication.* Boston: G. K. Hall, 1989.

Twentieth century and contemporary

Alfonsi, Ferdinando. *Dictionary of Italian-American Poets.* American University Studies. Series II, Romance Languages and Literature. 112. New York: Peter Lang, 1989.

Baughman, Ronald, ed. *American Poets.* Vol. 3 in *Contemporary Authors: Bibliographical Series.* Detroit: Gale, 1986.

Conte, Joseph, ed. *American Poets Since World War II: Fourth Series.* Dictionary of Literary Biography 165. Detroit: Gale Research, 1996.

_____. *American Poets Since World War II: Fifth Series.* Dictionary of Literary Biography 169. Detroit: Gale Research, 1996.

_____. *American Poets Since World War II: Sixth Series.* Dictionary of Literary Biography 193. Detroit: Gale Research, 1998.

Davis, Lloyd, and Robert Irwin. *Contemporary American Poetry: A Checklist.* Metuchen, N.J.: Scarecrow, 1975.

Green, Scott E. *Contemporary Science Fiction, Fantasy, and Horror Poetry: A Resource Guide and Biographical Directory.* New York: Greenwood Press, 1989.

Greiner, Donald J., ed. *American Poets Since World War II.* Dictionary of Literary Biography 5. Detroit: Gale Research, 1980.

Gwynn, R. S., ed. *American Poets Since World War II: Second Series.* Dictionary of Literary Biography 105. Detroit: Gale Research, 1991.

_____. *American Poets Since World War II: Third Series.* Dictionary of Literary Biography 120. Detroit: Gale Research, 1992.

Haralson, Eric L., ed. *Encyclopedia of American Poetry: The Twentieth Century.* Chicago: Fitzroy Dearborn, 2001.

Leo, John R. *Modern and Contemporary*. Vol. 2 in *Guide to American Poetry Explication*. Boston: G. K. Hall, 1989.

McPheron, William. *The Bibliography of Contemporary American Poetry, 1945-1985: An Annotated Checklist*. Westport: Meckler, 1986.

Moramarco, Fred, and William Sullivan. *Containing Multitudes: Poetry in the United States Since 1950*. Critical History of Poetry Series. New York: Twayne, 1998.

Quartermain, Peter, ed. *American Poets, 1880-1945: First Series*. Dictionary of Literary Biography 45. Detroit: Gale Research, 1986.

_____. *American Poets, 1880-1945: Second Series*. Dictionary of Literary Biography 48. Detroit: Gale Research, 1986.

_____. *American Poets, 1880-1945: Third Series*. Dictionary of Literary Biography 54. Detroit: Gale Research, 1987.

Shucard, Alan, Fred Moramarco, and William Sullivan. *Modern American Poetry, 1865-1950*. Boston: Twayne, 1989.

African American: biographical

Harris, Trudier, ed. *Afro-American Writers Before the Harlem Renaissance*. Dictionary of Literary Biography 50. Detroit: Gale, 1986.

_____. *Afro-American Writers from the Harlem Renaissance to 1940*. Dictionary of Literary Biography 51. Detroit: Gale, 1987.

Harris, Trudier, and Thadious M. Davis, eds. *Afro-American Poets Since 1955*. Dictionary of Literary Biography 41 Detroit: Gale, 1985.

African American: indexes of primary works

Chapman, Dorothy Hilton, comp. *Index to Black Poetry*. Boston, G. K. Hall, 1974.

Frankovich, Nicholas and David Larzelere, eds. *The Columbia Granger's Index to African-American Poetry*. New York: Columbia University Press, 1999.

African American: dictionaries, histories, handbooks

French, William P., et al. *Afro-American Poetry and Drama, 1760-1975: A Guide to Information Sources*. American Literature, English Literature, and World Literatures in English: An Information Guide Series 17. Detroit: Gale, 1979.

Sherman, Joan R. *Invisible Poets: Afro-Americans of the Nineteenth Century*. 2d ed. Urbana: University of Illinois Press, 1989.

Wagner, Jean, and Kenneth Douglas, trans. *Black Poets of the United States: From Paul Laurence Dunbar to Langston Hughes*. Urbana: University of Illinois Press, 1973.

African American: women writers

Chapman, Dorothy Hilton, comp. *Index to Poetry by Black American Women*. Bibliographies and Indexes in Afro-American and African Studies 15. New York: Greenwood, 1986.

Asian American

Chang, Juliana, ed. *Quiet Fire: A Historical Anthology of Asian American Poetry, 1892-1970*. New York: The Asian American Writers' Workshop, 1996.

Cheung, King-Kok, ed. *An Interethnic Companion to Asian American Literature*. New York: Cambridge University Press, 1997.

Cheung, King-Kok, and Stan Yogi. *Asian American Literature: An Annotated Bibliography*. New York: MLA, 1988.

Latino

Bleznick, Donald William. *A Sourcebook for Hispanic Literature and Language: A Selected, Annotated Guide to Spanish, Spanish-American, and United States Hispanic Bibliography, Literature, Linguistics, Journals, and Other Source Materials*. 3d ed. Lanham, Md.: Scarecrow Press, 1995.

Candelaria, Cordelia. *Chicano Poetry: A Critical Introduction*. Westport, Conn.: Greenwood Press, 1986.

Eger, Ernestina N. *A Bibliography of Criticism of Contemporary Chicano Literature*. Berkeley: Chicano Library Publications, University of California, 1982.

Kanellos, Nicolás, ed. *Biographical Dictionary of Hispanic Literature in the United States: The Literature of Puerto Ricans, Cuban Americans, and other Hispanic writers*. New York: Greenwood Press, 1989.

Lomelí, Francisco A., and Carl R. Shirley, eds. *Chicano Writers: First Series*. Dictionary of Literary Biography 82. Detroit: Gale Research, 1989.

_____. *Chicano Writers: Second Series*. Dictionary of Literary Biography 122. Detroit: Gale Research, 1992.

_____. *Chicano Writers: Third Series*. Dictionary of

Literary Biography 209. Detroit: Gale Group, 1999.

Martínez, Julio A., and Francisco A. Lomelí, eds. *Chicano Literature: A Reference Guide*. Westport, Conn.: Greenwood Press, 1985.

Native American

Howard, Helen Addison. *American Indian Poetry*. Twayne's United States Authors Series 334. Boston: Twayne, 1979.

Littlefield, Daniel F., Jr., and James W. Parins. *A Biobibliography of Native American Writers, 1772-1924*. Native American Bibliography Series 2. Metuchen, N.J.: Scarecrow, 1981.

_____. *A Biobibliography of Native American Writers, 1772-1924: Supplement*. Native American Bibliography Series 5. Metuchen, N.J.: Scarecrow, 1985.

Ruoff, A. LaVonne Brown. *American Indian Literatures: An Introduction, Bibliographic Review, and Selected Bibliography*. New York: Modern Language Association, 1990.

Roemer, Kenneth M., ed. *Native American Writers of the United States*. Dictionary of Literary Biography 175. Detroit: Gale Research, 1997.

Wiget, Andrew. *Native American Literature*. Twayne's United States Authors Series 467. Boston: Twayne, 1985.

_____, ed. *Dictionary of Native American Literature*. Garland Reference Library of the Humanities 1815. New York: Garland, 1994.

Whitson, Kathy J. *Native American Literatures: An Encyclopedia of Works, Characters, Authors, and Themes*. Santa Barbara, Calif.: ABC-CLIO, 1999.

Regional poetry

Bain, Robert, and Joseph M. Flora, eds. *Contemporary Poets, Dramatists, Essayists, and Novelists of the South: A Bio-bibliographical Sourcebook*. Westport Conn.: Greenwood Press, 1994.

Jantz, Harold S. *The First Century of New England Verse*. Worcester, Mass.: American Antiquarian Society, 1944.

Women writers

Davidson, Phebe, ed. *Conversations with the World: American Women Poets and Their Work*. Pasadena, Calif.: Trilogy Books, 1998.

Drake, William. *The First Wave: Women Poets in America, 1915-1945*. New York: Macmillan, 1987.

Reardon, Joan, and Kristine A. Thorsen. *Poetry by American Women, 1900-1975: A Bibliography*. Metuchen, N.J.: Scarecrow, 1979.

_____. *Poetry by American Women, 1975-1989: A Bibliography*. Metuchen, N.J.: Scarecrow, 1990.

WELSH POETRY IN ENGLISH

(*see also in the foreign-language section:* CELTIC LANGUAGES)

Conran, Anthony. *Frontiers in Anglo-Welsh Poetry*. Cardiff: University of Wales Press, 1997.

FOREIGN-LANGUAGE POETRY

GENERAL REFERENCE SOURCES

Biographical sources

Jackson, William T. H., ed. *European Writers*. 14 vols. New York: Scribner, 1983-1991.

Kunitz, Stanley, and Vineta Colby, eds. *European Authors, 1000-1900: A Biographical Dictionary of European Literature*. New York: Wilson, 1967.

Magill, Frank N., ed. *Critical Survey of Poetry: Foreign Language Series*. 5 vols. Englewood Cliffs, N.J.: Salem Press, 1984.

_____. *Critical Survey of Poetry: Supplement*. Englewood Cliffs, N.J.: Salem Press, 1987.

Serafin, Steven, ed. *Twentieth-Century Eastern European Writers: First Series*. Dictionary of Literary Biography 215. Detroit: Gale Group, 1999.

Serafin, Steven R. *Encyclopedia of World Literature in the Twentieth Century*. 3d ed. 4 vols. Detroit: St. James Press, 1999.

_____. *Twentieth-Century Eastern European Writers: Second Series*. Dictionary of Literary Biography 220. Detroit: Gale Group, 2000.

_____. *Twentieth-Century Eastern European Writers: Third Series*. Dictionary of Literary Biography 232. Detroit: Gale Group, 2001.

Solé, Carlos A., ed. *Latin American Writers*. 3 vols. New York: Scribner, 1989.

Criticism

Coleman, Arthur. *A Checklist of Interpretation, 1940-1973, of Classical and Continental Epics and Metrical Romances*. Vol. 2 in *Epic and Romance Criticism*. 2 vols. Seringtown: Watermill, 1974.

Jason, Philip K., ed. *Masterplots II: Poetry Series, Revised Edition*. 8 vols. Pasadena, Calif.: Salem Press, 2002.

Krstovic, Jelena, ed. *Hispanic Literature Criticism*. Detroit: Gale Research, 1994. Excerpts from criticism.

The Year's Work in Modern Language Studies. London: Oxford University Press, 1931. Annual review of scholarship.

Dictionaries, histories, handbooks

Auty, Robert, et al. *Traditions of Heroic and Epic Poetry*. 2 vols. Vol. 1, *The Traditions*; Vol. 2, *Characteristics and Techniques*. Publications of the Modern Humanities Research Association 9, 13. London: Modern Humanities Research Association, 1980, 1989.

Bede, Jean-Albert, and William B. Edgerton, eds. *Columbia Dictionary of Modern European Literature*. 2d ed. New York: Columbia University Press, 1980.

France, Peter, ed. *The Oxford Guide to Literature in English Translation*. New York: Oxford University Press, 2000. First part includes a chapter on the history and issues involved in translating poetry into English; second part surveys and evaluates what has been translated in specific languages.

Henderson, Lesley, ed. *Reference Guide to World Literature*. 2d ed. 2 vols. New York: St. James Press, 1995. Includes some contemporary writers, but focus is historical.

Oinas, Felix, ed. *Heroic Epic and Saga: An Introduction to the World's Great Folk Epics*. Bloomington: Indiana University Press, 1978.

Ostle, Robin, ed. *Modern Literature in the Near and Middle East, 1850-1970*. Routledge/SOAS Contemporary Politics and Culture in the Middle East Series. New York: Routledge, 1991.

Prusek, Jaroslav, ed. *Dictionary of Oriental Literatures*. 3 vols. Vol. 1, *East Asia*, edited by Z. Shupski; Vol. 2, *South and South-East Asia*, edited by D. Zbavitel; Vol. 3, *West Asia and North Africa*, edited by J. Becka. New York: Basic Books, 1974.

Pynsent, Robert B., ed. *Reader's Encyclopedia of Eastern European Literature*. New York: HarperCollins, 1993.

Weber, Harry B., George Gutsche, and P. Rollberg, eds. *The Modern Encyclopedia of East Slavic, Baltic, and Eurasian Literatures*. 10 vols. Gulf Breeze, Fla.: Academic International Press, 1977.

Indexes of primary works

Hoffman, Herbert H. *Hoffman's Index to Poetry: European and Latin American Poetry in Anthologies*. Metuchen, N.J.: Scarecrow Press, 1985.

Poetics

Gasparov, M. L. *A History of European Versification*. Translated by G. S. Smith and Marina Tarlinskaja. New York: Oxford University Press, 1996.

Wimsatt, William K., ed. *Versification: Major Language Types: Sixteen Essays*. New York: Modern Language Association, 1972.

AFRICAN LANGUAGES

(see also in the English-language section: GENERAL REFERENCE SOURCES (POSTCOLONIAL); AFRICA AND THE CARIBBEAN; *in the Foreign-language section:* FRANCOPHONE; SPANISH AND PORTUGUESE*)*

Limb, Peter, and Jean-Marie Volet. *Bibliography of African Literatures*. Lanham, Md.: Scarecrow Press, 1996. Includes African language, Arabic, Anglophone, Francophone, and Lusophone (Portuguese) literatures.

Elimimian, Isaac Irabor. *Theme and Style in African Poetry*. Lewiston, N.Y.: E. Mellen, 1991.

Herdeck, Donald E., ed. *African Authors: A Companion to Black African Writing, 1300-1973*. Dimensions of the Black Intellectual Experience. Washington, D.C.: Black Orpheus Press, 1973.

Killam, Douglas, and Ruth Rowe, eds. *The Companion to African Literatures*. Bloomington: Indiana University Press, 2000.

ARABIC

Allen, Roger. *An Introduction to Arabic Literature*. Cambridge, England: Cambridge University Press, 2001.

Badawi, M. M. *A Critical Introduction to Modern Arabic Poetry*. New York: Cambridge University Press, 1975.

_____. *Modern Arabic Literature.* New York: Cambridge University Press, 1992.

Frolov, D. V. *Classical Arabic Verse: History and Theory of ʿarud.* Boston: Brill, 2000.

Meisami, Julie Scott, and Paul Starkey, eds. *Encyclopedia of Arabic Literature.* New York: Routledge, 1998.

CARIBBEAN

(*see also in the English-language section:* AFRICA AND THE CARIBBEAN; *in the Foreign-language section:* DUTCH AND FLEMISH; FRANCOPHONE; SPANISH AND PORTUGUESE)

Arnold, A. James, ed. *A History of Literature in the Caribbean.* 3 vols. Vol. 1, *Hispanic and Francophone Regions*; Vol. 2, *English and Dutch-Speaking Countries*; Vol. 3, *Cross-Cultural Studies.* Comparative History of Literatures in European Languages 10. Philadelphia: J. Benjamins, 1994.

Berrian, Brenda F., and Aart Broek. *Bibliography of Women Writers from the Caribbean, 1831-1986.* Washington, D.C.: Three Continents Press, 1989. Includes Anglophone, Francophone, Dutch, and Spanish-language writers.

Fenwick, M. J. *Writers of the Caribbean and Central America: A Bibliography.* Garland Reference Library of the Humanities 1244. New York: Garland, 1992.

Goslinga, Marian. *Caribbean Literature: A Bibliography.* Scarecrow Area Bibliographies 15. Lanham, Md.: Scarecrow Press, 1998. Includes Anglophone, Dutch, Francophone, Spanish.

Herdeck, Donald E., ed. *Caribbean Writers: A Bio-Bibliographical-Critical Encyclopedia.* Washington, D.C.: Three Continents Press, 1979. Includes Anglophone, Dutch, Francophone, Papiamento, Spanish, Sranen.

CELTIC LANGUAGES

(*see also in the English-language section:* IRISH POETRY IN ENGLISH; SCOTTISH POETRY IN ENGLISH; WELSH POETRY IN ENGLISH)

Irish Gaelic

McBreen, Joan, ed. *The White Page = An Bhileog Bhʾan: Twentieth-Century Irish Women Poets.* Cliffs of Moher, County Clare, Ireland: Salmon, 1999.

Scottish Gaelic

Gifford, Douglas, and Dorothy McMillan. *A History of Scottish Women's Writing.* Edinburgh: Edinburgh University Press, 1997.

Glen, Duncan. *The Poetry of the Scots: An Introduction and Bibliographical Guide to Poetry in Gaelic, Scots, Latin, and English.* Edinburgh: Edinburgh University Press, 1991.

Thomson, Derick S. *An Introduction to Gaelic Poetry.* 2d ed. Edinburgh: Edinburgh University Press, 1989.

Welsh

Jarman, A. O. H., and Gwilym Rees Hughes, eds. *A Guide to Welsh Literature.* 6 vols. Cardiff: University of Wales Press, 1992-2000.

Lofmark, Carl. *Bards and Heroes: An Introduction to Old Welsh Poetry.* Felinfach: Llanerch, 1989.

Williams, Gwyn. *An Introduction to Welsh Poetry, from the Beginnings to the Sixteenth Century.* London: Faber and Faber, 1953.

CHINESE

Chang, Kang-i Sun, and Haun Saussy, eds. *Women Writers of Traditional China: An Anthology of Poetry and Criticism.* Stanford, Calif.: Stanford University Press, c. 1999.

Haft, Lloyd, ed. *The Poem.* Vol. 3 in *A Selective Guide to Chinese literature, 1900-1949.* New York: E. J. Brill, 1989.

Lynn, Richard John. *Guide to Chinese Poetry and Drama.* 2d ed. Boston, Mass.: G. K. Hall, 1984.

Nienhauser, William, Jr., ed. *The Indiana Companion to Traditional Chinese Literature.* Bloomington: Indiana University Press, 1986.

Wu-chi, Liu. *An Introduction to Chinese Literature.* Bloomington: Indiana University Press, 1966.

Yip, Wao-lim, ed. and trans. *Chinese Poetry: Major Modes and Genres.* Berkeley: University of California Press, 1976.

CLASSICAL GREEK AND LATIN

Albrecht, Michael von. *Roman Epic: An Interpretive Introduction.* Boston: Brill, 1999.

Briggs, Ward W. *Ancient Greek Authors.* Dictionary of Literary Biography 176. Detroit: Gale Research, 1997.

_____. *Ancient Roman Writers*. Dictionary of Literary Biography 211. Detroit: Gale Group, 1999.

Dihle, Albrecht, and Clare Krojzl, trans. *A History of Greek Literature: From Homer to the Hellenistic Period*. New York: Routledge, 1994.

Kessels, A. H. M., and W. J. Verdenius, comps. *A Concise Bibliography of Ancient Greek Literature*. 2d ed. Apeldoorn, Netherlands: Administratief Centrum, 1982.

Lefkowitz, Mary R. *The Lives of the Greek Poets*. Baltimore, Md.: Johns Hopkins University Press, 1981.

DUTCH AND FLEMISH

Meijer, Reinder P. *Literature of the Low Countries: A Short History of Dutch Literature in the Netherlands and Belgium*. New ed. Boston: Nijhoff, 1978.

Nieuwenhuys, Robert. *Mirror of the Indies: A History of Dutch Colonial Literature*. Translated by Frans van Rosevelt, edited by E. M. Beekman. Library of the Indies. Amherst: University of Massachusetts Press, 1982.

Vermij, Lucie, and Martje Breedt Bruyn. *Women Writers from the Netherlands and Flanders*. Amsterdam: International Feminist Book Fair Press/Dekker, 1992.

Weevers, Theodoor. *Poetry of the Netherlands in Its European Context, 1170-1930*. London: University of London-Athlone Press, 1960.

FRANCOPHONE
General

Gilroy, James P., ed. *Francophone Literatures of the New World*. Denver, Colo.: Dept. of Foreign Languages and Literatures, University of Denver, 1982. Includes French Canadian literature.

Africa and the Caribbean

Blair, Dorothy S. *African Literature in French: A History of Creative Writing in French from West and Equatorial Africa*. New York: Cambridge University Press, 1976.

Haigh, Sam, ed. *An Introduction to Caribbean Francophone Writing: Guadeloupe and Martinique*. New York: Berg, 1999.

Hurley, E. Anthony. *Through a Black Veil: Readings in French Caribbean Poetry*. Trenton, N.J.: Africa World Press, 2000.

Larrier, Renée Brenda. *Francophone Women Writers of Africa and the Caribbean*. Gainesville: University Press of Florida, 2000.

Ojaide, Tanure. *Poetic Imagination in Black Africa: Essays on African Poetry*. Durham, N.C.: Carolina Academic Press, 1996. Addresses Anglophone, Francophone, and Lusophone literatures.

Parekh, Pushpa Naidu, and Siga Fatima Jagne. *Postcolonial African Writers: A Bio-bibliographical Critical Sourcebook*. Westport, Conn.: Greenwood Press, 1998.

France: bibliographies

Kempton, Richard. *French Literature: An Annotated Guide to Selected Bibliographies*. New York: Modern Language Association of America, 1981.

France: biographical sources

Beum, Robert, ed. *Nineteenth-Century French Poets*. Dictionary of Literary Biography 217. Detroit: Gale Group, 2000.

Sinnreich-Levi, Deborah, and Ian S. Laurie, eds. *Literature of the French and Occitan Middle Ages: Eleventh to Fifteenth Centuries*. Dictionary of Literary Biography 208. Detroit: Gale Group, 1999.

France: criticism

Coleman, Kathleen. *Guide to French Poetry Explication*. New York: G. K. Hall, 1993.

France: dictionaries, histories, handbooks

Aulestia, Gorka. *The Basque Poetic Tradition*. Translated by Linda White. Reno: University of Nevada Press, 2000.

Bishop, Michael. *Nineteenth-Century French Poetry*. Twayne's Critical History of Poetry Series. New York: Twayne, 1993.

Brereton, Geoffrey. *An Introduction to the French Poets, Villon to the Present Day*. 2d rev. ed. London: Methuen, 1973.

Dolbow, Sandra W. *Dictionary of Modern French Literature: From the Age of Reason Through Realism*. New York: Greenwood Press, 1986.

France, Peter, ed. *The New Oxford Companion to Literature in French*. New York: Clarendon Press, 1995.

Gaunt, Simon, and Sarah Key, eds. *The Troubadours: An Introduction*. New York: Cambridge University Press, 1999.

Levi, Anthony. *Guide to French Literature.* 2 vols. Chicago: St. James Press, 1992-1994.

Switten, Margaret Louise. *Music and Poetry in the Middle Ages: A Guide to Research on French and Occitan Song, 1100-1400.* New York: Garland, 1995.

Thomas, Jean-Jacques, and Steven Winspur. *Poeticized Language: The Foundations of Contemporary French Poetry.* University Park: Pennsylvania State University Press, 1999.

France: women writers

Sartori, Eva Martin, and Dorothy Wynne Zimmerman. *French Women Writers: A Bio-bibliographical Source Book.* New York: Greenwood Press, 1991.

French Canadian

(see also in the English-language section: Canada)

Platnick, Phyllis. *Canadian Poetry: Index to Criticisms, 1970-1979 = Poésie canadienne: Index de critiques, 1970-1979.* Ontario: Canadian Library Association, 1985.

GERMAN
Biographical sources

Hardin, James, ed. *German Baroque Writers, 1580-1660.* Dictionary of Literary Biography 164. Detroit: Gale Research, 1996.

_____. *German Baroque Writers, 1661-1730.* Dictionary of Literary Biography 168. Detroit: Gale Research, 1996.

Hardin, James, and Will Hasty, eds. *German Writers and Works of the Early Middle Ages, 800-1170.* Dictionary of Literary Biography 148. Detroit: Gale, 1995.

Hardin, James, and Siegfried Mews, eds. *Nineteenth-Century German Writers to 1840.* Dictionary of Literary Biography 133. Detroit: Gale Research, 1993.

_____. *Nineteenth-Century German Writers, 1841-1900.* Dictionary of Literary Biography 129. Detroit: Gale, 1993.

Hardin, James, and Max Reinhart eds. *German Writers of the Renaissance and Reformation 1280-1580.* Dictionary of Literary Biography 179. Detroit: Gale Group, 1997.

_____. *German Writers and Works of the High Middle Ages, 1170-1280.* Dictionary of Literary Biography 138. Detroit: Gale, 1994.

Hardin, James, and Christoph E. Schweitzer, eds. *German Writers from the Enlightment to Sturm und Drang, 1720-1764.* Dictionary of Literary Biography 97. Detroit: Gale Research, 1990.

_____. *German Writers in the Age of Goethe, Sturm und Drang to Classicism.* Dictionary of Literary Biography 94. Detroit: Gale Research, 1990.

_____. *German Writers in the Age of Goethe, 1789-1832.* Dictionary of Literary Biography 90. Detroit: Gale Research, 1989.

Dictionaries, histories, handbooks

Browning, Robert M. *German Poetry from 1750 to 1900.* New York: Continuum, 1984.

_____. *German Poetry in the Age of the Enlightenment: From Brockes to Klopstock.* University Park: Pennsylvania State University Press, 1978.

Faulhaber, Uwe K., and Penrith B. Goff. *German Literature: An Annotated Reference Guide.* New York: Garland, 1979.

Hanak, Miroslav John. *A Guide to Romantic Poetry in Germany.* New York: Peter Lang, 1987.

Hutchinson, Peter, ed. *Landmarks in German Poetry.* New York: Peter Lang, 2000.

Mathiew, Gustave, and Guy Stern, eds. *Introduction to German Poetry.* New York: Dover Publications, 1991.

GREEK
(see also CLASSICAL GREEK AND LATIN*)*

Demaras, Konstantinos. *A History of Modern Greek Literature.* Translated by Mary P. Gianos. Albany: State University of New York Press, 1972.

Saïd, Suzanne and Monique Trédé. *A Short History of Greek Literature.* Translated by Trista Selous et al. New York: Routledge, 1999.

Van Dyck, Karen. *Kassandra and the Censors: Greek Poetry Since 1967.* Ithaca, N.Y.: Cornell University Press, 1998.

HEBREW AND YIDDISH
Biblical Hebrew

Alonso Schokel, Luis. *A Manual of Hebrew Poetics.* Subsidia Biblica 11. Rome: Editrice Pontificio Istituto Biblico, 1988.

Alter, Robert. *The Art of Biblical Poetry.* New York: Basic Books, 1985.

Gevirtz, Stanley. *Patterns in the Early Poetry of Israel.* Chicago: University of Chicago Press, 1963.

Kugel, James L. *The Great Poems of the Bible: A Reader's Companion with New Translations.* New York: Free Press, 1999.

O'Connor, M. *Hebrew Verse Structure.* Winona Lake, Ind.: Eisenbrauns, 1980.

Petersen, David L., and Kent Harold Richards. *Interpreting Hebrew Poetry.* Minneapolis: Fortress Press, 1992.

Watson, Wilfred G. E. *Classical Hebrew Poetry: A Guide to Its Techniques.* 2d ed. Sheffield, England: JSOT Press, 1986.

Nonbiblical Hebrew

Burnshaw, Stanley, T. Carmi, and Ezra Spicehandler, eds. *The Modern Hebrew Poem Itself: From the Beginnings to the Present, Sixty-nine Poems in a New Presentation.* With new afterword, "Hebrew Poetry from 1965 to 1988." Cambridge: Harvard University Press, 1989.

Pagis, Dan. *Hebrew Poetry of the Middle Ages and the Renaissance.* Berkeley: University of California Press, 1991.

Yiddish

Liptzin, Solomon. *A History of Yiddish Literature.* Middle Village, N.Y.: Jonathan David, 1985.

Madison, Charles Allan. *Yiddish Literature: Its Scope and Major Writers.* New York: F. Ungar, 1968.

Wiener, Leo. *The History of Yiddish Literature in the Nineteenth Century.* 2d ed. New York: Hermon Press, 1972.

Zinberg, Israel. *Old Yiddish Literature from its Origins to the Haskalah Period.* Translated and edited by Bernard Martin. Cincinnati: Hebrew Union College Press, 1975.

INDIAN AND SOUTH ASIAN LANGUAGES

(*see also* ARABIC; PERSIAN; VIETNAMESE)

Dimock, Edward C., Jr., et al. *The Literatures of India: An Introduction.* Chicago: University of Chicago Press, 1974.

Gerow, Edwin. *Indian Poetics.* Wiesbaden: Harrassowitz, 1977.

Lienhard, Siegfried. *A History of Classical Poetry: Sanskrit, Pali, Prakrit.* Wiesbaden: Harrassowitz, 1984.

Mahmud, Shabana. *Urdu Language and Literature: A Bibliography of Sources in European Languages.* New York: Mansell, 1992.

Natarajan, Nalini, ed. *Handbook of Twentieth-Century Literatures of India.* Westport, Conn.: Greenwood Press, 1996.

Rajan, P. K., and Swapna Daniel, eds. *Indian Poetics and Modern Texts: Essays in Criticism.* New Delhi: S. Chand, 1998.

Sadiq, Mohammed. *A History of Urdu Literature.* Delhi: Oxford, 1984.

Saran, Saraswiti. *The Development of Urdu Poetry.* New Delhi: Discovery Publishing House, 1990.

ITALIAN

Bondanella, Peter, and Julia Conaway Bondanella, eds. *Dictionary of Italian Literature.* Rev. ed. Westport, Conn.: Greenwood Press, 1996.

De Stasio, Giovanna Wedel, Glauco Cambon, and Antonio Illiano, eds. *Twentieth-Century Italian Poets: First Series.* Dictionary of Literary Biography 114. Detroit: Gale Research, 1992.

_____. *Twentieth-Century Italian Poets: Second Series.* Dictionary of Literary Biography 128. Detroit: Gale Research, 1993.

Dombroski, Robert S. *Italy: Fiction, Theater, Poetry, Film since 1950.* Middle Village, N.Y.: Council on National Literatures, 2000.

Italian Poets of the Twentieth Century. Florence, Italy: Casalini Libri, 1997.

Kleinhenz, Christopher. *The Early Italian Sonnet: The First Century, 1220-1321.* Collezione di Studi e Testi n.s. 2. Lecce, Italy: Milella, 1986.

JAPANESE

Carter, Steven D., ed. *Medieval Japanese Writers.* Dictionary of Literary Biography 203. Detroit: Gale Group, 1999.

Hisamatsu, Sen'ichi, ed. *Biographical Dictionary of Japanese Literature.* New York: Harper & Row, 1976.

Miner, Earl Roy, Hiroko Odagiri, and Robert E. Morrell. *The Princeton Companion to Classical Japanese Literature.* Princeton, N.J.: Princeton University Press, 1985.

Rimer, J. Thomas. *A Reader's Guide to Japanese Literature.* 2d ed. New York: Kodansha International, 1999.

Rimer, J. Thomas, and Robert E. Morrell. *Guide to Japanese Poetry.* Asian Literature Bibliography Series. 2d ed. Boston, Mass.: G. K. Hall, 1984.

KOREAN

Kim, Jaihiun. *Modern Korean Poetry.* Fremont, Calif.: Asian Humanities Press, 1994.

_____. *Traditional Korean Verse Since the 1900's.* Seoul, Korea: Hanshin, 1991.

Korean Poetry: An Anthology with Critical Essays. Seoul: Korean Culture & Arts Foundation, 1984.

Lee, Young-gul. *The Classical Poetry of Korea.* Seoul, Korea: Korean Culture and Arts Foundation, 1981.

McCann, David R. *Form and Freedom in Korean Poetry.* New York: Brill, 1988.

Who's Who in Korean Literature. Korean Culture & Arts Foundation. Elizabeth, N.J.: Hollym, 1996.

PERSIAN (FARSI)

Husain, Iqbal. *The Early Persian Poets of India (A.H. 421-670).* Patna: Patna University, 1937.

Jackson, A. V. Williams. *Early Persian Poetry, from the Beginnings Down to the Time of Firdausi.* New York: Macmillan, 1920.

Meisami, Julie Scott. *Medieval Persian Court Poetry.* Princeton, N.J.: Princeton University Press, 1987.

Thackston, W. M. *A Millennium of Classical Persian Poetry: A Guide to the Reading and Understanding of Persian Poetry from the Tenth to the Twentieth Century.* Bethesda, Md.: Iranbooks, 1994.

Thiesen, Finn. *A Manual of Classical Persian Prosody: With Chapters on Urdu, Karakhanidic, and Ottoman Prosody.* Wiesbaden: O. Harrassowitz, 1982.

SCANDINAVIAN LANGUAGES: DANISH, ICELANDIC, NORWEGIAN, SWEDISH

General

Zuck, Virpi, ed. *Dictionary of Scandinavian Literature.* New York: Greenwood Press, 1990.

Danish

Borum, Poul. *Danish Literature: A Short Critical Survey.* Copenhagen: Det Danske Selskab, 1979.

Rossel, Sven H., ed. *A History of Danish Literature.* Lincoln: University of Nebraska Press, 1992.

Stecher-Hansen, Marianne, ed. *Twentieth-Century Danish Writers.* Dictionary of Literary Biography 214. Detroit: Gale Group, 1999.

Icelandic

Beck, Richard. *History of Icelandic Poets, 1800-1940.* Ithaca, N.Y.: Cornell University Press, 1950.

Norwegian

Naess, Harald S. *A History of Norwegian Literature.* Lincoln: University of Nebraska Press, 1993.

Swedish

Scobbie, Irene. *Aspects of Modern Swedish Literature.* 2d ed. Norwich, England: Norvik Press, 1999.

Forsås-Scott, Helena. *Swedish Women's Writing, 1850-1995.* Atlantic Highlands, N.J.: Athlone, 1997.

Warme, Lars G. *A History of Swedish Literature.* Lincoln: University of Nebraska Press, 1996.

SLAVIC LANGUAGES

General

Jakobson, Roman, C. H. van Schooneveld, and Dean S. Worth, eds. *Slavic Poetics: Essays in Honor of Kiril Taranovsky.* Slavistic Printings and Reprintings 267. The Hague: Mouton, 1973.

Mihailovich, Vasa D., comp. and ed. *Modern Slavic Literatures.* 2 vols. Vol. 1, *Russian Literature*; Vol. 2, *Bulgarian, Czechoslovak, Polish, Ukrainian, and Yugoslav Literatures.* New York: F. Ungar, 1972. Excerpts from criticism.

Tschizewskij, Dmitrij. *Comparative History of Slavic Literatures.* Translated by Richard Noel Porter and Martin P. Rice, edited by Serge A. Zenkovsky. Nashville, Tenn.: Vanderbilt University Press, 1971.

Albanian

Elsie, Robert. *Dictionary of Albanian Literature.* Westport Conn.: Greenwood Press, 1986.

_____. *Studies in Modern Albanian Literature and Culture.* East European Monographs 455. New York: Distributed by Columbia University Press, 1996.

Pipa, Arshi. *Contemporary Albanian Literature.* East

European Monographs 305. New York: Distributed by Columbia University Press, 1991.

Ressuli, Namik. *Albanian Literature*. Edited by Eduard Lico. Boston: Pan-Albanian Federation of America Vatra, 1987.

Bulgarian

Matejic, Mateja, et al. *A Biobibliographical Handbook of Bulgarian Authors*. Translated by Predrag Matejic, edited by Karen L. Black. Columbus, Ohio: Slavica Publishers, 1981.

Czech

French, Alfred. *The Poets of Prague: Czech Poetry Between the Wars*. New York: Oxford University Press, 1969.

Novák, Arne. *Czech Literature*. Translated by Peter Kussi, edited by William E. Harkins. Joint Committee on Eastern Europe Publication Series 4. Ann Arbor: Michigan Slavic Publications, 1976.

Polish

Czerwinski, E. J., ed. *Dictionary of Polish Literature*. Westport, Conn.: Greenwood Press, 1994.

Russian

Cornwell, Neil, ed. *Reference Guide to Russian Literature*. Chicago: Fitzroy Dearborn, 1998.

Poggioli, Renato. *The Poets of Russia, 1890-1930*. Cambridge: Harvard University Press, 1960.

Rydel, Christine A., ed. *Russian Literature in the Age of Pushkin and Gogol*. Poetry and Drama. Dictionary of Literary Biography. 205. Detroit: Gale Group, 1999.

Tschizewskij, Dmitrij. *History of Nineteenth-Century Russian Literature*. Translated by Richard Noel Porter, edited by Serge A. Zenkovsky. Nashville, Tenn.: Greenwood Press, 1974.

Wachtel, Michael. *The Development of Russian Verse: Meter and Its Meanings*. New York: Cambridge University Press, 1998.

Ukrainian

Cyzevkyj, Dmytro. *A History of Ukrainian Literature: From the Eleventh to the End of the Nineteenth Century*. Translated by Dolly Ferguson, Doreen Gorsline, and Ulana Petyk, edited by George S. N. Luckyi. 2d ed. New York: Ukrainian Academic Press, 1997. Includes an overview of the twentieth century.

Piaseckyj, Oksana. *Bibliography of Ukrainian Literature in English and French: Translations and Critical Works, 1950-1986*. University of Ottawa Ukrainian Studies 10. Ottawa: University of Ottawa Press, 1989.

SPANISH AND PORTUGUESE
General

Bleznick, Donald William. *A Sourcebook for Hispanic Literature and Language: A Selected, Annotated Guide to Spanish, Spanish-American, and United States Hispanic Bibliography, Literature, Linguistics, Journals, and Other Source Materials*. 3d ed. Lanham, Md.: Scarecrow Press, 1995.

Newmark, Maxim. *Dictionary of Spanish Literature*. Westport, Conn.: Greenwood Press, 1972.

Sefami, Jacobo, comp. *Contemporary Spanish American Poets: A Bibliography of Primary and Secondary Sources*. Bibliographies and Indexes in World Literature 33. Westport, Conn.: Greenwood Press, 1992.

Woodbridge, Hensley Charles. *Guide to Reference Works for the Study of the Spanish Language and Literature and Spanish American Literature*. 2d ed. New York: Modern Language Association of America, 1997.

Africa

Ojaide, Tanure. *Poetic Imagination in Black Africa: Essays on African Poetry*. Durham, N.C.: Carolina Academic Press, 1996. Covers Anglophone, Francophone, and Lusophone literatures.

Parekh, Pushpa Naidu, and Siga Fatima Jagne. *Postcolonial African Writers: A Bio-bibliographical Critical Sourcebook*. Westport, Conn.: Greenwood Press, 1998. Addresses a few Lusophone writers.

Caribbean

Fenwick, M. J. *Writers of the Caribbean and Central America: A Bibliography*. Garland Reference Library of the Humanities 1244. New York: Garland, 1992.

James, Conrad, and John Perivolaris, eds. *The Cultures of the Hispanic Caribbean*. Gainesville: University Press of Florida, 2000.

Martinez, Julia A., ed. *Dictionary of Twentieth-Century Cuban Literature*. Westport Conn.: Greenwood Press, 1990.

Mexico and Central America

Cortes, Eladio. *Dictionary of Mexican Literature*. Westport, Conn.: Greenwood Press, 1992.

Dauster, Frank N. *The Double Strand: Five Contemporary Mexican Poets*. Lousiville: University Press of Kentucky, 1987.

Foster, David William. *Mexican Literature: A Bibliography of Secondary Sources*. 2d ed. Metuchen, N.J.: Scarecrow Press, 1992.

_____, ed. *Mexican Literature: A History*. Austin: University of Texas Press, 1994.

González Peña, Carlos. *History of Mexican Literature*. Translated by Gusta Barfield Nance and Florence Johnson Dunstan. 3d rev. ed. Dallas: Southern Methodist University Press, 1968.

Nicholson, Irene. *A Guide to Mexican Poetry, Ancient and Modern*. Minutiae Mexicana series. Mexico: Editorial Minutiae Mexicana, 1968.

South America

Brotherston, Gordon. *Latin American Poetry: Origins and Presence*. New York: Cambridge University Press, 1975.

Perrone, Charles A. *Seven Faces: Brazilian Poetry Since Modernism*. Durham: Duke University Press, 1996.

Rowe, William. *Poets of Contemporary Latin America: History and the Inner Life*. New York: Oxford University Press, 2000.

Smith, Verity, ed. *Encyclopedia of Latin American Literature*. Chicago: Fitzroy Dearborn, 1997.

Stern, Irwin, ed. *Dictionary of Brazilian Literature*. Westport, Conn.: Greenwood Press, 1988.

Spain and Portugal

Bellver, C. G. *Dictionary of the Literature of the Iberian Peninsula*. Cranbury, N.J.: Associated University Presses, 2001.

Florit, Eugenio, ed. *Introduction to Spanish Poetry*. New York: Dover Publications, 1991.

Foster, David Williams, Daniel Altamiranda, and Carmen de Urioste, eds. *Spanish Literature: 1700 to the Present*. Spanish Literature 3. New York: Garland, 2000.

Penna, Michael L., ed. *Twentieth-Century Spanish Poets: First Series*. Dictionary of Literary Biography 108. Detroit: Gale, 1991.

Pérez, Janet. *Modern and Contemporary Spanish Women Poets*. New York: Prentice Hall International, 1996.

Winfield, Jerry Phillips. *Twentieth-Century Spanish Poets: Second Series*. Dictionary of Literary Biography 134. Detroit: Gale Research, 1994.

TURKISH

Andrews, Walter G., Jr. *An Introduction to Ottoman Poetry*. Minneapolis: Bibliotheca Islamica, 1976.

Gibb, E. J. W. *A History of Ottoman Poetry*. 6 vols. Cambridge, England: Published and distributed by the Trustees of the "E. J. W. Gibb Memorial," 1963-1984.

VIETNAMESE

Thông, Huynh Sanh, ed. and trans. *An Anthology of Vietnamese Poems: From the Eleventh Through the Twentieth Centuries*. New Haven, Conn.: Yale University Press, 1996.

Vietnamese Poetry and History. In *Crossroads: An Interdisciplinary Journal of Southeast Asian Studies* 7, no. 2. DeKalb, Ill.: Center for Southeast Asian Studies, Northern Illinois University, 1992.

INDEXES

GEOGRAPHICAL INDEX

Meredith, George, 2556
Merton, Thomas, 2576
Middleton, Christopher, 2610
Milton, John, 2641
Morris, William, 2693
Nashe, Thomas, 2738
Newcastle, duchess of, 2768
Oldham, John, 2813
Owen, Wilfred, 2874
Patmore, Coventry, 2922
Pearl-Poet, The, 2947
Pope, Alexander, 3061
Prince, F. T., 3091
Prior, Matthew, 3096
Quarles, Francis, 3115
Ralegh, Sir Walter, 3136
Reed, Henry, 3157
Rochester, earl of, 3235
Rosenberg, Isaac, 3260
Rossetti, Christina, 3264
Rossetti, Dante Gabriel, 3269
Sackville, Thomas, 3311
Sassoon, Siegfried, 3359
Scott, Sir Walter, 3391
Sedley, Sir Charles, 3402
Service, Robert W., 3427
Shakespeare, William, 3442
Shelley, Percy Bysshe, 3458
Sidney, Sir Philip, 3478
Sidney, Sir Robert, 3487
Silkin, Jon, 3493
Sitwell, Edith, 3521
Skelton, John, 3529
Smart, Christopher, 3555
Smith, Stevie, 3567
Southey, Robert, 3623
Southwell, Robert, 3630
Spender, Stephen, 3635
Spenser, Edmund, 3643
Stevenson, Robert Louis, 3703
Suckling, Sir John, 3724
Surrey, earl of, 3730
Swift, Jonathan, 3742
Swinburne, Algernon Charles, 3750

Taylor, Edward, 3799
Tennyson, Alfred, Lord, 3815
Thomas, Dylan, 3834
Thomas, Edward, 3842
Thomson, James (1700-1748), 3846
Thomson, James (1834-1882), 3850
Tomlinson, Charles, 3865
Traherne, Thomas, 3880
Vaughan, Henry, 3970
Waller, Edmund, 4078
Watts, Isaac, 4106
Wilde, Oscar, 4162
Wordsworth, William, 4202
Wyatt, Sir Thomas, 4245
Young, Edward, 4301
Zweig, Stefan, 4318

GREECE. *See also* **LESBOS**
Greek Poetry in Antiquity, 4684
Greek Poetry Since 1820, 4695
Anacreon, 79
Archilochus, 123
Callimachus, 580
Cavafy, Constantine P., 653
Elytis, Odysseus, 1201
Foscolo, Ugo, 1315
Hesiod, 1706
Hikmet, Nazim, 1725
Homer, 1804
Kazantzakis, Nikos, 2005
Leonidas of Tarentum, 2218
Pindar, 3004
Ritsos, Yannis, 3220
Sappho, 3342
Seferis, George, 3407
Theocritus, 3824
Theognis, 3830

GUADELOUPE
Perse, Saint-John, 2967

HONG KONG
Chin, Marilyn, 721

HUNGARY
Hungarian Poetry, 4716
Ady, Endre, 15
Arany, János, 116
Babits, Mihály, 184
Illyés, Gyula, 1912
Petőfi, Sándor, 2981
Radnóti, Miklós, 3126
Rakosi, Carl, 3130
Vörösmarty, Mihály, 4034

INDIA
Commonwealth Poetry, 4443
Indian English Poetry, 4728
Durrell, Lawrence, 1150
Kipling, Rudyard, 2071
Seth, Vikram, 3432
Tagore, Rabindranath, 3765

INDONESIA
Lee, Li-Young, 2209

IRAN. *See also* **PERSIA**
Firdusi, 1286
Hafiz, 1577
Omar Khayyám, 2833
Sa'di, 3317

IRELAND. *See also* **NORTHERN IRELAND**
Æ, 20
Allingham, William, 55
Beckett, Samuel, 230
Boland, Eavan, 398
Clarke, Austin, 746
Colum, Padraic, 798
Darley, George, 975
Goldsmith, Oliver, 1465
Heaney, Seamus, 1647
Joyce, James, 1983
Kavanagh, Patrick, 2000
Kinsella, Thomas, 2063
MacBeth, George, 2364
MacNeice, Louis, 2421
Mangan, James Clarence, 2467

CATEGORIZED INDEX

The Categorized Index covers three primary subject areas: Cultural/Group Identities, Historical Periods/Literary Movements, and Poetic Forms and Themes.

Cultural/Group Identities

Historical Periods/Literary Movements

Poetic Forms and Themes

SUBJECT INDEX

Poésies, 1387; "Symphony in White Major," 1390, 4631

Gavlovič, Hugolín, 4915; *Valaská škola*, 4916

Gawain Poet. *See* Pearl-Poet, The

Gawain tradition, 4481, 4502

Gay, John, 1392-1399, 4536, 4543; *Fables*, 1396, 4535; *Shepherd's Week, The*, 1396; *Trivia*, 1397; "Wine," 1396

"Gazing at Yellow Crane Mountain" (Li Bo), 2268

GDR. *See* East German poetry

Gdzie wschodzi słońce i kędy zapada (Miłosz), 2638

Gebir (Landor), 2166

"Gedicht, Das." *See* "Poem, The" (Novalis)

Gedichten, gezangen en gebeden (Gezelle), 1408

"Geese, The" (Graham), 1495

Geijer, Erik Gustaf, 4879; *Manhem*, 4879; *Odalbonden*, 4879; *Siste kämpen, Den*, 4879; *Vikingen*, 4879

Geistliche Lieder. See *Devotional Songs* (Novalis)

Gelman, Juan, 4797

Gender criticism, 4357-4363

"General Prologue, The" (Chaucer), 718

"General William Booth Enters into Heaven" (Lindsay), 2282

Generation 68, 4307

Generation of '27, 4938-4939

Generation of 1930 (Greece), 4704, 4708

Generation of '98, 4938-4939

Generation of Peace, A (Ehrhart), 1170

"Generations" (Gurney), 1552

Generative metrics, 4376

Genezis z ducha (Słowacki), 3553

Génie, Le (Lebrun), 4624

Genius of the Crowd, The (Bukowski), 533

"Gente spaesata." *See* "Displaced People" (Pavese)

"Gentle Reader" (Jacobsen), 1926

Gentle Weight Lifter, The (Ignatow), 1907

Geoffrey of Monmouth, 4481, 4821; *History of the Kings of Britain*, 4481

Geoffroi de Breteuil, 4716

"Geographer: For Link (Luther Thomas Cupp) 1947-1974" (Hacker), 1573

Geography of Lograire, The (Merton), 2581

Geography of the Near Past (Young, A.), 4298-4299

"George" (Randall), 3146

George Washington Poems, The (Wakoski), 4055

George, Stefan, 1399-1405, 4669; *Algabal*, 1403; "In the Subterranean Kingdom," 1403; *Seventh Ring, The*, 1404; *Year of the Soul, The*, 1403

Georgian poetry and Rupert Brooke, 492

Georgian poets, 4558. *See also* Categorized Index

Georgics (Vergil), 3986, 4811

Gerlach, Harald, 4468

German Democratic Republic. *See* East German poetry

German Expressionism, 4671

German language, 4976

German poetry, 4649-4683; eighteenth century, 4658; nineteenth century, 4664; twentieth century, 4669; medieval, 4478, 4649; Nordic parallels, 4871; Reformation, 4656; Renaissance, 4655. *See also* East German poetry; Germany in Geographical Index; West German poetry

"German Requiem, A" (Fenton), 1271

"Gerontion" (Eliot), 1191

Gertrudis (Foix), 1301

Gerusalemme conquistata. See *Jerusalem Conquered* (Tasso)

Gerusalemme liberata. See *Jerusalem Delivered* (Tasso)

Gesammelten Gedichte, Die (Zweig), 4322

Ge-sar epic, 4948

Gestundete Zeit, Die (Bachmann), 194, 4676

Getting Home Alive (Morales *and* Levin Morales), 4830

Gezelle, Guido, 1405-1412; *Dichtoefeningen*, 1408; *XXXIII Kleengedichtjes*, 1409; *Driemaal XXXIII kleengedichtjes*, 1410; *Gedichten, gezangen en gebeden*, 1408; *Rijmsnoer*, 1411; *Tijdkrans*, 1410

Ghazal, defined, 4991

Ghose, Aurobindo. *See* Aurobindo, Sri

Ghose, Kasiprasad, 4730

Ghose, Manmohan, 4733

Ghost of Eden, The (Twichell), 3907

Giacometti's Dog (Becker), 227

Giambi ed epodi (Carducci), 604

Gibran, Kahlil, 1412-1419; *Forerunner, The*, 1416; *Procession, The*, 1416; *Prophet, The*, 1416; *Sand and Foam*, 1417

"Gift, The" (Lee), 2210

Gift, A (Slavitt), 3541

"Gift of Gravity, The," 303. See also *Wheel, The* (Berry)

Gilbert, Kevin, 4446

Gilbert, Nicolas-Joseph-Laurent, 4625

John the Good (French king), 4477

Johnson, Colin, 4447

Johnson, Emily Pauline, 4839

Johnson, James Weldon, 4392

Johnson, Marguerite. *See* Angelou, Maya

Johnson, Robert, 4399; *God's Trombones*, 4399

Johnson, Ronald, 1957-1962; *Ark*, 1961; *Book of the Green Man, The*, 1959; "Emerson, on Goethe," 1959; *RADI OS I-IV*, 1960; *Songs of the Earth*, 1960; *To Do as Adam Did*, 1961; *Valley of the Many-Colored Grasses*, 1958

Johnson, Samuel, 1962-1970, 4332, 4533, 4539; *Dictionary of the English Language*, 4536; *Irene*, 1968; *Life of Cowley*, 4334; *Life of Milton*, 4333; *Life of Pope*, 4333; *Lives of the Poets, The*, 4333; *London, 1966*, 4542; *Vanity of Human Wishes, The*, 1967, 4537, 4542

Jokond ile Si-Ya-U (Hikmet), 1729

Jokotoba preface (Japanese literary device), 4778

Jónás könyve (Babits), 187

Jónasson, Jóhannes B. *See* Kötlum, Jóhannes úr

Jones, Everett LeRoi. *See* Baraka, Amiri

Jones, Sir William, 4728, 4975

Jongleurs, 4924

Jonson, Ben, 1970-1979, 4519, 4522, 4530; "On My First Daughter," 4524; *Timber*, 1973; "To Penshurst," 1976, 4523

Jonsson, Thorsteinn. *See* Hamri, Thorsteinn frá

Jordan, June, 1979-1983; *Kissing God Goodbye*, 1982; *Naming Our Destinies*, 1982; "Poem About My Rights, A," 1982; *Some Changes*, 1981

Jørgensen, Johannes, 4883, 4886

"Journal for My Daughter" (Kunitz), 2124

"Journal of the Year of the Ox, A" (Wright, C.), 4225

Journals of Susanna Moodie, The (Atwood), 159

"Journey, The" (Boland), 405

Journey and Other Poems, The (Boland), 404

Journey and Other Poems, The (Winters), 4190

"Journey to Stalingrad" (Fühmann), 4471

"Journey Toward Poetry" (Sarton), 3354

Joyce, James, 1983-1989, 4563; *Chamber Music*, 1985; "Ecce Puer," 1988; *Pomes Penyeach*, 1987

József, Attila, 4723

Juan Chi. *See* Ruan Ji

Jubilation (Tomlinson), 3871

Judah ha-Levi, 1989-1993; "Ode to Zion," 1992

Judit (Della Valle), 4749

Judita (Marulić), 4451

Jueju (Chinese poetic form), 4432

Jugendstil, 4669. *See also* Categorized Index

Juglares, 4924-4925

Juhasz, Ferenc, 4725

Juhász, Gyula, 4723

Julian and Maddalo (Shelley), 3461

"Julian M. to A. G. Rochelle" (Brontë), 487

Juliana (Cynewulf), 927-928

"Julia's Petticoat" (Herrick), 1701

"June 1940" (Spender), 3639

Jung, Carl G., 4346, 4563, 4986; "Psychology and Literature," 4346

Jungian criticism, 4346

"Jüngling und die Spinne, Der" (Hofmannsthal), 1760

Jungmann, Josef, 4459

"Junior Life Saving" (Kumin), 2113

"Junk Shop, The" (Coulette), 829

Jussawala, Adil, 4735

Justice, Donald, 1993-1999; *Departures*, 1996; "First Death," 1998; *New and Selected Poems*, 1998; *Night Light*, 1996; *Selected Poems*, 1997; *Summer Anniversaries, The*, 1994

Juvenal, 4815

Juvenalian satire, 4514

Juvencus, 4819

Juvenilia (Carducci), 603

Kabaphēs, Kōnstantionos Petrou. *See* Cavafy, Constantine P.

Ka-bzhas form, 4951

Kadai languages, 4978

"Kaddish" (Ginsberg), 1423

Kahlau, Heinz, 4468

Kaichōon (Ueda Bin), 4788

Kaila, Tiina, 4903

Kailas, Uuno, 4890

Kakekotoba technique (Japanese poetry), 4778

Kakinomoto Hitomaro, 4774

Kaksikymmenta ja yksi (Haavikko), 1569

Kalevala epic, 4873

Kalvos, Andreas, 4697

Kama Mabuchi, 4785